International Criminal Law

International Criminal Law

Cases and Materials

Fourth Edition

Jordan J. Paust
UNIVERSITY OF HOUSTON
LAW CENTER

M. Cherif Bassiouni
DePAUL UNIVERSITY COLLEGE OF LAW

Michael Scharf
CASE WESTERN RESERVE
SCHOOL OF LAW

Leila Sadat
WASHINGTON-ST. LOUIS
SCHOOL OF LAw

Jimmy Gurulé
NOTRE DAME LAW SCHOOL

Bruce Zagaris
OF THE D.C. BAR

CAROLINA ACADEMIC PRESS
Durham, North Carolina

ISBN: 978-1-59460-905-3
LCCN: 2012948790

Carolina Academic Press
700 Kent Street
Durham, North Carolina 27701
Telephone (919) 489-7486
Fax (919) 493-5668
www.cap-press.com

Printed in the United States of America

Summary Table of Contents

Table of Contents

Part Three • Offenses

Preface

In this coursebook, editors with academic, governmental, and private practice backgrounds combine their various experiences and viewpoints to produce a fairly thorough coverage of international and transnational criminal law — with special emphasis on responsibilities (both individual and state); jurisdictional considerations; U.S. and Canadian fora and competencies; extradition, rendition and related matters; international cooperative efforts; international prosecutorial fora; various international crimes; and various matters of defense.

As we submit materials for publication, we are aware that current events will require supplementation especially of Chapter Seven. Opening statements are being made in the *Tadic* case before the International Criminal Tribunal for the Former Yugoslavia (ICTY). Indictments have been issued concerning alleged crimes in Rwanda and we expect new developments in connection with the International Criminal Tribunal for Rwanda (ICTR) by the time of publication. Additionally, there are historic efforts being made to create a permanent International Criminal Court. Regional international criminal tribunals are also being contemplated, offering new areas of practice and concern. The United Kingdom has recently announced its intention to prosecute an alleged Nazi war criminal under legislation that has not been used for decades. The U.S. and Canada have yet to make adequate efforts in this regard. Nonetheless, major concern with terrorism and drug trafficking have propelled our two countries into greater efforts and new cooperative arrangements, especially concerning so-called narco-terrorism, organized crime, and money laundering. Recurrent problems, and strains, remain with respect to processes of extradition and kidnapping. Civil claims also proceed in domestic courts, as in the case of *Kadic v. Karadzic* in the U.S. Second Circuit. In short, there are exciting new developments that will shape international criminal law for decades.

We are pleased to offer the first major coursebook for students in Canada, the United States, and elsewhere on International Criminal Law and expect that with its publication professors in areas of international law and/or criminal law will increasingly participate in a growing field of law that is clearly part of the needed curriculum for the next century.

The Editors
May of 1996

This third edition of the coursebook has been updated and revised, especially in view of developments in the International Criminal Tribunals for the Former Yugoslavia and for Rwanda and at the Rome Conference in 1998, leading to the creation of the Statute of the International Criminal Court (ICC) and its functioning. There are numerous notes and case extracts from decisions of the ICTY and ICTR. Most of the documents are found in the Documents Supplement accompanying this third edition.

With recent developments, this course has become all the more important as a supplement to any international law program.

The Editors
July 2006

This fourth edition has been extensively updated and revised, especially in view of more recent events and case trends in the ICTY and ICTR in connection with types of criminal responsibility and the core crimes of Genocide, other Crimes Against Humanity, and War Crimes. Additional subtitles with respect to forms of responsibility also appear in Chapter Two, Section One and in a few other places. A table of cases for the fourth edition will be available online through www.cap-press.com.

The Editors
October 2012

Acknowledgments and Permissions

We wish to acknowledge our many students who helped over the years to shape our views and professional efforts, as well as our many colleagues here and abroad who contributed similarly to this overall work product. We also acknowledge permissions from the following authors and/or publishers with respect to use of various materials listed below:

American Law Institute:

excerpts from the *Restatement (Third) Foreign Relations Law of the United States* (1987)

American Society of International Law:

remarks of Telford Taylor & Cherif Bassiouni, in 80 *Proceedings, American Society of International Law* 56, 59, 63, 70–72 (1986)

Burmester, The Recruitment and Use of Mercenaries in Armed Conflicts, 72 *American Journal of International Law* 37, 43–44, 49–50, 52, 54 (1978)

remarks of Jordan Paust & Malvina Halberstam, in 77 *Proceedings, American Society of International Law* 186–91 (1983)

Bruce Zagaris, Introductory Note, and Rules of Procedure and Evidence of the ICT for Former Yugoslavia, in 33 I.L.M. 484 (1994)

The *Tiede* case (U.S. Ct. Berlin), in 19 I.L.M. 179 (1980)

Commission on the Responsibility of the Authors of the War and on Enforcement of Penalties, Report Presented to the Preliminary Peace Conference, March 29, 1919, in 14 *American Journal of International Law* 95 (1920)

Case Western Reserve Journal of International Law:

Jordan Paust, Aggression Against Authority: The Crime of Oppression, Politicide And Other Crimes Against Human Rights, 18 *Case Western Reserve Journal of International Law* 283 (1986)

Michael P. Scharf, Symposium: "Terrorism on Trial": Defining Terrorism as the Peacetime Equivalent of War Crimes: Problems and Prospects, 36 *Case Western Reserve Journal of International Law* 359, 360-63 (2004)

Columbia Journal of Transnational Law:

John F. Murphy, The Future of Multilateralism and Efforts to Combat International Terrorism, 25 *Columbia Journal of Transnational Law* 35, 41–53 (1986)

Leila Sadat Wexler, The Interpretation of the Nuremberg Principles by the French Court of Cassation: From Touvier to Barbie and Back Again, 32 *Columbia Journal of Transnational Law* 289, 347-56, 358-62, 366-67, 379-80 (1994)

Houston Journal of International Law:

Jordan Paust, Universality and the Responsibility to Enforce International Criminal Law: No U.S. Sanctuary for Alleged Nazi War Criminals, 11 *Houston Journal of International Law* 337–40 (1989)

Human Rights Quarterly:

Hurst Hannum, International Law and Cambodian Genocide: The Sounds of Silence, 11 *Human Rights Quarterly* 82 (1989)

International Committee of the Red Cross:

Jean S. Pictet, IV *Commentary, Geneva Convention Relative to the Protection of Civilian Persons in Time of War* (1958)

International Law Reports:

Universal Jurisdiction (Austria) Case, in 28 Int'l L. Rep. 341 (1958)

Matter of Barbie, in 78 Int'l L. Rep. 125 (1988), and Note

Law and Contemporary Problems:

Michael Scharf, Beyond the Rhetoric of Comparative Interest Balancing, 50 *Law and Contemporary Problems* 95 (1987)

Los Angeles Daily Journal:

Christine Stevens, International Law Can't Be Activists' Defense Judge Says, L.A. Daily Journal, Feb. 29, 1988, at 9, col. 1

Martinus Nijhoff Publishers:

M. C. Bassiouni (ed.), *A Draft International Criminal Code and Draft Statute for an International Criminal Tribunal* 109–10, 146–50 (1987)

Michigan Journal of International Law:

Jordan Paust, On Human Rights: The Use of Human Right Precepts in U.S. History and the Right to an Effective Remedy in Domestic Courts, 10 *Michigan Journal of International Law* 543, 618–20 (1989)

———, Congress and Genocide: They're Not Going to Get Away With It, 11 *Michigan Journal of International Law* 90, 94–100 (1989)

———, Customary International Law: Its Nature, Sources and Status as Law of the United States, 12 *Michigan Journal of International Law* 59, 63–74 (1990)

New York Law School Journal of Human Rights:

Jordan Paust, Threats to Accountability After Nuremberg: Crimes Against Humanity, Leader Responsibility and National Fora, 12 *New York Law School Journal of Human Rights* 547 (1995)

Notre Dame Law Review:

Leila Nadya Sadat, Exile, Amnesty, and International Law, 81 *Notre Dame Law Review* 955, 958-70 (2006)

Russell & Volkenng:

Barbara Tuchman, *The Guns of August* 127, 151–53 (1962)

Sijthoff & Noordhoff:

M. C. Bassiouni (ed.), *International Criminal Law* 152–54 (1980)

Texas Law Review:

Jordan Paust, After My Lai: The Case for War Crime Jurisdiction Over Civilians in Federal District Courts, 50 *Texas Law Review* 6, 10–28 (1971)

Transnational Publishers, Inc.:

M. C. Bassiouni (ed.), 1 *International Criminal Law* 167–70 (1986); 2 *International Criminal Law* 413–24 (1986)

Leila Nadya Sadat, *The International Criminal Court and the Transformation of International Law: Justice for the New Millennium* 1-8, 146-52 (2002)

United Nations Association of the United States of America:

Senate Lends Consent to Genocide Convention, vol. XII-7 UNA/USA Washington Weekly Report 1-3 (21 Feb. 1986)

Deborah Scroggins, The U.N. War Crimes Files: A Question of Access, in The InterDependent, Oct./Nov. 1987, at 1, 6

University of North Carolina Press:

Peter D. Trooboff (ed.), *Law and Responsibility in Warfare — The Vietnam Experience* 226–27 (1975) (comments of Telford Taylor)

Vanderbilt Journal of Transnational Law:

Paust & Blaustein, War Crimes Jurisdiction and Due Process: The Bangladesh Experience, 11 *Vanderbilt Journal of Transnational Law* 1–38 (1978)

Virginia Journal of International Law:

Jordan Paust, Federal Jurisdiction Over Extraterritorial Acts of Terrorism and Nonimmunity for Foreign Violators of International Law Under the FSIA and the Act of State Doctrine, 23 *Virginia Journal of International Law* 191 (1983)

Washington and Lee Law Review

Michael P. Scharf, From the eXile Files: An Essay on Trading Justice for Peace, 63 *Washington and Lee Law Review* 339, 342-49 (2006)

Whittier Law Review:

Jordan Paust, Responding Lawfully to International Terrorism: The Use of Force Abroad, 8 *Whittier Law Review* 711, 711–12, 727–28 (1986)

International Criminal Law

Part One

General Nature, Responsibilities, and State Competencies to Enforce

Chapter 1

General Nature of International Criminal Law

Section 1
General Nature and Sources of ICL

International criminal law [hereinafter ICL] is reflected in the convergence of two disciplines: the penal aspects of international law and the international aspects of national criminal law. *See* M. Cherif Bassiouni, *An Appraisal of the Growth and Development of International Criminal Law*, 45 Rev. Int'l de Droit Penal 405 (1974).

International crimes have also been called *delicti jus gentium* (crimes against humanity). These terms were first developed under Roman law for application to people within the Roman Empire, although ICL concepts have related historic bases in other and earlier cultures. They were applied by publicists in the 1600s to pirates and others. *See, e.g.,* Leslie Green, *Terrorism and the Law of the Sea,* in International Law at a Time of Perplexity 209, 252–53 (Yoram Dinstein ed. 1989); Alfred Rubin, *The Law of Piracy,* 15 Den. J. Int'l L. & Pol. 173 (1987). U.S. Founders, often citing European scholars like Grotius, Vattel, Ayala, and Gentili, referred to them also as "crimes against mankind" and crimes "against the whole world," and their perpetrators as "enemies of the whole human family." See Jordan Paust, *Universality and the Responsibility to Enforce International Criminal Law: No U.S. Sanctuary for Alleged Nazi War Criminals,* 11 Hous. J. Int'l L. 337, 340 (1989). International crimes engaged in by individuals and prosecuted or recognized early in U.S. history included war crimes; piracy; breaches of neutrality, territorial infractions, and other offences against peace; violence against foreign officials; terroristic publications; poisoners, incendiaries and assassins by profession; banditti and brigands; unlawful capture of vessels; slave trading; violations of passports; violation of safe-conducts; counterfeiting of foreign currency; and, as the Supreme Court recognized in Talbot v. Janson, 3 U.S. (3 Dall.) 133, 159–61 (1795), "all ... trespasses committed against the general law of nations." Paust, *The Reality of Private Rights, Duties, and Participation in the International Legal Process,* 25 Mich. J. Int'l L. 1229, 1237–39 (2004). Since then, specific types of customary and treaty-based international crimes have substantially increased in number.

A. Penal Aspects of International Law: International Crimes

1. International crimes are criminally sanctionable violations of international law and are created directly only by international law. Their creation occurs today mostly through international agreements, but they are also created by customary law. *See* M. Cherif Bassiouni, International Crimes: Digest/Index of International Instruments 1815–1985 (2 vols. 1985). Thus, generally there are two basic types of international criminal law: (1) international agreements, and (2) customary international law. International agreements are technically binding only upon the signatories to such agreements (which in the past have included states, nations, international organizations, and other entities) and their nationals (or possibly also those with a significant nexus with a signatory to an agreement, such as resident aliens). In general, it does not matter that the international agreement is termed a treaty, convention, covenant, protocol, or something else. It is an international agreement, subject to international law concerning such agreements. According to some, general principles of law are also a possible source of international criminal law. *See* M. Cherif Bassiouni, *A Functional Approach to General Principles of International Law*, 11 Mich. J. Int'l L. 768 (1990). For others, general principles of law common to most domestic legal processes can at least evidence normative content and can certainly shape international legal content. At the very least, they may fill gaps where international law is unclear. These are the same sources as those expressly within the jurisdictional competence of the International Court of Justice, as set forth in Article 38 of its Statute, appended to the United Nations Charter.[1]

International agreements may also reflect customary international law, in whole or in part, either at the time of formation or later. Unlike international agreements as such, customary international law is universally obligatory. Thus, what was at one time an international agreement binding merely signatories and their nationals can later become customary law for the entire international community. The 1907 Hague Convention No. IV Respecting the Laws and Customs of War on Land is a well-known example of this transformation. As recognized by the International Military Tribunal at Nuremberg in 1946, rights and duties reflected in the treaty had become customary international law at least by 1939 at the outset of World War II (some 32 years later) and, thus, binding on Germany (as a party) and some of Germany's allies that had not been parties and their nationals despite the refusal of some states to ratify the treaty and a clause in the treaty making it applicable only during armed conflicts among signatories. In view of the name of the treaty, it is also likely that portions thereof were recognizably customary at the time of formation. *See, e.g.,* Anthony D'Amato, International Law: Process and Prospect 123–47 (1987); Clive Parry, The Sources and Evidences of International Law 62–67 (1965); Richard R. Baxter, *Multilateral Treaties as Evidence of Customary International Law*, 41 Brit. Y.B. Int'l L. 275 (1968); *infra* Chapter Eight.

2. What is "custom" or the customary law of nations? Article 38 of the Statute of the International Court of Justice recognizes that customary international law is evidenced by "a general practice accepted as law." See also Restatement of the Foreign Relations Law of the United States § 102(2) and Comments b & c (3 ed. 1987)[hereinafter Re-

---

1. It should be noted that the International Court of Justice (or ICJ) does not have jurisdiction to prosecute individual violators of international law. Its competence generally involves advisory opinions at the request of certain U.N. entities and cases arising between states. See Statute of the I.C.J., art. 36.

STATEMENT]. Thus, custom is comprised of two elements: (a) general patterns of practice or behavior (what people do), and (b) general acceptance as law (what people think) or general patterns of legal expectation or *opinio juris* (*i.e.*, expectations generally shared that something is legally required or appropriate). Both elements or patterns must exist or coincide. See North Sea Continental Shelf Cases (Federal Republic of Germany v. Denmark; Federal Republic of Germany v. Netherlands), 1969 I.C.J. 3, 44; *United States v. La Jeune Eugenie*, 26 F. Cas. 832 (C.C.D. Mass. 1821); *The Antelope*, 23 U.S. 66 (1825); and *Charge to Grand Jury*, 30 F. Cas. 1026 (C.C.D. Ga. 1859).

Fairly obviously, customary law can be dynamic—a law reflected in a dynamic process of behavior and expectation. What once was custom can change to non-custom if one or both of the elements are no longer extant, and what once was not customary law can grow into customary law recognizable, for example, by a judicial tribunal. *See, e.g., The Paquete Habana*, 175 U.S. 677 (1900); *Hilton v. Guyot*, 159 U.S. 113, 163 (1895); *The Scotia*, 81 U.S. (14 Wall.) 170, 187–88 (1871) ("Undoubtedly, no single nation can change the law of the sea. That law is of universal obligation, and no statute of one or two nations can create obligations for the world. Like all the laws of nations, it rests upon the common consent of civilized communities. It is of force, not because it was prescribed by any superior power, but because it has been generally accepted as a rule of conduct. Whatever may have been its origin, whether in the usages of navigation or in the ordinances of maritime states, or in both, it has become the law of the sea only by the concurrent sanction of those nations who may be said to constitute the commercial world.... They all became the law of the sea, not on account of their origin, but by reason of their acceptance as such.... Changes in nautical rules have taken place. How have they been accomplished, if not by the concurrent assent, express or understood, of maritime nations? ... This is not giving to the statutes of any nation extraterritorial effect. It is not treating them as general maritime laws, but it is recognition of the historical fact that by common consent of mankind, these rules have been acquiesced in as of general obligation. Of that fact we think we may take judicial notice. Foreign municipal laws must indeed be proved as facts, but it is not so with the law of nations."); *cf. Thirty Hogsheads of Sugar v. Boyle*, 13 U.S. (9 Cranch) 191, 198 (1815) (Marshall, C.J.); 1 Op. Att'y Gen. 30, 32 (1793). Moreover, the traditional view is that custom rests upon the general patterns of legal expectation (*opinio juris*) of humankind, not merely that of their representatives (*i.e.*, nation-states). *See, e.g., The Scotia, supra; The Prize Cases*, 67 U.S. (2 Black) 635, 670 (1863) ("founded on the common consent as well as the common sense of the world"); *Ware v. Hylton*, 3 U.S. (3 Dall.) 199, 227 (1796) ("established by the general consent of mankind"); IV W. BLACKSTONE, COMMENTARIES ON THE LAW OF ENGLAND 66 (1765).

The preamble to the 1907 Hague Convention No. IV Respecting the Laws and Customs of War on Land contained an early recognition that the "law of nations ... [results] from the usages established among civilized peoples, from the laws of humanity, and from the dictates of the public conscience." (see the Documents Supplement). Similar phrases appear in the 1949 Geneva Conventions. *See, e.g.,* Article 158 of the 1949 Geneva Convention Relative to the Protection of Civilian Persons in Time of War [hereinafter Geneva Civilian Convention], in the Documents Supplement.

It should be noted that "usage" as such is merely long-term practice, not law (unless conjoined with relevant patterns of *opinio juris*).

As materials below demonstrate, there are two other higher-level categories of international law. One category has been termed *obligatio erga omnes*, which are obligations owing not merely to certain states and their nationals, but to all of humankind. *See, e.g., infra* Chapter Three, Section 1, especially concerning the 1949 Geneva Conventions. Another category, termed *jus cogens*, involves customary peremptory norms that preempt any other inconsistent international law. The prohibition of genocide, for example, is a well-recognized part of customary *jus cogens*. So are the customary prohibitions of torture or cruel, inhuman, or degrading treatment; forced disappearance of persons; and slavery and the slave trade. *See, e.g.*, RESTATEMENT, *supra*, § 702, Comments d, n and Reporters' Note 1 (in Chapter Three, Section 1). For this reason, an agreement to commit or tolerate genocide or the other prohibited conduct noted above would be trumped by the *jus cogens* prohibition, and such an agreement would be void *ab initio* as a matter of law.

Jordan J. Paust, *Customary International Law: Its Nature, Sources and Status as Law of the United States*

12 MICH. J. INT'L L. 59, 63–74 (1990), revised in INTERNATIONAL LAW AS LAW OF THE UNITED STATES 4–7 (2 ed. 2003)

Of further significance is the fact that relevant patterns of legal expectation, perhaps contrary to Blackstone, need only be generally shared in the international community. Universality or unanimity are not required. Yet, for fuller exposition and understanding it is suggested that the researcher identify not merely how widespread a particular pattern of expectation is or has been, but also how intensely held or demanded a particular norm is or has been within the community. Awareness of the *degree* and *intensity* of general acceptance provides a more realistic approach to the identification and clarification of normative content and should aid those who must apply customary international law in making informed and rational choices. It would also be useful to know how long such patterns of expectation have existed, although a prior stability evident through time is no guarantee of continued acceptance in the future and time is not otherwise a determinative factor. It is possible, of course, to have a relatively recently widespread and intensely held expectation that something is legally appropriate or required and that such a pattern of *opinio juris* could form one of the components of a new rule of customary international law, one that will even be more stable in the future.

It is also significant that the behavioral element of custom (*i.e.*, general practice) is similarly free from the need for total conformity, and it rests not merely upon the practice of States as such but ultimately upon the practice of all participants in the international legal process. Thus, a particular nation-state might disagree whether a particular norm is customary and might even violate such a norm, but it would still be bound if the norm is supported by patterns of generally shared legal expectation and conforming behavior extant in the community. If the patterns of violation become too widespread, however, one of the primary bases of customary law can be lost. Similarly, if it is no longer generally expected that a norm is legally appropriate or required, the other base of customary law can be lost. When either base is no loner generally extant, there can be no conjoining of general patterns of legal expectation and behavior and, for such a social moment at least, a prior customary law will no longer be operative.

Since each nation-state, indeed each human being, is a participant in both the attitudinal and behavioral aspects of dynamic customary international law, each may initiate a change in such law or, with others, reaffirm its validity. Indeed, such a law at least, born of what people think and do is constantly reviewed and "re-enacted" in the social process, changed, or terminated. In the long-term, one wants to view such law with a movie camera; and yet at any given social moment (or at the time of a particular decision or activity), the existence of a customary international law will be dependent upon relevant patterns of expectation and behavior then extant.

These recognitions are also critical for the researcher's task. In one sense, they simplify that task since one need only identify patterns of what real people generally think and do. Yet, in another sense, researching customary law is significantly complicated by the fact that each person ultimately is a participant in the shaping of customary law and thus each viewpoint and every sort of human interaction could be relevant....

... [I]t is often impossible for one researcher to identify every relevant pattern of expectation and behavior. However, far less than perfect investigation has been accepted by courts and others, especially if documentation of such patterns is with reference to "judicial decisions, ... the works of jurists and commentators, and [documented] ... acts and usages of ... nations." Any evidence of customary norms and relevant patterns of expectation or behavior can be useful. In fact, in addition to judicial opinions and the works of textwriters, U.S. courts have considered treaties and other international agreements; domestic constitutions or legislation; executive orders, declarations or recognitions; draft conventions or codes; reports, resolutions or decisions of international organizations; and even the testimony or affidavits of textwriters.

Since any such evidence of expectation and behavior can be useful, it is also particularly misleading to ask whether a United Nations General Assembly resolution can be a source of customary law. A more realistic question, for example, might be whether a nearly unanimous resolution concerning the content or application of a norm of international law evidences a pattern of generally shared legal expectation or *opinio juris*. The very act of voting on a resolution is in some sense also an instance of behavior, but the most relevant forms of behavior will probably involve other patterns of action and inaction outside the U.N. plaza. Importantly also, U.N. resolutions have been utilized by U.S. courts as aids in identifying the content of customary international law....

With respect to general practice, it is also important to note that "inaction" or compliance because of a choice to not violate a norm may often be more relevant than the nonconforming practice of a few violators of the norm, and yet such a practice may be difficult to measure.... Too often textwriters argue that the death of a norm, even a treaty norm, has occurred because of the actions of a few States. Instead, what should be investigated are the patterns of expectation more generally extant (including those even of such law violators), and the actions and inactions of all participants. It is also too simplistic to argue that law violations which, in a relatively unorganized community, have not been subject to effective sanctions have, therefore, necessarily led to the demise of a customary norm. It would be ludicrous to argue, for example, that when a law-violating elite of a State knows that its actions are prohibited by customary law, when others generally expect that such conduct is an remains illegal, and when violations are scarce, the customary norm is obviated by a failure effectively to ensure sanctions against such an elite. Even in a relatively organized community the lack of effective sanctions against several law violators (*e.g.*, those who commit murder) does not necessarily lead one to the conclusion that a norm (*e.g.*, the prohibition of murder) has thereby been obviated.

[Editors' note: An early international criminal law case after formation of the U.N. Charter recognized the authoritativeness of certain General Assembly resolutions. See *United States v. Altstoetter*, 3 TRIALS OF WAR CRIMINALS 983 (1948) ("The General Assembly is not an international legislature but it is the most authoritative organ in existence for the interpretation of world opinion."). Concerning use of two General Assembly resolutions (found in the Documents Supplement) as aids for identification and clarification of human rights protected through a treaty, the U.N. Charter, consider the following case extract]

Filartiga v. Pena-Irala
630 F.2d 876, 881–84 (2d Cir. 1980)

I

The appellants, plaintiffs below, are citizens of the Republic of Paraguay. Dr. Joel Filartiga, a physician, describes himself as a longstanding opponent of the government of President Alfredo Stroessner, which has held power in Paraguay since 1954. His daughter, Dolly Filartiga, arrived in the United States in 1978 under a visitor's visa, and has since applied for permanent political asylum. The Filartigas brought this action in the Eastern District of New York against Americo Norberto Pena-Irala (Pena), also a citizen of Paraguay, for wrongfully causing the death of Dr. Filartiga's seventeen-year old son, Joelito. Because the district court dismissed the action for want of subject matter jurisdiction, we must accept as true the allegations contained in the Filartigas' complaint and affidavits for purposes of this appeal.

The appellants contend that on March 29, 1976, Joelito Filartiga was kidnapped and tortured to death by Pena, who was then Inspector General of Police in Asuncion, Paraguay. Later that day, the police brought Dolly Filartiga to Pena's home where she was confronted with the body of her brother, which evidenced marks of severe torture. As she fled, horrified, from the house, Pena followed after her shouting, "Here you have what you have been looking for so long and what you deserve. Now shut up." The Filartigas claim that Joelito was tortured and killed in retaliation for his father's political activities and beliefs.

Shortly thereafter, Dr. Filartiga commenced a criminal action in the Paraguayan courts against Pena and the police for the murder of his son. As a result, Dr. Filartiga's attorney was arrested and brought to police headquarters where, shackled to a wall, Pena threatened him with death. This attorney, it is alleged, has since been disbarred without just cause.

During the course of the Paraguayan criminal proceeding, which is apparently still pending after four years, another man, Hugo Duarte, confessed to the murder. Duarte, who was a member of the Pena household, claimed that he had discovered his wife and Joelito in *flagrante delicto*, and that the crime was one of passion. The Filartigas have submitted a photograph of Joelito's corpse showing injuries they believe refute this claim. Dolly Filartiga, moreover, has stated that she will offer evidence of three independent autopsies demonstrating that her brother's death "was the result of professional methods of torture." Despite his confession, Duarte, we are told, has never been convicted or sentenced in connection with the crime.

In July of 1978, Pena sold his house in Paraguay and entered the United States under a visitor's visa. He was accompanied by Juana Bautista Fernandez Villalba, who had lived with him in Paraguay. The couple remained in the United States beyond the term of their visas, and were living in Brooklyn, New York, when Dolly Filartiga, who was then living in Washington, D. C., learned of their presence. Acting on information provided by Dolly the Immigration and Naturalization Service arrested Pena and his companion, both of whom were subsequently ordered deported on April 5, 1979 following a hearing. They had then resided in the United States for more than nine months.

Almost immediately, Dolly caused Pena to be served with a summons and civil complaint at the Brooklyn Navy Yard, where he was being held pending deportation. The complaint alleged that Pena had wrongfully caused Joelito's death by torture and sought compensatory and punitive damages of $10,000,000. The Filartigas also sought to enjoin Pena's deportation to ensure his availability for testimony at trial. The cause of action is stated as arising under "wrongful death statutes; the U.N. Charter; the Universal Declaration on Human Rights; the U.N. Declaration Against Torture; the American Declaration of the Rights and Duties of Man; and other pertinent declarations, documents and practices constituting the customary international law of human rights and the law of nations," as well as 28 U.S.C. § 1350, Article II, sec. 2 and the Supremacy Clause of the U. S. Constitution. Jurisdiction is claimed under the general federal question provision, 28 U.S.C. § 1331 and, principally on this appeal, under the Alien Tort Statute, 28 U.S.C. § 1350.

... The Filartigas submitted the affidavits of a number of distinguished international legal scholars, who stated unanimously that the law of nations prohibits absolutely the use of torture as alleged in the complaint. Peña, in support of his motion to dismiss on the ground of *forum non conveniens*, submitted the affidavit of his Paraguayan counsel, Jose Emilio Gorostiaga, who averred that Paraguayan law provides a full and adequate civil remedy for the wrong alleged. Dr. Filartiga has not commenced such an action, however, believing that further resort to the courts of his own country would be futile....

II

Appellants rest their principal argument in support of federal jurisdiction upon the Alien Tort Statute, 28 U.S.C. § 1350, which provides: "The district courts shall have original jurisdiction of any civil action by an alien for a tort only, committed in violation of the law of nations or a treaty of the United States." Since appellants do not contend that their action arises directly under a treaty of the United States, a threshold question on the jurisdictional issue is whether the conduct alleged violates the law of nations. In light of the universal condemnation of torture in numerous international agreements, and the renunciation of torture as an instrument of official policy by virtually all of the nations of the world (in principle if not in practice), we find that an act of torture committed by a state official against one held in detention violates established norms of the international law of human rights, and hence the law of nations.

The Supreme Court has enumerated the appropriate sources of international law. The law of nations "may be ascertained by consulting the works of jurists, writing professedly on public law; or by the general usage and practice of nations; or by judicial decisions recognizing and enforcing that law." *United States v. Smith*, 18 U.S. (5 Wheat.) 153, 160–61 (1820).... In *Smith*, a statute proscribing "the crime of piracy (on the high seas) as defined by the law of nations," 3 Stat. 510(a) (1819), was held sufficiently determinate in meaning to afford the basis for a death sentence. The *Smith* Court discovered among the works of Lord Bacon, Grotius, Bochard and other commentators a genuine consensus that rendered the crime "sufficiently and constitutionally defined." *Smith*, supra, 18 U.S. (5 Wheat.) at 162.

The Paquete Habana, 175 U.S. 677 (1900), reaffirmed that

> where there is no treaty, and no controlling executive or legislative act or judicial decision, resort must be had to the customs and usages of civilized nations; and, as evidence of these, to the works of jurists and commentators, who by years of labor, research and experience, have made themselves peculiarly well acquainted with the subjects of which they treat. Such works are resorted to by judicial tribunals, not for the speculations of their authors concerning what the law ought to be, but for trustworthy evidence of what the law really is.

Id. at 700. Modern international sources confirm the propriety of this approach....

The United Nations Charter (a treaty of the United States) makes it clear that in this modern age a state's treatment of its own citizens is a matter of international concern. It provides:

> With a view to the creation of conditions of stability and well-being which are necessary for peaceful and friendly relations among nations ... the United Nations shall promote ... universal respect for, and observance of, human rights and fundamental freedoms for all without distinctions as to race, sex, language or religion.

Id. Art. 55. And further:

> All members pledge themselves to take joint and separate action in cooperation with the Organization for the achievement of the purposes set forth in Article 55.

Id. Art. 56.

While this broad mandate has been held not to be wholly self-executing ... this observation alone does not end our inquiry. For although there is no universal agreement as to the precise extent of the "human rights and fundamental freedoms" guaranteed to all by the Charter, there is at present no dissent from the view that the guaranties include, at a bare minimum, the right to be free from torture. This prohibition has become part of customary international law, as evidenced and defined by the Universal Declaration of Human Rights, General Assembly Resolution 217 (III)(A) (Dec. 10, 1948) which states, in the plainest of terms, "no one shall be subjected to torture." The General Assembly has declared that the Charter precepts embodied in this Universal Declaration "constitute basic principles of international law." G.A.Res. 2625 (XXV) (Oct. 24, 1970).

Particularly relevant is the Declaration on the Protection of All Persons from Being Subjected to Torture, General Assembly Resolution 3452 (1975).... Th[is] Declaration expressly prohibits any state from permitting the dastardly and totally inhuman act of torture. Torture, in turn, is defined as "any act by which severe pain and suffering, whether physical or mental, is intentionally inflicted by or at the instigation of a public official on a person for such purposes as ... intimidating him or other persons." The Declaration goes on to provide that "[w]here it is proved that an act of torture or other cruel, inhuman or degrading treatment or punishment has been committed by or at the instigation of a public official, the victim shall be afforded redress and compensation, in accordance with national law." This Declaration, like the Declaration of Human Rights before it, was adopted without dissent by the General Assembly....

These U.N. declarations are significant because they specify with great precision the obligations of member nations under the Charter. Since their adoption, "[m]embers can no longer contend that they do not know what human rights they promised in the Charter to promote".... [T]he Universal Declaration ..."is ... an authoritative statement of the international community." ...

Turning to the act of torture, we have little difficulty discerning its universal renunciation in the modern usage and practice of nations. *Smith*, supra, 18 U.S. (5 Wheat.) at 160–61. The international consensus surrounding torture has found expression in numerous international treaties and accords. *E. g., American Convention on Human Rights*, Art. 5 ("No one shall be subjected to torture or to cruel, inhuman or degrading punishment or treatment"); International Covenant on Civil and Political Rights; European Convention for the Protection of Human Rights and Fundamental Freedoms, Art. 3. The substance of these international agreements is reflected in modern municipal — i.e. national — law as well. Although torture was once a routine concomitant of criminal interrogations in many nations, during the modern and hopefully more enlightened era it has been universally renounced. According to one survey, torture is prohibited, expressly or implicitly, by the constitutions of over fifty-five nations, including both the United States and Paraguay. Our State Department reports a general recognition of this principle:

There now exists an international consensus that recognizes basic human rights and obligations owed by all governments to their citizens.... There is no doubt that these rights are often violated; but virtually all governments acknowledge their validity.

Department of State, *Country Reports on Human Rights for 1979*, Introduction at 1. We have been directed to no assertion by any contemporary state of a right to torture its own or another nation's citizens. Indeed, United States diplomatic contacts confirm the universal abhorrence with which torture is viewed:

In exchanges between United States embassies and all foreign states with which the United States maintains relations, it has been the Department of State's general experience that no government has asserted a right to torture its own nationals. Where reports of torture elicit some credence, a state usually responds by denial or, less frequently, by asserting that the conduct was unauthorized or constituted rough treatment short of torture.

Memorandum of the United States as *Amicus Curiae* at 16 n.34.

Having examined the sources from which customary international law is derived the usage of nations, judicial opinions and the works of jurists16 we conclude that official torture is now prohibited by the law of nations. The prohibition is clear and unambiguous, and admits of no distinction between treatment of aliens and citizens.... The treaties and accords cited above, as well as the express foreign policy of our own government, all make it clear that international law confers fundamental rights upon all people vis-a-vis their own governments. While the ultimate scope of those rights will be a subject for continuing refinement and elaboration, we hold that the right to be free from torture is now among them....

IV

... In the twentieth century the international community has come to recognize the common danger posed by the flagrant disregard of basic human rights and particularly the right to be free of torture. Spurred first by the Great War, and then the Second, civilized nations have banded together to prescribe acceptable norms of international behavior. From the ashes of the Second World War arose the United Nations Organization, amid hopes that an era of peace and cooperation had at last begun. Though many of these aspirations have remained elusive goals, that circumstance cannot diminish the true progress that has been made. In the modern age, humanitarian and practical considerations have combined to lead the nations of the world to recognize that respect for fundamental human rights is in their individual and collective interest. Among the rights universally proclaimed by all nations, as we have noted, is the right to be free of physical torture. Indeed, for purposes of civil liability, the torturer has become like the pirate and slave trader before him *hostis humani generis*, an enemy of all mankind. Our holding today, giving effect to a jurisdictional provision enacted by our First Congress, is a small but important step in the fulfillment of the ageless dream to free all people from brutal violence.

Notes and Questions

1. Although the *Filartiga* case is a civil case, it is instructive regarding both the formation of customary international legal norms and their application by municipal courts. Because international criminal law is a discipline that partakes of both public international law principles and criminal law doctrines, an understanding of the status of inter-

national legal norms and their application is important. The Alien Tort Statute referred to in the case, 28 USC § 1350, has often served as a means by which international criminal law norms have been incorporated by reference into U.S. domestic law. See Chapter Four, Section 3.

2. *Filartiga* and the many civil law cases brought in national courts by victims of international crimes of violence under domestic laws, such as the Alien Tort Statute (ATS) and the Torture Victim Protection Act (TVPA) have given rise to an active area of the law, whereby civil lawsuits seek to remedy criminal wrongdoing. The primary remedy is money damages, but punitive damages have been awarded in U.S. cases. Since the defendants are sometimes governments and high-level officials, the cases are often highly visible and nonimmunity normally rests on an *ultra vires* rationale such as that used by the International Military Tribunal at Nuremberg with respect to claims to immunity from criminal sanctions, *e.g.*, that crimes under international law are not lawful "public," "official," or "sovereign" acts entitled to immunity. *See, e.g.*, Jordan J. Paust, Jon M. Van Dyke, Linda A. Malone, International Law and Litigation in the U.S. 411–500, 822–33 (3 ed. 2009). The lawsuits sometimes result in other actions against the victims, such as deportation due to the publicity over the litigation. Occasionally, the executive and legislative branches of governments become involved in the policies affording such lawsuits and remedies. *See, e.g.*, Ralph G. Steinhardt, International Civil Litigation: Cases and Materials on the Rise of Intermestic Law (2002). How actively should governments encourage civil actions by victims for international crimes?

3. All sources of ICL must satisfy certain "principles of legality". For Professor Bassiouni, this is reflected in the Latin phrase: *nullum crimen sine lege, nulla poena sine lege* (no crime without law, no punishment without law). *See also* Articles 22–23 of the Statute of the International Criminal Court (ICC), in the Documents Supplement; *cf. id.* arts. 10, 21. Others prefer substitution of the word *jus* for *lege* in order to emphasize sources and normative bases other than written law,[2] especially since some confuse the term *lege* with *lex* (or at least *lex scripta*). But the principles of legality in international criminal law differ from those of many legal systems in that they are less rigorous than, for example, positivist legal systems. *See United States v. List*, 11 Trials of War Criminals 757, 1239 (1948) ("It is not essential that a crime be specifically defined"); M. Cherif Bassiouni, Crimes Against Humanity in International Criminal Law 123–76 (1999). *See also* Anthony D'Amato, *The Moral Dilemma of Positivism*, 20 Val. U.L. Rev. 43 (1985), wherein he states: "Not only do positivists insist upon separating law from morality, but they also appear to be unable to deal with moral questions raised by law once the two are separated." *Id.* at 43. *Contra* H.L.A. Hart, *Positivism and the Separation of Law and Morals*, 71 Harv. L. Rev. 593 (1958). *But cf.* Lon Fuller, *Positivism and Fidelity to Law: A Reply to Professor Hart*, 71 Harv. L. Rev. 630 (1958). Of course, there are other relevant jurisprudential orientations. *See, e.g.*, Myres McDougal, Harold Lasswell & W. Michael Reisman, *Theories About International Law: Prologue to a Configurative Jurisprudence*, 8 Va. J. Int'l L. 189 (1968); Lung-chu Chen, An Introduction to Contemporary International Law (1989).

4. An early 20th Century assumption derived from a rigid positivist approach to sovereignty (not fully shared and contrary to 18th and early 19th Century orientations) was that international criminal law is only declarative of certain legal obligations and that

---

2. *See also* Dig. Jul. I. 3.32 ("since *leges* themselves are binding on us for no other reason than that they have been received by the judgment of the people, it is proper that those [legal] things of which the people have approved without any writing shall also be binding on everyone.").

only states can enforce them. Since WWII, a more realistic and progressive approach has been reaffirmed, namely, that international criminal law is binding upon states, individuals, and other actors irrespective of how it is enforced, and that it can be enforced directly through international tribunals, as evidenced by the International Military Tribunal at Nuremberg (IMT) and the International Military Tribunal for the Far East at Tokyo (IMTFE). *See* Chapters Three and Six.

Importantly, international law has never been merely state-to-state and formal actors in addition to the state have included nations, peoples, tribes, free cities, belligerents, insurgents, and others. See Paust, *Nonstate Actor Participation in International La and the Pretense of Exclusion*, 51 Va. J. Int'l L. 977 (2011). International criminal law has been especially attentive to the duties of individuals under customary and treaty-based international law and individuals have had responsibility for international criminal conduct over the last few hundred years.

Enforcement of ICL through criminal sanctions has, however, been entrusted primarily to states that incorporate international criminal law proscriptions in their national criminal justice systems and enforce them domestically. To complement enforcement, it is the customary duty of states to initiate prosecution or to extradite those reasonably accused of international crime. This duty derived from a formula developed by Hugo Grotius calling for "*aut dedere … aut punire*" (hand over or punish). *See* Hugo Grotius, De Jure Belli ac Pacis, Bk. II, Chp. XXI, §§ III 8 IV (1624); English translation: The Law of War and Peace 526–529 (Classics of International Law, Francis W. Kelsey trans. 1925). Professor Bassiouni amended that maxim to *aut dedere aut judicare,* since the goal of adjudication is to prosecute and not merely to punish. *See* M. Cherif Bassiouni & Edward M. Wise, Aut Dedere Aut Judicare: The Duty to Prosecute or Extradite (1995). However, the assumption that international criminal law is only enforced through states (a process Professor Bassiouni terms "indirect" enforcement, as opposed to enforcement through international bodies) is not correct. A direct international enforcement system also exists, as evidenced, for example, by the *ad hoc* international criminal tribunals at Nuremberg and Tokyo established by the Allies after WWII (the IMT at Nuremberg and the IMT for the Far East) and those established in 1993 by the United Nations Security Council for the Former Yugoslavia (the ICTY) and in 1994 for Rwanda (the ICTR). *See* Chapter Six. A permanent International Criminal Court (ICC) with limited jurisdiction has also been created under the "Rome" Statute for an International Criminal Court. *See* Chapter Six, Section 10, and the Documents Supplement. Concerning the ICC's limited jurisdiction, see *id*. preamble and arts. 1, 5, 10, 22 (3). The Statute was adopted at a conference in Rome on July 17, 1998, culminating years of effort to create a permanent tribunal.[3]

---

3. Concerning the new ICC under the Statute adopted at Rome, see materials cited in Chapter Seven, Section 8. For earlier efforts, *see generally* M. Cherif Bassiouni, *Establishing an International Criminal Court: Historical Survey*, 149 Mil. L. Rev. 44 (1995); James Crawford, *Prospects for an International Criminal Court*, 48 Current L. Probs. 303 (1995); Paul D. Marquardt, *Law Without Borders: The Constitutionality of an International Criminal Court*, 33 Colum. J. Trans. L. 73 (1995); M. Cherif Bassiouni, A Draft International Criminal Code and Draft Statute for an International Criminal Tribunal 1–21 (1987); *Draft Statute for an International Commission of Criminal Inquiry and a Draft Statute for an International Criminal Court,* International Law Association, 60th Conference, Montreal, Aug. 29–Sept. 4, 1982, in Report of the 60th Conference of the International Law Association (1983); M. Cherif Bassiouni & Daniel Derby, *Final Report on the Establishment of an International Criminal Court for the Implementation of the Apartheid Convention and Other Relevant Instruments,* 7 Hofstra L. Rev. 523 (1981); Benjamin Ferencz, An International Criminal Court (2 vols. 1980); Benjamin Ferencz, An International Criminal Court (2 vols. 1980);

5. Since international crimes are created directly by and are part of treaty-based and customary international law, the question arises whether there should be a limited or proper subject-matter of these crimes. The writings of scholars on this specific issue are limited, although many have covered more general aspects of this topic.[4]

During a study of numerous international criminal law instruments, Professor Bassiouni recognized that international crimes can be identified on the basis of one or more of the following ten "penal characteristics." They are:

1. Explicit recognition of proscribed conduct constituting an international crime, or a crime under international law, or a crime (27);

2. Implicit recognition of the penal nature of the act by establishing a duty to prohibit, prevent, prosecute, punish, or the like (191);

3. Criminalization of the proscribed conduct (76);

4. Duty or right to prosecute (72);

5. Duty or right to punish the proscribed conduct (99);

6. Duty or right to punish or extradite (48);

Julius Stone & Robert Woetzel, Toward a Feasible International Criminal Court (1970); Fannie Klein & Daniel Wilkes, *United Nations Draft Statute for an International Criminal Court: An American Evaluation*, in International Criminal Law 526 (Gerhard O.W. Mueller & Edward M. Wise eds. 1965); Bienvenido C. Ambion, *Organization of a Court of International Criminal Jurisdiction*, 29 Philippines L.J. 345 (1954); Leila Sadat, *The Proposed Permanent International Criminal Court: An Appraisal*, 29 Cornell Int'l L.J. 665 (1996) (formerly Wexler); Quincy Wright, *Proposal for an International Criminal Court*, 46 Am. J. Int'l L. 60 (1952); Vespesian V. Pella, *Towards an International Criminal Court*, 44 Am. J. Int'l L. 37 (1950); Vespesian V. Pella, *Plan d'un Code Repressif Mondial*, 6 Rev. Int'l de Droit Pénal 1948 (1935); symposium, *Projet de Statut pour la Création d'une Chambre Criminelle au Sein de la Court Permanente de Justice Internationale*, 5 Rev. Int'l de Droit Pénal (1928) (presented by the International Association of Penal Law to the League of Nations in 1927); *Project of the International Association of Penal Law*, in Actes du Premier Congrés International de Droit Pénal, Bruxelles, 26–29 June 1926 (1927); Vespasian V. Pella, *The International Parliamentary Union, XXII Conference, held in Berne and Geneva, 1924*, in L'Union Interparlimentaire Compte Rendu de la XXII Conference Tenue a Berne et a Genève en 1924, Publie par le Bureau Interparliamentaire; Compte Rendu de la XXIII Conference Tenue a Washington et a Ottawa en 1925 (1926).

4. *See, e.g.,* M. Cherif Bassiouni, *The History of the Draft Code of Crimes Against the Peace and Security of Mankind*, 27 Israel L. Rev. 1–21 (1993), *reprinted in* Commentaries on the International Law Commission's 1991 Draft Code of Crimes Against the Peace and Security of Mankind, 11 Nouvelles Etudes Pénales 1 (1993); Farhad Malekian, International Criminal Law: The Legal and Critical Analysis of International Crimes (2 vols. 1991); M. Cherif Bassiouni, A Draft International Criminal Code and Draft Statute for an international Criminal Tribunal (1987); Robert Friedlander, *The Enforcement of International Criminal Law: Fact or Fiction?*, 17 Case W. Res. J. Int'l L. 79 (1985); *see also* 52 Rev. Int'l de Droit Pénale (1984), symposium issue on Draft International Criminal Code; Robert Friedlander, *The Foundations of International Criminal Law: A Present Day Inquiry*, 15 Case W. Res. J. Int'l L. 13 (1983); Leslie C. Green, *Is There an International Criminal Law?*, 21 Alberta L. Rev. 251 (1983); Leslie C. Green, *New Trends in International Criminal Law*, 11 Israel Y.B. Int'l L. 9 (1981); Yoram Dinstein, *International Criminal Law*, 3 Israel Y.B. Int'l L. 9 (1981); Leslie C. Green, *An International Criminal Code — Now?*, 3 Dalhousie L.J. 560 (1976); Quincy Wright, *The Scope of International Criminal Law: A Conceptual Framework*, 15 Va. J. Int'l L. 561 (1975); Georg Schwarzenberger, *The Problem of International Criminal Law*, 3 Current Leg. Probs. 263 (1950), *reprinted in* International Criminal Law 3–36 (Gerhard O.W. Mueller & Edward M. Wise eds. 1965); Gerhard O.W. Mueller & Douglas J. Besharov, *Evolution and Enforcement of International Criminal Law*, in ICL, *supra*, at 59; Edward M. Wise, *International Crimes and Domestic Criminal Law*, 38 DePaul L. Rev. 923 (1989).

7. Duty or right to cooperate in prosecution, punishment (including judicial assistance in penal proceedings) (67);

8. Establishment of a criminal jurisdiction basis (or theory of criminal jurisdiction or priority in criminal jurisdiction) (71);

9. Reference to the establishment of an international criminal court or international tribunal with penal characteristics (or prerogatives) (21);

10. Elimination of the defense of superior orders (16).

The numbers in parentheses represent the frequency of appearance of a characteristic in 312 international instruments surveyed in 1985. *See* M. Cherif Bassiouni, International Crimes: Digest/Index of International Instruments 1815–1985 (2 vols. 1985). Which "penal characteristic" is most prevalent? How might customary international law supplement these instruments? *See also* Article 21(1)(b) and (3).

A survey of conventions containing these characteristics from 1815 to date reveals that there are more than 318 such instruments which can be placed in 24 general categories. They are listed below under the heading of the protected interest that they reflect, although one might place particular crimes also in different categories (*e.g.*, hostage-taking under human rights):

A. Protection of Peace

    1. Aggression

B. Humanitarian Protection During Armed Conflicts, the Regulation of Armed Conflicts, and the Control of Weapons

    2. War Crimes

    3. Unlawful Use of Weapons; Unlawful Emplacement of Weapons

    4. Mercenarism

C. Protection of Fundamental Human Rights

    5. Genocide

    6. Crimes Against Humanity

    7. *Apartheid*

    8. Slavery and Related Crimes

    9. Torture

    10. Unlawful Human Experimentation

D. Protection Against Terror-Violence

    11. Piracy

    12. Aircraft Hijacking and Sabotage of Aircrafts

    13. Threat and Use of Force Against Internationally Protected Persons

    14. Taking of Civilian Hostages

    15. Attacks upon Commercial Vessels and Hostage-Taking on Board Such Vessels

E. Protection of Social Interests

    16. Drug Offenses

    17. International Traffic in Obscene Publications

F. Protection of Cultural Interests

     18. Destruction and/or Theft of National Treasurers

G. Protection of the Environment

     19. Environmental Protection

     20. Theft of Nuclear Materials

H. Protection of Communication Means

     21. Unlawful Use of the Mails

     22. Interference with Submarine Cables

I. Protection of Economic Interests

     23. Falsification and Counterfeiting

     24. Bribery of Foreign Public Officials

See M. Cherif Bassiouni, A Draft International Criminal Code and Draft Statute for an International Criminal Tribunal 41–42 (1987). It should be noted that when that text was published, only 312 conventions existed covering 22 crimes. Since then, additional conventions were adopted, bringing the number of crimes to more than 28 (newer crimes include Mercenarism, Attacks upon Commercial Vessels, Hostage-Taking on board such vessels, terrorist bombings (in the International Convention for Suppression of Terrorist Bombings), organized crime, corruption, and the financing of terrorism proscribed in the International Convention for Suppression of Financing of Terrorism).

According to Professor Bassiouni, among these categories of crimes, only a few must be the product of "state action," while a few cannot (such as piracy) and most can also be perpetrated by private actors. Others disagree that there is any international crime under customary international law that can only be committed by state actors and point to the fact that there have been many actors in the international legal process besides the state as well as the fact that crimes against peace (sometimes labeled as acts of aggression) had been committed by private actors (*e.g.*, *Henfield's* Case in 1793, addressed in Chapter Four) and crimes against humanity had been committed by private actors (see Chapter Nine, Section 1; Chapter Ten (genocide can be committed by private actors and it is a special type of crime against humanity). According to Professor Bassiouni, this may explain why the varying number of instruments applicable to each category of crimes does not reflect the same number of penal characteristics. Also according to Professor Bassiouni, crimes that necessarily require "state action" are of a political nature and have the least number of penal characteristics, as if to weaken enforcement provisions, such as what many consider to be the modern crime of aggression. *But see* Chapter Seven.[5] Conversely, those crimes which often have the least political content, like drug trafficking, are the object of many international instruments that have the largest number of penal and enforcement characteristics. Another way of categorizing is through the perspective of whose criminal responsibility is most likely at stake (recognizing, however, that most treaty-based crimes expressly reach, for example, "any person" and rarely do any exclude state actors expressly or by implication—see Chapter Two, *passim*). According to Professor Bassiouni, crimes which often implicate the responsibility of heads of state and senior political and military leaders are the ones less likely to be drafted with many penal and enforcement characteristics, while those which often do not bear upon such leader responsibility have

---

5. The concept of aggression has previously been related to conduct of private actors and, from a policy-oriented perspective, may also reach conduct of other actors such as insurgents. Consider, for example, Bosnian-Serb acts of aggression against Croatia. More generally, crimes against peace can be perpetrated by various actors. See Chapter Seven.

the most penal and enforcement characteristics. *See* M. CHERIF BASSIOUNI, *The Theory of International Criminal Law: Characteristics of International Criminal Law Conventions*, in 1 INTERNATIONAL CRIMINAL LAW: CRIMES 1–14 (M. Cherif Bassiouni ed. 1986). Notable exceptions appear to be the 1948 Genocide Convention, the 1949 Geneva Conventions, and the newer Torture Convention. See Chapters Eight, Ten, and Eleven. A group of distinguished experts recently drafted a proposed International Convention of the Protection and Punishment of Crimes Against Humanity that would combine the strong penal and enforcement characteristics of crimes requiring state action with the *jus cogens* norm prohibiting crimes against humanity. *See* FORGING A CONVENTION FOR CRIMES AGAINST HUMANITY (Leila Nadya Sadat, ed., 2011).

6. Most international criminal proscriptions also protect certain fundamental human rights. An examination of the 24 crimes listed above reveals the nexus between the protection of human rights and the criminalization of their violation. *See* M. Cherif Bassiouni, *The Enforcement of Human Rights Through International Criminal Law and by Means of an International Criminal Tribunal*, in HUMAN RIGHTS: AN AGENDA FOR THE NEXT CENTURY 347 (Louis Henkin & John Lawrence Hargrove eds. 1994); M. Cherif Bassiouni, *The Proscribing Function of International Criminal Law in the Processes of International Protection of Human Rights*, 9 YALE J. WORLD PUB. ORD. 193, 214 (1982); Chapter Eleven.

7. Many of the crimes listed above are also based in customary international law (such as war crimes, crimes against humanity, and piracy) and also fall under general principles of law, though, for some, like Professor Bassiouni, the latter source is questionable because it is least susceptible of satisfying the requirements of the "principles of legality". *See* paras. 2–3 above. If crimes listed in instruments are also crimes under customary international law, how might customary international law supplement the "penal characteristics" involved? One should note also that customary international law is a necessary background for purposes of interpretation of any international instrument. *See, e.g.*, Vienna Convention on the Law of Treaties, 1155 U.N.T.S. 331, art. 31 (3) (c) ("There shall be taken into account ... (c) any relevant rules of international law....").

Most contemporary scholars and states also expect that some of these crimes, like aggression in violation of the U.N. Charter, Article 2 (4); genocide; crimes against humanity; war crimes; piracy; slavery and the slave trade; forced disappearance; and torture or cruel, inhuman, or degrading treatment are now part of customary *jus cogens*. *See* RESTATEMENT §§ 102, Comment k, 404, 702; Human Rights Committee, General Comment No. 24, U.N. Doc. CCPR/C/21/Rev.1/Add.6 (1994); Kenneth Randall, *Universal Jurisdiction Under International Law*, 66 TEX. L. REV. 785 (1988); Jordan Paust, *Universality and the Responsibility to Enforce International Criminal Law*, 11 HOUS. J. INT'L L. 337 (1989). Professor Paust adds: "[U]niversal enforcement has been recognized over 'crimes against mankind,' crimes 'against the whole world' and the 'enemies of the whole human family,' or those persons who become *hostes humani generis* by the commission of international crimes." *Id.* at 340. *See also* Chapter Three, Section 1.

8. An analysis of the 24 categories of crimes reveals that some of them can affect more directly the peace and security of humankind or shock human conscience while others might affect a more limited international interest and may or may not have a transnational element (see Section 2 below). According to Professor Bassiouni:

> The former include the four major core crimes of aggression, genocide, crimes against humanity, and war crimes. The latter include aircraft hijacking, taking of hostages, traffic in drugs and unlawful use of the mails. The difference between them is in the protected interest. This has led to a distinction between in-

ternational crimes *stricto senso*, which are the ones involving threats to peace and security and those which shock human conscience, and international crimes *largo senso*, sometimes referred as transnational crimes, which are those that affect a narrower international interest and involve an inter-state element. The problem with such a distinction is that the latter classification overlaps with domestic crimes whose commission also involves an inter-state element.

Consider also Section 2 below. Which crimes do not have to actually directly affect "peace and security," "shock human conscience," or have a transnational element, but which nonetheless reach an international "interest"? What about local piracy? counterfeiting of foreign currency? hostage-taking (see the Convention on the Taking of Hostages in the Documents Supplement)?

9. Presently, international crimes are deemed to apply only to individual perpetrators (including private juridical entities such as corporations), although the notion of state criminal responsibility has long been advocated by a number of scholars and international criminal law contains various types of duties of states, violations of which can result in political, diplomatic, economic, and juridic sanctions against states. *See* FARHAD MALEKIAN, CRIMINAL RESPONSIBILITY OF STATES (1985). Professor Bassiouni maintains:

> The doctrinal debates among penalists and among publicists, as well as between penalists and publicists, on the question of the criminal responsibility of states offer an abundance of arguments for these and other propositions that conclude for and against the penal responsibility of legal entities, be they private (organizations) or public entities (including states and their organs). Nevertheless, all such positions now accept in some form or another the principle that a legal entity, be it private or public, can, through its policies and operations, transgress a norm resulting in a given harm for which the law, whether national or international, provides at the very least damages and other remedies that could be both compensatory and punitive. Thus the real distinction left with respect to the inquiry concerning the international penal responsibility of legal entities is how to label it, define it, and enforce it. As such the *rationae personae* for international crimes is that it applies both to individuals and legal entities, but with the *caveat* that the same principles of accountability and punishability differ as between individuals and legal entities.
>
> It must be noted, however, that since legal entities are legal abstractions whose policies and operations are made and carried out by individuals, some further refinement needs to be made in distinguishing between the criminal responsibility of individuals and that of legal entities. But that question goes more to the means and methods of labeling, establishing and assessing responsibility and the resulting sanctions and remedies (however labeled) than to the questions of whether any responsibility can befall a legal entity. In short, the gap between proponents and opponents of responsibility for legal entities under international law is for all practical purposes narrowing somewhat in contemporary legal doctrine.

See M. CHERIF BASSIOUNI, A DRAFT INTERNATIONAL CRIMINAL CODE AND DRAFT STATUTE FOR AN INTERNATIONAL CRIMINAL TRIBUNAL 47–48 (1987).

Governments are reluctant to allow progress on the question of criminal responsibility of states, even if it only means that state criminal responsibility results in fines, injunctions from unlawful conduct, or the return of spoils. After WWI, Germany was made to pay reparations to the Allies, and after WWII, Germany's territorial boundaries were changed by the Allies. The state can also be liable for international crimes under the principle of "state responsibility" and subject to possible political, diplomatic, economic, and juridic sanctions. *See, e.g.*, Case Concerning Application of the Convention on the Prevention and Punishment of the Crime of Genocide (Bosnia and Herzegovina v. Yugoslavia), 1996 I.C.J. 595, para. 32; *The Prosecutor v. Furundzija*, ICTY-95-17-1 (10 Dec. 1998). Since 1979, the ILC has been working on Draft Principles of State Responsibility, and Article 19 of the 1980 Draft provided for state criminal responsibility (which is not to be confused in any way with a delimiting test of individual responsibility), but significant controversy regarding Article 19 led to its deletion from the 2001 Draft Articles,[6] which now contain a much different proviso in Chapter III of Part Two of the Draft, "Serious Breaches of Obligations Under Peremptory Norms of General International Law:"

Article 40. Application of this chapter

1. This chapter applies to the international responsibility which is entailed by a serious breach by a State of an obligation arising under a peremptory norm of general international law.

2. A breach of such an obligation is serious if it involves a gross or systematic failure by the responsible State to fulfill the obligation.

Article 41. Particular consequences of a serious breach of an obligation under this chapter

1. States shall cooperate to bring to an end through lawful means any serious breach within the meaning of article 40.

2. No State shall recognize as lawful a situation created by a serious breach within the meaning of article 40, nor render aid or assistance in maintaining that situation.

3. This article is without prejudice to the other consequences referred to in this Part and to such further consequences that a breach to which this chapter applies may entail under international law.

The "other consequences" referred to in article 41(3) include restitution, compensation, and satisfaction ("acknowledgment of the breach, an expression of regret, a formal apology, or another appropriate modality"). Unlike former article 19, which gave examples of acts that might be international crimes (such as breaching the responsibility to prohibit aggression, colonial domination, or massive pollution), Chapter III declines to give such examples.

10. In terms of corporate criminal responsibility, there has been some evolution during the past decade. Although the IMT at Nuremberg found organizations like the SS and SA to be criminal, the Rome Statute for the International Criminal Court did not include the possibility of corporate criminal liability for the crimes within the ICC Statute. Nonetheless, relying upon the Nuremberg precedent, many scholars have argued that the principle of corporate criminal responsibility at the international level exists, as it does at the domestic level in certain legal systems like the U.S. *See* M. Cherif Bassiouni, A Draft International Criminal Code and Draft Statute for an International Crimi-

---

6. For a discussion of this controversial article, *see* Report of the International Law Commission on the work of its forty-sixth session, 48 U.N. GAOR, Supp. No. 10, at 358–64, UN Doc. A/48/10 (1994) [hereinafter 1994 ILC Report]; and Report of the International Law Commission on the work of its forty-seventh session, 49 U.N. GAOR, Supp. No. 10, at __, UN Doc. A/CN.4/469 & Adds. 1, 2, 3 (1995).

NAL TRIBUNAL 46–52 (1987). Recently, several jurisdictions have amended their criminal codes to provide for corporate criminal liability, including France and the Netherlands. *See* Code Penal [C. Pen.] art. 121–2 (Fr.) (translated in Leonard Orland and Charles Cachera, *Essay and Translation: Corporate Crime and Punishment in France: Criminal Responsibility of Legal Entities* (Personnes Morales) *under the New French Criminal Code* (Nouveau Code Penal), 11 CONN. J. INT'L L. 111 (1995)); Article 51 DPC (Netherlands) (translated in B.F. Keulen & E. Gritter, *Corporate Criminal Liability in the Netherlands*, 14.3 ELECTRONIC J. COMP. L. (Dec. 2010), available at http://www.ejcl.org/143/art143-9.pdf). For a discussion of corporate criminal liability systems in Western Europe, see Sara Sun Beale & Adam G. Safwat, *What Developments in Western Europe Tell Us About American Critiques of Corporate Criminal Liability*, 8 BUFF. CRIM. L. REV. 89, 105–136 (2004). See also Luca Enriques, *Bad Apples, Bad Oranges: A Comment from Old Europe on Post-Enron Corporate Governance Reforms*, 38 WAKE FOREST L. REV. 911, 912–926 (2003). For this reason, *the Proposed International Convention on the Prevention and Punishment of Crimes Against Humanity* includes a proviso on corporate responsibility for crimes against humanity for national legal systems which provide for corporate criminal liability more generally. Article 8, para. 6, of the *Proposed International Convention* in FORGING A CONVENTION FOR CRIMES AGAINST HUMANITY 370 (2011).

This issue has come up in the United States in the context of numerous alien tort statute cases in which plaintiffs have successfully alleged corporate civil liability for the commission of international crimes. In fact, twenty United States Supreme Court cases have already recognized that corporations and companies can have duties and rights under customary and treaty-based international law. *See, e.g.*, Paust, *Nonstate Actor Participation in International Law and the Pretense of Exclusion*, 51 VA. J. INT'L L. 977, 986–89 (2011), also documented many lower federal court cases. However, the matter is before the Supreme Court once again. *See Kiobel v. Royal Dutch Petroleum*, Chapter 2, Subsection B, Note 2. Non-U.S. cases also exist with respect to corporate liability. *See, e.g.*, Paust, *Human Rights Responsibilities of Private Corporations*, 35 VAND. J. TRANSNAT'L L. 801, 809–10 (2002). *See also* HENRY WHEATON, ELEMENTS OF INTERNATIONAL LAW 54–55 § 4 (3 ed. 1846); HENRY WHEATON, ELEMENTS OF INTERNATIONAL LAW 28 (6th ed. 1855); Chiméne I. Keitner, *Conceptualizing Complicity in Alien Tort Cases*, 60 HASTINGS L.J. 61 (2008); Rebecca M. Bratspies, *"Organs of Society": A Plea for Human Rights Accountability for Transnational Enterprises and Other Business Entities*, 13 MICH. ST. J. INT'L L. 9, 28 (2005); Richard L. Herz, *The Liberalizing Effects of Tort: How Corporate Complicity Liability Under the Alien Tort Statute Advances Constructive Engagement*, 21 HARV. HUM. RTS. J. 207, 208 (2008).

B. International Aspects of National Criminal Law: Enforcement

11. Individual states cannot, by mere declaration, create an international crime. Yet, states have the duty to enforce international criminal law through customary international law as well as the obligations they assume by treaty. *See supra* para. 2; Chapter Two, Section 3. Enforcement by states is reflected in the principle *aut dedere aut judicare*. Accordingly, states have the duty to initiate prosecution or to extradite. *See supra* paras. 3 and 4; Chapter Two, Section 3. Both duties are premised on the assumption that states shall carry out these processes effectively, in good faith, and fairly. The duty to prosecute is co-existent with that of extradition. However, a state can argue that lack of effective or

fair prosecution is a ground to refuse extradition (leaving it with the duty to initiate prosecution) or to give priority to extradition over domestic prosecution, as the case may be. This issue is pending before the U.N.'s International Court of Justice in a case filed by Belgium against Senegal, in which Belgium argued that Senegal breached its international legal obligations by not prosecuting or extraditing Hissène Habré, former president of Chad, for human rights violations. See Chapters Two, Section 3, and Five.

12. In some states, national criminal law is entrusted with the task of enforcing international criminal law by means of domesticating international legal proscriptions (*e.g.*, incorporating them indirectly through domestic legislation) and then prosecuting, extraditing and lending assistance to other states in their investigation, prosecution and enforcement endeavors. In others, international law (either custom or treaty-based) has been incorporated directly for purposes of criminal prosecution. See Chapter Four. States undertake to cooperate through a variety of means, but cooperative actions are ultimately tied to their internal laws and practices. This area of law has been termed inter-state cooperation in penal matters as well as mutual legal assistance. *See* M. Cherif Bassiouni, *Policy Considerations on Inter-State Cooperation in Criminal Matters*, in PRINCIPLES AND PROCEDURES FOR A NEW TRANSNATIONAL CRIMINAL LAW 807 (A. Eser & O. Lagodny eds. 1992), *reprinted in* 1992 PACE Y.B. INT'L L. The modalities in question include: extradition and other forms of rendition, legal assistance, transfer of penal proceedings, transfer of prisoners, recognition and enforcement of foreign penal judgments, seizure and forfeiture of assets deriving from criminal activities. See Chapters Five and Six. These modalities apply not only to the 24 categories of international crimes listed above, but also to domestic crimes when the state which has custody and enforcement jurisdiction seeks the cooperation of another state with respect to investigation, prosecution or enforcement of such crimes. *See, e.g.*, 2 INTERNATIONAL CRIMINAL LAW: PROCEDURE (M. Cherif Bassiouni ed. 1987).

13. Conventions proscribing international crimes (*i.e.*, the 315 instruments mentioned above) will frequently contain one or more of these modalities. But there are also specialized conventions which deal exclusively with such modalities. Regional conventions developed by the Council of Europe and the Organization of American States deal with each one of these modalities. *See* EKKEHART MULLER-RAPPARD & M. CHERIF BASSIOUNI, EUROPEAN INTER-STATE CO-OPERATION IN PENAL MATTERS (2 vols., 2d rev. ed. 1992) (also containing the table of ratifications, reservations, and other information concerning such agreements). In addition, many states have developed specialized legislation on all or some of these modalities. Some treat these modalities in an integrated fashion (*i.e.*, Austria, Germany, Switzerland), which allows more flexibility and effectiveness than the piece-meal approach used by other states like the U.S.

14. National legislation on modalities of inter-state cooperation in penal matters may form the exclusive basis for inter-state practices, but many states, like the U.S., require the existence of a treaty in addition to national legislation. *See, e.g.*, 18 U.S.C. § 3184 on the need for a treaty in addition to legislation for extradition from the U.S.; M. CHERIF BASSIOUNI, INTERNATIONAL EXTRADITION IN U.S. LAW AND PRACTICE, Chp. 2 (3d rev. ed. 1996); Chapter Five. Nevertheless, states may also cooperate in penal matters on the basis of reciprocity or comity.

Notes and Questions

1. In *United States v. Arjona*, 120 U.S. 479, 487–88 (1887), the Supreme Court declared: "A right secured by the law of nations to a nation, or its people, is one the United

States as the representatives of this nation are bound to protect ... if the thing made punishable ... [by Congress] is one which the United States are required by their international obligations to use due diligence to prevent, it is an offence against the law of nations." Do you agree, is the definition too broad?

2. Is the following definition of international crimes sufficient or too limited?

"An international offense is conduct internationally proscribed for which there is an international duty for states to criminalize the said conduct, prosecute or extradite and eventually punish the transgressor, and to cooperate internationally for the effective implementation of these purposes and duties."

M.C. Bassiouni, A Draft International Criminal Code and Draft Statute for an International Criminal Tribunal 55 (1987).

His study notes that not each duty or purpose is specified in a relevant international instrument and that the phrases "international crime" or "crime under international law" appear in only 27 of 312 international instruments analyzed (*id.* at 35), but that there are ten types of "penal characteristics" evidenced in such instruments (which may contain only one, or more, of the characteristics). *Id.* at 25–26, 29. The most prevalent type is "[i]mplicit recognition of the penal nature of the act by establishing a duty to prohibit, prevent, prosecute, punish, or the like." *Id.* at 29.

3. Must an international crime affect the international community? Is it sufficient that an international crime has the potential to affect? Does a minor act of armed robbery at sea off the coast of Vietnam that fits the definition of piracy affect (or have the potential to affect) the international community more than armed robbery of a bank and 100 people inside that is located in London and captured live on CNN?

Indeed, is it sufficient that more generally the international community has demonstrated its concern and has proscribed certain conduct? Can that concern reach single acts within a single state once thought to be essentially domestic affairs? *See also Advisory Opinion on Tunis and Morocco Nationality Decrees,* [1923] P.C.I.J., Ser. B, No. 4., at 24, 30; Myres McDougal, Harold Lasswell & Lung-chu Chen, Human Rights and World Public Order 210–11, 922 n.295 (1980). What drives international law (or law more generally (although even they can be interrelated), effects or *opinio juris*?

4. Should there be a proper subject-matter of international crimes? Should international criminal law be codified? What are the dangers posed by codification? What are the dangers posed by not doing so? Can state elites be trusted with such efforts? Is their participation unavoidable?

5. Does international criminal responsibility apply only to individuals or does it extend to states, other actors, and organizations? What standards of responsibility and guilt should apply, and what sanctions? Is it fair or preferable to levy collective fines or to impose reparations on a people? What additional facts would you like to know?

6. What is the legally enforceable nature of the maxim *aut dedere aut judicare*? Does the duty to initiate prosecution have precedence over that of extradition, or are they coextensive? What unarticulated premises or assumptions exist that may condition such duties? See also Chapter Two, Section 3.

7. A listing of, citation to, and list of signatories to many of the treaties that the U.S. is a signatory to can be found in a U.S. Dep't of State publication, Treaties in Force. Many treaties can also be found in the United Nations Treaty Series (U.N.T.S.) at www.un.org/Depts/overview. Lists of signatories to many human rights treaties can also be found at www.unhchr.ch.

8. One of the dynamic developments in international criminal law is the increasing role of non-governmental organizations (NGOs). Increasingly, groups such as Transparency International, Amnesty International, Human Rights Watch, Global Integrity, and Greenpeace are focusing on both relevant policy and cases. They are networking with law enforcement officials, legislators, and international organizations. They are increasingly conducting investigations of war crimes, and even bringing cases concerning transnational corruption—both to foster change and to educate the public and policy officials. *See, e.g.,* Philippe Bernard, *L'enquête sur les "biens mal acquis" por trois potentats d'Afrique sera rouverte (The inquiry about the "goods wrongfully acquired" by three African leaders is reversed),* Le Monde, Nov. 11, 2010 (discussing criminal cases brought by Transparency International and SHERPA, and the decision on November 9, 2010, whereby the French Supreme Court ruled in favor of the plaintiffs, authorizing a judicial inquiry on the manner in which the assets of three African Presidents and their families were acquired). The role of NGOs is important in the construction of international criminal law enforcement networks. These organizations increasingly provide an opportunity for legal professionals desiring to work in the field of international criminal law.

Section 2
Distinctions between International and Transnational Crimes

As noted above, international crimes are based in international law and are either set forth in international agreements or reflected in customary international law. By contrast, transnational crimes need not be based in international law as such, although both international agreements and custom can be relevant to issues concerning jurisdiction, enforcement, due process, judicial cooperation, the serving of sentences, and the like. Technically, transnational crimes are those with a transnational element. Further, international crimes do not require a transnational element, although often one or more exist. For example, genocide committed by officials against groups of their own people wholly within the territory of one country is an international offense even though no transnational elements exist. The same point can pertain with respect to other international crimes such as other crimes against humanity, slavery, apartheid, terrorism, and other human rights-related crimes.

A conspiracy to rob a bank in Canada may have transnational elements, such as the existence of co-conspirators and preparation in the United States, whereas final execution of the conspiracy occurs in Canada. Bank robbery as such, however, is not normally more than a domestic offense (*i.e.,* it is merely an offense against the laws of a country). Yet, there may be transnational aspects with respect to particular infractions and even violations of the domestic laws of two or more states. With increasing ease of travel and communication, it is likely that adequate enforcement of domestic criminal laws will increasingly involve attention to transnational aspects of law enforcement. As materials in this book demonstrate, there are many such aspects, and legal problems and solutions are often interrelated with international criminal law enforcement.

Another form of interconnection has involved the domestic prosecution of international crimes under domestic laws. At times, domestic legislation refers to the international crime, mirrors the elements of the international offense, or even incorporates international law by reference (see Chapter Four, Section 3). It may happen, however, that domestic prosecutors prefer to use more ordinary domestic legislation (such as a prohibition of murder, battery, or rape) to prosecute what is also an infraction of international law. In any event, one should not confuse domestic offenses as such with international crimes, however transnational in purpose or effect either set of infractions might be in a given circumstance.

Notes and Questions

1. Professor Bassiouni claims that international crimes will either have a "transnational" element (*e.g.,* a foreign perpetrator or victim or transnational acts or effects) or one of two "international" elements: (1) "a threat to the peace and security of mankind" or "a significant international interest", or (2) "shocking" or "egregious" conduct tested by "commonly shared values of the world community". M.C. Bassiouni, A Draft International Criminal Code and Draft Statute for an International Criminal Tribunal 36, 45 (1987). Thus, he does not argue that every international crime must involve a threat to peace and security or "egregious" conduct, or that each must involve a "transnational" element. Is the only necessary criterion, then, that there be an "international interest"? Is there any potential limit of such interests? Notice how international criminal law endeavors to effectuate a partition between national and international jurisdiction, just as U.S. constitutional law does so in terms of state and federal jurisdiction over criminal activity. Does the repartition of competencies between national and international jurisdictions have a constitutional basis in international law? If so, what would the source of that international "constitution" or *grundnorm* be? *See* Leila Nadya Sadat, *Exile, Amnesty, and International Law*, 81 Notre Dame L. Rev. 955 (2006); see also Bardo Fassbender, *The United Nations Charter As Constitution of the International Community*, 36 Colum. J. Transnat'l L. 529 (1998).

2. Nonetheless, some have argued that an international crime must be more egregious in character or effect than a domestic infraction as such. Do you suspect that this might be so? Why? Yet, is piracy necessarily egregious or heinous, or more so than a domestic counterpart? Is the counterfeiting of foreign currency, violation of passports, rape during war as opposed to rape in other contexts, pillage of property (a war crime in the context of an armed conflict), theft of archaeologic treasures, every aircraft hijacking, acts of mercenarism, or participation in a breach of neutrality (*see, e.g., Henfield's Case,* in Chapter Four, Section 2)?

Others might suggest that international crimes must be systematic or widespread, but this would not be correct. For example, one act of pillaging or one misuse of a Red Cross flag during war, one act of piracy, one act of slave trading, one act of mercenarism, one relevant violation of passports, one assassination of a diplomat, one act of genocide, or one act of hostage-taking is sufficient. It may be dangerous to generalize concerning all international infractions, although identification of common features, and differences, may be useful as you proceed through the following chapters.

Role-Playing Problem Concerning an Amnesty Agreement

Assume that it is June, 2010. The de facto military leaders of Surelica, Raoul Pedras and Philippe Bimbo (to be role-played by _____) are meeting at Governors Island New York with the leaders of the exiled democratically elected Government, Jean-Betrand Ariola and Roberto Maldonado (to be roll-played by _____). The goal of the meeting is to try to work out a peace agreement whereby the military leaders will step down and allow the democratically elected government of President Ariola to return to power. Acting as mediators at this meeting are Dante Caputo of the U.N. and Lawrence Pezzullo of the U.S. (to be roll-played by _____). The key sticking point in the negotiations is the question of amnesty for members of the Surelican military regime who allegedly engaged in assassination, torture, and other acts in violation of international law against local and foreign persons in Surelica.

Those assigned this problem should read the extract from Professor Sadat and Professor Scharf's articles, below, as well as Chapter Two, Section 3, at this time. Also consider the following questions: (a) What is likely to be each side's opening position on the question of amnesty? (b) What legal and policy rationales support these positions? Consider also U.N. Charter, preamble and arts. 2, 55(c) and 56 (in the Documents Supplement), (c) What compromises might be possible? (d) What are the legal and policy obstacles to such compromises? (e) Are such compromises desirable? (f) What inducements might be used by the U.N. or the U.S. to help the sides reach an agreement? (g) Are these desirable? Note that domestic amnesties or pardons are not binding on other states or nations.

More generally, is peace over time likely without justice or accountability? What consequences might occur if there is no justice or accountability, might social tensions be exacerbated and social violence erupt? Will leaders who order or commit numerous acts of murder and torture be reluctant to continue doing so? Does amnesty or "safe-haven" status encourage retributive assassination or transborder criminalnapping? What effects might occur with respect to international criminal law? For example, if relevant multilateral treaties with numerous signatories, such as the Convention Against Torture, require signatory states to initiate prosecution or to extradite those reasonably accused of crimes covered by the treaties, will amnesty agreements in violation of such duties have unwanted impacts on the sanctity of treaties, on international criminal law, and overall peace and security—much less justice and accountability? Should the U.S. participate in such a process? Should the U.N.? Does the U.N. Security Council have a special overriding power? See U.N. Charter, arts. 24(2), 25, 39–42, 48, 103. After setting up the ICTY and ICTR and with the creation of the ICC, would Security Council-backed amnesty agreements have adverse consequences? Given such developments, will amnesty agreements be "bumps along the road" to the ICC?

Leila Nadya Sadat, *Exile, Amnesty, and International Law*
81 Notre Dame L. Rev. 955, 958–970 (2006)*

Recently, it seemed as if exile and amnesty had become fashionable again. Before the U.S. invasion of Iraq, Saddam Hussein was offered the opportunity to leave Iraq to save his country. Donald Rumsfeld, U.S. Secretary of Defense, suggested that the "senior leadership" in Iraq and their families should be afforded safe haven in some other country to avoid the prospect of war. Later that year, Charles Taylor, President of Liberia, was convinced to accept exile in Nigeria. Shortly thereafter, Haiti's President Jean Bertrand Aristide was deposed and took up residence in South Africa.

Exile can of course be tantamount to imprisonment for those obliged to endure it. Napoleon was sent by the British to St. Helena (after escaping his first offshore prison at Elba), where he lived in considerably reduced circumstances and ultimately perished, apparently poisoned by arsenic in the wallpaper of his chamber. Indeed, banishment was a

* Reprinted with permission. © *Notre Dame Law Review*, University of Notre Dame. We bear responsibility for any errors in reprinting and editing.

significant punishment in a world without satellite television, internet access, cellular telephones or even regular mail service, and where travel to and from remote locations was infrequent (or nonexistent) and often dangerous. Modern exile, however, is considerably more pleasant. Although banished from kin and country, today's exiles often bring with them generous bank accounts and retire to live with a small retinue somewhere peaceful, and often quite attractive. Ferdinand Marcos found a haven in Hawaii; Haiti's "Baby Doc" Duvalier fled to the south of France; Ethiopia's Mengistu Haile Miriam sought refuge in Zimbabwe; and Uganda's Idi Amin recently died after many years living peaceably in Saudi Arabia.

During the second half of the twentieth century, offering exile or amnesty to individuals accused of human rights atrocities collided with the erection of a new system of international criminal justice. While exile might still be an option for individuals accused of general venality—tax fraud, corruption, or embezzlement—the notion of allowing the perpetrators of human rights atrocities to go unpunished appears to have become normatively unacceptable. Fueled by the horrors of the Second World War, inspired by the relative success of the Nuremberg trials and nourished by the aspirations of democratization and the new rhetoric of international human rights that followed the establishment of the United Nations, the "impunity" paradigm came to be replaced by calls for accountability and a demand for the investigation and criminal prosecution of those who ordered or committed human rights atrocities. Indeed, requiring accountability for past crimes has been posited by both scholars and practitioners as a remedy to impunity, as well as a necessary, if not sufficient, predicate for the reestablishment of peace. Accordingly, the establishment of the International Criminal Tribunals for Rwanda (ICTR) and the Former Yugoslavia (ICTY), the Special Court for Sierra Leone (SCSL), and the Special War Crimes Panels for East Timor was conceived of by the international community, and perhaps particularly by the United States, as a means (although not the means) to reestablish peace and stability, foster a transition to democratic principles of government, and establish general principles of international law to deter future atrocities. The negotiation and establishment of the International Criminal Court (ICC) treaty in 1998 drew heavily from this emerging practice, and seemed to offer the imprimatur of permanence to a then experimental concept.

Yet, even as the ad hoc tribunals have continued their work and the International Criminal Court has commenced its activities, many challenges to international criminal accountability remain. Some are practical in nature: the desire to trade peace for justice in order to end a conflict more quickly, even if temporarily; the overwhelming task of bringing cases against hundreds or even thousands of individuals implicated in the commission of genocide or other mass atrocities; and even the passage of time, which may cause authorities to hesitate in pursuing justice or extinguish otherwise valid cases through the application of statutes of limitations. Others question the entire international criminal justice endeavor itself, arguing that criminal trials may be counterproductive in fostering reconciliation, or that justice, to be effective, must be local, rather than international, in character. Finally, the fledgling international justice system has encountered political and ideological objections from those concerned with its constraint of state power. The U.S. objections to the International Criminal Court fall into this category, predicated as they are on the argument that international norms on accountability (particularly as embodied in the International Criminal Court Treaty) are problematic insofar as they might affect the conduct of U.S. foreign affairs, or impinge upon U.S. citizens' ability to travel abroad with impunity.

These challenges notwithstanding, there is substantial countervailing evidence that the notion of accountability has gained considerable traction in international and domestic state practice, as this Article makes clear. The SCSL Appeals Chamber ruled, for example, in 2004 that the Lomé Accord, which granted amnesty to the perpetrators of crimes committed during the conflict in Sierra Leone, could not deprive the SCSL of jurisdiction given that the crimes within the SCSL's statute were crimes subject to universal jurisdiction. Similarly, the amnesties granted in Chile during Pinochet's regime and in Argentina during Argentina's "dirty war" have been recently set aside, both by courts and legislatures in those countries, as well as by courts asked to consider them abroad. Even governments advocating exile initially, such as the Bush administration's offer to Saddam Hussein, have subsequently sought accountability in the form of criminal trials or other redress. Most recently, the Sudanese government, many of whose members have been accused of serious crimes under international law, has not argued that accountability is a poor idea; instead, the government has argued that it should be able to bring prosecutions itself, rather than having the Darfur situation referred to the International Criminal Court.

Although other courts have issued opinions relevant to the present inquiry, the cluster of recent cases arising out of the Latin American experience, combined with new decisions from international courts, offer an extraordinary example of transnational legal process in which municipal and international courts have engaged in a dialogue of international norm creation. These opinions suggest that amnesties are not only increasingly unacceptable as a matter of law, but particularly as regards top-level perpetrators, may be socially and politically unacceptable as well....

[T]his Article challenges the conventional wisdom that "swapping justice for peace" is morally and practically acceptable. Instead, I argue that international negotiators offering exile are neither morally nor legally justified in doing so. Indeed, although it is beguiling to imagine that offering exile to Saddam Hussein would save thousands of lives, or that the Lord's Resistance Army of Uganda would have laid down its weapons in return for automatic immunity, the evidence suggests the contrary: that warlords and political leaders capable of committing human rights atrocities are not deterred by the amnesties obtained, but emboldened. As will be discussed below, the cases of Sierra Leone, the Former Yugoslavia, and Haiti suggest that amnesties for top-level perpetrators imposed from above or negotiated at gunpoint do not lead to the establishment of peace— but at best create a temporary lull in the fighting. Indeed, amnesty deals typically foster a culture of impunity in which violence becomes the norm, rather than the exception.

.... [The question here addresses only] the problem of amnesties for the commission of jus cogens crimes—crimes covered by peremptory norms of international law—which may not be set aside by conflicting municipal laws. This is why the question of amnesties is problematic, especially before international courts.... [T]he legal effect of any particular grant of amnesty or exile will be determined, in part, by the forum before which the amnesty is invoked. In particular, the treatment of amnesties before international courts and tribunals is quite different than their effect before domestic or municipal courts.... .[C]ourts have correctly recognized (even if not explicitly) that an adjudication of international crimes before an international court involves the direct exercise of universal international jurisdiction, and is not the same as a domestic court's exercise of universal inter-state jurisdiction. This transformation was most clearly present in the quasi-revolutionary jurisdictional referral mechanisms present in the ICC Statute, which allow the Security Council to apply, in a manner unbounded by geography and state sovereignty, the substantive criminal law in the Court's Statute. The same idea was recognized by the ICJ in the Yerodia case, by the ICTY in the Furundzija case, and most recently by the Special Court for Sierra Leone. All three opinions recognized the impossibility of effectively invoking an immunity created by national law before an international tribunal.

> [One must] ... distinguish between "domestic" (granted as a matter of municipal law by the territorial state) and "transnational" amnesties (generally de facto amnesty received by individuals upon the condition that they leave the territorial state and take up residence elsewhere). In each case, the question raised is whether a particular amnesty is effective in the territorial state (where the offenses were committed), in a custodial state (where the "accused" may be found), or before an international court or tribunal. While both theory and practice dovetail nicely on the consideration of domestic and transnational amnesties before both state and international courts, the question whether the international community itself, whether by treaty or an act of the Security Council, may amnesty crimes so that even the territorial state is deprived of jurisdiction is a very difficult one.... This question has become of particular importance given the recent practice of the Security Council in exempting U.S. nationals, in particular, from the jurisdiction of the International Criminal Court, as well as the territorial jurisdiction of states receiving U.N. missions.
>
> With regard to domestic amnesties, although effective in the state where granted, their effectiveness clearly diminishes with time. As regards a custodial state ... courts in that jurisdiction should treat the amnesty as presumptively invalid; a presumption that can be overcome if the state granting the amnesty in question did so pursuant to a process that did not undermine the quest for accountability as a whole. The same is true in reverse for transnational amnesties, which have no effect in the territorial state, but may at least temporarily protect an accused so long as he remains in exile. Any third state, however, would not be bound by the grant of asylum in the state of exile. Drawing from both U.S. and European practice, [one can ask] ... whether international law needs an Erie doctrine, or at least some manner of systematically addressing the treatment of international law in municipal courts.

Notes

1. In Prosecutor v. Kallon & Kamara, Case Nos. SCSL-2004-15-AR72(E), SCSL-2004-16-AR72(E), Decision on Challenge to Jurisdiction: Lomé Accord Amnesty, ¶ 67 (Mar. 13, 2004), the Special Court for Sierra Leone stated,

> Where jurisdiction is universal, a State cannot deprive another State of its jurisdiction to prosecute the offender by the grant of amnesty. It is for this reason unrealistic to regard as universally effective the grant of amnesty by a State in regard to grave international crimes in which there exists universal jurisdiction. A State cannot bring into oblivion and forgetfulness a crime, such as a crime against international law, which other States are entitled to keep alive and remember.

2. Several national and international criminal tribunals have dealt with these questions of amnesty. See Prosecutor v. Kallon & Kamara, *supra* note 1; Prosecutor v. Furundzija, Case No. IT-95-17/1-T, Judgment (Dec. 10, 1998); Arrest Warrant of 11 April 2000 (Dem. Rep. Congo v. Belg.), 2002 I.C.J. 1 (Feb. 14). The SCSL reaffirmed Kallon and Kamara a few months later in Prosecutor v. Kondewa, Case No. SCSL-2004-14-AR72(G), Decision on Lack of Jurisdiction/Abuse of Process: Amnesty Provided by the Lome Accord (May 25, 2004). In Latin America, the Supreme Court of Argentina held that Argentina's amnesty laws were unconstitutional because they prevented Argentina from complying with obligations under international treaties, as regards *jus cogens* norms against forced

disappearances, Supreme Court of Argentina: Case of Julio Hector Simon, Int'l L. Brief, June 28, 2005, (discussing Corte Suprema de Justicia [CSJN], 14/6/2005, "In re Simon, Julio Hector / recurso de hecho," No. 17.768 (Arg.), available at http://www.clarin.com/diario/2005/06/14/um/fallopuntofinal.doc), and that crimes against humanity, including genocide, torture, execution and forced disappearances, are not subject to any statute of limitations due to their status as serious crimes under international law. Supreme Court of Argentina: Judgment in the Case of Enrique Lautaro Arancibia Clavel Confirming the Non-Applicability of Statutory Limitations to Crimes Against Humanity, Int'l L. Brief, Aug. 31, 2004, (discussing Corte Suprema de Justicia [CSJN], 24/8/2004, "In re Clavel, Enrique Lautaro / recurso de hecho," No. 259 (Arg.), available at http://www.derechos.org/nizkor/arg/doc/arancibia1.html). Similarly, courts in Chile have sidestepped Pinochet's self-granted amnesty, permitting Pinochet and others to be indicted and, in the case of some individuals, convicted of crimes committed during the Pinochet regime. *See generally* Naomi Roht-Arriaza, The Pinochet Effect: Transnational Justice in the Age of Human Rights 81 (2005).

3. The Ugandan government enacted the Ugandan Amnesty Act in 2000, providing amnesty from prosecution—including for war crimes—to members of the Lord's Resistance Army. The amnesty act resulted in the pardoning of 13,000 members of the LRA before it expired in May 2012. Nonetheless, the situation in Uganda was still so bad that the Ugandan government asked the International Criminal Court Prosecutor to open an investigation into the commission of atrocities there in 2004. Warrants were issued several alleged leaders of the LRA. None of the warrants have yet been executed, leading some to question if the Ugandan Amnesty might affect ICC prosecutions. See Manisuli Ssenyonjo, Accountability of *Non-State Actors in Uganda for War Crimes and Human Rights Violations: Between Amnesty and the International Criminal Court*, 10 J. Conflict Security L. 405 (2005).

Michael P. Scharf, *From the eXile Files: An Essay on Trading Justice for Peace*
63 Wash. & Lee L. Rev. 339, 342–349 (2006)

A. Interests Favoring Exile, Asylum, and Amnesty

Notwithstanding the popular catch phrase of the 1990s—"no peace without justice"—achieving peace and obtaining justice are sometimes incompatible goals—at least in the short term. In order to end an international or internal conflict, negotiations often must be held with the very leaders who are responsible for war crimes and crimes against humanity. When this is the case, insisting on criminal prosecutions can prolong the conflict, resulting in more deaths, destruction, and human suffering.

Reflecting this reality, during the past thirty years, Angola, Argentina, Brazil, Cambodia, Chile, El Salvador, Guatemala, Haiti, Honduras, Ivory Coast, Nicaragua, Peru, Sierra Leone, South Africa, Togo, and Uruguay have each, as part of a peace arrangement, granted amnesty to members of the former regime that committed international crimes within their respective borders.[1] With respect to five of these countries—Cambodia,

---

1. *See* Steven Ratner, *New Democracies, Old Atrocities: An Inquiry in International Law*, 87 Geo. L.J. 707, 722–23 (1999) (mentioning the governments in transitional democracies that have passed amnesty laws); Roht-Arriaza, *supra* note 8, at 461 (noting grants of amnesty in Argentina, Chile, Uruguay, Guatemala, and El Salvador); Michael P. Scharf, *The Letter of the Law: The Scope of the International Legal Obligation to Prosecute Human Rights Crimes*, 59 Law & Contemp. Probs. 41, 41 (1996) (discussing these countries' amnesty programs).

El Salvador, Haiti, Sierra Leone, and South Africa — "the United Nations itself pushed for, helped negotiate, or endorsed the granting of amnesty as a means of restoring peace and democratic government."

In addition to amnesty (which immunizes the perpetrator from domestic prosecution), exile and asylum in a foreign country (which puts the perpetrator out of the jurisdictional reach of domestic prosecution)[2] is often used to induce regime change, with the blessing and involvement of significant states and the United Nations. Peace negotiators call this the "Napoleonic Option," in reference to the treatment of French emperor Napoleon Bonaparte who, after his defeat at Waterloo in 1815, was exiled to St. Helena rather than face trial or execution. More recently, a number of dictators have been granted sanctuary abroad in return for relinquishing power. Thus, for example, Ferdinand Marcos fled the Philippines for Hawaii; Baby Doc Duvalier fled Haiti for France; Mengisthu Haile Miriam fled Ethiopia for Zimbabwe; Idi Amin fled Uganda for Saudi Arabia; General Raoul Cedras fled Haiti for Panama; and Charles Taylor fled Liberia for exile in Nigeria — a deal negotiated by the United States and U.N. envoy Jacques Klein.

As Payam Akhavan, then Legal Adviser to the Office of the Prosecutor of the International Criminal Tribunal for the Former Yugoslavia, observed a decade ago: "[I]t is not unusual in the political stage to see the metamorphosis of yesterday's war monger into today's peace broker."[3] This is because, unless the international community is willing to use force to topple a rogue regime, cooperation of the leaders is needed to bring about peaceful regime change and put an end to violations of international humanitarian law. Yet, it is not realistic to expect them to agree to a peace settlement if, directly following the agreement, they would find themselves or their close associates facing potential life imprisonment.

This conclusion finds support in the observations of the 2004 Report of the International Truth and Reconciliation Commission for Sierra Leone:

> The Commission is unable to condemn the resort to amnesty by those who negotiated the Lomé Peace Agreement [which provides amnesty to persons who committed crimes against humanity in Sierra Leone]. The explanations given by the Government negotiators, including in their testimonies before the Truth and Reconciliation Commission, are compelling in this respect. In all good faith, they believed that the RUF [insurgents] would not agree to end hostilities if the Agreement were not accompanied by a form of pardon or amnesty....

> The Commission is unable to declare that it considers amnesty too high a price to pay for the delivery of peace to Sierra Leone, under the circumstances that prevailed in July 1999. It is true that the Lomé Agreement did not immediately return the country to peacetime. Yet it provided the framework for a process that pacified the combatants and, five years later, has returned Sierra Leoneans to a context in which they need not fear daily violence and atrocity.

---

2. In cases of exile, the state where the offense occurred (the territorial state) cannot commence proceedings as it does not have physical custody over the accused, and the sanctuary state is generally prevented from prosecuting or extraditing by the doctrine of head of state immunity. *See, e.g.,* Regina v. Bow St. Metro. Stipendiary Magistrate, *ex parte* Pinochet Ugarte (No. 3), [2000] 1 A.C. 147, 242 (H.L. 1999) (U.K.) (noting that the doctrine "protects all acts which the head of state has performed in the exercise of the functions of government").

3. Payam Akhavan, *The Yugoslav Tribunal at a Crossroads: The Dayton Peace Agreement and Beyond,* 18 Hum. Rts. Q. 259, 271 (1996).

In brokering the Charles Taylor exile deal, the United States and United Nations were particularly encouraged by the success of similar amnesty/exile for peace arrangements relating to Haiti and South Africa in the 1990s. From 1990-1994, Haiti was ruled by a military regime headed by General Raol Cedras and Brigadier General Philippe Biamby, which executed over 3000 civilian political opponents and tortured scores of others. The United Nations mediated negotiations at Governors Island in New York Harbor, in which the military leaders agreed to relinquish power and permit the return of the democratically elected President (Jean-Bertrand Aristide) in return for a full amnesty for the members of the regime and a lifting of the economic sanctions imposed by the U.N. Security Council[5]. Under pressure from the United Nations mediators, Aristide agreed to the amnesty clause of the Governors Island Agreement[6]. The Security Council immediately "declared [its] readiness to give the fullest possible support to the Agreement signed on Governors Island,"[7] which it later said constitutes "the only valid framework for the resolution of the crisis in Haiti."[8] When the military leaders initially failed to comply with the Governors Island Agreement, on July 31, 1994, the Security Council took the extreme step of authorizing an invasion of Haiti by a multinational force[9]. On the eve of the invasion on September 18, 1994, a deal was struck, whereby General Cedras agreed to retire his command and accept exile in response to a general amnesty voted into law by the Haitian parliament and an offer by Panama to provide him asylum.[10]

The amnesty deal had its desired effect: The democratically elected Aristide was permitted to return to Haiti and reinstate a civilian government, the military leaders left the country for sanctuary in Panama, much of the military surrendered their arms, and most of the human rights abuses promptly ended—all with practically no bloodshed or resistance. Although the situation in Haiti has once again deteriorated, with a wave of violent protests and strikes erupting in 2004, the more recent problems were due largely to President Aristide's mismanagement and corruption, not the fact that the military leaders escaped punishment ten years earlier.

South Africa stands as another success story, indicating the potential value of trading justice for peace. From 1960 to 1994, thousands of black South Africans were persecuted and mistreated under that country's apartheid system. With the prospect of a bloody civil war looming over negotiations, "[t]he outgoing leaders made some form of amnesty for

---

5. *See* The Secretary-General, *The Situation of Democracy and Human Rights in Haiti*, U.N. Doc. S/26063, A/47/975 (July 12, 1993) (reproducing the text of the Governors Island Agreement). The Governors Island Agreement was supplemented by a document known as the New York Pact, which was signed by the two sides on July 16, 1993. Paragraph 4 of the New York Pact provides that "[t]he political forces and parliamentary blocs undertake to ensure that the following laws are passed, on the bases of an emergency procedure: … (ii) Act concerning the amnesty." The Secretary-General, *The Situation of Democracy and Human Rights in Haiti* annex, ¶ 4, U.N. Doc. S/26297, A/47/1000 (Aug. 13, 1993).

6. *See* Irwin P. Stotzky, *Haiti: Searching for Alternatives*, *in* IMPUNITY AND HUMAN RIGHTS IN INTERNATIONAL LAW AND PRACTICE 188 (Naomi Roht-Arriaza ed., 1995) (describing Aristide's opposition to granting amnesty to "common criminals" and his ultimate capitulation in the face of tremendous pressure). Professor Stotzky of the University of Miami School of Law served as Aristide's legal adviser while Aristide was in exile in the United States.

7. Letter from the President of the Security Council to the Secretary-General, U.N. SCOR, 48th Sess. at 120, U.N. Doc. S/INF/49 (July 15, 1993).

8. Statement of the President of the Security Council, U.N. SCOR, 48th Sess., 3298th mtg. at 126, U.N. Doc. S/INF/49 (Oct. 25, 1993).

9. S.C. Res. 940, ¶ 4, U.N. Doc. S/RES/940 (July 31, 1994).

10. *Haitian Lawmakers Pass Partial Amnesty to Pressure Cedras*, COMM. APPEAL (Memphis), Oct. 8, 1994, at A1.

those responsible for the regime a condition for the peaceful transfer to a fully democratic society."[11] The leaders of the majority black population decided that the commitment to afford amnesty was a fair price for a relatively peaceful transition to full democracy[12]. In accordance with the negotiated settlement between the major parties, on July 19, 1995, the South African Parliament created a Truth and Reconciliation Commission, consisting of a Committee on Human Rights Violations, a Committee on Amnesty, and a Committee on Reparation and Rehabilitation[13]. Under this process, amnesty would be available only to individuals who personally applied for it and who disclosed fully the facts of their apartheid crimes. After conducting 140 public hearings and considering 20,000 written and oral submissions, the South African Truth Commission published a 2739-page report of its findings on October 29, 1998[14]. Most observers believe the amnesty in South Africa headed off increasing tensions and a potential civil war.

It is a common misconception that trading amnesty or exile for peace is equivalent to the absence of accountability and redress[15]. As in the Haitian and South African situations described above, amnesties can be tied to accountability mechanisms that are less invasive than domestic or international prosecution. Ever more frequently in the aftermath of an amnesty- or exile-for-peace deal, the concerned governments have made monetary reparations to the victims and their families, established truth commissions to document the abuses (and sometimes identify perpetrators by name), and have instituted employment bans and purges (referred to as "lustration") that keep such perpetrators from positions of public trust[16]. While not the same as criminal prosecution, these mechanisms do encompass much of what justice is intended to accomplish: prevention, deterrence, punishment, and rehabilitation. Indeed, some experts believe that these mechanisms do not just constitute "a second best approach" when prosecution is impracticable, but that in many situations they may be better suited to achieving the aims of justice.[17]

B. Factors Favoring Prosecution

Although providing amnesty and exile to perpetrators may be an effective way to induce regime change without having to resort to force, there are several important countervailing considerations favoring prosecution that suggest amnesty/exile should be a bargaining tool of last resort reserved only for extreme situations. In particular, prosecuting leaders responsible for violations of international humanitarian law is necessary to discourage future human rights abuses, deter vigilante justice, and reinforce respect for law and the new democratic government.

While prosecutions might initially provoke resistance, many analysts believe that national reconciliation cannot take place as long as justice is foreclosed. As Professor Cherif Bassiouni, then Chairman of the U.N. Investigative Commission for Yugoslavia, stated in

---

11. MARTHA MINOW, BETWEEN VENGEANCE AND FORGIVENESS 52 (1998).

12. *Id.* at 55.

13. National Unity and Reconciliation Act 34 of 1995 §§ 2, 12, 16 & 23.

14. The text of the South African Truth Commission's Report is available on the Internet at www.info.gov.za/otherdocs/2003/trc.

15. *See* William W. Burke-White, *Reframing Impunity: Applying Liberal International Law Theory to an Analysis of Amnesty Legislation*, 42 HARV. INT'L L.J. 467, 482 (2001) (classifying amnesties into four categories, from least to most legitimate: (1) "Blanket Amnesties"; (2) "Locally Legitimized, Partial Immunities"; (3) "Internationally Legitimized, Partial Immunities"; and (4) "Constitutional Immunity").

16. NAOMI ROHT-ARRIAZA, IMPUNITY AND HUMAN RIGHTS IN INTERNATIONAL LAW AND PRACTICE 282–91(1995).

17. *See* MINOW, *supra*, at 9 (contending that prosecutions "are slow, partial, and narrow").

1996, "[i]f peace is not intended to be a brief interlude between conflicts," then it must be accompanied by justice.[18]

Failure to prosecute leaders responsible for human rights abuses breeds contempt for the law and encourages future violations. The U.N. Commission on Human Rights and its Sub-Commission on Prevention of Discrimination and Protection of Minorities have concluded that impunity is one of the main reasons for the continuation of grave violations of human rights throughout the world[19]. Fact finding reports on Chile and El Salvador indicate that the granting of amnesty or de facto impunity has led to an increase in abuses in those countries.[20]

Further, history teaches that former leaders given amnesty or exile are prone to recidivism, resorting to corruption and violence and becoming a disruptive influence on the peace process. From his seaside villa in Calabar, Nigeria, for example, Charles Taylor orchestrated a failed assassination plot in 2005 against President Lansana Conte of Guinea, a neighboring country that had backed the rebel movement that forced Taylor from power.[21]

What a new or reinstated democracy needs most is legitimacy, which requires a fair, credible, and transparent account of what took place and who was responsible. Criminal trials (especially those involving proof of widespread and systematic abuses) can generate a comprehensive record of the nature and extent of violations, how they were planned and executed, the fate of individual victims, who gave the orders, and who carried them out. While there are various means to develop the historic record of such abuses, the most authoritative rendering of the truth is possible only through the crucible of a trial that accords full due process. Supreme Court Justice Robert Jackson, the Chief Prosecutor at Nuremberg, underscored the logic of this proposition when he reported that the most important legacy of the Nuremberg trials was the documentation of Nazi atrocities "with such authenticity and in such detail that there can be no responsible denial of these crimes in the future."[22] According to Jackson, the establishment of an authoritative record of abuses that would endure the test of time and withstand the challenge of revisionism required proof of "incredible events by credible evidence."[23]

In addition to truth, there is a responsibility to provide justice. While a state may appropriately forgive crimes against itself, such as treason or sedition, serious crimes against persons, such as rape and murder, are an altogether different matter. Holding the viola-

---

18. M. Cherif Bassiouni, *Searching for Peace and Achieving Justice: The Need for Accountability,* 59 Law & Contemp. Probs. 9, 13 (1996).

19. U.N. Econ. & Soc. Council [ECOSOC], Comm'n on Human Rights, Working Group on Enforced or Involuntary Disappearances, *Report on the Consequences of Impunity,* ¶ 344, U.N. Doc. E/CN.4/1990/13 (Jan. 24, 1990), *reprinted in* 3 Transitional Justice: How Emerging Democracies Reckon with Former Regimes 18, 19 (N. Kritz ed., 1995).

20. U.N. Econ. & Soc. Council [ECOSOC], *Protection of Human Rights in Chile,* ¶ 341, U.N. Doc. A/38/385 (Oct. 17, 1983).

21. *See* Lizza, *supra* note 6, at 10 (citing an intelligence report prepared by investigators for the Special Court for Sierra Leone). In response, the U.N. Security Council adopted Resolution 1532, which required all states to freeze Charles Taylor's assets in order to prevent him from further engaging "in activities that undermine peace and stability in Liberia and the region." S.C. Res. 1532, pmbl., U.N. Doc. S/RES/1532 (Mar. 12, 2004).

22. Report from Justice Robert H. Jackson, Chief of Counsel for the United States in the Prosecution of Axis War Criminals, to the President (Oct. 7, 1946), *in* 20 Temple L.Q. 338, 343 (1946).

23. Report from Justice Robert H. Jackson, Chief of Counsel for the United States in the Prosecution of Axis War Criminals, to the President (June 7, 1945), *in* 39 Am. J. Int'l L. 178, 184 (Supp. 1945).

tors accountable for their acts is a moral duty owed to the victims and their families. Prosecuting and punishing the violators would give significance to the victims' suffering and serve as a partial remedy for their injuries. Moreover, prosecutions help restore victims' dignity and prevent private acts of revenge by those who, in the absence of justice, would take it into their own hands.[24]

While prosecution and punishment can reinforce the value of law by displacing personal revenge, failure to punish former leaders responsible for widespread human rights abuses encourages cynicism about the rule of law and distrust toward the political system. To the victims of human rights crimes, amnesty or exile represents the ultimate in hypocrisy: While they struggle to put their suffering behind them, those responsible are allowed to enjoy a comfortable retirement. When those with power are seen to be above the law, the ordinary citizen will never come to believe in the principle of the rule of law as a fundamental necessity in a society transitioning to democracy.

Finally, where the United Nations or major countries give their imprimatur to an amnesty or exile deal, there is a risk that leaders in other parts of the world will be encouraged to engage in gross abuses. For example, history records that the international amnesty given to the Turkish officials responsible for the massacre of over one million Armenians during World War I encouraged Adolf Hitler some twenty years later to conclude that Germany could pursue his genocidal policies with impunity. In a 1939 speech to his reluctant General Staff, Hitler remarked, "Who after all is today speaking about the destruction of the Armenians?"[25] Richard Goldstone, the former Prosecutor of the International Criminal Tribunal for the former Yugoslavia, has concluded that "the failure of the international community to prosecute Pol Pot, Idi Amin, Saddam Hussein and Mohammed Aidid, among others, encouraged the Serbs to launch their policy of ethnic cleansing in the former Yugoslavia with the expectation that they would not be held accountable for their international crimes."[26] When the international community encourages or endorses an amnesty or exile deal, it sends a signal to other rogue regimes that they have nothing to lose by instituting repressive measures; if things start going badly, they can always bargain away their responsibility for crimes by agreeing to peace.

Notes and Questions

1. Can you identify other interests or policies at stake? Do amnesties tend to encourage leaders to commit international crimes?

2. Note that under Article 53(2)(c) of the Statute of the International Criminal Court (ICC) the Prosecutor can decide that "[a] prosecution is not in the interests of justice," although this type of decision is subject to review by the Pre-Trial Chamber of the ICC. See *id*. art. 53(3)(b). How does this prosecutorial discretion relate to the object and purpose of the treaty evident in the preamble in phrases such as: "[a]ffirming that the most serious crimes of concern to the international community as a whole must not go unpunished and that their effective prosecution must be ensured" and "[d]etermined to put

---

24. Haitian citizens, for example, have committed acts of violence against the former members of the brutal military regime who were given amnesty for their abuses. Gary Borg, *Former Haitian General is Gunned Down in Street*, Chi. Trib., Oct. 4, 1995, at 4.

25. Adolf Hitler, Speech to Chief Commanders and Commanding Generals (Aug. 22, 1939), *quoted in* M. Cherif Bassiouni, Crimes Against Humanity in International Criminal Law 176 n.96 (1992).

26. Michael Scharf, *The Case for a Permanent International Truth Commission*, 7 Duke J. Comp. & Int'l L. 375, 398 n.128 (1997).

an end to impunity for the perpetrators of these crimes"? *See also id.* art. 27. Is "justice" possible without accountability?

3. Does the criminal justice system tend to focus on roles and interests of perpetrators and victims as opposed to those of relatively innocent and non-innocent "bystanders"? Consider Laurel E. Fletcher, *From Indifference to Engagement: Bystanders and International Criminal Justice*, 26 MICH. J. INT'L L. 1013 (2005).

4. For further reading, consider: M. CHERIF BASSIOUNI, CRIMES AGAINST HUMANITY IN INTERNATIONAL CRIMINAL LAW 212, 219–24 (1992) ("'Crimes against humanity' is a category of international crimes and as such, a general duty exists to prosecute or extradite. This duty ... has become a *civitas maxima* and a rule of customary international criminal law"); IMPUNITY AND HUMAN RIGHTS IN INTERNATIONAL LAW AND PRACTICE (N. Roht-Arriaza, ed. 1995); M. Cherif Bassiouni, *Searching for Peace and Achieving Justice: The Need for Accountability,* 59 LAW & CONTEMP. PROBS. 9 (1996); Carla Edelenbos, *Human Rights Violations: A Duty to Prosecute?,* 7 LEIDEN J. INT'L L. 5, 15 (1994); Dianne F. Orentlicher, *Settling Accounts: The Duty to Prosecute Human Rights Violations of a Prior Regime,* 100 YALE L.J. 2537 (1991); Naomi Roht-Arriaza, *State Responsibility to Investigate and Prosecute Grave Human Rights Violations in International Law,* 78 CAL. L. REV. 451 (1990); Leila Nadya Sadat, *Exile, Amnesty and International Law,* 81 NOTRE DAME L. REV. 955 (2006) (raising the question whether amnesty deals are violative of international law and/or immoral); Michael P. Scharf, *The Letter of the Law: The Scope of the International Legal Obligation to Prosecute Human Rights Crimes,* 59 LAW & CONTEMP. PROBS. 1 (1996); Michael P. Scharf, *Swapping Amnesty for Peace: Was there a Duty to Prosecute International Crimes in Haiti,* 31 TEX. INT'L L.J. 1 (1996); Elizabeth B. Ludwin King, *Amnesties in A Time of Transition,* 41 GEO. WASH. INT'L L. REV. 577 (2010); Lisa J. Laplante, *Outlawing Amnesty: The Return of Criminal Justice in Transnational Justice Schemes,* 49 VA. J. INT'L L. 915 (2009); Kate Allan, *Prosecution and Peace: A Role for Amnesty Before the ICC?,* 39 DENV. J. INT'L L. & POL'Y 239 (2011).

5. We address this matter again in Chapter Two, Section 3, with respect to the absolute responsibility of states under customary and treaty-based international law to either initiate prosecution of or to extradite those reasonably accused of international crime and the fact that domestic amnesties and pardons are not binding on other states or international entities.

Chapter 2

Individual, State and Other Responsibilities

Section 1
Individual Responsibility

A. Private Individuals, Officials, and Heads of State

1. An Introduction to General Types of Responsibility

Who can be held responsible for violations of international criminal law? Can private individuals commit international crimes? Can public officials, including heads of state and diplomats, be prosecuted? Do leaders have a responsibility to assure compliance with international law by those under their effective control? Can one be prosecuted for complicity or other forms of connection to an international crime primarily committed by others? Are there limits to any such responsibility and related defenses? Does sovereign immunity pertain with respect to international crime? Do domestic laws or superior orders limit individual responsibility or provide excuses for international crime?

Opinion and Judgment of the International Military Tribunal at Nuremberg
(October 1, 1946)

It was submitted that international law is concerned with the actions of sovereign States, and provides no punishment for individuals; and further, that where the act in question is an act of State, those who carry it out are not personally responsible, but are protected by the doctrine of the sovereignty of the State. In the opinion of the Tribunal, both these submissions must be rejected. That international law imposes duties and liabilities upon individuals as well as upon States has long been recognized. In the recent case of *Ex parte Quirin* (1942, 317 U.S. 1), before the Supreme Court of the United States, persons were charged during the war with landing in the United States for purposes of spying and sabotage. The late Chief Justice Stone, speaking for the court, said: "From the very beginning of its history this court has applied the law of war as including that part of the law of nations which prescribes for the conduct of war, the status, rights, and duties of enemy nations as well as enemy individuals."

He went on to give a list of cases tried by the courts, where individual offenders were charged with offences against the laws of nations, and particularly the laws of war. Many other authorities could be cited, but enough has been said to show that individuals can be punished for violations of international law. Crimes against international law are committed by men, not by abstract entities, and only by punishing individuals who commit such crimes can the provisions of international law be enforced.

The provisions of Article 228 of the Treaty of Versailles already referred to illustrate and enforce this view of individual responsibility.

The principle of international law, which under certain circumstances, protects the representatives of a State, cannot be applied to acts which are condemned as criminal by international law. The authors of these acts cannot shelter themselves behind their official position in order to be freed from punishment in appropriate proceedings. Article 7 of the Charter expressly declares: "The official position of defendants, whether as heads of state, or responsible officials in government departments, shall not be considered as freeing them from responsibility, or mitigating punishment."

On the other hand the very essence of the Charter is that individuals have international duties which transcend the national obligations of obedience imposed by the individual State. He who violates the laws of war cannot obtain immunity while acting in pursuance of the authority of the State if the State in authorizing action moves outside its competence under international law.

Principles of the Nuremberg Charter and Judgment

Formulated by the International Law Commission, and adopted by G.A. Res. 177 (II)(a), 5 U.N. GAOR, Supp. No. 12, at 11–14, para. 99, U.N. Doc. A/1316 (1950)

I.   Any person who commits an act which constitutes a crime under international law is responsible therefor and liable to punishment.

II. The fact that internal law does not impose a penalty for an act which constitutes a crime under international law does not relieve the person who committed the act from responsibility under international law.

III. The fact that a person who committed an act which constitutes a crime under international law acted as Head of State or responsible Government official does not relieve him from responsibility under international law....

VII. Complicity in the commission of a crime against peace, a war crime, or a crime against humanity as set forth in Principle VI is a crime under international law.

Report of the Secretary-General Pursuant to Paragraph 2 of Security Council Resolution 808

(1993) paras. 52–59, U.N. Doc. S/25704 (3 May 1993), adopted by the U.N. Security Council in Res. 827 (25 May 1993), establishing the Statute for the International Tribunal for Prosecution of Persons Responsible for Serious Violations of International Humanitarian Law Committed in the Territory of the Former Yugoslavia.

Article 6

Personal jurisdiction

The International Tribunal shall have jurisdiction over natural persons pursuant to the provisions of the present Statute.

Individual criminal responsibility

53. An important element in relation to the competence *ratione personae* (personal jurisdiction) of the International Tribunal is the principle of individual criminal responsibility. As noted above, the Security Council has reaffirmed in a number of resolutions that persons committing serious violations of international humanitarian law in the former Yugoslavia are individually responsible for such violations.

54. The Secretary-General believes that all persons who participate in the planning, preparation or execution of serious violations of international humanitarian law in the former Yugoslavia contribute to the commission of the violation and are, therefore, individually responsible.

55. Virtually all of the written comments received by the Secretary-General have suggested that the statute of the International Tribunal should contain provisions with regard to the individual criminal responsibility of heads of State, government officials and persons acting in an official capacity. These suggestions draw upon the precedents following the Second World War. The Statute should, therefore, contain provisions which specify that a plea of head of State immunity or that an act was committed in the official capacity of the accused will not constitute a defence, nor will it mitigate punishment.

56. A person in a position of superior authority should, therefore, be held individually responsible for giving the unlawful order to commit a crime under the present statute. But he should also be held responsible for failure to prevent a crime or to deter the unlawful behaviour of his subordinates. This imputed responsibility or criminal negligence is engaged if the person in superior authority knew or had reason to know that his subordinates were about to commit or had committed crimes and yet failed to take the necessary and reasonable steps to prevent or repress the commission of such crimes or to punish those who had committed them.

57. Acting upon an order of a Government or a superior cannot relieve the perpetrator of the crime of his criminal responsibility and should not be a defence. Obedience to superior orders may, however, be considered a mitigating factor, should the International Tribunal determine that justice so requires. For example, the International Tribunal may consider the factor of superior orders in connection with other defences such as coercion or lack of moral choice.

58. The International Tribunal itself will have to decide on various personal defences which may relieve a person of individual criminal responsibility, such as minimum age or mental incapacity, drawing upon general principles of law recognized by all nations.

59. The corresponding article of the statute would read:

Article 7

Individual criminal responsibility

1. A person who planned, instigated, ordered, committed or otherwise aided and abetted in the planning, preparation or execution of a crime referred to in articles 2 to 5 of the present Statute, shall be individually responsible for the crime.

2. The official position of any accused person, whether as Head of State or Government or as a responsible Government official, shall not relieve such person of criminal responsibility nor mitigate punishment.

3. The fact that any of the acts referred to in articles 2 to 5 of the present Statute was committed by a subordinate does not relieve his superior of criminal responsibility if he knew or had reason to know that the subordinate was about to commit such acts or had

done so and the superior failed to take the necessary and reasonable measures to prevent such acts or to punish the perpetrators thereof.

4. The fact that an accused person acted pursuant to an order of a Government or of a superior shall not relieve him of criminal responsibility, but may be considered in mitigation of punishment if the International Tribunal determines that justice so requires.

The Prosecutor v. Blagojevic & Jokic

IT-02-60-T (Trial Chamber, Judgement on Motions for Acquittal Pursuant to Rule 98 *bis*) (5 April 2004)

[footnote material appears in the text]

25. "Planning" means that one or more persons design the commission of a crime at both the preparatory and execution phases. Prosecutor v. Akayesu, ICTR-96-4-T (Judgment, 2 Sept. 1998), para. 480, reiterated in Prosecutor v. Krstic, IT-98-33-T (Judgment, 2 Aug. 2001), para. 601, in Prosecutor v. Blaskic, IT-95-14-T (Judgment, 3 Mar. 2000), para. 279, in Prosecutor v. Kordic & Cerkez, IT-95-14/2-T (Judgment, 26 Feb. 2001), para. 386.

26. "Instigating" means prompting another to commit an offence. Blaskic, para. 280, Krstic, para. 601, Kordic, para. 387, Akayesu, para. 482.

27. "Ordering" entails a person in a position of authority using that position to command another to commit an offence. Krstic, para. 601.

28. Planning, instigating and ordering require that the accused has criminal intent, either direct or indirect. Regarding planning: Blaskic, para. 278; Kordic, para. 386. Regarding instigating, see Kvocka, IT-98-30/1 (Trial Judgment, 15 Dec. 2000), para. 252. Regarding ordering, see Blaskic, para. 282.

29. "Committing" supposes that the accused carries out, physically or otherwise directly, the *actus reus* of the crime. Prosecutor v. Tadic, IT-95-1-A (Appeals Chamber, 15 July 1999), para. 189. This can be achieved individually or jointly with others. Co-perpetration and the theory of joint criminal enterprise are modes of joint commission that have been recognised in the Tribunal's jurisprudence. Regarding co-perpetration as a form of commission, see Prosecutor v. Stakic, IT-97-24-T (Judgment, 31 July 2003), para. 439.

Notes and Questions

1. Nearly all of the international criminal law treaties address crimes committed, for example, by "any person," *i.e.*, regardless of status. *See also* JORDAN J. PAUST, INTERNATIONAL LAW AS LAW OF THE UNITED STATES 8, 48–50, 201, 264–70, 289–91, 393, 407–09, *passim* (1996); Jordan J. Paust, *The Other Side of Right: Private Duties Under Human Rights Law*, 5 HARV. H.R.J. 51, 56–59 (1992); Sharon A. Williams, *The Role of the Individual in International Criminal Law: An Overview*, (Special Edition) QUEEN's L.J., International Law: Critical Choices for Canada 1985–2000, at 505 (1986); *Kadic v. Karadzic*, 70 F.3d 232, 239–43 (2d Cir. 1995) (private individuals can commit piracy, slave trade, war crimes, and genocide); *Adra v. Clift*, 195 F. Supp. 857, 864 (D. Md. 1961) (*quoting* 1 HYDE, INTERNATIONAL LAW § 11A, at 33–34 (2 ed. 1945): "regardless of the character of the actors"); materials in Chapter Seven Sections 2 A–B, and other cases throughout this book. The Genocide Convention seems more particular in this regard. Article IV reads: "Persons committing genocide ... shall be punished whether they are constitutionally responsible rulers, public officials or private individuals." Article III of the Geno-

cide Convention also states: "The following acts shall be punishable: (a) Genocide; (b) Conspiracy to commit genocide; (c) Direct and public incitement to commit genocide; (d) Attempt to commit genocide; (e) complicity in genocide." See also Article III of the International Convention on the Suppression and Punishment of the Crime of "Apartheid". These general developments are consistent with trends since the trial of Peter von Hagenbach in 1474 for crimes committed during his administration of territories on the upper Rhine (see Chapter Six, Section 1). *Compare* Articles 25–27 of the Statute of the ICC, in the Documents Supplement. Under international law more generally, any person may be tried for the commission of an international crime. Consider especially the Opinion and Judgment of the I.M.T. at Nuremberg (Oct. 1, 1946) ("It was submitted that international law is concerned with the actions of sovereign States, and provides no punishment for individuals, and further, that where the act in question is an act of State, those who carry it out are not personally responsible, but are protected by the doctrine of the sovereignty of the State.... both submissions must be rejected. That international law imposes duties and liabilities upon individuals as well as upon States has long been recognized.... Crimes against international law are committed by men, not by abstract entities.... The Principle of international law, which under certain circumstances, protects the representatives of a State, cannot be applied to acts which are condemned as criminal by international law. The authors of these acts cannot shelter themselves behind their official position.... He who violates the laws of war cannot obtain immunity while acting in pursuance of the authority of the State if the State in authorizing action moves outside its competence under international law.").

2. In *United States v. von Leeb* (The High Command Case), U.S. Military Tribunal, 1948, XI Trials of War Criminals 462 (1950), the tribunal affirmed:

> "International law operates as a restriction and limitation on the sovereignty of nations. It may also limit the obligations which individuals owe to their states, and create for them international obligations which are binding upon them to an extent that they must be carried out even if to do so violates a positive law or directive of the state."

See also 9 Op. Att'y Gen. 356, 357 (1859) ("a law which operates on the interests and rights of other States or peoples must be made and executed according to the law of nations. A sovereign who tramples upon the public law of the world cannot excuse himself by pointing to a provision in his own municipal code."); *see also Johnson v. Eisentrager*, 339 U.S. 763, 765, 789 (1950) (no public official immunity exists for war crimes); *The Santissima Trinidad*, 20 U.S. (7 Wheat.) 283, 350–55 (1822) ("If ... he [a foreign sovereign] comes personally within our limits, although he generally enjoy a personal immunity, he may become liable to judicial process in the same way, and under the same circumstances, as public ships of the nation [that violate international law]"); *The Prosecutor v. Furundzija*, ICTY-95-17/1, at para. 140 (10 Dec. 1998); *The Prosecutor v. Milosevic*, ICTY-99-37-PT, at paras. 26–34 (Nov. 8, 2001) (the ICTY Chamber famously ruled that Milosevic had no immunity from alleged international crimes as a head of state and that Article 7 of the Statute of the ICTY, which rejects head of state immunity, "reflects a rule of customary international law"). In *The Prosecutor v. Tadic*, ICTY-94-1-AR72 (2 Oct. 1995), the Appeals Chamber of the International Criminal Tribunal for Former Yugoslavia recognized: "It would be a travesty of law and a betrayal of the universal need for justice, should the concept of State sovereignty be allowed to be raised successfully against human rights. Borders should not be considered as a shield against the reach of the law and as a protection for those who trample underfoot the most elementary rights of humanity." *Id.* para. 58.

3. If a relevant treaty, code, or documentation of custom does not mention individual responsibility, much less criminal sanctions, are criminal sanctions nevertheless appropriate under international law? *See, e.g.*, Opinion of the I.M.T. at Nuremberg (*infra* Chapters Six and Seven); *Henfield's Case* (*infra* Chapter Four, Section 2).

4. U.S. Dep't of Army FM 27-10, The Law of Land Warfare at 183, paras. 510–511 (1956) recognizes the Nuremberg principles of nonimmunity for government officials and the lack of a defense based on domestic law "for an act which constitutes a crime under international law." With respect to criminal responsibility, the Field Manual adds:

Section II. Crimes Under International Law

498. Crimes Under International Law

Any person, whether a member of the armed forces or a civilian, who commits an act which constitutes a crime under international law is responsible therefor and liable to punishment. Such offenses in connection with war comprise:

a. Crimes against peace.

b. Crimes against humanity.

c. War crimes.

Although this manual recognizes the criminal responsibility of individuals for those offenses which may comprise any of the foregoing types of crimes, members of the armed forces will normally be concerned only with those offenses constituting "war crimes."

499. War Crimes

The term "war crime" is the technical expression for a violation of the law of war by any person or persons, military or civilian. Every violation of the law of war is a war crime.

500. Conspiracy, Incitement, Attempts and Complicity

Conspiracy, direct incitement, and attempts to commit, as well as complicity in the commission of, crimes against peace, crimes against humanity, and war crimes are punishable.

5. Do you agree with the *Blagojevic & Jokic* statements about planning, instigating, ordering, and committing? In *The Prosecutor v. Semanza*, ICTR-97-20-A (Appeals Chamber, 20 May 2005), para. 257, it was recognized that although a person could not be found guilty of dereliction of duty because the person lacked sufficient authority over perpetrators of the crime of rape, the accused can be prosecuted for "instigating" rape by others. In *The Prosecutor v. Kordic & Cerkez*, IT-95-14/2 (Appeals Chamber Judgment, 17 Dec. 2004), para. 32, the Appeals Chamber declared that a person can be guilty of "instigating" by instigating another person to commit an act or omission with the awareness of the substantial likelihood that a crime will be committed in the execution of that instigation and that instigating with such awareness has to be regarded as "accepting" that crime. The Appeals Chamber also stated that "planning" can occur if the person plans an act or omission with the awareness of the substantial likelihood that a crime will be committed in the execution of that plan and that planning with such awareness has to be regarded as accepting that crime. *Id.* para. 31. With respect to "incitement," see also U.N. S.C. Res. 1296, S/RES/1296, para. 17 (19 April 2000) (the Security Council "reaffirms its condemnation of all incitements to violence against civilians in situations of armed conflict, further reaffirms the need to bring to justice individuals who incite or otherwise cause such violence....").

In *The Prosecutor v. Blaskic*, IT-95-14-T-A (Appeals Chamber Judgment, 29 July 2004), para. 40, declared that "ordering" can involve a lower *mens rea* standard than "direct intent" and include "awareness of a higher likelihood of risk and a volitional element" than plain reckless disregard, adding: "A person who orders an act or omission with the awareness of the substantial likelihood that a crime will be committed in the execution of that order, has the requisite *mens rea* for establishing liability under Article 7(1) [of the Statute of the ICTY] pursuant to ordering. Ordering with such awareness has to be regarded as accepting that crime." *Id.* para. 42.

6. In The *Prosecutor v. Kordic & Cerkez*, IT-95-14/2-A (Appeals Chamber Judgment, 17 Dec. 2004), para. 311, it was declared: "The *nullum crimen sine lege* [no crime without law] principle does not require that an accused knew that specific legal definition of each element of a crime he committed. It suffices that he was aware of the [relevant] factual circumstances."

7. With respect to a potentially wide range of individual responsibility under customary international law applicable in time of armed conflict, consider also the following List of War Crimes prepared by the Responsibilities Commission of the Paris Peace Conference in 1919 (members: U.S., British Empire, France, Italy, Japan, Belgium, Greece, Poland, Roumania, Serbia). Are the crimes listed defined? Are elements of each crime set forth? Often, international criminal law instruments lack definitions of criminal proscriptions, much less elements of particular crimes. How would you further clarify or supplement the content of the proscriptions in the 1919 list? What types of *mens rea* are likely to pertain with respect to each crime (*e.g.*, knowledge, wanton or reckless disregard, criminal negligence)?

1. Murder and massacres—systematic terrorism.

2. Putting hostages to death.

3. Torture of civilians.

4. Deliberate starvation of civilians.

5. Rape.

6. Abduction of girls and women for the purpose of enforced prostitution.

7. Deportation of civilians.

8. Internment of civilians under inhuman conditions.

9. Forced labour of civilians in connection with the military operations of the enemy.

10. Usurpation of sovereignty during military occupation.

11. Compulsory enlistment of soldiers among the inhabitants of occupied territory.

12. Attempts to denationalize the inhabitants of occupied territory.

13. Pillage.

14. Confiscation of property.

15. Exaction of illegitimate or of exorbitant contributions and requisitions.

16. Debasement of the currency and issue of spurious currency.

17. Imposition of collective penalties.

18. Wanton devastation and destruction of property.

19. Deliberate bombardment of undefended places.

20. Wanton destruction of religious, charitable, educational and historic buildings and monuments.

21. Destruction of merchant ships and passenger vessels without warning and without provision for the safety of passengers and crew.

22. Destruction of fishing boats and relief ships.

23. Deliberate bombardment of hospitals.

24. Attack and destruction of hospital ships.

25. Breach of other rules relating to the Red Cross.

26. Use of deleterious and asphyxiating gases.

27. Use of explosive or expanding bullets and other inhuman appliances.

28. Directions to give no quarter.

29. Ill-treatment of wounded and prisoners of war.

30. Employment of prisoners of war on unauthorized works.

31. Misuse of flags of truce.

32. Poisoning of wells.

[Item added by the War Crimes Commission]

33. Indiscriminate mass arrests.

The Report of the 1919 Commission also contained a concluding section stating: "All persons…, however high their position may have been, without distinction of rank, including Chiefs of States, who have been guilty of offences against the laws and customs of war or the laws of humanity, are liable to criminal prosecution…." See Chapter Seven, Section 2. *Compare* Articles 25 and 27 of the Statute of the ICC; Article 7 of the Statute of the ICTY; Article 6 of the Statute of the ICTR; Rule 48 of the 1953 U.N. Rules of Criminal Procedure (Korea); Articles 6–7 of the Charter of the IMT at Nuremberg; Article V of the Charter of the IMT for the Far East; Article II of Control Council Law No. 10—each in the Documents Supplement—and the 1919 Treaty of Versailles, which publicly arraigned the Kaiser of Germany for international crimes alleged during World War I (in Chapter Seven, Section 2). Also consider the trial of von Hagenbach in 1474 (addressed in Chapter Six, Section 1).

2. Responsibility and Domestic Immunities of Officials and Heads of State

As many of the instruments addressed in Section 1 demonstrate in part, there has been no immunity for former and sitting officials and heads of state in international criminal law instruments. In fact, there have been prosecutions of numerous officials and many heads of state for customary and treaty-based international crimes.

In 1999, the English House of Lords had to consider whether a former head of state had criminal responsibility for, among other crimes, the international crime of torture documented in part in the 1984 Convention Against Torture and Other Cruel, Inhuman or Degrading Treatment and Punishment. In March of 1999, the majority of the English House of Lords decided that former Chilean head of state Augusto Pinochet Ugarte was extraditable on charges of torture committed since 1988, when Chile, Spain, and the U.K. had ratified the International Convention Against Torture and other Cruel, Inhuman or Degrading Treatment or Punishment (in the Documents Supplement) and the U.K. had also incorporated the treaty through the Criminal Justice Act of 1988. Spain and other countries had requested extradition of Pinochet for prosecution of various international crimes. We will visit this case again in Chapter Five, Section 1, concerning extradition. At this time, consider the following extracts from opinions of some of the Lord Justices on the question of head of state immunity with respect to international crime.

Regina v. Bartle and the Commissioner of Police for the Metropolis and Others, *Ex Parte* Pinochet

House of Lords (24 March 1999)

Browne-Wilkinson, L.J.

... [I]mmunity enjoyed by a head of state in power and an ambassador in post is a complete immunity attaching to the person of the head of state or ambassador and rendering him immune from all actions or prosecutions whether or not they relate to matters done for the benefit of the state. Such immunity is said to be granted *ratione personae.*

What then when the ambassador leaves his post or the head of state is deposed?....

The continuing partial immunity of the ambassador after leaving post is of a different kind from that enjoyed *ratione personae* while he was in post. Since he is no longer the representative of the foreign state he merits no particular privileges or immunities as a person. However in order to preserve the integrity of the activities of the foreign state during the period when he was ambassador, it is necessary to provide that immunity is afforded to his *official* acts during his tenure in post.... This limited immunity, *ratione materiae*, is to be contrasted with the former immunity *ratione personae* which gave complete immunity to all activities whether public or private.

In my judgment at common law a former head of state enjoys similar immunities, *ratione materiae*, once he ceases to be head of state. He too loses immunity *ratione personae* on ceasing to be head of state....

Can it be said that the commission of a crime which is an international crime against humanity and *jus cogens* is an act done in an official capacity on behalf of the state? I believe there to be strong ground for saying that the implementation of torture as defined by the Torture Convention *cannot be a state function* [emphasis added]....

The jurisdiction being established by the Torture Convention and the Hostages Convention is one where existing domestic courts of all the countries are being authorised and required to take jurisdiction....

Immunity *ratione materiae* applies not only to ex-heads of state and ex-ambassadors but to all state officials who have been involved in carrying out the functions of the state.... Therefore the whole elaborate structure of universal jurisdiction over torture committed by officials is rendered abortive and one of the main objectives of the Torture Convention—to provide a system under which there is no safe haven for torturers—will have been frustrated. In my judgment all these factors together demonstrate that the notion of continued immunity for ex-heads of state is inconsistent with the provisions of the Torture Convention....

Hope of Craighead, L.J.

... The fact that acts done for the state have involved conduct which is criminal does not remove the immunity.... A head of state needs to be free to promote his own state's interests during the entire period when he is in office without being subjected to the prospect of detention, arrest or embarrassment in the foreign legal system of the receiving state....

There are only two exceptions to this approach which customary international law has recognised. The first relates to criminal acts which the head of state did under the colour of his authority as head of state but which were in reality for his own pleasure or benefit.... The second relates to acts the prohibition of which has acquired the status under international law of *jus cogens*....

... The Torture Convention does not contain any provision which deals expressly with the question whether heads of state or former heads of state are or are not to have immunity from allegations that they have committed torture....

It would also be a strange result if the provisions of the Convention could not be applied to heads of state who, because they themselves inflicted torture or had instigated the carrying out of acts of torture by their officials, were the persons primarily responsible for the perpetration of these acts....

The *jus cogens* character of the immunity enjoyed by serving heads of state *ratione personae* suggests that, on any view, that immunity was not intended to be affected by the Convention....

These considerations suggest strongly that it would be wrong to regard the Torture Convention as having by necessary implication removed the immunity *ratione materiae* from former heads of state in regard to every act of torture of any kind which might be alleged against him falling within the scope of Article 1....

I would not regard this as a case of waiver. Nor would I accept that it was an implied term of the Torture Convention that former heads of state were to be deprived of their immunity *ratione materiae* with respect to all acts of official torture as defined in Article 1. It is just that the obligations which were recognised by customary international law in the case of such serious international crimes by the date when Chile ratified the Convention are so strong as to override any objection by it on the ground of immunity *ratione materiae* to the exercise of the jurisdiction over crimes committed after that date which the United Kingdom had made available.

I consider that the date as from which the immunity *ratione materiae* was lost was 30 October 1988, which was the date when Chile's ratification of the Torture Convention on 30 September 1988 took effect. Spain had already ratified the Convention.... The Convention was ratified by the United Kingdom on 8 December 1988 following the coming into force of section 134 of the Criminal Justice Act 1988....

Hutton, L.J.

... The alleged acts of torture by Senator Pinochet were carried out under colour of his position as head of state, but they cannot be regarded as functions of a head of state under international law when international law expressly prohibits torture as a measure which a state can employ in any circumstances whatsoever and has made it an international crime....

In my opinion there has been no waiver of the immunity of a former head of state in respect of his functions as head of state. My conclusion that Senator Pinochet is not entitled to immunity is based on the view that the commission of acts of torture is not a function of a head of state, and therefore in this case the immunity to which Senator Pinochet is entitled as a former head of state does not arise in relation to, and does not attach to, acts of torture....

Therefore I consider that a single act of torture carried out or instigated by a public official or other person acting in a official capacity constitutes a crime against international law, and that torture does not become an international crime only when it is committed or instigated on a large scale. Accordingly I am of opinion that Senator Pinochet cannot claim that a single act of torture or a small number of acts of torture carried out by him did not constitute international crimes and did not constitute acts committed outside the ambit of his functions as head of state....

Saville of Newdigate, L.J.

So far as the states that are parties to the Convention are concerned, I cannot see how, so far as torture is concerned, this immunity can exist consistently with the terms of that Convention. Each state party has agreed that the other state parties can exercise jurisdiction over alleged official torturers found within their territories, by extraditing them or referring them to their own appropriate authorities for prosecution; and thus to my mind can hardly simultaneously claim an immunity from extradition or prosecution that is necessarily based on the official nature of the alleged torture....

Millett, L.J.

... The Republic of Chile accepts that by 1973 the use of torture by state authorities was prohibited by international law, and that the prohibition had the character of *jus cogens* or obligation *erga omnes*. But it insists that this does not confer universal jurisdiction or affect the immunity of a former head of state *ratione materiae* from the jurisdiction of foreign national courts.

In my opinion, crimes prohibited by international law attract universal jurisdiction under customary international law if two criteria are satisfied. First, they must be contrary to a peremptory norm of international law so as to infringe a *jus cogens*. Secondly, they must be so serious and on such a scale that they can justly be regarded as an attack on the international legal order. Isolated offences, even if committed by public officials, would not satisfy these criteria....

In my opinion, the systematic use of torture on a large scale and as an instrument of state policy had joined piracy, war crimes and crimes against peace as an international crime of universal jurisdiction well before 1984. I consider that it had done so by 1973....

The definition of torture, ... in the Convention..., is in my opinion entirely inconsistent with the existence of a plea of immunity *ratione materiae*. The offence can be committed *only* by or at the instigation of or with the consent or acquiescence of a public official or other person acting in an official capacity. The official or governmental nature of the act, which forms the basis of the immunity, is an essential ingredient of the offence. No rational system of criminal justice can allow an immunity which is co-extensive with the offence....

In future those who commit atrocities against civilian populations must expect to be called to account if fundamental human rights are to be properly protected. In this context, the exalted rank of the accused can afford no defence....

Phillips of Worthmatravers, L.J.

... There are some categories of crime of such gravity that they shock the consciousness of mankind and cannot be tolerated by the international community. Any individual who commits such a crime offends against international law. The nature of these crimes is such that they are likely to involve the concerted conduct of many and liable to involve the complicity of the officials of the state in which they occur, if not of the state itself....

... [N]o established rule of international law requires state immunity *ratione materiae* to be accorded in respect of prosecution for an international crime. International crimes and extra-territorial jurisdiction in relation to them are both new arrivals in the field of public international law. I do not believe that state immunity *ratione materiae* can co-exist with them....

Notes and Questions

1. Which arguments or points are most persuasive? Why?

2. When Millet stated that in his opinion international crimes over which there is universal jurisdiction "must be contrary to a peremptory norm ... *jus cogens*," do you suspect he was correct? *See* Chapter Three, Section 1. When Millet stated that such crimes must also "be so serious and on such a scale that they can justly be regarded as an attack on the international legal order" and that "isolated offences" do not constitute such international crimes, was he correct? Recall Chapter One and consider, for example, the crimes of piracy, aircraft hijacking, aircraft sabotage, assaults on foreign ambassadors, breaches of neutrality, isolated war crimes, the definition of genocide in Article II of the Genocide Convention, and other crimes by private and public perpetrators. When he noted that immunity "finds its rationale" in state equality and the doctrine of noninterference in "internal affairs" of other states, can you posit an argument that, in view of such a rationale, acts of genocide and other human rights violations should be nonimmune?

3. Do any of the international instruments or opinions appearing or noted so far distinguish between notions *ratione personae* and *ratione materiae* in connection with alleged head of state immunity? Do any international legal instruments? What is the consistent recognition concerning head of state or other public official responsibility in each of the above instruments or opinions? Why, do you imagine, were such instruments and opinions not addressed? Note that the Rome Statute of the ICC is the latest international criminal instrument to reject head of state immunity. See *id.* art. 27.

Do you think that acts of a head of state that are international crimes under customary or treaty-based international law are immune? Recall the prior set of Notes and Questions. Do you think that only crimes *jus cogens* are nonimmune? Or do you agree with Lord Hope that head of state immunity from international crime is a *jus cogens* norm (does he cite anything for such a radical notion)? Do you think that a head of state is immune from prosecution for crimes such as hostage-taking, torture, or aircraft sabotage, if a relevant treaty recognizes international criminal responsibility for "any person" or "a person" who commits such a crime if the treaty does not also address head of state or public official immunity or nonimmunity? Also recall the portion of the Opinion and Judgment of the I.M.T. at Nuremberg quoted above on the lack of official "immunity," and lack of state competence, for acts made "criminal by international law." Is nonimmunity for international crime based merely on express provisions of Charters and treaties?

Are there other indications of ahistorical statements in the *Pinochet* opinions?

4. On June 17, 1881, a Swiss Consul General and president of the German-American Bank of Washington was indicted for a federal crime. The Swiss Confederation requested that he resign as Consul General on June 15th. He did so on June 20th. On application for a writ of certiorari, the U.S. Supreme Court denied the writ, which "is not a writ of right, but discretionary with the court." *Ex parte* Hitz, 111 U.S. 766, 767-768 (1884).

5. In February of 2000, a Senegalese court indicted a former dictator of Chad, Hissein Habre, on torture charges and placed him under house arrest. The former head of state had been living in exile in Senegal since his ouster in 1990. Private litigants had joined the proceedings. Belgium had sought Habre's extradition, and the I.C.J. held hear-

ings on the case in March 2012. See Questions Relating to the Obligation to Prosecute of Extradite (*Belgium v. Senegal*).

6. For extensive consideration of state practice in prosecuting heads of state, *see, e.g.*, ELLEN L. LUTZ & CAITLIN REIGER, PROSECUTING HEADS OF STATE (2009). Their study was instrumental in connection with the following summary of prosecutions of heads of state, diplomats, and other public officials.

Jordan J. Paust, Genocide in Rwanda, State Responsibility to Prosecute or Extradite, and Nonimmunity for Heads of State and Other Public Officials

34 HOUS. J. INT'L L. 57, 75–80 (2011)

Numerous high level officials were prosecuted after World War II,[1] and in 1950 the United States Supreme Court affirmed the customary norm that no form of immunity exists for war crimes in violation of the Geneva Conventions.[2] Also near that time, a court in France rightly recognized, as had other tribunals, that a diplomat is not immune with respect to crimes under international law and that the court cannot "subordinate the prosecution [of war crimes] to the authorization of the country where the guilty person belongs."[3] In 1961, top Nazi official Adolph Eichmann was convicted in Israel for international crimes over which there was universal jurisdiction.[4] In 1974, Greece convicted two former heads of state for bloody attacks and torture that were in violation of human rights.[5] In 1985, Argentina convicted former President Lambruschini for conduct in violation of human rights.[6] In the 1980s and 90s, civil suits against former Philippine head of state Ferdinand Marcos were allowed for violations of international law after denial of claims to immunity;[7] and in 1990 Panamanian leader Manuel Noriega was convicted in a U.S. court for international drug trafficking, among other crimes despite claims to im-

---

1. *See, e.g.*, this chapter and chapter 6, section 3; Trial of Hans Albin Rauter, 14 L. REPTS. OF TRIALS OF WAR CRIM, 89 (1949) (highest SS officer in the Netherlands, convicted in a Dutch tribunal of crimes against humanity); *In re* Kappler, Military Tribunal of Rome, 1948 ANN. DIG. 471, 472 (1948) (head of German Police and Security in Rome).

2. Johnson v. Eisentrager, 339 U.S. 763, 765, 789 (1950).

3. French case of Abetz, in 46 AM. J. INT'L L. 161, 162 (1952). A Subsequent Nuremberg case prosecuted by the U.S. also recognized that diplomatic immunity applies only to legitimate acts of state and not to violations of international law. United States v. Weizsacker, *et al.* (The Ministries Case), 16 INT'L L. REPTS. 344, 361 (1949); 12, 13 & 14 TRIALS OF WAR CRIMINALS BEFORE THE NUERNBERG TRIBUNALS UNDER CONTROL COUNCIL LAW NO. 10 (1950-51).

4. *See, e.g.*, Attorney General v. Eichmann, 36 INT'L L. REPTS. 277, 310 (Sup. Ct. Israel 1962) (his criminal acts "in point of international law ... are completely outside the 'sovereign' jurisdiction of the State that ordered or ratified their commission, and therefore those who participated in such acts must personally account for them and cannot shelter behind the official character of their task or mission").

5. *See, e.g.*, ELLEN L. LUTZ & CAITLIN REIGER, PROSECUTING HEADS OF STATE 15 (2009); Ellen L. Lutz, *Prosecutions of Heads of State in Europe*, in *id.* at 25, 28–29.

6. *See, e.g.*, LUTZ & REIGER, *supra* note 5, at 295. Argentina would convict two other former presidents in 2010. *See infra* note 26.

7. *See, e.g.*, Hilao v. Estate of Marcos, 103 F.3d 767 (9th Cir. 1996); *In re* Estate of Ferdinand E, Marcos Human Right Litigation, 25 F.3d 1467, 1470–71 (9th Cir. 1994), *cert. denied*, 513 U.S. 1126 (1995); Republic of the Philippines v. Marcos, 806 F.2d 344 (2d Cir. 1986); *In re* Estate of Ferdinand Marcos, 910 F. Supp. 1460 (D. Haw. 1995); Republic of the Philippines v. Marcos, 665 F. Supp. 793, 797 (N.D. Cal. 1987).

munity.[8] In 1993, Bolivia, Germany, and Mali convicted former heads of state for conduct violative of human rights.[9] In 1995, another former head of state of Germany was convicted;[10] and in 1996, South Korea convicted two former heads of state for conduct violative of human rights.[11] In 1998, the ICTR convicted former Rwanda President Jean Kambanda of genocide, incitement to genocide, and complicity in genocide.[12] In 1999, the U.K. House of Lords found former dictator of Chile Augusto Pinochet Ugarte to be extraditable and nonimmune for torture.[13] In 2001, the ICTY famously ruled that the lack head of state immunity for alleged international crimes reflected in the Statute of the ICTY is "a rule of customary international law."[14]

Also in 2001, the Republic of the Congo convicted former President Lissouba in absentia for conduct violative of human rights.[15] In 2004, a Rwandan court convicted former President Pasteur Bizimungu, although the trial was highly criticized as being politically motivated and he was later pardoned.[16] In 2005, Spain's Constitutional Tribunal allowed a criminal complaint against Guatemalan police chiefs, generals, and others to proceed on the basis of universal jurisdiction over international crimes;[17] and in 2006 arrest warrants were issued and extradition was sought for two former Presidents and a former Minister of Defense of Guatemala.[18] Iraqi leader Saddam Hussein was convicted by an Iraqi Special Tribunal for Crimes Against Humanity in 2006 and was subsequently hanged.[19] In

---

8. *See, e.g.*, United States v. Noriega, 746 F. Supp. 1506 (S.D. Fla. 1990), *aff'd*, 117 F.3d 1212 (11th Cir. 1997), *reh'g and reh'g en banc denied*, 128 F.3d 734 (1997), *cert. denied*, 523 U.S. 1060 (1998). In 2009, he was also found to be extraditable to France. Noriega v. Pastrana, 564 F.3d 1290 (11th Cir. 2009), *cert. denied*, 130 S.Ct. 1002 (2010), *reh'g denied*, 130 S.Ct. 1949 (2010). More recently, former Guatemalan President Alfonso Portillo was charged in the U.S. with international money laundering, a judge in Guatemala had found him to be extraditable, and he is now on trial. *See, e.g.*, William Booth & Nick Miroff, *A New Fight, A Familiar Battlefield*, Wash. Post, Feb. 10, 2011, at A1; *Ex-President Indicted*, L.A. Times, Jan. 26, 2010, at 15.

9. *See, e.g.*, Lutz & Reiger, *supra* note 5, at 296 (former head of state of Bolivia Luis García Meza), 300 (former head of state of East Germany Erich Honecker), 302 (former President of Mali Moussa Traore); Lutz, *supra* note 5, at 30–31.

10. *See, e.g.*, Lutz & Reiger, *supra* note 5, at 300 (former head of state of East Germany Egon Krenz); Lutz, *supra* note 5, at 31.

11. *See, e.g.*, Lutz & Reiger, *supra* note 5, at 304 (former Presidents Chum Doo Hwan and Roh Tae Woo).

12. The Prosecutor v. Jean Kambanda, ICTR-97-23-S (4 Sept. 1998).

13. *See, e.g.*, Regina v. Bartle and the Commissioner of Police for the Metropolis and Others (*Ex parte* Pinochet), House of Lords (Mar. 24, 1999), extract in this chapter.

14. The Prosecutor v. Milosevic, ICTY-99-37-PT, at paras. 26–34 (8 Nov. 2001). *See also* The Prosecutor v. Plavsic, ICTY-00-39&40/1-S (Sentencing Judgment, Feb. 27, 2003) (Bosnian Serb group's President plead guilty to one count of a persecution-type of crime against humanity).

15. *See, e.g.*, Lutz & Reiger, *supra* note , at 302.

16. *See, e.g.*, Mark A. Drumbl, *Prosecution of Genocide v. The Fair Trial Principle*, 8 J. Int'l Crim. Just. 289, 298 (2010); Leslie Haskell & Lars Waldorf, *The Impunity Gap of the International Criminal Tribunal of Rwanda: Causes and Consequences*, 34 Hastings Int'l & Comp. L. Rev. 49, 69 n.111 (2011).

17. *See, e.g.*, chapter three, end of section 1.

18. *See, e.g.*, Lutz & Reiger, *supra* note 5, at 298; Wolfgang Kaleck, *From Pinochet to Rumsfeld: Universal Jurisdiction in Europe 1998-2008*, 30 Mich. J. Int'l L. 927, 956–57 (2009) (they were arrested by Guatemala but charges were later dropped by Guatemala); Naomi Roht-Arriaza, *Making the State Do Justice: Transnational Prosecutions and International Support for Criminal Investigations in Post-Armed Conflict Guatemala*, 9 Chi. J. Int'l L. 79 (2008).

19. *See, e.g.*, Christopher Torchia, *Saddam Says Farewell Online*, Hous. Chron., Dec. 28, 2006, at A1; James Glanz, *Hussein Ruling Sets Execution Within 30 Days*, N.Y. Times, Dec. 27, 2006, at A1.

2007, France convicted a former diplomat from Tunisia for torture;[20] and the Netherlands, Suriname, and Uruguay began trials of former heads of state.[21] In 2008, the son of the former President of Liberia, himself an official, was convicted of torture in a U.S. federal court;[22] Hissêne Habré, the former leader of Chad, was sentenced in absentia by a court in Chad and Senegal is presently in the process of prosecuting him;[23] and a high court in Ethiopia affirmed the conviction in absentia of a former head of state for conduct violative of human rights.[24] In April 2009, former head of state of Peru Alberto Fujimori was found guilty of human rights violations, including torture, kidnappings, and forced disappearance.[25] In April and December 2010, two former presidents of Argentina were sentenced by Argentinian courts for the kidnaping and torturing persons that occurred during Argentina's "dirty war."[26] Earlier, Germany had sought extradition of one of the former presidents for teroristic crimes against humanity.[27] In March 2010, the U.S. Supreme Court ruled that a suit against former Somali defense minister and prime minister Mohamed Ali Samantar was not barred by U.S. legislation concerning foreign state immunity.[28]

Presently, Omar al-Bashir, the head of state of the Sudan, is under an arrest warrant issued by the ICC in connection with a case that was referred to the ICC by the U.N. Security Council.[29] Additionally, in February 2011 the Security Council referred the case of possible crimes against humanity committed in Libya by head of state Muammar Gaddafi (Qaddafi) and others to the ICC for investigation.[30] In April 2012, the Special Court for

---

20. *See, e.g.*, Kaleck, *supra* note 18, at 937. Concerning the lack of diplomatic immunity for international crimes, *see also supra* note 3.

21. *See, e.g.*, Lutz & Reiger, *supra* note 5, at 299 (Dutch trial of former President Bouterse for conduct violative of human rights and smuggling, and proceedings in Suriname, but he became President of Suriname again in 2010; and Uruguay's pre-trial arrest of Bordaberry for conduct violative of human rights, and he was sentenced to 30 years in March 2010); Naomi Roht-Arriaza, *Prosecuting Heads of State in Latin America*, in Lutz & Reiger, *supra* note 5, at 61.

22. *See, e.g.*, Carmen Gentile, *Son of Ex-President of Liberia Gets 97 Years*, N.Y. Times, Jan. 9, 2009, at A14; Yolanne Almanzar, *Son of Ex-President of Liberia Convicted of Torture*, N.Y. Times, Oct. 31, 2008, at A16 (Charles ("Chuckie") McArthur Emmanuel convicted in a federal court in Miami).

23. *See, e.g.*, Kaleck, *supra* note 18, at 935–36; *Chad: Ex-President Sentenced to Death*, N.Y. Times, Aug. 16, 2008, at A9; Human Rights Watch, *African Union: Press Senegal on Habré Trial* (Jan. 8, 2009), available at http://www.hrw.org/en/news/2009/01/08/african-union-press-senegal-habr-trial?print.

24. *See, e.g.*, Lutz & Reiger, *supra* note 5, at 301 (former head of state Mengistu Haile Mariam).

25. *See, e.g.*, *Fujimori's Instructive Fall*, N.Y. Times, Apr. 14, 2009, at A22; Maria McFarland Sanchez-Moreno, *Our Own Strongman*, N.Y. Times, Apr. 11, 2009, at A17; Joshua Partlow, *Peru's Fujimori Gets 25 Years*, Hous. Chron., Apr. 8, 2009, at A10. *See also* Kaleck, *supra* note 18, at 968–70 (regarding the role of regional institutions and Chile's 2007 decision to extradite Fujimori to Peru).

26. *See, e.g.*, *Argentina: Ex-Dictator Sentenced in Murders*, N.Y. Times, Dec. 23, 2010 (former President Jorge Rafael Videla sentence to life); Charles Newbery & Alexei Barrionuevo, *Argentine Ex-President Gets 25 Years for Role in "Dirty War,"* N.Y. Times, Apr. 21, 2010, at A8 (former President Reynaldo Benito Bignone sentenced to 25 years).

27. *See, e.g.*, Kaleck, *supra* note 18, at 950–51 (ex-President Videla).

28. Samantar v. Yousuf, _ U.S. _ ; 130 S.Ct. 2276, 2282 (2010) (denying immunity under 28 U.S.C. §§ 1330, 1602, *et seq.*).

29. *See, e.g.*, Ariel Zirulnick, *From Libya's Qaddafi to Sudan's Bashir*, Christian Sci. Mon., Mar. 3, 2011; Marlise Simons, *Sudan's Leader May Be Accused of Genocide*, N.Y. Times, Feb. 3, 2010, at A10; Lisa Bryant, Voice of America, *Appeals Court Says ICC Could Charge Sudan President With Genocide*, Feb. 3, 2010, 2010 WLNR 2282680.

30. *See, e.g.*, U.N. S.C. Res. 1970, para. 4 (2011), U.N. Doc. S/RES/1970 (Feb. 26, 2011) ("Decides to refer the situation in the Libyan Arab Jamahiriya since 15 February 2011 to the Prosecutor of the International Criminal Court"); Edward Wyatt, *Security Council Refers Libya to Criminal Court*, N.Y. Times, Feb. 27, 2011, at A14; *ICC: No Immunity for Perpetrators of Crimes Against Humanity in Libya*, Jurist (Feb. 28, 2011), available at http://jurist.org/paperchase/2011/02/icc-no-immunity-for-per-

Sierra Leone convicted former President of Liberia Charles Taylor for aiding and abetting war crimes and crimes against humanity. He received a sentence of 50 years.

Note

1. Karl Dönitz (Doenitz) was sentenced to 10 years in prison by the International Military Tribunal at Nuremberg. From April 29 to May 23, 1945, he was the President and Head of State of Germany, the successor of Adolf Hitler. He was released from prison Oct. 1, 1956.

Case Concerning the Arrest Warrant of 11 April 2000 (Democratic Republic of the Congo v. Belgium), International Court of Justice
February 14, 2002

The Court, delivers the following Judgment:

1. On 17 October 2000 the Democratic Republic of the Congo (hereinafter referred to as "the Congo") filed in the Registry of the Court an Application instituting proceedings against the Kingdom of Belgium (hereinafter referred to as "Belgium") in respect of a dispute concerning an "international arrest warrant issued on 11 April 2000 by a Belgian investigating judge ... against the Minister for Foreign Affairs in office of the Democratic Republic of the Congo, Mr. Abdulaye Yerodia Ndombasi."

In that Application the Congo contended that Belgium had violated the "principle that a State may not exercise its authority on the territory of another State," the "principle of sovereign equality among all Members of the United Nations, as laid down in Article 2, paragraph 1, of the Charter of the United Nations," as well as "the diplomatic immunity of the Minister for Foreign Affairs of a sovereign State, as recognized by the jurisprudence of the Court and following from Article 41, paragraph 2, of the Vienna Convention of 18 April 1961 on Diplomatic Relations."

13. On 11 April 2000 an investigating judge of the Brussels Tribunal de première instance issued "an international arrest warrant in absentia" against Mr. Abdulaye Yerodia Ndombasi, charging him, as perpetrator or co-perpetrator, with offences constituting grave breaches of the Geneva Conventions of 1949 and of the Additional Protocols thereto, and with crimes against humanity.

At the time when the arrest warrant was issued Mr. Yerodia was the Minister for Foreign Affairs of the Congo....

15. In the arrest warrant, Mr. Yerodia is accused of having made various speeches inciting racial hatred during the month of August 1998. The crimes with which Mr. Yerodia was charged were punishable in Belgium under the Law of 16 June 1993 "concerning the Punishment of Grave Breaches of the International Geneva Conventions of 12 August 1949 and of Protocols I and II of 8 June 1977 Additional Thereto," as amended by the Law of 10 February 1999 "concerning the Punishment of Serious Violations of International Humanitarian Law" (hereinafter referred to as the "Belgian Law"). Article 7 of the Belgian Law provides that "The Belgian courts shall have jurisdiction in respect of the of-

---

petrators-of-crimes-against-humanity.php. Later, the Security Council stressed "that those responsible for or complicit in attacks targeting the civilian population, including aerial and naval attacks, must be held to account." U.N. S.C. Res. 1973, prmbl. (2011), U.N. Doc. S/RES/1973 (17 Mar. 2011).

fences provided for in the present Law, wheresoever they may have been committed." In the present case, according to Belgium, the complaints that initiated the proceedings as a result of which the arrest warrant was issued emanated from 12 individuals all resident in Belgium, five of whom were of Belgian nationality. It is not contested by Belgium, however, that the alleged acts to which the arrest warrant relates were committed outside Belgian territory, that Mr. Yerodia was not a Belgian national at the time of those acts, and that Mr. Yerodia was not in Belgian territory at the time that the arrest warrant was issued and circulated. That no Belgian nationals were victims of the violence that was said to have resulted from Mr. Yerodia's alleged offences was also uncontested.

Article 5, paragraph 3, of the Belgian Law further provides that "[i]mmunity attaching to the official capacity of a person shall not prevent the application of the present Law."....

19. From mid-April 2001, with the formation of a new Government in the Congo, Mr. Yerodia ceased to hold the post of Minister of Education. He no longer holds any ministerial office today....

45. ... [I]n its Application instituting these proceedings, the Congo originally challenged the legality of the arrest warrant of 11 April 2000 on two separate grounds: on the one hand, Belgium's claim to exercise a universal jurisdiction and, on the other, the alleged violation of the immunities of the Minister for Foreign Affairs of the Congo then in office. However, in its submissions in its Memorial, and in its final submissions at the close of the oral proceedings, the Congo invokes only the latter ground.

46. As a matter of logic, the second ground should be addressed only once there has been a determination in respect of the first, since it is only where a State has jurisdiction under international law in relation to a particular matter that there can be any question of immunities in regard to the exercise of that jurisdiction. However, in the present case, and in view of the final form of the Congo's submissions, the Court will address first the question whether, assuming that it had jurisdiction under international law to issue and circulate the arrest warrant of 11 April 2000, Belgium in so doing violated the immunities of the then Minister for Foreign Affairs of the Congo.

47. The Congo maintains that, during his or her term of office, a Minister for Foreign Affairs of a sovereign State is entitled to inviolability and to immunity from criminal process being "absolute or complete," that is to say, they are subject to no exception. Accordingly, the Congo contends that no criminal prosecution may be brought against a Minister for Foreign Affairs in a foreign court as long as he or she remains in office, and that any finding of criminal responsibility by a domestic court in a foreign country, or any act of investigation undertaken with a view to bringing him or her to court, would contravene the principle of immunity from jurisdiction. According to the Congo, the basis of such criminal immunity is purely functional, and immunity is accorded under customary international law simply in order to enable the foreign State representative enjoying such immunity to perform his or her functions freely and without let or hindrance. The Congo adds that the immunity thus accorded to Ministers for Foreign Affairs when in office covers all their acts, including any committed before they took office, and that it is irrelevant whether the acts done whilst in office may be characterized or not as "official acts."

48. The Congo states further that it does not deny the existence of a principle of international criminal law, deriving from the decisions of the Nuremberg and Tokyo international military tribunals, that the accused's official capacity at the time of the acts cannot, before any court, whether domestic or international, constitute a "ground of ex-

emption from his criminal responsibility or a ground for mitigation of sentence." The Congo then stresses that the fact that an immunity might bar prosecution before a specific court or over a specific period does not mean that the same prosecution cannot be brought, if appropriate, before another court which is not bound by that immunity, or at another time when the immunity need no longer be taken into account. It concludes that immunity does not mean impunity.

49. Belgium maintains for its part that, while Ministers for Foreign Affairs in office generally enjoy an immunity from jurisdiction before the courts of a foreign State, such immunity applies only to acts carried out in the course of their official functions, and cannot protect such persons in respect of private acts or when they are acting otherwise than in the performance of their official functions.

50. Belgium further states that, in the circumstances of the present case, Mr. Yerodia enjoyed no immunity at the time when he is alleged to have committed the acts of which he is accused, and that there is no evidence that he was then acting in any official capacity. It observes that the arrest warrant was issued against Mr. Yerodia personally.

51. The Court would observe at the outset that in international law it is firmly established that, as also diplomatic and consular agents, certain holders of high-ranking office in a State, such as the Head of State, Head of Government and Minister for Foreign Affairs, enjoy immunities from jurisdiction in other States, both civil and criminal. For the purposes of the present case, it is only the immunity from criminal jurisdiction and the inviolability of an incumbent Minister for Foreign Affairs that fall for the Court to consider.

52. A certain number of treaty instruments were cited by the Parties in this regard. These included, first, the Vienna Convention on Diplomatic Relations of 18 April 1961, which states in its preamble that the purpose of diplomatic privileges and immunities is "to ensure the efficient performance of the functions of diplomatic missions as representing States." It provides in Article 32 that only the sending State may waive such immunity. On these points, the Vienna Convention on Diplomatic Relations, to which both the Congo and Belgium are parties, reflects customary international law. The same applies to the corresponding provisions of the Vienna Convention on Consular Relations of 24 April 1963, to which the Congo and Belgium are also parties.

The Congo and Belgium further cite the New York Convention on Special Missions of 8 December 1969, to which they are not, however, parties. They recall that under Article 21, paragraph 2, of that Convention:

> "The Head of the Government, the Minister for Foreign Affairs and other persons of high rank, when they take part in a special mission of the sending State, shall enjoy in the receiving State or in a third State, in addition to what is granted by the present Convention, the facilities, privileges and immunities accorded by international law."

These conventions provide useful guidance on certain aspects of the question of immunities. They do not, however, contain any provision specifically defining the immunities enjoyed by Ministers for Foreign Affairs. It is consequently on the basis of customary international law that the Court must decide the questions relating to the immunities of such Ministers raised in the present case.

53. In customary international law, the immunities accorded to Ministers for Foreign Affairs are not granted for their personal benefit, but to ensure the effective performance of their functions on behalf of their respective States. In order to determine the extent of these immunities, the Court must therefore first consider the nature of the functions ex-

ercised by a Minister for Foreign Affairs. He or she is in charge of his or her Government's diplomatic activities and generally acts as its representative in international negotiations and intergovernmental meetings. Ambassadors and other diplomatic agents carry out their duties under his or her authority. His or her acts may bind the State represented, and there is a presumption that a Minister for Foreign Affairs, simply by virtue of that office, has full powers to act on behalf of the State (see, for example, Article 7, paragraph 2 (a), of the 1969 Vienna Convention on the Law of Treaties). In the performance of these functions, he or she is frequently required to travel internationally, and thus must be in a position freely to do so whenever the need should arise. He or she must also be in constant communication with the Government, and with its diplomatic missions around the world, and be capable at any time of communicating with representatives of other States. The Court further observes that a Minister for Foreign Affairs, responsible for the conduct of his or her State's relations with all other States, occupies a position such that, like the Head of State or the Head of Government, he or she is recognized under international law as representative of the State solely by virtue of his or her office. He or she does not have to present letters of credence: to the contrary, it is generally the Minister who determines the authority to be conferred upon diplomatic agents and countersigns their letters of credence. Finally, it is to the Minister for Foreign Affairs that chargés d'affaires are accredited.

54. The Court accordingly concludes that the functions of a Minister for Foreign Affairs are such that, throughout the duration of his or her office, he or she when abroad enjoys full immunity from criminal jurisdiction and inviolability. That immunity and that inviolability protect the individual concerned against any act of authority of another State which would hinder him or her in the performance of his or her duties.

55. In this respect, no distinction can be drawn between acts performed by a Minister for Foreign Affairs in an "official" capacity, and those claimed to have been performed in a "private capacity," or, for that matter, between acts performed before the person concerned assumed office as Minister for Foreign Affairs and acts committed during the period of office. Thus, if a Minister for Foreign Affairs is arrested in another State on a criminal charge, he or she is clearly thereby prevented from exercising the functions of his or her office. The consequences of such impediment to the exercise of those official functions are equally serious, regardless of whether the Minister for Foreign Affairs was, at the time of arrest, present in the territory of the arresting State on an "official" visit or a "private" visit, regardless of whether the arrest relates to acts allegedly performed before the person became the Minister for Foreign Affairs or to acts performed while in office, and regardless of whether the arrest relates to alleged acts performed in an "official" capacity or a "private" capacity. Furthermore, even the mere risk that, by travelling to or transiting another State a Minister for Foreign Affairs might be exposing himself or herself to legal proceedings could deter the Minister from travelling internationally when required to do so for the purposes of the performance of his or her official functions ...

56. The Court will now address Belgium's argument that immunities accorded to incumbent Ministers for Foreign Affairs can in no case protect them where they are suspected of having committed war crimes or crimes against humanity. In support of this position, Belgium refers in its Counter-Memorial to various legal instruments creating international criminal tribunals, to examples from national legislation, and to the jurisprudence of national and international courts.

Belgium begins by pointing out that certain provisions of the instruments creating international criminal tribunals state expressly that the official capacity of a person shall not be a bar to the exercise by such tribunals of their jurisdiction.

Belgium also places emphasis on certain decisions of national courts, and in particular on the judgments rendered on 24 March 1999 by the House of Lords in the United Kingdom and on 13 March 2001 by the Court of Cassation in France in the Pinochet and Qaddafi cases respectively, in which it contends that an exception to the immunity rule was accepted in the case of serious crimes under international law.... As to the French Court of Cassation, Belgium contends that, in holding that, "under international law as it currently stands, the crime alleged [acts of terrorism], irrespective of its gravity, does not come within the exceptions to the principle of immunity from jurisdiction for incumbent foreign Heads of State," the Court explicitly recognized the existence of such exceptions....

58. The Court has carefully examined State practice, including national legislation and those few decisions of national higher courts, such as the House of Lords or the French Court of Cassation. It has been unable to deduce from this practice that there exists under customary international law any form of exception to the rule according immunity from criminal jurisdiction and inviolability to incumbent Ministers for Foreign Affairs, where they are suspected of having committed war crimes or crimes against humanity.

The Court has also examined the rules concerning the immunity or criminal responsibility of persons having an official capacity contained in the legal instruments creating international criminal tribunals, and which are specifically applicable to the latter (see Charter of the International Military Tribunal of Nuremberg, Art. 7; Charter of the International Military Tribunal of Tokyo, Art. 6; Statute of the International Criminal Tribunal for the former Yugoslavia, Art. 7, para. 2; Statute of the International Criminal Tribunal for Rwanda, Art. 6, para. 2; Statute of the International Criminal Court, Art. 27). It finds that these rules likewise do not enable it to conclude that any such an exception exists in customary international law in regard to national courts.

59. It should further be noted that the rules governing the jurisdiction of national courts must be carefully distinguished from those governing jurisdictional immunities: jurisdiction does not imply absence of immunity, while absence of immunity does not imply jurisdiction. Thus, although various international conventions on the prevention and punishment of certain serious crimes impose on States obligations of prosecution or extradition, thereby requiring them to extend their criminal jurisdiction, such extension of jurisdiction in no way affects immunities under customary international law, including those of Ministers for Foreign Affairs. These remain opposable before the courts of a foreign State, even where those courts exercise such a jurisdiction under these conventions.

60. The Court emphasizes, however, that the immunity from jurisdiction enjoyed by incumbent Ministers for Foreign Affairs does not mean that they enjoy impunity in respect of any crimes they might have committed, irrespective of their gravity. Immunity from criminal jurisdiction and individual criminal responsibility are quite separate concepts. While jurisdictional immunity is procedural in nature, criminal responsibility is a question of substantive law. Jurisdictional immunity may well bar prosecution for a certain period or for certain offences; it cannot exonerate the person to whom it applies from all criminal responsibility.

61. Accordingly, the immunities enjoyed under international law by an incumbent or former Minister for Foreign Affairs do not represent a bar to criminal prosecution in certain circumstances.

First, such persons enjoy no criminal immunity under international law in their own countries, and may thus be tried by those countries' courts in accordance with the relevant rules of domestic law.

Secondly, they will cease to enjoy immunity from foreign jurisdiction if the State which they represent or have represented decides to waive that immunity.

Thirdly, after a person ceases to hold the office of Minister for Foreign Affairs, he or she will no longer enjoy all of the immunities accorded by international law in other States. Provided that it has jurisdiction under international law, a court of one State may try a former Minister for Foreign Affairs of another State in respect of acts committed prior or subsequent to his or her period of office, as well as in respect of acts committed during that period of office in a private capacity.

Fourthly, an incumbent or former Minister for Foreign Affairs may be subject to criminal proceedings before certain international criminal courts, where they have jurisdiction. Examples include the International Criminal Tribunal for the former Yugoslavia, and the International Criminal Tribunal for Rwanda, established pursuant to Security Council resolutions under Chapter VII of the United Nations Charter, and the future International Criminal Court created by the 1998 Rome Convention. The latter's Statute expressly provides, in Article 27, paragraph 2, that "[i]mmunities or special procedural rules which may attach to the official capacity of a person, whether under national or international law, shall not bar the Court from exercising its jurisdiction over such a person."....

62. Given the conclusions it has reached above concerning the nature and scope of the rules governing the immunity from criminal jurisdiction enjoyed by incumbent Ministers for Foreign Affairs, the Court must now consider whether in the present case the issue of the arrest warrant of 11 April 2000 and its international circulation violated those rules....

70. The Court notes that the *issuance*, as such, of the disputed arrest warrant represents an act by the Belgian judicial authorities intended to enable the arrest on Belgian territory of an incumbent Minister for Foreign Affairs on charges of war crimes and crimes against humanity. The fact that the warrant is enforceable is clearly apparent from the order given to "all bailiffs and agents of public authority ... to execute this arrest warrant".... and from the assertion in the warrant that "the position of Minister for Foreign Affairs currently held by the accused does not entail immunity from jurisdiction and enforcement." The Court notes that the warrant did admittedly make an exception for the case of an official visit by Mr. Yerodia to Belgium, and that Mr. Yerodia never suffered arrest in Belgium. The Court is bound, however, to find that, given the nature and purpose of the warrant, its mere issue violated the immunity which Mr. Yerodia enjoyed as the Congo's incumbent Minister for Foreign Affairs. The Court accordingly concludes that the issue of the warrant constituted a violation of an obligation of Belgium towards the Congo, in that it failed to respect the immunity of that Minister and, more particularly, infringed the immunity from criminal jurisdiction and the inviolability then enjoyed by him under international law.

71. The Court also notes that Belgium admits that the purpose of the international *circulation* of the disputed arrest warrant was "to establish a legal basis for the arrest of Mr. Yerodia ... abroad and his subsequent extradition to Belgium." The Respondent maintains, however, that the enforcement of the warrant in third States was "dependent on some further preliminary steps having been taken" and that, given the "inchoate" quality of the warrant as regards third States, there was no "infringe[ment of] the sovereignty of the [Congo]." It further points out that no Interpol Red Notice was requested until 12 September 2001, when Mr. Yerodia no longer held ministerial office.

The Court cannot subscribe to this view. As in the case of the warrant's issue, its international circulation from June 2000 by the Belgian authorities, given its nature and purpose, effectively infringed Mr. Yerodia's immunity as the Congo's incumbent Minister for Foreign Affairs and was furthermore liable to affect the Congo's conduct of its international relations. Since Mr. Yerodia was called upon in that capacity to undertake travel in the performance of his duties, the mere international circulation of the warrant, even in the absence of "further steps" by Belgium, could have resulted, in particular, in his arrest while abroad. The Court observes in this respect that Belgium itself cites information to the effect that Mr. Yerodia, "on applying for a visa to go to two countries, [apparently] learned that he ran the risk of being arrested as a result of the arrest warrant issued against him by Belgium," adding that "[t]his, moreover, is what the [Congo] ... hints when it writes that the arrest warrant 'sometimes forced Minister Yerodia to travel by roundabout routes.'" Accordingly, the Court concludes that the circulation of the warrant, whether or not it significantly interfered with Mr. Yerodia's diplomatic activity, constituted a violation of an obligation of Belgium towards the Congo, in that it failed to respect the immunity of the incumbent Minister for Foreign Affairs of the Congo and, more particularly, infringed the immunity from criminal jurisdiction and the inviolability then enjoyed by him under international law....

76.... The warrant is still extant, and remains unlawful, notwithstanding the fact that Mr. Yerodia has ceased to be Minister for Foreign Affairs. The Court accordingly considers that Belgium must, by means of its own choosing, cancel the warrant in question and so inform the authorities to whom it was circulated....

78. For these reasons,

THE COURT, ...

(2) By thirteen votes to three,

Finds that the issue against Mr. Abdulaye Yerodia Ndombasi of the arrest warrant of 11 April 2000, and its international circulation, constituted violations of a legal obligation of the Kingdom of Belgium towards the Democratic Republic of the Congo, in that they failed to respect the immunity from criminal jurisdiction and the inviolability which the incumbent Minister for Foreign Affairs of the Democratic Republic of the Congo enjoyed under international law;

> IN FAVOUR: *President* Guillaume; *Vice-President* Shi; *Judges* Ranjeva, Herczegh, Fleischhauer, Koroma, Vereshchetin, Higgins, Parra-Aranguren, Kooijmans, Rezek, Buergenthal; *Judge* ad hoc Bula-Bula;

> AGAINST: *Judges* Oda, Al-Khasawneh; *Judge* ad hoc Van den Wyngaert;

(3) By ten votes to six,

Finds that the Kingdom of Belgium must, by means of its own choosing, cancel the arrest warrant of 11 April 2000 and so inform the authorities to whom that warrant was circulated.

> IN FAVOUR: *President* Guillaume; *Vice-President* Shi; *Judges* Ranjeva, Herczegh, Fleischhauer, Koroma, Vereshchetin, Parra-Aranguren, Rezek; *Judge* ad hoc Bula-Bula;

> AGAINST: *Judges* Oda, Higgins, Kooijmans, Al-Khasawneh, Buergenthal; *Judge* ad hoc

> Van den Wyngaert.

Dissenting Opinion of Judge Van Den Wyngaert

I. Introductory Observations

1. I have voted against paragraphs (2) and (3) of the *dispositif* of this Judgment. International law grants no immunity from criminal process to incumbent Foreign Ministers

suspected of war crimes and crimes against humanity. There is no evidence for the proposition that a State is under an obligation to grant immunity from criminal process to an incumbent Foreign Minister under customary international law. By issuing and circulating the warrant, Belgium may have acted contrary to international comity. It has not, however, acted in violation of an international legal obligation (Judgment, para. 78 (2)).

Surely, the warrant based on charges of war crimes and crimes against humanity cannot infringe rules on immunity *today*, given the fact that Mr. Yerodia has now ceased to be a Foreign Minister and has become an ordinary citizen. Therefore, the Court is wrong when it finds, in the last part of its *dispositif*, that Belgium must cancel the arrest warrant and so inform the authorities to which the warrant was circulated (Judgment, para. 78 (3)).

I will develop the reasons for this dissenting view below. Before doing so, I wish to make some general introductory observations....

3. Belgium has, at present, very broad legislation that allows victims of alleged war crimes and crimes against humanity to institute criminal proceedings in its courts. This triggers negative reactions in some circles, while inviting acclaim in others. Belgium's conduct (by its Parliament, judiciary and executive powers) may show a lack of *international courtesy*. Even if this were true, it does not follow that Belgium actually violated (customary or conventional) international law. *Political wisdom* may command a change in Belgian legislation, as has been proposed in various circles. *Judicial wisdom* may lead to a more restrictive application of the present statute, and may result from proceedings that are pending before the Belgian courts. This does not mean that Belgium has acted in violation of international law by applying it in the case of Mr. Yerodia. I see no evidence for the existence of such a norm, not in conventional or in customary international law for the reasons set out below.

4. The Judgment is shorter than expected because the Court, which was invited by the Parties to narrow the dispute, did not decide the question of (universal) jurisdiction, and has only decided the question of immunity from jurisdiction, even though, logically the question of jurisdiction would have preceded that of immunity....

5. This case was to be a test case, probably the first opportunity for the International Court of Justice to address a number of questions that have not been considered since the famous *"Lotus"* case of the Permanent Court of International Justice in 1927.

In technical terms, the dispute was about an arrest warrant against an incumbent Foreign Minister. The warrant was, however, based on charges of war crimes and crimes against humanity, which the Court even fails to mention in the *dispositif*. In a more principled way, the case was about how far States can or must go when implementing modern international criminal law. It was about the question what international law requires or allows States to do as "agents" of the international community when they are confronted with complaints of victims of such crimes, given the fact that international criminal courts will not be able to judge *all* international crimes. It was about balancing two divergent interests in modern international (criminal) law: the need of international accountability for such crimes as torture, terrorism, war crimes and crimes against humanity and the principle of sovereign equality of States, which presupposes a system of immunities....

II. Immunities

.... 11. I disagree with the proposition that incumbent Foreign Ministers enjoy immunities on the basis of customary international law for the simple reason that there is no evidence in support of this proposition. Before reaching this conclusion, the Court should have examined whether there is a rule of customary international law to this effect. It is not sufficient to compare the rationale for the protection from suit in the case of diplomats, Heads of State and Foreign Ministers to draw the conclusion that there is a rule of customary international law protecting Foreign Ministers: identifying a common raison d'être for a protective rule is one thing, elevating this protective rule to the status of customary international law is quite another thing. The Court should have first examined whether the conditions for the formation of a rule of customary law were fulfilled in the case of incumbent Foreign Ministers. In a surprisingly short decision, the Court immediately reaches the conclusion that such a rule exists. A more rigorous approach would have been highly desirable.

12. In the brevity of its reasoning, the Court disregards its own case law on the subject on the formation of customary international law. In order to constitute a rule of customary international law, there must be evidence of State practice *(usus)* and *opinio juris* to the effect that this rule exists....

A "negative practice" of States, consisting in their abstaining from instituting criminal proceedings, cannot, in itself, be seen as evidence of an *opinio juris*. Abstinence may be explained by many other reasons, including courtesy, political considerations, practical concerns and lack of extraterritorial criminal jurisdiction. Only if this abstention was based on a conscious decision of the States in question can this practice generate customary international law. An important precedent is the 1927 *"Lotus"* case, where the French Government argued that there was a rule of customary international law to the effect that Turkey was *not* entitled to institute criminal proceedings with regard to offences committed by foreigners abroad. The Permanent Court of International Justice rejected this argument....

24. On the subject of war crimes and crimes against humanity, the Court reaches the following decision: it holds that it is unable to decide that there exists under customary international law any form of exception to the rule according immunity from criminal process and inviolability to incumbent Ministers for Foreign Affairs, where they are suspected of having committed war crimes or crimes against humanity (Judgment, para. 58, first subparagraph)....

25. I strongly disagree with these propositions. To start with, as set out above, the Court starts from a flawed premise, assuming that incumbent Foreign Ministers enjoy full immunity from jurisdiction under customary international law. This premise taints the rest of the reasoning. It leads to another flaw in the reasoning: in order to "counterbalance" the postulated customary international law rule of "full immunity," there needs to be evidence of another customary international law rule that would negate the first rule. It would need to be established that the principle of international accountability has also reached the status of customary international law. The Court finds no evidence for the existence of such a rule in the limited sources it considers and concludes that there is a violation of the first rule, the rule of immunity....

27. Apart from being wrong in law, the Court is wrong for another reason. The more fundamental problem lies in its general approach, that disregards the whole recent movement in modern international criminal law towards recognition of the principle of individual accountability for international core crimes. The Court does not completely ignore this, but it takes an extremely minimalist approach by adopting a very narrow interpretation of the "no immunity clauses" in international instruments. Yet, there are many codifications of this principle in various sources of law, including the Nuremberg Prin-

ciples and Article IV of the Genocide Convention. In addition, there are several United Nations resolutions and reports on the subject of international accountability for war crimes and crimes against humanity.

In legal doctrine, there is a plethora of recent scholarly writings on the subject. Major scholarly organizations, including the International Law Association and the Institut de droit international have adopted resolutions and newly established think tanks, such as the drafters of the "Princeton principles" and of the "Cairo principles" have made statements on the issue. Advocacy organizations, such as Amnesty International, Avocats sans Frontières, Human Rights Watch, The International Federation of Human Rights Leagues (FIDH) and the International Commission of Jurists, have taken clear positions on the subject of international accountability. This may be seen as the opinion of civil society, an opinion that cannot be completely discounted in the formation of customary international law today. In several cases, *civil society* organizations have set in motion a process that ripened into international conventions. Well-known examples are the 1968 Convention on the Non-Applicability of Statutory Limitations to War Crimes and Crimes against Humanity, which can be traced back to efforts of the International Association of Penal Law, the 1984 Convention against Torture and Other Cruel, Inhuman or Degrading Treatment or Punishment, probably triggered by Amnesty International's Campaign against Torture, the 1997 Treaty banning landmines, to which the International Campaign to Ban Landmines gave a considerable impetus and the 1998 Statute for the International Criminal Court, which was promoted by a coalition of non-governmental organizations.

28. The Court fails to acknowledge this development, and does not discuss the relevant sources. Instead, it adopts a formalistic reasoning, examining whether there is, under customary international law, an international crimes exception to the–wrongly postulated–rule of immunity for incumbent Ministers under customary international law (Judgment, para. 58). By adopting this approach, the Court implicitly establishes a hierarchy between the rules on immunity (protecting incumbent Foreign Ministers) and the rules on international accountability (calling for the investigation of charges against incumbent Foreign Ministers charged with war crimes and crimes against humanity).

By elevating the former rules to the level of customary international law in the first part of its reasoning, and finding that the latter have failed to reach the same status in the second part of its reasoning, the Court does not need to give further consideration to the status of the principle of international accountability under international law. As a result, the Court does not further examine the status of the principle of international accountability. Other courts, for example the House of Lords in the *Pinochet* case and the European Court of Human Rights in the *Al-Adsani* case, have given more thought and consideration to the balancing of the relative normative status of international *jus cogens* crimes and immunities.

Notes and Questions

1. Do you agree with the majority or the dissent? Is there immunity of any person of any status in any international criminal instrument that has been identified so far? Do you suspect that the majority was aware of the many prosecutions of heads of state noted in materials set forth before this I.C.J. extract?

2. For more on the rejection of claims of immunity or amnesty, refer to Sadat, *Exile, Amnesty, and International Law* and notes 1–2, *supra* Chapter One.

3. Because the Congo failed to include an objection to jurisdiction in its final filings, the ICJ was unable to rule on the question of whether Belgium's claim of universal juris-

diction was legitimate. Nonetheless, President Guillaume issued a separate opinion finding that Belgium's claim of universal jurisdiction was not legitimate while Judges Higgins, Kooijmans, and Buergenthal issued an opinion finding that Belgium's arrest warrant did fall within "that small category" of grave crimes against humanity where universal jurisdiction is appropriate. *See* Chapter Three, Section 1.

4. Consider the following, from The Prosecutor v. Omar Hassan Ahmad Al Bashir, *Decision on the Prosecution's Application for a Warrant of Arrest*, Case No. ICC-02/05-02/09 (4 March 2009):

41. Furthermore, in light of the materials presented by the Prosecution in support of the Prosecution Application, and without prejudice to a further determination of the matter pursuant to article 19 of the Statute, the Chamber considers that the current position of Omar Al Bashir as Head of a state which is not a party to the Statute, has no effect on the Court's jurisdiction over the present case.

42. The Chamber reaches this conclusion on the basis of the four following considerations. First, the Chamber notes that, according to the Preamble of the Statute, one of the core goals of the Statute is to put an end to impunity for the perpetrators of the most serious crimes of concern to the international community as a whole, which "must not go unpunished." [Preamble of the Statute, paras. 4 and 5. No. ICC-02/05-01/09 15/95 4 March 2009 ICC-02/05-01/09-3 04-03-2009 15/146 CBPT]

43. Second, the Chamber observes that, in order to achieve this goal, article 27(1) and (2) of the Statute provide for the following core principles:

(i) "This Statute shall apply equally to all persons without any distinction based on official capacity;"

(ii) " … official capacity as a Head of State or Government, a member of Government or parliament, an elected representative or a government official shall in no case exempt a person from criminal responsibility under this Statute, nor shall it, in and of itself, constitute a ground for reduction of sentence;" and

(iii) "Immunities or special procedural rules which may attach to the official capacity of a person, whether under national or international law, shall not bar the Court from exercising its jurisdiction over such a person."

44. Third, the consistent case law of the Chamber on the applicable law before the Court has held that, according to article 21 of the Statute, those other sources of law provided for in paragraphs (l)(b) and (l)(c) of article 21 of the Statute, can only be resorted to when the following two conditions are met: (i) there is a lacuna in the written law contained in the Statute, the Elements of Crimes and the Rules; and (ii) such lacuna cannot be filled by the application of the criteria of interpretation provided in articles 31 and 32 of the Vienna Convention on the Law of the Treaties and article 21(3) of the Statute.

45. Fourth, as the Chamber has recently highlighted in its 5 February 2009 "Decision on Application under Rule 103," by referring the Darfur situation to the Court, pursuant to article 13(b) of the Statute, the Security Council of the United Nations has also accepted that the investigation into the said situation, as well as any prosecution arising therefrom, will take place in accordance with the statutory framework provided for in the Statute, the Elements of Crimes and the Rules as a whole.

5. Note that, per dicta, the majority stated that head of state immunity does not apply before an international criminal tribunal such as the ICTY, ICTR, and ICC. Addressing this dicta, the Special Court for Sierra Leone recognized that it was an international tribunal and that as a consequence it could properly indict Liberian President Charles Taylor for Crimes Against Humanity. The ICTY had already ruled that Milosevic could not take advantage of any claimed head of state immunity.

For views contrary to the majority, *see also* the dissenting opinion of Judge Al-Khasawneh, at paras. 1 (there is a "total absence of precedents with regard to the immunities of Foreign Ministers from criminal process"), 6–7, 11, *reprinted in* 41 I.L.M. 595 (2002); Adam Day, *Crimes Against Humanity as a Nexus of Individual and State Responsibility: Why the ICJ Got Belgium v. Congo Wrong*, 22 Berk. J. Int'l L. 489 (2004); Micaela Frulli, *The ICJ Judgment on the Belgium v. Congo Case (14 February 2002): A Cautious Stand on Immunity from Prosecution for International Crimes*, 3 German L.J. 3, 4 (2002); David S. Koller, *Immunities of Foreign Ministers: Paragraph 61 of the Yerodia Judgment as it Pertains to the Security Council and the International Criminal Court*, 20 Am. U. Int'l L. Rev. 7, 15 (2004); Abdul Tejan-Cole, *A Big Man in a Small Cell: Charles Taylor and the Special Court for Sierra Leone*, in Ellen Lutz & Caitlin Reiger, Prosecuting Heads of State 205, 222–24 (2009); Alberto Luis Zuppi, *Immunity v. Universal Jurisdiction: The Yerodia Ndombasi Decision of the International Court of Justice*, 63 La. L. Rev. 309 (2003). The majority opinion stated that the immunity afforded was not a substantive immunity, and did not imply impunity for acts that are criminal under international law. Specifically, the majority stated that "[w]hile jurisdictional immunity is procedural in nature, criminal responsibility is a question of substantive law. Jurisdictional immunity may well bar prosecution for a certain period or for certain offences; it cannot exonerate the person to whom it applies from all [criminal] responsibility." *Id.* para 60. Moreover, there is no immunity in an international criminal tribunal. *Id.* para. 61.

6. Read Article 1 of the Convention Against Torture, in the Documents Supplement. Who is expressly covered? Is there immunity expressed in any form? Is the treaty really "silent" on nonimmunity? Whether or not it is "silent," would customary international law reflected in the instruments noted above be useful background for interpretive purposes? Recall Vienna Convention on the Law of Treaties, art. 31 (3) (c), quoted in Chapter One.

7. Do Article 2(3)(a) of the International Covenant on Civil and Political Rights (ICCPR) and Article 25 (1) of the American Convention on Human Rights, in the Documents Supplement, provide further indicia of relevant legal expectations concerning nonimmunity for violations of human rights in the Americas? Consider also Article IX of the Inter-American Convention on the Forced Disappearance of Persons, in the Documents Supplement.

8. Concerning lack of former head of state immunity in the U.S., *see also United States v. Noriega*, 117 F.3d 1206, 1212 (11th Cir. 1997); *Jimenez v. Aristeguieta*, 311 F.2d 547 (5th Cir. 1962); Paust, Van Dyke, Malone, International Law and Litigation in the U.S. 460, 510, 861–80 (3 ed. 2009).

B. Membership in Organizations and Groups

Introduction

Membership in an organization declared to be criminal under international law can raise issues with respect to individual and group responsibility. In general, mere membership in such an organization does not directly create individual criminal responsibility. However, membership in such an organization can be part of relevant features of context and, coupled with other facts, might be relevant to personal responsibility as a (1) complicitor, (2) conspirator, or (3) member of a joint criminal enterprise with respect to international crimes directly committed by others. Membership can be part of circumstantial evidence with respect to proof of relevant connections and standards of *mens rea*. Consider what types of connection to the direct perpetrator of a crime is needed for each of these three general categories of relational responsibility and consider what type of *mens rea* is needed for each, *e.g.*, from intent, knowledge, wanton or reckless disregard, awareness, and negligence or foreseeability.

Domestically, Italy and the United States tend to criminalize membership in organized crime groups, while most countries require proof of some form of complicitous or conspiratorial involvement.

Organizations were declared to be "criminal" at the I.M.T. at Nuremberg for certain purposes. One purpose or result is explained below. Another involved the need to outlaw certain organizations for purposes of military government or occupation and still another purpose related to the need to control the assets of such criminal organizations. This latter purpose can also be related to responsibilities of groups or states, as well as individuals, to make reparations or to pay money damages for violations of international law. One aspect of the law of "state responsibility," for example, involves monetary sanctions that might pertain when a state violates international law.

Telford Taylor, Final Report to the Secretary of the Army on the Nuernberg War Crimes Trials under Control Council Law No. 10
at 69–70 (1949)

... Control Council Law No. 10 also "recognized" as a distinct punishable offense "membership in categories of a criminal group or organization declared criminal by the International Military Tribunal." The IMT did in fact declare several of the Nazi organizations (notably the SS and the Leadership Corps of the Nazi Party) criminal in character, but at the same time stated that the declaration should not apply to "persons who had no knowledge of the criminal purposes or acts of the organization ... unless they were personally implicated ... Membership alone is not enough to come within the scope of these declarations." Thus, membership was not really made a distinct and self-sufficient crime but rather was one of the ways by which an individual might be proved guilty of complicity in one or more of the four substantive categories of crimes just described.

As stated above, it was determined during the early part of 1946 that the so-called "membership cases" would, for the most part, be handled as a part of the denazification program. The punishment of membership in these organizations (within the limits of the IMT declaration) was, therefore, only an incidental purpose of the Nuernberg trials. In the three cases entirely devoted to activities of the SS (the "Pohl," "RuSHA," and "Einsatz" cases), substantially all of the defendants were SS officers, and accordingly were charged with membership as well as with the specific offenses described in the other counts of the indictments. In three other cases (the "Medical," "Justice," and "Ministries" cases) a majority of the defendants were members of one or more of the criminal organizations, and were likewise indicted accordingly. In two additional cases (the "Flick" and "Farben" cases) the "membership" charge was relatively unimportant, and in the remaining four trials (the "Milch," "Hostage," "Krupp," and "High Command" cases) it played no part whatsoever.

Notes and Questions

1. Concerning the fact that mere membership in the military is not a crime, *see, e.g.,* *Johnson v. Eisentrager,* 339 U.S. 763, 793 (1950) (Black, J., dissenting) ("legitimate 'acts of warfare,' however murderous, do not justify criminal conviction.... [I]t is no 'crime' to be a soldier"), citing *Ex parte Quirin,* 317 U.S. 1, 30–31 (1942); *United States v. Valentine,* 288 F. Supp. 957, 987 (D.P.R. 1968) ("Mere membership in the armed forces could not under any circumstances create criminal liability."), citing *Ford v. Surget,* 97 U.S. 594, 605–06 (1878). A related precept is combatant immunity. Combatant immunity provides immunity for combatants for lawful acts of war during a belligerency or international armed conflict. *See, e.g.,* Paust, *War and Enemy Status After 9/11: Attacks on the Laws of War,* 28 YALE J. INT'L L. 325, 330–32 (2003).

2. Concerning the liability of corporations and other organizations for international crime, also see 3 INTERNATIONAL CRIMINAL LAW: ENFORCEMENT 21, 104, 230 (M. Cherif Bassiouni ed. 1987); Johan D. van der Vyver, *Prosecution and Punishment of the Crime of Genocide,* 23 FORDHAM INT'L L.J. 286, 291, 297–98 (1999). Corporations have also been recognizably subject to civil sanctions for violations of international law. *See, e.g., Wiwa v. Royal Dutch Petroleum Co.,* 226 F.3d 88, 92 (2d Cir. 2000); *Weisshaus v. Swiss Bankers Ass'n,* 225 F.3d 191 (2d Cir. 2000); *Presbyterian Church of Sudan v. Talisman Energy, Inc.,* 374 F. Supp.2d 331 (S.D.N.Y. 2005); *In re Agent Orange Prod. Liab. Litig.,* 373 F. Supp.2d 7 (E.D.N.Y. 2005); *Estate of Rodriquez v. Drummond Co.,* 256 F. Supp.2d 1250 (N.D. Ala. 2003); *Burger-Fisher v. Degussa Corp.,* 65 F. Supp.2d 248, 272–73 (D.N.J. 1999); *Iwanowa v. Ford Motor Co.,* 57 F. Supp.2d 41, 60–62 (D.N.J. 1999); *Doe v. Unocal Corp.,* 963 F. Supp. 880 (C.D. Cal. 1997); *Jota v. Texaco, Inc.,* 157 F.3d 153 (2d Cir. 1998); 26 Op. Att'y Gen. 250, 252–53 (1907); Jordan J. Paust, *Nonstate Actor Participation in International Law and the Pretense of Exclusion,* 51 VA. J. INT'L L. 979, 986–89 (2011) (documenting these and other cases as well as 20 U.S. Supreme Court cases that have recognized that corporations and companies can have duties and rights under international law); PAUST, VAN DYKE, MALONE, INTERNATIONAL LAW AND LITIGATION IN THE U.S. 18–20 (3 ed. 2009). Vessels have also been subject to criminal fines and seizure for violations of international law, such as involvement in the slave trade and piracy and violation of the laws of neutrality and war. *See, e.g.,* Paust, *Nonstate Actor Participation, supra* at 990–92.

3. There is a possibility that some will blur the distinction between "criminal organization" responsibility and "collective punishment." As the above material demonstrates, guilt must be personal, although one can be guilty of complicitous involvement in violations of international law. Today, human rights norms prohibit collective punishment or the punishment of persons not for their acts or omissions, but for those of others.

This prohibition is evidenced in many related prohibitions. For example, norms of human rights in time of armed conflict clearly recognize the prohibition of collective punishment. *See, e.g.,* 1949 Geneva Convention Relative to the Protection of Civilian Persons in Time of War, Article 33, 75 U.N.T.S. 287, 6 U.S.T. 3516 (1955); the 1919 list of war crimes, *supra;* 1907 Hague Convention No. IV, Respecting the Laws and Customs of War on Land. Annex, Article 50, 36 Stat. 2277, T.S. No. 539, declared customary international law at Nuremberg, I Trials Major War Crimes 253–54 (1947); *see also id.* at 221. Human Rights law also recognizes the prohibition against "collective expulsion of aliens."

See, e.g., 1969 American Convention on Human Rights, Article 22(9), in the Documents Supplement; 1950 European Convention on Human Rights, 313 U.N.T.S. 221, Protocol No. 4, Article 4; Declaration on the Human Rights of Individuals Who Are Not Citizens of the Country in Which They Live, G.A. Res. 40/144, 40 U.N. GAOR, Supp. No. 53, at 252, U.N. Doc. A/40/53 (1985).

It is also important to recognize that any form of collective punishment would violate the right of individuals to human dignity (*e.g.*, the Universal Declaration of Human Rights, Article 1) and would necessarily deprive individuals of their right to be treated as individuals and to recognition "as a person before the law." *See id.* at Article 6. This would necessarily violate the right of the individual to be "presumed innocent." *See id.* at Article 11. This would subject the individual to "inhuman or degrading treatment or punishment." *Id.* at Article 5. *See also* International Covenant on Civil and Political Rights, arts. 2 (1), 4, 5, 9 (1), 22, 26, in the Documents Supplement.

Clearly an affirmation of individual worth and dignity, which is also recognized in the preamble to the United Nations Charter, requires that individuals be punished only for what they as an individual have done. As Justice Murphy rightly warned in another context: "to infer that examples of individual disloyalty prove group disloyalty and justify discriminatory action against the entire group is to deny that under our system of law individual guilt is the sole basis for deprivation of rights ... [and] to adopt one of the cruelest of the rationales used by our enemies to destroy the dignity of the individual and to encourage and open the door to discriminatory actions against other minority groups in the passions of tomorrow." *Korematsu v. United States*, 323 U.S. 214, 240 (1944) (Murphy, J., dissenting).

4. United States cases also recognize that collective punishment is impermissible and that governmental schemes premised upon action which "in essence comprehends the collective punishment of [individual] persons" must be condemned under the fifth amendment. *See Communist Party of the United States v. United States*, 384 U.S. 957, 967 (1967); *see also In re Yamashita*, 327 U.S. 1, 21 n.8 (1946). For similar reasons, federal courts have long condemned any governmental action or decree that smacks of "guilt by association." *See, e.g., Healy v. James*, 408 U.S. 169, 186 (1972); *United States v. Robel*, 389 U.S. 258, 265 (1967); *Keyishian v. Board of Regents*, 385 U.S. 589, 607 (1967); *NAACP v. Overstreet*, 384 U.S. 118, 122 (1966) (Douglas, J., dissenting); *Elfbrandt v. Russell*, 384 U.S. 11, 19 (1966); *Uphaus v. Wyman*, 360 U.S. 72, 79 (1959); *Adler v. Board of Education*, 342 U.S. 485, 508 (1952) (Douglas, J., dissenting); *Bridges v. Wixon*, 326 U.S. 135, 163 (1945) (Murphy, J., concurring). As our courts have said repeatedly, guilt must be personal, collective guilt is alien to our jurisprudence and to American values. *See, e.g., Schware v. Board of Bar Examiners*, 353 U.S. 232, 246 (1957); *Joint Anti-Fascist Refugee Committee v. McGrath*, 341 U.S. 123, 178 (1951) (Douglas, J., concurring); *Bridges v. Wixon*, 326 U.S. 135 (1945); *Schneidermann v. United States*, 320 U.S. 118, 154 (1943).

5. Would it be appropriate to prosecute members of al Qaeda on the basis of membership in a criminal organization? Would all members be rightly prosecuted for complicity or conspiracy to commit aircraft hijacking and the attacks on the World Trade Center on September 11, 2001? Later, also consider the tests used by the ICTY and other tribunals concerning individual responsibility for participation in a joint criminal enterprise.

6. Consider also *Switkes v. Laird*, 316 F. Supp. 358, 365 (S.D.N.Y. 1970) ("If war crimes are being committed in Indochina, not every member of the armed forces is an accomplice in those crimes"). What does a prosecutor have to prove in order to demonstrate accomplice responsibility? Consider the next subsection.

C. Complicity

Paust, *My Lai and Vietnam*...

57 Mɪʟ. L. Rᴇᴠ. 99, 165–69 (1972)

Individual Guilt and the Law of War

A. The Standards of Accountability

[P]articipation alone in even a criminal war does not constitute a sufficient basis for personal criminal guilt. As Telford Taylor asserts in disagreeing with Richard Falk's argument that guilt comes with knowledgeable participation in a criminal war, "the Nuremberg judgments ... have no such wide embrace. Those convicted at both Nuremberg and Tokyo of 'crimes against peace' were all part of the inner circles of leadership, and the Nuremberg acquittals of generals and industrialists cut directly against Professor Falk's argument." It was stated at Nuremberg that although the criminality of an organization can be analogous to the concept of conspiracy, membership alone in a criminal organization is not enough. Persons with "no knowledge of the criminal purposes or acts of the organization and those who were drafted by the State for membership," should at any rate be excluded from criminal prosecution "unless they were personally implicated in the commission of" criminal acts.

Furthermore, the Nuremberg Tribunal declared that membership in the armed forces or even an elite command structure is not a sufficient basis for prosecution absent personal guilt. It added that the German General Staff and High Command was neither an "organization" nor a "group" within the meaning of the normative precepts under consideration, and that the individual could not know he was joining a "group" or "organization" for such did not exist.

The Tokyo Tribunal "did not maintain that every member of the Japanese armed forces committed murder, or a punishable crime, in World War II. Common soldiers are entitled to presume the justice of their nation's war because they are almost always not in possession of sufficient facts to make a proper judgment," and should not be declared criminals per se "even though the war itself was actually criminal." Furthermore, the crime of conspiracy "is not possible if a person is in such ignorance of the factual situation that he does not know he is entering into a criminal agreement or plan, and if he may not be held to the duty of knowledge as a reasonable man."

B. Complicity

There can be a crime of complicity, but complicity does not include the actions of all those contributing to the crime "in the normal exercise of their duties." Complicity involves more than a contribution, it involves a necessary guilty intent. We should not forget, however, that society can act to remove from the armed forces those individuals who though lacking any subjective mental guilt or moral wrong-doing have nevertheless demonstrated a dangerous quality which society can ill-afford to be exercised.

There have been few efforts at defining the international standards of complicity. During the Diplomatic Conference on the 1949 Geneva Conventions it was even decided that such matters "should be left to the judges who would apply the national laws" enacted to punish grave breaches of the Conventions. J. Pictet in his commentary states that in the Convention law there is:

> joint responsibility of the author of an act and the man who orders it to be done.
> It will be possible to prosecute them both as accomplices. There is no mention,
> however, of the responsibility which might be incurred by persons who do not

intervene to prevent or to put an end to a breach of the Convention. In several cases of this type the Allied courts brought in a verdict of guilty. In view of the Convention's silence on this point, it will have to be determined under municipal law....

One of the U.S. standards in 1914 was that where an entire "body of troops, systematically disregards the law of war, *e.g.*, by refusal of quarter, any individuals belonging to it who are taken prisoner may be treated as *implicated* in the offense." (emphasis supplied.) During the Korean War a standard was expressed in the United Nations Command order that anyone who commits an offense "or who aids, abets, counsels, commands, permits, induces, or procures its commission, is a principal." Winthrop also referred to a complicitous offense through "taking part in" maltreatment or failure in the care of prisoners, but it is not clear by what criteria one was judged in the early days.

After World War II there were several convictions for complicitous conduct though judgments did not go into great detail in describing the guidelines used. In the *Trial of Lt. Gen. Kurt Maelzer*,[7] the general was found guilty of exposing prisoners in his custody to acts of violence, insults and public curiosity by ordering American and British prisoners of war to be paraded in the streets of Rome in 1944. According to witnesses, the population threw stones and sticks at the prisoners. The general's guilt was hinged partially on the joint action of exposure and public infliction of injury. A similar result was reached in the *Borkum Island* case when civilians brutalized and killed U.S. fliers who had been paraded through the streets of the Island in 1944.[8] Some members of the German guard who *stood by* as the civilians inflicted injury and death were convicted along with the commander who ordered the parading of troops and the Burgomeister and four civilians who took part in the incident. In the *Trial of Major Rauer and Six Others*,[9] four officers charged with being "concerned in" the killing of allied prisoners were convicted after the judge advocate pointed out that the prosecution had maintained that none of the killings could have occurred without the connivance, direction and complicity of the commander and his adjutant under the circumstances. At least three other cases found persons guilty of complicity,[10] but more revealing language is found in *The Alamo Trial*,[11] there the defendants were found to have known that the purpose of their assembly in the woods was to kill prisoners of war and civilian detainees. The report on the trial stated that under the circumstances:

> If people were all *present together* at the same time, *taking part in a common enterprise* which was unlawful, each one in their own way *assisting the common purpose* of all, they were equally guilty in law. [emphasis supplied.]

One had commanded the group, one did the actual shooting, and another "assisted by staying at the car and preventing strangers from disturbing the other two while they were engaged in the crime."[12]

---

7. 11 L.R T.W.C. 53 (1949).

8. Case No. 12-489, United States v. Kurt Goebell, *et al* (Dachau, Germany), see Report, Survey of the Trials of War Crimes Held at Dachau Germany ("The Simpson Report" to the Secretary of the Army) at 2–3 (Sept. 14, 1948 [hereinafter cited as The Simpson Report].

9. 4 L.R.T.W.C. 113, 116 (1948).

10. United States v. Milch, 2 T.W.C. 355, 854, 867 (1949); Trial of Gustav Becker, Wilhelm Weber and Eighteen Others, 7 L.R.T.W.C. 67, 70 (1948); the Trial of Franz Holstein and Twenty-three Others, 8 L.R.T.W.C. 22, 31–33 (1949). *See also* The Simpson Report at 2 (U.S. v. Otto Pauly, *et al.*), 4 (Beck and Weinreich), and 5 (Engelneiderhammer).

11. 1 L.R.T.W.C. 35, 43 (1947).

12. *Id.* See allegation that two American officers "stood by and watched and made no attempt to stop the mistreatment" of suspects being interrogated by South Vietnamese interpreters concerning the problem of defining and investigating complicity in the commission of war crimes in the Vietnamese

Although not entirely revealing of the measurement of guilt, these cases and pronouncements evidence an international norm of complicitous guilt which should be relevant to war crimes prosecutions in the future. It seems that in no case has mere presence at an incident been sufficient to constitute a crime. But what further conduct would constitute aiding and abetting the commission of war crimes or some accessory responsibility is not known with sufficient exactitude for "line-drawing" purposes. We know that some sort of criminal intent is necessary for a criminal prosecution involving complicitous conduct, but it seems that the intent can be minimally shown by circumstantial factors. There seem to be no charges for complicitous conduct arising from Vietnam war crimes or prohibited acts. In the trial of Captain Kotouc for finger maiming it seems that no such charges were brought; nor even charges of the lesser offenses of assault or conduct in violation of Article 17 of the 1949 Geneva Prisoner of War Convention of such a nature as to bring discredit upon the armed forces. Captain Kotouc was acquitted in April 1971, apparently on the ground that the maiming itself was accidental. Similarly, no such charges, or even charges of dereliction of duty, appear in the Medina trial.[13]

Although there were apparent failures of some American advisors to intervene to suggest to our allies that troops desist from violating the law, apparently no action has been taken against any U.S. advisor. It has been suggested in excuse that American advisors "did not have *command* authority over the Vietnamese,"[14] but past cases clearly demonstrate that one need not have command authority to violate standards of criminal complicity. Additionally, it is no excuse that those who commit the actual injury are allies when the crime of complicity has been committed.

Notes and Questions

1. Instead of the word "complicity" or the phrase "aided and abetted," some treaties use the word "accomplice". Is there a meaningful difference? Article 4(1) of the Convention Against Torture uses the phrase "complicity or participation in torture." *See also* Article III of the International Convention on the Suppression and Punishment of the Crime of "Apartheid" ("participate in, directly incite or conspire in ... Directly abet, encourage or co-operate in the commission of the crime...."). *Compare* Article 25 (3) (b)-(d) of the Statute of the ICC.

---

conflict. *U.S. Admits Violations of Geneva Code in Treatment of PWs*, Philadelphia Inquirer, Nov. 2, 1969, at 2. *Medina Says South Vietnam's Police Killed 2 He Is Accused of Murdering*, N.Y. Times, Aug. 12, 1970 at 10; and *Finger Maiming Is Laid to Kotouc*, N.Y. Times, Apr. 27, 1971, at 10 (allegations of complicitous conduct with South Vietnamese).

13. It is arguable, however, that actual dereliction of duty (an offense under article 92 of the UCMJ) is punishable under the charge of murder in violation of article 118 of the UCMJ where such conduct led directly to the death of the relevant persons. A dereliction of duty of such a nature as to evince a wanton disregard for human life and which is inherently dangerous to others could constitute the conduct relevant to a murder charge (dereliction would become the relevant act or omission). Furthermore, it is arguable that in such a case the dereliction of duty would be a lesser included offense to such a murder charge (article 79, UCMJ). Also included in the charge of murder are the lesser offenses of voluntary or involuntary manslaughter (article 119, UCMJ) and negligent homicide (article 134, UCMJ). *Cf.* events which took place concerning the prosecution of Captain Medina in: *101 of 102 Medina Murder Counts Cut*, Wash. Post, Sep. 18, 1971, at A1 and A4. Captain Medina was eventually found innocent of the remaining charges; Wash. Post, Sep. 23, 1971, at A1. The charge to the jury in the Medina case has been questioned by Telford Taylor, *see The Course of Military Justice*, N.Y. Times, Feb. 2, 1972, at 37 M.

14. *See The Herbert Case and the Record*, ARMY, Feb. 1972, at 6, 9–10.

2. Early U.S. cases and opinions addressing various forms of individual responsibility appear *infra* in Chapter Four, Sections 2–5 and 7. In general, 18 U.S.C. §2 treats a person aiding and abetting as a principal: "Whoever commits an offense against the United States or aids, abets, counsels, commands, induces or procures its commission, is punishable as a principle." Some special statutes provide punishments for aiders and abetters that differ from those for principals.

3. At least three significant cases before the International Criminal Tribunal for Rwanda involved convictions for complicitous behavior. In *The Prosecutor v. Jean-Paul Akayesu*, ICTR-96-4-T (2 Sept. 1998, Akayesu, a mayor or bourmestre of the commune Taba, was convicted for "direct and public incitement to commit genocide" (Count 4), but was found not guilty of "complicity in Genocide" (Count 2) because he was actually found guilty of committing genocide (Count 1) and the Trial Chamber had stated that "the same person could certainly not be both the principal perpetrator of, and accomplice to, the same offence ... [and that] the Chamber deems it necessary, in the instant case, to rule on Counts 1 and 2 simultaneously, so as to determine, as far as each proven fact is concerned, whether it constituted genocide or complicity in genocide." See *id*. paras. 26, 45–47, 56, and findings. With respect to the *mens rea* element concerning an accomplice to genocide (which itself requires a specific intent identified in Article II of the Convention), the Trial Chamber declared: "an accused is an accomplice in genocide if he knowingly aided and abetted or provoked a person or persons to commit genocide, knowing that this person or persons were committing genocide...." *Id*. para. 46. Do you agree with such a test? Is it a defense that an accused did not know that relevant conduct was genocide? Is that a defense under Articles II or III of the Genocide Convention with respect to a primary perpetrator, *i.e.*, one who commits genocide?

In *The Prosecutor v. Jean Kambanda*, ICTR-97-23-S (4 Sept. 1998, at www.un.org/ictr, Kambanda, an ex-Prime Minister, was found guilty of both "direct and public incitement to commit genocide" and "complicity in genocide" even though he was also found guilty of acts of genocide, since the complicitous acts were not the same acts supporting conviction of genocide as such. See *id*. para. 40. The portion of the opinion addressing the facts emphasized, for example, his refusal to act despite his participation in "meetings of the Council of Ministers, cabinet meetings and meetings of prefects where the course of massacres were actively followed," the circumstance where "he was personally asked to take steps to protect children who had survived the massacre at a hospital and he did not respond," another circumstance involving directives that "encouraged and reinforced" those committing massacres, and his "clear support" of a radio station "with the knowledge that it was a radio station whose broadcasts incited killing, the commission of serious bodily injury or mental harm to, and persecution of Tutsi and moderate Hutu." See *id*. para. 39.

In *The Prosecutor v. Georges Anderson Nderubumwe Rutaganda*, ICTR-96-3-T (6 Dec. 1999), the Trial Chamber found "that aiding and abetting alone is sufficient to render the accused criminally liable. In both instances, it is not necessary that the person aiding and abetting another to commit an offence be present during the commission of the crime. The relevant act of assistance may be geographically and temporally unconnected to the actual commission of the offence. The Chamber holds that aiding and abetting include all acts of assistance in either physical form or in the form of moral support; nevertheless, it emphasizes that any act of participation must substantially contribute to the commission of the crime. The aider and abettor assists or facilitates another in the accomplishment of a substantive offence." *Id*. at para. 43.

4. The Appeals Chamber of the ICTY in the Judgment of *The Prosecutor v. Tadic*, ICTY-94-1-AR72 (15 July 1999), also contains extensive discussion of complicity. See *id.* paras. 178–237, *reprinted in* 38 I.L.M. 1518, 1552–1566 (1999). *Tadic* was quoted in part in Barrueto v. Larios, 205 F. Supp.2d 1325, 1333 (S.D. Fla. 2002).

5. *Compare* Article 25 (3) (c) and (d) of the Statute of the ICC, in the Documents Supplement. Does it limit responsibility as an accomplice? See Johan D. van der Vyver, *Prosecution and Punishment of the Crime of Genocide*, 23 FORDHAM INT'L L.J. 286, 312–14 (1999), also addressing *The Prosecutor v. Tadic*, which declared that "assisting and abetting includes all acts of assistance by words or acts that lends encouragement or support, as long as the requisite intent is present" and added that if the accused "knowingly participated ... and his participation directly and substantially affected the commission of" the principal offense, the accused can be criminally culpable. ICTY-94-1-T (Judgment), at paras. 689, 692 (7 May 1997). Did the other precedents require direct and substantial affectation of the principal offense? Did Article 7 of the Statute of the ICTY? General trends in decision, with some notable exceptions, affirm that for accomplice liability the conduct of the accused does not have to cause the direct perpetrator's crime or directly or substantially contribute to the crime, but can merely aid or facilitate.

6. In *The Prosecutor v. Blagojevic & Jokic*, IT-02-60-T (Trial Chamber, Judgment on Motions for Acquittal Pursuant to Rule 98 *bis*, 5 April 2004), para. 30, the Trial Chamber stated: "Aiding and abetting" means rendering a substantial contribution to the commission of a crime. *Krstic*, para. 601; *Prosecutor v. Aleksovski*, IT-95-14/1-A (Appeals Chamber, 24 Mar. 2000), para. 162. The aider and abettor must have knowledge that his acts assist the commission of the crime. *Prosecutor v. Tadic*, IT-95-1-T (Judgment, 7 May 1997), para. 674; *Prosecutor v. Delalic*, IT-96-21-T (Judgment, 16 Nov. 1998), para. 326; *Prosecutor v. Aleksovski*, IT-95-14/1-T (Judgment, 25 June 1999), para. 61. Actually, in *Aleksovski* the Trial Chamber used a must have been aware standard: "By being present during the mistreatment, and yet not objecting to it notwithstanding its systematic nature and the authority he had over its perpetrators, the accused was necessarily aware that such tacit approval would be construed as a sign of his support and encouragement. He thus contributed substantially to the mistreatment." *Id.* para. 87. Later, in the Trial Judgement, the Trial Chamber stated that aiding and abetting genocide requires that the alleged perpetrator (1) carried out an act which consisted of practical assistance, encouragement or moral support to the principal that had a "substantial effect" on the commission of the crime, (2) had knowledge that his or her own acts assisted in the commission of the specific crime by the principal offender, and (3) knew that the crime was committed with the specific intent required for genocide [see Chapter Ten]. *Id.* para. 782 (17 Jan. 2005). This approach was affirmed by the Appeals Chamber in *The Prosecutor v. Kvocka, et al.*, IT-98-30/1-A (Appeals Chamber Judgment, 28 Feb. 2005), para. 90, noting that an aider and abettor must make a substantial contribution to the crime.

In *The Prosecutor v. Furundzija*, IT-95-17/1-T (Trial Chamber) (10 Dec. 1998), the Trial Chamber preferred that "assistance must have a substantial effect." *Id.* para. 234. In paras. 236–249, it was recognized that "mere knowledge that his actions assist ... is sufficient" (para. 236), "knowledge rather than intent" to assist is sufficient (para. 237), and "knowledge that his actions will assist" is sufficient (para. 245). Thus, one need not have a purpose to assist if one is aware that one's conduct will assist. With respect to the particular crime committed, *Furundzija* declared:

> 245.... the clear requirement in the vast majority of the cases is for the accomplice to have knowledge that his actions will assist.... This is particularly apparent from all the cases in which persons were convicted for having driven victims and perpetrators to the site of an execution. In those cases the prosecution did not

prove that the drive drove for the purpose of assisting in the killing, that is, with an intention to kill. It was the knowledge of the criminal purpose of the executioners that rendered the drive liable as an aider and abettor. Consequently, if it were not proven that a driver would reasonably have known that the purpose of the trip was an unlawful execution, he would be acquitted.

246. Moreover, it is not necessary that the aider and abettor should know the precise crime that was intended and which in the event was committed. If he is aware that one of a number of crimes will probably be committed, and one of those crimes is in fact committed, he has intended to facilitate the commission of that crime, and is guilty as an aider and abettor.

In *The Prosecutor v. Blaskic*, IT-95-14-T-A (Appeals Chamber, 29 July 2004), para. 50, it was recognized that "it is not necessary that the aider and abettor ... know the precise crime that was intended and which ... was committed. If he is aware that one of a number of crimes will probably be committed, and one of those crimes is in fact committed, he has intended to facilitate the commission of that crime, and is guilty as an aider and abettor."

7. At the International Military Tribunal for the Far East concerning the *Trial of Koiso*, an ex-Prime Minister, guilt was established where the accused knew that treatment of prisoners "left much to be desired" and he had asked for a full inquiry but did not resign from office or act more affirmatively to stop illegal treatment. 2 JUDGMENT OF THE IMT FOR THE FAR EAST 1778–79 (1948).

8. However, the ICC has a different rule. See Rome Statute for the ICC, art. 25(3)(c), using a test "for the purpose of facilitating." Is this different than when a person intends to engage in conduct with knowledge or awareness that such conduct can or will assist?

9. During an admitted Bush-Cheney "program" of secret detention (an international crime and war crime in time of armed conflict) and "coercive" or "tough" interrogation (a violation of several types of international criminal law, see Chapters Eight and Eleven), several attorneys drafted and/or wrote memos to facilitate such a program. Would any of the lawyers who did so be reasonably accused of complicity with respect to the crimes committed during such a program? Consider:

"[A]ny person who aids and abets torture has liability as a complicitor or aider and abettor before the fact, during the fact, or after the fact. Liability exists whether or not the person knows that his or her conduct is criminal or that the conduct of the direct perpetrator of torture is criminal or even constitutes torture as such. Under customary international law, a complicitor or aider and abettor need only be aware that his or her conduct (which can include inaction) would or does assist a direct perpetrator or facilitates conduct that is criminal. In any case, ignorance of the law is no excuse. Especially relevant in this respect are the criminal memoranda and behavior of various German lawyers in the German Ministry of Justice, high level executive positions outside the Ministry, and the courts in the 1930s and 1940s that were addressed in informing detail in *United States v. Altstoetter* (The Justice Case). Clearly, several memo writers and others during the Bush Administration abetted the "common, unifying" plan to use "coercive interrogation" and their memos and conduct substantially facilitated its effectuation. Therefore, prosecution or extradition of several former members of the Bush Administration for criminal complicity would be on firm ground."

Jordan J. Paust, *The Absolute Prohibition of Torture and Necessary and Appropriate Sanctions*, 43 VALP. U. L. REV. 1535, 1544–45 (2009).

D. Conspiracy

Some of the materials above demonstrate that there has been attention to individual responsibility as a co-conspirator, that conspiracy is not unknown in international criminal law. However, few international criminal law instruments expressly refer to conspiracy. Early instruments include the Charter of the I.M.T. at Nuremberg (Article 6) (1945), the Charter of the I.M.T. for the Far East (Article 5) (1946), Allied Control Council Law No. 10 (Article II (1)(a) (1946) (conspiracy with respect to crimes against peace), and the Principles of the Nuremberg Charter and Judgment (Article VI (a)(ii)) (1950) (conspiracy with respect to crimes against peace). Since then, at least seven international agreements address conspiracy as a form of criminal responsibility: (1) the Convention on the Prevention and Punishment of the Crime of Genocide, Article III (a) ("Conspiracy to commit genocide") (1948); (2) the International Convention on the Suppression and Punishment of the Crime of "Apartheid," Article III (a) ("conspire in the commission of" relevant acts) (1973); (3) the U.N. Convention Against Illicit Traffic in Narcotic Drugs and Psychotropic Substances, Article 3(1)(c)(iv) ("conspiracy to commit") (1988); (4) the Single Convention on Narcotic Drugs, Article 36(2)(a)(ii) (1961); (5) the Convention for the Suppression of the Illicit Traffic in Dangerous Drugs, Article 2(c) ("Conspiracy to commit") (1936); (6) the Supplementary Convention on the Abolition of Slavery, the Slave Trade, and Institutions and Practices of Slavery, Article 6(1) ("conspiracy to accomplish any such acts") (1956); and (7) the Council of Europe Convention on Laundering, Search, Seizure and Confiscation of the Proceeds from Crime, Article 6(d) ("conspiracy to commit") (1990).

When reading chapters herein that address specific crimes in more detail, such as crimes against peace or genocide, consider what tests have been applied with respect to responsibility for conspiracy.

The Prosecutor v. Karemera and Ngirumpatse
ICTR-98-44-T (Trial Chamber Judgment) (2 Feb. 2012)

Before: Judge Dennis C.M. Byron, presiding

Judge Gberdao Gustave Kam

Judge Vagn Joensen

3.2 Conspiracy to Commit Genocide

3.2.2 Law

1577. Conspiracy to commit genocide is "an agreement between two or more persons to commit the crime of genocide." The factual element of the crime is the entering into an agreement to commit genocide and the mental element the same as for genocide, namely that the individuals involved in the conspiracy must possess the specific intent to destroy, in whole or in part, a national, ethnical, racial or religious group, as such. As an inchoate offence, the crime is completed at the time the agreement is concluded regardless of whether genocide is actually committed as a result of the agreement.

1578. The existence of a formal or express agreement is not needed to prove the charge of conspiracy. It can be inferred from circumstantial evidence, as long as the existence of conspiracy to commit genocide is the only reasonable inference. In particular, an agreement can be inferred from the concerted or coordinated actions of a group of individuals. Given the requirements of "concerted or coordinated," it is insufficient to simply show similarity of conduct.

1579. As for the mental element, although there is no numeric threshold, the perpetrator must act with the intent to destroy at least a substantial part of the group. The perpetrator does not have to be solely motivated by a criminal intent to commit genocide, nor does the existence of personal motive prevent him from having the specific intent to commit genocide.

1580. In the absence of direct evidence, a perpetrator's intent to commit genocide can be inferred from relevant facts and circumstances that lead beyond any reasonable doubt to the existence of the intent. Factors that may give rise to the specific intent include the general context, the perpetration of other culpable acts systematically directed against the same group, the scale of atrocities committed, the systematic targeting of victims on account of their membership in a protected group, or the repetition of destructive and discriminatory acts....

3.2.3 Deliberations

1582. At the outset, the Chamber emphasises that the question under consideration is not whether there was a plan or conspiracy to commit genocide in Rwanda. Rather, it is whether the Prosecution has proven beyond a reasonable doubt, based on the evidence in this case, that Karemera and Ngirumpatse committed the crime of conspiracy to commit genocide.

Participants in the Alleged Conspiracy

1583. Another general matter relates to the participants in the alleged conspiracy. The Prosecution argues that the Accused conspired amongst themselves and with other named civilian and military authorities. There is no requirement that the Chamber conclude that the Accused conspired with all alleged co-conspirators named in the Indictment. It suffices if the Prosecution can establish that Karemera and Ngirumpatse conspired with at least each other, or one other person with whom they are alleged to have planned to commit genocide....

4. Cumulative Convictions

4.1 Introduction

1707. The Chamber has found that the evidence supports findings under different statutory provisions on the basis of the same conduct. The Appeals Chamber has held that cumulative convictions are permissible where each crime has a materially distinct element not contained in the other. An element is materially distinct from another if it requires proof of a fact not required by the other element. Where this test is not met, a conviction will be entered only under the more specific provision. The more specific offence subsumes the less specific one because the commission of the former necessarily entails the commission of the latter.

1708. In light of these legal principles, the Chamber turns to consider whether it may enter cumulative convictions based on its findings with respect to the policy of the Interim Government after 18 April 1994.

4.2 Genocide and Conspiracy to Commit Genocide

1709. With respect to the civil defence policy of the Interim Government, the Chamber has found that the evidence supports findings of the crime of genocide and conspiracy to commit genocide, which are treated as distinct crimes under Articles 2(3)(a) and 2(3)(b), respectively. The actus reus for the crimes is materially distinct. While the crime of genocide requires one of the enumerated acts in Article 2(2) to have been committed, the crime of conspiracy to commit genocide merely requires the act of entering into an agreement to commit genocide. Therefore, the underlying acts or omissions upon which the crimes are based are distinct. Accordingly, as noted recently by the Trial Chamber in Gatete and the ICTY Trial Chamber in Popović et al. ("Popović"), convictions for genocide and conspiracy to commit genocide are not necessarily cumulative because the conduct relevant to the crime of conspiracy is the agreement, which is not a requisite element for genocide.

1710. The Trial Chamber in Popović, however, noted that the basis of the concern regarding multiple convictions for the same act is one of fairness to the accused and further observed that the purpose of criminalising an inchoate offence such as conspiracy is to prevent the commission of the substantive offence. Thus, once the substantive offence is committed, the justification for punishing the prior conspiracy is less compelling, especially when proof of the substantive offence is the main piece of evidence from which an inference of a prior illegal agreement is drawn and upon which the conspiracy is based.

1711. In Popović, the Trial Chamber's findings for both genocide and conspiracy to commit genocide were based on the accused's participation in a joint criminal enterprise to murder with genocidal intent. Accordingly, it decided to follow the approach set forth by the Musema Trial Chamber and concluded that entering a conviction for the substantive offence of genocide rendered a conviction for conspiracy redundant, noting that the position most favourable to the accused must be paramount.

1712. In Gatete, the Chamber was faced with a similar scenario because it had inferred that Gatete had entered into an agreement to commit genocide from the evidence establishing that he had participated in a joint criminal enterprise to commit genocide. In light of those circumstances, and noting that a conviction for genocide, and not also conspiracy to commit genocide did not lessen the accused's criminal culpability, the Chamber decided to follow the approach taken by the Popović Trial Chamber and entered a conviction for genocide but not for conspiracy to commit genocide.

1713. In this case, the Chamber is faced with a situation analogous to Gatete and Popović. It has inferred that the Accused entered into an agreement to commit genocide from evidence regarding the policy of the Interim Government after 18 April 1994, which establishes that they participated in a joint criminal enterprise to destroy the Tutsi population in Rwanda. Accordingly, the Chamber concurs with the Musema, Popović, and Gatete Trial Chambers that the position most favourable to the accused must be paramount. Considering that the full criminality of the Accused is accounted for by a conviction for genocide, the Chamber finds that a further conviction for the inchoate crime of conspiracy would be duplicative and unfair to the Accused.

Chapter VII: Verdict

1714. For the reasons set out in this Judgement, having considered all evidence and arguments, the Trial Chamber finds unanimously that

Edouard Karemera is guilty as follows:

Count 1: of Conspiracy to Commit Genocide

Count 2: of Direct and Public Incitement to Commit Genocide

Count 3: of Genocide

[Counts 5–7]

1715. On the basis of the principles relating to cumulative convictions, the Chamber does not enter a conviction against Karemera for the count of conspiracy to commit genocide.

Matthieu Ngirupatse is guilty as follows:

Count 1: of Conspiracy to Commit Genocide

Count 2: of Direct and Public Incitement to Commit Genocide

Count 3: of Genocide

[Counts 5–7]

1716. On the basis of the principles relating to cumulative convictions, the Chamber does not enter a conviction against Ngirumpatse for the count of conspiracy to commit genocide.

Notes and Questions

1. The ICTR has found evidence to support a finding that a conspiracy to commit genocide existed but has, nevertheless, in its recent jurisprudence declined to convict on conspiracy charges where a defendant is also convicted of the predicate offense. In *The Prosecutor v. Jean-Baptiste Gatete*, ICTR-2000-61-T (March 31, 2011), the Trial Chamber said a conspiracy conviction would be redundant "given that a conviction for genocide, and not also conspiracy to commit genocide, in no way lessens the Accused's criminal culpability." *Id.* para. 661. *See also id.* paras. 654–662 (surveying case law on cumulative convictions and noting that, when the ICTR or ICTY has addressed this issue, it has declined to convict for conspiracy). The first such case at the ICTR was *The Prosecutor v. Alfred Musema*, Case No. ICTR-96-13-A (Jan. 27, 2000), in which the Trial Chamber applied the definition of conspiracy most favorable to the accused—namely, that "an accused cannot be convicted of both genocide and conspiracy to commit genocide on the basis of the same acts." Ruth Kok, *Prosecutor v. Musema, Commentary*, in 6 ANNOTATED LEADING CASES OF INTERNATIONAL CRIMINAL TRIBUNALS 614, 622 (2003). Kuk notes that this decision was inconsistent with ICTR precedents at the time; however, as the Trial Chamber noted in *Gatete*, the judgment in *Musema* was the first where conspiracy to commit genocide was clearly defined and subsequent cases at both the ICTR and ICTY have followed the *Musema* precedent.

2. Both Karemera and Ngirumpatse were civilian, not military, officials. What effect, if any, does this have on their culpability? Consider the following excerpt from *Musema*, ICTR-96-13-T (Jan. 27, 2000):

> 140. The influence at issue in a superior—subordinate command relationship often appears in the form of psychological pressure. This is particularly relevant to the case at bar, insofar as Alfred Musema was a socially and politically prominent person in Gisovu *Commune*.

> 141. It is also significant to note that a civilian superior may be charged with superior responsibility only where he has effective control, be it *de jure* or merely *de facto*, over the persons committing violations of international humanitarian law....

> 143. Such power of control, even if it is merely *de facto*, generally implies "indirect subordination," which ... extends beyond the commander's duty to his direct subordinate to "other persons under his responsibility," to prevent violations of the Geneva Conventions

3. In *The Prosecutor v. Musema*, ICTR-96-13-T (Trial Chamber) (27 Jan. 2000), the Trial Chamber chose a definition of conspiracy that require merely an agreement, that when there are acts in furtherance, such is an aggravated form of conspiracy:

185. The Chamber notes that the crime of conspiracy to commit genocide covered in the Statute is taken from the Genocide Convention. The *"Travaux Préparatoires"* of the Genocide Convention suggest that the rationale for including such an offence was to en-

sure, in view of the serious nature of the crime of genocide, that the mere agreement to commit genocide should be punishable even if no preparatory act has taken place. Indeed, during the debate preceding the adoption of the Convention, the Secretariat advised that, in order to comply with General Assembly resolution 96 (I), the Convention would have to take into account the imperatives of the prevention of the crime of genocide:

> "This prevention may involve making certain acts punishable which do not them-selves constitute genocide, for example, certain material acts preparatory to geno-cide, an agreement or a conspiracy with a view to committing genocide, or systematic propaganda inciting to hatred and thus likely to lead to genocide."

186. The Chamber notes that Common Law systems tend to view *"entente"* or conspir-acy as a specific form of criminal participation, punishable in itself. Under Civil Law, con-spiracy or *"complot"* derogates from the principle that a person cannot be punished for mere criminal intent*("résolution criminelle"*) or for preparatory acts committed. In Civil Law systems, conspiracy (*complot*) is punishable only where its purpose is to commit certain crimes considered as extremely serious, such as, undermining the security of the State.

187. With respect to the constituent elements of the crime of conspiracy to commit geno-cide, the Chamber notes that, according to the *"Travaux Préparatoires"* of the Genocide Convention, the concept of conspiracy relied upon the Anglo-Saxon doctrine of con-spiracy. In its Report, the Ad hoc Committee states that conspiracy "is a crime under Anglo-American law": Ad Hoc Committee Report (1948) 8. This reflected the assump-tions made during debates on conspiracy. The French representative initially observed that conspiracy was a foreign concept to French law. The U.S. representative, speaking as Chair, explained that "in Anglo-Saxon law 'conspiracy' was an offence consisting in the agree-ment of two or more persons to effect any unlawful purpose". Venezuela's representative later remarked that in Spanish the word "conspiration" meant a conspiracy against the Government and that the English term "conspiracy" was rendered in Spanish by *"aso-ciación"* (association) for the purpose of committing a crime. The representative of Poland observed that in Anglo-Saxon law the word "complicity" extended only to "aiding and abetting" and that the offence described as "conspiracy" did not involve complicity. Poland recalled that the Secretariat draft made separate provision for complicity and conspiracy. In the Sixth Committee debates, Mr. Maktos of the United States of America stated that "conspiracy" had "a very precise meaning in Anglo-Saxon law; it meant the agreement between two or more persons to commit an unlawful act". Mr. Raafat of Egypt noted that the notion of conspiracy had been introduced into Egyptian law and "meant the con-nivance of several persons to commit a crime, whether the crime was successful or not".

188. For its part, the United Nations War Crimes Commission defined conspiracy as follows:

> "The doctrine of conspiracy is one under which it is a criminal offence to con-spire or to take part in an allegiance to achieve an unlawful object, or to achieve a lawful object by unlawful means."

189. Civil Law distinguishes two types of *actus reus,* qualifying two "levels" of *'complot'* or conspiracy. Following an increasing level of gravity, the first level concerns (*le complot simple*) simple conspiracy, and the second level (*le complot suivi d'actes matériels*) conspiracy followed by material acts. Simple conspiracy is usually defined as a concerted agreement to act, decided upon by two or more persons (*résolution d'agir concertée et arrêtée entre deux ou plusieurs personnes*) while the conspiracy followed by preparatory acts is an ag-gravated form of conspiracy where the concerted agreement to act is followed by prepara-tory acts. Both forms of *'complot'* require that the following three common elements of

the offence be met: (1) an agreement to act [*la résolution d'agir*]; (2) concerted wills [*le concert de volontés*]; and (3) the common goal to achieve the substantive offence [*l'objectif commun de commettre l'infraction principale*].

190. Under Common Law, the crime of conspiracy is constituted when two or more persons agree to a common objective, the objective being criminal.

191. The Chamber notes that the constitutive elements of conspiracy, as defined under both systems, are very similar. Based on these elements, the Chamber holds that conspiracy to commit genocide is to be defined as an agreement between two or more persons to commit the crime of genocide....

194. The Chamber is of the view that the crime of conspiracy to commit genocide is punishable even if it fails to produce a result, that is to say, even if the substantive offence, in this case genocide, has not actually been perpetrated.

4. With respect to conspiracy to commit genocide, see also Professor Jens David Ohlin, *Incitement and Conspiracy to Commit Genocide*, in THE UN GENOCIDE CONVENTION: A COMMENTARY 207, 218–19 (Paola Gaeta ed. 2009) ("conspiracy is an inchoate offence, and a completed genocide need not occur in order for a conviction to obtain. This is consistent with the common law understanding of conspiracy, i.e., that once the individuals in question make the criminal agreement, the crime has in fact occurred.... The agreement need not be an express or formal one but may be inferred from the 'concerted or coordinated action on the part of the group of individuals,'" quoting *The Prosecutor v. Nahimana*, ICTR-99-52-A (Appeals Chamber, 12 Jan. 2007) para. 897).

5. With respect to the next subsection, what is the difference between responsibility for conspiracy and that pertaining with respect to the first type of joint criminal enterprise responsibility? Both require a relevant underlying agreement.

6. Consider whether conspiracy and joint criminal enterprise responsibility are reflected in whole or in part in Article 25(3)(d) of the Rome Statute of the International Criminal Court. Is it possible for the ICC to prosecute conspiracy to commit genocide, which is covered in Article III (b) of the Genocide Convention?

E. Joint Criminal Enterprise Responsibility

Joint criminal enterprise (JCE) responsibility requires an underlying agreement and, unlike ordinary conspiracy, conduct of the accused that contributes to the effectuation of the agreement or common purpose. Ordinary accomplice liability is different because there is no requirement of an underlying agreement between the complicitor and the direct perpetrator of a relevant international crime. There are three types of JCE responsibility that have been identified and they are differentiated basically on the basis of the type of *mens rea* of the person being prosecuted for contributing to the agreement or common purpose and, in each case, another member of the joint criminal enterprise will actually be the direct perpetrator of a relevant crime, such as a war crime, genocide, or another type of crime against humanity.

JCE responsibility was applied as an independent basis for criminal responsibility by the ICTY during the trial of Dusko Tadic with respect to crimes committed in the former Yugoslavia. While the theory behind this form of criminal responsibility that is connected with a group's purpose and behavior had been applied as early as the post-World War II trials, the *Tadic* decision formally labeled this independent type of responsibility and articulated the three types of JCE responsibility.

JCE I responsibility exists when the accused knowingly participates in at least one aspect of the common design and knows or is aware that the group intends to commit the specific crime that a direct perpetrator and member of the group actually commits. As some of the cases state, the accused must share the same criminal intention of the members of the group, but it should be added that the criminal intention that must be shared is with respect to the specific crime that is actually committed by a direct perpetrator. This type of JCE responsibility is closest to conspiracy but, as noted, ordinary conspiracy does not require conduct that contributes to or furthers the common purpose.

JCE II responsibility has its genesis in the so-called "concentration camp" cases that involved prosecutions for crimes committed during World War II. The specific requirements for JCE II responsibility are (1) the existence of an organized system of ill-treatment of detainees; (2) the accused's awareness of the nature of the system; and (3) the fact that the accused knowingly participated in some way in effectuating or contributing to the system, e.g., by encouraging, aiding and abetting, or otherwise participating in the realization of the common criminal design.

JCE III responsibility requires the existence of an underlying agreement or common purpose but, unlike JCE I, does not require that the accused intend or know that the crime committed by a direct perpetrator and member of the group will be committed. Instead, it is sufficient if the crime committed by the direct perpetrator is one that is reasonably foreseeable, that it might reasonably occur as a consequence of the underlying agreement or common purpose.

For some, JCE III responsibility is problematic. Some critics contend that an accused member should not be liable with respect to a crime committed by a direct perpetrator that the accused did not intend or know would occur. We consider below an extract from a Cambodian tribunal in 2010 that rejected JCE III-type responsibility with respect to crimes against humanity and war crimes committed in Cambodia between 1975 and 1979. For others, since one accused of JCE III responsibility can probably be prosecuted for complicity if the accused is found to have knowingly engaged in conduct that the accused knew or was aware could or would facilitate the crime of a direct perpetrator, there may not be a problem with prosecutions of accused for JCE III-type responsibility, especially given the fact that the latter requires an extra element of an underlying agreement or common purpose between the accused and the direct perpetrator and mere complicity does not (recall subsection C above, especially the extract from *The Prosecutor v. Blaskic*). When a person is aware that the crime committed by a direct perpetrator is one that could be committed, proof of such awareness might be based on circumstantial evidence that a reasonable person under the circumstances should have been aware. This would be close to the element for JCE III responsibility with respect to *mens rea* concerning the actual crime committed, *i.e.*, that it be a reasonably foreseeable outcome of the joint criminal enterprise.

1. *Trends in Decision*

The Prosecutor v. Blagojevic & Jokic
IT-02-60-T (Trial Chamber, Judgment on Motions for Acquittal
Pursuant to Rule 98 *bis*) (2 April 2004)

29.... .Regarding joint criminal enterprise as a form of commission, see *Prosecutor v. Krnojelac*, IT-97-25-A (Appeals Chamber, 5 Nov. 2003), para. 29. The *Stakic* Trial Judgement has defined commission as follows: "the accused participated, physically or otherwise directly or indirectly [Indirect perpetration in German law refers to the "perpetrator behind the perpetrator". This term is often used in the context of white collar crimes and other forms of organised crime.], in the material elements of the crime charged through positive acts or, based on a duty to act, omissions, whether individually or jointly with others. The accused himself need not have participated in all aspects of the alleged criminal conduct." Stakic, Trial Judgment, para. 439. Joint criminal enterprise is defined by three objective elements: first, there must be a plurality of persons; second, a common plan, design or purpose must exist, which amounts to or involves the commission of a crime provided in the Statute; and third, the accused must have participated in the common design. *Prosecutor v. Vasiljevic*, IT-98-32-A (Appeals Chamber, 25 Feb. 2004), para. 100. This participation need not involve the commission of a specific crime but may take the form of assistance in, or contribution to, the execution of the common plan or purpose. Tadic, Appeal Judgment, para. 277. The Appeals Chamber has distinguished three categories of joint criminal enterprise on the basis of the *mens rea* required. In the first category, all perpetrators share the same criminal intention; the accused must voluntarily participate in at least one aspect of the common design and, even if not personally effecting the crime(s), must nevertheless intend the result. The second category refers to the so-called "concentration camp" cases and is not applicable to this case. Under the third category, a member of a joint criminal enterprise is held responsible for the criminal acts committed by other such members when these criminal acts, while falling outside the scope of the common design, were natural and foreseeable consequences of effecting the common design. Tadic, Appeal Judgment, para. 196.

Notes and Questions

1. The following cases provide further details regarding ICTY use of "joint criminal enterprise" responsibility:

The first category involves "cases where all co-defendants, acting pursuant to a common design, possess the same criminal intention; for instance, the formulation of a plan among the co-perpetrators to kill, where, in effecting this common design (and even if each co-perpetrator carries out a different role within it), they nevertheless all possess the intent to kill. The objective and subjective prerequisites for imputing criminal responsibility to a participant who did not, or cannot be proved to have, effected the killing are as follows: (i) The accused must voluntarily participate in one aspect of the common design (for instance, by inflicting non-fatal violence upon the victim, or by providing material assistance to or facilitating the activities of his co-perpetrators), and (ii) The accused, even if not personally effecting the killing, must nevertheless intend the result." *The Prosecutor v. Tadic*, IT-94-1-A (Appeals Chamber Judgment) (15 July 1999), para. 196. Addressing the first category, *The Prosecutor v. Brdanin*, IT-99-36-T (Trial Chamber Judgment) (1 Sept. 2004), para. 264, stated that the accused must have: "(i) voluntarily participated in one of the aspects of the common plan, and (ii) intended the criminal result, even if not physically perpetrating the crime … [and] all participants in the joint criminal enterprise share the same criminal intent … [although] it is not necessary for the prosecution to establish that every participant agreed to every one of the crimes committed. However, it is necessary for the prosecution to prove that between the member … physically committing the material crime charged and the person held responsible under the joint criminal enterprise for that crime, there was a common plan to commit at least that particular crime." Daryl A. Mundis & Fergal Gaynor, *Current Developments at the Ad Hoc International Criminal Tribunals*, 3 J. Int'l Crim. Justice 268, 278 (2005).

The third category is proven "only if (i) the crime charged was a natural and foreseeable consequence of the execution of that enterprise, and (ii) the accused was aware that such a crime was a possible consequence of the execution of that enterprise, and, with that awareness, participated in that enterprise. The first is an objective element of the crime, and does not depend upon the state of mind of the accused. The second is the subjective state of mind of the accused which the Prosecutor must establish." *Brdanin, supra* para. 265. "An accused convicted of a crime under the third category ... need not be shown to have intended to commit the crime or even to have known with certainty that the crime was to be committed. Rather, it is sufficient that the accused entered into a joint criminal enterprise to commit a different crime with the awareness that the commission of that agreed upon crime made it reasonably foreseeable to him that the crime charged would be committed by other members of the joint criminal enterprise, and it was committed." *The Prosecutor v. Brdanin*, IT-99-36-A (Appeals Chamber, Decision on Interlocutory Appeal on Defence Motion for Acquittal) (19 Mar. 2004), para. 5.

Radoslav Brdanin had been a Bosnian Serb political leader in the Krajina region. He was indicted and convicted for several crimes (including persecutions as crimes against humanity involving torture, deportation, and inhumane acts of forcible transfer; wilful killing and torture as grave breaches of the Geneva Conventions; wanton destruction of cities, towns or villages, or devastation not justified by military necessity (a war crime); and destruction or wilful damage done to institutions dedicated to religion (a war crime)), but was not convicted for participation in a joint criminal enterprise where there was insufficient evidence of an agreement or understanding between him and relevant direct perpetrator and evidence presented allowed various inferences to be drawn. *Brdanin* (Trial Chamber), *supra* paras. 351–354, adding: "the mere espousal of the Strategic Plan [by the Bosnian Serbian leadership, regional political leaders, the Bosnian Serbian army and paramilitary forces, and others to permanently remove non-Serbian persons from certain areas and to link those areas to Serbian-populated areas] by the Accused on the one hand and many of the Relevant Physical Perpetrators on the other hand is not equivalent to an arrangement between them to commit a concrete crime. Indeed, the Accused and the Relevant Physical Perpetrators could espouse the Strategic Plan and form a criminal intent to commit crimes with the aim of implementing the Strategic Plan independently from each other, and without having an understanding or entering into any agreement between them to commit a crime. Moreover, the fact that the acts and conduct of an accused facilitated or contributed to the commission of a crime by another person and/or assisted in the formation of that person's criminal intent is not sufficient to establish beyond reasonable doubt that there was an understanding or an agreement between the two to commit that particular crime. An agreement between two persons to commit a crime requires a mutual understanding or arrangement with each other to commit a crime."

What is the difference between mere complicity or aiding and abetting and criminal responsibility for participation in a joint criminal enterprise? In *The Prosecutor v. Kvocka, et al.*, IT-98-30/1-A (Appeals Chamber Judgment) (28 Feb. 2005), para. 90, stated: "Where the aider and abettor only knows that his assistance is helping a single person to commit a single crime, he is only liable for aiding and abetting that crime. This is so even if the principal perpetrator is part of a joint criminal enterprise involving the commission of further crimes. Where, however, the accused knows that his assistance is supporting the crimes of a group of persons involved in a joint criminal enterprise and shares that intent, then he may be found criminally responsible for the crimes committed in furtherance of that common purpose as a co-perpetrator." The Appeals Chamber added that a theory of "aiding and abetting a joint criminal enterprise" is incorrect and that aiding and abetting "generally involves a lesser degree of individual criminal responsibility than co-participation in a joint criminal enterprise." *Id.* paras. 91–92.

Previously, in *The Prosecutor v. Milutinovic, et al.*, IT-99-37-AR72 (Appeals Chamber, Decision on Dragoljub Ojdanic's Motion Challenging Jurisdiction—Joint Criminal Enterprise) (21 May 2003), the Appeals Chamber noted: "Whilst conspiracy requires a showing that several individuals have agreed to commit a certain crime or set of crimes, a joint criminal enterprise requires, in addition to such a showing, that the parties to that agreement took action in furtherance of that agreement" and that "while mere agreement is sufficient in the case of conspiracy, the liability of a member of a joint criminal enterprise will depend on the commission of criminal acts in furtherance of that enterprise." *Id.* para. 23. The Chamber added: "Criminal liability pursuant to joint criminal enterprise is not a liability for mere membership or for conspiring to commit crimes.…" *Id.* para. 26.

2. In *United States v. Altstoetter* (The Justice Case), *supra*, having noted that the defendant "joined and retained his membership in the SS on a voluntary basis" and that the crimes of the SS were "of so wide a scope that no person of the defendant's intelligence, and one who had achieved" a high rank in the SS "could have been unaware of its illegal activities," the tribunal declared: "Surely, whether or not he took part in such activities or approved them, he must have known of that part which was played by an organization of which he was an officer."

3. Does Article 25(3)(d)(ii) of the Rome Statute of the ICC allow the ICC to prosecute an accused for conduct that would fit within JCE I-type responsibility? Does Article 25(3)(d)(i) allow the ICC to prosecute an accused for conduct that would fit within JCE III-type responsibility, since the accused's conduct need only "be made with the aim of furthering the criminal activity or criminal purpose of the group" and need not be made with knowledge of the intention of the group or the direct perpetrator to commit the specific crime that occurs? If so, and given the fact that the ICC will continue to have such competence, is it likely that the decision of the Cambodian tribunal addressed below will have much impact?

4. Is JCE responsibility mirrored in Article 2(3)(c) of the 1997 International Convention for the Suppression of Terrorist Bombings? in Article 2(5)(c) of the 1999 International Convention for the Suppression of the Financing of Terrorism? Both treaties are in the Documents Supplement.

5. For further and partly critical attention to the doctrine of joint criminal enterprise, *see, e.g.*, Allison Marston Danner & Jenny S. Martinez, *Guilty Associations: Joint Criminal Enterprise, Command Responsibility, and the Development of International Criminal Law*, 93 Cal. L. Rev. 75 (2005); Wayne Jordash & Penelope Vany Tuyl, *Failure to Carry the Burden of Proof: How Joint Criminal Enterprise List its Way at the Special Court for Sierra Leone*, 8 J. Int'l Crim. Just. 591, 597–98 (2010) (discussing the "doctrinal confusion and overreaching at the Special Court" regarding the application of JCE); Jens David Ohlin, *Joint Intentions to Commit International Crimes*, 11 Chi. J. Int'l L. 693 (2011) (arguing for eliminating JCE III).

2. The Cambodia Decision in 2010

In the name of the Cambodian people and the United Nations and pursuant to the Law on the Establishment of the Extraordinary Chambers in the Courts of Cambodia for the Prosecution of Crimes Committed During the Period of Democratic Kampuchea

Criminal Case File No. 002/19-09-2007-ECCC/OCIJ (PTC38)
Decision on the Appeals Against the Co-Investigative Judges Order on Joint
Criminal Enterprise (JCE) (May 20, 2010)

I. Procedural Background

1. These Appeals are filed in the context of the ongoing judicial investigation against NUON Chea, IENG Sary, IENG Thirith, KHIEU Samphan and KAING Guek Eav alias "Duch" relating to charges of crimes against humanity and grave breaches of the Geneva Conventions dated 12 August 1949, offences defined and punishable under Articles 5, 6, 29(new) of the Law on the Establishment of the Extraordinary Chambers in the Courts of Cambodia, dated 27 October 2004 ("ECCC Law").

2. On 28 July 2008, the Defence for IENG Sary filed before the Co-Investigating Judges ("OCIJ") a Motion Against the Application at the ECCC of the Form of Liability Known as Joint Criminal Enterprise ("JCE") ("IENG Sary Motion"), requesting the OCIJ to declare JCE inapplicable before the ECCC on the basis that 1) such application would violate the principle of legality because JCE was not acknowledged as customary international law before or during the period of 1975-1979, nor is it presently recognized as such and 2) JCE is not specified in the ECCC Establishment Law, nor is it part of Cambodian law or recognized by any international convention enforceable before the ECCC....

4. In the Impugned Order, the OCIJ made the following legal findings concerning the Appeals:

a) Although Article 29 of the ECCC Law does not expressly refer to JCE, it is a mode of liability articulated as a form of commission in the ICTY *Tadic* Appeal Judgment, which defines three categories of JCE, all of which have the same *actus reus* but a different *mens rea;*

b) The principle of legality requires an assessment of whether JCE was applicable law at the time of the crimes charged. The applicable test is whether "the criminal liability in question was sufficiently foreseeable" and "the law providing for such liability [was] sufficiently accessible at the relevant time;

c) "[T]he application of international customary law before the ECCC is a corollary from the finding that the ECCC holds indicia of an international court applying international law";

d) "Considering the international aspects of the ECCC" and the fact that "the jurisprudence relied upon in articulating JCE pre-existed the events under investigation at the ECCC..., there is a basis under international law for applying JCE" before the ECCC and

e) "[P]ursuant to principles of interpretation of autonomous legal *'regimes'*..., the modes of liability for international crimes can only be applied to the international crimes".

5. The OCIJ therefore decided that JCE does not apply to national crimes, and regarding international crimes, it rejected "the request insofar as the *actus reus* and *mens rea*" for JCE I and II and the *actus reus* for JCE III, confirming the applicability of those principles before the ECCC. It partially granted "the request insofar as the only *mens rea* for JCE III applicable before the ECCC is the subjective acceptance of the natural and foreseeable consequences of the implementation of the common plan"....

IV. Merit of the Appeal

37. The Pre-Trial Chamber recalls that its finding in Case 001, that JCE is one "mode of liability to describe a factual situation where crimes are committed jointly by two or more perpetrators [... is] relevant to determining whether this mode of liability can be applied before the ECCC". In the same decision, the Pre-Trial Chamber stated that three categories of JCE are distinguished and derive from the ICTY Appeals Chamber's interpretation of the post-Second World War jurisprudence on "common plan" liability. The basic form of JCE (JCE I) exists where the participants act on the basis of a common design or enterprise, sharing the same intent to commit a crime. The systemic form (JCE II) exists where the participants are involved in a criminal plan that is implemented in an institutional framework, such as an internment camp, involving an organized system of ill-treatment. The Pre-Trial Chamber notes that JCE II is a variant of JCE I. The extended form (JCE III) exists where one of the participants engages in acts that go beyond the common plan but those acts constitute a natural and foreseeable consequence of the realization of the common plan.

38. The objective elements (*actus reus*) are the same for all three forms of JCE, namely: (i) a common plan (The Pre-Trial Chamber notes that the plan in question must amount to or involve the commission of a crime within the jurisdiction of the court), (ii) involving a plurality of persons, and (iii) an individual contribution by the charged person or the accused to the execution of the common plan. The Pre-Trial Chamber notes that although the accused need not have performed any part of the *actus reus* of the perpetrated crime, it is required that he/she has "participated in furthering the common purpose at the core of the JCE". Not every type of conduct would amount to a significant enough contribution to entail the individual criminal responsibility of the accused based on his/her participation in a JCE.

39. The subjective element (*mens rea*) varies according to the form of JCE. JCE I requires a shared intent to perpetrate the crime(s). JCE II requires personal knowledge of the system of ill-treatment *and the intent to further it*. JCE III requires an intention to participate in the criminal plan or purpose of the JCE and to contribute to its execution, "with responsibility arising for extraneous crimes where the accused could foresee their commission and willingly took that risk"—in other words, "being aware that such crime was a possible consequence of the execution of that enterprise, and with that awareness, [deciding] to participate in that enterprise"....

54. The *Tadic* Appeals Judgment was the first decision of an International Tribunal to trace the existence and evolution of the doctrine of JCE in customary international law. It found that "the consistency and cogency of the case law and the treaties [it] referred to..., as well as their consonance with the general principles on criminal responsibility laid down both in the Statute and general international criminal law and in national legislation, warrant the conclusion that case law reflects customary rules of international criminal law". Therefore, the Impugned Order logically refers to the above ICTY seminal decision on JCE as persuasive authority for its conclusion that, "[c]onsidering the international aspects of the ECCC and the fact that the jurisprudence relied upon in articu-

lating JCE pre-existed the events under investigation at the ECCC, there is a basis under international law for applying JCE before the ECCC".

55. To reach its finding, the interpreted the ICTY Statute on the basis of its purpose as set out in the report of the United Nations Secretary-General to the Security Council. It also considered the specific characteristics of many crimes perpetrated in war. In this respect, the Pre-Trial Chamber concurs with the approach in *Tadic* that the development of the forms of responsibility applicable to violations of international criminal law has to be seen in light of the very nature of such crimes, often carried out by groups of individuals acting in pursuance of a common criminal design. In the words of *Tadic*, "although only some members of the group may physically perpetrate the criminal act..., the participation and contribution of the other members of the group is often vital in facilitating the commission of the offence in question. It follows that the moral gravity of such participation is often no less—or indeed no different—from that of those actually carrying out the acts in question". These crimes differ from ordinary crimes not only in scale, but also due to the fact that they often take place during conflict. In contrast to ordinary crimes, which are usually perpetrated by an individual or a small group of individuals, these crimes are often only made possible by the involvement of state organs pursuing criminal policies and using all available means to those criminal ends.

56. In order to determine the status of customary law in this area, *Tadic* studied in detail the case law relating to ten war crimes cases tried after the Second World War. It further considered the relevant provisions of two international Conventions which reflect the views of many States in legal matters (Article 2(3)(c) of the International Convention for the Suppression of Terrorist Bombings, Article 25 of the Statute of the International Criminal Court. Moreover, the Appeals Chamber referred to national legislation and case law, noting that the notion of "common purpose", established in international criminal law, has foundations in many national systems, while acknowledging that it was not necessarily established that most of the countries actually have the same notion of common purpose....

69. In the light of the London Charter, Control Council Law No. 10, international cases and authoritative pronouncements, the Pre-Trial Chamber has no doubt that JCE I and JCE II were recognized forms of responsibility in customary international law at the time relevant for Case 002. This is the situation irrespective of whether it was appropriate for *Tadic* to rely on the ICC draft Statute and on the International Convention for the Suppression of Terrorist Bombing....

74. The Pre-Trial Chamber turns now to the third and, undeniably, more controversial form of JCE: its extended form (JCE III).

(iii) JCE III, extended form of JCE

75. The Appeals argue that the *Tadic* Appeals Chamber conclusion that JCE III is firmly based in customary international law is unsupported and does not comply with the requirement that customary international law can only be determined with reference to consistent, widespread state practice and *opinio juris*.[15] As a result, its application before

---

15. Ieng Sary Appeal, para. 40 and n.105, where the Appellant refers to Shane Darcy, *Imputed Criminal Liability and the Goals of International Justice*, 20 LEIDEN J. INT'L L. 377, 384–85 (2007), according to which for the third category of JCE:

the Appeals Chamber relied on a few Italian decisions and a small number of trials before the Allied military courts, mostly concerning instances of mob violence, which relied on such a doctrine. It is doubtful that the employment by a few states of this expanded form of common plan liability at that time gave it the status of customary law, particularly seeing that none of the treaties adopted in the post war period recognized the concept. The Ap-the ECCC would violate the principle of legality.[16] The Appellant stresses that to reach the above conclusion, *Tadic* relied on cases such as the *Borkum Island Case* and the *Essen Lynching Case*. In these cases the military courts only issued a simple guilty verdict and made no extensive legal finding on the issue of common criminal plan or mob beatings. Thus, *Tadic* was "left to quote the words of the ... military prosecutor and *infer* that the judges adopted [his] reasoning".[17] In addition, *Tadic* "relied in large part on unpublished cases, mostly from Italy ... which has adopted a unitary system whereby any person who intervenes in the commission of a crime is liable as a perpetrator, whereas most national criminal law systems have adopted an approach that makes a distinction between perpetrators or principals to the crime and accessories to the crime or secondary parties. Furthermore, only one of the Italian cases (*D'Ottavio et al.*) could provide support for JCE III".[18] The Appellant noted Ambos' argument on the Italian cases as follows: "[i]n this trial — in contrast to the trials before British and U.S. American military tribunals — no international law was relied upon, but exclusively the national law ... was applied. In addition, this case law is not uniform since the Italian Supreme Court ... has adopted two dissenting decisions."[19]

76. The OCP respond that many advanced jurisdictions recognized modes of co- perpetration similar to JCE III, [including] conspiracy, the felony murder doctrine, the concept of *association de malfaiteurs* and numerous other doctrines of co-perpetration".[20] According to the OCP, the argument that the finding in *Tadic* on JCE forming part of customary international law was based on too few cases from too few jurisdictions ignores substantial evidence that supports the ICTY Appeals Chamber's finding.

77. Having reviewed the authorities relied upon by *Tadic* in relation to the extended form of JCE (JCE III), the Pre-Trial Chamber is of the view that they do not provide sufficient evidence of consistent state practice or *opinio juris* at the time relevant to Case 002. The Pre-Trial Chamber concludes that JCE III was not recognized as a form of responsibility applicable to violations of international humanitarian law for the following reasons.

---

peals Chamber found some limited support for the third category in domestic criminal laws, but noted, however, that the major systems do not all treat the notion in the same way. Critics argue that a large number of jurisdictions do not support liability for crimes outside the scope of the agreed objective for those persons who participate in a common plan. *See* also leng Thirith Appeal, para. 38, alleging that "there was no basis for JCE III in Cambodia in 1975-1979", as well as para. 44, alleging that the Impugned Order erroneously found that JCE III apply before the ECCC, because "JCE III was not enacted in Cambodian law in 1975-1979".

16. Ieng Sary Appeal, para. 2 e)

17. Ieng Sary Appeal, paras. 44–45, referring to Jens David Ohlin, *Three Conceptual Problems with the Doctrine of Joint Criminal Enterprise,* 5 J. INT'L CRIM. JusT. 69, 75, n.lO (2007). The Appellant also refers to Powles, according to which the *Essen Lynching* and *Borkum Island* Cases on which *Tadic* relied do not "provide unambiguous support for the liability pursuant to the extended form of JCE" and in particular in the first case, "there is possibly a question mark as to whether the court held anyone who did not possess the intent to kill guilty of murder" because the Prosecution pleaded that the accused should be found guilty of murder as they had the intent to kill and they were indeed convicted for murder. Ieng Sary Appeal, para. 40, n.l 05, referring to Steven Powles, *Joint Criminal Enterprise: Criminal Liability by Prosecutor Ingenuity and Judicial Creativity?*, 2 J. INT'L CRIM. JUST. 606, 615–616 {2004).

18. Ieng Sary Appeal, para. 40.

19. Ibid., referring to Kai Ambos Amicus Brief, p. 29.

20. Co-Prosecutors' Joint Response, para. 33, referring to Co-Prosecutors' Supplementary Observations, para. 10, nn.22–26.

78. The Pre-Trial Chamber notes that the Nuremberg Charter and Control Council Law No. 10 do not specifically offer support for the extended form of JCE (JCE III). The Pre-Trial Chamber does not find that the two additional international instruments referred to by *Tadic,* which were not in existence at the time relevant to Case 002, could serve as a basis for establishing the customary law status of JCE III in 1975-1979.

79. As to the international case law relied upon by *Tadic,* the Pre-Trial Chamber notes that facts of *Borkum Island* and *Essen Lynching* may indeed be directly relevant to JCE III. However, in the absence of a reasoned judgment in these cases, one cannot be certain of the basis of liability actually retained by the military courts. In the first case,[21] the accused included a number of senior officers, a number of privates, the mayor of Borkum, a number of policemen, a civilian and the leader of the Reich Labour Corps. All the accused "were charged with war crimes, in particular both with 'wilfully, deliberately and wrongfully encourag[ing], aid[ing], abett[ing] and participat[ing] in the killing' of the airmen and with 'wilfully, deliberately and wrongfully encourag[ing], aid[ing], abett[ing] and participat[ing] in assaults upon' the airmen".[22] Based on its review of the Prosecution's submissions, *Tadic* considered that "the Prosecutor substantially propounded a doctrine of common purpose which presupposes that all the participants in the common purpose shared the same criminal intent, namely, to commit murder".[23] Then, in the absence of a reasoned verdict, it assumed that "the court upheld the common design doctrine, but in a different form, for it found some defendants guilty of both the killing and assault charges[24] while others were only found guilty of assault".[25] In addition, the court inferred that: "all the accused found guilty were held responsible for pursuing a criminal common design, the intent being to assault the prisoners of war. However, some of them were also found guilty of murder, even where there was no evidence that they had actually killed the prisoners. Presumably, this was on the basis that the accused, whether by virtue of their status, role or conduct, were in a position to have predicted that the assault would lead to the killing of the victims by some of those participating in the assault."[26]

80. The Pre-Trial Chamber does not infer from these circumstances that the mode of liability based on which the military court convicted Akkerman, Krolikovski, Schmitz, Wentzel, Seiler and Goebbel for murder was an extended form of JCE (JCE III). In light of the fact that the Prosecution pleaded that all accused shared the intent that the airmen be killed, the court may as well have been satisfied that these six individuals possessed such intent rather than having merely foreseen this possible outcome.

---

21. In this case, seven crew members of a U.S. Flying Fortress, forced down on the German Island of Borkum, were taken prisoner and forced to march, beaten by members of the Reich Labour Corps, then by civilians on the street and, again beaten by civilians while the escorting guards, took part in the beating. This was after the Mayor of Borkum incited the mob to kill them and before the airmen were shot and killed by German soldiers when reaching the city hall.

22. *Tadic* Appeal Judgement, para. 210, referring to Charge Sheet, in U.S. National Archives Microfilm Publications, I ("Charge Sheet").

23. *Tadic* Appeal Judgement, para. 211.

24. *Tadic* Appeal Judgement, para. 212, referring to Charge Sheet, pp. 1280–1286, n.268, where "(t)he accused Akkerman, Krolikovski, Schmitz, Wentzel, Seiler and Goebbel were all found guilty on both the killing and assault charges and were sentenced to death, with the exception of Krolikovski, who was sentenced to life imprisonment.

25. *Tadic* Appeal Judgement, para. 212, referring to Charge Sheet, pp. 1280–1286, n.269, where "(t)he accused Pointner, Witzke, Geyer, Albrecht, Weber, Rommel, Mammenga and Heinemann were found guilty only of assault and received terms of imprisonment ranging between 2 and 25 years.

26. *Tadic* Appeal Judgement, para. 213.

81. In the second case,[27] *Tadic* "assumed" that the court accepted the Prosecution's position. The Appeals Chamber inferred from the arguments of the parties and the guilty verdict "that the court upheld the notion that the accused were found guilty took part, in various degrees, in the killing; not all of them intended to kill but all intended to participate in the unlawful treatment of the prisoners of war and were found guilty of murder, because they were 'concerned in the killing'". It was also inferred that "the court assumed that the convicted persons who simply struck a blow or implicitly incited the murder would have foreseen that others would kill the prisoners". This final inference seems safer than the previous one, although there is no indication in the case that the Prosecutor even explicitly relied on the concept of common design and this case alone would not warrant a finding that JCE III exists in customary international law.

82. *Tadic* also relied on several cases brought before Italian courts after World War II concerning war crimes committed between 1943 and 1945. These crimes were committed by civilians or military personnel belonging to the armed forces of the so-called "*Repubblica Sociale Italiana*" ("RSI"). The RSI was a *de facto* government under German control established by the Fascist leadership in central and northern Italy following the declaration of war by Italy against Germany on 13 October 1943. The crimes were committed against prisoners of war, Italian partisans or members of the Italian army fighting against the Germans and the RSI. These cases, in which domestic courts applied domestic law, do not amount to international case law and the Pre-Trial Chamber does not consider them as proper precedents for the purpose of determining the status of customary law in this area.

83. For the foregoing reasons, the Pre-Trial Chamber does not find that the authorities relied upon in *Tadic,* and as a result those relied upon in the Impugned Order, constitute a sufficiently firm basis to conclude that JCE III formed part of customary international law at time relevant to Case 002.

Notes and Questions

1. The ECCC Pretrial Chamber did not find the Borkum Island and Essen Lynching cases, which were relied upon by the ICTY in *Tadic,* to be persuasive authority for the proposition that JCE III was part of customary law before or during the period of 1975-79. Why not? Were the prior cases based merely on complicity? The ECC Pretrial Chamber also rejected the argument in *Tadic* that the post-WW II Italian cases support JCE III in customary law. What is the ECCC Pretrial Chamber's view of the Italian cases?

2. In *Prosecutor v. Radoslav Brdanin*, IT-99-36-A (Appeals Chamber, Judgment) (Apr. 3, 2007), the Appeals Chamber of the ICTY concluded that the defendants could be liable for the actions of the criminal perpetrators even if the actual perpetrators were not part of the JCE. Under this view, the co-defendants formed a JCE to commit international crimes. However, these crimes were perpetrated by other individuals and there was no overarching joint enterprise that connected all of the crimes together. *Id.* para. 411. Do you agree with this aspect of the Appeals Chamber's application of JCE III?

3. Does Article 25(3)(d) of the Rome Statute support criminal liability under JCE III? Article 25(3)(d) penalizes an individual when such person intentionally contributes "to

---

27. In this case, a crowd of people participated in the beating of three airmen, resulting in their deaths and it was not possible to determine who had struck the fatal blow in each case.

the commission … of a crime by a group of persons acting with a common purpose" and either is made (i) "with the aim of furthering the criminal activity or criminal purpose of the group," or (ii) "in the knowledge of the intention of the group to commit the crime." Article 30 of the Rome Statute also indicates that "'knowledge' means *awareness* that a circumstance exists or a consequence will occur in the ordinary course of events." *Id.* art. 30 (3). Does Article 25(d)(i) cover JCE III-type responsibility because one need only have an aim to further the criminal activity or criminal purpose and not the specific crime actually engaged in by a direct perpetrator? Does Article 25(d)(ii) cover merely JCE I-type responsibility because one must have knowledge of the intention of the group to commit "the" crime actually engaged in? or does Article 30(3) shift knowledge to awareness and a lesser form of *mens rea* with respect to the specific crime actually engaged in by a direct perpetrator. Moreover, does Article 25(3)(d)(i) extend liability for foreseeable actions of co-participants in the criminal enterprise that fall outside the scope of the criminal plan?

4. Prominent Italian jurist, Antonio Cassese, had proposed a significant restriction on the application of JCE III. In order to remain consistent with the required mental element for international crimes, Cassese maintained that JCE III should not be used as a theory of criminal liability for offenses that require a showing of special or specific intent. *See* Antonio Cassese, *The Proper Limits of Individual Responsibility under the Doctrine of Joint Criminal Enterprise*, 5 J. INT'L CRIM. JUST. 109 (2007). Therefore, Cassese would not have applied JCE III to genocide, which requires proof that the accused acted with the intent to destroy the protected group in whole or in part. Would the logical extreme of Cassese's proposal entail only using JCE III in cases where the *mens rea* of the underlying offense is recklessness? Under the more restrictive application, could JCE III be used to convict for crimes against humanity?

F. Leader Responsibility

Despite the fact that collective punishment is impermissible and that guilt must be personal, a person can be guilty of an international crime based on such person's failure properly to supervise the conduct of others, to take reasonable action to prevent violations of international law, or to properly engage in sanctions against prior violations by subordinates. What tests of leader responsibility or dereliction of duty have been developed? Have they been applied to military and civilian leaders, to civilians who are not directly in "command"? What limits of such responsibility might pose a defense? Consider the following:

Judgment of the International Military Tribunal for the Far East (1948)

In general the responsibility for prisoners held by Japan may be stated to have rested upon:

(1) Members of the Government;

(2) Military or Naval Officers in command of formations having prisoners in their possession;

(3) Officials in those departments which were concerned with the well-being of prisoners;

(4) Officials, whether civilian, military, or naval, having direct and immediate control of prisoners.

It is the duty of all those on whom responsibility rests to secure proper treatment of prisoners and to prevent their ill-treatment by establishing and securing the continuous and efficient working of a system appropriate for these purposes. Such persons fail in this duty and become responsible for ill-treatment of prisoners if:

(1) They fail to establish such a system.

(2) If having established such a system, they fail to secure its continued and efficient working.

Each of such persons has a duty to ascertain that the system is working and if he neglects to do so he is responsible. He does not discharge his duty by merely instituting an appropriate system and thereafter neglecting to learn of its application. An Army Commander or a Minister of War, for example, must be at the same pains to ensure obedience to his orders in this respect as he would in respect of other orders he has issued on matters of the first importance.

Nevertheless, such persons are not responsible if a proper system and its continuous efficient functioning be provided for and conventional war crimes be committed unless:

(1) They had knowledge that such crimes were being committed and having such knowledge they failed to take such steps as were within their power to prevent the commission of such crimes in the future, or

(2) They are at fault in having failed to acquire such knowledge.

If such a person had, or should, but for negligence or supineness, have had such knowledge he is not excused for inaction if his Office required or permitted him to take any action to prevent such crimes. On the other hand it is not enough for the exculpation of a person, otherwise responsible for him to show that he accepted assurances from others more directly associated with the control of the prisoners if having regard to the position of those others, to the frequency of reports of such crimes, or to any other circumstances he should have been put upon further enquiry as to whether those assurances were true or untrue. That crimes are notorious, numerous and widespread as to time and place are matters to be considered in imputing knowledge.

A member of a Cabinet which collectively, as one of the principal organs of the Government, is responsible for the care of prisoners is not absolved from responsibility if, having knowledge of the commission of the crimes in the sense already discussed, and omitting or failing to secure the taking of measures to prevent the commission of such crimes in the future, he elects to continue as a member of the Cabinet. This is the position even though the Department of which he has the charge is not directly concerned with the care of prisoners. A Cabinet member may resign. If he has knowledge of ill-treatment of prisoners, is powerless to prevent future ill-treatment, but elects to remain in the Cabinet thereby continuing to participate in its collective responsibility for protection of prisoners he willingly assumes responsibility for any ill-treatment in the future.

Army or Navy Commanders can, by order, secure proper treatment and prevent ill-treatment of prisoners. So can Ministers of War and of the Navy. If crimes are committed against prisoners under their control, of the likely occurrence of which they had, or should have had, knowledge in advance, they are responsible for those crimes. If for example it is shown that within the units under his command conventional war crimes have been committed of which he knew or should have known, a commander who takes no adequate steps to prevent the occurrence of such crimes in the future will be responsible for such future crimes.

Departmental Officials having knowledge of ill-treatment of prisoners are not responsible by reason of their failure to resign; but if their functions included the administration of the system of protection of prisoners and if they had or should have had knowledge of crimes and did nothing effective, to the extent of their powers, to prevent their occurrence in the future then they are responsible for such future crimes....

Roling, J. (dissenting)

To hold an official criminally responsible for certain acts which he himself did not order or permit, it will be necessary that the following conditions are fulfilled:

1. That they knew or should have known the acts.

Not only the knowledge, but also the lack of knowledge resulting from criminal negligence matters. If his function and the duties involved place upon the official concerned the obligation to know what is happening, lack of knowledge—if he could have known provided only he was normally alert—cannot be claimed in defense.

2. That he had the power to prevent the acts.

It is a generally recognized fact that in every war war crimes are committed by soldiers of every army. No government or commander will be able to prevent all war crimes. There is criminal responsibility only where all possible steps to prevent war crimes have not been taken. But since it is a matter of common knowledge that war crimes are likely to be committed, the authority vested in an official position should be exercised with due regard to this possibility.

3. That he had the duty to prevent these acts.

One could argue that the duty exists, as soon as knowledge and power are apparent. International law may develop to this point. At this moment, however, one has to look for the specific obligation, placed on government officials or military commanders, which makes them criminally responsible for "omissions."

The scope of this responsibility is extensive. The majority judgment may be generally referred to with regard to the extension of its implications. I must be stated, however, that it seems that the judgment goes too far where it assumes the responsibility of every member of the government for the atrocities committed in the field or against POW or civilian internees.

Paust, *My Lai and Vietnam...*
57 Mil. L. Rev. 99, 175–84 (1972)

The Limits of Leader Responsibility

There are limits to leader responsibility. A commander is not criminally responsible for all that his troops "do or fail to do," and "advanced systems of criminal law accept the principle that guilt is personal."[1] Grotius and others near his time accepted the normative value "that no one who was innocent of wrong may be punished for the wrong done by another."[2] This notion seems to permeate present international law as evidenced in

---

1. See Wright, *International Law and Guilt by Association*, 43 Am. J. Int'l L. 746 (1949), attacking the system of reprisals as a symptom of lawlessness and barbarism (also "wars, reprisals and sanctions with punitive intent").

2. *Id.* at 751. But, at the same time, Grotius recognized that "a community or its rulers, may be held responsible for the crime of a subject if they know of it and do not prevent it when they could and should prevent it." II Grotius, De Jure Belli Ac Pacis 523 (C.E.I.P. ed., Kelsey trans. 1925). *See also* IV E. de Vattel, Le Droit Des Gens, Ou Principles de la Loi Naturelle 163 (C.E.I.P. ed., Fenwick trans. 1916). The writings of these two jurists add centuries of experience and expectation to the present norm.

rules against collective punishment. Indeed, in *United States v. von Leeb*, Judge Harding stated that responsibility is not unlimited and:

It is fixed according to the customs of war, international agreements, fundamental principles of humanity, and the authority of the commander which has been delegated to him by his own government. As pointed out heretofore, his criminal responsibility is personal.

A high commander cannot keep completely informed of the details of military operations of subordinates and most assuredly not of every administrative measure. He has the right to assume that details entrusted to responsible subordinates will be legally executed.... There must be *personal dereliction*. That can occur only where the act is directly traceable to him or where his failure to properly supervise his subordinates constitutes *criminal negligence* on his part. In the latter case it must be a personal neglect amounting to a wanton, immoral disregard of the action of his subordinates amounting to acquiescence.

It seems that the court stated that absent direct responsibility, as in the case of the commander issuing illegal orders, a commander, to be criminally liable, must have knowledge of the commission of patently criminal offenses or offenses he personally knows to be illegal or "wanton, immoral disregard," and must either (1) acquiesce in, (2) participate in, or (3) be criminally negligent in regard to the offenses. Other cases fit into a general rule that the commander can be held criminally responsible if he *had knowledge* or *should have had knowledge* of troop conduct in violation of the law of war *and*, then, *took no reasonable corrective action*. With regard to corrective action, prosecutions have been based partially on the failure to control troops, disregard of troop conduct, acquiescence in troop activity, dereliction of duty, general complicity (incitement, approval, aiding and abetting, accessory responsibility, conspiracy), failure to educate troops or suppress crime, failure to prosecute troops who violate the law, failure to enforce the law generally, failure to maintain troop discipline, failure to investigate incidents, failure to report incidents to higher authorities, and at least in one case failure to resign from office. Many of these are interrelated and are tied to dereliction of duty in the general sense of the phrase "failure to take reasonable corrective commander action."

The United States view, which is consistent with international normative precepts, can be found in FM 27-10, paragraphs 501 and 507(b) which state:

501. Responsibility for Acts of Subordinates

In some cases, military commanders may be responsible for war crimes committed by subordinate members of the armed forces, or other persons subject to their control. Thus, for instance, when troops commit massacres and atrocities against the civilian population of occupied territory or against prisoners of war, the responsibility may rest not only with the actual perpetrators but also with the commander. Such a responsibility arises directly when the acts in question have been committed in pursuance of an order of the commander concerned. The commander is also responsible if he has actual knowledge, or should have knowledge, through reports received by him or through other means, that troops or other persons subject to his control are about to commit or have committed a war crime and he fails to take the necessary and reasonable steps to insure compliance with the law of war or to punish violators thereof.

507(b)

… Commanding officers of United States troops must insure that war crimes committed by members of their forces against enemy personnel are promptly and adequately punished.

The Navy text states that the commander is responsible for acts of his subordinates when such acts are committed "by order, authorization, or acquiescence of a superior." The fact that the commander did not order, authorize, or acquiesce in illegal conduct does not relieve him from responsibility if "it is established that the superior failed to exercise his authority to prevent such acts and, in addition, did not take reasonable measures to discover and stop offenses already perpetrated."[3]

Early texts stated that commanders ordering illegal acts or "under whose authority they are committed" may be punished [quoting a 1914 U.S. text]. Article 71 of the 1863 Lieber Code [extracts in the Documents Supplement] stated that whoever intentionally inflicts additional wounds on an enemy already disabled "or who orders or encourages soldiers to do so, shall suffer death, if duly convicted, whether he belongs to the Army of the United States, or is an enemy.…" In 1866 General Halleck stated in his text that when atrocities are committed, associated with scenes of drunkenness, lust, rapine, plunder, cruelty, murder and ferocity, the atrocities and the commander responsible are not excused "on the ground that the soldiers could not be controlled.… An officer is generally responsible for the acts of those under his orders.… In the same way, rebel officers were responsible for the murder of our captured negro troops, whether or not by their orders."[4]

By 1916, it was stated that by Article 54 of the 1916 Articles of War a commander has a duty of insuring "to the utmost of his power, redress of all abuses and disorders which may be committed by an officer or soldier under his command.".…

The new Army Subject Schedule states that where a commander "fails to take reasonable steps to prevent such crimes or to punish those guilty of a violation," the commander at a minimum "is guilty of dereliction of duty." It is further stated that if you are a commander at any level you have the duty:

> to insure that all those in your command observe the law of war. You must require instruction in the law of war. You should insure that your troops know the applicable rules of engagement. You must insure that both your own orders and those of your subordinate commanders are clear and unmistakable … you must take positive steps to keep fully informed of what your men are doing or failing to do.… You should insure that your men are aware of the law of war, of their duty to disobey orders that would require them to commit acts in violation of that law, and of their obligation to report any such violation of which they become aware.… You should further prepare directives … and establish proce-

---

3. *Law of Naval Warfare*, at para 330b(4). *See also* III MANUAL OF MILITARY LAW, *The Law of War on Land* 178 (British War Office 1958) stating that the commander is responsible if he knew or should have known of illegality committed or about to be committed and he "fails to use the means at his disposal to ensure compliance with the law of war," and that the failure raises a presumption (not easily rebuttable) of connivance, authorization, encouragement, acquiescence, or subsequent ratification. It is also stated, "it is probable that the responsibility of the commander goes beyond the duty as formulated above. He is also responsible if he fails, *negligently* or *deliberately, to ensure by all the means at his disposal that the guilty are brought to trial, deprived of their command or ordered out of the theatre of war*, as may be appropriate" (emphasis added). *See id.* at 179 for references to Canadian, Dutch and French law. [see Chapter Six, Section 2 re: the Leipzig Trials and the criminal negligence standard]

4. HALLECK, ELEMENTS OF INTERNATIONAL LAW AND LAWS OF WAR 199 (1866). Recall the commander responsibility for U.S. troop action in Canada during the War of 1812.

dures ... you must follow up ... you must take necessary and effective corrective action.

The requirements are not unprecedented in international law. In *United States v. List* convictions were based on the duty of a commanding general to investigate incidents and the failure "to take effective steps to prevent their execution or recurrence." It was stated that responsibility is coextensive with the area of command, that the commander must take proper corrective steps including obtaining complete information, and that where want of knowledge resulted from the failure to investigate, keep informed, and "require additional reports where inadequacy appears on their face," the commander cannot plead his own dereliction of duty as a defense.

In *United States v. von Leeb* it was stated that there must be a personal command dereliction of duty as where there is a "failure to properly supervise his subordinates." A chief of staff does not become criminally responsible unless he participated in criminal orders or their execution within the command, since he has no command authority and can only call matters to the attention of higher-ups. In *In re Yamashita* [5] the U.S. Supreme Court stated that the commander had an "affirmative duty to take such measures as were within his power and appropriate in the circumstances to protect prisoners of war and the civilian population." The Court also stated:

> It is evident that the conduct of military operations by troops whose excesses are unrestrained by the orders or efforts of their commander would almost certainly result in violations which it is the purpose of the law of war to prevent. Its purpose would largely be defeated if the commander of an invading army could with impunity neglect to take reasonable measures for their protection.[6]

It seems little known that although the procedures used in the trial of General Yamashita were deplorable and worthy of condemnation, there were sufficient facts given to enable the board which reviewed the record of trial to conclude on the issue of command responsibility:

> Upon this issue a careful reading of all the evidence impels the conclusion that it demonstrates this responsibility. In the first place the atrocities were so numerous, involved so many people, and were so widespread that accused's professional ignorance is incredible. Then, too, their manner of commission reveals a striking similarity of pattern throughout.... In many instances there was evidence of prearranged planning of the sites of the executions.... [There was] direct proof of statements by the Japanese participants that they were acting pursuant to orders of higher authorities.... There was some evidence in the record tending to connect accused more directly with the commission of some of the atrocities. His own Staff Judge Advocate, Colonel Hishiharu, told him that there was a large number of guerrillas in custody and not sufficient time to try them.... It is also noteworthy that the mistreatment of prisoners of war at Ft. McKinley occurred while accused was present in his headquarters only a few hundred yards distant.... [7]

---

5. 327 U.S. 1, 16 (1946). *See also* Kadic v. Karadzic, 70 F.3d 232, 242 (2d Cir. 1995).

6. *Id.* at 15; *see also* United States v. List, 11 T.W.C. 757, 1254, 1257, stating, "Unless civilization is to give way to barbarism in the conduct of war, crime must be punished.... Those responsible ... must be held to account if international law is to be anything more than an ethical code, barren of any practical coercive deterrent."

7. *Review of the Record of Trial by a Military Commission of Tomoyuki Yamashita, General, Imperial Japanese Army*, Gen. H.Q., U.S. Army Forces, Pacific, Office of the Theatre Judge Advocate,

Notice of the commission of offenses can be either actual or constructive as where such a great number of offenses occurred that a reasonable man would conclude that the commander must have known of the offenses. In the *Trial of General Matsui*,[8] where it was disclosed that during a six to seven week period over 100,000 people had been killed, women raped and property stolen or burned, the court said, "From his own observations and from the reports of his staff he must have been aware of what was happening. He admits he was told to some degree of misbehavior of his Army." It was also stated with regard to an issue likely to arise out of the Vietnam trials, that he "did nothing, or nothing effective to abate these horrors. He did issue orders before the capture of the City enjoining propriety of conduct upon his troops and later he issued further orders to the same purport. These orders were of no effect as is now known and as he must have known."

In the *Trial of Kimura*, a commander knew of troop illegality but "took no disciplinary measures or other steps to prevent the commission of atrocities." He had given orders but the court stated:

> The duty of an army commander in such circumstances is not discharged by the mere issue of routine orders.... His duty is to take such steps and issue such orders as will prevent thereafter the commission of war crimes and to satisfy himself that such orders are being carried out. This he did not do. Thus he deliberately disregarded his legal duty to take adequate steps to prevent breaches of the laws of war.

In the *Trial of Hata*, it was disclosed that atrocities had been committed on such a large scale by troops under his command that the commander either knew of them and took no corrective action, or he was "indifferent and made no provision for learning whether orders ... were obeyed." In the *Trial of Koiso*, an ex-Prime Minister, it was stated that atrocities were so numerous that it is improbable that a man in his position would not have been well-informed. He knew that the treatment of prisoners "left much to be desired" and had asked for a full inquiry, but he did not resign from office or act more affirmatively to stop illegal activity. He was punished for "deliberate disregard of his duty."[9]

A World War I case denied liability for poor conditions of a prisoner camp under the defendant's command where he had reported conditions, made small improvements on his own, and where fault was found to exist not in him but with his superiors.[10] But responsibility is different where prisoners are mistreated or die due to the commander's dereliction in controlling his troop activity.[11] The Judgment of the International Military Tribunal for the Far East stated that the duty to prisoners is "not a meaningless obligation cast upon a political abstraction. It is a specific duty to be performed in the first case by those persons who constitute the Government." Such persons "fail in this duty

---

Dec. 26, 1945. *See also,* Wright, *Due Process and International Law,* 40 Am. J. Int'l L. 398, 405 (1946). Repetition of the myth that Yamashita was an innocent sacrificial lamb may be found in Falk, III The Vietnam War and Int'l Law 327, 332 (1972).

  8. II Judgment of the IMT for the Far East 1181 (1948).

  9. *Id.* at 1179. *See also* Trials of [Minister] Shigemitsu, *id.* at 1195, and [Prime Minister] Togo, *id.* at 1205.

  10. *Current Notes, German War Trials, Judgment in the Case of Emil Muller,* 16 Am. J. Int'l L. 628, 684 (1922). Concerning the post WWI Leipzig trials, see Chapter Six, Section 2.

  11. *Id. See also* Trial of Lt. Gen. Baba Masao, 11 L.R.T.W.C. 56, 57 (1949) *citing In re Yamashita,* 327 U.S. 1, 16 and other trials 11 L.R.T.W.C. 59, 60 (1949), 4 L.R.T.W.C. 97, 116 (1948), and the Simpson Report, *supra* at 1 (the Malmmedy massacre), 2, 8–9.

and become responsible" if they fail to establish a system of protection or "fail to secure its continued and efficient working." Department officials who meet the knowledge requirements as to illegal conduct and then do "nothing effective, to the extent of their powers, to prevent their occurrence in the future ... are responsible for such future crimes."

The existence of a number of separate criminal events does not demonstrate a desired or acceptable high command or governmental policy or even a failure of high level persons to seek to implement law. However, such may demonstrate a breakdown of law and policy implementation in actual field practice and thus necessitate greater emphasis on training and precautions. And that "command failure," where it occurs, may not be criminal in nature but only a result of poor command ability.

For example, fifteen minutes of classroom instruction on the law of war would be totally insufficient to provide the unit with the guidance needed for a proper response to difficult field situations as where a patrol of five encounters fifteen wounded enemy soldiers, or where a platoon leader desires to interrogate a suspect in order to obtain information he considers vital to his unit's security. Two hours of suggested (not consistently mandatory) classroom instruction will not even be sufficient to inform each soldier what is expected of him in actual field operations. That type of law implementation can only be achieved through actual field training on the handling of detainees during sweep operations, the proper evacuation of civilians, the proper burning of selected structures, the proper use of firepower in response to sniper-fire, the proper interrogation of suspects and utilization of such procedures as map-tracking to obtain combat information, the proper treatment of enemy wounded, the individual response to illegal orders or illegal conduct, and command control of troops on sweeps through friendly villages. Without this type of training each soldier must react to situations in a different manner depending upon his fear, frustration, and individual ability to maintain a moral sense in an environment lacking proper psychic landmarks or warnings and one in which the soldier's primary thought is to stay alive. No commander can control all situations, but without proper unit training in the actual handling of detainees and prisoners the atrocities of war become more predictable—perhaps to such an extent that a conclusion of command dereliction of duty would be proper.

In Vietnam, Captain Leonard Goldman was convicted of a violation of Article 92, UCMJ, for violation of directives and dereliction of duty in failing to enforce safeguards to protect female detainees in the custody of his unit under circumstances such as to afford the defendant notice of physical abuse and murder of detainees.[12] Many allegations relevant to command responsibility in the past or present abound.

---

12. *United States v. Goldman*, a general court-martial convened pursuant to CMAO 7 (Jun. 29, 1968), as amended by CMAO 12 (Jul. 2, 1968) H.Q. 23d Infantry Div. (Americal), Vietnam. Findings of guilty announced Sep. 8, 1968. But a Court of Military Review subsequently reversed a dereliction of duty finding, contrary to the SJA review, as the court was not convinced "beyond a reasonable doubt" that the trier of fact was correct in concluding that the accused actually knew that a member of his unit participated in the killing (he was told, however, that a "prisoner" shot the victim). The court stated that this knowledge did not impose a duty to file a report according to military directives and that this negligent failure to investigate did not mandate criminal penalties under the circumstances. *United States v. Goldman*, 16 Sep. 1970. See U.S. Dep't of the Army PAM. 27-71-17, *JALS* at 6 (Sep. 1971). There was apparently no decision on the international "should have known" test of commander criminal responsibility.

The Prosecutor v. Delalic, *et al.*

IT-96-21-T (Trial Chamber, Judgment) (16 Nov. 1998)

334. The distinct legal character of the two types of superior responsibility must be noted. While the criminal liability of a superior for positive acts follows from general principles of accomplice liability, as set out in the discussion of Article 7(1) [of the Statute of the ICTY] above, the criminal responsibility of superiors for failing to take measures to prevent or repress the unlawful conduct of their subordinates is best understood when seen against the principle that criminal responsibility for omissions is incurred only where there exists a legal obligation to act. As is most clearly evidenced in the case of military commanders by Article 87 of Additional Protocol I, international law imposes an affirmative duty on superiors to prevent persons under their control from committing violations of international humanitarian law, and it is ultimately this duty that provides the basis for, and defines the contours of, the imputed criminal responsibility under Article 7(3) of the Statute.

335. Although historically not without recognition in domestic military law, it is often suggested that the roots of the modern doctrine of command responsibility may be found in the Hague Conventions of 1907. It was not until the end of the First World War, however, that the notion of individual criminal responsibility for failure to take the necessary measures to prevent or to repress breaches of the laws of armed conflict was given explicit expression in an international context. In its report presented to the Preliminary Peace Conference in 1919, the International Commission on the Responsibility of the Authors of the War and on Enforcement of Penalties recommended that a tribunal be established for the prosecution of, *inter alia*, all those who, ordered, or with knowledge thereof and with power to intervene, abstained from preventing or taking measures to prevent, putting an end to or repressing violations of the laws or customs of war.

336. Such a tribunal was never realised, however, and it was only in the aftermath of the Second World War that the doctrine of command responsibility for failure to act received its first judicial recognition in an international context. Whilst not provided for in the Charters of the Nürnberg or Tokyo Tribunals, nor expressly addressed in Control Council Law No. 10, a number of States at this time enacted legislation recognising the principle. For example, Article 4 of the French Ordinance of 28 August 1944, Concerning the Suppression of War Crimes, provided:

> Where a subordinate is prosecuted as the actual perpetrator of a war crime, and his superiors cannot be indicted as being equally responsible, they shall be considered as accomplices in so far as they have organised or tolerated the criminal acts of their subordinates.

337. Similarly, Article IX of the Chinese Law of 24 October 1946, Governing the Trial of War Criminals, stated:

> Persons who occupy a supervisory or commanding position in relation to war criminals and in their capacity as such have not fulfilled their duty to prevent crimes from being committed by their subordinates shall be treated as the accomplices of such war criminals.

338. In a number of cases against German and Japanese war criminals following the Second World War, beginning with the trial of the Japanese General Tomoyuki Yamashita before a United States Military Commission in Manila, the principle of command responsibility for failure to act was relied upon by military courts and tribunals as a valid basis for placing individual criminal responsibility on superiors for the criminal acts of

their subordinates. Thus, the United States Supreme Court, in its well-known holding in *In Re Yamashita*, answered in the affirmative the question of whether the law of war imposed on an army commander a duty to take the appropriate measures within his power to control the troops under his command for the prevention of acts in violation of the laws of war, and whether he may be charged with personal responsibility for failure to take such measures when violations result. Similarly, the United States Military Tribunal at Nürnberg, in *United States v. Karl Brandt and others* (hereafter "Medical Case"), declared that "the law of war imposes on a military officer in a position of command an affirmative duty to take such steps as are within his power and appropriate to the circumstances to control those under his command for the prevention of acts which are violations of the law of war." Likewise, in *United States v. Wilhelm List et al.* (hereafter "Hostage Case") it was held that "a corps commander must be held responsible for the acts of his subordinate commanders in carrying out his orders and for acts which the corps commander knew or ought to have known about. Again, in *United States v. Wilhelm von Leeb et al.* (hereafter "High Command Case") the tribunal declared that:

> [u]nder basic principles of command authority and responsibility, an officer who merely stands by while his subordinates execute a criminal order of his superiors which he knows is criminal violates a moral obligation under international law. By doing nothing he cannot wash his hands of international responsibility.

339. While different aspects of this body of case law arising out of the Second World War will be considered in greater detail below as the Trial Chamber addresses the more specific content of the requisite elements of superior responsibility under Article 7(3), it is helpful here to further recall the finding made in the trial of the Japanese Admiral Soemu Toyoda before a military tribunal in Tokyo. Declaring that it had carefully studied, and followed, the precedents of other tribunals on the question of command responsibility, the tribunal, after setting out at some length what it considered to be the essential elements of this principle, concluded:

> In the simplest language it may be said that this Tribunal believes that the principle of command responsibility to be that, if this accused knew, or should by the exercise of ordinary diligence have learned, of the commission by his subordinates, immediate or otherwise, of the atrocities proved beyond a shadow of a doubt before this Tribunal or of the existence of a routine which would countenance such, and, by his failure to take any action to punish the perpetrators, permitted the atrocities to continue, he has failed in his performance of his duty as a commander and must be punished.

340. In the period following the Second World War until the present time, the doctrine of command responsibility has not been applied by any international judicial organ. Nonetheless, there can be no doubt that the concept of the individual criminal responsibility of superiors for failure to act is today firmly placed within the corpus of international humanitarian law. . . .

(ii) Discussion and Findings

354. The requirement of the existence of a "superior-subordinate" relationship which, in the words of the Commentary to Additional Protocol I, should be seen "in terms of a hierarchy encompassing the concept of control", is particularly problematic in situations such as that of the former Yugoslavia during the period relevant to the present case—situations where previously existing formal structures have broken down and where, during an interim period, the new, possibly improvised, control and command structures, may be ambiguous and ill-defined. It is the Trial Chamber's conclusion, the reasons for

which are set out below, that persons effectively in command of such more informal structures, with power to prevent and punish the crimes of persons who are in fact under their control, may under certain circumstances be held responsible for their failure to do so. Thus the Trial Chamber accepts the Prosecution's proposition that individuals in positions of authority, whether civilian or within military structures, may incur criminal responsibility under the doctrine of command responsibility on the basis of their *de facto* as well as *de jure* positions as superiors. The mere absence of formal legal authority to control the actions of subordinates should therefore not be understood to preclude the imposition of such responsibility.

a. The Responsibility of Non-Military Superiors

355. Before turning to the substance of the requisite superior-subordinate relationship, the Trial Chamber deems it appropriate first to set out its reasoning in relation to the question of the application of the principle enshrined in Article 7(3) to persons in non-military positions of authority.

356. It is apparent from the text of this provision that no express limitation is made restricting the scope of this type of responsibility to military commanders or situations arising under a military command. In contrast, the use of the generic term "superior" in this provision, together with its juxtaposition to the affirmation of the individual criminal responsibility of "Head[s] of State or Government" or "responsible Government official[s]" in Article 7(2), clearly indicates that its applicability extends beyond the responsibility of military commanders to also encompass political leaders and other civilian superiors in positions of authority. This interpretation is supported by the explanation of the vote made by the representative of the United States following the adoption of Security Council resolution 827 on the establishment of the International Tribunal. The understanding of the United States was expressed to be that individual criminal responsibility arises in the case of "the failure of a superior—whether political or military—to take reasonable steps to prevent or punish such crimes by persons under his or her authority". This statement was not contested. The same position was adopted by Trial Chamber I in its review of the Indictment pursuant to Rule 61 in *Prosecutor v. Milan Martic*, where it held that:

> [t]he Tribunal has particularly valid grounds for exercising its jurisdiction over persons who, through their position of political or military authority, are able to order the commission of crimes falling within its competence *ratione materiae* or who knowingly refrain from preventing or punishing the perpetrators of such crimes.

357. This interpretation of the scope of Article 7(3) is in accordance with the customary law doctrine of command responsibility. As observed by the Commission of Experts in its Final Report, while "[m]ost legal cases in which the doctrine of command responsibility has been considered have involved military or paramilitary accused, [p]olitical leaders and public officials have also been held liable under this doctrine in certain circumstances". Thus, the International Military Tribunal for the Far East (hereafter "Tokyo Tribunal") relied on this principle in making findings of guilt against a number of civilian political leaders charged with having deliberately and recklessly disregarded their legal duty to take adequate steps to secure the observance of the laws and customs of war and to prevent their breach. For example, while holding General Iwane Matsui criminally liable for the infamous "Rape of Nanking" by declaring that "[h]e had the power, as he had the duty, to control his troops and to protect the unfortunate citizens of Nanking. He must be held criminally responsible for his failure to discharge this duty", the tribunal was also prepared to place

359. In *United States v. Friedrich Flick and others*, the six accused, all leading civilian industrialists, were charged with the commission of war crimes and crimes against humanity in that they were said to have been principals in, accessories to, to have ordered, abetted, taken a consenting part in, or to have been connected with plans and enterprises involving the enslavement and deportation to slave labour of civilians from occupied territory, enslavement of concentration camp inmates and the use of prisoners of war in work having a direct relation to war operations. More specifically, it was alleged that the defendants sought and utilised such slave labour programmes by using tens of thousands of slave labourers in the industrial enterprises owned, controlled or influenced by them.

360. While acquitting four of the accused, the tribunal found the defendants Flick and Weiss guilty, as instances had been proved of Weiss' voluntary participation in the slave labour programme. Concerning Flick, the person controlling the industrial enterprise in question, and Weiss' superior, the judgement makes mention of no more than his "knowledge and approval" of Weiss' acts. Noting this absence of explicit reasoning, the United Nations War Crimes Commission has commented that it "seems clear" that the tribunal's finding of guilt was based on an application of the responsibility of a superior for the acts of his inferiors which he has a duty to prevent.

361. Similarly, civilian superiors were found criminally liable for the ill-treatment of forced labourers employed in the German industry in an appellate decision by the Superior Military Government Court of the French Occupation Zone in Germany, in the *Roechling* case. This case involved five accused, all holders of senior positions within the Roechling Iron and Steel Works in Voelklingen, four of whom were charged, *inter alia*, with having "employed under compulsion nationals of countries at that time occupied, prisoners of war, and deported persons, who were subjected to ill-treatment by [their] orders or with [their] consent". In its appeal judgement, the court clarified this charge by declaring that Herman Roechling and the other accused members of the Directorate of the Voelklingen works are not accused of having ordered this horrible treatment, but of having permitted it; and indeed supported it, and in addition, of not having done their utmost to put an end to these abuses.

362. Finding that three of the defendants had possessed sufficient authority to intervene in order to ensure an improvement in the treatment accorded to the deportees, the court proceeded to register findings of guilt on the basis of the accused's failure to act.

363. Thus, it must be concluded that the applicability of the principle of superior responsibility in Article 7(3) extends not only to military commanders but also to individuals in non-military positions of superior authority.

b. The Concept of Superior

364. The Trial Chamber now turns to the issue which lies at the very heart of the concept of command responsibility for failure to act, the requisite character of the superior-subordinate relationship.

365. As noted above, the Defence contends that the fundamental distinction to be drawn in this connection is that between commanders on the one hand, and other types of superiors (including non-commanders with higher rank than individuals committing the underlying offences) on the other. It explains this distinction by way of the following quotation:

> "Commanders" are those who can issue orders on their own authority and over their own names to troops in the units they command, whether large (division, corps) or small (platoon, company). But except in very small units, a comman-

der cannot function effectively without helpers, who bring him information about the condition of his troops, the whereabouts and intentions of the enemy, and other circumstances which together form the basis for his decisions and orders. These helping officers are a "staff", and if the unit is a large one and the staff correspondingly numerous, it is headed by a "Chief of Staff". This officer may be of high rank and his function very important, but he cannot issue orders (other than to his own staff subordinates) except by the authority and in the name of the unit commander.

366. This may be compared with the definition of the position and duties of a chief of staff which was given in the *High Command* case:

> Staff officers, except in limited fields, are not endowed with command authority. Subordinate staff officers normally function through the chiefs of staff. The chief of staff in any command is the closest officer, officially at least, to the commanding officer. It is his function to see that the wishes of his commanding officer are carried out. It is his duty to keep his commanding officer informed of the activities which take place within the field of his command. It is his function to see that the commanding officer is relieved of certain details and routine matters, that a policy having been announced, the methods and procedures for carrying out such policy are properly executed. His sphere and personal activities vary according to the nature and interests of his commanding officer and increase in scope dependent upon the position and responsibilities of such commander.

367. Consistent with these views, the United States Military Tribunals in the *Hostage* and *High Command* cases adopted the position that, while chiefs of staff may be held criminally responsible for their own positive acts, they cannot be held criminally responsible on the basis of command responsibility. Thus it was held in the *High Command* case that:

> [s]taff officers are an indispensable link in the chain of their final execution. If the basic idea is criminal under international law, the staff officer who puts that idea into the form of a military order, either himself or through subordinates under him, or takes personal action to see that it is properly distributed to those units where it becomes effective, commits a criminal act under international law....

368. While these two cases offer support for the view that the possession of powers of command is a necessary prerequisite for the imposition of command responsibility, it may be thought that the legal position is rendered less clear when the Tokyo Tribunal's conviction of Lieutenant General Akira Muto is taken into account. Muto had been a staff officer under General Iwane Matsui at the time of the "Rape of Nanking", and later served as Chief of Staff to General Yamashita in the Philippines. In discussing his responsibility in the former position, the tribunal held that, while there was no doubt that Muto knew of the atrocities, he could in his subordinate position take no steps to stop them, and could therefore not be held criminally liable for their commission. However, the tribunal took a different view of his responsibility in his position as Chief of Staff to Yamashita:

> "His position was now very different from that which he held during the so-called "Rape of Nanking". He was now in a position to influence policy. During his tenure of office as such Chief of Staff a campaign of massacre, torture and other atrocities was waged by the Japanese troops on the civilian population, and prisoners of war and civilian internees were starved, tortured and murdered. MUTO shares responsibility for these gross breaches of the Laws of War. We reject his defence that he knew nothing of these occurrences. It is wholly incredible."

369. In this case, then, a chief of staff, with no formal powers of command, was apparently held responsible on the basis of the doctrine of command responsibility. At least one prominent commentator on the subject relies on this case as support for the proposition that persons in non-command positions, such as advisers to a military unit, may be held criminally responsible on the basis of command responsibility. In this view, such a person, while lacking the authority to control the conduct of the forces in question, is still obliged to utilise all means available to prevent the perpetration of war crimes (such means may include protesting to the unit commander, notifying the next higher level of command, or, finally, seeking release from his position in the unit).

370. While the matter is, thus, not undisputed, it is the Trial Chamber's opinion that a position of command is indeed a necessary precondition for the imposition of command responsibility. However, this statement must be qualified by the recognition that the existence of such a position cannot be determined by reference to formal status alone. Instead, the factor that determines liability for this type of criminal responsibility is the actual possession, or non-possession, of powers of control over the actions of subordinates. Accordingly, formal designation as a commander should not be considered to be a necessary prerequisite for command responsibility to attach, as such responsibility may be imposed by virtue of a person's *de facto*, as well as *de jure*, position as a commander.

371. While the terms of the Statute offer little guidance in relation to this issue, it is clear that the term "superior" is sufficiently broad to encompass a position of authority based on the existence of *de facto* powers of control. The same term is employed in Article 86 of Additional Protocol I, which, in Article 87, further establishes that the duty of a military commander to prevent violations of the Geneva Conventions extends not only to his subordinates but also to "other persons under his control". This type of superior–subordinate relationship is described in the Commentary to the Additional Protocols by reference to the concept of "indirect subordination", in contrast to the link of "direct subordination" which is said to relate the tactical commander to his troops. Among the examples offered of such indirect subordination, this Commentary notes that:

> [i]f the civilian population in its own territory is hostile to prisoners of war and threatens them with ill-treatment, the military commander who is responsible for these prisoners has an obligation to intervene and to take the necessary measures, even though this population is not officially under his authority.

372. A survey of the existing judicial precedents demonstrates that commanders in regular armed forces have, on occasion, been held criminally responsible for their failure to prevent or punish criminal acts committed by persons not formally under their authority in the chain of command. Thus, in the *Hostage* and *High Command* trials it was accepted that commanders in charge of occupied territory may be held responsible for war crimes committed against civilians and prisoners of war in that area by troops not under their command. As the tribunal in the *Hostage* case declared:

> [t]he matter of subordination of units as a basis of fixing criminal responsibility becomes important in the case of a military commander having solely a tactical command. But as to the commanding general of occupied territory who is charged with maintaining peace and order, punishing crime and protecting lives and property, subordination are [sic] relatively unimportant. His responsibility is general and not limited to a control of units directly under his command.

373. Likewise, the finding in the *High Command* case that a commander may be held criminally liable for failing to prevent the execution of an illegal order issued by his superiors, which has been passed down to his subordinates independent of him, indicates

that legal authority to direct the actions of subordinates is not seen as an absolute requirement for the imposition of command responsibility. Similarly, the finding in the *Toyoda* case, whereby the tribunal rejected the alleged importance of what it called the "theoretical" division between operational and administrative authority, may be seen as supporting the view that commanders are under an obligation to take action to prevent the commission of war crimes by troops under their control despite a lack of formal authority to do so. An officer with only operational and not administrative authority does not have formal authority to take administrative action to uphold discipline, yet in the view of the tribunal in the *Toyoda* case; "[t]he responsibility for discipline in the situation facing the battle commander cannot, in the view of practical military men, be placed in any hands other than his own".

374. Again, in the *Pohl* trial, the finding of guilt against the accused Karl Mummenthey, an officer of the Waffen SS and business manager of a large establishment of industries employing concentration camp labour, is best read as predicated upon his possession of *de facto* powers of control. Charged with responsibility for the conditions to which labourers were exposed, Mummenthey based his defence in part on the contention that any mistreatment of prisoners was caused by concentration camp guards over whom he had no control (and, by implication, for which he therefore could not be held responsible). In rejecting this assertion the tribunal held:

> It has been Mummenthey's plan to picture himself as a private businessman in no way associated with the sternness and rigour of SS discipline, and entirely detached from concentration camp routine. The picture fails to convince. Mummenthey was a definite integral and important figure in the whole concentration camp set-up, and, as an SS officer, wielded military power of command. If excesses occurred in the industries under his control he was in a position not only to know about them, but to do something. From time to time he attended meetings of the concentration camp commanders where all items pertaining to concentration camp routine such as labour assignment, rations, clothing, quarters, treatment of prisoners, punishment, etc., were discussed.

375. Similarly, as noted above, the Tokyo Tribunal's conviction of General Akiro Muto for acts occurring during his tenure as Chief of Staff to General Yamashita demonstrates that it considered powers of influence not amounting to formal powers of command to provide a sufficient basis for the imposition of command responsibility.

376. The cases imposing responsibility for failure to act on civilians occupying positions of authority, also indicate that such persons may be held liable for crimes committed by persons over whom their formal authority under national law is limited or non-existent. Thus, it has been noted that the Tokyo Tribunal convicted Foreign Minister Koki Hirota on the basis of command responsibility for war crimes although he lacked the domestic legal authority to repress the crimes in question. The tribunal found Hirota derelict in his duty in not "insisting" before the cabinet that immediate action be taken to put an end to the crimes, language indicating powers of persuasion rather than formal authority to order action to be taken. Moreover, the *Roechling* case is best construed as an example of the imposition of superior responsibility on the basis of *de facto* powers of control possessed by civilian industrial leaders. While the accused in this case were found guilty, *inter alia*, of failing to take action against the abuse of forced labourers committed by the members of the Gestapo, it is nowhere suggested that the accused had any formal authority to issue orders to personnel under Gestapo command. Instead, the judgement employs the wording "sufficient" authority, a term not normally used in relation to formal powers of command, but rather one used to describe a degree of (in-

formal) influence. This view is further supported by the reasoning employed in the judgement of the court of first instance in this case, which, in response to the claim of one of the accused that he could not give orders to the plant police and the personnel of a punishment camp, as these were under the orders of the Gestapo, makes reference to his status as Herman Roechling's son-in-law — clearly a source of no more than *de facto* influence — as a factor affecting his authority to obtain an alleviation in the treatment of workers by the plant police.

377. While it is, therefore, the Trial Chamber's conclusion that a superior, whether military or civilian, may be held liable under the principle of superior responsibility on the basis of his *de facto* position of authority, the fundamental considerations underlying the imposition of such responsibility must be borne in mind. The doctrine of command responsibility is ultimately predicated upon the power of the superior to control the acts of his subordinates. A duty is placed upon the superior to exercise this power so as to prevent and repress the crimes committed by his subordinates, and a failure by him to do so in a diligent manner is sanctioned by the imposition of individual criminal responsibility in accordance with the doctrine. It follows that there is a threshold at which persons cease to possess the necessary powers of control over the actual perpetrators of offences and, accordingly, cannot properly be considered their "superiors" within the meaning of Article 7(3) of the Statute. While the Trial Chamber must at all times be alive to the realities of any given situation and be prepared to pierce such veils of formalism that may shield those individuals carrying the greatest responsibility for heinous acts, great care must be taken lest an injustice be committed in holding individuals responsible for the acts of others in situations where the link of control is absent or too remote.

378. Accordingly, it is the Trial Chamber's view that, in order for the principle of superior responsibility to be applicable, it is necessary that the superior have effective control over the persons committing the underlying violations of international humanitarian law, in the sense of having the material ability to prevent and punish the commission of these offences. With the caveat that such authority can have a *de facto* as well as a *de jure* character, the Trial Chamber accordingly shares the view expressed by the International Law Commission that the doctrine of superior responsibility extends to civilian superiors only to the extent that they exercise a degree of control over their subordinates which is similar to that of military commanders....

c. "Had reason to know"

387. Regarding the mental standard of "had reason to know", the Trial Chamber takes as its point of departure the principle that a superior is not permitted to remain wilfully blind to the acts of his subordinates. There can be no doubt that a superior who simply ignores information within his actual possession compelling the conclusion that criminal offences are being committed, or are about to be committed, by his subordinates commits a most serious dereliction of duty for which he may be held criminally responsible under the doctrine of superior responsibility. Instead, uncertainty arises in relation to situations where the superior lacks such information by virtue of his failure to properly supervise his subordinates.

388. In this respect, it is to be noted that the jurisprudence from the period immediately following the Second World War affirmed the existence of a duty of commanders to remain informed about the activities of their subordinates. Indeed, from a study of these decisions, the principle can be obtained that the absence of knowledge should not be considered a defence if, in the words of the Tokyo judgement, the superior was "at fault in having failed to acquire such knowledge".

389. For example, in the *Hostage* case the tribunal held that a commander of occupied territory is charged with notice of occurrences taking place within that territory. He may require adequate reports of all occurrences that come within the scope of his power and, if such reports are incomplete or otherwise inadequate, he is obliged to require supplementary reports to apprise him of all the pertinent facts. If he fails to require and obtain complete information, the dereliction of duty rests upon him and he is in no position to plead his own dereliction as a defence. Likewise, in the trial against Admiral Toyoda, the tribunal declared that the principle of command responsibility applies to the commander who "knew, or should have known, by use of reasonable diligence" of the commission of atrocities by his subordinates. Similarly, the tribunal in the *Pohl* case, describing Mummenthey's position as one of an "assumed or criminal naivete", held that the latter's assertions that he did not know what was happening in the labour camps and enterprises under his jurisdiction did not exonerate him, adding that "it was his duty to know". Again, in the *Roechling* case, the court, under the heading of "The defence of lack of knowledge", declared that:

> [n]o superior may prefer this defence indefinitely; for it is his duty to know what occurs in his organization, and lack of knowledge, therefore, can only be the result of criminal negligence.

390. While this body of precedent accordingly may be thought to support the position advocated by the Prosecution, the Trial Chamber is bound to apply customary law as it existed at the time of the commission of the alleged offences. Accordingly, the Trial Chamber must, in its construction of Article 7(3), give full consideration to the standard established by Article 86 of Additional Protocol I, in addition to these precedents.

391. Article 86 underwent considerable change during the drafting of the Protocol, and the Trial Chamber notes that the drafters explicitly rejected the proposed inclusion of a mental standard according to which a superior would be criminally liable for the acts of his subordinates in situations where he should have had knowledge concerning their activities. Thus, not only was the proposed ICRC draft, according to which superiors would be held responsible for the illegal acts of a subordinate "if they knew or should have known that he was committing or would commit such a breach and if they did not take measures within their power to prevent or repress the breach", rejected, but an amended version put forward by the United States employing the formulation "if they knew or should reasonably have known in the circumstances at the time" was also not accepted.

392. When considering the language of this provision as finally adopted, problems of interpretation arise if the English and French texts are compared. While the English text contains the wording "information which should have enabled them to conclude", the French version, rather than the literal translation "*des information qui auraient dû leur permettre de concluire*", is rendered "*des information leur permettant de concluire*" (literally: information enabling them to conclude). The proposition has been made that this discrepancy amounts to a distinction between the English text, which is said to embrace two requirements, one objective (that the superior had certain information) and one subjective (from this information available to the superior he should have drawn certain conclusions), and the French text containing only the objective element. The Trial Chamber notes, however, that this discrepancy in language was considered during the drafting of the Protocol, when it was expressly declared by delegates that the difference was not to be considered one of substance.

393. An interpretation of the terms of this provision in accordance with their ordinary meaning thus leads to the conclusion, confirmed by the *travaux préparatoires*, that

a superior can be held criminally responsible only if some specific information was in fact available to him which would provide notice of offences committed by his subordinates. This information need not be such that it by itself was sufficient to compel the conclusion of the existence of such crimes. It is sufficient that the superior was put on further inquiry by the information, or, in other words, that it indicated the need for additional investigation in order to ascertain whether offences were being committed or about to be committed by his subordinates. This standard, which must be considered to reflect the position of customary law at the time of the offences alleged in the Indictment, is accordingly controlling for the construction of the mens rea standard established in Article 7(3). The Trial Chamber thus makes no finding as to the present content of customary law on this point. It may be noted, however, that the provision on the responsibility of military commanders in the Rome Statute of the International Criminal Court provides that a commander may be held criminally responsible for failure to act in situations where he knew or should have known of offences committed, or about to be committed, by forces under his effective command and control, or effective authority and control.

(d) Necessary and Reasonable Measures

394. The legal duty which rests upon all individuals in positions of superior authority requires them to take all necessary and reasonable measures to prevent the commission of offences by their subordinates or, if such crimes have been committed, to punish the perpetrators thereof. It is the view of the Trial Chamber that any evaluation of the action taken by a superior to determine whether this duty has been met is so inextricably linked to the facts of each particular situation that any attempt to formulate a general standard *in abstracto* would not be meaningful.

395. It must, however, be recognised that international law cannot oblige a superior to perform the impossible. Hence, a superior may only be held criminally responsible for failing to take such measures that are within his powers. The question then arises of what actions are to be considered to be within the superior's powers in this sense. As the corollary to the standard adopted by the Trial Chamber with respect to the concept of superior, we conclude that a superior should be held responsible for failing to take such measures that are within his material possibility. The Trial Chamber accordingly does not adopt the position taken by the ILC on this point, and finds that the lack of formal legal competence to take the necessary measures to prevent or repress the crime in question does not necessarily preclude the criminal responsibility of the superior.

(e) Causation

396. As noted above in sub-section (a), the Defence asserts the existence of a separate requirement of causation. It is contended that, if the superior's failure to act did not cause the commission of the offence, the commander cannot be held criminally liable for the acts of his subordinates. The Defence submits that this applies also to a commander's failure to punish an offence, as it may be argued that inaction in the form of failure to punish is the cause of future offences.

397. In response, the Prosecution rejects the contention that causation is an element of the doctrine of superior responsibility. It submits that superiors may be held responsible if they fail to adequately take the steps within their powers to prevent or punish violations, and explains that this requirement does not entail proving that the superior's failure directly caused each violation. It argues that this point is reinforced by the fact that many superiors at different levels can be held responsible, within their spheres of competence, for the illegal acts of the same subordinates, irrespective of which superior's omission

may have resulted in the commission of the violations. It is further claimed that a causation requirement would undermine the "failure to punish" component of superior responsibility, which, it is pointed out, can only arise after the commission of the offence. It is noted that as a matter of logic a superior could not be held responsible for prior violations committed by subordinates if a causal nexus was required between such violations and the superior's failure to punish those who committed them.

398. Notwithstanding the central place assumed by the principle of causation in criminal law, causation has not traditionally been postulated as a *conditio sine qua non* for the imposition of criminal liability on superiors for their failure to prevent or punish offences committed by their subordinates. Accordingly, the Trial Chamber has found no support for the existence of a requirement of proof of causation as a separate element of superior responsibility, either in the existing body of case law, the formulation of the principle in existing treaty law, or, with one exception, in the abundant literature on this subject.

399. This is not to say that, conceptually, the principle of causality is without application to the doctrine of command responsibility insofar as it relates to the responsibility of superiors for their failure to prevent the crimes of their subordinates. In fact, a recognition of a necessary causal nexus may be considered to be inherent in the requirement of crimes committed by subordinates and the superior's failure to take the measures within his powers to prevent them. In this situation, the superior may be considered to be causally linked to the offences, in that, but for his failure to fulfil his duty to act, the acts of his subordinates would not have been committed.

400. In contrast, while a causal connection between the failure of a commander to punish past crimes committed by subordinates and the commission of any such future crimes is not only possible but likely, the Prosecution correctly notes that no such casual link can possibly exist between an offence committed by a subordinate and the subsequent failure of a superior to punish the perpetrator of that same offence. The very existence of the principle of superior responsibility for failure to punish, therefore, recognised under Article 7(3) and customary law, demonstrates the absence of a requirement of causality as a separate element of the doctrine of superior responsibility.

The Prosecutor v. Zlatko Aleksovski
IT-95-14/1-T, Judgment (25 June 1999)

69. Article 7 [of the Statute of the ICTY] makes clear that superior responsibility may be invoked if three concurrent elements are proved:

(i) a superior-subordinate relationship between the person against whom the claim is directed and the perpetrators of the offence;

(ii) the superior knew or had reason to know that a crime was about to be committed or had been committed;

(iii) the superior did not take all the necessary and reasonable measures to prevent the crime or to punish the perpetrator or perpetrators thereof.

70. The three constituent elements which are evident from the wording of Article 7(3) clearly draw from Article 86, paragraph 2, of Additional Protocol I and Article 6 of the Draft Code of the International Law Commission of 1996. They are repeated in Article 28 of the Rome Statute of the International Criminal Court.

71. The three constituent elements, as already shown in the *Celebici* case, are also those used by the Prosecutor and the Defence. However, the Prosecution and Defence

diverge in their interpretation of the content of each of the constituent elements. This will be discussed in more detail in the following sections. It seems appropriate however to begin by spelling out the nature of this legal principle before the content of the elements is determined.

[Concerning leader responsibility of civilians, the Trial Chamber stated:]

75.... The generic term "superior" in Article 7(3) of the Statute can be interpreted only to mean that superior responsibility is not limited to military commanders but may apply to the civilian authorities as well. The International Law Commission thus explains that "the reference to 'superiors' is sufficiently broad to cover military commanders or other civilian authorities who are in a similar position of command and exercise a similar degree of control with respect to their subordinates." This interpretation, which corresponds to the wording of the Statute, was also the one chosen for the final report of the Commission of Experts and is in line with customary international law as the Trial Chamber in the *Celebici* case already noted.

76. Superior responsibility is thus not reserved for official authorities. Any person acting *de facto* as a superior may be held responsible under Article 7(3). The decisive criterion in determining who is a superior according to customary international law is not only the accused's formal legal status but also his ability, as demonstrated by his duties and competence, to exercise control.... [Next, the Trial Chamber quoted from the *Celebici* case, and added:]

77. The level of control required to establish that the person against whom command authority is attributed has however been the subject of differing interpretations. The majority position taken in trials after the Second World War was that a superior -subordinate relationship was necessary to entail superior responsibility. In the *Toyoda* case, the level of control required was defined as "the actual authority over the offenders to issue orders to them not to commit illegal acts and to punish offenders". The *Pohl* case did not clearly establish the accused's responsibility only on the basis of his power to exert influence. Pohl, director of a company and Waffen SS officer, who used concentration camp prisoners, was held responsible for the mistreatment meted out to the prisoners not only because of the influence he could exercise over the organisation of the camp and the manner in which the prisoners were treated but also, it seems, because of his position as a Waffen SS officer. The Trial Chamber does acknowledge, however, that some cases appear to have adopted the less restrictive criterion of the mere power to influence. The Tokyo Tribunal held that the power of the accused staff officer Akira Muto was sufficient to entail his responsibility as a superior. The Minister of Foreign Affairs Koki Hirota was found responsible for not have "insisted" to the Government that measures be taken. In the *Roechling* case also, mere *de facto* influence was judged sufficient to establish that the accused was duty-bound to take measures to ensure that the mistreatment of prisoners was stopped.

78. This approach is appealing but raises the question of the nature of the powers in fact and in law which an accused's functions confer on him. Hierarchical power constitutes the very foundation of responsibility under the terms of Article 7(3) of the Statute. In order to entail his responsibility under Article 7(3), whatever his status, the accused must first have superior authority. In this respect, the International Law Commission's conclusion that civilian authorities are superiors if they exercise a degree of control with respect to their subordinates similar to that of a military person in an analogous command position is a particularly relevant analytical aid. In the opinion of the Trial Chamber, a civilian must be characterised as a superior pursuant to Article 7(3) if he has the ability *de jure* or *de facto* to issue orders to prevent an offence and to sanction the perpetrators

thereof. A civilian's sanctioning power must however be interpreted broadly. It should be stated that the doctrine of superior responsibility was originally intended only for the military authorities. Although the power to sanction is the indissociable corollary of the power to issue orders within the military hierarchy, it does not apply to the civilian authorities. It cannot be expected that a civilian authority will have disciplinary power over his subordinate equivalent to that of the military authorities in an analogous command position. To require a civilian authority to have sanctioning powers similar to those of a member of the military would so limit the scope of the doctrine of superior authority that it would hardly be applicable to civilian authorities. The Trial Chamber therefore considers that the superior's ability *de jure* or *de facto* to impose sanctions is not essential. The possibility of transmitting reports to the appropriate authorities suffices once the civilian authority, through its position in the hierarchy, is expected to report whenever crimes are committed, and that, in the light of this position, the likelihood that those reports will trigger an investigation or initiate disciplinary or even criminal measures is extant.

80.... [Regarding the standard "had reason to know"] ... Admittedly, as regards "indirect" responsibility, the Trial Chamber is reluctant to consider that a "presumption" of knowledge about a superior exists which would somehow automatically entail his guilt whenever a crime was allegedly committed. The Trial Chamber deems however that an individual's superior position *per se* is a significant indicium that he had knowledge of the crimes committed by his subordinates. The weight to be given to that indicium however depends inter alia on the geographical and temporal circumstances. This means that the more physically distant the commission of the acts was, the more difficult it will be, in the absence of other indicia, to establish that the superior had knowledge of them. Conversely, the commission of a crime in the immediate proximity of the place where the superior ordinarily carried out his duties would suffice to establish a significant indicium that he had knowledge of the crime, *a fortiori* if the crimes were repeatedly committed.

Notes and Questions

1. For additional reading, *see, e.g.*, Hays Parks, *Command Responsibility for War Crimes*, 62 Mil. L. Rev. 1 (1973); Waldemar A. Solf, *A Response to Telford Taylor's "Nuremberg and Vietnam: An American Tragedy"* in 4 The Vietnam War and International Law 421, 433 *ff.* (R. Falk ed. 1976); Greg R. Vetter, *Command Responsibility of Non-Military Superiors in the International Criminal Court*, 25 Yale J. Int'l L. 89 (2000). Professor Bassiouni also recognizes that the knew or should have known test for commander responsibility is the "applicable legal standard." M. Cherif Bassiouni, Crimes Against Humanity in International Criminal Law 372 (1992); *see also id.* at 385–87. Also recall Article 7 (3) of the Statute of the ICTY.

In view of the above, what do you think of the creation of different tests for military and "other" leaders set forth in Article 28 (1) and (2) of the Statute of the ICC (in the Documents Supplement)? Where might civilian leaders who cannot be convicted under the limited liability recognized in Article 28 (2) be prosecuted? *See also* Chapter Three, Section 1, on universal jurisdiction.

2. Does leader responsibility pertain only when there is a formal chain of command or leadership? See M. McDougal & F. Feliciano, Law and Minimum World Public Order 691 (1961) ("the term 'superior' has been interpreted to embrace in reference not only formal rank and authority but also effective physical or moral capacity to induce commission of an unlawful act" — citing The Einsatzgruppen Case, 2 T.W.C. at

480 (1947) and Trial of Sadaiche, 15 W.C.R. at 175). Recall the decision of the I.M.T. for the Far East, *supra. See also* In the Matter of a Proposal for a Formal Request for Deferral to the Competence of the Tribunal, ICTY (May 16, 1995), paras. 23–24, *infra* in Chapter Six, Section 9. The Appeals Chamber in *Delalic* affirmed the Trial Chamber's recognitions that *de facto* powers of control are sufficient for application of leader responsibility and that "customary law has specified a standard of effective control." *The Prosecutor v. Delalic*, IT-96-21-A (Appeals Chamber, Judgment), paras. 188, 190, 195–198, 266 (20 Feb. 2001).

Compare Article 28 of the Statute of the ICC, in the Documents Supplement. Does that latter article fully reflect customary international law concerning leader responsibility?

3. Should the failure of a leader to keep informed or to obtain needed information be a defense to dereliction of duty? Read Article 86 of Protocol I to the Geneva Conventions ("had information which should have enabled"). Are you convinced that Article 86 has changed customary international law? Did the ICTY in the *Celibici* case identify other *opinio juris* supporting its conclusion in that regard? or state practice?

In *The Prosecutor v. Tihomir Blaskic*, IT-95-14 (3 March 2000), the ICTY sentenced Croatian General Blaskic to 45 years imprisonment for war crimes and crimes against humanity involving his ordering of attacks on civilians and failing to supervise or punish subordinates. The ICTY Trial Chamber declared that lack of knowledge must be held against him when it was a result of negligence in discharge of his duties. The trial began in June 1997 and closing arguments were heard July 26-30, 1999. There were 104 witnesses called by the Prosecutor, 46 by the defense, and 9 by the Trial Chamber. *United States v. List* had made the same point about failure of a leader to acquire relevant knowledge.

4. In *The Prosecutor v. Brdanin*, IT-99-36-T (Trial Chamber Judgment, 1 Sept. 2004), the accused was acquitted of genocide and complicity in genocide due to lack of proof of relevant genocidal intent. However, the Trial Chamber noted that leader responsibility for genocide can exist where the superior knew or had reason to know that his or her subordinates (1) were about to commit or had committed genocide, and (2) that the subordinates possessed the required specific intent to commit genocide [see Genocide Convention, art. II, in the Documents Supplement], adding that it is not necessary to prove that the leader possessed genocidal intent. *Id.* para. 715.

5. What do you think of the propriety of the following instructions in the Medina trial (of Cpt. Medina, company commander of the U.S. troops at My Lai)?

Instructions from the Military Judge to the Court Members in *United States vs. Captain Ernest L. Medina*

In relation to the question pertaining to the supervisory responsibilities of a Company Commander, I advise you that as a general principle of military law and custom a military superior in command is responsible for and required, in the performance of his command duties to make certain the proper performance by his subordinates of their duties as assigned by him. In other words, after taking or issuing an order a commander must remain alert and make timely adjustments as required by a changing situation. Furthermore, a commander is also responsible if he has actual knowledge that troops or other persons subject to his control are in the process of committing or are about to commit a war crime and he wrongfully fails to take the necessary and reasonable steps to insure compliance with the law of war. You will observe that these legal requirements placed upon a commander require actual knowledge plus a wrongful failure to act. Thus mere presence at the scene without knowledge will not suffice. That is, the commander-subordinate relationship alone will not allow an inference of knowledge. While it is not necessary that a commander actually see an atrocity being committed, it is essential that he know that his subordinates are in the process of committing atrocities or are about to commit atrocities....

As to the offense of involuntary manslaughter, you are advised that the omission of the accused must not only constitute culpable negligence but it must also be a proximate cause of the death or deaths. In this regard, the deaths of the unknown number of unidentified Vietnamese persons, not less than 100, must have been the natural and probable consequence of the accused's alleged culpable omission. That is, if Captain Medina had ordered his men to stop shooting noncombatants after he became aware that such was occurring, no deaths or further deaths would have occurred, and that such deaths were not the result of an independent intervening cause in which the accused did not have knowledge, and which he could not have foreseen. If it appears that the alleged culpable omission of the accused was not the proximate cause of the deaths of the unknown number of unidentified Vietnamese persons, not less that 100, but that another cause intervened over which the accused had no knowledge or control, and but for which death would not have occurred, such intervening cause is a good defense to the charge of involuntary manslaughter. To put this rule in evidentiary perspective, there has been expert evidence offered that because of experiences of the men of Charlie Company prior to the day of 16 March 1968, and because of the pressures of the combat assault, Captain Medina could have experienced difficulty in maintaining control over his men. There has also been evidence offered to the contrary, tending to indicate that his subordinates were responsive to Captain Medina's orders. The burden is upon the Government to establish beyond reasonable doubt that there was no such independent intervening cause, but that the accused's alleged culpable negligence was a proximate cause of the deaths of the unknown number of unidentified Vietnamese persons, not less than 100. Consequently, unless you are satisfied beyond reasonable doubt that the alleged victims' deaths were not the result of the unresponsiveness of the men of Charlie Company to Captain Medina's orders, but was proximately caused by the accused's alleged culpably negligent omission, you must acquit the accused of the Additional Charge and its Specification.

[Cpt. Medina was later acquitted]

6. For apt criticism, *see, e.g.*, Joe Bishop, Justice Under Fire 291–92 (1974). Consider also: Telford Taylor, remarks, Law and Responsibility in Warfare 226–27 (P. Trooboff ed. 1975):

Now in my opinion that is wrong in law and wrong in common sense. One need go no further than the United States Army Field Manual 27-l0, The Law of Land Warfare, which was published in 1956. It provides explicitly that a military commander is responsible not only for criminal acts committed in pursuance of his orders, but also if he has "actual knowledge, *or should have* knowledge" of what is happening in his command (emphasis added). Paragraph 501 of the Army Field Manual makes it clear that such constructive knowledge of the commander may result "through reports received by him or through other means." It also specifies that criminal liability exists if the commander having such actual or constructive knowledge "fails to take the necessary and reasonable steps to insure compliance with the law of war or to punish violators thereof."

Quite apart from what is in the Army Field Manual, assume for a moment that this problem applied to a noncriminal case. Suppose the troops entering My Lai had encountered resistance, and suppose that because of improper use or selection of weaponry or improper tactics they had suffered heavy losses. When the battalion commander comes to inquire why this has happened, suppose then that the company commander says "Major, I didn't know that they were doing it." The immediate, logical answer would have come: "Captain, it's your business to know precisely that — that's what company commanders are for."

Apply this now to war crimes. A hypothetical captain knows that he has poorly trained troops who have suffered casualties, who are in a state of panic, who have come to hate the Vietnamese people, and who have been improperly indoctrinated about the purposes of the war. He thinks to himself: "I'm going into this village and I really don't know what will happen if those troops go in shooting and find themselves among the villagers. I guess I'd better not know too much until the operation has gone beyond the first encounter."

I suggest that the standard just enunciated is indefensibly narrow. I am not concerned about the punishment of Captain Medina. He must know that the deaths of the villagers were very directly due to his failure to control his troops. He must know that the image of the Army and of his country was tarnished by the coverup far beyond anything that could possibly have followed if the rules about reporting atrocities had been followed instead of disregarded. That is a heavy enough burden for anyone to bear.

What I am concerned about is the possible perpetuation of the standard for military officers specified in the Medina charge. This would, I think, undermine the very legitimate area of command responsibility.

I do not at all mean to suggest a standard of absolute liability for military leaders. But even in ordinary criminal law we have cases in which people have affirmative responsibility. Certainly command in the military is such a situation. An officer is, and should be, responsible for what he should have known about wrongful conduct of his men that he did nothing to prevent. I suggest in conclusion that in terms of individual responsibility — the problem that has been explored and exposed above all others by the recent succession of trials and nontrials, acquittals and convictions — if we are to rise above the rank of the enlisted man at all, the Medina charge is a very inhibiting ruling and an ultimately unsatisfactory solution.

7. If Captain Medina had been found generally immobilized and weeping near the My Lai killing areas, would such be relevant to dereliction? mitigation? Would such indicate that Medina's troops were "out of control," that he knew this to be the case?

8. Consider also Article 86, paragraph 2, of Protocol I to the Geneva Conventions: "The fact that a breach of the Convention or of this Protocol was committed by a subordinate does not absolve his superiors from penal disciplinary responsibility ... if they knew, or had information which should have enabled them to conclude in the circumstances at the time, that he was committing or was going to commit such a breach and if they did not take all feasible measures within their power to prevent or repress the breach."

Is this standard similar to the "knew or should have known" standard developed under customary international law? Does the Protocol cover a circumstance where a person had information from which, under the circumstances, a reasonable person should have known?

Notes and Questions

1. What a person "should have known," but did not actually know or consciously or maliciously disregard, or acquiesce in, could rest on a criminal negligence standard that addresses fault or dereliction under the circumstances, including what a reasonable person under the circumstances should have known.

2. In *The Prosecutor v. Bisengimana*, ICTR-00-60 (Trial Chamber Judgment, 13 April 2006), Paul Bisengimana, a *bourgmestre* was found guilty as a leader who, although not present, had reason to know of attacks by others under his effective authority at the Ruhanda Protestant Church and School in Rwanda and did not take steps to stop the murder, extermination, and crimes against humanity perpetrated.

3. Would it be possible to defend Mr. Waldheim regarding allegations of international criminal behavior on the ground that he was merely a staff officer? Would it be possible to defend Mr. Waldheim on the grounds that he personally did not kill any human being during World War II, did not personally order the killing of another human being, and was not in a position of command to do so? Would complicity be a possible charge nonetheless? *See also* Scroggins, in Section 3; The Prosecutor v. Musema, above.

4. For use of the knew or should have known test in connection with civil liability, *see, e.g., Xuncax v. Gramajo*, 886 F. Supp. 162, 171–72 & n.3 (D. Mass. 1995), also *quoting* Senate Report No. 249, 102d Cong., 1st Sess. 9 (1991). *See also Kadic v. Karadzic*, 70 F.3d 232, 242 (2d Cir. 1995). With respect to civil liability, see also Article 75 of the Statute of the ICC and Article 106 of the 1994 ICTY Rules of Procedure and Evidence–both in the Documents Supplement.

5. What is the normal *mens rea* standard concerning attempts, complicity or conspiracy? Must one specifically intend to commit a crime as such or to participate in a crime as such, as opposed to an intent to engage or participate in conduct (*i.e.*, the commission of an act) that constitutes a crime? In other words, must a prosecutor prove a specific intent to violate law as opposed to an intent to engage in conduct that happens to be violative of law? Is ignorance of the law generally an excuse?

6. In *Khouzam v. Ashcroft*, 361 F.3d 161, 165–66 (2d Cir. 2004), the circuit panel stated that acquiescence in torture can occur when there is "awareness" of torture and a failure to intervene.

7. While we are on subjects that raise little emotion, consider the following:

Paust, remarks, 77 PROCEEDINGS, AM. SOC. INT'L L. 186, 187–89 (1983)*

Perhaps closer to a Soviet approach to questions about human rights deprivations than he might wish President Reagan has said that the investigation into the massacre of Palestinian refugees at the Sabra and Shatilla camps in Beirut and the recent Israeli report on the responsibility of certain Israeli officials present "an internal problem, strictly an internal affair." But as any international lawyer should know, the President's remarks are fundamentally incorrect.

Indeed, one has to be legally ignorant to pretend that criminal responsibility under the laws of war and the Genocide Convention poses merely "an internal problem" and not a serious matter of international concern. Today, there is simply no question whether war crimes and genocide, as violations of customary international law, are serious crimes

---

* Reproduced with permission from 77 Proc., ASIL 186 (1983), © The American Society of International Law.

against humankind over which there is universal jurisdiction. Any state can prosecute the perpetrators, there is no statute of limitations concerning such crimes, and individual perpetrators are liable as well to civil suit for money damages on the basis of such violations or, at least, on the basis of the underlying violations of basic human rights (especially in view of article 8 of the Universal Declaration of Human Rights which expressly guarantees an effective remedy in national tribunals for a relevant human rights deprivation).

More encouraging has been the Israeli commission's exercise of its responsibility to investigate alleged criminal and/or moral responsibility of Israeli persons with regard to the massacres. We still await any similar Lebanese report. But Israeli and Lebanese responsibility under international law is not satisfied. Both Israel and Lebanon have yet to fulfill their duty under international law to search for and prosecute or extradite those persons within their territory who are reasonably suspected of having committed war crimes or genocide. And any sensitive human being concerned about human rights and other deprivations must be concerned about the continued lack of meaningful sanctions.

Personal responsibility of the Lebanese perpetrators of the massacres is clear; especially suspect is one Hobeicha, head of the Phalange intelligence and officer in charge of the Phalange participants in the massacres. With regard to alleged Israeli responsibility, the question of criminal responsibility may not be clear to all, but the recent Israeli report raises at least serious questions of leader or command responsibility and complicity in connection with war crimes, genocide, and violations of fundamental human rights.

As one might recall from World War II prosecutions, complicity in connection with war crimes includes aiding, abetting or permitting war crime activity by others. The standard recognized in the U.N. Command during the Korean War was that one who "aids, abets, counsels, commands, permits, induces, or procures" the commission of a war crime "is a principal." Article III(e) of the Genocide Convention, which most recognize as customary law, declares that "complicity in genocide" is itself punishable as an international crime. In one World War II case, the *Borkum Island* case, certain members of a German guard who stood by as civilians inflicted injury on or killed U.S. fliers being paraded through the streets were convicted along with the commander who ordered the parading of U.S. troops.

With regard to the Beirut massacres, the Israeli commission's report demonstrates in ways not previously known that Sharon and Eytan assumed command responsibility for the "purification" operation. They helped *plan* the operation, they *ordered* the operation to commence, they *coordinated* and *supported* the operation (with Eytan, in particular, meeting with Phalange leaders during the operation after receiving reports of the massacre), and Israeli officers *ordered* a halt to the operation. These actions raise not only the question of possible complicitous relationships and complicitous responsibility, but also command control and command responsibility under the law of war.

Some type of criminal intent is needed for the crime of complicity under international law, but, as shown by World War II prosecutions, such a requirement can be satisfied under the more general "knew or should have known" test. In no case is mere presence at an incident enough. There must be some aiding, abetting, permitting, etc., of the proscribed activity. Intent, however, can be minimally shown by circumstantial factors.

With regard to command responsibility, the question becomes whether those officers who assumed some control over the joint operation knew or should have known what was happening or what could take place while they took no reasonable corrective action under the circumstances. As a U.S. military publication notes: a commander is responsible "if he has actual knowledge, or should have knowledge, through reports received ... or through other means, that troops or other persons subject to his control are about to commit or have committed a war crime and he fails to take the necessary and reasonable steps to insure compliance with the law of war or to punish violators thereof."

As mentioned, Sharon and Eytan assumed command control of the overall operation and helped plan it, ordered it to commence, coordinated and supported it. Additionally, there are damaging recognitions in the Israeli report that the then-Defense Minister Sharon "bears personal responsibility" and that Sharon, Eytan and others should have known what was going to occur or was likely to occur but ordered the Phalange militia into the Palestinian camps at approximately 8:30 p.m. Tuesday, September 14th even knowing, in the words of the report, "that the combatants in Lebanon belittle the value of human life far beyond what is necessary and accepted in wars between civilized people, and that ... atrocities ... had been widespread in Lebanon since 1975." Other facts developed in the report demonstrate enough reason to suspect that certain Israeli officials at times knew or should have known what was happening or about to happen and yet took no reasonable corrective action before, during or even after the massacres. Since both Israel and Lebanon remain under a duty to search for and prosecute or extradite those persons within their territory who are reasonably suspected of having committed war crimes or genocide, it is clear that the Israeli report, however encouraging and courageous, is insufficient.

One must hope, then, that both Israel and Lebanon will carry through with their responsibilities under international law and that Israel, in particular, as a democratic state, will demonstrate to the world its commitment to law and to its own historic moral values. We all know that complicity in genocide and war crime activity is fundamentally anti-Jewish. If the Jewish state, Israel, cannot carry through with its obligation to prosecute or extradite, then who among us will or can? Some of the most important of international laws hang in the balance.

Halberstam, remarks, *id.* at 190–91* & Paust, remarks in response:

Professor Halberstam then turned to comment on points raised by Jordan Paust in the context of the Genocide Convention. She suggested that, to the extent that Professor Paust relied on the report of the Israeli Commission as acknowledging Israeli responsibility for the "operation" in Sabra and Shatilla, he was using the term "operation" differently from the Commission. Professor Halberstam said that Professor Paust seemed to use the term "the operation" to refer to the killing of women and children in the camps, while the report used the term with reference to the operation of going into the camps and cleaning out any guerrillas that might be in the camps. To the extent that the report did note Israeli responsibility, it was only the responsibility of failing to take additional precautions in view of the history of violence between the Arab groups. Further, Professor Halberstam went on, the Genocide Convention focuses on the killing of the members of a group for the purpose of exterminating that group. Professor Halberstam saw no indication of such a purpose in the activities of Israel in Lebanon, nor even in those of the Lebanese. It was true, she conceded, that the "intent" requirement set out in the Genocide Convention included the "knew or should have known" standard. That, however, was drafted with reference to the systematic long-term effort to round up and exterminate six million Jews in Europe, and thus it might seriously be questioned whether the "knew or should have known" standard was applicable to a one-day action in one refugee camp. In Professor Halberstam's view, the deaths in the refugee camps in Lebanon did not raise any responsibility for genocidal conduct.

---

* Reproduced with permission from 77 ASIL Proc. 186 (1983), © The American Society of International Law.

Professor Paust responded that he had used the word "operation" in the same sense as suggested by Professor Halberstam — *i.e.*, with regard to going into and controlling the camps and not with regard to a plan actually to kill the occupants. This, nevertheless, in his view, still raised the question of command responsibility and criminal liability, particularly under the "should have known" test. He pointed out, further, that the "knew or should have known" standard used after World War II had not been limited to prosecutions related to the Holocaust, but, as a part of customary law, was also used in the case of General Yamashita as well as in a number of other non-Holocaust-related prosecutions. Thus, the "should have known" standard could apply to more ordinary war crimes, including those that might take place on a single day or at a single time, as in the Sabra and Shatilla incidents.

8. In 1987, a civil suit was filed in the District of Columbia against an alleged perpetrator of war crimes, Brigadier General Amos Yaron, committed in Lebanon in September of 1982. See *Ali Aidi, et al. v. Yaron*, Civ. Action No. 87-1216, slip op. (D.D.C. 1987). The civil suit was held up by the following order: "As this Court finds that defendant's diplomatic immunity is intact and deserving of full recognition, the motion to quash service of process will be granted. Accordingly, there is no need to reach the separate motion to dismiss.... Ordered that the motion of defendant to quash service of process be, and hereby is, granted; and it is further Ordered that the motion of defendant to dismiss be, and hereby is, denied as moot; and it is further Ordered that the complaint be, and hereby is, dismissed."

In partial justification, the district court argued:

Plaintiffs note that there is no such exception to the shield of diplomatic immunity expressed in either the Diplomatic Relations Act of 1978 or in the Vienna Convention. They maintain, however, that the Vienna Convention and the Diplomatic Relations Act of 1978 merely codify the rules of customary international law on the issues of diplomatic privileges and immunities. These customs in turn, argue plaintiffs, dictate that no one should be shielded from prosecution for the commission of international crimes. Plaintiffs maintain that these customs are illustrated in the Nuremberg Charter, the U.S. Army Field Manual, and the Fourth Geneva Convention of 1949.

Assuming arguendo that the Vienna Convention and the Diplomatic Relations Act of 1978 meant to embody these customs of international law, that these customs create additional exceptions to the grant of immunity, and that these customs declare that immunity shall be dissolved in the case of war criminals, defendant would still be entitled to diplomatic immunity as this is not a suit charging Mr. Yaron with international crimes. This is a civil action seeking damages for alleged tortious conduct, wrongful death and personal injury. This is not a criminal tribunal. Without exception, plaintiffs rely on statements which argue for the abrogation of diplomatic immunity when the defendant is before a criminal tribunal charged with committing international crimes. This is not such a tribunal.

Moreover, Professor Paust is quoted on page eleven of this same brief as stating that "Diplomatic Agent[s] charged with the commission of an international crime" are not entitled to immunity (emphasis added)."

What do you think of the reasoning and conclusions of the district court? *See also* Amerada Hess Shipping Corp. v. Argentine Republic, 830 F. 2d 421 (2d Cir. 1987); *Draft Brief Concerning Claims to Foreign Sovereign Immunity and Human Rights: Nonimmunity for Violations of International Law Under the FSIA*, 8 Hous. J. Int'l L. 49 (1985); the *Barbie Trial*, Chapter Nine, Section 3; Jordan J. Paust, *Suing Saddam: Private Remedies for War Crimes and Hostage-Taking*, 31 Va. J. Int'l L. 351, 374–78 (1991).

Revised from: J. Paust, *Threats to Accountability After Nuremberg: Crimes Against Humanity, Leader Responsibility and National Fora*
12 N.Y.L.S. J. H.R. 547 (1995)

As the above demonstrates, besides responsibility as a principal (or primary perpetrator), conspirator, or complicitor, leaders can be charged with dereliction of duty or criminal negligence.[1] The widely-known customary standard with respect to criminal negligence has been termed the "should have known" standard whereby a leader is criminally responsible if: (1) he or she should have had knowledge of illegality that had occurred, was occurring, or was about to occur at the hands of subordinates, (2) he or she had an opportunity to act, and (3) such a person failed to take reasonable corrective action under the circumstances.[2] Whether a person should have had knowledge must be tested circumstantially and with respect to a reasonable person in the same general position as the accused. Thus, reasonable foreseeability is quite relevant.

Although slightly different, Article 7(3) of the Statute of the International Tribunal for the Former Yugoslavia can be interpreted to reflect the customary standard. The language in Article 7 recognizes responsibility if one "knew or had reason to know," and logically one "had reason to know" if under the circumstances one should have known. As the report of the Secretary-General states, such language relates to an "imputed responsibility or criminal negligence" and a "failure to prevent a crime or to deter the unlawful behavior of his subordinates ... or to punish those who had committed" crimes.

Dereliction of duty or criminal negligence standards allow prosecution under thresholds far less than actual knowledge, wilfulness, or recklessness. Thus, standards such as "wilfully blind", "deliberately", "knowingly took the serious risk" or "recklessly" pose too high a threshold concerning leader responsibility. Additionally, leader responsibility is a separate offense, independent of the *mens rea* element of the offense committed by the

---

1. *See, e.g.,* extract of Judgment of the International Military Tribunal for the Far East (1 Nov. 1948), *supra* ("fail", "neglects", "fault", "negligence or supiness"); *id.* (Roling, J., dissenting) ("criminal negligence"); United States v. von Leeb, 11 T.W.C. at 543–44 (1948) ("dereliction" and "criminal negligence"); United States v. List, 11 T.W.C. at 1256, 1271 ("is charged with notice ... dereliction of duty ... [and] cannot plead his own dereliction as a defense"); U.S. Dep't of Army Pam. No. 27-161-2, II International Law 241 (1961) (*quoting In re Yamashita*, 327 U.S. 1, 16 (1946): "'neglect to take reasonable measures ... an affirmative duty to take such measures as were within his power and appropriate in the circumstances....'"); III Manual of Military Law, The Law of War on Land 178 (British War Office 1958) ("negligently or deliberately"); Leipzig Trials, case of Major Crusius [reported in Chapter Six, Section 2]; U.S. Dep't of Army FM 27-10, *supra* at 178–79, para. 501; Army Subject Schedule 27-1, at 10, 15–17; Report of the Secretary-General, at para. 56 ("imputed responsibility or criminal negligence"); Indictment: The Prosecutor of the Tribunal v. Radovan Karadzic, Ratko Mladic, paras. 32–33, 35–36, 39, 41, 43, 45, 48 (July 24, 1995); In the Matter of a Proposal for a Formal Request for Deferral to the Competence of the Tribunal re: Radovan Karadzic, Ratko Mladic and Mico Stanisic, No. IT-95-5-D, paras. 4, 17, 22–25 (May 16, 1995); other cases addressed *supra*.

2. See *supra* note 1; Xuncax v. Gramajo, 886 F. Supp. 162, 171–72 & n.3 (D. Mass. 1995); M.C. Bassiouni, Crimes Against Humanity in International Law 372 (1992) ("The applicable legal standard ... is the objective standard of 'reasonableness' in light of the existing circumstances, *i.e.,* reasonableness in terms of ... knowledge that should have been known.") (*see also id.* 385–87); Anthony D'Amato, *National Prosecution for International Crimes,* 3 International Criminal Law — Enforcement 173 (M.C. Bassiouni ed. 1987); Anthony D'Amato, *Superior Orders vs. Command Responsibility,* 80 Am. J. Int'l L. 604, 607–08 & n.1 (1986); Telford Taylor, remarks in Law and Responsibility in Warfare 226–27 (P. Trooboff ed. 1975); *cf.* William Eckhardt, *"Command Criminal Responsibility: A Plea for a Workable Standard,"* 97 Mil. L. Rev. 1 (1982); Hays Parks, *supra*. Nonetheless, in *von Leeb* the *mens rea* standard concerning aggressive war was quite different. See 11 T.W.C. at 488–90.

primary perpetrator. For example, a primary perpetrator might commit the crime of murder of a detainee which crime involves the intentional killing of a detainee, and yet the superior can be responsible under the "should have known" test (for a separate offense of dereliction of duty and one with a *mens rea* element met by the criminal negligence standard).

Notes and Questions

1. Radovan Karadzic and Ratko Mladic were indicted on July 25, 1995, for their alleged role in the joint criminal enterprise to eliminate and remove Bosnian Muslims and Bosnian Croats from the territories claimed by Bosnian Serbs. Karadzic was the president and supreme commander of the armed forces of the "Republika Srpska," the territory claimed by the Serbs within Bosnia and Herzegovina. Mladic was a general and Commander of the Main Staff of the Bosnian Serb Army. This first indictment included charges of war crimes, genocide, other crimes against humanity, and more particularly: persecution, extermination, murder, deportation, inhumane acts, terror, unlawful attacks on civilians, and the taking of hostages. *See, e.g.*, The Prosecutor of the Tribunal v. Radovan Karadzic, Ratko Mladic, *Indictment*, Case No. IT-95-5/18, paras. 36, 45–46 (1995). The Indictment also expressly mentioned liability as direct perpetrators, leader responsibility, and aiding and abetting liability. By the time the accused were arrested in 2008 and 2011, respectively, the prosecutors amended the indictments to include only the most serious of the crimes. *See* The Prosecutor v. Radovan Karadzic, *Prosecution's Marked-Up Indictment*, Case No. IT-95-5/18-PT (19 October 2009); The Prosecutor v. Ratko Mladic, *Prosecution Submission of the Fourth Amended Indictment*, Case No. IT-09-92-PT (16 December 2011). Of particular interest are their indictments on the charge of sniping and shelling attacks against civilians, which could prove an important precedent should the ICC investigate the charges of attacks on civilians ordered by President Bashar al-Assad of Syria. *See* Statement to the General Assembly on behalf of Ms. Navi Pillay, UN High Commissioner for Human Rights, 7 June 2012, http://www.ohchr.org/EN/Countries/MENARegion/Pages/SYIndex.aspx.

Portions of the original Indictment with respect to attacks on civilians included:

36. As described in paragraph 26 of this indictment, which is incorporated in full herein, Bosnian Serb military forces fired upon civilian gatherings that were of no military significance, thereby causing injury and death to hundreds of civilians. Radovan Karadzic and Ratko Mladic, individually and in concert with others planned, instigated, ordered or otherwise aided and abetted in the planning, preparation or execution of unlawful attacks against the civilian population and individual civilians with area fire, weapons such as mortars, rockets and artillery or knew or had reason to know that the Bosnian Serb military forces were about to unlawfully attack the civilian population and individual civilians, or had already done so, and failed to take the necessary and reasonable steps to prevent such shelling or to punish the perpetrators thereof.

By these acts and omissions, Radovan Karadzic and Ratko Mladic committed:

Count 5: a violation of the laws or customs of war (deliberate attack on the civilian population and individual civilians) as recognized by Articles 3, 7(1) and 7(3) of the Statute of the Tribunal....

44. Since 5 April 1992, the City of Sarajevo has been besieged by forces of the Bosnian Serb army. Throughout this siege, there has been a systematic campaign of deliberate targeting of civilians by snipers of the Bosnian Serb military and their agents. The sniping campaign has terrorized the civilian population of Sarajevo and has resulted in

a substantial number of civilian casualties, killed and wounded, including women, children and elderly. Between 5 May 1992 and 31 May 1995, snipers have systematically, unlawfully and wilfully killed and wounded civilians in the area of Sarajevo, including but not limited to the following individuals:

KILLED

Children ... [naming 4] ...

Women ... [naming 8] ...

Elderly ... [naming 4] ...

Men ... [naming 4] ...

WOUNDED

Children ... [identifying 15] ...

Women ... [identifying 16] ...

Elderly ... [identifying 10] ...

Men ... [identifying 15] ...

45. Radovan Karadzic and Ratko Mladic individually and in concert with others planned, ordered, instigated or otherwise aided and abetted in the planning, preparation or execution of the sniping of civilians or knew or had reason to know that subordinates were sniping civilians and failed to take necessary and reasonable measures to prevent such acts or to punish the perpetrators thereof.

As to the deliberate attacks by sniper fire against the civilian population and individual civilians, which resulted in death and injury to said civilians, and acts and omissions related thereto, Radovan Karadzic and Ratko Mladic committed:

Count 10: a violation of the laws or customs of war (deliberate attack on the civilian population and individual civilians) as recognized by Articles 3, 7(1) and 7(3) of the Statute of the Tribunal.

As to the killing by sniper fire of these civilians, among others, and acts and omissions related thereto, Radovan Karadzic and Ratko Mladic committed:

Count 11: a crime against humanity as recognized by Articles 5(a) (murder), 7(1) and 7(3) of the Statute of the Tribunal.

As to the wounding by sniper fire of these civilians, among others, and acts and omissions related thereto, Radovan Karadzic and Ratko Mladic committed:

Count 12: a crime against humanity as recognized by Articles 5(I) (inhumane acts), 7(1) and 7(3) of the Statute of the Tribunal.

2. Concerning leader responsibility, see also Decision of 16 May 1995, *In the Matter of a Proposal for a Formal Request for Deferral*, paras. 4, 17, 22–25 (a decision generally concerning the primacy of the ICTY) in Chapter Six, Section 9.

3. In *The Prosecutor v. Akayesu*, ICTR (2 Sept. 1998), noted earlier, the Trial Chamber stated: "Article 6(3) [of the Statute of the ICTR] does not necessarily require the superior to have had knowledge of such ... [acts of subordinates] to render him criminally liable. The only requirement is that he had reason to know that his subordinates were about to commit or had committed and failed to take the necessary or reasonable measures to prevent such acts or punish the perpetrators thereof." *Id.* at para. 39. In *The Prosecutor v. Kambanda*, ICTR (4 Sept. 1998), noted above, the Trial Chamber accepted the defen-

dant's plea of guilty partly on the following facts relevant to leader responsibility: "Kambanda acknowledges that he knew or should have known that persons for whom he was responsible were committing crimes of massacre upon Tutsi and that he failed to prevent them or punish the perpetrators ... [and] admits that he was an eye witness to the massacres of Tutsi and also had knowledge of them from regular reports of prefets, and cabinet discussions." *Id.* at para. 39 (xii).

Section 2
Other General Defenses or Grounds for Excluding Responsibility

A. Viable Defenses

1. Superior Orders

[see also this chapter, Section 1, and *United States v. Calley* in Chapter Four, Section 7 C]

In re Eck and Others (*The Peleus*)

Hamburg, British Military Court, Oct. 20, 1945; (1945), 13 Am. Dig.

[Editors' note: The accused Eck, who was the commander of a German submarine, and four members of the crew, were charged jointly with the killing of survivors of the crew of the Allied merchant-vessel *Peleus*, which they had torpedoed on the night of March 13–14, 1944. It appeared that most of the members of the crew of the *Peleus* had succeeded in reaching two rafts and floating wreckage. The submarine having surfaced, one of the survivors of the *Peleus* was hailed and interrogated as to the name of the merchant-vessel, its destination, and other particulars. Several members of the crew of the submarine, acting under the orders of the accused Eck, then proceeded to open fire with a machine-gun and throw grenades at those survivors who were still in the water or on the rafts. All but three of the survivors were killed outright or subsequently died of their wounds. The three survivors who escaped death remained on the rafts for more than twenty-five days before they were rescued. The accused Eck pleaded that as commander of the submarine he did not act out of cruelty or revenge but as a matter of operational necessity for the purpose of alienating all traces of the *Peleus*. The four other accused pleaded that they acted in obedience to superior orders. The court held that the five accused were guilty.]

In the course of his summation the Judge Advocate stated:

... It is a fundamental usage of war that the killing of unarmed enemies is forbidden.... To fire so as to kill helpless survivors of a torpedoed ship is a grave breach against the law of nations. The right to punish persons who break such rules of war has equally been recognized for many years....

Let me remind you once more of what ought to be the starting-point of your consideration of this case, the principle of International Law, which is expressed in ... the *Llandovery Castle*.... No one as far as I know has ever challenged the accuracy of the principle which is expressed in the judgment of the Supreme Court of Germany in that case....

The principle is stated in the judgment in the following form: 'The firing on the boars was an offence against the law of nations. In war on land the killing of unarmed enemies is not allowed.... Similarly, in war at sea the killing of shipwrecked people who have taken refuge in lifeboats is forbidden.' My advice to you is that you are entitled to take that statement of the principle as the starting-point of your investigation of this case....

... Each one of the accused ... is entitled in this court to just as fair treatment at your hands and just as much consideration as if he were a citizen of an Alien nation....

... [The Commander of the U-boat] now says, the purpose of [the] firing was primarily the destruction of wreckage in order that every trace of the sinking might be obliterated.... He says he was under an operational necessity to do what he did because he had as his first duty to ensure that the submarine was protected against attack by Allied aircraft. He says that the only way of doing that was to take every possible step ... to destroy every trace of the sinking. If as a result of that survivors were killed it was unfortunate for them, but he was under the paramount necessity of protecting his boat and his crew.

The question whether or not any belligerent is entitled to kill an unarmed person for the purpose of saving his own life has been the subject of much discussion. It may be that circumstances can arise ... in which such a killing might be justified; but I suggest to you that you consider this case on the facts which have emerged from the evidence of Eck [the U-boat's captain]....

... Eck, does not rely upon the defence of superior orders. He stands before you taking the sole responsibility of the command which he issued upon himself.... It is quite clear that [the weapons] officer Hoffman did fire. He says: 'I fired on the rafts. The Kommandant gave me orders; he gave orders directly to me.... Now I am sitting here I do not think it was right to fire as I did.'...

That brings me to the discussion ... of what has been called superior orders, that is to say, orders coming from a higher authority which the accused is by the law and custom of his service obliged to obey.... The duty to obey is limited to the observance of orders which are lawful. There can be no duty to obey that which is not a lawful order....

... The fact that a rule of warfare has been violated in pursuance if an order of a belligerent government, or of an individual belligerent commander, does not deprive the act in question of its character as a war crime....

Undoubtedly a Court confronted with a plea of superior orders adduced in justification of a war crime is bound to take into consideration the fact that obedience of military orders not obviously unlawful is a duty of every member of the armed forces, and that the latter cannot in conditions of war discipline be expected to weigh scrupulously the legal merits of the order received. The question, however, is governed by the major consideration that members of the armed forces are bound to obey lawful orders only, and that they cannot therefore escape liability if in obedience to a command they commit acts which both violate unchallenged rules of warfare and outrage the general sentiment of humanity.... It is not fairly obvious to you that if in fact the carrying out of Eck's command involved the killing of these helpless survivors, it was not a lawful command, and that it must have been obvious to the most rudimentary intelligence that it was not a lawful command, and that those who did the shooting are not to be excused for doing it upon the ground of superior orders? ...

Let me now ... deal with the case of [the medical officer] ... [He] says: 'I was ordered to shoot and I did shoot in pursuance of that order.' He admitted in the witness box that he, being a medical officer, was exempted by the regulations of the German Navy from using weapons for the purpose of offence. He enjoys all the privileges which doctors enjoy under International Law in relation to the fighting services of any country. He certainly knew of the exemptions which he enjoyed under the regulations of the particular service to which he belonged. Yet, knowing that, [he] fired with a machine-gun in the circumstances of which you have heard. It is for you to say what you think about it....

... The engineer-officer of this submarine ... was minded to protest the order which the Kommandant gave, and did in fact protest, telling him that he did not agree with it....

But having made his protest, having gone below..., he then comes up on deck.... He saw [the fifth accused, a leading seaman] using the machine-gun. He pushed him away and fired it himself, fired it, as he says, in order that there might be no question of a person to whom he had recently been speaking meaning one of those who had been interrogated, being killed by a bullet fired by the hand of such an undesirable person as he believed [this accused] to be. That, you may think, is a very odd explanation indeed. Whether it is true or not, you may still think that [this officer] might fall within the description of the charge-sheet of a person concerned in the killing of members of the crew of the steamship, because he voluntarily took upon himself at least the possibility of killing somebody on one of those pieces of wreckage, or on a raft.

It is for you to say what you think about it. It is for you to say how much importance is to be attached to the fact that he did make that protest whether it can provide him with a complete answer to this charge....

In re Von Leeb and Others

(German High Command Trial), United States Military Tribunal at Nuremberg, Germany, October 28, 1948, 15 I.L.R. 376 (1949), 11 Trials of War Crimes (1950)

[Editors' note: Referring to §§ 4(a) and (b) of Control Council Law No. 10, Art. II, the Tribunal stated:]

These two paragraphs are clear and definite. They relate to the crimes defined in Control Council Law No. 10, Art. II, Secs. 1(a), 1(b) and 1(c). All of the defendants in this case held official positions in the armed forces of the Third Reich. Hitler from 1938 on was Commander-in-Chief of the Armed Forces and was the Supreme Civil and Military Authority in the Third Reich, whose personal decrees had the force and effect of law. Under such circumstances to recognize as a defence to the crimes set forth in Control Council Law No. 10 that a defendant acted pursuant to the order of his government or of a superior would be in practical effect to say that all the guilt charged in the Indictment was the guilt of Hitler alone because he alone possessed the law-making power of the State and the supreme authority to issue civil and military directives. To recognize such a contention would be to recognize an absurdity.

It is not necessary to support the provision of Control Council Law No. 10 Art. II, Secs. 4(a) and (b), by reason, for we are bound by it as one of the basic authorities under which we function as a Judicial Tribunal. Reason is not lacking.

Inasmuch as one of the reiterated arguments advanced is the injustice of even charging these defendants with being guilty of the crimes set forth in the Indictment, when they were, it is said, merely soldiers and acted under governmental directives and superior orders which they were bound to obey, we shall briefly note what we consider sound reasons for the rejection of such a defence.

The rejection of the defence of superior orders without its being incorporated in Control Council Law No. 10 that such defence shall not exculpate would follow of necessity from our holding that the acts set forth in Control Council Law No. 10 are criminal not because they are therein set forth as crimes but because they then were crimes under International Common Law. International Common Law must be superior to [national law] and where it conflicts with, take precedence over National Law or directives issued by any national governmental authority. A directive to violate International Criminal Common Law is therefore void and can afford no protection to one who violates such law in reliance on such a directive....

The State being but an inanimate corporate entity or concept, it cannot as such make plans, determine policies, exercise judgments, experience fear or be restrained or deterred from action except through its animate agents and representatives.... Nor can it be permitted even in a dictatorship that the dictator, absolute though he may be, shall be the scapegoat on whom the sins of all his governmental and military subordinates are wished; and that, when he is driven into a bunker and presumably destroyed, all the sins and guilt of his subordinates shall be considered to have been destroyed with him.

The defendants in this case who received obviously criminal orders were placed in a difficult position, but servile compliance with an order clearly criminal for fear of some disadvantage or punishment not immediately threatened cannot be recognized as a defence. To establish the defence of coercion or necessity in the face of danger there must be a showing of circumstances such that a reasonable man would apprehend that he was in such imminent physical peril as to deprive him of freedom to choose the right and refrain from the wrong. No such situation has been shown in this case.

Furthermore, it is not a new concept that superior orders are no defence for criminal action. Article 47 of the German Military Penal Code, adopted in 1872, was as follows:

If through the execution of an order pertaining to the service, a penal law is violated, then the superior giving the order is alone responsible. However, the obeying subordinate shall be punished as accomplice (Teilnehmer):

(1) if he went beyond the order given to him,

(2) if he knew that the order of the superior concerned an act which aimed at a civil or military crime or offence.

The amendment of this in 1940 omitted the last two words 'to him' in Section 1 above in Section 2 changed the words, 'civil or military crime or offence', to 'general or military crime or offence'. If this amendment had any effect, it extended rather than restricted the scope of the preceding act.

It is interesting to note that an article by Goebbels, the Reich Propaganda Minister, which appeared in the *Voelkischer Beobachter*, the official Nazi publication, on 28th May 1944, contained the following correct statement of the law:

It is not provided in any military law that a soldier in the case of a despicable crime is exempt from punishment because he passes the responsibility to his superior, especially if the orders of the latter are in evident contradiction to all human morality and every international usage of warfare.

In re Ohlendorf and Others (Einsatzgruppen Trial)

United States Military Tribunal at Nuremberg, April 10, 1948, 15 I.L.R. 656 (1948)

[Editors' note: the Prosecutor in this case was Ben Ferencz]

... (7)*Plea of Superior Orders*—Those of the defendants who admit of participation in the mass killings which are the subject of this trial, plead that they were under military orders and, therefore, had no will of their own. As intent is a basic prerequisite to responsibility of crime, they argue that they are innocent of criminality since they performed the admitted executions under duress, that is to say, Superior Orders. The defendants formed part of a military organization and were, therefore, subject to the rules which govern soldiers. It is axiomatic that a military man's first duty is to obey. If the defendants were soldiers and as soldiers responded to the command of their superiors to kill certain people, how can they be held guilty of crime? This is the question posed by the defendants. The answer is not a difficult one. The obedience of a soldier is not the obedience of an automaton. A soldier is a reasoning agent. He does not respond, and is not expected to respond, like a piece of machinery. It is a fallacy of widespread consumption that a soldier is required to do everything his superior officer orders him to do. A very simple illustration will show to what absurd extreme such a theory could be carried. If every military person were required, regardless of the nature of the command, to obey unconditionally, a sergeant could order the corporal to shoot the lieutenant, the lieutenant could order the sergeant to shoot the captain, the captain could order the lieutenant to shoot the colonel, and in each instance the executioner would be absolved of blame. The mere statement of such a proposition is its own commentary. The fact that a soldier may not, without incurring unfavourable consequences, refuse to drill, salute, exercise, reconnoiter, and even go into battle, does not mean that he must fulfil every demand put to him. In the first place, an order to require obedience must relate to military duty. An officer may not demand of a soldier for instance, that he steal for him. And what the superior officer may not militarily demand of his subordinate, the subordinate is not required to do. Even if the order refers to a military subject it must be one which the superior is authorized under the circumstances to give. The subordinate is bound only to obey the lawful orders of his superior and if he accepts a criminal order and executes it with a malice of his own, he may not plead Superior Orders in mitigation of his offense. If the nature of the ordered act is manifestly beyond the scope of the superior's authority, the subordinate may not plead ignorance of the criminality of the order. If one claims duress in the execution of an illegal order it must be shown that the harm caused by obeying the illegal order is not disproportionally greater than the harm which would result from not obeying the illegal order. It would not be an adequate excuse, for example, by not obeying it he himself would risk a few days of confinement. Nor if one acts under duress, may he, without culpability, commit the illegal act once the duress ceases.

The International Military Tribunal, in speaking of the principle to be applied in the interpretation of criminal Superior Orders, declared that: 'The true test, which is found in varying degrees in the criminal law of most nations, is not the existence of the order, but whether moral choice was in fact possible'. The Prussian Military Code, as far back as 1845, recognized this principle of moral choice when it stated that a subordinate would be punished if, in the execution of an order, he went beyond its scope or if he executed an order knowing that it 'related to an act which obviously aimed at a crime'. This provision was copied into the Military Penal Code of the kingdom of Saxonia in 1867, and of Baden in 1870. Continuing even extending the doctrine of conditional obedience, the Bavarian Military Penal Code of 1869 went so far as to establish the responsibility of the subordinate as the rule, and his irresponsibility as the exception. The Military Penal Code of the Austro-Hungarian Monarchy of 1855 provided: 'Art. 158. A subordinate who does not carry out an order is not guilty of a violation of his duty of subordination if: (a) the order is obviously contrary to loyalty due to the Prince of the Land; (b) if the order pertains to an act or omission in which evidently a crime or an offense is to be recognized'. In 1872 Bismarck attempted to delimit subordinate responsibility by legislation, but the

Reichstag rejected his proposal and instead adopted the following as Article 47 of the German Military Penal Code: 'Art. 47: If through the execution of an order pertaining to the service, a penal law is violated, then the superior giving the order is alone responsible. However, the obeying subordinate shall be punished as accomplice: (1) if he went beyond the order given to him, or (2) if he knew that the order of the superior concerned an act which aimed at a civil or military crime or offense.' This law was never changed, except to broaden its scope by changing the word 'civil' to 'general', and as late as 1940 one of the leading commentators of the Nazi period, Professor Schwinge, wrote: 'Hence, in military life, just as in other fields, the principle of absolute, *i.e.,* blind obedience, does not exist'. Yet, one of the most generally quoted statements on this subject is that a German soldier must obey orders though the heavens fall. The statement has become legendary. The facts prove that it is a myth.... To plead Superior Orders one must show an excusable ignorance of their illegality. The sailor who voluntarily ships on a pirate craft may not be heard to answer that he was ignorant of the probability he would be called upon to help in the robbing and sinking of other vessels. He who willingly joins an illegal enterprise is charged with the natural development of the unlawful undertaking. What S.S. man could say that he was unaware of the attitude of Hitler towards Jewry? ... But it is stated that in military law even if the subordinate realizes that the act he is called upon to perform is a crime, he may not refuse its execution without incurring serious consequences, and that this, therefore, constitutes duress. Let it be said at once that there is no law which requires that an innocent man must forfeit his life or suffer serious harm in order to avoid committing a crime which he condemns. The threat, however, must be imminent, real and inevitable. No court will punish a man who, with a loaded pistol at his head, is compelled to pull a lethal lever.

Nor need the peril be that imminent in order to escape punishment. But were any of the defendants coerced into killing Jews under the threat of being killed themselves if they failed in their homicidal mission? The test to be applied is whether the subordinate acted under coercion or whether he himself approved of the principle involved in the order. If the second proposition be true, the plea of Superior Orders fails. The doer may not plead innocence to a criminal act ordered by his superior if he is in accord with the principle and intent of the superior. When the will of the doer merges with the will of the superior in the execution of the illegal act, the doer may not plead duress under Superior Orders. If the mental and moral capacities of the superior and subordinate are pooled in the planning and execution of an illegal act, the subordinate may not subsequently protest that he was forced into the performance of an illegal undertaking. Superior means superior in capacity and power to force a certain act. It does not mean superiority only in rank. It could easily happen in an illegal enterprise that the captain guides the major, in which case the captain could not be heard to plead Superior Orders in defense of his crime. If the cognizance of the doer has been such, prior to the receipt of the illegal order, that the order is obviously but one further logical step in the development of a program which he knew to be illegal in its very inception, he may not excuse himself from responsibility for an illegal act which could have been foreseen by the application of the simple law of cause and effect.... One who embarks on a criminal enterprise of obvious magnitude is expected to anticipate what the enterprise will logically lead to. In order successfully to plead the defense of Superior Orders the opposition of the doer must be constant. It is not enough that he mentally rebel at the time the order is received. If at any time after receiving the order he acquiesces in its illegal character, the defense of Superior Orders is closed to him. [The Tribunal also referred to the judgment of the German Supreme Court in the case of the *Llandovery Castle* (Annual Digest, 1923–24, Case No. 235)].

United States v. Staff Sergeant (E-6) Walter Griffen

RA 17542182, U.S. Army, Company D, 1st Battalion (Airborne), 8th Cavalry,
1st Cavalry Division (Airmobile), APO San Francisco 96490, CM 416805, petition for review by USCMA denied, 39 CMR 293

Porcella, Judge Advocate: In this contested case, the accused was found guilty of acting jointly with others in committing an unpremeditated murder in violation of Article
118 of the Uniform Code of Military Justice. After reducing the period of confinement
from ten years, the convening authority approved a sentence of total forfeitures, confinement at hard labor for seven years and reduction to the lowest enlisted grade.

In their assignment of errors, counsel for the appellant contend that the law officer
erred prejudicially in failing to instruct the court on the applicable law of the defense of
obedience to superior orders. In considering this contention, we will recite those facts
which appear pertinent to our disposition of the case.

On 4 April 1967, in Vietnam, a platoon of the 1st Cavalry Division was providing security for an engineer element near Bong Son. About 10 o'clock in the morning, members of the platoon apprehended an indigenous male of military age who, after evacuation
and interrogation by a higher echelon, was "confirmed" to be a member of the hostile
Viet Cong. Later that day, as the platoon was preparing to cross a large, open rice paddy,
a security element on the right flank found an unarmed male native about 40 to 45 years
old in a bunker. He was brought to the command post area, and a helicopter was requested for his evacuation. Meanwhile, the accused noticed that activities of his platoon
were being observed by a native he suspected might be a member of the Viet Cong. A patrol was dispatched to apprehend him. However, the search was unsuccessful. While the
patrol was reconnoitering by fire and discharging grenades in bunkers, one of its members was injured by a secondary explosion. Using radio communications, overheard by
several witnesses, Lieutenant Patrick the platoon leader, conversed with Captain Ogg, the
company commander. He arranged for the air evacuation of the wounded man but was
told this prisoner would not be evacuated by helicopter. The precise conversation concerning
the disposition of the prisoner is not clear. However, the understanding of Captain Ogg's
order appears to have been that the prisoner should be killed. There is evidence that Lieutenant Patrick gave the accused a direct order to the same effect. Specialist Garcia, the
medical technician attached to the platoon, removed the prisoner from the command
post area and escorted him, his hands tied behind his back, to an embankment, where
the accused and Private First Class Woods each fired several shots at him with M-16 rifles. The prisoner expired as a result. His body contained numerous fragments from M-
16 bullets.

The accused testified, in part, to the following effect: He overheard Captain Ogg state
in his radio transmission that the prisoner should be killed. Then Lieutenant Patrick
said: "Sergeant Griffen, take him down the hill and shoot him. Come back and let me
know." The accused admitted firing his rifle at the prisoner and thereafter reporting
back to Lieutenant Patrick. He committed the act because he had been ordered to do so
and for the safety of his men. He believed the order to be legal because his platoon
leader, a lieutenant, had once been relieved when a prisoner who had been securely tied
escaped during the night. Also, he felt that the security of the platoon would have been
violated if the prisoner were kept, since their operations had already been observed by
another suspect. In addition, several months earlier, all the members of his platoon had
either been killed or wounded in that same general area after their positions had been
observed.

Prior to argument, the defense submitted a proposed instruction on obedience of orders as a defense to the offense charged. The law officer did not give the requested instruction. Rather, he instructed the court as follows on this subject:

"Now, the general rule is that the acts of a subordinate, done in good faith in compliance with his supposed duty or orders, are justifiable. This justification does not exist, however, when those acts are manifestly, beyond the scope of his authority, or the order is such that a man of ordinary sense and understanding would know it to be illegal."

"I tell you as a matter of law that if instructions or orders were received over that radio or were given to the accused in this case to kill the prisoner suspect who was helpless there before them, such an order would have been manifestly an illegal order. You are advised as a matter of law, any such command, if in fact there was such a command, was an illegal order."

"A soldier or airman is not an automation but a reasoning agent who is under a duty to exercise judgment in obeying the orders of a superior officer to the extent, that where such orders are manifestly beyond the scope of the issuing officer's authority and are so palpably illegal on their face that a man of ordinary sense and understanding would know them to be illegal, then the fact of obedience to the order of a superior officer will not protect a soldier for acts committed pursuant to such illegal orders. This is the law in regard to superior orders."

In deciding the issues in this case, we will assume that a superior officer ordered the accused to kill the native male then in the platoon's custody.

The intentional killing of another person without premeditation is a felony, unpremeditated murder (UCMJ, Art 118, 10 USC § 918). However, a homicide committed in the proper performance of a legal duty is justifiable and not a crime. Thus, killing to prevent the escape of a prisoner if no other reasonably apparent means are adequate or killing an enemy in battle are cases of justifiable homicide (MCM, US, 1951, § 197b). Conversely, the killing of a docile prisoner taken during military operations is not justifiable homicide. In this connection, section 85, Department of the Army Field Manual 27-10, Law of Land Warfare, July 1956, promulgates the following doctrine:

85. Killing of Prisoners

> A commander may not put his prisoners to death because their presence retards his movements or diminishes his power of resistance by necessitating a large guard, or by reason of their consuming supplies, or because it appears certain that they will regain their liberty through the impending success of their forces. It is likewise unlawful for a commander to kill his prisoners on grounds of self-preservation, even in the case of airborne or commando operations, although the circumstances of the operation may make necessary rigorous supervision of and restraint upon the movement of prisoners of war.

The general rule is that the acts of a subordinate, done in good faith in compliance with his supposed duty or orders are, subject to certain qualifications, justifiable (MCM, US, 1951, § 197b). In his authoritative work, Winthrop stated:

"That the act charged as an offense was done in obedience to the order—verbal or written—of a military superior, is, in general, a good defense at military law."

" … Where the order is apparently regular and lawful on its face, he is not to go behind it to satisfy himself that his superior has proceeded with authority, but is to obey it according to its terms, the only exceptions recognized to the rule of obedience being cases of orders so manifestly beyond the legal power of discretion of the commander as to admit of no rational doubt of their unlawfulness." (Winthrop, Military Law and Precedents, 2d Ed. (1920 Reprint) 296–297.)

The Manual for Courts-Martial, U.S., 1921 (x. 415, page 355) stated:

> To justify from a military point of view a military inferior in disobeying the order of a superior, the order must be one requiring something to be done which is palpably a breach of law and a crime or an injury to a third person, or is of a serious character (not involving unimportant consequences only) and if done would not be susceptible of being righted. An order requiring the performance of a military duty or act can not be disobeyed with impunity unless it has one of these characteristics.

The Manual for Courts-Martial, United States, 1951 (§ 197B, p. 351), contains the following discussion relating to the defense of duty or orders as justification for a homicide:

> ... the acts of a subordinate, done in good faith in compliance with his supposed duties or orders are justifiable. This justification does not exist, however, then those acts are manifestly beyond the scope of his authority, or the order is such that a man of ordinary sense and understanding would know it to be illegal ... (emphasis supplied.)

(Substantially similar provisions appeared in the MCM, USA, 1928, § 148a and MCM, USA, 1949, § 179a.)

In CM 326604, *Gusik*, 76 Board of Review 265, 279, the Board of Review said:

> It will be seen, therefore, that, indispensable to the shield of immunity from criminal responsibility afforded one for homicide committed pursuant to lawful orders of his superior, and in the performance of a public duty, are the following:
>
> (a) That the order or authority was lawful or of such character that he had a right under the circumstances to believe and did believe it to be lawful,
>
> (b) That he acted reasonably within the scope of such authority, and
>
> (c) Not with malice, cruelty, or by willful oppression flowing from a wicked heart.

A well known treatise contains the following comments (36 Am. Jur. Homicide § 72, p. 208):

> ... But an order which is illegal in itself and not justified by the rules and usages of War, or which is, in its substance, clearly illegal, so that a man of ordinary sense and understanding would know as soon as he heard the order read or given that it was illegal, will afford no protection for a homicide, provided the act with which he may be charged has all the ingredients in it which may be necessary to constitute the same a crime in law.

... United States doctrine expressed in Department of the Army Field Manual 27-10, The Law of Land Warfare, July 1956, is as follows:

> The fact that the law of war has been violated pursuant to an order of a superior authority, whether military or civil, does not deprive the act in question of its character of a war crime, nor does it constitute a defense in the trial of an accused individual, unless he did not know and could not reasonably have been expected to know that the act ordered was unlawful. In all cases where the order is held not to constitute a defense to an

allegation of war crime, the fact that the individual was acting pursuant to orders may be considered in mitigation of punishment.

Having considered the foregoing authorities, we accept the foregoing principle for application in this case (§ 197b, MCM, US, 1951, quoted *supra*): The act of a subordinate, done in good faith in compliance with the supposed order of a superior, is not justifiable when the order is such that a man of ordinary sense and understanding would know it to be illegal. (See ACM 7321, *Kinder*, 14 CMR 742, 773 (1954)).

We now turn to the question: Did the law officer err in failing to give an appropriate instruction on justification as a defense to a homicide committed in good faith compliance with the order of a superior? As previously noted, the defense counsel made a request for such an instruction, but the law officer instructed contradictorily. He informed the court to the effect that if an order to kill the prisoner had been given, it would have been manifestly illegal.

A law officer is required to give an appropriate instruction when there is some evidence that will allow a reasonable inference that a defense is in issue (*United States v. Black*, 12 USCMA 571, 31 CMR 157 (1961)). Evaluating the record, we find the evidence clear and convincing that an unarmed, unresisting prisoner whose hands were bound behind his back was killed at close range by rifle fire discharged by the accused and another soldier. We note no evidence which could provide an inference suggestive of self-defense, or that the killing was to prevent the escape of the prisoner, or for that matter, any other justification or excuse for the killing. Also, there are strong moral, religious, and legal prohibitions in our society against killing others which should arouse the strongest scruples against killings of this kind. In fact, it is difficult to conceive of a military situation in which the order of a superior would be more patently wrong. Accordingly, we view the order as commanding an act so obviously beyond the scope of authority of the superior officer and so palpably illegal on its face as to admit of no doubt of its unlawfulness to a man of ordinary sense and understanding. As there was no evidence which would have allowed a reasonable inference that the accused justifiably killed the prisoner pursuant to the order of a superior officer, it follows, as a matter of law, that this defense was not in issue, the law officer did not err by refusing to give an instruction on it, and that the law officer properly instructed the court that such an order would have been manifestly illegal.

With respect to the law officer's instructions on sentence, appellate defense counsel contend and government appellate counsel concede that the failure of the law officer to instruct the court-martial that it could adjudge reduction in grade as punishment rendered that portion of the sentence excessive. We find the contention meritorious and will act appropriately (*United States* v. *Crawford*, 12 USCMA 203, 30 CMR 203 (1961)).

Further, with respect to the sentence, we observe that the accused was caught up in a rapidly moving sequence of events at the time of the incident. This factor lends mitigating weight to his assertion that he acted without reflection and in honest obedience of a superior's orders. In addition, the accused had approximately eight years of prior service at the time of trial and there were no previous convictions introduced against him. Also, no punitive discharge was adjudged. The staff judge advocate notes in his review, that the accused testified for the prosecution in a subsequent homicide trial of another soldier involving the same incident and that he is "intrinsically remorseful and has a fervent desire to be rehabilitated." He also notes that the two officers involved in this offense were acquitted. Other records of trial before this board of review show that Specialist-Five Raul Garcia was tried by a general court-martial for the same offence and that his approved sentence provides for bad conduct discharge, total forfeitures, confinement at hard labor for three years, and reduction. Private First Class David L. Woods was similarly tried. His approved sentence is confinement at hard labor for twelve months, total forfeitures, and reduction to the lowest enlisted grade.

In view of the foregoing, the board of review finds the findings of guilty and sentence as approved by proper authority correct in law and fact and determines on the basis of the entire record that only so much of the sentence as provides for confinement at hard labor for two years and forfeiture of all pay and allowances should be approved. The sentence is modified accordingly. The findings of guilty and the sentence as thus modified are affirmed.

Porcella, Myers (concurs) and Miller (concurs) Judge Advocates, 2 July 1968.

U.S. Dep't of Army FM 27-10, The Law of Land Warfare
at 182–83, para. 509 (1956)

509. Defense of Superior Orders

a. The fact that the law of war has been violated pursuant to an order of a superior authority, whether military or civil, does not deprive the act in question of its character of a war crime, nor does it constitute a defense in the trial of an accused individual, unless he did not know and could not reasonably have been expected to know that the act ordered was unlawful. In all cases where the order is held not to constitute a defense to an allegation of war crime, the fact that the individual was acting pursuant to orders may be considered in mitigation of punishment.

b. In considering the question whether a superior order constitutes a valid defense, the court shall take into consideration the fact that obedience to lawful military orders is the duty of every member of the armed forces; that the latter cannot be expected, in conditions of war discipline, to weigh scrupulously the legal merits of the orders received; that certain rules of warfare may be controversial; or that an act otherwise amounting to a war crime may be done in obedience to orders conceived as a measure of reprisal. At the same time it must be borne in mind that members of the armed forces are bound to obey only lawful orders (*e.g., UCMJ, Art. 92*).

Paust, *My Lai and Vietnam . . .*
57 Mil. L. Rev. at 171–75 (as revised)

Another Army text stated:

> The plea is valid if the accused does not and should not have known that the order was illegal. Many courts use the language "illegal on its face" to express the proposition that the illegality of the order must be obvious before the accused should be held liable for an act committed pursuant to that order. The reasoning is justified on the grounds that soldiers acting in wartime are trained to follow orders of their superiors relatively automatically, and would not normally be expected to question those orders except where their invalidity was fairly obvious.[3]

A newer Army Subject Schedule is in line with the above. In describing culpability in group situations, it states that acting under superior orders "is no defense to criminal

---

3. U.S. Dep't of Army Pamphlet No. 27-161-2, II International Law 251 (1961). *See also id.* at 244; U.S. Dep't of Navy, Law of Naval Warfare, para. 330b(1) (1955).

charges when the order is clearly illegal as in an order to kill a prisoner of war. While an American soldier must obey promptly all legal orders, he also must disobey an order which requires him to commit a criminal act in violation of the law of war." Furthermore, a soldier should not presume that an order asks for criminal conduct; rather the soldier should ask the superior for clarification and if the order as clarified is illegal, the soldier must try to have the order rescinded, disregard the order if the superior persists, and also report the incident to higher headquarters or an alternative source. This sometimes takes courage but if the soldier fails to disobey the illegal order, he/she can be tried and punished for committing a criminal act in violation of the law of war. The commander has a responsibility to see that troops obey the law of war. The soldier can only serve one's commander and one's nation by obeying lawful orders. No commander needs to have unlawful orders obeyed, and the commander must have them disobeyed if the commander is to carry out his/her own responsibilities.

It should be remembered that the average soldier is asked only to disobey (1) orders he/she personally *knows* to be illegal, and (2) orders which are *obviously* illegal such as that calling for the murder of captured detainees under force control, the deliberate attack with machine-gun fire on civilians when there is no military necessity for such, the torture or abuse of a prisoner in order to "get him to talk," or an order to place civilians ahead of a unit to "clear" a field of land mines. In doubtful cases, the responsibility rests with the superior giving the order, not the subordinate who obeys it—one can presume legality until an obviously illegal order arises.[4]

Contrary to the opinion of Telford Taylor, the defense of superior orders does not have its true base "in equity,"[5] but rather in a concept to spare soldiers from criminal prosecution in group action or chain action situations when the lower ranking soldier does not possess the requisite criminal mind or criminal culpability. It has its true base in *mens rea* (knew) and dangerous character (should have known)—though Telford Taylor was certainly correct that the existence of superior encouragement or force may be offered in mitigation of punishment, perhaps even to the point in extreme cases where "punishment" is nonexistent.[6] On subordinate criminal responsibility, Oppenheim added:

Undoubtedly, a Court confronted with the plea of superior orders adduced in justification of a war crime is bound to take into consideration the fact that obedience to military orders, not obviously unlawful is the duty of every member of the armed forces and that the latter cannot, in conditions of war discipline, be expected to weigh scrupulously the legal merits of the order received; that rules of warfare are often controversial and that an act otherwise amounting to a war crime may have been executed in obedience to orders received as a measure of reprisals.[7]

Of course, Oppenheim recognized the need to disobey and at least to seek clarification of orders "obviously unlawful."

---

4. *See* T. Taylor, Nuremberg and Vietnam: an American Tragedy 49–50, 52 (1970); United States v. List, 11 T.W.C. 757, 1236 (1948).

5. *See* Taylor, *supra* note 5, at 160; *cf.* his probable intent, at 49, where he distinguishes between knowledge and fear.

6. Consider also the separate defense of duress. *See* Taylor, *supra* note 151, at 50; *see also* United States v. List, 11 T.W.C. 757, 1237 (1948) ("no wrongful intent").

7. II L. Oppenheim, International Law 568–69 (7th ed. 1952). *See also* United States v. List, 11 T.W.C. 757, 1236 (1948), stating "if the illegality of the order was not known to the inferior, and he could not reasonably have been expected to know of its illegality, no wrongful intent necessary for the commission of a crime exists and the inferior will be protected."

Winthrop had earlier stated that, except in instances of palpable illegality, the inferior should presume that the order was lawful and such a person will not be prosecuted if he/she so acts. But if the order is manifestly beyond the legal power or discretion of the commander, an exception exists to the rule of obedience and the soldier can be liable for his/her conduct.[8] The United States has considered the doctrine of superior orders almost as long as the nation has existed, and except for minor interruption from 1914 until 1944 (cf. Winthrop above, 1920), the doctrine seems to have always coincided with that of international law and the recent phrase that a subordinate remains responsible for criminal conduct if he/she *knew* or *should have known* that what one was ordered to do was illegal.[9]

In the Korean conflict, the board of review in *United States v. Kinder*[10] made the following statement:

> It is the heart of the principle of law ... that a soldier or airman is not an automaton but a "reasoning agent" who is under a duty to exercise judgment in obeying the orders of a superior officer to the extent, that where such orders are manifestly

---

8. W. Winthrop, Military Law and Precedents 296–97 (2 ed. 1920); *see also id.* at 730 n. 31, *citing* Christian County Court v. Rankin & Tharp, 63 Ky. 502 (1866), where civil damages were imposed on a soldier for assisting, though under the orders of a superior, in the destruction by burning of a courthouse during the Civil War. For an English case in 1900 acquitting a soldier honestly doing his duty where the order was said to be not so manifestly illegal that he must have known it to be illegal, *see* Stephen, *Superior Orders as Excuse for Homicide*, 17 L.Q. Rev. 87, 88 (1901) (case of *Regina v. Smith*).

9. *See* Wilner, *Superior Orders as a Defense to Violations of International Criminal Law*, 26 Md. L. Rev. 127 (1966), adding historic terms to our inquiry as to what constitutes an obviously illegal order which the subordinate "shown have known" to be criminal. The terms or phrases used in the past were: plain, apparent, obvious, patent, palpable, manifest, clear, "known by most," and "one must instinctively feel." It is clear that the test is objective, not merely the subjective *knew* (though confusion and different standards did arise at times); furthermore, people who have acted with malice have been punished even absent a known or should have known proof (apparently punishing the guilty mind). As to the intervening practice of the United States from 1914 to 1944, *see* U.S. War Dep't, Rules of Land Warfare, para. 366, *cf.* para. 367 (1914), (GPO 1917), and FM 27-10, para. 347 (1940), changed on Nov. 15, 1944, by para. 345.1 to allow superior orders only as a partial defense (where the accused did not know and should not have known of the illegality connected with the order). It should be noted that from 1914–1944 there was only a change in the military manuals and a few military trials—no change existed in the decisions of the federal courts and the law seems to have remained despite temporal interruption through executive changes in enforcement policy. The language in Winthrop, *supra* note 9, at 296–97, strongly suggests that the United States followed a partial defense theory at least through 1920 even though conflicting language existed in the early texts from 1914–1944. It should be noted that the 1940 paragraph 347 merely stated that persons who commit offenses under the orders or sanction of their government or commanders "will not be punished." It does not say that such persons have not committed any crime. Therefore, it seems perfectly consistent to state that although individuals can also commit a crime while acting under the orders of a superior, the United States policy of 1940–1944 was not to punish such persons. *See* United States v. List, 11 T.W.C. 757, 1237 (1948) ("adopted it ... as a matter of policy"). For U.S., foreign and international standards past and present, see Spaight, Air Power and War Rights 57–58 (3d ed. 1947); Dinstein, The Defense of Obedience to Superior Orders in International Law (1965); II Oppenheim, *supra* note 8, at 568–72; Greenspan, The Modern Law of Land Warfare 490–96 (1959); M. McDougal, F. Feliciano, Law and Minimum World Public Order 692–98 (1962); Netherland's case reported at 50 Am. J. Int'l L. 968, 969 (1956); a German case at 57 Am. J. Int'l L. 139, 140 (1963); Sack, *Punishment of War Criminals and the Defense of Superior Orders*, 60 L. Q. Rev. 63 (1944); Dunbar, *Some Aspects of the Problem of Superior Orders in the Law of War*, 63 Jurid. Rev. 234 (1951); Norene, "Obedience to Orders as a Defense to a Criminal Act" (unpublished JAG School thesis, 1971).

10. 14 C.M.R. 742, 776 (AFBR 1954). See Manual for Courts-Martial, United States, 1969 (Revised Edition), para. 216d; and *Trial of Accused War Criminals*, Sec. 6, Rule 46; Order of General MacArthur, General H.Q., U.N. Command, Tokyo, Japan, AG000.5 (Oct. 28, 1950).

beyond the scope of the issuing officer's authority and are so palpably illegal on their face that a man of ordinary sense and understanding would know them to be illegal, then the fact of obedience to the order of a superior officer will not protect a soldier for acts committed pursuant to such illegal orders.

During the Vietnamese conflict, at least two cases ruled that the defense request for an instruction on the defense of superior orders can be denied where it is determined as a matter of law that the order in question was obviously or palpably illegal.[11] Instructions were also given on the defense of superior orders in the cases of *United States v. Hutto*[12] and *United States v. Calley*.[13] The instructions were different, but both were of such a nature as to comply with the general standard of "knew or should have known,"[14] and to define "*manifestly* illegal or unlawful" as that which a person of ordinary sense and understanding would know, if under the same or similar circumstances, to be unlawful.[15]

Notes and Questions

1. What is the test proffered in Article 33 of the Statute of the ICC? See the Documents Supplement. Is it preferable? Also *compare* Article 7 (4) of the Statute of the ICTY.

2. Duress

U.S. Dep't of Army, II International Law
247–48 (1962)

Plea of duress. The plea of duress is likely to be used in a case where a subordinate has committed a war crime because of command of his superior officer. The plea, as asserted

---

11. *See* United States v. Schultz, 18 U.S.C.M.A. 133, 39 C.M.R. 133 (1969); and United States v. Griffen, 29 C.M.R. 586 (ABR 1968).

12. General court-martial convened pursuant to CMAO 37 (Sept. 17, 1970), HQ Third U.S. Army. Findings of not guilty announced Jan. 15, 1971.

13. General court-martial convened pursuant to CMAO 70 (Nov. 24, 1969), HQ U.S. Army Infantry Center, Fort Benning, Georgia. Findings of guilty announced Mar. 29, 1971. For further details of *the Calley case, see* United States v. Calley, 46 C.M.R. 1131 (1973), *aff'd*, 22 U.S.C.M.A. 534, 48 C.M.R. 19 (1973); Chapter Four, Section 7 C; THE MILITARY IN AMERICAN SOCIETY—CASES AND MATERIALS 6-77 to 6-96 (D. Zillman, A. Blaustein, E. Sherman, *et al.* eds., Matthew Bender 1978).

14. The instructions are partially quoted in Norene, *supra* note 10, at 68–77, 79–81. In the *Hutto* case the judge stated, "You must resolve from the evidence and the law whether or not the order as allegedly given was *manifestly illegal on its face, or* if you are not satisfied beyond a reasonable doubt that the alleged order was manifestly illegal on its face, whether or not the order, even though illegal, as I have ruled it was, was *known to the accused*, Sgt. Hutto *to be illegal* or that by carrying out the alleged order Sgt. Hutto knew he was committing an illegal and criminal act" (emphasis added); and again, "unless you find beyond a reasonable doubt that the order given to the accused in this case was manifestly unlawful as I have defined the term, you must acquit the accused unless you find beyond a reasonable doubt that the accused had actual knowledge that the order was unlawful or that obedience of that order would result in the commission of an illegal and criminal act. In the *Calley* case the judge stated, "acts of a subordinate done in compliance with an unlawful order given him by his superior are excused ... unless the superior's order is one which a man of ordinary sense and understanding would, under the circumstances, know to be unlawful, or if the order in question is actually known to the accused to be unlawful"; and "Unless you find beyond reasonable doubt that the accused acted with actual knowledge that the order was unlawful you must proceed to determine whether, under the circumstances, a man of ordinary sense and understanding would have known the order was unlawful."

15. *Id.* at 71, 74 (*Hutto* case).

in the case of alleged war crimes, is subject to a number of limitations which are generally similar to those imposed under municipal law. The general theory behind this plea is aptly stated in the case of *United States v. Ohlendorf* in which the court said:

> But it is stated that in military law *even if the subordinate realises that the act he is called upon to perform is a crime*, he may not refuse its execution without incurring serious consequences, and that this, therefore, constitutes duress. Let it be said at once that there is no law which requires that an innocent man must forfeit his life or suffer serious harm in order to avoid committing a crime which he condemns. The threat, however, must be imminent, real and inevitable. No court will punish a man who, with a loaded pistol at his head, is compelled to pull a lethal lever. Nor need the peril be that imminent in order to escape punishment.

In the *Von Leeb Case* the court made this statement with respect to the plea of duress:

> The defendants in this case who received obviously criminal orders were placed in a difficult position, but servile compliance with orders clearly criminal for fear of some disadvantage or punishment not immediately threatened cannot be recognized as a defence. To establish the defence of coercion or necessity in the face of danger there must be a showing of circumstances such that a reasonable man would apprehend that he was in such imminent physical peril as to deprive him of freedom to choose the right and refrain from the wrong.

In order successfully to use the defense, the defendant must have an honest belief that he is to be subjected to a serious wrong if he does not carry out the act in question. Furthermore, this threatened harm must be more serious than the harm which will result to others from the act to be performed.

Paust, *My Lai and Vietnam...*
57 MIL. L. REV. at 169–70

Duress as a defense to violations of the law of war does not seem entirely relevant to complicitous criminality, but a discussion of the standard is important in our general inquiry into group conduct and defenses. When a soldier does an act known to be in violation of the law of war, he cannot plead duress as a defense unless there is "a showing of circumstances such that a reasonable man would apprehend that he was in such imminent physical peril as to deprive him of his freedom to choose the right and refrain from the wrong". It would not be sufficient to argue that the sergeant or lieutenant wouldn't want the soldier to disobey their order. There must be an honest belief of an immediate threat of physical harm. "Servile compliance with orders clearly criminal for fear of some disadvantage or punishment not immediately threatened cannot be recognized as a defense." It has also been stated that the threatened harm "must be more serious than the harm which will result to others from the act to be performed."

M. C. Bassiouni, A Draft International Criminal Code and Draft Statute for an International Criminal Tribunal
109 (1987)

Section 4. *Coercion*

4.0 A person acts under coercion when he is compelled by another under an imminent threat of force or use of force directed against him or another, to engage in conduct which may otherwise constitute a crime which he would not otherwise engage in, provided that such coerced conduct does not produce a greater harm than the one likely to be suffered and is not likely to produce death.

Report of the International Law Commission on the work of its forty-sixth session

2 May–22 July, 1994, 49 U.N. GAOR, Supp. No. 10, U.N. Doc. A/49/10, at 185–187:

177. The Special Rapporteur, in his twelfth report, expressed agreement with those Governments which, in their written responses, had considered that the concept of defences and that of extenuating circumstances should be dealt with separately. The two concepts, the Special Rapporteur said, were not in the same category. While defences stripped an act of its criminal character, extenuating circumstances did not remove that criminal character, but merely reduced the offender's criminal responsibility. In other words, defences related to the existence or non-existence of a crime, extenuating circumstances related to the penalty. The Special Rapporteur also shared the view that defences, because they sought to prove that no crime existed, should be defined in the Code in the same way that crimes were defined in the Code according to the *nullum crimen sine lege* principle. He therefore proposed a new draft article 14 to deal with the issue of defences, namely, self-defence, coercion and state of necessity.

The Special Rapporteur explained that the self-defence referred to here was not the self-defence provided for in Article 51 of the Charter of the United Nations. Article 51 removed the wrongfulness of a specific act and therefore exempted the State committing that act from international responsibility. However, because self-defence constituted an exception to the international responsibility of the State, it also relieved the leaders of that State of international criminal responsibility for the act concerned. As for the concepts of coercion and state of necessity, the judicial precedents of the International Military Tribunals established by the Charter of the Nurnberg Tribunal of 8 August 1945 and by Law No. 10 of the Control Council for Germany had admitted those concepts with the following reservations and conditions: (a) coercion and state of necessity must constitute a present or imminent danger; (b) an accused person who invokes coercion or state of necessity must not have helped, by his own behaviour, to bring about coercion or the state of necessity; and (c) there should be no disproportion between what was preserved and what was sacrificed in order to avert the danger. The Special Rapporteur also observed that this judicial practice, which had its origins in Anglo-American law, made no distinction between coercion and state of necessity.*

179. The idea of dealing with defenses in a separate article was generally welcomed in the Commission.

180. Criticism was nevertheless directed towards the wording of the new draft article 14 proposed by the Special Rapporteur. It was said that the new text was an oversimplification of the previous text and was likely to give rise to a regrettable confusion between self-defence in the case of an individual and that provided for in Article 51 of the Charter. Possible confusion between those two types of self-defence might well lead to serious consequences and made it necessary to clarify the text. It was also remarked that none of the defenses mentioned in the draft article could justify an act such as genocide and that

---

* The new draft article 14 proposed by the Special Rapporteur reads as follows:
"*Article 14 Self-defence, coercion and state of necessity*
There is no crime when the acts committed were motivated by self-defence, coercion or state of necessity.

the starkness of the text might suggest that such crimes were justifiable. It was suggested that the ambiguity of the article might be lessened somewhat by embodying in the article the conditions for its invocation mentioned by the Special Rapporteur in the body of his report (see para. 178 above). The Commission should, it was said, formulate a more specific text on self-defence, coercion and necessity, otherwise the defences would not be of much practical value to the accused.

181. It was further remarked that the draft article proposed by the Special Rapporteur should be split into two, as two different concepts were involved. An act done under self-defence was not illegal, whereas, in the case of coercion and state of necessity, fault was removed but not wrongfulness. Also, it was suggested that the defence of mistake should have a place in the draft, even though it was unlikely to be invoked frequently in a Code of Crimes against the Peace and Security of Mankind. "Insanity" and "consent" were also mentioned as defences which the Commission might consider in order to decide whether it would be advisable to include them in the Draft Code.

182. In addition, some members expressed a certain reluctance to accept the idea that defences should exist for crimes as serious as crimes against the peace and security of mankind.

183. The Special Rapporteur pointed out that in the new draft article which he had proposed in his twelfth report, the word "defences" had been eliminated from the title of the draft article.

R. v. Imre Finta
[1994] 28 C.R. (4th) 265 (S.C.) (Canada)

Cory, J. (Gonthier and Major JJ., concurring)

The "Moral Choice" Test, Coercion and Necessity

The "moral choice test" used by the International Military Tribunal has been criticized as undermining Art. 8, which effectively requires a subordinate to ignore a manifestly illegal order regardless of the consequences. (See for example: M. Greenspan, *The Modern Law of Land Warfare* (1959), at 493.) However, other international legal scholars such as Professor Bassiouni (*supra* at p. 427) and Dinstein (in *The Defence of 'Obedience to Superior Orders' in International Law, supra*, at p. 152) assert that the moral choice test as enunciated by the International Military Tribunal "was meant to complement the provision of Article 8 and not to undermine its foundations". According to this interpretation, Bassiouni, *supra*, notes at p. 437 that:

> …'obedience to superior orders' is not a defense … to an international crime when the order is patently illegal and when the subordinate has a moral choice with respect to obeying or refusing to obey the order. But, if the subordinate is coerced or compelled to carry out the order, the norms for the defense of coercion (compulsion) should apply. In such cases, the issue is not justification, but excuse or mitigation of punishment.

A person may be compelled to obey superior orders either because of natural causes which place the individual in a condition of danger (necessity) or because of pressure which is brought to bear on him or her by another person (coercion). Bassiouni *supra*, at p. 439 explains

> The two sources of compulsion though different may lead a person to harm another in order to avoid a greater or equal personal harm. Both are a concession to the instinct of human survival, but both are limited for policy and moral-ethical reasons, by positive and natural law.…

The defence of obedience to superior orders based on compulsion is limited to "imminent, real, and inevitable" threats to the subordinate's life (*The Einsatzgruppen Case*, 4 Trials of War Criminals 470 (1948)). As J. L. Bakker has pointed out in "The Defense of Obedience to Superior Orders: The *Mens Rea* Requirement" (1989), 17 *Am J. Crim. Law* 55, the problem is to determine when threats become so imminent, real, and inevitable that they rise to the level of compulsion that disables a subordinate from forming a culpable state of mind.

I agree with Bakker, when she states, at pp. 72 and 73:

> ... a moral choice is available where subordinates have the freedom to choose between right and wrong courses of conduct without suffering detrimental consequences. Subordinates who choose to obey an illegal order when they could have disobeyed without suffering adverse consequences are guilty of criminal action.

> Otto Ohlendorf, commanding officer of one of the notorious *Einsatzgruppen* (death wagons) [sic], executed more than 90,000 "undesirable elements composed of Russians, gypsies, Jews and others" on the basis of an order that he recognized as "wrong," although he refused to consider "whether it was moral or immoral(.)" In view of his acknowledged unwillingness to exercise moral judgment, the tribunal refused him a plea of obedience to superior orders.

Bakker suggests that it is only when the soldier faces an imminent, real and inevitable threat to his or her life that the defence of compulsion may be used as a defence to the killing of innocent people. "Stern punishment" or demotion would not be sufficient. She states at p. 74:

> Whether a subordinate's belief in the existence of an imminent, real and inevitable threat to his life is justified should be a function of circumstances surrounding the subordinate faced with an illegal order. A number of circumstances may be considered including age, education, intelligence, general conditions in which subordinates find themselves, length of time spent in action, nature of the hostilities, the type of enemy confronted, and opposing methods of warfare.

> Circumstances that go directly to the state of mind of the offender confronted with a moral choice include the announced penalty for disobeying orders, the probable penalty for disobedience, the typical subordinate's reasonable beliefs about the penalty, the subordinate's belief as to what the penalty is, and any alternatives available to the subordinate to escape execution of the penalty....

The element of moral choice was, I believe, added to the superior orders defence for those cases where, although it can readily be established that the orders were manifestly illegal and that the subordinate was aware of their illegality, nonetheless, due to circumstances such as compulsion, there was no choice for the accused but to comply with the orders. In those circumstances the accused would not have the requisite culpable intent.

I would add this to the comments of the text writers. The lower the rank of the recipient of an order the greater will be the sense of compulsion that will exist and the less will be the likelihood that the individual will experience any real moral choice. It cannot be forgotten that the whole concept of the military is to a certain extent coercive. Orders must be obeyed. The question of moral choice will arise far less in the case of a private accused of a war crime or a crime against humanity than in the case of a general or other high ranking officer.

Questions

1. Justice Cory also declared that even if the order was manifestly unlawful the following circumstances gave obedience to superior orders "an air of reality":

1) Finta's position in a para-military police organization;

2) the existence of war;

3) an imminent invasion by Soviet forces;

4) the Jewish sentiment in favor of the Allied forces;

5) the general, publicly stated belief in newspapers in Hungary that Jews were subversive and disloyal to the war effort in Hungary;

6) the expression in newspapers, cited by one of the witnesses, of approval of the deportation of Hungarian Jews;

7) the organizational activity involving the entire Hungarian state and their ally, Germany, in the internment and deportation;

8) the open and public manner of the confiscations under an official, hierarchical sanction;

9) the deposit of seized property with the National treasury or the Szeged Synagogue.

Do you agree that these are relevant aspects of circumstance, but not excuses per se? Did Finta still have a choice?

2. Do you find it preferable or realistic that for a defense of duress to exist the harm threatened must be more serious than the harm that results? Should death never result from proper application of a defense of duress? If a person under duress is ordered to kill three captured persons (and his superior is threatening him with imminent death if he does not comply), should the defense of duress be denied? Consider the following case:

Prosecutor v. Dražen Erdemović

IT-96-22-A (Appeals Chamber, Judgment) (7 Oct. 1997)

Before: Judge Antonio Cassese, Presiding

Judge Gabrielle Kirk McDonald

Judge Haopei Li

Judge Ninian Stephen

Judge Lal Chand Vohrah

I. Introduction

1. The Appeals Chamber of the International Tribunal for the Prosecution of Persons Responsible for Serious Violations of International Humanitarian Law Committed in the Territory of the Former Yugoslavia since 1991 ("the International Tribunal") is seised of an appeal lodged by Dražen Erdemović ("the Appellant") against the Sentencing Judgement rendered by Trial Chamber I on 29 November 1996 ("Sentencing Judgement"). By this Sentencing Judgement, the Trial Chamber sentenced the Appellant to 10 years' imprisonment, following his guilty plea to one count of a crime against humanity, for his participation in the execution of approximately 1,200 unarmed civilian Muslim men at the Branjevo farm near the town of Pilica in eastern Bosnia on 16 July 1995, in the aftermath of the fall of the United Nations 'safe area' of Srebrenica....

3. The Appellant was indicted on 29 May 1996 on one count of a crime against humanity and on an alternative count of a violation of the laws or customs of war. The Indictment alleged the following facts:

1. On 16 April 1993, the Security Council of the United Nations, acting pursuant to Chapter VII of the United Nations Charter, adopted resolution 819, in which it demanded that all parties to the conflict in the Republic of Bosnia and Herzegovina treat Srebrenica and its surroundings as a safe area which should be free from any armed attack or any other hostile act. Resolution 819 was reaffirmed by Resolution 824 on 6 May 1993 and by Resolution 836 on 4 June 1993.

2. On or about 6 July 1995, the Bosnian Serb army commenced an attack on the UN "safe area" of Srebrenica. This attack continued through until 11 July 1995, when the first units of the Bosnian Serb army entered Srebrenica.

3. Thousands of Bosnian Muslim civilians who remained in Srebrenica during this attack fled to the UN compound in Potocari and sought refuge in and around the compound.

4. Between 11 and 13 July 1995, Bosnian Serb military personnel summarily executed an unknown number of Bosnian Muslims in Potocari and in Srebrenica.

5. Between 12 and 13 July 1995, the Bosnian Muslim men, women and children, who had sought refuge in and around the UN compound in Potocari were placed on buses and trucks under the control of Bosnian Serb military personnel and police and transported out of the Srebrenica enclave. Before boarding these buses and trucks, Bosnian Muslim men were separated from Bosnian Muslim women and children and were transported to various collection centers around Srebrenica.

6. A second group of approximately 15,000 Bosnian Muslim men, with some women and children, fled Srebrenica on 11 July 1995 through the woods in a large column in the direction of Tuzla. A large number of the Bosnian Muslim men who fled in this column were captured by or surrendered to Bosnian Serb army or police personnel.

7. Thousands of Bosnian Muslim men who had been either separated from women and children in Potocari or who had been captured by or surrendered to Bosnian Serb military or police personnel were sent to various collection sites outside of Srebrenica including, but not limited to a hangar in Bratunac, a soccer field in Nova Kasaba, a warehouse in Kravica, the primary school and gymnasium of "Veljko Lukić-Kurjak" in Grbavci, Zvornik municipality and divers fields and meadows along the Bratunac-Milići road.

8. Between 13 July 1995 and approximately 22 July 1995, thousands of Bosnian Muslim men were summarily executed by members of the Bosnian Serb army and Bosnian Serb police at divers locations including, but not limited to a warehouse at Kravica, a meadow and a dam near La_ete and divers other locations.

9. On or about 16 July 1995, Dražen Erdemović and other members of the 10th Sabotage Detachment of the Bosnian Serb army were ordered to a collective farm near Pilica. This farm is located northwest of Zvornik in the Zvornik Municipality.

10. On or about 16 July 1995, Dražen Erdemović and other members of his unit were informed that bus loads of Bosnian Muslim civilian men from Srebrenica, who had surrendered to Bosnian Serb military or police personnel, would be arriving throughout the day at this collective farm.

11. On or about 16 July 1995, buses containing Bosnian Muslim men arrived at the collective farm in Pilica. Each bus was full of Bosnian Muslim men, ranging from approximately 17 to 60 years of age. After each bus arrived at the farm, the Bosnian Muslim men were removed in groups of about 10, escorted by members of the 10th Sabotage Detachment to a field adjacent to farm buildings and lined up in a row with their backs facing Dražen Erdemović and members of his unit.

12. On or about 16 July 1995, Dražen Erdemović, did shoot and kill and did participate with other members of his unit and soldiers from another brigade in the shooting and killing of unarmed Bosnian Muslim men at the Pilica collective farm. These summary executions resulted in the deaths of hundreds of Bosnian Muslim male civilians.

4. At his initial appearance on 31 May 1996, the Appellant pleaded guilty to the count of a crime against humanity. The Appellant added this explanation to his guilty plea:

Your Honour, I had to do this. If I had refused, I would have been killed together with the victims. When I refused, they told me: "If you are sorry for them, stand up, line up with them and we will kill you too." I am not sorry for myself but for my family, my wife and son who then had nine months, and I could not refuse because then they would have killed me. That is all I wish to add.

The Trial Chamber accepted the Appellant's guilty plea and dismissed the second count of a violation of the laws or customs of war....

8. In his testimony before the Trial Chamber, the Appellant described in detail the facts alleged in paragraphs 9 to 12 of the Indictment (see paragraph 3, supra). The Trial Chamber summed up his testimony on these facts as follows:

On the morning of 16 July 1995, Dražen Erdemović and seven members of the 10th Sabotage Unit of the Bosnian Serb army were ordered to leave their base at Vlasenica and go to the Pilica farm north-west of Zvornik. When they arrived there, they were informed by their superiors that buses from Srebrenica carrying Bosnian Muslim civilians between 17 and 60 years of age who had surrendered to the members of the Bosnian Serb police or army would be arriving throughout the day.

Starting at 10 o'clock in the morning, members of the military police made the civilians in the first buses, all men, get off in groups of ten. The men were escorted to a field adjacent to the farm buildings where they were lined up with their backs to the firing squad. The members of the 10th Sabotage Unit, including Dražen Erdemović, who composed the firing squad then killed them. Dražen Erdemović carried out the work with an automatic weapon. The executions continued until about 3 o'clock in the afternoon.

The accused estimated that there were about 20 buses in all, each carrying approximately 60 men and boys. He believes that he personally killed about seventy people.

And further on:

Dražen Erdemović claims that he received the order from Brano Gojković, commander of the operations at the Branjevo farm at Pilica, to prepare himself along with seven members of his unit for a mission the purpose of which they had absolutely no knowledge. He claimed it was only when they arrived on-site that the members of the unit were informed that they were to massacre hundreds of Muslims. He asserted his immediate refusal to do this but was threatened with instant death and told "If you don't wish to do it, stand in the line with the rest of them and give others your rifle so that they can shoot you." He declared that had he not carried out the order, he is sure he would have been killed or that his wife or child would have been directly threatened. Regarding this, he claimed to have seen Milorad Pelemis ordering someone to be killed because he had refused to obey. He reported that despite this, he attempted to spare a man between 50 and 60 years of age who said that he had saved Serbs from Srebrenica. Brano Gojković then told him that he did not want any surviving witness to the crime.

Dražen Erdemović asserted that he then opposed the order of a lieutenant colonel to participate in the execution of five hundred Muslim men being detained in the Pilica public building. He was able not to commit this further crime because three of his comrades supported him when he refused to obey....

10. The Trial Chamber, having accepted the Appellant's plea of guilty to the count of a crime against humanity, sentenced the Appellant to 10 years' imprisonment. This term of imprisonment was imposed by the Trial Chamber having regard to the extreme gravity of the offence and to a number of mitigating circumstances.

(a) The extreme gravity of the crime

The Trial Chamber took the view that the objective gravity of the crime was such that "there exists in international law a standard according to which a crime against humanity is one of extreme gravity demanding the most severe penalties when no mitigating circumstances are present."

(b) The mitigating circumstances

As regards the mitigating circumstances contemporaneous with the crime, that is the "state of mental incompetence claimed by the Defence [and] the extreme necessity in which [the Appellant] allegedly found himself when placed under duress by the order and threat from his hierarchical superiors as well as his subordinate level within the military hierarchy," the Trial Chamber considered that these were insufficiently proven since the Appellant's testimony in this regard had not been corroborated by independent evidence....

C. The Scope of the Appeals Chamber's Judicial Review: Issues Raised Proprio Motu and Preliminary Questions

16. The Appeals Chamber has raised preliminary issues *proprio motu* pursuant to its inherent powers as an appellate body once seised of an appeal lodged by either party pursuant to Article 25 of the Statute.... In pursuance of its *proprio motu* examination of the validity of the Appellant's guilty plea, the Appeals Chamber addressed three preliminary questions to the parties in a Scheduling Order dated 5 May 1997:

(1) In law, may duress afford a complete defence to a charge of crimes against humanity and/or war crimes such that, if the defence is proved at trial, the accused is entitled to an acquittal?

(2) If the answer to (1) is in the affirmative, was the guilty plea entered by the accused at his initial appearance equivocal in that the accused, while pleading guilty, invoked duress?

(3) Was the acceptance of a guilty plea valid in view of the mental condition of the accused at the time the plea was entered? If not, was this defect cured by statements made by the accused in subsequent proceedings?

III. Reasons

17. In answering the preliminary questions surrounding the validity of the Appellant's plea, the members of the Appeals Chamber differ on a number of issues, both as to reasoning and as to result. Consequently, the views of each of the members of the Appeals Chamber on particular issues are set out in detail in Separate Opinions which are attached to this Judgement and merely summarised here.

18. The Appeals Chamber, for the reasons set out in the Joint Separate Opinion of Judge McDonald and Judge Vohrah, unanimously finds that the Appellant's plea was voluntary.

19. For the reasons set out in the Joint Separate Opinion of Judge McDonald and Judge Vohrah and in the Separate and Dissenting Opinion of Judge Li, the majority of the Appeals Chamber finds that duress does not afford a complete defence to a soldier charged with a crime against humanity and/or a war crime involving the killing of innocent human beings. Consequently, the majority of the Appeals Chamber finds that the guilty plea of the Appellant was not equivocal....

20. However, the Appeals Chamber, for the reasons set out in the Joint Separate Opinion of Judge McDonald and Judge Vohrah, finds that the guilty plea of the Appellant was not informed and accordingly remits the case to a Trial Chamber other than the one which sentenced the Appellant in order that he be given an opportunity to replead. Judge Li dissents from this view for the reasons set out in his Separate and Dissenting Opinion.... Joint Separate Opinion of Judge McDonald and Judge Vohrah

III. Can Duress Be A Complete Defence in International Law to the Killing of Innocents?

32. As to the first preliminary question addressed to the parties in this appeal ... the issue may be stated more specifically as follows: In law, may duress afford a complete defence to a soldier charged with crimes against humanity or war crimes where the soldier has killed innocent persons?....

1. The relationship between superior orders and duress

34. Superior orders and duress are conceptually distinct and separate issues and often the same factual circumstances engage both notions, particularly in armed conflict situations. We subscribe to the view that obedience to superior orders does not amount to a defence *per se* but is a factual element which may be taken into consideration in conjunction with other circumstances of the case in assessing whether the defences of duress or mistake of fact are made out....

As obedience to superior orders may be considered merely as a factual element in determining whether duress is made out on the facts, the absence of a superior order does not mean that duress as a defence must fail....

A. The Applicable Law

40. The sources of international law are generally considered to be exhaustively listed in Article 38 of the Statute of the International Court of Justice ("ICJ Statute")....

B. Customary International Law *(Article 38(1)(b) of ICJ Statute)*

41. The Prosecution submits that "under international law duress cannot afford a complete defence to a charge of crimes against humanity and war crimes when the underly-

ing offence is the killing of an innocent human being." The Prosecution contends that the relevant case-law of the post-Second World War military tribunals does not recognise duress as a defence to a charge involving the killing of innocent persons. Given also that there is no conventional international law which resolves the question of duress as a defence to murder, it is the submission of the Prosecution that customary international law, as contained in the decisions of the post-World War Two military tribunals, clearly precludes duress as such a defence. Although the Prosecution does not confine its arguments to the specific question as to whether duress is a complete defence for a soldier who has been charged under international law with killing innocent persons, we would, however, so limit our inquiry in this appeal....

1. No customary international law rule can be derived on the question of duress as a defence to the killing of innocent persons

46. The Prosecution strongly contends that the opinions of the post-World War Two military tribunals on the question of duress as a defence to murder have become part of customary international law. It matters not, the Prosecution urges, that this custom was based originally on common law authorities....

47. A number of war crimes cases have been brought to our attention as supporting the position that duress is a complete defence to the killing of innocent persons in international law [the Appeals Chamber discussed cases from several jurisdictions]....

(b) No consistent and uniform state practice underpinned by *opinio juris*

49. Although some of the above mentioned cases may clearly represent the positions of national jurisdictions regarding the availability of duress as a complete defence to the killing of innocent persons, neither they nor the principles on this issue found in decisions of the post-World War Two military tribunals are, in our view, entitled to be given the status of customary international law. For a rule to pass into customary international law, the International Court of Justice has authoritatively restated in the *North Sea Continental Shelf cases* that there must exist extensive and uniform state practice underpinned by *opinio juris sive necessitatis*. To the extent that the domestic decisions and national laws of States relating to the issue of duress as a defence to murder may be regarded as state practice, it is quite plain that this practice is not at all consistent....

55. [I]t is our considered view that no rule may be found in customary international law regarding the availability or the non-availability of duress as a defence to a charge of killing innocent human beings. The post-World War Two military tribunals did not establish such a rule. We do not think that the decisions of these tribunals or those of other national courts and military tribunals constitute consistent and uniform state practice underpinned by *opinio juris sive necessitatis*.

C. General principles of law recognised by civilised nations (Article 38(1)(c) of ICJ Statute)

56. It is appropriate now to inquire whether the "general principles of law recognised by civilised nations," established as a source of international law in Article 38(1)(c) of the ICJ Statute, may shed some light upon this intricate issue of duress....

57. A number of considerations bear upon our analysis of the application of "general principles of law recognised by civilised nations" as a source of international law. First, although general principles of law are to be derived from existing legal systems, in particular, national systems of law, it is generally accepted that the distillation of a "general principle of law recognised by civilised nations" does not require the comprehensive survey of all legal systems of the world.

... Second, it is the view of eminent jurists, including Baron Descamps, the President of the Advisory Committee of Jurists on Article 38(1)(c), that one purpose of this article is to avoid a situation of *non-liquet,* that is, where an international tribunal is stranded by an absence of applicable legal rules. Third, a "general principle" must not be confused with concrete manifestations of that principle in specific rules....

1. Duress as a complete defence

(a) Civil law systems

59. The penal codes of civil law systems, with some exceptions, consistently recognise duress as a complete defence to all crimes. The criminal codes of civil law nations provide that an accused acting under duress "commits no crime" or "is not criminally responsible" or "shall not be punished." We would note that some civil law systems distinguish between the notion of necessity and that of duress. Necessity is taken to refer to situations of emergency arising from natural forces. Duress, however, is taken to refer to compulsion by threats of another human being. Where a civil law system makes this distinction, only the provision relating to duress will be referred to.

France

In the French Penal Code, promulgated on 22 July 1992, Article 122-2 provides that:

> No person is criminally responsible who acted under the influence of a force or compulsion which he could not resist.

It is apparent from this article that French law recognises duress as a general defence which leads to acquittal. The effect of the application of this provision is, speaking figuratively, the destruction of the will of the person under compulsion....

(b) Common law systems

England

60. In England, duress is a complete defence to all crimes except murder, attempted murder and, it would appear, treason. Although there is no direct authority on whether duress is available in respect of attempted murder, the prevailing view is that there is no reason in logic, morality or law in granting the defence to a charge of attempted murder whilst withholding it in respect of a charge of murder.

United States and Australia

The English position that duress operates as a complete defence in respect of crimes generally is followed in the United States and Australia with variations in the federal state jurisdictions as to the precise definition of the defence and the range of offences for which the defence is not available....

(c) Criminal Law of Other States

[The opinion surveyed the law of Japan, China, Morocco, Somalia, and Ethiopia]

2. Duress as a mitigating factor

62. The penal legislation of Poland and Norway concerning the punishment of war criminals explicitly rejects duress as a defence to war crimes in general and provides that circumstances of duress may at most be considered in mitigation of punishment. Article 5 of the Polish Law Concerning the Punishment of War Criminals of 11 December 1946 provides:

> The fact that an act or omission was caused by a threat, order or command does not exempt from criminal responsibility.

In such a case, the court may mitigate the sentence taking into consideration the circumstances of the perpetrator and the deed.

(a) The excepted offences in some national systems

63. In numerous national jurisdictions, certain offences are excepted from the application of the defence of duress. Traditional common law rejects the defence of duress in respect of murder and treason. Legislatures in many common law jurisdictions, however, often prescribe a longer list of excepted offences.

64. Despite these offences being excluded from the operation of duress as a defence, the practice of courts in these jurisdictions is nevertheless to mitigate the punishment of persons committing excepted offences unless there is a mandatory penalty of death or life imprisonment prescribed for the offence....

Mitigating factors may relate to the seriousness of the offence, and in particular, may reflect the culpability of the offender. It is clearly established in principle and practice that where an offender is close to having a defence to criminal liability, this will tend to reduce the seriousness of the offence....

65. Courts in civil law jurisdictions may also mitigate an offender's punishment on the ground of duress where the defence fails....

3. What is the general principle?

66. Having regard to the above survey relating to the treatment of duress in the various legal systems, it is, in our view, a general principle of law recognised by civilised nations that an accused person is less blameworthy and less deserving of the full punishment when he performs a certain prohibited act under duress. We would use the term "duress" in this context to mean "imminent threats to the life of an accused if he refuses to commit a crime" and do not refer to the legal terms of art which have the equivalent meaning of the English word "duress" in the languages of most civil law systems.... Mitigation is also relevant in two other respects. Firstly, punishment may be mitigated in respect of offences which have been specifically excepted from the operation of the defence of duress by the legislatures of some jurisdictions. Secondly, courts have the power to mitigate sentences where the strict elements of a defence of duress are not made out on the facts....

4. What is the applicable rule?

67. The rules of the various legal systems of the world are, however, largely inconsistent regarding the specific question whether duress affords a complete defence to a combatant charged with a war crime or a crime against humanity involving the killing of innocent persons. As the general provisions of the numerous penal codes set out above show, the civil law systems in general would theoretically allow duress as a complete defence to all crimes including murder and unlawful killing. On the other hand, there are laws of other legal systems which categorically reject duress as a defence to murder. Firstly, specific laws relating to war crimes in Norway and Poland do not allow duress to operate as a complete defence but permit it to be taken into account only in mitigation of punishment. Secondly, the Ethiopian Penal Code of 1957 provides in Article 67 that only "absolute physical coercion" may constitute a complete defence to crimes in general. Where the coercion is "moral," which we would interpret as referring to duress by threats, the accused is only entitled to a reduction of penalty. This reduction of penalty may extend, where appropriate, even to a complete discharge of the offender from punishment. Thirdly, the common law systems throughout the world, with the exception of a small minority of jurisdictions of the United States which have adopted without reservation Sec-

tion 2.09 of the United States Model Penal Code, reject duress as a defence to the killing of innocent persons.

(a) The case-law of certain civil law jurisdictions

68. We would add that although the penal codes of most civil law jurisdictions do not expressly except the operation of the defence of duress in respect of offences involving the killing of innocent persons, the penal codes of Italy, Norway, Sweden, Nicaragua, Japan, and the former Yugoslavia require proportionality between the harm caused by the accused's act and the harm with which the accused was threatened....

69. In addition, the provisions governing duress in the penal codes of Germany and the former Yugoslavia suggest the possibility that soldiers in an armed conflict may, in contrast to ordinary persons, be denied a complete defence because of the special nature of their occupation....

(b) The principle behind the rejection of duress as a defence to murder in the common law

70. Murder is invariably included in any list of offences excepted by legislation in common law systems from the operation of duress as a defence. The English common law rule is that duress is no defence to murder, either for a principal offender or a secondary party to the crime....

71. Given that duress has been held at common law not to negate *mens rea*, the availability of the defence turns on the question whether, in spite of the elements of the offence being strictly made out, the conduct of the defendant should be justified or excused. The second aspect of the common law stance against permitting duress as a defence to murder is the assertion in law of a moral absolute. This moral point has been pressed consistently in a long line of authorities in English law and is accepted by courts in other common law jurisdictions as the basis for the rejection of duress as a defence to murder....

(c) No consistent rule from the principal legal systems of the world

72. It is clear from the differing positions of the principal legal systems of the world that there is no consistent concrete rule which answers the question whether or not duress is a defence to the killing of innocent persons. It is not possible to reconcile the opposing positions and, indeed, we do not believe that the issue should be reduced to a contest between common law and civil law.

We would therefore approach this problem bearing in mind the specific context in which the International Tribunal was established, the types of crimes over which it has jurisdiction, and the fact that the International Tribunal's mandate is expressed in the Statute as being in relation to "serious violations of international humanitarian law."

D. The Rule Applicable to this Case

1. A normative mandate for international criminal law

73. We accept the submission of the Prosecution during the hearing of 26 May 1997 that

> even in ... a scenario where the killing of one life may save ten ... there may be sound reasons in law not to permit a complete defence but to compensate for the lack of moral choice through other means such as sentencing. I think this is exactly the thinking behind the Common Law position ... there is no categorical reason for saying that duress must necessarily apply. It may or may not be based on one's expectations of what is reasonable under the circumstances, based on

one's expectations of the harm which creation of such defence may create for such a society at large.

Certainly the avoidance of the harm to society which the acceptance or admission of duress as a defence to murder would cause was very much a consideration with regard to the English position....

75. [T]he law should not be the product or slave of logic or intellectual hair-splitting, but must serve broader normative purposes in light of its social, political and economic role. It is noteworthy that the authorities we have just cited issued their cautionary words in respect of domestic society and in respect of a range of ordinary crimes including kidnapping, assault, robbery and murder. Whilst reserving our comments on the appropriate rule for domestic national contexts, we cannot but stress that we are not, in the International Tribunal, concerned with ordinary domestic crimes. The purview of the International Tribunal relates to war crimes and crimes against humanity committed in armed conflicts of extreme violence with egregious dimensions. We are not concerned with the actions of domestic terrorists, gang-leaders and kidnappers. We are concerned that, in relation to the most heinous crimes known to humankind, the principles of law to which we give credence have the appropriate normative effect upon soldiers bearing weapons of destruction and upon the commanders who control them in armed conflict situations. The facts of this particular case, for example, involved the cold-blooded slaughter of 1200 men and boys by soldiers using automatic weapons. We must bear in mind that we are operating in the realm of international humanitarian law which has, as one of its prime objectives, the protection of the weak and vulnerable in such a situation where their lives and security are endangered.... If national law denies recognition of duress as a defence in respect of the killing of innocent persons, international criminal law can do no less than match that policy since it deals with murders often of far greater magnitude. If national law denies duress as a defence even in a case in which a single innocent life is extinguished due to action under duress, international law, in our view, cannot admit duress in cases which involve the slaughter of innocent human beings on a large scale. It must be our concern to facilitate the development and effectiveness of international humanitarian law and to promote its aims and application by recognising the normative effect which criminal law should have upon those subject to them....

77. Practical policy considerations compel the legislatures of most common law jurisdictions to withhold the defence of duress not only from murder but from a vast array of offences without engaging in a complex and tortuous investigation into the relationship between law and morality....

78. We do not think our reference to considerations of policy are improper. It would be naive to believe that international law operates and develops wholly divorced from considerations of social and economic policy. There is the view that international law should distance itself from social policy and this view has been articulated by the International Court of Justice in the *South West Africa Cases* 165., where it is stated that "[l]aw exists, it is said, to serve a social need; but precisely for that reason it can do so only through and within the limits of its own discipline." We are of the opinion that this separation of law from social policy is inapposite in relation to the application of international humanitarian law to crimes occuring during times of war. It is clear to us that whatever is the distinction between the international legal order and municipal legal orders in general, the distinction is imperfect in respect of the criminal law which, both at the international and the municipal level, is directed towards consistent aims. At the municipal level, criminal law and criminal policy are closely intertwined. There is no reason why this should be any different in international criminal law. We subscribe to the views of Professor Rosalyn Higgins (as she then was) when she argued:

Reference to the 'correct legal view' or 'rules' can never avoid the element of choice (though it can seek to disguise it), nor can it provide guidance to the preferable decision. In making this choice one must inevitably have consideration for the humanitarian, moral, and social purposes of the law.... Where there is ambiguity or uncertainty, the policy-directed choice can properly be made.

It appears that the essence of this thesis is not that policy concerns dominate the law but rather, where appropriate, are given due consideration in the determination of a case. This is precisely the approach we have taken to the question of duress as a defence to the killing of innocent persons in international law. Even if policy concerns are entirely ignored, the law will nevertheless fail in its ambition of neutrality "for even such a refusal [to acknowledge political and social factors] is not without political and social consequences. There is no avoiding the essential relationship between law and politics."

2. An exception where the victims will die regardless of the participation of the accused?

79. It was suggested during the hearing of 26 May 1997 that neither the English national cases nor the post-World War Two military tribunal decisions specifically addressed the situation in which the accused faced the choice between his own death for not obeying an order to kill or participating in a killing which was inevitably going to occur regardless of whether he participated in it or not. It has been argued that in such a situation where the fate of the victim was already sealed, duress should constitute a complete defence. This is because the accused is then not choosing that one innocent human being should die rather than another. In a situation where the victim or victims would have died in any event, such as in the present case where the victims were to be executed by firing squad, there would be no reason for the accused to have sacrificed his life. The accused could not have saved the victim's life by giving his own and thus, according to this argument, it is unjust and illogical for the law to expect an accused to sacrifice his life in the knowledge that the victim/s will die anyway. The argument, it is said, is vindicated in the Italian case of *Masetti*. which was decided by the Court of Assize in L'Aquila. The accused in that case raised duress in response to the charge of having organised the execute of two partisans upon being ordered to do so by the battalion commander. The Court of Assize acquitted the accused on the ground of duress and said:

> ... the possible sacrifice [of their lives] by Masetti and his men [those who comprised the execution squad] would have been in any case to no avail and without any effect in that it would have had no impact whatsoever on the plight of the persons to be shot, who would have been executed anyway even without him [the accused].

We have given due consideration to this approach which, for convenience, we will label "the *Masetti* approach." For the reasons given below we would reject the *Masetti* approach.

3. Rejection of utilitarianism and proportionality where human life must be weighed

80. The *Masetti* approach proceeds from the starting point of strict utilitarian logic based on the fact that if the victim will die anyway, the accused is not at all morally blameworthy for taking part in the execution; there is absolutely no reason why the accused should die as it would be unjust for the law to expect the accused to die for nothing. It should be immediately apparent that the assertion that the accused is not morally blameworthy where the victim would have died in any case depends entirely again upon a view of morality based on utilitarian logic. This does not, in our opinion, address the true rationale for our rejection of duress as a defence to the killing of innocent human beings.

The approach we take does not involve a balancing of harms for and against killing but rests upon an application in the context of international humanitarian law of the rule that duress does not justify or excuse the killing of an innocent person. Our view is based upon a recognition that international humanitarian law should guide the conduct of combatants and their commanders. There must be legal limits as to the conduct of combatants and their commanders in armed conflict. In accordance with the spirit of international humanitarian law, we deny the availability of duress as a complete defence to combatants who have killed innocent persons. In so doing, we give notice in no uncertain terms that those who kill innocent persons will not be able to take advantage of duress as a defence and thus get away with impunity for their criminal acts in the taking of innocent lives....

4. Mitigation of punishment as a clear, simple and uniform approach

85. Finally, we think, with respect, that it is inaccurate to say that by rejecting duress as a defence to the killing of innocent persons, the law "expects" a person who knows that the victims will die anyway to throw his life away in vain.... The law, in our view, does not "expect" a person whose life is threatened to be hero and to sacrifice his life by refusing to commit the criminal act demanded of him. The law does not "expect" that person to be a hero because in recognition of human frailty and the threat under which he acted, it will mitigate his punishment. In appropriate cases, the offender may receive no punishment at all....

E. Our conclusions

88. After the above survey of authorities in the different systems of law and exploration of the various policy considerations which we must bear in mind, we take the view that duress cannot afford a complete defence to a soldier charged with crimes against humanity or war crimes in international law involving the taking of innocent lives. We do so having regard to our mandated obligation under the Statute to ensure that international humanitarian law, which is concerned with the protection of humankind, is not in any way undermined.

[The opinion remitted the case to another Trial Chamber to replead with full knowledge of the consequences of a guilty plea].

Separate and Dissenting Opinion of Judge Cassese

I. The Notion of a Guilty Plea (or: the Extent to Which an International Criminal Court can Rely upon National Law for the Interpretation of International Provisions)

A. General Remarks

1. It is my contention that the provisions of the Statute of the International Tribunal ("Statute") and the Rules of Procedure and Evidence ("Rules") — respectively Article 20, paragraph 3, and Rule 62 — dealing with the guilty or not-guilty plea, do not necessarily imply a reference to the legislation and case-law of common-law countries.

Such reference to national law is not indispensable, for the notion of "guilty plea" can be constructed fairly easily on the strength of the Statute. Reference to national law, if at all necessary, can only be made to take account, with all due caution, of the wealth of distinctions propounded by national courts. This reference to national law might cast some light on the possible implications and ramifications of the notion, but ultimately that notion must be autonomously construed on the basis of the international provisions of the Statute.

2. I shall dwell on this matter because it has an importance largely transcending the specific question under discussion. The point at issue is the extent to which an interna-

tional criminal court may or should draw upon national law concepts and transpose these concepts into international criminal proceedings.

To my mind notions, legal constructs and terms of art upheld in national law should not be automatically applied at the international level. They cannot be mechanically imported into international criminal proceedings. The International Tribunal, being an international body based on the law of nations, must first of all look to the object and purpose of the relevant provisions of its Statute and Rules.

3. This approach is dictated by three fundamental considerations. Firstly, the traditional attitude of international courts to national-law notions suggests that one should explore all the means available at the international level before turning to national law.

On this score it should be noted that international courts have consistently held that even in the case of international rules embodying national-law notions, an effort must be made to construe those notions in the light of the object and purpose of the international rules or of their general spirit. Reliance on legal notions or concepts as laid down in a national legal system can only be justified if international rules make explicit reference to national law or if such reference is necessarily implied by the very content and nature of the concept.

An instance of implied reference to national law can be seen in the customary international rule whereby a State can exercise the right of diplomatic protection, or institute international judicial proceedings, on behalf of its nationals. To apply this international rule, namely to determine whether or not a specific individual has the nationality of a State, the international judge must perforce look into and apply the national legislation of the relevant State.

Whenever reference to national law is not commanded expressly, or imposed by necessary implication, resort to national legislation is not warranted....

One might wonder why international courts show such great caution in drawing upon national law when establishing the meaning of national law concepts and terms. Indeed, such caution might be regarded as inconsistent with the fact that the whole body of international law owes so much to national or municipal rules: as is well known, over the years international norms have greatly borrowed from the internal law of sovereign States, particularly from national private law. However, this historical spilling over from one set of legal systems into the law of nations does not detract from these legal systems (those of States on the one side, and international law, on the other) being radically different: their structure is different, their subjects are different, as are their sources and enforcement mechanisms. It follows that normally it would prove incongruous and inappropriate to apply in an inter-State legal setting a national law concept as such, that is, with its original scope and purport. The body of law into which one may be inclined to transplant the national law notion cannot but reject the transplant, for the notion is felt as extraneous to the whole set of legal ideas, constructs and mechanisms prevailing in the international context. Consequently, the normal attitude of international courts is to try to assimilate or transform the national law notion so as to adjust it to the exigencies and basic principles of international law.

4. The second consideration militating in favour of using great circumspection before transposing national law notions into international law is inextricably bound up with the very subject-matter under discussion. A note of warning about importing national concepts "lock, stock and barrel" into the international field, was sounded by such eminent international judges as McNair and Fitzmaurice. Both judges were referring to private law concepts. Their view should a fortiori apply to criminal law. International criminal procedure results from the gradual decanting of national criminal concepts and rules into the international receptacle. However, international criminal procedure does not originate from a uniform body

of law. It substantially results from an amalgamation of two different legal systems, that obtaining in common-law countries and the system prevailing in countries of civil-law (although for historical reasons, there currently exists at the international level a clear imbalance in favour of the common-law approach)....

5. The third reason discouraging a mechanical importation of notions from national law into international criminal proceedings is that such a process may alter or distort the specificity of these proceedings. International trials exhibit a number of features that differentiate them from national criminal proceedings. All these features are linked to the fact that international criminal justice is dispensed in a general setting markedly different from that of national courts: international criminal courts are not part of a State apparatus functioning on a particular territory and exercising an authority of which courts partake. International criminal courts operate at the inter-State level. They discharge their functions in a community consisting of sovereign States. The individuals over whom these courts exercise their jurisdiction are under the sway and control of sovereign States. Many important consequences follow from this state of affairs. Here I shall confine myself to stressing only the most striking one: an international criminal court has no direct means at its disposal of enforcing its orders, summonses, and other decisions; to compel individuals under the sovereignty of a State to comply with its injunctions, it must rely on the cooperation of that State. To lose sight of this fundamental condition, and thus simply transplant into international law notions originating in national legal systems, might be a source of great confusion and misapprehension. The philosophy behind all national criminal proceedings, whether they take a common-law or a civil-law approach, is unique to those proceedings and stems from the fact that national courts operate in a context where the three fundamental functions (law-making, adjudication and law enforcement) are discharged by central organs partaking of the State's direct authority over individuals. That logic cannot be simply transposed onto the international level: there, a different logic imposed by the different position and role of courts must perforce inspire and govern international criminal proceedings.

6. The foregoing considerations warrant, I submit, the following propositions. Any time international provisions include notions and terms of art originating in national criminal law, the interpreter must first determine whether these notions or terms are given a totally autonomous significance in the international context, i.e., whether, once transposed onto the international level, they have acquired a new lease of life, absolutely independent of their original meaning. If the result of this enquiry is in the negative, the international judge must satisfy himself whether the transplant onto the international procedure entails for the notion or term an adaptation or adjustment to the characteristic features of international proceedings. This exploration should be undertaken by examining whether the general context of international proceedings and the object of the provisions regulating them delineate with sufficient precision the scope and purpose of the notion and its role in the international setting. Only if this enquiry leads to negative conclusions is one warranted to draw upon national legislation and case-law and apply the national legal construct or terms as they are conceived and interpreted in the national context.

As a rule of thumb it can be said that normally neither the first nor the third hypothetical situation arises; it is more plausible and in keeping with the purpose and spirit of international proceedings that the second one will prevail.

A case in point is the notion of a "guilty plea," as I shall endeavour to show below....

B. Notion and Requirements of Duress

14. Duress, namely acting under a threat from a third person of severe and irreparable harm to life or limb, entails that no criminal responsibility is incurred by the person

acting under that threat. Duress is often termed "necessity," both in national legislation and in cases relating to war crimes or crimes against humanity. I too will have occasion to use these two terms as equivalent. However, as rightly pointed out in the British Manual of Military Law, from a technical viewpoint, necessity proper also covers situations other than those where one is faced with threats or compulsion of a third party, for instance the condition where a person "in extremity of hunger kills [another person] to eat him." In other words, necessity is a broader heading than duress, encompassing threats to life and limb generally and not only when they emanate from another person....

44. [T]he case-law seems to make an exception for those instances where — on the facts — it is highly probable, if not certain, that if the person acting under duress had refused to commit the crime, the crime would in any event have been carried out by persons other than the accused. The commonest example of such a case is where an execution squad has been assembled to kill the victims, and the accused participates, in some form, in the execution squad, either as an active member or as an organiser, albeit only under the threat of death. In this case, if an individual member of the execution squad first refuses to obey but has then to comply with the order as a result of duress, he may be excused: indeed, whether or not he is killed or instead takes part in the execution, the civilians, prisoners of war, etc., would be shot anyway. Were he to comply with his legal duty not to shoot innocent persons, he would forfeit his life for no benefit to anyone and no effect whatsoever apart from setting a heroic example for mankind (which the law cannot demand him to set): his sacrifice of his own life would be to no avail. In this case the evil threatened (the menace to his life and his subsequent death) would be greater than the remedy (his refraining from committing the crime, i.e., from participating in the execution).

In sum, the customary rule of international law on duress, as evolved on the basis of case-law and the military regulations of some States, does not exclude the applicability of duress to war crimes and crimes against humanity whose underlying offence is murder or unlawful killing. However, as the right to life is the most fundamental human right, the rule demands that the general requirements for duress be applied particularly strictly in the case of killing of innocent persons.

45. In evaluating the factual circumstances which may be relevant to duress, according to a trend discernible in the case-law, there may arise the need to distinguish between the various ranks of the military or civilian hierarchy....

46. Furthermore, a trial court adjudicating a plea of duress might also want to take into account another factor, namely whether and to what extent the person assertedly acting under duress willed the commission of the offence. For this purpose the court might enquire whether the person allegedly acting under duress confessed at the earliest possible opportunity to the act he had committed and denounced it to the relevant authorities. If the person at issue refrained from so doing, the inference might be warranted that he acquiesced in, and thus willed, the act which he perpetrated under duress.

6. Concluding considerations

47. I contend that the international legal regulation of duress in case of murder, as I have endeavoured to infer it from case-law and practice, is both realistic and flexible. It also takes account of social expectations more than the rule suggested by the Prosecution and that propounded by the majority.

Law is based on what society can reasonably expect of its members. It should not set intractable standards of behaviour which require mankind to perform acts of martyrdom, and brand as criminal any behaviour falling below those standards....

49. What I have argued so far leads me to the conclusion that international criminal law on duress is not ambiguous or uncertain. Here lies the main point of my disagreement with the Appeals Chamber's majority. Admittedly, when duress is urged as a defence for a war crime or a crime against humanity where the underlying offence is the killing of innocent persons, it proves particularly difficult for the international judge to establish whether the relevant facts are present and the necessary high requirements laid down in law are satisfied. But this is a matter for the trial judge to look into. However difficult and tricky his judicial investigation, he is not left empty-handed by law: on the contrary, he can draw from international law fairly accurate guidelines, spelled out in a number of national cases dealing with war crimes and crimes against humanity....

It should therefore be no surprise that I do not share the views of the majority of the Appeals Chamber, according to which, since international criminal law is ambiguous or uncertain on this matter, it is warranted to make a policy-directed choice and thus rely on "considerations of social and economic policy." I disagree not only because, as I have already repeatedly stated, in my view international law is not ambiguous or uncertain, but also because to uphold in this area of criminal law the concept of recourse to a policy-directed choice is tantamount to running foul of the customary principle *nullum crimen sine lege*. An international court must apply *lex lata*, that is to say, the existing rules of international law as they are created through the sources of the international legal system. If it has instead recourse to policy considerations or moral principles, it acts *ultra vires*.

In any event, even assuming that no clear legal regulation of the matter were available in international law, arguably the Appeals Chamber majority should have drawn upon the law applicable in the former Yugoslavia. In the former Yugoslavia and in the present States of the area the relevant criminal law provides that duress (called "extreme necessity") may amount to a total defence for any crime, whether or not implying the killing of persons. A national of one of the States of that region fighting in an armed conflict was required to know those national criminal provisions and base his expectations on their contents. Were *ex hypothesi* international criminal law really ambiguous on duress or were it even to contain a gap, it would therefore be appropriate and judicious to have recourse—as a last resort—to the national legislation of the accused, rather than to moral considerations or policy-oriented principles. In the specific instance under discussion, where the State at stake is one of the former Yugoslavia, this approach would also be supported by the general maxim in *dubio pro reo* (which in this case should be in *dubio pro accusato*).

Question

1. What is the test proffered in Article 31(1)(d) of the Statute of the ICC? Is it preferable? Is it realistic?

3. Self-Defense and Defense of Others

U.S. Dep't of Army, II International Law
246 (1962)

Self-defense. The plea of self-defense may be successfully put forward in war crimes trials in much the same circumstances as in trials held under municipal law. In the case of *United States v. Krupp*, the Court implied that it would accept a defense of self-defense defined as executing "the repulse of a wrong" and even a defense of necessity which is "the invasion of a right." Another case was the trial of Weiss and Mundo before the United States General Military Government Court at Ludwigsburg, Germany, November 1945. Here two German policemen were acquitted of shooting a captured American airman whom they believed to be drawing a gun.

M. C. Bassiouni, A Draft International Criminal Code and Draft Statute for an International Criminal Tribunal
109–10 (1987)

Section 2. *Self-Defense (Individual)*

2.0 Self-defense consists in the use of force against another person which may otherwise constitute a crime when and to the extent that the actor reasonably believes that such force is necessary to defend himself or anyone else against such other person's imminent use of unlawful force, and in a manner which is reasonably proportionate to the threat or use of force.

Commentary:

While the civil law system would view the conditions of exoneration listed in this Article as a questionable combination of principles of responsibility and legal defences, it was felt that a single Article containing all conditions which ultimately result in exoneration from responsibility, irrespective of their doctrinal or dogmatic basis should be placed together, as it gives these aspects a sense of cohesion and practical use by an international tribunal.

The self-defense provision, [above in] Section 2, is based on that contained in Article 2(2)a of the European Convention for the Protection of Human Rights and Fundamental Freedoms as well as on the language used in the *Model Penal Code*. The requirement that the defender reasonably believe that forceful response is necessary is a common law requirement which is superfluous for civil law systems. On the other hand, the introduction of the requirement that the response be to an "imminent" use of unlawful force may be viewed under the common law as surplusage.

Questions

1. What is the test proffered in Article 31(1)(c) of the Statute of the ICC? Is it preferable or realistic? What does "in a manner proportionate to the degree of danger to the person" mean?

2. If four persons clearly threaten another person with imminent death by gunfire, can that other person lawfully kill the four persons in self-defense?

4. Mistake of Fact
U.S. Dep't of Army, II International Law
246 (1962)

Mistake of fact. The German commander in Finland carried out a "scorched earth" policy under the mistaken impression that he was being pursued by Russian troops. The court commented as follows:

> ... The destruction was as complete as an efficient army could do it. Three years after the completion of the operation, the extent of the devastation was discernible to the eye. While the Russians did not follow up the retreat to the extent anticipated, there are physical evidences that they were expected to do so.

Gun emplacements, foxholes, and other defense installations are still perceptible in the territory. In other words there are mute evidences that an attack was anticipated.

There is evidence in the record that there was no military necessity for this destruction and devastation. An examination of the facts in retrospect can well sustain this conclusion. But we are obliged to judge the situation as it appeared to the defendant at the time. If the facts were such as would justify the action by the exercise of judgment, after giving consideration to all the factors and existing possibilities, even though the conclusion reached may have been faulty, it cannot be said to be criminal. After giving careful consideration to all the evidence on the subject, we are convinced that the defendant cannot be held criminally responsible although when viewed in retrospect, the danger did not actually exist.

[quoting *United States v. List*]

Questions

1. What is the mistake of fact test proffered in Article 32 of the Statute of the ICC ("only if it negates the mental element required by the crime")? Is it preferable?

2. What other defenses or general limits of responsibility are found in the Statute of the ICC? See Articles 26, 30–31. Are they preferable? Concerning mental incapacity, *see, e.g., The Prosecutor v. Delalic,* Judgment, IT-96-21-T (16 Nov. 1998); Peter Krug, *The Emerging Mental Incapacity Defense in International Criminal Law: Some Initial Questions of Implementation,* 94 Am. J. Int'l L.317 (2000). Note that Article 31 lists "[g]rounds for excluding criminal responsibility." These are not defenses per se and under this jurisprudential approach an accused may still be guilty but not criminally responsible.

B. Defenses Not Accepted

1. Propriety under Domestic Law

[recall Principle II of the Nuremberg Principles, in this chapter, Section 1]

U.S. Dep't of Army, II International Law
249 (1962)

Act was done in accordance with municipal law. This plea did not constitute a defense. It was treated by the courts in much the same fashion as the plea of superior orders, that is admissible as a circumstance possibly justifying mitigation of sentence.

Allied Control Council Law No. 10 authorized punishment for crimes against humanity "whether or not in violation of the domestic law in the country where perpetrated."

Field Manual 27-10 has summarized the rule as follows:

The fact that domestic law does not impose a penalty for an act which constitutes a crime under international law does not relieve the person who committed the act from responsibility under international law.

2. *Tu Quoque*

U.S. Dep't of Army, II International Law
238 (1962)

Tu Quoque. This doctrine which means literally "you also", was urged by the Germans in justification of their acts. They argued that at least one (the U.S.S.R.) and possibly more of the prosecuting nations had themselves waged aggressive wars contemporaneous with those of the Reich. The court answered as follows:

Under general principles of law an accused does not exculpate himself from a crime by showing that another committed a similar crime either before or after the alleged commission of the crime by the accused.

[citing *United States v. von Leeb*]

J. Pictet, IV Commentary
15–16, 228 (ICRC 1958)

Article 1 — Respect for the Convention

The High Contracting Parties undertake to respect and to ensure respect for the present Convention in all circumstances.

A clause of this kind appeared, in a slightly different form, in the 1929 Conventions. Its prominent position at the beginning of each of the 1949 Conventions gives it increased importance. By undertaking at the very outset to respect the clauses of the Convention, the Contracting Parties drew attention to the special character of that instrument. It is not an engagement concluded on a basis of reciprocity, binding each party to the contract only in so far as the other party observes its obligations. It is rather a series of unilateral engagements solemnly contracted before the world as represented by the other Contracting Parties. Each State contracts obligations *vis-a-vis* itself and at the same time *vis-a-vis* the others. The motive of the Convention is such a lofty one, so universally recognized as an imperative call of civilization, that the need is felt for its assertion, as much out of respect for it on the part of the signatory State itself as in the expectation of such respect from an opponent, indeed perhaps even more for the former reason than for the latter....
..In the event of a Power failing to fulfil its obligations, the other Contracting Parties (neutral, allied or enemy) may, and should endeavour to bring it back to an attitude of respect for the Convention. The proper working of the system of protection provided by the Convention demands in fact that the Contracting Parties should not be content merely to apply its provisions themselves, but should do everything in their power to ensure that the humanitarian principles underlying the Conventions are applied universally ... [t]he words "in all circumstances" mean that as soon as one of the conditions of application for which Article 2 provides, is present, no Contracting Party can offer any valid pretext, legal or otherwise, for not respecting the Convention in its entirety. The words in question also mean that the application of the Convention does not depend on the character of the conflict. Whether a war is "just" or "unjust", whether it is a war of aggression or of resistance to aggression ...

[re: Article 33 of the Geneva Civilian Convention]

... The principle of the prohibition of reprisals against persons has now become part of international law in respect of all persons, whether they are members of the armed forces or civilians protected by the Geneva Conventions ...

The prohibition of reprisals is closely connected with the provisions which, by ensuring that the Convention is applied in all circumstances, give it the character of a primary duty based essentially on the protection of the human person. This paragraph, like the first one, marks a decisive step forward in the affirmation and defence of rights of individuals and there is no longer any question of such rights being withdrawn or attenuated as a result of a breach for which those individuals bear no responsibility. Finally, reprisals constituted a collective penalty bearing on those who least deserved it. Henceforth, the penalty is made individual and only the person who commits the offence may be punished. The importance of this development and its embodiment in the new Geneva Convention is clear ...

The prohibition of reprisals is a safeguard for all protected persons, whether in the territory of a Party to the conflict or in occupied territory. It is absolute and mandatory in character and thus cannot be interpreted as containing tacit reservations with regard to military necessity.

The solemn and unconditional character of the undertaking entered into by the States Parties to the Convention must be emphasized. To infringe this provision with the idea of restoring law and order would only add one more violation to those with which the enemy is reproached.

Note

1. During the war in Afghanistan, President George Bush ordered humane treatment of detainees merely "in a manner consistent with the principles of Geneva" and then only "to the extent appropriate and consistent with military necessity." Memorandum of President George W. Bush (Feb. 7, 2002), available at http://wid.ap.org/documents/iraq/040824finalreport.pdf. Addressing the authorization, Professor Paust has written that this order is unlawful for three reasons: "(1) far more than the "principles" of Geneva law apply, (2) it is not "appropriate" to deny treatment required by Geneva law, and (3) alleged military necessity does not justify the denial of treatment required by Geneva law. The memorandum's language limiting protection "to the extent appropriate" is potentially one of the broadest putative excuses for violations of Geneva law. Necessarily, the President's memorandum of February 7, 2002, authorized and ordered the denial of treatment required by the Geneva Conventions and, therefore, necessarily authorized and ordered violations of the Geneva Conventions, which are war crimes." Jordan J. Paust, *Executive Plans and Authorizations to Violate International Law Concerning Treatment and Interrogation of Detainees*, 43 Columbia J. Transnat'l L. 811, 828 (2005), available at http://columbia.edu/cu/jtl/Vol_43_3_files/Paust.pdf. *See also id.* at 814–16.

3. Double Jeopardy Between Different Sovereigns

Under customary international law, no double jeopardy attaches regarding prosecutions by different sovereigns. *See also* International Covenant on Civil and Political Rights, art. 14(7), 999 U.N.T.S. 171. How should the International Covenant's prohibition of double jeopardy operate in a federal system like the United States, with relatively different "sovereign" federal and state entities? Some prohibitions of double jeopardy apply through special treaty provisions applicable among the signatories.

4. Official Status or Immunity
Control Council Law No. 10
art. II, 4 (a):

The official position of any person, whether as Head of State or as responsible official in a Government Department does not free him from responsibility for a crime or entitle him to mitigation of punishment.

[see also Chapter Two, Section 1; Chapter Three, Section 1; Chapter Six]

Note

1. If anything, official position can be relevant with respect to individual responsibility under the customary law of leader responsibility involving dereliction of duty. *See, e.g.,* this chapter, Section 1 and ICC Statute, art. 27. Recall that neither formal command responsibility nor a direct chain of command is required concerning leader responsibility. Further, a leader can be a military or civilian leader. Concerning civilians, *see, e.g.,* Paust, *My Lai and Vietnam: Norms, Myths and Leader Responsibility,* 57 MIL. L. REV. 99, 182–83 (1972), revised in *Superior Orders and Command Responsibility*, in 3 INTERNATIONAL CRIMINAL LAW: ENFORCEMENT 84–85 (M.C. Bassiouni ed. 1987); 1919 Report of the Responsibilities Commission, in Chapter Seven, Section 2; indictment of Karadzic, in this chapter, Section 1; *see also* trials of German civilians under Control Council Law No. 10, in Chapter Four, Section 8; the indictment per treaty of William II of Germany in Article 227 of the 1919 Treaty of Peace with Germany, in Chapter Seven, Section 2; trials of von Hagenbach (1474), Barbie (France), Touvier (France); indictments of Rutaganda (ICTR) and Akayesu (ICTR), in Chapter Six, Section 9. Moreover, an official status is not required. Additionally, a leader can be responsible independently of the law of leader responsibility if such a person engages in conspiratorial or complicitous behavior. See this chapter, Section 1.

Section 3
State Responsibility

Jordan J. Paust, *Universality and the Responsibility to Enforce International Criminal Law: No U.S. Sanctuary for Alleged Nazi War Criminals*
11 HOUS. J. INT'L L. 337, 337–40 (1989)

Today it is generally recognized that customary international law of a peremptory nature places an obligation on each nation-state to search for and bring into custody and to initiate prosecution of or to extradite all persons within its territory or control who are reasonably accused of having committed, for example, war crimes, genocide, breaches of neutrality, and other crimes against peace.

With respect to war crimes in particular, there has been a long history of expectation that war crimes are offenses against humankind over which there is universal jurisdiction and a universal duty to prosecute. For over two hundred years, the United States has generally shared such expectations and has imposed criminal sanctions against our own nationals and those of other countries, here and abroad, in military commissions and other fora, for violations of the laws of armed conflict. Additionally, there are numerous recognitions outside the United States of such jurisdictional competence and responsibility. As an example, the 1919 Report presented to the Preliminary Peace Conference by the Commission on the Responsibility of the Authors of the War and on Enforcement of Penalties affirmed:

> Every belligerent has, according to international law the power and authority to try the individuals alleged to be guilty of ... violations of the Laws and Customs of War, if such persons have been taken prisoner or have otherwise fallen into its power. Each belligerent has, or has power to set up, ... an appropriate tribunal, military or civil, for the trial of such cases.

Similarly, from the late 1960s to the early 1970s there were a series of United Nations General Assembly resolutions evidencing expectations about universal jurisdiction and the duty to engage in criminal sanction efforts. For example, in a 1973 resolution on principles of international cooperation in the detection, arrest, extradition, and punishment of persons guilty of war crimes and crimes against humanity, it was rightly affirmed:

> 1. War crimes and crimes against humanity, wherever they are committed, shall be subject to investigation and the persons against whom there is evidence that they have committed such crimes shall be subject to tracing, arrest, trial and, if found guilty, to punishment....

> 3. States shall co-operate with each other on a bi-lateral and multi-lateral basis with a view to halting and preventing war crimes and crimes against humanity, and take the domestic and international measures necessary for that purpose.

> 4. States shall assist each other in detecting, arresting and bringing to trial persons suspected of having committed such crimes and, if they are found guilty, in punishing them....

> 7. States shall not grant asylum to any person with respect to whom there are serious reasons for considering that he has committed a crime against peace, a war crime or a crime against humanity.

In other resolutions it was also affirmed that a refusal "to cooperate in the arrest, extradition, trial and punishment" of such persons is contrary to the United Nations Charter "and to generally recognized norms of international law."

The responsibility of nation-states to enforce such laws has also been recognized more particularly with respect to the 1949 Geneva Conventions, which would not be applicable directly to events prior to 1949, but which contain certain general recognitions considered to be part of customary law. Common article l of the Geneva Conventions addresses the duty of all signatories "to respect and to ensure respect" for the Conventions "in all circumstances." Another common article (*e.g.*, article 146 of the Geneva Civilian Convention) recognizes in pertinent part:

> Each High Contracting Party shall be under the obligation to search for persons alleged to have committed, or to have ordered to be committed, ... grave breaches, and shall bring such persons, regardless of their nationality, before its own courts. It may also, if it prefers, and in accordance with the provisions of its own legislation, hand such persons over for trial to another High Contracting party concerned, provided such High Contracting Party has made out a *prima facie* case.

> Each High Contracting party shall take measures necessary for the suppression of all acts contrary to the provisions of the present Convention other than … grave breaches.…

As Geneva law affirms, there is no exception to the duty to search for those reasonably accused of having committed relevant violations and to initiate prosecution or to extradite. There is, as with customary law, no power in any single state to grant asylum or some other form of immunity with respect to crimes against the international community. There is, as with customary law, no power to avoid such responsibility because of some domestic law or political concern. And, as the Geneva Conventions expressly note, there is no power in any state "to absolve itself" or any other state by agreement or elsewise. As Pictet adds in his commentaries, such enforcement responsibilities under humanitarian law are "absolute." And as the 1956 U.S. Army Field Manual 27-10, *The Law of Land Warfare* [para. 506 b], recognized more generally, the sanctions or "principles" documented in the Geneva Conventions "are declaratory of the obligations of belligerents under customary international law to take measures for the punishment of war crimes committed by *all* persons …" that is, regardless of the nationality of victims, or the place of occurrence (emphasis added). [see also FM 27-10, *supra* at para. 507 a, addressing "universality of jurisdiction" under customary international law.]

Letter dated 24 April 1996 from the President of the International Tribunal for the Prosecution of Persons Responsible for Serious Violations of International Humanitarian Law Committed in the Territory of the Former Yugoslavia since 1991 Addressed to the President of the Security Council
U.N. Doc. S/1996/319 (25 Apr. 1996)

I have the honour to report to the Security Council the refusal of the Federal Republic of Yugoslavia (Serbia and Montenegro) to cooperate with the International Tribunal, as required by resolutions of the Council and the Tribunal's own Statute. The occasion for making this report is the failure of the said Republic to execute arrest warrants against three accused Mile Mrksic, Miroslav Radic and Veselin Sljivancanin — all of whom are on its territory and who are charged with the murder of 260 civilians and other unarmed men following the fall of the city of Vukovar in November 1991. On 3 April 1996, Trial Chamber I of the International Tribunal certified that the failure to effect service of the indictment was due to the refusal of the Federal Republic of Yugoslavia (Serbia and Montenegro) to cooperate with the Tribunal, and entrusted the President of the Tribunal with notifying the Security Council thereof, in accordance with the procedure of Rule 61 (E). Accordingly, I now make this report to the Security Council.

The refusal of the Federal Republic of Yugoslavia (Serbia and Montenegro) to cooperate with the International Tribunal should be seen in its broadest context. The International Tribunal was established by the Security Council in 1993 to respond to the appalling crimes that were taking place before the very eyes of the world in the former Yugoslavia. As the Tribunal was established by virtue of Chapter VII of the Charter of the United Nations, all Member States are under an obligation to assist it, notably by complying with its orders. The cooperation of the States of the former Yugoslavia is particularly imperative: without such cooperation, few accused would ever be delivered to The Hague to stand trial. To this day, however, the Federal Republic of Yugoslavia (Serbia and Montenegro) has not executed a single arrest warrant addressed to it.

In this case, the accused whom the Federal Republic of Yugoslavia (Serbia and Montenegro) has failed to arrest, have, moreover, been commended and promoted by the said Republic for those same deeds which the Prosecutor charges as crimes against humanity, violations of the laws or customs of war and grave breaches of the Geneva Conventions of 1949. In the words of the Prosecutor in his final submission in this case, the said Republic has

> " ... promoted, supported and continued to pay an indicted war criminal [Sljivancanin] and to maintain him as a senior officer in their army, and if [...] reports are correct, they now even have him training officer cadets. Can there be any more flagrant way of showing their disregard and even contempt for their obligations as a Member State of the United Nations, obligations they recently reaffirmed by entering into the Dayton Accords?" (Transcript of the Hearing of 28 March 1996, pp. 45 and 46)

The Trial Chamber endorsed the spirit of this remark when confirming the indictment against the three accused.

As President of the International Tribunal for the Former Yugoslavia, it is my duty to bring non-compliance by the Federal Republic of Yugoslavia (Serbia and Montenegro) with the Tribunal's orders to the attention of the Security Council so that it can decide upon the appropriate response.

(Signed) Antonio CASSESE

President

Paust, *My Lai and Vietnam: Norms, Myths and Leader Responsibility*
57 MIL. L. REV. 99, 118–23 (1972)

The Myth of Political Excuse

There are many evidences of the principle that domestic laws or juridical acts cannot dissipate international criminal responsibility. For example, the Allied Control Council Law No. 10 (31 Jan. 1946) provided in Article II.5 that no statute of limitation, pardon, grant of immunity or amnesty under the Nazi regime would be admitted as a bar to trial or punishment. Recently the United Nations General Assembly stated that no statutory limitation would apply to war crimes, crimes against humanity, or genocide. The Principles of the Nuremberg Charter and Judgment recognized that governmental orders cannot free a person from criminal responsibility (so governmental acts could hardly do the same), and that even though domestic law "does not impose a penalty for an act which constitutes a crime under international law it does not relieve the person who committed the act from responsibility under international law." And in 1919 the Commission on the Responsibility of the Authors of the War and on Enforcement and Penalties took note of the rule that "no trial or sentence by a court of the enemy country shall bar trial and sentence by the tribunal or by a national court belonging to one of the Allied or Associated States." An example of the same reasoning can be found in the French case of *Abetz* where it was held that diplomatic immunity was not relevant to a war crimes prosecution since the legal basis of prosecution rests with offenses against the community of nations and as such any domestic interference through grants of immunity would "subordinate the prosecution to the authorization of the country to which the guilty person belongs."

A local grant of immunity could well be no more in conformity with community expectations than a refusal to prosecute for some other reason. A more serious problem would involve "fake" prosecutions which were designed to result in lesser crime convictions or in an acquittal where it is known that more serious charges could not be proven but the decision is made to prosecute unprovable higher offenses so that the defendant ultimately avoids conviction for the commission of other offenses. Furthermore, a refusal to prosecute can be a violation of the international obligations under the Conventions (1) to bring to trial *all* persons alleged to have committed or ordered to be committed "grave breaches" of the Conventions, (2) to take such measures necessary for the suppression of all acts contrary to the provisions of the Convention other than grave breaches, and (3) to respect and to ensure respect for the Conventions in all circumstances. The violation of such obligations on the part of the United States or North Vietnam would most likely be violations by the state itself, though this subject shall be considered later in connection with individual criminal responsibility for a failure to execute the law and to suppress violations, since individuals may be guilty as well.

Michael P. Scharf, *The Amnesty Exception to the Jurisdiction of the International Criminal Court*
32 CORNELL INT'L L. J. 507, 514–521 (1999)*

Crimes Defined in International Conventions

The prerogative of a state to issue an amnesty for an offense can be circumscribed by treaties to which the state is a party. There are several international conventions that clearly provide for a duty to prosecute the humanitarian or human rights crimes defined therein, including in particular the grave breaches provisions of the 1949 Geneva Conventions, and the Genocide Convention. When these Conventions are applicable, the granting of amnesty to persons responsible for committing the crimes defined therein would constitute a breach of a treaty obligation for which there can be no excuse or exception. It is important to recognize, however, that these Conventions were negotiated in the context of the cold war and by design apply only to a narrow range of situations....

General Human Rights Conventions

General Human Rights Conventions include the International Covenant on Civil and Political Rights, the European Convention for the Protection of Human Rights and Fundamental Freedoms, and the American Convention on Human Rights. [see the Documents Supplement] Although these treaties do not expressly require States to prosecute violators, they do obligate states to "ensure" the rights enumerated therein. There is growing recognition in the jurisprudence of the treaty bodies responsible for monitoring enforcement of these conventions and the writings of respected commentators that the duty to ensure rights implies a duty to hold specific violators accountable.[1]

Yet, a careful examination of the jurisprudence of these bodies suggests that methods of obtaining specific accountability other than criminal prosecutions would meet the requirement of "ensuring rights." This jurisprudence indicates that a state must fulfill five

---

    1. Dianne F. Orentlicher, *Settling Accounts, supra*, 100 YALE L.J. at 2568; Thomas Buergenthal, *To Respect and To Ensure: State Obligations and Permissible Derogations*, in THE INTERNATIONAL BILL OF RIGHTS 77 (L. Henkin, ed. 1981) ("obligation to 'ensure' rights creates affirmative obligations on the state—for example, to discipline its officials"); Yoram Dinstein, *The Right to Life, Physical Integrity, and Liberty*, in THE INTERNATIONAL BILL OF RIGHTS 77 (L. Henkin, ed. 1981) (Parties to the Covenant arguably must exercise due diligence to prevent intentional deprivation of life by individuals, "as well as to apprehend murderers and to prosecute them in order to deter future takings of life").

obligations in confronting gross violations of human rights committed by a previous regime: (1) investigate the identity, fate and whereabouts of victims; (2) investigate the identity of major perpetrators; (3) provide reparation or compensation to victims; (4) take affirmative steps to ensure that human rights abuse does not recur; and (5) punish those guilty of human rights abuse. Punishment can take many non-criminal forms, including imposition of fines, removal from office, reduction of rank, and forfeiture of government or military pensions and/or other assets.

Customary International Law: Crimes Against Humanity

... Unlike Grave Breaches of the Geneva Conventions and the crime of genocide [which expressly require signatories to initiate prosecution of or to extradite those accused of crimes covered therein], there exists no treaty requiring States to prosecute crimes against humanity, which are purely a creature of customary international law. Traditionally, those who committed crimes against humanity were treated like pirates, as *hostis humani generis* (an enemy of all humankind), and any state, including their own, could punish them through its domestic courts. In the absence of a treaty containing the *aut dedere aut judicare* (extradite or prosecute) principle, this so called "universal jurisdiction" is [according to the writer] generally thought to be permissive, not mandatory.[2] Yet, several commentators and human rights groups have ... taken the position that customary international law not only establishes permissive jurisdiction over perpetrators of crimes against humanity, but also requires their prosecution and conversely prohibits the granting of amnesty to such persons.

There are strong jurisprudential reasons for recognizing such a rule. The perpetrator of crimes against humanity incurs criminal responsibility and is subject to punishment as a direct consequence of international law notwithstanding the national laws of any state or states to the contrary. This unique characteristic of crimes under international law makes it questionable whether any state or group of states would be competent to negate this responsibility. Moreover, the notion of granting amnesty for crimes against humanity would be inconsistent with the principles of individual criminal responsibility recognized in the Nuremberg Charter and Judgment. The fundamental purpose of these

---

2. [Editors' note:] Professor Scharf thus argues that there is a right but not a duty to prosecute customary international crimes that lack such treaty-based duties. He also argues that the same right/not duty to prosecute exists with respect to violations of the Geneva Conventions that are not "grave breaches" of the Conventions. Scharf, *The ICC's Jurisdiction over the Nationals of Non-Party States: A Critique of the U.S. Position*, 63 Law & Contemp. Probs. (2000), citing Howard S. Levie, Terrorism in War: The Law of War Crimes 192-93 (1993); B.V.A. Roling, *The Law of War and the National Jurisdiction Since 1945*, 100 Recueil des Cours 325, 342 (1960) (suggesting an explanation "might" be that the Conventions create an obligation to prosecute grave breaches but only a right to prosecute others (citing no authority for such), which others are nonetheless war crimes, yet the "Conventions *demand* ... measures *shall* be taken for their suppression."(emphasis added)); Waldemar A. Solf, Edward R. Cummings, *A Survey of Penal Sanctions under Protocol I to the Geneva Conventions of August 12, 1949*, 9 Case W. Res. J. Int'l L. 205, 217 (1977) (stating other breaches "*may* be breaches ... which are not subject to universal jurisdiction for purposes of the extradition provisions...," (emphasis added) citing no authority, but adding: "Nevertheless, these acts remain serious crimes under customary law."); Theodor Meron, *International Criminalization of Internal Atrocities*, 89 Am. J. Int'l L.554, 569 (1995), which provides no citation in support of the viewpoint: "the Geneva Conventions created the obligation of *aut dedere aut judicare* only with regard to grave breaches...." Concerning crimes against humanity, Professor Meron notes that the U.S. has "emphasized that states have a continuing responsibility to prosecute those who commit crimes against humanity." *Id.* at 569 n.82, citing U.N. Doc. A/AC.244/1/Add.2, para. 23 (1995). Concerning the duty to prosecute or repress other breaches of the Geneva Conventions, see materials that follow and Chapter Eight, Section 2A.

principles is to remove any possibility of immunity for persons responsible for such crimes, from the most junior officer acting under the orders of his superior to the most senior government officials, including the head of state.

… [T]hose who argue that customary international law precludes amnesty for crimes against humanity base their position on non-binding General Assembly Resolutions,[3] hortative declarations of international conferences,[4] and international conventions that are not widely ratified,[5] rather than on any extensive state practice consistent with such a rule.

Commentators often cite the [1967] Declaration on Territorial Asylum as the earliest international recognition of a legal obligation to prosecute perpetrators of crimes against humanity. The Declaration provides that "states shall not grant asylum to any person with respect to whom there are serious reasons for considering that he has committed a … crime against humanity." Yet, according to the historic record of this resolution, "[t]he majority of members stressed that the draft declaration under consideration was not intended to propound legal norms or to change existing rules of international law, but to lay down broad humanitarian and moral principles upon which States might rely in seeking to unify their practices relating to asylum." This evidences that, from the onset, the General Assembly resolutions concerning crimes against humanity were not intended to create any binding duties.

In addition to this contrary legislative history, the trouble with an approach to proving the existence of customary international law that focuses so heavily on words is "that it is grown like a flower in a hot-house and that it is anything but sure that such creatures will survive in the much rougher climate of actual state practice." To the extent any state practice in this area is widespread, it is the practice of granting amnesties or de facto

---

3. *See, e.g., Declaration on Territorial Asylum*, G.A. Res. 2312, 22 U.N. GAOR Supp. (No. 16) at 81, U.N. Doc. A/6716 (1967); *United Nations Resolution on War Criminals*, G.A. Res. 2712, 25 U.N. GAOR Supp. (No. 28) at 78–79, U.N. Doc. A/8028 (1970) (adopted by a vote of 55 in favor to 4 against with 33 abstentions) (Condemns crimes against humanity and "calls upon the States concerned to bring to trial persons guilty of such crimes"); G.A. Res. 2840, 26 U.N. GAOR Supp. (No. 29), at 88, U.N. Doc. A/8429 (1971) (adopted by a vote of 71 in favor to none against with 42 abstentions) (affirming that a State's refusal "to cooperate in the arrest, extradition, trial and punishment" of persons accused or convicted of crimes against humanity is "contrary to the United Nations Charter and to generally recognized norms of international law"); *Principles of International Cooperation in the Detection, Arrest, Extradition, and Punishment of Persons Guilty of War Crimes and Crimes Against Humanity*, G.A. Res. 3074, GAOR Supp. (No. 30) at 79, U.N. Doc. A/9030 (1973) (adopted by a vote of 94 in favor to none against with 29 abstentions) (Crimes against humanity "shall be subject to investigation and the persons against whom there is evidence that they have committed such crimes shall be subject to tracing, arrest, trials and, if found guilty, to punishment"); *Principles on the Effective Prevention and Investigation of Extra-Legal, Arbitrary and Summary Executions*, G.A. Res. 1989/65 (1989) (states shall bring to justice those accused of having participated in extra-legal, arbitrary or summary executions); *Declaration on the Protection of All Persons From Enforced Disappearances*, G.A. Res. 47/133 (1992) (equating disappearances to a crime against humanity and requiring states to try any person suspected of having perpetrated an act of enforced disappearance). It is noteworthy that large numbers of countries abstained during voting on the above listed resolutions, and thereby did not manifest their acceptance of the principles enumerated therein.

4. The final Declaration and Programme of Action of the 1993 World Conference on Human Rights affirms that "[s]tates should abrogate legislation leading to impunity for those responsible for grave violations of human rights such as torture and prosecute such violations, thereby providing a firm basis for the rule of law." World Conference on Human Rights, Declaration and Programme of Action, Vienna, June 1993, U.N. Doc. A/Conf./57/23, second part.

5. Convention on the Non-Applicability of Statutory Limitations to War Crimes and Crimes Against Humanity, … 754 U.N.T.S. 73 [1968] … (ratified by just 39 states). Even if the Convention was more widely ratified, the prohibition on applying a statute of limitations to crimes against humanity is not the equivalent of a duty to prosecute such crimes.

impunity to those who commit crimes against humanity. That the United Nations itself has felt free of legal constraints in endorsing ... amnesty for peace deals in situations involving crimes against humanity confirms that customary international law has not yet crystallized in this area.

Notes and Questions

1. If the 1967 G.A. resolution was not meant to declare legal principles, does it follow that subsequent resolutions also did not do so? What percentage of states voted in favor of the 1973, 1989 and 1992 resolutions? How many states voted to approve the Statute of the ICC at the Rome conference? Does the Statute of the ICC allow immunity? See *id*. art. 27 (1) and (2), in the Documents Supplement. In 2006, the U.N. Security Council emphasized "the responsibility of States to comply with their relevant obligations to end impunity and to prosecute those responsible for war crimes, genocide, crimes against humanity and serious violations of international humanitarian law." U.N. S.C. Res. 1674, para. 8, U.N. Doc. S/RES/1674 (28 April 2006).

2. States such as Argentina and Chile had initially granted forms of amnesty to those involved with the disappearance of individuals (*see also* Chapter Eleven, Section 5). Such grants of amnesty are not binding under international law, nor do they preclude prosecutions or civil claims elsewhere that are based on international law. In fact, Spain has prosecuted persons responsible for torture, deaths and disappearances during Argentina's "dirty war" and Argentina has prosecuted former heads of state and others with respect to such crimes. See Section 2 above; Chapter Eleven. *See also* Sadat, *Exile, Amnesty and International Law*, in Chapter One; Diane F. Orentlicher, *Settling Accounts: The Duty to Prosecute Human Rights Violations of a Prior Regime*, 100 YALE L. J. 2537 (1991).

The Inter-American Court of Human Rights recognized in 2001 that amnesty laws cannot eliminate responsibility "for serious human rights violations such as torture, extrajudicial, summary or arbitrary execution and forced disappearance." Chumbipuma Aguirre, *et al*. v. Peru (Barrios Altos Case), Inter-American Court of Human Rights (March 14, 2001), para. 41. Also in 2001, the Inter-American Commission on Human Rights ruled that Chile's amnesty law preventing criminal investigation and prosecution of those involved in disappearance, torture, and extrajudicial killing impermissibly interfered with the human right of claimants to obtain reparations through civil courts. See IACHR Report No. 61/01, Case No. 11.771(Catalán Lincoleo v. Chile), Inter-American Commission on Human Rights, Apr. 16, 2001. For a full discussion, see Chapter One, Section 2.

3. Is the practice of granting amnesties "widespread"? In how many countries? *See also* Professor Scharf's commentary in Chapter One, Section 3 (addressing Argentina, Cambodia, Chile, El Salvador, Guatemala, Haiti, South Africa, Uruguay); Scharf, *The Letter of the Law: The Scope of the International Legal Obligations to Prosecute Human Rights Crimes*, 59 LAW & CONTEMP. PROBS. 41, 57–58 (1996).

There been efforts to abandon or limit impunity in Argentina, Cambodia, and Chile? *See, e.g.*, Kevin Whitelaw, *A Mission to Cambodia*, U.S. NEWS & WORLD RPT., May 8, 2000, at 33 (U.S. and U.N. officials demand international tribunal to address crimes in Cambodia); John Donnelly, *UN, Cambodia Near Deal on Khmer Rouge, Kerry Mediates Talks on Genocide Trials*, THE BOSTON GLOBE, April 30, 2000, at A4; *Cement for Society*, THE ECONOMIST, May 6, 2000 ("ex-officers face fresh charges of stealing babies from 'dirty war' prisoners who were then murdered"); Laura Oren, *Righting Child Custody Wrongs: The Children of the "Disappeared" in Argentina*, 14 HARV. H.R. J. 123 (2001), documenting the following: Jack Epstein, *Legacies of Terror*, Hous. Chron., May 10, 1998, at A1 (federal Congress enacts a symbolic repeal of the amnesty laws); several Agence France Presse stories from Nov. 1998 and Jan. and May 1999 (arrests of several officials from the dictatorship era on charges relating to child stealings). Prosecutions of former heads of state and other officials have occurred in Argentina, Cambodia, and Chile. See Paust, *Genocide in Rwanda, State Responsibility to Prosecute or Extradite, and Nonimmunity for Heads of State and Other Public Officials*, 34 Hous. J. Int'l L. 57, 75–80 (2011), extract appearing in Section 1. A. 2 in this Chapter.

4. Is domestic amnesty regarding an international crime a "ratification" of the international crime? Does it involve a "harboring" or "tolerating" of the alleged international criminal or provision of a "safe haven" for such a criminal? Consider also the case against Libya in Note 11 *infra*. Is it a form of state "complicity"? Consider *Henfield's Case* in Note 9 *infra*. What else would you like to know?

In 2003, the United Nations and the United States persuaded Nigeria to give asylum to then Liberian President Charles Taylor, who had been indicted for crimes against humanity by the Special Court for Sierra Leon (see Chapter Six). At the time, forces opposed to Taylor had taken over most of the country and were on the verge of attacking the capital city, Monrovia. Tens of thousands of civilian casualties were forecast. This set the stage of insertion of a U.N. peacekeeping mission that stabilized the country and set it on a possible path toward peace and democracy. Did the exile-asylum deal violate international law? Did it render Nigeria an accomplice to crimes? For an argument that it did not, *see, e.g.*, Michael Scharf, *From the eXile Files: An Essay on Trading Justice for Peace*, 63 Wash. & Lee L. Rev. 339 (2006). The agreement was short-lived. At the request of the newly elected President of Liberia in 2006, Taylor was handed over to the Special Court for Sierra Leone and was later transferred to the Hague for trial.

5. *See also* 1 Hyde, International Law § 11A. at 33–34 (2 ed. 1945) ("'regardless of the character of the actors … [there is a] duty to prevent or prosecute'"). Concerning the duty to insure prosecution and to prevent impunity, *see* Convention on the Nonapplicability of Statutory Limitations to War Crimes and Crimes Against Humanity, 754 U.N.T.S. 73 (26 Nov. 1968); European Convention on the Nonapplicability and Statutory Limitations to Crimes Against Humanity and War Crimes, E.T.S. No. 82 (25 Jan. 1974), *reprinted in* 13 I.L.M. 540 (1974); Article 29 of the Statute of the ICC, in the Documents Supplement. *See also* M Cherif Bassiouni & Edward M. Wise, Aut Dedere Aut Judicare 22–26, 51–53 (1995); M. Cherif Bassiouni, International Extradition: United States Law and Practice 5–11 (3 ed. 1997); Christine Van den Wyngaert, *War Crimes, Crimes Against Humanity, and Statutory Limitations*, in 3 International Criminal Law: Enforcement 8 (M. Cherif Bassiouni ed. 1987); Res. No. 7, Int'l Law Ass'n, Report of the Sixty-First Conference 7 (1985) ("States must try or extradite (*aut judicare aut dedere*) persons accused of acts of international terrorism. No state may refuse to try or extradite a person accused of an act of terrorism, war crime…, or a crime against humanity.…"); Lee A. Steven, *Genocide and the Duty to Extradite or Prosecute: Why the United States is in Breach of Its International Obligations*, 39 Va. J. Int'l L.425 (1999); Opinion of the Magistrate in *Ex parte* Pinochet, Belgian Tribunal of First Instance (8 Nov. 1998) ("We find that, before being codified in a treaty or statue, the prohibition of crimes against humanity was part of customary international law and of international *jus cogens*, and this norm imposes itself imperatively and *erga omnes* on our domestic legal order.… The general principle of international law *aut dedere aut judicare* … imports the necessity of combating impunity of crimes under international law and the responsibility of state authorities to ensure punishment of such crimes irrespective of the

place of commission."), *reprinted in* 93 Am. J. Int'l L.700, 702 (1999); *see also* U.N. G.A. Res. 96, U.N. Doc. A/64, at 189 (1946) (recognizing prior to creation of the treaty that genocide is a crime under international law and a duty exists to prosecute); U.N. S.C. Res. 1296, S/RES/1296, para. 17 (19 April 2000) (U.N. S.C. "reaffirms its condemnation of all incitements to violence against civilians in situations of armed conflict, further reaffirms the need to bring to justice individuals who incite or otherwise cause such violence…."); U.N. G.A. Res. 95, U.N. Doc. A/64, at 188 (1946); U.N. G.A. Res. 3, U.N. Doc. A/64, at 9 (1946); Jordan J. Paust, Albert P. Blaustein, *War Crimes Jurisdiction and Due Process: The Bangladesh Experience*, 11 Vand. J. Trans. L. 1, 20–27 (1978).

In 1625, Hugo Grotius explained:

> The state … ought to do one of two things…. it should either punish the guilty person as he deserves, or it should entrust him to the discretion of the party making the appeal. This latter course is rendition…. [A] people or king is not absolutely bound to surrender a culprit, but … either to surrender or to punish him.

Hugo Grotius, De Jure Belli ac Pacis bk. II, ch. XXI, in The Classics of International Law 526–28 (James Brown Scott ed., Francis W. Kelsy trans. 1925).

Also consider Resolution of 1781 of the Continental Congress, in Chapter Three, Section 1; *United States v. Klintock*, 18 U.S. (5 Wheat.) 144, 147–48 (1820) (piracy "is an offense against all. It is punishable in the Courts of all … [our courts] are authorized and bound to punish"); *Henfield's Case*, Charge of Justice Wilson, in Chapter Four, Section 2, *citing* E. de Vattel, The Law of Nations (1758) and W. Blackstone, Commentaries on the Laws of England (1765); *Ex parte dos Santos*, 7 F. Cas. 949, 953 (C.C.D. Va. 1835) (No. 4,016) (Vattel notes "duty of the sovereign to prevent his subjects from doing mischief to other states, and the consequent duty to punish or surrender."); *Republica v. De Longchamps*, 1 U.S. 111, 117 (Phila. 1784) ("it is now the interest as well as duty of the government, to animadvert upon … conduct [in violation of the law of nations] with becoming severity…."); 1 Op. Att'y Gen. 68, 69 (1797) ("violation of territorial rights … [is] an offence against the law of nations … [and] it is the interest as well as the duty of every government to punish with becoming severity all the individuals … who commit this offence."); Kent's Commentary on International Law 3, 427 (1866); W. Winthrop, Military Law and Precedents 778, 796 (2 ed. 1920) (it is a general obligation "[t]hat each belligerent shall duly punish all persons within his lines who may be guilty of violations of the laws of war…. [adding:]

> "In the event of violations of any of the laws of war…, the offenders, as a matter of both justice and policy, should be brought to punishment if they can be reached. As it is expressed in the Manual of the Institute [Project, Brussels Conference, pt. III, Penal Sanction 1874],— 'when infractions of the foregoing rules take place, the guilty persons should be punished, after trial, by the belligerent within whose power they are.' Offenders of this class have, with us, been brought to trial by Military Commission, and punished with death or imprisonment.").

Previous to Winthrop's recognition, the 1863 Lieber Code General Orders No. 100, Instructions for the Government of Armies of the United States in the Field (April 24, 1863), had recognized both individual responsibility and the need for criminal sanctions for infractions of the laws of war. *See, e.g., id.* arts. 11, 13, 37, 44, 59, 71 (in Chapter Eight, Section 2 B). Consider in particular:

Article 59

> A prisoner of war remains answerable for his crimes committed against the captor's army or people, committed before he was captured, and for which he has not been punished by his own authorities.

Article 71

> Whoever intentionally inflicts additional wounds on an enemy already wholly disabled, or kills such an enemy, or who orders or encourages soldiers to do so, shall suffer death, if duly convicted, whether he belongs to the Army of the United States, or is an enemy captured after having committed his misdeed.

6. Recall common article 1 of the 1949 Geneva Conventions: "The High Contracting Parties undertake to respect and to ensure respect for the present Convention in all circumstances." Are signatories and their nationals bound by Geneva law no matter what uniform their nationals wear or command structure they operate under, *e.g.,* even if they serve as advisers to allies or are part of a U.N. peacemaking force? Did U.S. and other troops (from Canada and some 17 other countries) in Korea cease to be bound by Geneva law merely because they operated under a U.N. flag? *See also* U.S. FM 27-10, THE LAW OF LAND WARFARE 7, para. 8a (1956); S. Lepper, *The Legal Status of Military Personnel in United Nations Peace Operations: One Delegate's Analysis,* 18 HOUS. J. INT'L L. 359, 398–407 (1996) (also addressing attacks on and protections for those serving on a U.N. mission); Chapter Six, Section 4. Such general and enveloping duties as those expressed and implied in common article 1 reach the nationals of signatories to treaties. *See generally* Paust, *The Other Side of Right: Private Duties Under Human Rights Law,* 5 HARV. H.R.J. 51, 51–2, 56–8 (1992), and references cited. Of course, U.N. entities are bound directly under the U.N. Charter, arts. 1(3) and 55(c) (*see also id.* art. 24(2)), to respect and to ensure respect for relevant human rights. See the Documents Supplement.

The power of NATO forces to comply with and enforce international law in Bosnia-Herzegovina is enhanced by Security Council competencies under Chapter VII of the U.N. Charter that have been allocated to NATO forces and by related Security Council resolutions calling for the enforcement of Geneva law in Bosnia-Herzegovina. There are express powers of arrest or detention, and others can be implied. The resolution setting up the International Criminal Tribunal (see Chapter Six, Section 9) expressly noted the Security Council's determination "to put an end to such crimes and to take effective measures to bring to justice the persons who are responsible...." Article 29 of the Statute of the Tribunal (in Chapter Six, Section 9), resting on Security Council competencies under Articles 25, 39 and 41 (and perhaps 42–43 and 48–49) of the U.N. Charter, requires that "States shall cooperate with the International Tribunal in the investigation and prosecution of persons accused ..." and, most importantly, that "States shall comply without undue delay with any request for assistance or an order issued by a Trial Chamber, including, but not limited to: the identification and location of persons ... the arrest or detention of persons ... [and] the surrender or the transfer of the accused to the International Tribunal." Decisions in the *Tadic* case (see Chapter Six, Section 9) generally affirm such powers and responsibilities. Under Article 103 of the U.N. Charter, such obligations preempt any unavoidably inconsistent competencies or obligations under other international agreements (such as the Dayton peace agreement). Do such powers pertain with respect to NATO forces in Kosovo since 1999? Will they apply under the Statute of the ICC? *See* the Documents Supplement.

Pictet noted that "repression of grave breaches [of the Geneva Conventions] was to be universal ... [with those reasonably accused] sought for in all countries," adding: "the obligation to prosecute and punish ... [is] absolute." IV COMMENTARY at 587, 590, 597, 602. With respect to common article 1 of the Geneva Conventions, Pictet adds that signatories "should do everything in their power to ensure that the humanitarian principles underlying the Conventions are applied universally." *Id.* at 16. Pictet also noted that other breaches of the Conventions are war crimes. See *id.* at 583 ("The Geneva Conventions form part of what are generally called the laws and customs of war, violations of which are ...'war crimes.'"), 594 (signatories "must also suppress all other acts contrary to the provisions of this Convention ... repression of breaches other than the grave breaches listed ... all breaches of the Convention should be repressed ... should institute judicial or disciplinary punishment for breaches of the Convention."), 602; *id.* vol. III, at 367–68 ("the 1929 Convention called for the punishment of *all* acts contrary to the provisions of the Convention ..." "*all* breaches of the present Convention should be repressed ... [national legislation] must include a general clause ... providing for the punishment of other breaches of the Convention.").

How might states more generally ensure respect for the Conventions?

7. One requirement is quite specific. Article 144 of the Geneva Civilian Convention, for example, recognizes:

> The High Contracting Parties undertake, in time of peace as in time of war to disseminate the text of the present Convention as widely as possible in their respective countries, and in particular, to include the study thereof in their programmes of military and, if possible, civil instruction, so that the principles thereof may become known to the entire population.
>
> Any civilian, military, police or other authorities, who in time of war assume responsibilities in respect of protected persons, must possess the text of the Convention and be specially instructed as to its provisions.

How extensive is civilian instruction concerning the Geneva Conventions? Do you think Canada and the United States are fully implementing nearly universal obligations under the Geneva Conventions? How might the electronic media be more effectively used? *See also* Jean-Jacques Surbeck, *Dissemination of International Humanitarian Law*, 33 Am. U.L. Rev. 125 (1983); Harry Almond, *The Teaching and Dissemination of the Geneva Conventions and International Humanitarian Law in the United States*, 31 Am. U.L. Rev. 981 (1982); Jordan J. Paust, *An International Structure for Implementation of the 1949 Geneva Conventions: Needs and Function Analysis*, 1 Yale Stud. in World Pub. Ord. 148 (1974).

8. Many international criminal law instruments also contain a requirement that state signatories enact any legislation needed to effectively prosecute crimes covered in the instrument. *See, e.g.,* Convention of the Prevention and Punishment of the Crime of Genocide, art. V; Geneva Civilian Convention, art. 146; International Convention Against the Taking of Hostages, art. 2; Convention Against Torture and Other Cruel, Inhuman or Degrading Treatment or Punishment, arts. 2(1) and 4–each in the Documents Supplement. We will consider this type of requirement also in Chapter Four and Chapter Five, Section 1 (in connection with dual criminality and the *Pinochet* case).

9. If a state did not initiate prosecution of one reasonably accused of international crime, it was recognized that the state could become an "accomplice" to illegality and be subject to various international sanctions. *See, e.g., Henfield's Case* and 1 Op. Att'y Gen. 68, 69 (1797) ("duty of every government to punish ... all the individuals ... who commit this offence"), in Chapter Four. *See also* Chapter Twelve. Today, state responsibility can also be fulfilled by extradition of the accused to another state or rendition to an international tribunal. See Chapter Six, Sections 9 & 10.

10. Concerning the denial of immunity or amnesty after an armed conflict, see also *infra* Chapter Four, Section 7 D (treaty re: South Africa and *Ex parte Mudd*); Chapter Seven, Section 2 B (World War I peace treaties); and materials throughout the book; Michael

Scharf, *Swapping Amnesty for Peace: Was there a Duty to Prosecute International Crimes in Haiti?*, 31 Tex. Int'l L.J. 1 (1996), and the many references cited; Paust, correspondence, 88 Am. J. Int'l L. 715 (1994); *cf.* Anthony D'Amato, *Peace and Accountability in Bosnia*, 88 Am. J. Int'l L. 500 (1994); *id.* at 94–95 (1995). Consider also Articles 1, 146, 148 of the 1949 Geneva Convention Relative to the Protection of Civilian Persons in Time of War, 75 U.N.T.S. 287; J. Pictet, IV Commentary at 587, 589–94, 597, 602–03; Universal Declaration of Human Rights, art. 14(2) (no right to seek asylum re: "prosecutions genuinely arising from non-political crimes or from acts contrary to the purposes and principles of the United Nations").

Professor Paust argues that "the quest for measured justice and opposition to amnesty is actually a reaffirmation of life, quality, sensitivity, and all that is opposed to the evil of despicable criminality. Listen to Beethoven's Eroica[6] and hear the grandeur of that reaffirmation and of a human opposition. Amnesty is misnamed, one more oppression, one less measure of human dignity."

Professor Sadat raises the question whether "amnesty deals" negotiated by large and powerful states are either legally or morally valid. *See* Leila Nadya Sadat, *Exile, Amnesty and International Law*, 81 Notre Dame L. Rev. 955 (2006), extract in Chapoter One.

11. If genocide, other crimes against humanity, and war crimes are criminal activities rather than politics by other means, why should perpetrators of such core international crimes be treated differently than those who commit other international crimes such as terrorism? When Usama bin Laden offered to cease his attacks on U.S. targets if his demands were met (and presumably his amnesty assured), the United States rejected the offer out of hand, arguing that no deals can be made with terrorists. If the U.S. stance is correct, why should governments permit or even encourage such agreements with alleged war criminals such a former Liberian President Charles Taylor (see Chapter Six, Section 8) or former Iraqi President Saddam Hussein (whom the U.S. once suggested should leave Iraq in order to save his country from military invasion) (see also Chapter Six, Section 7)? In late June, 2006, Saddam Hussein suggested that he could help to restore peace in Iraq. Should he be set free?

12. Note that the obligation of states to initiate prosecution or to extradite is in the alternative. Recall also Chapter One, Section 1. The question whether extradition should have priority over local prosecution appeared to be a central issue in the *Lockerbie* case before the International Court of Justice. Provisional measures were denied on April 14, 1992. In denying provisional measures, the Court issued two sets of opinions: one in the proceedings against the United Kingdom, the other in the proceedings against the United States.

> "The two men accused of blowing up Flight 103 are alleged to have acted as agents of the Libyan government. On November 14, 1991, they were simultaneously charged with criminal offenses both in the United Kingdom and the United States. Shortly thereafter, Libya started its own judicial investigation. The Libyan examining magistrate ordered the two suspects to be taken into custody, and asked the United Kingdom and United States to assist his investigation. On November 21, 1991, the United Kingdom and the United States issued a joint demand that Libya surrender the suspects for trial, allow access to other witnesses and evidence, accept responsibility for their actions, and pay compensation...."On

---

6. Concerning Beethoven's defiance of Napoleon, *see, e.g.,* J. Paust, International Law as Law of the United States 249 n.111 (2 ed. 2003).

January 17, 1992, Libya requested arbitration with the United Kingdom and the United States under article 14(1) of the Montreal Convention. Article 14(1) provides for submitting disputes involving the "application or interpretation" of the convention to arbitration; and, if the parties cannot agree about organizing arbitration, for referral of the dispute to the International Court of Justice. However, on January 21, 1992, the Security Council unanimously adopted Resolution 731 (1992), urging Libya "to provide a full and effective response" to the requests addressed to it. Then, on March 3, 1992, Libya instituted proceedings against the United Kingdom and the United States in the International Court of justice, asking for a declaration that Libya was in full compliance with its obligations under the Montreal Convention and that the United Kingdom and the United States had breached theirs by trying to coerce Libya into surrendering suspects whom it was entitled to try itself. Libya also sought provisional measures to prevent the respondents from taking further action to force Libya to hand over the suspects. The Court held hearings on the request for provisional measures on March 26–28, 1992.

"On March 31, 1992, before the Court could issue a decision on provisional measures, the Security Council adopted Resolution 748 (1992). This resolution characterized Libya's failure to respond to the requests addressed to it as a threat to international peace and security, and imposed sanctions on Libya, to remain in place until the Council determines that Libya has complied with those requests and with the demand that it renounce terrorism...."This argument takes it for granted that, under article 7 of the Montreal Convention, no special priority attaches to extradition. The requested state is perfectly free to reject a demand for extradition. On April 14, 1992, the ICJ, by a vote of 11–5, declined to indicate provisional measures. Question of Interpretation and Application of the 1971 Montreal Convention Arising from Aerial Incident at Lockerbie (Libya v. U.K.; Libya v. U.S.) 1992 I.C.J. 3, 1154 (Order of 14 Apr.). The five judges who dissented from the order denying provisional measures all agreed that, under the Montreal Convention, Libya was entitled to opt for prosecution instead of extradition. So did the four judges in the majority who addressed the question in a joint declaration.

"Libya, of course, is not merely the state where the alleged offenders have been located; it is also the state of which they are nationals. It could be regarded as having a specific jurisdictional interest of its own, on a par with that of the United kingdom or the United States. Moreover, its domestic law bars the extradition of nationals. In that respect, the decision to refuse extradition was not, at least on the surface, entirely a matter of free choice. Therefore, the case is not one in which a state whose jurisdiction is predicated solely on custody of an offender has claimed that it is completely free to choose whether to extradite or prosecute. The prevalent opinion among the judges who spoke to this issue seems to be, however, that none of this makes a difference: the Montreal Convention would not prohibit such a state from refusing extradition, so long as it took steps to submit the case to its competent authorities for the purpose of prosecution...."Judge Weeramantry observes that "Libya relies on the rule of customary international law, *aut dedere aut judicare*, as the governing principle which entitles it to try its own citizens, in the absence of an extradition treaty. He concludes that the Montreal Convention:

does not interfere with the principle of customary international law *aut dedere aut judicare*. Each Contracting State is however placed under a strict obligation, where it does not extradite an alleged offender, to submit the case to the competent authorities for prosecution (Art. 7). This principle *aut dedere aut judicare* is an important facet of a State's sovereignty over its nationals and the well-established nature of this principle in customary international law is evident from the following description: "The widespread use of the formula 'prosecute or extradite' either specifically stated, explicitly stated in a duty to extradite, or implicit in the duty to prosecute or criminalize, and the number of signatories to those numerous conventions, attests to the existing general *jus cogens* principle. (M. CHERIF BASSIOUNI, INTERNATIONAL EXTRADITION: UNITED STATES LAW AND PRACTICE, 1987, p. 22.)."

Excerpts from M. CHERIF BASSIOUNI & EDWARD M. WISE, AUT DEDERE AUT JUDICARE: THE DUTY TO PROSECUTE OR EXTRADITE IN INTERNATIONAL LAW 58–64 (1995). *See* Case Concerning Questions of Interpretation and Application of the 1971 Montreal Convention Arising from the Aerial incident at Lockerbie (Libyan Arab Jamahiriya v. United Kingdom), Provisional Measures, Order of 14 April 1991, [1991] I.C.J. 3; Case Concerning Questions of Interpretation and Application of the 1971 Montreal Convention Arising from the Aerial incident at Lockerbie (Libyan Arab Jamahiriya v. United States of America), Provisional Measures, Order of 14 April 1992, [1992] I.C.J. 114. The two sets of opinions are substantially identical.

In 1998, a special ad hoc Scottish Court in the Netherlands was set up to try two Libyan nationals accused of criminal involvement in the Lockerbie aircraft bombing. *See, e.g.,* 93 AM. J. INT'L L. 161 (1999); 38 I.L.M. 942 (1999). They were rendered to the tribunal and the trial began on May 3, 2000 and one person was convicted, later released from a Scottish prison and died in Libya.

13. Do you suspect that there are any violations of "state responsibility" to seek out and initiate prosecution of or extradite those reasonably accused of having committed war crimes evident in the following:

Deborah Scroggins, The U.N. War Crimes Files: A Question of Access

The InterDependent, Oct./Nov. 1987, at 1, 6:

For nearly 40 years the contents of the 36,800 files of the United Nations War Crimes Commission (UNWCC) have been shrouded in mystery, and it now appears that recent efforts to resolve that mystery will not see results for another month, and possibly longer. The files, compiled by the 17-nation Commission from 1944 to 1948 on alleged war criminals, suspects, and witnesses, gained prominent public attention in March of 1986, when it was disclosed that they contained information about the World War II activities of former U.N. Secretary-General Kurt Waldheim, at that time a presidential candidate in Austria.

Since then an often emotional debate has raged over whether the Commission's files—their use now restricted to U.N. member governments, and only on a confidential basis—should be made available to responsible groups and individuals, such as historians, journalists, and other researchers. Despite a much-heralded meeting of the Commission's member states called by Secretary-General Javier Perez de Cuellar for September 22 to 24, no decision has been taken on relaxing the stringent rules currently governing access to the files. And despite news reports that a majority of the original members had moved in recent months to support the opening of the files to scholarly research, representatives at the meeting returned home, without comment, for "consultations" with their governments until resumption of the session on October 14.

The struggle over access to the files first began when researchers at the World Jewish Congress (WJC) noticed a cross-reference number for the UNWCC beside Kurt Waldheim's name on the U.S. Army "Final Consolidated Wanted List." This list, which includes the names of and charges against all those on the UNWCC master list, had recently been declassified under the U.S. Freedom of Information Act. It revealed that one of the files accused Waldheim of "murder" and of "the putting to death of hostages" during his wartime service as a German intelligence officer stationed in Yugoslavia.

U.N. officials reacted swiftly and affirmatively to requests from the Austrian, Israeli, and U.S. governments for copies of Waldheim's file. But since then the Secretary-General has steadfastly resisted pressure from Israel, private Jewish groups, and historians to open any of the files to private citizens on his own authority, maintaining that the question of access is a matter of the 17 nations of the original Commission to decide.

The United Nations War Crimes Commission — composed of Australia, Belgium, China, Czechoslovakia, Denmark, France, Greece, India, Luxembourg, the Netherlands, New Zealand, Norway, Poland, South Africa, the U.K., the U.S., and Yugoslavia — was established in 1944 to help U.N. members track down war criminals. Although many of its records have long been open to scholars, those concerning individual cases have remained sealed since 1948, when the Commission concluded its work and they were handed over to the newly formed Secretariat. Each file contains the formal charges, supporting data, and a description of the evidence submitted by member governments to the UNWCC about an alleged war criminal. Once a government filed charges, the Commission sought to determine whether the evidence warranted placing the person's name on an international master list of suspected war criminals that it circulated during the four years it sat in London. The UNWCC master lists were then incorporated into national lists of wanted persons, such as the U.S. Army's Final Consolidated Wanted List.

Shortly after the Waldheim charges were exposed, Israel asked for blanket access to the Commission's files. U.N. officials explained the rules: They could only release copies of specifically requested individual files, and even these must be kept secret. Israel then ordered some 2,400 files selected at random from the UNWCC master list. These were turned over to Yad Vashem, the Holocaust memorial center in Jerusalem. Pronouncing the files "a treasure trove of new information about the Nazis," experts at Yad Vashem concluded that they "shed important new light on the extent of information that reached the West about the Holocaust before the war's end," on the personnel and organization of the Nazi extermination machine, and on the particular fate of millions who disappeared in the Holocaust. Israeli Ambassador to the U.N. Benjamin Netanyahu, citing the historical significance of Yad Vashem's findings and the inability of most governments to undertake the task of studying so massive a collection of files, requested in May 1986 and again one year later that the U.N. open the files. "The opening of the Archives is at heart not a matter of procedure," Netanyahu argued. "It is, rather, a supreme moral and historical imperative."

Nevertheless, with the exception of Australia, all the original members of the UNWCC, including the United States, continued to oppose the opening of the files, claiming that they contain hearsay and unproved allegations that could damage the reputations of innocent people. In a letter to Netanyahu, the Secretary-General asserted that the files must be handled on "the same basis of confidentiality as any other material being used in a criminal investigation. This derives from the fact that the material in the restricted records has not been submitted to judicial process or otherwise subjected to legal review." To this the Israelis respond that, first, the files have been subject to legal review—by the UNWCC itself. Second, since the Commission's master list is already publicly available in the U.S., confidentiality no longer applies. And, as Netanyahu has said, "Those who claim their innocence ought to be interested in clearing themselves with a full and open investigation."

One clue to the reluctance of Commission members to open the files may be found in the ongoing investigation of the Waldheim case. The first question many observers asked when Waldheim's background came to light was: How could members of the Security Council—all of which, with the possible exception of the Soviet Union, possessed a copy of the UNWCC master list—have been unaware of his activities during the war when they nominated him for Secretary-General? To this query, all governments involved, including the United States, responded that it had never occurred to them to investigate the background of Waldheim, at that time a distinguished Austrian diplomat.

New evidence, however, suggests that the U.S. government, at least, knew a great deal more about Waldheim than it admitted knowing when he was elected to the U.N. post. In 1980, Representative Stephen Solarz of New York wrote to the CIA to investigate charges about Waldheim's Nazi past that had been leveled against him in *The New Republic* that year. In its reply the CIA denied any knowledge of Waldheim's wartime career after 1941. But when the World Jewish Congress requested additional documentation this September under the Freedom of Information Act, the CIA acknowledged that it does possess a report on Waldheim by the Office of Strategic Services (OSS—the CIA's wartime predecessor) dated April 26, 1945. It now seems that Waldheim, who until last year denied that he had ever even served in Yugoslavia, turned himself in to American intelligence in Yugoslavia once the war was over. The debriefing he may have received about his intelligence work in what was to become a major battlefield of the cold war may explain why, as has been reported by *The New York Times*, the OSS gave Waldheim the clearance that enabled him to join the Austrian Foreign Service in occupied Austria.

Less clear are the reasons for the behavior of Israel, which may have been more aware of the significance of the UNWCC files than it was willing to admit in the past. Prior to the Waldheim affair, the U.N. had publicly released only three files from the War Crimes archives: on Adolf Eichmann, Joseph Mengele, and Klaus Barbie. Eichmann's file was released to Israel, at its specific request, in preparation for his trial in 1960, suggesting that the Israelis knew enough about the files to make use of them at the time. Yet, in 1980 when a professor at the City University of New York attempted to enlist the help of officials at the Israeli Mission to gain access to the files for a book on Italian war crimes, he was met with a stone wall. Michael Palumbo reveals that, at first, Israel's delegate, Shabtai Rosenne, claimed that the files were already open but that, when he saw that Palumbo knew they were not, he listed various obstacles to opening them, including the U.S. State Department and Waldheim himself. Later, when Palumbo contacted other war crimes experts and held a press conference, reported in *The New York Times*, about the need to open the files, Rosenne responded by calling Palumbo "a trouble-maker."

Palumbo, who is now writing a book about the Waldheim case scheduled to be published in the United Kingdom next June, is convinced that governments and the United Nations deliberately prevented his, and other, investigations because they knew that the files would yield embarrassing information about their postwar machinations. The Barbie trial revealed that Western intelligence services shielded Nazis who could provide them with useful information at the onset of the cold war. It is possible that the American and British governments may have encouraged the first U.N. Secretary-General, Trygve Lie, to close the files to conceal such cases—Waldheim's among then. On the other hand, Palumbo, who claims to have examined Waldheim's file and others, believes that many of them may have been invented by governments with the intent of blackmailing their cold war opponents. "I was the first person to call for the opening of the U.N. war crimes archives," says Palumbo, "but now that I have had a chance to look at some of them, I think they should remain closed. Perhaps hundreds of them were prepared by governments for the purposes of blackmail, including the one prepared by the Yugoslav government against Waldheim." Palumbo thinks that the original members of the UNWCC decided to close the Commission and the files when they realized that it was turning into an unreliable exercise in cold war public relations.

"We think these are all legitimate questions," says Steinberg of the World Jewish Congress. "That's why we want the files opened, so that historians and journalists can examine the entire record of the most dreadful period in human history in the hope of teaching us something." The Board of Governors of the United Nations Association expressed similar interest in "expanding access" to the files in a July 27 letter to the Secretary-General from UNA Board Chairman Orville Freeman.

The suspense may soon be over for Americans if the resumed session of the Commission's former members chooses to adopt a proposal by the U.S. whereby each government would establish its own criteria for citizen access to the files. According to State Department spokesmen, virtually any U.S. citizen would be able to gain access under the proposed rules. As the September 22 meeting began, only France, Poland, and India continued to maintain their public opposition to opening the archives. But since the meeting's close, a veil of silence has descended over the proceedings, and the U.S. and other Missions have refused to confirm or deny rumors that they are reconsidering their positions. In such an atmosphere of mystery, the one thing that seems certain is that the issue will not quickly fade away.

13. The InterDependent reported later:

> "After considerable debate," access will be given to individuals engaged in "bona fide" research ..."According to the new guidelines, governments themselves will now have blanket access to these files, and individual governments will establish the criteria by which their own citizens and residents may gain access to them. Approved applications will be transmitted to the Secretary-General by the country's permanent representative or observer. Applicants must also declare that (a) any published material based upon the file's contents will carry a statement to the effect that such information may be unsubstantiated and may not have been submitted to judicial review; (b) they accept responsibility for any claim which may result from their use of the files; and (c) they agree to hold harmless both the United Nations and the government that transmitted the application."

1980 Digest of United States Practice in International Law
263–64

Visa Ineligibility — Nazi Persecutions

On October 30, 1978, President Jimmy Carter signed Public Law 95-549, 92 Stat. 2065. section 101 of which amended section 212 (a) of the Immigration and Nationality Act of 1952 (8 U.S.C. 1182(a)) by making ineligible for visas, and excludable from admission into the United States, any alien who, between March 23, 1933, and May 8, 1945, had, under the direction of, or in association with, the Nazi government in Germany, or any government in any area occupied by its military forces, or any government established with its assistance of cooperation, or any government, which was its ally, ordered, incited, assisted, or otherwise participated in the persecution of any person because of race, religion, national origin, or political opinion. Section 102 of Public Law 95-549 precluded such aliens from being temporarily admitted as nonimmigrants in the discretion of the Attorney General (under section 212(d)(3) of the Immigration and Nationality Act (8 U.S.C. 1182(d)(3). Section 103 of Public Law 95-549 added such aliens to the general classes of deportable aliens under section 241(a) of the Immigration and Nationality Act (8 U.S.C. 1252(a)). Section 104 excluded such aliens from the provisions of section 243(h) of the Immigration and Nationality Act (8 U.S.C. 1253(h)), which authorizes the Attorney General to withhold deportation of any alien to any country in which in his opinion the alien would be subject to persecution on account of race, religion, or political opinion, for such period of time as the Attorney General deems necessary for that reason. Section 105 included such aliens within the classes of deportable aliens under deportation proceedings, as to whom section 244(e) of the Immigration and Nationality Act (8 U.S.C. 1254(e)) prohibits the Attorney General from granting voluntary departure in lieu of deportation.

Questions

1. In April, 2005, a federal court revoked the U.S. citizenship of John Hansl, 80, a former Nazi SS member and concentration camp guard for failing to revealing his prior conduct. DOJ stated that more than seventy people had be stripped of their U.S. citizenship since the Office of Special Investigations began its work in 1979.

2. Do U.S. efforts to denaturalize and deport, and in a few cases extradite, alleged Nazi war criminals meet U.S. responsibilities under international law to initiate prosecution of or to extradite all persons reasonably accused of having committed war crimes? See Paust, *Universality and the Responsibility to Enforce International Criminal Law: No U.S. Sanctuary for Alleged Nazi War Criminals,* 11 Hous. J. Int'l L. 337 (1989). The United States has never prosecuted alleged Nazi war criminals in its federal courts. Why has the United States refused?

3. Concerning Australian attempts and failures, *see, e.g.,* Graham T. Blewitt, *The Necessity for Enforcement of International Humanitarian Law,* 89 Proc., Am. Soc. Int'l L. 298, 299 (1995). Why has Australia refused?

4. What alternatives exist? See Chapters Four, Section 6; Five, Section 1; and Six, Section 8. Is it likely that states such as the United States and Australia will render persons accused of genocide, crimes against humanity, or war crimes to the ICC if such states ratify the "Rome" Statute? Can those accused of international crimes committed during World War II, the Korean War, or the Gulf War in the 1990s be prosecuted before the ICC? See Article 11 of the Statute, in the Documents Supplement.

Chapter 3

State Competencies

Section 1
Universal Jurisdiction

Introductory Note

There are several bases of jurisdictional competence of nation-states under international law. One of these, the universality principle, allows any state jurisdiction under international law to provide criminal or civil sanctions for violations of international law. Universal jurisdiction allows nation-state competence whenever an alleged offender is found within the state's territory or equivalent bases for enforcement of law (*e.g.*, its vessels, aircraft, space craft, or space stations, or in occupied territory or territory subject to international regimes or competencies (such as U.N. Security Council powers)). It does not matter where the alleged acts took place, who the alleged victims were, or whether there were any contacts with the forum state. Universal jurisdictional competence is just that—universal. A state's utilization of this competence to prosecute those reasonably accused of international crime will allow such state to fulfill its obligation under international law to initiate prosecution or extradite. Moreover, if universal jurisdiction pertains, it does not matter whether a criminal charge, cause of action, or statute is expressly related to international law.

There is a new type of related jurisdictional competence termed "universal by treaty" or "universal by consent." *See, e.g.*, International Convention Against the Taking of Hostages, art. 5(2), and Convention Against Torture and Other Cruel, Inhuman or Degrading Treatment or Punishment, art. 5(2), in the Documents Supplement. Such competence exists only among signatories to a multilateral treaty establishing a new international offense, and it reaches merely their nationals (or possibly others with a significant nexus to a signatory), at least until the offense becomes a part of customary international law. Once the crime reflected in a treaty becomes a crime under customary international law, any state has universal jurisdiction over such a crime. Today, both of these treaties reflect customary proscriptions. Universal by treaty is actually a form of consensual jurisdiction among the signatories. Examples of such treaties are considered below in connection with particular offenses, *e.g.*, aircraft sabotage and the taking of hostages in time of peace.

It is important whether or not a state like the United States has jurisdiction under international law. As the RESTATEMENT OF THE FOREIGN RELATIONS LAW OF THE UNITED STATES recognizes in §431, Comment a, "a state may not exercise authority to enforce law that it has no jurisdiction [under international law] to prescribe" and [s]uch assertion of jurisdiction ... may be objected to ... both by the affected person directly and by the other state concerned" (*i.e.*, the state of such person's nationality). *See also*, United States v. Darnaud, 25 F. Cas. 754, 759–60 (C.C.E.D. Pa.1855) (No. 14, 918) ("if the Congress … were to call upon the courts of justice to extend the jurisdiction of the United States beyond the limits … [set by the 'law of nations'], it would be the duty of courts of justice to decline…."); Jordan J. Paust, International Law as Law of the United States 11, 56–57 n.68, 415–16, 424 n.1 (2 ed. 2003).

Paust, *Federal Jurisdiction Over Extraterritorial Acts of Terrorism and Nonimmunity for Foreign Violators of International Law Under the FSIA and the Act of State Doctrine*
23 Va. J. Int'l L. 191, 211–14 (1983)

The universality principle provides for jurisdiction to enforce sanctions against crimes that have an independent basis in international law. In other words, the principle applies "to crimes that affect the international community and are against international law." Universal jurisdiction is thus technically jurisdiction to enforce, and the enforcement is actually made on behalf of the international community.

From the dawn of our own constitutional history, universal enforcement jurisdiction has been recognized over "crimes against mankind and the enemies of the whole human family," or those persons who are "hostes humani generis." It was also recognized more generally that violations of international law were subject to criminal sanction, and that civil or criminal sanctions for private violations of international law were often interchangeable, depending on whether an individual or government was seeking enforcement. The government has been successful in numerous instances in enforcing criminal sanctions against individuals for violations of international law. While prosecutions have occurred even in the absence of a domestic statute, it is now generally assumed that a federal statute is needed to impose domestic criminal sanctions on violators of international law. Thus, the same should be true with respect to universal jurisdiction to apply criminal sanctions against persons who have engaged in acts of terrorism in violation of international law.

A different question is whether or not a specific statutory offense prosecutable in federal court is also recognizably related to an international crime. If so, universal jurisdiction to enforce is possible whether or not the domestic statute expressly refers to an offense under international law. In the case of U.S. military prosecutions, for example, violations of international law have been prosecuted as offenses against the law of nations or, alternatively, as "ordinary" offenses under the Uniform Code of Military Justice. Similarly, there have been prosecutions in connection with acts of terrorism under federal law in which the court has explicitly referred to the universality principle despite the fact that relevant Congressional legislation was silent or nearly silent on the question.

Whether or not the conduct involved would constitute an offense under international law depends, of course, on international law. A number of terrorist offenses violate customary international law, although several violations relevant to international terrorism are based on treaty law of a relatively recent nature. It is useful to recall further that numerous types of conduct related to terrorism also violate international law. Thus, there are several international norms that are potentially relevant, and new efforts to enact U.S. legislation designed to control terrorism should expressly refer to violations of "international law" in order to cover all potential bases of illegality.

Notes

1. The types of international crimes or criminals recognized early in U.S. history included: violence against ambassadors; piracy; poisoners, assassins, incendiaries by profession; banditti; brigands; violation of passports; slave trading; breaches of neutrality; and war crimes. See *id.* at ns. 76–80, and references cited; J. PAUST, INTERNATIONAL LAW AS LAW OF THE UNITED STATES 12, 59–60 (2 ed. 2003). In 1836, Henry Wheaton wrote: "The judicial power of every independent state ... extends ... [t]o the punishment of piracy and other offences against the law of nations, by whomsoever and wheresoever committed." HENRY WHEATON, ELEMENTS OF INTERNATIONAL LAW 110 § 14 (1st ed. 1836).

2. Concerning piracy, also see *United States v. Furlong*, 18 U.S. (5 Wheat.) 184, 197 (1820) ("Robbery on the seas is considered as an offence within the criminal jurisdiction of all nations. It is against all, and punished by all ... within this universal jurisdiction."). This was the first U.S. case to use the phrase "universal jurisdiction." *Cf United States v. Smith*, 18 U.S. (5 Wheat.) 153, 161, 163 (1820) (piracy is "an offence against the universal law of society"); *United States v. Klintock*, 18 U.S. (5 Wheat.) 144, 147–48 (1820) (piracy "is an offense against all. It is punishable in the Courts of all ... [our courts] are authorized and bound to punish"); *Talbot v. Janson*, 3 U.S. (3 Dall.) 133, 159–60 (1795) (also affirming the widespread expectation that "all ... trespasses against the general law of nations, are enquirable and may be proceeded against in any nation where no special exemption can be maintained, either by the general law of nations, or by some treaty which forbids or restrains it."); *Ross v. Rittenhouse*, 2 U.S. (2 Dall.) 160, 162 (Pa. 1792) ("universal law"); *Respublica v. De Longchamps*, 1 U.S. (1 Dall.) 111, 113, 115 (Pa. 1784) (assault against a foreign consul is a "crime against the whole world," "crime against all other nations"); *United States v. La Jeune Eugenie*, 26 F. Cas. 832, 847–51 (C.C.D. Mass. 1821) (No. 15,551 (with respect to "an offence against the universal law of society," "no nation can rightly permit its subjects to carry it on, or exempt them ... [and] no nation can privilege itself to commit a crime against the law of nations."). In United States v. Hasan, 747 F. Supp.2d 599, 608 (E.D. Va. 2010), the court posited that the "paradigmatic universal offense" is "the offense of general piracy." The court held that "Article 101 of the UNCLOS reflects the modern customary international law definition of general piracy, which is applicable to 18 U.S.C. § 1651." *Id.* at 637.

3. As early as the 1600s, Grotius recognized that crimes against the law of nations are "offenses which affect human society at large ... and which other states or their rulers have a right to deal with." Grotius had also recognized the propriety of a "war" against a ruler who engages in a "manifest oppression" of his or her people, noting that such a military response was "undertaken to protect the subjects of another ruler from oppression" and to assure that they are not further denied "the right of all human society" to freedom from oppression. In that sense, "war" against the oppressor-ruler was a form of sanction strategy in response to acts of oppression that could affect human society at large. See H. GROTIUS, II ON THE LAW OF WAR AND PEACE, chs. 18 (sec. 6) 21 (sec. 3) 25 (sec. 8) (Francis W. Kelsey trans. 1925).

4. Consider the types of crimes recognized in the following instrument:

Resolution of 1781

21 Journals of the Continental Congress 1136–37:

On a report of a committee, consisting of Mr. [Edmund] Randolph, Mr. [James] Duane, Mr. [John] Witherspoon, appointed to prepare a recommendation to the states to enact laws for punishing infractions of the laws of nations:

The committee, to whom was referred the motion for a recommendation to the several legislatures to enact punishments against violators of the law of nations, report:

That the scheme of criminal justice in the several states does not sufficiently comprehend offenses against the law of nations:

That a prince, to whom it may be hereafter necessary to disavow any transgression of that law by a citizen of the United States, will receive such disavowal with reluctance and suspicion, if regular and adequate punishment shall not have been provided against the transgressor: That as instances may occur, in which, for the avoidance of war, it may be expedient to repair out of the public treasury injuries committed by individuals, and the property of the innocent to be exposed to reprisal, the author of those injuries should compensate the damage out of his private fortune.

Resolved, That it be recommended to the legislatures of the several states to provide expeditious, exemplary and adequate punishment:

First, For the violation of safe conducts or passports, expressly granted under the authority of Congress to the subjects of a foreign power in time of war:

Secondly, For the commission of acts of hostility against such as are in amity, league or truce with the United States, or who are within the same, under a general implied safe conduct:

Thirdly. For the infractions of the immunities of ambassadors and other public ministers, authorised and received as such by the United States in Congress assembled, by animadverting on violence offered to their persons, houses, carriages and property, under the limitations allowed by the usages of nations; and on disturbance given to the free exercise of their religion: by annulling all writs and processes, at any time sued forth against an ambassador, or other public minister, or against their goods and chattels, or against their domestic servants, whereby his person may be arrested: and,

Fourthly. For infractions of treaties and conventions to which the United States are a party.

The preceding being only those offences against the law of nations which are most obvious, and public faith and safety requiring that punishment should be co-extensive with such crimes:

Resolved, That it be farther recommended to the several states to erect a tribunal in each State, or to vest one already existing with power to decide on offences against the law of nations, not contained in the foregoing enumeration, under convenient restrictions.

Resolved, That it be farther recommended to authorise suits to be instituted for damages by the party injured, and for compensation to the United States for damage sustained by them from an injury done to a foreign power by a citizen.

5. Consider also this extract from 57 MIL. L. REV. at 129:

"brigands" had been outlawed at least since the time of Grotius (1612), Gentili (1620), and Pufendorf (1688). Earlier, Ayala (1582) stated that the old jurists assimilated the brigand with the pirate and that both were regarded as the "common enemy of all," and were subject to punishment by any sovereign. Gentili reiterated these views and stated that brigands have "broken the treaty of the human race." Furthermore, during the Revolutionary War all combat tactics were not considered legal and it was understood that the killing of prisoners would be considered a "gross and inhuman violation of the laws of nature and nations." It was further recognized that individuals could not on their own undertake to wage private war or violence absent state authority, that there were limits to allowable suffering, death and destruction, and that where laws existed the guerrillas could not disobey them with impunity.

6. And note:

> A publication that inspires a "foreign minister with fears of being killed by certain citizens of the United States, is, no doubt, a publication that may be made the subject of legal prosecution" for criminal libel ..." and in the case of a foreign public minister, the municipal law is strengthened by the law of nations...."

1 Op. Att'y Gen. 52, 52–53 (1794) (Bradford, Att'y Gen.). *See also Republica v. Cobbett*, F. WHARTON'S STATE TRIALS 322 (Pa. 1797) (criminal libel against King of Spain and Minister).

Demjanjuk v. Petrovsky
776 F.2d 571, 575–76, 581–83
(6th Cir. 1985), *cert. denied*, 475 U.S. 1016 (1986)

[Another portion of the opinion appears *infra* in Chapter Four, Section 4.]

Lively, J.

This international extradition case is before the court on appeal from the denial of a petition for a writ of habeas corpus, 612 F. Supp 571.

The petitioner, John Demjanjuk, is a native of the Ukraine, one of the republics of the Soviet Union. Demjanjuk was admitted to the United States in 1952 under the Displaced Persons Act of 1948 and became a naturalized United States citizen in 1958. He has resided in the Cleveland, Ohio area since his arrival in this country.

In 1981 the United States District Court for the Northern District of Ohio revoked Demjanjuk's certificate of naturalization and vacated the order admitting him to United States citizenship. See *United States v. Demjanjuk*, 518 F. Supp. 1362 (N.D. Ohio 1981), *aff'd per curiam*, 680 F.2d 32 (1982), *cert. denied*, 459 U.S. 1036 ... (1982). Chief Judge Battisti of the district court entered extensive findings of fact from which he concluded that the certificate and order "were illegally procured and were procured by willful misrepresentation of material facts under 8 U.S.C. § 1451(a)." 518 F. Supp. at 1386.

The district court found that Demjanjuk was conscripted into the Soviet Army in 1940 and was captured by the Germans in 1942. After short stays in several German POW camps and a probable tour at the Trawniki SS training camp in Poland, Demjanjuk became a guard at the Treblinka concentration camp, also in Poland, late in 1942. In his various applications for immigration to the United States the petitioner misstated his place of residence during the period 1938–1948 and did not reveal that he had worked for the SS at Treblinka or served in a German military unit later in the war. In the denaturalization proceedings Demjanjuk admitted that his statements concerning residence were false and that he had in fact served in a German military unit. He steadfastly denied that he had been at Trawniki or Treblinka, though documentary evidence placed him at Trawniki and five Treblinka survivors and one former German guard at the camp identified Demjanjuk as a Ukrainian guard who was known as "Ivan or Iwan Grozny," that is, "Ivan the Terrible."

Following the denaturalization order the government began deportation proceedings against Demjanjuk. While these proceedings were underway the State of Israel filed with the United States Department of State a request for the extradition of Demjanjuk. The United

States Attorney for the Northern District of Ohio, acting on behalf of the State of Israel, filed a complaint in the District court seeking the arrest of Demjanjuk and a hearing on the extradition request. Following a hearing the district court entered an order certifying to the Secretary of State that Demjanjuk was subject to extradition at the request of the State of Israel pursuant to a treaty on extradition between the United States and Israel signed December 10, 1962, effective December 5, 1963. Bond previously granted Demjanjuk was revoked and he was committed to the custody of the Attorney General of the United States pending the issuance of a warrant of surrender by the Secretary of State....

Before reaching the more technical arguments related to jurisdiction of the district court and the question of whether the crimes charged were within the treaty provisions, we deal with the sufficiency of the evidence. As noted, there are sworn testimony by affidavits from six witnesses who were at Treblinka in 1942 and 1943 who identified Demjanjuk. These witnesses stated that Demjanjuk was a guard who herded prisoners into the gas chambers and then actually operated the mechanism which filled the chambers with gas. In addition, several of the witnesses testified that they saw Demjanjuk beat and maim prisoners, some of whom died. Justice Holmes wrote in *Fernandez* that our task is to determine "whether there was *any* evidence warranting the finding that there was reasonable ground to believe the accused guilty." Surely the evidence in this case satisfied this lenient standard....

The Israeli statute under which Demjanjuk was charged deals with "crimes against the Jewish people," "crimes against humanity" and "war crimes" committed during the Nazi years. It is clear from the language defining the crimes, and other references to acts directed at persecuted persons and committed in places of confinement, that Israel intended to punish under this law those involved in carrying out Hitler's "final solution." This was made explicit in the prosecution of Adolph Eichmann in 1961. *Attorney General v. Eichmann*, 36 I.L.R. 277 (Sup. Ct. Israel 1962), reprinted in 2 Friedman, *The Law of War* at 1657–1687 (1972). Such a claim of extraterritorial jurisdiction over criminal offenses is not unique to Israel. For example, statutes of the United States provide for punishment in domestic district courts for murder or manslaughter committed within the maritime jurisdiction (18 U.S.C. § 1111) and murder or manslaughter of internationally protected persons wherever they are killed (18 U.S.C. § 1116(c)). We conclude that the reference in 18 U.S.C. § 3184 to crimes committed within the jurisdiction of the requesting government does not refer solely to territorial jurisdiction. Rather, it refers to the authority of a nation to apply its laws to particular conduct. In international law this is referred to as "jurisdiction to prescribe." Restatement § 401(1).

The law of the United States includes international law. *The Paquete Habana*, 175 U.S. 667, 712 (1900). International law recognizes a "universal jurisdiction" over certain offenses. Section 404 of the Restatement defines universal jurisdiction:

§ 404: Universal Jurisdiction to Define and Punish Selected Offenses

A state may exercise jurisdiction to define and punish certain offenses recognized by the community of nations as of universal concern, such as piracy, slave trade, attacks on or hijacking of aircraft, genocide, war crimes, and perhaps terrorism, even where none of the bases of jurisdiction indicated in § 402 is present.

This "universality principle" is based on the assumption that some crimes are so universally condemned that the perpetrators are the enemies of all people. Therefore, any nation which has custody of the perpetrators may punish them according to its law applicable to such offenses. This principle is a departure from the general rule that "the character of an act as lawful or unlawful must be determined wholly by the law of the country where the act is done." *American Banana Co. v. United Fruit Co.*, 213 U.S. 347, 356 ... (1909).

The wartime allies created the International Military Tribunal which tried major Nazi officials at Nuremberg and courts within the four occupation zones of post-war Germany which tried lesser Nazis. All were tried for committing war crimes, and it is generally agreed that the establishment of these tribunals and their proceedings were based on universal jurisdiction. *E.g.*, Sponsler, *The Universality Principle of Jurisdiction and the Threatened Trials of American Airmen*, 15 Loy. L. Rev. 43, 48–51 (1968–69).

Demjanjuk argues that the post-war trials were all based on the military defeat of Germany and that with the disestablishment of the special tribunals there are no courts with jurisdiction over alleged war crimes. This argument overlooks the fact that the post-war tribunals were not military courts, though their presence in Germany was made possible by the military defeat of that country. These tribunals did not operate within the limits of traditional military courts. They claimed and exercised a much broader jurisdiction which necessarily derived from the universality principle. Whatever doubts existed prior to 1945 have been erased by the general recognition since that time that there is a jurisdiction over some types of crimes which extend beyond the territorial limits of any nation.

Turning again to the Restatement, § 443 appears to apply to the present case:

> § 443. Jurisdiction to Adjudicate in Aid of Universal and Other Non-Territorial Crimes.
>
> A state's courts may exercise jurisdiction to enforce the state's criminal laws which punish universal crimes (§ 404) or other non-territorial offenses within the state's jurisdiction to prescribe (§§ 402–403).

Israel is seeking to enforce its criminal law for the punishment of Nazis and Nazi collaborators for crimes universally recognized and condemned by the community of nations. The fact that Demjanjuk is charged with committing these acts in Poland does not deprive Israel of authority to bring him to trial....

Though it was not explicitly argued, we have considered whether recognition of the power of Israeli courts to punish for war crimes committed outside of its national territory violates any right of Demjanjuk under the Constitution of the United States. Demjanjuk had notice before he applied for residence or citizenship in the United States that this country, by participating in post-war trials of German and Japanese war criminals recognized the universality principle. Israel has chosen to proceed under that principle, and we do not supervise the conduct of another judicial system. To do so "would directly conflict with the principle upon which extradition is based." *Jhirad v. Ferrandina*, 536 F.2d 478, 485 (2d Cir.) *cert. denied*, 429 U.S. 833 ... (1976). In the absence of any showing that Demjanjuk will be subjected to procedures "antipathetic to a federal court's sense of decency," *Gallina v. Fraser*, 278 F.2d 77, 79 (2d Cir.), *cert. denied*, 364 U.S. 851 ... (1960), this court will not inquire into the procedures which will apply after he is surrendered to Israel. There is absolutely no showing in this record that Israel will follow procedures which would shock this court's "sense of decency." *United States ex rel. Bloomfield v. Gengler*, 507 F.2d 925, 928 (2d Cir. 1974)....

Notes and Questions

1. Today, minimum human rights to due process under customary international law include those reflected in Article 14 of the International Covenant on Civil and Political Rights (ICCPR). See also Chapter Six; Hamdan v. Rumsfeld, 548 U.S. 557, 633 & n.66 (2006) (among "the barest of those trial protections that have been recognized by customary international law" are Article 14 of the ICCPR and Article 75 of Geneva Protocol I). This set of rights is what a court should use instead of its "sense of decency."

2. Demjanjuk was deported to Israel, convicted, and sentenced to death on April 25, 1988. Later, his conviction was overturned because he was not Ivan the Terrible, he was released and returned to the U.S. In 2008, was deported to Germany for trial and was convicted in May 2011 and sentenced to five years in prison. While awaiting appeal, he died in March 2012 at the age of 91.

Restatement of the Foreign Relations Law of the United States*
Comments and Reporters' Notes to § 404 (3 ed. 1987)

Comment:

a. Expanding class of universal offenses. This section, and the corresponding section concerning jurisdiction to adjudicate, § 423, recognize that international law permits any state to apply its laws to punish certain offenses although the state has no links of territory with the offense, or of nationality with the offender (or even the victim). Universal jurisdiction over the specified offenses is a result of universal condemnation of those activities and general interest in cooperating to suppress them, as reflected in widely-accepted international agreements and resolutions of international organizations. These offenses are subject to universal jurisdiction as a matter of customary law. Universal jurisdiction for additional offenses is provided by international agreements, but it remains to be determined whether universal jurisdiction over a particular offense has become customary law for states not party to such an agreement. See § 102, Comment f. A universal offense is generally not subject to limitations of time.

There has been wide condemnation of terrorism but international agreements to punish it have not, as of 1987, been widely adhered to, principally because of inability to agree on a definition of the offense. The United States and six states (all in Latin America) have adopted a Convention to Prevent and Punish the Acts of Terrorism Taking the Form of Crimes against Persons and Related Extortion that are of International Significance, 27 U.S.T. 3949, T.I.A.S. No. 8413 (1976). Universal jurisdiction is increasingly accepted for certain acts of terrorism, such as assaults on the life or physical integrity of diplomatic personnel, kidnapping, and indiscriminate violent assaults on people at large. See also § 477, Reporters' Note 6.

b. Universal jurisdiction not limited to criminal law. In general, jurisdiction on the basis of universal interests has been exercised in the form of criminal law, but international law does not preclude the application of non-criminal law on this basis, for example, by providing a remedy in tort or restitution for victims of piracy.

Reporters' Notes

1. *Offenses subject to universal jurisdiction.* Piracy has sometimes been described as "an offense against the law of nations," an international crime. Since there is no international penal tribunal, the punishment of piracy is left to any state that seizes the offender. *See, e.g., United States v. Smith,* 18 U.S. (5 Wheat.) 153, 161–62 (1820); 2 Moore, International Law § 951-68 (1906). Compare the power of Congress under Article I, Section 8 of the United States Constitution "to define and punish Piracies and Felonies committed on the high Seas, and Offences against the Law of Nations." Whether piracy is an international crime, or is rather a matter of international concern as to which international law accepts the jurisdiction of all states, may not make any important difference....

That genocide and war crimes are subject to universal jurisdiction was accepted after the Second World War, although apparently no state has exercised such jurisdiction in

---

circumstances where no other basis for jurisdiction under §402 was present. In the *Eich-mann* case, involving the principal executioner of Hitler's "final solution" during World War II, Israel relied on universal jurisdiction as well as other bases. See Attorney General of Israel v. Eichmann, 36 Int'l L. Rep. 277 (Sup. Ct. Israel 1962).... The principles of the Nuremberg Charter and Judgment were unanimously adopted by the United Nations General Assembly in 1946. G.A. Res. 95(1), 1(2) G.A.O.R. Resolutions, at 188. Genocide has also been unanimously condemned by resolution of the General Assembly, G.A. Res. 96(1), *ibid.* The Convention on the Prevention and Punishment of the Crime of Geno-cide, 1948, 78 U.N.T.S. 277 (1951), had, as of 1986, been adhered to be 100 states.... The Convention provides for trial by the territorial state or by an international penal tribunal to be established.... Universal jurisdiction to punish genocide is widely accepted as a principle of customary law. For genocide as a violation of customary law by a state, see §702(a).

International agreements have provided for general jurisdiction for additional offenses, *e.g.*, the Hague Convention for the Suppression of Unlawful Seizure of Aircraft, 22 U.S.T. 1641, T.I.A.S. 7192 (1971); the Montreal Convention for the Suppression of Unlawful Acts against the Safety of Civil Aviation, 24 U.S.T. 564, T.I.A.S. 7570 (1973); the Con-vention on the Prevention and Punishment of Crimes against Internationally Protected Persons including Diplomatic Agents, 28 U.S.T. 1975, T.I.A.S. 8532, 1035 U.N.T.S. 167 (1977); and the International Convention against the Taking of Hostages.... These agree-ments include an obligation on the parties to punish or extradite offenders, even when the offense was not committed within their territory or by a national. As of 1986, 121 states had become parties to the Hague Convention, 127 states to the Montreal Conven-tion, 69 to the Convention of the Prevention of Crimes against Internationally Protected Persons, and 29 to the Convention against the Taking of Hostages. The United States is party to each of these agreements. The International Convention on the Suppression and Punishment of the Crime of Apartheid, which came into force in 1976, declares that apartheid is a crime against humanity and subject to universal jurisdiction. As of Janu-ary 1, 1987, 86 states were parties to the Convention.... [The] Convention Against Tor-ture and Other Cruel, Inhuman and Degrading Treatment or Punishment ... in effect provides for universal jurisdiction.... Such agreements are effective only among the par-ties, unless customary law comes to accept these offenses as subject to universal jurisdic-tion. See Comment *a.* Articles on State Responsibility, prepared for the International Law Commission, would include a provision that an international crime may result from "a serious breach on a widespread scale of an international obligation of essential importance for safeguarding the human being, such as those prohibiting slavery, genocide and apartheid." Report of the International Law Commission, 33 U.N. GAOR Supp. No. 10, at 193 (1978). An international crime is presumably subject to universal jurisdiction.

Notes and Questions

1. Must there be "universal" condemnation for a prohibition to become customary in-ternational law? Recall Chapter One.

2. Has the U.S. Supreme Court ever ruled that Congress must adopt a relevant statute before those accused of an international crime can be prosecuted in federal courts? See *infra* Chapter Four, Sections 2–4. Further, the cases cited in the Restatement are not rel-evant to customary international crimes as such, much less treaty-based laws.

3. Other cases recognizing universal jurisdiction for criminal sanctions or extradition include: United States v. Yousef, 327 F.3d 56, 88–89, 96 (2d Cir. 2003) (universal by treaty,

Montreal Sabotage Convention; but "the indefinite category of 'terrorism' is not subject to universal jurisdiction." *Id.* at 79, see also *id.* at 86–87); United States v. Rezaq, 134 F.3d 1121, 1131, 1133 (D.C. Cir. 1998), *cert. denied*, 525 U.S. 834 (1998); United States v. Yunis, 924 F.2d 1086, 1092 (D.C. Cir. 1991); United States v. bin Laden, *et al.*, 92 F. Supp.2d 189, 215 n.42, 221–22 (S.D.N.Y. 2000); United States v. Yousef, 927 F. Supp. 673, 681–82 (S.D.N.Y. 1996), *aff'd in part*, 327 F.3d 56 (above); United States v. Yunis, 681 F. Supp. at 900–01, *aff'd*, 924 F.2d 1086 (above); 1 Op. Att'y Gen. 68, 69 (1797) ("violation of territorial rights ... [is] an offence against the law of nations ... [and] it is the interest as well as the duty of every government to punish...."). *See also* Anthony J. Colangelo, *The New Universal Jurisdiction: In Absentia Signaling Over Clearly Defined Crimes*, 36 GEO. J. INT'L L. 537 (2005) (discussing crimes that give rise to universal jurisdiction).

In United States v. Saac, 632 F.3d 1203, 1210–11 (11th Cir. 2011), the Eleventh Circuit affirmed the extraterritoriality of the Drug Trafficking Interdiction Act of 2008 ("DTVIA"), 18 U.S.C. §2285, under the universal principle. The DTVIA punishes whoever knowingly operates a "submersible vessel" without nationality and that is navigating in international waters with the intent to evade detection. The Court held that the "DTVIA targets criminal conduct that facilitates drug trafficking, which is 'condemned universally by law-abiding nations.'" Is mere "universal condemnation" the test for determining whether it is expected as a matter of international law that a crime is subject to universal jurisdiction? Murder is "condemned universally by law-abiding nations," but that does not mean that relevant *opinio juris* exists (*i.e.*, that it is widely expected that as a matter of international law murder is condemned), nor that universal jurisdiction would apply to all acts of murder.

4. In the absence of an international consensus on the definition of terrorism, is terrorism subject to universal jurisdiction? One commentator has cogently stated:

> In the words of the United States Court of Appeals for the Second Circuit in the recent *Yousef* opinion:
>
>> Unlike those offenses supporting universal jurisdiction under customary law–that is, piracy, war crimes, and crimes against humanity–that now have fairly precise definitions and that have achieved universal condemnation, "terrorism" is a term as loosely deployed as it is powerfully charged.... No consensus has developed on how to properly define "terrorism" generally.... [S]uch strenuous disagreement among States about what actions do or do not constitute terrorism ... [means that] terrorism–unlike piracy, war crimes, and crimes against humanity–does not provide a basis for universal jurisdiction.
>
> Thus the answer to the question of how to determine the customary definitional content of universal crimes is of increasing legal and practical importance.
>
> On my view..., that the answer lies in the substantive definitions of treaties, the international crime at issue in *Yousef*, which involved planting and exploding a bomb on a civilian aircraft–not abstractly "terrorism"–clearly would be subject to universal jurisdiction. The relevant international instrument, the 1971 Montreal Convention for the Suppression of Unlawful Acts Against the safety of Civil Aviation, not only evidences a custom of universal adjudicative jurisdiction by providing for extraterritorial and extra- national jurisdiction over alleged plane-bombers, it fills the prescriptive customary hole that so worried the Second Circuit by prescribing a definite international law articulation of the crime of plane-bombing. Thus while "terrorism' abstractly-labeled may not be subject to universal jurisdiction because of its definitional uncertainty, certainly clearly-defined acts of terrorism, like plane-bombing are.

Anthony J. Colangelo, *The Legal Limits of Universal Jurisdiction*, 47 Va. J. Int'l L. 149, 165–66 (2006). *See also* Colangelo, *The New Universal Jurisdiction, supra* (including certain acts of terrorism among those allowing universal jurisdiction).

Professor Christopher Blakesley also maintains that at least certain acts of terrorism are subject to universal jurisdiction:

Terrorism is quickly becoming a crime of universal jurisdiction.... For example, the Hague Convention grants all contracting parties jurisdiction over unlawful seizures of control of aircraft and obligates the party obtaining custody of the alleged hijackers to prosecute or extradite them and the Montreal Convention extends the Hague Convention to include acts of sabotage. The obligations in these treaties have likely become customary international law, as virtually all nations consider themselves legally obliged to abide by their rules. When this occurs, they become truly universal crimes.

Christopher L. Blakesley & Dan E. Stigall, *The Myopia of U.S. v. Martinelli: Extraterritorial Jurisdiction in the 21st Century*, 39 Geo. Wash. Int'l L. Rev. 1, 30 (2007).

As noted at the start of this Chapter, as soon as a treaty-based crime becomes a crime under customary international law, universal jurisdiction pertains. Do the prohibited acts reflected in fourteen major international instruments and protocols related to terrorism universal crimes over which there is universal jurisdiction? See Chapter Twelve. The crime set forth in each treaty listed in Reporters' Note 1 to Section 404 of the Restatement recognizably reflects customary international law today.

5. Must states either "punish" or extradite? Consider also *United States v. Yunis*, below.

6. U.S. legislation implementing the Convention Against Torture by providing criminal sanctions against torture is contained in 18 U.S.C. §2340A. The legislation is extraterritorial, applying to "[w]hoever outside the United States commits or attempts to commit torture" (subsection (a)), and jurisdiction includes the circumstance where "the alleged offender is present in the United States, irrespective of the nationality of the victim or alleged offender" (subsection (b) (2)). Would this legislation apply to U.S. nationals accused of torture at Guantanamo Bay, Cuba?

7. Note that if a new international tribunal is created to prosecute crimes that were already crimes under customary international law universal jurisdiction obtains with respect to such crimes and can be conferred by states creating the tribunal to the new tribunal. Recall *Demjanjuk* regarding formation of the International Military Tribunal at Nuremberg. In its Opinion and Judgment, the I.M.T. declared with respect to the creation of the international tribunal by the parties to the 1945 London Agreement creating the Charter, "[i]n doing so, they have done together what any one of them might have done singly...." Exercise of such a universal competence by the tribunal could not rightly be complained of by some other state. For these reasons, if the U.S. prefers not to ratify the new "Rome" Statute creating a permanent International Criminal Court (ICC), the U.S. cannot rightly complain about the exercise of any universal jurisdictional competence the ICC has under its constitutive treaty even if the U.S. is not a signatory to the treaty.

8. What is wrong with the following discussion of the universality principle?

United States v. Yunis
681 F. Supp. 896, 900–901 (D.D.C. 1988):

[Editors' note: Yunis, was treated as a national of Lebanon. The incident involved the hijacking of a Jordanian airliner on the ground in Beirut, Lebanon, and holding of crew and passengers, including three U.S. nationals, hostage during flights to Tunis, Tunisia (which would not allow the plane to land), Cyprus, Sicily, and Syria (which refused landing) and in Lebanon. Lebanon had ratified a relevant aircraft hijacking convention, but had not ratified the Hostage Taking Convention]

"The Universal and Passive Personal principle appear to offer potential bases for asserting jurisdiction over the hostage-taking and aircraft piracy charges against Yunis. However, his counsel argues that the Universal principle is not applicable because neither hostage-taking nor aircraft piracy are heinous crimes encompassed by the doctrine. He argues further, that the United States does not recognize Passive Personal as a legitimate source of jurisdiction The government flatly disagrees....

"*Universal Principle*

"The Universal principle recognizes that certain offenses are so heinous and so widely condemned that "any state if it captures the offender may prosecute and punish that person on behalf of the world community regardless of the nationality of the offender or victim or where the crime was committed." M. Bassiouni, II International Criminal Law, Ch. 6 at 298 (ed. 1986). The crucial question for purposes of defendant's motion is how crimes are classified as "heinous" and whether aircraft piracy and hostage taking fit into this category.

"Those crimes that are condemned by the world community and subject to prosecution under the Universal principal [sic] are often a matter of international conventions or treaties. *See Demjanjuk v. Petrovsky*, 776 F.2d 571, 582 (6th Cir. 1985) (Treaty against genocide signed by a significant number of states made that crime heinous; therefore, Israel had proper jurisdiction over Nazi war criminal under the Universal principle).

"Both offenses are the subject of international agreements. A majority of states in the world community including Lebanon, have signed three treaties condemning aircraft piracy: The Tokyo Convention, The Hague Convention, and The Montreal Convention. The Hague and Montreal Conventions explicitly rely on the principle of Universal jurisdiction in mandating that all states "take such measures as may be necessary to establish its jurisdiction over the offences ... where the alleged offender is present in its territory." Hague Convention Art. 4 § 2; Montreal Convention Art. 5 § 2. Further, those treaties direct that all "contracting states ... of which the alleged offender is found, ... shall, be obliged *without exception whatsoever and whether or not the offense was committed in its territory*, to submit the case to its competent authorities for the purpose of prosecution." Hague Convention Art. 7; Montreal Convention Art. 7. (emphasis added) These two provisions together demonstrate the international community's strong commitment to punish aircraft hijackers irrespective of where the hijacking occurred.

"The global community has also joined together and adopted the International Convention for the Taking of Hostages an agreement which condemns and criminalizes the offense of hostage taking. Like the conventions denouncing aircraft piracy, this treaty requires signatory states to prosecute any alleged offenders "present in its territory."

"In light of the global efforts to punish aircraft piracy and hostage taking, international legal scholars unanimously agree that these crimes fit within the category of heinous crimes for purposes of asserting universal jurisdiction. *See* M. Bassiouni, II International Criminal Law Ch. 2 at 31–32: McCredie, *Contemporary Uses of Force Against Terrorism*, 1986 Ga. J. of Int'l & Comp. L. 435, 439 (1986); Bazyler, *Capturing the Terrorist in the Wild Blue Yonder*, 8 Whittier L. Rev. 685, 687 (1986); Blakesley, *United States Jurisdiction over Extraterritorial Crime*, 73 J. of Crim. L. & Criminology 1109, 1140 (1982). In the Restatement (Revised) of Foreign Relations Law of the United States, a source heavily relied upon by the defendant, aircraft hijacking is specifically identified as a universal crime over which all states should exercise jurisdiction.

"Our Circuit has cited the Restatement with approval and determined that the Universal principle, standing alone, provides sufficient basis for asserting jurisdiction over an alleged offender. *See Tel-Oren v. Libyan Arab Republic*, 726 F.2d at 781, n.7, ("The premise of universal jurisdiction is that a state 'may exercise jurisdiction to define and punish certain offenses recognized by the community of nations as of universal concern,'... even where no other recognized basis of jurisdiction is present.") Therefore, under recognized principles of international law, and the law of this Circuit, there is clear authority to assert jurisdiction over Yunis for the offenses of aircraft piracy and hostage taking."

9. Concerning application of a new treaty creating a new offense to an offender who is not a national of a signatory to the treaty, consider Malvina Halberstam, *Terrorism on the High Seas: The Achille Lauro, Piracy and the IMO Convention on Maritime Safety*, 82 Am. J. Int'l L. 269, 271–72 & n.10 (1988). Yet, if widespread ratification of a new treaty that creates a new offense creates a new *opinio juris* (at least among the signatories) that it is not improper to exercise enforcement jurisdiction over an accused once such person enters the territory of a signatory, has customary international law changed? Does mere ratification of a treaty consenting to such competence among signatory states and their nationals constitute an *opinio juris* concerning the prosecution of nonsignatory nationals? If one can demonstrate an *opinio juris* that even prosecution of nonsignatory nationals is appropriate, is this enough to form new customary international law? What about practice? And is the prosecution of signatory nationals over time (and the absence of prosecution of nonsignatory nationals) sufficient practice? What if no such treaty had ever existed—how is customary international law created?

10. Consider also § 702 of the Restatement:

§ 702. Customary International Law of Human Rights

A state violates international law if, as a matter of state policy, it practices, encourages, or condones

(a) genocide,

(b) slavery or slave trade,

(c) the murder or causing the disappearance of individuals,

(d) torture or other cruel, inhuman or degrading treatment or punishment,

(e) prolonged arbitrary detention,

(f) systematic racial discrimination, or

(g) consistent patterns of gross violations of internationally recognized human rights.

The Restatement also identifies these international proscriptions as customary *jus cogens. Id.* Comments d, n and Reporters' Notes 1, 11. Thus, universal jurisdiction pertains. See *id.* § 404. Note that several of the above categories are also recognizably criminally sanctionable under international law (*e.g.,* genocide, the slave trade, torture); *see also* Chapter Eleven. A more expansive list of human rights *jus cogens* appears in General Comment No. 24 (1994) of the Human Rights Committee created under the International Covenant on Civil and Political Rights, para. 8, U.N. Doc. CCPR/C/21/REV.1/Add.6, *reprinted in* Paust, International Law as Law of the United States 376, 377 (2 ed. 2003); 34 I.L.M. 839 (1995). Concerning universal jurisdiction over torture, *obligatio erga omnes,* the *jus cogens* nature of the prohibition, and the lack of a statute of limitations or a political offense exception concerning extradition, see also *The Prosecutor v. Furundzija*, ICTY-95-17/1, at paras. 151–157 (10 Dec. 1998).

11. More generally, are violations of fundamental human rights also subject to universal criminal sanctions? Recall Chapter One; see *infra* Chapter Eleven.

12. Reporters' Note 12 to Section 702 of the RESTATEMENT adds: "Though it has not yet been authoritatively determined, violation by a state of [the] customary law of human rights ... may permit prosecution of individual officials responsible for such acts under the laws of any state, as an exercise of universal jurisdiction." In fact, Professor Bassiouni has recognized: "human rights ... seem to be the object of the largest number of instruments containing the largest number of penal provisions" whether they reach official or private perpetrators. M.C. BASSIOUNI, A DRAFT INTERNATIONAL CRIMINAL CODE AND DRAFT STATUTE FOR AN INTERNATIONAL CRIMINAL TRIBUNAL 33 (1987) (analyzing 312 international instruments). It has also been stated that "[t]he Nuremberg Charter applied a customary international law of human rights in charging the Nazi war criminals, *inter alia*, with crimes against humanity." LOUIS HENKIN, RICHARD PUGH, OSCAR SCHACHTER, HANS SMIT, INTERNATIONAL LAW 986 (2 ed. 1987). *See also* H. LAUTERPACHT, INTERNATIONAL LAW AND HUMAN RIGHTS 38–58, 61–62 (1968); RICHARD B. LILLICH, INTERNATIONAL HUMAN RIGHTS 896–99 (2 ed. 1991); MYRES S. McDOUGAL, HAROLD D. LASSWELL, LUNG-CHU CHEN, HUMAN RIGHTS AND WORLD PUBLIC ORDER 354–56, 535–36, 542–46 (1980); FRANK NEWMAN, DAVID WEISSBRODT, INTERNATIONAL HUMAN RIGHTS 663–64, 714–17 (1990); Paust, *The Other Side of Right: Private Duties Under Human Rights Law*, 5 HARV. H.R. J. 51 (1992); Chapter Eleven.

13. What legal bases exist in international law to demonstrate that particular matters are of international concern? Consider the following:

Paust, *Federal Jurisdiction Over Extraterritorial Acts of Terrorism....*
23 VA. J. INT'L L. 191, 221–32 (1983)

The General Principle of Nonimmunity

Perhaps the most general recognition of the nonimmunity of foreign States under international law is that contained in article 2(7) of the United Nations Charter. Although it merely declares that the United Nations is not authorized by the Charter "to intervene in matters which are essentially within the domestic jurisdiction of any state," it has been recognized that article 2(7) implicitly confirms competence to intervene in matters that are *not* "essentially within" the jurisdiction of a particular State and, moreover, that a State's violation of international law is precisely one of those circumstances that are not "essentially within" the domestic jurisdiction of a particular State. Thus even those violations of international law that occur entirely within a particular State's territory are of international concern and are not immune to responsive action by or on behalf of the international community.

This nonimmunity where violations of international law are involved is actually a reflection of customary international law. But it is the fact of nonimmunity, as distinguished from whether or not it is based on customary or treaty law, that is more important. And here it is enough to note that, however based, the principle of nonimmunity applies to violations of human rights and the laws of war and genocide, to violations of the prohibitions against apartheid and denials of self-determination, and, more specifically, to international terrorism.

A related aspect of the principle of nonimmunity has also been articulated by the International Court of Justice. The Court's oft-quoted dictum in *Barcelona Traction* affirmed that States owe certain obligations to the international community in general (as distinguished from those owed merely to another State or group of States), and these "are the concern of all States," that all States "have a legal interest in their protection," and that "they are obligations *erga omnes*." The Court then listed examples of these obligations, including those regarding outlawed acts of aggression, genocide and violations of basic human rights.

What makes this significant to the present study is that obligations *erga omnes* are precisely those international legal obligations that cannot be thwarted by the actions of one State alone and, in the case of international criminal activity, are not subject to grants of immunity from criminal sanction. Such a widely shared expectation flows from the fact that international crimes or other prohibitions of a universal nature involve violations of obligations owed to mankind generally, not merely to a particular State or group of States, and that the implementation of sanctions should be governed by universal standards.

For these reasons, domestic notions of "sovereign immunity" or "acts of State" should not be applied in domestic courts so as to thwart a universal sanctions effort directed at international criminal activity. Moreover, any attempt to avoid jurisdiction might have serious and damaging foreign policy implications, since legal obligations owed generally to mankind are at stake. It was declared early in U.S. courts that if an "offending citizen escapes into his own country, his nation should oblige him to repair the damage, if reparation can be made, or should punish him ... [and that if it should] refuse to do either, it renders itself in some measure an accomplice in the guilt, and becomes responsible for the injury." One might argue by analogy that any attempt to grant immunity or any refusal to exercise jurisdiction over foreign persons who are otherwise within a State's territorial jurisdiction would be similarly offensive. If, for example, a foreign government or official violated international law and one of our courts recognized a claim to immunity, the court's decision would have the undesirable effect of supporting illegality. The judiciary's commitment to law would be compromised and its decision to tolerate illegality would be functionally the same as though the court had been an accomplice of the offending government. But any attempt to grant such immunity would be ineffective under international law.

In the case of international terrorism, there are additional reasons why domestic notions of jurisdictional immunity are inconsistent with U.S. responsibility under international law and why a U.S. court's decision to grant immunity would play havoc with both the legal obligations and the foreign policy interests of the United States. When acts of terrorism occur in connection with serious war crimes or acts of genocide, the United States must [initiate prosecution] ... or extradite the alleged criminal or itself be subject to sanctions for a violation of international law. More generally, a refusal to prosecute or extradite an alleged international terrorist might encourage other countries to do the same in a later case when the United States sought the extradition or prosecution of a terrorist. In the appropriate circumstance it might even be argued that a refusal to prosecute constituted impermissible "assistance" or "toleration" of terrorist acts and was therefore in violation of the obligations of signatories to the U.N. Charter "to refrain from ... assisting ... terrorist acts in another State" or, more broadly, to refrain from acts that "tolerate subversive, terrorist or armed activities" of a certain sort. It is relevant that several recent treaties proscribe certain acts of terrorism and also set up their own requirements that all alleged violators be prosecuted or extradited unless there has been an affirmative and permissible grant of asylum by the government.

The general principle of nonimmunity for violations of international law has a more refined application to heads of State and other high governmental officials. The Nuremberg Principles recognize, for example, that in the case of war crimes or crimes against humanity "[a]ny person who commits an act which constitutes a crime under international law is responsible therefor and liable to punishment," and "[t]he fact that a person who committed an act which constitutes a crime under international law acted as Head of State or responsible Government official does not relieve him from responsibility under international law." As the International Military Tribunal at Nuremberg specifically held, "The principle of international law, which under certain circumstances protects the representatives of a state, cannot be applied to acts which are condemned as criminal by international law. The authors of these acts cannot shelter themselves behind their official position in order to be freed from punishment...." Similarly, the Nuremberg Principles stated that government orders cannot free a subordinate from criminal responsibility. The same should be true under U.S. domestic law.

A similar general recognition of nonimmunity for government officials applies to prohibitions against genocide and apartheid. And, as noted below, similar principles of nonimmunity have been applied in U.S. federal court decisions in connection with human rights claims and what might fairly be described as a terrorist assassination. It is also significant that no convention or draft convention attempting to control terrorism mentions any sort of exception for heads of State or other government officials who might violate those conventions. On the contrary, such conventions apply on their face to all persons or acts of terrorism therein mentioned. Moreover, in what was perhaps the earliest international trial of a "government official" for criminal government by terror in defiance of "the laws of God and man," there was no recognition at all of what we might term "sovereign immunity."

Of further interest is the fact that each of the categories of international law violation noted above are potentially relevant to terrorism. For example, the strategy of terrorism usually involves a violation of basic human rights, whether in times of conflict or relative peace. For this reason, any recognized principle of nonimmunity for human rights violations is potentially applicable to acts of terrorism.

In view of the above, I support the predominant notion that heads of State or other government officials who commit acts of terrorism or any other international crime must be denied any form of immunity at both the international and domestic level. Indeed, as noted above, I have already supported the more general and growing view that when a foreign state official violates international law, such an official must be denied immunity from domestic jurisdiction whether the putative claim to immunity is based on notions of "sovereign immunity" or "act of state." The fact that such violations involve international crime makes recognizing the need for such a denial all the more easy.

14. Concerning the nature of the 1949 Geneva Conventions as *obligatio erga omnes* and customary international law, *see, e.g.,* Paust, *Applicability of International Criminal Laws to Events in the Former Yugoslavia,* 9 Am. U.J. Int'l L. & Pol. 499, 502–03, 505 (1994); Jordan J. Paust, *Executive Plans and Authorizations to Violate International Law Concerning Treatment and Interrogation of Detainees,* 43 Columbia J. Transnat'l L. 811, 813–16 (2005).

15. For further discussion of nonimmunity from civil sanctions for violators of international law, *see, e.g., Kadic v. Karadzic,* 70 F.3d 232 (2d Cir. 1995); *Linder v. Portocarrero,* 963 F.2d 332, 336–37 (11th Cir. 1992), extract reproduced *infra* in Chapter Four, Section 7 D; Chapter Eight, Section 2 B; *Amerada Hess Shipping Corp. v. Argentine Republic,* 830 F.2d 421 (2d Cir. 1987); *Letelier v. Republic of Chile,* 488 F. Supp. 665, 673 (D.D.C.

1980); *The Santissima Trinidad*, 20 U.S. (7 Wheat.) 283, 352–53 (1822); *Draft Brief Concerning Claims to Foreign Sovereign Immunity and Human Rights: Nonimmunity for Violations of International Law Under the FSIA*, 8 Hous. J. Int'l L. 49 (1985); Note 13 below. *But see Argentine Republic v. Amerada Hess Shipping Corp.*, 488 U.S. 428 (1989) (narrow exceptions under C.J. Rehnquist's read of the FSIA regarding suits against foreign states or foreign state entities—*cf.* concurring opinions of Blackmun and Marshall). Even under the Rehnquist read, human rights infractions should meet the test. *See, e.g.,* J. Paust, International Law as Law of the United States 236–37, 321–22 (2 ed. 2003).

16. The general obligation of a nation-state to initiate prosecution of or to extradite alleged international criminals will also be considered later in connection with specific international offenses. Is the general obligation also that of the President of the United States? See U.S. Const., art. II, § 3; Paust, *After My Lai: The Case for War Crime Jurisdiction Over Civilians in Federal District Courts*, 50 Tex. L. Rev. 6, 6–8 (1971); *My Lai and Vietnam: Norms, Myths and Leader Responsibility*, 57 Mil. L. Rev. 99, 118–28 (1972); Chapter Four, Section 8.

17. For additional recognition of offenses over which there is universal jurisdiction, *see, e.g.*

Kenneth C. Randall, *Universal Jurisdiction Under International Law*, 66 Tex. L. Rev. 785, 834–38 (1988); Michael P. Scharf, *The ICC's Jurisdiction over the Nationals of Non-Party States: A Critique of the U.S. Position*, 63 Law & Contemp. Probs. (2000) (such crimes include: piracy, genocide, war crimes, crimes against humanity, torture, and certain acts of terrorism). Among the many cases he addressed were: *Hirsh v. State of Israel*, 962 F. Supp. 377, 381 (S.D.N.Y. 1997) ("A foreign state violates *jus cogens* when it participates in such blatant violations of fundamental human rights as genocide, slavery, murder, torture, prolonged arbitrary detention, and racial discrimination."); *Polyukhovich v. Commonwealth*, 172 C.L.R. 501 (Australia 1991) (universal jurisdiction exists over crimes against humanity and war crimes). He adds: "In recent years, domestic courts in Spain and the United Kingdom have determined that universal jurisdiction exists to prosecute the former President of Chile for acts of torture committed in Chile in the 1980s,[1] courts of Denmark and Germany have relied on the universality principle in trying Croatian and Bosnian Serb nationals for war crimes and crimes against humanity committed in Bosnia in 1992,[2] and courts in Belgium have cited the universality principle as a basis for issuing arrest warrants against persons involved in the atrocities in Rwanda in 1994."[3]

---

1. In the Pinochet Case, the U.K. House of Lords found the former President of Chile extraditable to Spain for prosecution under the universality principle enshrined in the Torture Convention. *Regina v. Bow Street Metropolitan Stipendiary Magistrate, ex parte Pinochet Ugarte*, [1999] 2 W.L.R. 272 (H.L.), reprinted in 38 ILM 430 (1999).

2. In the 1994 case of *Director of Public Prosecutions v. T*, the defendant was tried by a Denmark court for war crimes committed against Bosnians in the territory of the former Yugoslavia. *See* Mary Ellen O'Connell, *New International Legal Process*, 83 Am. J. Int'l L. 334, 341 (1999).

On April 30, 1999, the German Federal Supreme Court upheld the conviction of a Bosnian Serb convicted for committing acts of genocide in Bosnia. *See* 5 Int'l L. Update 52 (May 1999) (a press release on this case—Number 39/1999—is available on the German Federal Supreme Court's website: <www.unikarlsruhe.de/-bgh>.

The U.S. Second Circuit Court of Appeals similarly relied on universal jurisdiction in a tort case arising under the Alien Tort Claims Act and the Torture Victim Protection Act against Radovan Karadzic, the Bosnian Serb leader accused of crimes against humanity and war crimes in Bosnia. *Kadic. v. Karadzic*, 70 F.3d 232, 240 (2d Cir. 1995).

3. See Theodor Meron, *International Criminalization of Internal Atrocities*, 89 Am. J. Int'l L. 554, 576 (1995) (While several of the warrants involved the killing of Belgian peacekeepers, one of the warrants was issued against a Rwandan responsible for massacres of other Rwandans in Rwanda).

18. In 2005, Spain's Constitutional Tribunal reversed lower court dismissal of a complaint brought in the Audiencia Nacional (penal chamber) by various Guatemalans against Guatemalan generals, police chiefs and others for conduct engaged in against Mayan indigenous people and their supporters during the 1970s and 1980s involving alleged acts of genocide, torture, terrorism, summary execution, and unlawful detention — thus reinstating the claims. The Constitutional Tribunal based Spanish jurisdiction on universal jurisdiction. See Naomi Roht-Arriaza, Comment on the *Guatemala Genocide Case*, Judgment No. STC237/2005 (Constitutional Tribunal, (Second Chamber), 26 Sept. 2005), 100 Am. J. Int'l L. 207 (2006).

19. On October 15, 2005, two Afghan ex-generals, Mssrs. Hesam and Jalazoy, were convicted in the Netherlands for war crimes committed in Afghanistan during the communist rule in the 1980s. As noted in Chapter Four, in February 2000 a U.K. court of appeal upheld the conviction of Mr. Sawoniuk for war crimes committed in Belarus during the Nazi era.

Section 2
Other Bases of Jurisdiction

Regina v. Anderson
11 Cox Crime. Cas. 198 (U.K. Court of Criminal Appeals) (1868)

Bovill, C.J.

There is no doubt that the place where the offence was committed was within the territory of France, and that the prisoner was therefore subject to the laws of France, which the local authorities of that realm might have enforced if so minded; but at the same time, in point of law, the offence was also committed within British territory, for the prisoner was a seaman on board a merchant vessel, which, as to her crew and master, must be taken to have been at the time under the protection of the British flag, and, therefore, also amenable to the provisions of the British law. It is true that the prisoner was an American citizen, but he had with his own consent embarked on board a British vessel as one of the crew. Although the prisoner was subject to the American jurisprudence as an American citizen, and to the law of France as having committed an offence within the territory of France, yet he must also be considered as subject to the jurisdiction of British law, which extends to the protection of British vessels, though in ports belonging to another country.... On the whole I come to the conclusion that the prisoner was amenable to the British law and that the conviction was right....

Byles, J.

I am of the same opinion.... A British ship is, for the purposes of this question, like a floating island; and, when a crime is committed on board a British ship, it is within the jurisdiction of the Admiralty Court, and therefore of the Central Criminal Court, and the offender is as amenable to British law as if he had stood on the *Isle of Wight* and committed the crime....

Blackburn, J.

I am of the same opinion ... A ship on the high seas, carrying a national flag, is part of the territory of that nation whose flag she carries; and all persons on board her are to be considered as subject to the jurisdiction of the laws of that nation, as much so as if they had been on land within that territory. From the earliest times it has been held that the maritime courts have jurisdiction over offences committed on the high seas where great ships go, which are, as it were, common ground to all nations, and that the jurisdiction extends over ships in rivers or places where great ships go as far as the tide extends.

Notes

1. *Compare R. v. Leslie* (1860), 8 Cox Crim. Cas. 269. *See also R. v. Keyn* (1876), L.R. 2 Ex. D. 63, at p. 161; G. Marston, *Crimes on Board Foreign Merchant Ships at Sea: Some Aspects of English Practice,* 88 L.Q. Rev. 357 (1972); the *S.S. Lotus* (1927), P.C.I.J Ser. A, No. 10, where a Turkish vessel was assimilated to Turkish territory; and A.N. Sack, *Doctrine of Quasi-territoriality of Vessels and the Admiralty Jurisdiction over Crimes Committed on Board National Vessels in Foreign Ports,* 12 N.Y.U.L.Q. Rev. 628 (1935); and 13 N.Y.U.L.Q. Rev. 43. In 2012, the European Court of Human Rights affirmed that Italy's duties under the European Convention applied to conduct on an Italian vessel. Case of Hirsi Jamaa and Others v. Italy, Eur. Ct. H.R. (Grand Chamber, Feb. 23 2012). For U.S. cases recognizing that a flag vessel is the equivalent of flag territory, *see, e.g.,* Lauritzen v. Larsen, 345 U.S. 571 (1952); United States v. Flores, 289 U.S. 137, 155–59 (1933); Wilson v. McNamee, 102 U.S. 572, 574 (1880); United States v. Crews, 605 F. Supp. 730, 736 (S.D. Fla. 1985); United States v. Cooper, 25 F. Cas. 631 (C.C.D. Pa. 1800) (No. 14,865); S.S. Lotus(France v. Turkey). *See also* United States v. Davis, 25 F. Cas. 786, 787 (C.C.D. Mass. 1837) (No. 14,932) (also recognizing where shot fired from ship, jurisdiction also exists where the effects occurred, given intent to produce such effects).

2. As to air flight, *see, e.g.,* Chumney v. Nixon, 615 F.2d 389, 391 (6th Cir. 1980); United States v. Cordova, 89 F. Supp. 298, 302–03 (E.D.N.Y. 1950); Lissitzyn, *In Flight Crime and the United States Legislation,* 67 Am. J. Int'l L. 306 (1973). *See also* section 3 of the 1963 Tokyo Convention on Offences and Certain Other Acts Committed on Board Aircraft as well as section 3 on interference with civil aviation.

3. With respect to outer space, jurisdiction is given to the state of registration of the space craft, see article VIII of the Treaty on Principles Governing the Activities of States in the Exploration and Use of Outer Space, including The Moon and Other Celestial Bodies (1967); S. Gorove, *Criminal Jurisdiction in Outer Space,* 6 Int'l Law. 313 (1972).

4. Concerning crimes committed on sea ice, see F.M. Auburn, *International Law and Sea Ice Jurisdiction in the Arctic Ocean,* 22 Int'l & Comp. L. Rev. 552 (1973); D.A. Cruickshank, *"Arctic Ice and International Law: The Escamilla Case,* 10 West. Ont. L. Rev. 178 (1971); L.W. Aubrey, Jr., Note, *Criminal Jurisdiction over Arctic Ice Islands:* United States v. "Escamilla" (467 F.2d 341), 4 U.C.L.A. Alaska L. Rev. 419 (1975).

Prescriptive Jurisdiction

Revised from the original: *Federal Jurisdiction Over Extraterritorial Acts of Terrorism and Nonimmunity for Foreign Violators of International Law Under the FSIA and the Act of State Doctrine,* 23 Va. J. Int'l L. 191, 201–213 (1983) reprinted in Paust, International Law as Law of the United States 415–20 (2 ed. 2003)

A. *General Aspects of National Competence*

When one is presented with the general question whether there is jurisdiction in a U.S. court with regard to an international or transnational matter (implicating either civil or criminal sanctions), there are really two questions presented: (1) whether there are adequate bases for jurisdiction (or jurisdictional competencies) within the United States under international law, and (2), in the case of federal criminal jurisdiction, whether Congress has taken full advantage of the possible bases of jurisdiction under international law or, alternatively, whether jurisdiction is otherwise possible in federal court according to U.S. constitutional standards and is also supportable on one or more of the international bases. Merely stating the two questions should be sufficient to alert the reader to the fairly obvious fact that they are necessarily related.

Restated, this fairly obvious point compels recognition of the fact that a threshold inquiry should be whether or not there is a basis for jurisdiction under international law. If not, our courts must decline jurisdiction.[1] And conversely, if jurisdiction is possible under international law but is not permissible under the Constitution, it would be equally if not more obviously improper for a court to exercise jurisdiction. It is not surprising therefore that when certain federal courts have explored the propriety of judicial competence they have treated the two questions as one.[2]

Indeed, because international law is part of the supreme law of the land under article VI, clause 2 of the Constitution, and is also relevant to determining the scope of judicial power under article III, section 2 of Constitution, it is not only appropriate but incumbent on federal courts to address questions of international law. Further elaboration of this point is left to other writings on related aspects of the incorporation of international law under articles III and VI. It is useful for present purposes, however, to recall the famous statement by the Supreme Court in *The Paquete Habana:* "International law is part of our law, and must be ascertained and administrated by the courts of justice of appropriate jurisdiction as often as questions of right depending upon it are duly presented for their determination."[3] Although the Court was referring to normative rights, it was also addressing the question of Executive competence under international law to seize a foreign vessel in time of war and the power of the judiciary to ascertain and apply the law. Since it was first made, the statement has been applied to the incorporation of interna-

---

1. See RESTATEMENT (THIRD) FOREIGN RELATIONS LAW OF THE UNITED STATES §431(1) and Comment a (1987)[hereinafter cited as RESTATEMENT]. To proceed when no authority exists under international law could subject the United States to claims that it has violated international law. See Maier, *Extraterritorial Jurisdiction at a Crossroads: An Intersection Between Public and Private International Law,* 76 AM. J. INT'L L. 280, 292 (1982) ("Either prescription or enforcement of a rule without adequate jurisdiction violates international law.") (*citing* RESTATEMENT (SECOND) FOREIGN RELATIONS LAW OF THE UNITED STATES §8 (1965)). Further, as explained below, since international law is part of federal law and is also relevant to the exercise of judicial power under article III, §2 of the Constitution, the judiciary is bound to recognize limits on U.S. jurisdiction imposed by international law, such as that concerning "rights" and "duties." In this manner, international law, as incorporated in the Constitution, can aid in setting limits to what is constitutionally exercisable judicial authority. It can also enhance that authority.

2. *See, e.g.,* Rivard v. United States, 375 F.2d 882, 885 (5th Cir. 1967), *cert. denied sub nom.* Groleau v. United States, 389 U.S. 884 (1967); United States v. Layton, 509 F. Supp. 212, 215–16 (N.D. Cal. 1981); United States v. Rodriguez, 182 F. Supp. 479, 487 (S.D. Cal. 1960), *aff'd sub nom.* Rocha v. United States, 288 F.2d 545 (9th Cir. 1961), *cert. denied,* 366 U.S. 948 (1961).

The fact that a competence exists for the United States does not mean that it has been exercised by Congress where such must occur (*i.e.,* when law is not otherwise directly incorporable or incorporable indirectly through other means). Yet, the Supreme Court has recognized, it is also the case that Congress need not mention or otherwise disclose that a statute takes advantage of a competence or fulfills a duty under international law. *See, e.g.,* United States v. Arjona, 120 U.S. 479, 488 (1887). Thus, what is needed concerning the reach of a federal statute is not congressional recognition but the applicability of some prescriptive competence under international law.

3. 175 U.S. 677, 700 (1900).

tional law generally. Thus, whether or not international law permits jurisdiction is certainly relevant to U.S. courts, and customary principles of jurisdictional competence have been used by federal courts with respect to the enhancement and limitation of federal jurisdiction.[4] Indeed, it may be conceptually appropriate to say that "rights" are at stake where a defendant claims that a court does not have jurisdictional competence under the traditional rules of international law.[5] A court that agreed would actually be using international law as an aid to determining constitutionally exercisable judicial power.

B. *General Principles of Jurisdiction*

When federal courts have addressed the issue of jurisdictional competence, they have referred to five bases of jurisdiction under international law. These are (1) the territorial, (2) the nationality, (3) the protective, (4) the universality, and (5) the passive personality principles of jurisdiction. Although each of these principles could be relevant to extraterritorial acts, two of them, the passive personality and the nationality principles, require only brief attention in this study.

Under the passive personality (or victim) theory, a State has prescriptive jurisdiction over anyone anywhere who injures one of its nationals. Jurisdiction is based on the nationality of the victim. The United States, however, does not generally recognize this theory[6] — despite its recitation in certain case opinions — and there is doubt whether more than a handful of other States actually accept it as a valid principle of customary international law.[7] For this reason, U.S. federal courts should decline jurisdiction where it would rest solely on supposedly customary bases of the passive personality principle.

The nationality principle provides that a State has competence under international law to prescribe laws regulating the conduct of its nationals wherever they are. If, for example, the United States chose to proscribe terrorist acts of U.S. nationals both here and abroad,[8] the extraterritorial reach of such a law would not be in doubt as a matter of in-

---

4. *See, e.g.,* Cook v. United States, 288 U.S. 102, 120–21 (1933) (jurisdiction voided where government seized vessel in violation of treaty that had "imposed a territorial limitation upon" government's "own authority"); The Paquete Habana, 175 U.S. 677, 700 (1900) (customary international law must be applied in absence of controlling treaties or legislation); United States v. Toscanino, 500 F.2d 267, 276–79 (2d Cir.), *reh'g denied,* 504 F.2d 1380 (2d Cir. 1974); *see also* Rose v. Himely, 8 U.S. (4 Cranch) 241, 276–77 (1808) (foreign judicial decrees will be disregarded if foreign jurisdiction inconsistent with the law of nations); Demjanjuk v. Petrovsky, 776 F.2d 571, 582–83 (6th Cir. 1985), *cert. denied,* 475 U.S. 1016 (1986); United States v. Yunis, 681 F. Supp. 896, 899–903, 906 (D.D.C. 1988); Jordan J. Paust, *Customary International Law: Its Nature, Sources and Status as Law of the United States,* 12 Mich. J. Int'l L. 59, 88 & n.52 (1990) (other cases concerning customary principles of jurisdictional competence and their relation to the enhancement or limitation of federal jurisdiction).

5. *See* Restatement, *supra* note 1, §431, Comment a (lack of jurisdiction "may be objected to by both by [sic] the affected person directly and be the other state concerned."). Thus, at least, the individual certainly has "standing."

6. *But see* United States v. Yunis, 681 F. Supp. at 900, 902 & n.8(in context, with reference to treaty-based crimes). As an illustration, the United States should not accept an argument that it has competence under international law to prosecute an Italian national who kidnapped a U.S. General in Italy merely because the General was a U.S. national, or because some primary target such as the President was a U.S. national. See United States v. Columba-Colella, 604 F.2d 356, 360 (5th Cir. 1979)....

7. See ... DeSchutter, *Problems of Jurisdiction in the International Control and Repression of Terrorism,* in International Terrorism and Political Crimes 377, 383 (M. Bassiouni ed. 1975). States recognizing the passive personality principle include: Germany, Israel, Italy, Japan, Mexico, and Turkey....

8. The reference here is to "terrorist" acts in general. Obviously some legislation already exists that proscribes particular acts of terrorism committed by U.S. nationals abroad. *See, e.g.,* United States v. Layton, 509 F. Supp. at 222 (addressing 18 U.S.C. §351, concerning the murder of a Congressperson,

ternational law. It may therefore be useful to point out that where there are gaps in the extraterritorial reach of U.S. domestic law, one method of filling them, at least partly, would be to enact legislation based on the nationality principle.

C. *The Territorial Principle of Jurisdiction*

Two types of jurisdiction based on territorial principles have been recognized: (1) ordinary or subjective territorial jurisdiction, and (2) objective or "impact" territorial jurisdiction. Subjective territorial jurisdiction exists where acts are initiated in or, as is often the case, nearly all the events relevant to a particular case occur within the territorial confines of a State or on vessels, aircraft, spacecraft, or space stations subject to its "flag" jurisdiction. In contrast, objective territorial jurisdiction usually involves extraterritorial acts occurring totally outside the reach of ordinary or subjective territorial jurisdiction. Since the first type rarely involves external acts, it is not relevant to a consideration of extraterritorial activity. Moreover, the first type of territorial jurisdiction poses no real problem, since acts occurring within a State's territory are clearly subject to its jurisdiction absent some immunity. However, the objective or "impact" principle is worthy of more detailed attention.

Objective Territorial Jurisdiction

Under the principle of objective territorial jurisdiction it is possible to obtain jurisdiction over a foreign person, entity, or State based on certain types of conduct abroad.

The clearest case for jurisdiction is where acts occur partly outside and partly inside the United States. Where the case is less clear, the three factors most often considered by U.S. courts are: (1) acts, (2) intent, and (3) effects within the United States. But even if all the relevant acts occur outside the United States, it is still possible to obtain objective territorial jurisdiction. Thus, it is not always necessary that all three factors point in some way to the United States in a given case, nor do principles of international law or relevant factors have anything to do with domestic notions of "contact" with the forum. What is recognizably necessary for objective territorial jurisdiction is that at least two of the three factors identified above (or substitutes therefore) exist.

One example where jurisdiction would be recognized even though all the defendant's acts occurred outside the United States is where an agency relationship could be implied. Under this rationale a U.S. court would have jurisdiction if the defendant knowingly used an agent to consummate some plan or activity within the United States. "'The general rule of the law is that what one does through another's agency is to be regarded as done by himself.'"[9]

In establishing jurisdiction over the defendant it does not even matter whether the "agent" is a knowing or unknowing agent, or, using different categories, a "conscious or unconscious agent" or an "innocent agent."[10] What matters is that the defendant used the agent to further a plan or activity. Thus, a defendant standing outside the United States can be subject to U.S. jurisdiction if the defendant knowingly uses the U.S. mail service

---

and 18 U.S.C. §§ 1116–1117, concerning the murder of an internationally protected person).... Other relevant legislation is 10 U.S.C. §§ 918–19 (the murder and manslaughter provisions of the Uniform Code of Military Justice)....

9. Ford v. United States, 273 U.S. 593, 623 (1927). In a situation of this kind, where both intent and effect exist, the "act" factor will be supplied by the agency rationale. See Strassheim v. Daily, 221 U.S. 280, 284–85 (1911); Rivard v. United States, 375 F.2d 882, 885 (5th Cir. 1967).

10. See Ford v. United States, 273 U.S. at 621, 623.

to carry out a plan or activity within this country.[11] The same would follow from the use of other "innocent agents" to further criminal designs, for example, the use of telephone or wire services.[12] With respect to a hypothetical problem of a kidnapped U.S. General, if an Italian terrorist used the U.S. mail service to send a communiqué to several U.S. newspapers while ordering them to reprint it in the United States, the mail service could be viewed as an "innocent agent" acting within the country. The same would follow if the terrorist used the telephone or some other electronic medium, or even a government official, to communicate such a demand to the President and other government officials in the United States.

A slightly different rationale makes jurisdiction possible even though the defendant acts abroad and has not used an agent within the United States. This second rationale, known as the continuing act theory, allows jurisdiction where the defendant engages in an act or activity that the law views as continuing into the territory of another country. Thus, where a person stands in Mexico and shoots a person standing in the United States, the Mexican defendant cannot successfully argue that the United States does not have jurisdiction over him.[13] Jurisdiction exists in that case because there is an intent to produce an effect within the United States, an actual effect within the United States, and an "act" set in motion abroad that "continues" into the United States. Conceptually this is similar to the agency rationale.

The Supreme Court recognized the continuing act rationale in *Ford v. United States*,[14] where it quoted Judge John Bassett Moore of the Permanent Court of International Justice:

---

11. See Burton v. United States, 202 U.S. 344, 389 (1906) (*citing* Horner v. United States, 143 U.S. 207, 214 (1892)); *In re* Palliser, 136 U.S. 257, 266–68 (1890); Schoenbaum v. Firstbrook, 405 F.2d 200, 207 (2d Cir. 1968) (use of mails for security transactions). Other use of mails cases include Salinger v. Loisel, 265 U.S. 224, 234 (1924); Benson v. Henkel, 198 U.S. 1, 15 (1905); Hartzell v. United States, 72 F.2d 569, 576 (8th Cir. 1934); Horwitz v. United States, 63 F.2d 706, 708–09 (5th Cir. 1933), *cert. denied*, 289 U.S. 760 (1933); United States v. Steinberg, 62 F.2d 77, 78 (2d Cir. 1932); United States v. Hecht, 7 F.2d 133–34 (S.D.N.Y. 1924); United States v. Eisler, 75 F. Supp. 634, 637 (D.D.C. 1947); United States v. Archer, 51 F. Supp. 708, 710–11 (S.D. Cal. 1943); *see also* United States v. Lombardo, 241 U.S. 73, 77 (1916); Reass v. United States, 99 F.2d 752, 754 (4th Cir. 1938). Foreign cases include Morbarik Ali Ahmed v. State of Bombay, 24 I.L.R. 156 (1961) (Supreme Court of India 1957) (*citing* MacLeod v. Att'y Gen. of New South Wales, 1801 A.C. 455).

12. See Lamar v. United States, 240 U.S. 60, 65–66 (1916) (Holmes, J.) (*citing* Burton v. United States, 202 U.S. 344 (1906)). *But see* East Europe Domestic International Sales Corp. v. Terra, 467 F. Supp. 383 (S.D.N.Y. 1979), *aff'd*, 610 F.2d 806 (2d Cir. 1979) (finding no formal agency as such, but ignoring the unlitigated point about "innocent" agents). With regard to use of wire services or electronic communication cases, see Horwitz v. United States, 63 F.2d 706, 709 (radio communications); McBoyle v. United States, 43 F.2d 273, 275 (10th Cir. 1930) (telegraphic communications). For hypothetical examples of the use of "poisoned chocolates through the mails" and "stock fraud by mail," see J. SWEENEY, C. OLIVER & N. LEECH, [THE INTERNATIONAL LEGAL SYSTEM (2 ed. 1981)] , at 111–12. *See also id.* at 112 (discussing foreign cases).

13. See Burton v. United States, 202 U.S. 344, 388 (1906); *In re* Palliser, 136 U.S. 257, 265–66 (1890); Simpson v. State, 92 Ga. 41, 17 S.E. 984 (1893) (Georgia had jurisdiction over accused standing in South Carolina who fired bullet across state line in attempt to shoot person standing in Georgia—intent to produce effect in Georgia and effect in Georgia clearly present; the "act" in Georgia supplied by continuing act fiction); United States v. Davis, 25 F. Cas. at 787(addressed *supra* note 17).... For a case involving a claim to enjoin a shooting establishment that endangered adjoining territory, see Judgment of Nov. 1, 1900, Bundesgerichtes, Switz., 26 Entscheidungen des Schweizerischen Bundesgerichts, Antliche Sammlung [BG] I 444 [hereinafter cited as Swiss Case], cited in the Trail Smelter Case (U.S. v. Can.), 3 R. INT'L ARB. AWARDS 1905, 1963 (1949). For a reverse shooting situation involving Mexican claimants and U.S. government actors, see the Garcia Case (Mex. v. U.S.), 4 R. INT'L ARB. AWARDS 119 (1926), *reprinted in* H. STEINER & D. VAGTS, TRANSNATIONAL LEGAL PROBLEMS 283 (1968).

The principle that a man, who outside of a country wilfully puts in motion a force to take effect in it, is answerable at the place where the evil is done, is recognized in the criminal jurisprudence of all countries....

Its logical soundness and necessity received early recognition in the common law. Thus, it was held that a man who erected a nuisance in one county which took effect in another was criminally liable in the county in which the injury was done.[15]

Other courts have recognized objective territorial jurisdiction where acts outside the United States were intended to produce (intent) and actually did produce effects (effects) within the United States.[16] Courts have also recognized jurisdiction under an "effects" theory,[17] a "constructive presence" theory,[18] and a continuing act theory.[19] Courts have even recognized jurisdiction when the intent amounted to negligence, provided it was reasonably foreseeable that the effects would be felt within the United States. Thus, foreseeability can be a substitute for the intent element.

This negligence based version of the objective territorial principle formed the basis for both the U.S. competence to complain and Canada's responsibility for the damage in the famous *Trail Smelter Case.*[20] In *Trail Smelter*, the tribunal implicitly recognized the test earlier proposed by Judge Moore when it found that Canada owed a duty to protect the

---

14. 273 U.S. 593 (1927).

15. *Id.* at 623 (*quoting* 2 MOORE's INT'L L. DIG. 244 (1906)).

16. See United States v. Fernandez, 496 F.2d 1294, 1296 (5th Cir. 1974); United States v. Layton, 509 F. Supp. 212, 216 (N.D. Cal. 1981); United States v. Keller, 451 F. Supp. 631, 635 (D.P.R. 1978)....

17. See Hammond v. Sittel, 59 F.2d 683, 686 (9th Cir. 1932) (recognizing both the effects theory and the continuing act theory as bases for jurisdiction); Franklin Mint Corp. v. Franklin Mint, Ltd., 360 F. Supp. 478, 482 (E.D. Pa. 1973); Ramirez & Feraud Chili Co. v. Las Palmas Food Co., 146 F. Supp. 594, 600 (S.D. Cal. 1956), *aff'd*, 245 F.2d 875 (9th Cir. 1957), *cert. denied*, 355 U.S. 927 (1958); *see also* United States v. Thayer, 209 U.S. 39, 44 (1908) (even though case did not involve effects jurisdiction, Court acknowledged "the indisputable general proposition that a man sometimes may be punished where he has brought consequences to pass, although he was not there in person"). Although courts sometimes refer to an "effects" theory, it is evident that more than mere effects must occur (*e.g.*, an intent element (or substitute therefore, such as foreseeability, an aspect of negligence) or an act (or substitute therefore by fiction)). Foreign states are rightly critical of a *mere* "effects" theory. *See, e.g.*, BARRY E. CARTER & PHILLIP R. TRIMBLE, INTERNATIONAL LAW 733, 738 (2 ed. 1995); *but see* RESTATEMENT, *supra* note 1 § 402(1) (c) (conduct outside that "has *or* is intended to have ... effect"), Comm. d and Reporters' Note 2 (3 ed. 1987) (emphasis added). For purposes of international law, it should not matter whether a court recognized that more than mere effects occurred if in fact jurisdiction can be justified on the basis of act plus effect or intent plus effect.

18. See Hyde v. United States, 225 U.S. 347, 362 (1912) (noting that jurisdiction may be based on "a constructive presence in a State, distinct from a personal presence," Court saw "no reason why a constructive presence should not be assigned to conspirators as well as to other criminals"); Cochran v. Esola, 67 F.2d 743, 743 (9th Cir. 1933); Grayson v. United States, 272 F.2d 553, 557 (6th Cir. 1921), *cert. denied*, 257 U.S. 637 (1921).

19. See United States v. Freeman, 239 U.S. 117, 120 (1915); Brown v. Elliott, 225 U.S. 392, 400, 402 (1912); Reass v. United States, 99 F.2d 752, 754 (4th Cir. 1938); Moran v. United States, 264 F.2d 768, 770 (6th Cir. 1920); *see also* 1 Op. Att'y Gen. 123, 123 (1802) (Lincoln, Att'y Gen.) (theft of ship and goods can constitute a continuous act for jurisdictional purposes, and jurisdiction could exist "in every successive place to which the vessel was carried"). With regard to jurisdiction over those who broadcast from outside a territory and thus set radio waves in motion to take effect within the territory, see J. SWEENEY, C. OLIVER & N. LEECH, *supra*..., at 190. Radio transmissions are arguably similar to pollutant particles for purposes of the continuing act fiction.

20. (U.S. v. Can.), 3 R. INT'L ARB. AWARDS 1905 (1949).

United States "'against injurious acts by individuals from within its jurisdiction.'"[21] The tribunal recognized that the United States was competent to complain about acts engaged in by Canadians within Canada that caused injury "in or to the territory" of the United States "or the properties or persons therein, when the case is of serious consequence and injury is established by clear and convincing evidence."[22] What was involved in *Trail Smelter* was a continuing act—the activity that set the pollutant particles in motion—and injurious effects that were of "serious consequence." It did not matter that the particles were not "willfully" put in motion since it was clear there were pollutants and it was reasonably foreseeable that they would produce transnational effects.

Based on *Trail Smelter*, therefore, the three factors of act, intent, and effects can be met where (1) acts do not really occur as such in U.S. territory but the continuing act rationale applies, (2) willful intent does not exist but reasonable foreseeability does, and (3) effects—seemingly necessary—actually are felt within the territory. And if it was intentional that the effects should be felt, the case is even stronger, since intent plus effects can override the need for either an agency or continuing act circumstance.[23]

---

21. *Id.* at 1963 (*quoting* C. Eagleton, Responsibility of States in International Law 80 (1928)). For a discussion of other instances where "effects" are examined in the context of international responsibility, see J. Paust & A. Blaustein, The Arab Oil Weapon 141–45 (1977); Handl, *The Case for Mexican Liability for Transnational Pollution Damage Resulting from the Ixtoc I Oil Spill*, 2 Hous. J. Int'l L. 229 (1979)....

22. 3 R. Int'l Arb. Awards at 1965.

23. *See, e.g.*, Steele v. Bulova Watch Co., Inc., 344 U.S. 280, 288 (1952); Ford v. United States, 273 U.S. 593, 620–21 (1926); Strassheim v. Daily, 221 U.S. 280, 284–85 (1911) (a case involving all three elements: acts, intent, and effects); United States v. Pizzarusso, 388 F.2d 8, 10 (2d Cir. 1968), *cert. denied*, 392 U.S. 936 (1968); Rivard v. United States, 375 F.2d 882, 886–88 (5th Cir. 1967); United States v. Aluminum Co. of America, 148 F.2d 416, 443 (2d Cir. 1945) (despite dictum elsewhere in the opinion, a case emphasizing both the intent and effects elements); United States v. Layton, 509 F. Supp. 212, 215–16 (N.D. Cal. 1981); *In re* Grand Jury Investigation of the Shipping Indus., 186 F. Supp. 298, 313 (D.D.C. 1960); United States v. Imperial Chem. Indus., 100 F. Supp. 504, 557 (S.D.N.Y. 1951). For further examples of "effects" theory jurisdiction, see United States v. Sisal Sales Corp., 274 U.S. 268, 276 (1927); United States v. Fernandez, 496 F.2d 1294, 1296 (5th Cir. 1974); A.T. Cross Co. v. Sunil Trading Corp., 467 F. Supp. 47, 49 (S.D.N.Y. 1979); United States v. Keller, 451 F. Supp. 631, 635 (D.P.R. 1978); Menendez v. Faber, Coe & Gregg, Inc., 345 F. Supp. 527, 557–58 (S.D.N.Y. 1972), *modified*, 485 F.2d 1355 (2d Cir. 1973), *rev'd*, 425 U.S. 682 (1976); sources cited *supra* notes 28–31....

The Restatement avers that if there exists an intent to produce effects and some "activity" abroad demonstrates such an intent, "the fact that a plan or conspiracy was thwarted" and effects did not actually occur within a state "does not deprive the target state of jurisdiction...." See Restatement, *supra* note 1, §402, Comm. d. Use of this approach with respect to interrupted drug smuggling has been seemingly approved. *See, e.g.*, United States v. Columba-Colella, 604, F.2d 356, 358–59 (5th Cir. 1979) (dictum: "might be sufficient"). Those wishing to gain recognition of jurisdiction to prescribe in such cases, however, should inquire further whether there were some acts occurring within the target state under the agency (and conspiracy) rationale or whether acts or effects occurred in the past as part of a continuing pattern or process of smuggling. Presumably most smugglers have contacts within the target state either for sale or distribution of items attempted to be smuggled into the target country. Such contacts might be coconspirators, actual agents, and/or those communicated with from abroad through use of innocent agents in furtherance of a plan or conspiracy. Otherwise, the interruption of smuggling by an arrest outside U.S. territorial bases for jurisdiction negates both a continuing act of smuggling and effects within the U.S., leaving only the intent factor. Yet, must the state stand by and suffer a continuing act or predictable consequences in all such cases? In some circumstances it would be relatively easy to wait until acts in furtherance begin within areas under the state's control, but in others avoidance of serious consequences may require interruption outside such areas of control. In another context, if nuclear missiles are headed for its territory, the U.S. does not need consent of the government of "registry" to target the missiles.

It should be clear from the preceding discussion that the objective territorial principle can be quite important to any effort to control extraterritorial civil or criminal acts. In the case of the kidnapped U.S. General, objective territorial jurisdiction would allow prosecution of the Italian national whose terroristic conduct took place outside the United States: the acts of the postal service, telephone company, or other electronic media would be attributable to the accused, and they, as "agents," produced effects within the United States. In such a case, the critical elements of intent and effects would be met, as well as the third factor of acts partly within the United States. If the Italian national had sent a letter-bomb to another U.S. General that exploded within the United States, objective territorial jurisdiction under both the agency rationale (use of the mails) and the continuing act theory (accused set in motion a force to take effect within the United States and "serious consequences" were thereby produced) would clearly be permissible. Actually, all that would be required would be the existence of two out of three of the primary factors.

D. *The Protective Principle of Jurisdiction*

The protective principle is another useful basis for jurisdiction over extraterritorial civil or criminal acts. Even though all relevant acts occur outside the ordinary territorial jurisdiction of the United States, jurisdiction is possible under the protective principle if a significant national interest is at stake and it is not otherwise impermissible under international law to exercise jurisdiction.[24]

As recognized in an early study, relevant protective interests can involve threats to national security, territorial integrity, or political independence.[25] Other authors have also

---

The following chart identifies the general factors or their substitutes:
    continuing act
    act)
    agency
    objective territorial)
    intent)   foreseeability
    effect

24. *See, e.g.,* United States v. Pizzarusso, 388 F.2d 8, 10 (2d Cir. 1968), *cert. denied,* 392 U.S. 936 (1968); Rivard v. United States, 375 F.2d 882, 885–87 (5th Cir. 1967), *cert. denied, sub nom.,* Groleau v. United States, 389 U.S. 884 (1967); Rocha v. United States, 288 F.2d 545, 549 (9th Cir.), *cert. denied,* 366 U.S. 948 (1961); United States v. Zehe, 601 F. Supp. 196, 196–98 (D. Mass. 1985); United States v. Layton, 509 F. Supp. 212, 215–16 (N.D. Cal. 1981); United States v. Keller, 451 F. Supp. 631, 635 (D.P.R. 1978); United States v. Archer, 51 F. Supp. 708, 711 (S.D. Cal. 1943)....

As several of the U.S. cases noted above demonstrate, the protective principle has been applied to protect national interests concerning the sanctity of government documents despite the fact that these interests are not as clearly significant as security and self-defense interests.... Most all of the government documents cases are actually justifiable under the objective territorial principle because there is (1) an intent—at least in part—to produce an effect in the United States (or the foreseeability of such), (2) an effect in the United States (or the potential for an effect), and (3) the use of an "innocent agent" to further the intended plan or effect. It is also possible to use the continuing act rationale in government document cases, because they always involve an alien who "sets in motion" abroad a document to take effect—at least in part—in the United States. *See also* J. Sweeney, C. Oliver & N. Leech, *supra*..., at 118 (noting probable effects in the United States and a theory that effects occur when a alien enters the United States, but not mentioning the agency or continuing act fictions concerning the "act" element).

25. Harvard Draft, [Harvard Research in International Law, Draft Convention on Jurisdiction with Respect to Crime], art. 7; *see* United States v. Layton, 509 F. Supp. 212 (N.D. Cal. 1981) (threat to national security); United States v. Keller, 451 F. Supp. 631 (D.P.R. 1978) (invasion of territory); M. McDougal & W. Reisman, *supra* note 10, at 1319–20; Feller, *supra* note 10, at 26; Note, *Protective Principle of Jurisdiction Applied to Uphold Statute Intended to Have Extraterritorial Effect,* 62 Colum. L. Rev. 371, 372 (1962).

related the protective principle to self-defense. Thus, it would not be unreasonable to recognize the application of the protective principle to any violation of article 2(4) of the U.N. Charter directed against the United States. Moreover, in light of the increase in the number of terroristic threats against U.S. citizens abroad, there can be no doubt that the United States has significant security and protective interests at stake, at least when demands are made upon the U.S. government or the security of the United States is threatened. With respect the hypothetical problem about the kidnapped U.S. General, the national security interests might be of even greater magnitude. The fact that a U.S. General was involved as an instrumental target, and that the President and other U.S. government officials were being coerced as primary targets (no doubt with regard to important matters of national security and foreign affairs) would heighten the national security interests at stake.

There is a danger in pushing the protective theory too far, however, and I suspect that the better view is that actual effects should be felt, or be likely to be felt, before the protective principle could properly be seen to apply.[26] The national interests at stake, when viewed in context, should be of real significance; but these are matters best left to the courts for refinement. It is worth noting, however, that where both the objective territorial and the protective principles point to jurisdiction, the choice concerning application of the protective principle may be easier. An interesting example of such a case is *Schoenbaum v. Firstbrook*.[27] There, both protection from detrimental effects and use of the mails were mentioned, but jurisdiction seemed to rest on the effects doctrine alone.

The Case of the S.S. "LOTUS" (France v. Turkey)

P.C.I.J. Series A No 10; ICGJ 248 (P.C.I.J. 1927)

[Editors' Note: In August 1926, the French steamship *Lotus* crashed into and tore apart the Turkish ship *Boz-Kourt* on the high seas, resulting in the death of eight Turkish nationals. Lieutenant Demons had been on watch duty on the *Lotus* during the incident. Later, the *Lotus* proceeded to Constantinople, where the Turkish police arrested Demons on a charge of manslaughter. At trial, the Turkish court overruled Demons' objection to jurisdiction and sentenced him to imprisonment for eighty days and a fine. The Turkish prosecutor appealed the sentence, which suspended its execution until the appeal's completion.

The Turkish and French governments entered into an agreement referring the question of jurisdiction to the P.C.I.J. at The Hague. At the time of this decision, the Turkish criminal appeal was ongoing.]

I.

Before approaching the consideration of the principles of international law contrary to which Turkey is alleged to have acted—thereby infringing the terms of Article 15 of

---

26. *But see* United States v. Pizzarusso, 388 F.2d at 11 (offense complete when alien perjures himself at U.S. Consulate even without effect in United States); United States v. Keller, 451 F. Supp. at 635 (stating that no actual effect is necessary for protective principle).

27. *See, e.g.*, Schoenbaum v. Firstbrook, 405 F.2d 200 (2d Cir. 1968), where jurisdiction seemed to rest on the effects doctrine alone although the court suggested that protective interests might also be at stake. See *id.* at 206–08. It is important to note, however, that no specific jurisdictional principle was mentioned by the court, even though use of the mails provides a basis for application of the agency rationale and, thus objective territorial jurisdiction (provided, that is, that the other elements of intent and effect are present).

the Convention of Lausanne of July 24th, 1923, respecting conditions of residence and business and jurisdiction—, it is necessary to define … the position resulting from the special agreement. For, the Court having obtained cognizance of the present case by notification of a special agreement concluded between the Parties in the case, it is rather to the terms of this agreement than to the submissions of the Parties that the Court must have recourse in establishing the precise points which it has to decide. In this respect the following observations should be made: …

5. The prosecution was instituted in pursuance of Turkish legislation. The special agreement does not indicate what clause or clauses of that legislation apply. No document has been submitted to the Court indicating on what article of the Turkish Penal Code the prosecution was based; the French Government however declares that the Criminal Court claimed jurisdiction under Article 6 of the Turkish Penal Code, and far from denying this statement, Turkey, in the submissions of her Counter-Case, contends that that article is in conformity with the principles of international law. It does not appear from the proceedings whether the prosecution was instituted solely on the basis of that article.

Article 6 of the Turkish Penal Code, Law No. 765 of March 1st, 1926 (Official Gazette No. 320 of March 13th, 1926), runs as follows:

> "Any foreigner who, apart from the cases contemplated by Article 4, commits an offence abroad to the prejudice of Turkey or of a Turkish subject, for which offence Turkish law prescribes a penalty involving loss of freedom for a minimum period of not less than one year, shall be punished in accordance with the Turkish Penal Code provided that he is arrested in Turkey. The penalty shall however be reduced by one third and instead of the death penalty, twenty years of penal servitude shall be awarded."

> …"If the offence committed injures another foreigner, the guilty person shall be punished at the request of the Minister of Justice, in accordance with the provisions set out in the first paragraph of this article, provided however that:

> "(1) the article in question is one for which Turkish law prescribes a penalty involving loss of freedom for a minimum period of three years;

> "(2) there is no extradition treaty or that extradition has not been accepted either by the government of the locality where the guilty person has committed the offence or by the government of his own country."

Even if the Court must hold that the Turkish authorities had seen fit to base the prosecution of Lieutenant Demons upon the above-mentioned Article 6, the question submitted to the Court is not whether that article is compatible with the principles of international law; it is more general. The Court is asked to state whether or not the principles of international law prevent Turkey from instituting criminal proceedings against Lieutenant Demons under Turkish law. Neither the conformity of Article 6 in itself with the principles of international law nor the application of that article by the Turkish authorities constitutes the point at issue; it is the very fact of the institution of proceedings which is held by France to be contrary to those principles. Thus the French Government at once protested against his arrest, quite independently of the question as to what clause of her legislation was relied upon by Turkey to justify it. The arguments put forward by the French Government in the course of the proceedings and based on the principles which, in its contention, should govern navigation on the high seas, show that it would dispute Turkey's jurisdiction to prosecute Lieutenant Demons, even if that prosecution were based on a clause of the Turkish Penal Code other than Article 6, assuming for instance that the offence in question should be regarded, by reason of its consequences, to have been actually committed on Turkish territory.

II.

Having determined the position resulting from the terms of the special agreement, the Court must now ascertain which were the principles of international law that the prosecution of Lieutenant Demons could conceivably be said to contravene.

It is Article 15 of the Convention of Lausanne of July 24th, 1923, respecting conditions of residence and business and jurisdiction, which refers the contracting Parties to the principles of international law as regards the delimitation of their respective jurisdiction.

This clause is as follows:

> "Subject to the provisions of Article 16, all questions of jurisdiction shall, as between Turkey and the other contracting Powers, be decided in accordance with the principles of international law."

The French Government maintains that the meaning of the expression "principles of international law" in this article should be sought in the light of the evolution of the Convention. Thus it states that during the preparatory work, the Turkish Government, by means of an amendment to the relevant article of a draft for the Convention, sought to extend its jurisdiction to crimes committed in the territory of a third State, provided that, under Turkish law, such crimes were within the jurisdiction of Turkish Courts. This amendment, in regard to which the representatives of France and Italy made reservations, was definitely rejected by the British representative; and the question having been subsequently referred to the Drafting Committee, the latter confined itself in its version of the draft to a declaration to the effect that questions of jurisdiction should be decided in accordance with the principles of international law. The French Government deduces from these facts that the prosecution of Demons is contrary to the intention which guided the preparation of the Convention of Lausanne.

The Court must recall in this connection what it has said in some of its preceding judgments and opinions, namely, that there is no occasion to have regard to preparatory work if the text of a convention is sufficiently clear in itself. Now the Court considers that the words "principles of international law", as ordinarily used, can only mean international law as it is applied between all nations belonging to the community of States. This interpretation is borne out by the context of the article itself which says that the principles of international law are to determine questions of jurisdiction—not only criminal but also civil—between the contracting Parties, subject only to the exception provided for in Article 16. Again, the preamble of the Convention says that the High Contracting Parties are desirous of effecting a settlement in accordance "with modern international law", and Article 28 of the Treaty of Peace of Lausanne, to which the Convention in question is annexed, decrees the complete abolition of the Capitulations "in every respect". In these circumstances it is impossible—except in pursuance of a definite stipulation—to construe the expression "principles of international law" otherwise than as meaning the principles which are in force between all independent nations and which therefore apply equally to all the contracting Parties.

Moreover, the records of the preparation of the Convention respecting conditions of residence and business and jurisdiction would not furnish anything calculated to overrule the construction indicated by the actual terms of Article 15....

It should be added to these observations that the original draft of the relevant article, which limited Turkish jurisdiction to crimes committed in Turkey itself, was also discarded by the Drafting Committee; this circumstance might with equal justification give the impression that the intention of the framers of the Convention was not to limit this jurisdiction in any way.

The two opposing proposals designed to determine definitely the area of application of Turkish criminal law having thus been discarded, the wording ultimately adopted by common consent for Article 15 can only refer to the principles of general international law relating to jurisdiction.

III.

The Court, having to consider whether there are any rules of international law which may have been violated by the prosecution in pursuance of Turkish law of Lieutenant Demons, is confronted in the first place by a question of principle which, in the written and oral arguments of the two Parties, has proved to be a fundamental one. The French Government contends that the Turkish Courts, in order to have jurisdiction, should be able to point to some title to jurisdiction recognized by international law in favour of Turkey. On the other hand, the Turkish Government takes the view that Article 15 allows Turkey jurisdiction whenever such jurisdiction does not come into conflict with a principle of international law.

The latter view seems to be in conformity with the special agreement itself, No. 1 of which asks the Court to say whether Turkey has acted contrary to the principles of international law and, if so, what principles. According to the special agreement, therefore, it is not a question of stating principles which would permit Turkey to take criminal proceedings, but of formulating the principles, if any, which might have been violated by such proceedings.

This way of stating the question is also dictated by the very nature and existing conditions of international law.

International law governs relations between independent States. The rules of law binding upon States therefore emanate from their own free will as expressed in conventions or by usages generally accepted as expressing principles of law and established in order to regulate the relations between these co-existing independent communities or with a view to the achievement of common aims. Restrictions upon the independence of States cannot therefore be presumed.

Now the first and foremost restriction imposed by international law upon a State is that—failing the existence of a permissive rule to the contrary—it may not exercise its power in any form in the territory of another State. In this sense jurisdiction is certainly territorial; it cannot be exercised by a State outside its territory except by virtue of a permissive rule derived from international custom or from a convention.

It does not, however, follow that international law prohibits a State from exercising jurisdiction in its own territory, in respect of any case which relates to acts which have taken place abroad, and in which it cannot rely on some permissive rule of international law. Such a view would only be tenable if international law contained a general prohibition to States to extend the application of their laws and the jurisdiction of their courts to persons, property and acts outside their territory, and if, as an exception to this general prohibition, it allowed States to do so in certain specific cases. But this is certainly not the case under international law as it stands at present. Far from laying down a general prohibition to the effect that States may not extend the application of their laws and the jurisdiction of their courts to persons, property and acts outside their territory, it leaves them in this respect a wide measure of discretion which is only limited in certain cases by prohibitive rules; as regards other cases, every State remains free to adopt the principles which it regards as best and most suitable.

This discretion left to States by international law explains the great variety of rules which they have been able to adopt without objections or complaints on the part of other States; it is in order to remedy the difficulties resulting from such variety that efforts have been made for many years past, both in Europe and America, to prepare conventions the effect of which would be precisely to limit the discretion at present left to States in this respect by international law, thus making good the existing lacunæ in respect of jurisdiction or removing the conflicting jurisdictions arising from the diversity of the principles adopted by the various States.

In these circumstances, all that can be required of a State is that it should not overstep the limits which international law places upon its jurisdiction; within these limits, its title to exercise jurisdiction rests in its sovereignty.

It follows from the foregoing that the contention of the French Government to the effect that Turkey must in each case be able to cite a rule of international law authorizing her to exercise jurisdiction, is opposed to the generally accepted international law to which Article 15 of the Convention of Lausanne refers. Having regard to the terms of Article 15 and to the construction which the Court has just placed upon it, this contention would apply in regard to civil as well as to criminal cases, and would be applicable on conditions of absolute reciprocity as between Turkey and the other contracting Parties; in practice, it would therefore in many cases result in paralyzing the action of the courts, owing to the impossibility of citing a universally accepted rule on which to support the exercise of their jurisdiction....

Nevertheless, it has to be seen whether the foregoing considerations really apply as regards criminal jurisdiction, or whether this jurisdiction is governed by a different principle: this might be the outcome of the close connection which for a long time existed between the conception of supreme criminal jurisdiction and that of a State, and also by the especial importance of criminal jurisdiction from the point of view of the individual.

Though it is true that in all systems of law the principle of the territorial character of criminal law is fundamental, it is equally true that all or nearly all these systems of law extend their action to offences committed outside the territory of the State which adopts them, and they do so in ways which vary from State to State. The territoriality of criminal law, therefore, is not an absolute principle of international law and by no means coincides with territorial sovereignty.

This situation may be considered from two different standpoints corresponding to the points of view respectively taken up by the Parties. According to one of these standpoints, the principle of freedom, in virtue of which each State may regulate its legislation at its discretion, provided that in so doing it does not come in conflict with a restriction imposed by international law, would also apply as regards law governing the scope of jurisdiction in criminal cases. According to the other standpoint, the exclusively territorial character of law relating to this domain constitutes a principle which, except as otherwise expressly provided, would, *ipso facto*, prevent States from extending the criminal jurisdiction of their courts beyond their frontiers; the exceptions in question, which include for instance extraterritorial jurisdiction over nationals and over crimes directed against public safety, would therefore rest on special permissive rules forming part of international law.

Adopting, for the purposes of the argument, the standpoint of the latter of these two systems, it must be recognized that, in the absence of a treaty provision, its correctness depends upon whether there is a custom having the force of law establishing it. The same is true as regards the applicability of this system—assuming it to have been recognized as sound—in the particular case. It follows that, even from this point of view, before ascertaining whether there may be a rule of international law expressly allowing Turkey to prosecute a foreigner for an offence committed by him outside Turkey, it is necessary to begin by establishing both that the system is well-founded and that it is applicable in the particular case. Now, in order to establish the first of these points, one must, as has just been seen, prove the existence of a principle of international law restricting the discretion of States as regards criminal legislation.

Consequently, whichever of the two systems described above be adopted, the same result will be arrived at in this particular case: the necessity of ascertaining whether or not under international law there is a principle which would have prohibited Turkey, in the circumstances of the case before the Court, from prosecuting Lieutenant Demons. And moreover, on either hypothesis, this must be ascertained by examining precedents offering a close analogy to the case under consideration; for it is only from precedents of this nature that the existence of a general principle applicable to the particular case may appear. For if it were found, for example, that, according to the practice of States, the jurisdiction of the State whose flag was flown was not established by international law as exclusive with regard to collision cases on the high seas, it would not be necessary to ascertain whether there were a more general restriction; since, as regards that restriction—supposing that it existed—the fact that it had been established that there was no prohibition in respect of collision on the high seas would be tantamount to a special permissive rule.

The Court therefore must ... ascertain whether or not there exists a rule of international law limiting the freedom of States to extend the criminal jurisdiction of their courts to a situation uniting the circumstances of the present case.

IV.

The Court will now proceed to ascertain whether general international law, to which Article 15 of the Convention of Lausanne refers, contains a rule prohibiting Turkey from prosecuting Lieutenant Demons....

The arguments advanced by the French Government, other than those considered above, are, in substance, the three following:

> (1) International law does not allow a State to take proceedings with regard to offences committed by foreigners abroad, simply by reason of the nationality of the victim; and such is the situation in the present case because the offence must be regarded as having been committed on board the French vessel.

> (2) International law recognizes the exclusive jurisdiction of the State whose flag is flown as regards everything which occurs on board a ship on the high seas.

> (3) Lastly, this principle is especially applicable in a collision case....

As regards the first argument, the Court feels obliged in the first place to recall that its examination is strictly confined to the specific situation in the present case, for it is only in regard to this situation that its decision is asked for.

As has already been observed, the characteristic features of the situation of fact are as follows: there has been a collision on the high seas between two vessels flying different flags, on one of which was one of the persons alleged to be guilty of the offence, whilst the victims were on board the other.

This being so, the Court does not think it necessary to consider the contention that a State cannot punish offences committed abroad by a foreigner simply by reason of the nationality of the victim. For this contention only relates to the case where the nationality of the victim is the only criterion on which the criminal jurisdiction of the State is based.... [I]t is certain that the courts of many countries, even of countries which have given their criminal legislation a strictly territorial character, interpret criminal law in the sense that offences, the authors of which at the moment of commission are in the territory of another State, are nevertheless to be regarded as having been committed in the national territory, if one of the constituent elements of the offence, and more especially its effects, have taken place there. French courts have, in regard to a variety of situations, given decisions sanctioning this way of interpreting the territorial principle. Again, the Court does not know of any cases in which governments have protested against the fact that the criminal law of some country contained a rule to this effect or that the courts of a country construed their criminal law in this sense. Consequently, once it is admitted that the effects of the offence were produced on the Turkish vessel, it becomes impossible to hold that there is a rule of international law which prohibits Turkey from prosecuting Lieutenant Demons because of the fact that the author of the offence was on board the French ship. Since, as has already been observed, the special agreement does not deal with the provision of Turkish law under which the prosecution was instituted, but only with the question whether the prosecution should be regarded as contrary to the principles of international law, there is no reason preventing the Court from confining itself to observing that, in this case, a prosecution may also be justified from the point of view of the so-called territorial principle....

It has been sought to argue that the offence of manslaughter cannot be localized at the spot where the mortal effect is felt; for the effect is not intentional and it cannot be said that there is, in the mind of the delinquent, any culpable intent directed towards the territory where the mortal effect is produced. In reply to this argument it might be observed that the effect is a factor of outstanding importance in offences such as manslaughter, which are punished precisely in consideration of their effects rather than of the subjective intention of the delinquent. But the Court does not feel called upon to consider this question, which is one of interpretation of Turkish criminal law. It will suffice to observe that no argument has been put forward and nothing has been found from which it would follow that international law has established a rule imposing on States this reading of the conception of the offence of manslaughter....

The second argument put forward by the French Government is the principle that the State whose flag is flown has exclusive jurisdiction over everything which occurs on board a merchant ship on the high seas.

It is certainly true that—apart from certain special cases which are defined by international law—vessels on the high seas are subject to no authority except that of the State whose flag they fly. In virtue of the principle of the freedom of the seas, that is to say, the absence of any territorial sovereignty upon the high seas, no State may exercise any kind of jurisdiction over foreign vessels upon them. Thus, if a war vessel, happening to be at the spot where a collision occurs between a vessel flying its flag and a foreign vessel, were to send on board the latter an officer to make investigations or to take evidence, such an act would undoubtedly be contrary to international law.

But it by no means follows that a State can never in its own territory exercise jurisdiction over acts which have occurred on board a foreign ship on the high seas. A corollary of the principle of the freedom of the seas is that a ship on the high seas is assimilated to the territory of the State the flag of which it flies, for, just as in its own territory, that State exercises its authority upon it, and no other State may do so....

This conclusion could only be overcome if it were shown that there was a rule of customary international law which, going further than the principle stated above, established the exclusive jurisdiction of the State whose flag was flown. The French Government has endeavoured to prove the existence of such a rule, having recourse for this purpose to the teachings of publicists, to decisions of municipal and international tribunals, and especially to conventions which, whilst creating exceptions to the principle of the freedom of the seas by permitting the war and police vessels of a State to exercise a more or less extensive control over the merchant vessels of another State, reserve jurisdiction to the courts of the country whose flag is flown by the vessel proceeded against.

In the Court's opinion, the existence of such a rule has not been conclusively proved....

It only remains to examine the third argument advanced by the French Government and to ascertain whether a rule specially applying to collision cases has grown up, according to which criminal proceedings regarding such cases come exclusively within the jurisdiction of the State whose flag is flown....

The conclusion at which the Court has therefore arrived is that there is no rule of international law in regard to collision cases to the effect that criminal proceedings are exclusively within the jurisdiction of the State whose flag is flown.

This conclusion moreover is easily explained if the manner in which the collision brings the jurisdiction of two different countries into play be considered.

The offence for which Lieutenant Demons appears to have been prosecuted was an act — of negligence or imprudence — having its origin on board the *Lotus*, whilst its effects made themselves felt on board the *Boz-Kourt*. These two elements are, legally, entirely inseparable, so much so that their separation renders the offence non-existent. Neither the exclusive jurisdiction of either State, nor the limitations of the jurisdiction of each to the occurrences which took place on the respective ships would appear calculated to satisfy the requirements of justice and effectively to protect the interests of the two States. It is only natural that each should be able to exercise jurisdiction and to do so in respect of the incident as a whole. It is therefore a case of concurrent jurisdiction....

V.

Having thus answered the first question submitted by the special agreement in the negative, the Court need not consider the second question, regarding the pecuniary reparation which might have been due to Lieutenant Demons.

For These Reasons,

The Court, having heard both Parties, gives, by the President's casting vote — the votes being equally divided —, judgment to the effect

(1) that, following the collision which occurred on August 2nd, 1926, on the high seas between the French steamship *Lotus* and the Turkish steamship *Boz-Kourt*, and upon the arrival of the French ship at Stamboul, and in consequence of the loss of the *Boz-Kourt* having involved the death of eight Turkish nationals, Turkey, by instituting criminal proceedings in pursuance of Turkish law against Lieutenant Demons, officer of the watch on board the *Lotus* at the time of the collision, has not acted in conflict with the principles of international law, contrary to Article 15 of the Convention of Lausanne of July 24th, 1923, respecting conditions of residence and business and jurisdiction;

(2) that, consequently, there is no occasion to give judgment on the question of the pecuniary reparation which might have been due to Lieutenant Demons if Turkey, by pros-

ecuting him as above stated, had acted in a manner contrary to the principles of international law.

Dissenting Opinion by M. Loder.

Turkey, having arrested, tried and convicted a foreigner for an offence which he is alleged to have committed outside her territory, claims to have been authorized to do so by reason of the absence of a prohibitive rule of international law.

Her defence is based on the contention that under international law everything which is not prohibited is permitted.

In other words, on the contention that, under international law, every door is open unless it is closed by treaty or by established custom.

The Court in its judgment holds that this view is correct, well founded, and in accordance with actual facts.

I regret that I am unable to concur with the opinion of the Court.

It seems to me that the contention is at variance with the spirit of international law. This law is for the most part unwritten and lacks sanctions; it rests on a general consensus of opinion; on the acceptance by civilized States, members of the great community of nations, of rules, customs and existing conditions which they are bound to respect in their mutual relations, although neither committed to writing nor confirmed by conventions. This body of rules is called international law.

These rules may be gradually modified, altered or extended, in accordance with the views of a considerable majority of these States, as this consensus of opinion develops, but is seems to me incorrect to say that the municipal law of a minority of States suffices to abrogate or change them.

It also appears to me incorrect to claim that the absence of international disputes or diplomatic difficulties in regard to certain provisions of the laws of some States, which are at variance with generally accepted ideas, can serve to show the development or modification of such ideas.

International *disputes* only arise when a particular *application* of the laws in question shows them to be at variance with international law.

The family of nations consists of a collection of different sovereign and independent States.

The fundamental consequence of their independence and sovereignty is that no municipal law, in the particular case under consideration no criminal law, can apply or have binding effect outside the national territory.

This fundamental truth, which is not a custom but the direct and inevitable consequence of its premiss, is a logical principle of law, and is a postulate upon which the mutual independence of States rests.

The criminal law of a State applies in the first place to all persons within its territory, whether nationals or foreigners, because the right of jurisdiction over its own territory is an attribute of its sovereignty.

The criminal law of a State may extend to crimes and offences committed abroad by its nationals, since such nationals are subject to the law of their own country; but it *cannot* extend to offences committed by a foreigner in foreign territory, without infringing the sovereign rights of the foreign State concerned, since in that State the State enacting the law has no jurisdiction.

Nor can such a law extend in the territory of the State enacting it to an offence committed by a foreigner abroad should the foreigner happen to be in this territory after the commission of the offence, because the guilty act has not been committed within the area subject to the jurisdiction of that State *and the subsequent presence of the guilty person* cannot have the effect of *extending the jurisdiction of the State.*

It seems to me clear that such is the logical consequence of the fundamental principle above enunciated. It however is also clear that this consequence can be overridden by some convention to the contrary effect or by some exception generally and even tacitly recognized by international law.

Like all exceptions, however, such an exception must be strictly construed and cannot be substituted for the well-established rule, to which it is an exception.

Now, the rule has gradually undergone an important modification in the legislation of a somewhat large majority of civilized States, a modification which does not seem to have encountered objections and which may be regarded as having been accepted. This modification tends to except from the strict rule governing the jurisdiction over offences committed by foreigners abroad such offences, in so far as they are directed against the State itself or against its security or credit. The injured State may try the guilty persons according to its own law if they happen to be in its territory or, if necessary, it may ask for their extradition.

Apart from this exception, the rule holds good.

The so-called system of "protection" which Turkey claims to be entitled to apply and which is tantamount to the abrogation of the rule itself, is very far from being accepted by the great majority of States and is not in my opinion in harmony with positive international law.

The alleged offence with which M. Demons is charged by Turkey, namely, involuntary manslaughter, does not fall within the scope of the exception which I have mentioned. Turkey admits that she is applying the so-called system of "protection" in pursuance of her municipal law and she holds that she is authorized to do so because she has found nowhere a positive and accepted rule prohibiting her from so doing.

It will appear from the foregoing that I am of opinion that for this reason alone, Turkey must be held to have acted in contravention of the principles of international law....

The Court has been made cognizant of a definite occurrence; it has to give judgment upon a particular case. This case is the collision between the French ship *Lotus* and the Turkish ship *Boz-Kourt*....

[Turkey] argues that this offence took place on board the *Boz-Kourt* because it was there that the effects of [Demons'] alleged negligence were felt.

She therefore contends that the wrongful act having taken place on board the Turkish ship, its author is amenable to the jurisdiction of the Turkish Courts.

If this argument be sound, in point of fact the deduction made from it is correct and the accusation of having acted contrary to the principles of international law at once falls to the ground, because every State is entitled to prosecute and sentence any foreigner who commits an offence within its territory. And the vessel *Boz-Kourt* must be regarded as Turkish territory.

The question of the localization of the offence is therefore of capital importance for the purposes of the decision of the dispute before the Court.

It is clear that the place where an offence has been committed is necessarily that where the guilty person is when he commits the act. The assumption that the place where the effect is produced is the place where the act was committed is in every case a legal fiction. It is, however, justified where the act and its effect are indistinguishable, when there is a direct relation between them; for instance, a shot fired at a person on the other side of a frontier; a parcel containing an infernal machine intended to explode on being opened by the person to whom it is sent. The author of the crime intends in such cases to inflict injury at a place other than that where he himself is.

But the case which the Court has to consider bears no resemblance to these instances. The officer of the *Lotus*, who had never set foot on board the *Boz-Kourt*, had no intention of injuring anyone, and no such intention is imputed to him. The movements executed in the navigation of a vessel are only designed to avoid an accident.

Only an investigation by naval experts into the circumstances can show whether the manner in which the ship was navigated is to be regarded as contrary to the regulations or negligent in some respect, or whether some unforeseen movement by the other vessel contributed to the accident—and this investigation is a matter solely for the naval authorities of the country of the person responsible for navigating the ship.

In these circumstances, it seems to me that the legal fiction whereby the act is held to have been committed at the place where the effect is produced must be discarded....

The general rule that the criminal law of a State loses its compelling force and its applicability in relation to offences committed by a foreigner in foreign territory, a rule derived from the basic principle of the sovereignty and independence of States, has indeed undergone modifications and has been made subject to exceptions restricting its scope by the mutual consent of the different Powers in so far as territory properly so called is concerned.

But according to a generally accepted view, this is not the case as regards the high seas. There the law of the flag and national jurisdiction have retained their indisputable authority to the exclusion of all foreign law or jurisdiction. I lay special stress on the word "foreign". A guilty person on board a ship flying the flag of a State other than the one to which he owes allegiance, may of course be indicted and sentenced by the State of which he is a national. In that case, but only then, there will be concurrent jurisdiction.

But that is not M. Demons' case.

A merchant ship being a complete entity, organized and subject to discipline in conformity with the laws and subject to the control of the State whose flag it flies, and having regard to the absence of all territorial sovereignty upon the high seas, it is only natural that as far as concerns criminal law this entity should come under the jurisdiction of that State. This applies with especial force to the case now before the Court. The accusation against Lieutenant Demons is that whilst navigating his ship he gave an order for a wrong manœuvre.

The rules for navigation which he was obliged to follow were those contained in his national regulations. He was responsible to his national authorities for the observance of these rules. It was solely for these authorities to consider whether the officer had observed these rules, whether he had done his duty, and, if not, whether he had neglected their observance to such a degree as to have incurred criminal responsibility.

It consequently seems to me that Turkey, in arrogating to herself jurisdiction over the acts of a foreign officer doing duty on the high seas on a ship carrying a foreign flag, has acted in contravention of the principle of international law set out above.

On these grounds I regret that I am unable to concur with the Court in its present judgment....

Dissenting Opinion by Mr. Moore.

On the present judgment as a whole, the vote, as appears by the judgment itself, stood six to six, and, the Court being equally divided, the President gave, under Article 55 of the Statute, a casting vote, thus causing the judgment as it stands to prevail. I was one of the dissenting six; but I wish at the outset to state that my dissent was based solely on the connection of the pending case with Article 6 of the Turkish Penal Code, which I will discuss in due course. In the judgment of the Court that there is no rule of international law by virtue of which the penal cognizance of a collision at sea, resulting in loss of life, belongs exclusively to the country of the ship by or by means of which the wrong was done, I concur, thus making for the judgment on that question, as submitted by the *compromis*, a definitely ascertained majority of seven to five. But, as I have reached my conclusions, both on the general question and on the point on which I dissent, by a somewhat independent course of reasoning, I deem it to be my duty to deliver a separate opinion....

Notes and Questions

1. When the Court stated that a state "cannot exercise its power in any form in the territory of another state" except by international custom or a convention, the Court was addressing enforcement jurisdiction that generally "is certainly territorial." Here, Turkey was enforcing its law within its territory and the dispute concerned the reach of Turkish prescriptive jurisdiction.

2. The Court noted that a state's use of prescriptive jurisdiction must "not overstep the limits which international law places upon its jurisdiction." Today, how does this compare with § 431 of the RESTATEMENT?

3. Note that France had argued against jurisdiction based merely on the nationality of the victims. Was Turkish jurisdiction based merely on the victim or passive personality theory?

4. When the Court focused on "the territorial principle" and its acceptance when conduct is initiated abroad "if one of the constituent elements of the offence, and more especially its effects, have taken place" in the forum state or "were produced on the Turkish vessel" (which is the equivalent of Turkish territory), from today's perspective, what form of territorial jurisdiction was being addressed? What elements did the Court address when noting that there "was an act—of negligence or imprudence—having its origin on board the *Lotus*, whilst its effects made themselves felt on board the *Boz-Kourt*"? Given that the *Lotus* crashed into the *Boz-Kourt*, was the act continuous? Did French territory enter into Turkish territory? Was the Lieutenant's negligence a proper substitute for intent?

5. Note that Demons would be due some amount of pecuniary reparation, as an individual, if Turkey did not have jurisdiction.

United States v. Yunis
681 F. Supp. 896, 899–900, 901–03 (D.D.C. 1988)

The parties agree that there are five traditional bases of jurisdiction over extraterritorial crimes under international law:

> *Territorial*, wherein jurisdiction is based on the place where the offense is committed;
>
> *National*, wherein jurisdiction is based on the nationality of the offender;

Protective, wherein jurisdiction is based on whether the national interest is injured;

Universal, wherein jurisdiction is conferred in any forum that obtains physical custody of the perpetrator of certain offenses considered particularly heinous and harmful to humanity.

Passive personal, wherein jurisdiction is based on the nationality of the victim.

These general principles were developed in 1935 by a Harvard Research Project in an effort to codify principles of jurisdiction under international law. *See Harvard Research in International Law, Jurisdiction with Respect to Crime*, 29 Am. J. Int'l L. 435, 445 (Supp. 1935). Most courts, including our Court of Appeals, have adopted the Harvard Research designations on jurisdiction. *See, e.g., Tel-Oren v. Libyan Arab Republic*, 726 F.2d 774, 781, n.7 (D.C. Cir. 1984), *cert. denied*, 470 U.S. 1003 ... (1985); *Chua Han Mow. v. United States*, 730 F.2d 1308, 1311 (9th Cir. 1984), *cert. denied*, 470 U.S. 1031 ... (1985); *Rivard v. United States*, 375 F.2d 882, 885 (5th Cir.), *cert. denied*, 389 U.S. 884 ... (1967)....

Passive Personal Principle

This principle authorizes states to assert jurisdiction over offenses committed against their citizens abroad. It recognizes that each state has a legitimate interest in protecting the safety of its citizens when they journey outside national boundaries. Because American nationals were on board the Jordanian aircraft, the government contends that the Court may exercise jurisdiction over Yunis under this principle. Defendant argues that this theory of jurisdiction is neither recognized by the international community nor the United States and is an insufficient basis for sustaining jurisdiction over Yunis.

Although many international legal scholars agree that the principle is the most controversial of the five sources of jurisdiction, they also agree that the international community recognizes its legitimacy. Most accept that "the extraterritorial reach of a law premised upon the ... principle would not be in doubt as a matter of international law." Paust, Jurisdiction and Nonimmunity, 23 Va. J. of Int'l Law, 191, 203 (1983). More importantly, the international community explicitly approved of the principle as a basis for asserting jurisdiction over hostage takers. As noted above, the Hostage Taking Convention set forth certain mandatory sources of jurisdiction. But it also gave each signatory country discretion to exercise extraterritorial jurisdiction when the offense was committed "with respect to a hostage who is a national of that state if that state considers it appropriate." Art. 5(a) (d). Therefore, even if there are doubts regarding the international community's acceptance, there can be no doubt concerning the application of this principle to the offense of hostage taking, an offense for which Yunis is charged. See M. Bassiouni, II International Criminal Law ch. 4 at 120.

Defendant's counsel correctly notes that the Passive Personal principle traditionally has been an anathema to United States lawmakers. But his reliance on the Restatement (Revised) of Foreign Relations Laws for the claim that the United States can never invoke the principle is misplaced. In the past, the United States has protested any assertion of such jurisdiction for fear that it could lead to indefinite criminal liability for its own citizens. This objection was based on the belief that foreigners visiting the United States should comply with our laws and should not be permitted to carry their laws with them. Otherwise Americans would face criminal prosecutions for actions unknown to them as illegal. However, in the most recent draft of the Restatement, the authors noted that the theory "has been increasingly accepted when applied to terrorist and other organized attacks on a state's nationals by reason of their nationality, or to assassinations of a state's ambassadors, or government officials." Restatement (Revised) §402, comment g (Tent. Draft No. 6). *See also* McGinley, The Achille Lauro Affair-Implications for International Law,

52 Tenn. L. Rev. 691, 713 (1985). The authors retreated from their wholesale rejection of the principle, recognizing that perpetrators of crimes unanimously condemned by members of the international community, should be aware of the illegality of their actions. Therefore, qualified application of the doctrine to serious and universally condemned crimes will not raise the specter of unlimited and unexpected criminal liability.

Finally, this case does not present the first time that the United States has invoked the principle to assert jurisdiction over a hijacker who seized an American hostage on foreign soil.[12] The government relied on this very principle when it sought extradition of Muhammed Abbas Zaiden, the leader of the terrorists who hijacked the Achille Lauro vessel in Egyptian waters and subsequently killed Leon Klinghoffer, an American citizen. As here, the only connection to the United States was Klinghoffer's American citizenship. Based on that link, an arrest warrant was issued charging Abbas with hostage taking, conspiracy and piracy. *Id.* at 719; *See also* N. Y. Times, Oct. 16, 1985, at 1 col. 6.— — — — —

[Additional footnotes from *Yunis*]

[court's note] 13. Only recently, the Justice Department announced it had withdrawn the arrest warrant issued against Abbas after reviewing the outstanding indictment and weighing the fact that the defendant had been convicted and sentenced in absentia in an Italian Court. *See* Wash. Post, Jan. 17, 1988.

[court's note] 14. The government also argues that a third doctrine, the Protective principle, offers grounds for asserting jurisdiction over Yunis. Because this principle gives states wide latitude in defining the parameters of their jurisdiction, the international community has strictly construed the reach of this doctrine to those offenses posing a direct, specific threat to national security. *See* Blakesley, *United States Jurisdiction over Extraterritorial Crime*, 73 J. Crim. L. & Criminology at 1136, Bassiouni, II *International Criminal Law* ch. 2 at 21. Recently, some academicians have urged a more liberal interpretation of the protective principle when applied to terroristic activities. Given "the increase in the number of terroristic threats against United States nationals abroad, there can be no doubt that the United States has significant security and protective interests at stake." Paust, *Federal Jurisdiction Over Extraterritorial Acts of Terrorism*, 23 Va. J. of Int'l Law 191, 210 (1983).

In this case, the hijackers never made any demands upon the United States government nor directly threatened its security. Indeed, it was almost happenstance that three American nationals were on board the aircraft. Given the regional focus of the hijacking, a court would have to adopt an expansive view of the principle to assert jurisdiction over Yunis. Since jurisdiction is available under the universality and passive personality principle, there is no reason to reach out and rely on the protective principle as well.

Questions

1. Did the district court correctly quote the extract from Paust on the victim theory?

2. Does it result from the court's qualification of the victim theory that it is swallowed by another principle? Without such a limitation, are the fears of potentially indefinite liability under the victim theory for actions unknown to be illegal in the country of nationality still valid?

---

12. At least one Court has explicitly relied on the passive personality principle to assert jurisdiction over foreigners committing crimes against U.S. nationals overseas. *United States v. Benitez*, 741 F.2d 1312, 1316 (11th Cir. 1984) (Columbian charged with conspiracy to murder DEA agent). ("The nationality of the victims, who are United States Government agents, clearly supports jurisdiction.")

3. A more recent case accepting the victim theory as valid in the context of an airplane hijacking in the Mediterranean during which a U.S. citizen was killed is United States v. Rezaq, 134 F.3d 1121 (D.C. Cir.1998) (the opinion quoted from the Restatement § 402, cmt. g (1987): "The principle has not been generally accepted for ordinary torts or crimes, but it is increasingly accepted as applied to terrorist and other organized attacks on a state's nationals by reason of their nationality....""). *Rezaq* also used the principle of universal jurisdiction.

4. The protective principle has also been held to apply to offenses committed under the Espionage Act, 18 U.S.C. §§ 792–799. Espionage is a pure crime against the state (a "pure" political offense with respect to extradition), like treason or a military offense of absence without leave. In *United States v. Zehe*, 601 F. Supp. 196 (D. Mass. 1985), the United States prosecuted an East German citizen for acts of espionage committed outside the borders of the United States. In upholding the extraterritorial application of the Espionage Act, the court asserted that the protective principle grants Congress the authority to punish crimes directed against the United States regardless of the perpetrator's nationality or the locus of the offense:

> The defendant concedes that under principles of international law recognized by United States courts, Congress is competent to punish criminal acts, wherever and by whomever committed, that threaten national security or directly obstruct governmental functions. Espionage against the United States, because it is a crime that, by definition, threatens this country's security, can be punished by Congress even if committed by a noncitizen outside the United States.

Id. at 198.

5. For other cases using the protective principle, *see, e.g.*, United States v. Yousef, 327 F.3d 56, 93–94 (2d Cir. 2003) (terroristic aircraft sabotage and threats to U.S. national security, also using universal jurisdiction); United States v. Campbell 798 F. Supp.2d 293, 308–09 (D.D.C. 2011) (upholding extraterritorial jurisdiction based on the protective principle, finding that "[b]ribery in connection with contracts backed by U.S. financing is illegal precisely because it implicates and adversely affects the interests and purse of the United States"); United States v. Ayesh, 762 F. Supp.2d 832, 841(E.D. Va. 2011) (use of protective principal justified because statutes "which target government theft and corruption, certainly advance an important national interest that cannot be understated"). In United States v. Saac, 632 F.3d 1203, 1211 (11th Cir. 2011), the Eleventh Circuit upheld the extraterritorial reach of the Drug Trafficking Vessel Interdiction Act of 2008 ("DTVIA"), 18 U.S.C. § 2285, reasoning: "Those who engage in conduct the DTVIA targets threaten our nation's security by evading detection while using submersible vessels to smuggle illegal drugs or other contraband, such as illegal weapons, from one country to another, and often into the United States." However, what if the "submersible vessel" is not transporting illicit drugs at the time of the interdiction or, if transporting illegal drugs, the drugs are destined for another country? In either case, the conduct would not threaten the nation's security. Therefore, the protective principle would not apply.

Joyce v. Director of Public Prosecutions
[1946] A.C. 347 (U.K. House of Lords)

[Editors' note: The *Joyce* case is of importance for international law because it deals with questions such as the allegiance owed by aliens, the right of a state to assume jurisdiction over acts committed by them abroad, and the nature of the diplomatic protection of citizens and aliens. The case is also important from the point of view of criminal law since it involves the crime of treason. Finally, it deals with a constitutional question concerning the nature and extent of allegiance.]

Lord Jowitt, L.C.... The appellant [William Joyce] was born in the U.S.A., in 1906, the son of a naturalised American citizen who had previously been a British subject by birth. He thereby became himself a natural-born American citizen. At about three years of age he was brought to Ireland, where he stayed until 1921, when he came to England. He stayed in England until 1939.... On July 4, 1933, he applied for a British passport, describing himself as a British subject by birth, born in Galway. He asked for the passport for the purpose of holiday touring in [Europe]....

On some day after Aug. 24, 1939, the appellant left the realm.... Upon his arrest in 1945 there was found upon his person a "work book" issued by the German State on Oct. 4, 1939, from which it appeared that he had been employed by the German Radio Company of Berlin, as an announcer of English news from Sept. 18, 1939.... It was proved to the satisfaction of the jury that he had at the dates alleged in the indictment broadcast propaganda on behalf of the enemy. He was found guilty accordingly.... [T]he question for consideration is bound up with the question of allegiance. Allegiance is owed to their Sovereign Lord the King by his natural born subjects; so it is by those who, being aliens, become his subjects by denisation or naturalisation (I will call them all 'naturalized subject'); so it is by those who, being aliens, resident within the King's realm. Whether you look to the feudal law for the origin of this conception or find it in the elementary necessities of any political society, it is clear that fundamentally it recognizes the need of the man for protection and of the sovereign lord for service. '*Protectio trahit subjectioinem et subjectio protectionem.*' All who were brought within the King's protection were ad fidem regis: all owed him allegiance. The topic is discussed with much learning in *Calvin's* case.

The natural-born subject owes allegiance from his birth, the naturalized subject from his naturalization, the alien from the day when he comes within the realm. By what means and when can they cast off allegiance? The natural-born subject cannot at common law at any time cast it off. '*Nemo potest exurer patriam*' is a fundamental maxim of the law from which relief was given only by recent statutes. Nor can the naturalized subjects at common law. It is in regard to the alien resident within the realm that the controversy in this case arises. Admittedly he owes allegiance while he is so resident, but it is argued that his allegiance extends no further. Numerous authorities were cited by the learned counsel for the appellant in which it is stated without any qualification or extension that an alien owes allegiance so long as he is within the realm and it has been argued with great force that the physical presence of the alien actor within the realm is necessary to make his act treasonable. It is implicit in this argument that during absence from the realm, however brief, an alien ordinarily resident within the realm cannot commit treason; he cannot in any circumstances by giving aid and comfort to the King's enemies outside the realm be guilty of a treasonable act.

My Lords, in my opinion this which is the necessary and logical statement of the appellant's case is not only at variance with the principle of the law, but is inconsistent with authority which your Lordships cannot disregard. I refer first to authority. It is said in Foster's Crown Cases (3rd ed.), p. 183 — 'Local allegiance is founded in the protection a foreigner enjoyeth for his person, his family or effects, during his residence here; and it ceaseth, whenever he withdraweth with his family and effects'.... And if such alien, seeking the protection of the Crown, and having a family and effects here, should during a war with his native country, go thither, and there adhere to the King's enemies for purposes of hostility, he might be dealt with as a traitor. For he came and settled here under the protection of the Crown; and, though his person was removed for a time, his effects and family continued still under the same protection. This rule was laid down by all the judges assembled at the Queen's command January 12, 1707.... In my view therefore it is the law that in the case supposed in the resolution of 1707 an alien may be guilty of treason for an act committed outside the realm.... There is no evidence that the appellant left a family or effects behind him when he left this realm. I do not for this purpose regard parents or brother or sisters as a family. But though there was no continuing protection for his family or effects, of him too it must be asked, whether there was not such protection still afforded by the sovereign as to require of him the continuance of his allegiance. The principle which runs through feudal law and what I may perhaps call constitutional law requires on the one hand protection, on the other fidelity: a duty of the sovereign lord to protect, a duty of the liege or subject to be faithful. Treason, 'trahison', is the betrayal of a trust: to be faithful to the trust is the counterpart of the duty to protect....

... The material facts are these, that being for long resident here and owing allegiance he applied for and obtained a passport and, leaving the realm, adhered to the King's enemies. It does not matter that he made false representations as to his status, asserting that he was a British subject by birth, a statement that he was afterwards at pains to disprove. It may be that when he first made the statement, he thought it was true. Of this there is no evidence. The essential fact is that he got the passport and I now examine its effect. The actual passport issued to the appellant has not been produced, but its contents have been duly proved. The terms of a passport are familiar. It is thus described by Lord Alverstone, C.J., in *R. v. Brailsford*, [1905] 2 K.B. 730: 'It is a document issued in the name of the sovereign on the responsibility of a minister of the Crown to a named individual, intended to be presented to the governments of foreign nations and to be used for that individual's protection as a British subject in foreign countries'. By its terms it requests and requires in the name of His Majesty all those whom it may concern to allow the bearer to pass freely without let or hindrance and to afford him every assistance and protection of which he may stand in need. It is, I think true that the possession of a passport by a British subject does not increase the sovereign's duty of protection, though it will make his path easier. For him it serves as a voucher and means of identification. But the possession of a passport by one who is not a British subject gives him rights and imposes upon the sovereign obligations which would otherwise not be given or imposed. It is immaterial that he has obtained it by misrepresentation and that he is not in law a British subject. By the possession of that document he is enabled to obtain in a foreign country the protection extended to British subjects. By his own act he has maintained the bond which while he was within the realm bound him to his sovereign. The question is not whether he obtained British citizenship by obtaining the passport, but whether by its receipt he extended his duty of allegiance beyond the moment when he left the shores of this country. As one owing allegiance to the King he sought and obtained the protection of the King for himself while abroad.... What is this protection upon which the claim to fidelity is founded? To me, my Lords, it appears that the Crown in issuing a passport is assuming an onerous burden, and the holder of the passport is acquiring substantial privileges.... Armed with that document the holder may demand from the State's representatives abroad and from the officials of foreign governments that he be treated as a British subject, and even in the territory of a hostile state may claim the intervention of the protecting power.... ... The document speaks for itself. It was capable of affording the appellant protection. He applied for it and obtained it, and it was available for his use.... This point therefore also fails.

Lords Wright, Macmillan and Simonds concurred in this opinion.

Per Lord Porter (dissenting) ... It must be remembered that the matter to be determined is not whether the appellant took upon himself a new allegiance, but whether he continued an allegiance which he had owed for some twenty-four years, and a lesser amount of evidence may be required in the latter than in the former case. I cannot think that such a resident can in war-time pass to and from this country to a foreign jurisdiction and be permitted by our laws to adhere to the enemy there without being amenable to the law of treason. I agree with your Lordships also in thinking that if an alien is under British protection he occupies the same position when abroad as he would occupy if he were a British subject. Each of them owes allegiance, and in so doing each is subject to the jurisdiction of the British Crown. 'The law of nations', says Oppenheim, *International Law*, vol. I, p. 266 (5th ed.), 'does not prevent a state from exercising jurisdiction within its own territory over its subjects travelling or residing abroad, since they remain under its personal supremacy.' Moreover, in *R. v. Casement*, [1917] 1 K.B. 98, the point was directly decided in the case of a British subject who committed the act of adhering to the King's enemies abroad, and the decision was not seriously controverted before your Lordships. But my Lords, though the renewing of a passport might in a proper case lead to the conclusion that the possessor, though absent from the country, continued to owe allegiance to the British Crown, yet in my view the question whether that duty was still in existence depends upon the circumstances of the individual case and is a matter for the jury to determine. In the present case, as I understand him, the learned judge ruled that in law the duty of allegiance continued until the protection given by the passport came to an end—i.e. in a year's time—or at any rate until after the first act of adhering to the enemy, which I take to be the date of the appellant's employment as broadcaster by the German State on September 18, 1939. The Court of Criminal Appeal take, I think the same view, but since your Lordships, as I understand, think otherwise, I must set out the facts as I see them. The appellant, admittedly an American subject, but resident within this realm for some twenty-four years, applied for and obtained a passport, as a British subject, in 1933. This document continued to be effective for five years, and was renewed in 1938 and again on August 24, 1939. Extensions are normally granted for one year, and that given to the appellant followed the normal course. It would, I think, not be an unnatural inference that he used it in leaving England and entering Germany, but in fact nothing further was proved as to the appellant's movements, save that his appointment as broadcaster by the German State, dated September 18, 1939, was found in his possession when he was captured, and that at any rate by December 10 he had given his first broadcast. Nothing is known as to the passport after its issue, and it has not since been found.

Notes and Questions

1. Was it a defense that Joyce was following German law or that he might have been compelled to do so?

2. Does the nationality principle justify British jurisdiction in the *Joyce* case? For a U.S. case involving a U.S. citizen convicted of treason "by working as a radio speaker, announcer, script writer and broadcaster for the Imperial Japanese Government" from 1943–1945, see D'Aquino v. United States, 192 F.2d 338 (9th Cir.1951).

3. Would the objective territorial principle justify British jurisdiction in the *Joyce* case?

4. Would the protective principle apply in this case? The protective principle generally reaches crimes against the state that are known as "pure" political offenses in the context of extradition—offenses such as espionage, subversion, sedition, and treason—since they involve threats to significant national security interests. Yet, could any alien abroad (*e.g.*, including those with no connection with the forum) rightly be prosecuted for treason? Why would treason be treated differently than espionage with respect to aliens hav-

ing no connection with the forum? For an Italian case involving a resident alien convicted of treason with respect to conduct in Italy, see *Re* Penati, Court of Cassation, 1946, [1946] Ann. Dig. 74 (No. 30). The Inter-American Court of Human Rights found that Peru could prosecute foreign nationals under a law proscribing "treason" when the crimes alleged were actually forms of terrorism and, thus, there was no violation of the "right to nationality" under Article 20 of the American Convention on Human Rights. See Castillo Petruzzi, Merits, Judgment, para. 102, Inter-Am. Ct. H.R. (30 May 1999). Prosecution before a military tribunal, however, had involved several human rights violations. *Id.*

Are some forms of subversion and sedition protected under international law? Recall the 1984 General Assembly resolution concerning the Apartheid regime in South Africa, in Chapter One. What about subversive speech? See also Note 5, below.

5. Assume that during the "Cold War" a U.S. national working in West Germany for Radio Free Europe had participated in broadcasts into Eastern Europe that Czechoslovakia had thought were subversive and criminally sanctionable. The U.S. national was later arrested in Czechoslovakia. Is there jurisdiction to prescribe? Some states have argued that if an activity is a basic "freedom" engaged in in the territory of origin, that subsequent prosecution is impermissible. *See, e.g.*, 1935 Harvard Research in International Law, art. 7, in 29 Am. J. Int'l L. 435 (Supp. 1935). Was that what was involved in the *Joyce* case? in *D'Aquino*, in Note 2 above?

Can you make a similar argument based on human rights law? *See, e.g.*, Universal Declaration of Human Rights, Article 19 (*but see id.*, art. 29(2)); International Covenant on Civil and Political Rights, Article 19. Does it matter that the right to participate in transnational speech is a derogable human right? What test pertains with respect to claims to derogate? In the *Joyce* case, what state could rightly claim power to derogate from a right of transnational free speech? Where was the speech? When comparing general principles of jurisdiction under customary international law and customary human rights law, are there any priorities to consider? See also U.N. Charter, art. 103.

United States v. Georgescu

723 F. Supp. 912 (E.D.N.Y. 1989)

Weinstein, J.

Over the mid-Atlantic on a Scandinavian Airlines flight from Copenhagen, Denmark to John F. Kennedy International Airport in Queens, the defendant, a Romanian national, allegedly accosted a nine year old girl who is a national of Norway by placing his hand on her genitals. He was indicted for committing a criminal sexual act while in the special aircraft jurisdiction of the United States. 18 U.S.C. § 2241 (c) (Supp. V 1987), 49 U.S.C. § 1472 (k) (1) (Supp. V 1987). In this case of first impression, he moves to dismiss, claiming lack of jurisdiction in United States courts. His motion must be denied for the reasons stated below.

Statutory Language

Section 2241 of chapter 109A of title 18 of the United States Code deals with sexual abuse of a child under the age of twelve, making it a crime punishable by up to life imprisonment. It provides in part:

> Whoever in the special maritime and territorial jurisdiction of the United States ... knowingly engages in a sexual act with another person who has not attained the age of 12 years, or attempts to do so, shall be fined ...,imprisoned for any term of years or life, or both.

18 U.S.C. § 2241 (c) (Supp. V 1987).

The special maritime and territorial jurisdiction of the United States is defined in section 7 of title 18. Insofar as relevant, it covers only American owned aircraft, 18 U.S.C. § 7(5) (1982), and offenses "against a national of the United States." 18 U.S.C. § 7 (7) (Supp. V 1987). Neither applies here. Title 18 deals with crimes and criminal procedure generally. Many crimes are defined in the substantive titles of the Code.

Subsequent legislation, incorporated in the transportation title of the United States Code, title 49, established a new "special aircraft jurisdiction." Congress authorized the exercise of this jurisdiction over specified crimes, including sexual abuse crimes defined under chapter 109A of title 18. This provision reads:

> Whoever, while aboard an aircraft *within the special aircraft jurisdiction* of the United States, *commits an act which, if committed within the special maritime and territorial jurisdiction of the United States*, as defined in section 7 of Title 18, would be in violation of ... chapter 109A ... of such Title 18 shall be punished as provided therein.

49 U.S.C. App. § 1472 (k) (1) (Supp. V 1987) (emphasis added).

The broad definition of "special aircraft jurisdiction of the United States" includes a foreign aircraft scheduled to stop in the United States if it actually lands here. The statute states:

> (38) The term "special aircraft jurisdiction of the United States includes—
>
> (d) any other aircraft outside the United States—
>
> (i) that has its next scheduled destination ... in the United States, if that aircraft next actually lands in the United States....
>
> while that aircraft is in flight, which is from the moment when all external doors are closed following embarkation until the moment when one such door is opened for disembarkation....

49 U.S.C. App. § 1301 (38) (d) (Supp. V 1987). This definition covers the aircraft of the foreign airline aboard which the defendant and his alleged victim were traveling; Kennedy Airport was the next scheduled destination and the aircraft actually landed there....

Legislative History

The statutory language is clear enough so as to need no buttressing from legislative history. In fact, language and history are in accord. The history of the statutes regarding crimes committed aboard aircraft makes plain the congressional design to criminalize and create jurisdiction over specified acts committed in non-United States airspace aboard foreign carriers bound for and landing in the United States, including aggravated sexual abuse as defined in section 2241 of title 18....

The crimes made punishable in this expanded jurisdiction included rape, carnal knowledge of a female under 16, and lewd or obscene acts. Pub. L. No. 87-197, 75 Stat. 466, 466 (1961); H.R. Rep. No. 958, 87th Cong., 1st Sess. 13–14. Defendant's claim that the current version of this statute was intended to apply only to such crimes when committed in connection with a hijacking is untenable. The House report for this 1961 version stated, "The crimes referred to would be punishable regardless of whether there was any connection between the specific crime and the offense of aircraft piracy." H.R. Rep. No. 958, 87th Cong., 1st Sess. 10–11.

In 1969, the Senate consented to the ratification of the multilateral Convention on Of-fences and Certain other Acts Committed on Board Aircraft, [hereinafter Tokyo Con-vention] ... The purpose of the Tokyo Convention was in part to encourage countries to punish crimes and certain non-criminal acts committed aboard aircraft. The Tokyo Con-vention allows parties to exercise jurisdiction over crimes committed aboard foreign air-craft in foreign or international airspace.... When the Senate consented to ratification, it was aware of the Tokyo Convention's broad jurisdictional provisions. The President's message of transmittal of the Tokyo Convention to the Senate pointed out the concurrent jurisdiction provision. S. Exec. Doc. L, 90th Cong., 2d Sess. 3 & 6 (1968). In its report, the Senate reprinted testimony of the deputy legal advisor to the Department of State, who noted that the Tokyo Convention "would permit the United States to continue to exercise jurisdiction over acts aboard foreign aircraft flying to, in, or from the United States." S. Exec. Rep. No. 3, 91st Sess. 7 (1969).

In 1970, Congress enacted legislation regarding crimes committed aboard aircraft, in part to implement the Tokyo Convention. The 1970 legislation supplanted the vague no-tion of "in flight in air commerce" with a new jurisdictional definition, "special aircraft jurisdiction." The statute defined special aircraft jurisdiction to include

> (c) any other aircraft (i) within the United States or (ii) outside the United States which has its next scheduled destination or last point of departure in the United States provided that in either case it next actually lands in the United States....

The special aircraft jurisdiction was amended in 1974 to comply with the Convention for the Suppression of Unlawful Seizure of Aircraft (Hijacking), Dec. 16, 1970 ... [here-inafter Hague Convention]. See Pub. L. No. 93-366, 88 Stat. 409, 409–10 (1974). The amended definition added clause (ii) (italicized below) to the existing clause (i), to include, in relevant part, any aircraft outside the United States

> (i) that has its next scheduled destination ... in the United States, if that aircraft next actually lands in the United States; or *(ii) having "an offense" as defined in the [Hague Convention] committed aboard, if that aircraft lands in the United States with the alleged offender still aboard ...*

Pub. L. No. 93-366, 88 Stat. 409, 410 (1974) (emphasis added). The amended definition added Hague Convention offenses committed aboard foreign aircraft not scheduled to land in the United States, but that do in fact land there. The purpose of the amendment was to implement the Hague Convention by "extend[ing] the definition to include ... categories of aircraft not now covered by existing law." H.R. Rep. No. 93-885, 93rd Cong., 2d Sess. 11; H.R. Conf. Rep. No. 93-1194, 93d Cong., 2d Sess. 14. Jurisdiction over for-eign aircraft that are scheduled to and do in fact land in the United States was retained unchanged from the original statute.

The definition of special aircraft jurisdiction reached its present form in 1984, when Congress amended the statute to cover certain offenses defined in the Convention for the Suppression of Unlawful Acts Against the Safety of Civil Aviation (Sabotage) art. 1, §§ 1(d), 1(e), (1971) [Montreal Convention]. See Pub. L. No. 98-473, 98 Stat. 1837, 2189 (1984). Clause (iii) (italicized below) was added to the existing clauses (i) and (ii) so that the spe-cial aircraft jurisdiction now includes, in relevant part:

> (d) any other aircraft outside the United States
>
> > (i) that has its next scheduled destination or last point of departure in the United States, if that aircraft actually lands in the United States;

(ii) having "an offense" as defined in the [Hague Convention] committed aboard, if that aircraft lands in the United States with the alleged offender still aboard; or

(iii) *regarding which an offense as defined in [certain parts of the Montreal Conventional is committed if the aircraft lands in the United States with an alleged offender still on board;*

49 U.S.C. App. § 1472 (k) (1) (Supp. V 1987) (emphasis added). This amendment is analogous to the 1974 amendment in that it adds to the ambit of jurisdiction certain Montreal Convention offenses committed aboard foreign aircraft not scheduled to land in the United States, but actually landing there. The amendment "expands the protection accorded to aircraft ... by establishing criminal jurisdiction over certain aircraft-related offenses." S. Rep. No. 98-619, 98th Cong., 2d Sess. 1. And, like the 1974 amendment, it leaves intact jurisdiction over specified crimes committed on foreign aircraft scheduled to land and actually landing in the United States.

Defendant insists that the special aircraft jurisdiction should be read to cover foreign aircraft only when Hague or Montreal Convention offenses are committed on board. In other words, he contends, subsection (d) (i) does not stand on its own, but requires in addition the occurrence of (d) (ii) or (d) (iii). There is nothing in the legislative history to indicate that Congress meant to qualify the broad jurisdiction over crimes aboard foreign aircraft that it conferred in the 1961 and 1970 criminal provisions. Rather, the 1974 and 1984 amendments left the earlier provision intact while it expanded jurisdiction to include Hague or Montreal offenses committed aboard foreign aircraft that make *unscheduled* landings in the United States.

In 1986, Congress added chapter 109A of title 18 to the list of crimes punishable under 49 U.S.C. § 1472 (k) (1). See Pub. L. No. 99-646, 100 Stat. 3592, 3624 (1986). The statute now reads:

Whoever, while aboard an aircraft within the special aircraft jurisdiction of the United States, commits an act which, if committed within the special maritime and territorial jurisdiction of the United States, as defined in section 7 of Title 18, would be in violation of section 113, 114, 661, 662, 1111, 1112, 1113, chapter 109A, or 2111 of such Title 18 shall be punished as provided therein.

49 U.S.C. App. § 1472 (k) (1) (Supp. V 1987). Adding a reference to chapter 109A—and thus to section 2241 of title 18 under which defendant is charged—did not change the pattern of the underlying jurisdictional statute. Thus, the knowing engagement or attempted engagement in a sexual act with a child under the age of 12, aboard a foreign aircraft in non-United States airspace that is next scheduled to land and actually lands in the United States, is a federal crime punishable in a United States court....

The special aircraft jurisdiction statute was originally created to comply with treaty obligations under the Tokyo Convention. While the Tokyo Convention was intended primarily to deal with the punishment of air piracy, it was also designed to cover any other criminal offense. Article 1 defines the Tokyo Convention's scope as covering:

a) offences against penal law;

b) acts which, whether or not they are offences, may or do jeopardize the safety of the aircraft or of persons or property therein or which jeopardize good order and discipline on board.

The record of the drafting conference reports that the secretary general of the conference stated that the Convention was intended to apply to all penal offences "irrespective of whether or not they affected the safety of the aircraft." 1 International Civil Aviation Organization, *International Conference on Air Law, Tokyo, August-September 1963* 16 (1966)....

The Tokyo Convention's primary goal was to encourage nations to exercise jurisdiction over crimes committed aboard aircraft registered in that nation. Nevertheless, the Tokyo Convention explicitly provides for jurisdiction over crimes committed aboard aircraft of foreign registry. Article 3(3) provides, "This Convention does not exclude any criminal jurisdiction exercised in accordance with national law." See S.Exec. Doc. L, 90th Cong. 2d Sess. 3 & 6 (1968) (President and Secretary of State note that Tokyo Convention allows exercise of jurisdiction over crimes committed on foreign aircraft); S.Exec.Rep. No. 3, 91st Cong., 1st Sess. 7 (1969) (Senate Foreign Relations Committee report on Tokyo Convention noting jurisdiction over foreign aircraft); S. Rep. No. 91-1083, 91st Cong., 2d Sess. 2 (1970), *reprinted* in 1970 U.S.Code Cong. & Admin.News 3996, 3997 (report accompanying legislation creating special aircraft jurisdiction, noting the Convention's provision of concurrent jurisdiction); 1 P. Keenan, A. Lester, P. Martin & J. McMahon, *Shawcross and Beaumont on Air Law* 704 (3d ed. 1966) ("The principle of concurrent jurisdiction is retained."); id. at 705 ("[T]here is nothing in the Convention to prevent a State with only remote contacts from exercising jurisdiction.").

Defendant contends that jurisdiction over foreign aircraft is limited by article 4 of the Tokyo Convention. The limitations of article 4 apply to attempts to "interfere with an aircraft in flight to exercise ... criminal jurisdiction." Interference means forcing the aircraft to land, or unduly delaying the flight. *International Conference on Air Law, Tokyo, August-September 1963* 100–05 (1966); N. Matte, *Treatise on Air-Aeronautical Law* 339–40 (1981); 1 P. Keenan, A. Lester, P. Martin & J. McMahon, *supra*, at 705; Mendelsohn, *In-Flight Crime: The International and Domestic Picture Under the Tokyo Convention*, 53 Va.L.Rev. 509, 518 (1967). There is no contention or evidence that the defendant's flight was in any way diverted, delayed or forced to land in order to arrest him or aid in his prosecution.

When the Senate ratified the Tokyo Convention, it was made aware of the broad jurisdiction that the Convention allowed. A deputy legal advisor to the Department of State told the Senate in hearings on the matter that the Convention "would permit the United States to continue to exercise jurisdiction over acts aboard foreign aircraft flying to, in, or from the United States." S. Exec. Rep. No. 3, 91st Cong., 1st Sess. 7 (1969).

The Tokyo Convention's concurrent jurisdiction provisions reflect the international legal community's acceptance of broad bases for jurisdiction over criminal offenses occurring on aircraft. *See generally Restatement, supra* § 402 Comment h, at 240–41, § 403 Reporters' Note 9, at 253–54 (suggesting that acts aboard aircraft be considered a basis of jurisdiction independent of traditional bases in international law, and approving the exercise of criminal jurisdiction over an offense committed on foreign aircraft, especially if the offense involved the use of force). *See also* N. Matte, *Treatise on Air-Aeronautical Law* 332 (1966). Numerous other signatories to the Tokyo Convention have passed statutes conferring jurisdiction over crimes committed aboard foreign aircraft....

See, e.g., Code de L'Aviation Civile, Loi No. 72-623, 5 juillet 1972, art. L. 121-8, J.O. 7179 (July 9, 1972), Gazette du Palais (Legislation) 360 (2e Semestre 1972), translated in N. Leech, C. Oliver & J. Sweeney, *The International Legal System* 278 (1973) (French statute conferring jurisdiction based on place of landing); 2 Codes Belges (Penal) Aeronautique, 27 juin 1937, art. 36 (J. Servais & E. Mechelynck, 26e Supp. May 1 1983), 2 Les Codes Larcier (Penal) Navigation Aerienne, 27 juin 1937, art. 36 (1985), translated in 1

Senate Comm. on Com., Air Laws and Treaties of the World 257–58 (Comm.Print 1965) (Belgian code conferring jurisdiction based on place of landing, or location of accused in Belgium). *See also* Civil Aviation Act 1982, c. 16, §92(3) (United Kingdom statute conferring jurisdiction based on location of accused in United Kingdom); 2 International Civil Aviation Organization, International Conference on Air Law, Tokyo, August-September 1963 38–39 (proposal considered at Tokyo Convention conference to establish place of landing as the highest priority basis of jurisdiction; in the end, the Tokyo Convention did not include any priority ranking of jurisdiction).

Extension of jurisdiction to include criminal acts committed against foreign nationals aboard a foreign airliner bound for, and actually landing, at a United States airport makes good sense. The pilot can radio ahead for assistance, federal agents can be present to take the culprit into custody at once and the witnesses to the crime will be immediately available. If the United States did not exercise its jurisdiction, there is no guarantee that any other country would do so, since the Tokyo Convention does not oblige a state to prosecute alleged offenders. Mendelsohn, *In-Flight Crime: The International and Domestic Picture Under the Tokyo Convention*, 53 Va.L.Rev. 509, 516 (1967). For would-be criminals, it may have an inhibiting effect to know that upon landing they may be immediately apprehended and prosecuted....

Power of Courts to Refuse Jurisdiction

Despite this court's reservations about the wisdom of further prosecution in this country, it lacks the power to refuse jurisdiction on equitable grounds. The court is empowered to dismiss a criminal 'case only for unnecessary delay, Fed.R.Crim.P. 48 (b), failure to comply with the time limits set by the Speedy Trial Act, 18 U.S.C. §3161 (1982) or lack of jurisdiction or the failure of the indictment to charge an offense, Fed.R.Crim.P. 12(b) (2). See 1 C. Wright, *Federal Practice and Procedure* §3, at 12 (1982) (Rule 48 (b) and Speedy Trial Act); United States v. Weinstein, 511 F.2d 622, 627 (2d Cir.), *cert. denied*, 422 U.S. 1042, (1975) (Rule 12(b) (2), and generally noting the limited power of the court to act *sua sponte*); United States v. Dooling, 406 F.2d 192 (2d Cir.), *cert. denied*, 395 U.S. 911 (1969) (Rule 48(b), and generally noting that "inherent power of a district court 'to do justice'" is limited). In this case, where jurisdiction exists, the indictment properly charges an offense, and the prosecution is timely, the court must allow the case to proceed. The decision on whether to prosecute or refrain and leave prosecution to another country is entirely one for the prosecutor, guided by the Departments of Justice and State.

Questions

1. What basis(es) for jurisdiction in the United States existed in international law? Was there territorial jurisdiction? Did the offense continue into the United States or was it completed abroad? Was the suffering of the child within the U.S. foreseeable? If so, why might that be relevant? Would this satisfy the need for and intent to produce effects within the U.S. and effects within the U.S.?

2. Was the criminal sexual act a violation of international law? Including human rights law? *See, e.g.*, the International Covenant on Civil and Political Rights, in the Documents Supplement. Whether or not there was a universal jurisdictional basis for enforcement of the U.S. statute, was there consent to jurisdiction by treaty or a competence under "universal by treaty"? What role did the Tokyo Convention play in this regard? Romania had ratified the Tokyo Convention. If it had not, would that have made a difference?

United States v. Noriega

746 F. Supp. 1506, 1509–10, 1512–19, 1525–28 (S.D. Fla. 1990)

Hoeveler, J.

This Cause comes before the Court on the several motions of Defendants General Manuel Antonio Noriega and Lt. Col. Luis Del Cid to dismiss for lack of jurisdiction the indictment which charges them with various narcotics-related offenses.

The case at bar presents the Court with a drama of international proportions, considering the status of the principal defendant and the difficult circumstances under which he was brought before this Court. The pertinent facts are as follows:

On February 14, 1988, a federal grand jury sitting in Miami, Florida returned a twelve-count indictment charging General Manuel Antonio Noriega with participating in an international conspiracy to import cocaine and materials used in producing cocaine into and out of the United States. Noriega is alleged to have exploited his official position as head of the intelligence branch of the Panamanian National Guard, and then as Commander-in-Chief of the Panamanian Defense Forces, to receive payoffs in return for assisting and protecting international drug traffickers, including various members of the Medellin Cartel, in conducting narcotics and money laundering operations in Panama.

Specifically, the indictment charges that General Noriega protected cocaine shipments from Colombia through Panama to the United States; arranged for the transshipment and sale to the Medellin Cartel of ether and acetone, including such chemicals previously seized by the Panamanian Defense Forces; provided refuge and a base for continued operations for the members of the Medellin Cartel after the Colombian government's crackdown on drug traffickers following the murder of the Colombian Minister of Justice, Rodrigo Lara-Bonilla; agreed to protect a cocaine laboratory in Darien Province, Panama; and assured the safe passage of millions of dollars of narcotic proceeds from the United States into Panamanian banks. Noriega also allegedly traveled to Havana, Cuba and met with Cuban president Fidel Castro, who, according to the indictment, mediated a dispute between Noriega and the Cartel caused by the Panamanian troops' seizure of a drug laboratory that Noriega was paid to protect. All of these activities were allegedly undertaken for General Noriega's own personal profit. Defendant Del Cid, in addition to being an officer in the Panamanian Defense Forces, was General Noriega's personal secretary. He is charged with acting as liaison, courier, and emissary for Noriega in his transactions with Cartel members and other drug traffickers.

Because of the activities alleged, Defendants are charged with engaging in a pattern of racketeering activity, in violation of the RICO statutes, 18 U.S.C. §§ 1962(c) and 1962(d); conspiracy to distribute and import cocaine into the United States, in violation of 21 U.S.C. § 963; and distributing and aiding and abetting the distribution of cocaine, intending that it be imported into the United States, in violation of 21 U.S.C. § 959 and 18 U.S.C. § 2. Defendant Noriega is further charged with aiding and abetting the manufacture of cocaine destined for the United States, in violation of 21 U.S.C. § 959 and 18 U.S.C. § 2; conspiring to manufacture cocaine intending that it be imported into the United States, in violation of 21 U.S.C. § 963; and causing interstate travel and use of facilities in interstate commerce to promote an unlawful activity, in violation of 18 U.S.C. § 1952(a) (3) and 18 U.S.C. § 2. Subsequent to the indictment, the Court granted General Noriega's motion to allow special appearance of counsel, despite the fact that Noriega was a fugitive and not before the Court at that time. Noriega's counsel then moved to dismiss the indictment on the ground that United States laws could not be applied to a foreign leader whose alleged illegal activities all occurred outside the territorial bounds of the United States. Counsel further argued that Noriega was immune from prosecution as a head of state and diplomat, and that his alleged narcotics offenses constituted acts of state not properly reviewable by this Court....

Jurisdiction Over The Offense

... Where a court is faced with the issue of extraterritorial jurisdiction, the analysis to be applied is 1) whether the United States has the power to reach the conduct in question under traditional principles of international law; and 2) whether the statutes under which the defendant is charged are intended to have extraterritorial effect. As Noriega concedes, the United States has long possessed the ability to attach criminal consequences to acts occurring outside this country which produce effects within the United States. *Strassheim v. Daily*, 221 U.S. 280, 285 (1911); *Restatement (Third) of the Foreign Relations Law of the United States* [hereinafter *Restatement (Third)*] § 402(1) (c). For example, the United States would unquestionably have authority to prosecute a person standing in Canada who fires a bullet across the border which strikes a second person standing in the United States. See *Restatement (Third)* § 402, Comment d. "All the nations of the world recognize 'the principle that a man who outside of a country willfully puts in motion a force to take effect in it is answerable at the place where the evil is done ...'" *Rivard v. United States*, 375 F.2d 882, 887 (5th Cir.) (citations omitted), *cert. denied*, 389 U.S. 884 (1967). The objective territorial theory of jurisdiction, which focuses on the effects or intended effects of conduct, can be traced to Justice Holmes' statement that "[a]cts done outside a jurisdiction, but intended to produce or producing effects within it, justify a State in punishing the cause of the harm as if he had been present at the effect, if the State should succeed in getting him within its power." *Strassheim v. Daily*, 221 U.S. at 285 [Editors' note: *Strassheim* actually involved all three factors of intent, acts, and effects]. See also *Church v. Hubbart*, 6 U.S. (2 Cranch) 187, 234 (1804) ("[a nation's] power to secure itself from injury may certainly be exercised beyond the limits of its territory."). Even if the extraterritorial conduct produces no effect within the United States, a defendant may still be reached if he was part of a conspiracy in which some co-conspirator's activities took place within United States territory. *United States v. Baker*, 609 F.2d 134, 138 (5th Cir. 1980). The former Fifth Circuit, whose decisions establish precedent for this Court, has on numerous occasions upheld jurisdiction over foreigners who conspired to import narcotics into the United States but never entered this country nor personally performed any acts within its territorial limits, as long as there was proof of an overt act committed within the United States by a co-conspirator. *See United States v. Postal*, 589 F.2d 862 (5th Cir.), *cert. denied*, 444 U.S. 832 (1979); *United States v. Cadena*, 585 F.2d 1252 (5th Cir. 1978); *United States v. Winter*, 509 F.2d 975 (5th Cir.), *cert. denied*, 423 U.S. 825 (1975); *Rivard v. United States, supra.*

More recently, international law principles have expanded to permit jurisdiction upon a mere showing of intent to produce effects in this country, without requiring proof of an overt act or effect within the United States. See *United States v. Wright-Barker*, 784 F.2d 161, 168 (3rd Cir. 1986); *United States v. Postal*, 589 F.2d at 886, n. 39; *United States v. Columba-Colella*, 604 F.2d at 358, 360. According to the *Restatement (Third)*:

> Cases involving intended but unrealized effect are rare, but international law does not preclude jurisdiction in such instances, subject to the principle of reasonableness. When the intent to commit the proscribed act is clear and demonstrated by some activity, and the effect to be produced by the activity is substantial and foreseeable, the fact that a plan or conspiracy was thwarted does not deprive the target state of jurisdiction to make its law applicable. § 402, Comment d.

In the drug smuggling context, the 'intent doctrine' has resulted in jurisdiction over persons who attempted to import narcotics into the United States but never actually succeeded in entering the United States or delivering drugs within its borders. The fact that no act was committed and no repercussions were felt within the United States did not preclude jurisdiction over conduct that was clearly directed at the United States. *United States v. Wright-Barker, supra* ("The purpose of these [narcotics laws] is to halt smugglers *before* they introduce their dangerous wares into and distribute them in this country.") (emphasis in original); *United States v. Quemener*, 789 F.2d 145, 156 (2d Cir.), *cert. denied*, 479 U.S. 829 (1986); *United States v. Loalza-Vasquez*, 735 F.2d 153, 156 (5th Cir. 1984); *United States v. Baker*, 609 F.2d at 138–39.

These principles unequivocally support jurisdiction in this case. The indictment charges Noriega with conspiracy to import cocaine into the United States and alleges several overt acts performed within the United States in furtherance of the conspiracy. Specifically, the indictment alleges that co- conspirators of Noriega purchased a Lear jet in Miami, which was then used to transport drug proceeds from Miami to Panama. Moreover, Noriega's activities in Panama, if true, undoubtedly produced effects within this country as deleterious as the hypothetical bullet fired across the border. The indictment alleges that, as a result of Noriega's facilitation of narcotics activity in Panama, 2,141 pounds of cocaine were illegally brought into Miami from Panama. While the ability of the United States to reach and proscribe extraterritorial conduct having effects in this country does not depend on the amount of narcotics imported into the United States or the magnitude of the consequences, the importation of over 2,000 pounds of cocaine clearly has a harmful impact and merits jurisdiction. Finally, even if no overt acts or effects occurred within the territorial borders, the object of the alleged conspiracy was to import cocaine into the United States and therefore an intent to produce effects is present.

The defendant's argument that the exercise of jurisdiction over his alleged activities in Panama is unreasonable is simply unsupportable in light of established principles of international law and the overwhelming case law in this Circuit upholding jurisdiction under similar circumstances.[13] Other than asserting his status as a foreign leader, which presents a different question from the one posed here, Noriega does not distinguish this case from those cited above. He cites the principle of reasonableness recently articulated in the *Restatement (Third)* § 403, but fails to say how extending jurisdiction over his conduct would be unreasonable. In fact, the defendant's invocation of a reasonableness requirement supports rather than undermines the application of jurisdiction in the present case. Thus, for example, Noriega quotes the following language from the *Restatement*:

---

13. Defendant's citation to *United States v. Bank of Nova Scotia* for the proposition that extraterritorial jurisdiction must be exercised delicately does not balance in his favor. In that case, which involved a grand jury subpoena served upon a Canadian-chartered bank located in the Bahamas, the Eleventh Circuit acknowledged that enforcing the subpoena might provoke international friction but nonetheless held that it "simply cannot acquiesce in the proposition that United States criminal investigations must be thwarted whenever there is a conflict with the interest of other states." 691 F.2d 1384, 1391 (11th Cir. 1982) (*quoting In re* Grand Jury Proceedings (Field), 532 F.2d 404, 410 (5th Cir.), *cert denied*, 429 U.S. 940 (1976)), *cert. denied*, 462 U.S. 1119 (1982)). *Bank of Nova Scotia* is therefore in accord with the cases cited above.

Similarly unpersuasive in Defendant's reference to a legal treatise arguing that the effects doctrine should not be applied to extraterritorial conduct resulting in "more or less remote repercussions." *See* Jennings,, *Extraterritorial Jurisdiction and the United States Antitrust Laws*, 33 Brit. Y.B.C.L. 146, 159 (1957). Since Noriega is alleged to have conspired to import narcotics *into* the United States, the delivery of over 2,000 pounds of cocaine into Miami—far from being a 'remote repercussion' of the conspiracy—is in fact a direct and intended result of his alleged activities in Panama.

> In applying the principle of reasonableness, the exercise of criminal (as distinguished from civil) jurisdiction in relation to acts committed in another state may be perceived as particularly intrusive....
>
> It is generally accepted by enforcement agencies of the United States government that criminal jurisdiction over activity with substantial foreign elements should be exercised more sparingly than civil jurisdiction over the same activity, and only upon strong justification.

Restatement (Third) § 403, Reporters' Note 8. However, the same section of the *Restatement* establishes that narcotics offenses provide the strong justification meriting criminal jurisdiction: "Prosecution for activities committed in a foreign state have generally been limited to serious and universally condemned offenses, such as treason or traffic in narcotics, and to offenses by and against military forces. In such cases the state in whose territory the act occurs is not likely to object to regulation by the state concerned." *Id.* (citations omitted). The *Restatement* therefore explicitly recognizes the reasonableness of extending jurisdiction to narcotics activity such as that alleged here. See also *United States v. Wright-Barker*, 784 F.2d at 168 (construing § 403 to permit jurisdiction over extraterritorial narcotics trafficking). Even if another state were likely to object to jurisdiction here, the United States has a strong interest in halting the flow of illicit drugs across its borders. In assessing the reasonableness of extraterritorial jurisdiction, one of the factors to be considered is the character of the activity to be regulated, including the importance of regulation to the regulating state and the degree to which the desire to regulate is generally accepted. *Restatement (Third)* § 403(1) (c). The consensus of the American public on the need to stem the flow of drugs into this country is well publicized and need not be elaborated upon in detail. Further, the Court notes that the United States has an affirmative duty to enact and enforce legislation to curb illicit drug trafficking under the Single Convention on Narcotics Drugs, 18 U.S.T. 1409, T.I.A.S. No. 6298, New York, March 30, 1961, ratified by the United States, 1967, amended 26 U.S.T. 1441, T.I.A.S. No. 8118. See *In re Grand Jury Proceedings Bank of Nova Scotia*, 740 F.2d 817, 830–31 (11th Cir. 1984), *cert. denied*, 469 U.S. 1106 (1985) (discussing the Single Convention on Narcotics Drugs). Given the serious nature of the drug epidemic in this country, certainly the efforts of the United States to combat the problem by prosecuting conduct directed against itself cannot be subject to the protests of a foreign government profiting at its expense. In any case, the Court is not made aware of any instance in which the Republic of Panama objected to the regulation of drug trafficking by the United States. In sum, because Noriega's conduct in Panama is alleged to have resulted in a direct effect within the United States, the Court concludes that extraterritorial jurisdiction is appropriate as a matter of international law.

This conclusion does not end the Court's analysis, however, since a further requirement is that the criminal statutes under which the defendant is charged be intended to apply to conduct outside the United States. Noriega is charged with violations of 21 U.S.C. § 959 (distributing a controlled substance with the knowledge that it would be unlawfully imported into the United States); 21 U.S.C. § 952 (importing a controlled substance into the United States from a place outside thereof); 21 U.S.C. § 963 (conspiring to commit the above offenses); and 18 U.S.C. § 2 (aiding and abetting the violation of § 959). The indictment also alleges that Noriega participated in a pattern of racketeering activity consisting of the above crimes, in violation of the Racketeer Influenced and Corrupt Organizations Act (RICO), §§ 1962(c) and 1962(d), and caused the travel and use of facilities in interstate and foreign commerce in furtherance of a narcotics conspiracy, in violation of 18 U.S.C. § 1952(a) (3).

Section 959, prohibiting the distribution of narcotics intending that they be imported into the United States, is clearly meant to apply extraterritorially. The statute expressly states that it is "intended to reach acts of manufacture or distribution committed outside the territorial jurisdiction of the United States." 21 U.S.C. § 959(c). The remaining statutes, by contrast, do not on their face indicate an express intention that they be given extraterritorial effect. Where a statute is silent as to its extraterritorial reach, a presumption against such application normally applies. *United States v. Benitez*, 741 F.2d 1312, 1316–17 (11th Cir. 1984), *cert. denied*, 471 U.S. 1137 (1985). However, "such statutes may be given extraterritorial effect if the nature of the law permits it and Congress intends it. Absent an express intention on the face of the statutes to do so, the exercise of that power may be inferred from the nature of the offenses and Congress' other legislative efforts to eliminate the type of crime involved." United *States v. Baker*, 609 F.2d at 136. (citing *United States v. Bowman*, 260 U.S. 94, 97–98 (1922).

With respect to 21 U.S.C. § 952, it is apparent from the very nature of the offense that the statute was intended to reach extraterritorial acts. Section 952 makes it unlawful to import narcotics "into the United States from *any place outside* thereof.." (emphasis added). Because importation by definition involves acts originating outside of the territorial limits of the United States, the Court can only infer that § 952 applies to conduct which begins abroad; any interpretation to the contrary would render the statute virtually meaningless. *United States v. Cadena*, 585 F.2d at 1259. With jurisdiction over the substantive violations of §§ 959 and 952 established, jurisdiction over the conspiracy and aiding and abetting counts likewise follows. Since a conspiracy to commit an offense is closely related to the offense itself, courts have regularly inferred the extraterritorial reach of the § 963 conspiracy statute on the basis of a finding that the substantive statutes apply abroad. *See, e.g., Chua Han Mow v. United States*, 730 F.2d 1308, 1311 (9th Cir. 1984), *cert. denied*, 470 U.S. 1031 (1985); *United States v. Baker*, 609 F.2d at 139. The same must be said for an aiding and abetting charge; if anything, the act of aiding and abetting is even more intimately connected to the underlying crime. In short, the Court perceives no sound jurisdictional reason for distinguishing the conspiracy and aiding and abetting charges from the substantive offense for purposes of extraterritorial application. Section 963 and 18 U.S.C. § 2 must therefore be given extraterritorial effect as well.

Whether the RICO and Travel Act statutes reach conduct abroad is a more difficult question. None of the cases cited by the parties address this point and the Court is unaware of any case reaching the issue.[14] The question of these statutes' extraterritorial ef-

---

14. In *Republic of Philippines v. Marcos (Marcos II)*, the Philippine government brought a RICO action against deposed president Ferdinand Marcos and his wife Imelda for allegedly converting funds belonging to the Philippine people for their own personal use. The indictment charged that some of the funds were invested in properties in the United States and that other monies and valuables were transported to Hawaii upon the Marcos' arrival there. On the question of RICO's applicability, the court in dicta suggested that the Marcos' alleged conduct in the Philippines could not be reached but did not ultimately decide the issue since it upheld jurisdiction based upon the Marcos' alleged transportation of stolen property into the United States. The holding in that case thus provides little, if any, guidance on the issue. 818 F.2d 1473, 1478–79 (9th Cir. 1987), *op. withdrawn, reh. gr., rev'd on other grounds on reh. en banc, Republic of Philippines v. Marcos (Marcos III)*, 862 F.2d 1355 (9th Cir. 1988), *cert. denied*, — U.S.—, 109 S.Ct. 1933 (1989).

fect is therefore a matter of apparent first impression. For the reasons stated below, the Court finds that RICO, 18 U.S.C. §§ 1962(c) and (d), and the Travel Act, 18 U.S.C. § 1952(a) (3), apply to conduct outside the United States.

Section 1962(c) makes it unlawful for "any person associated with any enterprise engaged in, or the activities of which affect, interstate or foreign commerce, to conduct or participate ... in the conduct of such enterprise's affairs through a pattern of racketeering activity ..." 18 U.S.C. § 1962(c) (emphasis added). Section 1962(d) similarly makes it illegal for "any person to conspire to violate" Section 1962(c). 18 U.S.C. § 1962(d) (emphasis added). These prohibitions are on their face all-inclusive and do not suggest parochial application. Indeed, if any statute reaches far and wide, it is RICO.... [The court also addressed "the overall purpose of the Act" and found it to be extraterritorial. Regarding the Travel Act, the court recognized that it was enacted as "an attempt to reach criminal activities uniquely broad and transitory ... beyond state and national borders," and that "the Act itself indicates no ... territorial limitations."].

Jurisdiction over Defendant's extraterritorial conduct is therefore appropriate both as a matter of international law and statutory construction....

Notes and Questions

Prescriptive Jurisdiction

1. Quite obviously, *Noriega* rested in part on objective territorial jurisdiction. Could the court have been better explained why in view of relevant acts, intent, and effects? Were acts within the United States attributable to Noriega? Clearly, there was an intent to produce effects and, over the years, there were numerous effects within the United States

2. Could U.S. jurisdiction have also rested on protective and universal jurisdiction?

3. Professor Christopher Blakesley has been highly critical of application of the objective territorial principle to justify jurisdiction in narcotics conspiracy cases where no overt act was committed within the territory of the forum state (and no actual effects occur):

> [A] conspiracy outside the sovereign territory, by definition, cannot have any effect within the territory as it is an inchoate offense; it has no effect at all, until the substantive offense to which the parties are conspiring has occurred within the sovereign territory (or has occurred outside the territory with its own effects impacting within the territory).

Blakesley, *United States Jurisdiction Over Extraterritorial Crime,* 73 J. Crim. & Criminology 1109, 1131 (1982). *But see* Restatement § 402, Comm. d.

Do you agree with either Professor Blakesley or the Restatement?

4. Despite the Restatement, "intent" alone is not sufficient under international law. Can you make a more sophisticated claim for jurisdiction in interrupted smuggling cases? Look for other factors like the agency circumstance or a process of smuggling involving also prior acts and effects.

5. Noriega had also argued that he was entitled to "prisoner of war" status and that, therefore, he could only be tried in a U.S. military tribunal, according to military procedures, and that, since "hostilities" had ended, he must be "repatriated" back to Panama. Was Noriega really entitled to prisoner of war status if the U.S. was in Panama with the consent of the lawfully elected government? Were there "hostilities"? *See also* common Article 2 to the 1949 Geneva Conventions and Chapter Eight, Section 1 *infra.* U.S. courts defer to the Executive concerning recognition of foreign states and foreign governments.

The district court denied Noriega's claims that the district court lacked jurisdiction, that procedures must be different, and that he must be "repatriated," while also noting that "[u]nder 18 U.S.C. §3231, federal district courts have concurrent jurisdiction with military courts over all violations of the laws of the United States committed by military personnel." *See also* Chapter Six, Section 5; 1949 Geneva Convention Relative to the Treatment of Prisoners of War, arts. 82, 84–85, 87, 102, 105, in the Documents Supplement.

On the legality of Noriega's capture in Panama, consider Chapter Five, Sections 2 and 4; *The Panamanian Revolution: Diplomacy, War and Self-Determination in Panama: Self-Determination and Intervention in Panama,* and *Extraterritorial Law Enforcement and the "Receipt" and Trial of Noriega,* 84 Proc., Am. Soc. Int'l L. 182–202, 236–56 (1990); Paust, *After* Alvarez-Machain: *Abduction, Standing, Denials of Justice, and Unaddressed Human Rights Claims,* 67 St. John's L. Rev. 551, 566–67 & n.57 (1993).

After serving his sentence, Noriega was extradited to France for prosecution there. He had claimed that the Geneva Conventions precluded such an extradition, but U.S. courts denied his claim. See Noriega v. Pastrana, 564 F.3d 1290 (11th Cir. 2009), cert. denied, 130 S.Ct. 1002 (2010), reh'g denied, 130 S.Ct. 1942 (2010).

6. Professor Blakesley has proposed three ways in which extraterritorial jurisdiction can obtain with respect to inchoate crimes: (1) a hybrid approach which combines the protective and universal principles, (2) providing an exception under the objective territorial principle for narcotics conspiracies, and (3) by replacing the customary principles with a "rule of reasonableness" seen in §403 of the Restatement. See C.L. Blakesley, Terrorism, Drugs, International Law, and the Protection of Human Liberty 169–70 (1992). Do you agree? If so, which of the three approaches advanced should be adopted? If "reasonableness" is your preference, how should "reasonableness" be defined for purposes of asserting extraterritorial jurisdiction over an inchoate offense? Is it "reasonable" to assert such jurisdiction merely on the basis of intent to cause harmful effects, or is more at stake? Must the forum state wait until there is a detrimental impact?

Extraterritoriality of Federal Statutes

7. Congress' intent to apply a statute extraterritorially may be clear from the explicit language of the statute. For example, in *Noriega,* the court stated that 21 U.S.C. §959, which criminalizes the distribution of narcotics intending that they be imported into the United States, is clearly meant to apply extraterritorially. The statute expressly states that it is "intended to reach acts of manufacture or distribution committed outside the territorial jurisdiction of the United States." 21 U.S.C. §959(c). However, the issue of extraterritorial jurisdiction becomes more complicated when the statute fails to address its extraterritorial reach. When the statute is silent on the matter some prefer a presumption against extraterritorial application. *See* Morrison v. Nat'l Australia Bank, Ltd., 139 S.Ct. 2869 2877 (2010) (Scalia, J.) (reiterating the "longstanding principle of American law 'that legislation of Congress, unless a contrary intent appears, is meant to apply only within the territorial jurisdiction of the United States,'" *quoting* EEOC v. Arabian American Oil Co., 499 U.S. 244, 248 (1991), *but see id.* at 2891–92 (Stevens, J., concurring) (noting that the presumption is merely a "flexible rule of thumb" and that it does not require that clear intent of extraterritoriality exist within a statute)); Sale v. Haitian Centers Council, Inc., 509 U.S. 155, 188 (1993); Argentine Republic v. Amerada Hess Shipping, 488 U.S. 428, 440 (1991); United States v. Bowman, 260 U.S. 94, 98 (1922) (if a statute's prohibitions are "to be extended to [apply to acts] committed outside of the strict territorial jurisdiction, it is natural for Congress to say so in the statute, and failure to do so will negate the

purpose of Congress in this regard"); United States v. Delgado-Garcia, 374 F.3d 1337, 1344 (D.C. Cir. 2004) ("we presumptively read the text of congressional statutes not to apply extraterritorially, unless there are contextual reasons for reading the text otherwise"); United States v. Larsen, 952 F.2d 1099 (9th Cir. 1991); United States v. Benitez, 741 F.2d 1312, 1316–17 (11th Cir. 1984), *cert. denied*, 471 U.S. 1137 (1985); United States v. Cotten, 471 F.2d 744, 750 (9th Cir.), *cert. denied*, 411 U.S. 936 (1973). *See also* JIMMY GURULÉ, COMPLEX CRIMINAL LITIGATION: PROSECUTING DRUG ENTERPRISES AND ORGANIZED CRIME 444–46 (2d ed. 2000).

The judicially-created principle of construction has not been without controversy and has not been applied with respect to every form of legislation and every underlying jurisdictional basis and type of constitutionally-based power. For example, in United States v. Bowman, 260 U.S. 94 (1922), the Supreme Court recognized that the ordinary presumption has exceptions that can depend in part "upon the power and jurisdiction of a government to punish crime under the law of nations" and the judiciary may infer congressional intent to provide for extraterritorial jurisdiction for "criminal statutes which are, as a class, not logically dependent on their locality for the Government's jurisdiction, but are enacted because of the right of the Government to defend itself against obstruction, or fraud wherever perpetrated, especially if committed by its own citizens, officers, or agents." *Bowman*, 260 U.S. at 97–98. In *Bowman*, the Supreme Court reasoned:

> The necessary locus [of a crime], when not specifically defined, depends upon the purpose of Congress as evinced by the description and nature of the crime and upon the territorial limitations upon the power and jurisdiction of a government to punish crime under the law of nations. Crimes against private individuals or their property, like assaults, murder, burglary, larceny, robbery, arson, embezzlement, and frauds of all kinds, which affect the peace and good order of the community, must of course be committed within the territorial jurisdiction of the government where it may properly exercise it. If punishment of them is to be extended to include those committed outside of the strict territorial jurisdiction, it is natural for Congress to say so in the statute, and failure to do so will negative the purpose of Congress in this regard....

> But the same rule of interpretation should not be applied to criminal statutes which are, as a class, not logically dependent on their locality for the Government's jurisdiction, but are enacted because of the right of the Government to defend itself against obstruction, or fraud wherever perpetrated, especially if committed by its own citizens, officers, or agents. Some such offenses can only be committed within the territorial jurisdiction of the Government because of the local acts required to constitute them. Others are such that to limit their locus to the strictly territorial jurisdiction would be greatly to curtail the scope and usefulness of the statute and leave open a large immunity for frauds as easily committed by citizens on the high seas and in foreign countries as at home. In such cases, Congress has not thought it necessary to make specific provision in the law that the locus shall include the high seas and foreign countries, but allows it to be inferred from the nature of the offense.

Id. at 97–98. Clearly, the description and nature of the substantive law addressed and jurisdictional competence under the law of nations can limit the relevance of the ordinary presumption.

In United States v. Delgado-Garcia, 374 F.3d 1337 (D.C. Cir. 2004), the Circuit panel inferred congressional intent to apply 8 U.S.C. §§ 1324(a)(1) and (a)(2) extraterritorially, which punish conspiracy to encourage or induce aliens to come into the U.S. knowing that it would violate U.S. law and attempt to bring unauthorized aliens into the U.S. The court reasoned that § 1324(a) "protects the borders of the United States against illegal immigration" and would naturally "reach those outside the borders." *Id.* at 1345. *See also* United States v. Frank, 599 F.3d 1221, 1230, 1233 (11th Cir. 2010) (using nationality jurisdiction under international law and *Bowman* and finding the exercise of extraterritorial jurisdiction appropriate for 18 U.S.C. § 2251A, selling or buying of children); United States v. Campbell, 798 F. Supp.2d 293, 305, 308–09 (D.D.C. 2011) (same result for18 U.S.C. § 666(a)(1)(B), solicitation of a bribe by an agent of an organization receiving more than $10,000 in federal funds and expressly relying on *Bowman* and the fact that protective jurisdiction under customary international law exists); United States v. Ayesh, 762 F. Supp.2d 832, 839–41 (E.D. Va. 2011) (finding the protective principle supports "the exercise of extraterritorial jurisdiction appropriate for 18 U.S.C. §§ 641 and 208(a), which criminalize conversion and theft of federal financial assets and conflicts of interest in federal contracting); United States v. Finch, No. 10-333, 2010 WL 3938176, at *3–4 (D. Haw. Sept. 30, 2010) (noting that *Morrison* did not overrule *Bowman* and invoking *Bowman* and protective jurisdiction to find 18 U.S.C. § 201, prohibiting bribery or fraud committed against the U.S. or its officers, extended extraterritorially); United States v. Martinez, 599 F. Supp.2d 784, 799 (W.D. Texas 2009) (Congress intended 18 U.S.C. § 2423(a) and (b) to apply extraterritorially, which punish transporting a person under 18 years of age in interstate or foreign commerce with the intent that the individual engage in prostitution or any illicit sexual conduct). *See also* Christopher L. Blakesley & Dan E. Stigall, *The Myopia of U.S. v. Martinelli: Extraterritorial Jurisdiction in the 21st Century,* 39 Geo. Wash. Int'l L. Rev. 1, 36–39 (2007) (discussing the application of *Bowman* by the federal circuit courts of appeal).

8. *Bowman* concerned a criminal indictment charging three defendants who were U.S. citizens with conspiracy to defraud a corporation in which the U.S. was a stockholder, *i.e.,* the United States Shipping Board Emergency Fleet Corporation, after defendants submitted a false claim for fuel oil for one of its steamships. *United States v. Bowman,* 260 U.S. at 95. Does the rule in *Bowman* apply with equal force to non-U.S. citizens? In United States v. Delgado, 374 F.3d at 1345–46, the court held that "the citizenship of the defendants is irrelevant." *See also Ayesh,* 762 F. Supp.2d at 840 (finding *Bowman* applies equally to non-U.S. citizens).

9. Has the Supreme Court implicitly overruled the *Bowman* exception to the presumption against the extraterritorial application of Congressional statutes? *See* Morrison v. Nat'l Austl. Bank, Ltd., 130 S.Ct. 2869 (2010) (dismissing civil action brought under the Securities and Exchange Act of 1934 by Australian stockholders against Australian bank for fraud involving over-valuation of an American asset). In *Morrison,* the Court posited: "When a statute gives no clear indication of an extraterritorial application, it has none." *Id.* at 2878. "[W]e apply the presumption in all cases, preserving a stable background against which Congress can legislate with predictable effects." *Id.* at 2881 (emphasis added). *But see Morrison,* 130 S.Ct. at 2891–92 (Stevens, J., concurring) (quoted in Note 7 above); Sarei v. Rio Tinto, PLC, 671 F.3d 736, 743–46, 758–60, 763–65 (9th Cir. 2011) (extraterritoriality of the Alien Tort Statute (ATS) is appropriate where universal jurisdiction would obtain over violations of international law of a universal nature and concern); *Sarei,* 671 F.3d at 772, 776–79 (Pregerson, J., concurring) ("universal customary international law" supports extraterritoriality); *Sarei,* 671 F.3d at 780–83 (McKeown, J., concurring) (statutory focus of violations of international law supports extraterritoriality of the ATS); Doe v. Exxon Mobil Corp., 654 F.3d 11, 20–22 (D.C. Cir. 2011) (the ATS has

"obvious extraterritorial reach," "universal jurisdiction" pertains, and *Morrison* does not control); U.S. v. Campbell, 798 F. Supp. 2d at 303 & n.3, 308–09 (declining to follow *Morrison* in the context of a criminal statute supported by protective jurisdiction, finding that despite the strong wording in *Morrison* of a presumption against extraterritorial application in all cases, *Bowman* has never been explicitly limited or overruled, and noting that "it has been cited and applied by Circuit courts multiple times in recent years" and that "[m]any courts since *Morrison* have continued to find that *Bowman* presents an exception ... or have otherwise found no tension between the two cases"); United States v. Galvis-Pena, 2011 WL 7268437, at *5–7 (N.D. Ga. 2011) (applying "*Bowman* exception" and emphasizing "the inherently international scope of drug trafficking or smuggling"); United States v. Hijazi, 2011 WL 2838172, at *22, *24, *29 (C.D. Ill. 2011) (applying the protective principle under international law and *Bowman* to support a finding of extraterritorial application of the Major Fraud Act, 18 U.S.C. § 1031, and wire fraud statute, 18 U.S.C. § 1343, and finding no due process concerns where nexus exists and principles of international law support jurisdiction); Note 7 above; *see also* United States v. Belfast, 611 F.3d 783, 811, 813–14 (11th Cir. 2010) (applying *Bowman* despite *Morrison*).

10. In *United States v. Usama bin Laden, et al.*, 92 F. Supp.2d 189 (S.D.N.Y. 2000), a federal criminal indictment charging "fifteen defendants with conspiracy to murder United States nationals, to use weapons of mass destruction against United States nationals, to destroy United States buildings and property, and to destroy United States defense utilities. The Indictment also charged defendants Mohamed Sadeek Odeh, Mohamed Rashed Daoud al-'Owhali, and Khalfan Khamis Mohamed, among others, with numerous crimes in connection with the August 1998 bombings of the United States Embassies in Nairobi, Kenya, and Dar es Salaam, Tanzania, including 223 counts of murder. The Indictment also charges defendant Wadih el Hage with numerous perjury and false statement counts. Six of the Defendants are presently in the custody of the Bureau of Prisons: Mamdouh Mahmud Salim, Ali Mohamed, Wadih El Hage, Mohamed Rashed Daoud Al-Owhali, Khalfan Khamis Mohamed, and Mohamed Sadeek Odeh ("Odeh")." *Id.* at 192.

In *bin Laden*, the district court stated that "the Supreme Court has established a limited exception to this standard approach for 'criminal statutes which are, as a class, not logically dependent on their locality for the Government's jurisdiction, but are enacted because of the right of the government to defend itself against obstruction, or fraud wherever perpetrated.... ' *United States v. Bowman*, 260 U.S. 94, 98 ... (1922). As regards statutes of this type, courts may infer the requisite intent 'from the nature of the offense' described in the statute, and need not examine its legislative history." *Id.* at 193. The opinion then noted that "*Bowman* rests on two factors: (1) the right of the United States to protect itself from harmful conduct–irrespective of the locus of this conduct, and (2) the presumption that Congress would not both (a) enact a statute designed to serve this protective function, and ... (b) undermine this protective intention by limiting the statute's application to United States territory." *Id.* at 194. The court added: "the underlying *Bowman* rationale ... depends on the right of the United States to defend itself from harmful conduct regardless of its locus, and a presumption that Congress would not undercut the effectiveness of statutes intended to serve this protective purpose by limiting them to United States territory and United States nationals." *Id.* at 197, adding, *id.* at 196, "[t]he *Bowman* rule would appear to be most directly related to the protective principle" of prescriptive jurisdiction under international law.

Applying the *Bowman* rationale and using other indicia of congressional intent, the court concluded that "Congress intended each of the following statutory provisions to reach conduct by foreign nationals on foreign soil: 18 U.S.C. § 844(f) (1), (f) (3), (h) and (n);

18 U.S.C. §924(c); 18 U.S.C. §930(c); 18 U.S.C. §1114; and 18 U.S.C. §2155." *Id.* at 198. With respect to U.S. jurisdiction to prescribe under international law, supporting various congressional enactments used as bases for numerous counts in the indictments, the district court concluded that §844 (f) (3) "is justified by the protective principle–to reach all of the deaths caused by the two embassy bombings"; §2332a(a) (1) and (a) (3) "are justified, respectively, by the passive personality principle and the protective principle–to reach all of the deaths caused by the two embassy bombings"; §930 (c) "is based on the protective principle"; §1114 "is based on the protective principle"; and §1116 "is based on the universality principle, see *United States v. Layton*, 509 F. Supp. 212, 221–24 (N.D. Cal. 1981)–to reach the murders of Internationally Protected Persons in connection with the two embassy bombings." *Id.* at 215 n.42. Addressing the Antiterrorism Act (18 U.S.C. §2331, *et seq.*; see Chapter Twelve), the court also noted: "In penalizing extraterritorial conspiracies to kill nationals of the United States, Section 2332(b) is clearly designed to protect a vital United States interest. And, indeed, Congress expressly identified this protective function as the chief purpose of Section 2332." *Id.* at 221. Are each of the enactments also justified under the universal principle in view of customary human rights at stake and the international community's condemnation of all acts of terrorism as criminal (see Chapter Twelve, Section 2)? Later, on another motion, the district court noted that two of the named defendants "as well as some unindicted co-conspirators, are also said to have committed acts in furtherance of the conspiracy while inside the United States." *Id.*, 93 F. Supp.2d 484 (S.D.N.Y. 2000). What additional principle of jurisdiction therefore applies?

11. 18 U.S.C. §7 (3) reads: "The term 'special maritime and territorial jurisdiction of the United States,' as used in this title includes: ... (3) Any lands reserved or acquired for the use of the United States, and under the exclusive or concurrent jurisdiction thereof, or any place purchased or otherwise acquired by the United States by consent of the legislature of the State in which the same shall be, for the erection of a fort, magazine, arsenal, dockyard, or other needful building." In 1996, Congress recognized that the 12 mile territorial sea of the United States, "for purposes of Federal criminal jurisdiction is part of the United States..., and is within the special maritime and territorial jurisdiction of the United States...." Act of April 24, 1996, P. L. 104-132, Title IX, §901 (a), 110 Stat. 1317.

In view of the presumption against extraterritoriality, should §7 (3) be construed to be extraterritorial? to reach acts within a U.S. embassy in foreign territory? to reach acts within an apartment in foreign territory that happens to be rented by the Government of the United States as private living areas for embassy or consular staff and their family members? Under international law, utilizable as an interpretive background, would the U.S. have territorial jurisdiction over acts occurring in a U.S. embassy in foreign territory? in an apartment in foreign territory? One case held that §7 (3) reaches acts in a U.S. embassy abroad. *United States v. Erdos*, 474 F.2d 157 (4th Cir. 1973) (Erdos killed a person in the U.S. embassy in the new Republic of Equatorial Guinea. Both were U.S. nationals, Erdos was the senior diplomat and his victim was also an embassy employee.). Was the court correct? See also RESTATEMENT §466, cmts. a (re: diplomatic or consular premises: "That premises are inviolable does not mean that they are extraterritorial. Acts committed on those premises are within the territorial jurisdiction of the receiving state....") and c ("Applying general principles, this section declares that premises and related property are subject to the host state's jurisdiction to prescribe, adjudicate, or enforce law except by means or in circumstances where an exercise of jurisdiction would violate the premises or interfere with their use for the designated purposes...."). Legislative history demonstrates that the constant concern in the House and Senate debates involved inquiry into concurrent and exclusive jurisdictional competencies of the federal government and various States within the United States as well as potential clashes and gaps between them. See 42 CONG. REC. 586–89 (Jan. 10, 1908), 1184–95 (Jan. 28, 1908). The title of the new legislation openly demonstrates a limitation to the "Territorial Jurisdiction of the United States" when admiralty or maritime jurisdiction does not pertain. *Id.* at 1184. Indeed, legislative history speaks clearly against extraterritoriality. See *id.* at 1185–86 (remarks of Senator Heyburn regarding then Section 269 (3), while introducing Senate Bill S. 2982); Jordan J. Paust, *Non-Extraterritoriality of "Special Territorial Jurisdiction" of the United States: Forgotten History and the Errors of* Erdos, 24 YALE J. INT'L L. 305 (1999).

Addressing each of the above in great detail, the district court in *United Sates v. bin Laden* agreed that *Erdos* was incorrect and ruled that counts in the indictment under 18 U.S.C. § 1111, addressing murders committed "within the special maritime and territorial jurisdiction of the United States," as defined in 18 U.S.C. § 7, must be dismissed, since the killing of persons at the U.S. embassy compounds in Nairobi, Kenya and Dar es Salaam, Tanzania would not be covered by § 7(3). 92 F. Supp.2d at 204–15. Reasoning similarly and citing similar and some of the same sources, the Second Circuit held that § 7 (3) does not apply extraterritorially to conduct occurring on a U.S. military installation in Germany. See *United States v. Gatlin*, 216 F.3d 207 (2d Cir. 2000). However, a panel from the Ninth Circuit split on the issue, the majority considering that § 7(3) is extraterritorial. See *United States v. Cory*, 232 F.3d 1166 (9th Cir. 2000). What is the better conclusion?

Due Process Claims

12. When faced with a claim that due process requires a sufficient nexus or minimum contacts with the U.S., especially in view of *United States v. Davis*, 905 F.2d 245, 248–49 (9th Cir. 1990), *cert. denied*, 498 U.S. 1047 (1991), and *United States v. Caicedo*, 47 F.3d 370, 372 (9th Cir. 1995), the district court in *United States v. bin Laden* stated that they agreed with another Ninth Circuit case, *United States v. Peterson*, 812 F.2d 486, 493–94 (9th Cir. 1987), "that if the extraterritorial application of a statute is justified by the protective principle, such application accords with due process." 92 F. Supp.2d at 220. More generally, cases resting on nationality, protective, or universal jurisdiction (as opposed to merely objective territorial jurisdiction) do not find that due process has been violated. As noted in *Caicedo*, "[p]rinciples of international law are 'useful as a rough guide' in determining whether application of the statute would violate due process.... The First, Second, Fourth, Fifth and Eleventh Circuits agree that the United States may exercise jurisdiction consistent with international law over drug offenders apprehended aboard stateless vessels on the high seas without demonstrating any nexus to the United States.... stateless vessels ... are 'international pariahs ... [that] subject themselves to the jurisdiction of all nations.... A nexus requirement, imposed as a matter of due process, makes sense when the 'rough guide' of international law also requires a nexus ... [but not] where defendant attempts to avoid the law of all nations...." 47 F.3d at 372.

In *Daliberti v. Republic of Iraq*, 97 F. Supp.2d 38 (D.D.C. 2000), the district court rejected a due process—minimum contacts claim by Iraq with respect to alleged state sponsored terrorism subject to civil suit, since "'states are on notice that state sponsorship of terrorism is condemned by the international community'" (quoting *Flatow v. Islamic Republic of Iran*, 999 F. Supp. 1, 23 (D.D.C. 1998)), "nations that operate in a manner inconsistent with international norms should not expect to be granted the privilege of immunity from suit," states that sponsor terrorism have "adequate warning" of possible U.S. sanctions, including lawsuits in U.S. courts, and it is "reasonable that foreign states be held accountable in the courts of the United States for terrorist actions perpetrated against U.S. citizens anywhere." 97 F. Supp.2d at 52–54.

13. More generally, federal circuits are divided on whether the test for due process requires a "sufficient nexus" to the United States, commonly understood as real effects or consequences accruing in the country, or the prosecution is neither arbitrary or capricious. Several circuits reason that "[i]n order to apply extraterritorially a federal criminal statute to a defendant consistently with due process, there must be a sufficient nexus between the defendant and the United States so that such application would not be arbitrary or fundamentally unfair." United States v. Davis, 905 F.2d 245, 248–49 (9th Cir. 1990); *see also* United States v. Yousef, 327 F.3d 56, 111 (2d Cir. 2003); United States v. Mohammad-Omar, 323 Fed. Appx. 259, 261 (4th Cir. 2009) (unpublished); United States v. Hijazi 2011 WL 2838172, *5 (C.D. Ill.). In contrast, other circuits require only that extraterritorial prosecution be neither arbitrary nor fundamentally unfair, and are not concerned with whether a sufficient nexus exists. *See* United States v. Martinez-Hildago, 993 F.2d 1052, 1056 (3d Cir. 1993) (rejecting the sufficient nexus test and finding there was "nothing fundamentally unfair" about the defendant's prosecution); United States v. Cardales, 168 F.3d 548, 553 (1st Cir. 1999) ("To satisfy due process, our application of the [criminal statute] must not be arbitrary or fundamentally unfair."); United States v. Suerte, 291 F.3d 366, 375–77 (5th Cir. 2002) (rejecting sufficient nexus requirement in favor of the "arbitrary and fundamentally unfair" test). *See also* Anthony J. Colangelo, *Constitutional Limits on Extraterritorial Jurisdiction: Terrorism and the Intersection of National and International Law,* 48 HARV. INT'L L.J. 121, 162–65 (2007) (discussing competing tests for determining due process).

Do you prefer the "sufficient nexus" or "arbitrary or fundamentally unfair" test for determining whether due process is satisfied? Or do you prefer the rationale in *Caicedo* and other cases that support the view that if jurisdiction rests on protective or universal jurisdictional competence due process is satisfied? *See* Yousef, 327 F.3d at 112 (finding no due process violation because "it cannot be argued seriously that the defendants' conduct was so unrelated to American interests as to render their prosecution in the United States arbitrary and fundamentally unfair); United States v. Bin Laden, 92 F. Supp.2d 189, 220 (S.D.N.Y. 2000) ("if the extraterritorial application of the statute is justified by the protective principle, such application accords with due process"); *see also* United States v. Brehm, 2011 WL 1226088, at *4–5 (E.D. Va. Mar. 30, 2011) (finding no due process violation because defendant's conduct abroad directly impacted U.S. interests in Afghanistan). Which due process test is more favorable to the government or prosecution? In many circumstances, it may be that "[t]his difference is less real than apparent; the existence of a nexus is what makes the prosecution neither arbitrary nor fundamentally unfair." United States v. Shanani-Jahromi, 286 F. Supp.2d 723, 728 n.9 (E.D. Va. 2003). Could the *Caicedo* approach using prescriptive competence under international law allow avoidance of arbitrariness and confusion?

An Alleged Rule of Reasonableness

14. The RESTATEMENT's alleged rule of "reasonableness," preferring an ad hoc "balancing" of factors or contacts approach that might function to limit federal jurisdiction, has not generally been followed by U.S. courts, especially if jurisdiction is possible under the protective or nationality principles (it does not apply when universal jurisdiction pertains. See also Note 18, below). Section 403's list of factors include: "(a) the link of the activity to the territory of the regulating state, i.e., the extent to which the activity ... has substantial direct, and foreseeable effect upon or in the territory; ... (c) the character of the activity to be regulated; (d) the existence of justified expectations that might be protected or hurt by the regulation; ... (f) the extent to which the regulation is consistent with the traditions of the international system; [and] (g) the extent to which another state may have an interest in regulating the activity."

Foreign courts are not known to give up jurisdiction under such a theory, and no U.S. prosecution is known to have been dismissed because of a comity factors theory. In fact, the alleged "rule" is not a requirement of international law, nor is it a reflection of general practice in the U.S. or abroad. It is merely a controversial assertion based on "comity" factors or "choice of law" theory and would operate as a self-denying limit on jurisdictional competencies that pertain under international law. In addition to *United States v. Georgescu*, *supra*, *see, e.g.*, note 10 below; *Hartford Fire Ins. Co. v. California*, 113 S.Ct. 2891 (1993); *In re Estate of Marcos Litigation*, 978 F.2d 493, 499–500 (9th Cir. 1992) ("no nexus to this country" required, "no limitation"); *United States v. Yunis*, 924 F.2d 1086, 1091 (D.C. Cir. 1991) (may prosecute international crimes "even absent any special connection between the state and the offense"); *Laker Airways v. Sabena*, 731 F.2d 909, 949–51 (D.C. Cir. 1984) (adding: "there is no evidence that interest balancing represents a rule of international law"); *Filartiga v. Pena-Irala*, 630 F.2d 876, 878, 885 (2d Cir. 1980); *Forti v. Suarez-Mason*, 672 F. Supp. 1531 (N.D. Cal. 1987). *See also Demjanjuk v. Petrovsky*, 776 F.2d 571, 581–83 (6th Cir. 1985); *Adra v. Clift*, 195 F. Supp. 857, 864 (D. Md. 1961) (*quoting* 1 HYDE, INTERNATIONAL LAW § 11A, at 33–34 (2 ed. 1945): even though "'no connection therewith'"); BARRY E. CARTER & PHILLIP R. TRIMBLE, INTERNATIONAL LAW 738, 759, 760 (re: nationality) (2 ed. 1995); JORDAN J. PAUST, INTERNATIONAL LAW AS LAW OF THE UNITED STATES 440–41n.76 (2 ed, 2003); David J. Gerber, *Beyond Balancing: International Law Restraints on the Reach of National Laws*, 10 YALE J. INT'L L. 185, 205–06, 208–09 (1984); Berta Esperanza Hernandez, *RIP to IRP—Money Laundering and Drug Trafficking Controls Score a Knockout Victory over Bank Secrecy*, 18 N.C. J. INT'L L. & COMM. REG. 235, 254 (1993) (U.S. courts generally find U.S. interests outweigh foreign interests); Phillip R. Trimble, *The Supreme Court and International Law: The Demise of Restatement Section 403*, 89 AM. J. INT'L L. 53, 55–57 (1995) (adding: "there is no such general practice and hence no customary international law like that advanced in section 403" and "[t]he Souter majority [in *Hartford Fire Insurance Co.*] did not refuse to apply international law. It simply declined to apply section 403 ... the decision itself ... rejects section 403."); *cf.* Andreas F. Lowenfeld, *Conflict, Balancing of Interests, and the Exercise of Jurisdiction to Prescribe: Reflections on the Insurance Antitrust Case*, *id.* at 48. Some courts have used section 403. *See, e.g.*, United States v. Clark, 435 F.3d 1100, 1106 (9th Cir. 2006); United States v. Vasquez-Velasco, 15 F.3d 833, 840 (9th Cir. 1994); United States v. Martinez 599 F. Supp.2d 784, 800 (W.D. Tex. 2009).

15. The U.S. Supreme Court offered criticism of such an approach in *McCulloch v. Sociedad Nacional de Marineros de Honduras*, 372 U.S. 10, 19 (1963) ("Application of the sanctions of the Act ... on a purely *ad hoc* weighing of contacts basis ... would inevitably lead to embarrassment in foreign affairs and be entirely infeasible in actual practice"); *cf.* *Hartford Fire Ins. Co. v. California*, 113 S.Ct. at 2920–21 (Scalia, J., dissenting). If used, what weight should be given to what factors? What if there are combinations of prescriptive jurisdictional competence for the forum state? Wouldn't such an approach be haphazard, inflexible and "unreasonable" concerning policies at stake, and unpredictable, leaving others without adequate guidance or notice whether jurisdiction might be exercised? *See also* Michael Scharf, *Beyond the Rhetoric of Comparative Interest Balancing*, 50 L. & CONTEMP. PROBS. 95 (1987):

The Deficiencies of Comparative Interest Balancing

Vagueness is but one of the many deficiencies inherent in comparative interest balancing which render it an impractical approach to the problem of extraterritorial discovery conflicts. A second major problem with comparative interest balancing is that courts are simply unable to ascertain and to evaluate accurately the interests of the foreign states that are to be weighed against those of the United States. The Restatement (second) required an assessment of the "vital national interest" of the foreign state, and the Restatement (Revised) calls for an inquiry as to "the extent to which compliance with an order to produce the requested information would affect important substantive policies or interests of the state." Yet, unlike the United States Department of State, the judiciary possesses neither the special training nor the resources necessary to analyze the economic, political, and social interests that underlie a foreign state's policies of nondisclosure. Several courts have acknowledged that the judiciary lacks the "institutional resources," the expertise, and perhaps even the authority to "adequately chart the competing problems and priorities that inevitably define the scope of any nation's interest in a legislated remedy."

The Act of State doctrine presents a further barrier to the evaluation of the foreign interests underlying blocking legislation. The doctrine, which prevents an American court from sitting in judgment of the public acts of another country, directly conflicts with the position taken by the Restatement (Revised) that foreign "statutes that frustrate [discovery] need not be given the same deference by courts of the United States as substantive rules of law at variance with the law of the United States." One court has recently rejected this assertion by the Restatement (Revised), noting that it is "somewhat presumptuous, to gauge the importance of the Blocking Statute to France." This view was also highlighted in recent litigation in which the United Kingdom stated that it is as politically intolerable for leaders of foreign democracies to have their official policies evaluated, balanced, and coerced by U.S. courts as it would be for American leaders to have important U.S. policies and interests evaluated, judged, and coerced in foreign courts.

Even assuming domestic courts have the ability and authority to gauge vital foreign interests, they cannot reliably and impartially balance the foreign interests against those of the United States. In *Laker Airways v. Sabena, Belgian World Airlines*, Judge Malcolm Wilkey of the D.C. Circuit Court of Appeals argued that domestic courts are incapable of sitting as international tribunals and evenhandedly balancing national interests. He concluded that "courts inherently find it difficult neutrally to balance competing foreign interests." Given the vagueness of existing comparative interest balancing approaches, it is small wonder that a court might be encouraged to assert the primacy of U.S. interests. A court is likely to have difficulty, especially in a case involving U.S. nationals, in denying jurisdiction, unless it can base its decision on a concrete legal principle that clearly prohibits the exercise of such jurisdiction. Comparative interest balancing provides no such concrete principle.

Finally, judicial use of comparative interest balancing is contrary to the political question doctrine which removes certain issues from the scope of judicial review. In *Baker v. Carr*, the Supreme court extensively reviewed the history and evolution of the political question doctrine and explained that when the resolution of questions touching foreign relations turns on standards that defy judicial application, or involves the exercise of discretion demonstrably committed to the executive or legislature, such questions are nonjusticiable political questions. The preceding discussion has illustrated that comparative interest balancing incorporates "purely political factors" which the court is neither qualified to evaluate comparatively nor capable of properly balancing.

Appraisal of the national interests of a foreign state is therefore more appropriately a political rather than a judicial judgment. In accordance with the political question doctrine, a court should refrain from subscribing to a formulation whose standards are neither judicially discoverable nor manageable.

16. In *Societe Nationale Industrielle Aerospatiale v. United States District Court for the Southern District of Iowa*, 482 U.S. 522 (1987), the Court suggested use of a "comity" factors approach concerning compulsion of evidence from abroad. Nonetheless, it noted that U.S. courts can order a foreign party to produce evidence located abroad, and this even in the face of a foreign state "blocking statute" or a claim of "foreign sovereign compulsion" and a foreign state *amicus* brief. Are attempts to resolve conflicts concerning concurrent jurisdictional competencies best left to resolutions through international agreements and those favored under customary international law? *See also Wilson v. Girard*, 354 U.S. 524 (1957); *Wildenhus's Case*, 120 U.S. 1 (1886). Who could obtain tradeoffs for the United States, the courts or the Executive?

17. Congress has also ignored such an approach to jurisdiction, especially with respect to international crimes. Consider the Torture Victim Protection Act, P.L. 256, 106 Stat. 73 (1992); the "Terrorism" Act, 18 U.S.C. §§ 2331–2337; the Hostage Taking Act, 18 U.S.C. § 1203; the Torture Act, 18 U.S.C. § 2340A (b) (2); the Protection of Internationally Protected Persons Act, 18 U.S.C. § 112(a), (b) and (e); The Destruction of Aircraft Act, 18 U.S.C. § 32.

18. The alleged rule of reasonableness would only apply to jurisdictional competencies under § 402. It does *not* apply to universal jurisdiction under § 404. Should such a limiting approach, developed from the field of conflict of laws, have anything to do with international crimes over which there is universal jurisdictional competence and responsibility? Cases in the U.S. addressing violations of international law have ruled that no nexus with the U.S. is required. *See, e.g.*, United States v. Yousef, 327 F.3d 56, 79 (2d Cir. 2003); *In re* Estate of Marcos Litigation, 978 F.2d 493, 499–500 (9th Cir.1992) ("no nexus to this country" is required, "no limitation"); United States v. Yunis, 924 F.2d 1086, 1091–92 (D.C. Cir.1991) (may prosecute international crimes "even absent any special connection between the state and the offense"); Filartiga v. Pena–Irala, 630 F.2d 876, 878, 885 (2d Cir.1980); Forti v. Suarez–Mason, 672 F.Supp. 1531 (N.D. Cal.1987); see also Demjanjuk v. Petrovsky, 776 F.2d 571, 581–83 (6th Cir.1985); Restatement § 404, cmt. a ("international law permits any state to apply its laws to punish certain offenses although the state has no links of territory with the offense, or of nationality with the offender (or even the victim)."); Daliberti v. Republic of Iraq, 97 F. Supp.2d 38, 52–54 (D.D.C. 2000) (re: terrorism and international law). With respect to international crimes, what law is ultimately being enforced? *See also* Restatement of the Foreign Relations Law of the United States § 404, Comm. a ("international law permits any state to apply its laws to punish certain offenses although the state has no links of territory with the offense, or of nationality with the offender (or even the victim)."); Jordan J. Paust, *An Introduction to and Commentary on Terrorism and the Law*, 19 Conn. L. Rev. 697, 718–20 (1987); *but see* Christopher L. Blakesley, *Jurisdiction as Legal Protection Against Terrorism*, 19 Conn. L. Rev 895, 909–11, 922, *passim* (1987). For early views, see *Talbot v. Janson*, 3 U.S. (3 Dall.) 133, 159–61 (1795), quoted *infra*, Chapter Four, Section 5. With respect to conflict of laws as such, see Louise Weinberg, *Against Comity*, 80 Geo. L.J. 53 (1991).

If a U.S. court uses an ad hoc approach and does not permit prosecution, how can the United States live up to its international obligations with respect to international crimes? Should such international law, as law of the United States, condition the court's approach to jurisdiction?

Part Two

Incorporation and Enforcement

Chapter 4

U.S. Incorporation, Competencies and Fora

Introductory Problem

While studying the materials in this chapter, students might also find it useful to consider the following hypothetical problem.

I. Ben Schlechtermann, an alleged Nazi war criminal, has been arrested recently in the United States and charged with the commission of war crimes and crimes against humanity in Poland during World War II. Schlechtermann alleges that the United States has no jurisdiction under international or domestic law over such alleged offenses for the following reasons:

    a)   such crimes and individual responsibility did not exist as a matter of international law until after World War II;

    b)   prosecution of the accused would be merely "victor's justice" and would constitute a denial of fundamental due process guarantees;

    c)   the Executive has no power to prosecute such alleged crimes once a war is over;

    d)   use of a new military commission for such purposes would be ex post facto;

    e)   no relevant extraterritorial U.S. statute applies to acts of the accused abroad (*nullum crimen sine lege*);

    f)   no treaty can be self-executing in the U.S. for the purpose of criminal sanctions;

    g)   only treaties, not customary international law, can be applied as supreme federal law or "law of the land";

    h)   there is no jurisdiction over such alleged crimes in the U.S. federal district courts and no other federal court has such jurisdictional competence.

Section 1
The United States Constitution (extracts)

[read the extracts in the Documents Supplement]

Notes and Questions

1. See *Ware v. Hylton*, 3 U.S. (3 Dall.) 199, 237, 244 (1796) ("national or federal judges are bound by duty and oath to the same conduct" as state judges under Art. VI, cl. 2).

2. Article I, Section 1 declares: "All legislative Powers herein granted...." Does this imply that "legislative" powers are also granted elsewhere in the Constitution? What other lawmaking powers might there be?

3. Treaties are mentioned in several parts of the U.S. Constitution. The "law of nations," a phrase used as an equivalent to international law, is mentioned once. Does this mean that customary laws of nations (as opposed to treaty-based international law) are not operative through the Constitution except where the phrase is expressly mentioned or do not relate to powers or provisions aligned with the phrase "treaties"? See J. Paust, International Law as Law of the United States 7–11 (2 ed. 2003).

4. Is the following exposition of background materials helpful in answering the last question?

An early draft of Article III of the U.S. Constitution also declared that "the Judiciary [shall] have authority to hear and determine ... by Way of Appeal ... all cases in which foreigners may be interested in the Construction of any Treaty ... or on the Law of Nations...." Document VII of the Committee of Detail, reproduced in II The Records of the Federal Convention of 1787, at 157 (M. Farrand ed. 1937). The draft was dropped, possibly because the federal judiciary was given far more than mere appellate jurisdiction and Document VII was conditioned on an appellate competence. *See also id.* vol. III, at 608 (appeal of "all Causes wherein Questions shall arise on the Construction of Treaties made by U.S. — or on the Law of Nations") (the Pinckney Plan), 117 ("as well as the trial of questions arising on the law of nations, the construction of treaties, or....") (1787 Pinckney plan); vol. II, at 136 (the Pinckney Plan), 143 (legislative power to punish "offences against the law of nations"), 168 (same in Committee of detail Doc. IX), 182 (Madison's report), 316, 570, 595, 614–15; vol. I, at 292, 244, 238 ("foreigners where treaties are in their favor"), 22. *See also* Hamilton, The Federalist No. 80 (1788) ("cases arising upon treaties and the laws of nations" are appropriate); The Federalist No. 22 (1787) ("treaties of the United States, to have any force at all, must be considered as part of the law of the land. Their true import, as far as respects individuals, must, like all other laws, be ascertained by judicial determinations."); IV J. Elliot, The Debates in the Several State Conventions on the Adoption of the Federal Constitution, as Recommended by the General Convention at Philadelphia in 1787 158 (1901) (Davie in North Carolina in 1788: "It was necessary that treaties should operate as laws on individuals. They ought to be binding upon us the moment they are made. They involve in their nature not only our own rights, but those of foreigners" and should be protected by the federal judiciary); *id.* at 267 (Rutledge in South Carolina in 1788: "every treaty was law paramount, and must operate ... this treaty is binding in our courts and in England" re: private duties); *id.* at 277–79 (Pinckney: treaties are "paramount to the laws of the land," create individual rights and duties, and have the force of law); Preyer, *Jurisdiction to Punish: Federal Authority, Federalism and the Common Law of Crimes in the Early Republic*, 4 Law & Hist. Rev. 223, 232 (1986) ("law of nations" was "within the federal judicial power ... within the language of Article III...."); Robert Palmer, *The Federal Common Law of Crime*, 4 Law & Hist. Rev. 267, 276–78 (1986) (adding: "Livermore stated that the only reason why inferior federal courts should be established was to enforce the law of nations").

In 1781, the Continental Congress had recommended to the states that they enact laws to punish offenses against the law of nations. See 21 JOURNALS OF THE CONTINENTAL CONGRESS 1136–37 (G. Hunt ed. 1912), reproduced in Chapter Three, Section 1. The 1781 resolution listed certain violations and ended with a general clause incorporating all "offences against the law of nations, not contained in the foregoing enumeration." *Id.* at 1137. *See also* 29 JOURNALS OF THE CONTINENTAL CONGRESS 655 (Res. of Aug. 1785); Note, *Enforcing the Customary International Law of Human Rights in Federal Courts*, 74 CAL. L. REV. 127, 129–30 n.15 (1986).

According to Madison, one of Randolph's concerns about the confederation involved the following defect: "that they could not cause infractions of treaties or of the law of nations, to be punished." See J. MADISON, NOTES OF DEBATES IN THE FEDERAL CONVENTION OF 1787, at 29 (notes on Randolph's remarks of May 29, 1787). *See also* III J. ELLIOT, *supra*, at 507 (Nicholas in Virginia in 1788 recounting British punishment of an "offence against the law of nations").

Section 2
Early U.S. Cases and Opinions

Nathan v. Commonwealth of Virginia
1 U.S. (1 Dall.) 77, 78 (Common Pleas, Philadelphia County 1781)

The Pennsylvania Attorney General had argued:

"The [English] statute of Ann was read, with the history of the outrage that gave birth to it; which act declares that all process against the person, or goods, or domestics of an ambassador shall be null and void, and all concerned in issuing or serving it, should be punished as infractors of the laws of nations.

"That this statute was not introductory of any rule, but barely declaratory of the laws of nations. That there was nothing new in it, except the clause prescribing a summary mode of punishment. That it was a part of the common law of the land before, and consequently extended to Pennsylvania."

Respublica v. De Longchamps
1 U.S. (1 Dall.) 111, 113, 115 (Pa. 1784)

[Editors' note: While on the streets of Philadelphia, one De Longchamps became embroiled in a heated argument with the Consul of France. During the argument, De Longchamps struck the cane of the foreign consul, for which he was charged in the following indictment: assault on a French Minister "in violation of the laws of nations, against the peace and dignity of the United States and of the commonwealth of Pennsylvania."]

M'Kean, C.J.: "This is a case of the first impression in the United States. It must be determined on the principles of the laws of nations, which form a part of the municipal laws of Pennsylvania ..."The first crime in the indictment is an infraction of the law of nations. This law, in its full extent, is part of the law of this state, and is to be collected from the practice of different nations, and the authority of writers.

"The person of a public minister is sacred and inviolable. Whoever offers any violence to him, not only affronts the sovereign he represents, but also hurts the common safety and well-being of nations;—he is guilty of a crime against the whole world.

"All the reasons [apply likewise to the Minister's house] … to invade its freedom is a crime against the state and all other nations."

Notes and Questions

1. De Longchamps was convicted and given a criminal fine, jail sentence (of two years with seven years probation), and had to post a security bond. See *id.* at 111, 117.

2. After the decision, a resolution of the Continental Congress did "highly approve the action." See 27 J. CONT. CONG. 502–04.

3. Was the early expectation that written laws are necessary for prosecution of violators of the laws of nations?

4. After ratification of the U.S. Constitution, was an infraction of the law of nations still indictable in our courts? In U.S. courts?

1 Op. Att'y Gen.
26, 27 (June 26, 1792) (Randolph, Att'y Gen.)

"The law of nations, although not specially adopted by the constitution or any municipal act, is essentially a part of the law of the land. Its obligation commences and runs with the existence of a nation, subject to modifications on some points of indifference. Indeed a people may regulate it so as to be binding upon the departments of their own government, in any form whatever; but with regard to foreigners, every change is at the peril of the nation which makes it. Impliedly, however, the law of nations is considered by the act affixing penalties to certain crimes as being in force, and some of its subjects are thrown under particular provisions … what would be the consequence of finding this to be the case; and what ought to be done to avenge an infraction of the law of nations, which may not be punishable under any merely municipal law? … [But here] The arrest of the domestic servant of a public minister is declared illegal by the act … [and here] Congress appear to have excluded every resort to the law of nations. This must be the effect of their regulations, or else the offender would be punishable both under that and the law of nations; or at least under either, at the will of the prosecutor. But this cannot be conceived [here] as the sense of the legislature.…"

Notes and Questions

1. Does the above opinion indicate that Congress can obviate altogether a crime under the law of nations? What is the relevant constitutional power of Congress?

2. During the debates as to ratification, Wilson was reported to have stated: "To pretend to define the law of nations which depended on the authority of all the Civilized Nations of the World, would have a look of arrogance." See II FARRAND, RECORDS, at 65. *See also* Palmer, *The Federal Common Law of Crime, supra,* at 277 n.63:

"Allowing the judiciary to punish offenses against the law of nations without prior congressional definition was congruent with constitutional original intent," also *quoting* Representative Marshall in 10 ANNALS OF CONG. 607 (Mar. 7, 1800) re: Art. I, sec. 8, cl. 10: "'[T]his clause of the Constitution cannot be considered, […] as affecting acts which are piracy under the law of nations'" (Marshall adding that "the judicial power of the United States [under Art. III] extends to … piracy under the law of nations…, punishable by every nation" and that such power had been exercised by courts "under the Confederation … although there was no express power in Congress to define and punish the offence."

3. When courts and others had stated that the law of nations has been a part of the "common" or "municipal" law and part of the "law of the land," was its status merely that of common law? *See, e.g.,* PAUST, *supra* at 9, 39–43 n.50. Does such law bind the government, including Congress and the President, in addition to individuals? In addition to the above materials, consider the following:

United States v. Smith
18 U.S. (5 Wheat.) 153, 161 (1820)

"The common law … recognizes and punishes piracy as an offence, not against its own municipal code, but as an offence against the law of nations.…"

Ross v. Rittenhouse
2 U.S. (2 Dall.) 160, 162 (Pa. 1792)

[A resolution of the Continental Congress of January 15, 1780 had resolved] "that the trials in the Court of Appeals be according to the usage of nations, *and not by Jury*." This has been the practice in most nations, but the law of nations … is enforced by … the *municipal law* of the country; which … may … facilitate or improve the execution of its decisions, by any means they shall think best, provided the great universal law remains unaltered. (emphasis in original)

11 Op. Att'y Gen.
297, 299–300 (1865) (Speed, Att'y Gen.)

That the law of nations constitutes a part of the laws of the land, must be admitted. The laws of nations are expressly made laws of the land by the Constitution, when it says that "Congress shall have power to define and punish piracies and felonies committed on the high seas, and offences against the laws of nations." To *define* is to give the limits or precise meaning of a word or thing in being; to make is to call into being. Congress has power to *define*, not to make, the laws of nations; but Congress has the power to make rules for the government of the army and navy. From the very face of the Constitution, then, it is evident that the laws of nations do constitute a part of the laws of the land. But very soon after the organization of the federal government, Mr. Randolph, the Attorney General, said: "The law of nations, although not specifically [sic] adopted by the Constitution, is essentially a part of the law of the land. Its obligation commences and runs with the existence of a nation, subject to modification on some points of indifference." (See Opin. Attorney General, vol. 1, p. 27.) The framers of the Constitution knew that a nation could not maintain an honorable place amongst the nations of the world that does not regard the great and essential principles of the law of nations as a part of the law of the land. Hence

Congress may define those laws, but cannot abrogate them, or, as Mr. Randolph says, may "modify on some points of indifference."

That the laws of nations constitute a part of the laws of the land is established from the face of the Constitution, upon principle and by authority. But the laws of war constitute much the greater part of the law of nations. Like the other laws of nations, they exist and are of binding force upon the departments and citizens of the Government, though not defined by any law of Congress. No one that has ever glanced at the many treatises that have been published in different ages of the world by great, good, and learned men, can fail to know that the laws of war constitute a part of the law of nations, and that those laws have been prescribed with tolerable accuracy. Congress can declare war. When war is declared, it must be, under the Constitution, carried on according to the known laws and usages of war amongst civilized nations. Under the power to define those laws, Congress cannot abrogate them or authorize their infraction. The Constitution does not permit this Government to prosecute a war as an uncivilized and barbarous people.

As war is required by the framework of our Government to be prosecuted according to the known usages of war amongst the civilized nations of the earth, it is important to understand what are the obligations, duties, and responsibilities imposed by war upon the military. Congress, not having defined, as under the Constitution it might have done, the laws of war, we must look to the usage of nations to ascertain the powers conferred in war, on whom the exercise of such powers devolve, over whom, and to what extent do those powers reach, and in how far the citizen and the soldier are bound by the legitimate use thereof.

9 Op. Att'y Gen.

356, 362–63 (1859) (Black, Att'y Gen.)

(The public law of nations "must be paramount to local law in every question where local laws are in conflict" and "[w]hat you will do must of course depend upon the law of our own country, as controlled and modified by the law of nations")

1 Op. Att'y Gen.

566, 570–71 (1821) (Wirt, Att'y Gen.)

The President is the executive officer of the laws of the country; these laws are not merely the constitution, statutes, and treaties of the United States, but those general laws of nations which ... impose on them, in common with other nations, the strict observance of a respect for their natural rights and sovereignties ... This obligation becomes one of the laws of the country; to the enforcement of which, the President, charged by his office with the execution of all our laws, ... is bound to look.

See also III ELLIOT, DEBATES, *supra*, at 502 (Nicholas in Virginia, 1788: "the law of nations ... was superior to any act or law of any nation"); *Shanks v. Dupont*, 28 U.S. (3 Pet.) 242, 248 (1830) (Story, J., op.); *Heathfield v. Chilton*, 4 Burrow 2015, 98 E.R. 50 (K.B. 1767) (act of Parliament cannot "alter" the law of nations, which is part of English law).

Further references:

RESTATEMENT OF THE FOREIGN RELATIONS LAW OF THE UNITED STATES §§ 102, 103, 111, 114–115, 702 & Comment c, Reporters' Note 12 (3 ed. 1987); Henkin, *The President and International Law*, 80 AM. J. INT'L L. 930, 933 (1986), *citing* Henkin, *International Law as Law in the United States*, 82 MICH. L. REV. 1555, 1561 (1984) (not mere "common law"); Lobel, *The Limits of Constitutional Power: Conflicts Between Foreign Policy and International Law*, 71 Va. L. Rev. 1071, 1089, *passim* (1985); Paust, *Rediscovering the Relationship Between Congressional Power and International Law: Exceptions to the Last in Time Rule and the Primacy of Custom*, 28 Va. J. Int'l L. 393 (1988); *Customary International Law: Its Nature, Sources and Status as Law of the United States*, 12 Mich. J. Int'l L. 59 (1990).

4. Representative Marshall, the year before he joined the Supreme Court, had recognized that Article I, Section 8, clause 10 of the Constitution "cannot be considered, as affecting acts which are piracy under the law of nations" and that where, under customary international law, the people of the United States themselves have no competence to act, "that clause can never be construed to make to the Government a grant of power, which the people making it do not themselves possess," and thus that Congress has no power to act in violation of such law, nor "consequently ... [could such power be transferred] to their courts...." 10 Annals of Cong. 607; *see also id.* at 611; *The Antelope*, 23 U.S. (10 Wheat.) 66, 99 & n.6 (1825) (argument of counsel, *citing* House committee reports) (congressional act cannot "increase or diminish the list of offenses punishable by the law of nations"); *Miller v. The Ship Resolution*, 2 U.S. (2 Dall.) 1, 3–4 (1781) (congressional act "cannot change the law of nations"); Justice Wilson's 1791 charge to a grand jury (customary law of nations cannot be altered or abrogated by domestic law), in II The Works of James Wilson 803, 813–14 (R. McCloskey ed. 1967).

5. Justice Story stated in 1814 that a penalty of "forfeiture under the ... act, was absorbed in the more general operation of the law of war." See *The Sally*, 12 U.S. (8 Cranch) 382, 384 (1814) (Story, J., opinion). Does this mean that the customary law of war has a higher, absorbing effect?

6. It was expected quite early that statutes must be interpreted so as to be consistent with international law. *See, e.g.*, *The Charming Betsy*, 6 U.S. (2 Cranch) 64, 117–18 (1804) ("An Act of Congress ought never to be construed to violate the law of nations if any other possible construction remains, and, consequently, can never be construed to violate ... rights ... further than is warranted by the law of nations...."); *Talbot v. Seeman*, 5 U.S. (1 Cranch) 1, 43 (1801); 1 Op. Att'y Gen. 26, 27 (1792); *see also id.* at 53 (stating that the municipal law is strengthened by the law of nations); *Ross v. Rittenhouse*, 2 U.S. (2 Dall.) 160, 162 (Pa. 1792); *The Resolution*, 2 U.S. (2 Dall.) 1, 4 (1781); 11 Op. Att'y Gen. 297, 299–300 (1865); 9 Op. Att'y Gen. 356, 362–63 (1859); *The Ship Rose*, 36 Ct. Cl. 290, 301 (1901); *The Schooner Nancy*, 27 Ct. Cl. 99, 109 (1892); *Rutgers v. Waddington*, Mayor's Court of the City of New York (1784) (cited in 2 American Legal Records, Select Cases of the Mayor's Court of New York City 1674–1784, at 302 (R. Morris ed. 1935)) (construing the 1783 N.Y. Trespass Act consistently with the Treaty of Peace), discussed in 1 The Law Practice of Alexander Hamilton 413–14 (J. Goebel ed. 1964); G. Wood, The Creation of the American Republic 1776–1787, at 457–58 (1969); *United States v. Flores*, 289 U.S. 137, 159 (1933); *but see Mississippi Poultry Ass'n, Inc. v. Madigan*, 992 F.2d 1359, 1367 (5th Cir. 1993) ("loath ... to extend this maxim to multilateral trade agreements."); *United States v. Yunis*, 924 F.2d 1086, 1091 (D.C. Cir. 1991) (dictum: duty of courts merely to enforce statutes, "not to conform" them "to norms of customary international law"). In 1814, the Supreme Court also recognized that "[i]n expounding ... [the U.S.] constitution, a construction ought not lightly to be admitted which would" produce an effect contrary to or "which would fetter" results under customary international law. See *Brown v. United States*, 12 U.S. (8 Cranch) 110, 125 (1814). This approach has been utilized especially in connection with human rights.

Today, the rule of construction has been retained by the Supreme Court. Additionally, there has been built into such a rule a stronger primacy for international treaty law, since an unavoidable clash between a treaty and an act of Congress will not even arise unless there is a clear and unequivocal evidence of congressional intent to supersede the treaty. *See, e.g., Trans World Airlines, Inc. v. Franklin Mint Corp.*, 466 U.S. 243, 252 (1984); *McCulloch v. Sociedad Nacional de Marineros de Honduras*, 372 U.S. 10, 21–22 (1963); *Cook v. United States*, 288 U.S. 102, 120 (1933); *United States v. Payne*, 264 U.S. 446, 448 (1924); *Chew Heong v. United States*, 112 U.S. 536, 539–40, 549–50 (1884); *United States v. The Palestine Liberation Organization*, 695 F. Supp. 1456, 1465, 1468 (S.D.N.Y. 1988). This is generally referred to as the *Cook* rule, which one applies after using the *Charming Betsy* rule.

7. When Congress has exercised its power "to define and punish" under Article 1, sec. 8, cl. 10 of the Constitution, how have relevant offenses been described or categorized, as offenses "against the United States," as offenses "against the Laws of the United States," or as offenses against the law of nations or law of war? *See, e.g., United States v. Arjona*, 120 U.S. 479, 488 (1887); *Ex parte Quirin*, 317 U.S. 1, 27–30 (1942) [*infra* Section 3]; *United States v. Smith*, 18 U.S. (5 Wheat.) 153, 158–62 (1820) [*infra* Section 3]; *see also* 11 Op. Att'y Gen. 297, 299–300 (1865) [*supra*]; *cf.* An Act for the Punishment of Certain Crimes Against the United States, sec. 28, 1 Stat. 112, 118 (1790) (making it a crime to "assault, strike, wound, imprison, or in any manner infract the law of nations, by offering violence to the person of an ambassador or other public minister").

Henfield's Case

11 F. Cas. 1099 (C.C.D. Pa. 1793) (No. 6,360)

[Editors' note: The British Minister Plenipotentiary to the United States, Mr. Hammond, sent a letter to Secretary of State Jefferson complaining of the outfitting of two privateers in Charleston, South Carolina under French Commissions, carrying six guns, and being navigated by forty-five men, "for the most part, citizens of the United States," which constitute alleged breaches of neutrality. He also asked the Executive to repress such practices. Thereafter, Secretary Jefferson wrote to Mr. Rawle to apprehend and prosecute such U.S. citizens according to law. In turn, Mr. Rawle wrote to Mr. Baker that he had received information that one Gideon Henfield of Massachusetts was an officer of a privateer fitted out in Charleston that had been a British vessel taken as prize and stated that he had "received orders to prosecute, in every instance, those who commit breaches of neutrality ... during the present war between the European powers," and that he should prosecute Henfield if the information is correct.]

This charge, though not delivered to the particular grand jury by whom the bill against Henfield was found, was prepared for the purpose of settling the law generally as applying to the class of offenders, of whom Henfield was one, and in this light it is here introduced....

A charge delivered by the Honourable John Jay, Esquire, Chief Justice of the United States, to the grand jury impanelled for the court of the United States, holden for the Middle circuit in the district of Virginia, at the capitol in the city of Richmond, on the 22d day of May, 1793.

Gentlemen of the Grand Jury: That citizens and nations should [so] use their own as not to injure others, is an ancient and excellent maxim; and is one of those plain precepts of common justice, which it is the interest of all, and the duty of each to obey, and that not only in the use they may make of their property, but also of their liberty, their power and other blessings of every kind....

By their constitution and laws, the people of the United States have expressed their will, and their will so expressed, must sway and rule supreme in our republic. It is in obedience to their will, and in pursuance of their authority, that this court is now to dispense their justice in this district; and they have made it your duty, gentlemen, to inquire whether any and what infractions of their laws have been committed in this district, or on the seas, by persons in or belonging to it. Proceed, therefore, to inquire accordingly, and to present such as either have, or shall come to your knowledge. That you may perceive more clearly the extent and objects of your inquiries, it may be proper to observe, that the laws of the United States admit of being classed under three heads of descriptions. 1st. All treaties made under the authority of the United States. 2d. The laws of nations. 3dly. The constitution, and statutes of the United States.

Treaties between independent nations, are contracts or bargains which derive all their force and obligation from mutual consent and agreement; and, consequently, when once fairly made and properly concluded, cannot be altered or annulled by one of the parties, without the consent and concurrence of the other. Wide is the difference between treaties and statutes—we may negotiate and make contracts with other nations, but we can neither legislate for them, nor they for us; we may repeal or alter our statutes, but no nation can have authority to vacate or modify treaties at discretion. Treaties, therefore, necessarily become the supreme law of the land, and so they are very properly declared to be by the sixth article of the constitution. Whenever doubts and questions arise relative to the validity, operation or construction of treaties, or of any articles in them, those doubts and questions must be settled according to the maxims and principles of the laws of nations applicable to the case. The peace, prosperity, and reputation of the United States, will always greatly depend on their fidelity to their engagements; and every virtuous citizen (for every citizen is a party to them) will concur in observing and executing them with honour and good faith....

As to the laws of nations—they are those laws by which nations are bound to regulate their conduct towards each other, both in peace and war. Providence has been pleased to place the United States among the nations of the earth, and therefore, all those duties, as well as rights, which spring from the relation of nation to nation, have devolved upon us. We are with other nations, tenants in common of the sea—it is a highway for all, and all are bound to exercise that common right, and use that common highway in the manner which the laws of nations and treaties require. On this occasion, it is proper to observe to you, gentlemen, that various circumstances and considerations now unite in urging the people of the United States to be particularly exact and circumspect in observing the obligation of treaties, and the laws of nations, which as has been already remarked, form a very important part of the laws of our nation. I allude to the facts and injunctions specified in the president's late proclamation; it is in these words: "Whereas, it appears that a state of war exists between Austria, Prussia, Sardinia, Great Britain, and the United Netherlands of the one part, and France of the other, and the duty and interest of the United States, require that they should with sincerity and good faith, adopt and pursue a conduct friendly and impartial towards the belligerent powers: I have, therefore, thought fit by these presents, to declare the disposition of the United States to observe the conduct aforesaid towards these powers respectively, and to exhort and warn the citizens of the United States, carefully to avoid all acts and proceedings whatsoever, which may in any manner tend to contravene such disposition. I do hereby make known, that whosoever of the citizens of the United States, shall render himself liable to punishment or forfeiture, under the law of nations, by committing, aiding, or abetting hostilities against any of the said powers, or by carrying to them those articles which are deemed contraband, by the modern usage of nations, will not receive the protection of the United States against such punishment or forfeiture; and further, that I have given instructions to those officers to whom it belongs, to cause prosecutions to be instituted against all persons who shall within the cognizance of the courts of the United States, violate the law of nations, with respect to the powers at war, or any of them."

By this proclamation, authentic and official information is given to the citizens of the United States: — That war actually exists between the nations mentioned in it: That they are to observe a conduct friendly and impartial towards the belligerent powers: That offenders will not be protected, but on the contrary, prosecuted and punished. The law of nations, considers those as neutral nations "who take no part in the war, remaining friends to both parties, and not favouring the arms of one to the detriment of the other;" and it declares that a "nation, desirous safely to enjoy the conveniences of neutrality, is in all things to show an exact impartiality between the parties at war; for should he, when under no obligation, favour one to the detriment of the other, he cannot complain of being treated as an adherent and confederate of his enemy, of which no nation would be the dupe if able to resent it." The proclamation is exactly consistent with and declaratory of the conduct enjoined by the law of nations. It is worthy of remark that we are at peace with all these belligerent powers not only negatively in having war with none of them, but also in a more positive and particular sense by treaties with four of them.

By the first article of our treaty with France it is stipulated that "there shall be a firm, inviolable and universal peace, and true and sincere friendship between his Most Christian Majesty, his heirs and successors, and the United States; and between the countries, islands, cities and towns situate under the jurisdiction of his Most Christian Majesty and of the United States, and the people and inhabitants of every degree, without exception of persons or places." By the first article of our treaty with the United Netherlands, it is stipulated that "there shall be a firm, inviolable and universal peace, and sincere friendship between their High Mightinesses, the Lords and States General of the United Netherlands and the United States of America, and between the subjects and inhabitants of the said parties, and between the countries, islands and places situate under the jurisdiction of the said United Netherlands and the United States of America, their subjects and inhabitants of every degree, without exception of persons or places." The definitive treaty of peace with Great Britain begins with great solemnity, in the words following: "In the name of the most holy and undivided Trinity." By the seventh article of this treaty it is stipulated that "there shall be a firm and perpetual peace between his Britannic Majesty, and the United States, and between the subjects of the one and the citizens of the other." By the first article of our treaty with Prussia it is stipulated that "there shall be a firm, inviolable and universal peace and sincere friendship between his Majesty, the King of Prussia, his heirs, successors and subjects on the one part, and the United States of America and their citizens on the other, without exception of persons or places." ...

While the people of other nations do no violence or injustice to our citizens, it would certainly be criminal and wicked in our citizens, for the sake of plunder, to do violence and injustice to any of them. The president, therefore, has with great propriety declared "that the duty and interest of the United States require that they should, with sincerity and good faith, adopt and pursue a conduct friendly and impartial towards the belligerent powers." ...

It is on these and similar principles that whoever shall render himself liable to punishment or forfeiture, under the law of nations, by committing, aiding or abetting hostilities forbidden by his country, ought to lose the protection of his country against such punishment or forfeiture. But this is not all, it is not sufficient that a nation should only withdraw its protection from such offenders, it ought also to prosecute and punish them....

From the observations which have been made, this conclusion appears to result, viz.: That the United States are in a state of neutrality relative to all the powers at war, and that it is their duty, their interest, and their disposition to maintain it: that, therefore, they who commit, aid, or abet hostilities against these powers, or either of them, offend against the laws of the United States, and ought to be punished; and consequently, that it is your duty, gentlemen, to inquire into and present all such of these offences, as you shall find to have been committed within this district. What acts amount to committing or aiding, or abetting hostilities, must be determined by the laws and approved practice of nations, and by the treaties and other laws of the United States relative to such cases....

Charge of Judge Wilson, as president of a special court of the United States, for the Middle circuit and Pennsylvania district, holden at the court house, in the city of Philadelphia, on the 22d day of July, 1793, to the grand jury of said court:

Gentlemen of the Grand Jury: It is my duty to explain to you the very important occasion on which this court is specially convened, and to state the points of law not less important to the application of which that occasion gives rise.

To the judge of the Pennsylvania district information was given on oath, that certain citizens of the United States had acted in several capacities as officers on board an armed schooner, said to be commissioned by France as a cruiser or private ship-of-war; and with others on board that schooner did capture and make prize of several ships or vessels belonging to his Britannic Majesty, and otherwise assist in an hostile manner in annoying the commerce of the subjects of his said Britannic Majesty, who is at peace with the United States, contrary to their duty as citizens of the United States. On receiving this information the judge issued his warrant for apprehending the persons against whom complaint was made, that they might answer for their doings in the premises, and be dealt with according to law. That legal proceedings in this and some other business might be had speedily, one of the judges of the supreme court of the United States and the judge of the Pennsylvania district issued their warrant, directing that on this day, and at this place a special session of the circuit court for this district should be held, and that grand and traverse jurors should be summoned to attend it. As the court however is authorized generally to try criminal causes, if any other crimes or offences cognizable in it be laid before you or are in your knowledge, it is your duty to present them.... under our national constitution, treaties compose a portion of the public and supreme law of the land, and for their construction and enforcement are brought openly before the tribunals of our country. Of those tribunals juries form an essential part; under the construction given by those juries, treaties will suffer neither in their importance nor in their sanctity....

Under all the obligations due to the universal society of the human race, the citizens of a state still continue. To this universal society it is a duty that each nation should contribute to the welfare, the perfection and the happiness of the others. If so, the first degree of this duty is to do no injury. Among states as well as among men, justice is a sacred law. This sacred law prohibits one state from exciting disturbances in another, from depriving it of its natural advantages, from calumniating its reputation, from seducing its citizens, from debauching the attachment of its allies, from fomenting or encouraging the hatred of its enemies. Vatt. Law Nat. 127. But nations are not only prohibited from doing evil, they are also commanded to do good to one another. On states as well as individuals the duties of humanity are strictly incumbent; what each is obliged to perform for others, from others it is entitled to receive. Hence the advantage as well as the duty of humanity.... Let such be held responsible, when they can be rendered amenable for the consequences of their crimes and disorders. If the offended nation have the criminal in its power, it may without difficulty punish him, and oblige him to make satisfaction. Vatt. Law Nat. 145. When the offending citizen escapes into his own country, his nation should oblige him to repair the damage, if reparation can be made, or should punish him according to the measure of his offence. Vatt. Law Nat. 75; Burrows, 1480; 4 Bl. Comm. 68,69. If the nation refuse to do either, it renders itself in some measure an accomplice in the guilt, and becomes responsible for the injury. Vatt. Law Nat. 145. To what does this responsibility lead? To reprisal certainly (Vatt. Law Nat. 251); and if so, probably to war (Id. 2; 4 Bl. Comm. 68, 69). And should the fortunes or the lives of millions be placed in either of those predicaments by the conduct of one citizen, or of a few citizens? Vatt. Law Nat. 2, 89. Humanity and reason say no. The constitution of the United States says no....

Judge Wilson (with whom were Judge Iredell and Judge Peters) charged the jury as follows:

This is, gentlemen of the jury, a case of the first importance. Upon your verdict the interests of four millions of your fellow-citizens may be said to depend. But whatever be the consequence, it is your duty, it is our duty, to do only what is right....

The questions of law coming into joint consideration with the facts, it is the duty of the court to explain the law to the jury, and give it to them in direction. It is the joint and unanimous opinion of the court, that the United States, being in a state of neutrality relative to the present war, the acts of hostility committed by Gideon Henfield are an offence against this country, and punishable by its laws. It has been asked by his counsel, in their address to you, against what law has he offended? The answer is, against many and binding laws. As a citizen of the United States, he was bound to act no part which could injure the nation; he was bound to keep the peace in regard to all nations with whom we are at peace. This is the law of nations; not an ex post facto law, but a law that was in existence long before Gideon Henfield existed. There are also, positive laws, existing previous to the offence committed, and expressly declared to be part of the supreme law of the land. The constitution of the United States has declared that all treaties made, or to be made, under the authority of the United States, shall be part of the supreme law of the land. I will state to you, gentlemen, so much of the several treaties in force between American and any of the powers at war with France, as applies to the present case. The first article of the treaty with the United Netherlands, declares that there shall be a firm, inviolable, and universal peace and sincere friendship between the States General of the United Netherlands and the United States of America, and between the subjects and inhabitants of the said parties. The seventh article of the definitive treaty of peace between the United States and Great Britain, declares that there shall be a firm and perpetual peace between his Britannic Majesty and the United States, and between the subjects of the one and the citizens of the other. And the first article of the treaty with Prussia declares that there shall be a firm, inviolable, and universal peace and sincere friendship between his Majesty the King of Prussia and his subjects, on the one part, and the United States of America and their citizens on the other. It may be observed, that the treaty would not be less sufficient in relation to the present question, if "subjects" and "citizens" had not been mentioned. These treaties were in the most public, the most notorious existence, before the act for which the prisoner is indicted was committed.

The jury retired about nine on Saturday evening, and came into court again about half-past eleven, when they informed the court they had not agreed. They were desired to retire again, which they did, and returned on Monday morning, having delivered into the hands of Judge Wilson a privy verdict on Sunday morning, soon after the adjournment of the court.

One of the jurymen now expressed some doubts, which occasioned the judges separately to deliver their sentiments on the points of law adverted to in the charge on Saturday evening, each of them assenting to the same, particularly as to the change of political relation in the defendant, from his having been some time absent from home previous to his entering on board the privateer.

The jury again retired, and the court adjourned. At half-past four the court was convened, and the jury presented a written verdict, which the court refused to receive, as being neither general nor special. Another adjournment took place, and about seven o'clock a verdict of "Not guilty" was delivered.[7]

Notes and Questions

1. Duponceau, who had argued for the defense, made the following statement after the case:

> "Judge Wilson, who presided at this trial, in his charge to the jury, took the ground of its being also an offence at common law, of which the law of nations was a part, and maintained the doctrine that the common law was to be looked to for the definition and punishment of the offence. This ground had not been adverted to in argument, or, at least, very slightly. But it would seem that the common law considered as a municipal system had nothing to do with this case.

---

7. Chief Justice Marshall (Life of Washington, vol. 2, pp. 273, 274) thus notices the result: "The administration received additional evidence of the difficulty that would attend an adherence to the system which had been commenced in the acquittal of Gideon Henfield. A prosecution had been instituted against this person, who had enlisted in Charleston on Board a French privateer equipped in the port, which had brought her prizes into the port of Philadelphia. This prosecution had been directed under the advice of the attorney general, who was of opinion that persons of this description were punishable for having violated subsisting treaties, which by the constitution are the supreme law of the land, and that they were also indictable at common law, for disturbing the peace of the United States. It could not be expected that the Democratic party would be inattentive to an act so susceptible of misrepresentation. Their papers sounded the alarm, and it was universally asked, 'What law had been offended, and under what statute was the indictment supported? Were the American people already prepared to give to a proclamation the force of a legislative act, and to subject themselves to the will of the executive? But if they were already sunk to such a state of degradation, were they to be punished for violating a proclamation which had not been published when the offence was committed, if indeed it could be termed an offence to engage with France, combating for liberty against the combined despots of Europe.'" "As the trial approached, a great degree of sensibility was displayed, and the verdict in favour of Henfield was celebrated with extravagant marks of joy and exultation. It bereaved the executive of the strength to be derived from an opinion, that punishment might be legally inflicted on those who should openly violate the rules prescribed for the preservation of neutrality; and exposed that department to the obloquy of having attempted a measure which the laws would not justify." The verdict was considered by Washington of such moment, as to lead him to enumerate it as a principal reason to be considered in the question of calling an extra session of congress, respecting which he asked the opinion of his cabinet on August 3, 1793. See 10 Wash. Writ. by Sparks. 362.

The law of nations, being the common law of the civilized world, may be said, indeed, to be a part of the law of every civilized nation; but it stands on other and higher grounds than municipal customs, statutes, edicts, or ordinances. It is binding on every people and on every government. It is to be carried into effect at all times under the penalty of being thrown out of the pale of civilization, or involving the country into a war. Every branch of the national administration, each within its district and its particular jurisdiction, is bound to administer it. It defines offences and affixes punishments, and acts everywhere *proprio rigore*, whenever it is not altered or modified by particular national statutes, or usages not inconsistent with its great and fundamental principles. Whether there is or not a national common law in other respects this universal common law can never cease to be the rule of executive and judicial proceedings until mankind shall return to the savage state. Judge Wilson, therefore, in my opinion, rather weakened than strengthened the ground of the prosecution in placing the law of nations on the same footing with the municipal or local common law and deriving its authority exclusively from the latter. It was considering the subject in its narrowest point of view."

Reprinted in 11 F. Cas. at 1122. Do you agree with Mr. Duponceau? Note that Jay and Wilson gave separate charges and Duponceau was responding to Wilson's in Philadelphia. Also, both addressed treaties as supreme federal law.

2. Chief Justice Jay's recognition that customary laws of nations are a necessary background for the interpretation ("validity, operation or construction") of treaties has generally been followed. *See, e.g., McCulloch v. Sociedad Nacional de Marineros de Honduras*, 372 U.S. 10, 20–21 & n. 12 (1963); *Santovincenzo v. Egan*, 284 U.S. 30, 40 (1931); *Geofroy v. Riggs*, 133 U.S. 258, 271 (1890); *United States v. Rauscher*, 119 U.S. 407, 419–20, 429 (1886); *The Pizarro*, 15 U.S. (2 Wheat.) 227, 246 (1817); *Ware v. Hylton*, 3 U.S. (3 Dall.) 199, 261 (1796) ("The subject of treaties … is to be determined by the law of nations"); *see also Trans World Airlines v. Franklin Mint Corp.*, 466 U.S. 243, 261 (1984); *Jordan v. Tashiro*, 278 U.S. 123, 127 (1928); *Tucker v. Alexandroff*, 183 U.S. 424, 437 (1902); *Society for the Propagation of the Gospel in Foreign Parts v. New Haven*, 21 U.S. (8 Wheat.) 464, 490 (1823).

3. Justice Wilson's charge to the grand jury and the indictment recognized that private violations of the law of nations can constitute an act of "aggression" and a crime against "peace." See 11 F. Cas. at 1108–15. *See also id.* at 1107 (points of Rawle, dist. att'y: his "aggression" on them, "actual aggression is charged"); 1 Op. Att'y Gen. 68, 69 (1797) ("the peace of Mankind"); 1 Op. Att'y Gen. 57, 58 (1795) ("against the public peace"). Are these recognitions relevant to modern prosecutions of aggression war or crimes against peace? Consider these points when studying Chapter Seven.

4. What was the controversy noted in footnote 7 in *Henfield's* case? What did Justice Wilson say in response to the question of "what law has he offended"?

5. In 1794, Congress passed neutrality legislation to provide criminal sanctions for such offenses against the law of nations. 18 U.S.C. § 25, now § 960, reads:

> "Expedition against friendly nation
>
> "Whoever, within the United States, knowingly begins or sets on foot or provides or prepares a means for or furnishes the money for, or takes part in, any military or naval expedition or enterprise to be carried on from thence against the territory or dominion of any foreign prince or state, or of any colony, dis-

trict, or people with whom the United States is at peace, shall be fined not more than $3,000 or imprisoned not more than three years, or both."

Other sections that may be relevant include §§ 956–959 and 961–967. This material will also be addressed in Chapter Seven.

See also Quincy Wright, *The Law of the Nuremberg Trial*, 41 Am. J. Int'l L. 38, 246 (1947).

5. 18 U.S.C. § 960 does not mention "treaties" or the "law of nations." Nonetheless, are such laws relevant to an adequate interpretation of the statute? Also compare the following:

1 Op. Att'y Gen.
57, 58 (July 6, 1795) (Bradford, Att'y Gen.)

" ... acts of hostility committed by American citizens against such as are in amity with us, being in violation of a treaty, and against the public peace, are offences against the United States, so far as they were committed within the territory or jurisdiction thereof; and, as such, are punishable by indictment in the district or circuit courts.

" ... there can be no doubt that the company or individuals who have been injured by these acts of hostility have a remedy by a civil suit in the courts of the United States; jurisdiction being expressly given to these courts in all cases where an alien sues for a tort only, in violation of the law of nations, or a treaty of the United States...." ... the President [Washington]..., by his proclamation of the 22d of April, 1793 [Proc. of Neutrality, No. 3, *reprinted in* 11 Stat. 753 [App. 1859)], warned all of the United States against all such proceedings; declaring that all those who should render themselves liable to punishment under the laws of nations, by committing, aiding, or abetting hostilities against any of the said parties, would not receive the protection of the United States against such punishment; and that he had given instructions to those officers to whom it belongs to cause proceedings to be instituted against all persons who should, within the [jurisdictional] cognizance of the courts of the United States, violate the laws of nations with respect to the powers at war, or any of them."

1 Op. Att'y Gen.
61, 62 (Jan. 20, 1796) (Lee, Att'y Gen.)

re: breach of neutrality by an individual: "Forfeiture of the goods and ship, is the penalty annexed to such acts by the law of nations...."

1 Op. Att'y Gen.
68, 69 (Jan. 26, 1797) (Lee, Att'y Gen.)

The constitution [art. I, sec. 8, cl. 10] gives to Congress, in express words, the power of passing a law for punishing a violation of territorial rights, it being an offence against the law of nations, and of a nature very serious in its consequence. That the peace of mankind may be preserved, it is the interest as well as the duty of every government to punish with becoming severity all the individuals of the State who commit this offence. Congress has passed no act yet upon the subject, and Jones and his associates are only liable to be prosecuted in our courts at common law for the misdemeanor; and if convicted, to be fined and imprisoned. The common law has adopted the law of nations in its fullest extent, and made it a part of the law of the land.

6. Had legislation been necessary in *Henfield's Case* to incorporate relevant laws of nations? or treaties? Did Justice Wilson's statement that treaties, "for their construction and enforcement [,] are brought openly before the tribunals of our country" reflect Chief Justice Jay's approach to such a question and the meaning of Article III, Section 2, clause 1 of the Constitution?

7. What was the intent and effect of the President's proclamation? What is the relevant power of the President under Article II of the Constitution?

8. Was it thought to be necessary that treaties or laws of nations mention individual duties, elements of crimes, or even the possibility of criminal (or civil) sanctions?

Section 3
Incorporation by Reference

If a statute had referred to "treaties" or to the "law of nations," would such a terse reference be a constitutionally sufficient exercise of congressional power to "define and punish"—or a vague and improper attempted incorporation of international law for criminal sanction purposes? Consider the following case extracts addressing other international crimes:

United States v. Smith
18 U.S. (5 Wheat.) 153, 158–62 (1820) (Story, J.)

[Editors' note: Then, as now, relevant U.S. federal legislation simply refers to piracy "under the law of nations." See 18 U.S.C. § 1651. Interestingly, Canadian legislation also refers to "any act that, by the law of nations, is piracy." See Criminal Code of Canada Sec. 74. (1).]

The first point made at the bar is, whether this enactment be a constitutional exercise of the authority delegated to Congress upon the subject of piracies. The constitution declares that Congress shall have power "to define and punish piracies and felonies committed on the high seas, and offenses against the law of nations." The argument which has been urged in behalf of the prisoner is, that Congress is bound to define, in terms, the offense of piracy, and is not at liberty to leave it to be ascertained by judicial interpretation. If the argument be well founded, it seems admitted by the counsel that it equally applies to the 8th section of the act of Congress of 1790, ch. 9, which declares, that robbery and murder committed on the high seas shall be deemed piracy; and yet, notwithstanding a series of contested adjudications on this section, no doubt has hitherto been breathed of its conformity to the constitution.

In our judgment, the construction contended for proceeds upon too narrow a view of the language of the constitution. The power given to Congress is not merely "to define and punish piracy;" if it were, the words "to define" would seem almost superfluous, since the power to punish piracies would be held to include the power of ascertaining and fixing the definition of the crime. And it has been very justly observed, in a celebrated commentary, that the definition of piracies might have been left without inconvenience to the law of nations, though a legislative definition of them is to be found in most municipal codes. But the power is also given "to define and punish felonies on the high seas, and offenses against the law of nations." The term "felonies" has been supposed, in the same work, not to have a very exact and determinate meaning in relation to offenses at the common law committed within the body of a county. However this may be, in relation to offenses on the high seas, it is necessarily somewhat indeterminate, since the term is not used in the criminal jurisprudence of the admiralty in the technical sense of the common law. Offenses, too, against the law of nations, cannot, with any accuracy, be said to be completely ascertained and defined in any public code recognized by the common consent of nations. In respect, therefore, as well to felonies on the high seas as to offenses against the law of nations, there is a peculiar fitness in giving the power to define as well as to punish; and there is not the slightest reason to doubt that this consideration had very great weight in producing the phraseology in question.

But supposing Congress were bound in all the cases included in the clause under consideration to define the offense, still there is nothing which restricts it to a mere logical enumeration in detail of all the facts constituting the offense. Congress may as well define by using a term of a known and determinate meaning as by an express enumeration of all the particulars included in that term. That is certain which is by necessary reference made certain. When the act of 1790 declares, that any person who shall commit the crime of robbery, or murder, on the high seas, shall be deemed a pirate, the crime is not less clearly ascertained than it would be by using the definitions of these terms as they are found in our treatises of the common law. In fact, by such a reference, the definitions are necessarily included, as much as if they stood in the text of the act. In respect to murder, where "malice aforethought" is of the essence of the offense, even if the common law definition were quoted in express terms, we should still be driven to deny that the definition was perfect, since the meaning of "malice aforethought" would remain to be gathered from the common law. There would then be no end to our difficulties, or our definitions, for each would involve some terms which might still require some new explanation. Such a construction of the constitution is, therefore, wholly inadmissible. To define piracies, in the sense of the constitution, is merely to enumerate the crimes which shall constitute piracy; and this may be done either by a reference to crimes having a technical name, and determinate extent, or by enumerating the acts in detail, upon which the punishment is inflicted.

It is next to be considered, whether the crime of piracy is defined by the law of nations with reasonable certainty. What the law of nations on this subject is, may be ascertained by consulting the works of jurists, writing professedly on public law; or by the general usage and practice of nations; or by judicial decisions recognizing and enforcing that law. There is scarcely a writer on the law of nations who does not allude to piracy as a crime of a settled and determinate nature; and whatever may be the diversity of definitions, in other respects, all writers concur in holding that robbery, or forcible depredations upon the sea, animo furandi, is piracy. The same doctrine is held by all the great writers on maritime law, in terms that admit of no reasonable doubt. The common law, too, recognizes and punishes piracy as an offense, not against its own municipal code, but as an offense against the law of nations (which is part of the common law), as an offense against the universal law of society, a pirate being deemed an enemy of the human race.... And it is manifest from the language of Sir William Blackstone, in his comments on piracy, that he considered the common law definition as distinguishable in no essential respect from that of the law of nations. So that, whether we advert to writers on the common law, or the maritime law, or the law of nations, we shall find that they universally treat of piracy as an offense against the law of nations, and that its true definition by that law is robbery upon the sea. And the general practice of all nations in punishing all persons, whether natives or foreigners, who have committed this offense against any persons whatsoever, with whom they are in amity, is a conclusive proof that the offense is supposed to depend, no upon the particular provisions of any municipal code, but upon the law of nations, both for its definition and punishment. We have, therefore, no hesitation in declaring that piracy, by the law of nations, is robbery upon the sea, and that it is sufficiently and constitutionally defined by the fifth section of the act of 1819.

Ex parte Quirin
317 U.S. 1, 27–30 (1942)

[Editors' note: No federal statute existed to specifically implement the laws of war until the 1916 Articles of War addressed herein. Today, the same language in the 1916 statute addressed by the Court appears in 10 U.S.C. §§ 818, 821.]

From the very beginning of its history this Court has recognized and applied the law of war as including that part of the law of nations which prescribes, for the conduct of war, the status, rights and duties of enemy nations as well as of enemy individuals. By the Articles of War, and especially Article 15, Congress has explicitly provided, so far as it may constitutionally do so, that military tribunals shall have jurisdiction to try offenders or offenses against the law of war in appropriate cases. Congress, in addition to making rules for the government of our Armed Forces, has thus exercised its authority to define and punish offenses against the law of nations by sanctioning, within constitutional limitations, the jurisdiction of military commissions to try persons for offenses which, according to the rules and precepts of the law of nations, and more particularly the law of war, are cognizable by such tribunals. And the President, as Commander in Chief, by his Proclamation in time of war has invoked that law. By his Order creating the present Commission he has undertaken to exercise the authority conferred upon him by Congress, and also such authority as the Constitution itself gives the Commander in Chief, to direct the performance of those functions which may constitutionally be performed by the military arm of the nation in time of war.

An important incident to the conduct of war is the adoption of measures by the military command not only to repel and defeat the enemy, but to seize and subject to disciplinary measures those enemies who in their attempt to thwart or impede our military effort have violated the law of war. It is unnecessary for present purposes to determine to what extent the President as Commander in Chief has constitutional power to create military commissions without the support of Congressional legislation. For here Congress has authorized trial of offenses against the law of war before such commissions. We are concerned only with the question whether it is within the constitutional power of the national government to place petitioners upon trial before a military commission for the offenses with which they are charged. We must therefore first inquire whether any of the acts charged is an offense against the law of war cognizable before a military tribunal, and if so whether the Constitution prohibits the trial. We may assume that there are acts regarded in other countries, or by some writers on international law, as offenses against the law of war which would not be triable by military tribunal here, either because they are not recognized by our courts as violations of the law of war or because they are of that class of offenses constitutionally triable only by a jury. It was upon such grounds that the Court denied the right to proceed by military tribunal in *Ex parte Milligan, supra.* But as we shall show, these petitioners were charged with an offense against the law of war which the Constitution does not require to be tried by jury.

It is no objection that Congress in providing for the trial of such offenses has not itself undertaken to codify that branch of international law or to mark its precise boundaries, or to enumerate or define by statute all the acts which that law condemns. An Act of Congress punishing "the crime of piracy as defined by the law of nations" is an appropriate exercise of this constitutional authority, Art. I, sec. 8, cl. 10, "to define and punish" the offense since it has adopted by reference the sufficiently precise definition of international law. *United States v. Smith*, 5 Wheat. 153, 5 L.Ed. 57; see *The Marianna Flora*, 11 Wheat. 1, 40, 41, 6 L.Ed. 405; *United States v. The Malek Adhel*, 2 How. 210, 232, 11 L.Ed. 239; *The Ambrose Light*, D.C., 25 F. 408, 423, 428; 18 U.S.C. § 481, 18 U.S.C.A. § 481. Similarly by the reference in the 15th Article of War to "offenders or offenses that ... by the law of war may be triable by such military commissions", Congress has incorporated by reference, as within the jurisdiction of military commissions, all offenses which are defined as such by the law of war (compare *Dynes v. Hoover*, 20 How. 65, 82, 15 L.Ed. 838), and which may constitutionally be included within that jurisdiction. Congress had the choice of crystallizing in permanent form and in minute detail every offense against the law of war, or of adopting the system of common law applied by military tribunals so far as it should be recognized and deemed applicable by the courts. It chose the latter course.

See also *Filartiga v. Pena-Irala*, 630 F.2d 876, 880 (2d Cir. 1980) (recognizing that 28 U.S.C. § 1350 (which incorporates relevant international law for civil sanctions with the following language: "a tort..., committed in violation of the law of nations or a treaty of the United States") is "sufficiently determinate" and "'sufficiently and constitutionally defined'").

Section 4
New Statutes and New Fora

If a statute incorporates customary international law by reference, can a prosecution properly occur with respect to crimes committed before enactment of the statute? Is there an "ex post facto" or "*nullum crimen sine lege*" (versus "*jus*") defense?

Attorney General of Israel v. Eichmann
[1965]
45 Pesakim Mehoziim 3 (Israel, Jerusalem d. ct. 1961); 36 Int'l L. Rep. 18 (1968), *aff'd*, [1962] 16 Piske Din 2033 (Israel Supreme Court), 36 Int'l L. Rep. 277 (1968):

Our jurisdiction to try this case is based on the Nazis and Nazi Collaborators (Punishment) Law, *a statutory law the provisions of which are unequivocal*. The Court has to give effect to the law of the Knesset, and we cannot entertain the contention that this law conflicts with the principles of international law. For this reason alone Counsel's first contention must be rejected....

But we have also perused the sources of international law, including the numerous authorities mentioned by learned Counsel in his comprehensive written brief upon which he based his oral pleadings, and by the learned Attorney-General in his comprehensive oral pleadings, and failed to find any foundation for the contention that Israeli law is in conflict with the principles of international law. On the contrary, we have reached the conclusion that the law in question conforms to the best traditions of the law of nations.

The power of the State of Israel to enact the law in question or Israel's right to punish is based, with respect to the offences in question, from the point of view of international law, on a dual foundation: The universal character of the crimes in question and their specific character as being designated to exterminate the Jewish people. In what follows we shall deal with each of these two aspects separately....

The abhorrent crimes defined in this law are crimes not under Israel law alone. These crimes which afflicted the whole of mankind and shocked the conscience of nations are grave offenses against the law of nations itself ('*delicta juris gentium*'). Therefore, so far from international law negating or limiting the jurisdiction of countries with respect to such crimes, in the absence of an International Court the international law is in need of the judicial and legislative authorities of every country, to give effect to its penal injunctions and to bring criminals to trial. The authority and jurisdiction to try crimes under international law are universal....

The question whether the Israel Legislature may enact a criminal law with retroactive effect was considered in the first criminal case heard in this District Court after the establishment of the State and in the first appeal lodged with the Supreme Court of Israel, Criminal Appeal I/48, *Sylvester v. Attorney-General* (I Pesakim, 513, 528). Justice Smoira, the First President of the Supreme Court, said, *inter alia*:

"As regards the distinction between retroactive laws and *ex post facto* laws ... I now turn to the judgment of Mr. Justice Willes in *Phillips v. Eyre* (1871) L.R. 6 Q.B. I, at p. 25), in which he said:

> "'Mr. Justice Blackstone [I Comm. 46] describes laws *ex post facto* of this objectionable class as those by which "after an action indifferent in itself is committed, the legislation then for the first time declares it to have been a crime, and inflicts a punishment upon the person who has committed it. Here it is impossible that the party could foresee that an action, innocent when it was done, should be afterwards converted to guilt by a subsequent law; he had therefore no cause to abstain from it, and all punishment for not abstaining must of consequence be cruel and unjust"....

[The District Court also added (*id*. at para. 27):]

The Netherlands Law of July 10, 1947, which amends the preceding Law (of October 22, 1943) may serve as an example of *municipal retroactive legislation*, in adding Article 27A, which provides:

> "Any person who, during the present war, while in the military service of the enemy, is guilty of a war crime or any crime against humanity as defined in Article 6, subsection (b) or (c), of the Charter annexed to the London Agreement of August 8, 1945 ... shall, if such crime contains at the same time the elements of an act punishable according to Netherlands law, receive the punishment laid down for such act."

On the strength of such retroactive adoption of the definition of crimes contained in the Nuremberg Charter, the Senior Commander of the S.S. and Police in Holland, one Rauter, was sentenced to death by a special tribunal, and his appeal was dismissed in 1949 by the Special Court of Cassation (see L.R.T.W.C., XIV, pp. 89 *ff*). The double plea of "*nullum crimen, nulla poena sine lege*" was dismissed by the Court of Cassation on the grounds that the Netherlands legislator had abrogated this rule (which is expressly laid down in Section I of the Netherlands Criminal Law) with respect to crimes of this kind, and that indeed the rule was not adequate for these crimes. At p. 120 (*ibid*.) it is stated:

"From what appears above it follows that neither Article 27(A) of the Extraordinary Penal Law Decree nor Article 6 of the Charter of London (to which the said Netherlands provision refers) had, as the result of a change of view as to its legality, declared *after the event* to be a crime an act which was hitherto permitted; ... These provisions have merely defined in more detail the jurisdiction, as well as the limits of penal liability and the imposition of punishment, in respect of acts which already before their commission were not permitted by international law but were regarded as crimes...."In so far as the appellant considers punishment unlawful because his actions, although illegal and criminal, lacked a legal sanction provided against them precisely outlined and previously prescribed, this objection also fails.

"The principle that no act is punishable except in virtue of a legal penal provision which had preceded it, has as its object the creation of a guarantee of legal security and individual liberty, which legal interests would be endangered if acts about which doubts could exist as to their deserving punishment were to be considered punishable after the event.

"This principle, however, has no absolute character, in the sense that its operation may be affected by other principles with the recognition of which equally important interests of justice are concerned.

"These latter interests do not tolerate that extremely serious violations of the generally accepted principles of international law, the criminal ... character of which was already established beyond doubt at the time they were committed, should not be considered punishable on the sole ground that a previous threat of punishment was lacking. It is for this reason that neither the London Charter of 1945 nor the Judgment of the International Military Tribunal (at Nuremberg) in the case of the Major German War Criminals have accepted this plea, which is contrary to the international concept of justice, and which has since been also rejected by the Netherlands legislator, as appears from Article 27(A) of the Extraordinary Penal Law Decree."

The courts in Germany, too, have rejected the contention that the crimes of the Nazis were not prohibited at the time and that their perpetrators did not have the requisite criminal intent. The judgment of the Supreme Federal Tribunal of January 29, 1952 (I St/R 563/51 (BGH 562 234)) declares that the expulsion of the Jews, the object of which was the death of the deportees, was a continuous crime of murder committed by the principal planners and executants, a matter of which all other executants must have been conscious, since it cannot be accepted that they were unaware of the basic principles on which human society is based and which are the common legacy of all civilized nations.

See also BGH I St.R 404/60 (NIV 1961, 276), a judgment of December 6, 1960, which deals with the murder of mentally-sick persons on Hitler's orders. The judgment says, *inter alia* (pp. 277, 278) that in 1940 at the latest, it was clear to every person not too naive, and certainly to all who were part of the leadership establishment, that the Nazi regime did not shrink from the commission of crimes, and that whoever took part in these crimes could not argue that he had mistakenly assumed that a forbidden act was permissible, when these crimes violated basic principles of the rule of law.

[On appeal, the Supreme Court of Israel stated in 1962:]

[T]he deeds for which the appellant was convicted must be regarded as having been prohibited by the law of nations since "time immemorial", and that from this aspect the enactment of the Law of 1950 was not in any way in conflict with the maxim *nulla poena*, nor did it violate the principle inherent therein....

... [I]n enacting the said Law the Knesset only sought to set out the principles of international law and embody its aims. The two propositions on which we propose to rely will therefore be as follows:

(1) The crimes created by the Law and of which the appellant was convicted must be deemed today as having always borne the stamp of international crimes, banned by the law of nations and entailing individual criminal responsibility.

(2) It is the peculiarly universal character of these crimes that vests in every State the authority to try and punish anyone who participated in their commission.

Demjanjuk v. Petrovsky
776 F.2d 571, 582–83 (6th Cir. 1985), *cert. denied*, 475 U.S. 1016 (1986)

Israel is seeking to enforce its criminal law for the punishment of Nazis and Nazi collaborators for crimes universally recognized and condemned by the community of nations. The fact that Demjanjuk is charged with committing these acts in Poland does not deprive Israel of authority to bring him to trial.

Further, the fact that the State of Israel was not in existence when Demjanjuk allegedly committed the offenses is no bar to Israel's exercising jurisdiction under the universality principle. When proceeding on that jurisdictional premise, neither the nationality of the accused or the victim(s), nor the location of the crime is significant. The underlying assumption is that the crimes are offenses against the law of nations or against humanity and that the prosecuting nation is acting for all nations. This being so, Israel or any other nation, regardless of its status in 1942 or 1943, may undertake to vindicate the interest of all nations by seeking to punish the perpetrators of such crimes.

Notes

1. Other portions of this opinion appear *supra* in Chapter Three, Section 1. Demjanjuk was deported to Israel, convicted there and sentenced to death on April 25, 1988. Later, his conviction was overturned, he was released and, in 1993, returned to the United States.

2. *See also* Edward Sherman, "Songmy 2: Some Knotty Legal Questions," N.Y. Times, Feb. 21, 1970 ("legislation to provide for trial in federal court of servicemen who have been discharged ... would merely give the Federal court jurisdiction to try crimes already on the books"); 11 Op. Att'y Gen. 297, 299–300 (extract reprinted *supra*), 306; statements of Duponceau & Rep. Marshall, *supra*; *Triquet v. Bath*, 3 Burrow 1478 (K.B. 1764) (act only created new punishment).

3. After the Civil War, it was noted that: "Where an accused is charged with a violation of the laws of war, as laid down in paragraph 86 of General Orders No. 100, of War Department, of April 24, 1863 [the Lieber Code], it is no defence that the actual offence for which he was tried was committed before the date of the General Orders; the latter being merely a publication and affirmance of the law as it had previously existed." Digest of Opinions of JAG, Army 244 (1866).

4. When Congress enacts new legislation proscribing what are also international crimes, Congress need not describe the offenses "as offenses against the law of nations." See *United States v. Arjona*, 120 U.S. 479, 488 (1887); *United States v. White*, 27 F. 200, 202–03 (C.C.E.D. Missouri 1886).

Section 5
Prosecuting Without a Statute

Today, is a statute which incorporates customary or treaty-based international law necessary for criminal sanction purposes? Despite earlier cases noted above, today must Congress exercise its power "to define and punish" before lawful prosecution can commence? Consider the following:

A. Custom

The Three Friends
166 U.S. 1, 53 (1897) (Fuller, C.J.)

"The act of 1794, which has been generally recognized as the first instance of municipal legislation in support of the obligations of neutrality.... And though law of nations had been declared by Chief Justice Jay, in his charge to the grand jury at Richmond, May 22, 1793 (Whart. St. Tr. 49, 56), and by Mr. Justice Wilson, Mr. Justice Iredell, and Judge Peters, on the trial of Henfield in July of that year (Whart. St. Tr. 66, 84) to be capable of being enforced in the courts of the United States criminally, as well as civilly, without further legislation, yet it was deemed advisable to pass the act in view of controversy over that position, and, moreover, in order to provide a comprehensive code in prevention of acts by individuals...."

By 1812, the United States Supreme Court had ruled that there were to be no "common law" crimes. See *United States v. Hudson & Goodwin*, 11 U.S. (7 Cranch) 31, 32–3 (1812); 1 Op. Att'y Gen. 209, 210 (1818) (same re: fraud case). In no such case, however, was there any mention of treaties or the law of nations. Further, as noted above, customary international law, although a part of the law of the land and common law, was considered to be more than mere common law and to be of significant federal concern and even constitutionally based. Recall the 1865 opinion of the Attorney General and the Supreme Court's dictum in *United States v. Smith* (1820) and in *Ex parte Quirin* (1942) (and note that there had been no statute incorporating the laws of war until 1916 although war crimes had been prosecuted prior to that date), *supra*. Chief Justice Fuller, however, recognizes a prior "controversy" over the matter around 1794. Yet cases and opinions after that date (as noted above and in subsequent pages) continued to apply customary international law or to recognize its potential application without reference to a statute. In most cases since the early 1800s, however, criminal prosecution has also been supported by statute. Yet in some cases, U.S. courts allowed indictments alternatively under a statute or under the law of nations.

United States v. Hand
26 F. Cas. 103 (C.C.C. Pa. 1810) (No. 15,297)

—assault on charge d' affaires of Russia (found not guilty)

Washington, Cir. Judge, charging jury:

2 counts, indictment: (1) statute & (2) "infracting the law of nations"

See also United States v. Liddle, 26 F. Cas. 936 (C.C.D. Pa. 1808) (assault; statute & law of nations); *id.* at 938 (degree of punishment rests with the court); *United States v. Ortega*, 24 U.S. (11 Wheat.) 467 (1826) (Cir. Ct. has jurisdiction, not U.S. Sup. Ct. (because the victim was not an ambassador), over defendant for violating law of nations by offering violence to King of Spain's chargé d' affairs—defendant was indicted for: (1) "infracting the law of nations," and (2) violating a statute). Note that *Ortega* was after the 1812 decision of *Hudson & Goodwin*.

There was certainly no mention of such a controversy in Attorney General Lee's opinion of 1797 (1 Op. Att'y Gen. 68, 69) or in the following related judicial opinion:

Talbot v. Janson

3 U.S. (3 Dall.) 133, 159–61 (1795) (Iredell, J., concurring)

" ... all piracies and trespasses committed against the general law of nations, are enquirable, and may be proceeded against, in any nation where no special exemption can be maintained, either by the general law of nations, or by some treaty which forbids or restrains it ..." ... [Such] is not merely an offence against the nation of the individual committing the injury, but also against the law of nations, and, of course, cognizable in other countries ..."

"This is so palpable a violation of our own law (I mean the common law, of which the law of nations is a part, as it subsisted either before the act of Congress on the subject, or since that has provided a particular manner of enforcing it,) as well as the law of nations generally; that I cannot entertain the slightest doubt, but that upon the case of the libel, *prima facie*, the District Court has jurisdiction."

Consider also the following dictum:

Morris v. United States

161 F. 672, 675 (8th Cir. 1908)

"Without reviewing the authorities, as this would be but a work of supererogation, the following summary may be regarded as the settled law within the federal jurisdiction: (1) There are no crimes or offenses cognizable in the federal courts, outside of maritime or international law or treaties, except such as are created and defined by acts of Congress...."

Of further interest:

14 Op. Att'y Gen.

249 (1873)

[Editors' note: a military tribunal convicted some Modoc Indians for law of war violations though Congress had not enacted a statute, the Attorney General adding:]

"All the laws and customs of civilized warfare may not be applicable to an armed conflict with the Indian tribes upon our Western frontiers, but the circumstances attending the assassination of Canby and Thomas are such as to make their murder as much a violation of the laws of savage as of civilized warfare, and the Indians concerned in it fully understood the baseness and treachery of their act."

See also U.S. Dep't of Army Field Manual FM 27-10, The Law of Land Warfare, para. 505(e) (1956):

"Law Applied. As the international law of war is part of the law of the land in the United States, enemy personnel charged with war crimes are tried directly under international law without recourse to the statutes of the United States."

Note

1. Prosecutions of persons for war crimes occurred in military tribunals during various wars prior to the creation of the legislation in 1916 that was addressed in *Ex parte Quirin, supra.*

B. Treaties

Can a federally prosecutable crime be created by treaty alone, without additional domestic legislation? Most commentators seem to think that a treaty cannot be directly operative for criminal prosecutions and that all federally prosecutable crimes must be based on congressional legislation. This is a common assumption today, but for some it is arguable that the question remains open. In early cases, such as *Respublica v. De Longchamps* and *Henfield's Case*, the direct incorporation of international law, without congressional or other implementing legislation, was entirely permissible and expected. Furthermore, the Supreme Court has not specifically ruled whether direct incorporation of treaties for criminal prosecutions is permissible. *Cf* the opening paragraph in the extract from *Ex parte Quirin, supra.*

Consider the following materials:

The Over the Top
5 F.2d 838, 845 (D. Conn. 1925)

In support of its contention, the government cites and relies upon *United States v. The Pictonian*, 3 F. (2d) 145, recently decided in the Eastern district of New York, where it was held that the American-British Treaty did, as to ships of British registry, extend the operation of the criminal laws of the United States to the shifting line designated in the treaty. I have carefully read Judge Campbell's opinion and find myself unable to agree with its reasoning. The learned judge speaks of the treaty as self-executing. The significance of the phrase in this connection is somewhat obscure. As a treaty, there was no need of congressional legislation to make it effective, and in this sense all treaties are self-executing. But if it was the intent of the government to make it a crime for a ship of British registry to unlade liquor within a sea zone on our coast, traversable in one hour, then that intent was not effectuated by the mere execution of the treaty. It is not the function of treaties to enact the fiscal or criminal law of a nation. For this purpose no treaty is self-executing. Congress may be under a duty to enact that which has been agreed upon by treaty, but duty and its performance are two separate and distinct things. Nor is there any doubt that the treaty making power has its limitations. What these are has never been defined, perhaps never need by defined. Certain it is that no part of the criminal law of this country has ever been enacted by treaty.

Edwards v. Carter

580 F.2d 1055, 1057–58 (D.C. Cir. 1978), *cert. denied*, 436 U.S. 907 (1978)

The grant of authority to Congress under the property clause states that "The Congress shall have Power…," *not* that only the Congress shall have power, or that Congress shall have *exclusive* power. In this respect the property clause is parallel to Article I, sec. 8, which also states that "The Congress shall have power …"

Many of the powers thereafter enumerated in sec. 8 involve matters that were at the time the Constitution was adopted, and that are at the present time, also commonly the subject of treaties. The most prominent example of this is the regulation of commerce with foreign nations, Art. 1, sec. 8, cl. 3, and appellants do not go so far as to contend that the treaty process is not a constitutionally allowable means for regulating foreign commerce. It thus seems to us that, on its face, the property clause is intended not to restrict the scope of the treaty clause, but, rather, is intended to permit Congress to accomplish through legislation what may *concurrently* be accomplished through other means provided in the Constitution [*e.g.*, the treaty power].

Notes and Questions

1. How does the *Edwards* rationale add to inquiry whether Article I, §8, cl. 10, is an exclusive or concurrent congressional power? If it is merely concurrent, and "the treaty process is … a constitutionally allowable means for regulating" international crime, what might follow? Recall *Henfield's Case*.

2. In the 1865 opinion of the Attorney General on the laws of war, *supra*, a difference was recognized between congressional power with respect to international crimes (*i.e.*, to "define") and ordinary federal crimes (*i.e.*, "to make"). From this does it follow that Congress must "make" ordinary federal crimes but need not enact a statute in order for the United States to prosecute international crimes?

3. *See also United States v. Kelly*, 2 Extrater. Cases, 665, 669–70 (U.S.C. China 1923) (treaty prohibiting contraband trade can be self-executing for criminal sanction purposes); *Morris v. United States*, 161 F. 672 (8th Cir. 1908), *supra*; *United States v. Tiede*, U.S. Ct. for Berlin, 1979, *infra*; *United States v. Worrall*, 2 U.S. (2 Dall.) 384, 391 (Chase, J.), 395 (Peters, J.) (C.C.D. Pa. 1798); *Henfield's Case, supra* (on treaties); 1 Op. Att'y Gen. 57, 58 (1795) (violation of treaty).

4. Further references include:

McDougal & Arens, *The Genocide Convention and the Constitution*, 3 Vand. L. Rev. 683, 690–91 (1950) (adding: "No good reason has been, or can be, given to justify treating this one particular power of the Congress, the power 'to define and punish … offenses against the law of nations,' as exclusive….");

Paust, Self-Executing Treaties, 82 Am. J. Int'l L. 760 (1988) (rediscovered predominant view of the Founders was that all treaties are self-executing (except those which, by their terms considered in context, are not) and such is the express language of Article VI, clause 2 of the Constitution. "Merely because the full Congress has an express power to make a law should not be relevant to inquiry whether a treaty is 'self-executing,' since the Senate and President also have an express power to make treaty law and each treaty is supreme law of the land. The mere existence of a concurrent power does not obviate either the existence or the exercise of another." One exception seems to be the congressional power to declare war.);

RESTATEMENT OF THE FOREIGN RELATIONS LAW OF THE UNITED STATES, Comment i to § 111 (3 ed. 1987) ("It has been commonly assumed that an international agreement ... could not itself become part of the criminal law of the United States, but would require Congress to enact an appropriate statute before an individual could be tried or punished for the offense.").

5. If treaties are not inherently non-self-executing for criminal sanction purposes, the next question becomes whether or not a particular treaty is self-executing according to acceptable criteria (*e.g.*, using language of the treaty considered in context and intent of the signatories' tests). *See also* Paust, *Self-Executing Treaties, supra*; and RESTATEMENT, *supra*, § 111.

Section 6
Federal District Court Jurisdiction

If a federal statute incorporates international law for criminal sanction purposes but does not mention jurisdictional competence in federal district courts, is federal district court jurisdiction possible? As we read in *Ex parte Quirin*, the older 1916 Articles of War (now 10 U.S.C. §§ 818, 821), which were (and are) laws of the United States, incorporated the laws of war and Congress thus exercised its power to define and punish offenses against the law of nations. Can these laws be prosecuted in the federal district courts? Consider the following:

Judicial Courts Act
1 Stat. 73, 76, 79, §§ 9, 11 (1789)

Under a system of district and circuit court jurisdiction, the circuit courts shared "exclusive cognizance of all crimes and offences under the authority of the United States, (a) except as this act otherwise provides, or the laws of the United States shall otherwise direct, and concurrent jurisdiction with the district courts of the crimes and offences cognizable therein" — which include "all crimes and offences that shall be cognizable under the authority of the United States...."

Questions: what is the meaning of "all crimes and offences under the authority of the United States"? Do such include violations of customary laws of nations? of treaties made under the authority of the United States (see Article III, section 2, clause 1 and Article VI, clause 2 of the Constitution)? Does this statute act in part as implementing legislation with respect to treaty-based crimes? Recall *Ex parte Quirin, supra. See* Edwin D. Dickenson, *The Law of Nations as Part of the Law of the United States*, 101 U. PA. L. REV. 26, 46–47 (1952) ("covered by" the 1789 statute).

18 U.S.C. § 3231

"The district courts of the United States shall have original jurisdiction, exclusive of the courts of the States, of all offenses against the laws of the United States.

"Nothing in this title shall be held to take away or impair the jurisdiction of the courts of the several States under the laws thereof."

Question: what is the meaning of "offenses against the laws of the United States"? Obviously these include those listed in title 18 of the United States Code. Are there others?

Paust, *After My Lai: The Case for War Crime Jurisdiction Over Civilians in Federal District Courts*

50 Tex. L. Rev. 6, 10–28 (1971), *reprinted in* IV The Vietnam War and International Law 447 (R. Falk ed., ASIL 1976)*

[Editors' note: The first part of the article recognized possible use of (1) military courts-martial, and (2) military commissions for the prosecution of violations of the laws of war, 10 U.S.C §§ 818 and 821 (set forth in footnotes below) expressly recognizing jurisdiction over violations of the laws of war in such military tribunals. Questions remaining involved whether that law reaches alleged civilian perpetrators and former servicemembers who allegedly committed war crimes while in service, and whether such persons could also be prosecuted in federal district courts. Historically, civilians had been subject to prosecution in military tribunals during times of armed conflict. If peace had been formally proclaimed, civilians apparently could not have been prosecuted in courts-martial in view of *Reid v. Covert,* 354 U.S. 1 (1957), although it is not clear that *Reid* would apply to law of war violations as opposed to ordinary crimes. Military commissions also might not have been available in time of peace.]

It appears settled that by the Articles of War[1] Congress enacted domestic criminal law to punish violators of the law of war.[2] In *Ex parte Quirin* the Supreme Court stated that Congress had explicitly provided in the Articles of War that military tribunals have the power to try offenses against the law of war in appropriate cases. Traditionally, military law is said to derive its constitutional source from the enumerated power of Congress to make rules for the regulation of the armed forces. In *Ex parte Quirin,* however, the Supreme Court concluded that Congress had not only exercised this enumerated power in enacting the Articles of War but had also exercised the separate power to define and punish offenses against the law of nations. The Court also made it clear that Congress could "define and

---

* Copyright 1971 by the Texas Law Review Association. Reprinted by permission.

1. Act of Aug. 29, ch. 418, sec. 3, 39 Stat. 650, 652–53 (Articles 12 and 15) [footnotes have been renumbered].

2. *In re* Yamashita, 327 U.S. 1, 7–8 (1946); *Ex parte* Quirin, 317 U.S. 1, 28, 30 (1942); United States v. Schultz, 1 U.S.C.M.A. 512, 519, 4 C.M.R. 104, 111 (1952). Congress actually incorporated the law of war into United States law. *See* U.N. Doc. E/CN. 4/927/Add. 1 (1967) (United States stated that the law of war is "incorporated into" United States law by Article 18 of the U.C.M.J.). Instead of creating a separate codification for the law of war, Congress chose to exercise its power to "define and punish" the law of war as "offenses" against United States law by merely "incorporating" (or "adopting") international law into domestic law. *In re* Yamashita, 327 U.S. 1, 7–8 (1946); *Ex parte* Quirin, 317 U.S. 1, 28, 30 (1942); United States v. Schultz 1 U.S.C.M.A. 512, 4 C.M.R. 104 (1952). "Congress [has] incorporated by reference … all offenses which are defined as such by the law of war." *Id.* at 519, 4 C.M.R. at 111. It is apparently unimportant that Congress chose to exercise its constitutional power to "define and punish" the offenses against the law of war in Title 10 and the offenses of piracy and felonies committed on the high seas or on special federal territory in another title of the United States Code. The law of nations is much broader than the law of war, which is only part of the law of nations. Apparently Congress has not completely exercised its power to implement all of the law of nations by federal statute.

punish" without specific codification.... Since the present Articles 18[3] and 21[4] of the Uniform Code of Military Justice (U.C.M.J.) contain the same language found in Articles 12 and 15 of the old Articles of War, it seems safe to conclude that Congress reenacted the law of war as domestic criminal law when it codified the Articles of War into the U.C.M.J. in 1950 and when it subsequently amended the U.C.M.J. in 1964. This is consistent with the rule that interpretations in force when a statute is reenacted are deemed to have tacit congressional approval. The cases of *Ex parte Quirin* and *In re Yamashita* had interpreted the language of Articles 12 and 15 to create domestic criminal law, and Congress chose not to modify this judicial interpretation when it subsequently reenacted these sections.

If this analysis is correct, then domestic criminal law does exist for the prosecution of violations of the law of war. Since the specific provisions of the U.C.M.J. that deal with the law of war have been held to create an offense against the laws of the United States, enacted under the power of Congress to define and punish offenses against the law of nations, the status of the other provisions of the U.C.M.J. is irrelevant. The law of war, invoked by Articles 18 and 21, will thus remain a part of the criminal law of the United States even if the general penal provisions of the U.C.M.J. are interpreted to be mere regulations enacted under the power to regulate the armed forces.

Once it is established that the substantive provisions of the international law of war have been incorporated into domestic criminal law, two important issues remain. First, those who may be held accountable must be identified. The primary inquiry here deals with the amenability of civilians to the law of war. Secondly, the proper tribunals to apply the law of war must be determined.

II. Applicability of the Law of War to Civilians

This criminal law as enacted by Congress is applicable by its terms to "any person who by the law of war is subject to trial by a military tribunal." Apparently this allows prosecution of certain civilians as well as ex-soldiers and soldiers for violations of the law of war. Although most of the penal provisions of the U.C.M.J. are only applicable to military persons and although cases concerning the application of military law seem to turn on a question of military status, Congress apparently intended to apply certain provisions of the U.C.M.J. in Title 10 of the United States Code to civilians. The Supreme Court has dramatically curtailed the power of courts-martial to try servicemen for offenses not related to military service. This contraction of court-martial jurisdiction consequently restricts the application of the general provisions of the U.C.M.J. But it seems

---

3. Article 18 provides:

> Subject to section 817 of this title (article 17), general courts-martial have jurisdiction to try persons subject to this chapter for any offense made punishable by this chapter and may, under such limitations as the President may prescribe, adjudge any punishment not forbidden by this chapter, including the penalty of death when specifically authorized by this chapter. General courts-martial also have jurisdiction to try any person who by the law of war is subject to trial by a military tribunal and may adjudge any punishment permitted by the law of war....

10 U.S.C. § 818 (1970).

4. Article 21 provides:

> The provisions of this chapter conferring jurisdiction upon courts-martial do not deprive military commissions, provost courts, or other military tribunals of concurrent jurisdiction with respect to offenders or offenses that by statute or by the law of war may be tried by military commissions, provost courts, or other military tribunals.

10 U.S.C. § 821 (1970).

that the Supreme Court has cut back on the attempted application of the U.C.M.J. to civilians only in connection with laws based upon the congressional power to regulate the armed forces and on the general jurisdictional sections of the U.C.M.J. The Court has not specifically excluded jurisdiction over civilians under Articles 18 and 21 of the Code, and Article 18 concerns an entirely different body of law, based on an entirely different Congressional power.

It is important to emphasize that Article 18 creates a law not purely military and not purely civilian in nature, but a law designed to punish all offenses against the law of war. The international nature of this law and its corresponding obligations makes it a different creature from either domestic regulations for the government of troop conduct or traditional civilian criminal law. It is a body of international law developed by civilized nations of the world for the prosecution of any person who violates the commandments of the world community. The international scope of the law of war is not diminished by the requirement of our constitutional system that this law be implemented in the United States by congressional legislation. Furthermore, the law of war is implemented under the power to define and punish offenses against the law of nations and remains separate from enactments under the power to regulate the armed forces even though Congress has chosen to codify the law of war in the U.C.M.J., sandwiched between enactments of pure "military law." Recent proposals by Senator Ervin to reenact the law of war and to expressly extend federal court jurisdiction to civilians who commit war crimes would also be included in the U.C.M.J.

The difference between the source of congressional power for enactments of pure "military law" and the source of power for violations of the law of war not only allows an important distinction to be made concerning the line of cases culminating in *O'Callahan v. Parker*, but also allows a distinction to be made concerning cases indicating that courts-martial have exclusive jurisdiction over offenses under pure "military law." *Toth v. Quarles* and *O'Callahan v. Parker* dealt with "military law" and the power to regulate the armed forces, whereas *Ex parte Quirin* concerned the international law of war and the power to define and punish offenses against the law of nations.

Winthrop pointed out that the law of war authorizes the arrest, trial, and punishment of American citizens who violate the law of war. A problem arose, however, from the historic statutory restriction of court-martial jurisdiction almost exclusively to members of the military force. This restriction on the power of courts-martial to try civilians led to the creation of the military commission, a tribunal separate from the court-martial and endowed with different powers.

Today we find a similar exclusion by judicial decision of court-martial jurisdiction over civilians concerning "military law," but the exclusion thus far concerns only military law as opposed to court-martial jurisdiction over all persons who violate the law of war under Article 18 of the U.C.M.J. History would seem to show that if the Supreme Court holds that a civilian may not be tried by court-martial or by military commission, the occasion would again arise for the trial of offenses against the law of war in a different tribunal. The substantive offense would remain, but a change of forum would be required.

Nevertheless, we have not yet reached that state, and Congress and the Supreme Court have left open the possibility of trial of civilians in a military commission. Furthermore, the law of war has been applied to civilians in the past, and this occurred regardless of decisions to exclude civilians from military jurisdiction under "military law." A distinction based on the difference in the nature of the laws involved was implied by language in *Ex parte Mudd,*[5] by dictum in *Hammond v. Squier,*[6] by the Court's declaration in *Ex parte Quirin,*[7] and by the ruling in *Colepaugh v. Looney.*[8]

Of further interest is the fact that approximately 2,000 cases were tried by military commission during the Civil War and Reconstruction. In a sense these cases dealt with the trial of our own nationals. Some of these, as in the case of Dr. Mudd, were civilians who were subject to military commission jurisdiction for violations of the law of war during that era. Also of interest would be the trial of United States civilians by military tribunals overseas under the body of international law governing occupation of foreign territory,[9] since jurisdiction rested in Articles 12 and 15 of the old Articles of War. The case of *Madsen v. Kinsella* is also important concerning the concurrent jurisdiction of military commissions over violations of the law of war[10] in that the existence of concurrent jurisdiction over these offenses in forums other than courts-martial points to the inaccuracy of any statement that court-martial jurisdiction is exclusive. Furthermore, statements that court-martial jurisdiction is exclusive disregard the express conferral of concurrent jurisdiction in 10 U.S.C. § 821.[11]

The *Schultz*[12] case reaffirmed a statement in *Hammond v. Squier* that the law of war grants to military tribunals no power to try American nationals for "purely military offenses" when they are not subject to "military law."[13] The court went on to state, however, that nothing precludes a military tribunal from prosecuting a civilian for a violation of the law of war. Furthermore, the court held that under Article 12 of the Articles of War general courts-martial have the same jurisdiction over violations of the law of war as other military tribunals, and that such jurisdiction extends to civilians who are subject to the law of war "without regard to whether they may also be subject to military law." ...

III. Jurisdiction in the Federal District Courts

A. Concurrent Judicial Action under Constitutional Normative Requirements

Arguably, although Congress has the power to make rules for the regulation of the armed forces under Article I, Section 8, Clause 14, of the Constitution and although Congress may also create courts inferior to the Supreme Court under Article I, Section 8, Con-

---

5. 17 F. Cas. 954 (No. 9,899) (S.D. Fla. 1868) (manuscript opinion). *See also* 11 Op. Att'y Gen. 297 (1865).

6. 51 F. Supp. 227, 232 (W.D. Wash. 1943).

7. 317 U.S. 1, 37 (1942). The Court declared that the petitioner's status as a United States citizen and civilian would not affect the military commission's jurisdiction to prosecute violations of the law of war.

8. 235 F.2d 429 (10th Cir. 1956), *cert denied,* 352 U.S. 1014 (1957). *See also* Reid v. Covert, 354 U.S. 1 (1957); Toth v. Quarles, 350 U.S. 11 (1955); United States v. Schultz, 1 U.S.C.M.A. 512, 519–23, 4 C.M.R. 104, 111–15 (1952)....

9. *See, e.g.,* Madsen v. Kinsella, 343 U.S. 341, 358 n.23 (1952). The Court states that the occupation court in Germany tried some 1000 cases a month including twenty-five to thirty cases involving United States civilians. *See also* Rose v. McNamara, 375 F.2d 924 (D.C. Cir.), *cert. denied,* 389 U.S. 856 (1967).

10. 343 U.S. 341, 354–55 (1952).

11. Cases cited.... Assertions that court-martial jurisdiction is exclusive appear only in cases applying pure "military law" as opposed to cases dealing with the international law of war implemented under Article 18 of the present U.C.M.J. *See also In re* Bush, 84 F. Supp. 873 (D.D.C. 1949) (writ of habeas corpus).

12. United States v. Schultz, 1 U.S.C.M.A. 512, 4 C.M.R. 104 (1952).

13. *Id.* at 522, 4 C.M.R. 104 at 114, *citing* Hammond v. Squier, 51 F. Supp. 227, 231 (W.D. Wash. 1943); *see also* 2 JUDGE ADVOCATE GENERAL OF THE ARMY, DIGEST OP. 939 (1953).

gress may not create a quasi-constitutional executive forum with *exclusive* judicial powers concerning the enforcement of acts of Congress once it has also created a judicial forum.

Article III, Section 2, of the Constitution states that the *"judicial power shall extend to all Cases*, in Law or Equity, *arising under* this Constitution, *the Laws of the United States, and Treaties made ..."* (emphasis supplied). Under Article III, Section 2, there exists a dual basis for arguing that the judicial power under Article III extends to the prosecution of offenses against the law of nations incorporated into domestic law: this prosecution involves cases arising under the laws of the United States and, in most instances, would also involve treaties made by the United States. The combination of Article III, Section 2 judicial power bases in the case of violation of the law of war is certainly more solid than in attempts to extend judicial power to "regulations" prescribed by Congress to govern our domestic armed forces—the pure "military law" of the U.C.M.J. It should be noted that federal courts had early declared that judicial power extends to violations of international law, though there has been greater reluctance to extend into the realm of executive troop regulations or pure "military law"....

This does not necessarily mean that an executive forum cannot exist, nor that Congress cannot cut back the judicial power of particular inferior courts within the judicial system. It seems, however, that when a matter involves the judicial power an executive forum cannot itself exercise "judicial power" functions to the exclusion of those forums in which the judicial power has been vested by reason of Article III, Section 1. In other words, Congress cannot constitutionally preclude all judicial action within Article III courts concerning the enforcement of the laws of the United States, since an attempted cutback of every judicial involvement in a "judicial power" function, when Congress also grants executive power to carry out similar functions, would in that total context constitute a direct interference with the judicial power....

Indeed, a judicial-power forum exists in the federal district courts, and Congress granted to the federal courts jurisdiction over "all offenses against the laws of the United States" in 18 U.S.C. § 3231. Judicial power extends to all cases arising under the laws of the United States and therefore extends to "all offenses against the laws of the United States" as "cases arising under" those laws. Therefore, federal courts have the judicial power to prosecute all offenses against the laws of the United States. The only question seems to be whether Congress has cut back on this power and, if it has, whether it can do so constitutionally by exclusive executive jurisdiction.... Courts-martial are not justified by the Executive branch as Article III courts and are said to have no part of the judicial power. Assuming this to be correct, we need not analyze the power of Congress to limit Supreme Court review of criminal cases from an inferior court created with judicial power under Article III. It is sufficient to point out that courts-martial could not exercise exclusive judicial powers since they possess no judicial power in the first place.

It follows that the federal courts, since they alone contain the *judicial* power under Article III and the judicial power *extends* to all cases arising under the laws of the United States, have at least "concurrent" jurisdiction concerning enforcement of the laws of the United States....

B. Congressional Conferral of Federal Court Jurisdiction

Besides the argument that Congress could not preclude some sort of concurrent judicial action in this area, there exists an argument that Congress has conferred original jurisdiction over all offenses against the laws of the United States by 18 U.S.C. § 3231 (originally the Judicial Courts Act of Sept. 24, 1789) in the federal district courts, and has never expressly declared that Title 10 offenses, which are offenses against the laws of the United States, are not prosecutable in federal courts. Furthermore, the specific grant of jurisdiction to the military forums, in Articles 18 and 21 of the U.C.M.J., neither impliedly deprives the civil courts of the concurrent jurisdiction they already possess nor makes military jurisdiction exclusive....

... [F]ederal district courts already possess jurisdiction to entertain prosecutions for violations of the law of war under 10 U.S.C. §§ 818 and 821 by reason of the jurisdiction conferred on the district courts to entertain original jurisdiction over *all* offenses against the laws of the United States under 18 U.S.C. § 3231. Congress did not expressly exclude federal court jurisdiction in enacting the U.C.M.J. in 1950 and again in 1968. Express exclusion is necessary under 18 U.S.C. § 3231, and, therefore, the original jurisdiction of the civil courts to prosecute all offenses against the laws of the United States continues to exist. Since a violation of the law of war is an offense against the laws of the United States, it can be prosecuted in the federal district courts, which are the normal and preferred forums for all United States prosecutions.

Notes and Questions

1. Some within the Executive branch have argued that it is not possible presently for the U.S. to prosecute alleged World War II Nazi war criminals, so they must be extradited to other countries if they are to prosecuted at all. *But see* Section 7 B. Do you agree? If it is not possible, is the United States complying with its responsibilities under international law; and why has there been no effort to obtain new retroactive legislation?

For a general discussion of United States treatment of Nazi war criminals in the U.S., see Lippman, *The Denaturalization of Nazi War Criminals in the United States: Is Justice Being Served?*, 7 Hous. J. Int'l L. 169 (1985); Moeller, *United States Treatment of Alleged Nazi War Criminals: International Law, Immigration Law and the Need for International Cooperation*, 25 Va. J. Int'l L. 793 (1985); *see also* Paust, *Universality and the Responsibility to Enforce International Criminal Law: No U.S. Sanctuary for Alleged Nazi War Criminals*, 11 Hous. J. Int'l L. 337 (1989).

2. In 1990 President Bush and the U.S. DOD. indicated that the U.S. was preparing a war crimes file on the President of Iraq. Can the U.S. prosecute the President of Iraq in a U.S. federal district court?

3. Note that 10 U.S.C. § 818 also incorporates penalties by reference (*i.e.*, "any punishment permitted by the law of war...."). How would one identify these? How had they been identified before?

4. A newer federal statute implements part of the responsibilities of the United States to prosecute violations of the 1949 Geneva Conventions and incorporates various international laws by reference. Concerning such responsibilities, recall Chapter Two, Section 3.

The War Crimes Act
18 U.S.C. § 2441 (as amended 2006)

(a) Offense. Whoever, whether inside or outside the United States, commits a war crime, in any of the circumstances described in subsection (b), shall be fined under this title or imprisoned for life or any term of years, or both, and if death results to the victim, shall also be subject to the penalty of death.

(b) Circumstances. The circumstances referred to in subsection (a) are that the person committing such war crime or the victim of such war crime is a member of the Armed

Forces of the United States or a national of the United States (as defined in section 101 of the Immigration and Nationality Act [8 U.S.C. § 1101].

(c) Definition. As used in this section the term "war crime" means any conduct –

(1) defined as a grave breach in any of the international conventions signed at Geneva 12 August 1949, or any protocol to such convention to which the United States is a party;

(2) prohibited by Article 23, 25, 27, or 28 of the Annex to the Hague Convention IV, Respecting the Laws and Customs of War on Land, signed 18 October 1907;

(3) which constitutes a grave breach of common Article 3 (as defined in subsection (d)) when committed in the context of and in association with an armed conflict not of an international character; or

(4) of a person who, in relation to an armed conflict and contrary to the provisions of the Protocol on Prohibitions or Restrictions on the Use of Mines, Booby–Traps and Other Devices as amended at Geneva on 3 May 1996 (Protocol II as amended on 3 May 1996), when the United States is a party to such Protocol, willfully kills or causes serious injury to civilians.

(d) Common Article 3 Violations–

(1) Prohibited Conduct. In subsection (c)(3), the term "grave breach of common Article 3" means any conduct (such conduct constituting a grave breach of common Article 3 of the international conventions done at Geneva August 12, 1949), as follows:

(A) Torture.– The act of a person who commits, or conspires or attempts to commit, an act specifically intended to inflict severe physical or mental pain or suffering (other than pain or suffering incidental to lawful sanctions) upon another person within his custody of physical control for the purpose of obtaining information or a confession, punishment, intimidation, coercion, or any reason based on discrimination of any kind.

(B) Cruel of Inhuman Treatment.– The act of a person who commits, or conspires or attempts to commit, an act intended to inflict severe or serious physical or mental pain or suffering (other than pain or suffering incidental to lawful sanctions), including serious physical abuse, upon another within his custody or control.

(C) Performing Biological Experiments.– The act of a person who subjects, or conspires or attempts to subject, one or more persons within his custody or physical control to biological experiments without a legitimate medical or dental purpose and in so doing endangers the body or health of such person or persons.

(D) Murder.– The act of a person who intentionally kills, or conspires or attempts to kill, or kills whether intentionally or unintentionally in the course of committing any other offense under this subsection, one or more persons taking no active part in the hostilities, including those placed out of combat by sickness, wounds, detention, or any other cause.

(E) Mutilation or Maiming.– The act of a person who intentionally injures, or conspires or attempts to injure, or injures whether intentionally or unintentionally in the course of committing any other offense under this subsection, one or more persons taking no active part in the hostilities, including those placed out of combat by sickness, wounds, detention, or any other cause, by disfiguring the person or persons by any mutilation thereof or by permanently disabling any member, limb, or organ of his body, without any legitimate medical or dental purpose.

(F) Intentionally Causing Serious Bodily Injury.– The act of a person who intentionally causes, or conspires or attempts to cause, serious bodily injury to one or more persons, including lawful combatants, in violation of the law of war.

(G) Rape.– The act of a person who forcibly or with coercion or threat of force wrongfully invades, or conspires or attempts to invade, the body of a person by penetrating, however slightly, the anal or genital opening of the victim with any part of the body of the accused, or with any foreign object.

(H) Sexual Assault or Abuse.– The act of a person who forcibly or with coercion or threat of force engages, or conspires or attempt to engage, in sexual contact with one or more persons, or causes, or conspires or attempts to cause, one or more persons to engage in sexual conduct.

(I) Taking Hostages.– The act of a person who, having knowingly seized or detained one or more persons, threatens to kill, injure, or continue to detain such person or persons with the intent of compelling any nation, person other than the hostage, or group of persons to act or refrain from acting as an explicit or implicit condition for the safety or release of such person or persons.

(2) Definitions. In the case of an offense under subsection (a) by reason of subsection (c)(3)–

(A) the term "severe mental pain or suffering" shall be applied for purposes of paragraphs (1)(A) and (1)(B) in accordance with the meaning given the term in section 2340(2) of this title;

(B) the term "serious bodily injury: shall be applied for purposes of paragraph (1)(F) in accordance with the meaning given that term in section 113(b)(2) of this title;

(C) the term "sexual contact" shall be applied for purposes of subsection (1)(G) in accordance with the meaning given that term in section 2246(3) of this title;

(D) the term "serious physical pain and suffering" shall be applied for purposes of paragraph (1)(B) as meaning bodily injury that involves–

(i) a substantial risk of death;

(ii) extreme physical pain;

(iii) a burn or physical disfigurement of a serious nature (other than cuts, abrasions, or bruises); or

(iv) significant loss of impairment of the function of a bodily member, organ, or mental faculty; and

(E) the term "serious mental pain or suffering" shall be applied for purposes of subsection (1)(B) in accordance with the meaning given the term "severe mental pain or suffering" (as defined in section 2340(2) of this title), except that–

(i) the term "serious" shall replace the term "severe" where it appears; and

(ii) as to conduct occurring after the date of the enactment of the Military Commissions Act of 2006, the term "serious and non-transitory mental harm (which need not be prolonged)" shall replace the term "prolonged mental harm" where it appears.

(3) Inapplicability of Certain Provisions With Respect to Collateral Damage or Incident of Lawful Attack. The intent specified for the conduct stated in subparagraphs (D), (E), and (F) or paragraph (1) precludes the applicability of those subparagraphs to an offense under subsection (a) by reasons of subsection (c)(3) with respect to–

(A) collateral damage; or

(B) death, damage, or injury incident to a lawful attack.

(4) Inapplicability of Taking Hostages to Prisoner Exchange. Paragraph (1)(1) does not apply to an offense under subsection (a) by reason of subsection (c)(3) in the case of a prisoner exchange during wartime.

(5) Definition of Grave Breaches. The definitions in this subsection are intended only to define the grave breaches of common Article 3 and not the full scope of United States obligations under that Article.

Notes and Questions

1. There are four 1949 Geneva Conventions: Geneva Convention for the Amelioration of the Condition of the Wounded and Sick in Armed Forces in the Field, 12 August 1949, 75 U.N.T.S. 31; Geneva Convention for the Amelioration of the Condition of Wounded, Sick and Shipwrecked Members of Armed Forces at Sea, 12 August 1949, 75 U.N.T.S. 85; Geneva Convention Relative to the Treatment of Prisoners of War, 12 August 1949, 75 U.N.T.S. 135 [hereinafter GPW]; Geneva Convention Relative to the Protection of Civilian Persons in Time of War, 12 August 1949, 75 U.N.T.S. 287 [hereinafter GC and Geneva Civilian Convention]. Each convention has an article identifying "grave breaches" of that convention. Those concerning GPW and GC follow:

GPW, art. 130: Grave breaches to which the preceding Article relates shall be those involving any of the following acts, if committed against persons or property protected by the Convention: wilful killing, torture or inhuman treatment, including biological experiments, wilfully causing great suffering or serious injury to body or health, compelling a prisoner of war to serve in the forces of the hostile power or wilfully depriving a prisoner of war of the rights of fair and regular trial prescribed in this Convention.

GC, art. 147: Grave breaches to which the preceding Article relates shall be those involving any of the following acts, if committed against persons or property protected by the present Convention: wilful killing, torture or inhuman treatment, including biological experiments, wilfully causing great suffering or serious injury to body or health, unlawful deportation or transfer or unlawful confinement of a protected person, compelling a protected person to serve in the forces of a hostile Power or wilfully depriving a protected person of the rights of fair and regular trial prescribed in the present Convention, taking of hostages and extensive destruction and appropriation of property, not justified by military necessity and carried out unlawfully and wantonly.

2. Note that the new legislation generally incorporates Geneva provisions by reference. However, the 2006 amendment (in the 2006 Military Commissions Act) changed subsection (c)(3), which had previously covered (from 2000 to 2006) "any conduct ... [in]

violation of common Article 3" in any armed conflict, and added a controversial subsection (d) that provides special definitions that do not mirror trends in decision under the laws of war, relevant human rights law, and the Convention Against Torture. *See, e.g.,* Paust, *Above the Law: Unlawful Executive Authorizations Regarding Detainee Treatment, Secret Renditions, Domestic Spying, and Claims to Unchecked Executive Power,* 2007 UTAH L. REV. 345, 407–12 (2007). For example, the definition of torture in the Convention Against Torture can reach the torture of any person for any purpose. Further, under international law cruel treatment is different than merely inhuman treatment and relevant intent need only be to engage in conduct that the community considers to be cruel or inhuman. However, what is the effect of subsection (d)(5)?

Many other states also incorporate the laws of war, crimes against humanity, and genocide by reference. *See, e.g.,* Jordan J. Paust, *It's No Defense:* Nullum Crimen, *International Crime and the Gingerbread Man,* 60 ALBANY L. REV. 657 (1997) (addressing legislation in Australia, Bangladesh, Belgium, Canada, Ethiopia, Finland, France, Germany, Great Britain, Israel, Mexico, the Netherlands, Sweden, Yugoslavia); *cf.* Christopher Blakesley, Report, *reprinted in* 25 DENV. J. INT'L L. & POL. 233 (1997); Edward Wise, Report, *id.* at 313. What are some of the customary types of crimes against humanity that exist in the Charters of the International Military Tribunals at Nuremberg and at Tokyo, in the Documents Supplement? Would al Qaeda attacks on the World Trade Center in New York in 2001 fit within the definitions? Would they fit within Article 7 of the Rome Statute of the ICC?

3. Under the new legislation, is it possible to prosecute former Nazis accused of war crimes? Is it possible to prosecute Bosnian–Serbs accused of war crimes committed against other Bosnians?

4. Article 146 of the 1949 Geneva Convention Relative to the Protection of Civilian Persons in Time of War, 75 U.N.T.S. 287, creates an obligation "to enact any legislation necessary to provide effective penal sanctions for persons committing … any … grave breaches"? Has the new legislation met that obligation? How might those accused not covered by the new legislation be prosecuted for violations of the laws of war in the United States?

5. Is it possible under the new legislation for the U.S. to comply with another obligation in Article 146 of the Geneva Civilian Convention to "take measures necessary for the suppression of all acts contrary to the … Convention other than grave breaches"? How can these be prosecuted?

6. 18 U.S.C. § 3261 also allows prosecution of criminal offenses committed by certain members of the Armed Forces and by persons employed by or accompanying the Armed Forces outside the United States.

Section 7
Military Commissions and Courts-Martial

A. Military Commissions

In re Yamashita
327 U.S. 1, 5–13 (1946) (Stone, C.J., opinion)

No. 61 Miscellaneous is an application for leave to file a petition for writs of habeas corpus and prohibition in this Court. No. 672 is a petition for certiorari to review an order of the Supreme Court of the Commonwealth of the Philippines (28 U.S.C. § 349, denying petitioner's application to that court for writs of habeas corpus and prohibition. As both applications raise substantially like questions, and because of the importance and novelty of some of those presented, we set the two applications down for oral arguments as one case.

From the petitions and supporting papers it appears that prior to September 3, 1945, petitioner was the Commanding General of the Fourteenth Army Group of the Imperial Japanese Army in the Philippine Islands. On that date he surrendered to and became a prisoner of war of the United States Army Forces in Baguio, Philippine Islands. On September 25th, by order of respondent, Lieutenant General Wilhelm D. Styer, Commanding General of the United States Army Forces, Western Pacific, which command embraces the Philippine Islands, petitioner was served with a charge prepared by the Judge Advocate General's Department of the Army, purporting to charge petitioner with a violation of the law of war. On October 8, 1945, petitioner, after pleading not guilty to the charge, was held for trial before a military commission of five Army officers appointed by order of General Styer. The order appointed six Army officers, all lawyers, as defense counsel. Throughout the proceedings which followed, including those before this Court, defense counsel have demonstrated their professional skill and resourcefulness and their proper zeal for the defense with which they were charged.

On the same date a bill of particulars was filed by the prosecution, and the commission heard a motion made in petitioner's behalf to dismiss the charge on the ground that it failed to state a violation of the law of war. On October 29th the commission was reconvened, a supplemental bill of particulars was filed, and the motion to dismiss was denied. The trial then proceeded until its conclusion on December 7, 1945, the commission hearing two hundred and eighty-six witnesses, who gave over three thousand pages of testimony. On that date petitioner was found guilty of the offense as charged and sentenced to death by hanging.

These petitions for habeas corpus set up that the detention of petitioner for the purpose of the trial was unlawful for reasons which are now urged as showing that the military commission was without lawful authority or jurisdiction to place petitioner on trial, as follows:

(a) That the military commission which tried and convicted petitioner was not lawfully created, and that no military commission to try petitioner for violations of the law of war could lawfully be convened after the cessation of hostilities between the armed forces of the United States and Japan;

(b) that the charge preferred against petitioner fails to charge him with a violation of the law of war;

(c) that the commission was without authority and jurisdiction to try and convict petitioner because the order governing the procedure of the commission permitted the admission in evidence of depositions, affidavits and hearsay and opinion evidence, and because the commissions rulings admitting such evidence were in violation of the 25th and 38th Articles of War (10 U.S.C. §§ 1496, 1509, and the Geneva Convention (47 Stat. 2021), and deprived petitioner of a fair trial in violation of the due process clause of the Fifth Amendment;

(d) that the commission was without authority and jurisdiction in the premises because of the failure to give advance notice of petitioner's trial to the neutral power representing the interests of Japan as a belligerent as required by Article 60 of the Geneva Convention, 47 Stat. 2021, 2051.

On the same grounds the petitions for writs of prohibition set up that the commission is without authority to proceed with the trial.

The Supreme Court of the Philippine Islands, after hearing argument, denied the petition for habeas corpus presented to it, on the ground, among others, that its jurisdiction was limited to an inquiry as to the jurisdiction of the commission to place petitioner on trial for the offense charged, and that the commission, being validly constituted by the order of General Styer, had jurisdiction over the person of petitioner and over the trial for the offense charged.

In *Ex parte Quirin*, 317 U.S. 1, we had occasion to consider at length the sources and nature of the authority to create military commissions for the trial of enemy combatants for offenses against the law of war. We there pointed out that Congress, in the exercise of the power conferred upon it by Article I, sec. 8, Cl. 10 of the Constitution to "define and punish … Offenses against the Law of Nations …," of which the law of war is a part, had by the Articles of War (10 U.S.C. §§ 1471–1593) recognized the "military commission" appointed by military command, as it had previously existed in United States Army practice, as an appropriate tribunal for the trial and punishment of offenses against the law of war. Article 15 declares that "the provisions of these articles conferring jurisdiction upon courts-martial shall not be construed as depriving military commissions … or other military tribunals of concurrent jurisdiction in respect of offenders or offenses that by statute or by the law of war may be triable by such military commissions … or other military tribunals." See a similar provision of the Espionage Act of 1917, 50 U.S.C. § 38. Article 2 includes among those persons subject to the Articles of War the personnel of our own military establishment. But this, as Article 12 indicates, does not exclude from the class of persons subject to trial by military commissions "any other person who by the law of war is subject to trial by military tribunals," and who, under Article 12, may be tried by court martial, or under Article 15 by military commission.

We further pointed out that Congress, by sanctioning trial of enemy combatants for violations of the law of war by military commission, had not attempted to codify the law of war or to mark its precise boundaries. Instead, by Article 15 it had incorporated, by reference, as within the preexisting jurisdiction of military commissions created by appropriate military command, all offenses which are defined as such by the law of war, and which may constitutionally be included within that jurisdiction. It thus adopted the system of military common law applied by military tribunals so far as it should be recognized and deemed applicable by the courts, and as further defined and supplemented by the Hague Convention, to which the United States and the Axis powers were parties.

We also emphasized in *Ex parte Quirin*, as we do here, that on application for habeas corpus we are not concerned with the guilt or innocence of the petitioners. We consider here only the lawful power of the commission to try the petitioner for the offense charged. In the present cases it must be recognized throughout that the military tribunals which Congress has sanctioned by the Articles of War are not courts whose rulings and judgments are made subject to review by this Court. See *Ex parte Vallandigham*, 1 Wall. 243; *In re Vidal*, 179 U.S. 126; *cf. Ex parte Quirin*, *supra*, 317 U.S. 39. They are tribunals whose determinations are reviewable by the military authorities either as provided in the military orders constituting such tribunals or as provided by the Articles of War. Congress conferred on the courts no power to review their determinations save only as it has granted judicial power "to grant writs of habeas corpus for the purpose of an inquiry into the cause of the restraint of liberty." 28 U.S.C. §§ 451, 452. The courts may inquire whether the detention complained of is within the authority of those detaining the petitioner. If the military tribunals have lawful authority to hear, decide and condemn, their action is not subject to judicial review merely because they have made a wrong decision on disputed facts. Correction of their errors of decision is not for the courts but for the military authorities which are alone authorized to review their decisions. See *Dynes v. Hoover*, 20 How. 65, 81; *Runkle v. United States*, 122 U.S. 543, 555, 556; *Carter v. McClaughry*, 183 U.S. 365; *Collins v. McDonald*, 258 U.S. 416. *Cf. Matter of Moran*, 203 U.S. 96, 105.

Finally, we held in *Ex parte Quirin, supra*, 317 U.S. 24, 25, as we hold now, that Congress be sanctioning trials of enemy aliens by military commission for offenses against the law of war had recognized the right of the accused to make a defense. *Cf. Ex parte Kawato*, 317 U.S. 69. It has not foreclosed their right to contend that the Constitution or laws of the United States withhold authority to proceed with the trial. It has not withdrawn, and the Executive branch of the government could not, unless there was suspension of the writ, withdraw from the courts the duty and power to make such inquiry into the authority of the commission as may be made by habeas corpus.

With these governing principles in mind we turn to the consideration of the several contentions urged to establish want of authority in the commission. We are not here concerned with the power of military commissions to try civilians. See *Ex parte Milligan*, 4 Wall. 2, 132; *Sterling v. Constantin*, 287 U.S. 378; *Ex parte Quirin, supra*, 371 U.S. 45. The Government's contention is that General Styer's order creating the commission conferred authority on it only to try the purported charge of violation of the law of war committed by petitioner, an enemy belligerent, while in command of a hostile army occupying United States territory during time of war. Our first inquiry must therefore be whether the present commission was created by lawful military command and, if so, whether authority could thus be conferred on the commission to place petitioner on trial after the cessation of hostilities between the armed forces of the United States and Japan.

The authority to create the Commission. General Styler's order for the appointment of the commission was made by him as Commander of the United States Armed Forces, Western Pacific. His command includes, as part of a vastly greater area, the Philippine Islands, where the alleged offenses were committed, where petitioner surrendered as a prisoner of war, and where, at the time of the order convening the commission, he was detained as a prisoner in custody of the United States Army. The Congressional recognition of military commissions and its sanction of their use in trying offenses against the law of war to which we have referred, sanctioned their creation by military command in conformity to long established American precedents. Such a commission may be appointed by any field commander, or by any commander competent to appoint a general court martial, as was General Styer, who had been vested with that power by order of the President. 2 Winthrop, Military Law and Precedents, 2d Ed., 1302; *cf.* Article of War 8.

Here the commission was not only created by a commander competent to appoint it, but his order conformed to the established policy of the Government and to higher military commands authorizing his action. In a proclamation of July 2, 1942 (56 Stat. 1964, 10 U.S.C.A. § 1554 note), the President proclaimed that enemy belligerents who, during time of war, enter the United States, or any territory possession thereof, and who violate the law of war, should be subject to the law of war and to the jurisdiction of military tribunals. Paragraph 10 of the Declaration of Potsdam of July 6, 1945, declared that " ... stern justice shall be meted out to all war criminals including those who have visited cruelties upon prisoners." U.S. Dept. of State Bull., Vol. XIII, No. 318, pp. 137, 138. This Declaration was accepted by the Japanese government by its note of August 10, 1945. U.S. Dept. of State Bull., Vol. XIII, No. 320, p.205.

By direction of the President, the Joint Chiefs of Staff of the American Military Forces, on September 12, 1945, instructed General MacArthur, Commander in Chief, United States Army Forces, Pacific, to proceed with the trial, before appropriate military tribunals, of such Japanese war criminals "as have been or may be apprehended." By order of General MacArthur of September 24, 1945, General Styer was specifically directed to proceed with the trial of petitioner upon the charge here involved. This order was accompanied by detailed rules and regulations which General MacArthur prescribed for the trial of war criminals. These regulations directed, among other things, that review of the sentence imposed by the commission should be by the officer convening it, with "authority to approve, mitigate, remit, commute, suspend, reduce or otherwise alter the sentence imposed," and directed that no sentence of death should be carried into effect until confirmed by the Commander in Chief, United States Army Forces, Pacific.

It thus appears that the order creating the commission for the trial of petitioner was authorized by military command, and was in complete conformity to the Act of Congress sanctioning the creation of such tribunals for the trial of offenses against the law of war committed by enemy combatants. And we turn to the question whether the authority to create the commission and direct the trial by military order continued after the cessation of hostilities.

An important incident to the conduct of war is the adoption of measures by the military commander, not only to repel and defeat the enemy, but to seize and subject to disciplinary measures those enemies who, in their attempt to thwart of impede our military effort, have violated the law of war. *Ex parte Quirin, supra*, 317 U.S. 28. The trial and punishment of enemy combatants who have committed violations of the law of war is thus not only a part of the conduct of war operating as a preventive measure against such violations, but is an exercise of the authority sanctioned by Congress to administer the system of military justice recognized by the law of war. That sanction is without qualification as to the exercise of this authority so long as a state of war exists—from its declaration until peace is proclaimed ... The war power, from which the commission derives its existence, is not limited to victories in the field, but carries with it the inherent power to guard against the immediate renewal of the conflict, and to remedy, at least in ways Congress has recognized, the evils which the military operations have produced....

We cannot say that there is no authority to convene a commission after hostilities have ended to try violations of the law of war committed before their cessation, at least until peace has been officially recognized by treaty or proclamation of the political branch of the Government. In fact, in most instances the practical administration of the system of military justice under the law of war would fail if such authority were thought to end with the cessation of hostilities. For only after their cessation could the greater number of offenders and the principal ones be apprehended and subjected to trial.

No writer on international law appears to have regarded the power of military tribunals, otherwise competent to try violations of the law of war, as terminating before the formal state of war has ended. In our own military history there have been numerous instances in which offenders were tried by military commission after the cessation of hostilities and before the proclamation of peace, for offenses against the law of war committed before the cessation of hostilities.

The extent to which the power to prosecute violations of the law of war shall be exercised before peace is declared rests, not with the courts, but with the political branch of the Government, and may itself be governed by the terms of an armistice or the treaty of peace. Here, peace has not been agreed upon or proclaimed. Japan, by her acceptance of the Potsdam Declaration and her surrender, has acquiesced in the trials of those guilty of violations of the law of war. The conduct of the trial by the military commission has been authorized by the political branch of the Government, by military command, by international law and usage, and by the terms of the surrender of the Japanese government....

We therefore conclude that the detention of petitioner for trial and his detention upon his conviction, subject to the prescribed review by the military authorities were lawful, and that the petition for certiorari, and leave to file in this Court petitions for writs of habeas corpus and prohibition should be, and they are

Denied.

Writs denied.

Mr. Justice Jackson took no part in the consideration or decision of these cases.

Murphy, J. (dissenting)

The significance of the issue facing the Court today cannot be overemphasized. An American military commission has been established to try a fallen military commander of a conquered nation for an alleged war crime. The authority for such action grows out of the exercise of the power conferred upon Congress by Article I, sec. 8, cl. 10 of the Constitution to "define and punish ... Offenses against the Law of Nations...." The grave issue raised by this case is whether a military commission so established and so authorized may disregard the procedural rights of an accused person as guaranteed by the Constitution, especially by the due process clause of the Fifth Amendment....

The Court, in my judgment, demonstrates conclusively that the military commission was lawfully created in this instance and that petitioner could not object to its power to try him for a recognized war crime. Without pausing here to discuss the third and fourth issues, however, I find it impossible to agree that the charge against the petitioner stated a recognized violation of the laws of war....

B. Post WWII Executive Recognitions

U.S. Dep't of Army, FM 27-10, The Law of Land Warfare
180–81, para. 505 d & e (1956)

d. How Jurisdiction Exercised. War crimes are within the jurisdiction of general courts-martial (UCMJ, Art. 18), military commissions, provost courts, military government courts, and other military tribunals (UCMJ, Art. 21) of the United States, as well as of international tribunals.

e. Law Applied. [quoted *supra* Section 5].

Paust, *My Lai and Vietnam: Norms, Myths and Leader Responsibility*
57 Mil. L. Rev. 99, 123–24 (1972)

A further inquiry here concerns the duty of a High Contracting Party to enact "any legislation necessary to provide effective penal sanctions" for grave breaches of the Conventions. The United States had adopted the 1949 Geneva Conventions with the views of the Department of Justice in mind. The Justice Department stated that:

> A review of existing legislation reveals no need to enact further legislation in order to provide effective penal sanctions for those violations of the Geneva Conventions which are designated as grave breaches.

The present author concurs with that view, but in 1962 it was challenged in at least one law review article. In 1966 and 1967 the United States official position at the United Nations was that Congress has the power, and has from time to time exercised that power, to enact legislation for the creation of military tribunals for the trial of offenses against the law of war. This could be interpreted as stating that no need for further legislation exists since Congress can create a forum for effective penal sanctions and then prosecute within that forum the offenses which already exist under the law of war. Furthermore, in 1967 the United States said:

> The Uniform Code of Military Justice provides, in article 18, that "General courts-martial shall also have jurisdiction to try any person who by the law of war is subject to trial by a military tribunal and may adjudge any punishment permitted by the law of war." Thus, the law of war is incorporated into United States military law. The law of war includes the provisions of the 1949 Geneva Convention which became part of United States law upon its adherence.

This can be interpreted as stating that United States law, by Congressional enactment, has already implemented the law of war and that offenses against the law of war as implemented become violations of the laws of the United States. Furthermore, the statement does not preclude jurisdiction in another forum.

Notes and Questions

1. Is the "necessary legislation" or "domestic implementation" clause quoted from article 146 of the Geneva Civilian Convention one that necessarily precludes "self-executing" status for the Convention? *See, e.g.,* Iwasawa, *The Doctrine of Self-Executing Treaties in the United States: A Critical Analysis*, 26 Va. J. Int'l L. 627, 658–61 (1986); Paust, *Self-Executing Treaties*, 82 Am. J. Int'l L. 760 (1988); Comment, *Criteria for Self-Executing Treaties*, 1968 U. Ill. L. F. 238, 241 & n.20 (1968). *See also supra* Section 6. *But see Tel-Oren v. Libyan Arab Republic*, 726 F.2d 774, 818–19 (D.C. Cir. 1984) (Bork, J., concurring); *Linder v. Calero*, 747 F. Supp. 1452, 1463 (S.D. Fla. 1990), *rev'd on other gds., Linder v. Portocarrero*, 963 F.2d 332 (11th Cir. 1992).

2. Should U.S. soldiers, and civilians, be tried in a foreign military commission during an armed conflict? An enemy military commission? Why? Would an international tribunal such as the new ICC serve the interests of warring states if each holds alleged war criminals from an enemy state? If the U.S. does not ratify the "Rome Statute" creating the ICC, will U.S. soldiers be subject to ICC jurisdiction? *See, e.g,* Jordan J. Paust, *The Reach of ICC Jurisdiction Over Non-Signatory Nationals*, 33 Vand. J. Trans. L. 1 (2000).

3. Can use of regional or international tribunals reduce concerns about impartiality and fairness that have been raised with respect to use of national military commissions? Would use of regular civilian tribunals such as U.S. federal district courts, also reduce similar concerns connected with ad hoc military tribunals?

4. Are national military commissions still viable options for prosecution of some international crimes? Are U.S. military commissions limited to "time of war" and/or military occupation? See *Madsen v. Kinsella*, 343 U.S. 341, 348 (1952); *Johnson v. Eisentrager*, 339 U.S. 763, 786 (1950).

5. Professors Bassiouni, Paust, and Sadat, among others, made the following points about limitations on use of military commissions in a *Amici* brief before the U.S. Supreme Court in *Hamdan v. Rumsfeld*, No. 05-184 (Jan. 5, 2006):

A. Limitations With Respect to Place

The President's power as Commander-in-Chief to set up a military commission and its jurisdictional competence apply only during an actual war (to which the laws of war apply), and within a war zone (*i.e.*, an actual theater of war) or a war-related occupied territory. *See, e.g., The Grapeshot*, 76 U.S. 129, 132–33 (1869) (jurisdiction exists "wherever the insurgent power was overthrown"); WILLIAM WINTHROP, MILITARY LAW AND PRECEDENTS 836 (2d. 1920); Jordan J. Paust, *Antiterrorism Military Commissions: Courting Illegality*, 23 MICH. J. INT'L L. 1, 5 & n.14, 25 n.70, 26–27 (2001) [hereinafter Paust, *Military Commissions*]; *see also Madsen v. Kinsella*, 343 U.S. 341, 346–48 (1952) (military commissions are "war courts," "related to war," and are proper in a war-related occupied enemy territory "in time of war"); *Duncan v. Kahanamoku*, 327 U.S. 304, 324 (1946) (jurisdiction exists in "occupied enemy territory"); *id.* at 326 (Murphy, J., concurring) (jurisdiction exists "[o]nly when a foreign invasion or civil war actually closes the courts"); *In re Yamashita*, 327 U.S. 1, 11, 20 n.7 (1946) (a military commission is a "war court" prosecuting the "law of war" and in that instance was created by a military commander in charge of the U.S. Army Forces, Western Pacific, theater of war and war-related occupied territory "so long as a state of war exists." *Id.* at 912); *Coleman v. Tennessee*, 97 U.S. 509, 515 (1878) ("when ... in the enemy's country"); *id.* at 517 (when occupation of enemy territory occurs). As Colonel Winthrop recognized in his classic study of military law: "A military commission ... can legally assume jurisdiction only of offences committed within the field of command of the convening commander," and regarding military occupation, "cannot take cognizance of an offence committed without such territory.... The place must be the theater of war or a place where military government or martial law may be legally exercised; otherwise a military commission ... will have no jurisdiction...." WINTHROP, *supra*, at 836.

Contrary to the opinion of the Court of Appeals in this case, the military commission set up within the United States during World War II and recognized in *Ex parte Quirin* had been created during war in what was then an actual theater of war for prosecution of enemy belligerents for violations of the laws of war that occurred within the United States (in Florida and New York) and within the convening authority's field of military command — the Eastern Defense Command of the United States Army. 317 U.S. 1, 22 n.1 (1942).

What is unavoidably problematic with respect to military commission jurisdiction at Guantanamo, Cuba is the fact that the U.S. military base at Guantanamo is neither in an actual theater of war nor in a war-related occupied territory. *See, e.g.*, Paust, *Military Commissions, supra*, at 25 n.70. *See also Rasul v. Bush*, 124 S.Ct. 2686 (2004) (Kennedy, J., concurring) (correctly describing Guantanamo as territory "far removed from any hostilities"). Consequently, a military commission at Guantanamo is not properly constituted and is without lawful jurisdiction. Also, alleged violations of the laws of war by detainees during a war with the Taliban in Afghanistan did not occur in Cuba.

Further, the District Court properly recognized other jurisdictional limits: (1) "[t]he President may establish military commissions only for offenders or offenses triable by military tribunal under the laws of war," (2) "limits [are] now set for military commissions" by Congress "by Article 21" of the U.C.M.J. (by 10 U.S.C. § 818, 821), and (3) approval "does not extend past 'offenders or offenses that by statute or by the law of war may be tried by military commissions.'" *Hamdan v. Rumsfeld*, 344 F. Supp.2d 152, 158–59 (D.D.C. 2004)....

B. Limitations With Respect to Time

The President's power and a military commission's jurisdiction are limited in terms of time to a circumstance of actual war until the point when peace is finalized. *See, e.g.*, *Madsen v. Kinsella*, 343 U.S. 341, 346–48 (1952) (recognizing that military commission power is "related to war" and acknowledging them as "war courts"); *In re Yamashita*, 327 U.S. 1, 11–13 (1946) (adding *id.* at 20 n.7: a military commission is a "war court"); *Ex parte Quirin*, 317 U.S. 1, 28 (1942); *The Grapeshot*, 76 U.S. (9 Wall.) 129, 132–33 (1869); *Cross v. Harrison*, 57 U.S. 164, 190 (1853) (permitting jurisdiction until a "treaty of peace"); 24 Op. Att'y Gen. 570, 571 (1903); 11 Op. Att'y Gen. 297, 298 (1865); Paust, Bassiouni, *et al.*, International Criminal Law 309–10 (2 ed. 2000); Winthrop, *supra*, at 86, 831 (jurisdiction is tied to the war powers, "exclusively war-court"), 837 ("An offence ... must have been committed within the period of the war or of the exercise of military government.... jurisdiction ... cannot be maintained after the date of a peace...."). As Major General Henry Halleck wrote, military commissions "have jurisdiction of cases arising under the laws of war," adding: "[they] are war courts and can exist only in time of war." Halleck, *Military Tribunals and Their Jurisdiction*, 5 Am. J. Int'l L. 958, 965–66 (1911). Similarly, in 1865 Attorney General Speed formally advised the President:

> A military tribunal exists under and according to the Constitution in time of war. Congress may prescribe how all such tribunals are to be constituted, what shall be their jurisdiction, and mode of procedure. Should Congress fail to create such tribunals, then, under the Constitution, they must be constituted according to the laws and usages of civilized warfare. They may take cognizance of such offences as the laws of war permit.... In time of peace neither Congress nor the military can create any military tribunals, except such as are made in pursuance of that clause of the Constitution which gives to Congress the power "to make rules for the government of the land and naval forces."

11 Op. Att'y Gen. 297, 298 (1865).

Thus, relevant presidential power is tied to a war circumstance and law of war competencies such as the ability of a war-related occupying power to set up a military commission in war-related occupied territory to try violations of the laws of war in accordance with the laws of war. Congress can regulate the jurisdiction and procedure of military commissions, but must do so consistently with international law. Specifically, the requirements of international law "are of binding force upon the departments and citizens of the Government, though not defined by any law of Congress" and neither Congress nor the Executive can "abrogate them or authorize their infraction." *See, e.g.*, 11 Op. Att'y Gen. at 298–300; *Madsen v. Kinsella*, 343 U.S. 341, 348–49 (1952); *see also Dooley v. United States*, 182 U.S. 222, 231 (1901) (describing executive military powers as "'regulated and limited ... directly from the laws of war'"), *quoting* 2 Henry W. Halleck, International Law 444 (1st ed. 1861); Jordan J. Paust, International Law as Law of the United States 106–07, 169–73 (2 ed. 2003), and cases cited [hereinafter Paust, *Treatise*]; Paust, *Detainees*, ... [43 Columbia J. Transnat'l L. 811 (2005)] at 856–61. Additionally, federal statutes must be interpreted and applied consistently with international law. *See, e.g.*, *United States v. Flores*, 289 U.S. 137, 159 (1933); *Cook v. United States*, 288 U.S. 102, 120 (1933); *The Charming Betsy*, 6 U.S. (6 Cranch) 64, 117–18 (1804); *Talbot v. Seeman*, 5 U.S. (1 Cranch) 1, 43 (1801); 11 Op. Att'y Gen. at 299–300 (1865); 9

Op. Att'y Gen. 356, 362–63 (1859) ("law ... must be made and executed according to the law of nations"); Paust, *Treatise, supra*, at 99, 120, 124–25 nn.2–3.

6. The *Amici* brief noted another concern with respect to President Bush's military commissions at Guantanamo:

"[a] serious violation of the separation of powers exists with respect to the attempt by the President in his 2001 Military Order to preclude any judicial review of U.S. military commission decisions concerning offenses against the laws of war and other international crimes over which there is concurrent jurisdictional competence in federal district courts. See U.S. Dep't Defense, Military Commission Order No. 1 [Mar. 21, 2002], § 7(B) (1)–(2); *see also id.* §§ 6 H (4)–(6), 7 B. He cannot do so lawfully. *See, e.g.*, Paust, *Military Commissions, supra*, at 10–11, 15; Paust, *Judicial Power*, [44 HARV. INT'L L.J. 503 (2003)] at 518–24. Additionally, under Article I, Section 8, clause 9 of the United States Constitution, Congress merely has power "[t]o constitute Tribunals inferior to the Supreme Court" and, thus, tribunals subject to ultimate control by the Supreme Court. *See* James E. Pfander, *Federal Courts: Jurisdiction-Stripping and the Supreme Court's Power to Supervise Inferior Tribunals*, 78 TEX. L. REV. 1433, 1454–56 (2000). For this reason, the congressional authorization for creation of military commissions in 10 U.S.C. § 821 is necessarily subject to the constitutional restraint contained in Article I, Section 8, clause 9 and the President's attempt to preclude any form of judicial review is constitutionally improper whether or not a military commission has support in a general congressional authorization. The Supreme Court has already recognized the propriety of habeas review concerning detention at Guantanamo. *Rasul v. Bush*, 542 U.S. 466 (2004); see also Paust, *Judicial Power, supra*, at 517 & n.47, 519–20 n.67." *Amici* brief, *id.* at 17.

7. President Bush created the military commissions at Guantanamo by presidential order. Military Order of Nov. 13, 2001, 66 Fed. Reg. 57,833 (Nov. 16, 2001). The Department of Defense subsequently issued a series of military commission orders addressing the make-up of the commissions, review panels, rules of evidence, and other matters. Problems with respect to the military commissions created by President Bush for Guantanamo include concerns about customary and treaty-based human rights to due process. *See, e.g.*, Paust, *Military Commissions, supra* at 10–18; Paust, *Antiterrorism Military Commissions: The Ad Hoc DOD Rules of Procedure*, 23 MICH. J. INT'L L. 677, 678–90 (2002); *see also* Michal R. Belknap, *A Putrid Pedigree: The Bush Administration's Military Tribunals in Historical Perspective*, 38 CAL. W.L. REV. 433 (2002); Mark A. Drumbl, *Victimhood in Our Neighborhood: Terrorist Crime, Taliban Guilt, and the Symmetries of the International Legal Order*, 81 N.C. L. REV. 1, 10–12, 58–59 (2002); Harold Hongju Koh, *The Case Against Military Commissions*, 91 AM. J. INT'L L. 337, 338–39 (2002); Detlev F. Vagts, *Which Courts Should Try Persons Accused of Terrorism?*, 14 EUR. J. INT'L L. 313, 322 (2003). Consider also Paust, *Post-9/11 Overreaction and Fallacies Regarding War and Defense, Guantanamo, the Status of Persons, Treatment, Judicial Review of Detention, and Due Process in Military Commissions*, 79 NOTRE DAME L. REV. 1335, 1361–64 (2004):

"Since 9/11, we have witnessed the deliberate creation of rules of procedure for U.S. military commissions that would violate human rights and Geneva law guarantees and create war crime civil and criminal responsibility for those directly participating in their creation and application if the military commission rules are not changed and are utilized. We have seen a refusal to even disclose the names of persons detained and Executive claims are made before our courts and media that human beings have no human rights or Geneva law protections, no right of access to an attorney or to their Consulate, and no right of access to a court of law to address the propriety of their detention without trial. Present Department of Defense rules for military commissions would assure denial of the human rights to trial before a regularly constituted, competent, independent, and impartial court; to counsel of one's choice and to effective representation; to fair procedure and fair rules of evidence; to review by a competent, independent, and impartial court of law; and to various other human rights."

Hamdan v. Rumsfeld
548 U.S. 557 (2006)

Stevens, J. announced the judgment of the Court and delivered the opinion of the Court with respect to Parts I through IV, Parts VI through VI-D-iii, Part VI-D-v, and Part VII, and an opinion with respect to Parts V and VI-D-iv, in which Souter, J., Ginsburg, J., and Breyer, J. join.

Petitioner Salim Ahmed Hamdan, a Yemeni national, is in custody at an American prison in Guantanamo Bay, Cuba. In November 2001, during hostilities between the United States and the Taliban (which then governed Afghanistan), Hamdan was captured by militia forces and turned over to the U.S. military. In June 2002, he was transported to Guantanamo Bay. Over a year later, the President deemed him eligible for trial by military commission for then-unspecified crimes. After another year had passed, Hamdan was charged with one count of conspiracy "to commit ... offenses triable by military commission." ... Hamdan filed petitions for writs of habeas corpus and mandamus to challenge the Executive Branch's intended means of prosecuting this charge. He concedes that a court-martial constituted in accordance with the Uniform Code of Military Justice (UCMJ), 10 U.S.C. § 801 *et seq.* (2000 ed. and Supp. III), would have authority to try him. His objection is that the military commission the President has convened lacks such authority, for two principal reasons: First, neither congressional Act nor the common law of war supports trial by this commission for the crime of conspiracy — an offense that, Hamdan says, is not a violation of the law of war. Second, Hamdan contends, the procedures that the President has adopted to try him violate the most basic tenets of military and international law, including the principle that a defendant must be permitted to see and hear the evidence against him.

The District Court granted Hamdan's request for a writ of habeas corpus. 344 F. Supp.2d 152 (D.C. 2004). The Court of Appeals for the District of Columbia Circuit reversed. 415 F.3d 33 (2005). Recognizing, as we did over a half-century ago, that trial by military commission is an extraordinary measure raising important questions about the balance of powers in our constitutional structure, *Ex parte* Quirin, 317 U.S. 1, 19 ... (1942), we granted certiorari. 546 U.S. _ (2005).

For the reasons that follow, we conclude that the military commission convened to try Hamdan lacks power to proceed because its structure and procedures violate both the UCMJ and the Geneva Conventions. Four of us also conclude, see Part V, *infra*, that the offense with which Hamdan has been charged is not an "offens[e] that by ... the law of war may be tried by military commissions." 10 U.S.C. § 821.

I

On September 11, 2001, agents of the al Qaeda terrorist organization hijacked commercial airplanes and attacked the World Trade Center in New York City and the national headquarters of the Department of Defense in Arlington, Virginia. Americans will never forget the devastation wrought by these acts. Nearly 3,000 civilians were killed.

Congress responded by adopting a Joint Resolution authorizing the President to "use all necessary and appropriate force against those nations, organizations, or persons he determines planned, authorized, committed, or aided the terrorist attacks ... in order to prevent any future acts of international terrorism against the United States by such nations, organizations or persons." Authorization for Use of Military Force (AUMF), 115 Stat. 224, note following 50 U.S.C. § 1541 (2000 ed., Supp. III). Acting pursuant to the AUMF, and having determined that the Taliban regime had supported al Qaeda, the President ordered the Armed Forces of the United States to invade Afghanistan. In the ensuing hostilities, hundreds of individuals, Hamdan among them, were captured and eventually detained at Guantanamo Bay.

On November 13, 2001, while the United States was still engaged in active combat with the Taliban, the President issued a comprehensive military order intended to govern the "Detention, Treatment, and Trial of Certain Non-Citizens in the War Against Terrorism," 66 Fed. Reg. 57833 (hereinafter November 13 Order or Order). Those subject to the November 13 Order include any noncitizen for whom the President determines "there is reason to believe" that he or she (1) "is or was" a member of al Qaeda or (2) has engaged or participated in terrorist activities aimed at or harmful to the United States. *Id.*, at 57834. Any such individual "shall, when tried, be tried by military commission for any and all offenses triable by military commission that such individual is alleged to have committed, and may be punished in accordance with the penalties provided under applicable law, including imprisonment or death." *Ibid*. The November 13 Order vested in the Secretary of Defense the power to appoint military commissions to try individuals subject to the Order, but that power has since been delegated to John D. Altenberg, Jr., a retired Army major general and longtime military lawyer who has been designated "Appointing Authority for Military Commissions."

On July 3, 2003, the President announced his determination that Hamdan and five other detainees at Guantanamo Bay were subject to the November 13 Order and thus triable by military commission. In December 2003, military counsel was appointed to represent Hamdan. Two months later, counsel filed demands for charges and for a speedy trial pursuant to Article 10 of the UCMJ, 10 U.S.C. § 810. On February 23, 2004, the legal adviser to the Appointing Authority denied the applications, ruling that Hamdan was not entitled to any of the protections of the UCMJ. Not until July 13, 2004, after Hamdan had commenced this action in the United States District Court for the Western District of Washington, did the Government finally charge him with the offense for which, a year earlier, he had been deemed eligible for trial by military commission.

The charging document, which is unsigned, contains 13 numbered paragraphs. The first two paragraphs recite the asserted bases for the military commission's jurisdiction-namely, the November 13 Order and the President's July 3, 2003, declaration that Hamdan is eligible for trial by military commission. The next nine paragraphs, collectively entitled "General Allegations," describe al Qaeda's activities from its inception in 1989 through 2001 and identify Osama bin Laden as the group's leader. Hamdan is not mentioned in these paragraphs.

Only the final two paragraphs, entitled "Charge: Conspiracy," contain allegations against Hamdan. Paragraph 12 charges that "from on or about February 1996 to on or about November 24, 2001," Hamdan "willfully and knowingly joined an enterprise of persons who shared a common criminal purpose and conspired and agreed with [named members of al Qaeda] to commit the following offenses triable by military commission: attacking civilians; attacking civilian objects; murder by an unprivileged belligerent; and terrorism." ... There is no allegation that Hamdan had any command responsibilities, played a leadership role, or participated in the planning of any activity.

Paragraph 13 lists four "overt acts" that Hamdan is alleged to have committed some-time between 1996 and November 2001 in furtherance of the "enterprise and conspir-acy": (1) he acted as Osama bin Laden's "bodyguard and personal driver," "believ[ing]" all the while that bin Laden "and his associates were involved in" terrorist acts prior to and including the attacks of September 11, 2001; (2) he arranged for transportation of, and actually transported, weapons used by al Qaeda members and by bin Laden's body-guards (Hamdan among them); (3) he "drove or accompanied [O]sama bin Laden to various al Qaeda-sponsored training camps, press conferences, or lectures," at which bin Laden encouraged attacks against Americans; and (4) he received weapons training at al Qaeda-sponsored camps. *Id.*, at 65a–67a.

After this formal charge was filed, the United States District Court for the Western District of Washington transferred Hamdan's habeas and mandamus petitions to the United States District Court for the District of Columbia. Meanwhile, a Combatant Sta-tus Review Tribunal (CSRT) convened pursuant to a military order issued on July 7, 2004, decided that Hamdan's continued detention at Guantanamo Bay was warranted because he was an "enemy combatant." Separately, proceedings before the military commission commenced.

On November 8, 2004, however, the District Court granted Hamdan's petition for habeas corpus and stayed the commission's proceedings. It concluded that the President's authority to establish military commissions extends only to "offenders or offenses triable by military [commission] under the law of war," 344 F. Supp.2d, at 158; that the law of war includes the Geneva Convention (III) Relative to the Treatment of Prisoners of War, Aug. 12, 1949 ... (Third Geneva Convention); that Hamdan is entitled to the full protections of the Third Geneva Convention until adjudged, in compliance with that treaty, not to be a prisoner of war; and that, whether or not Hamdan is properly classified as a prisoner of war, the mil-itary commission convened to try him was established in violation of both the UCMJ and Common Article 3 of the Third Geneva Convention because it had the power to convict based on evidence the accused would never see or hear. 344 F. Supp.2d, at 158–172.

The Court of Appeals for the District of Columbia Circuit reversed. Like the District Court, the Court of Appeals declined the Government's invitation to abstain from con-sidering Hamdan's challenge. *Cf.* Schlesinger v. Councilman, 420 U.S. 738 ... (1975). On the merits, the panel rejected the District Court's further conclusion that Hamdan was en-titled to relief under the Third Geneva Convention. All three judges agreed that the Geneva Conventions were not "judicially enforceable," 415 F.3d, at 38, and two thought that the Conventions did not in any event apply to Hamdan, *id.*, at 40–42; *but see id.*, at 44 (Williams, J., concurring). In other portions of its opinion, the court concluded that our decision in *Quirin* foreclosed any separation-of-powers objection to the military com-mission's jurisdiction, and held that Hamdan's trial before the contemplated commission would violate neither the UCMJ nor U.S. Armed Forces regulations intended to imple-ment the Geneva Conventions. 415 F.3d, at 38, 42–43.

On November 7, 2005, we granted certiorari to decide whether the military commis-sion convened to try Hamdan has authority to do so, and whether Hamdan may rely on the Geneva Conventions in these proceedings.

II

On February 13, 2006, the Government filed a motion to dismiss the writ of certio-rari. The ground cited for dismissal was the recently enacted Detainee Treatment Act of 2005 (DTA), Pub.L. 109–148, 119 Stat. 2739. We postponed our ruling on that motion pending argument on the merits ... and now deny it.

The DTA, which was signed into law on December 30, 2005, addresses a broad swath of subjects related to detainees. It places restrictions on the treatment and interrogation of detainees in U.S. custody, and it furnishes procedural protections for U.S. personnel accused of engaging in improper interrogation. DTA §§ 1002–1004, 119 Stat. 2739–2740. It also sets forth certain "procedures for status review of detainees outside the United States." § 1005, *id.*, at 2740. Subsections (a) through (d) of § 1005 direct the Secretary of Defense to report to Congress the procedures being used by CSRTs to determine the proper classification of detainees held in Guantanamo Bay, Iraq, and Afghanistan, and to adopt certain safeguards as part of those procedures.

Subsection (e) of § 1005, which is entitled "Judicial Review of Detention of Enemy Combatants," supplies the basis for the Government's jurisdictional argument. The subsection contains three numbered paragraphs. The first paragraph amends the judicial code as follows:

"(1) In general.-Section 2241 of title 28, United States Code, is amended by adding at the end the following: ...

"'(e) Except as provided in section 1005 of the Detainee Treatment Act of 2005, no court, justice, or judge shall have jurisdiction to hear or consider-

"'(1) an application for a writ of habeas corpus filed by or on behalf of an alien detained by the Department of Defense at Guantanamo Bay, Cuba; or

"'(2) any other action against the United States or its agents relating to any aspect of the detention by the Department of Defense of an alien at Guantanamo Bay, Cuba, who-

"'(A) is currently in military custody; or

"'(B) has been determined by the United States Court of Appeals for the District of Columbia Circuit in accordance with the procedures set forth in section 1005(e) of the Detainee Treatment Act of 2005 to have been properly detained as an enemy combatant.'" § 1005(e), *id.*, at 2741–2742.

Paragraph (2) of subsection (e) vests in the Court of Appeals for the District of Columbia Circuit the "exclusive jurisdiction to determine the validity of any final decision of a [CSRT] that an alien is properly designated as an enemy combatant." Paragraph (2) also delimits the scope of that review. See §§ 1005(e)(2)(C)(i)–(ii), *id.*, at 2742.

Paragraph (3) mirrors paragraph (2) in structure, but governs judicial review of final decisions of military commissions, not CSRTs. It vests in the Court of Appeals for the District of Columbia Circuit "exclusive jurisdiction to determine the validity of any final decision rendered pursuant to Military Commission Order No. 1, dated August 31, 2005 (or any successor military order)." § 1005(e)(3)(A), *id.*, at 2743. Review is as of right for any alien sentenced to death or a term of imprisonment of 10 years or more, but is at the Court of Appeals' discretion in all other cases. The scope of review is limited to the following inquiries:

"(i) whether the final decision [of the military commission] was consistent with the standards and procedures specified in the military order referred to in subparagraph (A); and

"(ii) to the extent the Constitution and laws of the United States are applicable, whether the use of such standards and procedures to reach the final decision is consistent with the Constitution and laws of the United States." § 1005(e)(3)(D), *ibid.*

Finally, § 1005 contains an "effective date" provision, which reads as follows:

"(1) In general.-This section shall take effect on the date of the enactment of this Act.

"(2) Review of Combatant Status Tribunal and Military Commission Decisions.- Paragraphs (2) and (3) of subsection (e) shall apply with respect to any claim whose review is governed by one of such paragraphs and that is pending on or after the date of the enactment of this Act." § 1005(h), *id.*, at 2743–2744.

The Act is silent about whether paragraph (1) of subsection (e) "shall apply" to claims pending on the date of enactment.

The Government argues that §§ 1005(e)(1) and 1005(h) had the immediate effect, upon enactment, of repealing federal jurisdiction not just over detainee habeas actions yet to be filed but also over any such actions then pending in any federal court-including this Court. Accordingly, it argues, we lack jurisdiction to review the Court of Appeals' decision below.

Hamdan objects to this theory on both constitutional and statutory grounds. Principal among his constitutional arguments is that the Government's preferred reading raises grave questions about Congress' authority to impinge upon this Court's appellate jurisdiction, particularly in habeas cases. Support for this argument is drawn from *Ex parte Yerger*, 8 Wall. 85 ... (1869), in which, having explained that "the denial to this court of appellate jurisdiction" to consider an original writ of habeas corpus would "greatly weaken the efficacy of the writ," *id.*, at 102–103, we held that Congress would not be presumed to have effected such denial absent an unmistakably clear statement to the contrary. See *id.*, at 104–105; *see also* Felker v. Turpin, 518 U.S. 651 ... (1996); Durousseau v. United States, 6 Cranch 307, 314 ... (1810) (opinion for the Court by Marshall, C.J.) (The "appellate powers of this court" are not created by statute but are "given by the constitution"); United States v. Klein, 13 Wall. 128 ... (1872). *Cf. Ex parte* McCardle, 7 Wall. 506, 514 ... (1869) (holding that Congress had validly foreclosed one avenue of appellate review where its repeal of habeas jurisdiction, reproduced in the margin, could not have been "a plainer instance of positive exception"). Hamdan also suggests that, if the Government's reading is correct, Congress has unconstitutionally suspended the writ of habeas corpus.

We find it unnecessary to reach either of these arguments. Ordinary principles of statutory construction suffice to rebut the Government's theory—at least insofar as this case, which was pending at the time the DTA was enacted, is concerned.

The Government acknowledges that only paragraphs (2) and (3) of subsection (e) are expressly made applicable to pending cases, see § 1005(h)(2), 119 Stat. 2743–2744, but argues that the omission of paragraph (1) from the scope of that express statement is of no moment. This is so, we are told, because Congress' failure to expressly reserve federal courts' jurisdiction over pending cases erects a presumption against jurisdiction, and that presumption is rebutted by neither the text nor the legislative history of the DTA.

A like inference follows a fortiori from Lindh [v. Murphy, 521 U.S. 320 (1997)] in this case. "If ... Congress was reasonably concerned to ensure that [§§ 1005(e)(2) and (3)] be applied to pending cases, it should have been just as concerned about [§ 1005(e)(1)], unless it had the different intent that the latter [section] not be applied to the general run of pending cases." *Id.*, at 329. If anything, the evidence of deliberate omission is stronger here than it was in *Lindh*. In Lindh, the provisions to be contrasted had been drafted separately but were later "joined together and ... considered simultaneously when the language raising the implication was inserted." *Id.*, at 330. We observed that Congress' tandem review and approval of the two sets of provisions strengthened the presumption that the relevant omission was deliberate. *Id.*, at 331; *see also* Field v. Mans, 516 U.S. 59, 75 ... (1995) ("The more apparently deliberate the contrast, the stronger the inference, as applied, for example, to contrasting statutory sections originally enacted simultaneously in relevant respects"). Here, Congress not only considered the respective temporal reaches of paragraphs (1), (2), and (3) of subsection (e) together at every stage, but omitted paragraph (1) from its directive that paragraphs (2) and (3) apply to pending cases only after having rejected earlier proposed versions of the statute that would have included what is now paragraph (1) within the scope of that directive. *Compare* DTA § 1005(h)(2), 119 Stat. 2743–2744, *with* 151 Cong. Rec. S12655 (Nov. 10, 2005) (S. Amdt. 2515); see *id.*, at S14257–S14258 (Dec. 21, 2005) (discussing similar language proposed in both the House and the Senate). Congress' rejection of the very language that would have achieved the result the Government urges here weighs heavily against the Government's interpretation....

[S]ubsections (e)(2) and (e)(3) grant jurisdiction only over actions to "determine the validity of any final decision" of a CSRT or commission. Because Hamdan, at least, is not contesting any "final decision" of a CSRT or military commission, his action does not fall within the scope of subsection (e)(2) or (e)(3). There is, then, no absurdity.

The Government's more general suggestion that Congress can have had no good reason for preserving habeas jurisdiction over cases that had been brought by detainees prior to enactment of the DTA not only is belied by the legislative history, ... but is otherwise without merit. There is nothing absurd about a scheme under which pending habeas actions-particularly those, like this one, that challenge the very legitimacy of the tribunals whose judgments Congress would like to have reviewed-are preserved, and more routine challenges to final decisions rendered by those tribunals are carefully channeled to a particular court and through a particular lens of review.

Finally, we cannot leave unaddressed Justice Scalia's contentions that the "meaning of § 1005(e)(1) is entirely clear," and that "the plain import of a statute repealing jurisdiction is to eliminate the power to consider and render judgment-in an already pending case no less than in a case yet to be filed.... Only by treating the *Bruner* rule as an inflexible trump (a thing it has never been ...) and ignoring both the rest of § 1005's text and its drafting history can one conclude as much. Congress here expressly provided that subsections (e)(2) and (e)(3) applied to pending cases. It chose not to so provide—after having been presented with the option—for subsection (e)(1). The omission is an integral part of the statutory scheme that muddies whatever "plain meaning" may be discerned from blinkered study of subsection (e)(1) alone. The dissent's speculation about what Congress might have intended by the omission not only is counterfactual..., but rests on both a misconstruction of the DTA and an erroneous view our precedents....

For these reasons, we deny the Government's motion to dismiss.

III

Relying on our decision in *Councilman*, 420 U.S. 738..., the Government argues that, even if we have statutory jurisdiction, we should apply the "judge-made rule that civilian courts should await the final outcome of on-going military proceedings before entertaining an attack on those proceedings." ... Like the District Court and the Court of Appeals before us, we reject this argument....

Councilman identifies two considerations of comity that together favor abstention pending completion of ongoing court-martial proceedings against service personnel. See New v. Cohen, 129 F.3d 639, 643 (C.A.D.C.1997); *see also* 415 F.3d, at 36–37 (discussing *Councilman* and *New*). First, military discipline and, therefore, the efficient operation of the Armed Forces are best served if the military justice system acts without regular interference from civilian courts. See *Councilman*, 420 U.S., at 752. Second, federal courts should respect the balance that Congress struck between military preparedness and fairness to individual service members when it created "an integrated system of military courts and review procedures, a critical element of which is the Court of Military Appeals, consisting of civilian judges 'completely removed from all military influence or persuasion.... '" *Id.*, at 758 (quoting H.R.Rep. No. 491, 81st Cong., 1st Sess., p. 7 (1949)). Just as abstention in the face of ongoing state criminal proceedings is justified by our expectation that state courts will enforce federal rights, so abstention in the face of ongoing court-martial proceedings is justified by our expectation that the military court system established by Congress—with its substantial procedural protections and provision for appellate review by independent civilian judges—"will vindicate servicemen's constitutional rights," 420 U.S., at 758. See *id.*, at 755–758.

The same cannot be said here; indeed, neither of the comity considerations identified in *Councilman* weighs in favor of abstention in this case. First, Hamdan is not a member of our Nation's Armed Forces, so concerns about military discipline do not apply. Second, the tribunal convened to try Hamdan is not part of the integrated system of military courts, complete with independent review panels, that Congress has established. Unlike the officer in *Councilman*, Hamdan has no right to appeal any conviction to the civilian judges of the Court of Military Appeals (now called the United States Court of Appeals for the Armed Forces, see Pub.L. 103–337, 108 Stat. 2831). Instead, under Dept. of Defense Military Commission Order No. 1 (Commission Order No. 1), which was issued by the President on March 21, 2002, and amended most recently on August 31, 2005, and which governs the procedures for Hamdan's commission, any conviction would be reviewed by a panel consisting of three military officers designated by the Secretary of Defense. Commission Order No. 1 §6(H)(4). Commission Order No. 1 provides that appeal of a review panel's decision may be had only to the Secretary of Defense himself, §6(H)(5), and then, finally, to the President, §6(H)(6).

We have no doubt that the various individuals assigned review power under Commission Order No. 1 would strive to act impartially and ensure that Hamdan receive all protections to which he is entitled. Nonetheless, these review bodies clearly lack the structural insulation from military influence that characterizes the Court of Appeals for the Armed Forces, and thus bear insufficient conceptual similarity to state courts to warrant invocation of abstention principles.[14]

In sum, neither of the two comity considerations underlying our decision to abstain in *Councilman* applies to the circumstances of this case. Instead, this Court's decision in *Quirin* is the most relevant precedent. In *Quirin*, seven German saboteurs were captured upon arrival by submarine in New York and Florida. 317 U.S., at 21. The President convened a military commission to try the saboteurs, who then filed habeas corpus petitions in the United States District Court for the District of Columbia challenging their trial by commission. We granted the saboteurs' petition for certiorari to the Court of Appeals before judgment. See *id.*, at 19. Far from abstaining pending the conclusion of

---

14. [Court's fn.19] Justice Scalia chides us for failing to include the District of Columbia Circuit's review powers under the DTA in our description of the review mechanism erected by Commission Order No. 1.... Whether or not the limited review permitted under the DTA may be treated as akin to the plenary review exercised by the Court of Appeals for the Armed Forces, petitioner here is not afforded a right to such review. See ... § 1005(e)(3), 119 Stat. 2743.

military proceedings, which were ongoing, we convened a special Term to hear the case and expedited our review. That course of action was warranted, we explained, "[i]n view of the public importance of the questions raised by [the cases] and of the duty which rests on the courts, in time of war as well as in time of peace, to preserve unimpaired the constitutional safeguards of civil liberty, and because in our opinion the public interest required that we consider and decide those questions without any avoidable delay." *Ibid.*

As the Court of Appeals here recognized, *Quirin* "provides a compelling historical precedent for the power of civilian courts to entertain challenges that seek to interrupt the processes of military commissions." 415 F.3d, at 36. The circumstances of this case, like those in *Quirin*, simply do not implicate the "obligations of comity" that, under appropriate circumstances, justify abstention. Quackenbush v. Allstate Ins. Co., 517 U.S. 706, 733 ... (1996) (Kennedy, J., concurring).

Finally, the Government has identified no other "important countervailing interest" that would permit federal courts to depart from their general "duty to exercise the jurisdiction that is conferred upon them by Congress." *Id.*, at 716 (majority opinion). To the contrary, Hamdan and the Government both have a compelling interest in knowing in advance whether Hamdan may be tried by a military commission that arguably is without any basis in law and operates free from many of the procedural rules prescribed by Congress for courts-martial-rules intended to safeguard the accused and ensure the reliability of any conviction. While we certainly do not foreclose the possibility that abstention may be appropriate in some cases seeking review of ongoing military commission proceedings (such as military commissions convened on the battlefield), the foregoing discussion makes clear that, under our precedent, abstention is not justified here. We therefore proceed to consider the merits of Hamdan's challenge.

IV

The military commission, a tribunal neither mentioned in the Constitution nor created by statute, was born of military necessity. See W. Winthrop, Military Law and Precedents 831 (rev. 2d ed. 1920) (hereinafter Winthrop). Though foreshadowed in some respects by earlier tribunals like the Board of General Officers that General Washington convened to try British Major John Andre for spying during the Revolutionary War, the commission "as such" was inaugurated in 1847. *Id.*, at 832; G. Davis, A Treatise on the Military Law of the United States 308 (2d ed. 1909) (hereinafter Davis). As commander of occupied Mexican territory, and having available to him no other tribunal, General Winfield Scott that year ordered the establishment of both "'military commissions'" to try ordinary crimes committed in the occupied territory and a "council of war'" to try offenses against the law of war. Winthrop 832....

When the exigencies of war next gave rise to a need for use of military commissions, during the Civil War, the dual system favored by General Scott was not adopted. Instead, a single tribunal often took jurisdiction over ordinary crimes, war crimes, and breaches of military orders alike. As further discussed below, each aspect of that seemingly broad jurisdiction was in fact supported by a separate military exigency. Generally, though, the need for military commissions during this period—as during the Mexican War—was driven largely by the then very limited jurisdiction of courts-martial: "The occasion for the military commission arises principally from the fact that the jurisdiction of the court-martial proper, in our law, is restricted by statute almost exclusively to members of the military force and to certain specific offences defined in a written code." *Id.*, at 831 (emphasis in original).

Exigency alone, of course, will not justify the establishment and use of penal tribunals not contemplated by Article I, § 8 and Article III, § 1 of the Constitution unless some other part of that document authorizes a response to the felt need. See *Ex parte* Milligan, 4 Wall. 2, 121 ... (1866) ("Certainly no part of the judicial power of the country was conferred on [military commissions]"); *Ex parte* Vallandigham, 1 Wall. 243, 251 ... (1864); *see also Quirin*, 317 U.S., at 25 ("Congress and the President, like the courts, possess no power not derived from the Constitution"). And that authority, if it exists, can derive only from the powers granted jointly to the President and Congress in time of war. See *id.*, at 26–29; *In re* Yamashita, 327 U.S. 1, 11 ... (1946).

The Constitution makes the President the "Commander in Chief" of the Armed Forces, Art. II, § 2, cl. 1, but vests in Congress the powers to "declare War ... and make Rules concerning Captures on Land and Water,"Art. I, § 8, cl. 11, to "raise and support Armies," *id.*, cl.12, to "define and punish ... Offences against the Law of Nations," *id.*, cl.10, and "To make Rules for the Government and Regulation of the land and naval Forces," *id.*, cl.14. The interplay between these powers was described by Chief Justice Chase in the seminal case of *Ex parte* Milligan:

"The power to make the necessary laws is in Congress; the power to execute in the President. Both powers imply many subordinate and auxiliary powers. Each includes all authorities essential to its due exercise. But neither can the President, in war more than in peace, intrude upon the proper authority of Congress, nor Congress upon the proper authority of the President.... Congress cannot direct the conduct of campaigns, nor can the President, or any commander under him, without the sanction of Congress, institute tribunals for the trial and punishment of offences, either of soldiers or civilians, unless in cases of a controlling necessity, which justifies what it compels, or at least insures acts of indemnity from the justice of the legislature." 4 Wall., at 139–140.

Whether Chief Justice Chase was correct in suggesting that the President may constitutionally convene military commissions "without the sanction of Congress" in cases of "controlling necessity" is a question this Court has not answered definitively, and need not answer today. For we held in *Quirin* that Congress had, through Article of War 15, sanctioned the use of military commissions in such circumstances. 317 U.S., at 28 ("By the Articles of War, and especially Article 15, Congress has explicitly provided, so far as it may constitutionally do so, that military tribunals shall have jurisdiction to try offenders or offenses against the law of war in appropriate cases"). Article 21 of the UCMJ, the language of which is substantially identical to the old Article 15 and was preserved by Congress after World War II, reads as follows:

"Jurisdiction of courts-martial not exclusive.

"The provisions of this code conferring jurisdiction upon courts-martial shall not be construed as depriving military commissions, provost courts, or other military tribunals of concurrent jurisdiction in respect of offenders or offenses that by statute or by the law of war may be tried by such military commissions, provost courts, or other military tribunals." 64 Stat. 115.

We have no occasion to revisit *Quirin*'s controversial characterization of Article of War 15 as congressional authorization for military commissions.... Contrary to the Government's assertion, however, even *Quirin* did not view the authorization as a sweeping mandate for the President to "invoke military commissions when he deems them necessary." ... Rather, the *Quirin* Court recognized that Congress had simply preserved what power, under the Constitution and the common law of war, the President had had before 1916 to convene military commissions—with the express condition that the President and those under his command comply with the law of war. See 317 U.S., at 28–29.[15] That much is evidenced by the Court's inquiry, following its conclusion that Congress had authorized military commissions, into whether the law of war had indeed been complied with in that case. See *ibid.*

The Government would have us dispense with the inquiry that the *Quirin* Court undertook and find in either the AUMF or the DTA specific, overriding authorization for the very commission that has been convened to try Hamdan. Neither of these congressional Acts, however, expands the President's authority to convene military commissions. First, while we assume that the AUMF activated the President's war powers, see Hamdi v. Rumsfeld, 542 U.S. 507 ... (2004) (plurality opinion), and that those powers include the authority to convene military commissions in appropriate circumstances, see *id.*, at 518; *Quirin*, 317 U.S., at 28–29; *see also Yamashita*, 327 U.S., at 11, there is nothing in the text or legislative history of the AUMF even hinting that Congress intended to expand or alter the authorization set forth in Article 21 of the UCMJ. *Cf. Yerger*, 8 Wall., at 105 ("Repeals by implication are not favored").

Likewise, the DTA cannot be read to authorize this commission. Although the DTA, unlike either Article 21 or the AUMF, was enacted after the President had convened Hamdan's commission, it contains no language authorizing that tribunal or any other at Guantanamo Bay. The DTA obviously "recognize[s]" the existence of the Guantanamo Bay commissions in the weakest sense, ... because it references some of the military orders governing them and creates limited judicial review of their "final decision[s]," DTA § 1005(e)(3), 119 Stat. 2743. But the statute also pointedly reserves judgment on whether "the Constitution and laws of the United States are applicable" in reviewing such decisions and whether, if they are, the "standards and procedures" used to try Hamdan and other detainees actually violate the "Constitution and laws." *Ibid*.

Together, the UCMJ, the AUMF, and the DTA at most acknowledge a general Presidential authority to convene military commissions in circumstances where justified under the "Constitution and laws," including the law of war. Absent a more specific congressional authorization, the task of this Court is, as it was in *Quirin*, to decide whether Hamdan's military commission is so justified. It is to that inquiry we now turn.

V

The common law governing military commissions may be gleaned from past practice and what sparse legal precedent exists. Commissions historically have been used in three situations. See Bradley & Goldsmith, Congressional Authorization and the War on Terrorism, 118 Harv. L. Rev. 2048, 2132–2133 (2005); Winthrop 831–846; Hearings on H.R. 2498 before the Subcommittee of the House Committee on Armed Services, 81st Cong., 1st Sess., 975 (1949). First, they have substituted for civilian courts at times and in places where martial law has been declared. Their use in these circumstances has raised constitutional questions, see Duncan v. Kahanamoku, 327 U.S. 304 ... (1946); Milligan, 4 Wall., at 121–122..., but is well recognized. See Winthrop 822, 836–839. Second, commissions have been established to try civilians "as part of a temporary military government over occupied enemy territory or territory regained from an enemy where civilian government cannot and does not function." Duncan, 327 U.S., at 314; see Milligan, 4 Wall., at 141–142 ...

---

15. [Court's fn.23] Whether or not the President has independent power, absent congressional authorization, to convene military commissions, he may not disregard limitations that Congress has, in proper exercise of its own war powers, placed on his powers. See Youngstown Sheet & Tube Co. v. Sawyer, 343 U.S. 579, 637 ... (1952) (Jackson, J., concurring). The Government does not argue otherwise.

(Chase, C.J., concurring in judgment) (distinguishing "martial law proper" from "military government" in occupied territory). Illustrative of this second kind of commission is the one that was established, with jurisdiction to apply the German Criminal Code, in occupied Germany following the end of World War II. See Madsen v. Kinsella, 343 U.S. 341, 356 ... (1952).

The third type of commission, convened as an "incident to the conduct of war" when there is a need "to seize and subject to disciplinary measures those enemies who in their attempt to thwart or impede our military effort have violated the law of war," *Quirin*, 317 U.S., at 28–29, has been described as "utterly different" from the other two. Bickers, Military Commissions are Constitutionally Sound: A Response to Professors Katyal and Tribe, 34 Tex. Tech. L. Rev. 899, 902 (2002-2003). Not only is its jurisdiction limited to offenses cognizable during time of war, but its role is primarily a factfinding one — to determine, typically on the battlefield itself, whether the defendant has violated the law of war. The last time the U.S. Armed Forces used the law-of-war military commission was during World War II. In *Quirin*, this Court sanctioned President Roosevelt's use of such a tribunal to try Nazi saboteurs captured on American soil during the War. 317 U.S. 1. And in *Yamashita*, we held that a military commission had jurisdiction to try a Japanese commander for failing to prevent troops under his command from committing atrocities in the Philippines. 327 U.S. 1. *Quirin* is the model the Government invokes most frequently to defend the commission convened to try Hamdan. That is both appropriate and unsurprising. Since Guantanamo Bay is neither enemy-occupied territory nor under martial law, the law-of-war commission is the only model available. At the same time, no more robust model of executive power exists; *Quirin* represents the high-water mark of military power to try enemy combatants for war crimes.

The classic treatise penned by Colonel William Winthrop, whom we have called "the 'Blackstone of Military Law,'" Reid v. Covert, 354 U.S. 1, 19, n.38 ... (1957) (plurality opinion), describes at least four preconditions for exercise of jurisdiction by a tribunal of the type convened to try Hamdan. First, "[a] military commission, (except where otherwise authorized by statute), can legally assume jurisdiction only of offenses committed within the field of the command of the convening commander." Winthrop 836. The "field of command" in these circumstances means the "theatre of war." *Ibid*. Second, the offense charged "must have been committed within the period of the war." *Id.*, at 837. No jurisdiction exists to try offenses "committed either before or after the war." *Ibid*. Third, a military commission not established pursuant to martial law or an occupation may try only "[i]ndividuals of the enemy's army who have been guilty of illegitimate warfare or other offences in violation of the laws of war" and members of one's own army "who, in time of war, become chargeable with crimes or offences not cognizable, or triable, by the criminal courts or under the Articles of war." *Id.*, at 838. Finally, a law-of-war commission has jurisdiction to try only two kinds of offense: "Violations of the laws and usages of war cognizable by military tribunals only," and "[b]reaches of military orders or regulations for which offenders are not legally triable by court-martial under the Articles of war." *Id.*, at 839.

All parties agree that Colonel Winthrop's treatise accurately describes the common law governing military commissions, and that the jurisdictional limitations he identifies were incorporated in Article of War 15 and, later, Article 21 of the UCMJ. It also is undisputed that Hamdan's commission lacks jurisdiction to try him unless the charge "properly set[s] forth, not only the details of the act charged, but the circumstances conferring jurisdiction." *Id.*, at 842.... The question is whether the preconditions designed to ensure that a military necessity exists to justify the use of this extraordinary tribunal have been satisfied here.

The charge against Hamdan, described in detail in Part I, *supra*, alleges a conspiracy extending over a number of years, from 1996 to November 2001. All but two months of that more than 5-year-long period preceded the attacks of September 11, 2001, and the enactment of the AUMF—the Act of Congress on which the Government relies for exercise of its war powers and thus for its authority to convene military commissions. Neither the purported agreement with Osama bin Laden and others to commit war crimes, nor a single overt act, is alleged to have occurred in a theater of war or on any specified date after September 11, 2001. None of the overt acts that Hamdan is alleged to have committed violates the law of war.

These facts alone cast doubt on the legality of the charge and, hence, the commission; as Winthrop makes plain, the offense alleged must have been committed both in a theater of war and during, not before, the relevant conflict. But the deficiencies in the time and place allegations also underscore-indeed are symptomatic of-the most serious defect of this charge: The offense it alleges is not triable by law-of-war military commission. See *Yamashita*, 327 U.S., at 13 ("Neither congressional action nor the military orders constituting the commission authorized it to place petitioner on trial unless the charge proffered against him is of a violation of the law of war").

There is no suggestion that Congress has, in exercise of its constitutional authority to "define and punish ... Offences against the Law of Nations,"U.S. Const., Art. I, § 8, cl.10, positively identified "conspiracy" as a war crime. As we explained in *Quirin*, that is not necessarily fatal to the Government's claim of authority to try the alleged offense by military commission; Congress, through Article 21 of the UCMJ, has "incorporated by reference" the common law of war, which may render triable by military commission certain offenses not defined by statute. 317 U.S., at 30. When, however, neither the elements of the offense nor the range of permissible punishments is defined by statute or treaty, the precedent must be plain and unambiguous. To demand any less would be to risk concentrating in military hands a degree of adjudicative and punitive power in excess of that contemplated either by statute or by the Constitution. *Cf.* Loving v. United States, 517 U.S. 748, 771 ... (1996) (acknowledging that Congress "may not delegate the power to make laws"); Reid, 354 U.S., at 23–24 ("The Founders envisioned the army as a necessary institution, but one dangerous to liberty if not confined within its essential bounds"); The Federalist No. 47, p. 324 (J. Cooke ed. 1961) (J. Madison) ("The accumulation of all powers legislative, executive and judiciary in the same hands ... may justly be pronounced the very definition of tyranny").

This high standard was met in *Quirin*; the violation there alleged was, by "universal agreement and practice" both in this country and internationally, recognized as an offense against the law of war. 317 U.S., at 30; see *id.*, at 35–36 ("This precept of the law of war has been so recognized in practice both here and abroad, and has so generally been accepted as valid by authorities on international law that we think it must be regarded as a rule or principle of the law of war recognized by this Government by its enactment of the Fifteenth Article of War" (footnote omitted)). Although the picture arguably was less clear in *Yamashita*, compare 327 U.S., at 16 (stating that the provisions of the Fourth Hague Convention of 1907, 36 Stat. 2306, "plainly" required the defendant to control the troops under his command), with 327 U.S., at 35 (Murphy, J., dissenting), the disagreement between the majority and the dissenters in that case concerned whether the historic and textual evidence constituted clear precedent—not whether clear precedent was required to justify trial by law-of-war military commission.

At a minimum, the Government must make a substantial showing that the crime for which it seeks to try a defendant by military commission is acknowledged to be an offense against the law of war. That burden is far from satisfied here. The crime of "conspiracy" has rarely if ever been tried as such in this country by any law-of-war military commission not exercising some other form of jurisdiction, and does not appear in either the Geneva Conventions or the Hague Conventions-the major treaties on the law of war. Winthrop explains that under the common law governing military commissions, it is not enough to intend to violate the law of war and commit overt acts in furtherance of that intention unless the overt acts either are themselves offenses against the law of war or constitute steps sufficiently substantial to qualify as an attempt. See Winthrop 841 ("[T]he jurisdiction of the military commission should be restricted to cases of offence consisting in overt acts, *i.e.*, in unlawful commissions or actual attempts to commit, and not in intentions merely")....

The Government cites three sources that it says show otherwise. First, it points out that the Nazi saboteurs in *Quirin* were charged with conspiracy. See Brief for Respondents 27. Second, it observes that Winthrop at one point in his treatise identifies conspiracy as an offense "prosecuted by military commissions." *Ibid.* (citing Winthrop 839, and n.5). Finally, it notes that another military historian, Charles Roscoe Howland, lists conspiracy "'to violate the laws of war by destroying life or property in aid of the enemy'" as an offense that was tried as a violation of the law of war during the Civil War. Brief for Respondents 27–28 (citing C. Howland, Digest of Opinions of the Judge Advocates General of the Army 1071 (1912) (hereinafter Howland)). On close analysis, however, these sources at best lend little support to the Government's position and at worst undermine it. By any measure, they fail to satisfy the high standard of clarity required to justify the use of a military commission.

That the defendants in *Quirin* were charged with conspiracy is not persuasive, since the Court declined to address whether the offense actually qualified as a violation of the law-of-war—let alone one triable by military commission. The *Quirin* defendants were charged with the following offenses:

"[I.] Violation of the law of war.

"[II.] Violation of Article 81 of the Articles of War, defining the offense of relieving or attempting to relieve, or corresponding with or giving intelligence to, the enemy.

"[III.] Violation of Article 82, defining the offense of spying.

"[IV.] Conspiracy to commit the offenses alleged in charges [I, II, and III]."317 U.S., at 23.

The Government, defending its charge, argued that the conspiracy alleged "constitute[d] an additional violation of the law of war." *Id.*, at 15. The saboteurs disagreed; they maintained that "[t]he charge of conspiracy can not stand if the other charges fall." *Id.*, at 8. The Court, however, declined to resolve the dispute. It concluded, first, that the specification supporting Charge I adequately alleged a "violation of the law of war" that was not "merely colorable or without foundation." *Id.*, at 36. The facts the Court deemed sufficient for this purpose were that the defendants, admitted enemy combatants, entered upon U.S. territory in time of war without uniform "for the purpose of destroying property used or useful in prosecuting the war." That act was "a hostile and warlike" one. *Id.*, at 36, 37. The Court was careful in its decision to identify an overt, "complete" act. Responding to the argument that the saboteurs had "not actually committed or attempted to commit any act of depredation or entered the theatre or zone of active military operations" and therefore had not violated the law of war, the Court responded that they had actually "passed our military and naval lines and defenses or went behind those lines, in civilian dress and with hostile purpose." *Id.*, at 38."The offense was complete when with that purpose they entered—or, having so entered, they remained upon—our territory in time of war without uniform or other appropriate means of identification." *Ibid.*

Turning to the other charges alleged, the Court explained that "[s]ince the first specification of Charge I sets forth a violation of the law of war, we have no occasion to pass on the adequacy of the second specification of Charge I, or to construe the 81st and 82nd Articles of War for the purpose of ascertaining whether the specifications under Charges II and III allege violations of those Articles or whether if so construed they are constitutional." *Id.*, at 46. No mention was made at all of Charge IV—the conspiracy charge.

If anything, *Quirin* supports Hamdan's argument that conspiracy is not a violation of the law of war. Not only did the Court pointedly omit any discussion of the conspiracy charge, but its analysis of Charge I placed special emphasis on the completion of an offense; it took seriously the saboteurs' argument that there can be no violation of a law of war—at least not one triable by military commission—without the actual commission of or attempt to commit a "hostile and warlike act." *Id.*, at 37–38.

That limitation makes eminent sense when one considers the necessity from whence this kind of military commission grew: The need to dispense swift justice, often in the form of execution, to illegal belligerents captured on the battlefield. See S.Rep. No. 130, 64th Cong., 1st Sess., p. 40 (1916) (testimony of Brig. Gen. Enoch H. Crowder) (observing that Article of War 15 preserves the power of "the military commander in the field in time of war " to use military commissions.... The same urgency would not have been felt vis-à-vis enemies who had done little more than agree to violate the laws of war. *Cf.* 31 Op. Atty. Gen. 356, 357, 361 (1918) (opining that a German spy could not be tried by military commission because, having been apprehended before entering "any camp, fortification or other military premises of the United States," he had "committed [his offenses] outside of the field of military operations"). The *Quirin* Court acknowledged as much when it described the President's authority to use law-of-war military commissions as the power to "seize and subject to disciplinary measures those enemies who in their attempt to thwart or impede our military effort have violated the law of war." 317 U.S., at 28–29....

Winthrop and Howland are only superficially more helpful to the Government. Howland, granted, lists "conspiracy by two or more to violate the laws of war by destroying life or property in aid of the enemy" as one of over 20 "offenses against the laws and usages of war" "passed upon and punished by military commissions." Howland 1071. But while the records of cases that Howland cites following his list of offenses against the law of war support inclusion of the other offenses mentioned, they provide no support for the inclusion of conspiracy as a violation of the law of war. See *ibid.*... Winthrop, apparently recognizing as much, excludes conspiracy of any kind from his own list of offenses against the law of war. See Winthrop 839–840.

Winthrop does, unsurprisingly, include "criminal conspiracies" in his list of "[c]rimes and statutory offenses cognizable by State or U.S. courts" and triable by martial law or military government commission. See *id.*, at 839. And, in a footnote, he cites several Civil War examples of "conspiracies of this class, or of the first and second classes combined." *Id.*, at 839, n.5.... The Government relies on this footnote for its contention that conspiracy was triable both as an ordinary crime (a crime of the "first class") and, independently, as a war crime (a crime of the "second class"). But the footnote will not support the weight the Government places on it.

As we have seen, the military commissions convened during the Civil War functioned at once as martial law or military government tribunals and as law-of-war commissions.... Accordingly, they regularly tried war crimes and ordinary crimes together. Indeed, as Howland observes, "[n]ot infrequently the crime, as charged and found, was a combination of the two species of offenses." Howland 1071; *see also* Davis 310, n.2; Winthrop 842. The example he gives is "'murder in violation of the laws of war.'" Howland 1071–1072. Winthrop's conspiracy "of the first and second classes combined" is, like Howland's example, best understood as a species of compound offense of the type tried by the hybrid military commissions of the Civil War. It is not a stand-alone offense against the law of war. Winthrop confirms this understanding later in his discussion, when he emphasizes that "overt acts" constituting war crimes are the only proper subject at least of those military tribunals not convened to stand in for local courts. Winthrop 841, and nn.22, 23 ... (citing W. Finlason, Martial Law 130 (1867)).

Justice Thomas cites as evidence that conspiracy is a recognized violation of the law of war the Civil War indictment against Henry Wirz, which charged the defendant with "'[m]aliciously, willfully, and traitorously ... combining, confederating, and conspiring [with others] to injure the health and destroy the lives of soldiers in the military service of the United States ... to the end that the armies of the United States might be weakened and impaired, in violation of the laws and customs of war.'" (dissenting opinion) (quoting H.R. Doc. No. 314, 55th Cong., 3d Sess., 785 (1865). As shown by the specification supporting that charge, however, Wirz was alleged to have personally committed a number of atrocities against his victims, including torture, injection of prisoners with poison, and use of "ferocious and bloodthirsty dogs" to "seize, tear, mangle, and maim the bodies and limbs" of prisoners, many of whom died as a result. *Id.*, at 789–790. Crucially, Judge Advocate General Holt determined that one of Wirz's alleged co-conspirators, R.B. Winder, should not be tried by military commission because there was as yet insufficient evidence of his own personal involvement in the atrocities: "[I]n the case of R.B. Winder, while the evidence at the trial of Wirz was deemed by the court to implicate him in the conspiracy against the lives of all Federal prisoners in rebel hands, no such specific overt acts of violation of the laws of war are as yet fixed upon him as to make it expedient to prefer formal charges and bring him to trial." *Id.*, at 783....

Finally, international sources confirm that the crime charged here is not a recognized violation of the law of war. As observed above, none of the major treaties governing the law of war identifies conspiracy as a violation thereof. And the only "conspiracy" crimes that have been recognized by international war crimes tribunals (whose jurisdiction often extends beyond war crimes proper to crimes against humanity and crimes against the peace) are conspiracy to commit genocide and common plan to wage aggressive war, which is a crime against the peace and requires for its commission actual participation in a "concrete plan to wage war." 1 Trial of the Major War Criminals Before the International Military Tribunal: Nuremberg, 14 November 1945–1 October 1946, p. 225 (1947). The International Military Tribunal at Nuremberg, over the prosecution's objections, pointedly refused to recognize as a violation of the law of war conspiracy to commit war crimes, *see, e.g.,* 22 *id.*, at 469, and convicted only Hitler's most senior associates of conspiracy to wage aggressive war, see S. Pomorski, Conspiracy and Criminal Organization, in the Nuremberg Trial and International Law 213, 233–235 (G. Ginsburgs & V. Kudriavtsev eds. 1990). As one prominent figure from the Nuremberg trials has explained, members of the Tribunal objected to recognition of conspiracy as a violation of the law of war on the ground that "[t]he Anglo-American concept of conspiracy was not part of European legal systems and arguably not an element of the internationally recognized laws of war." T. Taylor, Anatomy of the Nuremberg Trials: A Personal Memoir 36 (1992); *see also id.*, at 550 (observing that Francis Biddle, who as Attorney General prosecuted the defendants in *Quirin*, thought the French judge had made a "'persuasive argument that conspiracy in the truest sense is not known to international law'").[16]

… The charge's shortcomings are not merely formal, but are indicative of a broader inability on the Executive's part here to satisfy the most basic precondition-at least in the absence of specific congressional authorization-for establishment of military commissions: military necessity. Hamdan's tribunal was appointed not by a military commander in the field of battle, but by a retired major general stationed away from any active hostilities. *Cf.* Rasul v. Bush, 542 U.S., at 487 (Kennedy, J., concurring in judgment) (observing that "Guantanamo Bay is … far removed from any hostilities"). Hamdan is charged not with an overt act for which he was caught redhanded in a theater of war and which military efficiency demands be tried expeditiously, but with an agreement the inception of which long predated the attacks of September 11, 2001 and the AUMF. That may well be a crime, but it is not an offense that "by the law of war may be tried by military commissio[n]." 10 U.S.C. §821. None of the overt acts alleged to have been committed in furtherance of the agreement is itself a war crime, or even necessarily occurred during time of, or in a theater of, war. Any urgent need for imposition or execution of judgment is utterly belied by the record; Hamdan was arrested in November 2001 and he was not charged until mid-2004. These simply are not the circumstances in which, by any stretch of the historical evidence or this Court's precedents, a military commission established by Executive Order under the authority of Article 21 of the UCMJ may lawfully try a person and subject him to punishment.

VI

Whether or not the Government has charged Hamdan with an offense against the law of war cognizable by military commission, the commission lacks power to proceed. The UCMJ conditions the President's use of military commissions on compliance not only with the American common law of war, but also with the rest of the UCMJ itself, insofar as applicable, and with the "rules and precepts of the law of nations," *Quirin*, 317 U.S., at 28—including, *inter alia*, the four Geneva Conventions signed in 1949. See *Yamashita*, 327 U.S., at 20–21, 23–24. The procedures that the Government has decreed will govern Hamdan's trial by commission violate these laws.

A

The commission's procedures are set forth in Commission Order No. 1, which was amended most recently on August 31, 2005—after Hamdan's trial had already begun.

---

16. [Court's fn.40] *See also* 15 United Nations War Crimes Commissions, Law Reports of Trials of War Criminals 90–91 (1949) (observing that, although a few individuals were charged with conspiracy under European domestic criminal codes following World War II, "the United States Military Tribunals" established at that time did not "recognis[e] as a separate offence conspiracy to commit war crimes or crimes against humanity"). The International Criminal Tribunal for the former Yugoslavia (ICTY), drawing on the Nuremberg precedents, has adopted a "joint criminal enterprise" theory of liability, but that is a species of liability for the substantive offense (akin to aiding and abetting), not a crime on its own. See Prosecutor v. Tadic, Judgment, Case No. IT-94-1-A (ICTY App. Chamber, July 15, 1999); see also Prosecutor v. Milutinovic, Decision on Dragoljub Ojdanic's Motion Challenging Jurisdiction-Joint Criminal Enterprise, Case No. IT-99-37-AR72, para. 26 (ICTY App. Chamber, May 21, 2003) (stating that "[c]riminal liability pursuant to a joint criminal enterprise is not a liability for … conspiring to commit crimes").

Every commission established pursuant to Commission Order No. 1 must have a presiding officer and at least three other members, all of whom must be commissioned officers. § 4(A)(1). The presiding officer's job is to rule on questions of law and other evidentiary and interlocutory issues; the other members make findings and, if applicable, sentencing decisions. § 4(A)(5). The accused is entitled to appointed military counsel and may hire civilian counsel at his own expense so long as such counsel is a U.S. citizen with security clearance "at the level SECRET or higher." §§ 4(C)(2)–(3).

The accused also is entitled to a copy of the charge(s) against him, both in English and his own language (if different), to a presumption of innocence, and to certain other rights typically afforded criminal defendants in civilian courts and courts-martial. See §§ 5(A)-(P). These rights are subject, however, to one glaring condition: The accused and his civilian counsel may be excluded from, and precluded from ever learning what evidence was presented during, any part of the proceeding that either the Appointing Authority or the presiding officer decides to "close." Grounds for such closure "include the protection of information classified or classifiable ... ; information protected by law or rule from unauthorized disclosure; the physical safety of participants in Commission proceedings, including prospective witnesses; intelligence and law enforcement sources, methods, or activities; and other national security interests." § 6(B)(3). Appointed military defense counsel must be privy to these closed sessions, but may, at the presiding officer's discretion, be forbidden to reveal to his or her client what took place therein. *Ibid.*

Another striking feature of the rules governing Hamdan's commission is that they permit the admission of any evidence that, in the opinion of the presiding officer, "would have probative value to a reasonable person." § 6(D)(1). Under this test, not only is testimonial hearsay and evidence obtained through coercion fully admissible, but neither live testimony nor witnesses' written statements need be sworn. See §§ 6(D)(2)(b), (3). Moreover, the accused and his civilian counsel may be denied access to evidence in the form of "protected information" (which includes classified information as well as "information protected by law or rule from unauthorized disclosure" and "information concerning other national security interests," §§ 6(B)(3), 6(D)(5)(a)(v)), so long as the presiding officer concludes that the evidence is "probative" under § 6(D)(1) and that its admission without the accused's knowledge would not "result in the denial of a full and fair trial." § 6(D)(5)(b). Finally, a presiding officer's determination that evidence "would not have probative value to a reasonable person" may be overridden by a majority of the other commission members. § 6(D)(1).

Once all the evidence is in, the commission members (not including the presiding officer) must vote on the accused's guilt. A two-thirds vote will suffice for both a verdict of guilty and for imposition of any sentence not including death (the imposition of which requires a unanimous vote). § 6(F). Any appeal is taken to a three-member review panel composed of military officers and designated by the Secretary of Defense, only one member of which need have experience as a judge. § 6(H)(4). The review panel is directed to "disregard any variance from procedures specified in this Order or elsewhere that would not materially have affected the outcome of the trial before the Commission." *Ibid.* Once the panel makes its recommendation to the Secretary of Defense, the Secretary can either remand for further proceedings or forward the record to the President with his recommendation as to final disposition. § 6(H)(5). The President then, unless he has delegated the task to the Secretary, makes the "final decision." § 6(H)(6). He may change the commission's findings or sentence only in a manner favorable to the accused. *Ibid.*

B

Hamdan raises both general and particular objections to the procedures set forth in Commission Order No. 1. His general objection is that the procedures' admitted deviation from those governing courts-martial itself renders the commission illegal. Chief among his particular objections are that he may, under the Commission Order, be convicted based on evidence he has not seen or heard, and that any evidence admitted against him need not comply with the admissibility or relevance rules typically applicable in criminal trials and court-martial proceedings.

The Government objects to our consideration of any procedural challenge at this stage on the grounds that (1) the abstention doctrine espoused in *Councilman*, 420 U.S. 738…, precludes pre-enforcement review of procedural rules, (2) Hamdan will be able to raise any such challenge following a "final decision" under the DTA, and (3) "there is … no basis to presume, before the trial has even commenced, that the trial will not be conducted in good faith and according to law."… The first of these contentions was disposed of in Part III, *supra*, and neither of the latter two is sound.

First, because Hamdan apparently is not subject to the death penalty (at least as matters now stand) and may receive a sentence shorter than 10 years' imprisonment, he has no automatic right to review of the commission's "final decision" before a federal court under the DTA. See § 1005(e)(3), 119 Stat. 2743. Second, contrary to the Government's assertion, there is a "basis to presume" that the procedures employed during Hamdan's trial will violate the law: The procedures are described with particularity in Commission Order No. 1, and implementation of some of them has already occurred. One of Hamdan's complaints is that he will be, and indeed already has been, excluded from his own trial.… Under these circumstances, review of the procedures in advance of a "final decision"—the timing of which is left entirely to the discretion of the President under the DTA—is appropriate. We turn, then, to consider the merits of Hamdan's procedural challenge.

C

In part because the difference between military commissions and courts-martial originally was a difference of jurisdiction alone, and in part to protect against abuse and ensure evenhandedness under the pressures of war, the procedures governing trials by military commission historically have been the same as those governing courts-martial. *See, e.g.,* 1 The War of the Rebellion 248 (2d series 1894) (General Order 1 issued during the Civil War required military commissions to "be constituted in a similar manner and their proceedings be conducted according to the same general rules as courts-martial in order to prevent abuses which might otherwise arise"). Accounts of commentators from Winthrop through General Crowder—who drafted Article of War 15 and whose views have been deemed "authoritative" by this Court, Madsen, 343 U.S., at 353—confirm as much. As recently as the Korean and Vietnam wars, during which use of military commissions was contemplated but never made, the principle of procedural parity was espoused as a background assumption. See Paust, Antiterrorism Military Commissions: Courting Illegality, 23 Mich. J. Int'l L. 1, 3–5 (2001-2002).

There is a glaring historical exception to this general rule. The procedures and evidentiary rules used to try General Yamashita near the end of World War II deviated in significant respects from those then governing courts-martial. See 327 U.S. 1. The force of that precedent, however, has been seriously undermined by post-World War II developments. *Yamashita*, from late 1944 until September 1945, was Commanding General of the Fourteenth Army Group of the Imperial Japanese Army, which had exercised control over the Philippine Islands. On September 3, 1945, after American forces regained control of the Philippines, Yamashita surrendered. Three weeks later, he was charged with violations of the law of war. A few weeks after that, he was arraigned before a military commission convened in the Philippines. He pleaded not guilty, and his trial lasted for two months. On December 7, 1945, Yamashita was convicted and sentenced to hang. See *id.*, at 5; *id.*, at 31–34 (Murphy, J., dissenting). This Court upheld the denial of his petition for a writ of habeas corpus.

The procedures and rules of evidence employed during Yamashita's trial departed so far from those used in courts-martial that they generated an unusually long and vociferous critique from two Members of this Court. See *id.*, at 41–81 (Rutledge, J., joined by Murphy, J., dissenting). Among the dissenters' primary concerns was that the commission had free rein to consider all evidence "which in the commission's opinion 'would be of assistance in proving or disproving the charge,' without any of the usual modes of authentication." *Id.*, at 49 (Rutledge, J.).

The majority, however, did not pass on the merits of Yamashita's procedural challenges because it concluded that his status disentitled him to any protection under the Articles of War (specifically, those set forth in Article 38, which would become Article 36 of the UCMJ) or the Geneva Convention of 1929, 47 Stat.2021 (1929 Geneva Convention). The Court explained that Yamashita was neither a "person made subject to the Articles of War by Article 2" thereof, 327 U.S., at 20, nor a protected prisoner of war being tried for crimes committed during his detention, *id.*, at 21.

At least partially in response to subsequent criticism of General Yamashita's trial, the UCMJ's codification of the Articles of War after World War II expanded the category of persons subject thereto to include defendants in *Yamashita*'s (and Hamdan's) position, and the Third Geneva Convention of 1949 extended prisoner-of-war protections to individuals tried for crimes committed before their capture. See 3 Int'l Comm. of Red Cross, Commentary: Geneva Convention Relative to the Treatment of Prisoners of War 413 (1960) (hereinafter GC III Commentary) (explaining that Article 85, which extends the Convention's protections to "[p]risoners of war prosecuted under the laws of the Detaining Power for acts committed prior to capture," was adopted in response to judicial interpretations of the 1929 Convention, including this Court's decision in *Yamashita*). The most notorious exception to the principle of uniformity, then, has been stripped of its precedential value.

The uniformity principle is not an inflexible one; it does not preclude all departures from the procedures dictated for use by courts-martial. But any departure must be tailored to the exigency that necessitates it. See Winthrop 835, n.81. That understanding is reflected in Article 36 of the UCMJ, which provides:

> "(a) The procedure, including modes of proof, in cases before courts-martial, courts of inquiry, military commissions, and other military tribunals may be prescribed by the President by regulations which shall, so far as he considers practicable, apply the principles of law and the rules of evidence generally recognized in the trial of criminal cases in the United States district courts, but which may not be contrary to or inconsistent with this chapter.

> "(b) All rules and regulations made under this article shall be uniform insofar as practicable and shall be reported to Congress." 70A Stat. 50.

Article 36 places two restrictions on the President's power to promulgate rules of procedure for courts-martial and military commissions alike. First, no procedural rule he adopts may be "contrary to or inconsistent with" the UCMJ—however practical it may seem. Second, the rules adopted must be "uniform insofar as practicable." That is, the rules applied to military commissions must be the same as those applied to courts-martial unless such uniformity proves impracticable.

Hamdan argues that Commission Order No. 1 violates both of these restrictions; he maintains that the procedures described in the Commission Order are inconsistent with the UCMJ and that the Government has offered no explanation for their deviation from the procedures governing courts-martial, which are set forth in the Manual for Courts-Martial, United States (2005 ed.) (Manual for Courts-Martial). Among the inconsistencies Hamdan identifies is that between § 6 of the Commission Order, which permits exclusion of the accused from proceedings and denial of his access to evidence in certain circumstances, and the UCMJ's requirement that "[a]ll ... proceedings" other than votes and deliberations by courts-martial "shall be made a part of the record and shall be in the presence of the accused."10 U.S.C.A. § 839(c) (Supp. 2006). Hamdan also observes that the Commission Order dispenses with virtually all evidentiary rules applicable in courts-martial.

The Government has three responses. First, it argues, only 9 of the UCMJ's 158 Articles— the ones that expressly mention "military commissions"—actually apply to commissions, and Commission Order No. 1 sets forth no procedure that is "contrary to or inconsistent with" those 9 provisions. Second, the Government contends, military commissions would be of no use if the President were hamstrung by those provisions of the UCMJ that govern courts-martial. Finally, the President's determination that "the danger to the safety of the United States and the nature of international terrorism" renders it impracticable "to apply in military commissions ... the principles of law and rules of evidence generally recognized in the trial of criminal cases in the United States district courts," November 13 Order § 1(f), is, in the Government's view, explanation enough for any deviation from court-martial procedures....

Hamdan has the better of this argument. Without reaching the question whether any provision of Commission Order No. 1 is strictly "contrary to or inconsistent with" other provisions of the UCMJ, we conclude that the "practicability" determination the President has made is insufficient to justify variances from the procedures governing courts-martial. Subsection (b) of Article 36 was added after World War II, and requires a different showing of impracticability from the one required by subsection (a). Subsection (a) requires that the rules the President promulgates for courts-martial, provost courts, and military commissions alike conform to those that govern procedures in Article III courts,"so far as he considers practicable." 10 U.S.C. § 836(a).... Subsection (b), by contrast, demands that the rules applied in courts-martial, provost courts, and military commissions—whether or not they conform with the Federal Rules of Evidence—be "uniform insofar as practicable." § 836(b).... Under the latter provision, then, the rules set forth in the Manual for Courts-Martial must apply to military commissions unless impracticable.

The President here has determined, pursuant to subsection (a), that it is impracticable to apply the rules and principles of law that govern "the trial of criminal cases in the United States district courts," § 836(a), to Hamdan's commission. We assume that complete deference is owed that determination. The President has not, however, made a similar official determination that it is impracticable to apply the rules for courts-martial. And even if subsection (b)'s requirements may be satisfied without such an official determination, the requirements of that subsection are not satisfied here.

Nothing in the record before us demonstrates that it would be impracticable to apply court-martial rules in this case. There is no suggestion, for example, of any logistical difficulty in securing properly sworn and authenticated evidence or in applying the usual principles of relevance and admissibility. Assuming arguendo that the reasons articulated in the President's Article 36(a) determination ought to be considered in evaluating the impracticability of applying court-martial rules, the only reason offered in support of that determination is the danger posed by international terrorism. Without for one moment underestimating that danger, it is not evident to us why it should require, in the case of Hamdan's trial, any variance from the rules that govern courts-martial.

The absence of any showing of impracticability is particularly disturbing when considered in light of the clear and admitted failure to apply one of the most fundamental protections afforded not just by the Manual for Courts-Martial but also by the UCMJ itself: the right to be present. See 10 U.S.C.A. § 839(c) (Supp. 2006). Whether or not that departure technically is "contrary to or inconsistent with" the terms of the UCMJ, 10 U.S.C. § 836(a), the jettisoning of so basic a right cannot lightly be excused as "practicable."

Under the circumstances, then, the rules applicable in courts-martial must apply. Since it is undisputed that Commission Order No. 1 deviates in many significant respects from those rules, it necessarily violates Article 36(b).

… The military commission was not born of a desire to dispense a more summary form of justice than is afforded by courts-martial; it developed, rather, as a tribunal of necessity to be employed when courts-martial lacked jurisdiction over either the accused or the subject matter. See Winthrop 831. Exigency lent the commission its legitimacy, but did not further justify the wholesale jettisoning of procedural protections.…

D

The procedures adopted to try Hamdan also violate the Geneva Conventions. The Court of Appeals dismissed Hamdan's Geneva Convention challenge on three independent grounds: (1) the Geneva Conventions are not judicially enforceable; (2) Hamdan in any event is not entitled to their protections; and (3) even if he is entitled to their protections, *Councilman* abstention is appropriate. Judge Williams, concurring, rejected the second ground but agreed with the majority respecting the first and the last. As we explained in Part III, *supra*, the abstention rule applied in *Councilman*, 420 U.S. 738…, is not applicable here. And for the reasons that follow, we hold that neither of the other grounds the Court of Appeals gave for its decision is persuasive.

i

The Court of Appeals relied on Johnson v. Eisentrager, 339 U.S. 763 … (1950), to hold that Hamdan could not invoke the Geneva Conventions to challenge the Government's plan to prosecute him in accordance with Commission Order No. 1. *Eisentrager* involved a challenge by 21 German nationals to their 1945 convictions for war crimes by a military tribunal convened in Nanking, China, and to their subsequent imprisonment in occupied Germany. The petitioners argued, *inter alia*, that the 1929 Geneva Convention rendered illegal some of the procedures employed during their trials, which they said deviated impermissibly from the procedures used by courts-martial to try American soldiers. See *id.*, at 789. We rejected that claim on the merits because the petitioners (unlike Hamdan here) had failed to identify any prejudicial disparity "between the Commission that tried [them] and those that would try an offending soldier of the American forces of like rank," and in any event could claim no protection, under the 1929 Convention, during trials for crimes that occurred before their confinement as prisoners of war. *Id.*, at 790.

Buried in a footnote of the opinion, however, is this curious statement suggesting that the Court lacked power even to consider the merits of the Geneva Convention argument:

"We are not holding that these prisoners have no right which the military authorities are bound to respect. The United States, by the Geneva Convention of July 27, 1929, 47 Stat.2021, concluded with forty-six other countries, including the German Reich, an agreement upon the treatment to be accorded captives. These prisoners claim to be and are entitled to its protection. It is, however, the obvious scheme of the Agreement that responsibility for observance and enforcement of these rights is upon political and military authorities. Rights of alien enemies are vindicated under it only through protests and intervention of protecting powers as the rights of our citizens against foreign governments are vindicated only by Presidential intervention." *Id.*, at 789, n.14.

The Court of Appeals, on the strength of this footnote, held that "the 1949 Geneva Convention does not confer upon Hamdan a right to enforce its provisions in court." 415 F.3d, at 40.

Whatever else might be said about the *Eisentrager* footnote, it does not control this case. We may assume that "the obvious scheme" of the 1949 Conventions is identical in all relevant respects to that of the 1929 Convention,[17] and even that that scheme would, absent some other provision of law, preclude Hamdan's invocation of the Convention's provisions as an independent source of law binding the Government's actions and furnishing petitioner with any enforceable right.[18] For, regardless of the nature of the rights conferred on Hamdan, *cf.* United States v. Rauscher, 119 U.S. 407 ... (1886), they are, as the Government does not dispute, part of the law of war. See *Hamdi*, 542 U.S., at 520–521 (plurality opinion). And compliance with the law of war is the condition upon which the authority set forth in Article 21 is granted.

ii

For the Court of Appeals, acknowledgment of that condition was no bar to Hamdan's trial by commission. As an alternative to its holding that Hamdan could not invoke the Geneva Conventions at all, the Court of Appeals concluded that the Conventions did not in any event apply to the armed conflict during which Hamdan was captured. The court accepted the Executive's assertions that Hamdan was captured in connection with the United States' war with al Qaeda and that that war is distinct from the war with the Taliban in Afghanistan. It further reasoned that the war with al Qaeda evades the reach of the Geneva Conventions. See 415 F.3d, at 41–42. We, like Judge Williams, disagree with the latter conclusion.

The conflict with al Qaeda is not, according to the Government, a conflict to which the full protections afforded detainees under the 1949 Geneva Conventions apply because Article 2 of those Conventions (which appears in all four Conventions) renders the full protections applicable only to "all cases of declared war or of any other armed conflict which may arise between two or more of the High Contracting Parties." 6 U.S. T., at 3318.

---

17. [Court's 548 U.S. at 627 fn.57] *But see, e.g.,* 4 Int'l Comm. of Red Cross, Commentary: Geneva Convention Relative to the Protection of Civilian Persons in Time of War 21 (1958) (hereinafter GCIV Commentary) (the 1949 Geneva Conventions were written "first and foremost to protect individuals, and not to serve State interests"); GCIII Commentary 91 ("It was not ... until the Conventions of 1949 ... that the existence of 'rights' conferred in prisoners of war was affirmed").

18. [Court's fn.58] *But see* generally Brief for Louis Henkin *et al.* as Amici Curiae; 1 Int'l Comm. for the Red Cross, Commentary: Geneva Convention for the Amelioration of the Condition of the Wounded and Sick in Armed Forces in the Field 84 (1952) ("It should be possible in States which are parties to the Convention ... for the rules of the Convention to be evoked before an appropriate national court by the protected person who has suffered a violation"); GCII Commentary 92; GCIV Commentary 79.

Since Hamdan was captured and detained incident to the conflict with al Qaeda and not the conflict with the Taliban, and since al Qaeda, unlike Afghanistan, is not a "High Contracting Party"—*i.e.*, a signatory of the Conventions, the protections of those Conventions are not, it is argued, applicable to Hamdan.

We need not decide the merits of this argument because there is at least one provision of the Geneva Conventions that applies here even if the relevant conflict is not one between signatories. Article 3, often referred to as Common Article 3 because, like Article 2, it appears in all four Geneva Conventions, provides that in a "conflict not of an international character occurring in the territory of one of the High Contracting Parties, each Party to the conflict shall be bound to apply, as a minimum," certain provisions protecting "[p]ersons taking no active part in the hostilities, including members of armed forces who have laid down their arms and those placed hors de combat by ... detention." *Id.*, at 3318. One such provision prohibits "the passing of sentences and the carrying out of executions without previous judgment pronounced by a regularly constituted court affording all the judicial guarantees which are recognized as indispensable by civilized peoples." *Ibid.*

The Court of Appeals thought, and the Government asserts, that Common Article 3 does not apply to Hamdan because the conflict with al Qaeda, being "'international in scope,'" does not qualify as a "'conflict not of an international character.'" 415 F.3d, at 41. That reasoning is erroneous. The term "conflict not of an international character" is used here in contradistinction to a conflict between nations. So much is demonstrated by the "fundamental logic [of] the Convention's provisions on its application." *Id.*, at 44 (Williams, J., concurring).... Common Article 3 ... affords some minimal protection, falling short of full protection under the Conventions, to individuals associated with neither a signatory nor even a nonsignatory "Power" who are involved in a conflict "in the territory of" a signatory. The latter kind of conflict is distinguishable from the conflict described in Common Article 2 chiefly because it does not involve a clash between nations (whether signatories or not). In context, then, the phrase "not of an international character" bears its literal meaning. *See, e.g.,* ... Commentary on the Additional Protocols to the Geneva Conventions of 12 August 1949, p. 1351 (1987) ("[A] non-international armed conflict is distinct from an international armed conflict because of the legal status of the entities opposing each other").

Although the official commentaries accompanying Common Article 3 indicate that an important purpose of the provision was to furnish minimal protection to rebels involved in one kind of "conflict not of an international character," *i.e.*, a civil war, see GC III Commentary 36–37, the commentaries also make clear "that the scope of the Article must be as wide as possible," *id.*, at 36.[19] In fact, limiting language that would have rendered Common Article 3 applicable "especially [to] cases of civil war, colonial conflicts, or wars of religion," was omitted from the final version of the Article, which coupled broader scope of application with a narrower range of rights than did earlier proposed iterations. See GC III Commentary 42–43.

---

19. [Court's 548 U.S. at 631 fn.63] See also GCIII Commentary 35 (Common Article 3 "has the merit of being simple and clear.... Its observance does not depend upon preliminary discussions on the nature of the conflict"); GCIV Commentary 51 ("[N]obody in enemy hands can be outside the law"); U.S. Army Judge Advocate General's Legal Center and School, Dept. of the Army, Law of War Handbook 144 (2004) (Common Article 3 "serves as a 'minimum yardstick of protection in all conflicts, not just internal armed conflicts'" (quoting Nicaragua v. United States, 1986 I.C.J. 14, para. 218, 25 I.L.M. 1023)); Prosecutor v. Tadic,Case No. IT-94-1, Decision on the Defence Motion for Interlocutory Appeal on Jurisdiction, para. 102 (ICTY App. Chamber, Oct. 2, 1995) (stating that "the character of the conflict is irrelevant" in deciding whether Common Article 3 applies).

iii

Common Article 3, then, is applicable here and, as indicated above, requires that Hamdan be tried by a "regularly constituted court affording all the judicial guarantees which are recognized as indispensable by civilized peoples." 6 U.S. T., at 3320 (Art. 3, para. 1(d)). While the term "regularly constituted court" is not specifically defined in either Common Article 3 or its accompanying commentary, other sources disclose its core meaning. The commentary accompanying a provision of the Fourth Geneva Convention, for example, defines "'regularly constituted'" tribunals to include "ordinary military courts" and "definitely exclud[e] all special tribunals." GC IV Commentary 340 (defining the term "properly constituted" in Article 66, which the commentary treats as identical to "regularly constituted"); *see also Yamashita*, 327 U.S., at 44 (Rutledge, J., dissenting) (describing military commission as a court "specially constituted for a particular trial"). And one of the Red Cross' own treatises defines "regularly constituted court" as used in Common Article 3 to mean "established and organized in accordance with the laws and procedures already in force in a country." Int'l Comm. of Red Cross, 1 Customary International Humanitarian Law 355 (2005); *see also* GC IV Commentary 340 (observing that "ordinary military courts" will "be set up in accordance with the recognized principles governing the administration of justice").

The Government offers only a cursory defense of Hamdan's military commission in light of Common Article 3.... As Justice Kennedy explains, that defense fails because "[t]he regular military courts in our system are the courts-martial established by congressional statutes." (opinion concurring in part). At a minimum, a military commission "can be 'regularly constituted' by the standards of our military justice system only if some practical need explains deviations from court-martial practice." As we have explained, see Part VI-C, *supra*, no such need has been demonstrated here.[20]

iv

Inextricably intertwined with the question of regular constitution is the evaluation of the procedures governing the tribunal and whether they afford "all the judicial guarantees which are recognized as indispensable by civilized peoples." 6 U.S. T., at 3320 (Art. 3, para. 1(d)). Like the phrase "regularly constituted court," this phrase is not defined in the text of the Geneva Conventions. But it must be understood to incorporate at least the barest of those trial protections that have been recognized by customary international law. Many of these are described in Article 75 of Protocol I to the Geneva Conventions of 1949, adopted in 1977 (Protocol I). Although the United States declined to ratify Protocol I, its objections were not to Article 75 thereof. Indeed, it appears that the Government "regard[s] the provisions of Article 75 as an articulation of safeguards to which all persons in the hands of an enemy are entitled." Taft, The Law of Armed Conflict After 9/11: Some Salient Features, 28 Yale J. Int'l L. 319, 322 (2003). Among the rights set forth in Article 75 is the "right to be tried in [one's] presence." Protocol I, Art. 75(4)(e).[21]

---

20. [Court's fn.65] Further evidence of this tribunal's irregular constitution is the fact that its rules and procedures are subject to change midtrial, at the whim of the Executive. See Commission Order No. 1, § 11 (providing that the Secretary of Defense may change the governing rules "from time to time").

21. [Court's fn.66] Other international instruments to which the United States is a signatory include the same basic protections set forth in Article 75. *See, e.g.*, International Covenant on Civil and Political Rights, Art. 14, para. 3(d), Mar. 23, 1976, 999 U.N.T.S. 171 (setting forth the right of an accused "[t]o be tried in his presence, and to defend himself in person or through legal assistance of his own choosing"). Following World War II, several defendants were tried and convicted by military commission for violations of the law of war in their failure to afford captives fair trials before imposition and execution of sentence. In two such trials, the prosecutors argued that the defendants' failure to apprise accused individuals of all evidence against them constituted violations of the law of

We agree with Justice Kennedy that the procedures adopted to try Hamdan deviate from those governing courts-martial in ways not justified by any "evident practical need," and for that reason, at least, fail to afford the requisite guarantees. We add only that, as noted in Part VI-A, *supra*, various provisions of Commission Order No. 1 dispense with the principles, articulated in Article 75 and indisputably part of the customary international law, that an accused must, absent disruptive conduct or consent, be present for his trial and must be privy to the evidence against him. See §§ 6(B)(3), (D). That the Government has a compelling interest in denying Hamdan access to certain sensitive information is not doubted. *Cf.* (Thomas, J., dissenting). But, at least absent express statutory provision to the contrary, information used to convict a person of a crime must be disclosed to him....

[I]n undertaking to try Hamdan and subject him to criminal punishment, the Executive is bound to comply with the Rule of Law that prevails in this jurisdiction.

The judgment of the Court of Appeals is reversed, and the case is remanded for further proceedings. It is so ordered.

Breyer, J., with whom Kennedy, J., Souter, J., and Ginsburg, J. join, concurring.

The dissenters say that today's decision would "sorely hamper the President's ability to confront and defeat a new and deadly enemy." (opinion of Thomas, J.). They suggest that it undermines our Nation's ability to "preven[t] future attacks" of the grievous sort that we have already suffered. That claim leads me to state briefly what I believe the majority sets forth both explicitly and implicitly at greater length. The Court's conclusion ultimately rests upon a single ground: Congress has not issued the Executive a "blank check." *Cf.* Hamdi v. Rumsfeld, 542 U.S. 507, 536 ... (2004) (plurality opinion). Indeed, Congress has denied the President the legislative authority to create military commissions of the kind at issue here. Nothing prevents the President from returning to Congress to seek the authority he believes necessary.

Where, as here, no emergency prevents consultation with Congress, judicial insistence upon that consultation does not weaken our Nation's ability to deal with danger. To the contrary, that insistence strengthens the Nation's ability to determine-through democratic means-how best to do so. The Constitution places its faith in those democratic means. Our Court today simply does the same.

Kennedy, J., with whom Souter, J., Ginsburg, J., and Breyer, J. join as to Parts I and II, concurring in part.

Military Commission Order No. 1, which governs the military commission established to try petitioner Salim Hamdan for war crimes, exceeds limits that certain statutes, duly enacted by Congress, have placed on the President's authority to convene military courts. This is not a case, then, where the Executive can assert some unilateral authority to fill a void left by congressional inaction. It is a case where Congress, in the proper exercise of its powers as an independent branch of government, and as part of a long tradition of legislative involvement in matters of military justice, has considered the subject of military tribunals and set limits on the President's authority. Where a statute provides the conditions for the exercise of governmental power, its requirements are the result of a deliberative and reflective process engaging both of the political branches. Respect for laws derived from the customary operation of the Executive and Legislative Branches gives some assurance of stability in time of crisis. The Constitution is best preserved by reliance on standards tested over time and insulated from the pressures of the moment.

---

war. See 5 U.N. War Crimes Commission 30 (trial of Sergeant-Major Shigeru Ohashi), 75 (trial of General Tanaka Hisakasu).

These principles seem vindicated here, for a case that may be of extraordinary importance is resolved by ordinary rules. The rules of most relevance here are those pertaining to the authority of Congress and the interpretation of its enactments.

It seems appropriate to recite these rather fundamental points because the Court refers, as it should in its exposition of the case, to the requirement of the Geneva Conventions of 1949 that military tribunals be "regularly constituted"—a requirement that controls here, if for no other reason, because Congress requires that military commissions like the ones at issue conform to the "law of war," 10 U.S.C. § 821. Whatever the substance and content of the term "regularly constituted" as interpreted in this and any later cases, there seems little doubt that it relies upon the importance of standards deliberated upon and chosen in advance of crisis, under a system where the single power of the Executive is checked by other constitutional mechanisms. All of which returns us to the point of beginning—that domestic statutes control this case. If Congress, after due consideration, deems it appropriate to change the controlling statutes, in conformance with the Constitution and other laws, it has the power and prerogative to do so.

I join the Court's opinion, save Parts V and VI-D-iv. To state my reasons for this reservation, and to show my agreement with the remainder of the Court's analysis by identifying particular deficiencies in the military commissions at issue, this separate opinion seems appropriate.

Trial by military commission raises separation-of-powers concerns of the highest order. Located within a single branch, these courts carry the risk that offenses will be defined, prosecuted, and adjudicated by executive officials without independent review. *Cf.* Loving v. United States, 517 U.S. 748, 756–758, 760 ... (1996). Concentration of power puts personal liberty in peril of arbitrary action by officials, an incursion the Constitution's three-part system is designed to avoid. It is imperative, then, that when military tribunals are established, full and proper authority exists for the Presidential directive....

In § 821 Congress has addressed the possibility that special military commissions—criminal courts other than courts-martial—may at times be convened. At the same time, however, the President's authority to convene military commissions is limited: It extends only to "offenders or offenses" that "by statute or by the law of war may be tried by" such military commissions. *Ibid....* The Government does not claim to base the charges against Hamdan on a statute; instead it invokes the law of war. That law, as the Court explained in *Ex parte Quirin*, 317 U.S. 1 (1942), derives from "rules and precepts of the law of nations"; it is the body of international law governing armed conflict. *Id.*, at 28. If the military commission at issue is illegal under the law of war, then an offender cannot be tried "by the law of war" before that commission.

The Court is correct to concentrate on one provision of the law of war that is applicable to our Nation's armed conflict with al Qaeda in Afghanistan and, as a result, to the use of a military commission to try Hamdan.... *see also* 415 F.3d 33, 44 (C.A.D.C. 2005) (Williams, J., concurring). That provision is Common Article 3 of the four Geneva Conventions of 1949. It prohibits, as relevant here, "[t]he passing of sentences and the carrying out of executions without previous judgment pronounced by a regularly constituted court affording all the judicial guarantees which are recognized as indispensable by civilized peoples." *See, e.g.*, Article 3 of the Geneva Convention (III) Relative to the Treatment of Prisoners of War, Aug. 12, 1949, [1955] 6 U.S.T. 3316, 3318, T.I.A.S. No. 3364. The provision is part of a treaty the United States has ratified and thus accepted as binding law. See *id.*, at 3316. By Act of Congress, moreover, violations of Common Article 3 are considered "war crimes," punishable as federal offenses, when committed by or against

United States nationals and military personnel. See 18 U.S.C. § 2441. There should be no doubt, then, that Common Article 3 is part of the law of war as that term is used in § 821.

The dissent by Justice Thomas argues that Common Article 3 nonetheless is irrelevant to this case because in Johnson v. Eisentrager, 339 U.S. 763 ... (1950), it was said to be the "obvious scheme" of the 1929 Geneva Convention that "[r]ights of alien enemies are vindicated under it only through protests and intervention of protecting powers," *i.e.*, signatory states, *id.*, at 789, n.14. As the Court explains ... this language from *Eisentrager* is not controlling here. Even assuming the *Eisentrager* analysis has some bearing upon the analysis of the broader 1949 Conventions and that, in consequence, rights are vindicated "under [those Conventions]" only through protests and intervention, 339 U.S., at 789, n.14, Common Article 3 is nonetheless relevant to the question of authorization under § 821. Common Article 3 is part of the law of war that Congress has directed the President to follow in establishing military commissions.... Consistent with that view, the *Eisentrager* Court itself considered on the merits claims that "procedural irregularities" under the 1929 Convention "deprive[d] the Military Commission of jurisdiction." 339 U.S., at 789, 790.

In another military commission case, *In re* Yamashita, 327 U.S. 1 ... (1946), the Court likewise considered on the merits-without any caveat about remedies under the Convention-a claim that an alleged violation of the 1929 Convention "establish[ed] want of authority in the commission to proceed with the trial." *Id.*, at 23, 24. That is the precise inquiry we are asked to perform here.

Assuming the President has authority to establish a special military commission to try Hamdan, the commission must satisfy Common Article 3's requirement of a "regularly constituted court affording all the judicial guarantees which are recognized as indispensable by civilized peoples,"6 U.S. T., at 3318. The terms of this general standard are yet to be elaborated and further defined, but Congress has required compliance with it by referring to the "law of war" in § 821. The Court correctly concludes that the military commission here does not comply with this provision.

Common Article 3's standard of a "regularly constituted court affording all the judicial guarantees which are recognized as indispensable by civilized peoples," *ibid.*, supports, at the least, a uniformity principle similar to that codified in § 836(b). The concept of a "regularly constituted court" providing "indispensable" judicial guarantees requires consideration of the system of justice under which the commission is established, though no doubt certain minimum standards are applicable. See ... 1 Int'l Committee of the Red Cross, Customary International Humanitarian Law 355 (2005) (explaining that courts are "regularly constituted" under Common Article 3 if they are "established and organised in accordance with the laws and procedures already in force in a country").

The regular military courts in our system are the courts-martial established by congressional statutes. Acts of Congress confer on those courts the jurisdiction to try "any person" subject to war crimes prosecution. 10 U.S.C. § 818. As the Court explains, moreover, while special military commissions have been convened in previous armed conflicts — a practice recognized in § 821 — those military commissions generally have adopted the structure and procedure of courts-martial....

In addition, whether or not the possibility, contemplated by the regulations here, of midtrial procedural changes could by itself render a military commission impermissibly irregular, *supra* n.65; *see also* Military Commission Order No. 1, § 11 (Aug. 31, 2005), App. to Brief for Petitioner 46a–72a (hereinafter MCO), an acceptable degree of independence from the Executive is necessary to render a commission "regularly constituted" by the standards of our Nation's system of justice. And any suggestion of Executive power to interfere with an ongoing judicial process raises concerns about the proceedings' fairness. Again, however, courts-martial provide the relevant benchmark. Subject to constitutional limitations, see *Ex parte* Milligan, 4 Wall. 2 … (1866), Congress has the power and responsibility to determine the necessity for military courts, and to provide the jurisdiction and procedures applicable to them. The guidance Congress has provided with respect to courts-martial indicates the level of independence and procedural rigor that Congress has deemed necessary, at least as a general matter, in the military context.

At a minimum a military commission like the one at issue—a commission specially convened by the President to try specific persons without express congressional authorization—can be "regularly constituted" by the standards of our military justice system only if some practical need explains deviations from court-martial practice. In this regard the standard of Common Article 3, applied here in conformity with §821, parallels the practicability standard of §836(b). Section 836, however, is limited by its terms to matters properly characterized as procedural—that is, "[p]retrial, trial, and post-trial procedures"—while Common Article 3 permits broader consideration of matters of structure, organization, and mechanisms to promote the tribunal's insulation from command influence. Thus the combined effect of the two statutes discussed here—§§836 and 821—is that considerations of practicability must support departures from court-martial practice. Relevant concerns, as noted earlier, relate to logistical constraints, accommodation of witnesses, security of the proceedings, and the like, not mere expedience or convenience. This determination, of course, must be made with due regard for the constitutional principle that congressional statutes can be controlling, including the congressional direction that the law of war has a bearing on the determination.

These principles provide the framework for an analysis of the specific military commission at issue here....

It is no answer that, at the end of the day, the Detainee Treatment Act of 2005 (DTA), 119 Stat. 2739, affords military-commission defendants the opportunity for judicial review in federal court. As the Court is correct to observe, the scope of that review is limited, DTA §1005(e)(3)(D), *id.*, at 2743; and the review is not automatic if the defendant's sentence is under 10 years, §1005(e)(3)(B), *ibid*. Also, provisions for review of legal issues after trial cannot correct for structural defects, such as the role of the Appointing Authority, that can cast doubt on the factfinding process and the presiding judge's exercise of discretion during trial. Before military-commission defendants may obtain judicial review, furthermore, they must navigate a military review process that again raises fairness concerns. At the outset, the Appointing Authority (unless the Appointing Authority is the Secretary of Defense) performs an "administrative review" of undefined scope, ordering any "supplementary proceedings" deemed necessary. MCO No. 1 §6(H)(3). After that the case is referred to a three-member Review Panel composed of officers selected by the Secretary of Defense. §6(H)(4); MCI No. 9, §4(B) (Oct. 11, 2005), available at www.defenselink.mil/news/Oct2005/d20051014MCI9.pdf. Though the Review Panel may return the case for further proceedings only if a majority "form[s] a definite and firm conviction that a material error of law occurred," MCO No. 1, §6(H)(4); MCI No. 9, §4(C)(1)(a), only one member must have "experience as a judge," MCO No. 1, §6(H)(4); nothing in the regulations requires that other panel members have legal training. By comparison to the review of court-martial judgments performed by such independent bodies as the Judge Advocate General, the Court of Criminal Appeals, and the Court of Appeals for the Armed Forces, 10 U.S.C. §§862, 864, 866, 867, 869, the review process here lacks structural protections designed to help ensure impartiality.

These structural differences between the military commissions and courts-martial—the concentration of functions, including legal decisionmaking, in a single executive official; the less rigorous standards for composition of the tribunal; and the creation of special review procedures in place of institutions created and regulated by Congress—remove safeguards that are important to the fairness of the proceedings and the independence of the court. Congress has prescribed these guarantees for courts-martial; and no evident practical need explains the departures here. For these reasons the commission cannot be considered regularly constituted under United States law and thus does not satisfy Congress' requirement that military commissions conform to the law of war.

Apart from these structural issues, moreover, the basic procedures for the commissions deviate from procedures for courts-martial, in violation of §836(b). As the Court explains, ... the Military Commission Order abandons the detailed Military Rules of Evidence, which are modeled on the Federal Rules of Evidence in conformity with §836(a)'s requirement of presumptive compliance with district-court rules.

Instead, the order imposes just one evidentiary rule: "Evidence shall be admitted if ... the evidence would have probative value to a reasonable person," MCO No. 1, §6(D)(1). Although it is true some military commissions applied an amorphous evidence standard in the past, *see, e.g.,* 1 Law Reports 117–118 (discussing World War II military commission orders); Exec. Order No. 9185, 7 Fed. Reg. 5103 (1942) (order convening military commission to try Nazi saboteurs), the evidentiary rules for those commissions were adopted before Congress enacted the uniformity requirement of 10 U.S.C. §836(b) as part of the UCMJ, see Act of May 5, 1950, ch. 169, 64 Stat. 107, 120, 149. And while some flexibility may be necessary to permit trial of battlefield captives like Hamdan, military statutes and rules already provide for introduction of deposition testimony for absent witnesses, 10 U.S.C. §849(d); R.C.M. 702, and use of classified information, Military Rule Evid. 505. Indeed, the deposition-testimony provision specifically mentions military commissions and thus is one of the provisions the Government concedes must be followed by the commission at issue. That provision authorizes admission of deposition testimony only if the witness is absent for specified reasons, §849(d)—a requirement that makes no sense if military commissions may consider all probative evidence. Whether or not this conflict renders the rules at issue "contrary to or inconsistent with" the UCMJ under §836(a), it creates a uniformity problem under §836(b).

The rule here could permit admission of multiple hearsay and other forms of evidence generally prohibited on grounds of unreliability. Indeed, the commission regulations specifically contemplate admission of unsworn written statements, MCO No. 1, §6(D)(3); and they make no provision for exclusion of coerced declarations save those "established to have been made as a result of torture," MCI No. 10, §3(A) (Mar. 24, 2006), available at www. defenselink.mil/news/Mar2006/d20060327MCI10.pdf; *cf.* Military Rule Evid. 304(c)(3) (generally barring use of statements obtained "through the use of coercion, unlawful influence, or unlawful inducement"); 10 U.S.C. §831(d) (same). Besides, even if evidence is deemed nonprobative by the presiding officer at Hamdan's trial, the military-commission members still may view it. In another departure from court-martial practice the military commission members may object to the presiding officer's evidence rulings and determine themselves, by majority vote, whether to admit the evidence. MCO No. 1, §6(D)(1); *cf.* R. C. M. 801(a)(4), (e)(1) (providing that the military judge at a court-martial determines all questions of law).

As the Court explains, the Government has made no demonstration of practical need for these special rules and procedures, either in this particular case or as to the military commissions in general, nor is any such need self-evident. For all the Government's regulations and submissions reveal, it would be feasible for most, if not all, of the conventional military evidence rules and procedures to be followed.

In sum, as presently structured, Hamdan's military commission exceeds the bounds Congress has placed on the President's authority in §§ 836 and 821 of the UCMJ. Because Congress has prescribed these limits, Congress can change them, requiring a new analysis consistent with the Constitution and other governing laws. At this time, however, we must apply the standards Congress has provided. By those standards the military commission is deficient.

III

In light of the conclusion that the military commission here is unauthorized under the UCMJ, I see no need to consider several further issues addressed in the plurality opinion by Justice Stevens and the dissent by Justice Thomas.

First, I would not decide whether Common Article 3's standard—a "regularly constituted court affording all the judicial guarantees which are recognized as indispensable by civilized peoples," 6 U.S. T., at 3320 (para. (1)(d))—necessarily requires that the accused have the right to be present at all stages of a criminal trial. As Justice Stevens explains, Military Commission Order No. 1 authorizes exclusion of the accused from the proceedings if the presiding officer determines that, among other things, protection of classified information so requires. See §§ 6(B)(3), (D)(5)....

I likewise see no need to address the validity of the conspiracy charge against Hamdan—an issue addressed at length in Part V of Justice Stevens' opinion.... Finally, for the same reason, I express no view on the merits of other limitations on military commissions described as elements of the common law of war in Part V of Justice Stevens' opinion....

With these observations I join the Court's opinion with the exception of Parts V and VI-D-iv.

Scalia, J., with whom Thomas, J. and Alito, J. join dissenting.

On December 30, 2005, Congress enacted the Detainee Treatment Act (DTA). It unambiguously provides that, as of that date, "no court, justice, or judge" shall have jurisdiction to consider the habeas application of a Guantanamo Bay detainee. Notwithstanding this plain directive, the Court today concludes that, on what it calls the statute's most natural reading, every "court, justice, or judge" before whom such a habeas application was pending on December 30 has jurisdiction to hear, consider, and render judgment on it. This conclusion is patently erroneous. And even if it were not, the jurisdiction supposedly retained should, in an exercise of sound equitable discretion, not be exercised....

... Because of "military necessity," a joint session of Congress authorized the President to "use all necessary and appropriate force," including military commissions, "against those nations, organizations, or persons [such as petitioner] he determines planned, authorized, committed, or aided the terrorist attacks that occurred on September 11, 2001." Authorization for Use of Military Force, § 2(a), 115 Stat. 224, note following 50 U.S.C. § 1541 (2000 ed., Supp. III). In keeping with this authority, the President has determined that "[t]o protect the United States and its citizens, and for the effective conduct of military operations and prevention of terrorist attacks, it is necessary for individuals subject to this order ... to be detained, and, when tried, to be tried for violations of the laws of war and other applicable laws by military tribunals." Military Order of Nov. 13, 2001, 3 CFR § 918(e) (2002)....

Thomas, J., with whom Scalia, J. joins, and with whom Alito, J. joins in all but Parts I, II-C-1, and III-B-2, dissenting.

For the reasons set forth in Justice Scalia's dissent, it is clear that this Court lacks jurisdiction to entertain petitioner's claims.... The Court having concluded otherwise, it is appropriate to respond to the Court's resolution of the merits of petitioner's claims because its opinion openly flouts our well-established duty to respect the Executive's judgment in matters of military operations and foreign affairs. The Court's evident belief that it is qualified to pass on the "[m]ilitary necessity," ... of the Commander in Chief's decision to employ a particular form of force against our enemies is so antithetical to our constitutional structure that it simply cannot go unanswered. I respectfully dissent.

I

Our review of petitioner's claims arises in the context of the President's wartime exercise of his commander-in-chief authority in conjunction with the complete support of Congress....

... As a plurality of the Court observed in *Hamdi*, the "capture, detention, and trial of unlawful combatants, by 'universal agreement and practice,' are 'important incident[s] of war,'" *Hamdi*, 542 U.S., at 518 (quoting *Quirin, supra*, at 28, 30 ...), and are therefore "an exercise of the 'necessary and appropriate force' Congress has authorized the President to use." *Hamdi*, 542 U.S., at 518; *id.*, at 587 (Thomas, J., dissenting). *Hamdi* 's observation that military commissions are included within the AUMF's authorization is supported by this Court's previous recognition that "[a]n important incident to the conduct of war is the adoption of measures by the military commander, not only to repel and defeat the enemy, but to seize and subject to disciplinary measures those enemies who, in their attempt to thwart or impede our military effort, have violated the law of war." *In re* Yamashita, 327 U.S. 1, 11 ... (1946); *see also Quirin, supra*, at 28–29; Madsen v. Kinsella, 343 U.S. 341, 354, n.20 ... (1952) ("'[T]he military commission ... is an institution of the greatest importance in the period of war and should be preserved'" (quoting S.Rep. No. 229, 63d Cong., 2d Sess., 53 (1914) (testimony of Gen. Crowder))).

... Accordingly, congressional authorization for military commissions pertaining to the instant conflict derives not only from Article 21 of the UCMJ, but also from the more recent, and broader, authorization contained in the AUMF....

Notes and Questions

1. Concerning the fact that the 1949 Geneva Conventions create individual rights, see (in addition to the Court's footnotes 57–58), Chapter Eight; Paust, *Judicial Power To Determine the Status and Rights of Persons Detained Without Trial*, 43 HARV. INT'L L.J. 503, 515–16 & n.43 (2003) [hereinafter Paust, *Judicial Power*].

2. Concerning application of common Article 2 of the Geneva Conventions and the customary laws of war in the theaters of war in Afghanistan and Iraq (even with respect to treatment of members of al Qaeda), points that the Court did not address, see Chapter Eight. The Court notes, however, that today common Article 3 reflects a customary set of minimum rights and protections even during an international armed conflict. *See* the Court's footnote 63. See also Paust, *Executive Plans and Authorizations to Violate International Law Concerning Treatment and Interrogation of Detainees*, 43 COLUMBIA J. TRANSNAT'L L. 811, 816 & n.19 (2005).

3. What role does Article 36 of the UCMJ (10 U.S.C. § 836) play in limiting the President's power to set up military commissions?

4. In dissent, Justice Alito stated:

"Common Article 3 thus imposes three requirements. Sentences may be imposed only by (1) a 'court' (2) that is 'regularly constituted' and (3) that affords 'all the judicial guarantees which are recognized as indispensable by civilized peoples.'...

"I see no need here to comment extensively on the meaning of the first and third requirements. The first requirement is largely self-explanatory, and, with respect to the third, I note only that on its face it imposes a uniform international standard that does not vary from signatory to signatory.

"The second element ('regularly constituted') is the one on which the Court relies, and I interpret this element to require that the court be appointed or established in accordance with the appointing country's domestic law. I agree with the Court ... that, as used in Common Article 3, the term 'regularly' is synonymous with 'properly.'...

"In order to determine whether a court has been properly appointed, set up, or established, it is necessary to refer to a body of law that governs such matters. I interpret Common Article 3 as looking to the domestic law of the appointing country because I am not aware of any international law standard regarding the way in which such a court must be appointed, set up, or established, and because different countries with different government structures handle this matter differently. Accordingly, 'a regularly constituted court' is a court that has been appointed, set up, or established in accordance with the domestic law of the appointing country."

Do you agree? When interpreting an international treaty, customary international law is a necessary background. *See, e.g.*, Vienna Convention on the Law of Treaties, art. 31(3)(c). Customary international law requires that a criminal justice system provide the right, among others, to have one's conviction and sentence reviewed by a competent, independent, and impartial higher tribunal according to law. *See, e.g.*, International Covenant on Civil and Political Rights, art. 14(5); Leila Nadya Sadat, The International Criminal Court and the Transformation of International Criminal Law 241, 150–51 (2002); Jordan J. Paust, *Antiterrorism Military Commissions: The Ad Hoc DOD Rules of Procedure*, 23 Mich. J. Int'l L. 677, 685–86 (2002) (also addressing the various procedural concerns noted in the Court's majority opinion, but from the perspective of customary and treaty-based international law); Paust, *Antiterrorism Military Commissions: Courting Illegality*, 23 Mich. J. Int'l L. 1, 10–11, 15 (2001) [hereinafter *Courting Illegality*]. This requirement was not provided for by the President's Order creating the military commissions.

As the majority opinion recognizes, common Article 3 incorporates by reference due process requirements reflected in customary international law. *See also Courting Illegality, supra* at 7 n.15, 12 n.26; Paust, *Judicial Power, supra* at 511 n.27. Consideration of the minimum due process requirements under customary international law reflected in Article 14 of the International Covenant on Civil and Political Rights is found in Chapter Six, Section 5.

5. Justice Alito also stated: "Article 66 [of the Geneva Civilian Convention] permits an occupying power to try civilians in its 'properly constituted, non-political military courts,' 6 U.S. T., at 3558. The commentary on this provision states:

'The courts are to be "regularly constituted". This wording definitely excludes all special tribunals. It is the ordinary military courts of the Occupying Power which will be competent.' 4 Int'l Comm. of Red Cross, Commentary: Geneva Convention Relative to the Protection of Civilian Persons in Time of War 340 (1958)....

"If 'special' means anything in contradistinction to 'regular,' it would be in the sense of 'special' as 'relating to a single thing,' and 'regular' as 'uniform in course, practice, or occurrence.'"

Knowing that the President's Order created military commissions that expressly applied only to alien defendants and, more particularly, only to members of al Qaeda or to those who engaged in or participated in terrorist activities against the U.S., do you think that the commissions were "special" and not "regular"? Do you think that they were to be "the ordinary military courts of the Occupying Power" (*i.e.*, the ordinary military courts of the United States) within the meaning of GC art. 66? After *Hamdan*, could Congress constitute a military commission that has jurisdiction only over certain aliens ever be "regularly constituted"?

6. Congress created the Military Commissions Act in 2006 and revised the legislation in 2009. This is the basis for prosecutions at GTMO since 2012. Are military commissions under such legislation "regularly constituted" or are they created *post hoc*? Are they "special courts" because they apply only for prosecution of certain aliens and with respect to certain violations of the laws of war? See also Jordan J. Paust, *Still Unlawful: The Obama Military Commissions, Supreme Court Holdings, and Deviant Dicta in the D.C. Circuit*, 45 CORNELL INT'L L.J. 367 (2012).

C. Courts-Martial

Calley v. Callaway
519 F.2d 184 (5th Cir. 1975), *cert. denied*, 425 U.S. 911 (1975)

Ainsworth, J.

In this habeas corpus proceeding we review the conviction by military court-martial of Lieutenant William L. Calley, Jr., the principal accused in the My Lai incident in South Vietnam, where a large number of defenseless old men, women and children were systematically shot and killed by Calley and other American soldiers in what must be regarded as one of the most tragic chapters in the history of this nation's armed forces.

Petitioner Calley was charged on September 5, 1969, under the Uniform Code of Military Justice, 10 U.S.C. § 801 *et seq.*, with the premeditated murder on March 16, 1968 of not less than 102 Vietnamese civilians at My Lai (4) hamlet, Song My village, Quang Ngai province, Republic of South Vietnam.[1] The trial by general court-martial began on November 12, 1970, at Fort Benning, Georgia, and the court members received the case on March 16, 1971. (The function of court members in a military court-martial is substantially equivalent to that of jurors in a civil court.) On March 29, 1971, the court-martial, whose members consisted of six Army officers, found Calley guilty of the premeditated murder of not fewer that 22 Vietnamese civilians of undetermined age and sex, and of as-

---

1. There was a Charge and an Additional Charge against Calley, each of which contained two Specifications. Specification 1 under the Charge accused Calley of the premeditated murder of not less that 30 Oriental human beings; Specification 2 accused him of the premeditated murder of not less than 70 Oriental human beings. Specification 1 under the Additional Charge accused Calley of the premeditated of one Oriental male human being; Specification 2 accused him of the premeditated murder of one Oriental human being approximately two years old, whose name and sex are unknown.

sault with intent to murder one Vietnamese child.[2] Two days later, on March 31, 1971, the court members sentenced Calley to dismissal from the service, forfeiture of all pay and allowances, and to confinement at hard labor for life. On August 20, 1971, the convening authority, the Commanding General of Fort Benning, Georgia, approved the findings and sentence except as to the confinement period which was reduced to twenty years. See Article 64 of the Uniform Code of Military Justice (U.C.M.J.), 10 U.S.C. sec. 864. The Army Court of Military Review then affirmed the conviction and sentence. *United States v. Calley*, 46 C.M.R. 1131 (1973).[3] The United States Court of Military Appeals granted a petition for review as to certain of the assignments of error, and then affirmed the decision of the Court of Military Review. *United States v. Calley*, 22 U.S.C.M.A. 534, 48 C.M.R. 19 (1973); see Art. 67(b)(3), U.C.M.J., 10 U.S.C. sec. 867(b)(3).[4] The Secretary of the Army reviewed the sentence as required by Art. 71(b), U.C.M.J., 10 U.S.C. sec. 871(b), approved the findings and sentence, but in a separate clemency action commuted the confinement portion of the sentence to ten years. On May 3, 1974 President Richard Nixon notified the Secretary of the Army that he had reviewed the case and determined that he would take no further action in the matter.[5]

On February 11, 1974, Calley filed a petition for a writ of habeas corpus in the United States District Court for the Middle District of Georgia against the Secretary of the Army and the Commanding General, Fort Benning, Georgia. At that time, the district court enjoined respondents from changing the place of Calley's custody or increasing the conditions of his confinement. On February 27, 1974, the district court ordered that Calley be released on bail pending his habeas corpus application. On June 13, 1974, this Court reversed the district court's orders, returning Calley to the Army's custody. *Calley v. Callaway*, 5 Cir., 1974, 496 F.2d 701. On September 25, 1974, District Judge Elliott granted Calley's petition for a writ of habeas corpus and ordered his immediate release. The Army appealed and Calley cross-appealed. At the Army's request a temporary stay of the district judge's order of immediate release was granted by a single judge of this Court. See Rule 27(c), Fed.R.App.P. This Court subsequently met *en banc*, upheld the release of Calley pending appeal, and ordered *en banc* consideration of the case. We reverse the district court's order granting a writ of habeas corpus and reinstate the judgment of the court-martial.[6]

I. Summary of the Facts

On March 16, 1968, in the small hamlet of My Lai, in South Vietnam, scores of unarmed, unresisting Vietnamese civilians were summarily executed by American soldiers.

---

2. The findings of the court members as to the charges were as follows: (1) under Specification 1 of the Charge, guilty of the premeditated murder of not less than one person; (2) under Specification 2 of the Charge, guilty of the premeditated murder of not less than 20 persons; (3) under Specification 1 of the Additional Charge, guilty as charged; (4) under Specification 2 of the Additional Charge, guilty of assault with intent to commit murder. Tr. at 5044.

3. The Court of Military Review is established by the Judge Advocate General, with one or more panels composed of three appellate military judges. See Art. 66, U.C.M.J., 10 U.S.C. sec. 866.

4. The Court of Military Appeals is established under article I of the U.S. Constitution and consists of three civilian judges appointed by the President. See Art. 67, U.C.M.J., 10 U.S.C. sec. 867.

5. [Editors' note: President Nixon had already ordered Calley's release from the stockade at Ft. Benning, Georgia, so that Calley would live in his bachelor officer quarters on post, with his girl friend, awaiting appeals. After exhaustion of all appeals, including the *habeas* petition, the Secretary of the Army released Calley on parole in 1974.]

6. The Army has granted Calley's application for parole and he has been released from confinement. This fact, however, does not deprive the federal courts of habeas corpus jurisdiction, for a person on parole is "in custody" for purposes of habeas corpus jurisdiction. *Jones v. Cunningham*, 371 U.S. 236 (1963). *See also* 28 U.S.C. sec. 2253, which grants this court jurisdiction to review on appeal the final order in a habeas corpus proceeding before a district judge.

A number of American soldiers were charged[7] but only First Lieutenant William Calley was convicted of murder in what has been called the My Lai incident and also the My Lai Massacre. The facts, which are largely undisputed, are set forth in considerable detail in the written opinions of the military courts, and will be summarized only to the extent necessary for our purposes.[8]

Lieutenant Calley, was the 1st platoon leader in C Company, 1st Battalion, 20th Infantry, 11th Light Infantry Brigade, and had been stationed in Vietnam since December of 1967. Prior to March 16, 1968, his unit had received little combat experience. On March 15, members of the unit were briefed that they were to engage the enemy in an offensive action in the area of My Lai (4). The troops were informed that the area had long been controlled by the Viet Cong, and that they could expect heavy resistance from a Viet Cong battalion which might outnumber them by more than two to one. The objective of the operation was to seize the hamlet and destroy all that could be useful to the enemy.

The attack began early in the morning of March 16. Calley's platoon was landed on the outskirts of My Lai after about five minutes of artillery and gunship fire. After cautiously approaching My Lai (4), C Company discovered only unarmed, unresisting old men, women and children eating breakfast or beginning the day's chores although intelligence reports had indicated the villagers would be gone to market. Encountering only civilians and no enemy soldiers, Calley's platoon, which was to lead the sweep through the hamlet, quickly became disorganized. Some soldiers undertook the destruction of livestock, foodstuffs and buildings as ordered. Others collected and evacuated the Vietnamese civilians and then proceeded systematically to slaughter the villagers.

Specification 1 of the first charge against Calley stemmed from events occurring at a collection point for civilians along a trail in the southern part of My Lai (4). This charge was also first in time of the charges against Calley. The remaining charges and specifications also followed in chronological sequence. The initial charge, with two specifications, related to two separate group killings at different locations. Private First Class Meadlo was guarding a group of between 30 and 40 unarmed old men, women and children at the trail location. Calley approached Meadlo and told him, "You know what to do," and left. Meadlo continued to stand guard over the villagers. Calley returned and yelled at Meadlo, "Why haven't you wasted them yet?" Meadlo replied that he thought Calley had meant merely to watch the villagers. Calley replied, "No, I mean kill them." First Calley and then Meadlo opened fire on the group, until all but a few children fell. Calley then

---

7. Information in the record, particularly in the volumes containing newspaper clippings and magazine articles, shows that a total of 12 infantrymen were formally charged with violations of the U.C.M.J. for their part in the My Lai incident. Some of these individuals went to trial and were acquitted, while the charges against others were dropped. A number of soldiers participating in the My Lai incident (as many as 22) could not be charged by the Army as they were civilians and no longer amenable to trial by court-martial for the acts while in uniform, under *Toth v. Quarles*, 350 U.S. 11 (1955).

8. The Army Court of Military Review was required to evaluate both the facts and all legal challenges raised by Calley. Article 66(c), U.C.M.J., 10 U.S.C. sec. 866(c) provides that the Court of Military Review

> may affirm only such findings of guilty, and the sentence or such part or amount of the sentence, as it finds correct in law and in fact and determines, on the basis of the entire record, should be approved. In considering the record, it may weigh the evidence, judge the credibility of witnesses, and determine controverted questions of fact, recognizing that the trial court saw and heard the witnesses.

The Court of Military Review, pursuant to Art. 67(b), U.C.M.J., 10 U.S.C. sec. 867(b), granted review of three of the 30 issues urged by petitioner on appeal. One of the issues considered by the Court of Military Appeals was the sufficiency of the evidence.

personally shot the remaining children. In the process, Calley expended four or five magazines from his M-16 rifle. Calley was charged with premeditated murder of not less than 30 human beings as a result of the killings at this location. Although numerous bodies, about 20, were shown at this point by photographs introduced in evidence, a pathologist testified that he could point to only one wound on one body which, in his opinion, was certain to have been instantly fatal. The court members found Calley guilty under this specification of the murder of not less than one human being.

After the killings along the trail at the southern edge of My Lai (4), Calley proceeded to the eastern portion of the hamlet. There, along an irrigation ditch, another and larger group of villagers was being held by soldiers. Meadlo estimated the group contained from 75 to 100 persons, consisting of old men, women and children. Calley then ordered Meadlo, stating: "We got another job to do, Meadlo." The platoon members with their weapons then began pushing these people into the ditch. They were yelling and crying as they knelt and squatted in the ditch. Calley ordered the start of firing into the people and he with Meadlo and others joined in the killing. Private First Class Dursi refused to follow Calley's order that he assist with the executions; he testified, "I couldn't go through with it. These little defenseless men, women, and kids." Specialist Fourth Class Maples refused Calley's request for Maples' machine gun to be used in the killing. A number of different groups of civilians were brought to the ditch, there to be slaughtered by the soldiers at point-blank range. A helicopter pilot[9] landed his craft near the ditch, and had a discussion with Calley. The pilot was able to evacuate some of the villagers from the scene. After speaking to the pilot, Calley returned to the ditch and resumed the killing, stating, "I'm the boss here." In all, Calley supervised and participated in killings at the ditch for about forty-five minutes to an hour, and personally expended between 10 and 15 magazines of ammunition. Calley was charged with the murder of not less than 70 human beings at the ditch; the court members found him guilty of the murder of not less than 20 persons.

After the incident at the ditch, Calley and Specialist Fourth Class Sledge encountered a forty- to fifty-year old man dressed in the white robes of a monk. After questioning the man whether he was a Viet Cong, Calley shot the man in the face, blowing half his head away. The court found Calley guilty of the premeditated murder of one male human being, as charged.

Sledge testified that immediately after the shooting of the monk:

> Someone hollered, "there's a child," you know, running back toward the village. Lieutenant Calley ran back, the little—I don't know if it was a girl or a boy— but it was a little baby, and he grabbed it by the arm and threw it into the ditch and fired.

Sledge stated he observed this from a distance of 20–30 feet. He testified one shot was fired by Calley at the child from a distance of 4 or 5 feet, but did not see whether it struck. Calley was charged with the premeditated murder of one human being approximately two years old; the court members found him guilty of assault with intent to commit murder on this charge. A total of two to four hours had elapsed between the time the attack on My Lai (4) began and the killing of the villagers was completed.

At trial and on appeal to the military courts, Calley's participation in most of the killings was conceded—those at both the trail and the ditch. Calley admitted ordering Meadlo to kill the villagers at the trail, and admitted that he fired into the people at the ditch with

---

9. [Editors' note: *See* TRENT ANGERS, THE FORGOTTEN HERO OF MY LAI: THE HUGH THOMPSON STORY (1999), also listing names of 504 people killed, *id.* at 223–26.

his gun's muzzle within 5 feet of the people kneeling or squatting there. He denied killing the monk, stating he merely "buttstroked" the man in the face with the butt of his rifle, and also denied killing the two-year-old child. The major emphasis of Calley's defense was that he was not legally responsible for the killings because there was an absence of malice on his part, that he thought he was performing his duty in the operation, having been ordered by Captain Medina to kill everyone in the village. Calley's principal defense, therefore, was his claim that the night before the attack on My Lai (4) and two times by radio while he was present in the village, he had received orders from Captain Medina to kill all villagers the soldiers encountered. Captain Medina, who was called at the request of the court members, stated that during the briefing on the night of March 15 he was asked by someone specifically whether women and children were to be killed. He testified that his answer was:

> No, you do not kill women and children. You must use common sense. If they have a weapon and are trying to engage you, then you can shoot back, but you must use common sense.

There was considerable dispute at the trial about this statement. Twenty of the 27 persons who were members of Calley's platoon on March 16 testified at the trial, along with others who were present at the briefing. Some stated that Medina's answer to the question was, "Yes, it means women and children," while most of these witnesses, however, had no recollection of orders by Medina at the briefing to kill women and children. The findings of guilty of the court members resolved what was a classic jury issue.

Calley further claimed that he had received orders by radio directing him to dispose of the Vietnamese and get on to other duties during the day of March 16 while he was in My Lai (4). Calley's testimony in this regard was not substantiated by the two persons who acted as radio operators to Captain Medina on March 16. One of the operators stated he had no recollection either way regarding such orders. The other operator stated positively that no orders to kill or waste civilians went out over the unit radio to Calley. Moreover, even if Calley had received the orders as claimed, he would not necessarily have been exonerated. The military judge properly instructed that an order to kill unresisting Vietnamese would be an illegal order, and that if Calley knew the order was illegal or should have known it was illegal, obedience to an order was not a valid defense. Thus, the military jury could have found either that the alleged order to kill was not issued, or, if it was, that the order was not a defense to the charges. The military courts found ample evidence to support either hypothesis.

With this review of the facts, we turn to the issues on appeal. District Judge Elliott's extensive written opinion concluded that Calley was entitled to a writ of habeas corpus for four principal reasons: (1) prejudicial pretrial publicity concerning the My Lai incident and Calley's participation therein deprived him of an opportunity to receive a fair and impartial trial; (2) the military judge's failure to subpoena certain witnesses requested by the defense deprived Calley of his right of confrontation and compulsory process and deprived him of due process; (3) the refusal of the House of Representatives to release testimony to the defense taken in executive session in its My Lai investigation deprived Calley of due process; and (4) the Charges, Specifications and Bill of Particulars under which Calley was tried did not adequately notify him of the charges against him nor fully protect him against possible double jeopardy.

II. Scope of Review of Court-Martial Convictions

We must first consider the extent to which a federal court is empowered to review court-martial convictions on petitions for habeas corpus. The Government contends that the district court exercised an impermissibly broad scope of review of Calley's claims. Relying on *Burns v. Wilson*, 346 U.S. 137 (1953), the Government argues that review by the federal courts is complete after a determination that the military courts have fully and fairly considered Calley's claims, and that, since that has been accomplished by the military courts, further review by way of habeas corpus proceedings is not appropriate.

A brief historical outline is helpful to a determination of this question. The first military habeas corpus case to reach the Supreme Court was *Ex parte Reed*, 100 U.S. 13 (1879). *Reed* held that a federal civil court's inquiry into a military court-martial conviction could extend only so far as to ascertain whether the military court was properly vested with jurisdiction "over the person and the case.... Having had such jurisdiction, its proceedings cannot be collaterally impeached for any mere error or irregularity, if there were such, committed within the sphere of its authority." 100 U.S. at 23. Subsequent Supreme Court decisions followed the jurisdictional test and emphasized that the scope of inquiry for federal courts was limited to whether the court-martial was properly constituted, whether it had jurisdiction over the person and the offense charged, and whether the sentence was authorized by law....

In general, federal courts would not consider due process attacks on court-martial convictions in habeas proceedings if it appeared that the military court properly possessed jurisdiction when it made its decision....

World War II provided an important impetus for federal courts to broaden habeas corpus review of military cases. When millions of persons suddenly became subject to military justice, greater concern seemed essential. As Chief Justice Warren said in this regard, "When the authority of the military has such a sweeping capacity for affecting the lives of our citizenry, the wisdom of treating the military establishment as an enclave beyond the reach of civilian courts almost inevitably is drawn into question." Warren, *supra*, 37 N.Y.U.L.Rev. at 188. *See also* Generous, Swords and Scales: The Development of the Uniform Code of Military Justice 14–15, 167–169 (1973). Military law thus had a breadth and impact not previously possessed, requiring greater supervision over the actions of courts-martial. More importantly, there was public concern over the harsh justice and severe sanctions employed by the military during the war. See Bishop, *supra* at 117–118; Generous, *supra*, at 14–21.

Thus federal courts, having expanded collateral attack in civilian habeas corpus cases, were confronted with new pleas by military defendants that the courts give cognizance to allegations that their convictions were invalid by virtue of constitutional, if not jurisdictional, deficiencies....

Determining the Proper Scope of Review

The cited cases establish the power of federal courts to review court-martial convictions to determine whether the military acted within is proper jurisdictional sphere. We are more concerned here, however, with the extent to which federal courts may review the validity of claims that error in the military trial deprived the accused of due process of law, when the military courts have previously considered and rejected the same contentions. We conclude from an extensive research of the case law that the power of federal courts to review military convictions of a habeas petition depends on the nature of the issues raised, and in this determination, four principal inquiries are necessary.

1. The asserted error must be of a substantial constitutional dimension....

Most habeas corpus cases have provided relief only where it has been established that errors of constitutional dimension have occurred. But the Supreme Court held in a recent decision that nonconstitutional errors of law can be raised in habeas corpus proceedings where "the claimed error of law was 'a fundamental defect which inherently results in a complete miscarriage of justice,'" and when the alleged error of law "'present[ed] exceptional circumstances where the need for the remedy afforded by the writ of habeas corpus is apparent.'" *Davis v. United States*, 417 U.S. 333, 346 (1974), *quoting Hill v. United States* 368 U.S. 424, 428 (1962). Thus, an essential prerequisite of any court-martial error we are asked to review is that it present a substantial claim of constitutional dimension, or that the error be so fundamental as to have resulted in a gross miscarriage of justice.

2. The issue must be one of law rather than of disputed fact already determined by the military tribunals. The second inquiry is whether the issue raised is basically a legal question, or whether resolution of the issue hinges on disputed issues of fact....

3. Military considerations may warrant different treatment of constitutional claims. The third inquiry is whether factors peculiar to the military or important military considerations require a different constitutional standard. Where a serviceman's assertion of constitutional rights has been determined by military tribunals, and they have concluded that the serviceman's position, if accepted, would have a foreseeable adverse effect on the military mission, federal courts should not substitute their judgment for that of the military courts. In this regard the Supreme Court stated in *Burns* that the law of civilian habeas corpus could not be assimilated to the law governing military habeas corpus because military law is *sui generis*. 346 U.S. at 139–140. This point was reemphasized in *Schlesinger v. Councilman*, 420 U.S. 738 (1975):

> This Court repeatedly has recognized that, of necessity, "[m]ilitary law ... is a jurisprudence which exists separate and apart from the law which governs in our federal judicial establishment." *Burns v. Wilson*, 346 U.S. 137, 140 (1953); *Parker v. Levy*, 417 U.S. 733, 744 (1974).

Id. at 746. *See also Parker v. Levy*, 417 U.S. 733, 758 (1974), where the Court noted that "[t]he fundamental necessity for obedience, and the consequent necessity for imposition of discipline, may render permissible within the military that which would be constitutionally impermissible outside it." The Supreme Court in *Burns* emphasized that "the rights of men in the armed forces must perforce be conditioned to meet certain overriding demands of discipline and duty, and the civil courts are not the agencies which must determine the precise balance to be struck in this adjustment." 346 U.S. at 140....

There are other reasons why federal courts should not intervene in basically military matters. Congress, with its power to create and maintain the armed forces and to declare war, and the President, with his power as Commander-in-Chief, have great powers and responsibilities in military affairs. Congress has a substantial role to play in defining the rights of military personnel, see *Burns, supra*, 346 U.S. at 140, and by enactment of the Uniform Code of Military Justice and the Military Justice Act of 1968 it has assumed that responsibility. *See also Schlesinger v. Councilman, supra*; *Hammond v. Lenfest*, 2 Cir., 1968, 398 F.2d 705, 710. A related reason is that an independent appellate court, the Court of Military Appeals composed of nonmilitary judges, has been established to review military convictions. That court has reaffirmed the fundamental premise that "the protections in the Bill of Rights, except those which are expressly or by necessary implication inapplicable, are available to members of our armed forces." *United States v. Jacoby*, 11 U.S.C.M.A. 428, 430–431, 29 C.M.R. 244 (1960); *see also United States v. Tempia*, 16 U.S.C.M.A. 629, 633, 37 C.M.R. 249 (1967); *United States v. Culp*, 14 U.S.C.M.A. 199, 33 C.M.R. 411 (1963); *Bishop, supra*, 61 Colum.L.Rev. at 56, 65–66. The Court of Military Appeals has, in many instances, extended the constitutional rights of servicemen beyond those accorded to civilians. Safeguarding the serviceman's rights is frequently best left to a body with special knowledge of the military system. *Schlesinger v. Councilman, supra*, 420 U.S. at 757.

4. The military courts must give adequate consideration to the issues involved and apply proper legal standards....

To summarize, the scope of review may be stated as follows:

Military court-martial convictions are subject to collateral review by federal civil courts on petitions for writs of habeas corpus where it is asserted that the court-martial acted without jurisdiction, or that substantial constitutional rights have been violated, or that exceptional circumstances have been presented which are so fundamentally defective as to result in a miscarriage of justice. Consideration by the military of such issues will not preclude judicial review for the military must accord to its personnel the protections of basic constitutional rights essential to a fair trial and the guarantee of due process of law. The scope of review for violations of constitutional rights, however, is more narrow than in civil cases. Thus federal courts should differentiate between questions of fact and law and review only questions of law which present substantial constitutional issues. Accordingly, they may not retry the facts or reevaluate the evidence, their function in this regard being limited to determining whether the military has fully and fairly considered contested factual issues. Moreover, military law is a jurisprudence which exists separately and apart from the law governing civilian society so that what is permissible within the military may be constitutionally impermissible outside it. Therefore, when the military courts have determined that factors peculiar to the military require a different application of constitutional standards, federal courts are reluctant to set aside such decisions....

Notice and Double Jeopardy

The district court also held that the Charges, Specifications and Bill of Particulars under which Calley was tried did not adequately notify him of the charges against him nor fully protect him against the possibility of double jeopardy. The court apparently found fair notice problems in the fact that the first and second Specifications of the Original Charge against Calley (the killings at the trail in the southern part of the hamlet and at the ditch in the eastern portion) covered multiple unnamed victims in a single specification. The double jeopardy problem discerned by the court was two-fold. First, quoting a hypothetical situation posed by Calley's counsel, the district court found that there was a risk that Calley might have been twice convicted for killing the same individual within the same trial. See 382 F. Supp. at 710. Second, the district court speculated that Calley might again be charged for other killings in Vietnam and might not be able accurately to plead former conviction. We find no merit in these conclusions.

Fair notice and double jeopardy issues involve requirements of both the Fifth and Sixth Amendments. See *United States v. Sanchez*, 5 Cir., 1975, 508 F.2d 388, 395. The Constitution requires that criminal charges be sufficiently specific (1) to apprise the defendant of what he must be prepared to meet at trial, and (2) to enable the defendant to show with accuracy the extent to which he may plead former acquittal or conviction in other proceedings brought against him for a similar offense. *Russell v. United States*, 369 U.S. 749, 763–764 (1962) and cases cited. We are satisfied that the charges against Calley, as amplified in the Bill of Particulars, met these requirements.

The charges set forth the time and place of the alleged offense. Under the Bill of Particulars, the prosecution set for the chronological sequence of the separate charges: the killings at the trail occurred first, followed by the killings at the ditch, and next followed by the murder of the monk and then the child. The Bill of Particulars specified the actual physical location: the killings at the trail were in the southern portion of the village, those at the ditch occurred in the eastern part of My Lai (4). The instructions of the military judge were detailed and thorough, and required the prosecution's proof to conform to these allegations in the Bill of Particulars. The killings of the monk and the child, for example, were required to be proven as occurring in sequence after the mass killings at the ditch. The effect of Judge Kennedy's instructions is most evident with regard to the alleged killings at the trail. While there was substantial evidence of extensive participation by Calley in the slaying of the estimated 30–40 persons at this location, the court members returned a verdict of guilty for "not less that one" murder. This was no doubt due to the instructions and the testimony of a pathologist that he could point to only one wound on one body which he was certain to have been instantly fatal. Also, in considering the fair notice requirement, we mention again that Calley did not deny his involvement and participation in the mass killings at the ditch and the trail. It is difficult to understand how a defendant is deprived of fair notice of the charges against him when he confirms that the alleged incidents happened and that he participated in them. We are convinced that there was no failure to provide Calley fair notice of the charges against him, nor is there any likelihood that there will be any double jeopardy problems.

Petitioner Calley's Cross Appeal

Calley urged several additional contentions before the district court which the district judge did not discuss in his opinion. Among these was Calley's contention that the Army lacked jurisdiction over his person because he was improperly retained on active duty by the Army beyond his scheduled separation date of September 6, 1969, and that the military has no authority to court-martial a serviceman after the date of his scheduled separation by so retaining him on active duty. We agree, however, with the Government that Calley was lawfully retained in active duty status, and that military jurisdiction having properly attached prior to September 6, 1969, it continued until disposition of the case. See 46 C.M.R. at 1138–1142. We have carefully considered Calley's other contentions and, in light of our discussion of the proper scope of review in part II, *supra*, conclude that the additional issues presented for review are beyond the scope of review of the federal courts.

Conclusion

This Court is convinced that Lieutenant Calley received a fair trial from the military court-martial which convicted him for the premeditated murder of numerous Vietnamese civilians at My Lai. The military courts have fully and fairly considered all of the defenses made by him and have affirmed that he is guilty. We are satisfied after a careful and painstaking review of this case that no violation of Calley's constitutional or fundamental rights has occurred, and that the findings of guilt were returned by impartial members based on the evidence presented at a fairly conducted trial.

There is no valid reason then for the federal courts to interfere with the military judgment, for Calley has been afforded every right under our American system of criminal justice to which he is entitled.

Accordingly, the order of the district court granting a writ of habeas corpus to Calley is

Reversed.

Bell, Circuit Judge, with whom Gewin, Thornberry, Morgan and Clark, Circuit Judges, join (dissenting).

Questions

1. Do you agree with the statements made in note 7 of the court's opinion? Were courts-martial available in time of war for prosecutions of war crimes as such? Compare *Reid v. Covert*, 354 U.S. 1 (1957). Were military commissions (if newly created)? At least since 1986, a member of the U.S. reserves might be ordered to active duty for trial by court martial with respect to an offense committed while previously on active duty. See 10 U.S.C. §§ 802(d), 803(a) (1986); *Murphy v. Garrett*, 29 M.J. 469 (CMA 1990).

2. Was Calley prosecuted merely for a violation of "military law"? Recall *Ex parte Quirin*.

3. Was the trial "basically [a] military matter"? merely a "military matter"?

4. Should U.S. civilians be tried by court-martial in time of war? Why? In 1957 in *Reid v. Covert*, the U.S. Supreme Court ruled that civilians cannot be tried in general courts-martial in time of peace.

D. Regular Uses of Such Fora and State Courts

Paust, *My Lai and Vietnam: Norms, Myths and Leader Responsibility*
57 Mil. L. Rev. 99, 112–17, 130–34 (1972)

The American Commitment to the International Law of War

The American experience demonstrates how widespread that consensus was in the late 18th Century, for this nation was founded with a basic respect for international law. Indeed, during the Revolutionary War itself, the American Congress showed "great solicitude to maintain inviolate the obligations of the law of nations, and to have infractions of it punished in the only way that was then lawful, by the exercise of the authority of the several states."[1] When the federation became stronger, "Congress, claiming cognizance of all matters arising upon the law of nations, professed obedience to that law 'according to the general usages of Europe.'"[2] An earlier Congressional Resolution had imposed the death penalty on alien spies "according to the law and usage of nations, by sentence of a general court-martial."[3] That power was exercised by a Board of General Officers appointed by General Washington to convict Major Andre of the British Army as a spy in violation of "the laws of war."[4] In 1794 Congress further defined "the setting on foot of a military expedition from American territory against a friendly country (filibustering) as an offense against the law of nations."[5] One year earlier the federal courts took jurisdic-

---

1. Kent's Commentaries, *supra*, at 427, *citing* 7 Journals of Congress 181; and *see* Wright, *The Law of the Nuremberg Trial*, 41 Am. J. Int'l L. 38, 259, n.66a (1947). The Continental Congress of the United States in several resolutions adopted, from 1779 to 1781, called upon States to provide for punishment of offenses against the law of nations. British soldiers had been tried in a colonial court for the Boston Massacre and defended by John Adams who obtained an acquittal.

2. Kent's Commentaries, *supra*, at 3, *citing*, Ordinance of Dec. 4, 1781, 7 Journals of Congress 185. *See also*, U.S. Const. art. 1, sec. 8, cl. 10. For prisoner practice *see* Report, Exchanges of Prisoners During the American Revolutionary War (Mass. Hist. Society 1861).

3. Resolution of August 12, 1776, *cited* at Warren, *Spies, And the Power of Congress to Subject Certain Classes of Civilians To Trial by Military Tribunal*, 53 Am. L. Rev. 195 (1919).

4. *See* Glueck, *By What Tribunal Shall War Offenders Be Tried?*, 56 Harv. L. Rev. 1059, 1064 n.13; Green, *The Military Commission*, 42 Am. J. Int'l L. 832 (1948); and Taylor at 21.

5. Wright, *The Law of the Nuremberg Trial*, *supra* note 41, at 246, *citing* 18 U.S.C. § 25 (1794).

tion over an offense against the law of nations involving the violation of principles of neutrality by a civilian, stating that though there had been no exercise of the power conferred upon Congress by the Constitution in this matter, the federal judiciary has jurisdiction.[6] There were also Congressional denunciations of the killing of our soldiers as a "gross and inhuman violation of the laws of nature and nations," and similar denunciations concerned the crime of violence against noncombatants.[7]

During the War of 1812, some stragglers from the American Army in Upper Canada needlessly burned some buildings at St. David's. The U.S. commander was summarily dismissed from the service. For a similar occurrence at Long Point the commander was "brought before a military inquiry by his own government [U.S.]."[8] And in 1818 there occurred the famous court-martial and execution of two Englishmen, Arbuthnot and Ambrister, for conduct as "accomplices of the savages" in carrying on war against the U.S. in a manner contrary to the laws and usages of war, and also in that "one of them was the mover and promoter of the war, which, without his interference and false promises to the Indians of support from the British Government, never would have happened."[9] Arbuthnot was charged and found guilty of: (1) exciting the Creek Indians to war against the U.S., and (2) aiding and comforting the enemy, and supplying them with the means of war. A murder charge was withdrawn as not within the jurisdiction of the tribunal. Ambrister was charged and found guilty of levying war against the United States by taking command of hostile Indians and ordering a party of them to give battle. General Jackson approved the findings and increased the punishment despite vocal opposition both at home and abroad. The text comments that this was "savage" warfare incited by the defendants whereby wives and children were brutally massacred, referring to an incident in 1817 when a boat of soldiers and their families was captured and survivors scalped while children were "snatched by the heels and their heads crushed by being dashed against the boat."[10] The incitement and complicity were further described as an example of inciting to armed violence against the law of nations the population of one territory (Spanish Florida) against that of another (the U.S.).[11] Today we might describe such conduct as crimes against peace, humanity, and the law of war in general.[12]

There was widespread public anger in Britain against the American trial, but the British Ministry stood behind the decision, "disregarding the first clamors of a powerful press, and first erroneous impulses of an almost universal public opinion," which might have led to war.[13] Jackson also stood behind the decision though his political opposition made the

---

6. Henfield's Case, 11 F. Cas. 1099 (No. 6,360) (Pa 1793); *see also* Paust, *After My Lai — The Case for War Crime Jurisdiction Over Civilians in Federal District Courts*, 50 Tex. L. Rev. 6 (1971). *See* United States v. Jones, 26 F. Cas. 653 (No. 15,494) (Pa. 1813), concerning the Congressionally implemented international crime of piracy.

7. *See* Winthrop at 791 n.14, 788 n.21, and 780 n.31.

8. Colby, *War Crimes*, 23 Mich. L. Rev. 482, 501–02 (1925). *See* Joint U.S., British Commission investigation of maltreatment of U.S. POWs and repatriation made in Wharton's Digest, *infra* note 9, at 331–32; and the denunciation of the burning of the Capitol and President's residence by President Madison in 1814 as a gross violation of the laws of war. *Id.* at 335–36.

9. *See* Wharton's III Digest of the International Law of the United States 326–29 (1886).

10. *Id.* at 327–28.

11. *Id. See also* President Jefferson's 4th Annual Message in 1804, *quoted* in Wharton's Digest, *supra* note 9, at 339.

12. Note that Wright, *supra* at 267 n.102, lists many examples of trials of persons "for *initiating* or *contributing to* the initiation of aggressive war in antiquity" (emphasis added). *See also id.* at 244 n.14, *citing* numerous articles on "aggressive war."

13. *Id.* at 329.

trial "a party issue" and "one of the chief grounds of opposition to General Jackson's election and to his subsequent administration."[14] America stood firm behind her early convictions of the need to follow the law of nations. During the Mexican War (1846–1848), in which "the behavior of our troops on foreign soil afforded instruction worthy to be pondered," members of the U.S. forces were rendered amenable to the law of war by virtue of General Scott's General Order No. 20.[15] However, the trials of Mexicans for breaches of the law of war seem to have outnumbered those of Americans.[16]

The Civil War brought with it the adoption of the 1863 Lieber Code and the use of the military commission for the trial of enemy belligerent and combatant and noncombatant civilians for offenses against the law of war.[17] U.S. troops were also tried and convicted but the records are scarce.[18] In 1865, however, an important pronouncement of present relevance was made:

> Under the Constitution and laws of the United States, should a commander be guilty of ... a flagrant breach of the law ... (he) would be punished after a military trial. The many honorable gentlemen who hold commissions in the army of the United States ... would keenly feel it as an insult to their profession of arms for any one to say that they could not or would not punish a fellow-soldier who was guilty of wanton cruelty to a prisoner, or perfidy towards the bearers of a flag of truce.[19]

Apparently superior officers felt that these crimes of violence were more than mere insults to the profession, for Article 44 of the 1863 Lieber Code provided:

> A soldier, officer or private, in the act of committing such violence, and disobeying a superior ordering him to abstain from it, may be lawfully killed on the spot by such superior.

* * *

Guerilla warfare became widespread in the Mexican War (1846–1848), but during the American Civil War the debate seemed at an end. Guerrillas operating without commission from their government were denounced and subject to trial as illegal combatants. The Lieber Code of 1863 stated that men who commit hostilities without commission and who "with intermitting returns to their homes and avocations" divest themselves of the "character or appearance of soldiers," are not entitled to prisoner of war status, and "shall be treated summarily as highway robbers or pirates." In 1865 reasons for the denial

---

14. Of course, the opposition failed and General Jackson showed rare courage of conviction in the finest of American tradition which we would do well to emulate today. The trial had generally been criticized for lack of due process rather than the unjustness of the result.

15. Colby, *War Crimes*, 23 MICH. L. REV. 482, 502 (1925); and Colby, *Courts-Martial and the Law of War*, 17 AM. J. INT'L L. 109, 111 (1923).

16. *Compare* WINTHROP at 832 *with id.* at 795 n.51; and *see* 14 Op. Att'y Gen. 249, 251 (1873).

17. *See also* WINTHROP at 776, 778–79, 780, 784, n.57, 787, and 791–92, last cited concerning the trials of Captain Wirz, Mr. Duncan and Major Gee for the maltreatment of prisoners. *See also* DIG. OPS. OF THE JAG, ARMY, 1067 n.6 and 1070–72 (1912); 11 Ops. Att'y Gen. 297 (1865); and DIG. OPS. OF THE JAG, ARMY, 132, 133–41 and 245–48 (1866). Concerning the granting of amnesty *see* WHARTON'S DIGEST, *supra* note 9, at 325.

18. *See* Note, *U. S. Navy War Crimes Trials (1945–1949)*, 5 WASHBURN L.J. 89, 91 (1965); DIG. OPS. OF THE JAG, ARMY, 462 469, para 1694 (1901); and Lieber Code, arts. 11, 13, 37, 44, 47 ("if committed by an American soldier") and 71 ("Whoever ... whether he belongs to the Army of the United States, or is an enemy ..."). The general nature of the Lieber Code, itself evidencing customary international law, showed the punishment orientation as well as a preventive law approach.

19. 11 Op. Att'y Gen. 297, 303–04 (1865).

of status and summary treatment were put forward in a manner defeating the notions that guerrilla warfare is new, that the laws of war did not consider guerrilla tactics in the development of positive rules, or that prisoner status was based on jealously guarded aristocratic privilege rather than on fundamental humanitarian concepts. The Attorney General, in approving military tribunal jurisdiction over certain war crimes prosecutions, stated:

> In all wars, and especially in civil wars, secret but active enemies are almost as numerous as open ones.... The horrors of war would indeed by greatly aggravated if every individual of the belligerent states were allowed to plunder and slay indiscriminately the enemy's subjects without being in any manner accountable for his conduct. Hence it is that, in land wars, irregular bands of marauders are liable to be treated as lawless banditti, not entitled to the protection of the mitigated usages of war as practiced by civilized nations.[20]

These notions were reiterated in 1866 when it was held that "[g]uerillas are triable by military commission for a 'violation of the laws and customs of war' in the commission of acts of violence, robbery, etc."[21] ...

American trials after the Civil War were few or hard to discover. In 1868 there was a state prosecution of a civilian for murder based on international standards of culpability,[22] and in 1873 there was a military tribunal conviction of some Modoc Indians for law of war violations.[23] The 19th Century saw a few other foreign trials for violations of the laws of war,[24] but the early 20th Century saw many more.[25] As earlier stated, before World War I most felt it sufficient to have the law of war enforced by each nation's own military system,[26] and the Americans were no exception since the trial of soldiers and civilians was preferred in a U.S. court-martial.[27]

During the conflict in the Philippines, a reported forty-four officers, soldiers and "camp followers" were tried for "cruelty, looting and like crimes" in a two-year period. Major Waller was acquitted for killing eleven Filipinos partially on the basis of superior orders

---

20. 11 Op. Atty Gen. 297, 306–07 (1865). The opinion also quoted an earlier speech by Patrick Henry in the case of Josiah Phillips at the Virginia Convention as being in favor of the summary execution of banditti who do not follow the law since they are "an enemy to the human name." *Id.* at 306.

21. Dig. Ops. of the Jag, Army, 141 and 246–47 (1866); *see* Halleck, Elements of International Law and Laws of War 174–75 (1866).

22. Minnesota v. Gut, 13 Minn. R. 341 (315), 356 (Minn. 1868). John Gut was convicted for the murder of Indians after they had been captured and imprisoned; it was not a defense to the charge that he was emotionally upset due to the loss of his best friend at the hands of the particular Indians. *Cf.* lack of trial for the Sand Creek massacre in 1864, or the massacre at Wounded Knee, S.D., in 1890 by U.S. troops. Robinson, A History of the Dakota or Sioux Indians (1904).

23. *See* 14 Op. Atty Gen. 249 (1873), punishing the acts though Congress had not made them a crime by statute. *See also* Winthrop at 786 and 788 n.91.

24. *See* Mundo & Stowell, II International Cases 222 (1916); Winthrop at 843 n.35; and an 1807 Scottish case *cited* at Dunbar, *Some Aspects of the Problem of Superior Orders in the Law of War*, 63 Jurid. Rev. 234, 238 (1951).

25. *E.g.*, a Russian court-martial of two Japanese officers: Regina v. Smith (1900), reported at Stephen, *Superior Orders As Excuse for Homicide*, 17 L.Q. Rev. 87 (1901); *see* Taylor at 24; the Leipzig trials of 1921, *see* Taylor at 24; 16 Am. J. Int'l L. 674 (1922); and Mullins, the Leipzig Trials (London 1921); and French and British prosecutions after World War I, *see* Colby, *War Crimes*, 23 Mich. L. Rev. 482, 496–97, and 504 (1925), citing cases, and at 487, stating that some war criminals had been shot without trial.

26. Colby, *supra* at 500.

27. *See* Colby, *Courts-Martial and the Laws of War*, 17 Am. J. Int'l L. 109, 111–13 (1923).

and the defense of not knowing that the orders were illegal because of Article 82 of the Lieber Code (seemingly allowing summary execution). Brigadier General Jacob Smith was convicted on the charge of "conduct to the prejudice of good order and military discipline" and his sentence of a reprimand and retirement from the service was upheld by President Theodore Roosevelt.[28] What is little known is that charges were dropped against an Army captain after he left the service because (1) the court-martial had no jurisdiction over an ex-serviceman, and (2) because a military commission lost jurisdiction upon the proclamation of peace.[29]

Since then, prosecutions of U.S. troops for violations of the law of war have been in military fora and generally for violations of our domestic law as in prosecutions for military offenses under the present Uniform Code of Military Justice. Trials occurred during World War I[30] and World War II, but it would be difficult to compile an accurate record due to the labeling of cases by military offense title, *e.g.*, the killing of civilians as a domestic murder prosecution even though probably also a violation of the law of war. The record keeping does not seem to have improved. One interesting case was *United States v. Aikins and Seevers*,[31] in which the defendants were convicted of murder in violation of the law of war, the law of belligerent occupation to be exact. The defendants' terms of enlistment had expired and a court-martial could not then exercise normal jurisdiction over them due to discharge from former status. Prosecution was based on Articles 12 and 15 of the 1916 Articles of War (similar to the present UCMJ, articles 18 and 21), which allowed a prosecution based on an offense against the law of war.

Similarly during the Korean War there were prosecutions under the UCMJ for offenses likely to have been violations of the law of war as well, specifically the law of belligerent occupation.[32] By coincidence or design the result in the *Aikins* case was repeated during the Korean War in the case of *United States v. Fleming*.[33] Prosecution for offenses against the law of war was allowed despite discharge from a prior enlistment.

In Vietnam the practice has been to prosecute under the UCMJ. It was recently disclosed that some 60 servicemen have been convicted of murdering civilians in Vietnam out of 117 charged, and that sentences were reduced in 247 cases of other crimes (unknown number) against Vietnamese civilians. At least one trial resulted in a finding of guilty on a charge of "cutting off an ear from the body of an unknown dead Viet Cong soldier, which conduct was of a nature of being discredit upon the Armed Forces of the United States as a violation of the Law of War."

---

28. *See* Greider, *The Point Where War Becomes Murder*, Wash. Post, Oct. 11, 1970; and *Vietnam Precedents in a Filipino Insurgency*, Wash. Post, Apr. 13, 1971, at A18.

29. 24 Op. Att'y Gen. 570, 571 (1903).

30. As a clue to U.S. prosecutions, see U.S. Army Training Manual, 27–250, *Cases on Military Government*, 79–80 (GPO 1943), stating that crimes did occur, became of considerable concern, and that in 1919 orders were issued for the reporting and investigating of all allegations. No evidence of trials appear here. Many of the WW II cases are still classified. *See also* Taylor *Nuremberg and Vietnam: Who Is Responsible for War Crimes?*, III The Vietnam War and International Law 379 (R. Falk ed.1972).

31. 5 B.R. 331, 360–61 (ABR 1949).

32. *See, e.g.*, prosecutions for murder, rape, robbery of civilians in occupied territory: United States v. Hanson, 1 C.M.R. 141 (ABR 1951); United States v. Rushing, 1 C.M.R. 328 (ABR 1951); and United States v. Abraham, 1 C.M.R. 424 (ABR 1951). *See also* Greider, *supra* note 28.

33. 2 C.M.R. 312, 315, 318 (ABR 1951).

Notes and Questions

1. Other nation-states also prosecute alleged war criminals in domestic tribunals. Consider the following reply of the Federal Republic of Germany of July 9, 1970 to the United Nations Secretary General, reported at U.N. Doc. A/8038 (1970):

> The statistics do not show 56,705 acknowledged Nazi criminals to be leading a carefree existence in the Federal Republic of Germany. What they do show, rather, is that of the approximately 75,000 persons whose alleged part in Nazi crimes has been investigated since the end of the Second World War by German or Allied prosecuting authorities, a total of 56,705 [were innocent, not proved with certainty necessary for trial, or died].... The seeming discrepancy [6,227 convictions to date] is attributable to the fact that a very wide-ranging group of "suspects" had to be included in the initial investigations.... Furthermore, it must be noted that it is the privilege of an independent judiciary to decide cases on their merits rather than on political grounds. To increase the number of convictions because the government wants it would be a regression to the very methods which the law courts in the Federal Republic of Germany consider a crime.

In 2001, Julius Viel, an 83-year-old former Nazi SS commander, was convicted and sentenced to twelve years in prison for murdering seven Jewish detainees at the Theresienstadt concentration camp in Nazi-occupied Czechoslovakia in 1945.

2. As a further illustration, it may be noted that in 1904 a Russian court-martial convicted two Japanese officers for disguising themselves as Chinese peasants to blow up a railway bridge in Manchuria during the Russo-Japanese War. The Japanese officers were later executed for their violations of the laws of war.

In this connection, consider also the following extract from Paust, *My Lai and Vietnam, supra,* at 131–32:

> It is interesting to note the recent practice of nations concerning the granting of status and treatment of irregular combatants. In the Algerian conflict and the Kenya uprising of the Mau Mau, France and Britain seem to have granted protected status similar to that given prisoners of war to irregular troops who had generally followed the law of war themselves. Those who had engaged in the indiscriminate use of force were in many cases executed. Israel seems to have followed the same practice in the 1969 case of *The Military Prosecutor v. Omar Mahmud Kassem.*[1] There the military court considered the requirement that the guerrilla himself observe the laws of war was critical, even admitting for purposes of the decision the fulfillment of the requirement as to arms and uniforms.[2] The court stated that lawful belligerency "is incompatible with disregard of the rules and customs of war," and concluded that the accused be denied prisoner of

---

1. INSTITUTE FOR LEGISLATIVE RESEARCH AND COMPARATIVE LAW, LAW AND COURTS IN THE ISRAEL-HELD AREAS, 17 (Hebrew Univ. of Jerusalem 1970); reviewed in 65 AM. J. INT'L L. 409 (1971). *See also* MERON, SOME LEGAL ASPECTS OF ARAB TERRORISTS' CLAIMS TO PRIVILEGED COMBATANCY (1970).

2. The Israeli military court would apparently accept green outfits with caps as fulfilling the uniform requirement on the desert. For an example of the great difficulty Ceylon is having in this regard *see Ceylon's Police and Army Fight Rebels with Terror,* New York Times, Apr. 25, 1971, at 2, stating, "The insurgents were seen wearing blue trousers and shorts during their initial raids ... [t]o try to ferret them out, the police have taken to stopping young men and ordering them to take down their trousers to see if they are wearing blue shorts...."

war status because, "the Popular Front for the Liberation of Palestine acts in complete disregard of the international consuetudinary law accepted by civilized nations."[3]

See also Ex parte Quirin, 317 U.S. at 30–38.

Also in the early 1900s, England had reserved the right to try those accused of having committed war crimes during the Boer War (1899–1902) in South Africa. Consider article 4 of the Treaty of Peace Between the Orange Free State and the South African Republic with Great Britain, 31 May 1902 (95 British & Foreign State Papers 160, *reprinted in* 60 Naval War College International Law Studies, Documents on Prisoners of war 66 (H. Levie ed. 1979):

> No proceedings, civil or criminal, will be taken against any of the burghers surrendering or so returning for any acts in connection with the prosecution of the war. The benefit of this clause will not extend to certain acts, contrary to usages of war, which have been notified by the Commander-in-Chief to the Boer Generals, and which shall be tried by court-martial immediately after the close of hostilities.

3. England enacted a War Crimes Act in 1991. A former British Rail ticket collector, Mr. Sawoniuk, at the age of 78, was the first person to face trial under the Act. A jury found him guilty of having committed Nazi war crimes some 57 years ago in his former hometown of Belarus while serving with local police, he was given two life sentences, and his conviction was upheld by a court of appeal on February 10, 2000. *See* The Gloucester Citizen, Feb. 10, 2000, at 8; *Convicted War Criminal Awaits Appeal Decision*, Press Assoc. Newsfile, Feb. 10, 2000.

4. Are civil sanctions also available against violators of the law of war? With or without a statutory base? With or without mention in international law of a cause of action and/or sanctions? See *Kadic v. Karadzic*, 70 F.3d 232 (2d Cir. 1995); *see also Matter of Barbie,* in Chapter Nine, Section 3 (re: related crimes against humanity); Chapter Eight, Section 2 B; M.C. Bassiouni, A Draft International Criminal Code and Draft Statute for an International Criminal Tribunal 106–08 (1987) (civil sanctions are generally available for international crimes); Paust, *Suing Karadzic*, 10 Leiden J. Int'l L.91 (1997). Also consider the following extract from Paust, *On Human Rights: The Use of Human Right Precepts in U.S. History and the Right to an Effective Remedy in Domestic Courts*, 10 Mich. J. Int'l L. 43, 618–20 (1989) [considering *Christian County Court v. Rankin & Tharp*, 63 Ky. 502, 505–06 (1866), and other cases]:

After ruling that the burning of a courthouse by Confederate soldiers was an unlawful act of war in violation of "the law of nations," the Supreme Court of Kentucky declared:

> There must be a remedy, and of that remedy the State judiciary has jurisdiction. There is nothing in the Federal Constitution which deprives a State court of power to decide a question of international law incidentally involved in a case over which it has jurisdiction; and for every wrong the common law ... provides an adequate remedy. To sustain this action, therefore, it is not necessary to invoke any statutory aid....

---

3. Israeli opinion, *supra* at 34. The opinion dismissed the problem of applying art. 4(A)(3) of the Geneva Prisoner of War Convention in a rather unsatisfactory manner at 24. *Cf.* III Pictet at 62–64; but the 1956 U.S. Army manual would apparently allow the same conclusion though it is not clear. *See* FM 27-10, paras. 74, 80–81; but *cf.* para. 70.

Wherefore, on international and common law principles, we adjudge that the petition in this case sets forth a good cause of action....

The Kentucky court also recognized such a cause of action and right to a remedy in several other cases. In one such case the court spoke of "a right to maintain this action for adequate damages," the propriety of "civil remedies for private wrongs," and the "tortious" nature of acts of soldiers in "violation of the law of international war," adding that the soldier's "act was illegal, and he is personally responsible in this action for all the consequences of his own unjustifiable and tortious act."

Analogous cases were decided by the Supreme Court of South Carolina in the 1780s with respect to unlawful acts occurring at the time of the American Revolution. Thus judicial recognition of the private right to a remedy for violations of international law predates the U.S. Constitution and relevant federal statues. In an early case in Pennsylvania, it was decided that no cause of action existed where there was no violation of the law of nations by the Continental Congress, the Pennsylvania Board of War, or General Schuyler, although plaintiff's counsel had rightly argued: "that every right must have a remedy is a principle of general law." Several years later, in 1824, and in response to what was found to be a violation of the law of nations by the U.S. seizure of a French vessel abroad, the U.S. Supreme Court entertained suit by a private party for damages while noting that if such a law is violated "justice demands that the injured party should receive a suitable redress." In 1828, Justice Story similarly remarked: "with reference to principles of international law, he has a right, both to the justice of his own and the foreign sovereign."

See also The Apollon, 22 U.S. (9 Wheat.) 362, 369–71, 374, 376–79 (1824); Kadic v. Karadzic, 70 F.3d 232 (2d Cir. 1995); RESTATEMENT OF THE FOREIGN RELATIONS LAW OF THE UNITED STATES § 404, Comment b (3 ed. 1987), reproduced in Chapter Three; Paust, Suing Saddam: Private Remedies for War Crimes and Hostage-Taking, 31 VA. J. INT'L L. 351 (1991); Paust, On Human Rights, supra, at 624 n.503 (other cases involving civil actions with respect to international crimes); Henfield's Case, in Chapter Four, Section 2 (re: breach of neutrality and possible damages); but see Tel-Oren v. Libyan Arab Republic, 726 F.2d 774, 779, 780 n.4 (D.C. Cir. 1984) (Edwards, J., concurring); id. at 799, 801, 809–10, 812, 822 (Bork, J., concurring); Linder v. Calero, 747 F. Supp. 1452 (S.D. Fla. 1990); Handel v. Artukovic, 601 F. Supp. 1421, 1425–27 (C.D. Cal. 1985). For further discussion of the errors in Tel-Oren, see Paust, On Human Rights, supra at 628–50.

How might prosecutions within international or domestic criminal courts interact with potential civil actions, including complex civil actions charging racketeering? See also Articles 75, 79 of the Statute of the ICC.

5. Linder was reversed on appeal to the Eleventh Circuit. Linder v. Portocarrero, 963 F.2d 332, 336–37 (11th Cir. 1992):

"There are no allegations in the amended complaint upon which to base the defendants' argument that the torture and murder of Linder took place during "a battle" or "skirmish". Rather it is specifically alleged that Linder was targeted, tortured and executed while he was a non-combatant civilian in the process of constructing a dam.

"The determinative question to be resolved in this case is the following: Even though a civil war was in progress and "the actions taken against Linder [torture and murder] were part of an overall design to wage attacks on foreign development workers at development sites like hydro-electric plants as a means of terrorizing the population of Nicaragua", does this immunize the defendants from tort liability for the torture and murder of Linder? We think not.

"Contrary to the district court's conclusion, there is no foreign civil war exception to the right to sue for tortious conduct that violates the fundamental norms of the customary laws of war. And even if there were a geographical foreign civil war exception to the right to sue for such tortious conduct, that exception would be inapplicable here. The amended complaint alleges that substantial tortious conduct took place in the Southern District of Florida. This is not a case where the tortious conduct occurred wholly or even principally outside the United States.

"All of the authorities agree that torture and summary execution—the torture and killing of wounded non-combatant civilians—are acts that are viewed with universal abhorrence. As the court said in *Filartiga v. Pena-Irala*, 630 F.2d 876, 890 (2nd Cir. 1980), "for purposes of civil liability, the torturer has become—like the pirate and slave trader before him—*hostis humani generis*, an enemy of all mankind." There is no exception for deliberately planned and heinous acts even during an armed conflict ..."The district court's reliance on *Underhill v. Hernandez*, 168 U.S. 250 ... (1897) and *La Amistad de Rues*, 18 U.S. (5 Wheat) 385 ... (1820) is misplaced. These cases stand only for the generally accepted premise that acts of *legitimate warfare* cannot be made the basis for individual liability, *Underhill* at 253, and that each belligerent has an undoubted right to exercise all the *rights of war* against the other, *La Amistad de Rues* at 390. They do not support the district court's findings that domestic tort actions are not appropriate remedies for injuries to noncombatants occurring outside of the United States during conflicts between belligerents."

6. Captain Henry Wirz, confederate commander of a prisoner of war camp at Andersonville, Georgia during the Civil War, was tried by a military commission in Washington, D.C. for crimes contrary to the laws and customs of war. He was later convicted, sentenced to death and, on November 11, 1865, executed. His employee, James Duncan, was also tried and sentenced to imprisonment at hard labor for fifteen years. See W. WINTHROP, MILITARY LAW AND PRECEDENTS 792 (2 ed. 1920).

Was trial in a military commission violative of the U.S. Constitution if an alternative federal court was available? Consider *Ex parte Milligan*, decided the next year, 71 U.S. (4 Wall.) 2 (1866); 8 Op. Att'y Gen. 396 (1857) (the normal forum for trial of soldiers for murder had been the state courts); and *Ex parte Mudd*, manuscript opinion of Judge Boynton, Sept. 9, 1868, otherwise reported at 17 F. Cas. 954 (S.D. Fla. 1868) (No. 9,899).

The latter case involved a petition for habeas corpus submitted by Dr. Samuel Mudd, Samuel Arnold and Edward Spangler, civilians who had been convicted by a military commission ("sitting in the City of Washington, in the Spring of 1865, ... [and sentenced] to military confinement at Fort Jefferson within this judicial District") of complicity in the assassination of President Lincoln. The primary thrust of Mudd's collateral attack was based upon the decision in *Ex parte Milligan*, 71 U.S. (4 Wall.) 2 (1866). Although the district court professed that " ... no decision was ever more willingly followed than would be the decision and reasoning [of *Milligan*] by this court in any case where that decision was in point," it denied relief without even a return of the writ and argument of both parties. In distinguishing *Ex parte Milligan* as not involving a violation of the law of war the court stated:

> "There is nothing in the opinion of the Court [in *Milligan*] or in the third article of the constitution ... to lead to the conclusion that if any army had been encamped in the state of Indiana (whether in the presence of the enemy or not) and any person a resident of Indiana or any other state (enlisted soldier or not) had not from any private animosity but from public reasons made his way into the Army lines and assassinated the Commanding General, such a person could

not have been legally tried for his military offense by a Military Tribunal and legally convicted and sentenced. The President was assassinated not from private animosity nor any other reason than a desire to impair the effectiveness of military operations.... It was not Mr. Lincoln who was assassinated but the commander-in-chief of the Army for military reasons. I find no difficulty therefore in classing the offense as a Military one, and with this opinion arrive at the necessary conclusion that the proper tribunal for the trial ... was a military one." M.S. Op. p.2.

In response to petitioner's second contention concerning the presidential proclamation of amnesty of July 4th, 1868, the court clarified its concept of the offense for which Mudd had been convicted:

"But that proclamation plainly excludes ... petitioners, whether they have been convicted or not. It pardons the crime of treason ... but it pardons no person who has transgressed the laws of war—no spy, no assassin, no person who has been guilty of barbarous treatment to prisoners.... Such a provision would refer to those prisoners who had made open and honorable war and transgressed the fearfully wide rules which war allows to be legal." MS. Op. at 2, 3.

7. Do you agree with the district court in *Mudd* that the offense was a "military" one? *See also* 11 Op. Att'y Gen. 297 (1865). General Lee had surrendered at Appomattox April 9, 1865, five days before Lincoln was shot. General Taylor surrendered May 4th. Confederate troops in Texas surrendered May 26, 1865.

8. As noted above, criminal and civil sanctions for violations of the law of war have occurred in state courts. In the cases noted, violations had occurred within the forum state. Is state (versus federal) jurisdiction nonetheless permissible under the universality principle with respect to violations of international law occurring abroad? On the universality principle, see Chapter Three *supra*.

How would piracy and violations of the law of neutrality occurring on the high seas have been prosecuted prior to 1789? *See* Sections 2 and 5 *supra*.

9. If former Panamanian dictator Noriega was entitled to prisoner of war status following the 1989 incursion of U.S. forces into Panama, should he have been tried for international drug trafficking offenses in a military tribunal? Could he, given *Ex parte Milligan*? Could he if "peace" had occurred at least by the time of his arrest in Panama? Recall *In re Yamashita*. More generally, see *United States v. Noriega*, 745 F. Supp. 1506, 1534 (S.D. Fla. 1990).

Section 8
U.S. Occupation Courts

Introductory Note

U.S. Dep't of Army Pamphlet No. 27-161-2
II International Law 224, 226–33 (1962)

The Subsequent Proceedings at Nuremberg (August 1946–April 1949). Allied Control Council Law No. 10, 20 December 1945, was promulgated in order to establish a uniform legal basis in Germany for the prosecution of war criminals and other similar offenders, other than those dealt with by the International Military Tribunal. The American courts established under this law tried twelve cases, known as "The Subsequent Proceedings." These twelve cases, plus the single cases tried by the International Military Tribunal at Nuremberg and the International Military Tribunal for the Far East make up the war crimes cases tried by international courts to which the United States was a party. The United States, acting alone, tried many more cases before military commissions....

Acting under this Control Council Law, the United States promulgated Military Government Ordinance No. 7. This ordinance provided that each tribunal was to consist of three members and an alternate. All were to be civilian lawyers from the United States. Six tribunals were formed composed of 18 judges and six alternates. These six tribunals heard twelve cases....

The Twelve Subsequent Proceedings

a. *U.S. v. Karl Brandt, et al.* (The Medical Case). The indictment named twenty-three defendants. The chief defendant, Karl Brandt, had, for a time, been one of Hitler's personal physicians and had risen to become Reich Commissioner for Health and Sanitation, the highest medical position in the Reich. The other defendants were the Chief of the Medical Service of the Luftwaffe, Chief Surgeon of the SS, Dean of the Medical Faculty of the University of Berlin, a specialist in tropical medicine, and lesser doctors in the military and civilian hierarchy. The principal count of the indictment charged the defendants with criminal responsibility for cruel and frequently murderous "medical experiments" performed without the victims' consent, on concentration camp inmates, prisoners of war, and others. The trial lasted from 9 December 1946 to 19 July 1947. The tribunal's judgment of 19 August 1947 convicted 16 defendants and acquitted seven. Karl Brandt, Gebhardt, Rudolf Brandt, Mrugowsky, Seivers, Brack, and Hoven were sentenced to hang. Imprisonment was given to Becker-Freyseng (20 years), Beiglboeck (10 years), Handloser (life), Schroeder (life), Genzken (life), Rose (life), Fischer (life), Oberheuser (20 years), and Poppendick (10 years). Rostock, Blome, Ruff, Romberg, Weltz, Schaefer, and Pokorney were acquitted.

b. *U.S. v. Joseph Altstoetter, et al.* (The Justice Case). The fourteen defendants were all officials, as judges, prosecutors, or ministerial officers, of the judicial system of Nazi Germany. The main point of the prosecution's charge was that the defendants were guilty of "judicial murder and other atrocities, which they committed by destroying law and justice in Germany, and then utilizing the emptied forms of legal process for persecution, enslavement, and extermination on a vast scale." The court, in its judgment, concluded that "The dagger of the assassin was concealed beneath the robe of the jurist." The sentences imposed were as follows: Schlegelberger (life), Klemm (life), Rothenberger (7 years), Lautz (10 years), Mettgenberg (10 years), Von Ammon (10 years), Joel (10 years), Rothaug (life), Oeschey (life), Altstoetter (5 years). Four of the fourteen defendants were acquitted. They were Bannickel, Petersen, Nebelung, and Cuhorst.

c. *U. S. v. Milch*. This is the first of two cases dealing with government ministers. It is also the only subsequent proceeding with only one defendant. Erhard Milch was indicted on the basis of his activity as member of the Central Planning Board, established by a Hitler decree of 29 October 1943. The chief of this Board, Albert Speer, was tried by the International Military Tribunal. This Board had authority to instruct Saukel, also tried by the IMT, to provide slave laborers for industries under its control. Milch was also accused of complicity in the medical experiments for the German Air Force.

The court's judgment, rendered on 16 April 1947, found Milch not guilty of implication in the medical experiments but guilty of complicity in the slave labor program. He was sentenced to life in prison.

d. *U.S. v. Ernst Weizsaecker, et al.* (The Ministries Case). This is the second of the two cases dealing with ministers. It was the longest and last of the Subsequent Proceedings. Seventeen months elapsed from the filing of the indictment to the rendering of the judgment, 15 Nov. 1947–14 April 1949. There were twenty-one defendants, eighteen of whom were ministers or high functionaries in the civil administration of the Third Reich. The defendants were the lower echelon of the higher dignitaries who sat in the dock before the IMT.

The indictment consisted of eight counts: crimes against peace (1 and 2), mistreatment of PW's, against only seven defendants (3), crimes against humanity before the war (4), crimes against humanity and war crimes after the war started (5), plunder of property in occupied areas (6), deportation of slave labor (7), membership in criminal organizations (8). Count Four was dismissed [re: crimes against humanity before 1939]. The trial continued on the remaining seven counts. The sentences were as follows:

Berger	25 years
Lammers	20 years
Veesenmayer	20 years
Koerner	15 years
Pleiger	15 years
Kehrl	15 years
Krosigk	10 years
Keppler	10 years
Darryl	7 years
Woermann	7 years
Dietrich	7 years
Weizsaecker	7 years
Rasche	7 years
Von Mayland	7 years
Schellenberg	6 years
Bohle	5 years
Puhl	5 years
Ritter	4 years
Meissner	NG
Stuckart	Time Served
Erdmannsdorff	NG

e. *U.S. v. Flick.* Three of the twelve cases concerned industrialists. They were the Flick, I.G. Farben, and Krupp trials. Flick was a powerful steel magnate and industrial promoter. He was indicted along with his five principal associates. The indictment contained five counts: (1) deportation of slave labor, (2) plunder of property in occupied areas, (3) crimes against humanity in the pre-war years, (4) financial support of the SS (two defendants only), and (5) membership in the SS (one defendant only). The indictment was filed on 8 February 1947 and the judgment rendered on 22 December 1947.

The results of this trial are as follows:

Defendant	Counts	1	2	3	4	5	Sentence
Flick		G	G		G		7 years
Weiss		G	NG				2.5 years
Steinbrinck		NG	NG		G	G	5 years
Burkart		NG	NG				Acquitted
Kaletsch		NG	NG				Acquitted
Terberger		NG	NG				Acquitted

[count three was dismissed]

f. *U.S. v. Krauch* (I.G. Farben Case). Twenty-four individuals were indicted, twenty of whom were members of I.G. Farben's governing body, the "Vorstand." The other four were important officers of the corporation. Twenty-three were actually tried. The indictment contained five counts: (1) crimes against peace (aggressive war), (2) plunder of property in occupied areas, (3) slave labor, (4) membership in the SS, and (5) conspiracy to wage aggressive war. The judgment of the tribunal was handed down in July 1948. All twenty-three of the defendants were acquitted on counts 1 and 5. All three who were indicted under Count 4 were acquitted. Only five were found guilty under Count 3: Krauch, Ambros, Buetifisch, Duemfeld, and Ter Meer. Nine were convicted and fourteen acquitted on Count 2. Ter Meer was the only defendant found guilty under two counts. Ten defendants were acquitted and thirteen convicted.

Sentences were as follows:

Ambros	8 years
Duemfeld	8 years
Ter Meer	7 years
Krauch	6 years
Buetifisch	6 years
Von Schnitzler	5 years
Schmitz	4 years
Ilgner	3 years
Haefliger	2 years
Oster	2 years
Buergin	2 years
Kugler	1.5 years
Jaehne	1.5 years

g. *U.S. v. Krupp.* This is the third and last trial of the industrialists. Gustav Krupp was indicted before the IMT. However, he was too infirm to stand trial. Here his forty-year-old son was indicted along with eleven other officials. The Krupp organization was the largest manufacturer in Germany. The indictment indicated that the officials of this firm were engaged in the slave labor program (Court Three) and in the economic plunder of occupied areas (Count Two) similar to the defendants in the *Flick* case. Two additional counts were added, that of crimes against peace (Count One) and conspiracy to commit crimes against peace (Count Four), because it was alleged that the Krupp firm took the lead in secret rearmament, supported Hitler's seizure of power, and cooperated willingly in the rearmament of Germany for foreign conquest.

The trial lasted from early December 1947 to the end of June 1948. On April 5, 1948 the Tribunal granted a motion for a finding of not guilty on Count One and Count Four. The following are the findings and sentences:

Defendant	Counts 2	3	Sentence
Alfried Krupp	G	G	12 yrs
Loeser	G	G	7 yrs
Houdremont	G	G	10 yrs
Mueller	G	G	12 yrs
Janssen	G	G	10 yrs
Ihn	NG	G	9 yrs
Eberhardt	G	G	9 yrs
Korschan	NG	G	6 yrs
Buelow	NG	G	12 yrs
Lehmann		G	6 yrs
Kupke		G	Time Served
Pfirsch	NG	NG	Acquitted

h. *U.S. v. Von Leeb* (The High Command Case). The cases of Generals Von Leeb and List comprise, from the military point of view, two of the most important of the twelve Subsequent Proceedings. Here were the trials of high military figures for the manner in which they conducted the war and the manner in which they governed unruly occupied areas.

The first was the trial of the high command of the German Army. Fourteen general officers were indicted under four counts: (1) crimes against peace, (2) war crimes, (3) crimes against humanity, and (4) conspiracy to commit these three crimes. The court dismissed charges 1 and 4. This was in line with the pattern in the Subsequent Proceedings. Rarely was an individual convicted of crimes against peace. The principal war crimes charged concerned the Commissar Order for the killing of Communist political advisors in the Russian Army, the Barbarossa Jurisdiction Order for the suppression of guerrilla warfare, the Commando Order for no quarter against British raiding parties, and the Night and Fog Decree for the secret deportation of individuals. Crimes against humanity (Count Three) dealt with the activities of race execution teams operating in areas controlled by the defendants. The following findings and sentences were handed down on 28 October 1948:

Defendant	Counts 2	3	Sentence
Von Leeb	NG	G	3 yrs
Schniewind	NG	NG	Acquitted
Sperrle	NG	NG	Acquitted
Kuechler	G	G	20 yrs
Hoth	G	G	15 yrs
Reinhardt	G	G	15 yrs
von Salmuth	G	G	20 yrs
Hollidt	G	G	5 yrs

Roques	G	G	20 yrs
Reinecke	G	G	Life
Warlimont	G	G	Life
Woehler	G	G	8 yrs
Lehmann	G	G	7 yrs

i. *U.S. v. List* (Hostages Case). This second military case dealt principally with the actions of the occupation authorities in Yugoslavia and Greece. A second element was the destruction of property during the evacuation of Finland and Norway. The case receives its name from the widespread use of hostages and reprisal prisoners in order to discourage partisan warfare in Yugoslavia and Greece.

Twelve German Army generals were indicted on four counts: (1) excess shooting of hostages, (2) plunder and destruction of property, (3) ill treatment of prisoners of war, and (4) slave labor. On 19 February 1948 the court handed down the following findings and sentences:

Defendant	Counts 1	2	3	4	Sentence
List	G	NG	G	NG	Life
Weichs	Not tried because of illness				
Rendulic	G	NG	G	G	20 years
Kuntze	G	NG	G	G	Life
Foertsch	NG	NG	NG	NG	Acquitted
Boehme	Suicide				
Felmy	G	G	NG	NG	15 years
Lanz	G	NG	G	NG	12 years
Dehner	G	NG	NG	NG	7 years
Leyser	NG	NG	G	G	10 years
Speidel	G	NG	NG	NG	20 years
Geitner	NG	NG	NG	NG	Acquitted

j. *The SS Cases.* The SS Cases comprise the three remaining Subsequent Proceedings. They were *U.S. v. Ohlendorf* ("Einsatzgruppen Case"), *U.S. v. Pohl* (Concentration Camps), and *U.S. v. Greifelt* (The RuSHA Case).

The Einsatzgruppen were extermination units whose mission was to kill minority races in occupied areas, particularly Jews and Gypsies. Twenty-two were indicted. Twenty-one were convicted of serious participation in this murder program. The remaining defendant was sentenced to time already served. The sentences were severe compared to those handed down by the other tribunals. However, the enormity of the crime called for such punishment. Fourteen were sentenced to hang, two to life in prison, three to twenty years, and the remaining two to ten years each.

Oswald Pohl and seventeen others were indicted principally for their administration of the concentration camps. Three were sentenced to hang, three to life in prison, two to 20 years, one to 15 years, and six to ten years each. Three were acquitted.

The third SS case, known as the *RuSHA* case is a peculiar mixture of race hatred and pseudo-science. *RuSHA* is the German abbreviation for the race and settlement Main Office, an SS agency. Its purpose was to strengthen biologically and territorially the German nation at the expense of conquered countries. Fourteen were indicted. One was acquitted. Of the remaining thirteen one was sentenced to life in prison, two to twenty-five years, one to twenty years, three to fifteen years, one to ten years, and five to time served.

Notes

1. These cases are reported in TRIALS OF WAR CRIMINALS BEFORE THE NUERNBERG MILITARY TRIBUNALS (Wash. GPO 1950–51).

2. Foreign war criminals convicted by U.S. tribunals received pardons or mitigated sentences from the U.S. High Commissioner on January 31, 1951. By 1958, all such persons had been released. See A. RUCKERL, THE INVESTIGATION OF NAZI WAR CRIMES, 1945–1978 135 n.6 (1980).

United States v. Tiede

Crim. Case No. 78-001A (U.S. Ct. for Berlin Mar. 14, 1979), 85 F.R.D. 227 (1979), *reprinted in* 19 I.L.M. 179 (1980)*

Herbert J. Stern,** opinion:

This is a criminal proceeding arising out of the alleged diversion of a Polish aircraft by the defendants from its scheduled landing in East Berlin to a forced landing in West Berlin.

United States authorities exercised jurisdiction over this matter and convened this Court. Court-appointed defense counsel have now moved for a trial by jury. The Prosecution objects, contending that these proceedings are not governed by the United States Constitution, but by the requirements of foreign policy and that the Secretary of State, as interpreter of that policy, has determined that these defendants do not have the right to a jury trial.

The special nature of this Court and the unusual position taken by the United States Attorney for Berlin require an extensive account and analysis of the history of the occupation of Berlin, the jurisdictional basis of this Court, and the limitations, if any, on the Secretary of State and the American authorities who govern the 1.2 million people who reside in the American sector of Berlin. The Court holds that the United States Constitution applies to these proceedings and that defendants charged with criminal offenses before the United States Court for Berlin have constitutional rights, including the right to a trial by jury.

I. Factual Background

On August 30, 1978, a Polish civilian aircraft on a scheduled flight from Gdansk, Poland, to Schoenefeld Airport in East Berlin, was diverted and forced to land at Tempelhof Airport in the United States sector of West Berlin. Following the landing, defendants Hans Detlef Alexander Tiede and Ingrid Ruske, together with Mrs. Ruske's twelve-year-old daughter, were detained by United States military authorities at a U.S. Air Force installation located at Tempelhof. On November 1, 1978, the United States Mission in Berlin

---

* Reproduced with permission from 19 I.L.M. (1980), © The American Society of International Law.

** Herbert J. Stern, United States Judge for the District of New Jersey, sitting as United States Judge for Berlin by appointment of the United States Ambassador to the Federal Republic of Germany.

advised the German authorities in West Berlin that it would exercise jurisdiction over the investigation and prosecution of any crimes committed in connection with the diversion of the Polish airliner. Mrs. Ruske was released from detention on November 3; her daughter had been released several weeks earlier.

The United States authorities, acting under the authority of Law No. 46, a law promulgated in 1955 by the former United States High Commissioner for Germany, then convened this Court. On November 30, 1978, the Honorable Dudley B. Bonsal was sworn in as United States Judge for Berlin. Judge Bonsal limited his function to the promulgation of rules of criminal procedure which govern the bringing of charges, pretrial proceedings, and trials in this Court. Judge Bonsal was succeeded by the Honorable Leo M. Goodman, who took the oath of office as United States Judge for Berlin on December 6, 1978.

On that day a complaint, supported by an affidavit executed by a U.S. Air Force investigating officer, was filed against the defendant Tiede. Based on the complaint, Judge Goodman issued a warrant for the arrest of Tiede. The warrant was executed the same day and Tiede was brought before Judge Goodman who advised him of his rights under the United States Constitution and explained to him the nature of the criminal complaint filed against him. In view of Tiede's indigency, Judge Goodman assigned a member of the Berlin criminal bar as counsel for Tiede. Following Tiede's presentment, and upon the defendant's request, Judge Goodman scheduled a preliminary hearing and arraignment for mid- January.

Also on December 6, a complaint with supporting affidavit was filed against the defendant Ruske, on the basis of which Judge Goodman caused a summons to be issued, commanding Mrs. Ruske to appear before the Court in mid-January for presentation and arraignment. German defense counsel was appointed by Judge Goodman for the defendant Ruske in late December.

On January 11, 1979, the author of this opinion became United State Judge for Berlin. The defendants were arraigned the next day. Prior to arraignment, this Court appointed American counsel for both defendants because the proceedings would be conducted under American procedural law, although German substantive law would apply. Defendants filed timely motions demanding a trial by jury.

II. Historical Background

A. *Overview of the Allied Occupation of Germany Since World War II*

1. *The Occupation of Germany*

In 1944, some eight months before final victory in the Second World War, the United States, the United Kingdom and the Soviet Union began preparing for the occupation of a defeated Germany. They formed the European Advisory Commission and agreed on the division of pre-War German territory into three zones of occupation and on the principle that Greater Berlin would be administered jointly by the Allies. A second agreement created the Allied administration structure for governing occupied Germany. Subsequently, the Provisional Government of the French Republic was invited to participate in the occupation of Germany, and the British and United States zones of occupation were re-divided to create a fourth, the French zone of occupation.

On June 5, 1945, the Allies declared the total defeat for Germany and assumed "supreme authority" over the country, "including all the powers possessed by the German Government, the High Command and any state, municipal or local government or authority." The Allied declaration expressly denied any intent to "effect the annexation of Germany." A Control Council, composed of the Commanders-in-Chief of the occupying forces of each of the Four Powers, headed the Allied administration. Its responsibilities were to coordinate the administration of the four zones, to legislate on matters affecting Germany as a whole, to supervise the German central administration, and to direct jointly the government of Berlin "through appropriate organs." Decisions of the Control Council were required to be unanimous. . . .

2. *The Occupation of Greater Berlin*

On September 12, 1944, the United States, the United Kingdom and the Soviet Union, in an exercise of their anticipated rights of conquest, agreed that:

> The Berlin Area (by which expression is understood the territory of, "Greater Berlin," as defined by the Law of 27th April, 1920) will by jointly occupied by armed forces of the U.S.A., U.K., and U.S.S.R., assigned by the respective Commanders-in-Chief.

A "Protocol on Zones of Occupation" divided Greater Berlin into separate sectors, each to be occupied by one of the Allied Powers. Further, an "Inter-Allied Governing Authority" (*Kommandatura* in Russian), was established "to direct jointly the administration of the 'Greater Berlin' area." On November 14, 1944, in the Agreement on Control Machinery, the Allies further agreed to establish a subordinate Inter-Allied technical staff "to serve the purpose of supervising and controlling the activities of the local organs of 'Greater Berlin,' which are responsible for its municipal services."

In the summer of 1945, United States, United Kingdom and French military forces moved into Berlin, which initially had been taken by Soviet military forces. On July 11, 1945, the "Allied Kommandatura" was established pursuant to the agreed arrangements for Greater Berlin. Subject to the Allied Kommandatura, which was responsible for the administration of the city as a whole and for the control of local German authorities, each sector had a military Sector Commandant who had authority to control and administer his particular sector. Each Sector Commandant also had the power to promulgate necessary sector legislation.

In the initial months after the establishment of the Allied Kommandatura, cooperation among the wartime Allies was maintained. By late 1946, however, the Soviet authorities increasingly began to obstruct the functioning of the Kommandatura and to impede the quadripartite control of Greater Berlin. Throughout 1947, relations between the Soviet Union and the Western Allies continued to deteriorate and, beginning on January 6, 1948, the Soviet authorities progressively restricted access to Greater Berlin from the Western zones of occupation. By mid-June, 1948, all land ties were cut off, and the Berlin blockade was established. In December, 1948, the Allied (Western) Kommandatura resumed operation on the theory that the Soviet withdrawal could not abrogate the original quadripartite agreement for Joint control over Greater Berlin, even though the decisions of the Allied (Western) Kommandatura could only be given effect in the Western sectors.

The Berlin blockade ended on May 12, 1949, following an agreement among the Four Powers to discuss the strained relations in the Council of Foreign Ministers. When no agreement was reached by that body, the three Western Powers began to cope with a *de facto* partition of Greater Berlin between the Soviet Sector and the three Western sectors. The Western Powers agreed that the agreement establishing the civilian Allied High Commission for the new German Federal Republic would "be applied as far as practicable to the Western Sectors of Berlin." The internal procedure for the Allied (Western) Kommandatura was accordingly revised to make clear its subordination to the newly-created civilian Allied High commission. . . .

The United States Court for Berlin

On April 28, 1955, only a few days before the occupation regime terminated in the rest of Germany, the U.S. High Commissioner promulgated Law No. 46 establishing the "United States Court for Berlin." The Law defines the jurisdiction of the Court, sets forth the applicable substantive law and provides for the appointment of judges and other principal court personnel by the United States Ambassador to the Federal Republic of Germany. Despite the fact that this Court was established in 1955, this is the first time in its 24-year history that the Court has been convened.

As previously noted, the President has delegated to the United States Ambassador to the Federal Republic of Germany his "supreme authority ... with respect to all responsibilities, duties, and governmental functions of the United States in all Germany [including Berlin] under the supervision of the Secretary of State and subject to the ultimate direction of the President." Thus, this court sits in Berlin as an instrumentality of the United States, executing the sovereign powers of the United States. As a matter of United States law, it is a court established pursuant to the powers granted to the President by Article II of the United States Constitution.

Article 3(1) of Law No. 46 provides that "the Court shall have original jurisdiction to hear and decide any criminal cases arising under any legislation in effect in the United States Sector for Berlin if the offense was committed within the area of Greater Berlin." The criminal jurisdiction of the Court is concurrent with that of the Berlin courts, except to the extent that the American Sector Commandant withdraws jurisdiction from the German courts in a given case. Thus, the Court exercises jurisdiction which is territorial in nature. If the American authorities choose to do so, they can arraign before this Court any person physically present in the American Sector of Berlin, regardless of such person's nationality, including—when authorized by the American Sector Commandant—members of the United States Armed Forces stationed in West Berlin. Pursuant to Article 5, convictions or sentences pronounced by the Court may be reviewed by the American Ambassador to the Federal Republic.

Article 3(5) confers broad powers upon the judges appointed to this Court, including the power "to establish consistently with the applicable legislation rules of practice and proceedings" for the Court. Pursuant to that authority, on November 30, 1978, Judge Bonsal promulgated as Rules of Criminal Procedure for the United States Court for Berlin a set of rules which, with one exception, adopted almost verbatim the Federal Rules of Criminal Procedure and the Federal Rules of Evidence; the exception related to jury trials. Thus, under the Rules of Criminal Procedure of this Court, the defendants here are not entitled to a trial by jury.

We now turn to the question of whether the Constitution of the United States, which might require a jury trial under these circumstances, applies to the proceedings in this court.

III. Application of the United States Constitution to These Proceedings

The Prosecution's basic position is that the United States Constitution does not apply to these proceedings because Berlin is a territory governed by military conquest. The Prosecution maintains that the question whether constitutional rights must be afforded in territories governed by United States authorities outside the United States depends on the nature and degree of association between such territories and the United States, and that the relationship between the United States and Berlin is such that the Constitution does not apply to proceedings in Berlin. Thus, it says:

> It is appropriate to visualize a hierarchy of types of United States involvement in the governance of overseas territories. For incorporated territories, which are

in many cases territories on their way toward full statehood, the full panoply of Constitutional rights is applicable. Next there are those territories, as yet unincorporated, which are guaranteed most or all Constitutional safeguards by virtue of act of Congress. Then there are unincorporated territories now governed by the *King* [*v. Morton*, 520 F.2d 1140] doctrine, where the constitutionality of Congressional failure to extend the provisions of the Bill of Rights is determined on the basis of a factual inquiry into the feasibility of applying the Bill of Rights at least as to American citizens. In all of these territories, the United States exercises sovereignty....

The very last in the hierarchy of types of United States governing authority overseas is United States occupation and control pursuant to conquest. In such a situation international law prescribes the limits of the occupant's power. Occupation does not displace the sovereignty of the occupied state, though for the time being the occupant may exercise supreme governing authority. Nor does occupation effect any annexation or incorporation of the occupied territory into the territory or political structure of the occupant, and the occupant's constitution and laws do not extend of their own force to the occupied territory.

It is this last sort of authority that the United States exercises in Berlin. Significantly, the occupation is multilateral in character: the Allied Kommandatura jointly exercises supreme governing authority, with each sector commandant exercising delegated authority within his own sector. The Allies have repeatedly disclaimed any intent to annex Berlin or extend their own political systems thereto. The explicit Allied philosophy, in accordance with international law, is to provide for the security of Berlin while at the same time affording to the people of Berlin the fullest possible rights of self-government through their own institutions.

As a corollary to this position, the Prosecution contends that everything which concerns the conduct of an occupation is a "political question" not subject to court review. Thus, it states in its brief:

Berlin is an occupied city. It is not United States territory. The United States presence there grows out of conquest, not the consent of the governed. The United States and the other Western Allies have, over time, made political judgments to turn over to the Berliners control of important institutions and functions of governance. But these decisions reflect political judgments, not legal necessity.

The Prosecution further argues that this Court is not an independent tribunal established to adjudicate the rights of the defendants and lacks the power to make a ruling contrary to the foreign policy interests of the United States. This, it contends follows from the fact that "United States occupation courts in Germany have been instruments of the United States occupation policy." According to the Prosecution, this political aspect was expressed by General Lucius D. Clay, the former United States Military Governor for Germany, who described his aspirations for the administration of justice in the United States area of occupation as follows:

We are trying to make our own judicial procedures an example of democratic justice and concern for the individual.

From the earliest point of the occupation of Germany, the Prosecution contends, the United States occupation courts functioned as an extension of American foreign policy....

Thus, the Prosecution maintains that any rights to which the defendants are entitled must be granted by Secretary of State Vance, or they do not exist at all:

> The basic point is this: a defendant tried in the United States Court for Berlin is afforded certain rights found in the constitution, but he receives these rights not by force of the Constitution itself…, but because the Secretary of State has made the determination that these certain rights should be provided.

Further, the Prosecution argues, such rights would be granted not because of constitutional dictates, but because they would be in accord with our longstanding foreign policy. It is said that throughout the occupation:

> the rules and procedures of the courts were revised by the occupation authorities to implement aspects of United States foreign policy, not by virtue of requirements arising under the United States Constitution or United States law.

Pursuing its thesis that this Court is nothing more than an implementing arm of the United States' foreign policy, the Prosecution instructs the Court that the Secretary of State has determined, as a matter of foreign policy, that the right to a jury trial should not be afforded to the defendants. The Prosecution's brief asserts:

> The conduct of occupation is fundamentally different from the exercise of civil government in the United States. The actions of an occupying power, from necessity, may be inconsistent with the wishes or attitudes of the occupied population. In short, the assumptions and values which underlie the great common law conception of trial by jury do not necessarily have a place in the conduct of an occupation. Whether it does in a particular situation is quintessentially a political question, to be determined by the officers responsible for the United States conduct of this occupation, *and not by this Court.*

The Court finds the Prosecution's argument to be entirely without merit. First, there has never been a time when United States authorities exercised governmental powers in any geographical area—whether at war or in times of peace—without regard for their own Constitution. *Ex parte Milligan*, 71 U.S. (4 Wall.) 2 (1866). Nor has there ever been a case in which constitutional officers, such as the Secretary of State, have exercised the powers of their office without constitutional limitations. Even in the long-discredited case of *In re Ross*, 140 U.S. 453 (1891), in which American consular officers were permitted to try United States citizens in certain "non-Christian" countries, the Court made its decision under the Constitution—not in total disregard of it. The distinction is subtle but real: The applicability of any provision of the Constitution is itself a point of constitutional law, to be decided in the last instance by the judiciary, not by the Executive Branch.

This fundamental principle was forcefully and clearly announced by the Supreme Court more than a century ago in *Ex parte Milligan*, 71 U.S. (4 Wall.) 2, 120–21 (1866):

> [The Framers of the American Constitution] foresaw that troublous times would arise, when rulers and people would become restive under restraint, and seek by sharp and decisive measures to accomplish ends deemed just and proper; and that the principles of constitutional liberty would be in peril, unless established by irrepealable law. The history of the world had taught them that what was done in the past might be attempted in the future. *The Constitution of the United States is a law for rulers and people, equally in war and in peace, and covers with the shield of its protection all classes of men, at all times, and under all circumstances.* No doctrine, involving more pernicious consequences, was ever invented

by the wit of man than that any of its provisions can be suspended during any of the great exigencies of government. Such a doctrine leads directly to anarchy or despotism, but the theory of necessity on which it is based is false; for the government, within the Constitution, has all the powers granted to it, which are necessary to preserve its existence; as has been happily proved by the result of the great effort to throw off its just authority. [Emphasis added.]

Although the Supreme Court was reviewing the power of military commissions organized by military authorities in the United States during the Civil War, the wisdom of the principle set forth above is nowhere better demonstrated than in this city, during this occupation, and before this Court.

The Prosecution's position, if accepted by this Court, would have dramatic consequences not only for the two defendants whom the United States has chosen to arraign before the Court, but for every person within the territorial limits of the United States Sector of Berlin. If the occupation authorities are not governed by the Constitution in this Court, they are not governed by the Constitution at all. And, if the occupation authorities may act free of all constitutional restraints, no one in the American Sector of Berlin has any protection from their untrammeled discretion. If there are no constitutional protections, there is no First Amendment, no Fifth Amendment or Sixth Amendment; even the Thirteenth Amendment's prohibition of involuntary servitude would be inapplicable. The American authorities, if the Secretary of State so decreed, would have the power, in time of peace and with respect to German and American citizens alike, to arrest any person without cause, to hold a person incommunicado, to deny an accused the benefit of counsel, to try a person summarily and to impose sentence—all as a part of the unreviewable exercise of foreign policy.

This court does not suggest that the American occupation authorities intend to carry the Prosecution's thesis to its logical conclusion. Nonetheless, people have been deceived before in their assessment of the intentions of their own leaders and their own government; and those who have left the untrammeled, unchecked power in the hands of their leaders have not had a happy experience. It is a first principle of American life—not only life at home but life abroad—that everything American public officials do is governed by, measured against, and must be authorized by the United States Constitution....

IV. The Requirements of the Constitution in These Proceedings

A. *The Question Presented*

The sole but novel question before the Court is whether friendly aliens, charged with civil offenses in a United States court in Berlin, under the unique circumstances of the continuing United States Occupation of Berlin, have a right to a jury trial. This Court is not concerned with the procedures to be used by a United States military commission trying a case in wartime or during the belligerent occupation of enemy territory before the termination of war. This case does not involve the theft or destruction of military property. Nor does in involve spying, an offense against Allied military authority or a violation of the laws of war. Further, this Court does not sit as an international tribunal, but only an American court.

The defendants are German citizens. It is of no moment whether they be deemed citizens of the Federal Republic or of the German Democratic Republic because the United States is at peace with, and maintains diplomatic relations with, both states. Thus, in law, the defendants are friendly aliens. They are not enemy nationals, enemy belligerents or prisoners of war. The defendants are charged with non-military offenses under German law which would have been fully cognizable in the open and functioning German courts in West Berlin, but for the withdrawal of the German courts' jurisdiction by the United States Commander.

The Court takes judicial notice that the occupation regime in existence in Greater Berlin in 1979 is unique in the annals of international relations. Berlin has played, and is destined to play in the future, a special role in the preservation of the free world. The genesis of the occupation is to be found in belligerent occupation, but the relationship between the "occupiers" and the "occupied" in Greater Berlin has undergone fundamental changes since Berlin was initially occupied in 1945 by force of arms.

West Berlin today is a thriving metropolis, a center of commerce, tourism and the arts, with a civilian administration adhering to the principles of democratic self-government, and with a minimum of control exerted by the Western occupying powers. What began as belligerent occupation of a vanquished enemy has turned into a "protective occupation" of a friendly and allied people. West Berliners stand firmly with the Western Allies in the struggle against the tyranny and alien ideology imposed upon the territories surrounding their beleaguered island of freedom....

[regarding *Reid v. Covert*, 354 U.S. 1 (1957)]

The logic of Mr. Justice Black's opinion with respect to the question whether the Constitution applies abroad—or in the vernacular of the time, "whether the Constitution follows the flag"—is, in this Court's view, irrefutable and deserves to be cited at length. The Justice began by postulating the obligation which the United States owes to its citizens:

> At the beginning we reject the idea that when the United States acts against citizens abroad it can do so free of the Bill of Rights. The United States is entirely a creature of the Constitution. Its power and authority have no other source. It can only act in accordance with all the limitations imposed by the Constitution. When the Government reaches out to punish a citizen who is abroad, the shield which the Bill of Rights and other parts of the Constitution provide to protect his life and liberty should not be stripped away just because he happens to be in another land. This is not a novel concept. To the contrary, it is as old as government. It was recognized long before Paul successfully invoked his right as a Roman citizen to be tried in strict accordance with Roman law.

Mr. Justice Black then referred to the relevant Constitutional provisions—Article III, section 2, and the Fifth and Sixth Amendments—and confirmed:

> The language of Art. III § 2 manifests that constitutional protections for the individual were designed to restrict the United States Government when it acts outside of this country, as well as here at home. After declaring that all criminal trials must be by jury, the section states that when a crime is "not committed within any State, the Trial shall be at such Place or Places as the Congress may by law have directed." If this language is permitted to have its obvious meaning, § 2 is applicable to criminal trials outside of the States as a group without regard to where the offense is committed or the trial held.... The Fifth and Sixth Amendments, like Art. III, § 2, are also all inclusive with their sweeping references to "no person" and to "all criminal prosecutions."

> This Court and other federal courts have held or asserted that various constitutional limitations apply to the Government when it acts outside the continental United States. While it been suggested that only those constitutional rights which are "fundamental" protect Americans abroad, we can find no warrant, in logic or otherwise, for picking and choosing among the remarkable collection of

"Thou Shalt Nots" which were explicitly fastened on all departments and agencies of the Federal Government by the Constitution, and its Amendments. Moreover, in view of our heritage and the history of the adoption of the Constitution and the Bill of Rights, it seems peculiarly anomalous to say that trial before a civilian judge and by, an independent jury picked from the common citizenry is not a fundamental right. 353 U.S. at 7–9.

As regards the continued vitality of the doctrine enunciated in *In re Ross, supra,* Mr. Justice Black said:

The *Ross* case is one of those cases that cannot be understood except in its peculiar setting; even then, it seems highly unlikely that a similar result would be reached today....

The *Ross* approach that the Constitution has no applicability abroad has long since been directly repudiated by numerous cases. That approach is obviously erroneous if the United States Government, which has no power except that granted by the Constitution, can and does try citizens for crimes committed abroad. Thus the *Ross* case rested, at least in substantial part, on a fundamental misconception and the most that can be said is support of the result reached there is that the consular court jurisdiction had a long history antedating the adoption of the Constitution.... At best, the *Ross* case should be left as a relic from a different era.

354 U.S. at 10–12....

The Significance of the Nature of the Tribunal

The Prosecution argues, however, that *Duncan* is inapplicable here because this Court is a type of Military commission and it claims defendants tried by a military commission have no right to a jury trial. In support of this contention, the Prosecution relies principally on *Ex pare Quirin,* 317 U.S. 1 (1942), and *Madsen v. Kinsella,* 343 U.S. 341 (1952). Although both cases are unquestionably relevant to these proceedings, an examination of them reveals that they do not support the Prosecution's contention.

In *Ex parte Quirin,* 317 U.S. 1 (1942), the Supreme Court considered habeas corpus petitions filed by German saboteurs who, in the summer of 1942, landed from German submarines on the Eastern seaboard of the United States armed with explosives and instructions from an officer of the German High Command to destroy American war industries and facilities. *Id.* at 21. They were apprehended and placed on trial before a military commission convened by the President specifically to try the petitioners, *id.* at 21–22, on charges, among others, that they, "being enemies of the United States and acting for ... the German Reich, a belligerent enemy nation, secretly and covertly passed, in civilian dress, contrary to the law of war....

The Supreme Court decided only the questions "whether it is within the constitutional power of the National Government to place petitioners upon trial before a military commission *for the offenses with which they are charged.*" *Id.* at 29 (emphasis supplied). The Court extensively reviewed the history of trials of violations of the laws of war, including trials held before the Constitution was enacted, and found that "these petitioners were charged with *an offense against the law of war which the Constitution does not require to be tried by jury.*" *Id.* at 29 (emphasis supplied). The Court held that:

[T]he Fifth and Sixth Amendments did not restrict whatever authority was conferred by the Constitution to try *offenses against the law of war* by military commission, and that *petitioners, charged with such an offense* not required to be tried by jury at common law, were lawfully placed on trial by the Commission without a jury.

317 U.S. at 45 (emphasis supplied).

The Court did not hold, as the Prosecution contends, that the *Quirin* petitioners need not be accorded trial by jury because the petitioners were being tried by a military commission rather than a civil court. If the Court intended such a holding, its long and thorough analysis of the history of trials of individuals tried for similar offenses would be entirely superfluous. Rather, the Court held that petitioners were not entitled to a jury trial because they were charged with violations of the laws of war. *Quirin* does *not* stand for the proposition that the nature of the tribunal dictates whether defendants must be accorded a trial by jury or that individuals tried before a military commission are never entitled to a jury. *Quirin* holds that whether an individual is entitled to a jury trial is determined by the nature of the crime with which he is charged.

The defendants here are not charged with violations of the laws of war. They are neither enemy aliens nor associated with the armed forces of an enemy. The defendants are friendly aliens charged with what may be characterized as "garden-variety" felonies in times of peace. Thus, under *Quirin*, neither the nature of this tribunal nor the crimes with which these defendants are charged permits this Court to deny the defendants a jury trial.

In *Madsen v. Kinsella*, 343 U.S. 341 (1952), the Supreme Court addressed a petition for a writ of habeas corpus filed by the wife of an air force lieutenant stationed in Germany who, in 1949, had been convicted of murdering her husband by the United States Court of the Allied High Commission for Germany, a predecessor of this Court. Mrs. Madsen challenged the jurisdiction of the court which convicted her, contending that she could only be tried by a regularly convened United States general court-martial. The issue before the Supreme Court was:

> whether a United States Court of the Allied High Commission for Germany had jurisdiction, in 1950, to try a civilian citizen of the United States, who was the dependent wife of a member of the United States Armed Forces, on a charge of murdering her husband in violation of § 211 of the German Criminal Code. The homicide occurred in October, 1949, within the United States Area of Control in Germany.

343 U.S. 342–43. The Court concluded that the military commission had jurisdiction over Mrs. Madsen.

The Court traced the history of United States military commissions and other United States tribunals in the nature of such commissions. Its discussion of the United States Military Government Courts for Germany, which became the United States Courts for the Allied High Commission for Germany, referred to the procedures used in those courts and included the following footnote:

> They did not provide for juries. The presentment or indictment of a grand jury required a federal capital case by the Fifth Amendment to the Constitution of the United States, under the terms of that Amendment, has no application to "cases arising in the land or naval forces...." The right of trial by jury required in federal criminal prosecutions by the Sixth Amendment is similarly limited. See *Ex parte Quirin*, 317 U.S. 1, 40, 43–45; *Ex parte Milligan*, 4 Wall. 2, 123, 138.

343 U.S. at 360 n. 26. The Prosecution seizes upon this footnote as conclusive authority that the Constitution does not require a jury trial in this Court.

In this Court's view, however, *Madsen v. Kinsella* does not support the Prosecution's thesis that a jury trial is never required in an occupation court. First, the statement of the issue in *Madsen*, as formulated by the Supreme Court, clearly indicates that the question of Mrs. Madsen's right to a trial by jury was neither presented nor considered. She never claimed the right to trial by jury. Indeed, Mrs. Madsen's claim was that she should have been tried by a general court-martial, pursuant to the Articles of War, which did *not* provide for trial by jury.

Second, the Court's reference to the absence of jury trials before occupation courts in Germany in 1949 is hardly dispositive of the issue here. Because *Madsen* was decided long before *Duncan v. Louisiana* declared the right to trial by jury to be a "fundamental" right under the Constitution, *Madsen* certainly cannot be considered conclusive authority that the Constitution does not require a jury trial in this Court in 1979.

Finally, when Mrs. Madsen was tried, the United States and Germany were technically still at war. The Constitution does not require that the "enemy" be accorded self-government or be taken into the bosom of the occupation authority. Occupation courts need not share their jurisdiction with "enemy" aliens, nor are "enemy" aliens to be permitted to nullify the provisions or proceedings of any arm of the occupation government.

However, "occupations" which survive not merely hostilities but also belligerency, and which are maintained to "protect" the occupied and to preserve their democratic institutions, are of an altogether different kind. Such occupations are asserted not *against* but *on behalf of* the "occupied." Such occupation authorities are not viewed as military representatives of a hostile power bivouacked in the Town Square; rather, they are benign forces of protection—like the police or military of the occupied country itself. Their role as protectors gives them no license to abuse the inhabitants. The Constitution of the United States does not permit an American policeman or an American soldier to disregard the rights of those on whose behalf they stand watch. . . .

F. *Constitutional Rights Afforded to Aliens*

Finally, the Prosecution seeks to distinguish most prior decisions dealing with the rights of accused in occupation courts and the instant proceeding on the ground that the prior adjudications concerned the rights to be afforded to American citizens, whereas the defendants here are aliens.

Although it is true that most of the cases discussed concerned prosecutions of American citizens abroad, the Court finds the purported distinction unpersuasive in the context of a trial of friendly aliens, accused of non-military offenses, in Berlin in 1979. The Prosecution conceded in oral argument that in its view aliens, as well as citizens, enjoyed the same "non-rights" in this Court; that is, neither need be afforded a trial by jury. More importantly, whatever distinction may still be permissible between citizens and friendly aliens in civil cases, the Fifth Amendment to the Constitution requires, in terms admitting of no ambiguity, that "no *person*" shall be deprived of life or liberty without due process of law; similarly, the Sixth Amendment protects all who are "*accused*", without qualification. Finally, it appears to the Court that the United States is precluded from treating these defendants less favorably than United States citizens, not only by its own Constitution, but also by an international agreement to which the United States is a party.

Article 15, paragraph 2, of the Convention on Offenses and Certain Other Acts Committed on Board Aircraft (The Tokyo Convention) provides in part that—

> [A] Contracting State in whose territory a person has been disembarked . . ., or delivered [by the aircraft commander], or has disembarked and is suspected of

having committed an act [of hijacking], shall accord to such person treatment which is no less favorable for his protection and security than that accorded to nationals of such Contracting State in like circumstances.

In its transmittal of the Tokyo Convention to the United States Senate for its advice and consent, the Executive Branch explained the meaning of the phrase "treatment which is no less favorable for his protection and security than that accorded to nationals of such Contracting State" in the following manner:

> By this formulation it is intended that persons in any form of custody or otherwise subject to the law of Contracting States should be entitled to avail themselves of the provisions of law of the State relating to the protection of nationals.

The testimony of the representative of the Department of State in Congressional hearings on the Tokyo Convention supports the conclusion that this provision should be interpreted broadly as requiring the United States "to accord the Offender all the rights and privileges that any criminal would have in this country." Indeed, the language of Article 15(2) was originally proposed by the United States delegation to the 1963 International Conference on Air Law, which approved the Tokyo Convention. At that time, the United States explained that the purpose of the proposed language was:

> To guarantee that any person who is subjected to any type of investigation or placed under any type of custody in a Contracting State is granted the same protection of his rights and immunities as nationals of such Contracting State.

Therefore, this Court believes that these defendants should be afforded the same constitutional rights that the United States would have to afford its own nationals when brought before this Court.

In sum, this Court does not hold that jury trials must be afforded in occupation courts *everywhere* and under *all* circumstances; the Court holds only that if the United States convenes a United States court in Berlin, under the present circumstances, and charges civilians with non-military offenses, the United States must provide the defendants with the same constitutional safeguards that it must provide to civilian defendants in any other United States court.

VI

Finally, the Court must address the Prosecution's suggestion that if the Court were to order a jury trial, the United States occupation authorities in Berlin may not implement the Court's order. The Prosecution states:

> These [jury questions] are all clearly matters within the exclusive purview of the Executive authorities—that is, the United States occupation authorities in Berlin—to consider and decide. They involve, foremost, policy questions on the conduct of the United States in the continuing occupation in Berlin.

> Without going further into the question of basic mechanics of directing a jury system, we submit with all due respect that because this Court lacks power to establish a jury system, both as a practical and as a political matter, it is simply not possible for a jury to be ordered in this case.

Whether Law No. 46 empowers this Court to issue whatever process is necessary to select, summon and empanel a jury is academic. The Court will not issue directives to the civilian population in the American Sector of Berlin which might be countermanded by the United States occupation authorities. The civilian population should not be subjected to inconsistent directives.

Pursuant to the authority vested in this Court by Article 3(5) of Law No. 46, the Court will simply amend the "Rules of Criminal Procedure for the United States Court for Berlin," originally promulgated on November 30, 1978, to provide for trial by jury, and will direct the Clerk of the Court that 500 veniremen drawn from a cross-section of the German population of the United States Sector of Berlin be summoned to appear at the start of the trial in May. Unless the United States occupation authorities state on the record that they will comply with, and implement the Court's directive, the charges lodged against these defendants will be dismissed.

Notes and Questions

1. After receiving a jury trial in accordance with U.S. constitutional guarantees, Tiede was convicted of some offenses but was sentenced by Judge Stern "to time served" while awaiting trial. See H. STERN, JUDGMENT IN BERLIN 350–351, 367–72 (1984). Judge Stern made it clear that he was not about to turn over persons for incarceration to a government that had demonstrated its unwillingness to follow law and had argued that judges, in Berlin, should merely follow orders.

For additional background, see Ed Gordon, *American Courts, International Law and "Political Questions" which Touch Foreign Relations*, 14 INT'L LAW. 297 (1980); Jordan Paust, *Is the President Bound by the Supreme Law of the Land?—Foreign Affairs and National Security Reexamined*, 9 HASTINGS CONST. L.Q. 719, 723–25, 729–30 (1982); RE-STATEMENT OF THE FOREIGN RELATIONS LAW OF THE UNITED STATES § 722, Reporters' Notes 15–16 (3 ed. 1987).

2. Is the President (and other members of the executive branch) bound by international law, including relevant due process guarantees (noted *infra*)? See U.S. Const. Art. II § 3; note 1 above and *compare* J. PAUST, INTERNATIONAL LAW AS LAW OF THE UNITED STATES 169–73 (2 ed. 2003); Paust, *Executive Plans and Authorizations to Violate International Law Concerning Treatment and Interrogation of Detainees*, 43 COLUMBIA J. TRANSNAT'L L. 811, 856–61 (2005) [hereinafter Paust, *Executive Plans*]; Paust, *The President Is Bound by International Law*, 81 AM. J. INT'L L. 377 (1987) *with* Charney, D'Amato, Glennon, Henkin and Kirgis in *Agora: May the President Violate Customary International Law?*, in 80 AM. J. INT'L L. 913 (1986) and 81 AM. J. INT'L L. 371 (1987). *See also* Paust, *Paquete and the President: Rediscovering the Brief for the United States*, 34 VA. J. INT'L L. (1994). Cases since *Paquete Habana* include: *Trans World Airlines v. Franklin Mint Corp.*, 466 U.S. 243, 261 (1984) (O'Connor, J.: power "delegated by Congress to the Executive Branch" as well as a relevant congressional-executive "arrangement" must not be "exercised in a manner inconsistent with ... international law."); *United States v. Curtiss-Wright Export Corp.*, 299 U.S. 304, 318 (1936) ("operations of the nation in ... ["foreign"] territory must be governed by treaties ... and the principles of international law."); *Valentine v. Neidecker*, 299 U.S. 5, 14 & n.12, 18 (1936); *Francis v. Francis*, 203 U.S. 233, 240, 242 (1906); *United States v. Ferris*, 19 F.2d 925, 926 (N.D. Cal. 1927) (executive seizure in violation of "international law" and treaty obviated jurisdiction and is "not to be sanctioned by any court"); *United States v. Yunis*, 681 F. Supp. 896, 906 (D.D.C. 1986) ("The government cannot act beyond the jurisdictional parameters set forth by principles of international law...."); *Fernandez v. Wilkinson*, 505 F. Supp. 787, 799–800 (D. Kan. 1980); *see also United States v. Verdugo-Urquidez*, 110 S.Ct. 1056, 1066 (1990) (Rehnquist, C. J., dictum re: U.S. use of armed force abroad and that "restrictions on searches and seizures which occur incident to such action ... [can] be imposed by ... treaty...."); *Ford v. United States*, 273 U.S. 593, 606 (1927); *United States v. Toscanino*, 500 F.2d 267,

276–79 (2d Cir.), *reh'g denied*, 504 F.2d 894, 906 n.10 (2d Cir. 1974); *but see Garcia-Mir v. Meese*, 788 F.2d 1446 (11th Cir. 1986) (executive acts were "controlling" under the circumstances despite claims under customary international law), *cert. denied sub nom. Ferrer-Mazorra v. Meese*, 107 S.Ct. 289 (1986). Every known case addressing the laws of war has recognized that the President and all within the Executive branch are bound by the laws of war. *See, e.g.*, Jordan J. Paust, *In Their Own Words: Affirmations of the Founders, Framers, and Early Judiciary Concerning the Binding Nature of the Customary Law of Nations*, 14 U.C. Davis J. Int'l L. & Pol'y 205, 240–45 (2008); Paust, *Executive Plans, supra* at 858–61.

3. As *Tiede* declares, the Constitution applies abroad to restrain Executive conduct. Do you agree that the restraints on Executive power thereby protect aliens? *Compare* Stephan, *Constitutional Limits on the Struggle Against International Terrorism: Revisiting the Rights of Overseas Aliens*, 19 Conn. L. Rev. 831 (1987) *with United States v. Toscanino*, 500 F.2d 267, 276–80 (2d Cir. 1974); *United States v. Yunis*, 681 F. Supp. 896, 916–18 (D.D.C. 1988); Restatement of the Foreign Relations Law of the United States §§ 433, Reporters' Notes 3–4, and 722, Reporters' Notes 15–16 (3 ed. 1987); Paust, *Antiterrorism Military Commissions: Courting Illegality*, 1, 18–20 (2001); Paust, *An Introduction to and Commentary on Terrorism and the Law*, 19 Conn. L. Rev. 697, 721–35 (1987).

Has *United States v. Verdugo-Urquidez*, 494 U.S. 259 (1990) changed the *Tiede, Toscanino* and *Yunis* approach? Does it only apply to the Fourth Amendment? Is the majority opinion in *Verdugo-Urquidez* correct? Consider the following extract from the majority opinion per Chief Justice Rehnquist concerning U.S. searches abroad and claimed rights of aliens under the Fourth Amendment:

> [The text of the Fourth Amendment], by contrast with the Fifth and Sixth Amendments, extends its reach only to "the people." Contrary to the suggestion of *amici curiae* that the Framers used this phrase "simply to avoid [an] awkward rhetorical redundancy," Brief for American Civil Liberties Union et al. as *Amici Curiae* 12, n.4, "the people" seems to have been a term of art employed in select parts of the Constitution. The Preamble declares that the Constitution is ordained and established by "the People of the United States." The Second Amendment protects "the right of the people to keep and bear Arms," and the Ninth and Tenth Amendments provide that certain rights and powers are retained by and reserved to "the people." *See also* U.S. Const., Amdt. 1 ("Congress shall make no law ... abridging ... *the right of the people* peaceably to assemble") (emphasis added); Art. I, §2, cl. 1 ("The House of Representatives shall be composed of Members chosen every second Year *by the People of the several States*") (emphasis added). While this textual exegesis is by no means conclusive, it suggests that "the people" protected by the Fourth Amendment, and by the First and Second Amendments, and to whom rights and power are reserved in the Ninth and Tenth Amendments, refers to a class of persons who are part of a national community or who have otherwise developed sufficient connection with this country to be considered part of that community ... The language of these Amendments contrasts with the words "person" and "accused" used in the Fifth and Sixth Amendments regulating procedure in criminal cases.

Can United States officials ever act lawfully in contravention of the Constitution? Also see generally *United States v. Curtiss-Wright Export Corp.*, 299 U.S. 304, 320 (1936); *United States v. Lee*, 106 U.S. 196, 220 (1882); Paust, International Law as Law of the United States 487–95, *passim* (2 ed. 2003).

4. In *Boumediene v. Bush*, 553 U.S. 723 (2008), the U.S. Supreme Court affirmed that constitutionally-based habeas corpus applies to persons detained at Guantanamo Bay, Cuba. The Court stated: "We hold these petitioners do have the habeas corpus privilege. Congress has enacted a statute, the Detainee Treatment Act of 2005 (DTA), 119 Stat. 2739, that provides certain procedures for review of the detainees' status. We hold that those procedures are not an adequate and effective substitute for habeas corpus. Therefore §7 of the Military Commissions Act of 2006 (MCA), 28 U.S.C.A. §2241(e) (Supp.2007), operates as an unconstitutional suspension of the writ....

"Our basic charter cannot be contracted away ... [by a lease with Cuba]. The Constitution grants Congress and the President the power to acquire, dispose of, and govern territory, not the power to decide when and where its terms apply. Even when the United States acts outside its borders its powers are not "absolute and unlimited" but are subject "to such restrictions as are expressed in the Constitution." Murphy v. Ramsey, 114 U.S. 15, 44 (1885)....

"[W]e conclude that at least three factors are relevant in determining the reach of the Suspension Clause: (1) the citizenship and status of the detainee and the adequacy of the process through which that status determination was made; (2) the nature of the sites where apprehension and then detention took place; and (3) the practical obstacles inherent in resolving the prisoner's entitlement to the writ....

"Guantanamo Bay ... is no transient possession. In every practical sense Guantanamo is not abroad; it is within the constant jurisdiction of the United States.... The Government presents no credible arguments that the military mission at Guantanamo would be compromised if habeas courts had jurisdiction to hear the detainees' claims. And in light of the plenary control the United States asserts over the base, none are apparent to us...."

See also Jordan J. Paust, Boumediene *and Fundamental Principles of Constitutional Power*, 21 REGENT U. L. REV. 351 (2008-2009).

5. In *Hirota v. MacArthur*, 338 U.S. 197, 198 (1948), it was stated that the tribunal in occupied Japan was one of the Allied powers set up by General MacArthur "as the agent of the Allied Powers" under the Joint Command, was "not a tribunal of the United States," and that "courts of the United States have no power or authority to review, to affirm, set aside or annul the judgments and sentences" of such international tribunals. In a concurring opinion (*id.* at 205), Justice Douglas suggested that a U.S. citizen would, however, have recourse via habeas corpus to U.S. courts with respect to U.S. action carrying out the decision of an international tribunal. Have *Reid* and *Tiede* expanded upon Justice Douglas's suggestion? Justice Douglas also recognized that the IMT for the Far East was created ultimately by executive agreement, the Moscow Agreement (December 27, 1945), which established a Far Eastern Commission composed of representatives of eleven nations with broad powers, including the power to prosecute crimes, and that the Commission "provided the Supreme Commander for the Allied Powers ... power to appoint special international military courts to try war criminals. *Id.* at 206–207. He also noted that the President's agreement was based partly on the President's Commander in Chief and "foreign relations" powers. *Id.* at 208; also see the earlier *Hirota* decision, 335 U.S. 876, 878 (1948), opinion of Justice Jackson (Commander in Chief, foreign affairs, and cooperative "commitment of the President"). Justice Douglas added: "The fact that the tribunal has been set up by the Allied Powers should not of itself preclude our inquiry. Our inquiry is directed ... to the conduct of our own officials. If an American General holds a prisoner, our process can reach him wherever he is. To that extent at least, the Constitution follows the flag. It is no defense for him to say that he acts of the Allied Powers.

He is an American citizen who is performing functions for our government. It is our Constitution which he supports and defends." *Id.* at 204.

6. With respect to *Tiede*, if hostilities had ended and peace was formally declared by 1951, constitutionally was the war power thereafter inoperative? *See also In re Yamashita, supra*; *Cross v. Harrison*, 57 U.S. (16 How.) 164, 190 (1853); 24 Op. Att'y Gen. 570, 571 (1903). The "occupation regime" terminated in 1955; but see the court's label ("protective occupation"). If not, with whom was the U.S. still at "war" with? If so, can Berlin be "occupied" territory?

If the war power was inoperative in Berlin, what constitutional power exists to authorize U.S. "governmental functions" in Berlin, including the retention of a U.S. Court for Berlin described as an Article II court? In *Tiede*, the court noted that "[i]n 1952 a series of agreements among the Three Powers and the Federal Republic of Germany, known collectively as the "Bonn Convention," were signed. These agreements, however, did not enter into force until May 5, 1955. On that date, the occupation regime in the Federal Republic of Germany was terminated ... The Bonn Convention however, did not provide for the termination of the occupation in Berlin. There, the occupation continued." Was the occupation in Berlin one that continued by Executive Agreement? If so, can the President, by Executive Agreement, set up a court on foreign territory? Does the agreement enhance presidential power because the President under the U.S. Constitution, Article II, section 3, must faithfully execute the law? See Jordan J. Paust, *Customary International Law: Its Nature, Sources and Status as Law of the United States*, 12 MICH. J. INT'L L. 59, 81–82 & n.39 (1990); *cf.* extracts from *Ex parte Milligan* and *Reid v. Covert, supra*. In *Reid v. Covert*, the Supreme Court also declared:

> No agreement with a foreign nation can confer power on the Congress, or on any other branch of Government, which is free from the restraints of the Constitution ... The prohibitions of the Constitution were designed to apply to all branches of the national Government and they cannot be nullified by the executive or by the Executive and the Senate combined.

See also Pollard v. Hagan, 44 U.S. (3 How.) 212, 225 (1845) ("It cannot be admitted that the King of Spain could, by treaty or otherwise, impart to the United States any of his royal prerogatives; and much less ... that they have the capacity to receive or power to exercise them"); Paust, *The Unconstitutional Detention of Prisoners by the United States Under the Exchange of Prisoner Treaties*, in INTERNATIONAL ASPECTS OF CRIMINAL LAW: ENFORCING UNITED STATES LAW IN THE WORLD COMMUNITY 204 (R. Lillich ed. 1981). If the Constitution confers power on the President to create tribunals by Executive Agreement or by treaty, or such agreements can enhance presidential power, have *Reid* and *Pollard* been met?

6. Constitutionally, how can the United States participate in an international criminal court in time of peace?

The International Military Tribunals considered in Chapter Six were created in time of war.

U.S. consular courts and the U.S. Court for China, operative abroad in time of peace, had been set up by congressional legislation. *See, e.g.*, 22 U.S.C. §§ 150–174 (repealed in 1956); §§ 191–200 (repealed in 1948).

Chapter 5

Obtaining Persons Abroad

Section 1
Extradition

Introductory Problem

For purposes of this problem, assume you are the clerk to a federal district judge in Massachusetts assigned the extradition case of *Ayer v. United States*. Assume also that Canada has a law which makes it a crime punishable by up to five years in prison for a person to publish a libel through means of mass distribution to the public (see s. 298 re: Defamatory Libel). Canada has no statute of limitations for this offense. Massachusetts does not have a criminal libel statute but recognizes a civil cause of action for libel, with an applicable 3 year statute of limitations.

The "relator" (or fugitive), James Ayer, is a U.S. citizen who is wanted by Canada on charges of criminal libel. Ayer is the author of Hess the Snake, a nonfiction book published four years ago and sold in stores throughout Canada, which details the shady dealings of a prominent Canadian lawyer, Theodore Hess, who has since been elected to Parliament and appointed Minister of Justice and Attorney-General of Canada.

Last year, Ayer moved to France, where he began work on his next novel, Hess the Devil, which has not yet been completed. A few months ago, Ayer was extradited by France to the United States on charges of tax evasion for failing to report the royalties for Hess the Snake. He was subsequently convicted and is currently serving a 5 year term in a Massachusetts prison.

Canada now wants the United States to extradite Ayer to Canada for trial on the criminal libel charges. Canada's extradition request contained: (1) a photograph of James Ayer; (2) a copy of the Canadian Defamatory Libel law; and (3) a copy of an indictment issued by a court in Ottawa three and a half years ago (the same day Theodore Hess was appointed Attorney General) which alleges that Ayer's book contains false and libelous statements about Theodore Hess.

Based on the materials in Section 1 of this chapter, how would you advise the judge to rule in this case? In particular, consider the following questions: Does Ayer have standing to challenge his extradition to Canada on the basis of the specialty doctrine? Would the specialty doctrine apply if France consented to Ayer's re-extradition to Canada? Would denial of Ayer's extradition be appropriate on the basis of lack of double criminality? Should Ayer's extradition be denied on the basis of the Massachusetts statute of limitations for civil libel actions? Should Ayer's extradition be denied on the basis of the political offense exception since the indictment appears to have been brought for political reasons? Finally, should an extradition judge allow Ayer to submit evidence proving that the unflattering statements in his book about Theodore Hess were all true?

A. The Process

M. Cherif Bassiouni (ed.), 2 International Criminal Law
417–22 (1986)

The Applicable Law to Extradition Proceedings

The national laws of the requested state will always be applicable. In the United States such laws consist of the United States Constitution, the applicable bilateral treaty, Title 18, United States Code, Sections 3181–3191, the jurisprudence of the federal courts interpreting the provisions of the applicable treaty and Sections 3181–3191 [see below], and, with respect to the requirement of "double criminality," federal criminal laws and the criminal laws of the state wherein the federal proceedings are conducted (which is where the relator has been arrested) on the basis of the extradition warrant.

There are still some pending constitutional questions concerning eventual conflicts between a treaty provision that may be contrary to or inconsistent with a constitutional right. So far none have arisen throughout the history of United States extradition, but at least some new treaties now raise that possibility. For example, the 1984 U.S.-Italy treaty does not specifically require "probable cause" for extradition, which is required by Title 18, Section 3184, and by the Fourth Amendment to the Constitution. Thus, under that treaty the standard of proof that the relator committed the crime charged could be deemed lesser than "probable cause," and in that case, the treaty would override the statue (Section 3184), but it would not override the United States Constitution (the Fourth Amendment).[1] If that were the case, then the United States Senate, which ratifies treaties, would have the power to amend, suspend, and alter the United States Constitution.

Rules of Procedure and Evidence

The procedural and evidentiary rules of the requested state shall apply in extradition proceedings. However, where an international legal right applies, it would supersede national laws. Thus, among the European states who signed the 1950 European Convention on Human Rights and Fundamental Freedoms, the provisions protecting individual rights and freedoms supersede national laws and are applicable by their own force and effect without the need for additional national legislation, except of course that which may be needed to ratify the Convention and make it nationally enforceable.[2]

In the United States the Constitution controls, and to the extent that the applicable bilateral treaty is not in conflict with the Constitution, its provisions shall be controlling, followed by the applicable federal statue, some aspects of the Federal Rules of Criminal Procedure and some aspects of the Federal Rules of Criminal Evidence. But since the United States considers extradition as *sui generis*, though partaking of a criminal nature, it considers it essentially subject to those procedural and evidentiary rules applicable to

---

1. See *United States v. Rauscher, supra* [all *supra* cites are in the original]; *see also United States ex. rel. Donnelly v. Mulligan*, 74 F.2d 220 (2d Cir. 1934) and *United States v. Romano, supra* [706 F.2d 370 (2d Cir. 1983)] wherein the court held that a relator may assert a "denial of justice" claim under international law which would be recognized in U.S. courts under certain conditions, *id*. at 375.

2. See Bassiouni, *Extradition*, Vol. II Chapter IX.

civil proceedings. Extradition cases are docketed as "miscellaneous," and *Habeas Corpus* review of extradition orders are docketed "civil." Thus, it is held that the Federal Rules of Criminal Procedure, and the Federal Rules of Criminal Evidence are not applicable to extradition hearings, with some exceptions, because such hearings are not for the purpose of determining guilt or innocence.

The U.S. government, acting on behalf of the requesting state, must only prove "probable cause" (Section 3184) and can do so by hearsay evidence, and by evidence that may not be admissible in criminal matters. The relator cannot introduce evidence to prove innocence, or even rebut the government's evidence, but may introduce evidence to "clarify" or "explain" the government's evidence. The relator cannot subpoena evidence or witnesses from the requesting state. Discovery is extremely limited,[3] and the right of confrontation and cross-examination" exists only where the government will present the testimony of a person present in the U.S. The sufficiency of the evidence shall be determined by the court in accordance with analogous "probable cause" hearings, which is that evidence satisfying the "ordinary reasonable person" test.

When the United States is a requested state, it receives first a request from the diplomatic agents of the requesting state, and transmits it through the United State's Attorney of the Federal District where the person sought is believed to be found or has been found. Thereafter, a judicial process initiates.

Extradition Proceedings

The Initial Stage — Bail: The initial stage in U.S. extradition proceedings is in the nature of a hearing before a U.S. magistrate or judge shortly after arrest of the person to determine whether the person arrested is the one named in the arrest warrant and to allow arguments by the relator for admission to bail. There is no recognized constitutional right to bail, but case law has established that a relator may be released on bail pending the determination of the relator's extraditability if that person can show "special circumstances" justifying bail.[4] Usually the principal factors are: seriousness of the charges, and the "ties" that such a person may have with the community. The government may argue in opposition to bail that "risk of flight" may prevent the U.S. from carrying out its treaty obligations toward the requesting state. In general, the same criteria used in criminal cases will be applied, but without the benefit of a constitutional right.

During these preliminary stages, which precede the hearing on extraditability, the relator will have the right to a court appointed counsel if such a person has no means to secure private counsel. The relator will then receive a copy of the extradition request and the documentation supporting it and will have a very limited right of discovery in the discretion of the court.

The Extradition Hearing: The hearing on extraditability is essentially in the nature of a "probable cause" hearing where the identity of relator is established, the criminal charges brought against that person are determined extraditable offenses within the meaning of the Treaty, that the charges satisfy the requirements of "double criminality" and any other

---

3. *In re Wadge*, 15 F. 864 (S.D.N.Y. 1883); *First Nat'l City Bank v. Aristeguieta*, 287 F.2d 219 (2d Cir. 19960); *Petrushanshky v. Maresco, supra*; the two *Jhirad v. Ferrandina*, and *Sabatier v. Dambrowski*, 435 F. Supp. 1250 (D.R.I. 1978), *affirmed*, 586 F.2d 866 (1st Cir. 1978).
4. *Wright v. Henkel*, 190 U.S. 40 (1903); *In re Mitchell*, 171 F. 289 (S.D.N.Y. 1909); *Fioconni v. Attorney General*, 462 F.2d 475 (2d Cir. 1972); *Peroff v. Hylton*, 542 F.2d 1247 (4th Cir. 1976), *cert. denied.* 429 U.S. 1062 (1977); *United States v. Williams*, 480 F. Supp. 482 (D.C. Mass. 1979); *Matter of Sindona*, 450 F. Supp. 672 (S.D.N.Y. 1978); *Caltagirone v. Grant, supra*; *Hu Yan-Lueng v. Soscia* and *United States v. Messina, supra*.

treaty and statutory requirements, that the evidence presented by the government in support of the request constitutes "probable cause," and that there are no grounds within the Treaty or the applicable statute for denial of extradition.[5]

The relator may not argue his innocence or present exculpatory evidence but can present evidence that "explains" or "clarifies" the evidence presented by the government with a view to show the absence of "probable cause" or its insufficiency.[6] While this stage of the proceedings is the one at which the opposing sides will be presenting evidence supporting "probable cause" and negatively "clarifying" it, the significant legal issue will usually be "double criminality" and the sufficiency of the evidence presented. In these respects, the jurisprudence of the courts will sometimes vary from circuit to circuit depending on the treaty in question and the crime charged....

Review of Extradition Orders

An order denying extradition is not reviewable on appeal at the government's motion,[7] but since such an extradition order is not a final order, the government can reintroduce a request even when based on the same, or substantially the same facts as were already adjudicated.[8]

A person found extraditable can have the order reviewed by means of a petition for a Writ of *Habeas Corpus*. Such a review, however, is neither an appeal nor a trial *de novo*, it is limited to the following issues: the proper identity of the relator, the existence of a treaty, the extraditability of the crime charged, "double criminality," the existence of "probable cause," the absence of any grounds for denial of extradition.[9] The reviewing court will rule on the questions of law involved in the issues stated above, and will examine the facts only insofar as they relate to these legal issues. The reviewing court will not substitute its judgement to the U.S. magistrate or judge who heard the case initially, unless on the face of the record it appears that such judge abused his judicial discretion, failed to apply the proper legal standards, committed error with respect to the sufficiency of the evidence supporting the existence of "probable cause" or failed to recognize one of the grounds for denial of extradition.

A *Habeas Corpus* hearing will be held before a U.S. judge, who would in fact be reviewing not only a magistrate's order, but also, sometimes, another judge's (of equal judicial stature) order. In some cases even the same judge will review his own decision.[10]

If a judge on such *Habeas Corpus* hearing upholds the order of extradition the relator can appeal to the U.S. Court of Appeals which will then only review the decision of the judge in the *Habeas Corpus* proceedings or the same legal grounds stated above. The relator may also, in case of an unfavorable judgment, file a motion for a rehearing *en banc* before the same circuit court, and also petition the United States Supreme Court on a petition for a Writ of *Certiorari*, which is rarely granted in extradition cases.

---

5. *Benson v. McMahon*, 127 U.S. 457 (1888).

6. For some major Supreme Court decisions: *Glucksman v. Henkel, supra*; *Collins v. Loisel, supra*; *Fernandez v. Phillips*, 268 U.S. 311 (1925); *Factor v. Laubenheimer*, 290 U.S. 276 (1933). For other major decisions, *see Sayne v. Shipley, supra*; *Jhirad v. Ferrandina, supra* note 47; *Garcia-Guillern v. United States, supra*; *Merino v. United States, supra*; *Greci v. Birknes*, 527 F.2d 956 (1st Cir. 1976); *Hooker v. Klein*, 573 F.2d 1360 (9th Cir. 1978); *United States v. Wiebe*, 733 F.2d 549 (8th Cir. 1984).

7. *In re Mackin*, 668 F.2d 122 (2d Cir. 1981).

8. *Id.*, and *Jhirad v. Ferrandina*, and *Jimenez v. Aristeguieta*, 290 F.2d 106 (5th Cir. 1961).

9. *Terlinden v. Ames, supra*; *Fernandez v. Philips, supra*; *Ornelas v. Ruiz*, 161 U.S. 502 (1896); *Wright v. Henkel, supra*; *Benson v. McMahon, supra*.

10. *David v. Attorney General*, 699 F.2d 411, 416 (7th Cir. 1983), *cert. denied*, 464 U.S. 832 (1983); *Demjanjuk v. Petrovsky, supra* at 577.

Should the judge in a Habeas Corpus order find the relator non-extraditable which is tantamount to a reversal of the order of extradition, the government may appeal that order to the U.S. Circuit Court, and if the decision is negative, the government can file a motion for a rehearing *en banc* before the same circuit court and in the event that decision is also negative it can file a petition for a Writ of *Certiorari* before the U.S. Supreme Court.

A petition for a Writ of *Habeas Corpus* and any eventual petitions by the relator must be accompanied by a petition for an order to stay the surrender. Otherwise, the relator may still be surrendered to the requesting state if the original order, even on review, has not been stayed.

At all levels of review, the question of bail may be reargued either by the relator or by the government.

A declaratory judgment or *mandamus* can be sought in limited cases. The former, as an alternative to review by means of *Habeas Corpus*,[11] the latter, only when there is a clear abuse of discretion by the court or the government.[12] Both are rare occurrences. Present proposals for amending U.S. extradition laws provide for review by appeal by the relator and the government.[13]

18 U.S.C. §§ 3181 *et seq.*

[Editors' note: In the United States, the statute that governs extradition is Title 18 of the United States Code, Sections 3181 through 3195, which is reproduced below.]

§ 3181. Scope and limitation of chapter

The provisions of this chapter relating to the surrender of persons who have committed crimes in foreign countries shall continue in force only during the existence of any treaty of extradition with such foreign government....

§ 3184. Fugitives from foreign country to United States

Whenever there is a treaty or convention for extradition between the United States and any foreign government, any justice or judge of the United States, or any magistrate [United States magistrate judge] authorized so to do by a court of the United States, or any judge of a court of record of general jurisdiction of any State, may, upon complaint made under oath, charging any person found within his jurisdiction, with having committed within the jurisdiction of any such foreign government any of the crimes provided for by such treaty or convention, issue his warrant for the apprehension of the person so charged, that he may be brought before such justice, judge, or magistrate, to the end that the evidence of criminality may be heard and considered. Such complaint may be filed before and such warrant may be issued by a judge or magistrate of the United States District court for the District of Columbia if the whereabouts within the United States of the person charged are not known or, if there is reason to believe the person will shortly enter the United States. If, on such hearing, he deems the evidence sufficient to sustain the charge under the provisions of the proper treaty or convention, he shall certify the same, together with a copy of all the testimony taken before him, to the

---

11. A declaratory judgment is an adequate procedural for the government and the relator to challenge some aspect of the judicial proceedings, and in the case of the relator, a substitutive means to challenge an extradition order instead of resorting to *Habeas Corpus*, see *Wacker v. Bisson*, 348 F.2d 602 (5th Cir. 1965).

12. *Mandamus* may also be resorted to in cases of clear usurpation of power or abuse of discretion. *In re Extradition of Ghandtchi*, 697 F.2d 1037 (11th Cir. 1983).

13. *See* Bassiouni, [17 Akron L. Rev. (1984)] *supra*, at 556–557.

Secretary of State, that a warrant may issue upon the requisition of the proper authorities of such foreign government, for the surrender of such person, according to the stipulations of the treaty or convention; and he shall issue his warrant for the commitment of the person so charged to the proper jail, there to remain until such surrender shall be made ...

§ 3186. Secretary of State to surrender fugitive

The Secretary of State may order the person committed under section 3184 or 3185 of this title to be delivered to any authorized agent of such foreign government, to be tried for the offense of which charged.

Such agent may hold such person in custody, and take him to the territory of such foreign government, pursuant to such treaty.

A person so accused who escapes may be retaken in the same manner as any person accused of any offense.

§ 3187. Provisional arrest and detention within extraterritorial jurisdiction

The provisional arrest and detention of a fugitive, under sections 3042 and 3183 of this title, in advance of the presentation of formal proofs, may be obtained by telegraph upon the request of the authority competent to request the surrender of such fugitive addressed to the authority competent to grant such surrender. Such request shall be accompanied by an express statement that a warrant for the fugitive's arrest has been issued within the jurisdiction of the authority making such request charging the fugitive with the commission of the crime for which his extradition is sought to be obtained.

No person shall be held in custody under telegraphic request by virtue of this section for more than ninety days.

§ 3188. Time of commitment pending extradition

Whenever any person who is committed for rendition to a foreign government to remain until delivered up in pursuance of a requisition, is not so delivered up in pursuance of a requisition, is not so delivered up and conveyed out of the United States within two calendar months after such commitment, over and above the time actually required to convey the prisoner from the jail to which he was committed, by the readiest way, out of the United States, any judge of the United States, or of any State, upon application made to him by or on behalf of the person so committed, and upon proof made to him that a reasonable notice of the intention to make such application has been given to the Secretary of State, may order the person so committed to be discharged out of custody, unless sufficient cause is shown to such judge why such discharge ought not to be ordered.

§ 3189. Place and character of hearing

Hearings in cases of extradition under treaty stipulation or convention shall be held on land, publicly, and in a room or office easily accessible to the public.

§ 3190. Evidence on hearing

Depositions, warrants, or other papers or copies thereof offered in evidence upon the hearing of any extradition case shall be received and admitted as evidence on such hearing for all the purposes of such hearing if they shall be properly and legally authenticated so as to entitle them to be received for similar purposes by the tribunals of the foreign country from which the accused party shall have escaped, and the certificate of the principal diplomatic or consular officer of the United States resident in such foreign country shall be proof that the same, so offered, are authenticated in the manner required....

§ 3195. Payment of fees and costs

All costs or expenses incurred in any extradition proceeding in apprehending, securing, and transmitting a fugitive shall be paid by the demanding authority.

All witness fees and costs of every nature in cases of international extradition, including the fees of the magistrate [United States magistrate judge], shall be certified by the judge or magistrate before whom the hearing shall take place to the Secretary of State of the United States, and the same shall be paid out of appropriations to defray the expenses of the judiciary or the Department of Justice as the case may be.

The Attorney General shall certify to the Secretary of State the amounts to be paid to the United States on account of said fees and costs in extradition cases by the foreign government requesting the extradition, and the Secretary of State shall cause said amounts to be collected and transmitted to the Attorney General for deposit in the Treasury of the United States.

Notes and Questions

1. As indicated in the extradition statute reproduced above, the United States may extradite only pursuant to an extradition treaty. *See also Valentine v. United States ex rel. Neidecker,* 299 U.S. 5 (1936); RESTATEMENT OF THE FOREIGN RELATIONS LAW OF THE UNITED STATES § 475, Cmnt. b and Reporters' Note 3 (3 ed. 1987). The Restatement's note 3 stated that *Valentine* held that "under existing law the Executive Branch may not exercise discretion to extradite a person unless authority to do so is expressly conferred by treaty." *Id.* Note 3; *cf* note 3 below. Nonetheless, it is permissible for the U.S. to receive an accused without a treaty-based extradition (if no international norms are violated). *Id.* Also, some countries do not need a treaty to extradite. *Id.* Cmnt. b.

As Secretary of State, Jefferson stated that the "delivery of fugitives from one country to another, as practiced by several nations, is in consequence of conventions settled between them, defining precisely the cases wherein such deliveries shall take place." Letter to President Washington, Nov. 7, 1791, in 8 JEFFERSON's WRITINGS 253–54 (1903). In 1792, he noted: "The unsuccessful strugglers against tyranny, have been the chief martyrs of treason laws in all countries" and they should not be extradited. Further, "[a]ll excess of punishment is a crime. To remit a fugitive to excessive punishment is to be accessory to the crime." *Id.* at 330–32.

2. The bilateral treaties of extradition to which the United States is a party are listed in 18 U.S.C. § 3181. For a current list, see the List of U.S. Bilateral Extradition Treaties, in the Documents Supplement. What countries are conspicuously absent from the list of bilateral treaties above? Why do you think the United States has refrained from entering into extradition treaties with these countries? Note in this regard that the United States is party to extradition treaties with such countries as Iraq, Pakistan, Singapore, Turkey, and Thailand, whose notions of due process and appropriate punishments for crimes are significantly different from that of the United States (although human rights law provides a set of minimum guarantees).

3. Can an executive agreement constitute a "treaty" for purposes of extradition from the U.S., *e.g.*, for purposes of §§ 3181 and 3184 of the U.S. legislation? The word "treaty" in some U.S. statutes has been interpreted to include executive agreements. *See, e.g.*, RESTATEMENT §§ 111, RN 4, 303, RN 1. The United States entered into two treaty-executive agreements with the International Criminal Tribunals for Former Yugoslavia and for Rwanda for the purpose of rendering accused to the Tribunals. The executive agreements

are based ultimately on the authority of the U.N. Charter and Security Council resolutions setting up the Tribunals and their competencies. *See generally*, Robert Kushen, Kenneth J. Harris, *Surrender of Fugitives by the United States to the War Crimes Tribunals for Yugoslavia and Rwanda*, 90 Am. J. Int'l L. 510 (1996); correspondence, *id.* vol. 91, at 90 (1997). Thus, they are treaty-executive agreements. The Statute of the International Criminal Court (ICC) or "Rome" Treaty provides for the "surrender" of persons to the ICC in Articles 89–102 of the treaty, see Documents Supplement.

In *Ntakirutimana v. Reno*, 184 F.3d 419 (5th Cir. 1999), *cert. denied*, 120 S.Ct. 977 (2000), Circuit Judge Garza ruled that the 1995 executive agreement with the ICTR, coupled with a 1996 statute "to implement the Agreement" (National Defense Authorization Act, Pub. L. 104–106, §1342, 110 Stat. 486 (1996)), provided a constitutional basis for extradition of Ntakirutimana, a former President of the Seventh Day Adventist Church for Rwanda, to the ICTR to stand trial on charges of genocide, complicity in genocide, conspiracy to commit genocide, crimes against humanity, and serious violations of Article 3 common to the Geneva Conventions and of Additional Protocol II thereto. The opinion noted that *Valentine* had stated that "'[t]here is no executive discretion to surrender ... unless that discretion is granted by law ... by an act of Congress or by the terms of a treaty'"; that *Valentine* concluded that the President's "'power, in the absence of [a] statute conferring an independent power, must be found in the terms of the treaty ...'"; and that *Valentine* "supports the constitutionality of using the Congressional-Executive Agreement to extradite...." *Id.* at 425.

4. An offense committed prior to the existence of an extradition treaty can be covered by the new treaty or new amendment (and without violating ex post facto prohibitions). *See, e.g., Factor v. Laubenheimer*, 290 U.S. 276, 304 (1933); *In re Giacomo*, 7 F. Cas. 366, 369–70 (C.C.S.D.N.Y. 1874) (No. 3,747); *Demjanjuk v. Petrovsky*, in Chapter Three, Section 1; Restatement §476, Cmnt. b; Paust, *Extradition and United States Prosecution of the* Achille Lauro *Hostage-Takers: Navigating the Hazards,* 20 Vand. J. Trans. L. 235, 238 n.9 (1987).

5. Bilateral treaties to which the United States is a party typically contain a list of extraditable offenses. When the treaty contains a list, the listed offenses are liberally construed to support extradition. Yet, under the customary "speciality" doctrine (read into any extradition treaty) the accused can be extradited, and then prosecuted, only for an offense for which the accused has been extradited (unless there has been a subsequent waiver by the requested or extraditing state). *See, e.g., United States v. Rauscher*, 119 U.S. 407, 411–12 (1886); *United States v. Puentes*, 50 F.3d 1567 (11th Cir. 1995) [in the extract below in Section B]; Restatement §477.

6. Since there is no duty under customary international law to extradite (Restatement §475, Cmnt. a), there is a need for consent of the requested state—either ad hoc (for countries that do not need a treaty-base to extradite) or by a bilateral or multilateral agreement. *See also Ex parte dos Santos*, 7 F. Cas. 949, 953–56 (C.C.D. Va. 1835) (No. 4,016) (no obligation to extradite absent a treaty); 1 Op. Att'y Gen. 521 (1821). Normally, there is a bilateral extradition treaty forming the basis of state consent.

7. The United States is a party to the Multilateral Convention on Extradition signed at Montevideo on Dec. 26, 1933, entered into force for the U.S. on Jan. 25, 1935. 49 Stat. 3111. Other state signatories include: Argentina, Chile, Colombia, Dominican Republic, Ecuador, El Salvador, Guatemala, Honduras, Mexico, Nicaragua, Panama.

8. Several other multilateral treaties exist which allow states to treat such an agreement as an extradition treaty. These are especially relevant to international criminal law.

See, e.g., Article 10(2) of the 1979 International Convention Against the Taking of Hostages (in Chapter Eleven). Article 10(1) adds that the offenses therein "shall be deemed to be included as extraditable offences in any extradition treaty existing between States Parties." See also RESTATEMENT § 475, Reporters' Note 5. Other such treaties include: the Hague Aircraft Hijacking Convention; the Montreal Aircraft Sabotage Convention; the Convention Against Torture; the 1988 U.N. Drug Convention; the International Convention for the Suppression of Terrorist Bombings; and the International Convention on the Suppression of the Financing of Terrorism, see the Documents Supplement. Newer treaties include the United Nations Convention on Transnational Organized Crime (also known as the Palermo Convention), which entered into force on Sept. 19, 2003; and other multilateral conventions with extradition articles such as the (OECD) Convention on Combating Bribery of Foreign Officials in International Business Transactions (Art. 10), the Inter-American Convention Against Corruption (Art. XIII), the U.N. Convention Against Corruption (Art. 45), and the Council of Europe Criminal Law Convention on Corruption (Art. 37).

9. The European Union has instituted the European Arrest Warrant (EAW) which is designed to facilitate the surrender of persons charged with crimes within the EU and dispenses with some of the normally required procedures for extradition. It is designed to meet the needs of justice, liberty and security within a single region. The facts described in an EAW must, at a minimum, comprise the essential elements of the punishable conduct so that the executing state can ascertain whether the principle of *ne bis in idem* (the principle against trying a person more than once for the same offense) is being violated. The "speciality" rule also requires a precise description of the individual offenses in the form sheet. However, the form sheet is not suited for use with respect to a multitude of offenses, especially in the case of both listed offenses and other offenses, which must be punishable in both legal systems. Although the EU is still working out some implementation issues, the ability to use a EAW will obviate some of the lengthy and more cumbersome procedures of extradition. For background, see Bruce Zagaris, *European Union Provides Recommendations on Implementing the European Arrest Warrant*, 21 INT'L L. REP. 94 (Mar. 2005), citing Council of European Union, Recommendations of the Conference "First Practical Experiences with the European Arrest Warrant," 14618/04, Brussels, Nov. 17, 2004.

10. Why do you think Congress in the extradition statute gave the Secretary of State the power to deny extradition even after an extradition court has found the accused "extraditable"? What does "extraditable" mean or imply? Consider the case of a present request for extradition from Cuba or Iran.

11. Based on the statute and discussion above, how can the accused challenge an extradition judge's ruling that he is extraditable? How can the Government challenge an extradition judge's ruling that the accused is not extraditable? Why isn't such a challenge by the prosecutor barred by the double jeopardy clause of the U.S. Constitution?

12. In United States v. Duarte-Acero, 208 F.3d 1282 (11th Cir. 2000), the Eleventh Circuit recognized that although the International Covenant on Civil and Political Rights guarantees the right to be free from double jeopardy, such does not apply to prosecutions by two different sovereigns [unless the prohibition is expressly part of a relevant extradition treaty], adding that the Rome Statute for the International Criminal Court (ICC) creates a different form of *non bis in idem* and noting the ICCPR Human Rights Committee's view in A.P. v. Italy (2 Nov. 1987) (no double jeopardy exists when Italy prosecutes a person convicted in Switzerland for acts arising out of the same conduct). Columbia had refused to extradite Duarte-Acero to the U.S. "apparently citing the *non bis in idem*

clause of the extradition treaty then in effect between the United States and Columbia" when he had already been prosecuted in Columbia. The defendant had been lured into Equador, where he was arrested.

13. Section 3187 of the extradition statute provides for "provisional arrest" and up to ninety days detention pending receipt of a fully documented formal request for extradition. Based on the statute, what documentation do you think needs to accompany a provisional arrest warrant? Does the U.S. Constitution require additional proof that the accused has committed the alleged crime? See RESTATEMENT § 478. Consider also the 1980 DIGEST OF UNITED STATES PRACTICE IN INTERNATIONAL LAW 220–223:

14. The probable cause standard applicable to an extradition hearing is the same as the standard used in federal preliminary hearings, meaning that the magistrate's role is merely "to determine whether there is competent evidence to justify holding the accused to await trial." Orindola v. Hackman, 478 F.3d 588 (4th Cir. 2007) (internal quotation marks omitted). Evidence considered by the magistrate at the extradition hearing "need not meet the standards for admissibility at trial" and "may be based upon hearsay in whole or in part." *Id.* at 608 (internal quotation marks omitted). At the extradition hearing, the fugitive can present evidence to challenge or explain away the government's evidence of probable cause. *See* Barapind v. Enomoto, 400 F.3d 744, 749 (9th Cir. 2005). "Generally, evidence that explains away or completely obliterates probable cause is the only evidence admissible at an extradition hearing, whereas evidence that merely controverts the existence of probable cause, or raises a defense, is not admissible." Mainero v. Gregg, 164 F.3d 1199, 1207 n.7 (9th Cir. 1999). Further, extradition courts do not make credibility determinations or weigh conflicting evidence in examining the government's probable cause evidence. *See Barapind v. Enomoto*, 400 F.3d at 750; Ordinola v. Hackman, 478 F.3d at 608. *See also* Caltagirone v. Grant, 629 F.2d 730 (2d Cir. 1980) (holding that the U.S.-Italy extradition treaty required a showing of probable cause not only on requests to the U.S. for formal extradition, but also on requests for provisional arrest pending submission of a formal extradition demand).

B. Standing and the "Speciality" Doctrine

United States v. Puentes
50 F.3d 1567 (11th Cir. 1995)

[Editors' note: The issue before the court was whether the accused, Ramon Puentes, had standing to raise the "specialty doctrine" in order to limit his prosecution in the United States to the specific charges for which he was extradited from Uruguay.]

The government correctly points out that this circuit has not squarely addressed the issue of whether a defendant has standing to assert a violation of an extradition treaty. When faced with appellants' challenges to extradition, this court has assumed, without deciding, that the appellants had standing to bring the claim. *See, e.g., United States v. Herbage*, 850 F.2d 1463, 1466 (11th Cir. 1988), *cert. denied*, 489 U.S. 1027 (1989); *United States v. Lehder-Rivas*, 955 F.2d 1510, 1520 n. 7 (11th Cir.), *cert. denied, Reed v. United States*, 113 S.Ct. 347 (1992)....

Under the doctrine of speciality, a nation that receives a criminal defendant pursuant to an extradition treaty may try the defendant only for those offenses for which the other nation granted extradition. *Herbage*, 850 F.2d at 1465; M. Bassiouni, *International Extradition: United States Law and Practice*, vol. 1, ch. 7, p. 359–60 (2d rev. ed. 1987)....

Extradition is "the surrender by one nation to another of an individual accused or convicted of an offense outside of its own territory, and within the territorial jurisdiction of the other, which, being competent to try and to punish him, demands the surrender." *Terlinden v. Ames*, 184 U.S. 270, 289 (1902). As a matter of international law, however, nations are under no legal obligation to surrender a fugitive from justice in the absence of a treaty. Bassiouni, at 319; *Factor v. Laubenheimer*, 290 U.S. 276, 287 (1933). An extradition treaty is, therefore, a cooperative agreement between two governments for the prosecution and punishment of criminal offenders. *See* Bassiouni, at 319. Extradition treaties typically specify certain offenses for which extradition will be granted as between the two respective nations. Upon receipt of an extradition request, the surrendering nation may examine the substance of each of the charges specified in the request, and may choose to grant extradition for only the extraditable offenses listed in the treaty....

In *United States v. Rauscher*, 119 U.S. 407 (1886), the Court drew a distinction between this country's treatment of a treaty and other countries in which a treaty is essentially a contract between two nations. Under our Constitution, the Court explained, a treaty is the law of the land and the equivalent of an act of the legislature. *Rauscher*, 119 U.S. at 418. The Court's opinion suggests that the rights described in the treaty are conferred on both the extradited individual and the respective governments. The Court stated:

> [A] treaty may also contain provisions which confer certain rights upon the citizens or subjects of one of the nations residing in the territorial limits of the other, which partake of the nature of municipal law, and *which are capable of enforcement as between private parties in the courts of the country*.... The Constitution of the United States places such provisions as these in the same category as other laws of Congress, by its declaration that "This Constitution and the laws made in pursuance thereof, and all treaties made or which shall be made under authority of the United States, shall be the supreme law of the land." A treaty, then, is a law of the land, as an Act of Congress is, whenever its provisions prescribe a rule by which the *rights of the private citizen or subject may be determined*. And when such rights are of a nature to be enforced in a court of justice, that court resorts to the treaty for a rule of decision for the case before it as it would to a statute.

Rauscher, 119 U.S. at 418–19 (quoting *Chew Heong v. United States*, 112 U.S. 536 (1884)) (emphasis added)....

All of the circuit courts of appeals have not embraced the holding we announce today. Other courts have held that an extradited individual lacks standing to assert the doctrine of specialty in the absence of an express objection on the part of the requested nation. Invariably, the courts that adhere to this rule consider the principle of specialty to be a matter of international law that inures solely to the benefit of the requested nation, protects its dignity and interests, and confers no rights on the accused. *Cf. Shapiro v. Ferrandina*, 478 F.2d 894, 906 (2d Cir.), *cert. dismissed*, 414 U.S. 884 (1973). These courts have taken the international law rule of construction that only nations may enforce treaty obligations, and inferred that an individual cannot, therefore, assert any rights under a treaty in our national courts. This analysis is flawed, we submit, because it ignores both the history of the concept of extradition and *Rauscher*.

As we stated earlier, extradition is not a part of customary international law. Therefore, in order to broaden the reach of their criminal justice systems, two nations may enter into a cooperative agreement for the exchange of criminal suspects: an extradition contract. *See Geoffroy v. Riggs*, 133 U.S. 258, 271, 10 S.Ct. 295, 298, 33 L.Ed. 642 (1890) (characterizing treaties as contracts between nations). The doctrine of specialty is but one of the provisions of this contract. Of course, the rights conferred under the contract ultimately belong to the contracting parties, the signatory nations. This does not mean, however, that provisions of the contract may not confer certain rights under the contract on a non-party who is the object of the contract. We believe that *Rauscher* clearly confers such a right on the extradited defendant. The extradited individual's rights, however, need not be cast in stone; rather, the individual may enjoy these protections only at the sufferance of the requested nation. The individual's rights are derivative of the rights of the requested nation. We believe that *Rauscher* demonstrates that even in the absence of a protest from the requested state, an individual extradited pursuant to a treaty has standing to challenge the court's personal jurisdiction under the rule of specialty. The courts which have adopted the contrary holding, in effect, consider the requested state's objection to be a condition precedent to the individual's ability to raise the claim. We believe the Supreme Court's recent opinion in *United States v. Alvarez-Machain*, 504 U.S. 655 (1992) seriously undermines any vitality that approach may have once possessed. [see Section 4 B, *infra*]

… *Alvarez-Machain* demonstrates the infirmity in the reasoning of those cases which require an affirmative protest by the requested nation in order for the extradited individual to contest personal jurisdiction under the rule of specialty.

We, therefore, hold that an individual extradited pursuant to an extradition treaty has standing under the doctrine of specialty to raise any objections which the requested nation might have asserted. The extradited individual, however, enjoys this right at the sufferance of the requested nation. As a sovereign, the requested nation may waive its right to object to a treaty violation and thereby deny the defendant standing to object to such an action.

R. v. Parisien

[1988] 1 S.C.R. 950 (Canada)

The appellant, a Canadian citizen, was arrested in Brazil on August 18, 1978 at the request of the Canadian government after a warrant for arrest on a charge of fraud had been laid against him in Canada. This was only one of many complaints about his alleged fraudulent activities. On August 29, 1978, four other charges of fraud were laid.

There was no extradition treaty between Canada and Brazil but Brazilian law permits extradition in the absence of treaty where the requesting state offers to reciprocate in respect of fugitives from Brazil. Canada agreed to reciprocate and for that purpose proclaimed Part II of the Canadian *Extradition Act*, R.S.C. 1970, c. E-21, to be in effect with respect to Brazil.

The Brazilian law also provides that no surrender shall take place unless the requesting state agrees that the person surrendered will not be imprisoned nor tried for other acts which occurred before the extradition request. By diplomatic note dated January 15, 1980, Canada agreed to this and a number of other conditions. As a result, the appellant was surrendered to Canada on January 25 of that year pursuant to the arrangement to face prosecution on the five counts of fraud. The conditions agreed to, of which only the first and fourth are relevant, are as follows:

The extraditee shall not be handed over unless the State undertakes the following:

I — that the extraditee will not be arrested or tried for other offenses prior to the request for extradition; …

IV — that the extraditee will not be handed over to any other State requesting him without the consent of Brazil; …

Immediately upon the appellant's return to Canada, he was charged with an additional forty-four offences, based on acts committed prior to his extradition. At a preliminary hearing in May, 1980, however, the Crown withdrew the additional charges. The appellant then pleaded guilty to the original five counts and was sentenced to eighteen months imprisonment. He was released on parole on January 26, 1981, and his sentence expired December 29, 1981.

At the preliminary hearing, Crown counsel notified the appellant that with Brazil's consent before the expiration of his sentence, or without Brazil's consent afterwards, the Crown would proceed with the further charges. Canada negotiated with Brazil to obtain its consent, but Brazil refused unless the appellant consented as well. As could be expected, the appellant's consent was not forthcoming.

On April 14, 1982, the appellant left Canada to visit Portugal and returned of his own free will within a month. On May 26, 1982, a new information was sworn charging him with thirty-nine offences, all of which were included in the forty-four charges laid upon the appellant's return to Canada from Brazil. These thirty-nine charges are the basis of these proceedings. On October 19, 1982, two other charges were laid which are not part of these proceedings but will likely be affected by the outcome....

Canada expressly provides that a fugitive shall not be tried or punished for a crime committed before his surrender unless he has been restored or given an opportunity to return to the state that surrendered him. Section 33 of the *Extradition Act* reads as follows:

> 33. Where any person accused or convicted of an extradition crime is surrendered by a foreign state, in pursuance of any extradition arrangement, he is not, until after he has been restored or has had an opportunity of returning to the foreign state within the meaning of the arrangement, subject, in contravention of any of the terms of the arrangement, to a prosecution or punishment in Canada for any other offence committed prior to his surrender, for which he should not, under the arrangement, be prosecuted.

Section 33 applies not only to surrenders made under formal general treaties, but to those made under informal arrangements as well. Section 2 of the *Extradition Act* broadly defines an "extradition arrangement" as including any arrangement for the surrender of fugitive criminals that applies between Canada and a foreign state, including the kind of ad hoc arrangement involved in this case ...

The court denied Parisien's appeal because once he was no longer in Canada he sought of his own accord to live in Canada and to enjoy the protection of Canadian laws. Hence, the court reasoned, he owed a duty of allegiance to Canada and was subject to those laws. The court found that without a doubt Parisien chose to stay in Canada, then left for a time, and returned despite the earlier warning that he would be prosecuted for the offenses for which he is now charged. The court concluded that Brazil's condition related to prosecutions that can occur by reasons of the surrender of a fugitive to the requesting state, not to cases where prosecution become possible because the accused decides to stay in the requesting state following prosecution.

United States v. Najohn
785 F.2d 1420 (9th Cir. 1986)

Najohn moved before trial to dismiss his indictment on the grounds that his prosecution and punishment would violate the specialty doctrine of federal extradition law. The district court denied his motion, and Najohn appealed. The appellate court affirmed on the merits because Switzerland has waived the specialty rule in this case.

Najohn was indicted in the Eastern District of Pennsylvania and charged with interstate transportation of stolen property in violation of 18 U.S.C. §2314 (1982), and a warrant for his arrest was issued. The United States Embassy in Berne, Switzerland, requested Najohn's extradition to the United States. Swiss authorities arrested Najohn, a Swiss court ordered his extradition to face the Pennsylvania charges, and Najohn was transported from Switzerland to Pennsylvania. Najohn pleaded guilty to one count of the Pennsylvania indictment and received a four year sentence.

While serving his sentence, Najohn was indicted in the Northern District of California and charged with interstate transportation of stolen property, *see* 18 U.S.C. §2315 (1982), and conspiracy *see* 18 U.S.C. §371 (1982). Najohn moved to dismiss the indictment on the ground that his trial on the California charges was barred by the extradition treaty between the United States and Switzerland, and by specific language in the Swiss court's extradition order. The district court found that the Swiss government had waived the treaty language relied on by Najohn and, on that basis, denied Najohn's motion to dismiss the Northern District of California indictment.

Although the doctrine of specialty would ordinarily protect Najohn from being tried for offenses other than the one for which he was originally extradited, the doctrine has a specific exception. "[T]he extradited party may be tried for a crime other than that for which he was surrendered *if the asylum country consents.*" *Berenguer v. Vance*, 473 F. Supp. 1195, 1197 (D.D.C. 1979) (emphasis in original); *see* M. Bassiouni, *International Extradition* ch. VII, §6-3, at 6–11 (1983) (specialty does not prevent requesting state from trying defendant for offense not listed as a basis for extradition if requested state consents). The government claims that the Swiss government has waived the principle of specialty. Najohn argues that the purported waiver is insufficient.

The only authorizations for this prosecution are a letter from the Magistrate of the District of Zurich requesting prosecution and a letter from the Swiss Embassy to the United States asking for prosecution and agreeing that the principle of specialty was suspended. Najohn argues that these are insufficient because the treaty, requiring that prosecution only be for the crimes for which extradition was sought, binds the United States regardless of the consent of the Swiss authorities.

Najohn also argued unsuccessfully that the statements contained in the documents approving further prosecution were insufficient because, unlike the order of extradition, they are not court-approved. The court observed that Najohn did not try to obtain a Swiss judgement prohibiting Swiss consent to further prosecution. Hence, the court regarded the statement of the executive branch as the last word of the Swiss government.

Notes and Questions

1. Do you agree with the holding in *Puentes*? Do you find the court's reliance on *Rauscher* and *Alvarez-Machain* compelling? As a Supreme Court decision, isn't *Rauscher* determinative? Professor Bassiouni has written that in his view, as a treaty right, it can be raised by the relator or extraditee irrespective of any protest by the original requested state. M. Cherif Bassiouni (ed.), 2 International Criminal Law 424 (1986), citing *Rauscher* and Johnson v. Browne, 205 U.S. 309 (1907), and other cases.

2. Is the court correct in its criticism of those circuits that hold that a defendant lacks standing to challenge his extradition on doctrine of specialty grounds absent a protest by

the asylum nation (*i.e.*, that individual rights are merely derivative)? The *Puentes* court stated:

> These courts have taken the international law rule of construction that only nations may enforce treaty obligations, and inferred that an individual cannot, therefore, assert any rights under a treaty in our national courts. This analysis is flawed, we submit, because it ignores both the history of the concept of extradition and *Rauscher*.

50 F.3d at 1574. Do you agree with the court's statement? See RESTATEMENT, §477, Cmnt. b; Paust, *After* Alvarez-Machain: *Abduction, Standing, Denials of Justice, and Unaddressed Human Rights Claims,* 67 ST. JOHN'S L. REV. 551, 555–58, 568–74 (1993). Is there a general "rule of construction" that treaties are agreements between contracting nations which confer no rights on private parties? *See generally id.*; J. PAUST, INTERNATIONAL LAW AS LAW OF THE UNITED STATES chpts. 2, 3, 5 (2 ed. 2003). Do extradition treaties confer rights on third parties, who are non-signatories (or their nationals) to the treaty?

Based on *Najohn*, what constitutes a sufficient waiver of the specialty doctrine by the surrendering State? If an individual is granted standing to raise an issue concerning speciality, is it logical that the matter can simply be waived by the requested state?

3. If the surrendering State can waive the specialty doctrine, should the accused have the right to assert it in the absence of a protest by the surrendering State? See RESTATEMENT §477, Comm. b. As noted in *Puentes,* several circuits have adopted the position that a criminal defendant lacks standing to challenge his extradition on doctrine of specialty grounds in the absence of an express objection by the requested nation. *See* United States v. Antonakeas, 255 F.3d 714, 719 (9th Cir. 2001) (appellant lacks standing to raise noncompliance with procedural provisions of the extradition treaty); United States v. Miro, 29 F.3d 194, 200 (5th Cir. 1994) (absent an objection by the extraditing country, defendant lacked standing to argue a violation of the specialty rule); *Matta-Ballesteros v. Henman,* 896 F.2d 255, 259 (7th Cir.) ("It is well established that individuals have no standing to challenge violations of international treaties in the absence of a protest by the sovereigns involved."), *cert. denied,* 498 U.S. 878 (1991); *United States v. Kaufman,* 874 F.2d 242, 242 (5th Cir.) ("only an offended nation can complain about the purported violation of an extradition treaty"), *cert. denied sub nom. Franks v. Harwell,* 493 U.S. 895 (1986); *Demjanjuk v. Petrovsky,* 776 F.2d 571, 584 (6th Cir. 1985) (same), *cert. denied,* 475 U.S. 1016 (1986); *United States v. Cordero,* 668 F.2d 32, 37 (1st Cir. 1981) ("[U]nder international law, it is the contracting foreign government, not the defendant, that would have the right to complain about a violation."); *Shapiro v. Ferrandina,* 478 F.2d 894, 906 (2d Cir.) ("the principle of specialty has been viewed as a privilege of the asylum state ... rather than a right accruing to the accused"), *cert. dismissed,* 414 U.S. 884 (1973). The circuits embracing this view reason that the principle of specialty is a privilege of the asylum state, designed to protect the interests of the surrendering nation, not a right accruing to the defendant.

In contrast, the Eighth, Ninth, Tenth, and Eleventh Circuits hold that the defendant may raise whatever objections the extraditing country is entitled to raise even absent an objection by the extraditing nation. *See United States v. Thirion,* 813 F.2d 146, 150 (8th Cir. 1987) (defendant may raise whatever objections to his prosecution that the surrendering country might have); *United States v. Andonian,* 29 F.3d 1432, 1435 (9th Cir. 1994) ("An extradited person may raise whatever objections the extraditing country is entitled to raise."); *accord United States v. Cuevas,* 847 F.2d 1417, 1426 (9th Cir. 1990), *cert. denied,* 489 U.S. 1012 (1989); *United States v. Najohn,* 785 F.2d 1420, 1421 (9th Cir.), *cert.*

denied, 479 U.S. 1009 (1986); *Abell-Silva*, 948 F.2d at 1172; *United States v. Levy*, 905 F.2d 326, 328 n. 1 (10th Cir. 1990) (same), *cert. denied*, 498 U.S. 1049 (1991); *United States v. Puentes*, 50 F.3d 1567, 1573 (11th Cir. 1995) ("[E]ven in the absence of a protest from the requested state, an individual extradited pursuant to a treaty has standing to challenge the court's personal jurisdiction under the rule of specialty."); *United States v. Herbage*, 850 F.2d 1463, 1466 (11th Cir. 1988) ("For purposes of this case, we assume, without deciding, that an individual has standing to allege a violation of the specialty principle."), *cert. denied*, 489 U.S. 1027 (1989). Thus, a substantial split in authority remains on the issue of standing to raise a challenge to the extradition treaty as such. *See also* Jimmy Gurulé, Complex Criminal Litigation: Prosecuting Drug Enterprises and Organized Crime § 10-2(a), at 486–489 (LEXIS Publ. 2d ed.) (2000); Paust, *After Alvarez-Machain*, *supra*.

4. If the only purpose of an extradition treaty is to protect the "sovereignty" interests or consent of the contracting nations, why should the defendant be accorded standing absent an express protest by the surrendering nation? Is that the only purpose? *See, e.g.,* Paust, *After* Alvarez-Machain, *supra* at 555–58, 568–74. Should silence or failure to object constitute a waiver by a state of any of its interests concerning a violation under the extradition treaty?

5. The doctrine of specialty prohibits the requesting nation from prosecuting the defendant for a "separate offense," meaning an offense other than that for which the defendant was extradited. What constitutes a "separate offense" within the meaning of the doctrine of specialty has been the subject of substantial litigation. The problem frequently arises when the government obtains a superseding indictment after the defendant has been extradited from the foreign country, which alleges additional offenses or overt acts expanding the scope of the criminal conspiracy. For example, if a defendant is extradited on an order of extradition authorizing prosecution on narcotics conspiracy and money laundering counts, and the government thereafter obtains a superseding indictment alleging additional overt acts committed in furtherance of the drug conspiracy and additional money laundering counts, does this constitute prosecution on a "separate offense" in violation of the rule of specialty?

The circuits have avoided a narrow and overly technical interpretation of what constitutes trial for a "separate offense." The courts have upheld extradition where the defendant was convicted of offenses of the "same or similar character" as those for which he was extradited. In *United States v. Paroutian*, 299 F.2d 468, 490–91 (2d Cir. 1962), the defendant was extradited on an indictment alleging various narcotics charges, but was tried on an indictment that included two drug counts not listed in the original indictment that formed the basis for extradition. While the Second Circuit agreed that trial on "some other offense totally unrelated to the traffic in narcotics" would violate the principle of specialty, the court found that additional drug charges would not have been considered separate offenses by the surrendering country. Since the defendant had been extradited on drug offenses, the court reasoned that the asylum country would have no reason to protest prosecution on additional counts charging the same offense.

The general test adopted by the federal circuits for determining "separate offense" is "whether the extraditing country would consider the acts for which the defendant was prosecuted as independent from those for which he was extradited." *United States v. Andonian*, 29 F.3d 1432, 1435 (9th Cir. 1994). When the challenged counts allege offenses of the "same character" as the crimes for which the defendant was extradited, the defendant's argument on doctrine of specialty grounds has been rejected by the courts. *See Andonian*, 29 F.3d at 1436. More generally, see Gurulé, *supra* at § 10-2(b), at 489–494.

6. If a fugitive is extradited to the United States on drug trafficking charges, would a subsequent criminal forfeiture action brought by the Government be barred by the specialty doctrine? This issue was considered by the court in *United States v. Saccoccia*, 58 F.3d 754 (1st Cir. 1995). The First Circuit held that the specialty doctrine did not bar a subsequent forfeiture action because "criminal forfeiture is a punishment, not a separate criminal offense." Do you agree with this holding?

Defendant argued that "an offense which is itself nonextraditable cannot serve as a predicate act in conjunction with other, extraditable offenses." The court rejected this argument. Why? *See also* United States v. Lomeli, 596 F.3d 496, 503 (8th Cir. 2010) (district court's consideration of Lomeli's criminal history in sentencing him for an extradited offense did not constitute punishment for non-extradited conduct and therefore did not violate the doctrine of specialty).

7. As you read the materials below, consider whether the question of standing should be handled differently with respect to the political offense exception or the issue of double or dual criminality (a customary doctrine that requires that the offense for which a person is extradited generally be a crime in both the requesting and requested state).

C. Grounds for Denial of Extradition

M.C. Bassiouni (ed.), 2 International Criminal Law
413–17 (1986)

Failure of the requesting state to meet the requirements of the extradition treaty whether it is substantive, such as the offense is extraditable and satisfies "double criminality," or whether it is procedural, providing the necessary documentation in the proper form and at the proper time, and providing evidence that meets the standard and sufficiency of "probable cause," will result in denial of extradition. In addition, however, there are a number of defenses, exceptions and exclusions which will likewise result in denial of extradition [if covered by a treaty]. They are:

1. "The political offense exception";
2. Exclusion for prosecution based on certain discriminatory grounds;
3. Offenses of a military character;
4. Offenses of a fiscal character;
5. Exclusion of nationals;
6. Double jeopardy;
7. Applicability of a statute of limitation;
8. Extinction of the cause of action by amnesty or pardon;
9. Immunity from prosecution;
10. Exclusions concerning certain penalties and treatment of offenders.

The Political Offense Exception: There are two types of offenses falling within the category of the "political offense exception:" The "purely political offense" and the "relative political offense." There is also an exception to this exception, namely international crimes which are excluded from the "political offense exception."

All U.S. extradition treaties contain a provision concerning the "political offense exception," but only the "purely political offense" has been consistently applied without question. These are offenses of opinion, political expression or those which otherwise do not involve the use of violence. They include, for example, such offenses of opinion, political expression or those which otherwise do not involve the use of violence. They include, for example, such offenses as treason and espionage.[33]

The "relative political offense" is one which involves violence as an incidence of the political motivation and goal of the actor, but which does not constitute wanton violence directed against innocent persons. The violence that befalls innocent and unintended targets must be initially directed against a permissible target, incidental to the political motives and goals of the actor, and performed in the context of a civil war, insurrection or uprising. These tests have originally been applied by U.S. courts who borrowed them from earlier English jurisprudence.[34] The more recent jurisprudence of the United States involved a number of cases in which Irish resisters belonging to the PIRA committed acts of violence; all of these cases resulted in the application of the exception,[35] while one case involving a Palestinian did not.[36]

While the "political offense exception" continues to attract great interest and attention in light of increased international terrorism,[37] it has not been the object of many decisions in the U.S. where the jurisprudence of the courts has been consistent and narrow in granting it.[38] Throughout the history of extradition, from Jay's Treaty of 1794 to 1986, there have been approximately 80 cases involving the "political offense" exception, approximately 20 in the last 30 years and it was granted only 5 times in the last 20 years [1956-1986]....

---

33. See *Chandler v. United States*, 171 F.2d 921 (1st Cir. 1948); see also Bassiouni, "Ideologically motivated Offenses and the Political Offense Exception in Extradition—a Proposed Juridical Standard for an Unruly Problem," 19 *De Paul L. Rev.* 217 (1969) and Garcia-Mora, "The Nature of the Political Offenses: A Knotty Problem of Extradition," 48 *Va. L. Rev.* 1226 (1962).

34. The cases relied upon by the U.S. were *In re Castioni* [1891] 1 Q.B., 149, followed by *In re Meunier* [1894] 2 Q.B., 415. U.S. Courts first followed these cases in *Re Ezeta*, 62 F. 972 (N.D. Col. 1894); *Ornelas v. Ruiz*, 161 U.S. 502 (1896); *Artukovic v. Boyle*, 107 F. Supp. 11 (S.D. Cal. 1952); *Ivancevic v. Artukovic*, 211 F.2d 565 (9th Cir. 1954); *Karadzole v. Artukovic*, 247 F.2d 198 (9th Cir. 1957); *United States v. Artukovic*, 170 F. Supp. 383 (S.D. Cal. 1950); *Ramos v. Diaz*, 179 F. Supp. 459 (S.D. Fla 1959); *Jiminez v. Aristeguieta*, 311 F.2d 547 (5th Cir. 1962), *cert. denied*, 373 U.S. 914 (1963); *Garcia-Guillern v. United States*, 450 F.2d 1189 (5th Cir. 1971), *cert. denied*, 405 U.S. 989 (1972) and in the cases cited *infra*.

35. The four major cases decided in the U.S. involving persons who committed acts of violence in the United Kingdom and Northern Ireland who were sought for extradition by the U.K. and whose extradition was denied, are: *In re McMullen*, [Magistrates Decisions No. 3-78-1099 M.B. at 3 (N.D. Calif., May 11, 1979)]; *In re Mackin* [Doc. S.C. 180 Cr. Misc., 47, (S.D.N.Y. Aug. 13, 1981) Government's app. dism. *In re Mackin*, 668 F.2d. 122 (2nd Cir. 1981)]; *Quinn v. Robinson* [C-82-6688 R.P.A. (N.D. Cal. Oct. 3, 1983), vacated and remanded, Quinn v. Robinson, 83 F.2d 776 (9th Cir. 1986) (9th Cir.)]; *In re Doherty* [599 F. Supp. 270 (S.D.N.Y. 1984), Government's Declaratory Judgement Petition Denied, 85 CIV. 935—C.F.H. (S.D.N.Y. June 25, 1985)]. *See also* Cantrell, " The Political Offense exception in International Extradition: a Comparison of the United States, Great Britain, and the republic of Ireland," 60 *Marquette L. Rev.* 777 (1977); and Banoff and Pyle "To Surrender Political Offenders: The Political Offense Exception to Extradition in the United States Law", 16 *J. Int'l L. & Pol.* 169 (1984). For a critical review of the doctrine and some of its applications, see Carbonneau, "The Political Offense Exception to Extradition and Transnational Terrorists." 1 *A.S.I.L.S. Int'l L. J.* 1 (1977); Hannay, " International Terrorism and the Political Offense Exception to Extradition," 18 *Colum. J. Transnat'l L.* 381 (1979), and Lubet and Czackes, "The Role of the American Judiciary in the Extradition of Political Terrorists," 71 *J. Crim.L. & Criminology* 193 (1980).

36. *Eain v. Wilkes*, 641 F.2d 504 (7th Cir. 1981), *cert. denied*, 454 U.S. 894 (1981).

37. See, C. Van Den Wijngaert, *The Political Offense Exception in Extradition* (1981); and M.C. Bassiouni, *International Terrorism and Political Crimes* (1975).

38. See *supra* notes 34–36.

Exclusion for prosecution based on certain discriminatory grounds: Usually, a requested state may not examine the process by which a requesting state reached the decision to seek extradition, or the legal process by which it secured the evidence in support of the extradition, or the process and evidence by means of which a person was ordered arrested, charged, or convicted of a crime. The requested state may also not, as part of its decision on the merits of extradition, inquire into the subsequent legal processes, treatment or penalties which the relator may be subjected to upon surrender. That is the "Rule of Non-Inquiry," also followed in the United States.[39] However, that rule limits only the judiciary in its determination of whether the relator is to be extradited, it does not bind or limit the Executive which retains "Executive Discretion" exercised by the president through the secretary of state which may manifest itself either in a denial of extradition, even after a judicial determination of extraditability, or in a "Conditional Extradition" (discussed below).

Offenses of a Military and Fiscal Nature: These are exclusions contained in most treaties, though in recent times, the U.S. has sought to include fiscal offenses, such as, tax evasion related to organized crime or tax evasion under mail fraud in its treaties....

Exclusion of Nationals: As a general rule, the U.S. does not exclude its nationals from extradition, even when other states with which it has extradition relations do so. However, the U.S. usually reserves the option not to extradite its nationals to states which consistently refuse to reciprocate. This option, however, is exercised by the Secretary of State as part of "Executive Discretion" (discussed below).

Double Jeopardy: While this defense is normally available, it will depend largely on the similarity of the charges for which the relator has been requested and for which he has been already prosecuted, acquitted or convicted thereof. Since, however, the Constitution which protects against double jeopardy is not deemed in this case to apply extraterritorially, and because of the doctrine of "separate sovereignties" which is recognized in the U.S. among sister-states and the federal government, the defense has had limited application, and it has been deemed essentially a treaty defense.[40]

Statute of Limitations and Extinction of the Cause of Action by Reason of Pardon or Amnesty: Most treaties specify that either the law of the requesting or requested state shall apply with respect to the applicability of a relevant statute of limitations, and extinction of the cause of action. It is therefore deemed a treaty defense to which the provisions of the treaty are applicable.

[Witness] Immunity from Prosecution: Because of the peculiar U.S. prosecutorial technique of granting immunity from prosecution and plea-bargaining, which are techniques

---

39. In *Neely v. Henkel*, 180 U.S. 109 (1901), the Supreme Court held that U.S. constitutional guarantees do not extend extraterritorially, and that became the basis of subsequent decisions which upheld the "rule of non-inquiry." However, recent cases have indicated in dicta that its application would not necessarily be without question. In *Gallina v. Fraser*, 278 F.2d 77 (2d Cir. 1960), *cert. denied*, 364 U.S. 851 (1960), the Court stated "We can imagine situations when the relator, upon extradition, would be subject to procedures or punishment too antipathetic to a federal court's sense of decency as to require re-examination of the principle set out above." *Id.* 78–79. The same position was restated in *Peroff v. Hylton, supra; United States ex. rel. Bloomfield v. Gengler, supra; United States v. Romano, supra*. See also *Escabedo v. United States, supra*, where the Court took a narrower view; *Arnbjornsdottir Mendler v. United States*, 721 F.2d 679 (9th Cir. 1983), which seems to follow *Gallina v. Fraser, id.* See also, *Digest of U.S. Practice in International Law* 410–11 (1978).[Paust, Achille Lauro *Hostage-Takers, supra* at 247–49]

40. In *Galanis v. Pallanck*, 568 F.2d 234 (2d Cir. 1977), where the Court held that it was a treaty right . See also *United States ex. rel. Bloomfield v. Gengler*, 507 F.2d 925 (2d Cir. 1974); and *Gusikoff v. United States*, 620 F.2d 459 (5th Cir. 1980).[Paust, Achille Lauro *Hostage-Takers, supra* at 242–44]

not recognized in most other systems of the world, certain problems arise with respect to enforceability of such agreements even when approved by the courts. The U.S. has, however, sought to enforce such agreements, grants of immunity and plea-bargains, in extradition proceedings even though these are not recognized exclusions or exceptions under any of the treaties the U.S. now has in force.

Exclusions Concerning Certain Penalties and Treatment of Offenders: Certain countries exclude extradition where the death penalty is enforceable for the offense charged, but the U.S. does not.

Notes and Questions

1. The United States considers that the doctrines of speciality and double or dual criminality and the political offense exception to extradition are customary international law. Thus, they are a necessary background for interpretation and application of any extradition treaty that does not obviate or limit their effect.

2. "Pure" political offenses, for which extradition can be refused, include "crimes against the state" such as treason, subversion (not involving violence), aiding the enemy (as such), and espionage. Are "military" crimes, such as disobedience of a lawful order and desertion, and "fiscal character" crimes (such as tax evasion, addressed by Professor Bassiouni, or failure to pay customs fees) merely a subset of "pure" political offenses? Article 13 of the International Convention for the Suppression of the Financing of Terrorism expressly excludes the possibility of refusal of "a request for extradition or for mutual legal assistance on the sole ground that ... [a covered offense] concerns a fiscal offence."

With respect to "relative" political offenses, there are splits within the Circuits in the U.S. and among states in the international community concerning tests for relative political offenses. Nonetheless, one widely accepted criterion requires that the offense be committed for a "political" motive.

3. With respect to political offenses, see also *Ex parte* Kentucky v. Dennison, 65 U.S. (24 How.) 66, 99–100 (1860) ("According to these usages, ... persons who fled on account of political offences were almost always excepted, and the nation ... exercises a discretion.... And the English Government has always refused to deliver up political offenders."); *In re* Metzger, 46 U.S. (5 How.) 176, 188 n.2 (1847) ("'it is generally admitted that extradition should not be granted in the case of political offenders, but only in the case of individuals who have committed crimes against the Law of Nature, the laws which all nations regard as the foundation of public and private security'"), quoting 1 PHILLIMORE, INTERNATIONAL LAW 413 (1854); *In re* Ezeta, *et al.*, 62 F. 972, 997–1003 (N.D. Cal. 1894); United States v. Watts, 14 F. 130, 135 (D. Cal. 1882) ("It has been urged that the right of asylum for political offenders is so universally recognized as sacred and inviolable that an infringement of it was ... not ... possible, but jurists ... are not always agreed as to what constitutes a political offense"); *In re* Sheazle, 21 F. Cas. 1214, 1215 (C.C.D. Mass. 1845) (No. 12,734) ("in case of mere political offences, it is seldom done"); Oliver v. Kauffman, 18 F. Cas. 657, 659 (C.C.E.D. Pa. 1850) (No. 10,497) ("law of nations which refuse to deliver up persons guilty of mere political offences").

4. When the U.S. requested extradition of various Achille Lauro boatjackers from Italy to stand trial for "piracy," Italy rightly refused extradition. "Piracy" under customary international law (and U.S. Supreme Court cases) is comprised of two elements: (1) robbery or similar depredation or violence for private ends, and (2) involving perpetrators who move from one vessel (or aircraft, etc.) to another and conduct that is directed against

the other vessel (or aircraft, etc.) or persons or property on board such vessel (or aircraft, etc.). The Achille Lauro boatjackers, who were from a Palestinian group, committed their acts for political purposes and did not transfer from one vessel to another to engage in their conduct. Thus, the conduct was not "piracy" and extradition for prosecution of "piracy" could be refused. *See, e.g.*, Paust, Achille Lauro *Hostage-Takers, supra* at 255–56. Moreover, one could argue that the political offense exception to extradition was relevant. After the incident, boatjacking became a treaty-based crime under the 1988 Convention for the Suppression of Unlawful Acts Against the Safety of Maritime Navigation, in the Documents Supplement.

5. Some international criminal law treaties expressly exclude use of the political offense exception to extradition. *See, e.g.*, the Genocide Convention (art. VII); the Apartheid Convention (art. XI(1)); the International Convention for the Protection of All Persons from Enforced Disappearance (art. 13(1); the Inter-American Convention on the Forced Disappearance of Persons (art. V); the International Convention for the Suppression of Terrorist Bombings (art. 11); and the International Convention for the Suppression of the Financing of Terrorism (art. 14). Does U.N. G.A. Res. 59/195, Human Rights and Terrorism, para. 10 [in the Documents Supplement], support preclusion of the political offense exception for those who planned, facilitated or participated in the commission of acts of terrorism? In Quinn v. Robinson, 783 F.2d 776 (9th Cir. 1986), the Ninth Circuit stated with respect to "[c]rimes against humanity, such as genocide": "we do not believe that the political offense exception ... should have been extended to protect those carrying out a governmental policy calling for acts of destruction whose 'nature and scope ... exceeded human imagination.'... They are certainly in our view excluded...."

6. Several international criminal law treaties contain a clause that provides consent in advance by treaty to use of "the law of the requested state" to avoid extradition. *See, e.g.*, International Convention Against the Taking of Hostages, art. 10 (2); Hague Convention on the Suppression of Unlawful Seizure of Aircraft (Hijacking), art. 8 (2). If the law of the requested state includes the political offense exception, extradition can be denied for the international crime of hostage-taking if it was committed for a political purpose and other criteria with respect to the test for "political offenses" under the law of the requested state are met. Does this make sense? Note that such treaties require that if the requested state does not extradite it must initiate prosecution of the international crime without any exception whatsoever. *See, e.g.*, Hostages Convention, art. 8 (1); Hague Hijacking Convention, art. 7.

7. Were the 9/11 attacks by al Qaeda on the World Trade Center in New York and the Pentagon "relative" political offenses for purposes of extradition? Might they implicate an exception to the political offense exception?

8. In November, 2005, Judge Enrico Manzi rejected an appeal by former CIA station chief in Milan, Seldon Lady, claiming diplomatic immunity with respect to the alleged kidnapping of an Egyptian cleric, Moustafa Hassan Nasr, in Milan on Feb. 17, 2003. Nasr, an alleged al Qaeda-supporting terrorist, was flown to Egypt and has been reportedly tortured there. The Italian judge ruled that consular official protection exists "always within the limits of international law. Within these limits, naturally, is the principle of the sovereignty of the host state that cannot allow on its territory the use of force by a foreign state that is outside every control of the political and judicial authorities." Italian prosecutors have been seeking the extradition of 22 alleged CIA operatives involved in the abduction. *See also* Bruce Zagaris, Italian Judge Orders Arrest of CIA Agents in Milan Kidnapping of Egyptian Cleric, 21 INT'L ENFORCEMENT L. REPRTR. no. 8, at 320 (Aug. 2005). On April 12, 2006, Italian Justice Minister Castelli said he would not request extradition

of the 22 CIA operatives. The Milan prosecutor Spataro said he would resubmit the ex-tradition to the incoming center-left government. See Bruce Zagaris, Italian Justice Min-ister Defers Extradition of C.I.A. Operatives, *id.* vol. 22, no. 6, at 226 (June 2006). On June 4, 2006, Marco Mancini, director of operations of Italy's SISMI (military secret ser-vice) was arrested on suspicion of involvement with the kidnapping and media announced that four U.S. citizens are now fugitives of justice in Italy with respect to the incident. See Christine Spolar, *Ex-spy: CIA, Italians Worked on Abduction; Arrest Warrant Targets 4 Ac-cused Americans*, CHICAGO TRIB., July 9, 2006, at 10.

On November 4, 2009, an Italian magistrate found 23 U.S. citizens guilty of kidnap-ping a Muslim cleric in Milan in 2003, making it the first time U.S. nationals were pros-ecuted for rendition with respect to suspected terrorists. The rendition was an alleged operation involving CIA agents and members of the Italian secret service to apprehend Hassan Mustafa Osama Nasr, also known as Abu Omar. Abu Omar was thereafter al-legedly brought to Egypt and tortured, under suspicion for participation in terrorism, without judicial review. One of the defendants, Sabrina De Sousa, has filed a civil suit against the CIA, the State Department, and others, claiming that she was entitled to full diplomatic immunity. In response the Department of Justice filed a motion to dismiss. Italy has not proactively tried to extradite the defendants. For more information *see* Erik Sapin, *Italy Convicts 23 Americans for Alleged Rendition of Terrorism Suspect*, 26 INT'L EN-FORCEMENT L. REP. 11 (Jan. 2010).

9. If the statute of limitations has run in the requesting country, is there simply no ju-risdiction in such country? In *Murphy v. United States*, 199 F.3d 599 (2d Cir. 1999), the court held that the fact that prosecution for indecent assault, gross indecency, and common as-sault would be barred by either the U.S. state or federal statute of limitations did not bar extradition of the accused to Canada, where there was no such statute of limitation.

10. Since the 1970s the U.S. has included fiscal offenses in extradition treaties. A trend ex-ists internationally to include fiscal offenses as an extraditable offense. One problem that may affect the extraditability of a tax case is whether the signatory countries criminalize the same types of tax offenses. The substantive distinctions between tax evasion and tax fraud may enable defense counsel to successfully argue that the crimes are sufficiently distinguishable that extradition should not be granted. Some extradition treaties include tax offenses and of-fenses "connected with" tax offenses (e.g., false statements, obstruction of justice, Continu-ing Criminal Enterprise (CCE),racketeering, wire fraud, and mail fraud. See Bruce Zagaris, U.S. Efforts to Extradite persons for Tax Offenses, 25 LOY. L.A. INT'L & COMP. L. REV. 653 (2003).

1971 Treaty on Extradition Between the Government of Canada and the Government of the United States of America

[read the treaty in the Documents Supplement, especially Articles 2, 4, 6, 12, and the Schedule]

1991 Protocol Amending the Treaty on Extradition

[read the Protocol in the Documents Supplement]

Notes and Questions

1. The most important provisions of the 1971 U.S.-Canada Extradition Treaty can be summarized as follows: Article 2 of the treaty (together with the annexed Schedule) spec-

ifies what is to be considered an extraditable offense. Article 3 provides that the treaty shall apply to extraterritorial offenses as well as offenses committed within the territory of the requesting state. Article 4 sets forth the following exceptions to the treaty: double jeopardy (known internationally as "non bis in idem"); statute of limitations; and the political offense exception. Article 5 grants the requested state the option of denying extradition of its residents who are under 18 years of age. Article 6 grants the requested state the option of denying extradition when the charge is punishable by death, unless the requesting state provides an assurance that the death penalty shall not be imposed. Article 9 specifies the documentation that is required for an extradition request and Article 10 sets forth the standard of proof applicable to the extradition proceedings. Article 11 governs provisional arrest. Article 12 codifies the "specialty doctrine."

2. Note that the original 1971 U.S.-Canada Extradition Treaty reproduced in the Documents Supplement contained a schedule of extraditable offenses. Pursuant to Article 2 of the Treaty, only crimes that were specifically listed in the Schedule were considered extraditable offenses. What serious crimes are missing from this list?

3. In 1988, the United States and Canada signed a Protocol to the treaty, which among other things substitutes a dual criminality clause for the schedule of offenses. A dual criminality clause permits extradition for any crime that is punishable in both countries by imprisonment or other detention for at least one year. This obviates the need to renegotiate or supplement the treaty as new offenses become punishable under the laws of both states. In addition, Article I of the Protocol allows the United States to request extradition of offenses including interstate mail fraud or interstate transportation in aid of racketeering enterprises even though the Canadian laws do not include analogous jurisdictional elements for similar underlying criminal behavior.

4. While the dual criminality principle employed in Article 2 of the Protocol Amending the US-Canada Extradition Treaty requires that the offense charged be punishable as a serious crime in both countries, the requesting and requested countries need not have identical penal statutes. *See generally* RESTATEMENT § 476, Cmnt. d and Reporters' Notes 1 & 2. In *Collins v. Loisel*, the Supreme Court opined:

> The law does not require that the name by which the crime is described in the two countries shall be the same; nor that the scope of the liability shall be coextensive, or, in other respects, the same in the two countries. It is enough if the particular act charged is criminal in both jurisdictions.

Collins v. Loisel, 259 U.S. 309, 312 (1922). The focus is on the "acts of the defendant, not on the legal doctrines of the country requesting extradition." *United States v. Sensi*, 879 F.2d 888, 893 (D.C. Cir. 1989). "If the acts upon which the charges of the requesting country are based are also proscribed by a law of the requested nation, the requirement of double criminality is satisfied." *Demjanjuk v. Petrovsky*, 776 F.2d 571, 579–80 (6th Cir. 1985), *cert. denied*, 475 U.S. 1016 (1986). The mere fact that the crime charged in the requesting state is not a crime under the laws of the asylum country does not defeat extradition, so long as the alleged acts are prohibited under foreign law. "The fact that a particular act is classified differently in the criminal law of the two states does not prevent extradition under the double criminality rule." *Sensi*, 879 F.2d at 893. *See also* In the Matter of the Extradition of Zhenly Ye Gon, 786 F. Supp.2d 61, 86 (D.D.C. 2011) (The "finding of dual criminality is valid even though the Mexican money laundering statute does not require a financial transaction, while the U.S. statute does.").

5. Professor Sharon Williams indicates in *The Double Criminality Rule Revisited*, 27 ISRAEL L. REV. 297 (1993), that the Supreme Court of Canada in the case *United States v.*

McVey II, [1992] 3 S.C.R. 475, clarified the approach to double criminality where the list approach is used by holding that " … what must be established is that the conduct of the fugitive would, if it had occurred in Canada, constitute a crime listed in the Treaty according to a name by which it is known under the law of Canada." A double listing under the name known in the requesting state as well is not necessary. Do you agree that Article 2 (1) of the 1971 Canada-United States Extradition Treaty that applied in the Canadian case did not require such a double listing? *See also* Williams, *Extradition From Canada Since the Charter of Rights, supra,* at 383–86.

6. Note that Article III of the Protocol Amending the U.S.-Canada Extradition Treaty reproduced in the Documents Supplement allows the requested State to grant extradition for an offense committed outside the requesting State even if the requested State's laws do not have a similar extraterritorial reach. What is the importance of this provision? In this regard, consider the following excerpt from the 1975 Digest of United States Practice in International Law 177:

> The Department of State informed the Embassy of the Federal Republic of Germany, in a note dated November 11, 1975, that it was not possible to comply with the Embassy's request for the provisional arrest for extradition to Germany of four foreign crewmen for the alleged murder on October 10, 1975, of four German officers on board the vessel *Mimi* on the high seas. The Department's note stated, in part:
>
> > The Department of State has carefully studied the facts of the case as developed by investigation, and the extradition treaty in force between the United States and the Federal Republic of Germany, and has determined that extradition is not possible in this case because of lack of dual criminality as required by Article I of the treaty. Although it appears that the Federal Republic of Germany would have jurisdiction by its internal law to prosecute fugitives for offenses committed against German citizens outside the territory of the Federal Republic of Germany, the United States under its law may prosecute for offenses committed outside its territory only if the offenses occurred within the special maritime and territorial jurisdiction of the United States as defined in section 7 of Title 18 of the *United States Code.* The United States has no jurisdiction to prosecute fugitives based upon United States citizenship of the victim of the offense.
>
> Dept of State File No. P75 0175-0032. The extradition treaty in force between the United States and the Federal Republic of Germany was signed July 12, 1930 (T.S. No. 836; 47 Stat. 1862; 8 Bevans 214; entered into force Apr. 26, 1931).

7. With respect to the request by Spain to the U.K. for extradition of former Chilean leader Pinochet (recall Chapter Two, Section 1), the Spanish magistrate, Judge Baltazar Garzón, issued orders seeking extradition for genocide, terrorism, and acts of torture that are a part of the crime of genocide. In November, 1988, the Criminal Division of the Spanish National Court (*Audiencia Nacional*) unanimously held that Spain had universal jurisdiction over crimes alleged in the extradition warrants. Article 23 (4) of the Judicial Branch Act of 1985 grants Spanish courts jurisdiction over acts committed abroad by either Spanish or foreign nationals when such acts are likely to be considered, according to the Spanish criminal legislation, any of the following crimes: genocide, terrorism, piracy, or "any other which according to international treaties or conventions must be prosecuted by Spain." The legislation does not specifically refer to torture or to crimes against humanity as such. The Spanish National Court held that the allegations of torture could be subsumed under

the concepts of genocide or terrorism. *See* María des Carmen Márquez Carrasco, Joaquín Alcaide Fernández, *In re Pinochet*, 93 Am. J. Int'l L. 690, 690–93 & ns.5, 14 (1999). Is the concluding phrase in Article 23 (4) sufficient to cover acts of torture committed in Chile? *See also* the Convention Against Torture and Other Cruel, Inhumane or Degrading Treatment or Punishment, in the Documents Supplement.

8. In the first decision of the House of Lords on November 25, 1998 (deciding 3-2 that Pinochet was not entitled to immunity regarding torture or hostage-taking), Lord Slynn noted that the Spanish request for extradition "set out a large number of alleged murders, disappearances and cases of torture ... in breach of Spanish law relating to genocide, to torture and to terrorism;" that Spain claimed universal jurisdiction under international law and internal legislation; but stated that the U.K.'s Genocide Act of 1969 did not enact Article IV of the Genocide Convention "as part of domestic law" (although Article IV covers heads of state). He added that the acts covered by the definition of genocide in Article II of the Convention were made a domestic criminal offense in the U.K. under the Genocide Act. See 37 I.L.M. at 1302, 1305, 1311, 1315 (1998). He also assumed that Article IV of the Convention makes heads of state liable to punishment (as opposed to merely recognizing nonimmunity or responsibility for any person). *Id.* at 1315. Lord Lloyd added that Parliament omitted Article IV from the English Act because it probably intended, "or at least contemplated," head of state immunity. *Id.* at 1324. Using such logic, would the omission of Article IV mean that no person can be responsible for genocide under the English Act, since Article IV addresses the responsibility of all persons, including other public officials and private persons? Such logic also leads to the conclusion that England is in breach of Articles I and V of the Genocide Convention (see Documents Supplement), as well as customary international law. *See* Chapters One and Two, Section 3. Article V expressly affirms the duty to enact legislation needed "to give effect to the provisions of the ... Convention and, in particular, to provide effective penalties for persons guilty...."

If a lack of dual criminality concerning domestic laws of the U.K. and Spain exits, should the U.K. rightly claim that it will not extradite Pinochet for genocide because of its breach of the Genocide Convention? and then add that Spain cannot thereafter prosecute Pinochet for genocide because of the doctrine of speciality? Should the consequence of such a breach enlarge a functional immunity for genocide in the U.K. to an immunity from prosecution for genocide in Spain because of the doctrines of dual criminality and speciality, thus imposing the consequences of the U.K.'s breach on other states? Would this not be inconsistent with a universal jurisdictional competence and responsibility concerning international crimes? Recall Chapters Two, Section 3 and Three, Section 1. Should there be an international crimes exception to the doctrines of dual criminality and speciality? Does universal responsibility under customary international law to either initiate prosecution or extradite override the doctrines?

9. General Pinochet was allowed to fly back to Chile on March 2, 2000, supposedly because of his lack of physical and mental capacity to stand trial. At the airport he walked among numbers of supporters, conversing with them. Later, he was denied immunity under domestic Chilean law and prosecution was initiated against him for several types of criminal activity.

10. Is there a due process right to a "speedy" extradition hearing or process? See *In re Matter of Extradition of Drayer*, 190 F.3d 410 (6th Cir. 1999) (holding that there is no such right).

11. Article 6 of the U.S.-Canada extradition treaty provides that the requested State may deny extradition if the offense is punishable by death unless the requesting State pro-

vides an assurance that the death penalty will not be imposed or executed. The European Court of Human Rights examined the requirements of a death penalty assurance in the 1989 *Soering Case*, 161 Eur. Ct. Hum. Rts. (Series A) (1989), 11 Eur. Hum. Rts. Rep. 439 (1989), 28 I.L.M. 1063 (1989). In examining the European Court of Human Rights' opinion excerpted below, consider the following questions: (1) Why was the initial assurance provided by the Virginia authorities deemed insufficient by the Court? (2) What is the legal basis of the Court's objection to Soering's extradition to the United States? and (3) Is the precedent likely to be confined to its unique facts (*i.e.*, the long length of detention on death row in Virginia, the abhorrent conditions on Virginia's death row, and the young age and poor mental state of the accused) or to be applied to bar extradition to the United States generally of persons accused of capital murder?

Soering Case
161 Eur. Ct. H.R. (Ser. A) (1989)

Procedure

1. The case was brought before the Court ... by the European Commission of Human Rights ("the Commission"), ... by the Government of the United Kingdom ... within ... the Convention for the Protection of Human Rights and Fundamental Freedoms ("the Convention"). It originated in an application ... against the United Kingdom lodged with the Commission under Article 25 by a German national, Mr. Jens Soering....

The object of the request ... was to obtain a decision from the Court as to whether or not the facts of the case disclosed a breach by the respondent State of its obligations under Articles 3, 6 and 13 of the Convention....

11. The applicant, Mr. Jens Soering, was born on August 1966 and is a German national. He is currently detained in prison in England pending extradition to the United States of America to face charges of murder in the Commonwealth of Virginia.

12. The homicides in question were committed in Bedford County, Virginia, in March 1985. The victims, William Reginald Haysom (aged 72) and Nancy Astor Haysom (aged 53) were the parents of the applicant's girlfriend, ... a Canadian national.... At the time the applicant.., aged 18..., [was a student] at the University of Virginia. [He] disappeared ... from Virginia in October 1985, but [was] arrested in England in April 1986 in connection with cheque fraud.

13. The applicant was interviewed in England between 5 and 8 June 1986 by a police investigator from the Sheriff's Department of Bedford County. In a sworn affidavit dated 24 July 1986 the investigator recorded the applicant as having admitted the killings....

14. [T]he government of the United States of America requested the applicant's ... extradition under the terms of the Extradition Treaty of 1972 between the United States and the United Kingdom....

15. [T]he British Embassy in Washington addressed a request to the United States' authorities in the following terms:

"Because the death penalty has been abolished in Great Britain, the Embassy has been instructed to seek an assurance, in accordance with the terms of ... the Extradition Treaty, that, in the event of Mr. Soering being surrendered and being convicted of the crimes for which he has been indicted..., the death penalty, if imposed, will not be carried out.

Should it not be possible on constitutional grounds for the United States Government to give such assurance, the United Kingdom authorities ask that the United States Government undertake to recommend to the appropriate authorities that the death penalty should not be imposed or, if imposed, should not be executed."

20. Mr. Updike swore an affidavit in his capacity as Attorney for Bedford County, in which he certified as follows:

"I hereby certify that should Jens Soering be convicted of the offence of capital murder as charged in Bedford County, Virginia ... a representation will be made in the name of the United Kingdom to the judge at the time of sentencing that it is the wish of the United Kingdom that the death penalty should not be imposed or carried out." ...

During the course of the present proceedings the Virginia authorities have informed the United Kingdom Government that Mr. Updike was not planning to provide any further assurances and intended to seek the death penalty in Mr. Soering's case because the evidence, in his determination, supported such action....

24.... [T]he Secretary of State signed a warrant ordering the applicant's surrender to he United States' authorities. However, the applicant has not been transferred to the United States by virtue of the interim measures indicated in the present proceedings firstly by the European Court....

25. On 5 August 1988 the applicant was transferred to a prison hospital where he remained until early November 1988 under the special regime applied to suicide-risk prisoners.

According to psychiatric evidence adduced on behalf of the applicant..., the applicant's dread of extreme physical violence and homosexual abuse from other inmates in death row in Virginia is in particular having a profound psychiatric effect on him. The psychiatrist's report records a mounting desperation in the applicant, together with objective fears that he may seek to take his own life.

36. There is no provision in the Extradition Acts relating to the death penalty, but Article IV of the United Kingdom-United States Treaty provides:

"If the offence for which extradition is requested is punishable by death under the relevant law of the requesting Party, but the relevant law of the requested Party does not provide for the death penalty in a similar case, extradition may be refused unless the requesting Party gives assurances satisfactory to the requested Party that the death penalty will not be carried out."

37. In the case of a fugitive requested by the United State who faces a charge carrying the death penalty, it is the Secretary of State's practice, pursuant to Article IV of the United Kingdom-United States Extradition Treaty, to accept an assurance from the prosecuting authorities of the relevant State that a representation will be made to the judge at the time of sentencing that it is the wish of the United Kingdom that the death penalty should be neither imposed nor carried out....

There has, however, never been a case in which the effectiveness of such an undertaking has been tested.

42. The sentencing procedure in a capital murder case in Virginia is a separate proceeding from the determination of guilt. Following a determination of guilt of capital murder, the same jury, or judge sitting without jury, will forthwith proceed to hear evidence regarding punishment. All relevant evidence concerning the offence and the defendant is admissible. Evidence in mitigation is subject to almost no limitation, while evidence of aggravation is restricted by statute ...

44. The imposition of the death penalty on a young person who has reached the age of majority—which is 18 years ... —is not precluded under Virginia law. Age is a fact to be weighed by the jury....

56.... The average time between trial and execution in Virginia, calculated on the basis of the seven executions which have taken place since 1977, is six to eight years. The delays are primarily due to a strategy by convicted prisoners to prolong the appeal proceedings as much as possible. The United States Supreme Court has not as yet considered or ruled on the "death row phenomenon" and in particular whether it falls foul of the prohibition of "cruel and unusual punishment" under the Eighth Amendment to the Constitution of the United States....

61. There are currently 40 people under sentence of death in Virginia. The majority are detained in Mecklenburg Correctional Center, which is a modern maximum security institution with a total capacity of 335 inmates....

63. The size of a death row inmate's cell is 3m by 2.2m. Prisoners have an opportunity for approximately 7 hours' recreation per week in summer and approximately 6 hours' per week, weather permitting, in winter. The death row area has two recreation yards, both of which are equipped with basketball courts and one of which is equipped with weights and weight benches. Inmates are also permitted to leave their cells on other occasions, such as to receive visits, to visit the law library or to attend the prison infirmary. In addition, death row inmates are given one hour out-of-cell time in the morning in a common area. Each death row inmate is eligible for work assignments, such as cleaning duties. When prisoners move around the prison they are handcuffed with special shackles around the waist.

When not in their cells, death row inmates are housed in a common area called "the pod." The guards are not within this area and remain in a box outside. In the event of disturbance or inter-inmate assault, the guards are not allowed to intervene until instructed to do so by the ranking officer present.

64. The applicant adduced much evidence of extreme stress, psychological deterioration and risk of homosexual abuse and physical attack undergone by prisoners on death row, including Mecklenburg Correctional Center. This evidence was strongly contested by the United Kingdom Government on the basis of affidavits sworn by administrators from the Virginia Department of Corrections....

68. A death row prisoner is moved to the death house 15 days before he is due to be executed. The death house is next to the death chamber where the electric chair is situated. Whilst the prisoner is in the death house he is watched 24 hours a day. He is isolated and has no light in his cell. The lights outside are permanently lit. A prisoner who utilizes the appeals process can be placed in the death house several times....

69. Relations between the United Kingdom and the United States of America on matters concerning extradition are conducted by and with the Federal and not the State authorities. However, in respect of offenses against State laws the Federal authorities have no legally binding power to provide, in an appropriate extradition case, an assurance that the death penalty will not be imposed or carried out. In such cases the power rests with the State. If a State does decide to give a promise in relation to the death penalty, the United States Government would have the power to give assurance to the extraditing Government that the State's promise will be honoured....

Proceedings Before the Commission

76. Mr. Soering's application ... was lodged with the Commission on 8 July 1988. In his application Mr. Soering stated his belief that, notwithstanding the assurance given to

the United Kingdom Government, there was a serious likelihood that he would be sentenced to death if extradited to the United States of America. He maintained that in the circumstances and, in particular, having regard to the "death row phenomenon" he would thereby be subjected to inhuman and degrading treatment and punishment contrary to Article 3 of the Convention. In his further submission his extradition to the United States would constitute a violation of Article 6 § 3 (c) because of the absence of legal aid in the State of Virginia to pursue various appeals. Finally, he claimed that, in breach of Article 13, he had no effective remedy under United Kingdom law in respect of his complaint under Article 3....

78. The Commission declared the application admissible on 10 November 1988.

In its report adopted on 19 January 1989 (Article 31) the Commission expressed the opinion that there had been a breach of Article 13 (seven votes to four) but no breach of either Article 3 (six votes to five) or Article 6 § 3 (c) (unanimously)....

As to the Law

I. Alleged Breach of Article 3

80. The applicant alleged that the decision by the Secretary of State for the Home Department to surrender him to the authorities of the United States of America would, if implemented, give rise to a breach by the United Kingdom of Article 3 of the Convention, which provides:

"No one shall be subjected to torture or to inhuman or degrading treatment or punishment."

A. *Applicability of Article 3 in cases of extradition*

81. The alleged breach derives from the applicant's exposure to the so-called "death row phenomenon." This phenomenon may be described as consisting in a combination of circumstances to which the applicant would be exposed if, after having been extradited to Virginia to face a capital murder charge, he were sentenced to death....

82. In its report ... the Commission reaffirmed "its case-law that a person's deportation or extradition may give rise to an issue under Article 3 of the Convention where there are serious reasons to believe that the individual will be subjected, in the receiving State, to treatment contrary to that Article."

The Government of the Federal Republic of Germany supported the approach of the Commission, pointing to a similar approach in the case-law of the German courts.

The applicant likewise submitted that Article 3 ... also embodies an associated obligation not to put a person in a position where he will or may suffer such treatment or punishment at the hands of other States.

83. The United Kingdom Government, on the other hand, contended that Article 3 should not be interpreted so as to impose responsibility ... for acts which occur outside its jurisdiction ... In the alternative, the United Kingdom Government submitted that the application of Article 3 in extradition cases should be limited to those occasions in which the treatment or punishment is certain, imminent and serious ...

86.... These considerations cannot, however, absolve the Contracting Parties from responsibility under Article 3 for all and any foreseeable consequences of extradition suffered outside their jurisdiction.

87. In interpreting the Convention regard must be had to its special character as a treaty for the collective enforcement of human rights and fundamental freedoms ... Thus, the object and purpose of the Convention as an instrument for the protection of individual

human beings require that its provisions be interpreted and applied so as to make its safeguards practical and effective....

88. ... The question remains whether the extradition of a fugitive to another State where he would be subjected or be likely to be subjected to torture or to inhuman or degrading treatment or punishment would itself engage the responsibility of a Contracting State under Article 3. The abhorrence of torture has such implications is recognized in Article 3 of the United Nations Convention Against Torture and Other Cruel, Inhuman or Degrading Treatment or Punishment, which provides that "no State Party shall ... extradite a person where there are substantial grounds for believing that he would be in danger of being subjected to torture". The fact that a specialized treaty should spell out in detail a specific obligation attaching to the prohibition of torture does not mean that an essentially similar obligation is not already inherent in the general terms of Article 3 of the European Convention. It would hardly be compatible with the underlying values of the Convention, the "common heritage of political traditions, ideals, freedoms and the rule of law" to which the Preamble refers, were a Contracting State knowingly to surrender a fugitive to another State where there were substantial grounds for believing that he would be in danger of being subjected to torture, however heinous the crime allegedly committed. Extradition in such circumstances, while not explicitly referred to in the brief and general wording of Article 3, would plainly be contrary to the spirit and intendment of the Article, and in the Court's view this inherent obligation not to extradite also extends to cases in which the fugitive would be faced in the receiving State by a real risk of exposure to inhuman or degrading treatment or punishment proscribed by that Article....

91. In sum, the decision by a Contracting State to extradite a fugitive may give rise to an issue under Article 3, and hence engage the responsibility of that State under the Convention, where substantial grounds have been shown for believing that the person concerned, if extradited, faces a real risk of being subjected to torture or to inhuman or degrading treatment or punishment in the requesting country. The establishment of such responsibility inevitably involves an assessment of conditions in the requesting country against the standards of Article 3 of the Convention. Nonetheless, there is no question of adjudicating on or establishing the responsibility of the receiving country, whether under general international law, under the Convention or otherwise. In so far as any liability under the Convention is or may be incurred, it is liability incurred by the extraditing Contracting State by reason of its having taken action which has a direct consequence the exposure of an individual to proscribed ill-treatment....

92. ... It therefore has to be determined on the above principles whether the foreseeable consequences of Mr. Soering's return to the United States are such as to attract the application of Article 3. This inquiry must concentrate firstly on whether Mr. Soering runs a real risk of being sentenced to death in Virginia, since the source of the alleged "death row phenomenon," lies in the imposition of the death penalty. Only in the event of an affirmative answer to this question need the Court examine whether exposure to the "death row phenomenon" in the circumstances of the applicant's case would involve treatment or punishment incompatible with Article 3.

1. Whether the applicant runs a real risk of a death sentence and hence of exposure to the "death row phenomenon"

98. ... Whatever the position under Virginia law and practice..., and notwithstanding the diplomatic context of the extradition relations between the United Kingdom and the United States, objectively it cannot be said that the undertaking to inform the judge

at the sentencing stage of the wishes of the United Kingdom eliminates the risk of the death penalty being imposed. In the independent exercise of his discretion the Commonwealth's Attorney has himself decided to seek and to persist in seeking the death penalty because the evidence, in his determination, supports such action.... If the national authority with responsibility for prosecuting the offence takes such a firm stance, it is hardly open to the Court to hold that there are no substantial grounds for believing that the applicant faces a real risk of being sentenced to death and hence experiencing the "death row phenomenon".

99. The Court's conclusion is therefore that the likelihood of the feared exposure to the applicant to the "death row phenomenon" has been shown to be such as to bring Article 3 into play.

2. *Whether in the circumstances the risk of exposure to the "death row phenomenon" would make extradition a breach of Article 3*

(a) *General considerations*

100. As is established in the Court's case-law, ill-treatment, including punishment, must attain a minimum level of severity if it is to fall within the scope of Article 3. The assessment of this minimum is, in the nature of things, relative; it depends on all the circumstances of the case, such as the nature and context of the treatment or punishment, the manner and method of its execution, its duration, its physical or mental effects and, in some instances, the sex, age and state of health of the victim....

Treatment has been held by the Court to be both "inhuman" because it was premeditated, was applied for hours at a stretch and "caused, if not actual bodily injury, at least intense physical and mental suffering", and also "degrading" because it was "such as to arouse in [its] victims feelings of fear, anguish and inferiority capable of humiliating and debasing them and possibly breaking their physical or moral resistance".... In order for a punishment or treatment associated with it to be "inhuman" or "degrading", the suffering or humiliation involved must in any event go beyond that inevitable element of suffering or humiliation connected with a given form of legitimate punishment.... In this connections, account is to be taken not only of the physical pain experienced but also, where there is a considerable delay before execution of the punishment, of the sentenced person's mental anguish of anticipating the violence he is to have inflicted on him.

101. Capital punishment is permitted under certain conditions by Article 2 § 1 of the Convention, which reads:

"Everyone's right to life shall be protected by law. No one shall be deprived of his life intentionally save in the execution of a sentence of a court following his conviction of a crime for which this penalty is provided by law."

In view of this wording, the applicant did not suggest that the death penalty *per se* violated Article 3. He, like the two Government Parties, agreed with the Commission that the extradition of a person to a country where he risks the death penalty does not in itself raise an issue under either Article 2 or Article 3. On the other hand, Amnesty International in their written comments ... argued that the evolving standards in Western Europe regarding the existence and use of the death penalty required that the death penalty should now be considered as an inhuman and degrading punishment within the meaning of Article 3.

102. Certainly, "the Convention is a living instrument which ... must be interpreted in the light of present-day conditions"; and, in assessing whether a given treatment or

punishment is to be regarded as inhuman or degrading for the purposes of Article 3, "the Court cannot but be influenced by the developments and commonly accepted standards in the penal policy of the member States of the Council of Europe in this field".... *De facto* the death penalty no longer exists in time of peace in the Contracting States to the Convention. In the few Contracting States which retain the death penalty in law for some peacetime offenses, death sentences, if ever imposed, are nowadays not carried out. This "virtual consensus in Western European legal systems that the death penalty is, under current circumstances, no longer consistent with regional standards of justice", to use the words of Amnesty International, is reflected in Protocol No. 6 to the Convention, which provides for the abolition of the death penalty in time of peace. Protocol No. 6 was opened for signature in April 1983, which in the practice of the Council of Europe indicates the absence of objection on the part of any of the Member States of the Organization; it came into force in March 1985 and to date has been ratified by thirteen Contracting States to the Convention, not however including the United Kingdom.

Whether these marked changes have the effect of bringing the death penalty *per se* within the prohibition of ill-treatment under Article 3 must be determined on the principles governing the interpretation of the Convention.

103.... Article 3 evidently cannot have been intended by the drafters of the Convention to include a general prohibition of the death penalty since that would nullify the clear wording of Article 2 § 1.

Subsequent practice in national penal policy, in the form of a generalized abolition of capital punishment, could be taken as establishing the agreement of the Contracting States to abrogate the exception provided for under Article 2 § 1 an hence to remove a textual limit on the scope for evolutive interpretation of Article 3. However, Protocol No. 6, as a subsequent written agreement, shows that the intention of the Contracting Parties as recently as 1983 was to adopt the normal method of amendment of the text in order to introduce a new obligation to abolish capital punishment in time of peace and, what is more, to do so by an optional instrument allowing each State to choose the moment when to undertake such an engagement. In these conditions, notwithstanding the special character of the Convention..., Article 3 cannot be interpreted as generally prohibiting the death penalty.

104. That does not mean however that circumstances relating to death sentence can never give rise to an issue under Article 3. The manner in which it is imposed or executed, the personal circumstances of the condemned person and a disproportionality to the gravity of the crime committed, as well as the conditions of detention awaiting execution, are examples of factors capable of bringing the treatment or punishment received by the condemned person within the proscription under Article 3. Present-day attitudes in the Contracting States to capital punishment are relevant for the assessment whether the acceptable threshold of suffering or degradation has been exceeded.

(b) *The particular circumstances ...*

　　i. *Length of detention prior to execution*

106. The period that a condemned prisoner can expect to spend on death row in Virginia before being executed is on average six to eight years.... This length of time awaiting death is, as the Commission and the United Kingdom noted, in a sense largely of the prisoner's own making in that he takes advantage of all avenues of appeal which are offered to him by Virginia law....

Nevertheless, just as some lapse of time between sentence and execution is inevitable if appeal safeguards are to be provided to the condemned person, so it is equally part of human nature that the person will cling to life by exploiting those safeguards to the full. However well-intentioned and even potentially beneficial is the provision of the complex of post-sentence procedures in Virginia, the consequence is that the condemned prisoner has to endure for many years the conditions on death row and the anguish and mounting tension of living in the ever-present shadow of death.

ii. *Conditions on death row*

107. As to conditions in Mecklenburg Correctional Center, where the applicant could expect to be held if sentenced to death, the Court bases itself on the facts which were uncontested by the United Kingdom Government, without finding it necessary to determine the reliability of the additional evidence adduced by the applicant, notably as to the risk of homosexual abuse and physical attack undergone by prisoners on death row....

... In this connection, the United Kingdom Government drew attention to the necessary requirement of extra security for the safe custody of prisoners condemned to death for murder. Whilst it might thus well be justifiable in principle, the severity of a special regime such as that operated on death row in Mecklenburg is compounded by the fact of inmates being subject to it for a protracted period lasting on average six to eight years.

iii. *The applicant's age and mental state*

108. At the time of the killings, the applicant was only 18 years old and there is some psychiatric evidence, which was not contested as such, that he "was suffering from [such] an abnormality of mind ... as substantially impaired his mental responsibility for his acts"....

Unlike Article 2 of the Convention, Article 6 of the 1966 International Covenant on Civil and Political Rights and Article 4 of the 1969 American Convention on Human Rights expressly prohibit the death penalty from being imposed on persons aged less than 18 at the time of commission of the offence. Whether or not such a prohibition be inherent in the brief and general language of Article 2 of the European Convention, its explicit enunciation in other, later international instruments, the former of which has been ratified by a large number of States Parties to the European Convention, at the very least indicates that as a general principle the youth of the person concerned is a circumstance which is liable, with others, to put in question the compatibility with Article 3 of measures connected with a death sentence.

It is in line with the Court's case-law ... to treat disturbed mental health as having the same effect for the application of Article 3....

Conclusion

111. For any prisoner condemned to death, some element of delay between imposition and execution of the sentence and the experience of severe stress in conditions necessary for strict incarceration are inevitable. The democratic character of the Virginia legal system in general and the positive features of Virginia trial, sentencing and appeal procedures in particular are beyond doubt. The Court agrees with the Commission that the machinery of justice to which the applicant would be subject in the United States is in itself neither arbitrary nor unreasonable, but, rather, respects the rule of law and affords not inconsiderable procedural safeguards to the defendant in a capital trial. Facilities are available on death row for the assistance of inmates, notably through provision of psychological and psychiatric services....

However, in the Court's view, having regard to the very long period of time spent on death row in such extreme conditions, with the ever present and mounting anguish of awaiting execution of the death penalty, and to the personal circumstances of the applicant, especially his age and mental state at the time of the offence, the applicant's extradition to the United States would expose him to a real risk of treatment going beyond the threshold set by Article 3. A further consideration of relevance is that in the particular instance the legitimate purpose of extradition could be achieved by another means which would not involve suffering of such exceptional intensity or duration.

Accordingly, the Secretary of State's decision to extradite the applicant to the United States would, if implemented, give rise to a breach of Article 3.

For these Reasons, the Court Unanimously

1. *Holds* that, in the event of the Secretary of State's decision to extradite the applicant to the United States of America being implemented, there would be a violation of Article 3 ...

Notes and Questions

1. After the European Court's decision, the prosecutor of Bedford County, Virginia, amended the charges to remove the offense of capital murder. The United Kingdom then extradited Mr. Soering to Virginia for trial. He was convicted of first-degree murder in June of 1990. See RICHARD B. LILLICH & HURST HANNUM, INTERNATIONAL HUMAN RIGHTS 768 (3 ed. 1995). What if the County prosecutor refused to avoid seeking the death penalty?

Would a U.S. Executive assurance to the U.K. (that a death penalty will not be sought or imposed) as part of a process of agreement constitute an Executive agreement and override the power of state entities within a federated system? *See* Malvina Halberstam, *The Constitutional Authority of the Federal Government in State Criminal Proceedings that Involve U.S. Treaty Obligations or Affect U.S. Foreign Relations*, 10 IND. INT'L & COMP. L. REV. 1 (1999). With respect to the primacy of Executive agreements over state law and power, see generally United States v. Pink, 315 U.S. 203 (1942). In the case of Pietro Venezia, Sentence No. 223-1996 (27 June 1996), the Supreme Court of Italy declared that the U.S.-Italy Extradition Treaty did not provide a sufficient guarantee that the accused would not suffer the death penalty (which is impermissible in Italy) because an agreement by federal prosecutors not to seek the death penalty was supposedly not binding on states within the U.S.

2. The human right to freedom from torture or cruel, inhumane or degrading treatment or punishment exception to extradition has been followed in "a long line of decisions by the [European] Commission and the Court." See LILLICH & HANNUM, *supra* at 759; Bader and others v. Sweden, ECHR 2005-II, No. 13284/04, para. 29 ("an alien must not be sent to a country where there are reasonable grounds for believing that he or she would be in danger of suffering capital or corporal punishment or of being subjected to torture or other inhuman or degrading treatment or punishment."); see also RESTATEMENT, *supra* §§ 475, Cmnt. g, 476, Cmnt. h, 711, RN 7. One related case is Chahal v. United Kingdom, Eur. Ct. H.R., No. 70/1995/576/662 (15 Nov. 1996). *Chahal* involved a potential deportation of a Sikh activist from the U.K. on grounds of "national security" and an assessment of a real risk of being tortured in India, a complicitous violation of Article 3 by the U.K. The European Court ruled that the U.K.'s limitation of judicial review of deportation orders failed to provide Mr. Chahal with an effective remedy as mandated by the European Convention on Human Rights. On applicability of the Convention to state

acts abroad or the effects abroad of state acts, see also Drozd & Janousek v. France and Spain, Case No. 21/1991/273/344. para. 91 (23 & 27 Jan. 1992); Cyprus v. Turkey, Eur. Cm. H.R., 1975 Y.B. Eur. Conv. Hum. Rts. 82, 118 (1976) (state duty exists to secure human rights protections "to all persons under their actual authority and responsibility, whether that authority is exercised within their own territory or abroad."); Juliane Kokott & Beate Rudolf, note re: *Loizidou v. Turkey*, 310 Eur. Ct. H.R. (ser. A) (1995), in 90 Am. J. Int'l L. 98 (1996). in 2001, Spain and other countries refused to render detainees to the U.S. for detention at Guantanamo Bay, Cuba because of alleged violations of human rights law that would occur there. See also Leila Zerrougui, *et al.*, Report, *Situation of Detainees at Guantanamo Bay*, Commission on Human Rights, 62nd sess., items 10 and 11 of the provisional agenda, U.N. Doc. E/CN.4/2006/120 (Feb. 15, 2006), para. 55 ("the Special Reporter takes the view that the United States practice of 'extraordinary rendition' constitutes a violation of article 3 of the Convention against Torture and article 7 of the ICCPR"); Council of Europe, Parliamentary Assembly, Res. 1433, *Lawfulness of Detentions by the United States in Guantanamo Bay* (26 Apr. 2005), para. 7 (vii) ("the United States has, by practising 'rendition' (removal of persons to other countries, without judicial supervision, for purposes such as interrogation or detention), allowed detainees to be subjected to torture and to cruel, inhuman or degrading treatment, in violation of the prohibition on *non-refoulement*."), in the Documents Supplement. *See generally* Leila Nadya Sadat, *Ghost Prisoners and Black Sites: Extraordinary Rendition Under International Law*, 57 Case W. Res. J. Int'l L. 309 (2006).

3. An issue may be raised under Article 6 of the European Convention for the Protection of Human Rights and Fundamental Freedoms where extradition may subject the fugitive to a "real risk" of suffering a flagrant denial of justice in the requesting country. In Othman (Abu Qatada) v. United Kingdom, Appl No. 8139/09 (Eur. Ct. H.R. Jan. 17, 2012), the European Court of Human Rights ruled that the UK may not deport Omar Othman (also known as Abu Qatada), an extremist preacher linked to al Qaeda, to Jordan, where there was a "real risk" that evidence obtained by torture of others would be used and admitted against Othman. *But see* Babar Ahmad v. United Kingdom, Appls. Nos. 24027/07, 11949/08, 36742/08, 66911/09 & 67354/09 (Eur. Ct. H.R. April 10, 2012), where the European Court of Human Rights held that Britain could legally extradite five suspects wanted in the U.S. on terrorism charges, including Abu Hamza al-Masri, an inflamatory Egyptian-born cleric incarcerated in the U.K and indicted for acts of terrorism in the U.S. The Court ruled that the human rights of the defendants would not be violated by their prospective captivity in a U.S. maximum security prison. The judges found that the conditions of incarceration would not constitute "inhuman or degrading treatment," concluding that while the inmates would be confined to their cells for the vast majority of their time, they would be provided with "services and activities (television, radio, newspapers, books, hobby and craft items, telephone calls, social visits, correspondence with families, group prayer) which went beyond what was provided in most prisons in Europe." *Id.* at para. 222.

 ·4. The Convention Against Torture and Other Cruel, Inhuman or Degrading Treatment or Punishment (CAT) requires that "[n]o State Party shall expel, return ('*refouler*') or extradite a person to another State where there are substantial grounds for believing that he would be in danger of being subjected to torture." In a Report of the U.N. Committee Against Torture, the Committee stated that a claim of the Bush Administration that the duties under Article 3 should not apply outside U.S. territory at Guantanamo Bay, Cuba was in error and that the United States "should apply the *non-refoulement* guarantee to all detainees in its custody, cease rendition of suspects, in particular by its intelligence agencies, to States where they face a real risk of torture, in order to comply with its obligations under article 3 of the Convention" and that that United States "should always ensure that suspects have the possibility to challenge decisions of *refoulement*". *Consideration of Reports Submitted by States Parties Under Article 19 of the Convention: Conclusions and Recommendations of the Committee against Torture, United States of America*, 36th sess., U.N. Doc. CAT/C/USA/CO/2 (18 May 2006), para. 20. Moreover, U.S. obligations apply "in all places of detention under its *de facto* effective control." *Id.* para. 24; see also *id.* paras. 14–15, 17–18, 22, 26, quoted in Chapter Eleven. With respect to the application of rights and duties under the International Covenant on Civil and Political Rights in any territory under the jurisdiction of a state or within the power or effective control of a state, see Chapter Eleven. The human rights duties of states under Articles 55(c) and 56 of the U.N. Charter apply universally, *e.g.*, without any territorial limitation.

5. In 1793, Thomas Jefferson informed the French Minister: "until a reformation of the criminal codes of most nations, to deliver fugitives from them would be to become their accomplices," quoted in *Ex parte* Kaine, 14 F. Cas. 78, 81 (C.C.S.D.N.Y. 1853) (No. 7,597).

6. Extradition can also be denied to a country where there is a real risk that the extraditee will be persecuted on account of his or her race, religion, nationality, ethnic origin, or political opinion. Customary and treaty-based human rights law requires the requested state to not be complicit in such persecution. Certain international criminal law treaties also expressly limit extradition in such circumstances. *See, e.g.*, International Convention for the Suppression of Terrorist Bombings, art. 12; International Convention for the Suppression of the Financing of Terrorism, art. 15; International Convention Against the Taking of Hostages, art. 9 (1); Convention Against Torture and Other Cruel, Inhuman or Degrading Treatment or Punishment, art. 3.

7. For an argument contrary to *Soering* with respect to the requirement that an extraditing state seek a so-called "death penalty assurance" (*i.e.*, an assurance that the death penalty will not be imposed in the receiving state), consider the following opinion of the Supreme Court of Canada.

Kindler v. Canada (Minister of Justice)
[1991] 2 S.C.R. 779

La Forest, J.

The appellant, Joseph John Kindler, was found guilty of murder, kidnapping and criminal conspiracy by a court of competent jurisdiction in the State of Pennsylvania. A sentencing hearing was held in accordance with Pennsylvania law and the jury, which found that the aggravating circumstances surrounding these offenses outweighed the mitigating circumstances, unanimously returned a sentence of death. The appellant escaped from custody before the sentence could be imposed and was arrested in the province of Quebec several months later. The United States requested the appellant's extradition pursuant to the 1976 *Extradition Treaty Between Canada and the United States of America*, Can. T.S. 1976 No. 3.

The broad question raised by this appeal is whether the decision of the Minister of Justice to surrender the appellant to the United States, without first seeking assurances that the death penalty will not be imposed or executed, violates the appellant's rights under the *Canadian Charter of Rights and Freedoms*.

The appellant framed his arguments both in terms of s. 7 [Everyone has the right to life, liberty and security of person and the right not to be deprived thereof except in accordance with the principles of fundamental justice] and s. 12 [Everyone has the right not to be subjected to any cruel and unusual treatment or punishment] of the *Charter*, but he more directly focused on s. 12, the provision that prohibits cruel and unusual punishment or treatment. But McLachlin J. quite rightly points out that s. 7 of the *Charter* is the appropriate provision under which the actions of the Minister are to be assessed. The Minister's actions do not constitute cruel and unusual punishment. The execution, if it ultimately takes place, will be in the United States under American law against an American citizen in respect of an offence that took place in the United States. It does not result from any initiative taken by the Canadian Government. Canada's connection with the matter results from the fact that the fugitive came here of his own free will, and the question to be determined is whether the action of the Canadian Government in returning him to his own country infringes his liberty and security in an impermissible way.

There can be no doubt that the appellant's right to liberty and security of the person is very seriously affected because he may face the death penalty following his return. The real question is whether surrender under these conditions violates the principles of fundamental justice. I should, at the outset, say that I agree with Cory J. that the procedure followed by the Minister did not offend these principles. So the question is whether these principles were violated in substantive aspects....

There are, of course, situations where the punishment imposed following surrender—torture, for example—would be so outrageous to the values of the Canadian community that the surrender would be unacceptable. But I do not think the surrender of fugitives who may ultimately face the death penalty abroad would in all cases shock the conscience of Canadians.... One could not imagine a similar vote on the question of whether to re-instate torture. And it must be emphasized that we are trying to assess the public conscience, not in relation to the execution of the death penalty in Canada, but in regard to the extradition of an individual under circumstances where the death penalty might be imposed in another country.... There is strong ground for believing that having regard to the limited extent to which the death penalty advances any valid penological objectives and the serious invasion of human dignity it engenders that the death penalty cannot, except in exceptional circumstances, be justified in this country. But that, I repeat, is not the issue.

Unlike the internal situation, the Minister's decision in the present case operates in a specific case where the particular facts are critical to constitutional evaluation. More important, it takes place in a global setting where the vast majority of the nations of the world retain the death penalty. There has, it is true, been a growing and, in my view, welcome trend among Western nations over the past fifty years to abolish the death penalty but some have gone against this trend, notably the United States, a fact of especial concern having regard to its size and proximity to this country. There are also a number of major international agreements mentioned by Cory J. supporting the trend for abolition but, except for the *European Protocol No. 6 to the Convention for the Protection of Human Rights and Fundamental Freedoms Concerning the Abolition of the Death Penalty*, Europ. T.S. No. 114, all fall short of actually prohibiting use of the death penalty. This contrasts with the overwhelming universal condemnation that has been directed at practices such as genocide, slavery and torture; *cf.*, for example, Articles 6 and 7 of the *International Covenant on Civil and Political Rights*, 999 U.N.T.S. 172.

There is thus, despite these trends, no international norm. Indeed, more directly reflective of international attitudes towards extraditing an individual to face the death penalty is the *Model Treaty on Extradition* brought forth at the Eighth United Nations Congress on the Prevention of Crime and the Treatment of Offenders as late as 1990 in Havana. Article 4 of the *Model Treaty on Extradition*, which lists "optional grounds" for refusing extradition, and provides for the same sort of discretion in obtaining assurances regarding the death penalty as is found in Article 6 of the *Canada-United States Extradition Treaty*, clearly contemplates the possibility of unconditional extradition under circumstances such as those found in the present case.

The Government has the right and duty to keep out and to expel aliens from this country if it considers it advisable to do so. This right, of course, exists independently of extradition. If an alien known to have a serious criminal record attempted to enter into Canada, he could be refused admission. And by the same token, he could be deported once he entered Canada.... If it were otherwise, Canada could become a haven for criminals and others whom we legitimately do not wish to have among us....

I can see no reason why the same general approach should not apply to extradition. One of the basic purposes of that procedure is to ensure that a specific kind of undesirable alien should not be able to stay in Canada. It is, no doubt, true that extradition and deportation do not always have the same purpose, for cases can arise where they serve different ends, and fairness may demand that one procedure be used rather than the other. But that is not this case, and I would be concerned about encouraging a resort to deportation rather than extradition with its inbuilt protections geared to the criminal process.

Thus the question with which we are presented here is whether it shocks the conscience to surrender individuals who have been charged with the worst sort of crimes to face capital prosecution in the United States. Absent proof of some mitigating circumstance, I do not think it does. This is especially true given that the failure to extradite without restrictions might lead to Canada becoming a more attractive destination for American fugitives in the future. It is also significant, as McLachlin J. notes, that the party requesting extradition in this case is the United States—a country with a criminal justice system that is, in many ways, similar to our own, and which provides substantial protections to the criminal defendant.

While the decisions of the executive are, of course, subject to judicial review, the jurisdiction of courts to interfere with the executive's exercise of discretion in this area "must be exercised with the utmost circumspection consistent with the executive's preeminent position in matters of external relations"; see *Argentina v. Mellino*, [1987] 1 S.C.R. 536, at pp. 557–58. The executive has a much greater expertise than the Court in the area of foreign relations, and is in a better position to evaluate many of the considerations which have been set forth above....

I therefore conclude that the decision to extradite the appellant without restrictions, which was taken with the view to deterring fugitives from seeking a safe haven in Canada to avoid the death penalty, was made in pursuit of a legitimate and, indeed, compelling social goal. Surrendering the appellant to the United States without restriction does not go beyond what is necessary to achieve that goal, for it is apparent that surrendering the appellant with the restriction that the death penalty would not be imposed would completely undermine the deterrent effect the government is seeking to achieve. As this Court has frequently noted, the social goal addressed is an important consideration in a s. 7 balancing....

I need only add a few words about the subsidiary grounds raised by the appellant. The appellant argues that the death penalty in its practical application is arbitrarily and indiscriminately imposed. That argument is really directed at the criminal justice system in the United States and, as made, would require extraterritorial application of the Charter; see *United States of America v. Cotroni, supra*, at p. 1501. There is nothing here to indicate that the alleged arbitrariness is in any way related to the fugitive. It has nothing to do with the policy of the Canadian Government to protect the Canadian public against dangerous criminals seeking haven here. There may conceivably be situations where certain types of arbitrary conduct may sufficiently "shock the conscience" as to trigger s. 7, but this has not been established here. It is worth noting as well that the United States Supreme Court is well aware of the arbitrariness issue and has shown a willingness to act to prevent it....

The appellant laid great stress on the "death row" phenomenon and the manner of execution.... The unwieldy and time-consuming nature of this generous appeal process has come under heavy criticism in the United States in recent years, and is the subject of efforts at reform.... the fact remains that a defendant is never forced to undergo the full appeal procedure, but the vast majority choose to do so. It would be ironic if delay caused by the appellant's taking advantage of the full and generous avenue of the appeals available to him should be viewed as a violation of fundamental justice.... As in *Soering, supra,* there may be situations where the age or mental capacity of the fugitive may affect the matter, but again that is not this case.

So far as the specific manner of execution, electrocution, is concerned, it must be said that regardless of the manner chosen, there is a certain horror inherent in execution. It is far from clear, however, that there are more humane methods as viable alternatives....

For these reasons, then, I am of the opinion that surrendering the appellant unconditionally would not violate the principles of fundamental justice under the circumstances of this case. I reach this conclusion principally for two reasons. First, I believe that extradition of an individual who has been accused of the worst form of murder, to face capital prosecution in the United States, could not be said to shock the conscience of the Canadian people nor to be in violation of the standards of the international community. Second, I find that it is reasonable to believe that extradition in this case does not go beyond what is necessary to serve the legitimate social purpose of preventing Canada from becoming an attractive haven for fugitives.

Notes and Questions

1. Note the concentration by Justice La Forest on the death penalty itself and the denial of direct applicability of section 12 of the Charter of Rights, as this would be extraterritorial in nature. This is in contrast to the *Soering* and *Loizidou v. Turkey* courts in their application of the European Convention. Consider the emphasis in *Kindler* on returning "American citizens" to the United States for the "worst sort of crime" committed there. Do you think it would make a difference to the section 7 analysis if the alleged or convicted offender was a Canadian citizen? As Professor Williams notes in *Extradition From Canada Since the Charter of Rights, supra,* at 393–94, "following the surrender of Kindler and Ng [*i.e.,* Ng Extradition (Canada) [1991] 2 S.C.R. 858] to the United States, both individuals applied to the United Nations Committee on Human Rights. They contended that Canada's extradition without assurances against the death penalty violated Canada's obligations under [Article 6, protecting the right to life, and Article 7, protecting against cruel, inhuman or degrading treatment or punishment] the International Covenant on Civil and Political Rights." In both cases, the Committee concluded that extradition did not violate Article 6. With respect to Article 7, the Committee found that prolonged periods on deathrow do not generally violate the article. For such a violation to occur, one must demonstrate specific personal consequences and other factors concerning conditions on deathrow, as well as the proposed method of execution. In Kindler's case, no violation of Article 7 was found, his counsel having made no submissions on such points.

In Charles Ng's case, the Committee found that in California execution is by asphyxiation by cyanide gas and that detailed information had been provided concerning the prolonged agony and suffering that would take place and, thus, that a violation was revealed. See *Kindler v. Canada,* CCPR/C/48/D/470/1991 (Nov. 11, 1993); *Ng v. Canada,* CCPR/C/49/D/469/1991 (Jan. 7, 1994); *see also* International Law Association, Report of the Sixty-Sixth Conference—Buenos Aires, Argentina 144, 150, 154–56, 161 (1994).

2. Another question that has arisen in the context of extradition from Canada to the United States is whether lengthy minimum mandatory sentences are compatible with the Canadian Charter of Rights guarantees contained in section 7. In three cases that are on appeal to the Supreme Court of Canada, the issue is whether the penalties that would be handed down violate the principles of fundamental justice in that they are disproportionate to what would be received for similar criminal conduct in Canada. See *Whitley,* (1995), 20 O.R. 794 (Ont. C.A.); *Ross,* (1993), 93 C.C.C. (3d) 500 (B.C.C.A); *Jamieson,* (1993), 93 C.C.C. (3d) 265 (Q.C.A.). Do you think that it should make a difference if the criminal conduct involves a cross border drug conspiracy that could be prosecuted in Canada or the United States? What if the fugitive is also a Canadian citizen?

3. Concerning non-extradition to countries that predictably will violate the human rights of an accused, *also see* Restatement §§ 475, Cmnt. g, 476, Cmnt. h; Report of the Sixty-Sixth Conference, *supra,* at 145–67; Paust, *Extradition and United States Prosecution of the* Achille Lauro *Hostage-Takers: Navigating the Hazards,* 20 Vand. J. Trans. L. 235, 247–49 (1987); *see also* Restatement §§ 702, 711.

D. The Political Offense Exception and Non-Inquiry

Introductory Problem

For purposes of this problem, assume you are the Legal Counsel on the staff of Senator Grimm (Republican, State of Confusion), a ranking member of the Senate Foreign Relations Committee, who is concerned about the outcome of a number of extradition cases that have been in the news in recent years. The Senator has prepared a rough draft of legislation that he wishes to introduce next month and he has asked you to critique the draft using the materials contained in this sub-section of the book. The draft follows:

Be it enacted by the Senate and House of Representatives of the United States of America, Congress assembled,

SEC. 1. SHORT TITLE

This Act may be cited as the Extradition Law Reform Act of 1997.

SEC. 2. ELIMINATION OF THE POLITICAL OFFENSE EXCEPTION TO EXTRADITION

For the purposes of extradition from the United States, the following shall not be regarded as an offense of a political character: murder of or assault on non-police or non-military personnel.

SEC. 3. REVERSAL OF THE RULE OF NON-INQUIRY

Notwithstanding any other provision of law, including any treaty, a request for extradition shall be denied if the person sought establishes to the satisfaction of the competent judicial authority by a preponderance of the evidence that the proceedings or punishment that await him or her in the foreign country do not comport with U.S. standards of due process or notions of fairness or with international human rights.

1. *The Political Offense Exception*

Letter, Secretary of State Marcy to Mr. Hulsemann of Austria

Sept. 26, 1853, in 2 WHARTON'S DIGEST 483 (1886):

"To surrender political offenders ... is not a duty, but, on the contrary, compliance with such a demand would be considered a dishonorable subserviency to a foreign power, and an act meriting the reprobation of mankind...."

Quinn v. Robinson

783 F.2d 776 (9th Cir. 1986)

Reinhardt, J.

Pursuant to 18 USC § 3184 (1982) and the governing treaty between the United States and the United Kingdom of Great Britain and Northern Ireland ("United Kingdom"), Extradition Treaty of June 8, 1972, United States-United Kingdom, 28 U.S.T. 227, T.I.A.S. No. 8468 [hereinafter cited as *Treaty*], the United Kingdom seeks the extradition of William Joseph Quinn, a member of the Irish Republican Army ("IRA"), in order to try him for the commission of a murder in 1975 and for conspiring to cause explosions in London in 1974 and 1975. After a United States magistrate found Quinn extraditable, Quinn filed a petition for a writ of habeas corpus. The district court determined that Quinn cannot be extradited because a long-standing principle of international law which has been incorporated in the extradition treaty at issue—the political offense exception—bars extradition for the charged offenses. The United States government, on behalf of the United Kingdom, appeals....

In the case before us, we find, for reasons we will explain in full, that the charged offenses are not protected by the political offense exception. We vacate the writ of habeas corpus and remand to the district court. We hold that Quinn may be extradited on the murder charge but that the district court must consider Quinn's remaining defense to the conspiracy charge before extradition is permitting for that offense....

Nor does the assignment to the judiciary of the initial determination of the applicability of the political offense exception deprive the executive branch of all discretion to determine that a person claiming the protection of that exception should not be extradited. The executive branch has the ultimate authority to decide whether to extradite the accused after a judicial determination that the individual is, in fact, extraditable. *Eain*, 641 F.2d at 516 (citing *In re Ezeta*, 62 F. 972 (N.D. Cal. 1894)); 18 U.S.C. § 3186 (1982). Although the Secretary of State's authority to refuse extradition is presumably constrained by our treaty obligations, the contours of executive branch discretion in this area have never been expressly delineated. Bassiouni, *supra* p. 4, at 756 (["T]he statute should probably be interpreted to grant the Secretary only limited discretion to differ from the courts in the matter of treaty interpretation. In fact, the Secretary has always based his refusal to surrender upon a determination that the treaty did not require extradition in that instance.... [T]he Secretary apparently considers his discretion only coextensive with the issues presentable at the extradition proceedings ... [and] has refused to surrender infrequently (only twice between 1940 and 1960)...."). Nevertheless, it is clear that the Secretary of State has sole discretion to determine whether a request for extradition should be denied because it is a subterfuge made for the purpose of punishing the accused for a political crime, *see In re Lincoln*, 228 F. 70 (E.D.N.Y. 1915), *aff'd*, 214 U.S. 65 ... (1916) (per curiam), or to refuse extradition on humanitarian grounds because of the procedures or treatment that await a surrendered fugitive, *Arnbjornsdottir-Mendler v. United States*, 721 F.2d 679, 683 (9th Cir. 1983); *Escobedo v. United States*, 623 F.2d 1098, 1105 (5th Cir.), *cert. denied*, 449 U.S. 1036 … (1980); 18 U.S.C. § 3186 (1982)….

IV. THE DEVELOPMENT OF THE POLITICAL OFFENSE EXCEPTION

A. Origin of the Exception

The political offense exception is premised on a number of justifications. First, its historical development suggests that it is grounded in a belief that individuals have a "right to resort to political activism to foster political change." Note, *American Courts and Modern Terrorism: The Politics of Extradition*, 13 N.Y.U. J. Int'l L. & Pol. 617, 622 (1981) [hereinafter cited as *Politics of Extradition*]; *see also In re Doherty*, 599 F. Supp. 270, 275 n. 4 (S.D.N.Y. 1984) ("The concept was first enunciated during an era when there was much concern for and sympathy in England for the cause of liberation for subjugated peoples.") (citation omitted). This justification is consistent with the modern consensus that political crimes have greater legitimacy than common crimes. *Politics of Extradition, supra.* 31, at 632. Second, the exception reflects a concern that individuals—particularly unsuccessful rebels—should not be returned to countries where they may be subjected to unfair trials and punishments because of their political opinions. *See* M. Bassiouni, *International Extradition and World Public Order* 425 (1974); C. Van den Wijngaert, *supra* P. 22, at 3; Garcia-Mora, *supra* p. 3, at 1226, 1238. Third, the exception comports with the notion that governments—and certainly their nonpolitical branches—should not intervene in the internal political struggles of other nations. *See* C. Van den Wijngaert, *supra* p. 22, at 3, 158, 204; *Politics of Extradition, supra* p. 31, at 622. [note omitted].

B. Comparative Legal Standards

None of the political offense provisions in treaties includes a definition of the word "political." I.A. Shearer, *supra* p. 22 at 168. Thus, the term "political offense" has received various interpretations by courts since the mid-nineteenth century. Garcia-Mora, *supra*, p. 3 at 1230–31; Wise, Book Review, 30 Am.J. Comp.L. 362, 363, (1982) (reviewing C. Van den Wijngaert, *The Political Offense Exception to Extradition* (1980); cf. M. Bassiouni, *supra* p. 32, at 371–72 (inability to define precisely the term "political offense" promotes a necessary flexibility of the concept). Not every offense that is politically motivated falls within the exception. Instead, courts have devised various tests to identify those offenses that comport with the justifications for the exception and that, accordingly, are not extraditable.

Within the confusion about definitions it is fairly well accepted that there are two distinct categories of political offenses: "pure political offenses" and "relative political offenses." *See Karadzole v. Artukovic*, 247 F.2d 198, 203 (9th Cir. 1957), vacated, 355 U.S. 393 78 S.Ct. 381, 2 L.Ed.2d 356 (1958) (mem.); *see generally* Garcia-Mora, *supra* p. 3, at 1230; *20th Century American Courts, supra* p. 30, at 1009. Pure political offenses are acts aimed directly at the government, *see* Lubet & Czackes, *supra* p. 3, at 1230. These offenses, which include treason, sedition, and espionage, Garcia-Mora, *supra* p. 3, at 1234; Lubet & Czackes, *supra* p. 3, at 200, do not violate the private rights of individuals, Garcia-Mora, *supra* p. 3, at 1237. Because they are frequently specifically excluded from the list of extraditable crimes given in a treaty, *see 20th Century American Courts, supra* p. 30, at 1009, courts seldom deal with whether these offenses are extraditable, *see id.*, and it is generally agreed that they are not, *see* Lubet & Czackes, *supra* p. 3, at 200 (citing *In re Ezeta*, 62 F. 972 (1894)).

The definitional problems focus around the second category of political offenses—the relative political offenses. These include "otherwise common crimes committed in

connection with a political act," Lubet & Czackes, *supra* p. 3, at 200, or"common crimes …
committed for political motives or in political context," *20th Century American Courts*,
supra p. 30, at 1009. Courts have developed various tests for ascertaining whether " the
nexus between the crime and the political act is sufficiently close … [for the crime to be
deemed] not extraditable." Lubet & Czackes, *supra* p. 3, at 200. The judicial approaches
can be grouped into three distinct categories: (1) the French "objective" test; (2) the Swiss
"proportionality" or "predominance" test; and (3) the Anglo-American "incidence" test.
See generally Carbonneau, The Political Offense Exception to Extradition and Transnational Terrorists: Old Doctrine Reformulated and New Norms Created, 1 Assoc. of Student Int'l L. Societies Int'l L.J. 1, 11–31 (1977); Garcia-Mora, *supra* p. 3, at 1239–56;
20th Century American Courts, *supra* p. 30, at 1009–17. More recent developments allow
for further distinctions between the British test and the test employed in the United States.
See generally Lubet & Czackes, *supra* p. 3, at 201–10.

The early French test, most clearly represented in *In re* Giovanni Gatti, [1947] Ann.Dig.
145 (No. 70) (France, Ct.App. of Grenoble), considered an offense non-extraditable only
if it directly injured the rights of the state. *See 20th Century American Courts*, *supra* p. 30,
at 1010. Applying this rigid formula, French courts refused to consider the motives of
the accused. Garcia-Mora, *supra* p. 3, at 1249–50. The test primarily protects only pure
political offenses, *see id.* at 1235–36 (discussing cases), and is useless in attempts to define whether an otherwise common crime should not be extraditable because it is connected with a political act, motive, or context. Id. at 1252. Because politically motivated
and directed acts may injure private as well as state rights, the objective test fails to satisfy the various purposes of the political offense exception. Politics of Extradition, *supra*
p. 31, at 629–30. Nevertheless, this test has one benefit: because it is so limited, it is not
subject to abuse; perpetrators of common crimes will not be protected because of alleged
political motivations. Id. at 630; Garcia-Mora, *supra* p. 3, at 1251.

In contrast to the traditional French test, Swiss courts apply a test that protects both
pure and relative political offenses. The Swiss test examines the political motivation of
the offender, *see* Garcia-Mora, *supra* p. 3, at 1251, but also requires (a) a consideration
of the circumstances surrounding the commission of the crime, *see* Carbonneau, *supra*
p. 34, at 23–26, and (b) either a proportionality between the means and the political
ends, *see 20th Century American Courts*, *supra* p. 30 at 1010–11, or a predominance of the
political elements over the common crime elements, *see* Garcia-Mora, *supra* p. 3, at 1254.

At least one commentator has suggested that the first condition of the Swiss test is a
requirement of a direct connection between the crime and the political goal—a condition that essentially requires the presence of a political movement. *See* Garcia Mora, *supra*
p. 3, at 1253 (citing Swiss cases). Others point out that the early Swiss requirement that
a crime be incident to a political movement has been explicitly rejected in later cases. *See,*
e.g., Carboneau, *supra* p. 34, at 26–28 (citing Swiss cases). More recent Swiss cases concentrate less on the accused's motive, relying instead almost entirely on an ends-means
test under which politically motivated conduct is protected by the exception only if the
danger created by the conduct is proportionate to the objectives, *i.e.*, if the means employed
are the only means of accomplishing the end and the interests at stake are sufficiently important to justify the danger and harm to others. *See* Carbonneau, *supra* p. 34, at 28–29
(citing Swiss cases).

The comprehensiveness and flexibility of the "predominance" or "proportionality"
test allows it to be conformed to changing realities of a modern world. *See* Garcia-Mora,
supra p. 3 at 1255. But because the relative value of the ends and the necessity of using
the chosen means must be considered, the criteria applied by Swiss courts incorporate

highly subjective and partisan political considerations within the balancing test. *See* C. Van den Wijngaert, *supra* p. 22 at 158; Politics of Extradition, *supra* p. 31, at 631. [note omitted]. The test explicitly requires an evaluation of the importance of the interests at stake, the desirability of political change, and the acceptability of the means used to achieve the ends. The infusion of ideological factors in the determination of which offenses are non-extraditable threatens both the humanitarian objectives underlying the exception and the concern about foreign non-intervention in domestic political struggles. Moreover, it severely undermines the notion that such determinations can be made by an apolitical, unbiased judiciary concerned primarily with individual liberty. *See supra* pp. 788–89.[1]

The "incidence" test that is used to define a non-extraditable political offense in the United States and Great Britain was first set forth by the Divisional Court in *In re* Castioni, [1891] 12 Q.B. 149 (1890). In that case, the Swiss government requested that Great Britain extradite a Swiss citizen who, with a group of other angry citizens, had stormed the palace gates and killed a government official in the process. *Id.* at 150–51. Castioni did not know the victim or have a personal grudge against him. The habeas court considered:

> [W]hether, upon the facts, it is clear that the man was acting as one of a number of persons engaged in acts of violence of a political object, and as part of the political movement and [up]rising in which he was taking part.

Id. at 159 (per Denman, J.). The court denied extradition, finding that Castioni's actions were "incidental to and formed a part of political disturbances," *id.* at 166 (per Hawkind, J.), and holding that common crimes committed "in the course" and "in the furtherance" of a political disturbance would be treated as political offenses, *id.* at 156 (per Denman, J.).

Although both the United States and Great Britain rely explicitly on Castioni, each has developed its own version of the incidence test. British courts proceeded first to narrow the exception in 1894. In *In re* Neunier, [1894] 2 Q.B 415, the court extradited a French anarchist charged with bombing a café and military barracks, *id.* at 415, concluding that anarchist action is not incident to a two-party struggle for political power, *id.* at 419 (per Cave, J.). The court held that the political offense exception protects those who seek to substitute one form of government for another, not those whose actions disrupt the social order and whose "efforts are directed primarily against the general body of citizens." *Id.*

---

1. A number of commentators have suggested that perhaps the most useful test for when the exception should apply can be derived from the theory of "ideological self-preservation." *See, e.g.*, M. Bassiouni, *International Extradition: United States Law & Practices* ch. VIII, at §2-74 to §2-77 (1983); C Van den Wijngaert, *supra* p. 22, at 157–58. The premise of this theory is that a political crime is justified if it is a form of self-defense, in that the means used to attempt to secure a fundamental right were limited to the least harmful means available. The commentators suggest that an objective test could be derived from this theory and would weigh (a) the nature of the rights violated by the state; (b) the nature of the state conduct that violated these rights; and (c) the nature of the individual conduct that violated the law of the state in an attempt to defend these rights. As one commentator has noted, *see* C. Van den Wijngaert, supra p. 22 at 158, this test resembles the Swiss proportionality test but, in addition to the balancing required by that test, it requires an evaluation of the conduct of the requesting nation. Despite the initial appeal of the theory of ideological self-preservation, we believe it is an inappropriate test. It is subject to all the criticisms to which the Swiss test is subject. Moreover, it requires the kind of evaluation of the conduct of another nation that violates the principle of non-intervention in the internal affairs of another state. *See id.* It thus runs counter to one of the primary tenets underlying the political offense exception, *see supra* pp. 792–93, are requires the judiciary to undertake a task for which it is particularly ill-suited, *see supra* pp. 788–89 & note 6.

The rigid "two-party" struggle" requirement of the British incidence test has not survived. More recently, British courts have taken other factors into account, noting that political offenses must be considered "according to the circumstances existing at the time." *Regina v. Governor of Brixton Prison* (ex parte Kolczynski), [1955] 1 Q.B. 540, 549 (1954) (per Cassels, J.). In *Kolczynski*, a British court refused to extradite Polish soldiers who were at risk of being punished for treason although the Polish government officially sought their extradition for common crimes. *See id*. at 543, 545. No political uprising existed at the time the crimes were committed. *Id*. at 544. Instead of a distinct uprising, the new British incidence test requires some "political opposition ... between fugitive and requesting State," *Schtraks v. Government of Israel*, [1964] A.C. 556, 591 (1962) (per Viscount Radcliffe), and incorporates an examination of the motives of the accused and the requesting country in those situations in which the offense is not part of an uprising, *see* Lubet & Czackes, *supra* p. 3, at 202–03. [note omitted].

C. Original Formulation of the United States Incidence Test

The United States, in contrast to Great Britain, has adhered more closely to the Castioni test in determining whether conduct is protected by the political offense exception. The seminal United States case in this area is *In re Ezeta*, 62 F. 972 (N.D. Cal. 1894), in which the Salvadoran government requested the extradition of a number of individuals accused of murder and robbery. The fugitives maintained that the crimes had been committed while they unsuccessfully attempted to thwart a revolution. *See id*. at 995. Extradition was denied because the acts were "committed during the progress of actual hostilities between contending forces," *id*. at 997, and were "closely identified" with the uprising "in an unsuccessful effort to suppress it," *id*. at 1002. However, an alleged act that occurred four months prior to the start of armed violence was held not to be protected by the incidence test despite the accused's contention that El Salvador's extradition request was politically motivated. *Id*. at 986. [note omitted].

As we noted at the outset, the Supreme Court has addressed the political offense issue only once. In *Ornelas v. Ruiz*, 161 U.S. 502, 16 S.Ct. 689, 40 L.Ed. 787 (1896), Mexico sought the extradition of an individual for murder, arson, robbery, and kidnapping committed in a Mexican border town, at or about the time revolutionary activity was in progress. *Id*. at 510, 16 S.Ct. at 692. The Court allowed extradition on the basis that the habeas court had applied an improper, non-deferential standard of review to the extradition court's findings. *Id*. at 511–12, 16 S.Ct. at 92–93. It continued by listing four factors pertinent to the political offense inquiry in the case: (1) the character of the foray; (2) the mode of attack; (3) the persons killed or captured: and (4) the kind of property taken or destroyed. *Id*. at 511, 16 S.Ct. at 692. It found that although the raid (in December 1892) may have been contemporaneous with a revolutionary movement (in 1891), it was not of a political character because it was essentially unrelated to the uprising. The Court noted that the purported political aspects of the crimes were negated "by the fact that immediately after this occurrence, though no superior armed force of the Mexican government was in the vicinity to hinder their advance into the country, the bandits withdrew with their booty across the river into Texas." *Id*.

Since *Ornelas*, lower American courts have continued to apply the incidence test set forth in *Castioni* and *Ezeta* with its two-fold requirement; (1) the occurrence of an uprising or other violent political disturbance[2] at the time of the charged offense, *see, e.g., Garcia-Guillern*

---

2. Although unnecessary to the resolution of the cases before them, a number of courts have stated that a "war" could qualify as the violent political disturbance for purposes of the incidence test. *See, e.g., Eain v. Wilkes*, 641 F.2d 504, 518 (7th Cir.), *cert denied*, 451 U.S. 894, 102 S.Ct. 390, 70 L.Ed.2d

v. United States, 450 F.2d 1189, 1192 (5th Cir. 1971), *cert. denied*, 405 U.S. 989, 92 S.Ct. 1251, 13 L.Ed.2d 455 (1972); *Ramos v. Diaz*, 179 F. Supp. 459, 462 (S.D. Fla. 1959),[3] and (2) a charged offense that is "incidental to" "in the course of," or "in furtherance of" the uprising, *see, e.g.*, Eain, 641 F.2d at 518; *Sindona v. Grant*, 619 F.2d 167, 173 (2d Cir. 1980); *Garcia-Guillern*, 450 F.2d at 1192. While the American view that an uprising must exist is more restrictive than the modern British view and while we, unlike the British, remain hesitant to consider the motives of the accused or the requesting state, *see* Lubet & Czackes, *supra* p. 3, at 203, 205, American courts have been rather liberal in their construction of the requirement that the act be "incidental to" an uprising, *see* Garcia-Mora, *supra* p. 3 at 1244.

The American approach has been criticized as being "both underinclusive and overinclusive," *see* Lubet & Czackes, *supra* p. 3, at 203, and as "yield[ing] anomalous ... results," *see 20th Century American Courts, supra* p. 30, at 1013–14. Although these criticisms have some merit, neither flaw in the American incidence test is serious. Some commentators have suggested that the test is underinclusive because it exempts from judicially guaranteed protection all offenses that are not contemporaneous with an uprising even though the acts may represent legitimate political resistance. *See, e.g.*, Lubet & Czackes, *supra* p. 3, at 203–04. For example, the attempted kidnapping of a Cuban consul, allegedly for the purpose of ransoming the consul for political prisoners held in Cuba, was held by a court not to be a political offense because the act was not "committed in the course of and incidental to a violent political disturbance." *Escobedo v. United States*, 623 F.2d 1098, 1104 (5th Cir.), *cert. denied*, 449 U.S. 1036, 101 S.Ct. 612, 66 L.Ed.2d 497 (1980).

There are several responses to the charge of underinclusiveness. First, in their critiques, the commentators fail to give sufficient weight to the existence of a number of ameliorative safeguards. For example, review of certifications of extradition by the Secretary of State, *see supra* pp. 789–90, serves partially to remedy any underinclusiveness problem. If a court finds the accused extraditable, the Secretary has, at the very least, broad discretion to review the available record and conduct a de novo examination of the issues and, if necessary, to consider matters outside the record in determining whether to extradite. *See* Lubet & Czackes, *supra* p. 3, at 199. The potential underinclusiveness dangers of the uprising requirement are also mitigated by the fact that purely political offenses are never extraditable. *See id.* at 206; *supra* pp. 793–94. Additionally, because of the rule of dual criminality, *see supra* pp. 782–83, individuals accused of offenses that constitute protected activity under the First Amendment will not be extradited. *See* Lubet & Czackes, *supra* p. 3, at 206. Second, it is questionable whether the incidence test is, in fact, underinclusive. While it does not protect all politically motivated offenses, it protects those

---

208 (1981); *Sindona v. Grant*, 619 F.2d 167, 173 (2d Cir.1980). Although the terms "rebellion," "revolution," "uprising," and "civil war" may for our purposes be treated as synonymous, none is for any purpose synonymous with the term "war." As we discuss further below, *see infra* note 33, we question the propriety of applying the incidence test in the same manner in the case of crimes occurring during wars as in the case of crimes occurring during uprisings.

3. American courts generally will take judicial notice of a state of uprising. *See, e.g., Karadzole v. Artukovic*, 247 F.2d 198, 204 (9th Cir. 1957) (noting that district court properly took judicial notice of struggle for political control in Croatia), *vacated and remanded*, 355 U.S. 393, 78 S.Ct. 381, 2 L.Ed.2d 356 (1958) (mem.); *Ramos v. Diaz*, 179 F. Supp. 459, 462 (S.D. Fla. 1959) (extradition court took judicial notice of revolutionary movement in Cuba); *In re McMullen*, No. 3-78-1099 MG, slip op. at 4 (N.D. Cal. May 11, 1979) (magistrate took judicial notice of uprising in Northern Ireland). *But see In re Abu Eain*, No. 79 M 175, slip op. at 13–14 (N.D.Ill. Dec. 18, 1979) (magistrate refused to take judicial notice of Middle East hostilities), *reprinted in Abu Eain v. Adams*, 529 F. Supp. 685, 688–95 (N.D.Ill. 1980).

acts that are related to a collective attempt to abolish or alter the government—the form of political offense that the exception was initially designed to protect, *see supra* pp. 792–93. Third, any effort to protect all crimes that are in some way politically motivated would either require the abandonment of the objective test for determining which offenses fall within the exception—in our view a most undesirable result—or would result in the protection of innumerable crimes that fall far outside the original purposes underlying the exception.

A number of commentators suggest, on the other hand, that the America test is overbroad because it makes non-extraditable some offenses that are not of a political character merely because the crimes took place contemporaneously with an uprising. *See* Garcia-Mora, *supra* p. 3, at 1246; Lubet & Czackes, *supra* p. 3, at 205; Politics of Extradition, *supra* p. 3, at 628. We think these commentators misunderstand the test. They all cite *Karadzole v. Artukovic*, 247 F.2d 198 (9th Cir. 1957)—"one of the most roundly criticized cases in the history of American extradition jurisprudence," *Eain v. Wilkes*, 641 F.2d 504, 522 (7th Cir.), *cert. denied*, 454 U.S. 894 ... (1981)—to support their argument. [note omitted]. In *Artukovic*, the Yugoslavian government sought the extradition of a former Minister of the Interior of the puppet Croatian government which took over a portion of Yugoslavia following the German invasion in April 1941. Artukovic was charged with directing the murder of hundreds of thousands of civilians in concentration camps between April 1941 and October 1942. Prior to a hearing by an extradition magistrate, the district court granted habeas relief, concluding that the charged offenses were non-extraditable political offenses. *Artukovic v. Boyle*, 140 F. Supp. 245, 246 (S.D.Cal. 1956). We affirmed, applying the Castioni language and noting that the offenses occurred during the German invasion of Yugoslavia and subsequent establishment of Croatia. *Karadzole v. Artukovic*, 247 F.2d 198, 202–04 (9th Cir. 1957). We considered but were unpersuaded by the argument that because war crimes are so barbaric and atrocious they cannot be considered political crimes, *see id.* at 204 and the United Nations resolutions called for the extradition of war criminals, *see id.* at 205.

The Supreme Court vacated our opinion in a one paragraph per curiam opinion and remanded for an extradition hearing pursuant to 18 U.S.C. § 3184. *See* 355 U.S. 393 (1958). The Court did not comment on the substantive issues and may well have based its order solely on the fact that the habeas court considered the legal questions involved in Artukovic's extradition before an extradition court had an opportunity to make the preliminary findings mandated by section 3184. *See United States v. Artukovic*, 170 F. Supp. 383, 393 (S.D.Cal. 1959). In his subsequent decision the magistrate denied extradition on the ground that there was insufficient evidence to establish probable cause of Artukovic's guilt, *see id.* at 392, but in dicta he adopted our vacated political offense analysis, *see id.* at 393. [note omitted].

We do not believe that *Artukovic* adequately supports the commentators' suggestion that the incidence test is overinclusive. We think it more likely that the problem lies not in the test itself but in the fact that we erred by applying it in that case.

The offenses with which Artukovic was charged fall within that very limited category of acts which have been labeled "crimes against humanity." In *Artukovic* we erroneously assumed that "crimes against humanity" was synonymous with "war crimes," and then concluded in a somewhat irrelevant fashion that not all war crimes automatically fall outside the ambit of the political offense exception. *See* 247 F.2d at 204. Our analysis was less than persuasive. We did not need then, and do not need now, to reach a conclusion about whether all war crimes fall outside the bounds of the exception. *Cf.* C.Van den Wijngaert, *supra* p. 22, at 1143 (suggesting that, under international law, states remain free to consider war crimes as political offenses). The offenses with which Artukovic was charged were crimes against humanity; it matters not whether or not they were also war crimes; either way, crimes of that magnitude are not protected by the exception.

Crimes against humanity, such as genocide, violate international law [note omitted] and constitute an "abuse of sovereignty" because by definition, they are carried out by or with the toleration of authorities of a state. [note omitted]. While some of the same offenses that violate the laws and customs of war [note omitted] are also crimes against humanity, crimes of the latter sort most notably include "murder, extermination, enslavement, ... or persecutions on political, racial, ethnic, national or religious grounds ..." of entire racial, ethnic national or religious groups. The Nurnberg (Nuremberg) Trial, 6 F.R.D. 69, 130 (Int'l Military Tribunal 1946). Various "inhumane acts ... committed after the beginning of [World War II] did not constitute war crimes, [but] ... constituted crimes against humanity." *Id.* at 131.

Wholly aside from the Artukovic court's confusion of "war crimes" and "crimes against humanity," we do not believe that the political offense exception, even if meant to protect the acts of representatives of a former government,[4] should have been extended to protect those carrying out a governmental policy calling for acts of destruction whose "nature and scope ... exceeded human imagination." Excerpts from Speech by German President, N.Y. Times, May 9, 1985, at 10, col. 1, 3 (excerpts from Speech to Parliament on May 8, 1985 by President Richard von Weizsacker, as translated by the West German Foreign Ministry) (noting that the Nazi genocide is "unparalleled in history"). These crimes are simply treated differently and are generally excluded from the protection of many normally applicable rules. *See, e.g.,* The Nurmberg (Nuremberg) Trial, 6 F.R.D. at 107–11 (individuals accused of these offenses can be tried before international tribunal because offenses violate international law). They are certainly in our view to be excluded from coverage under the political offense exception.

Accordingly, we do not consider the "underinclusiveness" and "overinclusiveness" problems of the incidence test to have been as severe as has been suggested by some of the commentators. Rather, we believe the incidence test, when properly applied, has served the purposes and objectives of the political offense exception well. More recently, a number of courts have begun to question whether, in light of changing political practices and realities, we should continue to use the traditional American version of that test. They have suggested that basic modifications may be required and, specifically, that certain types of conduct engaged in by some contemporary insurgent groups, conduct that we in our society find unacceptable, should be excluded from coverage. For the reasons we explain below, we believe that the American test in its present form remains not only workable but desirable; that the most significant problems that concern those advocating changes in the test can be dealt with without making the changes they propose; and the efforts to modify the test along the lines suggested would plunge our judiciary into a political morass and require the type of subjective judgments we have so wisely avoided until now.

---

4. The incidence test was originally intended to afford protection to individuals engaged in political resistance; the test was designed to identify a set of protestors, namely, those engaged in an uprising designed to change the existing government. *See supra* pp. 792–93. It is unclear whether this test applies to former government officials, *cf. In re Ezeta,* 62 F. 972, 1000 (N.D.Cal. 1894) (noting that most extradition cases involve acts committed against the government, and that such cases are only of *some* value when the pending case concerns acts that were committed by representatives of the then-existing government), and even whether the political offense exception is applicable at all to such individuals.

D. The Recent Political Offense Cases

Recently, the American judiciary has split almost evenly over whether the traditional American incidence test should be applied to new methods of political violence in two categories—domestic revolutionary violence and international terrorism—or whether fundamental new restrictions should be imposed on the use of the political offense exception.

In both *In re McMullen*, No. 3-78-1099 MG (N.D.Cal. May 11, 1979), and *In re Mackin*, No. 80 Cr. Misc 1 (S.D.N.Y. Aug. 13, 1981), extradition magistrates applied the traditional United States incidence test despite expressing serious concern over the nature of the charged offenses. In *McMullen*, the United Kingdom sought the extradition of a former PIRA member accused of murder in connection with the bombing of a military barracks in England. Finding that McMullen's acts took place during a state of uprising throughout the United Kingdom and were incidental to the political disturbance, the magistrate denied extradition noting that "[e]ven though the offense be deplorable and heinous, the criminal actor will be excluded from deportation if the crime is committed under these pre-requisites." Slip op. at 3. The magistrate's formulation of the test for the political offense exception in *Mackin* was similar. In that case, the United Kingdom's request for the extradition of an IRA member accused of murdering a British soldier in Northern Ireland was denied.

In contrast, although asserting that the existing incidence test "is sufficiently flexible to avoid [the] abuses [noted by commentators]," 641 F.2d at 519, and while ostensibly applying the traditional test, *see id.* at 515–16, 518, the Seventh Circuit in *Eain v. Wilkes*, 641 F.2d 504 (7th Cir.), *cert. denied*, 454 U.S. 894, 102 S.Ct. 390, 70 L.Ed.2d 208 (1981), superimposed a number of limitations on the exception that had not previously been a part of United States law. Abu Eain, a resident of the occupied West Bank and a member of the PLO, was accused by the State of Israel of setting a bomb that exploded in the Israeli city of Tierias in 1979, killing two boys and injuring more than thirty other people. A magistrate granted Israel's extradition request, the district court denied habeas corpus relief, and the Seventh Circuit affirmed.

First, the *Eain* court distinguished between conflicts that involved "on-going, organized battles between contending armies," 641 F.2d at 519, and conflicts that involved groups with "the dispersed nature of the PLO," *id.*, noting that in the former case, unlike the latter, a clear distinction can be drawn between the activities of the military forces and individual acts of violence. Second, although acknowledging that motivation is not determinative of the political character of an act, *see id.* at 520 (citing Lubet & Czackes, *supra* p. 3, at 203 n. 102), and characterizing its next requirement as that of a "direct link" between the offense and the conflict, *id.* at 521, the court examined the motivation for and political legitimacy of the act. The court appears to have concluded that, according to the evidence presented, the PLO's objectives were not politically legitimate: the PLO sought changes in "the Israeli political structure as an incident of the expulsion of a certain population from the country," *id.* at 520, and its activities were therefore more properly characterized as aimed at Israel's "social structure," *id.* Third, the court held simply that regardless what the political objective is, "the indiscriminate bombing of a civilian population is not recognized as a protected act." *Id.* at 521.

Thus, the Seventh Circuit in *Eain* redefined an "uprising" as a struggle between organized, non-dispersed military forces; made a policy determination regarding the legitimacy of given political objectives; and excluded violent acts against innocent civilians [note omitted] from the protection afforded by the exception. *Cf.* Note, *Terrorist Extradition and Political Offense Exception: An Administrative Solution*, 21 Va. J.Int'l L. 163,

177–78 (1980) (criticizing *Eain* magistrate's test because it invites ideological and foreign policy determinations by extradition courts). As part of its justification for the new limitations it imposed on the applicability of the exception, the *Eain* court expressed concern that, in the absence of these restrictions,

> nothing would prevent a safe haven in America ... Terrorists who have committed barbarous acts elsewhere would be able to flee to the United States and live in our neighborhoods and walk our streets forever free from any accountability for their acts. We do not need them in our society.... [T]he political offense exception ... should be applied with great care lest our country, become a social jungle....

Id. at 520.

The District Court for the Southern District of New York has recently rejected portions of the Eain analysis but accepted some of the new restrictions propounded by the Seventh Circuit. In *In re Doherty*, 599 F. Supp. 270 (S.D.N.Y. 1984), the court denied the United Kingdom's request that a PIRA member accused of attacking a convoy of British soldiers in Northern Ireland be extradited. The extradition court rejected the notion that the exception protects only "actual armed insurrections or more traditional and overt military hostilities." *Id.* at 275. Noting that "political struggles have been ... effectively carried out by armed guerrillas," *id.*, the court concluded that a dissident group's likelihood of success and its ability to effect changes by other than violent means were not determinative factors. *Id.* Nevertheless, the court agreed with the Seventh Circuit's tacit conclusion that the traditional incidence test is "hardly consistent with ... the realities of the modern world," *id.* at 274.

The *Doherty* court continued by approving of the *Eain* court's willingness to balance policy considerations so that the exception "does not afford a haven for persons who commit the most heinous atrocities for political ends." *Id.* at 275 n. 4. Although such issues were not raised in *Doherty*, the court stated explicitly that the exception would not protect bombings in public places, *id.* at 275; acts that "transcend the limits of international law," *id.*; acts "inconsistent with international standards of civilized conduct," *id.* at 274; harm to hostages, *id.* at 276; violations of the Geneva convention, *id.*; or the acts of "amorphous" or "fanatic" groups without structure, organization, or clearly defined political objectives, *id.* Thus, the *Doherty* court, like the *Eain* court, concluded that the traditional incidence test is insufficient to determine which offenses are protected by the exception. Both courts felt it necessary and appropriate to judge the political legitimacy of various ends and means and to exclude "illegitimate" acts from protection even if the incidence test were met. While not identifying their new limitations as such, both incorporated significant aspects of the Swiss ends-means or proportionality test into Anglo-American jurisprudence.

V. THE POLITICAL OFFENSE EXCEPTION AND THE REALITIES OF CONTEMPORARY POLITICAL STRUGGLES

A. The Political Reality: The Contours of Contemporary Activity

The recent lack of consensus among United States courts confronted with requests for the extradition of those accused of violent political acts committed outside the context of an organized military conflict reflects some confusion about the purposes underlying the political offense exception. *See supra* pp. 792–93. The premise of the analyses performed by modern courts favoring the adoption of new restrictions on the use of the exception is either that the objectives of revolutionary violence undertaken by dispersed forces and directed at civilians are by definition, not political, *see, e.g., Eain*, 641 F.2d at 519 ("Terrorist activity seeks to promote social chaos."), or that, regardless of the actors' objectives, the conduct is not politically legitimate because it "is inconsistent with international standards of civilized conduct," *Doherty*, 599 F. Supp. at 274. Both assumptions are subject to debate.

A number of courts appear tacitly to accept a suggestion by some commentators that begins with the observation that the political offense exception can be traced to the rise of democratic governments. *See* I.A. Shearer, *supra* p. 22, at 166; C. Van den Wijngaert, *supra* p. 22, at 100; Carbonneau, *supra* p. 34, at 5. Because of this origin, these commentators argue, the exception was only designed to protect the right to rebel against tyrannical governments, *see, e.g.*, Epps, *supra* p. 4, at 65, and should not be applied in an ideologically neutral fashion, *see, e.g.*, Carbonneau, *supra* p. 34, at 44; *see also In re Gonzales*, 217 F. Supp. 717, 721 n. 9 (S.D.N.Y. 1963) (evaluating whether acts in question "were blows struck in the cause of freedom against a repressive totalitarian regime") *But see* C. Van den Wijngaert, *supra* p. 22, at 102 (noting that democratic states may also suppress political conduct in the guise of criminality).

These courts then proceed to apply the exception in a non-neutral fashion but, in doing so, focus on and explicitly reject only the tactics, rather than the true object of their concern, the political objectives. *See* C. Van den Wijngaert, *supra* p. 22, at 102. The courts that are narrowing the applicability of the exception in this manner appear to be moving beyond the role of an impartial judiciary by determining tacitly that particular political objectives are not "legitimate."

We strongly believe that courts should not undertake such a task. The political offense test traditionally articulated by American courts, as well as the text of the treaty provisions, *see, e.g.*, Treaty, *supra* p. 781, at art. V(1)(c), is ideologically neutral. We do not believe it appropriate to make qualitative judgments regarding a foreign government or a struggle designed to alter that government. Accord *In re Doherty*, 599 F. Supp. 270, 277 (S.D.N.Y. 1984); *see generally supra* note 6. Such judgments themselves cannot be other than political and, as such, involve determinations of the sort that are not within the judicial role. *See supra* Section II.B.

A second premise may underlie the analyses of courts that appear to favor narrowing the exception, namely, that modern revolutionary tactics which include violence directed at civilians are not politically "legitimate." This assumption, which may well constitute an understandable response to the recent rise of international terrorism, skews any political offense analysis because of an inherent conceptual shortcoming. In deciding what tactics are acceptable, we seek to impose on other nations and cultures our own traditional notions of how internal political struggles should be conducted.

The structure of societies and governments, the relationships between nations and their citizens, and the modes of altering political structures have changed dramatically since our courts first adopted the *Castioni* test. Neither wars nor revolutions are conducted in as clear-cut or mannerly a fashion as they once were. Both the nature of the acts committed in struggles for self-determination, *see* M. Bassiouni, *International Extradition: United States Law & Practice*, ch VIII, at §§ 2-71 to 2-72, and the geographic location of those struggles have changed considerably since the time of the French and American revolutions. Now challenges by insurgent movements to the existing order take place most frequently in Third World countries rather than in Europe and North America. In contrast to the organized, clearly identifiable, armed forces of past revolutions, today's struggles are often carried out by networks of individuals joined only by a common interest in opposing those in power.

It is understandable that Americans are offended by the tactics used by many of those seeking to change their governments. Often these tactics are employed by persons who do not share our cultural and social values or mores. Sometimes they are employed by those whose views of the nature, importance, or relevance of individual human life differ radically from ours. Nevertheless, it is not our place to impose our notions of civilized strife on people who are seeking to overthrow the regimes in control of their countries in contexts and circumstances that we have not experienced, and with which we can identify only with the greatest difficulty. It is the fact that the insurgents are seeking to change their governments that makes the political offense exception applicable, not their reasons for wishing to do so or the nature of the acts by which they hope to accomplish that goal.

Politically motivated violence, carried out by dispersed forces and directed at private sector institutions, structures, or civilians, is often undertaken—like the more organized, better disciplined violence of preceding revolutions—as part of an effort to gain the right to self-government. *See Politics of Extradition, supra* p. 31, at 632–33. We believe the tactics that are used in such internal political struggles are simply irrelevant to the question whether the political offense exception is applicable.

B. Relationship Between the Justifications for the Exception, the Incidence Test, and Contemporary Political Realities

One of the principal reasons our courts have had difficulty with the concept of affording certain contemporary revolutionary tactics and protection of the political offense exception is our fear and loathing of international terrorism. *See, e.g., Eain,* 641 F.2d at 520. The desire to exclude international terrorists from the coverage of the political offense exception is a legitimate one; the United States unequivocally condemns all international terrorism. However, the restrictions that some courts have adopted in order to remove terrorist activities from coverage under the political offense exception are overbroad. As we have noted, not all politically motivated violence undertaken by dispersed forces and directed at civilians is international terrorism and not all such activity should be exempted from the protection afforded by the exception.

Although it was not accepted as international law, the position of the United States, not only on international terrorism but also on the extradition of international terrorists, was made clear in 1972 when it introduced its Draft Convention on Terrorism in the United Nations. *See* U.N. Draft Convention for the Prevention and Punishment of Certain Acts of International Terrorism: United States Working Paper, U.N. Doc. A/C.6/L.850 (September 25, 1972), *reprinted in* 1 R. Friedlander, *Terrorism: Documents of International and Local Control* 487 (1979). The Draft Convention calls either for trial of international terrorists in the State where found or for their extradition. *See id.* at art. 3; *see also* 1984 Act to Combat International Terrorism §201, Pub.L. 98-533, 96 Stat. 2706, 2709 (to be codified at 18 U.S.C. §3077) (reaffirming United States' position on the extradition of international terrorists).

The policy and legal considerations that underlie our responses to acts of international terrorism differ dramatically from those that form the basis for our attitudes toward violent acts committed as part of other nations' internal political struggles. The application of the political offense exception to acts of domestic political violence comports in every respect with both the original justifications for the exception and the traditional requirements of the incidence test. The application of that exception to acts of international terrorism would comport with neither. First, we doubt whether the designers of the exception contemplated that it would protect acts of international violence, regardless of the ultimate objective of the actors. Second, in cases of international terrorism, we are being asked to return the accused to the government in a country where the acts were committed: frequently that is not a government the accused has sought to change. In such cases there is less risk that the accused will be subjected to an unfair trial or punishment because of his political opinion. [note omitted]. Third, the exception was designed, in part, to protect against foreign intervention in internal struggles for political self-determination. When we extradite an individual accused on international terrorism, we are not interfering with any internal struggle; rather, it is the international terrorist who has interfered with the rights of others to exist peacefully under their chosen form of government.

There is no need to create a new mechanism for defining "political offenses" in order to ensure that the two important objectives we have been considering are met: (a) that international terrorists will be subject to extradition, and (b) that the exception will continue to cover the type of domestic revolutionary conduct that inspired its creation in the first place. While the precedent that guides us is limited, the applicable principles of law are clear. The incidence test has served us well and requires no significant modification. The growing problem of international terrorism, serious as it is, does not compel us to reconsider or redefine that test. The test we have used since the 1800's simply does not cover acts of international terrorism.

1. The "Incidence" Test

As all of the various tests for determining whether an offense is extraditable make clear, not every offense of a political character is non-extraditable. In the United States, an offense must meet the incidence test which is intended, like the tests designed by other nations, to comport with the justifications for the exception. We now explain the reasons for our conclusion that the traditional United States incidence test by its terms (a) protects acts of domestic violence in connection with a struggle for political self-determination, but (b) was not intended to and does not protect acts of international terrorism.

2. The "Uprising" Component

The incidence test has two components—the "uprising" requirement and the "incidental to" requirement. The first component, the requirement that there be an "uprising," "rebellion," or "revolution," has not been the subject of much discussion in the literature, although it is firmly established in the case law, *see supra* note 1. Most analyses of whether the exception applies have focused on whether the act in question was in furtherance of or incidental to a given uprising. Nevertheless, it is the "uprising" component that plays the key role in ensuring that the incidence test protects only those activities that the political offense doctrine was designed to protect.

As we have noted, the political offense doctrine developed out of a concern for the welfare of those engaged in a particular form of political activity—an effort to alter or abolish the government that controls their lives—and not out of a desire to protect all politically motivated violence. *See In re Ezeta*, 62 F. 972, 998 (N.D.Cal. 1894) ("'Any offense committed in the course of or furthering of civil war, insurrection, or political commotion.'") (quoting John Stuart Mill); *In re* Castioni, [1981] 1 Q.B. 149, 156 (1890) ("a sort of overt act in the course of acting in a political matter, a political rising, or a dispute between two parties in the State as to which is to have the government in its hands") (per Denman, J.).

The uprising component serves to limit the exception to its historic purposes. It makes the exception applicable only when a certain level of violence exists and when those engaged in that violence are seeking to accomplish a particular objective. The exception does not apply to political acts that involve less fundamental efforts to accomplish change or that do not attract sufficient adherents to create the requisite amount of turmoil. *See Escobedo v. United States*, 623 F.2d 1098 (5th Cir.), *cert. denied*, 449 U.S. 1036, 101 S.Ct. 612, 66 L.Ed.2d 497 (1980). Thus, acts such as skyjacking (an act that never been used by revolutionaries to bring about a change in the composition or structure of the government in their own country) fall outside the scope of the exception.

Equally important, the uprising component serves to exclude from coverage under the exception criminal conduct that occurs outside the country or territory in which the uprising is taking place. The term "uprising" refers to a revolt by indigenous people against their own government or an occupying power. That revolt can occur only within the country or territory in which those rising up reside. By definition acts occurring in other lands are not part of the uprising. The political offense exception was designed to protect those engaged in internal or domestic struggles over the form or composition of their own government, including, of course, struggles to displace an occupying power. It was not designed to protect international political coercion or blackmail, or the exportation of violence and strife to other locations—even to the homeland of an oppressor nation. Thus, an uprising is not only limited temporally, it is limited spatially. *See 20th Century American Courts, supra* p. 30 at 1021 n. 115.

In his concurring opinion, Judge Duniway points out that the limitation to acts occurring within the territory in which there is an uprising means that persons committing acts of piracy, terrorism, or other crimes on the high seas will be unable to invoke the protection of the political offense exception. His observation is correct. Just as skyjackers and other international terrorists are not protected under the exception, neither are persons who commit or threaten to commit violent crimes on the high seas. The political offense exception was never intended to reach such conduct.

While determining the proper geographic boundaries of an "uprising" involves a legal issue that ordinarily will be fairly simple to resolve, there may be some circumstances under which it will be more difficult to do so. We need not formulate a general rule that will be applicable to all situations. It is sufficient in this case to state that for purposes of the political offense exception an "uprising" cannot extend beyond the borders of the country or territory in which a group of citizens or residents is seeking to change their particular government or governmental structure.

It follows from what we have said that an "uprising" can exist only when the turmoil that warrants that characterization is created by nationals of the land in which the disturbances are occurring. Viewed in that light, it comes clear that had the traditional incidence test been applied in *Eain*, discussed *supra* pp. 801–01, the result would have been identical to that reached by the Seventh Circuit. When PLO members enter Israel and commit unlawful acts, there is simply no uprising for the acts to be incidental to. The plain fact is that the Israelis are not engaged in revolutionary activity directed against their own government. They are not seeking to change its form, structure, or composition through violent means. That the PLO members who commit crimes are seeking to destroy Israel as a state does not help bring them within the political offense exception. In the absence of an uprising, the violence engaged in by PLO members in Israel and elsewhere does not meet the incidence test and is not covered by the political offense exception. To the contrary, the PLO's worldwide campaign of violence, including the crimes its members commit in the state of Israel, clearly constitutes "international terrorism."

Moreover, Eain's conduct may have fallen outside the political offense exception for an additional, though related, reason. Not only was there no uprising in Israel, but Eain himself was not a national of that country. It is not clear whether, even when the violence is primarily conducted by nationals and thus an uprising may properly be found to exist, a foreign citizen who voluntarily joins the fray is protected by the exception. The exception was designed to protect those seeking to change their own government or to oust an occupying power that is asserting sovereignty over them. We question whether it should apply when the accused is not a citizen of the country or territory in which the uprising is occurring. In the absence of a tangible demonstration that he or she has more than a transitory connection with that land, the acts of a foreign national may simply not qualify for protection.

Although we find substantial merit to the argument that foreign nationals should be excluded from coverage under the political offense exception, the incidence test has never previously been analyzed in a manner that considers the question in any detail. Because of the conclusion we reach with respect to other issues in the case before us, there is no need for us to answer the question here. Accordingly, we leave its resolution to a subsequent time. It is enough for our purposes merely to note that the fact that Eain was not an Israeli might well have constituted another basis for holding that his conduct was not protected under the incidence test.

In short, the *Eain* and *Doherty* courts' objective that this country not become a haven for international terrorists can readily be met through a proper application of the incidence test. It is met by interpreting the political offense exception in light of its historic origins and goals. Such a construction excludes acts of international terrorism. There is no reason, therefore, to construe the incidence test in a subjective and judgmental manner that excludes all violent political conduct of which we disapprove. Moreover, any such construction would necessarily exclude some forms of internal revolutionary conduct and thus run contrary to the exception's fundamental purpose. For that reasons, we reject the *Eain* test and especially the concept that courts may determine whether particular forms of conduct constitute acceptable means or methods of engaging in an uprising.

3. The "Incidental to" Component

When describing the second requirement of the incidence test, the "incidental to" component, American courts have used the phrases "in the course of," "connected to," and "in furtherance of" interchangeably. We have applied a rather liberal standard when determining whether this part of the test has been met and have been willing to examine all of the circumstances surrounding the commission of the crime. *Garcia-Guillern v. United States*, 450 F.2d 1189, 1192 (5th Cir. 1971), *cert. denied*, 405 U.S. 989, 92 S.Ct. 1251, 31 L.Ed.2d 455 (1972); *Ramos v. Diaz*, 179 F. Supp. 459, 463 (S.D. Fla. 1959).

Commentators have criticized United States courts for applying the "incidental to" component too loosely or flexibly. *See supra* p. 797. We disagree with this criticism. To put the matter in its proper context, it is necessary to bear in mind that the offense must occur in the context of an "uprising." Acts "incidental to" an uprising are, as we have noted, limited by the geographic confines of the uprising. In addition, the act must be contemporaneous with the uprising. Moreover, the "incidental to" component is not satisfied by "any connection, however feeble, between a common crime and a political disturbance," Garcia-Mora, *supra* p. 3, at 1244. The act must be causally or ideologically related to the uprising. *See, e.g., Ornelas v. Ruiz*, L.Ed. 787 (1896) (concluding that rapid withdrawal of bandits after foray, in absence of threatening armed forces, suggested that acts were not incidental to uprising).

We believe the traditional liberal construction of the requirement that there be a nexus between the act and the uprising, *see supra* p. 797, is appropriate. There are various types of acts that, when committed in the course of an uprising, are likely to have been politically motivated. There is little reason, under such circumstances, to impose a strict nexus standard. Moreover, the application of a strict test would in some instances jeopardize the rights of the accused.

Under the liberal nexus standard, neither proof of the potential or actual effectiveness of the actions in achieving the group's political ends, *In re Castioni*, [1891] 1 Q.B. 149, 158–59 (1890) (refusing to consider whether the act was a wise mode of promoting the cause) (per Denman, J.), nor proof of the motive of the accused, *Eain*, 641 F.2d at 519, or the requesting nation, *Garcia-Guillern*, 450 F.2d at 1192; *Ramos v. Diaz*, 179 F. Supp. at 463, is required. Nor is the organization or hierarchy of the uprising group or the accused's membership in any such group determinative. *See Eain*, 641 F.2d at 519.

When extradition is sought, the "offender" at this stage in the proceedings has ordinarily only been accused, not convicted, of the offense. It would be inconsistent with the rights of the accused to require proof of membership in an uprising group. For example, the accused might be able to show that the acts were incidental to the uprising but might be unable to prove membership because he or she did not commit the offense or was not a member of the group. Furthermore, requiring proof of membership might violate the accused's Fifth Amendment rights both because it might force him to supply circumstantial evidence of guilt of the charged offense and because membership in the group itself might be illegal. Also, we question how one proves membership in an uprising group. Uprising groups often do not have formal organizational structures or document membership. In addition, it is entirely possible to sympathize with, aid, assist, or support a group, help further its objectives and its activities, participate in its projects, or carry on parallel activities of one's own, without becoming a member of the organization. Still, one may be acting in furtherance of an uprising.

On the other hand, a number of factors, though not necessary to the nexus determination, may play a part in evaluating the circumstances surrounding the commission of the offense. For example, proof of membership in an uprising group may make it more likely that the act was incidental to the uprising. *See, e.g., Ramos v. Diaz*, 179 F. Supp. at 463; *Castioni*, 1 Q.B. at 157–59 (per Denman, J.). The similarity of the charged offense to other acts committed by the uprising group, and the degree of control over the accused's acts by some hierarchy within the group, may give further credence to the claim that the act was incidental to the uprising. And while evidence of the accused's political motivation is not required and is usually unavailable, evidence that an act was "committed for purely personal reasons such as vengeance or vindictiveness," *In re Doherty*, 599 F. Supp. 270, 277 n. 7 (S.D.N.Y. 1984), may serve to rebut any presumption that a nexus exists. The exception is not designed to protect mercenaries or others acting for nonpolitical motives.

Under the liberal nexus test we have traditionally applied, or even under a strict nexus standard, there is no justification for distinguishing, as Doherty suggests, between attacks on military and civilian targets. The "incidental to" component, like the incidence test as a whole, must be applied in an objective, non-judgmental manner. It is for the revolutionaries, not the courts, to determine what tactics may help further their chances of bringing down or changing the government. All that the courts should do is determine whether the conduct is related to or connected with the insurgent activity. It is clear that various "non-military" offenses, including acts as disparate as stealing food to sustain the combatants, killing to avoid disclosure of strategies, or killing simply to avoid capture, may be incidental to or in furtherance of an uprising. To conclude that attacks on the military are protected by the exception, but that attacks on private sector institutions and civilians are not, ignores the nature and purpose of the test we apply, as well as realities of contemporary domestic revolutionary struggles. *See supra* pp. 804–05.

We should add that the spatial limitations imposed under the "uprising" component may not be circumvented by reliance on the "incidental to" component. As we said earlier, for the political offense exception to be applicable at all, the crime must have occurred in the country or territory in which the uprising was taking place, not in a different geographic location. *See supra* pp. 806–07.

VI. THE INCIDENCE TEST APPLIED TO THE CHARGED OFFENSES

.... In light of the justifications for the political offense exception, the formulation of the incidence test as it has traditionally been articulated, and the cases in which the exception has historically been applied, we do not believe it would be proper to stretch the term "uprising" to include acts that took place in England as a part of a struggle by nationals of Northern Ireland to change the form of government in their own land. Accordingly, we need not decide whether had an uprising occurred, the protection afforded by the exception would have been extended to one who, like Quinn, is a citizen of a different and uninvolved nation. Because the incidence test is not met, neither the bombing conspiracy nor the murder of Police Constable Tibble is a non-extraditable offense under the political offenses exception to the extradition treaty between the United States and the United Kingdom.

Notes and Questions

1. Noting that there are two types of political offenses (*i.e.,* "pure" and "relative"), what are the policies underlying the political offense exception as identified by the court in *Quinn v. Robinson*? What are the relative advantages and disadvantages of the French, Swiss, British and various U.S. tests for determining what constitutes a political offense. Which test is most consistent with the policies underlying the political offense exception?

2. What level or degree of violence is necessary to satisfy the "political uprising" component of the political offense exception? For cases finding a "political uprising," *see* Ordinola v. Hackman, 478 F.3d 588, 600 (4th Cir. 2007) ("agreeing that the alleged actions here occurred during the course of a violent political uprising. The Peruvian government and the Shining Path were engaged in a violent struggle for control of the country.... Approximately 50 percent of Peruvian territory and approximately 65 percent of the country's population [was] under a state of national emergency.... Clearly, then, it is appropriate to describe the situation in Peru at the time of Ordinola's alleged actions as 'a political revolt, an insurrection, or a civil war.') (citations omitted); Barapind v. Enomoto, 400 F.3d 744, 750 (9th Cir. 2005) ("There is no real doubt that the crimes Barapind is accused of committing occurred during a time of violent political disturbance in India. As the extradition court noted, '[t]ens of thousands of deaths and casualties' resulted between the mid-1980s and early 1990s as Sikh nationalists clashed with government officers and sympathizers in Punjab. Substantial violence was taking place, and the persons engaged in the violence were pursuing specific political objectives.") (citations omitted); Arambasic v. Ashcroft, 403 F. Supp. 2d 951, 960 (D.S.D. 2005) ("The goal of changing a government by indigenous people within the territory in which they resided is present in the case at hand.... The Croats in Croatia had coherent goals in setting up and maintaining new forms of political power. Likewise, the Serbs in Croatia had coherent goals in resisting the establishment of the new political power.") (citations omitted). *But see* Vo v. Benov, 447 F.3d 1235, 1242–43 (9th Cir. 2006) (declining to find a 'political uprising' because defendant "cannot show a sustained and widespread degree of violence that rises to the level of an uprising. The sum of a few skirmishes with the police, coupled with a handful of explosions and bombing attempts around the Pacific Rim and a keen desire to see the

downfall of the communist regime in his native land, does not amount to an uprising.") (citations omitted).

3. In *Barapind v. Enomoto*, 400 F.3d 744 (9th Cir. 2005), a deeply divided *en banc* court of appeals reaffirmed *Quinn v. Robinson*. In a strongly worded dissenting opinion, Circuit Judge Rymer stated: "we must overrule *Quinn*, because indiscriminate violence against innocent persons should not qualify for the political offense exception to extradition, even if politically motivated." *Id.* at 756. Instead, she argued that the statement of the Supreme Court's *Ornelas v. Ruiz* position should be followed:

> [W]e should overrule *Quinn's* elaboration of the "incidental to" prong and instead follow the approach articulated by the Supreme Court in *Ornelas v. Ruiz*, 161 U.S. 502, 511, 16 S.Ct. 689, 40 L.Ed. 787 (1896), by considering the "character of the foray, the mode of attacks, the persons killed or captured, and the kind of property taken or destroyed." *Id.* at 753.

In *Arambasic v. Ashcroft*, 403 F. Supp.2d 941, 963 (D.S.D. 2005), the court explicitly rejected *Quinn* and adopted the minority view in *Barapind*. Do you favor the *Quinn* approach or the position advanced by the dissent in *Barapind*?

4. There are significant splits in U.S. circuits (and among foreign states) as to which tests should be applied and how they can be applied in a given circumstance. See Restatement §476, Comm. g and Reporters' Notes 4 & 5. As the court in *Quinn v. Robinson* notes, several U.S. Courts have recently attempted to limit the application of the political offense exception in cases involving acts of terrorism. In *Eain v. Wilkes*, 641 F.2d 504, 520–21 (7th Cir. 1981), *cert. denied*, 454 U.S. 894 (1981), the court held that "the indiscriminate bombing of a civilian population is not recognized as a protected political act." In *In re Doherty*, 599 F. Supp. 270, 275 (S.D.N.Y. 1984), the court stated that the political offense exception would not protect bombings in public places, acts that transcend the limits of international law, acts inconsistent with international standards of civilized conduct, harm to hostages, violations of the Geneva Conventions, or the acts of fanatic groups without structure, organization or clearly defined political objectives. *See also Ahmad v. Wigen*, 910 F.3d 1063, 1066 (2d Cir. 1990) ("We agree that an attack on a commercial bus carrying civilian passengers on a regular route is not a political offense. Political motivation does not convert every crime into a political offense."); *Arambasic v. Ashcroft*, 403 F. Supp.2d 951, 963 (D.S.D. 2005) (torturing, disfiguring, and killing of imprisoned Croatian police officers by petitioner, a commander in the Republika Srpska army who took active part in the armed clashes with the Croatian police and Croatian army, were not crimes of a political character).

In *Matter of Extradition of Marzook*, 924 F. Supp. 565, 577 (S.D.N.Y. 1996), the court rejected a political offense exception with respect to indiscriminate killings of civilians which are "crimes abhorrent to human nature." In *Ordinola v. Hackman*, 478 F.3d 588 (4th Cir. 2007), Ordinola, a former member of a Peruvian military unit, was found to not benefit from the exception when his alleged offenses of relatively indiscriminate murder and forced disappearance were not "incidental to or in furtherance of a violent political uprising." The court in *Quinn v. Robinson*, however, did not believe such judicially imposed limitations on the traditional test for determining whether an act qualifies as a political offense were justified. Do you agree? What are the problems inherent in the tests employed by the Fourth and Seventh Circuits and Southern District of New York? What are the benefits in applying a violation of international law exception to the political offense exception? See M.C. Bassiouni, *supra*; Paust, Achille Lauro *Hostage-Takers*, *supra* at 245–47, and references cited.

5. The international community appears to reject the application of the political offense exception adopted in *Quinn* and to have sided with the courts in *Eain*, *Ahmad*, and

In re Doherty, excluding from the political offense exception criminal acts "inconsistent with international standards of civilized conduct," including violent acts directed against civilians. Earlier, Article VII of the Genocide Convention precluded use of the political offense exception for listed crimes and the same type of exclusion is found in Article XI (1) of the International Convention on the Punishment of the Crime of "Apartheid"; Article 13(1) of the International Convention for the Protection of All Persons from Enforced Disappearance; and Article V of the Inter-American Convention on the Forced Disappearance of Persons. See the Documents Supplement. More recently, the political offense exception has been denied for terrorist-related crimes. The International Convention for the Suppression of Terrorist Bombings precludes use of the political offense exception for conduct condemned under Article 2. Article 11 of the Terrorist Bombings Convention provides: "None of the offenses set forth in Article 2 shall be regarded, for purposes of extradition or mutual legal assistance, as a political offence or as an offence connected with a political offence or as an offence inspired by political motives. Accordingly, a request for extradition or for mutual legal assistance based on such an offence may not be refused on the sole ground that it concerns a political offence or an offence connected with a political offence or an offence inspired by political motives." An identical provision is included in Article 14 of the International Convention for the Suppression of the Financing of Terrorism, see the Documents Supplement. However, several older treaties expressly permit a denial of extradition under the laws of the requested state. *See, e.g.,* International Convention Against the Taking of Hostages, art. 10 (2). Each treaty requires the requested state to initiate prosecution if extradition is denied.

Article 2 of the Terrorist Bombings Convention condemns the use of an explosive or other lethal device "against a place of public use, a State or governmental facility, a public transportation system or an infrastructure " with the requisite "intent to cause death or serious bodily injury," or with "the intent to cause extensive destruction of such a place, facility or system, where such destruction results in or is likely to result in major economic loss." Does exempting crimes listed in Article 2 from the political offense exception mean that these crimes are not politically legitimate? Such crimes are "inconsistent with international standards of civilized conduct"? What if the killing of innocent civilians was committed by means other than use of an explosive device, such as beheading? Such conduct is not covered by the anti-Terrorist Bombing Convention. Should the court deny a request for extradition based on the political offense exception?

6. If police and military personnel can be lawful targets in an armed conflict, does this add to your consideration one way or the other? Consider Paust, *An Introduction to and Commentary on Terrorism and the Law,* 19 Conn. L. Rev. 697, 744 (1987).

7. The court in *Quinn v. Robinson* narrowly construed the geographic and temporal scope of the "uprising requirement" of the incidence test. Thus, it held that a bombing in London did not qualify for the political offense exception because it took place some distance from the "uprising," which was occurring in Northern Ireland. Do you agree with this interpretation? What are its implications for other situations? Not all courts apply an incidence or uprising test, especially in cases where persons are fleeing tyranny. Which approach do you prefer? *Compare* Steven Lubet, *Extradition Unbound: A Reply to Professors Blakesley and Bassiouni,* 24 Tex. Int'l L.J. 47, 50 (1989) *with* Jordan Paust, *An Introduction, supra,* at 745–46. What if Jews had killed a guard at a German concentration camp while escaping in 1940 — should they have been extradited back to Nazi Germany? Would they have had "political" motives sufficient to label the killing a relative political offense?

In its concluding paragraph, the court in *Quinn v. Robinson* suggested that the political offense exception might not be applicable to cases involving persons who are a "citizen of a different and uninvolved nation." What are the justifications for such a limitation? What problems might it create?

8. During the 1980s, congressional hearings were held to determine whether the extradition statute should be amended to exclude certain acts from the political offense exception. See Molner, *Extradition: Limitation of the Political Offense Exception,* 27 HARV. INT'L L. J. 266 (1986). When it became clear that Congress was unlikely to amend the extradition statute, the Executive Branch began to negotiate Supplementary Extradition Treaties with its "stable democratic allies" that exclude from the political offense exception cases involving murder, kidnapping, the hijacking of aircraft, aircraft sabotage, crimes against diplomats and other internationally protected persons, the taking of hostages, "maliciously wounding", "false imprisonment", and "possession of a firearm or ammunition by a person who intends either himself or through another person to endanger life," as well as offenses involving explosives. The United States has so far concluded such treaties with Canada, the United Kingdom, Belgium, Germany, and Spain. See Article IV of the Protocol Amending the U.S.-Canada Extradition Treaty reproduced above.

Why do you think Congress decided not to amend the extradition statute to limit the political offense exception to extradition? What are the problems with the ad hoc approach of negotiating supplementary treaties with so-called stable democratic allies? Are these treaty-based exclusions preferable? Do they reach too far and are they too inflexible? *Compare* Steven Lubet, *Taking the Terror Out of Political Terrorism: The Supplementary Treaty on Extradition Between the United States and the United Kingdom,* 19 CONN. L. REV. 863 (1987); *International Criminal Law and the "Ice-Nine" Error: A Discourse on the Fallacy of Universal Solutions,* 28 VA. J. INT'L L. 963 (1988) *with* M. Cherif Bassiouni, *The "Political Offense" Exception Revisited: Extradition Between the U.S. and the U.K.—A Choice Between Friendly Cooperation Among Allies and Sound Law and Policy,* 15 DEN. J. INT'L L. & POL. 255 (1987); Christopher Blakesley, *An Essay on Executive Branch Attempts to Eviscerate the Separation of Powers,* 2 UTAH L. REV. 451 (1987); Jordan Paust, *"Such a Narrow Approach" Indeed,* 29 VA. J. INT'L L. 413 (1989). In the United States, can it be lawful for a private citizen to carry a gun with an intent to perform an act that might "endanger life"? If so, should this sort of possession of a firearm be an automatic bar to use of the political offense exception? Should "false imprisonment"?

2. Non-Inquiry

Ahmed v. Wigen
726 F. Supp. 389 (E.D.N.Y. 1989)

Weinstein, J.

This case raises serious questions—some of them novel—about the United States' obligations under an extradition treaty and the court's role in ensuring that those extradited are treated fairly. As indicated below, two changes in law must now be recognized: The "political offense" bar to extradition is narrowed to exclude terrorism and acts of war against civilians. A correlative expansion is required in courts' power to ensure that those extradited are granted due process and are treated humanely. Petitioner has been afforded due process in this country, and adequate guarantees exist that he will be fairly treated in Israel, the country seeking his extradition to stand trial for alleged terrorist acts against its citizens....

Mahmoud El-Abed Ahmad seeks a writ of habeas corpus, 28 U.S.C. § 2241, to prevent his extradition to Israel to stand trial. On April 12, 1986, he allegedly attacked by firebombs and automatic weapons fire a passenger bus en route to Tel Aviv traveling between Israeli settlements in the occupied territory of the West Bank. Death of the bus driver and serious injury to one of the passengers resulted....

... Petitioner claimed that should he be extradited to Israel he would face procedures and treatment "antipathetic to a court's sense of decency." Because this ground had not been raised in any prior proceeding, petitioner requested an evidentiary hearing to demonstrate that the Israeli judicial system would not afford him due process and that he would be subject to conditions of detention and interrogation in violation of universally accepted principles of human rights.

The government opposed petitioner's request for a hearing. It asserted that the scope of habeas review is extremely narrow and that the rule of non-inquiry prohibited the court from inquiring into the integrity of the requesting state's judicial system. Neither side requested that the issue be referred to Judge Korman. The petition was referred to the present judge by random selection.

On May 16, 1989 this court ruled from the bench that it would consider petitioner's due process claim and permit both parties to submit further evidence on this and any other issue. The government sought a writ of mandamus from the Court of Appeals for the Second Circuit to prohibit the court from holding a hearing and from receiving evidence on the probable nature of the judicial procedures of the requesting nation in an extradition matter. On June 20, 1989 the Court of Appeals denied the writ of mandamus.

This court held evidentiary hearings in July and August of 1989 to supplement the record before Magistrate Caden and Judge Korman. Both parties submitted documentary evidence. Petitioner called four witnesses to testify on the Israeli judicial process and conditions of detention: Professor John Quigley, Abdeen M. Jabara, Heah Tsemel, Esq. and Sami Esmail. Preserving its objection to the proceedings, respondent called two witnesses, Professors Alan Dershowitz and Monroe Freedman, and submitted statements of United States officials who had observed trials in Israel. A representative of the Israeli government certified the protections petitioner would receive in Israel. *See* Appendix attached *infra*. The parties then fully briefed and argued the case in September, 1989.

In all, some fourteen days of evidentiary hearings, and extensive oral argument based upon full briefs and the court's own research, were devoted to this case. Petitioner has had a full opportunity to be heard....

Petitioner contends that should he be extradited to Israel, he would be subjected to torture and cruel and unusual punishment during interrogation to coerce him into confessing the acts alleged; he would not receive even "a semblance of due process" in the Israeli criminal justice system, particularly since any conviction would in all likelihood rest on either his or his alleged accomplices' coerced confessions; and, finally, he would be housed in indecent detention and prison facilities. He contends that extradition under these circumstances violates fundamental principles of due process and human rights.

The claim raises the question of whether a federal court may inquire into the fairness of a requesting country's criminal justice system, including its methods of interrogation, rules of evidence regarding confessions and conditions of detention. If so, the court must determine whether petitioner faces treatment and procedures on extradition so offensive to the court's sense of decency that the habeas corpus writ must be granted and extradition prohibited. This court is empowered to hold an evidentiary hearing to determine the nature of treatment probably awaiting petitioner in a requesting nation to determine whether he or she can demonstrate probable exposure to such treatment as would violate universally accepted principles of human rights.

It should be emphasized that by conducting such an inquiry, we do not make it "the business of our courts to assume the responsibility for supervising the integrity of the judicial system of another sovereign nation." *Jhirad v. Ferrandina*, 536 F.2d 478, 484–85 (2d Cir.), *cert. denied*, 429 U.S. 833 (1986). But neither can another nation use the courts of our country to obtain power over a fugitive intending to deny that person due process. We cannot blind ourselves to the foreseeable and probable results of the exercise of our jurisdiction. *Cf. Jhirad*, 536 F.2d at 485 (requiring demanding state to show that petitioner would not be prosecuted for a crime for which the statute of limitations had run); *Gallina v. Fraser*, 278 F.2d 77, 79 (2d Cir.), *cert. denied*, 364 U.S. 851 (1960) ("federal court's sense of decency" may limit extradition"); *In re Extradition of Burt*, 737 F.2d 1477, 1486–87 (7th Cir. 1984) ("fundamental conceptions of fair play and decency" and "particularly atrocious procedures or punishments" may be considered by the court); *Plaster v. United States*, 720 F.2d 340, 348, 354 (4th Cir. 1983) ("individual constitutional rights" must be weighed to determine if extradition would be "fundamentally unfair"); *United States ex rel. Bloomfield v. Gengler*, 507 F.2d 925, 928 (2d Cir. 1974), *cert. denied*, 421 U.S. 1001 (1975) (extradition may be "antipathetic to a federal court's sense of decency").

Reflective of our country's concern for the extraditee is the fact that our State Department has insisted that the requesting nation protect those extradited. It requires, for example, that as a condition of surrender a person found guilty in absentia be retried. *Gallina v. Fraser*, 278 F.2d 77, 78 (2d Cir.), *cert. denied*, 364 U.S. 851 (1960). Moreover, this court was informed that the State Department will observe the trial abroad to ensure that its conditions are fulfilled.

A. Due Process Exception to the Rule of Non-Inquiry

1. Generally

The theme that treaties and other international obligations should not inhibit fundamental individual rights policies of the United States is a powerful one. *Cf. Societe Nationale Industrielle Aerospatiale v. United States District Court, S.D. Iowa*, 482 U.S. 522, 554 (1987) (treaty interpreted to leave United States rules for discovery in civil cases intact); Henkin, *Rights: American and Human*, 79 Colum. L. Rev. 405, 411 (1979) (American rights are in some sense supreme because they "antecede the Constitution and are above government"). The inherent conflict between national sovereignty and obligations under treaties which appear to limit that sovereignty is well illustrated by the right of extraditing nations to refuse to violate their own sense of individual justice. *See Barr v. United States Dep't of Justice*, 819 F.2d 25, 27 (2d. Cir. 1987) (The "treaty may authorize only such governmental action as in conformity with the Constitution."); *Reid v. Covert*, 354 U.S. 1, 16–18 (1957) (supremacy of Constitution over particular treaty); L. Henkin, R. Pugh, O. Schachter & H. Smit, *International Law: Cases and Materials* 184–85 (2d ed. 1987).

Treaty obligations will sometimes need to be read and interpreted by the courts of a nation in the context of the fundamental law of the nation that entered into them. In the United States that law includes those principles embodied in the due process clauses of the fifth and fourteenth amendments of the Constitution guaranteeing extensive protections to the criminally accused. *Cf.* L. Henkin, *Foreign Affairs and the Constitution* 255 (1972) ("In regard to foreign relations ... 'due process of law' requires fair procedures for aliens as for citizens ... in civil as in criminal proceedings, before administrative bodies and in courts."). This principle, we emphasize, does not require us to impose the details of our Constitution or procedural system on a requesting country's judicial system. *See Neely v.*

Henkel, 180 U.S. 109, 122, 21 S.Ct. 302, 306, 45 L.Ed. 448 (1901). It does entail an obligation not to extradite people who face procedures or treatment that "shocks the conscience" of jurists acting under the United States Constitution and within our current legal ethos. *See Rosado v. Civiletti*, 621 F.2d 1179, 1195–96 (2d Cir.), *cert. denied*, 449 U.S. 856 (1980) ("Thus, although the Constitution cannot limit the power of a foreign sovereign to prescribe procedures for the trial and punishment of crimes committed within its territory, it does govern the manner in which the United States may join the effort."). *Cf. Rochin v. California*, 342 U.S. 165, 172 (1952).

As pointed out in Section III A(1), *supra*, international custom and treaties limiting attacks on civilians are not derogatory to our Constitution. Rather they expand and give substance to a developing enriched concept of rights of the individual that harmonizes with our own constitutional developments.

The introductory note to the subchapter on extradition of the Restatement points out, "The requested state retains an interest in the fate of a person it has extradited" as well as the probable fate of those whose extradition is sought. *Restatement, supra*, at 557. Extradition may be refused, for example, where requested nation has a substantial ground for believing that the person sought "would not receive a fair trial or would risk suffering other violations of human rights" in the requesting nation. *Id.* § 475 comment g, at 562, § 476 comment h. at 571. "Thus, while extradition treaties obligate the parties to extradite according to their terms, nearly all extradition treaties leave some room—at least by implication—for discretion by the requested state not to extradite in certain cases." *Id.* at 558. *See Sindona v. Grant*, 619 F.2d 167, 176 (2d Cir.1980) ("[T]he executive branch ... is empowered to make the final decision on extradition and has assumed the discretion to deny or delay extradition on humanitarian grounds."); S. Treaty Doc. No 100-20, 100th Cong. 2d Sess. 7 (1988) (executive has discretion to refuse to extradite if extraditee is in danger of being subject to torture); Kester, *Some Myths of United States Extradition Law*, 76 Geo.L.J. 1441, 1478 (1988).

Three independent protections are erected against this country's participation in the wrongful deed of surrendering fugitives to likely abuse by the requesting state. First, Congress and the executive branch do not enter into extradition treaties with countries in whose criminal justice system they lack confidence. *Restatement, supra*, at 558 (noting absence of extradition treaties with the U.S.S.R., People's Republic of China, North Korea and Iran). Second, when conditions change after an extradition treaty is concluded, without formal denunciation or suspension of the treaty, the executive of the requested state—here the Secretary of State—may refuse to extradite. *Id.*; S. Treaty Doc. No. 100-20, 100th Cong., 2d Sess. 7 (1988). Third, the courts in this country, constituting and independent branch of government, charged with defending the due process rights of all those who appear before them, may grant the accused prisoner a writ of habeas corpus blocking extradition.

2. United States Precedent

The existence, and ambit, of this third, court imposed, protection is not settled. Under the traditional rule of non-inquiry, claims of probable lack of due process in the requesting nation would fall within "the exclusive purview of the executive branch" and courts would not inquire into the procedures which await the accused upon extradition. *Sindona v. Grant*, 619 F.2d 167, 174 (2d Cir. 1980). *Accord, e.g., Garcia-Guillern v. United States*, 450 F.2d 1189 (5th Cir. 1971), *cert. denied*, 405 U.S. 989 (1972); *Peroff v. Hylton*, 542 F.2d 1249 (4th Cir. 1976), *cert. denied*, 429 U.S. 833 (1910) ("We are bound by the existence of an extradition treaty to assume that the trial will be fair.").

Despite this limiting line of cases, the courts, as an independent branch of government, have a duty to stand between the executive and the accused where a case of abdication of State Department responsibility for the protection of the accused has been made out. Courts may not compromise "that judicial integrity so necessary in the true administration of justice." *Mapp v. Ohio*, 367 U.S. 643, 660 (1961). The courts may not be parties to abusive judicial practices, even where sensitive foreign relations matters are concerned. *See Barr v. United States*, 819 F.2d 25, 27 n.2 (2d Cir. 1987) ("[It is a] recognized principle that, regardless of the degree of American government involvement in the conduct of a foreign sovereign, the federal courts will not allow themselves to be placed in the position of putting their imprimatur on unconscionable conduct.").

Despite the fact that the executive branch has a constitutional duty and right to conduct foreign policy, and the legislative and executive branches together have the duty and right to enter into treaties for extradition, the courts are not, and cannot be, a rubber stamp of the other branches of government in the exercise of extradition jurisdiction. They must, under article III of the Constitution, exercise their independent judgement in a case or controversy to determine the propriety of an individual's extradition. The executive may not foreclose the courts from exercising their responsibility to protect the integrity of the judicial process. A court must ensure that it is not used for purpose which do not comport with our constitution or principles of fundamental fairness.

The court's powers and responsibilities are necessarily greater in foreign extradition cases than in extradition between states of this country. *See Uniform Criminal Extradition and Rendition Act*, 11 U.L.A. §§ 3-107, 3-101, 3-102 (Supp. 1989). This is so because of the constitutional mandate for extradition between states of the United States. United States Constitution, art. IV, § 2, cl.2. Fairness of hearings or methods of incarceration in the requesting state are not inquired into by the courts of the extraditing state. *Sweeney v. Woodall*, 344 U.S. 86, 73 S.Ct. 139, 97 L.Ed. 114 (1952); *Pacileo v. Walker*, 449 U.S. 86 (1980). Nor do the governors have the same broad authority as the Secretary of State to refuse extradition. *Drew v. Thaw*, 235 U.S. 432 (1914); *Puerto Rico v. Branstad*, 483 U.S. 219 (1987). The reason for the reduced responsibility of a state extraditing to another state as compared to the United States extraditing to another nation is obvious: If a demanding state violates the rights of an extradited person, he or she can seek the protection of the fourteenth amendment of our federal Constitution. The person extradited to a foreign nation can generally seek only whatever protection that nation affords. *But cf.* Section II a(3), *infra* (discussion of European Court of Human Rights, *Soering* Case).

The Second Circuit has repeatedly acknowledged that it could "imagine situations where the [accused], upon extradition, would be subject to procedures or punishment so antipathetic to a federal court's sense of decency as to require reexamination" of the rule of non-inquiry. *Gallina v. Fraser*, 278 F.2d 77, 79 (2d Cir.), *cert. denied*, 364 U.S. 851 (1960). *Accord United States ex. rel. Bloomfield v. Gengler*, 507 F.2d 925, 928 (2d Cir. 1974), *cert. denied* 421 U.S. 1001 (1975); *Rosado v. Civiletti*, 621 F.2d 1179, 1195 (2d Cir.) *cert. denied*, 449 U.S. 856 (1980). *See also Demjanjuk v. Pertrovsky*, 776 F.2d 571, 583 (6th Cir. 1985), *cert. denied*, 475 U.S. 1016 (1986); *Arnbjornsdottir-Mendler v. United States*, 721 F.2d 679, 683 (9th Cir. 1983). The *Gallina* exception to the rule of non-inquiry has apparently yet to be invoked to prevent extradition since thus far no petitioner has persuasively demonstrated that extradition would expose him to unconscionable abuse. *see, e.g., Demjanjuk v. Petrovsky*, 776 F.2d at 583 ("There is absolutely no showing in this record that Israel will follow procedures which would shock this court's 'sense of decency.'"); *Arnbjornsdottir-Mendler v. United States*, 721 F.2d at 683 ("In light of Iceland's outstanding human rights' record and appellant's uncorroborated prediction of maltreatment, the district court had no obligation to hold an evidentiary hearing to consider the claim.").

3. International Precedent

The present status of international and human rights law on this issue is demonstrated by the *Soering Case*, decided by the European Court of Human Rights of the Council of Europe in Strasbourg on July 7, 1989. slip sheet 1/1989/161/217. There was strong evidence that Soering a West German citizen, had assisted in the commission of a homicide in Virginia. Soering was arrested in Great Britain and ordered extradited to Virginia, pursuant to a treaty between the United States and the United Kingdom. The European Court intervened upon Soering's application charging the United Kingdom with a breach of its obligations under various articles of the European Convention for the Protection of Human Rights and Fundamental Freedoms, Nov. 4, 1950, 213 U.N.T.S. 221, 224 (1955). In particular, Soering claimed that by ordering his extradition to Virginia, the United Kingdom would subject him to the risk of languishing for years on death row—a fate he contended would constitute a violation of article 3 of the Convention which provides: "No one shall be subjected to torture or to inhuman or degrading treatment or punishment." 213 U.N.T.S. at 224.

The European Court adopted the principle that the requested country bears a responsibility to measure the conditions in the requesting country against article 3 of the Convention "where substantial grounds have been shown for believing that the person concerned, if extradited, faces a real risk of being subjected to torture or to inhuman or degrading treatment or punishment in the requesting country." *Soering Case*, slip sheet at 27. The court found that although the Convention is not considered to be part of United Kingdom law, "the English courts can review the 'reasonableness' of an extradition decision in the light of" such factors. *Id.* at 38.

In an unanimous decision, the Court rejected extradition:

> [H]aving regard to the very long period of time spent on death row in such extreme conditions, with the ever present and mounting anguish of awaiting execution of the death penalty, … [Soering's] extradition to the United States would expose him to a real risk of treatment going beyond the threshold set by Art. 3.

Id. at 35. It based its decision upon evidence demonstrating that it would probably take at least six years to decide the defendant's fate after conviction and that there was a substantial possibility that he would experience the severely damaging psychological and physical conditions of death row for from six to eight years. *Id.* at 17. Apparently, the European Court believed that the protections of article 3 of the Convention are greater than those that would be provided by the courts of Virginia and the Supreme Court of the United States under our due process and cruel and unusual punishment clauses of the United States Constitution.

The *Soering* case arguably went too far in limiting extradition based upon probable conditions in the requesting country. Its decision perhaps can be justified as a matter of equity if not law on the ground that defendant would not go unwhipped of justice even were he not extradited to Virginia. He was a German national who could be tried for the crime in West Germany where the maximum penalty would be life imprisonment. That country was also seeking his extradition. *Id.* at 34 (majority found this possibility of extradition to a third country not "material," but given some weight in obtaining "a fair balance of interests").

In considering *Soering*, it is significant that the European Court of Human Rights recognized that a court's determination of whether to extradite entails a responsibility to consider the interests of the community in its safety from terrorists and other criminals. The Court declared:

> [I]nherent in the whole of the Convention is a search for a fair balance between the demands of the general interest of the community and the requirements of the protection of the individual's fundamental rights. As movement about the world becomes easier and crime takes on a larger international dimension, it is increasingly in the interest of all nations that suspected offenders who flee abroad should be brought to justice. Conversely, the establishment of safe havens for fugitives would not only result in danger for the State obliged to harbour the protected person but also tend to undermine the foundations of extradition. These considerations must also be included among the factors to be taken into account in the interpretation and application of the notions of inhuman and degrading treatment or punishment in extradition cases.

Id. at 27. Thus, just as national policies and international norms are taken into account by American courts ascertaining the scope of the political offense exception, *see* Section IIE(1) *supra*, so too must these considerations enter into the assessment of whether the likelihood of particular treatment in the requesting country constitutes such a violation of due process and fundamental fairness as to prevent extradition.

Soering constitutes an important precedent on the refusal to extradite because of anticipated torture, cruel conditions of incarceration or lack of due process at trial in the requesting country. It reflects a persuasive though non-binding international standard. *Cf. Demjanjuk v. Petrovsky*, 776 F.2d 571, 582 (6th Cir. 1985), *cert. denied*, 475 U.S. 1016 (1986) ("The law of the United States includes international law," *citing The Paquete Habana*, 175 U.S. 677, 712, 20 S.Ct. 290, 304, 44 L.Ed. 320 (1900)). *Cf.* United Nations Convention Against Torture and Other Cruel, Inhuman and Degrading Treatment or Punishment art. 3, GAOR A/39/506 (1984), 23 I.L.M. 1027, 1028 (1984) ("No State Party shall ... extradite a person to another State where there are substantial grounds for believing that he would be in danger of being subjected to torture."); S. Treaty Doc. No. 100-20, 100th Cong. 2d Sess. 7 (1988) (reprinting Convention, together with message of transmittal recommending ratification).

The opinion in *Soering* sets forth factors a court should consider in assessing the severity of ill-treatment, including "all the circumstances of the case, such as the nature and context of the treatment or punishment, the manner and method of its execution, its duration, its physical or mental effects and , in some instances, the sex, age and state of health of the victim." *Soering Case*, slip sheet at 30. The European Court of Human Rights has also given definition to the vague terms "inhuman and degrading treatment and punishment":

> Treatment has been held by the Court to be both "inhuman" because it was premeditated, was applied for hours at a stretch and "caused, if not actual bodily injury, at least intense physical and mental suffering," and also "degrading" because it was "such as to arouse in its victims feelings of fear, anguish and inferiority capable of humiliating and debasing them and possibly breaking their physical and moral resistance."

Id.

Torture and cruel and unusual punishment must be defined for our purposes as including threats and other inhuman psychological pressure may be even more painful and more effective than physical pressure in destroying person's dignity or in overcoming the will of the person interrogate, thus inducing false confessions. Even if the probable inhumane act is unauthorized by the requesting nation and is applied by those abusing power it could constitute a basis for non-extradition. *See Altun v. Federal Republic of Germany*, 36 Eur. Comm'n H.R. 209, 233–35 (1983) (in action challenging extradition, torture incidents considered even though Turkish government had discouraged them by prosecuting police officers responsible).

B. Burden of Proof

As a general rule our courts should rely on the State Department's initial approval and forwarding of the extradition request to the appropriate United States Attorney as certification that the requesting state may be relied upon to treat the accused fairly. *See* S. Treaty Doc. No. 100-20, 100th Cong., 2d Sess. 7 (1988) (Secretary of State should use its discretion to ensure that extraditee will not be subject to torture). The Department has better resources than the courts to make appropriate inquiries. Particularly since it is charged by Congress under sections 116(d) and 502B(b) of the Foreign Assistance Act of 1961 with making an annual review of human rights conditions through the world, the State Department may be assumed to be sensitive to the problem. *See, e.g.,* United States Dep't of State, 101st Cong., 1st Sess., *Country Reports on Human Rights Practices for 1988* (S.Prt. 101–3, 1989). There may, however, be instances where immediate political, military or economic needs of the United States induce the State Department to ignore the rights of the accused. Should such cases occur, the courts must be prepared to act.

There is presumption in favor of the State Department's and a foreign nation's good faith exercise of its powers. Nevertheless, "the presumption of fairness routinely accorded the criminal process of a foreign sovereign may require closer scrutiny if a [petitioner] persuasively demonstrates that extradition would expose him to procedures or punishments 'antipathetic to a federal court's sense of decency.'" *Rosado v. Civilleti,* 621 F.2d 1179, 1195 (2d Cir.), *cert. denied,* 449 U.S. 856 (1980). Because foreign policy is involved, the State Department's decision that extradition is proper will be given considerable weight. The burden of proof is on petitioner to come forward with a written submission showing a substantial probability that he or she can rebut the presumption of State Department propriety in assuming the fairness of the judicial process in the requesting country. *Cf.* Fed.R.Evid. 301 (shifting burden of coming forward). If petitioner makes such a threshold showing, the rule of non-inquiry yields and an evidentiary hearing may be conducted on the issue of probable due process to the accused in the requesting country. The Federal Rules of Evidence do not apply to such extradition hearings. Fed.R.Evid. 1101(d)(3).

In previous cases of extradition to Israel, the courts have repeatedly and uniformly found that the State Department properly concluded that Israeli courts would act fairly. *See, e.g., Demjanjuk v. Petrovsky,* 776 F.2d 571, 583 (6th Cir. 1985), *cert. denied,* 475 U.S. 1016 (1986); *Eain v. Wilkes,* 641 F.2d 504, 512 n. 9 (7th Cir.), *cert. denied,* 454 U.S. 894 (1981). Nevertheless, in the instant case, petitioner submitted reports of torture of those who were thought guilty of acts of violence against Israelis in the occupied territory, of trial by military rather than civilian courts, and of unacceptable conditions of imprisonment after conviction. These included the State Department's own report on human rights conditions in Israel which acknowledges that "where security concerns predominate, the strictures [against torture, and other cruel, inhuman or degrading treatment or punishment] have been violated." United States Dep't of State, 101st Cong., 1st Sess., *Country Reports on Human Rights Practices for 1988,* at 1367 (S.Prt. 101–3, 1989). The violations petitioner cited suffice to rebut the presumption. *Cf.* Fed.R.Evid. 301.

Notes and Questions

1. Besides Article 3(1) of the Torture Convention, quoted above, 3(2) requires "competent authorities" to "take into account all relevant considerations including, where ap-

plicable, the existence in the State concerned of a consistent pattern of gross, flagrant or mass violations of human rights." Article 7(3) also requires that "fair treatment at all stages of the proceedings" brought in connection with an offense obtain. Article 9 of the International Convention Against the Taking of Hostages requires that extradition "shall not be granted if the requested State Party has substantial grounds for believing: (a) That the request ... has been made for the purpose of prosecuting or punishing a person on account of his race, religion, nationality, ethnic origin or political opinion; or (b) That the person's position may be prejudiced (i) for any of the reasons mentioned in subparagraph (a)..., or (ii) for the reason that communication with him by the appropriate authorities of the State entitled to exercise rights of protection [*e.g.*, state of nationality] cannot be effected." In the case of refugees, Articles 1(A)(2) and 33(1) of the Convention Relating to the Status of Refugees provide similar protections and state responsibilities related to the need for inquiry. Also recall the treaties and reports addressing the principle of *nonrefoulement* in Notes earlier in this chapter.

2. Some prefer that there be a rule of non-inquiry and, as several courts prefer, that it be likened to the political question doctrine. Should there be a rule of non-inquiry? If so, should it have recognized limits or exceptions based in international law and/or constitutional law (which would relate to the competence and responsibility of the judiciary)? Some also prefer that such a rule relate more to political power and Executive discretion. For example, the Seventh Circuit has stated in connection with what some term the motivation prong of the rule:

> Evaluations of the motivation behind a request for extradition so clearly implicate the conduct of this country's foreign relations as to be a matter better left to the Executive's discretion.... Thus, the Judiciary's deference to the Executive on the "subterfuge" question is appropriate since political questions would permeate any judgment on the motivation of a foreign government.

Eain v. Wilkes, 641 F.2d 504, 507 (7th Cir.), *cert. denied*, 454 U.S. 894 (1981). As to the fair trial prong of the non-inquiry rule, the Ninth Circuit, in *Quinn v. Robinson*, stated similarly:

> We do not believe it appropriate to make qualitative judgments regarding a foreign government.... Such judgments themselves cannot be other than political and, as such, involve determinations of the sort that are not within the judicial role.

Quinn v. Robinson, 783 F.2d 776, at 804. If the rule of non-inquiry, as some prefer, is the extradition version of the political question doctrine, did Judge Weinstein's decision to conduct an inquiry into the fairness of the Israeli justice and penal system violate constitutional separation of powers principles or do such matters involve legal issues within Article III powers of the judiciary as opposed to questions concerning the general nature of a foreign government or "motivation" of such a government? Should human rights law, as law of the land, also be appropriate for judicial inquiry—indeed, mandatory in view of the customary human right to an effective remedy in domestic tribunals? *See generally* Paust, Achille Lauro *Hostage-Takers, supra* at 247–49; J. Paust, International Law as Law of the United States chpts. 1, 2, 5, *passim* (2 ed. 2003); Restatement §§ 475, Comm. g, 476 Comm. h, 702, 711, Reporters' Note 7; note 1 above. Didn't the United Kingdom try to argue a non-inquiry rule in the *Soering* case?

3. In *Ahmad v. Wigen*, Judge Weinstein assumed that the State Department's act of forwarding the extradition request to the appropriate United States Attorney constituted "certification that the requested State may be relied upon to treat the accused fairly." He hypothesized that "there may, however, be instances where immediate political, military

or economic needs of the United States induce the State Department to ignore the rights of the accused." He therefore held that an exception to the rule of non-inquiry is justified where "a case of abdication of State Department responsibility for the protection of the accused has been made out." Shortly after the opinion in *Ahmad v. Wigen* was published, the State Department submitted an affidavit in *In re Ranjit Singh Gill and Sukhmider Singh Sandhu v. Romolo J. Imundi, U.S. Marshal*, Dec. 88 Civ. 1530, U.S. District Court, S.D.N.Y. (Dec. 22, 1989):

"2. The process of extraditing a fugitive to a foreign country begins when a formal extradition request is presented to the Department by a diplomatic note from the requesting State's Embassy in Washington. Upon receiving the request with supporting documents properly certified by the U.S. Embassy in the requesting State, my office conducts a preliminary review of the materials to determine: (a) whether an extradition treaty is in effect between the requesting State and the United States, (b) whether the request appears to come within the scope of the applicable extradition treaty, and (c) whether, on the face of the supporting documents, there is no clearly-evident defense to extradition (for example, that the offense is manifestly a political offense or that the request is manifestly politically motivated). If the answers to these questions are yes, we transmit the request and documents to the Department of Justice for further review and, if appropriate, the commencement of judicial extradition proceedings.

"3. The Department of Justice review, conducted by the Office of International Affairs, is primarily intended to determine whether the supporting documents contain sufficient evidence to meet U.S. evidentiary requirements. If the Department of Justice considers that the documents are in order and the extradition request is well founded, it has the request and documents filed (generally, by a United States Attorney's Office) in the appropriate federal district court along with a complaint seeking a warrant for the fugitive's arrest. Upon issuance of the arrest warrant, the U.S. Marshals Service apprehends the person sought, if he can be found, and he is held pending the extradition hearing.

"4. A hearing on the merits of the extradition request is then held before a United States magistrate or a United States district judge sitting as an extradition magistrate. The Department of Justice, through the Office of the U.S. Attorney, will represent the legal interests of the requesting State at the hearing when it is obliged to do so by treaty or when the requesting State agrees to provide reciprocal representation for U.S. requests presented before its courts. If the extradition judge or magistrate confirms the identity of the fugitive and finds that probable cause exists to believe that he committed the offense charged (or that he has been convicted in the requesting State of the offense) and that no defense to extradition under the applicable treaty has been made, he will issue a certificate of extraditability and order that the fugitive be held in custody pending a final determination on his extradition by the Secretary of State. The judicial record in the case is then certified to the Secretary, pursuant to 18 U.S.C. Section 3184, for a decision by the Secretary on whether to authorize the surrender of the fugitive to the agents of the requesting State. *See* 18 U.S.C. Section 3186. This authority has been delegated to the Deputy Secretary of State; consequently, either the Secretary or the Deputy Secretary may exercise this authority.

"5. The fugitive may seek judicial review of the magistrate's finding by petitioning for a writ of habeas corpus, generally in the district court in which the extradition hearing was held. The district court's decision on the petition for a writ of habeas corpus is appealable to the United States Court of Appeals. Either party may seek review of a Court of Appeals decision by petitioning the Supreme Court for a writ of certiorari. the Secretary will not make a final determination on whether to extradite the fugitive until the completion of the judicial proceedings.

"6. Although the Department of Justice generally represents the interests of the requesting State during judicial extradition proceedings, this representation does not in any way constitute a decision by the United States, acting through the Secretary of State, to extradite the individual. The Secretary's decision on whether to extradite is made after final judicial action. However, if the court declines to issue a certificate of extraditability on grounds of lack of probable cause or a treaty-based defense, there will be no occasion for the Secretary to act.

"7. Upon the issuance of a certificate of extraditability and completion of judicial proceedings, the Secretary may consider *de novo* all issues properly raised before the court, and any new arguments either in favor of or against surrender that are presented to him by any interested party or which have otherwise come to the Department's attention. He may also consider any arguments which, although not new, are relevant and could not have been considered by the court, *e.g.*, whether the extradition request was politically motivated, or whether the fugitive is likely to be denied a fair trial or otherwise persecuted upon his return.

"8. The manner in which the Secretary may consider these issues will vary from case to case. Invariably, the Department of State will rely upon its knowledge and expertise of the judicial and penal conditions and practices of the requesting country. It may in some cases make specific inquiries relating to the individual fugitive or it may frame its judgement on the basis of its analysis of more general information.

"9. Based on an analysis of such information by all relevant offices within the Department, the Secretary may decide to surrender the fugitive to the requesting State, to deny surrender of the fugitive, or to surrender the fugitive subject to any conditions he deems reasonable or otherwise appropriate.

"10. The allegations raised by petitioners during the course of these judicial proceedings relating to their inability to receive a fair trial and claims of persecution upon extradition have not yet been presented to the Secretary for consideration. The Department is aware of the seriousness of the allegations and will consider them prior to the Secretary's final determination on extradition. In fact, my office has already sought to obtain relevant information from the Department's Country Office for India and from its Bureau of Human Rights and Humanitarian Affairs. Either petitioner is also free to submit to the Secretary in writing any material that he believes is relevant generally to the question of his extradition. If, upon completion of judicial proceedings, the courts have sustained the finding of extraditability, the Department would present all relevant issues to the Secretary for his consideration and decision.

"11. The foregoing demonstrates that petitioners' unsupported claims that the Secretary of State cannot and will not consider their allegations of persecution are unfounded...."

Based on the statements made in the affidavit, was Judge Weinstein correct in his assumption that the State Department's act of forwarding of the extradition request to the U.S. Attorney constituted the Department's certification that the accused would be treated fairly by the requesting state? When does the Department make a determination concerning the probable treatment of the accused upon surrender to the requesting state? Is this sufficient? See question 5 below. Judge Sweet in *Gill v. Imundi*, 747 F. Supp. 1028 (S.D.N.Y. 1990), stated that he was not confident with respect to the ability of the Executive to take human rights into account. *Id.* at 1050.

4. The Second Circuit reversed Judge Weinstein's ruling in *Ahmad v. Wigen*, 910 F.2d 1063 (2nd Cir. 1990):

> " ... We have no problem with the district court's rejection of Ahmad's remaining argument to the effect that, if he is returned to Israel, he probably will be mistreated, denied a fair trial, and deprived of his constitutional and human rights. We do, however, question the district court's decision to explore the merits of this contention in the manner that it did. The Supreme Court's above-cited cases dealing with the scope of habeas corpus review carefully prescribe the limits of such review. Habeas corpus is not a writ of error, and it is not a means of rehearing what the certification judge or magistrate already has decided. *Fernandez v. Phillips, supra*, 268 U.S. at 312, 45 S.Ct. at 542. A consideration of the procedures that will or may occur in the requesting country is not within the purview of a habeas corpus judge. *Gallina v. Fraser, supra*, 278 F.2d at 79. Indeed, there is substantial authority for the proposition that this is not a proper matter for consideration by the certifying judicial officer. In *Sindona v. Grant*, 619 F.2d 167, 174 (2d Cir. 1980), we said that "the degree of risk to [appellant's] life from extradition is an issue that properly falls within the exclusive purview of the executive branch." In *Jhirad v. Ferrandina, supra*, 536 F.2d at 484–85, we said that "[i]t is not the business of our courts to assume the responsibility for supervising the integrity of the judicial system of another sovereign nation." *See also Arnbjornsdottir-Mendler v. United States*, 721 F.2d 679, 683 (9th Cir. 1983); *Garcia-Guillern v. United States*, 450 F.2d 1189, 1192 (5th Cir. 1971), *cert. denied*, 405 U.S. 989 (1972); *Matter of Extradition of Tang Yee-Chun*, 674 F. Supp. 1058, 1068–69 (S.D.N.Y. 1987).
>
> "Notwithstanding the above described judicial roadblocks, the district court proceeded to take testimony from both expert and fact witnesses and received extensive reports, affidavits, and other documentation concerning Israel's law enforcement procedures and its treatment of prisoners. This, we think, was improper. The interests of international comity are ill-served by requiring a foreign nation such as Israel to satisfy a United States district judge concerning the fairness of its laws and the manner in which they are enforced. *Jhirad v. Ferrandina, supra*, 536 F.2d at 484–85. It is the function of the Secretary of State to determine whether extradition should be denied on humanitarian grounds. *Matter of Extradition of Tang Yee-Chun, supra*, 674 F. Supp. at 1068 (citing *Sindona v. Grant, supra*, 619 F.2d at 174). So far as we know, the Secretary never has directed extradition in the face of proof that the extraditee would be subjected to procedures or punishment antipathetic to a federal court's sense of decency. *See Arnbjornsdottir-Mendler v. United States, supra*, 721 F.2d at 683. Indeed, it is difficult to conceive of a situation in which a Secretary of State would do so."

5. Do you agree with the Second Circuit if human rights law (based in treaties and/or customary international law) is at stake as opposed to mere comity or political consider-

ations? *See generally* RESTATEMENT §§ 475, Comm. g, 476, Comm. h, 711, Reporters' Note 7. Under international law, can the United States knowingly or foreseeably subject a person to human rights violations? Should that person have a right to an effective remedy in U.S. courts, as required by international human rights law? If not, how can the United States comply with human rights provisions of the U.N. Charter (which are evidenced and defined by authoritative human rights instruments such as the Universal Declaration (article 8 of which provides the express right to an effective remedy in domestic tribunals), *see, e.g., Filartiga v. Pena-Irala,* 630 F.2d 876, 882 (2d Cir. 1980); J. PAUST, INTERNATIONAL LAW AS LAW OF THE UNITED STATES 224-29 (2 ed. 2003)), or other human rights treaties? In view of Article 103 of the Charter, obligations under the Charter prevail over any other inconsistent international agreements, such as an extradition treaty.

6. During the process of giving its advice and consent to ratification of the U.S.-U.K. Supplementary Extradition Treaty, the U.S. Senate amended the Treaty by adding Article 3, which in effect avoids non-inquiry in cases dealing with IRA terrorism:

Article 3

(a) Notwithstanding any other provision of this Supplementary Treaty, extradition shall not occur if the person sought establishes to the satisfaction of the competent judicial authority by a preponderance of the evidence that the request for extradition has in fact been made with a view to try or punish him on account of his race, religion, nationality, or political opinions, or that he would, if surrendered, be prejudiced at his trial or punished, detained or restricted in his personal liberty by reason of his race, religion, nationality, or political opinions.

(b) In the United States, the competent judicial authority shall only consider the defense to extradition set forth in paragraph (a) for offenses listed in Article 1 of this Supplementary Treaty. A finding under paragraph (a) shall be immediately appealable by either party to the United States district court, or court of appeals, as appropriate. The appeal shall receive expedited consideration at every stage. The time for filing a notice of appeal shall be 30 days from the date of the filing of the decision. In all other respects, the applicable provisions of the Federal rules of Appellate Procedure or Civil Procedure, as appropriate, shall govern the appeals process.

The First Circuit has characterized Article 3 as a compromise "placing most violent crimes beyond the political offense exception's reach but adding certain novel safeguards for the protection of potential extraditees." *In re Extradition of Howard,* 996 F.2d 1320, 1324 (1st Cir. 1993). Are these "novel" safeguards? Consider United Nations Charter, arts. 55(c), 56, 103; Universal Declaration of Human Rights, arts. 2, 8–10; 1966 Covenant on Civil and Political Rights, arts. 2, 9, 26; Convention Relating to the Status of Refugees, arts. 3, 4, 16, 32, 33—*but see id.* art. 1 F (such treaty rights not applicable re: a war crime, crime against humanity, "serious non-political crime", acts contrary to the purposes and principles of the U.N. Charter); RESTATEMENT §§ 475, Comm. g, 476, Comm. h, 711, Reporters' Note 7.

In light of the principles underlying the rule of non-inquiry, in *United States v. Smyth,* 61 F.3d 711 (9th Cir. 1995), the Ninth Circuit held that Article 3 must be interpreted with respect to likely treatment of the accused:

" ... the district court erred in relying extensively upon evidence of the general discriminatory effects of the Diplock system upon Catholics and suspected Republican sympathizers. That evidence does not relate to the treatment Smyth is likely to receive as a consequence of extradition, as required under Article 3(a)....

> Article 3(a) does not permit denial of extradition on the basis of an inquiry into the general political conditions extant in Northern Ireland. The history of the provision shows that it requires an individualized inquiry."

For a discussion of this issue, *see, e.g.*, Valerie Epps, Note, 90 Am. J. Int'l L. 296 (1996) (considering non-inquiry to be traditional and the U.S.-U.K. Supplementary Treaty to alter non-inquiry—but not addressing human rights claims or other treaties); Michael P. Scharf, *Foreign Courts on Trial: Why U.S. Courts Should Avoid Applying the Inquiry Provision of the Supplementary U.S.-U.K. Extradition Treaty*, 25 Stan. J. Int'l L. 257 (1989). Do you agree with the Ninth Circuit?

7. In *Munaf v. Geren*, 553 U.S. 674 (2008), which involved the transfer of prisoners from U.S. military custody in Iraq to Iraqi custody, the Court applied the rule against inquiry on the basis that the judiciary should not sit in judgment of executive determinations concerning future treatment. According to the Court, to do so would improperly "pass judgment on foreign justice systems and undermine the Government's ability to speak with one voice in this area." *Munaf*, 553 U.S. at 701. The Court stated that a limited humanitarian exception would apply when transferring prisoners from military custody, explaining that "this is not a more extreme case in which the Executive has determined that a detainee is likely to be tortured but decides to transfer him anyway." *Munaf*, 553 U.S. at 702. Arguably, the humanitarian exception should be applicable even more so in extradition cases than in military transfer cases, since the former have diminished concerns about foreign policy and military/national security concerns. *Cf. Kiyemba v. Obama*, 561 F.3d 509, 518, n.3 (D.C. Cir. 2009) (Kavanaugh, J., concurring) ("After *Munaf*, courts in extradition cases presumably may require—but must defer to—an express executive declaration that the transfer is not likely to result in torture."). Is this approach consistent with the fact that courts determine what the law requires, including what international law requires? Recall, for example, Article 3(1) of the Convention Against Torture. Do you suspect that Judge Kavanaugh is biased in this regard, since he was a lawyer in the White House during President George W. Bush's admitted "program" of unlawful secret detention and interrogation that had also involved the unlawful transfer of non-prisoners of war our of occupied territory for unlawful forms of interrogation by the CIA or members of foreign governments? See also Articles 49 and 147 of the Geneva Civilian Convention, in the Documents Supplement. Do courts have a responsibility to assure that the Executive does not violate laws of war and human rights laws that are binding on the United States and its nationals? How can courts do so if they follow a rule of non-inquiry?

Can a case be made for a more flexible application of the rule against non-inquiry and a narrower and more explicitly functional approach to serve the goals of the rule? *See, e.g.*, John T. Parry, *International Extradition, The Rule of Non-Inquiry, and the Problem of Sovereignty*, 90 Boston U.L. Rev. 1973, 1976 (2010). Doesn't the fact that courts inquire about the allegations of unfair trial, conditions of detention, and so forth mean that once the case with the right facts comes before them, courts will overlook the rule of non-inquiry?

8. On April 10, 2012, the European Court of Human Rights (ECHR) ruled that Britain can extradite five suspects to the United States to face terrorism charges. The individuals had challenged the extradition by claiming that life imprisonment in a U.S. maximum security facility amounted to a violation of their human rights. The conditions in U.S. prisons, according to the ECHR, did not constitute inhumane or degrading treatment. The individuals had been accused of a variety of terrorist acts, including kidnapping and the 1998 bombing of the U.S. embassy in Kenya. *Case of Babar Ahmad and Others v. United Kingdom*, European Court of Human Rights, Apr.

10, 2012. Significantly, the Court took evidence on the condition of detention at ADX Florence, a super-max prison, especially regarding solitary confinement, restrictions on recreation and outdoor exercise in prison, and detention and mental health may violate the prohibition against inhuman and degrading treatment, the length of sentences, and whether they violated the prohibition against inhuman and degrading treatment. The opinion illustrates that, notwithstanding the rule against non-inquiry, courts, (especially international human courts (such as the European Court of Human Rights), do scrutinize the criminal, detention, and penal practices of sovereign states in the context of extradition requests, but will inquire. Otherwise, would courts be complicit in foreseeable deprivations of human rights where there is evident a "real risk" of such deprivations?

Section 2
Rendition

Introduction

Rendition can involve acceptable conduct outside an extradition process or conduct that is violative of legal precepts or highly suspect. For example, deportation of an alien accused can be considered permissible or impermissible depending on various legal policies at stake and circumstances involved. *See generally* RESTATEMENT § 475, Reporters' Note 6; 74 PROC., AM. SOC. INT'L L. 274–89 (1980) (remarks of Evans, Kenney, Gordon and Editors Bassiouni and Zagaris).

A. By International Agreement

1. Commonwealth Countries

The surrender of fugitives to and from Commonwealth countries is called rendition and is governed by the Fugitive Offenders Act.[5] Under this legislation there is no list of extraditable offences, no provisions on double criminality or specialty, and no exemptions for political offenders. Why should there be differences such as these between Commonwealth rendition and non-Commonwealth extradition? The Law Reform Commission in Working Paper 37, entitled Extraterritorial Jurisdiction (1984), stated:

> While we cannot, in the course of this general study on jurisdiction, do more than scratch the surface of the large and complex subjects of extradition and rendition, we have seen enough to convince us of the need to modernize our statutes concerning these subjects. However, before that can be done, the federal Government will have to seek answers to questions such as: Should "political offence" be defined in legislation? Does Canada need two Acts? Would not one suffice? Is there any longer a need to differentiate between "extradition" and "rendition?" Should depositions from other countries admitted in evidence at extradition hearings in Canada be subject to the hearsay rule or be subject to their deponents being cross-examined?

---

5. R.S.C. 1985, c. F-32. See P. O'Higgins, *Extradition Within the Commonwealth*, 9 INT'L & COMP. L.Q. 486 (1960).

R. v. Taylor

June 29, 1988 (Ontario Provisional Ct.—Crim. Div.) (unreported)

Scullion, J.

This is an application by the accused, William Charles Taylor, for declaration holding that the *Fugitive Offenders Act* has no force or effect to the extent necessary to protect the integrity of the accused's rights and freedoms under the *Charter of Rights and Freedoms* in that the *Fugitive Offenders Act* breaches his rights under s. 6, 7, and 15 of the *Charter of Rights and Freedoms.*

On October 13th, 1987, an information was sworn in Great Britain against William Charles Taylor, accusing him of the following British offence: that he on divers days between the 1st of October, 1986, and the 27th of December, 1986, conspired with Albert Watt and Trevor Cubbon and others to have in the possession of the said Trevor Cubbon in England firearms and ammunition with intent to enable another person by means thereof to endanger life, contrary to s. 1 of the Criminal Law Act, 1977.

A warrant for Taylor's arrest was issued on the same day out of the Liverpool Magistrate's Court to arrest Taylor in Canada.

The said warrant was sent to this country and endorsed by a judge of the Supreme Court of Ontario on the 2nd of February, 1988, pursuant to the provisions of s. 8 of the *Fugitive Offenders Act* (R.S.C., 1970, F-32).

Taylor was thereafter arrested pursuant to the endorsed warrant and brought before this Court and remanded on bail pending a hearing and production of sufficient evidence to justify committal to prison (under s. 12 of the *Fugitive Offenders Act*) to await the further decision of the Governor General (under s. 15 of the *Fugitive Offenders Act*) as to whether or not he should be surrendered to Great Britain and be there dealt with according to law.

Taylor has now brought an application requesting this Court to make an order that the *Fugitive Offenders Act* or parts thereof be declared of no force or effect to the extent necessary to protect the integrity of Taylor's rights and freedoms under the Charter and that the rendition proceedings be stayed or quashed....

The accused raised the following questions: (1) Is the *Fugitive Offenders Act* or parts thereof inconsistent with the provisions of the *Charter* and, therefore, of no force and effect by reason of the fact that

(a) Nothing in the *Fugitive Offenders Act* precludes a receiving country from trying the fugitive for other offences. Section 40 of the *Extradition Act*, in essence, provides that there shall be no extradition of a person from Canada unless assurance is given to Canada that person will not be tried for any other offence.

(b) It is not an essential pre-condition to the operation of the *Fugitives Offenders Act* that the foreign offence alleged need to be an offence under Canadian law. In fact, s. 4 of the *Fugitive Offenders Act* explicitly provides that the foreign offence need not be an offence under Canadian law. There is a requirement under the *Extradition Act* and the case law under the Act that the foreign offence be an offence under Canadian law.

(c) Rendition is sought of Taylor on a foreign charge substantially similar to Canadian criminal offences alleged against him. The *Fugitive Offenders Act* allows for the receipt into evidence of affidavits upon which there can be no cross-examination.

In dealing with this matter, the following sections of the *Charter*, the *Extradition Act* and the *Fugitive Offenders Act* apply: [ss. 6(1), s. 7, 11(g)–(i) & s. 15(1) of the *Charter*; ss. 33 & 40 of the *Extradition Act*; and ss. 4, 12 & 17 of *The Fugitive Offenders Act*]

It is common ground that extradition under the *Extradition Act* and rendition under the *Fugitive Offenders Act* are parallel proceedings virtually functionally identical. However, Taylor argues that because the *Fugitive Offenders Act* does not have similar sections to s. 33 and s. 40 of the *Extradition Act*, then his rights granted under the *Charter* have been breached.

Similarly, the double criminality rule embodied in s. 4 of the *Fugitive Offenders Act* contrasts to the double criminality rule developed under the *Extradition Act*, which provides that a person is not extraditable unless the impugned conduct is criminal under Canadian and foreign law (regardless of whether the elements of the extradition crime must be identical in both states, see re Cohen (1904), 8 C.C.C. 251, S.C.C.; the *State of Washington* v. *Johnson*, an unreported decision of the Supreme Court of Canada, released February, 1988.)....

A reading of these authorities and an analysis of both the *Extradition Act* and the *Fugitive Offenders Act* does not lead me to believe that there has been a breach of the accused's rights under the *Charter* so fundamental as to cause me to declare the Act or parts thereof of no force and effect under s. 52 of the *Charter*. I am not convinced that the principle of speciality, that is, a fugitive may not be tried in the requesting state for an offence other than the one for which rendition was made is a fundamental right, as found in s. 6 of the *Charter*, nor by s. 7 of the *Charter* which guarantees every person's right to life, liberty and security of a person and the right not to be deprived thereof except in accordance with the principles of fundamental justice.

Although there is no specific provisions in the *Fugitive Offenders Act* (as there are in the *Extradition Act*, see s. 40 of that Act), to ensure that the principle of speciality will be respected by the requesting commonwealth country, there is a unique provision for the Court to make an order on an ad hoc basis if the Court deems just. This would permit the making of an order that a particular commonwealth country should provide assurances to Canada before surrender is made they will not try a particular fugitive for an offence other than the offence for which he is surrendered. It must be noted that in the case of Great Britain, such an order will not be necessary because under s. 14(2) of the *Fugitive Offenders Act* (1967), its courts are precluded from trying an accused who is surrendered to Great Britain and being tried for an offence other than the offence or offences for which he was surrendered. (see LaForest *Extradition to and from Canada. supra*, 225)

I am of the view that rendition of a fugitive, per se, does not deny his substantive rights to life, liberty and security of person guaranteed by s. 7 of the *Charter* nor does it constitute an abuse of process or otherwise breach a fugitive's procedural rights in a fundamentally unjust manner. (see *Mellino, supra*, 347; *Schmidt, supra*, 217–18)

The principle of double criminality evolved out of the recognized need to safeguard a fugitive's rights before extraditing him to a country where the laws and judicial system were fundamentally different from those of the requesting country and when surrendering him to a separate and distinctly foreign sovereign. However, our law evolved out of the common law of England, and the commonwealth members share a great deal in that common legal and political heritage. Amongst those shared characteristics are the relationship between legislative, executive and judicial branch of government, the adversarial system of criminal justice and procedure, the rules of evidence, prerogative writs including the writs of *habeas corpus, et cetera*, all of which is common ground that constitutes a basis for a measure of cooperation as to the rendering of fugitive criminals. That is not necessarily the case under the *Extradition Act*.

I am, therefore, satisfied that there has been no breach of the accused's rights under the *Charter*. However, if I should be wrong and there is a breach of the sections of the *Charter* enumerated by the accused, I must proceed to s. 1 of the *Charter*....

Keeping in mind the test set out by the Supreme Court of Canada in *R. v. Oakes, supra,* I am not satisfied that the need for rendition of persons allegedly committing crimes in one of the commonwealth countries renders the *Fugitive Offenders Act* unreasonable. As it was said in *R. v. Harrison*, (1918) 29 C.C.C. 420:

> "It is quite obvious that some additional care ought to be taken in the case of extraditing persons to foreign countries more than in facilitating criminal proceedings in the various parts of the Empire to which alone the *Fugitive Offenders Act* applies."

Again, in *Mellino, supra,* at p. 349:

> "Consequently, Parliament has felt free to expressly authorize the Courts not only to review on these grounds [s. 17] but to impose greater evidentiary, demands on those seeking surrender [under the Fugitive Offenders Act].
>
> These tasks, I might add, would generally be easier to perform than it would be at an extradition hearing because Commonwealth countries are heirs to the British criminal justice system."

I am satisfied that the protections afforded under s. 12 and 17 of the *Fugitive Offenders Act* provide broad and effective safeguards against any arbitrary removal of Her Majesty's fugitives from Canada and would hold that the Act is not unreasonable and can be demonstrably justified in a free and democratic society. Therefore, the application is refused.

Notes and Questions

1. Note that the United Kingdom amended its legislation in 1967. See Fugitive Offenders Act 1967, c. 68. This provides for a political offence exception, specialty and the other procedural safeguards known to extradition. Other Commonwealth countries have also amended their relevant statutes. Why has Canada not done so yet?

2. Note also that the Commonwealth Scheme for Rendition adopted in 1990 at a Commonwealth Conference, forms the basis for domestic rendition legislation, and provides for a range of safeguards that is as comprehensive or more so than most extradition arrangements.

2. Others

[see Statute for the International Criminal Tribunal for the Former Yugoslavia, Article 29, in the Documents Supplement]

Notes and Questions

1. In the United States, if an international agreement is required to "extradite" an accused (*see, e.g., Valentine v. United States ex rel. Neidecker,* 299 U.S. 5 (1936)), consider the effect of multilateral treaties like the 1979 International Convention Against the Taking of Hostages, art. 10(2) (re: substitute status), in Chapter Eleven, Section 4. See also

Report of the Secretary-General Pursuant to Paragraph 2 of Security Council Resolution 808 (1993), paras. 125–127, in Chapter Six, Section 9.

2. Should an accused have a right to seek a change of "venue" (while seeking a fair trial) by rendition to an international tribunal? What legal basis would exist to support such a defense claim? Could Article 29 of the Statute for the ICT for the Former Yugoslavia allow the Tribunal to play a role with respect to such claims?

3. Will some nation-states have to change their domestic laws? See Karin Oellers-Frahm, *Cooperation: The Indispensable Prerequisite to the Efficiency of International Criminal Tribunals,* 89 Proc., Am. Soc. Int'l L. 304 (1995).

B. Deportation as Disguised Extradition

Ruiz Massieu v. Reno
915 F. Supp. 681 (D.N.J. 1996)

Barry, J.

Plaintiff, Mario Ruiz Massieu, seeks a permanent injunction enjoining the deportation proceeding instituted against him pursuant to 8 U.S.C. § 1251(a)(4)(C)(i) and a declaration that the statute, which has not previously been construed in any reported judicial opinion, is unconstitutional. That statute, by its express terms, confers upon a single individual, the Secretary of State, the unfettered and unreviewable discretion to deport any alien lawfully within the United States, not for identified reasons relating to his or conduct in the United States or elsewhere but, rather, because that person's mere presence here would impact in some unexplained way on the foreign policy interests of the United States. Thus, the statute represents a breathtaking departure both from well established legislative precedent which commands deportation based on adjudications of defined impermissible conduct by the alien in the United States, and from well established precedent with respect to extradition which commands extradition based on adjudications of probable cause to believe that the alien has engaged in defined impermissible conduct elsewhere.

Make no mistake about it. This case is about the Constitution of the United States and the panoply of protections that document provides to the citizens of this country and those non-citizens who are here legally and, thus, here as our guests. And make no mistake about this: Mr. Ruiz Massieu entered this country legally and is not alleged to have committed any act within this country which requires his deportation. Nor, on the state of this record, can it be said that there exists probable cause to believe that Mr. Ruiz Massieu has committed any act outside of this country which warrants his extradition, for the government has failed in four separate proceedings before two Magistrate Judges to establish probable cause. Deportation of Mr. Ruiz Massieu is sought merely because he is here and the Secretary of State and Mexico have decided that he should go back.

The issue before the court is not whether plaintiff has the right to remain in this country beyond the period for which he was lawfully admitted; indeed, as a "non-immigrant visitor" he had only a limited right to remain here but the right to then go on his way to wherever he wished to go. The issue, rather, is whether an alien who is in this country legally can, merely because he is here, have his liberty restrained and be forcibly removed to a specific country in the unfettered discretion of the Secretary of State and without any meaningful opportunity to be heard. The answer is a ringing "no"....

[From March through December of 1995, the Government tried four times, each unsuccessfully, to extradite Ruiz Massiue]

With that, the government seemingly accepted defeat as to Mr. Ruiz Massieu's extraditability. It was then, however, that this case took a turn toward the truly Kafkaesque. On December 22, 1995, immediately after Magistrate Judge Chesler issued his opinion, Mr. Ruiz Massieu was taken into custody by the Immigration and Naturalization Service ("the INS") pursuant to a previously unserved and unannounced detainer dated September 29, 1995. In addition, he was served with an INS Order to Show Cause and Notice of Hearing. The notice advised Mr. Ruiz Massieu that he was ordered to show cause as to why he should not be deported because, the Secretary of State has made a determination that, pursuant to Section 241(a)(4)(C) of the Immigration and Nationality [sic] Act, 8 U.S.C. §1251(a)(4)(C), there is reasonable ground to believe your presence or activities in the United States would have potentially serious adverse foreign policy consequences for the United States ... No further explanation of the ground for Mr. Ruiz Massieu's alleged deportability was tendered.

Sometime after notice was served on Mr. Ruiz Massieu, the INS produced an October 2, 1995 letter addressed to Attorney General Janet Reno from Secretary of State Warren Christopher. [see attachment at end of case] The letter urged the Attorney General to effect Mr. Ruiz Massieu's "expeditious deportation" "to Mexico" based on the Secretary's conclusion that Mr. Ruiz Massieu's presence in the United States will have potentially serious adverse foreign policy consequences for the United States. *Id.* The letter referenced the "serious allegations" that are pending in Mexico against Mr. Ruiz Massieu and the recent strides that both governments have taken in "our ability to cooperate and confront criminality on both sides of the border." *Id.* At bottom, the Secretary's request was premised on the proposition that "our inability to return to Mexico Mr. Ruiz Massieu—a case the Mexican Presidency has told us is of the highest importance—would jeopardize our ability to work with Mexico on law enforcement matters. It might also cast a potentially chilling effect on other issues our two governments are addressing." *Id.*

The relevant deportation statute, §241(a)(4)(C)(i) of the Immigration and Naturalization Act ("INA"), provides simply that "an alien whose presence or activities in the United States the Secretary of State has reasonable ground to believe would have potentially serious adverse foreign policy consequences for the United States is deportable". 8 U.S.C. §1251(a)(4)(C)(i). Because an indication of the Secretary of State's belief is all that the statute by its terms requires, the October 2, 1995 letter, alone, comprised (and remains) the universe of evidence that the INS has offered to support its charge of Mr. Ruiz Massieu's deportability. A master calendar proceeding, the first stage of deportation hearings held pursuant to section 242 of the INA, was scheduled to begin on January 19, 1996. On January 17, 1996, however, Mr. Ruiz Massieu filed a complaint in this court requesting that the deportation proceedings be preliminarily and permanently enjoined, and that section 241(a)(4)(C) of the INA be declared unconstitutional.

The complaint contains three core constitutional claims: (1) the deportation proceeding evidences selective enforcement in retaliation for Mr. Ruiz Massieu's exercise of his First Amendment right to criticize the Mexican political system; (2) the deportation proceeding represents a "de facto" extradition and is an attempt to overrule, albeit indirectly, four federal court decisions, in violation of the separation of powers; and (3) section 241(a)(4)(C)(i) of the INA is unconstitutionally vague, in violation of the due process clause of the Fifth Amendment. The United States Department of Justice, on behalf of all defendants, has responded that section 241(a)(4)(C)(i) withstands constitutional attack both facially and as applied to Mr. Ruiz Massieu. In addition, it has taken the position that this court lacks jurisdiction to hear the case on the grounds that (1) what is at issue is a nonjusticiable political question; (2) Mr. Ruiz Massieu has failed to exhaust his administrative remedies under the INA; and (3) the doctrine of constitutional avoidance counsels against this court reaching the ultimate issues presented in Mr. Ruiz Massieu's complaint....

[The court determined that the district court has jurisdiction to hear plaintiff's due process claims, administrative exhaustion is not required, and the claims are ripe. Next, it address the political question claim of the Government]

The government contends that the dispute at issue is one over the foreign policy of the United States and, therefore, presents a nonjusticiable political question. According to the government, the wisdom of the Secretary's and the Attorney General's policy determinations cannot be reviewed by this or any other court. With the "wisdom" assertion, this court could not agree more. Neither the legislature's vast power over deportation issues, nor the executive department's exclusive control over matters of foreign policy, however, are enough to transform this dispute into a nonjusticiable political question.

Given the overtones of international diplomacy that infuse this case, it would not be unreasonable to think of this controversy in political terms. As the Supreme Court has emphatically stated, however, the presence of constitutional issues with significant political overtones does not automatically invoke the political question doctrine. Resolution of litigation challenging the constitutional authority of one of the three branches cannot be evaded by courts because the issues have political implications in the sense urged by [the government]. *INS v. Chadha*, 462 U.S. 919, 942–43 ... (1983). What is at issue in this case is not review of a foreign policy determination but, rather, the constitutionality of an act of Congress and the decision of the executive to enforce that act against an individual within this nation's borders, thus declaring that individual expendable. "No policy underlying the political question doctrine suggests that Congress or the Executive, or both acting in concert and in compliance with Art. I, can decide the constitutionality of a statute; that is a decision for the courts." *Id.* at 941–42. *See also Shahla v. INS*, 749 F.2d 561, 563 n.2 (9th Cir. 1984) (recognizing that while "the judicial branch must show deference to the political branches of government in foreign policy matters[,] nevertheless, we believe that the judicial branch may examine whether the political branches have used a foreign policy crisis as an excuse for treating aliens arbitrarily"). In short, this court finds the resolution of this constitutional controversy to be well within the role traditionally reserved for the judiciary....

This court now turns its attention to the substance of the challenge before it. In terms of due process, plaintiff attacks § 241(a)(4)(C)(i) of the INA on two distinct, though related, grounds. The first contention is that the statute is void for vagueness. The second is that, by its terms, the statute denies plaintiff, and any alien deported thereunder, a meaningful opportunity to be heard before being subjected to the severe deprivation of liberty that is deportation. Additionally, the court has sua sponte raised the issue of whether the statute is so devoid of standards that it represents an unconstitutional delegation of legislative power to the executive....

[The court determined that governmental power over aliens "is circumscribed by the constitutional constraints imposed on the exercise of all governmental authority." Next, it found the statute void for vagueness while noting:]

"Foreign policy" cannot serve as the talisman behind which Congress may abdicate its responsibility to pass only sufficiently clear and definite laws when those laws may be enforced against the individual. *See Shahla v. INS*, 749 F.2d 561, 563 n.2 (9th Cir. 1984) ("the judicial branch may examine whether the political branches have used a foreign policy crisis as an excuse for treating aliens arbitrarily"). Although the executive's discretionary authority over foreign affairs is well established, Congress cannot empower the executive to employ that authority against the individual except through constitutional means. See *Valentine v. United States ex rel. Neidecker*, 299 U.S. 5, 9 ... ("the Constitution creates no executive prerogative to dispose of the liberty of the individual. Proceedings against him must be authorized by law. There is no executive discretion to surrender him to a foreign government, unless that discretion is governed by law"). If the Constitution was adopted to protect individuals against anything, it was the abuses made possible through just this type of unbounded executive authority.

There can be no more graphic illustration of the exercise of unbounded executive authority than that seen in this case. In this case, the Secretary has determined that plaintiff is expendable—for "foreign policy" reasons which the Secretary need neither explicate nor defend—merely because Mexico wants plaintiff back. Had plaintiff overstayed his welcome, had he entered this country illegally, or had he committed a crime while here— all clearly defined grounds for deportation—he would be entitled to a host of protections, not the least of which would be notice of the prohibited conduct and a meaningful opportunity to be heard. Similarly, if it were believed that plaintiff had committed a crime in Mexico, his extradition would, presumably, have again been sought and, again, there would be no problem of vagueness and he would be entitled to substantial protections. Extradition, after all, is the time-tested mechanism used by this country and other civilized countries to send a criminal back, a mechanism that the government has unsuccessfully utilized vis-a-vis plaintiff in four separate court proceedings. § 241(a)(4)(C)(i) does an end run around and, indeed, subverts the extradition framework, which would never permit the return of an alien merely because he is considered undesirable by his government....

[Next, the court found that there was a denial of an opportunity to be heard]

In the final analysis, this court is convinced that a balancing of the appropriate factors tips well in plaintiff's favor. Absent a meaningful opportunity to be heard, the Secretary of State's unreviewable and concededly "unfettered discretion" to deprive an alien, who lawfully entered this country, of his or her liberty to the extent exemplified by this case is, in this court's view, unconstitutional. Accordingly, this court now holds that § 241(a)(4)(C)(i) of the INA, 8 U.S.C. § 1251(a)(4)(C)(i) is unconstitutional both on its face and as applied....

[The court also found that there was an unconstitutional delegation of legislative power to the Executive, and concluded:]

For the reasons stated above, this court now finds that § 241(a)(4)(C)(i) of the INA is unconstitutional. Accordingly, the deportation proceedings instituted against plaintiff, pursuant thereto, will be permanently enjoined.

ATTACHMENT

THE SECRETARY OF STATE

WASHINGTON

October 2, 1995

Dear Madam Attorney General:

I am writing to inform you that, pursuant to Section 241(a)(4)(C) of the Immigration and Nationality Act, 8 U.S.C. section 1251(a)(4)(C), I have concluded that the presence or Mario Ruiz Massieu in the United States would have potentially serious foreign policy consequences for the United States. Accordingly, I request that you take all steps possible, consistent with the Immigration and Nationality Act and other relevant law, to effect his deportation to Mexico.

My decision to invoke INA section 241(a)(4)(C) with respect to Mr. Ruiz Massieu is based on the following considerations: As you are well aware, the United States and Mexico have made tremendous progress in the past five years in strengthening one of our most important and vital bilateral relationships. The range of issues that unite our two nations—from combatting international drug trafficking, to addressing vexing problems of legal and illegal migration, to fortifying trade and investment in one of the world's largest and fastest growing markets—is complex and varied.

One aspect of our relationship that has received the utmost attention from both governments is our ability to cooperate to confront criminality on both sides of the border. We have seen successes on this front, but we continue to seek enhanced cooperation. With easy transit between the United States and Mexico and extensive and ever-increasing ties, this is an area of vital importance to the United States. Our inability to return to Mexico Mr. Ruiz Massieu—a case the Mexican presidency has told us is of the highest importance—would jeopardize our ability to work with Mexico on law enforcement matters. It might also cast a potentially chilling effect on other issues our two governments are addressing.

Furthermore, the case in question involves charges against the former second ranking law enforcement authority in Mexico and a man connected through his circle of family and friends to the center of power in Mexican politics. Serious allegations against such a high former official are unprecedented in modern Mexico. The case against Mr. Ruiz Massieu and the arrest and trial for related crimes of Mr. Raul Salinas, brother of the former President, were the dramatic and unequivocal signs of the determination of President Zedillo and his Attorney General to break the so-called "culture of impunity" that long protected corrupt politicians, officials and other powerful elite from being held accountable for their actions and crimes. President Zedillo's anti-corruption drive has resonated throughout Mexico and continues to receive strong support from the Mexican people.

The U.S. Government has consistently urged Mexico to take the steps towards reform in its justice system that President Zedillo is so forcefully pursuing. The ability to prosecute Mr. Ruiz Massieu and other powerful individuals in Mexico for the crimes of which they are accused is key to the success of Zedillo's pledge to transform totally the judicial and law enforcement system and to rid Mexico of corruption and abuse of power. Should the U.S. Government not return Mr. Ruiz Massieu to Mexico, our support of such reforms would be seen as hollow and self-serving and would be a major setback for President Zedillo and our combined efforts to chart a new and effective course of U.S.-Mexican relations.

Our efforts to remove Mr. Ruiz Massieu from the United States should be directed at achieving his direct return to Mexico. When apprehended in New Jersey, Mr. Ruiz Massieu was attempting to depart the United States just days after being called for questioning in Mexico with regard to the crimes with which he was subsequently charged. If our efforts to remove him from the United States result in his ability to depart to a destination other than Mexico, the U.S. Government will almost certainly be viewed by Mexican officials and the Mexican public as not only permitting, but also aiding his successful escape front justice.

Accordingly, I have concluded that Mr. Ruiz Massieu's presence in the United States would have potentially serious adverse foreign policy consequences for the United States, as provided for in INA Section 241(a)(4)(C). I request that you take all reasonable efforts to ensure Mr. Ruiz Massieu's expeditious deportation from the United States. Further, in light of the Mexican Government's interest in having Mr. Ruiz Massieu returned to Mexico, I also request that you do everything possible, consistent with the Immigration and Nationality Act, to effect his deportation to Mexico.

Sincerely,

Warren Christopher

Section 3
Luring (Trickery)

Regular rendition of a person, usually by extradition, occurs when an individual is surrendered by a requested country to a requesting state. Rendition is irregular when individuals are taken from one country to another as a criminal suspect against their free will and without the consent of the nation from which they were taken. Governments use deceit, fraud and tricks to lure individuals from the country of their residence to a location where there is jurisdiction to arrest the suspects. Unlike abduction by force, weapons are not used to get the suspect to the location where the arrest will occur. However, whether tricks can overbear the will of an individual just as much as a gun is a controversial issue. The United States has consistently upheld the legitimacy of the practice of luring, contrary to the beliefs of many other nations throughout the international community.

A. The United States Position on Luring: *Yunis* and *Mala Captus Bene Detentus*

The United States Government has continued to use "luring" as an alternative to extradition, and the U.S. court system has upheld the constitutionality of the practice. The United States has authorized law enforcement authorities to lure a defendant out of their homeland even when there is an existing extradition treaty with that nation.

United States v. Yunis
681 F. Supp. 909 (D.D.C. 1988), rev'd on other gds., *859 F.2d 953 (D.C. Cir. 1988)*

Defendant, Fawaz Yunis, a citizen of Lebanon, was lured out of his homeland, arrested in international waters off the coast of Cyprus, and forcibly brought to the United States to face charges of hostage taking and aircraft piracy. His counsel argues that the arresting officers failed to respect the defendant's constitutional rights when he was arrested and that they unlawfully secured inculpatory statements from him while he was being brought back to the United States. He has moved to dismiss the indictment on grounds that the circumstances surrounding the arrest were outrageous and violated defendant's due process rights. Counsel has also moved to suppress his client's inculpatory statements and written confession claiming that his rights were not voluntarily or knowingly waived....

Defendant's counsel has moved to dismiss the entire multi-count indictment on two grounds: first, the government's actions contravened its extradition treaty obligations with Lebanon and Cyprus, and second, the government used excessive and outrageous force when arresting defendant in violation of fifth amendment rights to due process. Both grounds present threshold questions of standing and jurisdiction: whether Yunis can assert violations of an extradition treaty absent objections or protests by either Lebanon or Cyprus, and whether the defendant, a nonresident alien, can invoke the protective cloak of our Constitution for actions committed beyond the territorial borders of the United States.

For the reasons set forth.... the Court concludes that individuals, alone, are not empowered to enforce extradition treaties. Therefore, it need not reach the issue whether the United States breached its treaty obligations. As to the fifth amendment claims, the Court determines that the Constitution applies abroad to aliens but that the government's actions did not rise to the level of "outrageousness" that "shocks the conscience" and warrants dismissal of the indictment....

Application of the Constitution to Foreign Aliens

Before the Court can determine whether the government's actions were so outrageous as to "shock the conscience" and violate defendant's due process rights, it must resolve the threshold inquiry: whether the constitutional restraints apply to governmental activity overseas. The Constitution is silent regarding its application overseas and the Supreme Court has never definitively resolved whether aliens are protected by the Constitution.[6]

Although the Supreme Court has never explicitly addressed whether the Constitution applies to aliens overseas, it has consistently reaffirmed the principle that our government is one of enumerated powers without authority to act beyond the limitations of the Constitution. This fundamental principle was heralded more than a century ago in *Ex parte Milligan*, 71 U.S. (4 Wall) 2 (1886). "The Constitution of the United States is a law for rulers and people, equally in war and in peace, and covers with the shield of its protection all classes of [persons], at all times, and under all circumstances." In other cases,

---

6. The most relevant Supreme Court decisions concerning the application of rights to overseas aliens are *Johnson v. Eisentrager*, 339 U.S. 763 (1950) and *Reid v. Covert*, 354 U.S. 1 (1957). In *Eisentrager*, American military authorities were involved in the arrest of criminals in China and their conviction and incarceration in Germany after World War II. Later, writs of habeas corpus were sought in American courts. In reflecting their application for relief, the Supreme Court wrote: "the Constitution does not confer a right of personal security or an immunity from military trial and punishment upon an alien enemy engaged in the hostile service of a government at war with the United States. *Id.* 339 U.S. at 785.

Some courts have interpreted *Eisentrager* broadly to prohibit any application of the Constitution overseas. Others have read the case more narrowly as denying constitutional rights to enemy aliens in occupied territories during a declared war.

Several years later, the Court ruled in a plurality opinion that citizens overseas enjoyed the full constitutional protections from acts of their government. *Reid v. Covert*, 354 U.S. 1 (1957) involved two women stationed with their husbands overseas military bases. Each killed her husband and was tried without a jury. The Court overturned the convictions holding that "the United States is entirely a creature of the Constitution. Its powers and authority have no other source. It can only act in accordance with all the limitations imposed by the Constitution." *Id.* at 5–6. Lower courts have interpreted *Reid* as holding that the reach of the Constitution does not stop at the border. Whenever the United States exercises its sovereignty outside the country, it must act in accordance with the limitations imposed by the Constitution. However, *Reid* involved U.S. citizens residing overseas. Since *Reid*, the Court has had no occasion to rule on the extra-territorial application of the Constitution to nonresident aliens. *See* Stephan, *Constitutional Limits on the Struggle against International Terrorism: Revisiting the Rights of Overseas Aliens*, 19 Conn. L. Rev. 831, 831–842 (1987).

the Supreme Court has held that the Constitution regulates and restricts the conduct of the federal government "whenever and wherever the sovereign power of that government is exerted." *Balzac v. Porto Rico*, 258 U.S. 298 (1922). Indeed, even in *United States v. Curtiss-Wright Export Corp.*, 299 U.S. 304 (1936), a case routinely cited for the proposition that executive powers are strongest in the realm of foreign affairs, the Court's opinion reads, "every ... government power, must be exercised in subordination to the applicable provisions of the Constitution." 299 U.S. at 320. Granting the United States unfettered powers to secure the arrest of a nonresident alien overseas runs directly contrary to the Court's theory of constituted powers. As Justice Louis Brandeis eloquently stated in *Olmstead v. United States*, 277 U.S. 438, 485 (1928) "To declare that in the administration of the criminal law the ends justify the means — to declare that the government may commit crimes in order to secure the conviction of a private criminal — would bring terrible retribution."

The majority of circuits have applied the Constitution extraterritorially and required the United States government to conform to constitutional proscriptions when acting overseas.[7] Similarly, *The Restatement (revised) of Foreign Relations Law* supports extending constitutional rights to aliens in certain cases.[8] Although our Court of Appeals has never explicitly embraced this trend,[9] this Court finds the majority view compelling and persuasive and concludes that the Constitution applies to circumscribe the activity of federal officials overseas.

Method of Arrest as a Violation of Defendant's Fifth Amendment Rights

Concluding that the Constitution extends to governmental activities overseas is only the starting point of the inquiry. The Court now turns to the fundamental question raised by defendant's motion: does the Constitution impose any restraints on the methods used to arrest a defendant and bring him within the jurisdiction of this Court.

---

7. *See, e.g., United States v. Pinto-Mejia*, 720 F.2d 248, 259, 261 (2d Cir. 1983); *United States v. Marino-Garcia*, 679 F.2d 1373, 1384 (11th Cir. 1982), *cert. denied*, 459 U.S. 1114, (1983); *United States v. Green*, 671 F.2d 46, 53 (1st Cir. 1982); *United States v. Williams*, 617 F.2d 1063, 1078 (5th Cir. 1980).

8. Notes to the RESTATEMENT provide that "although the matter has not been authoritatively adjudicated, at least some actions by the United States in respect of foreign nations outside the country are also subject to constitutional limitations." § 721, Comment m & Reporters' Note 16.

9. Indeed, the case law in this Circuit is quite murky. In a relatively early case, the Court explicitly refused to permit foreign aliens to raise constitutional objections. *Pauling v. McElroy*, 278 F.2d 252, 254 n. 3 (D.C. Cir.), *cert. denied*, 264 U.S. 835 (1960) (in dismissing a suit brought by overseas aliens to enjoin nuclear testing, the Court, held that overseas aliens have no standing to assert constitutional claims). In later cases, the Court appeared more receptive to granting aliens rights under the Constitution. *Dostal v. Haig*, 652 F.2d 173, 176 (D.C. Cir. 1981) (In rejecting challenge by Berlin citizens that Army violated their due process rights Court "accepted *arguendo* that the Bill of Rights is fully applicable to govern the conduct of U.S. officials in Berlin," but found no substantive violation); *Cardenas v. Smith*, 733 F.2d 909, 913 (D.C. Cir. 1984) (In conferring standing on a Colombian citizen objecting to the United States government's seizure of her Swiss bank account without any notice, the Court stated that "an injury endured abroad is not less of an injury for Article III standing purposes because it happened on foreign soil.").

However, in our Circuit's most recent treatment of the subject, it explicitly refused to rule on the application of the Bill of Rights to aliens overseas. In *Sanchez-Espinoza v. Reagan*, 770 F.2d 202, 208 (D.C. Cir. 1985), a case involving Nicaraguan citizens seeking compensation for injuries suffered at the hands of the United States supported Contradoros, the court wrote "[w]e do not reach the question whether the protections of the Constitution extend to noncitizens abroad." However, it ultimately refrained from exercising jurisdiction over the action under the political question doctrine. Neither aliens nor United States citizens were conferred standing to proceed with the case. Therefore, *Sanchez* can be interpreted as holding that an alien can not assert any greater rights under the Constitution than a United States citizen.

The Supreme Court in two decisions has developed well reasoned precedents that forcible abduction neither offends due process nor requires dismissal of an indictment. *Ker v. Illinois*, 119 U.S. 436 (1886) and *Frisbie v. Collins*, 342 U.S. 519 (1952). *Ker* involved a defendant who while residing in Peru was indicted for larceny in Illinois. He was forcibly abducted from Peru by a Pinkerton agent brought to Illinois, tried and convicted. *Frisbie* involved the forcible abduction—seizure, handcuffing and blackjacking—of a defendant from his home in Illinois to Michigan to stand trial for murder. The Court reasoned that "due process of law is satisfied when one present in court is convicted of a crime after having been fairly apprized of the charges against him and after trial in accordance with constitutional procedural safeguards. There is nothing in the Constitution that requires a court to permit a guilty person rightfully convicted to escape justice because he was brought to trial against his will." *Frisbie*, 342 U.S. at 522.

Despite intense criticism of the doctrine,[10] the Supreme Court has continued to reaffirm the *Ker-Frisbie* doctrine. *See Immigration & Naturalization Service v. Lopez-Mendoza*, 468 U.S. 1032 (1984); *United States v. Crews*, 445 U.S. 463, 474 (1980); *Stone v. Powell*, 428 U.S. 465 (1976); *Gerstein v. Pugh*, 420 U.S. 103, 119 (1975) ("Nor do we retreat from the established rule that illegal arrest or detention does not void a subsequent conviction.").

While defendant's counsel concedes that as a general rule, our jurisprudence has relied upon the safeguards of the system itself and has, on most occasions, turned a blind eye to the methods used to bring a person to Court, he nonetheless contends that this action falls into what is commonly referred to as the *Toscanino* exception, *United States v. Toscanino*, 500 F.2d 267 (2d Cir. 1974). There, the defendant also alleged that he was subjected to torture and abuse by United States officials. Reasoning that the government should not be given a carte blanche to bring defendants to the jurisdiction of the United States by torture and brutal force and then permitted to utilize the fruits of its own lawlessness, the Second Circuit ruled that a court in the name of due process is required to divest itself of jurisdiction "where it has been acquired as the result of the government's deliberate, unnecessary and unreasonable invasion of the accused's constitutional rights." *Toscanino*, 500 F.2d at 275.

The extensive torture suffered by the defendant in *Toscanino* is worthy of recitation to illustrate the benchmark for the type of outrageous conduct necessary to invoke the exception to *Ker-Frisbie* and warrant the radical remedy of dismissal. The government abducted defendant from Uruguay and subjected him to a series of torture: denial of sleep and nourishment for days at a time, forced walks for excessive hours accompanied by kicking and beating him when he could no longer stand, pinching his fingers with metal pliers, flushing alcohol into his eyes and nose and forcing other fluids up his anal passage, and finally, attaching electrodes to his extremities and genitals. 500 F.2d at 270. Even in face of that record, the trial court refused to dismiss the indictment, concluding that United States officials were not involved in that conduct. *United States v. Toscanino*, 398 F. Supp. 916 (E.D.N.Y. 1975).

Shortly after *Toscanino*, the Second Circuit stressed the narrowness of its holding and reaffirmed the vitality of the *Ker-Frisbee* doctrine. *United States v. ex rel. Lujan v. Gengler*, 510 F.2d 62 (2d Cir. 1975), *cert. denied*, 421 U.S. 1001 (1975). Although *Gengler* did not involve any allegations of torture—the defendant argued that federal officials lured him to neutral territory under fraudulent business pretenses—it stands for the proposition that

---

10. For an extensive list of articles criticizing the doctrine *see* M. BASSIOUNI, II INTERNATIONAL CRIMINAL LAW, Chapter 5, note 17 (1986 ed.).

absent "government conduct of a most shocking and outrageous character," dismissal is not warranted. *Id.* at 65. "Not every violation by prosecution or policy ... requires nullification of the indictment." *Id.* at 66.

Although most circuits have acknowledged the exception carved out by *Toscanino*, it is highly significant that *no* court has ever applied it to dismiss an indictment. They have uniformly treated *Toscanino* as a very narrow exception to *Ker-Frisbie*. See Shafer, *District Court Jurisdiction over Criminal Suspects Who were Abducted in Foreign Countries*, 64 A.L.R.Fed. 292.

Two distinct grounds have been relied upon in refusing to dismiss an indictment under the *Toscanino* exception: either courts conclude that the torturous activity did not rise to the level of outrageousness warranting dismissal, or conclude that United States officials were not directly involved in the torturous activity. In the first, the courts have used the allegations of torture in *Toscanino* as a threshold standard for outrageousness, and uniformly concluded that the government's conduct did not rise to that level of outrageousness, shocking the conscience and warranting dismissal. *See, U.S. v. Rosenthal*, 793 F.2d 1214, 1232 (11th Cir. 1986), *cert. denied*,—- U.S.—-, 107 S.Ct. 1377 (1987) (defendant abducted from Bahamas on narcotic charges, the court declined to adopt the *Toscanino* exception but even if applicable, found no evidence of conduct which shocked the conscience); *U.S. v. Darby*, 744 F.2d 1508 (11th Cir. 1986), *cert. denied*, 471 U.S. 1004 (1985) (Honduran citizen abducted from Honduras, driven at gunpoint to airport, and forced on plane for trial in United States; court held that defendant had not "alleged the sort of cruel, inhuman and outrageous treatment" to warrant dismissal); *U.S. v. Reed*, 639 F.2d 896 (2d Cir. 1981) (Bahamian defendant, residing in the Bahamas, deceitfully enticed by CIA agents to board a plane bound for Bimini; agents placed a cocked gun at his head and forced him to lie on aircraft floor for the duration of the flight and then twisted his arm as he exited plane; court found that use of revolver and threatening language not "gross mistreatment" warranting dismissal); *U.S. v. Cordero*, 668 F.2d 32 (1st Cir. 1981) (defendants arrested, abducted in Venezuela to face drug charges in Puerto Rico. In refusing to dismiss the indictment, the court concluded that although defendants were subjected to poor treatment, insulted and slapped when abducted and while in jail were poorly fed and forced to sleep on the floor, those conditions "are a far cry from deliberate torture warranting dismissal"). Several of the above cases involved serious allegations of torture and abuse. The fact that not *one* of the courts relied on *Toscanino* to dismiss the indictment highlights the extreme narrowness of that exception and underscores the force of the *Ker-Frisbie* doctrine.

In cases where defendants have urged the court to dismiss the indictment solely on the grounds that they were fraudulently lured to the United States, courts have uniformly upheld jurisdiction. *United States v. Wilson*, 732 F.2d 404, 411 (5th Cir.), *cert. denied*, 469 U.S. 1099 (1984). In *Wilson*, undercover agent persuaded defendant to leave his refuge in Libya. The court refused to dismiss the indictment concluding that "Wilson has simply been the victim of a nonviolent government trick ... any irregularity in a criminal defendant's apprehension will not vitiate proceedings against him." 721 F.2d. at 972.

In the second line of cases, where it was determined that the United States officials were not involved in the alleged brutality or torture, the courts saw no purpose in dismissing the indictment. *See United States v. Lopez*, 542 F.2d 283 (5th Cir. 1876) (United States agents played no role in alleged torture of defendant in Dominican Republic); *United States v. Lira*, 515 F.2d 68 (2nd Cir. 1975) (defendant charged with distribution of narcotics beaten and tortured with electrodes by Chilean police, no involvement by United States police). The purpose underlying the *Toscanino* rule is to deter police misconduct by barring the government from using the fruits of its deliberate lawlessness. When the United States is not involved in the torturous activity, no purpose would be served by dismissing the indictment.

In this action, there is no dispute that United States law enforcement officers were fully involved in the planning and execution of defendant's arrest. However, defendant has failed either to allege or to show any actions committed by these officers that meet the standard of outrageousness established by *Toscanino* and its progeny requiring this Court to divest itself of jurisdiction.

The record in this proceeding has been reviewed with care and the Court fails to find the type of cruel, inhumane and outrageous conduct that would warrant dismissal under *Toscanino*. That is not to say that the Court accepts the government's representations in its December 1, 1987 response to defendant's pretrial motion that Yunis "was treated with the greatest care and with due deference to whatever personal requests he made during the voyage from the Mediterranean to the United States." Even the government has admitted that "there may well have been in hindsight too much force brought upon Mr. Yunis' wrists" when he was forced down and thrown to the deck during the course of his arrest. Trans. of Motions Hearing, Dec. 23, 1987, at 38. Indeed, the two agents immediately involved believed that the amount of force and method used in effectuating the arrest were necessary to ensure that the defendant did not attempt to jump overboard.

Similarly, although the defendant may not have been given the best or even adequate medical care, the treatment provided was not so poor as to be "cruel and inhumane." The testimony of the three treating physicians, Drs. Braddock, Gore and Gabriel refuted the government's representations that the doctors remained at Yunis' "beckon call. [sic]" Trans. at 45 (Dec. 23, 1987). Indeed, despite the defendant's constant complaints concerning the condition of and the pain emitting from his fractured wrists, the orthopedist, Dr. Gore, did not examine Yunis until September 15, the third day into the naval voyage. When he conducted his initial examination of the defendant's wrists, he recommended ice treatment and elevation and at the motions hearing testified that in his judgment placing casts on the defendant's wrists without the use of x-ray would be "excessive and overkill." Tran. of Jan. 20, 1988 at 187.[11] Dr. Keith Gabriel, the physician who treated Yunis after he entered the United States, offered alternative advice. Given the defendant's symptoms and in the absence of x-ray facilities, he would have "at least offer[ed] the patient some type of immobilization, whether that might be a splint or a cast, or simply an adhesive wrapping, like an ace wrap." Trans. of test., Jan. 25, 1988, at 39. However, merely because the two doctors prescribed contrary treatment, does not transform Dr. Gore's at worst negligent diagnosis and prescription into malicious, inhumane conduct. Moreover, the defendant's nausea and sea sickness were certainly not the result of any deliberate actions by the government. Indeed, several of the FBI agents involved in the operation appeared to suffer from motion sickness.

Finally, even if the procedure employed in transporting the defendant by airplane from the Saratoga to the United States was extremely confining, it did not rise to the level of outrageousness that shocks the conscience. S.A. David Johnson, who was primarily responsible for the hostage rescue team, testified that it was necessary to tranquilize the defendant and place him in the Stokes later due to the size of the plane and the need to protect the aircraft and the personnel on board. Trans. of Johnson at 53.

Even if the Court were to accept each and every allegation of excessiveness made by the defendant, taken together, they simply do not rise to the deliberate torture and abuse al-

---

11. It is undisputed that there were no x-ray facilities on board the Butte.

leged in *Toscanino*. However, the defendant is not left without any relief from the government's allegedly illegal law enforcement practices. He is afforded all the procedural and substantive constitutional safeguards provided every criminal defendant facing trial.

Indeed, the discussion and resolution of defendant's motion to suppress, which follows, demonstrate the premise and significance of the *Ker-Frisbie* doctrine — that a defendant's rights to due process of law are satisfied by the protections afforded a defendant at trial.

Notes

1. On applicability of the U.S. Constitution abroad, *see also United States v. Tiede*, in Chapter Four, Section 8, and other portions of that section.

2. Courts have consistently upheld jurisdiction in cases where defendants move to dismiss their indictment based solely on the fact that they were lured to the United States. *See United States v. Reed*, 639 F.2d 896 (2d Cir. 1981) (upholding the constitutionality of Reed's arrest). Reed was enticed by Central Intelligence Agency agents to leave Bimini Island in the Bahamas. He was told that the private plane he boarded was destined for Nassau, not Florida. The court held that Reed's Fourth Amendment rights were not violated because a valid arrest warrant existed. There was also no due process violation or *Toscanino* exception because of a lack of brutal torture. *Reed*, 639 F.2d at 901.

In *United States v. Wilson*, 732 F.2d 404, 411 (5th Cir.), *cert. denied*, 469 U.S. 1099 (1984), an agent persuaded the defendant to leave Libya through deceit. The court refused to dismiss the indictment because Wilson was simply "the victim of a nonviolent government trick ... any irregularity in a criminal defendant's apprehension will not vitiate proceedings against him." *Yunis*, 681 F. Supp. at 919 (quoting *Wilson*, 721 F.2d at 972). Consequently, although United States agents were admittedly responsible for the planning and execution of Yunis' and Wilson's arrest, there was no extreme torture or abuse. Therefore, the arrest did not meet the standard of outrageousness required to fall within the *Toscanino* exception.

3. The United States has accepted the use of luring by its law enforcement officials to coerce a suspect to enter a locality where a valid arrest can occur. Under the *Ker-Frisbie* doctrine, such a practice is logically constitutional as it arrives at the same objective as forcible abduction, but by using tricks and not force. However, the practice of luring to bring a suspect into a different jurisdiction is not as readily accepted by other nations as it is by the United States.

B. International Consensus Against the Practice of Luring

1. State Viewpoints

Some nations are not in agreement with the United States that such irregular rendition is acceptable. States have often disapproved of luring as a means to bring a person into a jurisdiction and finds it as unacceptable as forcible abduction.

In the case of Mr. Kenneth Walker, a Canadian citizen, U.S. Customs officials utilized Barry Brokaw, a business associate of Walker's, to arrange a weapons deal with him. After many solicitations, Walker finally agreed to provide Brokaw with the requested arms. Walker was hesitant until he confirmed with "Prince," also a U.S. undercover agent, that Ecuador was a legal destination for arms sales. Walker did not learn that the weapons were really destined for Chile until he was indicted.

Later, Mr. Prince asked Walker to meet with him in New York, but Walker declined and suggested a meeting in Toronto. Finally, Prince convinced Walker to meet with him in the Bahamas with the promise of an all expenses paid trip. The U.S. agents arranged for Walker to receive his airline ticket at the last possible moment before departure. Walker did not learn that the flight had been routed through New York until he was aboard the plane. The United States agents knew they would have to lure Mr. Walker into the U.S., because there were not enough facts to extradite him from Canada or another country. Walker was subsequently arrested upon landing in New York.

After approximately six months in pre-trial detention, Walker pled guilty and was released on bond prior to sentencing. Mr. Walker chose not to return for sentencing. The U.S. Government requested his extradition. In an unprecedented response, after several exchanges of diplomatic correspondence, Canada refused to even convene a hearing on the extradition request, citing violations of Canadian law and sovereignty.

Mr. Walker brought a civil suit against the United States Government and the persons who participated in the operation. The U.S. claimed immunity. The Canadian trial court rejected the United States' assertion and found that a restraint on a person need not always be physical. As long as a person's will is overcome by force or fraud, the person has been "abducted." Here, a false imprisonment occurred at the point of total restraint when Mr. Walker boarded the airplane in Toronto based on the misrepresentations of the United States, because he could not change its destination.[1] Mr. Walker claims that he was tricked and lured against his will because of the planned arrangements for him to fly from Toronto to the Bahamas with a connection in New York, and such a practice was an abduction and therefore a violation of the Criminal Code of Canada, R.S.C. 1985, C-46, s. 279 (1)(b). However, the Canadian appellate courts reversed and held that the U.S. and other defendants were immune.

The Canadian response to the *Walker* incident is an indication of the reactions of a minority of nations to the use of luring in the practice of transnational law enforcement. In addition to filing a diplomatic note in formal protest of the actions of U.S. Customs officials in the arrest of Mr. Walker, the Canadian Government supported Mr. Walker during the litigation.

Cyprus and the Bahamas are two other nations that have objected to the use of luring by the United States Government as an alternative means to extradition. The U.S. indicted Mr. Hossein Alikhani for allegedly violating a U.S. statute prohibiting the export of certain goods to Libya.[2] Mr. Alikhani, a Cypriot citizen, learned of the U.S. embargo against Libya from Mr. Al Baumler, sales manager of Turbo Power and Marine Systems (TPMS), and as a result did not pursue any sales to the nation. However, a year after the incident, Baumler offered to supply parts to Alikhani while concealing his true identity as an informant of the U.S. Customs Service. A letter was sent by Baumler and other agents through a front company advising Alikhani how to perform the business deal while conforming to American law. Alikhani relied on this information in deciding to complete the business transaction with Mr. Baumler.

In October 1992, Baumler informed Mr. Alikhani that his presence was needed at a business meeting in the Bahamas. Alikhani accepted, and upon his arrival he was met by undercover agents at the Bahamian airport. At that time, Alikhani was told that he would

---

1. *Walker v. Bank of New York, Inc.,* (1993) 16 O.R. (3d) 596 (Gen. Div).
2. *See* Libyan Sanctions Regulations, 31 C.F.R. § 550 (1994).

travel to another Bahamian island, and he agreed to board the plane under that presumption. However, several minutes after takeoff when the plane was no longer in Bahamian airspace, the U.S. agents revealed their true identities and arrested Mr. Alikhani.

In response to the arrest of Mr. Alikhani, the Government of the Bahamas and the Government of Cyprus formally submitted diplomatic notes in protest of the abduction of Mr. Alikhani. After six months in pretrial detention, Mr. Alikhani made a plea agreement. [note omitted]. The U.S. Government, aware of the criticism of Alikhani's abduction by foreign governments, placed a provision in the plea bargain agreement forbidding any complaints by the defendant concerning the circumstances of his arrest. However, on his return to Cyprus, Mr. Alikhani has begun legal proceedings to make unenforceable the part of the plea bargain agreement wherein he agrees not to challenge his arrest and conviction.[3]

Both Alikhani and Walker have filed a petition to adjudicate the way in which the U.S. conducted the investigation and arrest.[4] However, because the U.S. Government has not ratified the Inter-American Convention on Human Rights, but is bound by the O.A.S. Charter as supplemented by the American Declaration, the plaintiffs can only bring their petition in the Inter-American Commission on Human Rights, which cannot directly compel enforcement or directly provide monetary relief. *Cf. Velasquez Rodriguez Case*, Inter-Am. Ct. H.R. (29 July 1988).

Court decisions of several countries have recently held that mere physical presence of a person before the court is not sufficient to confer jurisdiction. Common and civil law countries such as New Zealand, Britain, Zimbabwe, South Africa, and Switzerland have condemned the practice of abduction by giving the courts discretion not to exercise jurisdiction.[5] This trend could lead to an absolute bar on the exercise of jurisdiction where an abduction by force or deceit has occurred.

Some view the practice of abduction by fraud as a violation of territorial sovereignty and international law, violations that do pertain if forcible abduction without foreign state consent occurs.[6] The Restatement codifies the customary international law principle that a nation's agents may not use police powers and seize an individual from another nation without obtaining consent from the other nation's government, and even foreign state consent would not obviate human rights violations.[7]

---

3. *See Hossein Alikhani, et al. v. United States, et al.*, S.D. Fla. (Case No. 93-8513 CIV-ZLOCH).

4. Kenneth Walker, *et al.* v. United States, Inter-American H.R. Commission, filed July ___, 1995.

5. *See, e.g.*, R. v. Hartley [1978] 2 NZLR 199; S. v. Reahan 1992 (1) South African Criminal Law Reports 307 (ZS) at 317 (Zimbabwe); S. v. Ebrahim, in 31 I.L.M. 890 (Feb. 26, 1991); Bennett v. Horseferry Road Magistrates Court, 2 All E.R. 318 (1993). For an example of a civil law country jurisprudence on this matter, see the decision of the Swiss Federal Supreme Court of July 25, 1982, Eur. Grundr Zeitschrift (1983) 435; and 39 Swiss Yearbook of International Law (1983); *Resolutions Proposed by International Committees*, International Law Association, Buenos Aires Conference 17 (1994).

6. The international community is also very much opposed to United States practice of abduction by force. After the U.S. Supreme Court's *Alvarez-Machain* decision, which upheld jurisdiction of a defendant who was brought to the United States through the use of force, *United States v. Alvarez-Machain*, 504 U.S. 655 (1992), there was strong opposition by many foreign nations to the decision itself and, in general, to the use of abduction by force. Paul Hoffman, *Kidnapping Foreign Criminal Suspects*, 15 Whittier L. Rev. 419, 421 (1994).

7. *See* Restatement, §§ 432–433; Kristin Berdan Weissman, *Extraterritorial Abduction: The Endangerment of Future Peace*, 27 U.C. Davis L. Rev. 459, 474 (1994); also see Paust, *After* Alvarez-Machain; *Abduction, Standing, Denials of Justice, and Unaddressed Human Rights Claims*, 67 St. John's L. Rev. 551 (1993).

2. *Jurisprudence of the ICTY: The* Dokmanovic *Case*

In April 1996, the ICTY issued a sealed indictment against Slavko Dokmanovic, a Croatian Serb, for his complicity in the greatest single massacre of the 1991 war in Croatia, that of the execution of 261 people forcibly taken out of a hospital in Vukovar, eastern Croatia.[8] The same day the indictment was issued, an order for Dokmanovic's arrest was secretly transmitted to the United Nations Transitional Administration for Eastern Slavonia (UNTAES),[9] directing the U.N. forces to search for, arrest, and surrender Dokmanovic to the ICTY.

Unfortunately, by the time UNTAES received the order for Dokmanovic's arrest, he had moved from the Eastern Slavonia region of Croatia to the Federal Republic of Yugoslavia (FRY), which had failed to execute the warrants which remain outstanding for the arrest of the three co-accused in the Indictment against Dokmanovic.[10] The ICTY's Office of the Prosecutor (OTP) thus turned to plan B: In June 1997, Kevin Curtis, an OTP investigator, met with Dokmanovic at his home in the FRY in an effort to lure Dokmanovic into Eastern Slavonia for arrest by UNTAES. Curtis purported to set up a meeting between Dokmanovic and General Jacques Klein, the Transitional Administrator of Eastern Slavonia, for the stated purpose of arranging for possible compensation for Dokmanovic's property in Eastern Slavonia, which he had been forced to abandon. In accordance with this arrangement, on the afternoon of 27 June 1997, Dokmanovic crossed the border into Eastern Slavonia under what he believed was a promise of safe conduct, and voluntarily entered an UNTAES vehicle which was to take him to meet General Klein at the UNTAES base in the town of Erdut. Upon arriving at Erdut, UNTAES soldiers removed Dokmanovic from the vehicle at gunpoint and handcuffed him, while a member of the OTP advised him of his rights and the charges against him. Dokmanovic was then flown on board an UNTAES airplane to The Hague and handed over to the ICTY for trial.

In a pretrial motion, counsel for Dokmanovic argued that the manner of Dokmanovic's arrest was illegal, violating the Statute and Rules of the ICTY, the sovereignty of the FRY, and international law. In particular, the defense argued that "Dokmanovic was arrested in a 'tricky way,' which can only be interpreted as a 'kidnapping,'" and that "Dokmanovic's arrest violated the sovereignty of the FRY and international law because he was arrested in the territory of the FRY without the knowledge or approval of the competent State authorities." *Id.* at paras. 16–18.

While recognizing that some unconsented law enforcement activities (*i.e.*, abductions) would violate the principle of territorial integrity, the Trial Chamber in the *Dokmanovic* case held that luring would not do so. As the Trial Chamber noted, "the Prosecution freely concedes that it 'used trickery, it was a ruse'" and that "it was the intention of the Prosecution from day one to arrest Mr. Dokmanovic." *Id.* at para. 57. However, the Trial Chamber found "that such luring is consistent with principles of international law and the sovereignty of the FRY." *Id.* In so finding, the Trial Chamber stressed that "there was no actual physical violation of FRY territory in gaining custody of Mr. Dokmanovic." *Id.* at para. 77.

---

8. *The Prosecutor v. Slavko Dokmanovic*, Decision on the Motion for Release by the Accused Slavko Dokmanovic, ICTY-95-13a-PT, T. Ch. II (22 Oct. 1997). Dokmanovic was mayor of Vukovar, the capital of Eastern Slavonia, and administrator of the Ovcara area at the time of the massacre. He is charged with six counts of grave breaches of the Geneva Conventions, violations of the laws or customs of war and crimes against humanity for his role in the massacre.

9. UNTAES was established pursuant to Security Council Resolution 1037, S/RES/1037 (15 Jan. 1996), to administer the region of Eastern Slavonia pending its return to the control of Croatia.

10. The addition of Dokmanovic to the Indictment was not disclosed to the FRY.

Notes and Questions

1. Do you agree that luring is the legal equivalent of a forcible abduction? Does luring implicate a violation of a state's territorial sovereignty? What if the accused was predisposed to commit the crime and left the foreign jurisdiction for the purpose of committing the fabricated offense? Were the accused's human rights violated nonetheless?

2. For a critique of the *Dokmanovic* case, see Michael P. Scharf, *The Prosecutor v. Slavko Dokmanovic: Irregular Rendition and the ICTY*, 11 Leiden J. Int'l L. 369–382 (1998).

3. Is the ICTY correct that the luring of Dokmonovic was accomplished without any physical violation of FRY territory? Would your answer be different if the communications between the ICTY officials and the target of the luring were conducted exclusively over the phone, radio, e-mail, or fax, rather than in a face to face meeting in the territory of the FRY without the permission of FRY authorities?

4. The Trial Chamber sought to distinguish the many national cases in which courts have "frowned upon the notion of luring an individual into a jurisdiction to effectuate his arrest" on the ground that in such cases there existed an established extradition treaty that was circumvented (*Id.* at para. 74), while in the *Dokmanovic* case there was no extradition treaty in force between the FRY and the Tribunal. *Id.* at para. 67. Is this a valid distinction?

The rationale for the distinction is that the circumvention of an extradition treaty undermines the process of international law and fosters its disrespect.[11] The Trial Chamber's analysis, however, ignores the fact that transfer to the ICTY is not "extradition" as such and does not involve the same state concerns as extradition. The obligation of states to arrest and transfer the accused is a consequence of the establishment of the ICTY by the Security Council acting under Chapter VII of the United Nations Charter. As indicated in the Secretary-General's report on the Yugoslavia Tribunal, "an order by a Trial Chamber for the surrender or transfer of persons to the custody of the International Tribunal shall be considered to be the application of an enforcement measure under Chapter VII of the Charter of the United Nations." (see Chapter Six, Section 9 A, U.N. S.G. Report, at para. 126). There is no reference to extradition in the Secretary-General's report, the ICTY's Statute or its Rules of Procedure, and it was not envisaged that states would have to enter into extradition agreements with the ICTY as a prerequisite to surrendering indicted persons to the Tribunal.[12] Consequently, states have pursued different means to implement their responsibility to surrender indicted war criminals to the ICTY. Twenty states have enacted special legislation on cooperation. A handful of states have entered into truncated extradition agreements with the ICTY. Others have formally stated that no legislation or agreement is necessary to ensure full cooperation.[13] The FRY has neither enacted legislation nor entered into an agreement with the ICTY but has transferred persons to the tribunal on two occasions.

Prior to the luring operation, no request for the surrender of Dokmanovic was transmitted to the FRY, which was under a treaty obligation (Articles 25, 48 of the U.N. Charter) to comply with such a request irrespective of the nonexistence of an extradition agreement with the ICTY. For Professor Scharf, at least, the luring of Dokmanovic in lieu

---

11. See S. Evans, *International Kidnapping in a Violent World: Where the United States Ought to Draw the Line*, 137 Mil. L. Rev. 187, 197 (1992).

12. V. Morris & M. Scharf, An Insider's Guide to the International Criminal Tribunal for the Former Yugoslavia 210–213 (1995).

13. Such states include the Republic of Korea, the Russian Federation, Singapore and Venezuela.

of pursuing his surrender from the FRY through the formally established procedure,[14] therefore, raises the same concerns as if the ICTY had acted in circumvention of an operational extradition treaty. That the FRY failed to comply with its obligations to surrender persons to the Tribunal in the past does not alter this conclusion, since in the cases cited by the Trial Chamber, luring was likewise used in response to non-cooperation by the host state.

5. Some argue that luring violates human rights law and that it can lead to civil liability in tort. What human right would be relevant to luring, if any? Others disagree that luring violates human rights law. Further discussion can be seen in the prior edition of this casebook.

6. Some claim that a U.S. practice of luring alleged criminals from their country to an area of international or U.S. jurisdiction has deleterious ramifications with respect to how the U.S. criminal justice system is viewed in the international community. Further discussion can be seen in the prior edition of this casebook.

Section 4
Abductions

Introductory Problem

For purposes of this problem, assume you are the Assistant Attorney General, Office of Legal Counsel, U.S. Department of Justice. The Attorney General has asked your advice on whether he should authorize the FBI and CIA, with the assistance of the Department of Defense, to conduct an extraterritorial abduction of Usama bin Laden, the mastermind of the terrorist attacks of September 11 that resulted in the murder of approximately 3,000 innocent civilians at the World Trade Center, the Pentagon, and a field in Pennsylvania. Usama bin Laden is an exiled Saudi Arabian multi-millionaire, who is believed to have financed and planned terrorist operations against the United States, including the August 1998 bombings of the U.S. embassies in Kenya and Tanzania, and the 2000 bombing of the U.S.S. Cole. Usama bin Laden has been indicted (*United States v. Usama bin Laden, et al.*, F. Supp.2d (S.D.N.Y. 2000), and is now "Number One" on the FBI's "Most Wanted List." Bin Laden is believed to be hiding in the mountainous regions of Pakistan.

In 1985, 1989, 1991, and 1993, the U.N. General Assembly condemned "as criminal and unjustifiable, all acts, methods and practices of terrorism wherever and by whoever committed." See Chapter Twelve, Section 2. The U.N. Security Council has also condemned the abduction of Eichmann by Israeli agents and has condemned "unequivo-

---

14. The procedure set forth in the ICTY's Rules contemplates a request for surrender transmitted to state authorities, and in the event of non-compliance, a report to the Security Council, which would determine what further action is appropriate. *See* Statute of the ICTY, arts. 20(2), 21, in the Documents Supplement; *see also* Rules of Procedure and Evidence of the Yugoslavia Tribunal (11 Feb. 1994) (amended 5 May 1994 and 4 Oct. 1994, revised 30 Jan. 1995, further amended 3 May 1995, 15 June 1995, 6 Oct. 1995, 18 Jan. 1996, 23 Apr. 1996, 25 June 1996, 5 July 1996, and 3 Dec. 1996), Rule 55 (Execution of Arrest Warrants), Rule 56 (Cooperation of States), Rule 57 (Procedure after Arrest), Rule 59 (Failure to Execute a Warrant), Rule 59 *bis* (Transmission of Arrest Warrants), Rule 60 (Advertisement of Indictment), and Rule 61 (Procedure in Case of Failure to Execute a Warrant), U.N. Doc. IT/32/Rev.10.

cally ... all acts of abduction." See Section 5 A. The U.N. Security Council adopted Resolutions 1368 and 1373 condemning in the strongest possible terms the horrifying terrorist attacks of September 11, calling on the international community to work together urgently to bring to justice the perpetrators of these terrorist attacks. The Attorney General has asked you for an analysis of the legal and policy issues implicated by an extraterritorial abduction of bin Laden from Pakistan or any other country where he may be located. Consider also the last sections of this chapter.

Introduction

Where extradition is not possible because of the lack of a treaty or for some other reason, states have sometimes resorted to abductions without the consent of the state in which the fugitive is located. Such action raises several questions which are addressed in this Section, namely: does such action violate international law? And if it does, is the executive branch nevertheless constitutionally permitted to authorize action by its law enforcement agents in violation of international law? Most importantly, can a criminal defendant whose custody has been achieved in this manner contest the jurisdiction of the court? Should the illegal act by law enforcement officers or other persons from the prosecuting state result in the court divesting itself of jurisdiction? Is the kidnapping simply a violation of customary or conventional international law relating to the territorial sovereignty of the state of refuge that may be complained about by that state alone or are there also rights of the abductee at stake?

A. Unconsented to Extraterritorial Abductions Under International Law

In 1989, the Office of Legal Counsel (OLC) at the U.S. Department of Justice reversed its earlier opinion and concluded that the FBI has legal authority under domestic U.S. law to arrest persons in other countries without the consent of those countries.

William P. Barr, Assistant Attorney General, Office of Legal Counsel, United States Department of Justice, testified during a hearing On the Legality as a Matter of Domestic Law of Extraterritorial Law Enforcement Activities that Depart from International law, Before the Subcommittee on Civil and Constitutional Rights of the Committee on the Judiciary, United States House of Representatives, November 8, 1989. Mr. Barr explained that the U.S. faced increasingly serious threats to its domestic security from both international terrorist groups and narcotics traffickers and that some foreign governments had not acted to protect the U.S. from such dangers, while others actually act in complicity with these groups.

Mr. Barr explained that his 1989 opinion re-examined a 1980 opinion of the OLC that concluded apprehension by the FBI and other Executive Officials of a fugitive in a foreign country without that country's consent would most likely constitute a violation of customary international law and, hence, the FBI had no authority to do so.

Barr explained that, insofar as the 1980 Opinion expressed that the U.S., as a sovereign nation, has no authority under its own laws to conduct law enforcement operations in another country without the country's consent, it was flawed. He claimed that courts have repeatedly recognized that the executive and legislative branches may, in exercising their respective authority, depart from customary international law norms, although this is not correct and the only cases stating that Executive acts can be controlling arose in the mid-1908s in connection with control of aliens and immigration. *See, e.g.*, JORDAN J. PAUST, INTERNATIONAL LAW AS LAW OF THE UNITED STATES 176–77, 188–91 nn.66–70 (2 ed. 2003).

Barr explained that the 1980 Opinion failed to consider what the Executive claims is the President's inherent constitutional power to authorize law enforcement activities and his constitutional responsibility to "take Care that the Laws be faithfully executed," U.S. Const. Art. II, §2, which empower him to authorize agents of the Executive Branch to conduct extraterritorial arrests. Barr also claimed that the President's "foreign affairs" powers allow the President to violate customary international law, although no case is on point.

Abraham D. Sofaer, The Legal Adviser, U.S. Department of State, U.S. Department of State, also testified before the same Subcommittee and explained that international law permits extraterritorial "arrests" in situations that permit a valid claim of self-defense and that the principle of territorial integrity is not entitled to absolute deference in international law. *See* Note 8 below.

Notes and Questions

1. As a practical matter, why do you think the Department of Justice Office of Legal Counsel issued the 1989 opinion on extraterritorial arrests? Do you agree with the Barr position? *See* Matthew Purdy, *Congress slams Justice ruling on kidnap of suspects abroad*, HOUS. CHRON., Nov. 9, 1989, at 10A, col. 1 (Rep. Don Edwards adding: "I can think of no act of Congress or no provision of the Constitution that gives the United States the authority to be an international outlaw."). It was reported that "Sofaer said that the Justice Department considered only domestic law and not international law or U.S. foreign policy in determining its opinion." *Id.*

2. Is the position taken in the OLC opinion consistent with the principle that U.S. statutes are to be construed consistently with international law in the absence of a clear and unequivocal declaration of different congressional intent? *See* Chapter Four, Section 2. The FBI authorization statute gives it authority to "detect and prosecute" crimes and "to make arrests" without any geographic limitation. Should such a limitation be implied? If not, do you think that authority "to make arrests" abroad is necessarily authority to make arrests in violation of international or any other relevant law?

3. Barr's remarks referred to two decisions of Chief Justice Marshall, which Barr claimed recognized that while customary international law may provide rules of decision in the absence of a controlling executive or legislative act to the contrary, it does not absolutely restrict the Nation's sovereign capacity to act in the international arena. *Brown v. United States*, 12 U.S. (8 Cranch) 110, 128 (1814); *The Schooner Exchange v. M'Faddon*, 11 U.S. (7 Cranch) 116, 145–46 (1812). Do these cases actually support such an assertion? Did the Barr statement involve a misreading of *Brown*? Did *Brown* actually address customary international law, where quoted, or merely "usage" (which is merely long-term practice and not law)? Did Chief Justice Marshall, who recognized elsewhere that the President is bound by international law, ever use the phrase "controlling executive … act"? What did Justice Story recognize in his dissent about the reach of the laws of war (which the majority did not disagree with)? Did *Tag* or *The Over the Top* address executive acts as such as opposed to Congress' powers? What have been the actual trends in Founder, Framer, and judicial opinions and decisions (*i.e.*, what really has been "repeatedly recognized")? *See, e.g.*, PAUST, INTERNATIONAL LAW AS LAW OF THE UNITED STATES, *supra* at 169–73; Paust, *Executive Plans and Authorizations to Violate International Law Concerning Treatment and*

Interrogation of Detainees, 43 Columbia J. Transnat'l L. 811, 856–61 (2005), available at http://www.columbia.edu/cu/jtl/Vol_43_3_files/Paust.pdf; Paust, *International Law Before the Supreme Court: A Mixed Record of Recognition*, 45 Santa Clara L. Rev. 829, 839–40 n.53 (2005) ("That the president and every member of the executive branch are bound by the law of war has been well understood since the Founding" in an unswerving line of Supreme Court and other cases.). With respect to *The Schooner Exchange*, the Court recognized that customary international law allowed a discretion, as a matter of comity, in the United States to grant or refuse immunity for a foreign ship of war entering our waters, and although such ships had an implied waiver of our jurisdictional reach, the waiver of U.S. jurisdiction could be taken back. *See* 11 U.S. (7 Cranch) at 136–45; Republic of Austria v. Altmann, 124 S.Ct. 2240, 2247–48 (2004) ; Verlinden B.V. v. Central Bank of Nigeria, 461 U.S. 480, 486 (1983); Berg v. British and African Steam Navigation Co. (The Prize Ship "Appam"), 243 U.S. 124, 153–56 (1917); The Santissima Trinidad, 20 U.S. (7 Wheat.) 283, 350–55 (1822) (also addressing nonimmunity of a foreign public ship of war regarding violations of customary international law—see Chapter Two). *The Schooner Exchange* clearly did not hold or even suggest that either the United States or the President could violate customary international law.

4. Did *The Paquete Habana* actually recognize that the Executive can violate customary international law? What did the Government's and other briefs in the case recognize? What was the actual ruling? See Paust, *supra* at 171–72, 174–77, 189–90 n.67; *Paquete and the President: Rediscovering the Brief for the United States*, 34 Va. J. Int'l L. 981 (1994).

5. In view of the U.S. Constitution, art. II, sec. 3, does the President have a "constitutional authority" to not faithfully execute the law or a constitutionally-based duty to faithfully execute international law? See Paust, *supra* at 169–73.

6. On the split as to whether Congress can override customary international law domestically and the limited precedent on both sides, *see, e.g.,* Paust, *supra* at 106–07 (Congress is bound by the laws of war), 108–115 (sparse precedent on both sides of the question whether congress is bound more generally by customary international law).

7. On use of force, the U.N. Charter and self-defense, see also Section 5 below and Chapter Seven.

8. Former Legal Adviser Abraham D. Sofaer while testifying also explained that the doctrine of self-defense can justify a breach of territory integrity in certain cases. In that regard, he opined that the activities and threats of some drug traffickers may give rise to the right to resort to self-defense. *But see* the exact language set forth in Article 51 of the United Nations Charter, in the Documents Supplement (and addressed in Chapter Seven). The actual implications of nonconsensual arrest in foreign territory may vary with factors such as the seriousness of the offense for which the apprehended person is arrested; the citizenship of the offender; whether the foreign government had tried to bring the offenders to justice or would have consented to the arrest had it been asked; and the general tenor of bilateral relations with the U.S. Such operations pose risks to U.S. agents and to the risk of suits against the U.S. in the foreign country's courts for the illegal actions taken in that country. According to Sofaer's testimony, under what circumstances would an unconsented to extraterritorial abduction be consistent with international law? Even when international law allows such action, what risks do U.S. law enforcement agents entail when they engage in a transborder abduction? What risks do their superiors entail? What effect might such action have on the country's foreign relations?

9. When the 1989 OLC opinion was made public, the White House issued the following Press Statement:

THE WHITE HOUSE

Office of the Press Secretary

Notice to the Press

October 13, 1989

The Office of Legal Counsel at Justice prepared an opinion some months ago on the question of whether the FBI has legal authority under domestic U.S. law to arrest persons in other countries.

It is important to isolate the question of whether domestic legal authority exists from the separate question of whether the President will in fact authorize the use of that authority.

In any given case, the President must weigh his constitutional responsibilities for formulating and implementing both foreign policy and law enforcement policy.

An interagency process exists to insure that the President takes into account the full range of foreign policy and international law considerations as well as the domestic law enforcement issues raised by any specific case. There will be no arrests abroad that have not been considered through that interagency process.

The Executive Branch has never addressed the question of whether the 1990 abduction of Dr. Humberto Alvarez-Machain from Mexico (discussed below) was authorized through such an inter-agency process. Indeed, his abduction was apparently never authorized at high levels within the Executive branch. Dr. Alvarez-Machain was accused of participating in the torture and murder of DEA special agent Enrique Camarena-Salazar. Was the abduction of Alvarez-Machain consistent with the exception to the rule against violating the territorial sovereignty of another state as described in Abraham Sofaer's testimony? Is it possible that the abduction of Dr. Alvarez-Machain represented a breakdown in the inter-agency process envisaged above? If so, why do you think the Department of Justice would insist on taking the case all the way to the Supreme Court? Do you suspect that State or DOJ would be more attentive to international law?

10. If ever lawful outside the context of an actual armed attack on the United States, its embassies or nationals abroad or series of attacks, what role may the armed forces play in assisting in an extraterritorial abduction? In this regard, consider the case of *United States v. Yunis*, 681 F. Supp. 891 (D.D.C. 1988), in which the defendant argued that the involvement of the United States Navy in his apprehension abroad and transportation to the United States violated the Posse Comitatus Act. The Posse Comitatus Act, 18 U.S.C. Section 1385, provides that: "Whoever, except in cases and under circumstances expressly authorized by the Constitution or Act of Congress, willfully uses any part of the Army or the Air Force as a posse comitatus or otherwise to execute the laws shall be fined not more than $10,000 or imprisoned not more than two years, or both." The U.S. District Court for the District of Columbia rejected the defendant's claim, holding as follows:

"In this proceeding, the Navy's activities in the apprehension of Yunis were not the type prohibited by the Posse Comitatus Act, nor were they prohibited by the DOD military cooperation laws. The FBI was in charge of the operation at all times. At most, the Navy merely provided necessary support services. Navy personnel never participated in the arrest or interrogation of the defendant. Their equipment and staff already stationed in the Mediterranean were at the disposal of the FBI for only limited purposes, involving a passive role. Their limited role included: advising the FBI crew aboard the yacht (used in the capture of the defendant) on its location in international waters; providing a launch to transport the defendant from the FBI yacht to the Navy vessel—the U.S.S. Butte, supplying the defendant with shelter, clothes, food, and toiletries while on board the Navy launch and providing required medical attention; arranging a rendezvous between the Butte and the aircraft carrier—the U.S.S. Saratoga; piloting the Navy plane with the defendant and his FBI custodians from the Saratoga to the United States.

"It is clear from these facts that the Navy's activities did not constitute direct active involvement in the execution of the laws, nor did the use of military personnel pervade the activities of the civilian authorities. Rather, it was a civilian operation originating from within the FBI. By its very nature, the operation required the aid of military located in the area. Under the direction of the FBI, the Navy gave the necessary support in the form of equipment, supplies, and services. The furnishing of materials, work, and services, standing alone, is not a violation of the Posse Comitatus Act."

681 F. Supp. at 895.

B. Judicial Responses to Extraterritorial Abductions

The general stance of the judiciary in the United States, Canada and the United Kingdom has been that a fugitive should not succeed in escaping trial merely because he or she was brought illegally into the jurisdiction of the prosecuting state. This practice is evidenced in the Roman maxim, *mala captus bene detentus* (sometimes referred to as the "tough luck rule"), which means that the court once in possession of the accused has jurisdiction over the person and all that is required is a fair trial. An exception in U.S. cases has involved violations of treaty law. *See, e.g., Cook v. United States,* 288 U.S. 102 (1933); *United States v. Ferris,* 19 F.2d 925, 926 (N.D. Cal. 1927); *see also* (all re: customary international law) *The Apollon,* 22 U.S. (9 Wheat.) 362, 370–71, 376–79 (1824); *Motherwell v. United States ex rel. Alexandroff,* 107 F. 437, 446 (3d Cir. 1901) (Gray, J., concurring), *rev'd,* 183 U.S. 424 (1902). Although the U.S. Second Circuit Court of Appeals in *United States v. Toscanino* also declared that there exists an exception in cases in which the manner in which the fugitive is apprehended "shocks the conscience of the Court," this exception has not been applied subsequently to exclude jurisdiction.

United States v. Toscanino
500 F.2d 267 (2d Cir. 1974)

Mansfield, J.

Francisco Toscanino appeals from a narcotics conviction entered against him in the Eastern District of New York by Chief Judge Jacob Mishler after a jury trial. Toscanino was sentenced to 20 years in prison and fined $20,000. He contends that the court acquired jurisdiction over him unlawfully through the conduct of American agents who kidnapped him in Uruguay, used illegal electronic surveillance, tortured him and abducted him to the United States for the purpose of prosecuting him here. We remand the case to the district court for further proceedings in which the government will be required to respond to his allegations concerning the methods by which he was brought into the Eastern District and the use of electronic surveillance to gather evidence against him.

Toscanino, who is a citizen of Italy, and four others were charged with conspiracy to import narcotics into the United States in violation of 21 U.S.C. §§ 173 and 174 in a one count indictment returned by a grand jury sitting in the Eastern District on February 22, 1973. The other defendants were S. Nicolay, Segundo Coronel, Roberto Arenas and Umberto Coronel. Also named as a conspirator but not as a defendant was one Hosvep Caramian. At a joint trial of all the defendants (except for Nicolay who had fled to Argentina), which began on May 22, 1973, the only government witness against Toscanino was Caramian who testified that he met with Toscanino in Montevideo, Uruguay, during the summer of 1970 and agreed to find buyers for a shipment of heroin into the United States, which would be delivered by Nicolay. Caramian testified further that in November, 1970, he left Uruguay and came to the United States where he met with Arenas and the Coronel brothers who agreed to buy the heroin. On November 30, 1970, Caramian received part of Toscanino's shipment delivered by Nicolay in Miami, Florida, but ultimate distribution of the narcotics was intercepted by government agents who posed as buyers from Arenas and the Coronel brothers. Toscanino, testifying in his own behalf, denied any knowledge of these transactions. On June 5, 1973, the jury returned a verdict of guilty against him and all the other defendants.

Toscanino does not question the sufficiency of the evidence or claim any error with respect to the conduct of the trial itself. His principal argument, which he voiced prior to trial and again after the jury verdict was returned, is that the entire proceedings in the district court against him were void because his presence within the territorial jurisdiction of the court had been illegally obtained. He alleged that he had been kidnapped from his home in Montevideo, Uruguay, and brought into the Eastern District only after he had been detained for three weeks of interrogation accompanied by physical torture in Brazil....

The government prosecutor neither affirmed nor denied these allegations but claimed they were immaterial to the district court's power to proceed.

Toscanino alleged further that, prior to his forcible abduction from Montevideo, American officials bribed an employee of the public telephone company to conduct electronic surveillance of him and that the results of the surveillance were given to American agents and forwarded to government prosecutors in New York. According to Toscanino the telephone company employee was eventually arrested in Uruguay for illegal eavesdropping and was indicted and imprisoned. In connection with these later allegations Toscanino moved, pursuant to 18 U.S.C. § 3594, to compel the government to affirm or deny whether in fact there had been any electronic surveillance of him in Uruguay.

Toscanino's motion for an order vacating the verdict, dismissing the indictment and ordering his return to Uruguay was denied by the district court on November 2, 1973, without a hearing. Relying principally on the decisions of the Supreme Court in *Ker* v. *Illinois*, 119 U.S. 436, 7 S.Ct. 225, 30 L.Ed. 421 (1886), and *Frisbie* v. *Collins*, 342 U.S. 519, 72 S.Ct. 509, 96 L.Ed. 541 (1952), the court held that the manner in which Toscanino was brought into the territory of the United States was immaterial to the court's power to proceed, provided he was physically present at the time of trial....

In an era marked by a sharp increase in kidnapping activities, both here and abroad, *see, e.g.*, New York Times, Jan. 5, 1974, at 25, col. 6, Dec. 13, 1973, at 2, col. 5, Oct. 17, 1973, at 14, col. 5, we face the question, as we must in the state of the pleadings, of whether a federal court must assume jurisdiction over the person of a defendant who is illegally apprehended abroad and forcibly abducted by government agents to the United States for the purpose of facing criminal charges here. The answer necessitates a review and appraisal of two Supreme Court decisions, heavily relied upon by the government and by the district court, *Ker* v. *Illinois*, 119 U.S. 436, 7 S.Ct. 225, 30 L.Ed. 421 (1888), and *Frisbie* v. *Collins*, 342 U.S. 519, 72 S.Ct. 509, 96 L.Ed. 541 (1952). For years these two cases have been the mainstay of a doctrine to the effect that the government's power to prosecute a defendant is not impaired by the illegality of the method by which it acquires control over him. This teaching originated almost 90 years ago in *Ker*. While residing in Peru, Ker was indicted by an Illinois grand jury for larceny and embezzlement. At the request of the Governor of Illinois the President, invoking the current treaty of extradition between the United States and Peru, issued a warrant authorizing a Pinkerton agent to take custody of Ker from the authorities of Peru. The warrant, however was never served, probably for the reason that by the time the agent arrived there, armed forces of Chile, then at war with Peru, were in control of Lima. See Ker v. Illinois Revisited, 47 Am. J. Int'l L. 678 (1953). Instead Ker was forcibly abducted by the agent, placed aboard an American vessel and eventually taken to the United States, where he was tried and convicted in Illinois. The Supreme Court rejected Ker's argument that he was entitled by virtue of the treaty with Peru to a right of asylum there and held that the abduction of Ker did not violate the Due Process Clause of the Fourteenth Amendment (then less than 20 years old), which was construed as merely requiring that the party be regularly indicted and brought to trial "according to the forms and modes prescribed for such trials." The Court accordingly held that Ker might be tried by Illinois, regardless of the method by which it acquired control over him.

Sixty-six years later the Supreme Court again faced the question in *Frisbie* v. *Collins*, *supra*, in a slightly different context. There a Michigan state prisoner, petitioning for habeas corpus, alleged that he had been brought from Chicago, Illinois, to Michigan for trial only after he had been kidnapped, handcuffed and blackjacked in Chicago by Michigan police officers who had gone there to retrieve him. The prisoner claimed that his conviction in Michigan violated the Due Process Clause of the Fourteenth Amendment as well as the federal Kidnapping Act, 18 U.S.C. §1201, and was therefore a nullity. Rejecting the due process claim the Supreme Court explained.

> "This court has never departed from the rule announced in *Ker* v. *Illinois*, 119 U.S. 436, 444, [7 S.Ct. 225, 229, 30 L.Ed. 421], that the power of a court to try a person for crime is not impaired by the fact that he had been brought within the court's jurisdiction by reason of a 'forcible abduction.' No persuasive reasons are now presented to justify overruling this line of cases. They rest on the sound basis that due process of law is satisfied when one present in court is convicted of crime after being fairly apprized of the charges against him and after a fair trial in accordance with constitutional procedural safeguards."

Thus, under the so-called "Ker-Frisbie" rule, due process was limited to the guarantee of a constitutionally fair trial, regardless of the method by which jurisdiction was obtained over the defendant. Jurisdiction gained through an indisputably illegal act might still be exercised, even though the effect could be to reward police brutality and lawlessness in some cases.

Since *Frisbie* the Supreme Court, in what one distinguished legal luminary describes as a "constitutional revolution," see Griswold, The Due Process Revolution and Confrontation, 119 U. Pa. L. Rev. 711 (1971), has expanded the interpretation of "due process." No longer is it limited to the guarantee of "fair" procedure at trial. In an effort to deter police misconduct, the term has been extended to bar the government from realizing directly the fruits of its own deliberate and unnecessary lawlessness in bringing the accused to trial....

In light of these developments we are satisfied that the "Ker-Frisbie" rule cannot be reconciled with the Supreme Court's expansion of the concept of due process, which now protects the accused against pretrial illegality by denying to the government the fruits of its exploitation of any deliberate and unnecessary lawlessness on its part. Although the issue in most of the cases forming part of this evolutionary process was whether evidence should have been excluded (*e.g.*, *Mapp*, *Miranda*, *Wong Sun*, *Silverman*), it was unnecessary in those cases to invoke any other sanction to insure that an ultimate conviction would not rest on governmental illegality. Where suppression of evidence will not suffice, however, we must be guided by the underlying principle that the government should be denied the right to exploit its own illegal conduct, *Wong Sun* v. *United States*, 371 U.S. 471, 488, 83 S.Ct. 407, 9 L.Ed.2d 441 (1963), and when an accused is kidnapped and forcibly brought within the jurisdiction, the court's acquisition of power over his person represents the fruits of the government's exploitation of its own misconduct. Having unlawfully seized the defendant in violation of the Fourth Amendment, which guarantees "the right of the people to be secure in their persons ... against unreasonable ... seizures," the government should as a matter of fundamental fairness be obligated to return him to his *status quo ante*.

Faced with a conflict between the two concepts of due process, the one being the restricted version found in *Ker-Frisbie* and the other the expanded and enlightened interpretation expressed in more recent decisions of the Supreme Court, we are persuaded that to the extent that the two are in conflict, the *Ker-Frisbie* version must yield. Accordingly we view due process as now requiring a court to divest itself of jurisdiction over the person of a defendant where it has been acquired as the result of the government's deliberate, unnecessary and unreasonable invasion of the accused's constitutional rights. This conclusion represents but an extension of the well-recognized power of federal courts in the civil context to decline to exercise jurisdiction over a defendant whose presence has been secured by force or fraud. See *In re Johnson*, 167 U.S. 120, 126, 17 S.Ct. 735, 42 L.Ed. 103 (1896); *Fitzgerald Construction Co.* v. *Fitzgerald*, 137 U.S. 98, 11 S.Ct. 36, 34 L.Ed. 608 (1890).

If the charges of government misconduct in kidnapping Toscanino and forcibly bringing him to the United States should be sustained, the foregoing principles would, as a matter of due process, entitle him to some relief. The allegations include corruption and bribery of a foreign official as well as kidnapping, accompanied by violence and brutality to the person. Deliberate misconduct on the part of United States agents, in violation not only of constitutional prohibitions but also of the federal Kidnapping Act, *supra*, and of two international treaties obligating the United States Government to respect the territorial sovereignty of Uruguay, is charged. See U.N. Charter, art. 2; O.A.S. Charter, art. 17. The conduct alleged here satisfies those tests articulated by the Supreme Court in its most recent "entrapment" decision, *United States* v. *Russell*, 411 U.S. 432 (1973), where, in holding that due process did not bar prosecution for the manufacture and sale of an illegal drug, even though a government undercover agent had supplied a scarce chemical required for its synthesis, it noted that the government agent had violated no constitution prohibition or federal law and had committed no crime in infiltrating the defendant's drug enterprise. It furthermore appeared that the type of undercover activity engaged in there by the agent was necessary in order to gather essential evidence. Here, in contrast, not only were several laws allegedly broken and crimes committed at the behest of government agents but the conduct was apparently unnecessary, as the extradition treaty between the United States and Uruguay, see 35 Stat. 2028, does not specifically exclude narcotics violations so that a representative of our government might have been able to conclude with Uruguay a special arrangement for Toscanino's extradition. *Cf. Fiocconi* v. *Attorney General of United States*, 339 F. Supp. 1242, 1244 (S.D.N.Y. 1972).

In any event, since *Ker* and *Frisbie* involved state court convictions only, the views expressed in those cases would not necessarily apply to the present case, which is an appeal from a judgment entered by a federal district court. Here we possess powers not available to a federal court reviewing a state tribunal's resolution of constitutional issues. In this case we may rely simply upon our supervisory power over the administration of criminal justice in the district courts within our jurisdiction.... Clearly this power may legitimately be used to prevent district courts from themselves becoming "accomplices in wilful disobedience of law." See *McNabb, supra* at 345. Moreover the supervisory power is not limited to the admission or exclusion of evidence, but may be exercised in any manner necessary to remedy abuses of a district court's process. *Cf. Rea* v. *United States*, 350 U.S. 214, 76 S.Ct. 292, 100 L.Ed. 233 (1955). Drawing again from the field of civil procedure, we think a federal court's criminal process is abused or degraded where it is executed against a defendant who has been brought into the territory of the United States by the methods alleged here. *Cf. Commercial Mutual Accident Co.* v. *Davis*, 213 U.S. 245, 29 S.Ct. 445, 53 L.Ed. 782 (1909); *Fitzgerald Construction Co.* v. *Fitzgerald, supra.* We could not tolerate such an abuse without debasing "the processes of justice".

If distinctions are necessary, *Ker* and *Frisbie* are clearly distinguishable on other legally significant grounds which render neither of them controlling here. Neither case, unlike that here, involved the abduction of a defendant in violation of international treaties of the United States. *Frisbie* presented an alleged interstate abduction in which the appellant was clearly extraditable and an order returning him to his asylum state, Illinois, would have been an exercise in futility since Illinois would have been obligated to return him to Michigan for trial. U.S. Const. Art. IV, § 2, cl. 2; 18 U.S.C. § 3182. Although the appellant in *Ker* argued that his forcible abduction by the Pinkerton agent violated the extradition treaty between the United States and Peru, the Supreme Court disagreed, holding that the extradition treaty did not apply and that it would have been violated by the demanding state only if, after receiving a fugitive, it tried him for a crime other than that for which he was surrendered. See *United States v. Rauscher*, 119 U.S. 407, 7 S.Ct. 234, 30 L.Ed. 425 (1888). Here, in contrast, Toscanino alleges that he was forcibly abducted from Uruguay, whose territorial sovereignty this country has agreed in two international treaties to respect. The Charter of the United Nations, the members of which include the United States and Uruguay, see Department of State, Treaties in Force 402–03 (1973), obligates "All Members" to "refrain ... from the threat or use of force against the territorial integrity of political independence of any state...." See U.N. Charter, art. 2 para. 4. Additionally, the Charter of the Organization of American States, whose members also include the United States and Uruguay, see Department of State, Treaties in Force 359 (1973), provides that the "territory of a state is inviolable; it may not be the object, even temporarily, ... of ... measures of force taken by another state, directly or indirectly, on any grounds whatever ..." See O.A.S. Charter, art. 17.

That international kidnappings such as the one alleged here violate the U.N. Charter was settled as a result of the Security Council debates following the illegal kidnapping in 1960 of Adolf Eichmann from Argentina by Israeli "volunteer groups." In response to a formal complaint filed by the U.N. representative from Argentina pursuant to article 35 of the U.N. Charter[8] the Security Council, by eight votes to none (with two abstentions

---

8. Article 35 of the U.N. Charter permits member nations to bring "any dispute ... to the attention of the Security Council or of the General Assembly."

and one member—Argentina—not participating in the vote), adopted a resolution condemning the kidnapping and requesting "the Government of Israel to make appropriate reparation in accordance with the Charter of the United Nations and rules of international law...." U.N. Doc. S/4349 (June 23, 1960), quoted in W. Friedmann, O. Lissitzyn & R. Pugh, International Law: Cases and Materials 497 (1969). The resolution merely recognized a long standing principle of international law that abductions by one state of persons located within the territory of another violate the territorial sovereignty of the second state and are redressable usually by the return of the person kidnapped. See *The Vincenti Affair*, 1 Hackworth, *Digest of International Law* 624 (1920); *The Cantu Case*, 2 Hackworth 310 (1914); *The Case of Blatt and Converse*, 2 Hackworth 309 (1911).

Since the United States thus agreed not to seize persons residing within the territorial limits of Uruguay, appellant's allegations in this case are governed not by *Ker* but by the Supreme Court's later decision in *Cook* v. *United States*, 288 U.S. 102, 53 S.Ct. 305, 77 L.Ed. 641 (1933). In *Cook* officers of the United States Coast Guard boarded and seized a British vessel, the Mazel Tov, in violation of territorial limits fixed by a treaty then in force between the United States and Great Britain. The Supreme Court held that the government's subsequent libel for forfeiture of the vessel in the federal district court was properly dismissed, since under the treaty the forcible seizure was incapable of giving the district court power to adjudicate title to the vessel regardless of the vessel's physical presence within the court's jurisdiction.... Thus *Ker* does not apply where a defendant has been brought into the district court's jurisdiction by forcible abduction in violation of a treaty.... It derives directly from the Court's earlier decision in *United States* v. *Rauscher*, 119 U.S. 407, 7 S.Ct. 234, 30 L.Ed. 425 (1888), decided the same day as *Ker* and written by the same Justice. In *Rauscher*, the Court held that United States courts were barred from trying a fugitive, surrendered by Great Britain pursuant to a treaty of extradition, for a crime other than that for which he had been extradited, at least until he had been afforded an opportunity to return to the country from which he had been brought. In reaching this result the Court rejected the argument that even where a trial might be in violation of a treaty obligation, the defendant's exclusive remedy was an "appeal to the executive branches of the treaty governments for redress." See 119 U.S. at 430–432. See also *Johnson* v. *Browne*, 205 U.S. 309, 27 S.Ct. 639, 51 L.Ed. 816 (1907)....

The case is remanded to the district court for further proceedings not inconsistent with this opinion. Our remand should be construed as requiring an evidentiary hearing with respect to Toscanino's allegations of forcible abduction only if, in response to the government's denial, he offers some credible supporting evidence including specifically evidence that the action was taken by or at the direction of United States officials. Upon his failure to make such an offer the district court may, in its discretion, decline to hold an evidentiary hearing.

Notes and Questions

1. The RESTATEMENT has adopted the *Toscanino* exception. See RESTATEMENT §433 (2), Comm. c and Reporters' Note 3. The majority of textwriters are also opposed to *mala captus* practices. *See, e.g.,* M.C. BASSIOUNI, INTERNATIONAL EXTRADITION IN UNITED STATES LAW AND PRACTICE §2-9 (1983). In later cases such as *United States v. Herrera*, 504 F.2d 859 (5th Cir. 1974); *United States ex rel. Lujan v. Gengler*, 510 F. 2d 62 (2d Cir. 1975); *United States v. Lira*, 515 F.2d 68 (2d Cir 1975); and *United States v. Marschener*, 470 F. Supp. 201 (D. Conn. 1979), the *Toscanino* decision was distinguished and explained. It was distinguished in *Gengler* on the ground that although government agents do not have

a *carte blanche* to bring defendants from abroad to the United States by the use of torture, brutality and similar outrageous conduct, not every violation of law by the government or irregularity in the circumstances of a defendant's arrival in the jurisdiction is sufficient to vitiate the proceedings in a criminal court. There the conduct of the U.S. government agents was not outrageous and furthermore the offended state did not object to that conduct. In fact, the "*Toscanino* exception" failed as a basis for requiring the court to divest itself of jurisdiction in every case but *United States* v. *Caro-Quintero,* 745 F. Supp. 599 (C.D. Cal. 1990). That decision was later reversed by the U.S. Supreme Court in *United States* v. *Alvarez-Machain,* 504 U.S. 655 (1992), reproduced below.

2. Canadian courts in *R.* v. *Walton,* (1905), 10 C.C.C. 269, and *Re Hartnett and the Queen: Re Hudson and the Queen,* (1973), 1 O.R. (2d) 206, have applied the *mala captus bene detentus* maxim although, as indicated in the Brief submitted by Canada in *Alvarez-Machain* (reproduced below), it seems quite unlikely that they will have to address the question in future.

3. What policies underlie the *Ker-Frisbie* doctrine (the American version of the *mala captus bene detentus* maxim)? What policies underlie the *Cook, Rauscher,* and *Toscanino* exceptions to the doctrine?

4. In 1985, the U.N. Security Council recognized that "abductions are offenses of grave concern to the international community, having severe adverse consequences for the rights of the victims and for the promotion of friendly relations and co-operation among States," condemned "unequivocally all acts of ... abduction," and recognized the "obligation of all States in whose territory hostages or abducted persons are held urgently to take all appropriate measures to secure their safe release and to prevent the commission of acts of hostage-taking and abduction in the future." U.N. S.C. Res. 579 (1985), reprinted in 25 ILM 243 (1986).

5. The Human Rights Committee established under the International Covenant on Civil and Political Rights has also recognized that forcible abductions can violate the human rights of the abductee. Views of the Human Rights Committee on the Complaint of Lopez, 36 U.N. GAOR, Supp. No. 40, at 176–84, U.N. Doc. A/36/40 (1981); *see also id.* at 185–89; Restatement § 432, Reporters' Note 1; *id.* § 702 (c). The Human Rights Committee, in *Canon Garcia v. Ecuador* (Decision of May 11, 1991, U.N. Doc. CCPR/C/43/319/1988), has also found that Ecuador violated article 9 of the Covenant by participating in an abduction of a person to the U.S. accused of drug trafficking. In Europe, abductions are also considered to violate human rights protecting the individual from arbitrary deprivation of liberty. *See, e.g., Bozano v. France,* Ser. A, No. 111 (18 Dec. 1986), 9 EHRR 297 (1987), (2 Dec. 1991), 13 EHRR 428 (1991). In *Bozano,* the European Court found a violation of Article 5(1) of the European Convention on Human Rights in a context where the individual had been found to be not extraditable from France (to Italy, the requesting state) and the French Government nonetheless issued a deportation order and French police took him against his will to Switzerland where he was extradited to Italy to serve sentence after conviction in Italy in absentia. The Court noted that "'lawfulness'" "implies absence of any arbitrariness," that the deportation was a disguised form of extradition contrary to French judicial rulings, and that the individual's "deprivation of liberty ... was neither 'lawful'..., nor compatible with the 'right to security of person'" within the meaning of the Convention. *Id.* at paras. 58–60. In *Bennett v. Horseferry Road Magistrate's Court,* [1993] All ER 138 (House of Lords), jurisdiction was refused where a person had been deported from South Africa and deportation was used as disguised extradition. See also International Law Association, Report of the Sixty-Sixth Conference—Buenos Aires, Argentina 142, 162–65 (1994) (noting several of the above as well as cases in New Zealand, Zimbabwe, South Africa and Switzerland).

For a discussion of relevant human rights and "denial of justice" claims, *see, e.g.,* Paust, *After* Alvarez-Machain: *Abduction, Standing, Denials of Justice, and Unaddressed Human Rights Claims,* 67 St. John's L. Rev. 551, 560–67, 577–78 (1993), also recognizing exceptions under international law. *Id.* at 563–66, 574–80, and authorities cited. The exceptions include: (1) reasonably necessary international criminal-napping (when, on balance, it is not arbitrary, cruel, inhumane, degrading, unjust, or otherwise unlawful), (2) capture of a dictator, (3) permissible acts of self-defense under the U.N. Charter, and (4) permissible actions under Chapters VII and VIII of the U.N. Charter. Clearly, the last two exceptions are based directly in the U.N. Charter. The first two are probably still a minority viewpoint, especially given the Eichmann and abductions resolutions of the Security Council in 1960 and 1985. *See also* Section 5 A and B near the end of this chapter.

6. Is dismissing the case against the defendant an appropriate remedy for abuses committed by arresting agents? *Compare* Restatement § 432, Comm. c and Reporters' Note 3 *with* Paust, *supra* at 567–68, and authorities cited. What other remedies would be available to a defendant so apprehended? In this regard, note that Dr. Alvarez-Machain, who was abducted from Mexico, has sued DEA officials and the Department of Justice in U.S. federal court for $20 million in damages relating to his abduction. Barry Carter & Phillip Trimble, International Law 812 (2 ed. 1995). *See also* 28 U.S.C. § 1350; 1 Op. Att'y Gen. 68, 69 (1797); 1 Op. Att'y Gen. 57, 58 (1795); M.C. Bassiouni, *supra* at § 4-11 & n.32; Paust, *supra* at 558, 577.

7. The International Criminal Tribunal for the Former Yugoslavia (ICTY) had to face the issue whether its jurisdiction should be obviated because of the abduction of an accused in violation of his human rights by unknown individuals allegedly committed in collusion with the NATO-led Stabilization Force (SFOR) that gained custody of him. In The Prosecutor v. Nikolic, IT-94-2-AR73 (Appeals Chamber, Decision on Interlocutory Appeal Concerning Legality of Arrest, 5 June 2003), the decision was that jurisdiction would not be obviated, noting that the Trial Chamber had concluded that in this case the mistreatment "was not of such an egregious nature as to impede the exercise of jurisdiction." *Id.* para. 28. Yet, each decision must address the actual circumstances of mistreatment and, in the view of the Appeals Chamber, although setting aside jurisdiction of the international tribunal would be unusual, more serious mistreatment such as use of cruel, inhuman or degrading treatment or torture could obviate jurisdiction. See *id.* paras. 28–30; The Prosecutor v. Nikolic, IT-94-2-PT (Trial Chamber, Decision on Defence Motion Challenging the Exercise of Jurisdiction by the Tribunal, 9 Oct. 2002). The Appeals Chamber also addressed the Israeli *Eichmann* and French *Barbie* cases, noting that the domestic courts kept jurisdiction despite abductions of the accused. *Id.* para. 23. The Appeals Chamber stressed that its jurisdiction, like that of Israel and France, was being applied to crimes universally recognized. *Id.* para. 24, adding: "The damage caused to international justice by not apprehending fugitives accused of serious violations of international humanitarian law is comparatively higher than the injury, if any, caused to the sovereignty of a State by a limited intrusion in its territory, particularly when the intrusion occurs in default of the State's cooperation." *Id.* para. 26.

Does the ICTY decision support certain forms of international criminal-napping? or does it merely deny the remedy of preclusion of jurisdiction in certain cases?

8. The *Amici* Briefs of Canada and Mexico in the case of *United States v. Alvarez-Machain* are available in 31 I.L.M. 919 (1992) (Canada) and 31 I.L.M. 934 (1992) (Mexico).

United States v. Alvarez-Machain
504 U.S. 655 (1992)

Rehnquist, C.J.

The issue in this case is whether a criminal defendant, abducted to the United States from a nation with which it has an extradition treaty, thereby acquires a defense to the jurisdiction of this country's courts. We hold that he does not, and that he may be tried in federal district court for violations of the criminal law of the United States.

Respondent, Humberto Alvarez-Machain, is a citizen and resident of Mexico. He was indicted for participating in the kidnap and murder of United States Drug Enforcement Administration (DEA) special agent Enrique Camarena-Salazar and a Mexican pilot working with Camarena, Alfredo Zavala-Avelar. The DEA believes that respondent, a medical doctor, participated in the murder by prolonging agent Camarena's life so that others could further torture and interrogate him. On April 2, 1990, respondent was forcibly kidnapped from his medical office in Guadalajara, Mexico, to be flown by private plane to El Paso, Texas, where he was arrested by DEA officials. The District Court concluded that DEA agents were responsible for respondent's abduction, although they were not personally involved in it. *United States* v. *Caro-Quintero*, 745 F. Supp. 599, 602–604, 609 (C.D. Cal. 1990).

Respondent moved to dismiss the indictment, claiming that his abduction constituted outrageous governmental conduct, and that the District Court lacked jurisdiction to try him because he was abducted in violation of the extradition treaty between the United States and Mexico. *Extradition Treaty, May 4, 1978, [1979] United States-United Mexican States*, 31 U.S.T. 5059, T.I.A.S. No. 9656 (Extradition Treaty or Treaty). The District Court rejected the outrageous governmental conduct claim, but held that it lacked jurisdiction to try respondent because his abduction violated the Extradition Treaty. The district court discharged respondent and ordered that he be repatriated to Mexico. *Caro-Quintero, supra*, at 614.

The Court of Appeals affirmed the dismissal of the indictment and the repatriation of respondent, relying on its decision in *United States* v. *Verdugo-Urquidez*, 939 F.2d 1341 (9th Cir. 1991), cert. pending, No. 91-670. 946 F.2d 1466 (1991). In *Verdugo*, the Court of Appeals held that the forcible abduction of a Mexican national with the authorization or participation of the United States violated the Extradition Treaty between the United States and Mexico. Although the Treaty does not expressly prohibit such abductions, the Court of Appeals held that the "purpose" of the Treaty was violated by a forcible abduction, 939 F.2d, at 1350, which, along with a formal protest by the offended nation, would give a defendant the right to invoke the Treaty violation to defeat jurisdiction of the district court to try him. The Court of Appeals further held that the proper remedy for such a violation would be dismissal of the indictment and repatriation of the defendant to Mexico.

In the instant case, the Court of Appeals affirmed the district court's finding that the United States had authorized the abduction of respondent, and that letters from the Mexican government to the United States government served as an official protest of the Treaty violation. Therefore, the Court of Appeals ordered that the indictment against respondent be dismissed and that respondent be repatriated to Mexico. 946 F.2d, at 1467. We granted *certiorari* ... and now reverse.... In construing a treaty, as in construing a statute, we first look to its terms to determine its meaning.... The Treaty says nothing about the obligations of the United States and Mexico to refrain from forcible abductions of people from the territory of the other nation, or the consequences under the Treaty if such an abduction occurs. Respondent submits that Article 22(1) of the Treaty which states that it "shall apply to offenses specified in Article 2 [including murder] committed before and after this Treaty enters into force," 31 U.S.T., at 5073–5074, evidences an intent to make application of the Treaty mandatory for those offenses. However, the more natural conclusion is that Article 22 was included to ensure that the Treaty was applied to extraditions requested after the Treaty went into force, regardless of when the crime of extradition occurred.

More critical to respondent's argument is Article 9 of the Treaty which provides:

"1. Neither Contracting Party shall be bound to deliver up its own nationals, but the executive authority of the requested Party shall, if not prevented by the laws of that Party, have the power to deliver them up if, in its discretion, it be deemed proper to do so.

"2. If extradition is not granted pursuant to paragraph 1 of this Article, the requested Party shall submit the case to its competent authorities for the purpose of prosecution, provided that Party has jurisdiction over the offense." *Id.*, at 5065.

According to respondent, Article 9 embodies the terms of the bargain which the United States struck: if the United States wishes to prosecute a Mexican national, it may request that individual's extradition. Upon a request from the United States, Mexico may either extradite the individual, or submit the case to the proper authorities for prosecution in Mexico. In this way, respondent reasons, each nation preserved its right to choose whether its nationals would be tried in its own courts or by the courts of the other nation. This preservation of rights would be frustrated if either nation were free to abduct nationals of the other nation for the purposes of prosecution. More broadly, respondent reasons, as did the Court of Appeals, that all the processes and restrictions on the obligation to extradite established by the Treaty would make no sense if either nation were free to resort to forcible kidnapping to gain the presence of an individual for prosecution in a manner not contemplated by the Treaty. *Verdugo, supra*, at 1350.

We do not read the Treaty in such a fashion. Article 9 does not purport to specify the only way in which one country may gain custody of a national of the other country for the purposes of prosecution. In the absence of an extradition treaty, nations are under no obligation to surrender those in their country to foreign authorities for prosecution.... (United States may not extradite a citizen in the absence of a statute or treaty obligation). Extradition treaties exist so as to impose mutual obligations to surrender individuals in certain defined sets of circumstances, following established procedures. See 1 J. Moore, *A Treatise on Extradition and Interstate Rendition*, §72 (1891). The Treaty thus provides a mechanism which would not otherwise exist, requiring, under certain circumstances, the United States and Mexico to extradite individuals to the other country, and establishing the procedures to be followed when the Treaty is invoked.

The history of negotiation and practice under the Treaty also fails to show that abductions outside of the Treaty constitute a violation of the Treaty. As the Solicitor General notes, the Mexican government was made aware, as early as 1906, of the *Ker* doctrine, and the United States' position that it applied to forcible abductions made outside of the terms of the United States-Mexico extradition treaty. Nonetheless, the current version of the Treaty, signed in 1978, does not attempt to establish a rule that would in any way curtail the effect of *Ker*. Moreover, although language which would grant individuals exactly the right sought by respondent had been considered and drafted as early as 1935 by a prominent group of legal scholars sponsored by the faculty of Harvard Law School, no such clause appears in the current treaty.

Thus, the language of the Treaty, in the context of its history, does not support the proposition that the Treaty prohibits abductions outside of its terms. The remaining question, therefore, is whether the Treaty should be interpreted so as to include an implied term prohibiting prosecution where the defendant's presence is obtained by means other than those established by the Treaty. See *Valentine*, 299 U.S., at 17, 57 S.Ct., at 106 ("Strictly the question is not whether there had been a uniform practical construction denying the power, but whether the power had been so clearly recognized that the grant should be implied").

Respondent contends that the Treaty must be interpreted against the backdrop of customary international law, and that international abductions are "so clearly prohibited in international law" that there was no reason to include such a clause in the Treaty itself. Brief for Respondent 11. The international censure of international abductions is further evidenced, according to respondent, by the *United Nations Charter* and the *Charter of the Organization of American States. Id.*, at 17, 57 S.Ct., at 106. Respondent does not argue that these sources of international law provide an independent basis for the right respondent asserts not to be tried in the United States, but rather that they should inform the interpretation of the Treaty terms.

The Court of Appeals deemed it essential, in order for the individual defendant to assert a right under the Treaty, that the affected foreign government had registered a protest. *Verdugo*, 939 F.2d, at 1357 ("in the kidnapping case there must be a formal protest from the offended government after the kidnapping"). Respondent agrees that the right exercised by the individual is derivative of the nation's right under the Treaty, since nations are authorized, notwithstanding the terms of an extradition treaty, to voluntarily render an individual to the other country on terms completely outside of those provided in the Treaty. The formal protest, therefore, ensures that the "offended" nation actually objects to the abduction and has not in some way voluntarily rendered the individual for prosecution. Thus the Extradition Treaty only prohibits gaining the defendant's presence by means other than those set forth in the Treaty when the nation from which the defendant was abducted objects.

This argument seems to us inconsistent with the remainder of respondent's argument. The Extradition Treaty has the force of law, and if, as respondent asserts, it is self-executing, it would appear that a court must enforce it on behalf of an individual regardless of the offensiveness of the practice of one nation to the other nation. . . .

More fundamentally, the difficulty with the support respondent garners from international law is that none of it relates to the practice of nations in relation to extradition treaties. In *Rauscher*, we implied a term in the *Webster-Ashburton Treaty* because of the practice of nations with regard to extradition treaties. In the instant case, respondent would imply terms in the extradition treaty from the practice of nations with regards to international law more generally. Respondent would have us find that the Treaty acts as a prohibition against a violation of the general principle of international law that one government may not "exercise its police power in the territory of another state." Brief for Respondent 16. There are many actions which could be taken by a nation that would violate this principle, including waging war, but it cannot seriously be contended an invasion of the United States by Mexico would violate the terms of the extradition treaty between the two nations.

In sum, to infer from this Treaty and its terms that it prohibits all means of gaining the presence of an individual outside of its terms goes beyond established precedent and practice. In *Rauscher*, the implication of a doctrine of specialty into the terms of the *Webster-Ashburton Treaty* which, by its terms, required the presentation of evidence establishing probable cause of the crime of extradition before extradition was required, was a small step to take. By contrast, to imply from the terms of this Treaty that it prohibits obtaining the presence of an individual by means outside of the procedures the Treaty establishes requires a much larger inferential leap, with only the most general of international law principles to support it. The general principles cited by respondent simply fail to persuade us that we should imply in the *United States-Mexico Extradition Treaty* a term prohibiting international abductions.

Respondent and his amici may be correct that respondent's abduction was "shocking," Tr. of Oral Arg. 40, and that it may be in violation of general international law principles. Mexico has protested the abduction of respondent through diplomatic notes, App. 33–38, and the decision of whether respondent should be returned to Mexico, as a matter outside of the Treaty, is a matter for the Executive Branch. We conclude, however, that respondent's abduction was not in violation of the Extradition Treaty between the United States and Mexico, and therefore the rule of *Ker* v. *Illinois* is fully applicable to this case. The fact of respondent's forcible abduction does not therefore prohibit his trial in a court in the United States for violations of the criminal laws of the United States.

The judgment of the Court of Appeals is therefore reversed, and the case is remanded for further proceedings consistent with this opinion. So ordered.

Stevens, J. (dissenting)

The Court correctly observes that this case raises a question of first impression.... The case is unique for several reasons. It does not involve an ordinary abduction by a private kidnaper, or bounty hunter, as in *Ker* v. *Illinois*, 119 U.S. 436, 7 S.Ct. 225, 30 L.Ed. 421 (1886); nor does it involve the apprehension of an American fugitive who committed a crime in one State and sought asylum in another, as in *Frisbie* v. *Collins*, 342 U.S. 519, 72 S.Ct. 509, 96 L.Ed. 541 (1952). Rather, it involves this country's abduction of another country's citizen; it also involves a violation of the territorial integrity of that other country, with which this country has signed an extradition treaty.... The Extradition Treaty with Mexico is a comprehensive document containing 23 articles and an appendix listing the extraditable offenses covered by the agreement. The parties announced their purpose in the preamble: The two Governments desire "to cooperate more closely in the fight against crime and, to this end, to mutually render better assistance in matters of extradition." From the preamble, through the description of the parties' obligations with respect to offenses committed within as well as beyond the territory of a requesting party, the delineation of the procedures and evidentiary requirements for extradition, the special provisions for political offenses and capital punishment, and other details, the Treaty appears to have been designed to cover the entire subject of extradition. Thus, Article 22, entitled "Scope of Application" states that the "Treaty shall apply to offenses specified in Article 2 committed before and after this Treaty enters into force," and Article 2 directs that "[e]xtradition shall take place, subject to this Treaty, for wilful acts which fall within any of [the extraditable offenses listed in] the clauses of the Appendix." Moreover, as noted by the Court, ... Article 9 expressly provides that neither Contracting Party is bound to deliver up its own nationals, although it may do so in its discretion, but if it does not do so, it "shall submit the case to its competent authorities for purposes of prosecution."

Petitioner's claim that the Treaty is not exclusive, but permits forcible governmental kidnaping, would transform these, and other, provisions into little more than verbiage. For example, provisions requiring "sufficient" evidence to grant extradition (Art. 3), withholding extradition for political or military offenses (Art. 5), withholding extradition when the person sought has already been tried (Art. 6), withholding extradition when the statute of limitations for the crime has lapsed (Art. 7), and granting the requested State discretion to refuse to extradite an individual who would face the death penalty in the requesting country (Art. 8), would serve little purpose if the requesting country could simply kidnap the person. As the Court of Appeals for the Ninth Circuit recognized in a related case, "[e]ach of these provisions would be utterly frustrated if a kidnapping were held to be a permissible course of governmental conduct." *United States* v. *Verdugo-Urquidez*, 939 F.2d 1341, 1349 (1991). In addition, all of these provisions "only make sense if they are understood as requiring each treaty signatory to comply with those procedures whenever it wishes to obtain jurisdiction over an individual who is located in another treaty nation." *Id.*, at 1351.

It is true, as the Court notes, that there is no express promise by either party to refrain from forcible abductions in the territory of the other Nation.... Relying on that omission, the Court, in effect, concludes that the Treaty merely creates an optional method of obtaining jurisdiction over alleged offenders, and that the parties silently reserved the right to resort to self help whenever they deem force more expeditious than legal process. If the United States, for example, thought it more expedient to torture or simply to execute a person rather than to attempt extradition, these options would be equally available because they, too, were not explicitly prohibited by the Treaty. That, however, is a highly improbable interpretation of a consensual agreement, which on its face appears to have been intended to set forth comprehensive and exclusive rules concerning the subject of extradition. In my opinion, "the manifest scope and object of the treaty itself," *Rauscher,* 119 U.S. at 422..., plainly imply a mutual undertaking to respect the territorial integrity of the other contracting party....

... It is shocking that a party to an extradition treaty might believe that it has secretly reserved the right to make seizures of citizens in the other party's territory. Justice Story found it shocking enough that the United States would attempt to justify an American seizure of a foreign vessel in a Spanish port:

> "But, even supposing, for a moment, that our laws had required an entry of the Apollon, in her transit, does it follow, that the power to arrest her was meant to be given, after she had passed into the exclusive territory of a foreign nation? We think not. It would be monstrous to suppose that our revenue officers were authorized to enter into foreign ports and territories, for the purpose of seizing vessels which had offended against our laws. It cannot be presumed that Congress would voluntarily justify such a clear violation of the laws of nations." *The Apollon*, 9 Wheat. 362, 370–371, 6 L.Ed. 111 (1824) (emphasis added).

The law of nations, as understood by Justice Story in 1824, has not changed. Thus, a leading treatise explains: "A State must not perform acts of sovereignty in the territory of another State...."It is ... a breach of International Law for a State to send its agents to the territory of another State to apprehend persons accused of having committed a crime. Apart from other satisfaction, the first duty of the offending State is to hand over the person in question to the State in whose territory he was apprehended." 1 *Oppenheim's International Law* 295, and n. 1 (H. Lauterpacht 8th ed. 1955).

Commenting on the precise issue raised by this case, the chief reporter for the American Law Institute's *Restatement of Foreign Relations* used language reminiscent of Justice Story's characterization of an official seizure in a foreign jurisdiction as "monstrous:"

> "When done without consent of the foreign government, abducting a person from a foreign country is a gross violation of international law and gross dis-

respect for a norm high in the opinion of mankind. It is a blatant violation of the territorial integrity of another state; it eviscerates the extradition system (established by a comprehensive network of treaties involving virtually all states)."

... A critical flaw pervades the Court's entire opinion. It fails to differentiate between the conduct of private citizens, which does not violate any treaty obligation, and conduct expressly authorized by the Executive Branch of the Government, which unquestionably constitutes a flagrant violation of international law, and in my opinion, also constitutes a breach of our treaty obligations. Thus, at the outset of its opinion, the Court states the issue as "whether a criminal defendant, abducted to the United States from a nation with which it has an extradition treaty, thereby acquires a defense to the jurisdiction of this country's courts." *Ante*, at 2190. That, of course, is the question decided in *Ker* v. *Illinois*, 119 U.S. 436, 7 S.Ct. 225, 30 L.Ed. 421 (1886); it is not, however, the question presented for decision today.

The importance of the distinction between a court's exercise of jurisdiction over either a person or property that has been wrongfully seized by a private citizen, or even by a state law enforcement agent, on the one hand, and the attempted exercise of jurisdiction predicated on a seizure by federal officers acting beyond the authority conferred by treaty, on the other hand, is explained by Justice Brandeis in his opinion for the Court in *Cook* v. *United States*, 288 U.S. 102, 53 S.Ct. 305, 77 L.Ed. 641 (1933). That case involved a construction of a prohibition era treaty with Great Britain that authorized American agents to board certain British vessels to ascertain whether they were engaged in importing alcoholic beverages. A British vessel was boarded 11 miles off the coast of Massachusetts, found to be carrying unmanifested alcoholic beverages, and taken into port. The Collector of Customs assessed a penalty which he attempted to collect by means of libels against both the cargo and the seized vessel. The Court held that the seizure was not authorized by the treaty because it occurred more than 10 miles off shore. The Government argued that the illegality of the seizure was immaterial because, as in *Ker*, the Court's jurisdiction was supported by possession even if the seizure was wrongful. Justice Brandeis acknowledged that the argument would succeed if the seizure had been made by a private party without authority to act for the Government, but that a different rule prevails when the Government itself lacks the power to seize....

The same reasoning was employed by Justice Miller to explain why the holding in *Rauscher* did not apply to the *Ker* case. The arresting officer in *Ker* did not pretend to be acting in any official capacity when he kidnaped Ker. As Justice Miller noted, "the facts show that it was a clear case of kidnapping within the dominions of Peru, without any pretence of authority under the treaty or from the government of the United States." *Ker* v. *Illinois*, 119 U.S., at 443, 7 S.Ct., at 229 (emphasis added). The exact opposite is true in this case, as it was in *Cook*.

The Court's failure to differentiate between private abductions and official invasions of another sovereign's territory also accounts for its misplaced reliance on the 1935 proposal made by the Advisory Committee on Research in International Law. See *ante*, at 2194–2195, and n.13. As the text of that proposal plainly states, it would have rejected the rule of the *Ker* case. The failure to adopt that recommendation does not speak to the issue the Court decides today. The Court's admittedly "shocking" disdain for customary and conventional international law principles, see ante, at 2195, is thus entirely unsupported by case law and commentary.... As the Court observes at the outset of its opinion, there is reason to believe that respondent participated in an especially brutal murder of an American law enforcement agent. That fact, if true, may explain the Executive's intense interest in punishing respondent in our courts. Such an explanation, however, provides no justification for disregarding the Rule of Law that this Court has a duty to uphold. That the Executive may wish to reinterpret the Treaty to allow for an action that the Treaty in no way authorizes should not influence this Court's interpretation. Indeed, the desire for revenge exerts "a kind of hydraulic pressure ... before which even well settled principles of law will bend," ... but it is precisely at such moments that we should remember and be guided by our duty "to render judgment evenly and dispassionately according to law, as each is given understanding to ascertain and apply it." ... The way that we perform that duty in a case of this kind sets an example that other tribunals in other countries are sure to emulate.

The significance of this Court's precedents is illustrated by a recent decision of the Court of Appeal of the Republic of South Africa. Based largely on its understanding of the import of this Court's cases—including our decision in *Ker* v. *Illinois*—that court held that the prosecution of a defendant kidnaped by agents of South Africa in another country must be dismissed. *S* v. *Ebrahim*, S.Afr.L.Rep. (Apr.-June 1991). The Court of Appeal of South Africa—indeed, I suspect most courts throughout the civilized world—will be deeply disturbed by the "monstrous" decision the Court announces today. For every Nation that has an interest in preserving the Rule of Law is affected, directly or indirectly, by a decision of this character. As Thomas Paine warned, an "avidity to punish is always dangerous to liberty" because it leads a Nation "to stretch, to misinterpret, and to misapply even the best of laws." To counter that tendency, he reminds us:

> "He that would make his own liberty secure must guard even his enemy from oppression; for if he violates this duty he establishes a precedent that will reach to himself."....

Notes and Questions

1. What is the actual holding in *Alavarez-Machain*? Did the Supreme Court give federal law enforcement the "green light" to conduct extraterritorial abductions of foreign fugitives? Do you agree with the majority's opinion or the dissent in this case, or with portions thereof? Which arguments did you find most persuasive?

2. Using the majority's approach to interpretation of the bilateral extradition treaty and recalling the point of Justice Stevens concerning silence or omitted language, do you think that assassination is also permissible? If so, why? If not, why, and do you agree with the majority's interpretive approach? See also citations in note 4 below and articles 31 and 32 of the Vienna Convention on the Law of Treaties, U.N. Doc. A/CONF. 39/27 (1969) (utilizing especially "the ordinary meaning to be given to the terms of the treaty in their context and in light of its object and purpose" and "any relevant rules of international law").

3. Upon remand, the defendant argued that, the extradition treaty aside, the abduction nevertheless was a violation of other international laws and that *Ker*, therefore, did not control. *See United States v. Alvarez-Machain*, 971 F.2d 310 (9th Cir. 1992). The Court of Appeals, in a terse, unreasoned opinion, ruled that the Supreme Court's decision and its reliance on *Ker* precluded them from considering the issue. Ironically, after the question of jurisdiction in the case had been considered by the Supreme Court and twice by the Court of Appeals, the District Court ultimately ordered a directed verdict dismissing the charges against Alvarez-Machain on the ground that the prosecution had failed to

produce adequate proof of its charges. See Seth Mydons, *Judge Clears Mexican in Agent's Killing*, N.Y. Times, Dec. 15, 1992, at A20.

4. For differing views on the Supreme Court's holding in this case or related issues, *see, e.g.*, Secretaria de Relaciones Exteriores, Limits to National Jurisdiction vols. 1 and 2 (Mexico 1992 and 1993); Abraham Abramovsky, *Extraterritorial Abductions: America's Catch and Snatch Policy Run Amok*, 31 Va. J. Int'l L. 151 (1991); Richard Bilder, remarks, 86 Proc., Am. Soc. Int'l L. 451, 454 (1992); Valerie Epps, *Forcible Abduction, Jurisdiction And Treaty Interpretation*, Int'l Pract. Notebook No. 55, at 6 (1992); Joan Fitzpatrick, remarks, 86 Proc., Am. Soc. Int'l L. 451–52 (1992); Michael Glennon, *State-Sponsored Abduction: A Comment on* United States v. Alvarez-Machain, 86 Am. J. Int'l L. 746 (1992); Jimmy Gurulé, *Terrorism, Territorial Sovereignty, and the Forcible Apprehension of International Criminals Abroad*, 17 Hast. Int'l & Comp. L. Rev. 457 (1994); Malvina Halberstam, *In Defense of the Supreme Court Decision in* Alvarez-Machain, 86 *id.* at 736; correspondence, *id.* vol. 87 at 256; remarks, 86 Proc., Am. Soc. Int'l L. 453–54 (1992); Alan Kreczko, remarks, *id.* at 451–52, 454; Monroe Leigh, *Is the President Above Customary International Law?*, *id.* vol. 86 at 757; Jordan Paust, correspondence, *id.* vol. 87 at 252; Paust, *After* Alvarez-Machain, *supra*; John Quigley, *Government Vigilantes at Large: The Danger to Human Rights from Kidnapping of Suspected Terrorists*, 10 Hum. R.Q. 193 (1988); Hernan Ruiz-Bravo, *Monstrous Decision: Kidnapping Is Legal*, 24 Hast. Const. L.Q. 833 (1993); Ruth Wedgwood, remarks, 84 Proc., Am. Soc. Int'l L. 241 (1990).

5. Does *Alvarez-Machain* recognize a general right to abduct abroad, or was the matter framed much more narrowly? Refer to the specific jurisdictional issue outlined by the Chief Justice and his conclusion. Note that the Court stated that the abduction might be "shocking" but that, as a matter outside the treaty, it was a matter for the Executive Branch to decide whether the respondent should be returned to Mexico. *See also* references in note 4 above.

6. Has the Supreme Court's holding in *Alvarez-Machain* foreclosed application of the *Toscanino* exception to nonconsensual extraterritorial abductions? Recall that the court in *Toscanino*, although it also recognized a treaty exception to *Ker*, generally based its holding on two separate and independent grounds: (1) the due process clause of the Constitution; and (2) the supervisory power of federal courts over the administration of the federal criminal justice system. With respect to this second ground, the Court stated: "Clearly this power may legitimately be used to prevent district courts from themselves becoming 'accomplices in wilful disobedience of law.'" The District Court in *Alvarez-Machain* held that there was no evidence that the defendant had been tortured by his abductors, and the issue was not considered by the Supreme Court. 7. On June 29, 2004, the United States Supreme Court issued an opinion in the civil case brought by Humberto Alvarez-Machain, the Guadalajara, Mexico physician that the U.S. Drug Enforcement Administration (DEA) abducted from his home. *Sosa v. Alvarez-Machain*, 542 U.S. 692 (2004). The Court held that he was not entitled to a remedy under either the Federal Tort Claims Act (FTCA) (28 U.S.C. § 1346(b)(1), §§ 2671–2680) or the Alien Tort Claims Act (ATCA) (or Alien Tort Statute (ATS)) (28 U.S.C. § 1350). However, the Court did uphold the validity of the ATCA (ATS), although it cautioned the federal judiciary to use it sparingly in cases involving violations of customary international law known early in our history or that are sufficiently definable. With respect to the reach of *Sosa*, *see, e.g.*, Paust, *International Law Before the Supreme Court*, *supra* at 848–54. Justice Breyer's concurrence in part in *Sosa* recognized that actionable violations of customary international law include war crimes, torture, genocide, and other crimes against humanity. *See* 542 U.S. at 760.

Consider also the following case:

United States v. Matta-Ballesteros
71 F.3d 754 (9th Cir. 1995)

Poole, J.

Near dawn on April 5, 1988, Matta-Ballesteros was abducted from his home in Tegucigulpa, Honduras. Aided by Honduran Special Troops, or "Cobras," four United States Marshals bound his hands, put a black hood over his head, thrust him on the floor of a car operated by a United States Marshal, and drove him to a United States Air Force Base in Honduras. The Marshals then moved him to the United States, via the Dominican Republic. Within twenty-four hours of his armed abduction Matta-Ballesteros was a prisoner in the federal penitentiary at Marion, Illinois. The government does not dispute that he was forcibly abducted from his home in Honduras.

The government does dispute his account of how he was treated by his abductors. Matta-Ballesteros claims that while being transported bound and hooded to the United States Air Force Base he was beaten and burned with a stun gun at the direction of the Marshals. He claims that during his flight he was once again beaten and tortured by a stun gun applied to various parts of his body, including his feet and genitals....

Matta-Ballesteros argues that the extradition treaties between Honduras and the United States preclude his prosecution because of the recent Supreme Court ruling that treaties are self-executing and bestow rights upon individuals. *United States v. Alvarez-Machain*, 504 U.S. 655, 119 L. Ed. 2d 441, 112 S. Ct. 2188 (1992). However, *Alvarez-Machain* primarily holds that where the terms of an extradition treaty do not specifically prohibit the forcible abduction of foreign nationals, the treaty does not divest federal courts of jurisdiction over the foreign national. *Id.* at 664–66. *Alvarez-Machain* therefore dictates that, in the absence of express prohibitory terms, a treaty's self-executing nature is illusory.

The treaties between the United States and Honduras contain preservations of rights similar to those which *Alvarez-Machain* held did not sufficiently specify extradition as the only way in which one country may gain custody of a foreign national for purposes of prosecution. *Compare* 504 U.S. at 665–66 *with* 1909 Honduras-United States Extradition Treaty (37 Stat. 1616; 45 Stat. 2489), Art. VIII; 1933 Inter-Americas Extradition Treaty (49 Stat. 3111), Arts. II–IV, XXI. Nothing in the treaties between the United States and Honduras authorizes dismissal of the indictment against Matta-Ballesteros....

Though we may be deeply concerned by the actions of our government, it is clear in light of recent Supreme Court precedent that the circumstances surrounding Matta-Ballesteros's abduction do not divest this court of jurisdiction in this case. Since we have already concluded that the relevant treaty does not prohibit the abduction, "the rule in *Ker* applies, and the court need not inquire as to how respondent came before it." *Alvarez-Machain*, 504 U.S. at 662. In the shadow cast by *Alvarez-Machain*, attempts to expand due process rights into the realm of foreign abductions, as the Second Circuit did in *United States v. Toscanino*, 500 F.2d 267 (2d Cir. 1974), have been cut short....

This court has held, however, that we have inherent supervisory powers to order dismissal of prosecutions for only three legitimate reasons: (1) to implement a remedy for the violation of a recognized statutory or constitutional right; (2) to preserve judicial integrity by ensuring that a conviction rests on appropriate considerations validly before a jury; and (3) to deter future illegal conduct. *United States v. Simpson*, 927 F.2d 1088, 1090, *cert. denied*, 484 U.S. 898 ... (1987). *See also United States v. Hasting*, 461 U.S. 499, 505 ...

(1982); *United States v. Gatto*, 763 F.2d 1040, 1044 (9th Cir. 1985). We review dismissal based on the exercise of supervisory powers for an abuse of discretion. *United States v. Restrepo*, 930 F.2d 705, 712 (9th Cir. 1991).

The circumstances surrounding Matta-Ballesteros's abduction, while disturbing to us and conduct we seek in no way to condone, meet none of these criteria.... While it may seem unconscionable to some that officials serving the interests of justice themselves become agents of criminal intimidation, like the DEA agents in *Alvarez-Machain*, their purported actions have violated no recognized constitutional or statutory rights. They have likewise engaged in no illegal conduct which this court could attempt to deter in the future by invoking its supervisory powers.[5]....

Noonan, J. (concurring)

What This Case Is Not. This case does not involve the kidnapping by a private citizen of a defendant residing in a foreign country and wanted for an offense against the statute of a particular state of the United States and the subsequent placing of the kidnapped person on trial in the state's court. *Ker v. Illinois*, 119 U.S. 436 ... (1886).

This case does not involve the kidnapping of a defendant from one state of the United States by police officers of another one of the states, and his removal for trial to the officers' state. *Frisbie v. Collins*, 342 U.S. 519 ... (1952). This case does not involve the removal of the head of state of a foreign country by the military forces of the United States, acting at the direction of the President as Commander-in-Chief in an action found to be "military war," and the subsequent federal trial of the person removed. *United States v. Noriega*, 746 F. Supp. 1506, 1537 (S.D. Fla. 1990).

This case does not turn on the alleged violation of a treaty between the United States and the foreign country from which the defendant was removed to undergo trial in a federal court. *United States v. Alvarez-Machain*, 504 U.S. 655, 112 S. Ct. 2188, 119 L. Ed. 2d 441 (1992).

This case does not turn on an alleged violation of international customary law. *United States v. Alvarez-Machain*, 971 F.2d 310 (9th Cir. 1992).

This case does not turn on a protest by the sovereign of the country from which the defendant was abducted for trial in federal court; for there was no such protest. *Matta-Ballesteros v. Henman*, 896 F.2d 255, 259–260 (7th Cir. 1990).

This case does not turn on the Fourth Amendment rights of the abducted defendant. *Id.* at 262.

---

5. Matta-Ballesteros's abduction, even if we labeled it a "kidnapping," does not violate recognized constitutional or statutory provisions in light of *Alvarez-Machain*. Kidnapping also does not qualify as a *jus cogens* norm, such that its commission would be justiciable in our courts even absent a domestic law. *Jus cogens* norms, which are nonderogable and peremptory, enjoy the highest status within customary international law, are binding on all nations, and can not be preempted by treaty. *Committee of U.S. Citizens Living in Nicaragua v. Reagan*, 859 F.2d 929, 939–40 (D.C. Cir. 1988). While Art. 9 of the Universal Declaration of Human Rights does state that no one "shall be subjected to arbitrary arrest, detention or exile," G.A. Res. 217A(III), 3(1), U.N. GAOR Resolutions 71, U.N. Doc. A/810 (1948), kidnapping does not rise to the level of other *jus cogens* norms, such as torture, murder, genocide, and slavery. See *Siderman de Blake v. Republic of Argentina*, 965 F.2d 699, 717 (9th Cir. 1992), *cert. denied*, 113 S. Ct. 1812 (1993) ("We conclude that the right to be free from official torture is fundamental and universal, a right deserving of the highest status under international law, a norm of *jus cogens*.").

This case does not turn on the due process rights of the abducted defendant as in *United States v. Toscanino*, 500 F.2d 267 (2d Cir. 1974), a case qualified by *United States ex rel. Lujan v. Gengler*, 510 F.2d 62 (2d Cir. 1975), *cert. denied*, 421 U.S. 1001....

This case is not to be decided by stray dicta from the above cases; for what a court does not have before it a court does not authoritatively address. Emanations and intimations of the views of the opinion writer no doubt can be gathered from the dicta. They are not the holding of the court. They do not operate as binding decisional precedent....

That this act of kidnapping occurred is not disputed by the government. There is dispute as to how Matta was treated by his kidnappers and that treatment is not considered further here. Kidnapping in itself is a violent attack upon a human person—a sudden invasion of personal security, a brutal deprivation of personal liberty. Kidnapping in itself is a cruel act, and the cruelty is magnified when the victim's home is the place where the violent assault upon his liberty is made. Kidnapping committed in a foreign country becomes an offense against federal law when the victim is transported by the kidnappers into the United States. *United States v. Garcia*, 854 F.2d 340 (9th Cir. 1988). The kidnapping continues as long as the victim is not released by the abductors. *Id.* at 343....

If confirmation were wanted of the common view that humankind has of kidnapping it is furnished by Article 9 of the Universal Declaration of Human Rights which affirms that no one "shall be subjected to arbitrary arrest, detention or exile." G.A. Res. 217A(III), 3(1), U.N. GAOR Resolutions 71, U.N. Doc. A/810 (1948). United Nations Security Council Resolution 579 (1985) lumps "acts of abduction" with "acts of hostage-taking" as "manifestations of international terrorism" and "condemns unequivocally all acts of hostage-taking and abduction."....

The motive of the kidnappers—here no doubt well-meaning in their officiousness—does not qualify the violence of their conduct nor its impact on the person whom they kidnap. That the abductors were law enforcement officers of the United States, rather than some fanatic band, doubles the horror of their activity....

We are then confronted with a kidnapping, and we as judges are asked to be part of the kidnapping. We are asked to participate in two ways. First, the acts of the United States Marshals were directed to bringing Matta within the jurisdiction of the courts of the United States so that he might be tried for federal crimes and in particular for the crime of which he stands convicted in the Central District of California. The acts of the Marshals were not personal acts of revenge. Their purpose was to assure Matta's presence in the federal courts. Without the participation of the federal courts the kidnapping was purposeless. The federal courts are inextricably tied to the kidnapping because federal trial was the reason for abducting him.... [Nonetheless, Judge Noonan went on to state that because another Circuit upheld conviction in this case and defendant's presence in California is the result of that conviction, the Ninth Circuit should not dismiss the case].

Note and Questions

1. Note that the Honduran government apparently consented to the capture and transfer of Matta-Ballesteros and did not protest his arrest. Do you think that this was an "abduction" or "kidnapping" in foreign state territory? If not, does this distinguish the case from *Toscanino* and *Alvarez-Machain*? Is it more like *Noriega*? In light of the facts, was the detention "arbitrary" within the meaning of human rights law? If not, should prohibitions concerning "kidnappings" apply? If it was, are kidnappings violations of *jus cogens* norms?

and are such non-waivable by a state? Did the forcible apprehension of Matta-Ballesteros violate Honduras' territorial sovereignty? *See, e.g.*, RESTATEMENT § 432, Reporter's Note 1, § 702 (e), Comments h and n, Reporters' Notes 6 and 11; General Comment No. 24 of the Human Rights Committee, para. 8, U.N. Doc. CCPR/C/21/REV.1/Add.6 (1994), *reprinted in* PAUST, INTERNATIONAL LAW AS LAW OF THE UNITED STATES 376–78 (2 ed. 2003). In view of Judge Noonan's recognition of judicial "participation" in kidnappings, is there judicial responsibility under international law? Recall Chapter Two, Section 1 and *United States v. Altstoetter*. Also recall the views of the Human Rights Committee and the European Court of Human Rights noted *supra*.

Also, do you suspect that the Dominican Republic consented to the use of police powers within its territory with respect to movement of the accused to the U.S. "via the Dominican Republic"?

2. In *Alvarez-Machain*, Justice Stevens in his dissent referred to the South African case of *State* v. *Ebrahim* (1991), 2 S.A. Rep. 553(a); translation into English from Afrikaans in 31 I.L.M. 888 (1992). In that case, Ebrahim, a South African citizen by birth and since 1962 a member of the military wing of the African National Congress (ANC), was forcibly abducted from his home in Swaziland and taken across the border into South Africa. In 1964, he had been convicted of several acts of sabotage and had been sentenced to 15 years of imprisonment. Upon his release in 1979, he was restricted to Pinetown, Natal. In 1980, he fled to Swaziland. Upon his arrival in South Africa, he was formally arrested and later charged with treason. In his application for release, he submitted that his "abduction in Swaziland took place with the authority and knowledge of the South African Police or other agents of the South African state." It does not appear that the government of Swaziland protested at any time. The Court, based on a combination of Roman-Dutch law and English common law and referring in particular to the *Toscanino* case considered above, held that the South African trial court had no jurisdiction to hear the case on account of the abduction, and consequently his conviction and sentence were set aside.

3. In *United States* v. *Yunis*, 681 F. Supp. 909, 914–15 (D.D.C. 1988), the accused was lured from Lebanon to Cyprus by a friend who had been co-opted by the United States Drug Enforcement Administration and the CIA. He was arrested on a boat in international waters off the coast of Cyprus by an FBI agent who was posing as a drug dealer, for whom Yunis thought he would be working. Yunis was transferred to a U.S. Navy communications vessel, from there to the U.S. aircraft carrier "Saratoga" and finally by non-stop Navy jet to Andrews Air Force Base outside of Washington, D.C. Yunis' arrest had been authorized by a United States magistrate. He had, with others, hijacked a Royal Jordanian Airlines aircraft in Beirut, Lebanon, which was eventually blown up. The prosecution in the United States was founded on legislation contained in 18 U.S.C. § 2331 entitled "Terrorist Acts Against U.S. Nationals." Yunis was found guilty and sentenced to 30 years in prison. How is the *Yunis* case different from *Toscanino* and *Alvarez-Machain*? Would the flag or registry of the vessel that Yunis was lured onto be important for enforcement jurisdiction? Recall Chapter Three, Section 2; RESTATEMENT §§ 432–433; and see Paust, *After* Alvarez-Machain, *supra* at 568–69 n.65. Does it make a difference that Yunis was wanted for aircraft hijacking, sabotage, and hostage-taking? See Section 3 (Luring).

4. Alan J. Kreczko, the Deputy Legal Adviser of the U.S. Department of State, testified to a House Judiciary Subcommittee about the international reaction to the Supreme Court's opinion in *Alvarez-Machain*:

> The Supreme Court's decision has caused considerable concern among a wide range of governments, particularly in the Americas, but elsewhere as well. Many

governments have expressed outrage that the United States believes it has the right to decide unilaterally to enter their territory and abduct one of their nationals. Governments have informed us that they would regard such action as a breach of international law. They have also informed us that they would protect their nationals from such action, that such action would violate their domestic law, and that they would vigorously prosecute such violations. Some countries, as well, have told us that they believe that such actions would violate our extradition treaties with them. Some have also suggested that they will challenge the lawfulness of such abductions in international forums. Some have indicated that the decision could affect their parliaments' review of pending law enforcement agreements with the United States....

... [I]mmediately following the Supreme Court's decision, the White House issued a public statement, reaffirming that: "The United States strongly believes in fostering respect for international rules of law, including, in particular, the principles of respect for territorial integrity and sovereign equality of states. U.S. policy is to cooperate with foreign states in achieving law enforcement objectives...."

At the same time, we are not prepared categorically to rule out unilateral action. It is not inconceivable that in certain extreme cases, such as the harboring by a hostile foreign country of a terrorist who has attacked U.S. nationals and is likely to do so again, the President might decide that such an abduction is necessary and appropriate as a matter of the exercise of our right of self-defense. This necessary reservation of right for extreme cases doe not, however, detract from our strong support for the principles of sovereignty and territorial integrity generally. To reinforce this point, the White House statement also noted the Administration has in place procedures designed to ensure that U.S. law enforcement activities overseas fully take into account foreign relations and international law....

3 U.S. Dept. of State Dispatch 614 (1992).

Was this statement of the Clinton administration a change from the approach of William Barr? With respect to the Clinton administration claim of permissible "abduction" in extreme cases of self-defense when attacks are ongoing, see also the final sections of this chapter.

5. In light of "the diplomatic setbacks suffered by the United States subsequent to the Supreme Court's decision in the *Alvarez* case," Professor Anthony D'Amato wrote "this is one the Justice Department should have tried hard to lose." Do you agree? *See* A. D'Amato, International Law Anthology 249 (1994).

6. For other recommendations, *see, e.g.,* Paust, *After* Alvarez-Machain, *supra* at 565 n.56, 567 n.59, 575–76 n.96 (H.R. Comm. of the Am. Branch of the ILA), 575–77 (Prof. Paust's draft), 579–80 (draft U.N. G.A. Dec.).

7. Shortly after the *Alvarez-Machain* decision, members of the Iranian Parliament passed a draft law giving the President of Iran the right to arrest anywhere U.S. persons who take action against Iranian citizens or property anywhere in the world and bring them to Iran for trial. The bill provided that U.S. citizens would be tried by Iranian courts under Islamic law. The bill "aims at preserving the prestige and territorial integrity of the Islamic Republic, safeguarding the lives and properties of Iranian nationals abroad and defending the interests of the Islamic Republic." Barry Carter & Phillip Trimble, International Law 812 (2 ed. 1995). How do you think the United States would react if Iranian agents kidnapped a U.S. citizen from Washington, D.C. for trial in Iran?

8. With respect to judicial power and responsibilities, Professor Paust adds: "Certain extraordinary circumstances ... [noted above] pose reasonable exceptions to a flat prohibition of the use of force to arrest persons in foreign territory without foreign state consent. Nonetheless, absent such extraordinary circumstances, transnational abductions recognizably constitute violations of several international norms, including those providing relevant rights of the individual victim of an abduction.... all of this assumes an executive branch willing to abide by customary and treaty-based international law, and thus the mandate of Article II, Section 3 of the United States Constitution, and an executive branch capable of making fine point distinctions with respect to the context and relevant legal policies at stake. When it becomes evident that this is not the case, when the executive claims to be above the law and able to act in lawless disregard of its duty under the Constitution, the need for judicial review, indeed judicial supervisory power, becomes all the more necessary in a free society ... Ultimately, this quest for unbounded power threatens much more than law and justice or our own rights and liberties. Ultimately, this quest for power uncontrolled by law is subversive of constitutional democracy." Paust, *After* Alvarez-Machain, *supra* at 577–78.

Section 5
Other Uses of Force

A. Capture During War or in Self-Defense

[see Chapter Two, Section 3; Chapter Four, Sections 7 and 8; Chapter Seven]

Notes

1. Professor Paust has written: "I do not agree ... that every abduction or capture of a person in foreign state territory without foreign state consent is violative of international law more generally or is necessarily "arbitrary," "cruel," "inhuman," or "degrading" within the meaning of relevant human rights standards. For example, it may not be incompatible with principles of justice, "unjust," "unlawful" or otherwise "arbitrary" to abduct or capture an international criminal in a context when action is reasonably necessary to assure adequate sanctions against egregious international criminal activity." J. Paust, *After* Alvarez-Machain*: Abduction, Standing, Denials of Justice, and Unaddressed Human Rights Claims*, 67 St. John's L. Rev. 551, 564 (1993), also recognizing the permissibility of capture during self-defense operations. *See also* Statement of Paul Hoffman, lead counsel for *Alvarez-Machain*, *in* 79 A.B.A. J. 22 (1993); *United States v. Yunis*, 681 F. Supp. 896, 907 (D.D.C. 1988) (citing D. Cameron Findlay, *Abducting Terrorists Overseas for Trial in the United States: Issues of International and Domestic Law*, 23 Tex. Int'l L.J. 1 (1988)), *aff'd*, 924 F.2d 1086 (D.C. Cir. 1991); M. Halberstam, *In Defense of the Supreme Court Decision in Alvarez-Machain*, 86 Am. J. Int'l L. 736, 744–45 & n.58 (1992) ("illegally seized," but should not release accused or obviate jurisdiction); M. Halberstam, correspondence, 87 Am. J. Int'l L. 256, 257 (1993) ("Whether one who has committed monstrous crimes against humanity is tried or permitted to escape justice should not depend solely on the consent of the State that harbored him."). These are probably still minority viewpoints. What is your preference?

2. Professor Paust also wrote in the same article (*id*. at 566): "And it may not be 'arbitrary' or 'unjust' to capture an individual whose present activity forms part of a process of armed attack on a state in violation of the United Nations Charter and triggers a right of self-defense in response. Indeed, in the latter circumstance, abduction may provide a less violent and injurious option than general military strikes or targeting that is otherwise reasonably necessary and proportionate. Further, if a capture, arrest, and transfer is conducted as part of an armed activity authorized by the United Nations Security Council under its competence to address threats to the peace, breaches of the peace, or acts of aggression, such a capture may not be 'arbitrary' or 'unjust' and, in a given circumstance, may be permissible. The same conclusions may obtain when capture is part of a lawful exercise of regional power in accordance with Chapter VIII of the United Nations Charter." Do you agree? See also M. Halberstam, *In Defense, supra*, at 736 n.5 ("Not all abductions are violations of international law. Abduction of terrorists may be justified self-defense under Article 51 of the United Nations Charter and may thus not be in violation of international law."); M. Glennon, *State Sponsored Abduction: A Comment on United States v. Alvarez-Machain*, 86 Am. J. Int'l L. 746, 749, 755 (1992).

B. U.N. Security Council Powers

[see U.N. Charter, articles 24–25, 39–45, 48–49, 51, 52–53, 103 in the Documents Supplement]

Questions

1. What powers does the Security Council have to authorize the capture of alleged international criminals in the territory of a state? Can the Security Council lawfully order such a state to hand over the accused to another state or to an international tribunal? Do these powers override other international agreements? *See also* Article 29 (2)(e) of the Statute of the International Tribunal for the Former Yugoslavia, adopted by U.N. S.C. Res. 827 (25 May 1993) ("States shall comply without undue delay with any request for assistance or an order issued by a Trial Chamber, including ... the surrender or the transfer of the accused to the International Tribunal.").

2. In Questions of Interpretation and Application of the 1971 Montreal Convention Arising from the Aerial Incident at Lockerbie (Libya v. U.K.; Libya v. U.S.) 1992 I.C.J. 3, the International Court of Justice declined to grant Libya injunctive relief in view of Security Council orders to Libya to turn over those accused in connection with the Lockerbie bombing (of Pan Am 103 in 1988), although the Montreal Convention would allow Libya the discretion to prosecute (in good faith and in accordance with the Convention) in lieu of extradition and Libya claimed that it had the sovereign right to refuse to extradite its nationals. Should the Charter override the Montreal Convention? Does the Court have the power to second-guess a decision of the Security Council?

See generally T. Franck, *The "Powers of Appreciation": Who is the Ultimate Guardian of UN Legality?*, 86 Am. J. Int'l L. 519 (1992); C. Joyner & W. Rothbaum, *Libya and the Aerial Incident at Lockerbie: What Lessons for International Extradition Law*, 14 Mich. J. Int'l L. 222 (1993); G. Watson, *Constitutionalism, Judicial Review, The World Court*, 34 Harv. Int'l L. J. 1 (1993). *See also* The Prosecutor of the Tribunal v. Dusko Tadic, in Chapter Six, Section 9.

By special agreement, an ad hoc court was set up to try the Lockerbie accused in the Netherlands. The trial began on May 3, 2000. See also Chapter Two, Section 3; Chapter Twelve, Section 2 B.

3. Are there any limits to such Security Council powers? *See generally* Jose E. Alvarez, *Judging the Security Council,* 90 Am. J. Int'l L. 1 (1996); J. Paust, *Peace-Making and Security Council Powers: Bosnia-Herzegovina Raises International and Constitutional Questions,* 19 So. Ill. U.L.J. 131, 137–42 (1994); W.M. Reisman, correspondence, 87 Am. J. Int'l L. 589 (1993).

4. NATO authorized the use of military force in Kozovo in 1999. Can NATO do so under Articles 52-53 of the U.N. Charter? Can NATO forces in Kozovo arrest persons there who are reasonably accused of having committed genocide, other crimes against humanity, and/or war crimes? See also Chapter 7, Section D.

Chapter 6

International Prosecutorial Efforts and Tribunals

Section 1
Early Experience

Introductory Note

Most trials of violators of international law have been in domestic fora. In human history, it has been rare that a tribunal was formulated to try offenses against humankind. One notable early example occurred at Naples in 1268 when Conradin von Hohenstafen, Duke of Suabia, was tried for initiating an unjust war. It was also an early example of the trial and conviction of a political leader for an offense against peace. Von Hohenstafen was later executed for his misdeeds on October 29, 1268.

During the U.S. Revolutionary War, there were suggestions that the King of England and others be prosecuted for their "War against the natural rights of all Mankind." Consider the following:

> "The laying a Country desolate with Fire and Sword, declaring War against the rights of all Mankind, and extirpating the Defenders thereof from the Face of the Earth, is the Concern of every Man...." So wrote the American revolutionary Thomas Paine in February of 1776. The war against human rights of which he wrote had already led to the 1775 Declaration of the Causes and Necessity of Taking Up Arms, which had denounced Parliament's "cruel and impolitic purpose of enslaving the [colonials] ... by violence ...", the British government's "intemperate rage for unlimited domination", acts of "cruel aggression", and numerous "oppressive measures" that had reduced our political ancestors "to the alternative of causing an unconditional submission to the tyranny of irritated ministers, or resistance by force." As the world knows, our ancestors chose armed revolution as the self-help sanction response to aggression against the authority of the people, and our revolution served as a precursor for numerous others in the Americas, Europe, and elsewhere, even into the twentieth century.

Paust, *Aggression Against Authority: The Crime of Oppression, Politicide And Other Crimes Against Human Rights*, 18 Case West. Res. J. Int'l L. 283, 283–84 (1986).

Although the war against human rights and the crime of political oppression led to no criminal sanctions against the King of England and his retainers, an international trial would not have been completely unprecedented. For the oppression of persons under his charge and actions against the "laws of God and man," including responsibility for murder, rape, and pillage, the Burgundian Peter von Hagenbach was deprived of his knighthood and then executed with an order, "Let justice be done." The trial of von Hagenbach for the improper and terroristic administration of pledged territories on the Upper Rhine had occurred at Breisach in 1474 at the order of the Archduke of Austria and was presided over by twenty-eight judges from allied towns.

Notes

1. It should also be noted that von Hagenbach was tried before actual war in 1476, so it would be improper to label the case a normal "war crimes" trial. Von Hagenbach was found guilty of murder, rape, perjury and other crimes said to constitute violations of the "laws of God and man." He raised a defense of obedience to superior orders (from Duke Charles of Burgundy who had placed von Hagenbach in charge of territories on the upper Rhine of the Archduke of Austria that had been pledge to Charles) and asked for adjournment to obtain confirmation of such orders, but the defense was denied as being contrary to the law of God. It really does not matter whether the tribunal was in the strict sense a "war crimes" tribunal or an international tribunal. What is more important is the demonstrated consensus, not incompatible with the medieval "law of arms," that a leader must not administer trust territory improperly.

2. For further inquiry, see T. TAYLOR, NUREMBERG AND VIETNAM: AN AMERICAN TRAGEDY 81–82 (1970); G. SCHWARZENBERGER, II INTERNATIONAL LAW 462–66 (1968); *Matter of Barbie*, in Chapter Nine *infra*.

3. More generally during the Middle Ages, the Holy Roman Emperor failed to obtain sufficient authority to enforce the law of arms. Such application occurred in the councils and courts of the major sovereigns in Europe. Further, the Papacy had attempted to establish a right to hear claims concerning violations of the law of arms, but to no avail. For additional reading on the "law of arms," *see, e.g.*, KEEN, THE LAW OF WAR IN THE LATE MIDDLE AGES (1965); Paust, *My Lai and Vietnam*, 57 MIL. L. REV. 99, 109 (1972).

Section 2
Efforts During World War I Era

After World War I there were trials of war criminals in domestic courts, including trials of U.S. soldiers in U.S. military tribunals (see Chapter Four, Section 7 D *supra*). The French tried Captain Imhof on the Rhine. See N.Y. Times, June 2, 1920. An effort was made to obtain many of those accused of having committed such crimes from Germany for trial in Allied tribunals.

U.S. Department of the Army Pamphlet No. 27-161-2
II INTERNATIONAL LAW 221–22 (1962)

The Leipzig Trials (1921).

Pursuant to articles 228–230 of the Versailles Treaty [see Chapter Seven, Sec. 2B], Germany agreed to turn over suspected war criminals to the Allies for trial by Allied tribunals.

At the Paris Peace Conference on February 6, 1920, the Allies formally demanded of Germany the extradition of 896 Germans accused of violating the laws of war. England demanded 97 for trial, France and Belgium 344 each, Italy 29, Poland 47, Rumania 31, and Serbia 4. Kurt von Lersner, head of the German peace delegation, refused to accept the extradition list. The German Government was not very stable and compliance with the demand might have led to its overthrow. Von Lersner resigned from the Peace Conference and returned to Berlin.

As a compromise, the Allies, at the suggestion of Great Britain, agreed to accept an offer by Germany to try a selected number of individuals before the Criminal Senate of the Imperial Court of Justice of Germany. Forty-five names were selected. Of these forty-five only twelve were actually brought to trial, six at the insistence of the British, five accused by France, and one by Belgium....

The trial resulted in six convictions and six acquittals. Most of the acquittals resulted from a failure of the court to accept certain evidence as creditable. Disappointment was expressed not only over the comparatively light sentences meted out but also over the fact the trials dealt almost exclusively with the treatment of shipwrecked survivors of submarine activity and with the treatment of prisoners of war. No trials were held on the actual conduct of hostilities, such as the use of weapons and the destruction of life and property in combat. Another objection was the fact that the court itself was under pressure from the German press and German public opinion. Both were very hostile to the trials. For example, after the sentence was announced in the Llandovery Castle case the British observers had to leave by the side door under police escort.

The name of each accused, the charge, and the finding and sentence are as follows:

Sgt. Karl Heymen	Mistreatment of PW's	Guilty	10 months
Capt. Emil Muller	Mistreatment of PW's	Guilty	6 months
Pvt. Robert Neumann	Mistreatment of PW's	Guilty	6 months
Lt. Capt. Karl Neumann	Torpedoing the hospital ship, the Dover Castle	Not Guilty	
1st Lt. Ludwig Dithmar	Firing on survivors in lifeboats of hospital ship, Llandovery Castle	Guilty	4 Years
1st Lt. John Boldt	Firing on survivors in lifeboats of hospital ship, Llandovery Castle	Guilty	4 Years
Max Ramdahr	Mistreatment of Belgian children	Not Guilty	
Major Benno Crusius	Passing on the alleged order of Gen. Stenger	Guilty through Negligence	2 Years
1st Lt. Adolph Laule	Killing a PW	Not Guilty	
Lt. Gen. Hans Von Schock	Mistreatment of PW's	Not Guilty	
Maj. Gen. Benno Kruska	Mistreatment of PW's	Not Guilty	
Lt. Gen. Karl Stenger	Ordering the killing of prisoners of war	Not Guilty	

Notes

1. The existence of trial observers can be useful for several reasons, *e.g.*, to assure a serious effort to prosecute those reasonably accused of international crime, to assure greater concern for international community demands and expectations, and to assure a fair procedure and trial.

2. By 1919, the numerous offenses committed by Germans, Austrians, Turks, Bulgarians, and others led to the formulation of a list* of war crimes to be tried following World War I. The following are excerpts from the Report Presented to the Preliminary Peace Conference by the Commission on the Responsibility of the Authors of the War and on Enforcement of Penalties, pp. 8–9 (1919) (members of the commission were: United States, British Empire, France, Italy, Japan, Belgium, Greece, Poland, Romania, Serbia):

"Every belligerent has, according to international law, the power and authority to try the individuals alleged to be guilty of the crimes of which an enumeration has been given in Chapter II on Violations of the Laws and Customs of War, if such persons have been taken prisoners or have otherwise fallen into its power. Each belligerent has, or has power to set up, pursuant to its own legislation, an appropriate tribunal, military or civil, for the trial of such cases. These courts would be able to try the incriminated persons according to their own procedure, and much complication and consequent delay would be avoided which would arise if all such cases were to be brought before a single tribunal.... but no trial or sentence by a court of an enemy country shall bar trial and sentence by the tribunal or by a national court belonging to one of the Allied or Associated States."

Section 3
International Tribunals After World War II

A. The International Military Tribunal at Nuremberg

1. Opinion and Judgment as to Jurisdiction (October 1, 1946)

The jurisdiction of the Tribunal is defined in the Agreement and Charter, and the crimes coming within the jurisdiction of the Tribunal, for which there shall be individual responsibility, are set out in Article 6. The law of the Charter is decisive, and binding upon the Tribunal.

The making of the Charter was the exercise of the sovereign legislative power by the countries to which the German Reich unconditionally surrendered; and the undoubted right of these countries to legislate for the occupied territories has been recognized by the civilized world. The Charter is not an arbitrary exercise of power on the part of the victorious nations, but in the view of the Tribunal, as will be shown, it is the expression of international law existing at the time of its creation; and to that extent is itself a contribution to international law.

The Signatory Powers created this Tribunal, defined the law it was to administer, and made regulations for the proper conduct of the Trial. In doing so, they have done together what any one of them might have done singly; for it is not to be doubted that any nation has the right thus to set up special courts to administer law. With regard to the con-

---

* [The list appears *supra* in Chapter Two, Section 1]

stitution of the court, all that the defendants are entitled to ask is to receive a fair trial on the facts and law.

2. Individual Responsibility

Justice Jackson as chief prosecutor at Nuremberg:

"We are able to do away with domestic tyranny and violence and aggression by those in power against the rights of their own people only when we make all men answerable to law."

3. Decision of the International Military Tribunal at Nuremberg
In re Goering and Others
(October 1, 1946) INTERNATIONAL LAW REPORTS 203

On August 8, 1945, an Agreement was concluded in London between the Governments of Great Britain and Northern Ireland, of the United States of America, of France, and of the Union of Soviet Socialist Republics, acting in the interest of all the United Nations. That Agreement provided for the establishment of an international Military Tribunal for the trial of war criminals whose offences had no particular geographical location. The constitution, jurisdiction and function of the Tribunal were defined in the Charter annexed to the Agreement.

Article 6 of the Charter provided:

"The Tribunal established by the Agreement referred to in Article I hereof for the trial and punishment of the major war criminals of the European Axis countries shall have the power to try and punish persons who, acting in the interests of the European Axis countries, whether as individuals or as members of organizations, committed any of the following crimes.

"The following acts, or any of them, are crimes coming within the jurisdiction of the Tribunal for which there shall be individual responsibility:

(a) *Crimes against peace:* namely, planning, preparation, initiation or waging of a war of aggression, or a war in violation of international treaties, agreements or assurances, or participation in a common plan or conspiracy for the accomplishment of any of the foregoing;

(b) *War crimes:* namely, violations of the laws or customs of war. Such violations shall include, but not be limited to, murder, ill-treatment or deportation to slave labour or for any other purpose of civilian population of or in occupied territory, murder or ill-treatment of prisoners of war or persons on the seas, killing of hostages, plunder of public or private property, wanton destruction of cities, towns or villages, or devastation not justified by military necessity;

(c) *Crimes against humanity:* namely, murder, extermination, enslavement, deportation, and other inhumane acts committed against any civilian population, before or during the war, or persecutions on political, racial or religious grounds in execution of or in connection with any crime within the jurisdiction of the Tribunal, whether or not in violation of the domestic law of the country where perpetrated.

Leaders, organizers, instigators and accomplices participating in the formulation or execution of a common plan or conspiracy to commit any of the foregoing crimes are responsible for all acts performed by any persons in execution of such plan."

Article 7 provided:

"The official position of defendants, whether as Heads of State or responsible officials in Government Departments, shall not be considered as freeing them from responsibility or mitigating punishment."

Article 8 provided:

"The fact that the Defendant acted pursuant to order of his Government or of a superior shall not free him from responsibility, but may be considered in mitigation of punishment if the Tribunal determines that justice so requires."

Article 9 provided:

"At the trial of any individual member of any group or organization the Tribunal may declare (in connection with any act of which the individual may be convicted) that the group or organization of which the individual was a member was a criminal organization.

"After receipt of the Indictment the Tribunal shall give such notice as it thinks fit that the prosecution intends to ask the Tribunal to make such declaration and any member of the organization will be entitled to apply to the Tribunal for leave to be heard by the Tribunal upon the question of the criminal character of the organization. The Tribunal shall have power to allow or reject the application. If the application is allowed, the Tribunal may direct in what manner the applicants shall be represented and heard."

In accordance with Article 14 of the Charter an Indictment was, on October 18, 1945, presented to the Tribunal sitting in Berlin. It is convenient to summarize the four Counts of the Indictment.

Count One: The Common Plan or Conspiracy. — The accused were charged with participation in the formulation and execution of a common plan or conspiracy to commit crimes against peace, war crimes and crimes against humanity. It was alleged that the National Socialist Party was the central core of the common plan or conspiracy and that its objects included: (1) the abrogation of the Treaty of Versailles and the lifting of the restrictions upon the military rearmament and activity of Germany; (2) the acquisition, at the expense of neighbouring States, of the territories lost by Germany as a result of the First World War and other territories in Europe asserted to be occupied principally by so called "racial Germans". It was further alleged that on March 7, 1936, in violation of the Treaty of Versailles and of the Rhine Pact of Locarno of October 16, 1925, the Rhineland was reoccupied and fortified; that on March 12, 1938, German armed forces invaded Austria; that on March 15, 1939, in violation of the Pact concluded between the United Kingdom, France, Italy and Germany in Munich on September 29, 1938, which involved the cession of the Sudetenland by Czechoslovakia to Germany, armed forces of the latter country occupied the major part of Czechoslovakia not ceded to Germany by the Munich pact; that, having denounced the German-Polish Pact of 1934 on false grounds, demands were made for the cession of Polish territory; and that upon the refusal by Poland to yield, German armed forces invaded that country on September 1, 1939. It was also alleged that the accused participated in active preparations for an extension of the war in Europe, and that in accordance with those plans they caused the German armed forces to invade Denmark and Norway on April 9, 1940; Belgium, the Netherlands and Luxemburg on May 10, 1940; Yugoslavia and Greece on April 6, 1941; and Russia on June 22, 1941.

Count Two: Crimes against Peace. — The accused were charged with participation in the planning, preparation, initiation and waging of the wars of aggression enumerated in

Court One, which wars, it was alleged, were in violation of international treaties, agreement and assurances.

Count Three: War Crimes. — The accused were charged with responsibility for the commission of war crimes between September 1, 1939, and May 8, 1945, in Germany and in all the countries occupied by German armed forces since September 1, 1939, and Austria, Czechoslovakia and Italy, and on the high seas. The war crimes included those enumerated in Article 6(*b*) of the Charter set out above.

Count Four: Crimes against Humanity. — The accused were charged with responsibility for the commission of crimes against humanity during a period of years preceding May 8, 1945, in Germany and in the countries specified in Count Three. Those crimes included the murder and persecution of individuals on political, racial and religious grounds and of those persons who were, or who were suspected of being, opposed to the common plan alleged in Count One. It was stated in Count Four that the prosecution would rely upon the facts pleaded under Count Three as also constituting crimes against humanity.

> *Held:* that Goering and eighteen other accused were guilty of various charges.
> Three accused were acquitted.... .

II. Crimes Against Peace

(1) *War of Aggression as a Crime. The Principle of Retroactivity.* The Tribunal said: "The charges in the Indictment that the defendants planned and waged aggressive wars are charges of the utmost gravity. War is essentially an evil thing. Its consequences are not confined to the belligerent states alone, but affect the whole world. To initiate a war of aggression, therefore, is not only an international crime; it is the supreme international crime, differing only from other war crimes in that it contains within itself the accumulated evil of the whole. The first acts of aggression referred to in the Indictment are the seizure of Austria and Czechoslovakia, and the first war of aggression charged in the Indictment is the war against Poland begun on the lst [of] September, 1939. Before examining that charge it is necessary to look more closely at some of the events which preceded these acts of aggression. The war against Poland did not come suddenly out of an otherwise clear sky; the evidence has made it plain that this war of aggression, as well as the seizure of Austria and Czechoslovakia, was premeditated and carefully prepared, and was not undertaken until the moment was thought opportune for it to be carried through as a definite part of the preordained scheme and plan. For the aggressive designs of the Nazi Government were not accidents arising out of the immediate political situation in Europe and the world; they were a deliberate and essential part of Nazi foreign policy (at p.13).

> "It was urged on behalf of the defendants that a fundamental principle of all law — international and domestic — is that there can be no punishment of crime without a pre-existing law. '*Nullum crimen sine lege, nulla poena sine lege.*' It was submitted that *ex post facto* punishment is abhorrent to the law of all civilized nations, that no sovereign power had made aggressive war a crime at the time the alleged criminal acts were committed, that no statute had defined aggressive war, that no penalty had been fixed for its commission, and no court had been created to try and punish offenders.

> "In the first place, it is to be observed that the maxim *nullum crimen sine lege* is not a limitation of sovereignty, but is in general a principle of justice. To assert that it is unjust to punish those who in defiance of treaties and assurances have attacked neighbouring states without warning is obviously untrue, for in such circumstances the attacker must know that he is doing wrong, and so far from

it being unjust to punish him, it would be unjust if his wrong were allowed to go unpunished. Occupying the positions they did in the government of Germany, the defendants; or at least some of them, must have known of the treaties signed by Germany, outlawing recourse to war for the settlement of international disputes; they must have known that they were acting in defiance of all international law when in complete deliberation they carried out their designs of invasion and aggression. On this view of the case alone, it would appear that the maxim has no application to the present facts."

[Editors' note: The Tribunal found that as a result of the Kellogg-Briand Pact of 1928 renouncing war as an instrument of national policy, as reinforced by other treaties and resolutions, war "has become throughout practically the entire world … an illegal thing."

The Tribunal also found that the war initiated by Germany against Poland in September, 1939, was an aggressive war; that the invasions of Denmark and Norway were acts of aggressive war and not defensive; that the invasions of Belgium, Holland, and Luxembourg were "entirely without justification" and acts of aggressive war; and that the invasion of Russia was for the purpose of "economic exploitation" and "plain aggression."]

III. War Crimes and Total Warfare

(1) *War Crimes as Part of a System.* "The truth remains that war crimes were committed on a vast scale, never before seen in the history of war. They were perpetrated in all the countries occupied by Germany, and on the High Seas, and were attended by every conceivable circumstance of cruelty and horror. There can be no doubt that the majority of them arose from the Nazi conception of 'total war', with which the aggressive wars were waged. For in this conception of 'total war', the moral ideas underlying the conventions which seek to make war more humane are no longer regarded as having force or validity. Everything is made subordinate to the overmastering dictates of war. Rules, regulations, assurances and treaties all alike are of no moment and so, freed from restraining influence of international law, the aggressive war is conducted by the Nazi leaders in the most barbaric way. Accordingly, war crimes were committed when and wherever the Fuehrer and his close associates thought them to be advantageous. They were for the most parts the result of cold and criminal calculation...."

(2) *The Laws of War and the Hague Conventions. The General Participation Clause.* "The Tribunal is of course bound by the Charter in the definition which it gives both of war crimes and crimes against humanity. With respect to war crimes, however, as has already been pointed out, the crimes defined by Article 6, section (*b*), of the Charter were already recognized as war crimes under international law. They were covered by Articles 46, 50, 52 and 56 of the Hague Convention of 1907, and Articles 2, 3, 4, 46, and 51 of the Geneva Convention of 1929. That violations of these provisions constituted crimes for which the guilty individuals were punishable is too well settled to admit the argument.

"But it is argued that the Hague Convention does not apply in this case because of the 'general participation' clause in Article 2 of the Hague Convention of 1907. That clause provided:

'The provisions contained in the regulations (Rules of Land Warfare) referred to in Article I as well as in the present Convention do not apply except between contracting powers, and then only if all the belligerents are parties to the Convention.'

Several of the belligerents in the recent war were not parties to this Convention.

"In the opinion of the Tribunal it is not necessary to decide this question. The rules of land warfare expressed in the Convention undoubtedly represented an advance over existing international law at the time of their adoption. But the Convention expressly stated that it was an attempt to revise the general laws and customs of war', which it thus recognized to be then existing; but by 1939 these rules laid down in the Convention were recognized by all civilized nations, and were regarded as being declaratory of the laws and customs of war which are referred to in Article 6 (*b*) of the Charter...."

(3) *War Crimes and Crimes against Humanity.* "With regard to crimes against humanity, there is no doubt whatever that political opponents were murdered in Germany before the war, and that many of them were kept in concentration camps in circumstances of great horror and cruelty. The policy of terror was certainly carried out on a vast scale, and in many cases was organized and systematic. The policy of persecution, repression and murder of civilians in Germany before the war of 1939, who were likely to be hostile to the Government, was most ruthlessly carried out. The persecution of Jews during the same period is established beyond all doubt. To constitute crimes against humanity, the acts relied on before the outbreak of war must have been in execution of, or in connection with, any crime within the jurisdiction of the Tribunal. The Tribunal is of the opinion that revolting and horrible as many of these crimes were, it has not been satisfactorily proved that they were done in execution of, or in connection with, any such crime. The Tribunal therefore cannot make a general declaration that the acts before 1939 were crimes against humanity within the meaning of the Charter, but from the beginning of the war in 1939 war crimes were committed on a vast scale, which were also crimes against humanity; and in so far as the inhumane acts charged in the Indictment, and committed after the beginning of the war, did not constitute war crimes, they were all committed in execution of, or in connection with, the aggressive war, and therefore constituted crimes against humanity...."

"Reference should also be made to the policy which was in existence in Germany by the summer of 1940, under which all aged, insane, and incurable people, 'useless eaters', were transferred to special institutions where they were killed, and their relatives informed that they had died from natural causes. The victims were not confined to German citizens, but included foreign labourers who were no longer able to work, and were therefore useless to the German war machine. It has been estimated that at least some 275,000 people were killed in this manner in nursing homes, hospitals and asylums."....

[The Tribunal also found that such acts as the deportation to slave labor of inhabitants of occupied territories, murder and mistreatment of prisoners of war, murder of hostages, plunder and pillage of public and private property, and wanton destruction of cities and towns were war crimes in violation of the Hague Convention and customary international law.]

Notes

1. With respect to the recognition by the Tribunal that the states creating the Tribunal "have done together what any one of them might have done singly," and jurisdiction under international law, it should be noted that the London Agreement (to which the Charter was annexed) recognized that the IMT was set up "for the trial of war criminals whose offences have no particular geographical location." *Id.* Also consider Articles 10–11 of the Charter of the IMT at Nuremberg (in the Documents Supplement) noting that accused found in the territory of the U.K., U.S., France or the U.S.S.R. could also be prosecuted. *See also id.* art. 15.

2. The Judgment of the IMT at Nuremberg was given on September 30, 1946. Sentences were pronounced on October 1, 1946:

	Counts on which Convicted	Sentence
Hermann Wilhelm Goering	1,2,3,4	Death by hanging
Rudolf Hess	1,2	Imprisonment for life
Joachim von Ribbentrop	1,2,3,4	Death by hanging
Wihelm Keitel	1,2,3,4	"
Ernst Kaltenbrunner	3,4	"
Alfred Rosenberg	1,2,3,4	"
Hans Frank	3,4	"
Wilhelm Frick	2,3,4	"
Julius Streicher	4	"
Walter Funk	2,3,4	Imprisonment for life
Hjalmar Schacht	Not Guilty	
Karl Doenitz	2,3	Imprisonment for ten years
Erich Raeder	1,2,3	Imprisonment for life
Baldur von Schirach	4	Imprisonment for twenty years
Fritz Sauckel	3,4	Death by hanging
Alfred Jodl	1,2,3,4	"
Franz von Papen	Not Guilty	
Artur Seyss-Inquart	2,3,4	Death by hanging
Albert Speer	3,4	Imprisonment for twenty years
Constantin von Neurath	1,2,3,4	Imprisonment for fifteen years
Hans Fritzsche	Not Guilty	
Martin Bormann	3,4	Death by hanging

3. The full opinion and judgment is reprinted in 41 Am. J. Int'l L. 172 (1947), from which some of the above was extracted.

4. Admiral Karl Dönitz (Doenitz) had been President and Head of State of Germany from April 29 to May 23, 1945, as successor to Hitler.

B. The International Military Tribunal for the Far East

U.S. Dep't of the Army Pamphlet No. 27-161-2
II International Law 233–34 (1962)

This tribunal was the Far Eastern counterpart of the International Military Tribunal which sat at Nuremberg. However, it did not base its jurisdiction on documents pertinent to the European Tribunal such as the Inter-Allied Declaration signed at St. James's Palace, London, at 13 January 1942, the Moscow Declaration of Oct. 30, 1943, the London Agreement of 8 August 1945, and the Charter annexed thereto.

The basic policy for the trial and punishment of Japanese war criminals was the Potsdam Declaration of 26 July 1945 jointly issued by China, the United Kingdom, and the U.S.A. The U.S.S.R. subsequently adhered to it. By the Instrument of Surrender, signed on 2 September 1945, Japan accepted the provisions of the Potsdam Declaration. General MacArthur, as Supreme Commander of the Allied Powers, was then directed by the United States to proceed with the trial of Japanese war criminals. Though approved by other nations this action was unilateral on the part of the United States. General MacArthur, acting under the authority of the Moscow Conference of 26 December 1945, established the International Military Tribunal for the Far East on 19 January 1946. Because of the fundamentally international character of such a trial it was felt that the original United States directive should be followed by a truly allied directive. This was done on 3 April 1946 by a policy decision of the Far Eastern Advisory Commission entitled "Apprehension, Trial and Punishment of War Criminals in the Far East." Based on this policy decision a new directive was issued to General MacArthur on 23 April 1946.

The tribunal consisted of 11 judges, one each from Australia, Canada, China, France, Great Britain, India, Netherlands, New Zealand, Philippines, Soviet Union, and the United States.

Twenty-eight were indicted. Two died and one became ill. Trial proceeded as to the remaining twenty-five. All twenty-five were found guilty on one or more of 10 counts of the 55 count indictment. Seven were sentenced to hang, sixteen to life in prison, one to twenty years, and one to seven and one-half years in prison.

Notes

1. The ten counts and the number convicted under each one are as follows: *Count 1*, conspiracy to commit crimes against peace, 24 convicted; *Count 27*, aggressive war against China, 22 convicted; *Count 29*, aggressive war against the U.S.A., 18 convicted; *Count 31*, aggressive war against the British Commonwealth, 18 convicted; *Count 32*, aggressive war against the Netherlands, 18 convicted; *Count 33*, aggressive war against France, 2 convicted; *Count 35*, aggressive war against the U.S.S.R. in 1938, 2 convicted; *Count 36*, aggressive war against the U.S.S.R. in 1939, 3 convicted; *Count 54*, war crimes against pows and civilians in occupied areas, 5 convicted; *Count 55*, failure to correct or to prevent the commission of war crimes by subordinates, 7 convicted.

2. For further information, *see, e.g.*, THE TOKYO WAR CRIMES TRIAL—AN INTERNATIONAL SYMPOSIUM (C. Hosoya, N. Ando, Y. Onuma, R. Minear eds. 1986); Onuma, Yasuaki, "The Tokyo Trial—Beyond Victors' Justice," JAPAN ECHO, vol. XI, at 63 (1984).

3. At the Tokyo trials, all 25 prosecuted were found guilty. At Nuremberg, 3 were acquitted (some 12.5%). At the subsequent trials in Germany held by the U.S. under Control Council Law No. 10, some 35 out of 185 individuals were acquitted (nearly 20%).

4. For further thoughts on post-Nuremberg and Tokyo influences of the trials, *see, e.g.*, 80 PROCEEDINGS, AM. SOC. INT'L L. (1986), panel on "Forty Years After the Nuremberg and Tokyo Tribunals: The Impact of the War Crimes Trials on International and National Law."

5. What is also of special interest is the precedential value of sanction efforts at Nuremberg and Tokyo concerning crimes of aggression and oppression or violations of fundamental human rights in this post-Nuremberg era. Increasingly, there is attention paid to crimes of apartheid, crimes against self-determination, aggression against authority or politicide and political oppression, whether or not actual war exists. Even at Nuremberg, these trends were partly foretold. As the Chief Prosecutor, Justice Jackson, remarked in his opening statement: " … these prisoners represent sinister influences.… We will show them to be living symbols of racial hatreds, of terrorism and violence, and of the arrogance and cruelty of power."

C. Allied Control Council Law No. 10

Also occurring after World War II were the prosecutions in Europe of former enemies under Allied Control Council Law No. 10 promulgated by the occupying powers in 1945. Summaries of the U.S. proceedings under the Control Council Law appear earlier in Chapter Four, Section 8.

In his FINAL REPORT TO THE SECRETARY OF THE ARMY ON THE NUREMBERG WAR CRIMES TRIALS UNDER CONTROL COUNCIL LAW NO. 10 (1949), then General Telford Taylor wrote (at 136–38):

In general, Law No. 10 adopted the London Agreement as a model, although the language differed in numerous important particulars. Each of the four Zone Commanders was authorized to arrest suspected war criminals, and to establish "appropriate tribunals" for their trial. Elaborate provisions were included for the exchange of war crimes suspects among the four occupation zones, and for their delivery to other countries.

In the Soviet zone of occupation, so far as is known to the writer, little or nothing was ever done to carry Law No. 10 into effect. The British, in their zone, preferred to handle war crimes on a military court basis under the "Royal Warrant." In the French zone, at Rastatt (near Baden-Baden), one major trial under Law No. 10 and several of lesser interest have been held.

The principal defendant in the major trial was the well-known iron, steel, and coal magnate of the Saar, Hermann Roechling, who, interestingly enough, had been sought and tried *in absentia* as a war criminal by the French after the first World War.

In the American zone, a series of twelve trials have been held at Nuremberg under the provisions of Law No. 10. The tribunals before which these trials were conducted, constituted under the authority of Law No. 10, were established by the Military Governor (General McNarney) pursuant to Military Government Ordinance No. 7, promulgated on 18 October 1946. The twelve indictments named 185 individuals as defendants; the first indictment was filed on 25 October 1946, and the last of the twelve judgments was delivered on 14 April 1949.

While the international trials were taking place, a great number of other war crimes trials were held all over Europe before tribunals constituted by individual nations. Germans accused of war crimes against American troops (such as the perpetrators of the notorious "Malmedy massacre," and the participants in "lynchings" of American flyers) and the managing staffs of concentration camps overrun by American troops (Buchenwald, Flossenburg, Dachau) were tried at Dachau (in the American zone of occupation near Munich) before military tribunals established by the Judge Advocate's Department of the United States Army. In the British zone, German soldiers accused of atrocities or responsibility therefor (including some leading generals such as Falkenhorst and Student) and concentration camp personnel (Belsen) were tried before British military tribunals convoked pursuant to the "Royal Warrant." Field Marshal Kesselring and others were tried before similar British tribunals in Italy for atrocities against the Italian population (committed after the fall of Mussolini). Numerous German generals, SS and police leaders, and civilian officials were tried before tribunals in Belgium, Denmark, Greece, Holland, Norway, Poland, Russia, and Yugoslavia for atrocities committed in German-occupied territory. The European countries also tried their own pro-Nazi "traitors," such as "Lord Haw-Haw" in England, Graziani in Italy, and Petain in France.

War crimes trials were also under way in the Far East. Numerous Japanese officers and men were prosecuted for crimes against American troops and atrocities in the Philippines and elsewhere; the trials of Generals Yamashita and Homma are outstanding examples. Twenty-eight leading Japanese officials, military and civilian, were tried before the International Tribunal for the Far East. Eleven nations (Australia, Britain, Canada, China, France, India, the Netherlands, New Zealand, the Philippines, the Soviet Union, and the United States) were represented on the bench. This trial lasted over two years and resulted in the conviction, in November 1948, of all the defendants.

To summarize, the second World War has resulted in numerous war crimes trials of wide scope and great variety. It will be seen that they fall into three more or less definite categories. In the initial category are the first Nuremberg (IMT) trial and the Tokyo trial, conducted before tribunals composed of judges from four nations at Nuremberg and eleven at Tokyo, and constituted under *ad hoc* international agreements. The second includes the other Nuremberg trials and the Rastatt trials, held under international authority (Control Council Law No. 10) before tribunals established under the principal auspices of individual nations. The third is comprised of the thousands of trials held before national tribunals in Europe and the Far East. It might be said that such trials as those of Petain and "Lord Haw-Haw" comprise a fourth category.

* * *

The following is an extract of "**The Simpson Report**," a report of Sept. 14, 1948, with respect to some of the subsequent trials mentioned by General Taylor held at Dachau:

MEMORANDUM FOR: The Secretary of the Army 14 Sep. 1948

SUBJECT: Survey of the Trials of War Crimes Held at Dachau, Germany

1. Pursuant to Department of the Army orders (Tab A), the undersigned reported 30 July 1948 to the Commander-in-Chief, European Command, and informed him of their mission as set forth in those orders and amplified by Department of the Army radio 85938, 16 July 1948 (Tab B).

2. There were tried at Dachau 489 cases involving 1672 accused. The following tabulation reflects action taken as of 12 August 1948.

Number of accused convicted	1416
Number of accused acquitted	256
Number of death sentences approved	297
Number of death sentences disapproved	10
Number of life sentences approved	220
Number of disapproved sentences (including 10 death sentences)	69
Number of sentences reduced	138
Number of death sentences commuted	119
Number of death sentences executed	152

In view of the voluminous records (estimated to weigh 12-1/2 tons) appertaining to the trials of war crimes at Dachau, it was determined, after consultation with the Commander-in-Chief, European Command, to direct the survey principally but not exclusively to that portion of the records (65 cases) involving the 139 confirmed death sentences (underscored on Tab C) which remain unexecuted.

3. In the course of this survey there has been examined, in connection with each approved and unexecuted death sentence, the Review of the Deputy Judge Advocate for War Crimes, the recommendations of the Chief, War Crimes Branch, the recommendations

of the War Crimes Boards of Review, and the recommendations of the Judge Advocate, European Command, both with reference to the original proceeding as well as any petition for review or clemency subsequently filed. It would not have been possible to have made an examination of the entire record in each case within the time allotted; and, in view of the information furnished by the Chief, War Crimes Branch, (Tab D) and confirmed by the Judge Advocate, European Command, this was not necessary to accomplish this mission. The assumption made with reference to the correctness of the facts as stated in the reviews has been verified by a complete examination of the record in doubtful cases including, but not limited to, those in which the claim has been advanced that prosecution evidence was improperly obtained by pretrial investigation or otherwise.

In re Ohlendorf and Others (Einsatzgruppen Trial)

U.S. Military Tribunal at Nürnberg, 15 Int'l L. Rep. 656 (1948)

The Tribunal: ... (1) *Jurisdiction of the Tribunal: Control Council Law No. 10 and the Principle of "Nullem Crimen Sine Lege".* — The Tribunal said:

On December 20, 1945, the Allied Control Council, composed of representatives of the same four above-mentioned nations and constituting the highest legislative authority for Germany, enacted Law No. 10, concerning 'Punishment of Persons Guilty of War Crimes, Crimes Against Peace and Crimes Against Humanity'. This Tribunal came into being under the provisions of the Law, but while the Tribunal derives its existence from the authority indicated, its jurisdiction over the subject matter results from International Law valid long prior to World War II.... Control Council Law No. 10 is but the codification and systemization of already existing legal principles, rules and customs. Under the title of Crimes against Humanity, these rules and customs are the common heritage of civilized peoples, and, in so far as War Crimes are concerned, they have been recognized in various International Conventions, to which Germany was a party, and they have been International Law for decades if not centuries. As far back as 1631, Grotius, in his *De Jure Belli ac Pacis*, wrote: 'But ... far must we be from admitting the conceit of some, that the Obligation of all Right ceases in war; nor when undertaken ought it to be carried on beyond the Bounds of Justice and Fidelity'.... It is indeed fundamental in every system of civilized jurisprudence that no one may be punished for an act which was not prohibited at the time of its commission. But it must be understood that the *lex* referred to is not restricted to statutory law. Law does, in fact, come into being as the result of formal written enactment and thus we have codes, treaties, conventions and the like, but it may also develop effectively through custom and usage and through the application of Common Law. The latter methods are no less binding than the former.... Of course some fields of International Law have been codified to a substantial degree and one such subject is the law of Land Warfare which includes the Law of Belligerent Occupation because belligerent occupation is incidental to warfare. The Hague Regulations, for instance, represent such a codification. Article 46 of these Regulations provides with regard to invading and occupying armies that: 'Family honour and rights, the livers of persons and private property, as well as religious convictions, and practice must be respected'. This provision imposed obligations on Germany not only because Germany signed the Hague Convention on Land Warfare, but because it had become International Law binding on all nations.

But the jurisdiction of this Tribunal over the subject matter before it does not depend alone on this specific pronouncement of International Law. As already indicated, all nations have held themselves bound to the rules or laws of war which came into being through common recognition and acknowledgment. Without exception these rules universally condemn the wanton killing of non-combatants. In the main, the defendants in this case are charged with murder. Certainly no one can claim with the slightest pretense at reasoning that there is any taint of *ex post factoism* in the law or murder. Whether any individual defendant is guilty of unlawful killing is a question which will be determined later, but it cannot be said that prior to Control Council Law No. 10 there existed no law against murder. The killing of a human being has always been a potential crime which called for explanation. The person standing with drawn dagger over a fresh corpse must, by the very nature of justice, exonerate himself. This he may well do, advancing self-defense or legal authorization for the deed, or he may establish that the perpetrator of the homicide was one other than himself. It is not questioned that the defendants were close enough to mass killings to be called upon for an explanation—and to whom are they to render explanation so that their innocence or guilt may be determined? Is the matter of some one million non-military deaths to be denied judicial inquiry because a Tribunal was not standing by, waiting for the apprehension of the suspects?

The specific enactments for the trial of war criminals which have governed the Nuremberg trials, have only provided a machinery for the actual application of international law theretofore existing. In the comparatively recent *Saboteurs Case* (*Ex parte Quirin*, 317 U.S., 1, 1942) the Supreme Court of the United States affirmed that individual offenders against the rules and customs of war are amenable to punishment under the common law of nations without any prior designation of tribunal or procedure. In this connection reference may also be made to trials for piracy where, going back centuries, the offenders, regardless of nationality, were always tried in the arresting state without any previous designation of tribunal. Military Tribunals for years have tried and punished violators of the rules of land warfare outlined in the Hague Conventions even though the Convention is silent on the subject of courts.... There is no authority which denies any belligerent nation jurisdiction over individuals in its actual custody charged with violation of international law. And if a single nation may legally take jurisdiction in such instances, with what more reason may a number of nations agree, in the interest of justice, to try alleged violations of the international code of war? In spite of all that has been said in this and other cases, no one would be so bold as to suggest that what occurred between Germany and Russia from June 1941 to May 1945 was anything but war, and, being war, that Russia would not have the right to try the alleged violators of the rules of war on her territory and against her people. And if Russia may do this alone, certainly she may concur with other nations who affirm that right. Thus, Russia's participation in the formulation of Control Council Law No. 10 is in accordance with every recognized principle of international law, and any attack on that participation is without legal support. The Tribunal also finds and concludes that Control Council Law No. 10 is not only in conformity with International Law but is in itself a highly significant contribution to written International Law....

Section 4
Efforts of the United Nations Command in Korea and Procedural Guarantees

Introductory Note

During the Korean Conflict, some sites of alleged war crimes were investigated, and witnesses and prisoners were interrogated. Nonetheless, prisoners held by U.N. forces were repatriated and no U.N. trials took place. Although there were no trials under U.N. Military Commissions, the following material is of historic and precedential value.

GENERAL HEADQUARTERS UNITED NATIONS COMMAND
TOKYO, JAPAN

AG 000.5 (28 Oct 50) JA   28 October 1950

SUBJECT: Trial of Accused War Criminals

TO: Commanding General, Eighth Army, APO 301

  Commander, United States Naval Forces, Far East, Navy No. 1165

  Commanding General, Far East Air Forces, APO 925

  Commanding General, X Corps, APO 909

1. Trials of persons accused of violating the laws and customs of war in connection with the Korean conflict will be by Military Commission. Authority to convene such Military Commissions will be delegated by General Headquarters, United Nations Command, as the need arises. Charges and specifications, with supporting documentary proof and statements of witnesses, will be forwarded to the Commander-in-Chief, United Nations Command, Attention: Command Judge Advocate, with each request for the convening of a Military Commission.

2. Trials will be governed by the "Rules of Criminal Procedure for Military Commissions of the United Nations Command," dated 22 October 1950, a copy of which is forwarded herewith. Additional copies of the inclosure will be made available upon request.

BY COMMAND OF GENERAL MacARTHUR:
K. B. BUSH
Brigadier General, USA
Adjutant General

1 Incl

  Rules of Criminal procedure
  for Military Commissions of
  the United Nations Command

w/ANNEX "A"

GENERAL HEADQUARTERS
UNITED NATIONS COMMAND
TOKYO, JAPAN
PROMULGATION

By virtue of the authority vested in me as Commander-in-Chief, United Nations Command, I hereby promulgate the following articles designated "Articles Governing United Nations Prisoners of War," and I hereby declare and prescribe that, effective on and after 1 November 1951, the conduct of all prisoners of war detained by the United Nations Command shall be governed by these said articles.

Witness my hand and seal in the City of Tokyo, Honshu, Japan, this 23rd day of October, 1951.

/s/ M. B. RIDGWAY
/t/ M. B. RIDGWAY
General, United States Army

Commander-in-Chief
United Nations Command

[Read the 1953 U.N. Supplemental Rules of Criminal Procedure, in the Documents Supplement]

Notes and Questions

1. The 1950 Rules of Criminal Procedure for Military Commissions of the United Nations Command to be used for the trial of persons accused of violating the laws and customs of war in connection with the Korean conflict were substantially the same as the 1951 "Articles Governing United Nations Prisoners of War" for "postcapture" offenses (including postcapture violations of the law of war). The 1951 articles are printed here because of their great significance as historic documentations of due process expectation by a United Nations Command that was desirous of complying with the "new" due process guarantees of the 1949 Geneva Conventions. At the insistence of the North Koreans and with the "agreement" of parties to the prisoner of war repatriations, no trials under the U.N. rules were actually held. For evidence of U.S. cases, see Chapter Four, Section 7 D *supra*.

2. Would the U.N. rules produce a "fair" trial? Which rules would you change, how, and why?

3. Note that under the U.N. rules the accused was to have at least three weeks notice of charges before trial and at least two weeks to prepare for a defense. See Rules 27 and 53. At the International Military Tribunal at Nuremberg, the accused had thirty days to prepare for trial. General Yamashita, prosecuted in a U.S. military commission proceeding, was arraigned on October 8, 1945 and charged with 64 specifications. Trial began on October 29, 1945 with 59 additional specifications filed (which had been shown to defense counsel 3 days earlier). The trial was over on December 7, 1945.

4. The following extract on procedures taken at Nuremberg is from the Opinion and Judgment:

"The Trial which was conducted in four languages—English, Russian, French and German—began on the 20th November, 1945, and pleas of "Not Guilty" were made by all the defendants except Bormann.

"The hearing of evidence and the speeches of Counsel concluded on 31st August, 1946.

"Four hundred and three open sessions of the Tribunal have been held. Thirty-three witnesses gave evidence orally for the Prosecution against the individual defendants, and 61 witnesses, in addition to 19 of the defendants, gave evidence for the Defence.

"A further 143 witnesses gave evidence for the Defence by means of written answers to interrogatories.

"The Tribunal appointed Commissioners to hear evidence relating to the organisations, and 101 witnesses were heard for the Defence before the Commissioners, and 1,809 affidavits from other witnesses were submitted. Six reports were also submitted, summarising the contents of a great number of further affidavits.

"Thirty-eight thousand affidavits, signed by 155,000 people, were submitted on behalf of the Political Leaders, 136,213 on behalf of the SS, 10,000 on behalf of the SA, 7,000 on behalf of the SD, 3,000 on behalf of the General Staff and OKW, and 2,000 on behalf of the Gestapo.

"The Tribunal itself heard 22 witnesses for the organisations. The documents tendered in evidence for the prosecution of the individual defendants and the organizations numbered several thousands. A complete stenographic record of everything said in court has been made, as well as an electrical recording of all the proceedings.

"Copies of all the documents put in evidence by the Prosecution have been supplied to the Defence in the German language. The applications made by the defendants for the production of witnesses and documents raised serious problems in some instances, on account of the unsettled state of the country. It was also necessary to limit the number of witnesses to be called, in order to have an expeditious hearing, in accordance with Article 18(c) of the Charter. The Tribunal, after examination, granted all those applications which in their opinion were relevant to the defence of any defendant or named group or organisation, and were not cumulative. Facilities were provided for obtaining those witnesses and documents granted through the office of the General Secretary established by the Tribunal.

"Much of the evidence presented to the Tribunal on behalf of the Prosecution was documentary evidence, captured by the Allied armies in German army headquarters, Government buildings, and elsewhere. Some of the documents were found in salt mines, buried in the ground, hidden behind false walls and in other places thought to be secure from discovery. The case, therefore, against the defendants rests in a large measure on documents of their own making, the authenticity of which has not been challenged except in one or two cases."

For a different slant on the fairness of a "speedy" trial at Nuremberg, *see, e.g.,* Kranzbuhler, *Nuremberg Eighteen Years Afterwards*, 14 DePaul L. Rev. 333 (1965) (former defense counsel criticizing procedures and motives). Professor Bassiouni, among others, has also been critical of what he sees as a lack of specificity in customary crimes. See M.C. Bassiouni, A Draft International Criminal Code and Draft Statute for an International Criminal Tribunal 3, 24, 49, 53–54 (1987).

5. Which rules of procedure in the Charters of the IMTs at Nuremberg and for the Far East (see the Documents Supplement) appear problematic in terms of modern human rights law noted in the next section? Would Article 29 of the Charter of the IMT at Nuremberg allow the placing of an accused in double jeopardy?

6. What sort of advantages are there for a nation-state to prosecute its own nationals for international crimes?

7. Do any such advantages lend credence to claims of "victors' justice" with respect to prosecution of war crimes? Who will tend best to temper justice with mercy?

8. Does the fact that use of international (or even domestic) fora for prosecution of war crimes has been relatively rare make particular crimes less egregious or less criminal in nature?

9. What institutional alternatives exist for the better serving of common interests at stake? Which do you recommend and how can they be effectuated?

Further References:

M.C. Bassiouni, *supra*; R. Minear, Victors' Justice 1–33, 175–180 (1971); Against the Crime of Silence (J. Duffett ed. 1970); *In re Yamashita*, 327 U.S. 1, 31–40 (1956)

(Murphy J., dissenting). *See also* Gross, *The Punishment of War Criminals*, 11 Neth. Int'l L. Rev. 356 (1956); Q. Wright, *The Law of the Nuremberg Trial*, 41 Am. J. Int'l L. 38 (1947); W. Cowles, *Universality of Jurisdiction Over War Crimes*, 33 Cal. L. Rev. 177 (1945); E. Colby, *War Crimes*, 23 Mich. L. Rev. 482 (1925); M. McDougal & F. Feliciano, Law and Minimum World Public Order (1961).

10. Consider also: *United States v. Heilman*, 54 F. Supp. 414, 415 (N.D. Ohio 1943) ("We are at war because we know that there can be no security or freedom or peace anywhere until the perpetrators of such international crimes are brought into subjection to law.").

Section 5
Human Rights to Due Process

Today, customary and treaty-based human rights law provides additional procedural guarantees and relevant rights of an accused or detainee. Recall *Hamdan v. Rumsfeld*, 548 U.S. 557 (2006) (common Article 3 of the Geneva Conventions reflects a minimum set of customary procedural guarantees and incorporates ICCPR, art. 14 and Geneva Protocol I, art. 75, by reference), in Chapter 4, sec. 7 B. In addition to the rights, duties and prohibitions reflected in instruments noted below, one should consult regional human rights instruments such as the 1969 American Convention on Human Right, arts. 7 and 8); the 1950 European Convention for the Protection of Human Rights and Fundamental Freedoms, arts. 5 and 6; Protocol No. 7 to the European Convention, art. 2, *reprinted in* 24 I.L.M. 535 (1985); the 1981 African Charter on Human and Peoples' Rights (Banjul Charter), art. 7; and the 2004 Arab Charter on Human Rights, arts. 13, 15–16.

Universal Declaration of Human Rights
G.A. Res. 217A (1948)
[Read Articles 1–2, 5, and 7–11 of the Universal Declaration]

International Covenant on Civil and Political Rights
999 U.N.T.S. 171 (1966)
[Read Articles 2, 4, 7, 9–10, 14–15 and 26 of the International Covenant]

Notes and Questions

1. Do Article 11(1) of the Universal Declaration and Article 14(2) of the International Covenant explicitly require proof of guilt beyond a reasonable doubt? What might you check to see whether this is an implied legal standard? Also, do human rights instruments guarantee a right of cross-examination? Do they prohibit an appeal by a prosecutor of an acquittal?

2. If they apply, see also the 1949 Geneva Civilian Convention, arts. 31–33, 71–78, 75 U.N.T.S. 287; Geneva Protocol I, art. 75. Article 93 of the U.N. Standard Minimum Rules for the Treatment of Prisoners also recognizes the right of access to an attorney. Aliens also have a right of access to their consulate.

3. Concerning the trial of prisoners of war, consider Articles 82, 84, 87, 102, 105, 118–119, 129 of the 1949 Geneva Convention Relative to the Treatment of Prisoners of War (GPW), in the Documents Supplement. See also Article 85: Prisoners of war prosecuted under the laws of the Detaining Power for acts committed prior to capture shall retain, even if convicted, the benefits of the present Convention; J. PICTET, III COMMENTARY 416–22 (1960) (these apply to crimes under international law and other crimes under the law of the Detaining Power—assumes that "in general, acts not connected with the state of war" should be punishable "under the laws of both the Detaining Power and the Power of origin.").

In *United States v. Noriega*, 746 F. Supp. 1506 (S.D. Fla. 1990), addressed in Chapter Three, Section 2, former Noriega argued, among other claims, that he was entitled to "prisoner of war" status, that such a status obviated federal district court jurisdiction (because of Article 84 of the GPW and the fact that penalties must be the same as those for U.S. military personnel because of Article 87), and that he must be "repatriated" to Panama at the end of the "hostilities" (per Article 118). The district court denied these claims, finding especially that, if he had been a prisoner of war, Article 84 was met because federal district courts have a general concurrent jurisdictional competence with military tribunals under 18 U.S.C. §3231, and because Article 119 allowed the U.S. to retain jurisdiction even after a close of supposed "hostilities." Was the district court correct?

4. The Bush Administration's creation of military commissions at Guantanamo Bay, Cuba have sparked concerns about human rights to due process under DOD Rules of Procedure and Evidence, especially concerning the customary human rights reflected in Article 14 of the ICCPR. Recall the section on military commissions in Chapter Four. Compliance with the following portions of Article 14 are either not possible or highly problematic: Article 14(1), (3) (b), (e), (5). *See, e.g.*, Paust, *Antiterrorism Military Commissions: The Ad Hoc Rules of Procedure*, 23 MICH. J. INT'L L. 677 (2002); *see also* Mark A. Drumbl, *Victimhood in Our Neighborhood: Terrorist Crime, Taliban Guilt, and the Symmetries of the International Legal Order*, 81 N.C. L. REV. 1, 10–12, 58–59 (2002); Harold Hongju Koh, *The Case Against Military Commissions*, 91 AM. J. INT'L L. 337, 338–39 (2002); Detlev F. Vagts, *Which Courts Should Try Persons Accused of Terrorism?*, 14 EUR. J. INT'L L. 313, 322 (2003). As noted in Chapter Eight, customary rights to due process are incorporated by reference in common Article 3 of the 1949 Geneva Conventions, which is itself customary law applicable during any armed conflict. Recall *Hamdan v. Rumsfeld*, 548 U.S. 557 (2006).

Do the Obama military commissions at GTMO comply? Consider Paust, *Still Unlawful: The Obama Military Commissions, Supreme Court Holdings, and Deviant Dicta in the D.C. Circuit*, 45 CORNELL INT'L L.J. 367 (2012), available at http://ssrn.com/abstract=1997478.

Extract from Report of the Mission of the International Commission of Jurists, Inquiry into the Israeli Military Court System in the Occupied West Bank and Gaza

36–40 (1989), full report reprinted in 14 HAST. INT'L & COMP. L. REV. 1 (1990)

Attorney Notice, Visits and Time to Prepare

As noted above, attorney access to clients is severely limited by the processes of arrest and interrogation, and in some cases can be denied for weeks and months. Under Military Order No. 1220, detainees are supposedly entitled to see a lawyer immediately after arrest but, as noted above, there are two fifteen day provisions which can lead to an extended denial for thirty days, and there are other orders authorizing secret arrests. Lawyers do not see clients until after interrogation.

Defense attorneys complain that they are not always allowed reasonable access to their clients prior to a hearing or able reasonably to communicate with clients they do see, nor do they always have adequate time and facilities for preparation of the defense of clients. Sometimes they have to wait for hours outside a facility and then have only a few minutes to communicate with each client.

Rules are set by different base commanders as to when a lawyer can visit, how long, with or without guards, and so forth. In Gaza City at Ansar 2, lawyers are apparently allowed to see clients for one hour per week, as worked out in part by an agreement with the local bar association. Even then there can be problems getting through the gate. The camp commander at Ansar 2 affirmed that visits are controlled in accordance with an agreement whereby some ten to fifteen lawyers are admitted each day to see some 120 to 150 prisoners (or about ten prisoners each) — most times at a separate place. We saw one of the defense attorneys seated at a table with his client outside one of the buildings at the camp. At Ansar 2 there is supposed to be a new building built for attorneys to meet with clients, but there were delays in contracting out for such a building. When asked who built the camp commander's air-conditioned office, he stated that it had been built by the army. A military judge in Gaza stated that if he knows that a lawyer is having difficulty seeing a client at Ansar 2 he will phone to ensure access. The Legal Adviser in Gaza stated that the Ansar 2 commander is under orders to allow attorneys access and that one sees them in the camp moving around and signing up clients (also to obtain a "power of attorney" needed to view files located in the court complex).

Defense lawyers also complain about the lack of timely and accurate information concerning hearings. In Nablus defense attorneys complained about notice from a book in the office of the court secretary and that some dates for hearings are left blank. We saw attorneys using such a book in Nablus. There, attorneys also complain that they must talk with clients in a crowded hallway in the court complex because their room for such courthouse visits was taken for a computer (which was not yet in operation). They also complain that they can't use the telephone. The President of the Military Court in Nablus stated that a public telephone will be installed and that he is open to the Arab Lawyers' Committee and to individual complaints. A military judge in Gaza stated that he is also open to talking with attorneys, and the President of the Military Appeals Court stated that he finds it important to talk with defense lawyers and the court judges and that he schedules meetings on a regular basis at 5 p.m. one day every two weeks. A military judge in Ramallah added that he asks local lawyers to talk with him and had met twice with members of the Arab Lawyers' Committee in the last three months. He also stated that soon in Ramallah defense lawyers will have a building or room to meet with clients. At one point in Ramallah we saw a woman defense attorney whispering with her client while leaning against the wall outside the packed one-judge-courtroom, within sight and some ten feet of two military guards.

The Legal Adviser of Gaza was aware of the letter from Gaza defense attorneys early in 1989 (in February) but had already had a three-hour meeting with about five attorneys representing the bar association to work on problems (on April 3, 1989). He stated that defense attorneys have access to him, being out in the halls a few yards away to check posted lists in Arabic of clients (names and detainee numbers) and hearing dates, and that they can also call on the phone to see his deputy and six other officers who are available (in rooms off of a long hallway on the second floor where the defense lawyers were seen by members of the mission checking postings or files). A local defense lawyer acknowledged a series of meetings and the posting of "next week's trials" and added that he works with the secretary to re-schedule dates. Another, a representative of the Gaza Bar Association, stated that lawyers see a weekly list which they publish in a newspaper. He added that the process is still difficult for lawyers with several clients, especially visits in the prisons.

In terms of adequate time to prepare a defense, the Advocate General of the IDF stated that the military has had problems orchestrating witnesses (especially reservists), accused, and files, but that more speedy trials, within 48 hours, are posed as a solution. The Legal Adviser in Gaza admitted that there had been quick trials because of prior massive arrests. This was confirmed by other military lawyers. One judge in Ramallah, while berating defense counsel for arguing in English, allegedly for "propaganda" purposes (in front of members of the mission), added in open court that in his opinion trial delays are for the benefit of the defense lawyers because they are not always prepared.

Concerns, Conclusions and Recommendations

Article 11(1) of the Universal Declaration of Human Rights guarantees the right of all persons to a "trial at which he has all the guarantees necessary for his defence." Such guarantees obviously include the right to adequate representation by counsel of one's choice and adequate time and facilities to prepare for a defense. As Article 14(3), sub-paragraphs (b) and (d) [of the International Covenant] declare, an accused has the right "to defend himself in person or through legal assistance of his own choosing; to be informed, if he does not have legal assistance, of this right;" and, among other relevant rights, "[t]o have adequate time and facilities for the preparation of his defence and to communicate with counsel of his own choosing." Paragraph 93 of the U.N. Standard Minimum Rules for the Treatment of Prisoners adds that an untried prisoner shall be allowed to apply for legal advice "and to receive visits from his legal adviser with a view to his defence and to prepare and hand to him confidential instructions." The U.N. rules also state that interviews "may be within sight but not within the hearing of a police or institution official."

Article 72 of the Geneva Civilian Convention expresses these guarantees as follows: "They shall have the right to be assisted by a qualified advocate or counsel of their own choice who shall be able to visit them freely and shall enjoy the necessary facilities for preparing the defence." Pictet adds to his commentary:

> The defending counsel must be given … all the facilities and freedom of action necessary for preparing the defence. Above all, he must be allowed to study the written evidence in the case, to visit the accused and interview him without witnesses and to get in touch with persons summoned as witnesses.
>
> It will not always be easy for these rules to be observed during an occupation, in view of the psychological atmosphere, but they must nevertheless be observed scrupulously in all circumstances and in all places.

Importantly, the Geneva Convention also adds a notification requirement tied to due process guarantees outlined in Article 71. Although the notification requirement is expressed in terms of notification to a "Protecting Power," which Palestinians do not have under the circumstances, the notification requirement sets a minimum standard of three weeks notification. Article 71 states that such notification shall be at least "three weeks before the date of the first hearing" and that "unless, at the opening of the trial, evidence is submitted that the provisions of this Article are fully complied with, the trial shall not proceed." The three weeks notice provision includes notice of the accused, place of detention, specification of the charge or charges, and the court and place and date of the "first hearing." These provisions obviously relate to requirements that defense attorneys have adequate notice of charges and time to prepare a defense.

We find it informative of general expectations in this area that the 1953 U.N. Supplemental Rules of Criminal Procedure for Military Commissions of the United Nations Command in Korea contained similar requirements. Rule 26 stated that defense counsel were to have "the reasonably necessary facilities to prepare the defense of the accused" and "may, in particular, freely visit the accused and interview him in private" and "also confer with any witnesses for the defense, including prisoners of war." Rule 27(a) set a limitation on commencement of proceedings "of at least three weeks from the date of the receipt by the accredited Delegate of the International Committee of the Red Cross, the prisoners' representative, and the accused of the notice required" elsewhere to such persons; and Rule 27(b) set another minimum time limit with respect to defense counsel:

> No trial shall commence until the Advocate or Counsel conducting the defense
> on behalf of the accused shall have had at his disposal a period of at least two weeks
> to prepare the defense of the accused.

It is also informative in terms of due process standards that at the International Military Tribunal at Nuremberg, defense counsel were given at least thirty days to prepare a defense. It is also instructive that Article 146 of the G.C. [Geneva Civilian Convention] declares that "in all circumstances, the accused persons shall benefit by safeguards of proper trial and defence, which shall not be less favourable than those provided by Article 105 and those following of the Geneva Convention Relative to the Treatment of Prisoners of War of August 12, 1949" [GPW], since Article 105 of the GPW provides "a period of two weeks at least before the opening of the trial" as a minimum time "to prepare the defence."

We are concerned that there have been violations of each of the above mentioned standards in the past. In particular, we are deeply concerned about the denial of access by counsel for some fifteen or even thirty days after arrest, the denial of the right of counsel under Article 72 of the G.C. "to visit ... freely" with an accused, the denial of adequate facilities for attorney visits at military prison camps, the denial of adequate facilities for attorney visits and preparation at the military courts, and the denial of adequate time for the preparation of a defense. "Quick trials" within a few days (or even a week) of formal charges pose a special problem for an adequate defense and, in our opinion, violate a minimum of three weeks notification requirement found within Article 71 of the G.C.

As noted above, we have recommended far earlier access by counsel. We also recommend that more uniform rules concerning attorney visits be set after coordination with the Gaza Bar Association and the Arab Lawyers' Committee in the West Bank by the Advocate General and his staff. Defense counsel must be allowed to "visit ... freely" with an accused and have the time to prepare a defense. In this regard, we recommend also that the Advocate General ensure that no hearing on the plea occur until after an accused has had notice of three weeks of the formal charges against him and, if represented by counsel, that counsel of his choice has had at least three weeks to prepare a defense.

Further, we recommend that the willingness of both military and defense professionals to explore problems and find solutions be nurtured through regular contacts, at various levels. We are impressed by the desire of persons like the President of the Military Appeals Court to schedule bi-weekly meetings and we feel that such contacts can aid both sides in solving problems like the need for adequate facilities for the preparation of a defense. We are left quite unimpressed with excuses concerning delays in the construction or provision of defense facilities when the army is capable of providing air-conditioned offices for others.

Section 6
Efforts After the Independence of Bangladesh

Introduction

Jordan Paust & Albert Blaustein, *War Crimes Jurisdiction and Due Process: The Bangladesh Experience*

11 VAND. J. TRANSNAT'L L. 1, 2–5 (1978)

In April, 1973, the new state of Bangladesh announced its intention to proceed with the trial of 195 Pakistani nationals "for serious crimes, which include genocide, war crimes, crimes against humanity, breaches of article 3 of the Geneva Conventions, murder, rape, and arson." Although state trials of individuals accused of committing war crimes were still occurring, the Bangladesh trials promised to be particularly significant. Not since Nuremberg had there been a criminal inquiry into widespread acts of genocide, crimes against humanity, and war crimes. Deaths in Bangladesh, not to mention other egregious acts such as torture, terror, and rape, numbered in the millions. No post-Nuremberg proceedings, not even the Israeli prosecution of Eichmann or United States prosecutions of American servicemen, had involved such a wide range of international criminal charges. Some of the charges posed novel problems. One particular problem was determining how the prosecution of genocide or the prosecution of a violation of common article 3 of the 1949 Geneva Conventions was to proceed.

Equally important political questions surrounded the criminal charges. Although Bangladesh openly sought prosecution, her ally, India, held the 195 Pakistanis accused of committing the crimes as prisoners of war. Could prisoners of war be prosecuted for war crimes and other international law violations, or should they have been returned upon demand to their country of origin when the active hostilities ceased? Could India prosecute the accused for acts that occurred in what is now the state of Bangladesh? Could the new state of Bangladesh or Pakistan prosecute? Must any state that holds and controls prisoners either prosecute those accused of having committed serious violations of international law or extradite them to a state what will prosecute? Finally, would similar breaches of international law by India or Indian troops obviate any jurisdictional competence or duties of India or Bangladesh? ...

It would also be necessary to decide whether violations of human rights were prosecutable by the state whose nationals were the victims of substantial and intentional deprivations. Do general human rights protections apply in an armed conflict? What interrelationships exist between human rights, laws of armed conflict, and prohibitions of genocide? The Bangladesh trials would surely be significant for their precedential value, the analyses of the jurisdictional issues, and the final determinations on the competence to prosecute and to sanction. They would perhaps be as significant as Nuremberg. Equally interesting would be the application of international due process guarantees to safeguard the human rights of the accused before, during, and after the trials. No previous court had faced such issues squarely, and few national or international courts had specifically incorporated human rights into due process guarantees.

Four months later, in August of 1973, India, Pakistan, and Bangladesh reached an agreement for repatriation of the 91,000 Pakistani prisoners of war being held in India, save those 195 specifically accused of war crimes. Bangladesh had already passed the International Crimes (Tribunals) Act of July 19, 1973, providing for the trial of the accused, and the authors had been requested by Counsel for the Government of Bangladesh to prepare a memorandum on relevant points of law. This memorandum could be received by the tribunals as a "friend of the court" communication from the authors as representatives of the International League for the Rights of Man (now the International League for Human Rights). The authors were also to serve as trial observers and would use the memorandum as a basis for their observation of the trials and subsequent comment upon the proceedings and outcomes.

Bangladesh International Crimes (Tribunals) Act of July 19, 1973

[Read the Bangladesh Act, in the Documents Supplement]

Questions

1. Would the Bangladesh Tribunals have been fairer than those at Nuremberg, the Tokyo Tribunal, the U.N. Military Tribunals in Korea?

2. What sorts of evidence might have been received?

3. What penalties might a Tribunal have imposed?

Comments of Professors Paust and Blaustein on the International Crimes (Tribunals) Act of 1973

from Paust & Blaustein, War Crimes Jurisdiction and Due Process: A Case Study of Bangladesh 65–70 (1974)

First. Under paragraph 1(3), it is provided that the Act "shall come into force at once." This provision, however, (together with the list of "crimes" in paragraph 3(2)) merely creates the forum for the prosecution within Bangladesh of international crimes already "in force at the time" the acts in question were committed. This does not, of course, attempt to create new offenses. (See Geneva Convention Relative to the Treatment of Prisoners of War, 1949 [GPW], art. 99.) The Act merely categorizes the types of international offenses within the jurisdiction of the Tribunal provided for under the Act in order to have domestic prosecution of international crime.

Some question may arise under paragraph 3(2)(c) where the phrase "political group" is used. This is an addition to the language of the 1948 Genocide Convention. Nonetheless, the intent to destroy a "political group" by such measures as are set forth under paragraph 3(2)(c)(i-v) would indeed fall within the shared expectations of the community as to the reasonable interpretation of the nature of the crime of genocide. Moreover, such an interpretation would fall within the primary goals of the Genocide Convention. (See also UN GA Res. 96 (I) (1946) referring to "political" groups). Note also that a "national" group is not the equivalent of a "state" group and this phrase might, under certain circumstances, cover the same category of persons as a "political" group.

Second. The Act apparently applies both to enemy (Pakistani) prisoners of war and to the members of the armed forces of India and Bangladesh. This is set forth in the language of paragraph 3(1) applying the jurisdiction of the Tribunal to "any person" who is a member of "any armed" force—provided that the acts in question were committed within the territory of Bangladesh. This is consistent with GPW, art. 102, which provides that "a prisoner of war can be validly sentenced only if the sentence has been pronounced by the same courts according to the same procedure as in the case of members of the armed forces of the Detaining Power." The Tribunal set up under this Act would presumably try (under the same procedures) members of the armed forces of Bangladesh for any crimes of this character for which they may be accused.

It is not known (from this Act, certainly) how civilians or ex-servicemen would be prosecuted for crimes against humanity, crimes against peace, genocide, war crimes, violations of the Geneva Conventions (which are also war crimes), and violations of "other crimes under international law."

Third. While nothing in the Act is incompatible with the notice requirements of GPW, arts. 104–105, two sections of the Act are silent as to the length of notice—and thus require interpretation consistent with GPW.

Paragraph 6(1) provides that "the Government may, by notification in the *Official Gazette*, set up one or more Tribunals," etc. Paragraph 16(2) provides that "a copy of the formal charge ... shall be furnished to the accused person at a reasonable time before the trial," etc.

GPW, art. 104, reads in pertinent part:

"In any case in which the Detaining Power has decided to institute judicial proceedings against a prisoner of war, it shall notify the Protecting Power [or power of origin, Pakistan] as soon as possible and at least three weeks before the opening of the trial...."

The said notification shall contain the following information: ...

(3) Specification of the charge ... ;

(4) Designation of the court which will try the case, likewise the date and place fixed for the opening of the trial...."

This means that paragraph 6(1) publication by itself is not sufficient to meet the test of GWP, art. 104. Three weeks of notification is demanded; and it means that the word "reasonable" in paragraph 16(2) must be interpreted as not less than three weeks.

Fourth. Qualifications of the members of the Tribunal(s) are set forth in paragraph 6(2) of the Act.... Yet proper implementation of paragraph 6(2) would limit membership of a Tribunal to persons who are "independent and impartial" within the meaning of art. 10 of the 1948 Universal Declaration of Human Rights, art. 84 of the 1949 Geneva Prisoner of War Convention, and the common expectations encompassed in art. 14(1) of the 1966 Covenant on Civil and Political Rights.

There is of course no indication from the wording of the Act that persons appointed pursuant to paragraph 6(2) would not have the required impartiality and independence for a fair trial. On the other hand, paragraph 6(8) raises an obstacle to the full guarantee of impartiality. For paragraph 6(8) provides that "Neither the constitution of a tribunal nor the appointment of its chairman or member shall be challenged by the prosecution or by the accused persons or their counsel." Note, however, that there is no mention of the right to challenge the bench in either the Charter of the International Tribunal, Nuremberg, or in GPW—but such a right was provided for under Rules 25(f) and 30 promulgated by the United Nations Command, Korean conflict.

Another *possible* hindrance to the full guarantee of impartiality exists in the wording of paragraph 10(1)(h) ... While there is nothing in the language itself incompatible with international due process standards and while this provision is well within the due process guarantees of the 1948 Universal Declaration of Human Rights and the Geneva Convention, the powers granted the Tribunal here could possibly be abused.

Consideration might well be given to art. 14(3)(e) of the 1966 Covenant on Civil and Political Rights and art. 6(3)(d) of the European Convention on Human Rights which provide for a minimum guarantee to each accused that each shall be entitled to "examine, or have examined, the witnesses against him." Additionally, art. 24(g) of the Charter of the International Tribunal, Nuremberg, had guaranteed that the "prosecution and the defense shall interrogate and may cross-examine any witnesses and any defendant who gives testimony," even though under art. 24(f) the "Tribunal may put any question to any witness and to any defendant, at any time." (See also *id.*, art. 17). Moreover, Rule 25(e) of the 1951 United Nations Command, Korean conflict, had specifically granted the accused a right "to cross examine, personally or through Counsel, each adverse witness who personally appears before the Commission." [What is "adverse" would seem to depend upon actual circumstances during the trial.] The requirement in Article 8(2)(f) of the 1969 American Convention on Human Rights would, if applicable, allow the "right of the defense to examine witnesses present in the court."

Thus, while it is perfectly proper to have the Tribunal examine witnesses, the actual process must not be such as to deprive the accused of the opportunity to have the witness examined fully. In other words, the Tribunal must not implement paragraph 10(1)(h) in such a way as to deprive the accused of the opportunity for a fair defense to the charges. Similarly, the Tribunal must not implement this paragraph in such a way as to deprive the accused of his right under GPW, art. 105, to call witnesses, or under GPW, art. 99 to present his defense. It would seem difficult for a Tribunal to refuse a defense request (or a prosecution request) for cross-examination and still remain impartial and fair, but this would depend upon the actual circumstances....

Fifth. Pursuant to paragraph 9(4) of the Act:

"The submission of a list of witnesses and documents under subsection (3) [providing for three weeks notice] shall not preclude the prosecution from calling, with the permission of the Tribunal, additional witnesses or tendering any further evidence at any stage of the trial:

Provided that notice shall be given to the defence of the additional witnesses intended to be called or additional evidence sought to be tendered by the prosecution."

This should be implemented as far as possible in such a manner that the accused is notified "in good time before the opening of the trial" of at least the additional documents in order to assure compliance with GPW, art. 105, fourth paragraph.

Sixth. The Act provides, in various paragraphs, for the assistance of qualified counsel, for an interpreter, for the right to call witnesses and present a defense, etc., but proper compliance with Geneva law requires that the accused be actually informed of these rights — in due time before the beginning of trial. (Three weeks time is demanded to meet the standards of GPW, arts. 104–105.) (See III [J. Pictet] Commentary at 488.)

It is assumed that the accused will understand that the right to counsel includes the right to qualified counsel of his own choice within the meaning of GPW, art. 105. (See also art. 14(3)(b), (d) and (f) of the 1966 Covenant on Civil and Political Rights, and III Commentary at 486–487 and 492.)

Conclusion. It can be concluded that the International Crimes (Tribunals) Act adequately affords the accused the full guarantees of international due process to which they are entitled—far more guarantees than the minimal requirements demanded by international law. Despite the fact that certain provisions of the Act (as with the provisions of any due process act of any country) admit the possibility of abuse of process, the entire nature and spirit of the Act leads to the conclusion that there will be "a fair and public hearing by an independent and impartial Tribunal."

Questions

1. Do you agree with Professors Paust and Blaustein?

2. What other safeguards are now required under international law, if any? What others might you recommend?

Paust & Blaustein, *War Crimes Jurisdiction and Due Process: The Bangladesh Experience*

11 Vand. J. Transnat'l L. 1, 31–38 (1978)

Human Rights to Due Process of Law

It has been authoritatively declared [in *United States v. List*] that the killing of persons in the control of a party without a trial would be "nothing less than plain murder." Moreover, the 1949 Geneva Conventions reiterate this prohibition and a common provision states that "wilfully depriving a protected person of the rights of fair and regular trial as prescribed in the present Convention" constitutes a "grave breach" of the Conventions. Additionally, the Geneva Conventions require that those being prosecuted for a grave breach of the Conventions shall in all circumstances "benefit by safeguards of proper trial and defence, which shall not be less favourable than those provided by" articles 105 through 108 of the Geneva Prisoner of War Convention. If the accused is a prisoner of war, he is entitled to the procedural safeguards of the Geneva Prisoner of War Convention in articles 82 through 104. . . .

Alleged Violations by India Would Not Immunize International Crime or

Suspend Applicability of the Geneva Conventions

It has been argued that if one party breaches the Geneva Conventions, other parties can engage in counter-breaches, or that the Conventions are suspended as between them. This argument is based on the simplistic and incorrect assumption that a breach of the Geneva Conventions should be treated similarly to a breach of contract under domestic law or a breach of a bilateral treaty. A better analogy is to the criminal law, since all nations properly expect that one crime does not justify another. In the international legal process even the formalistic Vienna Convention on the Law of Treaties recognized in article 60(5) that such a limited perspective is totally unacceptable when the treaty provisions relate to the protection of the human person and the treaty is of humanitarian character. The Geneva Conventions, like the Genocide Convention, are undoubtedly examples of such treaties. Provisions designed to ensure universal sanctions relate to and are designed to ensure a more effective and universal protection of human beings. A breach by one party does not justify a counter-breach. Similarly, the breaching party is not relieved from further performance under the Conventions since a breach does not suspend the operation of the Conventions and a state cannot absolve itself or any other state of past or future performance by its actions.

Any doubt concerning the state of the law prior to the Conventions on this matter was, as Pictet's Commentary states, dispelled when the High Contracting Parties obligated themselves to respect and to ensure respect for the Conventions in all circumstances. Moreover, these obligations are not state-to-state (nor on a basis of reciprocity) but are obligations to all mankind, and the Conventions are of a much higher order than mere trade compacts or ordinary agreements between states. Even necessity does not justify a deviation from the provisions of the Conventions unless the applicable article so provides. The Advisory Opinion of the International Court of Justice on Reservations to the Genocide Convention is also relevant. The Court declared:

> The Convention was manifestly adopted for a purely humanitarian and civilizing purpose.... Consequently, in a convention of this type one cannot speak of individual advantages or disadvantages to States, or of the maintenance of a perfect contractual balance between rights and duties. The high ideals which inspired the Convention provide, by virtue of the common will of the parties, the foundation and measure of all its provisions.

The International Court also declared that "obligations of a State towards the international community as a whole" are "the concern of all States...." The Court also stated:

> [I]n view of the importance of the rights involved, all States can be held to have a legal interest in their protection; they are obligations *erga omnes*. Such obligations derive, for example, in contemporary international law, from the outlawing of acts of aggression, and of genocide, as also from the principles and rules concerning the basic rights of the human person ... [*e.g.*, the 1948 Universal Declaration and the 1949 Geneva Conventions].

Postscript

The international crimes trials never took place, not because of lack of jurisdiction but, as is too often the case, because of politics. The issues of international crime and criminal jurisdiction had become so intermeshed with post-war regional disputes and global politics that Bangladesh finally agreed in 1974 to allow India to repatriate the 195 alleged violators of international law to Pakistan, even though Pakistan did not agree to prosecute grave breaches of the 1949 Geneva Conventions or to sanction any relevant international crime.

Throughout the previous years (1972–73) India and Pakistan had been carrying on separate talks concerning the settlement of old boundary lines. India, Bangladesh, and Pakistan had been involved in talks concerning the return of civilians trapped during the fighting, the repatriation of prisoners of war, and other related matters. At the same time, the Government of Bangladesh was anxious to obtain formal recognition, United Nations membership, and international trade and assistance necessary for a new state's survival. All of these concerns, however, became so interconnected that political pressures finally forced Bangladesh to abandon any hope of carrying out the proposed prosecutions.

Pakistan, contrary to the letter and spirit of the 1949 Geneva Conventions, placed even more pressure on Bangladesh by refusing to release some 400,000 Bengalis (civilians and former members of Pakistan's armed forces) who were being held in Pakistan and utilized as pawns in a complicated power game. To add to the pressure, Pakistan refused to recognize Bangladesh and was joined by the People's Republic of China in an effort to bar admission of the new state to the United Nations. At the United Nations in 1972, China finally did bar Bangladesh from membership when she cast her first veto in the Security Council. Thereafter, Pakistan and China began joint plans for further action to force Bangladesh to allow a return of *all* the Pakistani war prisoners to Pakistan and to address other matters of common interest concerning the subcontinent.

China had justified its veto on the grounds that Bangladesh refused to allow repatriation of all the war prisoners in accordance with the 1949 Geneva Conventions. This was a curious twist of the Geneva Conventions, especially in view of the obligations of Bangladesh and India to prosecute those accused of grave breaches of the Conventions. China and Pakistan clearly had no intention to allow other states to fulfill their obligations to prosecute violations of international law. Political considerations were far more important than fulfillment of international legal responsibility.

On April 17, 1973, when Bangladesh announced its intention to prosecute, it still insisted that it had a right to impose criminal sanctions, at least on the 195 individuals accused of war crimes, genocide, and other violations. By mid-December, India and Pakistan had reached a new agreement. India would return *all* the Pakistani war prisoners and detainees to Pakistan, but Bangladesh still had not consented. The new India-Pakistan agreement also led to Pakistan's declaration on December 14th of its intention to drop the Pakistani suit against India before the International Court of Justice, a proceeding initiated on May 11, 1973, by Pakistan. The International Court of Justice accordingly removed the case from its list, thus providing the only judicial record of prior attempts to apply criminal sanctions against those accused of murders, tortures, assaults, and other conduct in violation of international human rights, laws of war, and prohibitions of genocide and crimes against humanity.

All was not finalized, however. Bangladesh still hoped that the trials would proceed as India and Bangladesh had earlier agreed. Nevertheless, in the next three months, the three states reached a major agreement paving the way for a settlement of post-war political and economic difficulties. As part of the agreement, the 195 Pakistani prisoners of war were to be returned to Pakistan. During negotiations, Bangladesh had insisted that Pakistan at least conduct its own trials of the accused and demanded some form of justice. On April 10th, however, all that had come from Pakistan was a qualified apology. The Government of Pakistan "condemned and deeply regretted any crimes that may have been committed." India had already repatriated some 80,000 prisoners, in accordance with the India-Pakistan agreement of December, 1973. Soon the others would also be returned.

Neither India, Pakistan, nor Bangladesh had lived up to their responsibilities under the 1949 Geneva Conventions to search out and prosecute, or extradite for prosecution, those accused of grave breaches of the Conventions—the most serious deprivations of human rights in time of armed conflict since the atrocities of World War II. Repatriation did not end such responsibility, it merely transferred primary prosecutorial responsibility to Pakistan where it remains today. On September 14, 1974, the state of Bangladesh was admitted to the United Nations.

Final Comments

There are many lessons in the Bangladesh experience. Our main concern, however, is with international law and the precedential value of the statutes, memoranda, and sanction efforts involved. The 1973 Bangladesh Act "to provide for the detention, prosecution and punishment of persons for genocide, crimes against humanity, war crimes and other crimes under international law" is of significant precedential value, despite the lack of an actual prosecution of Pakistani prisoners. The 1973 Bangladesh Act represents an important recognition and implementation of international due process guarantees for those accused of international crimes. This act goes beyond the Nuremberg guarantees. Furthermore, it is far more useful evidence of present legal expectation than the 1950 and 1951 United Nations Command rules of criminal procedure. Neither the 1973 Act nor the 1950–1951 rules appear to be widely studied. Neither appear in any international law text, although their import to the study of war crimes, genocide, crimes against humanity, and human rights to due process seems obvious.

The Bangladesh setting is important as a reflection of a modern, post-Nuremberg problem—the application of the laws of armed conflict, genocide and general human rights. The Bangladesh case offers a rich source of analysis of the application of modern international norms to both internal and international armed conflict, and an important basis for a post-Nuremberg approach to modern military conflicts. The Bangladesh experience offers a valuable context for exploration of the application of general human rights law to a people seeking self-determination and self-determination assistance by other states. Self-determination struggles, some claim, are the wars of the future—as groups of people seek political independence, economic independence, or the free integration or association with other political entities.

Notes and Questions

1. Did China violate its obligation under common article 1 of the 1949 Geneva Conventions "to respect and to ensure respect for" the Conventions "in all circumstances"? *See also* U.N. Charter, arts. 55(c), 56.

2. What special benefits and detriments would prosecution in the new International Criminal Court (ICC) pose? On the weakness of the state system for enforcement, *see, e.g.,* M.C. BASSIOUNI, A DRAFT INTERNATIONAL CRIMINAL CODE AND DRAFT STATUTE FOR AN INTERNATIONAL CRIMINAL TRIBUNAL 53, *passim* (1987).

3. Can domestic tribunals function also with foreign judges sitting over international criminal cases? What problems might exist in the United States with respect to the appointment of foreign and U.S. judges sitting on a U.S. military commission? A court-martial? Some other domestic forum?

4. For views on an international terrorism court, a regional criminal court, and a national court with foreign judges, *see, e.g.,* remarks of panelists, 20 VAND. J. TRANS. L. 358–59 (1987).

Section 7
The Iraqi High Tribunal

[See the Iraq High Criminal Court Law, Res. No. 10, in the Documents Supplement]

Michael P. Scharf, "Basic Information About the Iraqi High Tribunal"
from Grotian Moment: The War Crimes Trial Blog, http://law.case.edu/saddamtrial (2006)

What is the Iraqi High Tribunal?

The Iraqi High Tribunal (IHT) is a judicial body, which was established by the U.S.-appointed Iraqi Governing Council on December 10, 2003, and approved by the Iraqi Transitional National Assembly on August 11, 2005, to prosecute high level members of the former Iraqi regime who are alleged to have committed war crimes, crimes against humanity, genocide, and aggression. It is composed of two, five-person Trial Chambers, and a nine-person Appeals Chamber. Some have called the IHT an "internationalized domestic court" since its statute and rules of procedure are modeled upon the U.N. war crimes tribunals for the former Yugoslavia, Rwanda, and Sierra Leone, and its statute requires the IHT to follow the precedent of the U.N. tribunals. Its judges and prosecutors are to be assisted by international experts. But it is not fully international, since its seat is Baghdad, its Prosecutor is Iraqi, and its bench is composed exclusively of Iraqi judges.

What are the specific charges against Saddam Hussein?

Rather than join the defendants and offenses and hold a single, comprehensive trial like that at Nuremberg, the IHT decided to proceed with a dozen mini-trials. The first case to be brought against Saddam Hussein involved his role in the 1982 execution of 150 Iraqi civilians in Dujail, a predominantly Shiite town north of Baghdad, in response to a failed assassination attempt on Saddam. Several of his top deputies have also been charged in the massacre. Among other charges, Saddam Hussein stands accused of ordering the slaughter of some 5,000 Kurds with chemical gas in Halabja in 1988, killing or deporting more than 10,000 members of the Kurdish Barzani tribe in the 1980s, invading Kuwait in 1990, and drying rivers, killing hundreds of thousands of Marsh Arabs in response to their 1991 uprising. In addition to Saddam, eleven high-ranking Iraqi officials are in custody awaiting indictments, including Abid Hamid al-Tikriti, a former presidential secretary, Ali Hassan al-Majid ("Chemical Ali"), Saddam's cousin and adviser, and Tariq Aziz, the former deputy prime minister.

Under which body of laws are they being tried?

The IHT has jurisdiction over crimes committed in Iraq or abroad (*e.g.*, in Iran or Kuwait) between 1968 and 2003 by former regime members. The IHT's subject matter jurisdiction is comprised of a mix of international law crimes and domestic law crimes that existed prior to Saddam's ascension to power in 1968. The international law offenses are (1) war crimes, (2) the crime of aggression, and (3) the crime of genocide. The domestic law crimes are (1) manipulation of the judiciary; (2) wastage of national resources and squandering of public assets and funds; and (3) acts of aggression against an Arab country. The IHT's procedural law is comprised of a mix of international law procedures set forth in the IHT's Rules of Procedures, supplemented by the Rules of Procedure of the Iraqi Criminal Code. Traditional Islamic Law, "sharia," is not applied by the IHT. The IHT is empowered to imprison convicted persons for up to life or subject them to capital punishment (a penalty that is not available in trials before the existing international and hybrid tribunals).

Who are the judges on the tribunal?

The IHT is comprised of fifty investigative, trial, and appellate judges, all of them native Iraqis mostly of Shiite or Kurdish ethnic origin. The IHT Statute prohibits anyone from serving as a judge who was a member of the Baath party. Each judge was nominated and vetted by the Iraqi Governing Council with the assistance of the 20,000 member Iraqi Bar Association. Five judges will preside over each trial, and nine different judges will preside over each appeal. The names of most of the judges have not been disclosed for security reasons.

Notes and Questions

1. For a debate among experts regarding more than forty issues related to the IHT, see Grotian Moment: The Saddam Hussein Trial Blog, a website maintained by Case Western Reserve University School of Law (www.law.case.edu/saddamtrial). Issues include: Is the Tribunal legitimate? Is the death penalty appropriate? Should the trial be televised? Is the process fair? *See also* M. Cherif Bassiouni, *Post Conflict Justice in Iraq: An Appraisal of the Iraq Special Tribunal*, 38 (2) Cornell Int'l L.J. 327 (2005); *Symposium: Milosevic & Hussein on Trial*, 38 (3) Cornell Int'l L. J. 649–1021 (2005).

2. Why do you think the United States and Iraqi Government preferred to try Saddam Hussein before a domestic tribunal in Baghdad, rather than before the International Criminal

Court or a Security Council-established ad hoc international or UN-endorsed hybrid tribunal? For the argument that the trial would have been more legitimate before an international or hybrid tribunal, see Leila Sadat, "Neither Fish nor Fowl: Saddam Hussein and the Iraqi Special Tribunal, Indigenous Solution or (U.S.) Occupation Court?" (2005), in Grotian Moment: The International War Crimes Trial Blog (2005), http://www.law.case.edu/saddamtrial/documents/Leila_Sadat_Indigenous_Solution_or(U.S.)_Occupation_Court.pdf; Diane Marie Amann, "Saddam Hussein and the Impartiality Deficit in International Criminal Justice," in Grotian Moment: The International War Crimes Trial Blog (2005), http://www.law.case.edu/saddamtrial/documents/Saddam_Hussein_and_Impartiality_Deficit.pdf.

3. If the U.S. was effectively an occupying power during the creation of the IHT and a new Iraqi regime was not constituted under the Iraqi Constitution until later, is the IHT legitimate? Is it an independent, competent tribunal constituted under law? See Jordan J. Paust, *The United States As Occupying Power Over Portions of Iraq and Special Responsibilities Under the Laws of War*, 27 Suffolk Transnat'l L. Rev. 1, 20–23 (2003). Did the subsequent action by the democratically elected Iraqi National Legislature to approve a revised IHT Statute and the list of IHT judges "cure" these legitimacy problems by subsequent ratification?

The IHT's costs are covered by the new government of Iraq, which currently receives billions of dollars in financial assistance from the United States. The IHT was originally established with $75 million in U.S. government funds. The United States also set up the "Regime Crimes Liaison Office" (RCLO) in Baghdad to help the IHT with investigations, translation of legal materials, and training of judges and prosecutors. RCLO is run by the U.S. Department of Justice, and has worked in partnership with international NGOs such as the International Bar Association (based in London), the International Legal Assistance Consortium (based in Stockholm), the International Association of Penal Law (based in Siracusa, Sicily), and an Academic Consortium (including Case Western Reserve University School of Law, William and Mary School of Law, and University of Connecticut School of Law).

4. Due to the manner in which the Court was established, its funding, operation, jurisdiction, substantive law and procedural rules, the legitimacy of the Saddam Hussein Trial has been called into question by many experts. Professor Sadat raises some of these issues and mentions some possible solutions:

A. Should Judge Rahman be recused? "[T]he nationality or ethnicity of a particular judge is not enough, without more, to support otherwise unfounded allegations of bias. Indeed, if the test for recusal were that broad, almost any judge could be disqualified for a variety of reasons including social class (biased against or for the poor) or religion. So, the mere fact that the presiding judge in the Saddam trial is Kurdish should not and does not disqualify him. More disquieting, however, is that the judge hales from Halabja, and has family members who were killed by the attack there that was allegedly ordered by Saddam. Under the rules governing International Tribunals, the question is whether Judge Rahman can be said to have a 'personal interest in the case,' (*see, e.g.*, ICC Rule 34(1)(a)) because members of his family were the victim's of one of the defendant's alleged crimes, even if it is not the crime charged in the instant case."

B. Will the Sunnis accept the Judgment of the Court? "Under Saddam's regime, defense lawyers received the file of their clients the morning of the trial. This attitude appears to persist in the Iraqi High Criminal Court. Unless Saddam's defense team is allowed to put forward an effective defense, which might require that the proceedings be moved out of

Iraq for security reasons, the trial will never appear fair to the Sunnis—now or twenty years from now. Additionally, the judges need to issue written, reasoned decisions on preliminary motions relating to jurisdiction, venue, and particular defenses. Otherwise their out of hand dismissal of these motions—even if correct on the facts and the law—appears to be arbitrary and partial, rather than judicious and impartial. Finally, of the five initial judges sitting on the Saddam trial, three have now been replaced. This suggests political interference with the Court that is unlikely to sit well with constituencies already inclined to be skeptical about the proceedings. Further tinkering with the composition of the bench needs to stop if the proceedings are to retain any semblance of credibility."

Leila Nadya Sadat, *Fixing the Legitimacy Deficit in the Saddam Hussein Trial*, in SADDAM ON TRIAL: UNDERSTANDING AND DEBATING THE IRAQI HIGH TRIBUNAL 166 (Michael P. Scharf & Gregory S. McNeal eds. 2006). She adds: because the IHT Statute does not permit the Tribunal to hear cases involving allegations of abuses of coalition forces within its jurisdiction (such as the so-called Hadith massacre in November 2005), but is essentially limited to the trial of Iraqis, it has been viewed as dominated by U.S. influence by many observers.

5. There is no right to appeal IHT decisions to the ordinary Iraqi courts. There is possible appeal to a Cassation Panel within the tribunal process. Is this a violation of customary human rights law reflected in Article 14(5) of the ICCPR?

6. Various international human rights NGOs were initially critical of the IHT because its Statute (Article 19) provides that "the accused is presumed innocent until proven guilty before the Court," but does not explicitly state that the "beyond reasonable doubt" standard would be used. Supporters of the IHT argue that although the Statute does not stipulate the test for proving guilt, the Statute must be read together with the Iraqi Criminal Code and practice. Iraq, like more than one hundred other countries, uses the Civil Law inquisitorial system rather than the Common Law adversarial system. In Iraq, as in most Civil Law countries, guilt must be proved "to a moral certainty." Article 14(2) of the ICCPR does not express the standard of proof that is required under human rights law, but requires that an accused is innocent "until proved guilty according to law."

7. Some critics considered that it was a mistake to prosecute the Dujail case as the first case against Saddam Hussein, since only a few hundred people were killed in Dujail and Saddam Hussein stood accused of murdering hundreds of thousands of persons elsewhere. Nonetheless, Professor Scharf considers that it was appropriate to begin with the *Dujail* case for four reasons:

"First, the evidence for the Dujail prosecution was extremely strong. Eye witnesses (both victims and members of the armed forces) were available to testify; forensic evidence had been collected and preserved; and video and documents existed which prove the atrocity, as well as who ordered it and how it was carried out. And it is far easier to prove the elements of a crime against humanity (the charge in the *Dujail* case), than the elements of genocide (the charge in the *Anfal* case).

"Second, the *Dujail* case did not lend itself to as many defenses as the other charges. Saddam Hussein's lawyers could not argue that his subordinates acted without authority in Dujail, because Saddam could still be held responsible under the principle of command responsibility for failing to punish those subordinates for the atrocity. Though the defense team tried to argue that Saddam Hussein's actions were justified as self-defense in response to acts of terrorism, the prosecution was able to show that his response (razing the town, executing the townspeople, and destroying the surrounding date palm groves) was disproportionate and therefore unjustifiable.

"Third, one of Saddam Hussein's co-defendants in the *Dujail* case was the former head of the Revolutionary Court, who was charged with crimes against humanity in connection with ordering the execution of 148 Dujail townspeople after an unfair trial. He is the first judge since the Nuremberg-era *Altstoetter* case, which was made into the Academy Award-winning Movie "Judgment at Nuremberg," to be tried for using his court as a political weapon. The precedent of this trial will uniquely serve to discourage future judicial abuses in Iraq.

"Finally, it made a lot of sense to begin with a less important and less complex case because it enabled the Tribunal to focus on the broad legal challenges to the process which are brought by the defense. Once these are disposed of in the *Dujail* case, the principle of *res judicata* will prevent the Defense from re-litigating them in subsequent trials, enabling the Tribunal to focus entirely on the factual and legal complexities of those more difficult cases."

Michael Scharf, "Does it make good sense to start with the Dujail case, rather than a greater atrocity like the Anfal campaign?," from Grotian Moment: The Saddam Hussein Trial Blog, www.law.case.edu/saddamtrial (2006).

8. Do you think the due process provisions of the IHT Statute are sufficient to ensure a fair trial? *See* the Iraq High Criminal Court Law, Res. No. 10, in the Documents Supplement. *See also* Will Saddam Hussein Get a Fair Trial, Debate Between Dr. Curtis F.J. Doebbler [one of Saddam's U.S. lawyers] and Professor Michael P. Scharf, 37 Case Western J. Int'l. L. 21–40 (2005) (transcript of a debate that was broadcast nationally on C-SPAN on January 29, 2005). More generally, *see, e.g.*, Diane Marie Amann, *"The Only Thing Left Is Justice": Cherif Bassiouni, Saddam Hussein, and the Quest for Impartiality in International Criminal Law*, in The Theory and Practice of International Criminal Law: Essays in Honor of M. Cherif Bassiouni 365 (Leila Nadya Sadat & Michael P. Scharf eds. 2008). Note that many of the procedural guarantees are facially similar to those reflected in Article 14 of the ICCPR, which are considered to constitute a minimum set of customary human rights to due process. However, is there a guarantee of the right to confront witnesses against the accused, as required in Article 14(3)(e) of the ICCPR?, perhaps with the gloss of interpretation created in the ICTY and ICTR? Compare Section 9 of this chapter.

9. The phrase "Trial of the Century" has been employed with respect to major international war crimes trials, including the 1945 Nuremberg Trial, the 1961 Adolf Eichmann Trial, the 1987 Klaus Barbie Trial, the 1989 Nicolae Ceausescu Trial, and most recently the 2002-2005 Milosevic Trial. Do you think that the Saddam Hussein Trial will rank among these seminal cases? What criteria would you use to define the "trial of the century": The scale of the atrocities charged and/or proven? The high level status of the accused? The level of interest of the international community? The legal precedent that the trial provided? The effect of the trial on international peace and security? Can a trial that is criticized as unfair still be one of the trials of the century? For a debate on this question, see: "Issue # 10: Is the Saddam Hussein Trial one of the most important court cases of all time? Michael P. Scharf & Leila Nadya Sadat, *Is the Saddam Hussein Trial One of the Most Important Cases of all Time?*, in Saddam on Trial: Understanding and Debating the Iraqi High Tribunal 229, 230 (2006). Professor Sadat adds: is there something more important than media interest to the success, importance and legitimacy of a trial: "Criminal trials, whether of important and notorious individuals, or of small-time offenders accused of petty crimes, are nothing more than show trials, unless three criteria are met: The judges must be independent, well-qualified and impartial; the accused must be properly and effectively represented; and the proceedings must be fair. Using these criteria, it is

difficult not to be skeptical about the fairness, and therefore the ultimate significance, of the trial of Saddam Hussein."

10. With respect to developments and prospects more generally in connection with special domestic criminal tribunals, *see, e.g.*, Jenia Iontcheva Turner, *Nationalizing International Criminal Law*, 41 STANFORD J. INT'L L. 1 (2005).

Section 8
The Special Court for Sierra Leone: A Hybrid Model

The Special Court for Sierra Leone (SCSL) is a judicial body established by an agreement between the United Nations and the Government of Sierra Leone on January 16, 2002. The treaty was subsequently ratified by the Sierra Leone Parliament on March 7, 2002. The SCSL was established in order "to prosecute persons who bear the greatest responsibility for serious violations of international humanitarian law and Sierra Leonean law" committed since November 31, 1996 as part of the Sierra Leone armed conflict. The Special Court consists of the Chambers, the Prosecutor and the Registry. There are two Trial Chambers, each consisting of three judges, one appointed by the Government of Sierra Leone and two judges appointed by the Secretary-General of the United Nations. The Appeals Chamber consists of five judges, two of whom are appointed by the Government of Sierra Leone and three appointed by the Secretary-General. The Prosecutor operates as a separate organ of the Special Court and is assisted by a Sierra Leonean Deputy Prosecutor. The Registry is responsible for the overall administration of the Special Court. The expenses of the SCSL are borne by voluntary contributions from the international community.

What crimes can the Special Court prosecute?

The Special Court has the power to prosecute specifically enumerated international law crimes and domestic law crimes. The international law offences are (1) crimes against humanity, (2) war crimes, and (3) other serious violations of international humanitarian law. The Special Court also has subject matter jurisdiction over two violations of Sierra Leonean Law: offences relating to the abuse of girls under the Prevention of Cruelty to Children Act and offences relating to wanton destruction of property under the Malicious Damage Act. In the interpretation of international law, the Special Court is to be guided by the decisions of the International Tribunals for the Former Yugoslavia and for Rwanda. The decisions of the Supreme Court of Sierra Leone guide the interpretation and application of Sierra Leone laws. The SCSL has the power to imprison a convicted person for a specified number of years or to confiscate property, but, consistent with existing hybrid and international courts, the Special Court cannot impose the death penalty.

Who is being tried by the Special Court?

Currently, eleven persons stand indicted by the Special Court, representing all three of the country's former warring factions: the Revolutionary United Front (RUF), the Armed Forces Revolutionary Council (AFRC), and the Civil Defence Forces (CDF). Of the eleven indicted, ten are in the custody of the Special Court. Only the disposition of Johnny Paul Koroma remains uncertain. He was widely reported to have been killed in June 2003 but, as definitive evidence of his death was never provided, his indictment has not been dropped. Indictments of two leaders of the RUF, Foday Sankoh and Sam Bockarie were dropped after their deaths. Although all are individually charged, the members of each faction have been grouped. The Revolutionary United Front trial began on July 5, 2004, the Civil Defence Forces trial started on June 3, 2004, and the Armed Forces Revolutionary Council trial started on March 7, 2005. The charges against each faction include murder, rape, extermination, acts of terror, enslavement, pillaging, sexual slavery, and conscription of children into an armed force. In addition, the indictments against the RUF members include attacks on United Nations peacekeepers and humanitarian workers.

Notes and Questions

1. The SCSL is a good example of a so-called "hybrid court" which is neither completely international nor completely domestic in character. In addition to the SCSL, hybrid courts have been established in Kosovo and East Timor. Professor Dickinson comments: "Incorporating some aspects of the formal international criminal justice models while seeking to include local actors and develop local norms, the hybrid approach has been thought beneficial in addressing practical, on the ground dilemmas about criminal accountability for human rights abuses." What practical dilemmas can be more easily addressed by a hybrid court? What other benefits does a hybrid court offer? Are there any disadvantages? See Laura A. Dickinson, *The Promise of Hybrid Courts*, 97 Am. J. Int'l L. 295, 300 (2003).

2. Charles Taylor, the former president of Liberia, supported the Revolutionary Armed Front (RUF) by providing material and personnel, weapons and training—with the aim of destabilizing Sierra Leone and gaining access to its rich supply of diamonds. The RUF launched its first attack in March 1991, and according to numerous reports were quick to demonstrate its brutality. Taylor resigned as president of Liberia on August 11, 2003 under U.S. pressure and was granted asylum in Nigeria. After more than two years in exile, the new democratically elected president of Liberia submitted an official request to Nigeria for Taylor's extradition. One week later, on March 25, 2006, Nigeria agreed to release Taylor to stand trial at the Special Court of Sierra Leone. He was arrested on March 29, 2006 on the Cameroon border while trying to leave Nigeria and was transferred to the Special Court's custody.

Immediately upon receiving Taylor into its custody, the Special Court requested relocation of the trial to The Hague, citing concerns about stability in West Africa if the trial was held at the Special Court's headquarters in Freetown, Sierra Leone's capital. The Netherlands agreed to host the trial on the condition that a third country take Taylor if convicted. On June 15, 2006, after other European countries refused, the British government said that it was willing to imprison Taylor if he was convicted. Taylor was transferred to The Hague and was tried in the Special Court for Sierra Leone, having pled not guilty at his initial appearance before the Special Court on April 3, 2006. See Note 9 *infra*.

What are the advantages and disadvantages of hosting a trial away from the place of commission of the crimes? What measures should be taken to ensure that victims and their families have access to trial proceedings? What are the advantages and disadvantages of asking a third country to imprison Taylor or other war criminals? Why are other European countries unwilling to do so? Should the United States step up and offer to incarcerate international war criminals?

3. The decision whether or not to hold a tribunal at the location of the alleged crimes seems to involve a balance of a security risk and the desire to keep the perpetrator close to the victims. How do time, distance and the ruling nation's control of the area factor into this balance?

4. The jurisdiction of the Special Court extends to crimes committed after November 31, 1996, although the armed conflict in Sierra Leone began in 1991. The U.N. Report

of the Secretary General concluded that the 1996 date "would have the benefit of putting the Sierra Leone conflict in perspective without unnecessarily extending the temporal jurisdiction of the Special Court." U.N. S.G., *Report of the Secretary-General on the Establishment of a Special Court for Sierra Leone*, U.N. Doc. S/2000/915 (Oct. 4, 2000). What benefits might he have in mind? Can justice be served if crimes committed during the entire war are not tried?

5. The Lomé Peace Accord was a peace agreement between the warring parties signed on July 7, 1999. *See* Lomé Peace Agreement Between the Government of Sierra Leone and the Revolutionary United Front of Sierra Leone (July 7, 1999), *available at* http://www.sierra-leone.org/lomeaccord.html. Among its conditions, the accord granted amnesty to all RUF combatants. Two defendants argued that the amnesty granted under the Lomé Peace Agreement precluded their trial before the SCSL. Professor Sadat discussed the position of the defendants and the decision of the Special Court:

> The defendants argued that, notwithstanding the international nature of the crimes, the SCSL was bound to respect the amnesty granted by the Lomé Agreement because the Agreement was an international treaty, having been signed by six states and a number of international organizations [and entities], including the RUF. The SCSL disagreed ... [and] found that the agreement could not be characterized as an international instrument. Conversely, it held that article 10 of the Special Court's Statute, forbidding the Special Court from taking into consideration "an amnesty granted to any person falling within the jurisdiction of the Special Court in respect of [international] crimes [within the Special Court's jurisdiction] shall not be a bar to prosecution," did apply. Therefore, any amnesty granted to the accused had no effect.

Leila Nadya Sadat, *Exile, Amnesty and International Law*, 81 Notre Dame L. Rev. 955, 1015–16 (2006).

6. In 2000, a domestic Truth and Reconciliation Commission Act set up a truth commission in Sierra Leone "to create an impartial historical record of violations and abuses of human rights and international humanitarian law related to the armed conflict in Sierra Leone; to address impunity; respond to the needs of the victims; to promote healing and reconciliation; and to prevent a repetition of the violations and abuses suffered." Truth and Reconciliation Commission Act 2000, section 6(1) (Sierra Leone). Are these the same goals of the SCSL? For a discussion of the relationship between the Truth and Reconciliation Commission Act and the SCSL *see, e.g.*, William Schabas, *A Synergistic Relationship: The Sierra Leone Truth and Reconciliation Commission and the Special Court for Sierra Leone*, 15 Crim. L.F. 3–54 (2004).

7. On May 7, 2004, the Trial Chamber of the Special Court approved a motion by prosecutors to add a new crime against humanity of "forced marriage" to indictments against six defendants alleged to have been leaders of the former AFRC and RUF. Prosecutor David Crane described how women were abducted, forced to have sex and bear children, and threatened with death if they tried to escape. Angela Stephens, *Forced Marriage Pursued As Crime in Sierra Leone Tribunal Cases*, April 16, 2004, *available at* http://www.globalpolicy.org/intljustice/tribunals/sierra/2004/0416marriage.htm. See also Michael P. Scharf & Suzanne Mattler, *Forced Marriage: Exploring the Visibility of the Special Court for Sierra Leone's New Crime Against Humanity*, 3 African Perspectives on Int'l Crim. Justice (2005), available at http://papers.ssrn.com/so13/papers.cfm?abstract_id=824291. How does this crime fit within the rubric of crimes against humanity of "rape, sexual slavery, enforced prostitution, forced pregnancy and any other form of

sexual violence" enumerated in the SCSL's Statute? *See* Statute of the Special Court for Sierra Leone (January 16, 2002), *available at*, http://www.sc-sl.org/DOCUMENTS/tabid/176/Default.aspx. Does it matter that some of these women have chosen to remain in these marriages after the war ended and they were given the opportunity to leave?

8. On May 31, 2004, the Appeals Chamber of the Special Court ruled unanimously that Charles Taylor does not enjoy any immunity from prosecution by the Court as Head of State of Liberia at the time criminal proceedings were initiated, the Chamber noting that it is "an international criminal tribunal with an international mandate exercising jurisdiction over international crimes." The Prosecutor v. Charles Ghankay Taylor, No. SCSL-2003-01-1, Decision on Immunity form Jurisdiction (31 May 2004). Given the decision of the Appeals Chamber that it is an international tribunal, would the tribunals in Cambodia and East Timor arguably be international? Is the Iraqi High Tribunal merely domestic, like the previously attempted Bangladesh Tribunal?

9. On April 26, 2012, Taylor was found guilty on all eleven counts of war crimes and crimes against humanity, but the Trial Chamber found that he had aided and abetted the RUF and the Armed Forces Revolutionary Council (AFRC), not that he was proven guilty with respect to dereliction of duty or for providing unlawful orders. He became another in a growing set of heads of state and former heads of state who have been convicted in international tribunals and domestic courts for international crimes. Recall in particular the prosecution of Peter von Hagenbach in 1474 and the finding in the ICTY that under customary international law Milosevic was not immune from prosecution prior to his death.

10. For a discussion of the differences between the SCSL and the International Tribunals for the former Yugoslavia and for Rwanda, see Michael P. Scharf, ASIL Insights: *The Special Court for Sierra Leone* (October 2000), *available at* http://www.asil.org/insights/insigh53.htm. Issues include the composition of the courts, the primacy of the courts over national courts, and the subject matter jurisdiction of each court.

Section 9
The Ad Hoc International Criminal Tribunals for Former Yugoslavia and Rwanda

A. ICT for Former Yugoslavia

Report of the Secretary-General Pursuant to Paragraph 2 of Security Council Resolution 808 (1993)
U.N. Doc. S/25704 (May 3, 1993)

Introduction

1. By paragraph 1 of resolution 808 (1993) of 22 February 1993, the Security Council decided "that an international tribunal shall be established for the prosecution of persons responsible for serious violations of international humanitarian law committed in the territory of the former Yugoslavia since 1991".

2. By paragraph 2 of the resolution, the Secretary-General was requested "to submit for consideration by the Council at the earliest possible date, and if possible no later than

60 days after the adoption of the present resolution, a report on all aspects of this matter, including specific proposals and where appropriate options for the effective and expeditious implementation of the decision [to establish an international tribunal], taking into account suggestions put forward in this regard by Member States."

3. The present report is presented pursuant to that request.

4. Resolution 808 (1993) represents a further step taken by the Security Council in a series of resolutions concerning serious violations of international humanitarian law occurring in the territory of the former Yugoslavia.

5. In resolution 764 (1992) of 13 July 1992, the Security Council reaffirmed that all parties to the conflict are bound to comply with their obligations under international humanitarian law and in particular the Geneva Conventions of 12 August 1949, and that persons who commit or order the commission of grave breaches of the Conventions are individually responsible in respect of such breaches.

6. In resolution 771 (1992) of 13 August 1992, the Security Council expressed grave alarm at continuing reports of widespread violations of international humanitarian law occurring within the territory of the former Yugoslavia and especially in Bosnia and Herzegovina, including reports of mass forcible expulsion and deportation of civilians, imprisonment and abuse of civilians in detention centres, deliberate attacks on non-combatants, hospitals and ambulances, impeding the delivery of food and medical supplies to the civilian population, and wanton devastation and destruction of property. The Council strongly condemned any violations of international humanitarian law, including those involved in the practice of "ethnic cleansing", and demanded that all parties to the conflict in the former Yugoslavia cease and desist from all breaches of international humanitarian law. It called upon States and international humanitarian organizations to collate substantiated information relating to the violations of humanitarian law, including grave breaches of the Geneva Conventions, being committed in the territory of the former Yugoslavia and to make this information available to the Council. Furthermore, the Council decided, acting under Chapter VII of the Charter of the United Nations, that all parties and others concerned in the former Yugoslavia, and all military forces in Bosnia and Herzegovina, should comply with the provisions of that resolution, failing which the Council would need to take further measures under the Charter.

7. In resolution 780 (1992) of 6 October 1992, the Security Council requested the Secretary-General to establish an impartial Commission of Experts to examine and analyse the information as requested by resolution 771 (1992), together with such further information as the Commission may obtain through its own investigations or efforts, of other persons or bodies pursuant to resolution 771 (1992), with a view to providing the Secretary-General with its conclusions on the evidence of grave breaches of the Geneva Conventions and other violations of international humanitarian law committed in the territory of the former Yugoslavia.

8. On 14 October 1992 the Secretary-General submitted a report to the Security Council pursuant to paragraph 3 of resolution 780 (1992) in which he outlined his decision to establish a five-member Commission of Experts (S/24657). On 26 October 1992, the Secretary-General announced the appointment of the Chairman and members of the Commission of Experts.

9. By a letter dated 9 February 1993, the Secretary-General submitted to the President of the Security Council an interim report of the Commission of Experts (S/25274), which concluded that grave breaches and other violations of international humanitarian law had been committed in the territory of the former Yugoslavia, including wilful killing,

"ethnic cleansing", mass killings, torture, rape, pillage and destruction of civilian property, destruction of cultural and religious property and arbitrary arrests. In its report, the Commission noted that should the Security Council or another competent organ of the United Nations decide to establish an ad hoc international tribunal, such a decision would be consistent with the direction of its work.

10. It was against this background that the Security Council considered and adopted resolution 808 (1993). After recalling the provisions of resolutions 764 (1992), 771 (1992) and 780 (1992) and, taking into consideration the interim report of the Commission of Experts, the Security Council expressed once again its grave alarm at continuing reports of widespread violations of international humanitarian law occurring within the territory of the former Yugoslavia, including reports of mass killings and the continuation of the practice of "ethnic cleansing". The Council determined that this situation constituted a threat to international peace and security, and stated that it was determined to put an end to such crimes and to take effective measures to bring to justice the persons who are responsible for them. The Security Council stated its conviction that in the particular circumstances of the former Yugoslavia the establishment of an international tribunal would enable this aim to be achieved and would contribute to the restoration and maintenance of peace.

11. The Secretary-General wishes to recall that in resolution 820 (1993) of 17 April 1993, the Security Council condemned once again all violations of international humanitarian law, including in particular, the practice of "ethnic cleansing" and the massive, organized and systematic detention and rape of women, and reaffirmed that those who commit or have committed or order or have ordered the commission of such acts will be held individually responsible in respect of such acts.

12. The Security Council's decision in resolution 808 (1993) to establish an international tribunal is circumscribed in scope and purpose: the prosecution of persons responsible for serious violations of international humanitarian law committed in the territory of the former Yugoslavia since 1991. The decision does not relate to the establishment of an international criminal jurisdiction in general nor to the creation of an international criminal court of a permanent nature, issues which are and remain under active consideration by the International Law Commission and the General Assembly....

I. THE LEGAL BASIS FOR THE ESTABLISHMENT OF THE

INTERNATIONAL TRIBUNAL

18. Security Council resolution 808 (1993) states that an international tribunal shall be established for the prosecution of persons responsible for serious violations of international humanitarian law committed in the territory of the former Yugoslavia since 1991. It does not, however, indicate how such an international tribunal is to be established or on what legal basis.

19. The approach which, in the normal course of events, would be followed in establishing an international tribunal would be the conclusion of a treaty by which the States parties would establish a tribunal and approve its statute. This treaty would be drawn up and adopted by an appropriate international body (*e.g.*, the General Assembly or a specially convened conference), following which it would be opened for signature and ratification. Such an approach would have the advantage of allowing for a detailed examination and elaboration of all the issues pertaining to the establishment of the international tribunal. It also would allow the States participating in the negotiation and conclusion of the treaty fully to exercise their sovereign will, in particular whether they wish to become parties to the treaty or not.

20. As has been pointed out in many of the comments received, the treaty approach incurs the disadvantage of requiring considerable time to establish an instrument and then to achieve the required number of ratifications for entry into force. Even then, there could be no guarantee that ratifications will be received from those States which should be parties to the treaty if it is to be truly effective.

21. A number of suggestions have been put forward to the effect that the General Assembly, as the most representative organ of the United Nations, should have a role in the establishment of the international tribunal in addition to its role in the administrative and budgetary aspects of the question. The involvement of the General Assembly in the drafting or the review of the statute of the International Tribunal would not be reconcilable with the urgency expressed by the Security Council in resolution 808 (1993). The Secretary-General believes that there are other ways of involving the authority and prestige of the General Assembly in the establishment of the International Tribunal.

22. In the light of the disadvantages of the treaty approach in this particular case and of the need indicated in resolution 808 (1993) for an effective and expeditious implementation of the decision to establish an international tribunal, the Secretary-General believes that the International Tribunal should be established by a decision of the Security Council on the basis of Chapter VII of the Charter of the United Nations. Such a decision would constitute a measure to maintain or restore international peace and security, following the requisite determination of the existence of a threat to the peace, breach of the peace or act of aggression.

23. This approach would have the advantage of being expeditious and of being immediately effective as all States would be under a binding obligation to take whatever action is required to carry out a decision taken as an enforcement measure under Chapter VII.

24. In the particular case of the former Yugoslavia, the Secretary-General believes that the establishment of the International Tribunal by means of a Chapter VII decision would be legally justified, both in terms of the object and purpose of the decision, as indicated in the preceding paragraphs, and of past Security Council practice.

25. As indicated in paragraph 10 above, the Security Council has already determined that the situation posed by continuing reports of widespread violations of international humanitarian law occurring in the former Yugoslavia constitutes a threat to international peace and security. The Council has also decided under Chapter VII of the Charter that all parties and others concerned in the former Yugoslavia, and all military forces in Bosnia and Herzegovina, shall comply with the provisions of resolution 771 (1992), failing which it would need to take further measures under the Charter. Furthermore, the Council has repeatedly reaffirmed that all parties in the former Yugoslavia are bound to comply with the obligations under international humanitarian law and in particular the Geneva Conventions of 12 August 1949, and that persons who commit or order the commission of grave breaches of the Conventions are individually responsible in respect of such breaches.

26. Finally, the Security Council stated in resolution 808 (1993) that it was convinced that in the particular circumstances of the former Yugoslavia, the establishment of an international tribunal would bring about the achievement of the aim of putting an end to such crimes and of taking effective measures to bring to justice the persons responsible for them, and would contribute to the restoration and maintenance of peace.

27. The Security Council has on various occasions adopted decisions under Chapter VII aimed at restoring and maintaining international peace and security, which have involved the establishment of subsidiary organs for a variety of purposes. Reference may be made in this regard to Security Council resolution 687 (1991) and subsequent resolutions relating to the situation between Iraq and Kuwait.

28. In this particular case, the Security Council would be establishing, as an enforcement measure under Chapter VII, a subsidiary organ within the terms of Article 29 of the Charter, but one of a judicial nature. This organ would, of course, have to perform its functions independently of political considerations; it would not be subject to the authority or control of the Security Council with regard to the performance of its judicial functions. As an enforcement measure under Chapter VII, however, the life span of the international tribunal would be linked to the restoration and maintenance of international peace and security in the territory of the former Yugoslavia, and Security Council decisions related thereto.

29. It should be pointed out that, in assigning to the International Tribunal the task of prosecuting persons responsible for serious violations of international humanitarian law, the Security Council would not be creating or purporting to "legislate" that law. Rather, the International Tribunal would have the task of applying existing international humanitarian law.

30. On the basis of the foregoing considerations, the Secretary-General proposes that the Security Council, acting under Chapter VII of the Charter, establish the International Tribunal....

II. COMPETENCE OF THE INTERNATIONAL TRIBUNAL

31. The competence of the International Tribunal derives from the mandate set out in paragraph 1 of resolution 808 (1993). This part of the report will examine and make proposals regarding these fundamental elements of its competence: ratione materiae (subject-matter jurisdiction), ratione personae (personal jurisdiction), ratione loci (territorial jurisdiction) and ratione temporis (temporal jurisdiction), as well as the question of the concurrent jurisdiction of the International Tribunal and national courts....

A. Competence ratione materiae (subject-matter jurisdiction)

33. According to paragraph 1 of resolution 808 (1993), the international tribunal shall prosecute persons responsible for serious violations of international humanitarian law committed in the territory of the former Yugoslavia since 1991. This body of law exists in the form of both conventional law and customary law. While there is international customary law which is not laid down in conventions, some of the major conventional humanitarian law has become part of customary international law.

34. In the view of the Secretary-General, the application of the principle nullum crimen sine lege requires that the international tribunal should apply rules of international humanitarian law which are beyond any doubt part of customary law so that the problem of adherence of some but not all States to specific conventions does not arise. This would appear to be particularly important in the context of an international tribunal prosecuting persons responsible for serious violations of international humanitarian law.

35. The part of conventional international humanitarian law which has beyond doubt become part of international customary law is the law applicable in armed conflict as embodied in: the Geneva Conventions of 12 August 1949 for the Protection of War Victims; the Hague Convention (IV) Respecting the Laws and Customs of War on Land and the Regulations annexed thereto of 18 October 1907; the Convention on the Prevention and

Punishment of the Crime of Genocide of 9 December 1948; and the Charter of the International Military Tribunal of 8 August 1945.

36. Suggestions have been made that the international tribunal should apply domestic law in so far as it incorporates customary international humanitarian law. While international humanitarian law as outlined above provides a sufficient basis for subject-matter jurisdiction, there is one related issue which would require reference to domestic practice, namely, penalties (see para. 111 below).

Grave breaches of the 1949 Geneva Conventions

37. The Geneva Conventions constitute rules of international humanitarian law and provide the core of the customary law applicable in international armed conflicts. These Conventions regulate the conduct of war from the humanitarian perspective by protecting certain categories of persons: namely, wounded and sick members of armed forces in the field; wounded, sick and shipwrecked members of armed forces at sea; prisoners of war, and civilians in time of war.

38. Each Convention contains a provision listing the particularly serious violations that qualify as "grave breaches" or war crimes. Persons committing or ordering grave breaches are subject to trial and punishment....

39. The Security Council has reaffirmed on several occasions that persons who commit or order the commission of grave breaches of the 1949 Geneva Conventions in the territory of the former Yugoslavia are individually responsible for such breaches as serious violations of international humanitarian law....

Violations of the laws or customs of war

41. The 1907 Hague Convention (IV) Respecting the Laws and Customs of War on Land and the Regulations annexed thereto comprise a second important area of conventional humanitarian international law which has become part of the body of international customary law.

42. The Nurnberg Tribunal recognized that many of the provisions contained in the Hague Regulations, although innovative at the time of their adoption were, by 1939, recognized by all civilized nations and were regarded as being declaratory of the laws and customs of war. The Nurnberg Tribunal also recognized that war crimes defined in article 6(b) of the Nurnberg Charter were already recognized as war crimes under international law, and covered in the Hague Regulations, for which guilty individuals were punishable.

43. The Hague Regulations cover aspects of international humanitarian law which are also covered by the 1949 Geneva Conventions. However, the Hague Regulations also recognize that the right of belligerents to conduct warfare is not unlimited and that resort to certain methods of waging war is prohibited under the rules of land warfare....

Genocide

45. The 1948 Convention on the Prevention and Punishment of the Crime of Genocide confirms that genocide, whether committed in time of peace or in time of war, is a crime under international law for which individuals shall be tried and punished. The Convention is today considered part of international customary law as evidenced by the International Court of Justice in its Advisory Opinion on Reservations to the Convention on the Prevention and Punishment of the Crime of Genocide, 1951....

Crimes against humanity

47. Crimes against humanity were first recognized in the Charter and Judgement of the Nurnberg Tribunal, as well as in Law No. 10 of the Control Council for Germany. Crimes

against humanity are aimed at any civilian population and are prohibited regardless of whether they are committed in an armed conflict, international or internal in character....

48. Crimes against humanity refer to inhumane acts of a very serious nature, such as wilful killing, torture or rape, committed as part of a widespread or systematic attack against any civilian population on national, political, ethnic, racial or religious grounds. In the conflict in the territory of the former Yugoslavia, such inhumane acts have taken the form of so-called "ethnic cleansing" and widespread and systematic rape and other forms of sexual assault, including enforced prostitution....

B. Competence ratione personae (personal jurisdiction) and individual criminal responsibility

50. By paragraph 1 of resolution 808 (1993), the Security Council decided that the International Tribunal shall be established for the prosecution of persons responsible for serious violations of international humanitarian law committed in the territory of the former Yugoslavia since 1991. In the light of the complex of resolutions leading up to resolution 808 (1993) (see paras. 5–7 above), the ordinary meaning of the term "persons responsible for serious violations of international humanitarian law" would be natural persons to the exclusion of juridical persons.

51. The question arises, however, whether a juridical person, such as an association or organization, may be considered criminal as such and thus its members, for that reason alone, be made subject to the jurisdiction of the International Tribunal. The Secretary-General believes that this concept should not be retained in regard to the International Tribunal. The criminal acts set out in this statute are carried out by natural persons; such persons would be subject to the jurisdiction of the International Tribunal irrespective of membership in groups....

Individual criminal responsibility

53. An important element in relation to the competence ratione personae (personal jurisdiction) of the International Tribunal is the principle of individual criminal responsibility. As noted above, the Security Council has reaffirmed in a number of resolutions that persons committing serious violations of international humanitarian law in the former Yugoslavia are individually responsible for such violations.

54. The Secretary-General believes that all persons who participate in the planning, preparation or execution of serious violations of international humanitarian law in the former Yugoslavia contribute to the commission of the violation and are, therefore, individually responsible.

55. Virtually all of the written comments received by the Secretary-General have suggested that the statute of the International Tribunal should contain provisions with regard to the individual criminal responsibility of heads of State, government officials and persons acting in an official capacity. These suggestions draw upon the precedents following the Second World War. The Statute should, therefore, contain provisions which specify that a plea of head of State immunity or that an act was committed in the official capacity of the accused will not constitute a defence, nor will it mitigate punishment.

56. A person in a position of superior authority should, therefore, be held individually responsible for giving the unlawful order to commit a crime under the present statute. But he should also be held responsible for failure to prevent a crime or to deter the unlawful behaviour of his subordinates. This imputed responsibility or criminal negligence is engaged if the person in superior authority knew or had reason to know that his subordinates were about to commit or had committed crimes and yet failed to take the nec-

essary and reasonable steps to prevent or repress the commission of such crimes or to punish those who had committed them.

57. Acting upon an order of a Government or a superior cannot relieve the perpetrator of the crime of his criminal responsibility and should not be a defence. Obedience to superior orders may, however, be considered a mitigating factor, should the International Tribunal determine that justice so requires. For example, the International Tribunal may consider the factor of superior orders in connection with other defences such as coercion or lack of moral choice.

58. The International Tribunal itself will have to decide on various personal defences which may relieve a person of individual criminal responsibility, such as minimum age or mental incapacity, drawing upon general principles of law recognized by all nations....

C. Competence ratione loci (territorial jurisdiction) and ratione temporis (temporal jurisdiction)

60. Pursuant to paragraph 1 of resolution 808 (1993), the territorial and temporal jurisdiction of the International Tribunal extends to serious violations of international humanitarian law to the extent that they have been "committed in the territory of the former Yugoslavia since 1991".

61. As far as the territorial jurisdiction of the International Tribunal is concerned, the territory of the former Yugoslavia means the territory of the former Socialist Federal Republic of Yugoslavia, including its land surface, airspace and territorial waters.

62. With regard to temporal jurisdiction, Security Council resolution 808 (1993) extends the jurisdiction of the International Tribunal to violations committed "since 1991". The Secretary-General understands this to mean anytime on or after 1 January 1991. This is a neutral date which is not tied to any specific event and is clearly intended to convey the notion that no judgement as to the international or internal character of the conflict is being exercised....

D. Concurrent jurisdiction and the principle of *non-bis-in-idem*

64. In establishing an international tribunal for the prosecution of persons responsible for serious violations committed in the territory of the former Yugoslavia since 1991, it was not the intention of the Security Council to preclude or prevent the exercise of jurisdiction by national courts with respect to such acts. Indeed national courts should be encouraged to exercise their jurisdiction in accordance with their relevant national laws and procedures.

65. It follows therefore that there is concurrent jurisdiction of the International Tribunal and national courts. This concurrent jurisdiction, however, should be subject to the primacy of the International Tribunal. At any stage of the procedure, the International Tribunal may formally request the national courts to defer to the competence of the International Tribunal. The details of how the primacy will be asserted shall be set out in the rules of procedure and evidence of the International Tribunal.

66. According to the principle of *non-bis-in-idem*, a person shall not be tried twice for the same crime. In the present context, given the primacy of the International Tribunal, the principle of *non-bis-in-idem* would preclude subsequent trial before a national court. However, the principle of *non-bis-in-idem* should not preclude a subsequent trial before the International Tribunal in the following two circumstances:

(a) The characterization of the act by the national court did not correspond to its characterization under the statute; or

(b) Conditions of impartiality, independence or effective means of adjudication were not guaranteed in the proceedings before the national courts.

67. Should the International Tribunal decide to assume jurisdiction over a person who has already been convicted by a national court, it should take into consideration the extent to which any penalty imposed by the national court has already been served....

III. THE ORGANIZATION OF THE INTERNATIONAL TRIBUNAL

70. The International Tribunal should therefore consist of the following organs: the Chambers, comprising two Trial Chambers and one Appeals Chamber; a Prosecutor; and a Registry....

72. The Chambers should be composed of 11 independent judges, no 2 of whom may be nationals of the same State. Three judges would serve in each of the two Trial Chambers and five judges would serve in the Appeals Chamber....

83. The judges of the International Tribunal as a whole should draft and adopt the rules of procedure and evidence of the International Tribunal governing the pre-trial phase of the proceedings, the conduct of trials and appeals, the admission of evidence, the protection of victims and witnesses and other appropriate matters....

B. The Prosecutor

85. Responsibility for the conduct of all investigations and prosecutions of persons responsible for serious violations of international humanitarian law committed in the territory of the former Yugoslavia since 1 January 1991 should be entrusted to an independent Prosecutor. The Prosecutor should act independently as a separate organ of the International Tribunal. He or she shall not seek or receive instructions from any Government or from any other source....

IV. INVESTIGATION AND PRE-TRIAL PROCEEDINGS

93. The Prosecutor would initiate investigations ex officio, or on the basis of information obtained from any source, particularly from Governments or United Nations organs, intergovernmental and non-governmental organizations. The Prosecutor would assess the information received or obtained and decide whether there is a sufficient basis to proceed.

94. In conducting his investigations, the Prosecutor should have the power to question suspects, victims and witnesses, to collect evidence and to conduct on-site investigations. In carrying out these tasks, the Prosecutor may, as appropriate, seek the assistance of the State authorities concerned.

95. Upon the completion of the investigation, if the Prosecutor has determined that a prima facie case exists for prosecution, he would prepare an indictment containing a concise statement of the facts and the crimes with which the accused is charged under the statute. The indictment would be transmitted to a judge of a Trial Chamber, who would review it and decide whether to confirm or to dismiss the indictment.

96. If the investigation includes questioning of the suspect, then he should have the right to be assisted by counsel of his own choice, including the right to have legal assistance assigned to him without payment by him in any such case if he does not have sufficient means to pay for it. He shall also be entitled to the necessary translation into and from a language he speaks and understands.

97. Upon confirmation of the indictment, the judge would, at the request of the Prosecutor, issue such orders and warrants for the arrest, detention, surrender and transfer of persons, or any other orders as may be necessary for the conduct of the trial....

V. TRIAL AND POST-TRIAL PROCEEDINGS

A. Commencement and conduct of trial proceedings

99. The Trial Chambers should ensure that a trial is fair and expeditious and that proceedings are conducted in accordance with the rules of procedure and evidence and with full respect for the rights of the accused. The Trial Chamber should also provide appropriate protection for victims and witnesses during the proceedings.

100. A person against whom an indictment has been confirmed would, pursuant to an order or a warrant of the International Tribunal, be informed of the contents of the indictment and taken into custody.

101. A trial should not commence until the accused is physically present before the International Tribunal. There is a widespread perception that trials in absentia should not be provided for in the statute as this would not be consistent with article 14 of the International Covenant on Civil and Political Rights, which provides that the accused shall be entitled to be tried in his presence.

102. The person against whom an indictment has been confirmed would be transferred to the seat of the International Tribunal and brought before a Trial Chamber without undue delay and formally charged. The Trial Chamber would read the indictment, satisfy itself that the rights of the accused are respected, confirm that the accused understands the indictment, and instruct the accused to enter a plea. After the plea has been entered, the Trial Chamber would set the date for trial.

103. The hearings should be held in public unless the Trial Chamber decides otherwise in accordance with its rules of procedure and evidence.

104. After hearing the submissions of the parties and examining the witnesses and evidence presented to it, the Trial Chamber would close the hearing and retire for private deliberations....

B. Rights of the accused

106. It is axiomatic that the International Tribunal must fully respect internationally recognized standards regarding the rights of the accused at all stages of its proceedings. In the view of the Secretary-General, such internationally recognized standards are, in particular, contained in article 14 of the International Covenant on Civil and Political Rights....

C. Protection of victims and witnesses

108. In the light of the particular nature of the crimes committed in the former Yugoslavia, it will be necessary for the International Tribunal to ensure the protection of victims and witnesses. Necessary protection measures should therefore be provided in the rules of procedure and evidence for victims and witnesses, especially in cases of rape or sexual assault. Such measures should include, but should not be limited to the conduct of in camera proceedings, and the protection of the victim's identity....

D. Judgement and penalties

110. The Trial Chambers would have the power to pronounce judgements and impose sentences and penalties on persons convicted of serious violations of international humanitarian law. A judgement would be rendered by a majority of the judges of the Chamber and delivered in public. It should be written and accompanied by a reasoned opinion. Separate or dissenting opinions should be permitted.

111. The penalty to be imposed on a convicted person would be limited to imprisonment. In determining the term of imprisonment, the Trial Chambers should have re-

course to the general practice of prison sentences applicable in the courts of the former Yugoslavia.

112. The International Tribunal should not be empowered to impose the death penalty.

113. In imposing sentences, the Trial Chambers should take into account such factors as the gravity of the offence and the individual circumstances of the convicted person.

114. In addition to imprisonment, property and proceeds acquired by criminal conduct should be confiscated and returned to their rightful owners. This would include the return of property wrongfully acquired by means of duress. In this connection the Secretary-General recalls that in resolution 779 (1992) of 6 October 1992, the Security Council endorsed the principle that all statements or commitments made under duress, particularly those relating to land and property, are wholly null and void....

E. Appellate and review proceedings

116. The Secretary-General is of the view that the right of appeal should be provided for under the Statute. Such a right is a fundamental element of individual civil and political rights and has, *inter alia*, been incorporated in the International Covenant on Civil and Political Rights. For this reason, the Secretary-General has proposed that there should be an Appeals Chamber.

117. The right of appeal should be exercisable on two grounds: an error on a question of law invalidating the decision or, an error of fact which has occasioned a miscarriage of justice. The Prosecutor should also be entitled to initiate appeal proceedings on the same grounds.

118. The judgement of the Appeals Chamber affirming, reversing or revising the judgement of the Trial Chamber would be final. It would be delivered by the Appeals Chamber in public and be accompanied by a reasoned opinion to which separate or dissenting opinions may be appended.

119. Where a new fact has come to light which was not known at the time of the proceedings before the Trial Chambers or the Appeals Chamber, and which could have been a decisive factor in reaching the decision, the convicted person or the Prosecutor should be authorized to submit to the International Tribunal an application for review of the judgement....

F. Enforcement of sentences

121. The Secretary-General is of the view that, given the nature of the crimes in question and the international character of the tribunal, the enforcement of sentences should take place outside the territory of the former Yugoslavia. States should be encouraged to declare their readiness to carry out the enforcement of prison sentences in accordance with their domestic laws and procedures, under the supervision of the International Tribunal.

122. The Security Council would make appropriate arrangements to obtain from States an indication of their willingness to accept convicted persons. This information would be communicated to the Registrar, who would prepare a list of States in which the enforcement of sentences would be carried out.

123. The accused would be eligible for pardon or commutation of sentence in accordance with the laws of the State in which sentence is served. In such an event, the State concerned would notify the International Tribunal, which would decide the matter in accordance with the interests of justice and the general principles of law....

VI. COOPERATION AND JUDICIAL ASSISTANCE

125. As pointed out in paragraph 23 above, the establishment of the International Tribunal on the basis of a Chapter VII decision creates a binding obligation on all States to take whatever steps are required to implement the decision. In practical terms, this means that all States would be under an obligation to cooperate with the International Tribunal and to assist it in all stages of the proceedings to ensure compliance with requests for assistance in the gathering of evidence, hearing of witnesses, suspects and experts, identification and location of persons and the service of documents. Effect shall also be given to orders issued by the Trial Chambers, such as warrants of arrest, search warrants, warrants for surrender or transfer of persons, and any other orders necessary for the conduct of the trial.

126. In this connection, an order by a Trial Chamber for the surrender or transfer of persons to the custody of the International Tribunal shall be considered to be the application of an enforcement measure under Chapter VII of the Charter of the United Nations....

Annex
Statute of the International Tribunal

Having been established by the Security Council acting under Chapter VII of the Charter of the United Nations, the International Tribunal for the Prosecution of Persons Responsible for Serious Violations of International Humanitarian Law Committed in the Territory of the Former Yugoslavia since 1991 (hereinafter referred to as "the International Tribunal") shall function in accordance with the provisions of the present Statute.

[Editors' note: By a decision of the Security Council on May 25, 1993, the Tribunal was adopted along with the Statute of the Tribunal annexed to the Secretary-General's Report. S.C. Res. 827, S/RES/827 (1993), at para. 2, the Security Council adding in para. 4: "Decides that all States shall cooperate fully with the International Tribunal and its organs in accordance with the present resolution and the Statute of the International Tribunal and that consequently all States shall take any measures necessary under their domestic law to implement the provisions of the present resolution and the Statute, including the obligation of States to comply with requests for assistance or orders issued by a Trial Chamber under Article 29 of the Statute."]

[Read the Statute of the ICTY, in the Documents Supplement]

Rules of Procedure and Evidence
reprinted from 33 I.L.M. 484 (1994)*

[Reproduced from the text provided by the International Tribunal for the Prosecution of Persons Responsible for Serious Violations of International Humanitarian Law Committed in the Territory of Former Yugoslavia since 1991, U.N. Document IT/32 of March 14, 1994]

Introductory Note by Bruce Zagaris

On February 11, 1994, the International Tribunal for the Prosecution of Persons Responsible for Serious Violations of International Humanitarian Law Committed in the

---

* Reproduced with permission from 33 I.L.M. (1994), © The American Society of International Law.

Territory of Former Yugoslavia since 1991 adopted Rules of Procedure and Evidence, under which the Tribunal will operate. The Rules came into force on March 14, 1994. The Tribunal itself was established by Security Council Resolution 827 (1993) of May 25, 1993.

The Rules of Procedure and Evidence have historical significance for public international law in part because of the relative novelty of the Tribunal for War Crimes in Former Yugoslavia and perhaps, even more importantly, for the precedent they set for the establishment of a permanent International Criminal Court. For many years, the establishment of the latter Tribunal has been hindered by the perception that it would be impossible if not difficult to elaborate workable rules of procedure and evidence in view of the many legal systems of the world and the political issues of such a Tribunal.

The Rules complement the Statute establishing the Tribunal and provide for the operation of the Tribunal. They contain nine Parts as follows: 1) General Provisions; 2) Primacy of the Tribunal; Organization of the Tribunal; 4) Investigations and Rights of Suspects; 5) Pre-Trial Proceedings; 6) Proceedings Before Trial Chambers; 7) Appellate Proceedings; 8) Review Proceedings; and 9) Pardon and Commutation of Sentence.

Part One, "General Provisions," provides that the working language of the Tribunal will be English and French although an accused has the right to use his own language or by leave of the Chamber a language other than the two working languages or his own. A Chamber may exercise its functions at a place other than the Hague, which is the seat of the Tribunal, if the Tribunal's President authorizes it in the interests of justice.

The Rules may be amended, provided they are unanimously approved by the Judges. The ability to amend the Rules provides an internal dynamic that will facilitate the need to accommodate unforseen demands on the Tribunal.

Part Two provides for the operation of the principle of primacy of the Tribunal's concurrent jurisdiction with national courts under certain circumstances. For instance, the Prosecutor can propose to the Trial Chamber designated by the President that a formal request be made to the national court to defer to the competence of the Tribunal where it appears to the Prosecutor that in any such investigations or criminal proceedings instituted in the national courts of any state:

(i) the national court characterizes the act under investigation as an ordinary crime;

(ii) a lack of impartiality or independence exists, or the investigations or proceedings are designed to shield the accused from international criminal responsibility, or the case is not diligently prosecuted; or

(iii) the proceeding concerns matters closely related to significant factual or legal questions that may have implications for investigations or prosecutions before the Tribunal.

The Tribunal may also request a national court to defer to the competence of the Tribunal and, if within 60 days after a request for deferral has been made the national state fails to respond satisfactorily, the Tribunal may request the Tribunal's President to report the matter to the Security Council which can take whatever action it deems appropriate. The ability of the Tribunal to have competence over national courts and to enforce its right of having national courts defer proceedings is designed to ensure fairness, integrity, and efficiency. Already, the Bosnian courts have tried war crimes and the German Government has arrested and is considering prosecuting a Serb for war crimes in the former Yugoslavia.

Part Three, "Organization of the Tribunal," provides for Judges, the Tribunal's Presidency, the Registry, the Prosecutor, and the Bureau. The latter is composed of the President, Vice-President and the Presiding Judges of the Trial Chambers, and is to consider all major questions relating to the functioning of the Tribunal. The judges will rotate on a regular basis between the Trial Chambers and the Appeals Chamber.

A critical organ will be a Victims and Witnesses Unit that will be established under the authority of the Registrar and will have as its obligations to: recommend protective measures for victims and witnesses in accordance with Article 22 of the Statute; and provide counselling and support for them, especially in cases of rape and sexual assault.

Under Part Four, "Investigations and Rights of Suspects," a prosecutor may request any State to take provisional measures, such as arresting a suspect provisionally, seizing physical evidence, and taking all necessary measures to prevent the escape of a suspect or an accused, injury to or intimidation of a victim or witness, or the destruction of evidence.

The rights of suspects are set forth, including the right to the assistance of counsel, including the appointment of counsel and interpreters for indigents. No defendant or suspect can be questioned without the presence of counsel unless the defendant or suspect has voluntarily waived his right to counsel.

Part Five, "Pre-Trial Proceedings," sets forth procedure for indictments. When the Prosecutor is satisfied that sufficient evidence exists to provide reasonable grounds for believing that a suspect has committed a crime within the jurisdiction of the Tribunal, he must prepare and forward to the Registrar an indictment for confirmation by a Judge, together with supporting material. Upon receipt of the material from the Registrar, the judge will review the indictment and, after hearing from the Prosecutor, may confirm or dismiss each count or may adjourn the review. A Prosecutor may amend an indictment, without leave, at any time before its confirmation, and thereafter with leave of the Judge who confirmed it or, if at trial, with leave of the Trial Chamber.

Although indictments are to be made public, the judge may delay public disclosure of the indictment until it is served on the accused, if satisfied that the making of such an order is in the interests of justice. A judge or a Trial Chamber can issue such orders, summonses and warrants as may be necessary for the purposes of investigation or for the preparation or conduct of the trial.

The procedure for issuing and executing arrest warrants is set forth. A State must arrest and transfer the accused to the Tribunal. If it is unable to execute an arrest warrant, a State must transmit the reasons therefor. If it does not, the Tribunal may notify the Security Council accordingly. If a warrant of arrest has not been executed and the Prosecutor satisfies a judge that all reasonable steps have been taken to effect personal service and inform the accused of the indictment, including publication of newspaper advertisements, the Trial Chamber may hear evidence and, if there exist reasonable grounds for believing the accused has committed all or any of the crimes charged in the indictment, it will so determine. Once detained, an accused may not be released except by order of a Trial Chamber, only in exceptional circumstances, and only if it is satisfied that the accused will appear for trial and, if released, will not pose a danger to any victim, witness or other person.

Three rules make specific provision for disclosure of evidence by the prosecutor to the defense, for reciprocal disclosure, and disclosure of exculpatory evidence. In exceptional circumstances the Prosecutor can apply to a Trial Chamber to order the non-disclosure of the identity of a victim or witness who may be in danger or at risk until such person is brought under the protect of the Tribunal. Subject to measures that can be taken for the protection of victims or witnesses, their identity must be disclosed in sufficient time prior to the trial to permit adequate time for preparation of the defense.

In Part Six, "Proceedings Before Trial Chambers," a Chamber can, if it considers it desirable for the proper determination of the case, invite or grant leave to a State, organization or person to appear before it and make submissions on any issue the Chamber specifies. Human rights organizations can be expected to try actively to participate.

A Judge or Chamber can order appropriate measures for the privacy and protection of victims, provided that the measures are consistent with the rights of the accused. A Chamber can hold an ex parte proceeding to determine whether to order measures to prevent disclosure to the public or the media of the identity or location of a victim or a witness, or of persons related to or associated with him through various means.

A criticism of the Tribunal's Statute and the Rules is that they do not grant victims the right to plead and be represented by counsel. Such a right has been instrumental, for instance, in the French prosecution of Georges Ibrahim Abdallah for his role in the 1982 assassination of Charles R. Ray, a U.S. military attache. Because Ray's estate and family had representation and took a more aggressive stand throughout the case and did not have to worry about political considerations, their counsel was instrumental both in achieving a conviction and also in obtaining a judgment for monetary damages. Perhaps, the Tribunal's ability to invite or grant leave to an organization to appear before it will be creatively used to enable victims to have appropriate representation throughout the proceedings. [See Bruce Zagaris, "Abdallah Stands Trial and Is Sentenced to Life Imprisonment," 3 *Int'l Enforcement L. Rep.* 45 (Feb. 1987)].

In the rules for case presentation the Trial Chamber, if it finds the accused guilty of a crime and concludes from the evidence that unlawful taking of property by the accused was associated with it, it must make a specific finding to that effect in its judgement and may order restitution. Dissenting opinions are permitted.

Within Part Six, the Section on "Rules of Evidence" sets forth general rules and also detailed ones. For instance, evidence obtained directly or indirectly by means which constitute a serious violation of internationally protected human rights will not be admissible. In cases of sexual assault, three specific rules apply: no corroboration of the victim's testimony is required; consent will not be permitted as a defense; and prior sexual conduct of the victim will not be admitted in evidence.

The Section on "Sentencing Procedure," provides that a convicted person may be sentenced to imprisonment for a term up to and including life, taking into account the factors mentioned in Article 24(2) of the Statute. The place of imprisonment will be served in a State designated by the Tribunal from a list of States which have indicated their willingness to accept convicted persons.

After a judgement of conviction, the Prosecutor can convene a special hearing of the Trial Chamber to determine the restitution of the property or the proceeds thereof. The Chamber may order such provisional measures for the preservation and protection of the property or proceeds as it considers appropriate.

A victim or persons claiming through him can bring an action in a national court or other competent body to obtain compensation pursuant to relevant national legislation.

Part Seven, "Appellate Proceedings," allows for and sets forth procedure for appeals, including briefs, timing, and the status of the accused following appeal.

Part Eight sets forth "Review Proceedings," which may occur where a new fact has been discovered which was not known to the moving party at the time of the proceedings before a Trial Chamber or the Appeals Chamber, and could not have been discovered through the exercise of due diligence.

Part Nine, "Pardon and Commutation of Sentence," allows a State in which a convicted person is imprisoned to notify the Tribunal of eligibility of the person for pardon or commutation of sentence, which ultimately, the Tribunal's President determines, in consultation with the judges under the standards set forth in Rule 125.

The Rules of Procedure and Evidence will play a critical role in achieving success for the Tribunal. Indeed the Tribunal confronts formidable financial, legal, and political obstacles to success. The Rules are endeavoring to pioneer a path through the forest of impediments. Professionals, scholars, and policymakers should scrutinize the operation of the entire effort, as well as the component parts, since enforcement of international humanitarian law is an imperative which mankind no longer has the luxury to consider only for its academic interest....

[Read the extracts of the 1994 Rules of Procedure and Evidence of the ICTY, in the Documents Supplement]

Questions

1. Would you change any of the Rules? How can they be changed?

2. When is one a "suspect"? *See also* Christopher L. Blakesley, remarks, 88 PROC., AM. SOC. INT'L L. 244 (1994). When the Prosecution seeks an indictment? See Rules 41–42, 47, 52-53. When the Prosecutor asks one questions? When does the right to counsel pertain? See Rule 42. *Compare* Article 55 of the Statute of the ICC, also in the Documents Supplement.

3. Is Rule 92 consistent with the human rights standard that one is "presumed innocent until proved guilty"? *See, e.g.,* Universal Declaration of Human Rights, art. 11; International Covenant on Civil and Political Rights, art. 14(2).

4. What is a "serious" violation of human rights within the meaning of Rule 95? What rights might be relevant? Is inadmissibility concerning serious violations required by human rights law? Is it a compromise between those systems using an exclusionary rule and those that do not?

5. With respect to Rule 96, why was "consent" to sexual "assault" not allowed as a defense? Does this merely mean that consent can be considered with respect to the conclusion whether an "assault" has occurred, but that once that conclusion is reached consent is not a defense? If not, what does "assault" encompass? Are paragraphs ii and iii preferable? *See also* Jennifer Green, Rhonda Copelon, Patrick Cotter, Beth Stephens, *Affecting the Rules for the Prosecution of Rape and Other Gender-Based Violence Before the International Criminal Tribunal for the Former Yugoslavia: A Feminist Proposal and Critique,* 5 HAST. WOMEN's L.J. 171, 178, 191–94, 199–203, 217–19 (1994) (also offering useful commentary re: several rules); M. Cherif Bassiouni & Marcia McCormick, *Sexual Violence: An Invisible Weapon of War in the Former Yugoslavia* (Occas. Paper No. 1, DePaul Int'l H.R. Inst. 1996); 88 PROC., AM. SOC. INT'L L. 244 (Blakesley), 252–53 (Scharf), 255 (Paust), 256 (Johnson) (1994). Rule 96(ii) was changed in 1994 and a new section iii was added in 1995:

(ii) consent shall not be allowed as a defense if the victim

a) has been subjected to or threatened with or has had reason to fear violence, duress, detention or psychological oppression; or

b) reasonably believed that if she did not submit, another might be so subjected, threatened or put in fear.

(iii) before evidence of the victim's consent is admitted, the accused shall satisfy the Trial Chamber that the evidence is relevant and credible.

See Jennifer Green *et al., supra* at 231–32. If consent is considered, do you think it is at all likely that any woman detained in Bosnia-Herzegovina, especially in a camp, "consented" to sex with a member of enemy troops, police or guards? Concerning rape as a war crime, see also Chapter Eight, Section 2.

Compare Articles 63, 67–69 of the Statute of the ICC, in the Documents Supplement.

6. Rule 75 is part of the amalgam of common and civil law procedures. Also, recall that human rights law does not expressly confer a right of cross-examination of witnesses as such, but merely the right of confrontation of witnesses or, as expressed in Article 14(3)(e) of the Covenant on Civil and Political Rights, "[t]o examine, or have examined, the witnesses against him...." Monroe Leigh, quoted in the ABA Journal, at 58–59 (Apr. 1996), expressed concern with respect to witness testimony in forms that conceal the identify of the witness (*e.g.*, use of video forms of testimony involving the distortion of faces and voices to disguise witnesses). If one does not know the identity of a witness, some argue that adequate examination (or cross-examination, otherwise permitted under the Rules) will be thwarted. Others argue that other interests are at stake and that the two rules (Rules 75 and 85(B); see also Rules 79, 89, 90, 96) can be accommodated in given circumstances. In the *Tadic* case (see below), no victim protection unit had been created but the Trial Chamber issued a protective order to protect witness identities, Judge Stephen dissenting on the point concerning non-identification and fair trial standards. *See, e.g.,* Monroe Leigh, *The Yugoslav Tribunal: Use of Unnamed Witnesses Against the Accused,* 90 Am. J. Int'l L. 235 (1996). How would you respond? *Compare* Articles 67–69 of the Statute of the ICC, in the Documents Supplement.

7. "'[I]t is settled jurisprudence that ... hearsay evidence is admissible as long as it is of probative value' and that a Trial Chamber may rely on it." The Prosecutor v. Naletilic & Martinovic, IT-98-34-A (Appeals Chamber, 3 May 2006), para. 217, quoting The Prosecutor v. Semanza, ICTR-97-20-A (Appeal Chamber Judgment, 20 May 2005), para. 159. For an earlier critique of unrestricted use of hearsay evidence by the ICTY, *see, e.g.,* Michael P. Scharf, *Trial and Error: An Assessment of the First Judgment of the Yugoslavia War Crimes Tribunal,* 30 N.Y.J. Int'l L. & Pol. 167, 180–83 (1998).

8. Rule 106 (B) and (C) recognize a right to compensation, but would you rewrite Rule 106 (B) to include "pursuant to the relevant national constitution" to also allow direct use of customary international law or self-execution of treaties in accordance with a national constitution? On the right to civil remedies for war crimes, see Chapter Eight, Section 2 B. *Compare* Articles 75 and 109 of the Statute of the ICC, in the Documents Supplement.

9. Would ICTY Rule 106 (C)'s mandate be binding in a U.S. or Canadian court? The rule is part of a process intertwined with a "decision" of the U.N. Security Council, which is tied to U.N. member obligations under Articles 25, 39 and 41 of the Charter. See also *id.* Arts. 48–49.

10. Should accused have the right to act as their own attorney? *See* Michael P. Scharf & Christopher M. Rassi, *Do Former Leaders Have an International Right to Self-Representation in War Crimes Trials?,* 20 Ohio St.J. Dispute Res. 3 (2005); Michael P. Scharf, *Self-Representation Versus Assignment of Defence-Counsel before International Criminal Tribunals,* 4 J. Int'l Crim. Justice 31 (2006). Professor Scharf was critical of the ICTY's handling of several procedural issues during the trial of Milosevic. *See* Michael P. Scharf, *The Legacy of the Milosevic Trial,* 37 New England L. Rev. 915 (2003).

11. Is there any indication in human rights law that a prosecutor should not have a right of appeal? Do you favor such a right? *Compare* Articles 81–82 of the Statue of the ICC, in the Documents Supplement.

12. Would you have favored witness immunity for testimony or plea bargaining? *See* Steven J. Leeper, remarks, 88 Proc., Am. Soc. Int'l L. 248 (1994). *Compare* Articles 53(1)(c), (2)(c) and 54(3)(d) of the Statute of the ICC. Concerning actual trends in bargaining regarding guilty pleas and sentence reductions within the ICTR and ICTY, *see, e.g.*, Nancy Amoury Combs, *Procuring Guilty Pleas for International Crimes: The Limited Influence of Sentence Discounts*, 59 Vand. L. Rev. 69 (2006). For a critique of the use of plea-bargaining, *see, e.g.*, Michael P. Scharf, *Trading Justice for Efficiency: Plea-Bargaining and International Tribunals*, 2 J. Int'l Crim. Justice no. 4, at 1070 (2004).

13. The ICTY approved an indictment of Bega Beqaj for allegedly knowingly and wilfully interfering with the administration of justice by threatening, intimidating, and offering a bribe to, or otherwise interfering with witnesses or potential witnesses in The Prosecutor v. Limaj, IT-03-66-R77 (Indictment, 21 Oct. 2004). He was arrested in Kosovo on October 19, 2004 and transferred to the custody of the ICTY. Rule 77 of the ICTY Rules of Procedure and Evidence allows the ICTY to exercise its inherent power to hold persons in contempt, although contempt power is not expressed in the Statute of the ICTY. On January 31, 2000, the Appeals Chamber of the ICTY found that Milan Vujin, former defense counsel for Tadic, "put forward ... in support of the Rule 115 application a case which was known to him to be false in relation to the weight to be given to statements made ... an in relation to the responsibility of Goran Borovnica for the killing of the two Muslim policemen, and ... manipulated Witnesses A and B." For this infraction he was fined 15,000 Dutch guilders and the Registrar was directed "to consider striking" him off the list of assigned counsel and reporting his conduct to the professional body of which he belongs.

15. On February 9, 2000, the Appeals Chamber granted The Prosecutor's ground of appeal that the Trial Chamber erred in sentencing Zlatko Aleksovski, a commander of a prison at Kaonik, Croatia, to merely two and a half years of imprisonment with respect to individual and superior responsibility for war crimes, namely outrages upon personal dignity committed on detainees. Aleksovski was ordered returned to custody pending a final written judgment and "revised sentence."

16. For cases decided by the ICTY and other materials, see www.un.org/icty.

17. For further reading, *see, e.g.*, Substantive and Procedural Aspects of International Criminal Law (Gabrielle Kirk McDonald & Olivia Swaak-Goldman eds. 2000).

In the Matter of a Proposal for a Formal Request for Deferral to the Competence of the Tribunal Addressed to the Republic of Bosnia and Herzegovina in Respect of Radovan Karadzic, Ratko Mladic and Mico Stanisic

the International Criminal Tribunal for the Former Yugoslavia (May 16, 1995)

Before: Judge Karibi-Whyte, Presiding

Judge Odio Benito

Judge Jorda

Registrar: Mrs. Dorthee de Sampayo Garrido-Nijgh

DECISION

The Office of the Prosecutor:

Mr. Richard J. Goldstone Mr. Graham Blewitt Mr. Grant Niemann

Amicus Curiae: Ms. Vasvija Vidovic—Republic of Bosnia and Herzegovina

THE TRIAL CHAMBER

Considering the Application dated 21 April 1995 ("the Application"), filed by the Prosecutor of the International Criminal Tribunal for the Former Yugoslavia ("the International Tribunal"),

Noting that the Trial Chamber has been designated by the President of the International Tribunal pursuant to Rule 9 of the Rules of Procedure and Evidence ("the Rules") of the International Tribunal to determine the Application,

Having read and considered the Application and the Schedule ("the Schedule") annexed thereto,

Having granted leave to the representative of the Government of the Republic of Bosnia and Herzegovina to appear as amicus curiae, and having read and considered the submission of such representative,

Having heard both the Prosecutor and the representative of the Government of the Republic of Bosnia and Herzegovina at a public sitting held at The Hague on 15 May 1995,

HEREBY ISSUES ITS DECISION.

I—The Application

1. This is an application by Richard J. Goldstone, Prosecutor of the International Tribunal, made pursuant to Article 9(2) of the Statute of the International Tribunal in accordance with Rule 9 (iii) of the Rules. The Application is for the issue of a formal request from this Trial Chamber to the Government of the Republic of Bosnia and Herzegovina for the deferral to the competence of the International Tribunal of all investigations and criminal proceedings involving Radovan Karadzic, Ratko Mladic and Mico Stanisic being conducted by the Government of the Republic of Bosnia and Herzegovina in the territory of the former Yugoslavia since 1991, pursuant to Rule 10 of the Rules.

2. The Prosecutor states, and the Government of the Republic of Bosnia and Herzegovina has confirmed in both its written and oral submissions, that it is currently conducting investigations into war crimes and violations of the criminal laws of the Republic of Bosnia and Herzegovina. Criminal proceedings have been instituted by the Government of the Republic of Bosnia and Herzegovina against Radovan Karadzic, the Bosnian Serb

leader; Ratko Mladic, the military commander of the Bosnian Serb armed forces; and Mico Stanisic, in charge of Bosnian Serb internal affairs, in respect of alleged war crimes and violations of Articles 141, 142 and 151 of the Criminal Law of the Socialist Federal Republic of Yugoslavia as recognised by the Republic of Bosnia and Herzegovina, which include genocide, war crimes against the civilian population, and destruction of cultural and historic monuments.

3. Various documents cited in the Prosecutor's Application and mentioned at the hearing (documents dated 12 June 1992, 17 August 1992, 26 December 1992 and 20 September 1993) indicate that, one, the Higher Public Prosecutor's Office in Sarajevo submitted a request to the Higher Court in Sarajevo for the opening of an investigation in respect of these suspects, and secondly, the District Military Prosecutor's Office also lodged a request for an investigation involving the same individuals to a District Military Court relating to alleged offences which are within the jurisdiction of the Tribunal. The Prosecutor furthermore stated that contacts between the Ministry of Justice of the Republic of Bosnia and Herzegovina and the Prosecutor of the International Tribunal have enabled the investigative steps regarding the suspects to be outlined. It was confirmed at the hearing that national arrest warrants have been issued by the Government of the Republic of Bosnia and Herzegovina.

4. The Prosecutor states in the Schedule, and it was confirmed at the hearing, that he is conducting investigations into a wide range of violations which are within the jurisdiction of the Tribunal, in particular genocide, crimes against civilians, and the destruction of cultural and historical monuments. It was also confirmed at the hearing that those violations are identical to those in respect of which investigations are being carried out on Bosnian territory. A significant focus of these investigations relates to persons in positions of authority who are or were responsible for serious violations of international humanitarian law in the former Yugoslavia. The Prosecutor's view is that the matter of the individual criminal responsibility of the three persons in political, military or police leadership positions must be examined.

5. The Prosecutor has also initiated an investigation into the criminal responsibility of Radovan Karadzic, Ratko Mladic and Mico Stanisic arising out of indictments already issued by the International Tribunal against various named individuals for genocide, murder, rape, mistreatment of civilians, torture, and other offences allegedly committed in the running of detention camps.

6. Finally, the Prosecutor mentioned a significant investigation concerning the prolonged siege of Sarajevo (including attacks, considered unlawful, against civilian members of humanitarian organizations, United Nations peace-keeping forces and humanitarian-aid convoys).

7. The Prosecutor's investigations place the main focus on the positions of authority held by the three suspects who are allegedly guilty of serious violations of international humanitarian law in the territory of the former Yugoslavia. In the Schedule the involvement of Radovan Karadzic, Ratko Mladic and Mico Stanisic is described, as was confirmed by the representative of the Government of the Republic of Bosnia and Herzegovina at the hearing, as follows:

Radovan Karadzic is one of the main architects of the [Serbian Democratic Party] political programme, involving extreme nationalist and ethnic policies and objectives. Radovan Karadzic became the first president of the Bosnian Serb administration in Pale. The constitution of this administration provides that the president commands its armed forces. Radovan Karadzic exercises his power and control from Pale, a town near Sarajevo.

Radovan Karadzic has acted as and been dealt with internationally as the president of the Bosnian Serb administration in Pale. In that capacity, Radovan Karadzic has, *inter alia*, participated in international negotiations and has personally made agreements on such matters as cease-fires and humanitarian relief that have been implemented.

Ratko Mladic … is a career military officer … In the summer of 1991, he was appointed to command the 9th Corps of the Yugoslav People's Army (JNA) in Knin in the Republic of Croatia. Subsequently, he assumed command of the forces of the Second Military District of the JNA which effectively became the Bosnian Serb army. In that capacity he has negotiated, *inter alia*, cease-fire and prisoner exchange agreements that have been implemented.

Mico Stanisic … was the first minister of internal affairs of the Bosnian Serb administration in Pale. In that capacity, he was, *inter alia*, responsible for the regular and special police forces at the regional and local level in the territory under Bosnian Serb control. It is alleged that those forces were actively involved in organising a campaign of terror against the non-Serbian population of Bosnia and Herzegovina."

8. The legal basis for these investigations by the Prosecutor is Article 7 of the Statute of the International Tribunal concerning individual criminal responsibility, a concept discussed in paragraphs 55 and 56 of the Report of the Secretary-General of the United Nations dated 3 May 1993

9. Notwithstanding that national courts are vested with concurrent jurisdiction by Article 9 of the Statute of the International Tribunal, the Prosecutor, relying on Rule 9, is proposing that a formal request be issued to the Republic of Bosnia and Herzegovina, pursuant to Rule 10 of the Rules, to defer its investigations and criminal proceedings in respect of Radovan Karadzic, Ratko Mladic and Mico Stanisic, to the competence of the International Tribunal, and to provide the Prosecutor with all information concerning its investigations.

10. The Prosecutor states that the continuation by the Government of the Republic of Bosnia and Herzegovina of investigations similar to those being conducted by the Prosecutor could have significant implications for those investigations, as set out in the Schedule.

11. In particular, the Prosecutor refers to a number of matters which may have implications for his investigations or any subsequent prosecutions. Matters involving significant factual questions include:

(i) witnesses may be exposed to greater risks as their identities and evidence will already have been made public;

(ii) witnesses may be unwilling or unable to testify for a second time;

(iii) critical evidence stored in war zones in the Republic of Bosnia and Herzegovina could be damaged or lost before use by the International Tribunal;

(iv) witnesses may become confused as to the scope and authority of the two investigations;

(v) the International Tribunal is not a party to the conflict in the Republic of Bosnia and Herzegovina and has a better ability to obtain evidence worldwide;

(vi) deferral of these investigations may encourage Governments and other sources to furnish additional information to the International Tribunal that has thus far not been provided.

Those involving significant legal issues include:

(vii) issues relating to the principle of *non-bis-in-idem*;

(viii) there is the potential inadvertently to create inconsistent sworn evidence;

(ix) issues relating to possible trials in absentia which may be held in the Republic of Bosnia and Herzegovina;

(x) it would be undesirable and not in the interest of justice if the decisions of a national court and of the International Tribunal were to conflict.

12. The Government of the Republic of Bosnia and Herzegovina, appearing as amicus curiae, has indicated in both its written and oral submissions that it does not oppose the issue of a formal request by the Trial Chamber for the deferral of all investigations and criminal proceedings in respect of Radovan Karadzic, Ratko Mladic and Mico Stanisic.

II — Discussion

13. Article 8 of the Statute of the International Tribunal extends its territorial jurisdiction to the territory of the former Socialist Republic of Yugoslavia, including its land surface, airspace and territorial waters, beginning on 1 January 1991. Article 9 of the Statute provides as follows:

"1. The International Tribunal and national courts shall have concurrent jurisdiction to prosecute persons for serious violations of international humanitarian law committed in the territory of the former Yugoslavia since 1 January 1991.

"2. The International Tribunal shall have primacy over national courts. At any stage of the procedure, the International Tribunal may formally request national courts to defer to the competence of the International Tribunal in accordance with the present Statute and the Rules of Procedure and Evidence of the International Tribunal."

However, the right to primacy can only be exercised on a formal request to the national court to defer to the competence of the International Tribunal. The Rules provide the modus for the exercise of the right.

14. Rule 9 of the Rules provides as follows:

Where it appears to the Prosecutor that in any such investigations or criminal proceedings instituted in the courts of any State:

(i) ...

(ii) ...

(iii) what is in issue is closely related to, or otherwise involves, significant factual or legal questions which may have implications for investigations or prosecutions before the Tribunal, the Prosecutor may propose to the Trial Chamber designated by the President that a formal request be made that such court defer to the competence of the Tribunal.

15. To comply with the enabling provisions for grant of the Application, the Prosecutor must therefore establish that:

(a) national investigations or criminal proceedings have been instigated by the Republic of Bosnia and Herzegovina in respect of suspects including Radovan Karadzic, Ratko Mladic and Mico Stanisic; (b) investigations are currently being conducted by the Prosecutor into crimes within the jurisdiction of the International Tribunal, including the individual criminal responsibilities of persons in political, military and police leadership positions, including Radovan Karadzic, Ratko Mladic and Mico Stanisic; (c) what is in issue in the national investigations or criminal proceedings is closely related to, or otherwise involves, significant factual or legal questions which may have implications for the investigations of the Prosecutor and any subsequent proceedings before the International Tribunal.

16. The Trial Chamber notes that Radovan Karadzic, Ratko Mladic and Mico Stanisic are the subject of investigations instituted by the Government of the Republic of Bosnia and Herzegovina into the same alleged offences being investigated by the Prosecutor and that the investigations and any criminal proceedings that may be instituted by the national courts of the Republic of Bosnia and Herzegovina in respect of the matters listed in paragraphs 2 and 3 hereof, relate to the same issues. The Government of the Republic of Bosnia and Herzegovina does not contest these points.

17. The Trial Chamber further notes that the Prosecutor is investigating a wide range of allegations covering offences within the competence of the Tribunal including genocide, offences against civilians and destruction of cultural and historical monuments and that he is examining the individual criminal responsibilities of persons in political, military and police leadership positions, including Radovan Karadzic, Ratko Mladic and Mico Stanisic. It does indeed appear from the Application that the three named persons hold such positions of authority.

18. A reading of the Schedule clearly supports the claim that the investigations and proceedings instituted by the Government of the Republic of Bosnia and Herzegovina in respect of Radovan Karadzic, Ratko Mladic and Mico Stanisic involve significant factual or legal questions which have an impact on the investigations instituted by the Prosecutor in respect of serious violations of international humanitarian law in the territory of the former Yugoslavia. The Trial Chamber refers in particular to paragraphs 3.1 and 3.2 of the Schedule.

19. These issues are not disputed by the Government of the Republic of Bosnia and Herzegovina.

20. Consequently, the Trial Chamber is satisfied that the Prosecutor has shown that the investigations being carried out by the Prosecutor and by the Government of the Republic of Bosnia and Herzegovina in respect of Radovan Karadzic, Ratko Mladic and Mico Stanisic involve the same alleged crimes, in particular, genocide, offences against civilians and destruction of cultural and historical monuments and that the issues in any criminal proceedings that may be instituted by the Government of the Republic of Bosnia and Herzegovina in respect of such crimes would involve significant factual or legal questions which may have implications for investigation or prosecutions before the International Tribunal .

21. The Government of the Republic of Bosnia and Herzegovina has also made clear its intent to pursue its investigations of Radovan Karadzic, Ratko Mladic and Mico Stanisic and to proceed to trial in the absence of a formal request for deferral.

22. Proceedings in respect of persons in positions of authority before the International Tribunal derive expressly from Article 7 of the Statute of the International Tribunal and more particularly, from paragraphs 1, 2 and 3 thereof.

23. The punishment for the crimes allegedly committed by such individuals is also based on the general principles of international humanitarian law, and derives in particular from the precedents laid down by Nuremberg and Tokyo; furthermore, the principle of individual criminal responsibility of persons in positions of authority has been reaffirmed in a number of decisions taken by national courts, and adopted in various national and international legal instruments.

24. It follows from the above principle that the official capacity of an individual even de facto in a position of authority—whether as military commander, leader, or as one

in government—does not exempt him from criminal responsibility and would tend to aggravate it; and, moreover, it is that position of authority which would have enabled the suspects to plan, instigate, or order the crimes in respect of which the above-mentioned investigations have been conducted, or given them the means to prevent the said crimes, or at the least to punish their perpetrators.

25. Accordingly, more so than those just carrying out orders, they would thus undermine international public order; and therefore the International Tribunal established by the international community to restore that order is particularly well-founded to invoke its primacy over national courts, as acknowledged in Article 9(2) of the Statute of the International Tribunal.

26. The Trial Chamber has already concluded in paragraph 20 that the Prosecutor has established the grounds laid down in Rule 9(iii). In addition, the Trial Chamber notes that the International Tribunal is the appropriate forum to try the persons responsible for the kinds of crimes covered by the investigations currently being conducted by the Government of the Republic of Bosnia and Herzegovina in respect of Radovan Karadzic, Ratko Mladic and Mico Stanisic and to examine the individual criminal responsibilities of persons in political, military and police leadership positions. Indeed, it could be stated that it is one of the fundamental purposes of the International Tribunal to exercise its primacy in such cases.

27. The Trial Chamber is satisfied that deferral of the investigations and proceedings which are the subject of this Application is appropriate and, pursuant to Article 9 of the Statute and Rules 9 and 10, issues a formal request for deferral to the Government of the Republic of Bosnia and Herzegovina as hereinafter set forth.

III — Decision

The Trial Chamber Based on the Foregoing Determines As Follows:

considering all the matters before it and addressed in the public hearing, and considering the requirements contained in Rule 9(iii) of the Rules, the Trial Chamber consisting of Judge Karibi-Whyte, as Presiding Judge, Judge Odio Benito and Judge Jorda, being seized of the Application made by the Prosecutor,

Hereby Grants the said Application,

Formally Requests the Government of the Republic of Bosnia and Herzegovina, in respect of serious violations of international humanitarian law over which the International Tribunal has jurisdiction, as specified in Articles 2 to 5 of the Statute of the International Tribunal, that the courts of the Republic of Bosnia and Herzegovina defer to the competence of the International Tribunal in regard to their investigations and criminal proceedings involving Radovan Karadzic, Ratko Mladic and Mico Stanisic,

Invites the Government of the Republic of Bosnia and Herzegovina to take all necessary steps, both legislative and administrative, to comply with this Formal Request and to notify the Registrar of the International Tribunal of the steps taken to comply with this Formal Request, and

Requests that the Government of the Republic of Bosnia and Herzegovina forward to the International Tribunal the results of its investigations and a copy of the records and judgment, if any, of its national courts.

The Trial Chamber requests the Registrar of the International Tribunal to notify the Government of the Republic of Bosnia and Herzegovina of this its Decision and Formal Request.

The Prosecutor of the Tribunal v. Dusko Tadic

Decision on the Defence Motion on Jurisdiction (Aug. 10, 1995), the International Criminal Tribunal for the Former Yugoslavia, *revised and affirmed in part* by the Appeals Chamber (2 Oct. 1995) (before Judges Cassese, Li, Deschenes, Abi-Saab and Sidhwa)

IN THE TRIAL CHAMBER

Before: Judge McDonald, Presiding Judge Stephen, Judge Vohrah

Registrar: Mrs. Dorothee de Sampayo Garrido-Nijgh

The Office of the Prosecutor:

Mr. Grant Niemann, Mr. Alan Tieger, Mr. Michael Keegan, Ms. Brenda Hollis, Mr. William Fenrick

Counsel the Accused:

Mr. Michail Wladimiroff, Mr. Milan Vujin, Mr. Krstan Simic

DECISION

On 23 June 1995 the Defence filed a preliminary motion, pursuant to Rule 73 (A) (i) of the Rules of Procedure and Evidence ("the Rules") which provides for objections based on lack of jurisdiction, seeking dismissal of all of the charges against the accused. The Defence motion challenges the powers of the International Tribunal for the Prosecution of Person Responsible for Serious Violations of International Humanitarian Law Committed in the Territory of the Former Yugoslavia since 1991 ("the International Tribunal") to try the accused under three heads: the alleged improper establishment of the International Tribunal; the improper grant of primacy to the International Tribunal; and challenges to the subject-matter jurisdiction of the International Tribunal. The Prosecutor contends that none of these points is valid and that the International Tribunal has jurisdiction over the accused as charged. The Government of the United States of America has submitted a brief as amicus curiae.

The argument of the parties on this motion was heard on 25 and 26 July and judgment on the motion was reserved, to be delivered this day.

THE TRIAL CHAMBER, HAVING CONSIDERED the written submissions and oral arguments of the parties and the written submission of the amicus curiae,

REASONS FOR DECISION

I. The Establishment of the International Tribunal

A. Legitimacy of creation

1. The attack on the competence of the International Tribunal in this case is based on a number of grounds, some of which may be subsumed under one general heading: that the action of the Security Council in establishing the International Tribunal and in adopting the Statute under which it functions is beyond power; hence the International Tribunal is not duly established by law and cannot try the accused.

2. It is said that, to be duly established by law, the International Tribunal should have been created either by treaty, the consensual act of nations, or by amendment of the Charter of the United Nations, not by resolution of the Security Council. Called in aid of this general proposition are a number of considerations: that before the creation of the International Tribunal in 1993 it was never envisaged that such an ad hoc criminal tribunal

might be set up; that the General Assembly, whose participation would at least have guaranteed full representation of the international community, was not involved in its creation; that it was never intended by the Charter that the Security Council should, under Chapter VII, establish a judicial body, let alone a criminal tribunal; that the Security Council had been inconsistent in creating this tribunal while not taking a similar step in the case of other areas of conflict in which violations of international humanitarian law may have occurred; that the establishment of the International Tribunal had neither promoted, nor was capable of promoting, international peace, as the current situation in the former Yugoslavia demonstrates; that the Security Council could not, in any event, create criminal liability on the part of individuals and that this is what the creation of the International Tribunal did; that there existed and exists now no such international emergency as would justify the action of the Security Council; that no political organ such as the Security Council is capable of establishing an independent and impartial tribunal; that there is an inherent defect in the creation, after the event, of ad hoc tribunals to try particular types of offences and, finally, that to give the International Tribunal primacy over national courts is, in any event and in itself, inherently wrong....

5. The Trial Chamber has heard out the Defence in its submissions involving judicial review of the actions of the Security Council. However, this International Tribunal is not a constitutional court set up to scrutinise the actions of organs of the United Nations. It is, on the contrary, a criminal tribunal with clearly defined powers, involving a quite specific and limited criminal jurisdiction. If it is to confine its adjudications to those specific limits, it will have no authority to investigate the legality of its creation by the Security Council.

6. The force of criminal law draws its efficacy, in part, from the fact that it reflects a consensus on what is demanded of human behaviour. But it is of equal importance that a body that judges the criminality of this behaviour should be viewed as legitimate. This is the first time that the international community has created a court with criminal jurisdiction. The establishment of the International Tribunal has now spawned the creation of an ad hoc Tribunal for Rwanda. Each of these ad hoc Tribunals represents an important step towards the establishment of a permanent international criminal tribunal. In this context, the Trial Chamber considers that it would be inappropriate to dismiss without comment the accused's contentions that the establishment of the International Tribunal by the Security Council was beyond power and an ill-founded political action, not reasonably aimed at restoring and maintaining peace, and that the International Tribunal is not duly established by law.

7. Any discussion of this matter must begin with the Charter of the United Nations. Article 24(1) provides that the Members of the United Nations:

> "confer on the Security Council primary responsibility for the maintenance of international peace and security, and agree that in carrying out its duties under this responsibility the Security Council acts on their behalf."

The powers of the Security Council to discharge its primary responsibility for the maintenance of international peace and security are set out in Chapters VI, VII, VIII and XII of the Charter. The International Tribunal was established under Chapter VII. The Security Council has broad discretion in exercising its authority under Chapter VII and there are few limits on the exercise of that power. As indicated by the travaux préparatoires:

> "Wide freedom of judgment is left as regards the moment [the Security Council] may choose to intervene and the means to be applied, with sole reserve that it should act 'in accordance with the purposes and principles of the United Nations.'"

(See Statement of the Rapporteur of Committee III/3, Doc. 134, IIE/3/3, 11 U.N.C.I.O. Docs. 785 (1945).) The broad discretion given to the Security Council in the exercise of its Chapter VII authority itself suggests that decisions taken under this head are not reviewable.

8. For the Defence it is said that it is a basic human right of an accused to have a fair and public hearing by a competent, independent and impartial tribunal established by law. The Defence asserts that this right is protected by a panoply of principles of fundamental justice recognized by human rights law. There can be no doubt that the International Tribunal should seek to provide just such a trial; indeed, in enacting its Statute, care has been taken by the Security Council to ensure that this in fact occurs and the Judges of the International Tribunal, in framing its Rules, have also paid scrupulous regard to the requirements of a fair trial. For example, Article 21 of the Statute of the International Tribunal guarantees the accused the right to a fair trial and Article 20 obligates the Trial Chambers to ensure that trials are, in fact, fair. There are several other provisions to the same effect. However, it is one thing for the Security Council to have taken every care to ensure that a structure appropriate to the conduct of fair trials has been created; it is an entirely different thing in any way to infer from that careful structuring that it was intended that the International Tribunal be empowered to question the legality of the law which established it. The competence of the International Tribunal is precise and narrowly defined; as described in Article I of its Statute, it is to prosecute persons responsible for serious violations of international humanitarian law, subject to spatial and temporal limits, and to do so in accordance with the Statute. That is the full extent of the competence of the International Tribunal.

9. The Defence seeks to extend the competence of the International Tribunal to review the actions of the Security Council by reference to the Rules of the International Tribunal. It refers first to Rule 73(A)(i), which provides that preliminary motions by the accused can include: "objections based on lack of jurisdiction". That Rule relates to challenges to jurisdiction and is no authority for engaging in an investigation, not into jurisdiction, but into the legality of the action of the Security Council in establishing the International Tribunal. The Defence also points to Rule 91, False Testimony Under Solemn Declaration, as an example of the exercise by the International Tribunal of powers that are not explicitly provided for in its Statute. There is, however, no analogy to be drawn between the inherent authority of a Chamber to control its own proceedings and any suggested power to review the authority of the Security Council. Therefore, even were it conceivable that the Rules adopted by the Judges could extend the competence of the International Tribunal, the Rules referred to by the Defence do not support such an enlargement.

10. The Defence relies on, or at least refers to, what has been said by the International Court of Justice ("the Court") in three cases: Certain Expenses of the United Nations, 1962 I.C.J. 151, 168 (Advisory Opinion of 20 July) (the "Expenses Advisory Opinion"), Legal Consequences for States of the Continued Presence of South Africa in Namibia (South-West Africa) Notwithstanding Security Council Resolution 776, 1971 I.C.J. 16, 45 (Advisory Opinion of 21 June) (the "Namibia Advisory Opinion ") and Questions of Interpretation and Application of the 1971 Montreal Convention Arising from the Aerial Incident at Lockerbie (Libya v. U.S.), 1992 I.C.J. 114, 176 (Provisional Measures Order of 14 April) (the "Lockerbie decision"). In the first of these, the Expenses Advisory Opinion, the Court specifically stated that, unlike the legal system of some States there exists no procedure for determining the validity of acts of organs of the United Nations. It referred to proposals at the time of drafting of the Charter that such a power should be given to the Court and to the rejection of those proposals.

11. In the second of these cases, the Namibia Advisory Opinion, the Court dealt very specifically with this matter, stating that: "Undoubtedly, the Court does not possess powers of judicial review or appeal in respect of the decisions taken by the United Nations organs concerned".

12. Finally, in the Lockerbie decision, Judge Weeramantry, in his dissenting opinion, but in this respect not in dissent from other members of the Court, said that "it is not for this Court to sit in review on a given resolution of the Security Council" and, that in relation to the exercise by the Security Council of its powers under Chapter VII:

> "the determination under Article 39 of the existence of any threat to the peace ... is one entirely within the discretion of the Council.... the Council and no other is the judge of the existence of the state of affairs which brings Chapter VII into operation.... Once [such a determination is] taken the door is opened to the various decisions the Council may make under that Chapter."

13. These opinions of the Court clearly provide no basis for the International Tribunal to review the actions of the Security Council, indeed, they are authorities to the contrary.

14. In support of its submission that this Trial Chamber should review the actions of the Security Council, the Defence contends that the decisions of the Security Council are not sacrosanct". Certainly, commentators have suggested that there are limits to the authority of the Security Council. It has been posited that such limits may be based on Article 24(2), which provides that the Security Council: "shall act in accordance with the Purposes and Principles of the United Nations. The specific powers appointed to the Security Council for the discharge of these duties are laid down in Chapters VI, VII, VIII, and XII." One commentator interprets this provision to mean that the Security Council "cannot, in principle, act arbitrarily and unfettered by any restraints." (D. W. Bowett, The Law of International Institutions 33 (1982).) Another commentator has taken the position that although the Security Council has broad discretion in the field of international peace and security, it cannot "act arbitrarily or use the existence of a threat to the peace as a basis for action which ... is for collateral and independent purposes, such as the overthrow of a government or the partition of a State." (Ian Brownlie, The Decisions of Political Organs of the United Nations and the Rule of Law, in Essays in Honour of Wang Tieya 95 (1992).)

15. Support for the view that the Security Council cannot act arbitrarily or for an ulterior purpose is found in the nature of the Charter as a treaty delegating certain powers to the United Nations. In fact, such a limitation is almost a corollary of the principle that the organs of the United Nations must act in accordance with the powers delegated them. It is a matter of logic that if the Security Council acted arbitrarily or for an ulterior purpose it would be acting outside the purview of the powers delegated to it in the Charter.

16. Although it is not for this Trial Chamber to judge the reasonableness of the acts of the Security Council, it is without doubt that, with respect to the former Yugoslavia, the Security Council did not act arbitrarily. To the contrary, the Security Council's establishment of the International Tribunal represents its informed judgment, after great deliberation, that violations of international humanitarian law were occurring in the former Yugoslavia and that such violations created a threat to the peace. One commentator has noted the "careful, incremental approach" of the Security Council to the situation in the former Yugoslavia and described the establishment of the International Tribunal as a protracted, four-step process involving: "(1) condemnation; (2) publication; (3) investigation; and (4) punishment." (James C. O'Brien, The International Tribunal for Violations of International Humanitarian Law in the Former Yugoslavia, 87 Am. J. Int'l L. 639,

640–42 (1993).) First, with its resolution 764, adopted on 13 July 1992, the Security Council stressed that "persons who commit or order the commission of grave breaches of the [1949 Geneva] Conventions are individually responsible in respect of such breaches". Second, the Security Council publicized this condemnation by adopting, on 12 August 1992, resolution 771, which called upon States and other bodies to submit "substantiated information" to the Secretary-General, who would report to the Security Council recommending additional measures that might be appropriate. Third, by resolution 780 of 6 October 1992, the Security Council established the Commission of Experts to investigate these violations of international humanitarian law. The Security Council in due course received the report of the Commission of Experts, which concluded that grave breaches of the 1949 Geneva Conventions and other violations of international humanitarian law had been committed in the territory of the former Yugoslavia, including wilful killing, "ethnic cleansing," mass killings, torture, rape, pillage and destruction of civilian property, destruction of cultural and religious property and arbitrary arrests. (See Interim Report of the Commission of Experts, U.N. Doc. S/25274 (26 January 1993).) Finally, on 22 February 1993, by resolution 808, the Security Council decided that an international tribunal should be established and directed the Secretary-General to submit specific proposals for the implementation of that decision. On 25 May 1993, in resolution 827, the Security Council adopted the draft Statute and thus established the International Tribunal.

17. None of the hypothetical cases which commentators have suggested as examples of limits on the powers of the Security Council, whether imposed by the terms of the Charter or general principles of international law and, in particular, *jus cogens*, have any relevance to the present case. Moreover, even if there be such limits, that is not to say that any judicial body, let alone this International Tribunal, can exercise powers of judicial review to determine whether, in relation to an exercise by the Security Council of powers under Chapter VII, those limits have been exceeded....

19. It is not irrelevant that what the Security Council has enacted under Chapter VII is the creation of a tribunal whose jurisdiction is expressly confined to the prosecution of breaches of international humanitarian law that are beyond any doubt part of customary law, not the establishment of some eccentric and novel code of conduct or some wholly irrational criterion as the possession of white hair, as was instanced in argument by the Defence. Arguments based upon reductio ad absurdum may be useful to destroy a fallacious proposition but will seldom provide a firm foundation for the creation of a valid one....

21. The Security Council established the International Tribunal as an enforcement measure under Chapter VII of the United Nations Charter after finding that the violations of international humanitarian law in the former Yugoslavia constituted a threat to the peace. In making this finding, the Security Council acted under Article 39 of the Charter, which provides:

> "The Security Council shall determine the existence of any threat to peace, breach of peace, or act of aggression and shall make recommendations, or decide what measures shall be taken in accordance with Articles 41 and 42, to maintain or restore international peace and security."

22. When, in resolution 827, the Security Council stated that it was "convinced" that, in the "particular circumstances of the former Yugoslavia," the establishment of the International Tribunal would contribute to the restoration and maintenance of peace, the course it took was novel only in the means adopted but not in the object sought to be attained. The Security Council has on a number of occasions addressed humanitarian law

issues in the context of threats to the peace, has called upon States to comply with obligations imposed by humanitarian law and has on occasion taken steps to ensure such compliance. It has done so, for example. in relation to Southern Rhodesia in 1965 and 1966, South Africa in 1977, Lebanon on a number of occasions in the 1980's, Iran and Iraq in 1987, Iraq again in 1991, Haiti and Somalia in 1993 and, of course, Rwanda in 1994. In the last of these, the establishment of the Rwanda Tribunal by the Security Council followed its finding that the conflict there involved violations of humanitarian law and was a threat to the peace.

23. The making of a judgment as to whether there was such an emergency in the former Yugoslavia as would justify the setting up of the International Tribunal under Chapter VII is eminently one for the Security Council and only for it; it is certainly not a justiciable issue but one involving considerations of high policy and of a political nature. As to whether the particular measure of establishing the International Tribunal is, in fact, likely to be conducive to the restoration of peace and security is, again, pre-eminently a matter for the Security Council and for it alone and no judicial body, certainly not this Trial Chamber, can or should review that step.

24.... The validity of the decision of the Security Council to establish the International Tribunal rests on its finding that the events in the former Yugoslavia constituted a threat to the peace. This finding is necessarily fact-based and raises political, nonjusticiable issues. As noted by Judge Weeramantry, such a decision "entails a factual and political judgement and not a legal one". (The Lockerbie decision at 176.) A commentator has agreed, saying that "a threat to international peace and security is not a fixed standard which can be easily and automatically applied". (David L. Johnson, Note, Sanctions and South Africa, 19 Harv. Int'l L.J. 887, 901 (1978).) The factual and political nature of an Article 39 determination by the Security Council makes it inherently inappropriate for any review by this Trial Chamber.

25. The Defence contends that there has been a lack of consistency in the actions of the Security Council. Certainly the International Tribunal is the first of its kind to be created. However, the fact that the Security Council has not taken a similar step in other, earlier cases cannot in itself be of any relevance in determining the legality of its action in this case.

26. Article 41 of the Charter provides:

> "The Security Council may decide what measures not involving the use of armed force are to be employed to give effect to its decisions, and it may call upon the Members of the United Nations to apply such measures. These may include complete or partial interruption of economic relations and of rail, sea, air, postal, telegraphic, radio, and other means of communication, and the severance of diplomatic relations."

The Article, on its face, does not limit the discretion of the Security Council to take measures not involving the use of armed force.

27. That it was not originally envisaged that an ad hoc judicial tribunal might be created under Chapter VII, even if that be factually correct, is nothing to the point. Chapter VII confers very wide powers upon the Security Council and no good reason has been advanced why Article 41 should be read as excluding the step, very appropriate in the circumstances, of creating the International Tribunal to deal with the notorious situation existing in the former Yugoslavia. This is a situation clearly suited to adjudication by a tribunal and punishment of those found guilty of crimes that violate international humanitarian law. This is not, as the Defence puts it, a question of the Security Council

doing anything it likes; it is a seemingly entirely appropriate reaction to a situation in which international peace is clearly endangered.

28. The Defence argues that the establishment of the International Tribunal is not a measure contemplated by Article 41 because the examples included in that Article focus on economic and political measures, not judicial measures. As the Defence concedes, however, the list in that Article is not exhaustive. Once again, the decision of the Security Council in this regard is fraught with fact-based, policy determinations that make this issue non-justiciable.

29. Further, the Defence contends that the International Tribunal is not an appropriate measure under Article 41 because it has failed to restore peace in the former Yugoslavia. However, the accused is but the first and, as yet, the only accused to be brought before the International Tribunal, and it is wholly premature at this initial stage of its functioning to attempt to assess the effectiveness of the International Tribunal as a measure to restore peace, even were it the function of the International Tribunal to do so.

30. The Security Council discussions on the situation in the former Yugoslavia suggest two ways in which the International Tribunal would help in the restoring and maintaining of peace. First, several States expressed the view that the creation of the International Tribunal would deter further violations of international humanitarian law. (See Provisional Verbatim Record, U.N. SCOR, 48th Sess., 3175th mtg. at 8, 22, U.N. Doc. S/PV.3175 (22 February 1993); Provisional Verbatim Record, U.N. SCOR, 48th Sess., 3217th mtg. at 12, 19, U.N. Doc. S/PV.3217 (25 May 1993).)

31. Second, States took the position that the establishment of the International Tribunal would assist in the restoration of peace in the region....

32. Then it is said that international law requires that criminal courts be independent and impartial and that no court created by a political body such as the Security Council can have those characteristics. Of course, criminal courts worldwide are the creations of legislatures, eminently political bodies. The Court, in the Effect of Awards case, specifically held that a political organ of the United Nations—in that case, the General Assembly—could and had created "an independent and truly judicial body." (Effect of Awards of Compensation Made by the United Nations Administrative Tribunal, 1954 I.C.J. 47, 53 (Advisory Opinion of 13 July) (Effect of Awards").) The question whether a court is independent and impartial depends not upon the body that creates it but upon its constitution, its judges and the way in which they function. The International Tribunal has, as its Statute and Rules attest, been constituted so as to ensure a fair trial to an accused and it is to be hoped that the way its Judges administer their jurisdiction will leave no room for complaints about lack of impartiality or want of independence.

33. The fact that the Security Council has established an ad hoc tribunal is also said to reveal invalidity because it is said to deny to the accused the right conferred by Article 14 of the International Convention on the Protection of Civil and Political Rights ("ICCPR") to be tried by a tribunal "established by law". However, on analysis this introduces no new concept; it is but another way of expressing the general complaint that the creation of the International Tribunal was beyond the power of the Security Council.

34. It is noteworthy that, in the context of the International Covenant and its entitlement in Article 14 to trial by a "tribunal established by law", this phrase requires only that the tribunal be legally constituted. At the time Article 14 was being drafted, it was sought unsuccessfully to amend it to require that tribunals should be "pre-established". As Professor David Harris puts it in his article The Right to a Fair Trial in Criminal Proceedings as a Human Right, 16 I.C.L.Q. 353, 356 (1967):

"An amendment which sought to change the wording of the United Nations text to read 'pre-established' and so cover all ad hoc or special tribunals was firmly and successfully opposed, however, on the ground that this would make normal judicial reorganization difficult. Mention was also made of the Nuremberg and Tokyo Tribunals which were ad hoc and yet which, it is generally agreed, gave the accused a fair trial in a procedural sense in most respects.... the important consideration is whether a court observes certain other requirements once it begins to function, however it might be created."

35. It is also argued that Article 29 of Chapter VI of the Charter does not contemplate the creation by the Security Council of an international judicial body when it refers to the creation of subsidiary organs. The reasoning behind this submission is no more than an assertion that a judicial body cannot be an additional organ of some other body; yet Article 29 is expressed in the broadest terms and nothing appears to limit its scope to non-judicial organs. In any event, it is not under Chapter VI of the Charter that the Security Council has established this Tribunal; as the Statute of the International Tribunal declares in its opening paragraph, it is as a measure under Chapter VII that the Security Council has created this International Tribunal. Moreover, in the Effect of Awards case mentioned above, the Court specifically decided that the General Assembly had the power to create an administrative tribunal. (Effect of Awards case at 56–61.) If the General Assembly has the authority to create a subsidiary judicial body, then surely the Security Council can create such a body in the exercise of its wide discretion to act under Chapter VII.

36. Nor has any basis been established for denying to the Security Council the power of indirect imposition of criminal liability upon individuals through the creation of a tribunal having criminal jurisdiction. On the contrary, given that the Security Council found that the threat to the peace posed by the conflict in the former Yugoslavia arose because of large scale violations of international humanitarian law committed by individuals, it was both appropriate and necessary for the Security Council, through the International Tribunal, to act on individuals in order to address the threat to the peace. In this regard it is important that when, in its resolutions 731 and 748, the Security Council required the Libyan Government to surrender the two Libyan nationals who were accused of the Lockerbie bombing and imposed mandatory commercial and diplomatic sanctions to obtain Libya's compliance with its decision, it was, in substance, acting upon individuals, seeking, the extradition and trial of those Libyan nationals.

37. Reference was also made to the *jus de non evocando*, a feature of a number of national constitutions. But that principle, if it requires that an accused be tried by the regularly established courts and not by some special tribunal set up for that particular purpose, has no application when what is in issue is the exercise by the Security Council, acting under Chapter VII, of the powers conferred upon it by the Charter of the United Nations. Of course, this involves some surrender of sovereignty by the member nations of the United Nations but that is precisely what was achieved by the adoption of the Charter. In particular, that was achieved, in the case of action by the Security Council under Chapter VII, by Article 2(7) of the Charter and its reference to the application of enforcement measures under Chapter VII. The same observation applies to the contention that there is some vice involved in the conferring of primacy upon this Tribunal. That is no more than a means by which the Security Council seeks to give effect to the powers conferred upon it by Chapter VII. In any event it is by no means clear that an individual defendant has standing to raise this point.

38. The submission that there should have been involvement of the General Assembly in the creation of the International Tribunal can only have any meaning if what is sug-

gested is the creation of a tribunal by means of an amendment of the Charter. If, however, the International Tribunal can, as seems clear, be created under Chapter VII, the suggestion of an amendment of the Charter is as unnecessary, as it is impractical as a measure appropriate by way of a response to the current situation in the former Yugoslavia.

39. It was claimed on behalf of the accused that he was disadvantage by his removal from the jurisdiction of German courts to that of the International Tribunal since that denied him the opportunity under the optional Protocol to the ICCPR to have recourse to the Human Rights Committee to complain about the trial accorded him. No doubt this is so, since that right does not appear to apply to proceedings before international tribunals, but that is nothing to the point in any challenge to the jurisdiction of this Trial Chamber; it can only be remedied, if remedy is required, by a further Protocol to the ICCPR. A similar comment applies in the case of the European Convention on Human Rights, to which the Defence also refers. . . .

B. Primacy of the International Tribunal

41. The Trial Chamber deals next with the Defence argument that the primacy jurisdiction conferred upon the International Tribunal by Article 9(2) finds no basis in international law because the national courts of Bosnia and Herzegovina or, alternatively, of the entity known as the Bosnian Serb Republic, have primary jurisdiction to try the accused. This argument in effect again challenges the legality of the action of the Security Council in establishing the International Tribunal: the answer to this has already been provided above. The Trial Chamber is not entitled to engage in an exercise involving the review of a resolution passed by the Security Council. In any event, the accused not being a State lacks the locus standi to raise the issue of primacy, which involves a plea that the sovereignty of a State has been violated, a plea only a sovereign State may raise or waive and a right clearly the accused cannot take over from that State. (See Israel v. Eichmann, 36 I.L.R. 5, 62 (1961).) In this regard, it is pertinent to note that the challenge to the primacy of the International Tribunal has been made against the express intent of the two States most closely affected by the indictment against the accused—Bosnia and Herzegovia and the Federal Republic of Germany. The former, on the territory of which the crimes were allegedly committed, and the latter where the accused resided at the time of his arrest, have unconditionally accepted the jurisdiction of the International Tribunal and the accused cannot claim the rights that have been specifically waived by the States concerned. To allow the accused to do so would be to allow him to select the forum of his choice, contrary to the principles relating to coercive criminal jurisdiction. As to the entity known as the Bosnian Serb Republic, similarly, the accused as an individual, has no locus standi, for the reasons given above, to raise the issue of this entity's sovereignty rights should it have been endowed with all the attributes of statehood.

42. Before leaving this question relating to the violation of the sovereignty of States, it should be noted that the crimes which the International Tribunal has been called upon to try are not crimes of a purely domestic nature. They are really crimes which are universal in nature, well recognized in international law as serious breaches of international humanitarian law, and transcending the interest of any one State. The Trial Chamber agrees that in such circumstances, the sovereign rights of States cannot and should not take precedence over the right of the international community to act appropriately as they affect the whole of mankind and shock the conscience of all nations of the world. There can therefore be no objection to an international tribunal properly constituted trying these crimes on behalf of the international community. . . .

44. One final word before leaving this topic. The crimes with which the accused is charged form part of customary international law and existed well before the establish-

ment of the International Tribunal. If the Security Council in its informed wisdom, acting well within its powers pursuant to Article 39 and 41 under Chapter VII of the Charter, creates the International Tribunal to share the burden of bringing perpetrators of universal crimes to justice, the Trial Chamber can see no invasion into a State's jurisdiction because, as it has been rightly argued on behalf of the Prosecutor, they were never crimes within the exclusive jurisdiction of any individual State. In any event, Article 2(7) of the Charter, as has been noted above, prohibiting intervention by the United Nations in matters essentially within a State's domestic jurisdiction, is qualified in that "this principle shall not prejudice the application of enforcement measures under Chapter VII".

II. Subject-Matter Jurisdiction ...

A. Article 2: Grave Breaches of the Geneva Convention of 1949

46. The Statute of the International Tribunal confers jurisdiction by Articles 1 to 8 and supplements, and in one respect qualifies, that jurisdiction in Articles 9 and 10. However it is essentially Articles 1, 2, 3 and 5 with which this motion is concerned.

47. Article 1 does no more than confer power to prosecute for serious violations of international humanitarian law and confines that power, spatially, to breaches committed in the territory of the former Yugoslavia and, temporally, to the period since 1991. It further requires that the power thus conferred be exercised in accordance with the provisions of the Statute.

48. Article 2 confers subject-matter jurisdiction to prosecute in respect of grave breaches of the Geneva Conventions and identifies those breaches by the phrase, "namely the following acts against persons or property protected under the provisions of the relevant Geneva Conventions." There then follows an enumeration of acts, culled from the four Conventions and, with very slight variations, repeating and in effect consolidating, the terms of the grave breaches provisions to be found in varying form in each of those Conventions.

49. The Article has been so drafted as to be self-contained rather than referential, save for the identification of the victims of enumerated acts; that identification and that alone involves going to the Conventions themselves for the definition of "persons or property protected." In the present case it is not contended that the alleged victims in the several charges were not protected persons; in any event that will be a matter for evidence in due course.

50. What is contended is that for Article 2 to have any application there must exist a state of international conflict and that none in fact existed at any relevant time-or place. However, the requirement of international conflict does not appear on the face of Article 2. Certainly, nothing in the words of the Article expressly require its existence; once one of the specified acts is allegedly committed upon a protected person the power of the International Tribunal to prosecute arises if the spatial and temporal requirements of Article 1 are met.

51. The Report of the Secretary-General, (U.N. Doc. S/25704 (3 May 1993)) (the "Report") makes it clear, in paragraph 34, that it was intended that the rules of international law that were to be applied should be "beyond any doubt part of customary law", so that problems of non-adherence of particular States to any international Convention should not arise. Hence, no doubt, the specific reference to the law of the Geneva Conventions in Article 2 since, as the Report states in paragraph 35, that law applicable in armed conflict has beyond doubt become part of customary law. But there is no ground for treating Article 2 as in effect importing into the Statute the whole of the terms of the

Conventions, including the reference in common Article 2 of the Geneva Convention to international conflicts. As stated, Article 2 of the Statute is on its face, self-contained, save in relation to the definition of protected persons and things. It simply confers subject matter jurisdiction to prosecute what, if one were concerned with the Conventions, would indeed be grave breaches of those Conventions, but which are, in the present context, simple enactments of the Statute.

52. When what is in issue is what the Geneva Conventions contemplate in the case of grave breaches, namely their prosecution before a national court and not before an international tribunal, it is natural enough that there should be a requirement of internationality; a nation might well view with concern, as an unacceptable infringement of sovereignty, the action of a foreign court in trying an accused for grave breaches committed in a conflict internal to that nation. Such considerations do not apply to the International Tribunal, any more than do the references in the Conventions to High Contracting Parties and much else in the Conventions; all these are simply inapplicable to the International Tribunal. They do not apply because the International Tribunal is not in fact, applying conventional international law but, rather, customary international law, as the Secretary-General makes clear in his Report, and is doing so by virtue of the mandate conferred upon it by the Security Council. In the case of what are commonly referred to as "grave breaches", this conventional law has become customary law, though some of it may well have been conventional law before being written into the predecessors of the present Geneva Conventions.

53. It follows that the element of internationality forms no jurisdictional criterion of the offences created by Article 2 of the Statute of the International Tribunal. If it did, there are clear indications in the great volume of material before the Trial Chamber that the acts alleged in the indictment were in fact committed in the course of an international armed conflict. However, little of this material is such that judicial notice can be taken of it and none of it is in the form of, nor has it been tendered as, evidence. In these circumstances the Trial Chamber makes no finding regarding the nature of the armed conflict in question.

54. As a submission alternative to its principal submission that there was here an international armed conflict, the Prosecutor contended that certain agreements entered into were, in any event, such that they operated, pursuant to common Article 3 of the 1949 Geneva Conventions ("common Article 3"), "to bring into force, by means of special agreements", those provisions of the Conventions relating to serious breaches.

55. Those agreements, entered into under the auspices of the International Committee of the Red Cross on 22 and 23 May and on 1 October 1992, were accompanied by a programme of action agreed upon on 27 August 1992.

56. That these agreements had the effect contended for by the Prosecutor was contested by the Defence. In view of the conclusion of the Trial Chamber that Article 2 of our Statute expressly and directly confers jurisdiction to prosecute in respect of the commission of the acts enumerated in that Article, it is also unnecessary to express any conclusion regarding this alternative submission.

B. Article 3: Violations of the Laws or Customs of War

57. The Defence contends that the accused may not be tried for violations of laws or customs of war under Article 3 of the Statute because that article is based on the Hague Convention (IV) Respecting the Laws and Customs of War on Land and the regulations thereto of 18 October 1907 ("Hague Convention"), and the 1977 Protocol I, which apply only to an international conflict, and that none, in fact, existed at any relevant time or

place. The Prosecutor responds by asserting that the term "laws or customs of war" in Article 3 applies to both international and internal conflict and that the International Tribunal may apply the minimum standards of common Article 3 which are applicable to both international and internal armed conflicts. Since the Prosecutor seemingly does not seek to import Protocol I into Article 3 of the Statute, the Trial Chamber does not address that issue.

58. Having considered the position of the parties, the Trial Chamber finds that the character of the conflict, whether international or internal, does not affect the subject-matter jurisdiction of the International Tribunal under Article 3 to try persons who are charged with violations of laws or customs of war.

59. The interpretation of the scope of Article 2 of the Statute is applicable to the view of the Trial Chamber of its subject matter jurisdiction under Article 3. Contrary to the position of the Defence, nothing in the words of Article 3 expressly requires the existence of an international conflict. Indeed, with respect to Article 3, unlike Article 2, there is no mention of any convention. Article 3 simply provides that the International Tribunal "shall have the power to prosecute persons violating the laws or customs of war". A list of prohibitory acts are then set forth in the Article. It is clear that the list is illustrative and not exhaustive, for the list is preceded with the phrase, "such violations shall include, but not be limited to...."

60. The competence of the International Tribunal extends to serious violations of international humanitarian law that are a part of customary law. International humanitarian law includes international rules designed to solve humanitarian problems arising from international or non-international armed conflicts. (See Commentary on the Additional Protocols of 8 June 1977, at p. XXVII (ICRC 1987).) Even though the acts enumerated in Article 3 are from the Hague Convention, the term "laws or customs of war" should not be limited to international conflicts. Laws or customs of war include prohibitions of acts committed both in international and internal armed conflicts. Indeed, common Article 3 is clear evidence that customary international law limits the conduct of hostilities in internal armed conflicts. However, unlike contracting parties to treaties, the International Tribunal is not called upon to apply conventional law but instead is mandated to apply customary international law. Therefore, the element of internationality forms no jurisdictional criterion even if the Hague Convention was originally envisaged by the Contracting Parties to apply to international conflicts.

61. Violations of the laws or customs of war are commonly referred to as "war crimes". They can be defined as crimes committed by any person in violation of recognized obligations under rules derived from conventional or customary law applicable to the parties to the conflict. (See L.C. Green, The Contemporary Law of Armed Conflict 276 (1993), ("war crimes are violations of the laws and customs of the law of armed conflict and are punishable whether committed by combatants or civilians, including the nationals of neutral states"). See also, M.C. Bassiouni, A Draft International Criminal Code And Draft Statute For An International Criminal Tribunal 130 (1987) ("[w]ar crimes consist of conduct (acts or omissions) which is prohibited by the rules of international law applicable in armed conflict, conventions to which the parties to the conflict are Parties, and the recognized principles and rules of international law of armed conflict").)

62. In Article 6(b) of the Charter of the International Military Tribunal at Nuremberg, war crimes are defined as

"[V]iolations of the laws and customs of war. Such violations shall include, but not be limited to, murder, ill-treatment or deportation to slave labor or for any other purpose of civilian population of or in occupied territory, murder or ill-treatment of prisoners of war or persons on the seas, killing of hostages, plunder of public or private property, wanton destructions of cities, towns, or villages, or devastation not justified by military necessity."

63. Although the Statute of the International Military Tribunal limited its competence to the international armed conflict of World War II, historically laws or customs of war have not been limited by the nature of the conflict they regulate. The Lieber Code [extracts in the Documents Supplement], broadly recognized as the most famous early example of a national manual outlining the laws of war for the use of armed forces, and one of the first attempts to codify the laws of land warfare, was drafted to regulate the conduct of the United States armed forces during the American Civil War. (The Lieber Code, Instructions for the Government of Armies of the United States in the Field by Order of the Secretary of War, General Orders No. 100, Washington, D.C. (24 April 1863), reprinted in L. Friedman (ed.) 1 A Documentary History 158 (1972).) This Code, based on what Lieber regarded as the generally accepted law of his day, was used as the model for other manuals and greatly inspired later developments of the laws of war. Indeed, the drafters of the first proposal for a codification of the "laws or customs of war on land" in The Hague, relied heavily on the "Declaration of Brussels of 1874," which in turn, was strongly influenced by the Lieber Code. (See F. Kalshoven, Constraints on the Waging of War 13 (1987).) It is also an established principle of customary international law that the laws of war might become applicable to non-international armed conflicts of a certain intensity through the doctrine of "recognition of belligerency". (See, for example, 1956 United States Army Field Manual, which stipulated that "the customary law of war becomes applicable to civil war upon recognition of the rebels as belligerents", para. 11a.) Further, even in internal conflict situations where the recognition of belligerency was explicitly withheld, it has been recognized that some fundamental rules of the law of war would nevertheless apply, regardless of non-recognition of belligerency. (See A. Cassese "The Spanish Civil War and the Development of Customary Law Concerning Internal Armed Conflict", in Current Problems of International Law 313 (Cassese, ed.1975).) Additionally, under the International Law Commission's Draft Code on Crimes Against The Peace and Security of Mankind, the notion of "exceptionally serious war crimes", is defined to include certain conduct and no differentiation is made with respect to whether committed in the course of an international or non-international armed conflict. Members of the Security Council are also of the opinion that the term "laws or customs" is not limited to international armed conflicts. (See Statements of U.S., U.K. and French representatives to the Security Council following the adoption of resolution 827, U.N. Doc. S/PV.3217, 15 (May 25, 1993).)

64. The Trial Chamber concludes that Article 3 of the Statute provides a non-exhaustive list of acts which fit within the rubric of "laws or customs of war". The offences that it may consider are not limited to those contained in the Hague Convention and may arise during an armed conflict regardless of whether it is international or internal.

65. The Prosecutor affirmatively contends that the minimum standards contained in common Article 3 are incorporated in Article 3 of the Statute. The Trial Chamber finds that it has subject-matter jurisdiction under Article 3 because violations of laws or customs of war are a part of customary international law over which it has competence regardless of whether the conflict is international or national. However, the Trial Chamber considers that it is necessary to respond to the specific assertion by the Prosecutor that laws or customs of war include the obligations imposed by common Article 3. The Trial Chamber finds that common Article 3 imposes obligations that are within the subject-mat-

ter jurisdiction of Article 3 of the Statute because those obligations are a part of customary international law. Further, the Trial Chamber finds that violations of these prohibitions can be enforced against individuals. Imposing criminal responsibility upon individuals for these violations does not violate the principle of *nullum crimen sine lege*.

66. Common Article 3 prohibits the following acts when committed against persons taking no active part in the hostilities:

(a) violence to life and person, in particular murder of all kinds, mutilation, cruel treatment and torture;

(b) taking of hostages;

(c) outrages upon personal dignity, in particular humiliating and degrading treatment;

(d) the passing of sentences and the carrying out of executions without previous judgement pronounced by a regularly constituted court, affording all the judicial guarantees which are recognized as indispensable by civilized-people.

67. For the reasons discussed herein, the acts proscribed by common Article 3 constitute criminal offences under international law. The fact that common Article 3 is part of customary international law was definitively decided by the International Court of Justice in the Nicaragua case (Military and Paramilitary Activities (Nicar. v. U.S.)), 1986 I.C.J. 4 [paras. 218, 255](Merits Judgement of 27 June 1986) in which the Court, applying customary international law, determined that the rules contained in common Article 3 constitute a "minimum yardstick" applicable in both international and non-international armed conflicts, thus finding that these prohibitions are part of customary international law. As early as 1958 the view was already held that common Article 3:

" … merely demands respect for certain rules, which were already recognised as essential in all civilised countries, and embodied in the municipal law of the states in question, long before the Convention was signed…. no government can object to observing, in its dealings with internal enemies, whatever the nature of the conflict between it and them, a few essential rules which it in fact observes daily, under its own laws, even when dealing with common criminals." (Commentary on the Geneva Conventions of 12 August 1919: [No.] IV Geneva Convention Relative to the Protection of Civilian Persons in Time of War 36 (Pictet ed., 1958).)

A more recent commentator notes that " … the norms stated in Article 3(1)(a)-(c) are of such an elementary, ethical character, and echo so many provisions in other humanitarian and human rights treaties, that they must be regarded as embodying minimum standards of customary law also applicable to non-international armed conflicts." (Theodor Meron, Human Rights and Humanitarian Norms as Customary Law 35 (1991).) The customary status of common Article 3 is further supported by statements made by representatives to the Security Council following the adoption of resolution 827 adopting the Statute of the International Tribunal. The United States representative explicitly stated that she considered Article 3 of the Statute to include common Article 3 of the 1949 Geneva Conventions, and representatives from the United Kingdom and France made similar statements. (U.N. Doc. S/PV.3217 (25 May 1993), paras. 11, 15 and 19.)

68. The fact that acts proscribed by common Article 3 constitute criminal offences under international law is also evident from the fact that the acts within common Article 3 are criminal in nature. They are similar in content to acts prohibited by the grave breaches provisions, which clearly entail individual criminal liability. In addition, the type of acts listed in common Article 3 have been found in the past to result in individual criminal liability. For example, Article 44 of the Lieber Code *supra* provided for the

prohibition, criminal responsibility and punishment of persons committing acts which are of the type that would today fall within common Article 3. In addition, there have been national trials for individuals charged with violations similar to common Article 3. (See Jordan Paust, War Crimes Jurisdiction and Due Process: The Bangladesh Experience 11 *Vanderbilt Journal of Transnational Law* 1, 25 (1978).)

69. The customary international law doctrine of recognition of belligerency allows for the application to internal conflicts of the laws applicable to international armed conflict, thus ensuring that even in a non-international conflict individuals can be held criminally responsible for violations of the laws and customs of war. Additionally, some national military manuals and laws emphasise the criminal nature of acts within common Article 3. For example, the United States Army regards violations of common Article 3 as encompassed by the notion of war crimes, thus empowering it to prosecute captured military personnel for war crimes if they were accused of breaches of common Article 3. The German Military Manual describes violations of common Article 3 as "grave breaches of international humanitarian law," implying that violations of common Article 3 could form the basis for individual criminal responsibility. (See Theodor Meron, International Criminalization of Internal Atrocities, 89 *Am. J. Int'l L.* 554, 564–65 (1995).) Further, the criminal nature of the acts within common Article 3 is evident from the language of common Article 3 itself, which is clearly prohibitory and addresses fundamental offences such as murder and torture which are prohibited in all States:

> "Therefore, no person who has committed such acts … could claim in good faith that he/she did not understand that the acts were prohibited. And the principle *nullum crimen* is designed to protect a person only from being punished for an act that he or she reasonably believed to be lawful when committed." (*Id.* at 566.)

70. The individual criminal responsibility of the violator need not be explicitly stated in a convention for its provisions to entail individual criminal liability. This is evident from the use of the Fourth Hague Convention and the 1929 Geneva Prisoners of War Convention as the basis for prosecutions and convictions at Nuremberg, despite the fact that neither convention contains any reference to penal prosecution or individual liability for breaches.

71. A further indication that the acts proscribed by common Article 3 constitute criminal offences under international law is that, assuming arguendo that there is no clear obligation to punish or extradite violators of non-grave breach provisions of the Geneva Conventions, such as common Article 3, all States have the right to punish those violators. Therefore, individuals can be prosecuted for the violations of the acts listed and thus prosecution by the International Tribunal based on primacy does not violate the ex post facto prohibition. In addition, in the Nicaragua case, the Court recognised the applicability of common Article 1 of the Geneva Conventions to non-international armed conflicts. The requirement in common Article 1 that all Contracting Parties must respect and ensure respect for the Conventions may entail resort to penal measures.

72. In his Report, the Secretary-General states that "the application of the principle *nullum crimen sine lege* requires that the International Tribunal should apply rules of international humanitarian law which are beyond any doubt part of customary law". (UN Doc. S/25704, para. 34.) Article 15(1) of the ICCPR contains the prohibition against *nullum crimen sine lege*, and provides in relevant part that "[n]o one shall be held guilty of any criminal offence on account of an act or omission which did not constitute a criminal offence, under national or international law, at the time when it was committed". As is demonstrated from the above, common Article 3 is beyond doubt part of customary

international law, therefore the principle of *nullum crimen sine lege* is not violated by incorporating the prohibitory norms of common Article 3 in Article 3 of the Statute of the International Tribunal.

73. Additional support for the finding that there is no violation of the principle of *nullum crimen sine lege* is that by incorporating the prohibitory norms of common Article 3 into its national law, the former Yugoslavia has criminalized these offences. (See Art. 125 of the Criminal Code of the former Yugoslavia, which provides that the prohibition of war crimes against the civilian population applies to situations of "war, armed conflict or occupation," irrespective of the nature of the conflict, thus implying that situations of non-international armed conflict could be covered.)

74. For these reasons, the Trial Chamber finds that the character of the conflict, whether international or internal, does not affect the subject-matter jurisdiction of the Tribunal under Article 3. The term "laws or customs of war", applies to international and internal armed conflicts. The minimum standards of common Article 3 apply to the conflict in the former Yugoslavia and the accused's prosecution for those offences does not violate the principle of *nullum crimen sine lege.*

C. Article 5: Crimes Against Humanity

75. Crimes against humanity have been described by the Secretary-General in his Report (at paragraph 48) as those inhumane acts of a very serious nature committed as part of a widespread or systematic attack against any civilian population on national, political, ethnic, racial or religious grounds. The Statute then defines the jurisdiction of the International Tribunal over crimes against humanity in Article 5 of the Statute as follows:

> "The International Tribunal shall have the power to prosecute persons responsible for the following crimes when committed in armed conflict, whether international or internal in character, and directed against any civilian population:
>
> (a) murder; (b) extermination; (c) enslavement; (d) deportation; (e) imprisonment; (f) torture; (g) rape; (h) persecutions on political, racial and religious grounds; (i) other inhumane acts.

76. There is no question but that crimes against humanity form part of customary international law. They found expression in Article 6(c) of the Nuremberg Charter of 8 August 1945, Article II(l)(c) of Law No. 10 of the Control Council for Germany of 20 December 1945 and Article 5(c) of the Tokyo Charter of 26 April 1946, three major documents promulgated in the aftermath of World War II.

77. The Defence claims that "the Tribunal only has jurisdiction under Article 5 of the Statute if it involves crimes that have been committed in the execution of or in connection with an international armed conflict." It purports to find authority for this proposition requiring the existence of an armed conflict of an international nature in the Nuremberg Charter which, in its definition of crimes against humanity, spoke of inhumane acts committed "in execution of or in connection with any crime within the jurisdiction of the Tribunal …" and in the affirmation given to the principles of international law recognised by the Charter of the Nuremberg Tribunal and Judgement of the Tribunal in General Assembly resolution 95(1) of 1948. The Defence further contends that the broadening of the scope of Article 5 to crimes when committed in armed conflicts of an internal character offends the *nullum crimen* principle.

78. The Trial Chamber does not agree. The nexus in the Nuremberg Charter between crimes against humanity and the other two categories, crimes against peace and war crimes, was peculiar to the context of the Nuremberg Tribunal established specifically

"for the just and prompt trial and punishment of the major war criminals of the European Axis countries." (Nuremburg Charter, Article 1). As some of the crimes perpetrated by Nazi Germany were of such a heinous nature as to shock the conscience of mankind, it was decided to include crimes against humanity in order to enable the International Military Tribunal to try the major war criminals for the barbarous acts committed against German Jews, amongst others, who, as German nationals, were outside the protection of the laws of warfare which only prohibited violations involving the adversary or enemy populations. (See Antonio Cassese, International Law in a Divided World para. 169 (1986).)

79. That no nexus is required in customary international law between crimes against humanity and crimes against peace or war crimes is strongly evidenced by subsequent case law. The military tribunal established under Control Council Law No. 10 stated in the Einsatzgruppen case that:

> "Crimes against humanity are acts committed in the course of wholesale and systematic violation of life and liberty ... The International Military Tribunal, operating under the London Charter, declared that the Charter's provisions limited the Tribunal to consider only those crimes against humanity which were committed in the execution of or in connection with crimes against peace and war crimes. The Allied Control Council, in its Law No. 10, removed this limitation so that the present Tribunal has jurisdiction to try all crimes against humanity as long known and understood under the-general principles of criminal law." (4 Trials of War Criminals 499).

80. Further, the Special Rapporteur of the International Law Commission had this to say:

> "First linked to a state of belligerency ... the concept of crimes against humanity gradually came to be viewed as autonomous and is today quite separate from that of war crimes ... Crimes against humanity may be committed in time of war or in time of peace; war crimes can only be committed in time of war." (Seventh Report on the Draft Code of Crimes Against the Peace and Security of Mankind, [1989] 2 Yearbook of ILC, U.N. Doc., A/N/CN.4/SER. A/1986/Add. 1).

81. Finally, this view that crimes against humanity are autonomous is confirmed by the opus classicus on international law, Oppenheim's International Law, where special reference is made to the fact that crimes against humanity "are now generally regarded as a self-contained category, without the need for any formal link with war crimes ..." (R. Jennings and A. Watts, I Oppenheim's International Law 966 (1992)).

82. Even were it arguable that a nexus is required between crimes against humanity and war crimes, the element of internationality certainly forms no jurisdictional criterion because, as has been shown above, war crimes are prohibited under customary international law in armed conflicts both of an international and internal nature.

83. In conclusion, the Trial Chamber emphasises that the definition of Article 5 is in fact more restrictive than the general definition of crimes against humanity recognised by customary international law. The inclusion of the nexus with armed conflict in the article imposes a limitation on the jurisdiction of the International Tribunal and certainly can in no way offend the *nullum crimen* principle so as to bar the International Tribunal from trying the crimes enumerated therein. Because the language of Article 5 is clear, the crimes against humanity to be tried in the International Tribunal must have a nexus with an armed conflict, be it international or internal.

DISPOSITION The foregoing deals with the several objections to jurisdiction proper raised by the Defence as well as with the other objections not properly relating to jurisdiction but which instead put in issue the lawful creation and competence of the International Tribunal.

For the foregoing reasons, THE TRIAL CHAMBER, being seized of the Motion filed by the Defence, and PURSUANT TO RULE 72

HEREBY DISMISSES the motion insofar as it relates to primacy jurisdiction and subject-matter jurisdiction under Articles 2, 3 and 5 and otherwise decides it to be incompetent insofar as it challenges the establishment of the International Tribunal

HEREBY DENIES the relief sought by the Defence in its Motion on the Jurisdiction of the Tribunal.

/s/ Gabrielle Kirk McDonald, Presiding Judge

Dated this tenth day of August 1995

At The Hague

The Netherlands

[Seal of the Tribunal]

Notes

1. The article by Professor Paust concerning the Bangladesh experience was actually by Professors Paust and Blaustein, and other relevant pages include: 11 VAND. J. TRANS. L. at 2, 14–15, 28 n.101. On applicability of common article 3 breaches to the grave breach provisions of the Geneva Conventions, see also Paust, *Applicability of International Criminal Laws to Events in the Former Yugoslavia*, 9 AM. U. J. INT'L L. & POL. 499, 511–12 & ns.39–42 (1994); *but see* Theodor Meron, *International Criminalization of Internal Atrocities*, 89 AM. J. INT'L L. 554 (1995); and *see generally* Chapter Eight, Sections 1 & 2. On appeal, the majority of the judges in the Appeals Chamber of the ICT for the Former Yugoslavia decided that grave breach provisions do not cover violations of common Article 3. See Chapter Eight, Section 2 (decision of 2 Oct. 1995).

2. Most of the other conclusions of the Trial Chamber were affirmed on appeal in what became the first decision of the Appeals Chamber. The majority opinion of Judge Cassese used dictionary definitions of "jurisdiction" (a point of interest concerning a common or shared meaning), noted that it could not review the decisions of the Security Council as such although it could address its own creation and competence (Judge Li dissenting), decided that such issues were not barred by a political question doctrine, noted that Security Council powers have constitutional limits (especially in Article 24(2) of the U.N. Charter), noted that Articles 39 and 41 of the U.N. Charter provide the Security Council with a basis to set up the Tribunal, decided that the I.C.T. was established by law, decided (contrary to the Trial Chamber) that individuals have standing to raise the issue of jurisdictional primacy, decided that there is universal jurisdiction, decided by a vote of 4 to 1 (Judge Sidhwa dissenting) that the I.C.T. has subject matter jurisdiction, decided that under Article 3 the Statute of the Tribunal that the phrases laws of war and war crimes include violations of such law in internal armed conflicts (including common Article 3 of the Geneva Conventions, "the core of Additional Protocol II," and laws concerning certain tactics and weapons), decided that common Article 3 of the Geneva Conventions relates also to criminal responsibility, and decided that crimes against humanity can occur in times of relative peace and that such is "now a settled rule of customary in-

ternational law" (Cassese, *id.* at para. 141). Judge Li decided that the armed conflict is international in character (Li, *id.*, separate opinion, at paras. 14–19) but disagreed on the extent of Article 3 of the Statute of the Tribunal reach with respect to internal armed conflicts (*id.* at paras. 5–13). Judge Li dissented on the vote whether the Tribunal could address its own creation by the Security Council.

3. With respect to individual standing to address the issue of jurisdictional primacy, Judge Cassese's opinion (*id.* at para. 55) notes:

[After referring to *Eichmann* [concerning a lack of standing] and *United States v. Noriega*] "Authoritative as they may be, those pronouncements do not carry, in the field of international law, the weight which they may bring to bear upon national judiciaries. Dating back to a period when sovereignty stood as a sacrosanct and unassailable attribute of statehood, recently this concept has suffered progressive erosion at the hands of the more liberal focus at work in the democratic societies, particularly in the field of human rights."

4. Concerning limits to Security Council powers, recall Chapter Five, Section 5E.

5. Cases decided by the ICTY also appear in other chapters addressing, for example, war crimes, crimes against humanity, and genocide. For a general survey of trends in decision and developments, *see, e.g.,* Sean D. Murphy, *Process and Jurisprudence of the International Criminal Tribunal for the Former Yugoslavia*, 93 Am. J. Int'l L. 57 (1999); Kelly D. Askin, *Reflections on Some of the Most Significant Achievements of the ICTY*, 37 New England L. Rev. 903 (2003); Mark A. Drumbl, *Looking Up, Down and Across: The ICTY's Place in the International Legal Order*, 37 New England L. Rev. 1037 (2003); Leila Nadya Sadat, *The Legacy of the ICTY: The International Criminal Court*, 37 New England L. Rev. 1073 (2003); Michael P. Scharf, *The ICTY at Ten: A Critical Assessment of the Major Rulings on the International Criminal Tribunal Over the Past Decade: Foreword*, 37 New England L. Rev. 865 (2003). *See also* the multi-volume series entitled Annotated Leading Cases of International Criminal Tribunals (André Klip and Göran Sluiter, eds.).

6. On August 2, 2001, Trial Chamber I of the ICTY found former Bosnian Serb general Radislav Krstic guilty of genocide for his role in the systematic massacre of almost 8,000 Muslim men and boys in Srebrenica between the 13th and 19th of July 1995. The Chamber concluded that "the intent to kill all the Bosnian Muslim men of military age in Srebrenica constitutes an intent to destroy in part the Bosnian Muslim group within the meaning of Article 4 and therefore must be qualified as a genocide." *The Prosecutor v. Radislav Krstic*, IT-98-33 (Trial Chamber I, 2 August 2001), paras. 598–599. Ultimately, the Trial Chamber concluded that it was proven beyond all reasonable doubt that genocide, crimes against humanity and violations of the laws or customs of war were perpetrated against the Bosnian Muslims at the Srebrenica massacre, which is considered Europe's worst atrocity since World War II. Notably, this judgment was the ICTY's first conviction for genocide in connection with the Bosnian war. On April 19, 2004, the Appeals Chamber affirmed Krstic's conviction but reduced his sentence from forty-six years, as initially imposed by the Trial Chamber, to thirty-five years' imprisonment. *The Prosecutor v. Radislav Krstic*, IT-98-33-A (Appeals Chamber, 19 April 2004), para. 275.

7. On July 25, 1995, the ICTY indicted Generals Ratko Mladic and Radovan Karadzic for genocide as well as other crimes against humanity, including the 1995 Srebrenica massacre. These Serbian generals represent two of the highest level accused in terms of criminal responsibility, however, both remain at large and are the ICTY's most wanted fugitives. In 2001, former Yugoslav President Slobodan Milosevic was successfully brought before the ICTY to face charges. His trial was extensively covered by the media, and many crit-

icized the proceedings as too long. Following the close of the Prosecution's case and during the presentation of the defense's case, the proceedings were abruptly terminated on March 14, 2006, due the Milosevic's death on March 11, 2006. Milosevic was the first head of state to be tried for war crimes in an international court. For more commentary on the Milosevic trial, see Lawrence Douglas, *Justice denied at The Hague?; Milosevic's trial ends without a verdict, but history may not deem it a failure*, L.A. Times, Mar. 14, 2006, at 11; Molly Moore & Daniel Williams, *Milosevic Found Dead in Prison; Genocide Trial is Left Without a Final Judgment*, Wash. Post, Mar. 12, 2006, at A01; Michael P. Scharf, *The Legacy of the Milosevic Trial*, 37 New England L. Rev. 915 (2003); Marlise Simons, *The hoped-for legacy of the Milosevic trial; Letter from The Hague*, Int'l Herald Trib., Mar. 30, 2006, at 2.

B. ICT for Rwanda

U.N. S.C. Res. 955 (8 Nov. 1994)

[Read the Resolution and Annex, providing the Statute of the International Criminal Tribunal for Rwanda, in the Documents Supplement]

Notes

1. The seat of the ICTR is now in Arusha, Tanzania.

2. The case on jurisdictional competence of the ICTR similar to *Tadic* was The Prosecutor v. Joseph Kanyabashi, ICTR-96-15-T (June 1997).

3. For cases decided by the ICTR and other materials, see www.ictr.org/.

The Prosecutor of the Tribunal v. Georges Anderson Nderubumwe Rutaganda

Indictment, Case No. ICTR-96-3-I (12 Feb. 1996)

The Prosecutor of the International Criminal Tribunal for Rwanda, pursuant to his authority under Article 17 of the Statute of the Tribunal, charges:

GEORGES ANDERSON NDERUBUMWE RUTAGANDA

with GENOCIDE, CRIMES AGAINST HUMANITY and VIOLATIONS OF ARTICLE 3 COMMON TO THE GENEVA CONVENTIONS, as set forth below:

Background

1. On April 6, 1994, a plane carrying President Juvenal Habyarimana of Rwanda and President Cyprien Ntaryamira of Burundi crashed at Kigali airport, killing all on board. Following the deaths of the two Presidents, widespread killings having both political and ethnic dimensions, began in Kigali and spread to other parts of Rwanda.

The Accused

2. Georges RUTAGANDA, born in 1958 in Masango commune, Gitarama prefecture, was an agricultural engineer and businessman; he was general manager and proprietor of Rutaganda SARL. Georges RUTAGANDA was also a member of the National and Prefectoral Committees of the *Mouvement Republicain National pour le Developpement et la Democratie* (hereinafter, "MRND") and a shareholder of *Radio Television Libre des Mille*

Collines. On April 6, 1994, he was serving as the second vice president of the National Committee of the Interahamwe, the youth militia of the MRND.

General Allegations

3. Unless otherwise specified, all acts set forth in this indictment took place between 1 January 1994 and 31 December 1994 in the prefectures of Kigali and Gitarama, territory of Rwanda.

4. In each paragraph charging genocide, a crime recognized by Article 2 of the Statute of the Tribunal, the alleged acts were committed with intent to destroy, in whole or in part, a national, ethnical or racial group.

5. The victims in each paragraph charging genocide were members of a national, ethnical, racial or religious group.

6. In each paragraph charging crimes against humanity, crimes punishable by Article 3 of the Statute of the Tribunal, the alleged acts were committed as part of a widespread or systematic attack against a civilian population on political, ethnic or racial grounds.

7. At all times relevant to this indictment, a state of internal armed conflict existed in Rwanda.

8. The victims referred to in this indictment were, at all relevant times, persons taking no active part in the hostilities.

9. The accused is individually responsible for the crimes alleged in this indictment. Under Article 6(1) of the Statute of the Tribunal, individual criminal responsibility is attributable to one who plans, instigates, orders, commits or otherwise aids and abets in the planning, preparation or execution of any of the crimes referred to in Articles 2 to 4 of the Statute of the Tribunal.

Charges

10. On or about April 6, 1994, Georges RUTAGANDA distributed guns and other weapons to Interahamwe members in Nyarugenge commune, Kigali.

11. On or about April 10, 1994, Georges RUTAGANDA stationed Interahamwe members at a roadblock near his office at the "Amgar" garage in Kigali. Shortly after he left the area, the Interahamwe members started checking identity cards of people passing the roadblock. The Interahamwe members ordered persons with Tutsi identity cards to stand on one side of the road. Eight of the Tutsis were then killed. The victims included men, women and an infant who had been carried on the back of one of the women.

12. In April 1994, on a date unknown, Tutsis who had been separated at a roadblock in front of the Amgar garage were taken to Georges RUTAGANDA and questioned by him. He thereafter directed that these Tutsis be detained with others at a nearby building. Later, Georges RUTAGANDA directed men under his control to take 10 Tutsi detainees to a deep, open hole near the Amgar garage. On Georges RUTAGANDA's orders, his men killed the 10 Tutsis with machetes and threw their bodies into the hole.

13. From April 7 to April 11, 1994, thousands of unarmed Tutsi men, and women children and some unarmed Hutus sought refuge at the Ecole Technique Officielle ("ETO school") in Kicukiro sector, Kicukiro commune. The ETO school was considered a safe haven because Belgian soldiers, part of the United Nations Assistance Mission for Rwanda forces, were stationed there.

14. On or about April 11, 1994, immediately after the Belgians withdrew from the ETO school, members of the Rwandan armed forces, the gendarmerie and militia, including the Interahamwe, attacked the ETO school and, using machetes, grenades and guns, killed the people who had sought refuge there. The Interahamwe separated Hutus from Tutsis during the attack, killing the Tutsis. Georges RUTAGANDA participated in the attack at the ETO school, which resulted in the deaths of a large number of Tutsis.

15. The men, women and children who survived the ETO school attack were forcibly transferred by Georges RUTAGANDA, members of the Interahamwe and soldiers to a gravel pit near the primary school of Nyanza. Presidential Guard members awaited their arrival. More Interahamwe members converged upon Nyanza from many directions and surrounded the group of survivors.

16. On or about April 12, 1994, the survivors who were able to show that they were Hutu were permitted to leave the gravel pit. Tutsis who presented altered identity cards were immediately killed. Most of the remainder of the group were attacked and killed by grenades or shot to death. Those who tried to escape were attacked with machetes. Georges RUTAGANDA, among others, directed and participated in these attacks.

17. In April of 1994, on dates unknown, in Masango commune, Georges RUTAGANDA and others known to the Prosecutor conducted house-to-house searches for Tutsis and their families. Throughout these searches, Tutsis were separated from Hutus and taken to a river. Georges RUTAGANDA instructed the Interahamwe to track all the Tutsis and throw them into the river.

18. On or about April 28, 1994, Georges RUTAGANDA, together with Interahamwe members, collected residents from Kigali and detained them near the Amgar garage. Georges RUTAGANDA and the Interahamwe demanded identity cards from the detainees. A number of persons, including Emmanuel Kayitare, were forcibly separated from the group. Later that day, Emmanuel Kayitare attempted to flee from where he was being detained and Georges RUTAGANDA pursued him, caught him and struck him on the head with a machete and killed him.

19. In June 1994, on a date unknown, Georges RUTAGANDA ordered people to bury the bodies of victims in order to conceal his crimes from the international community.

Counts 1–2

(Genocide)

(Crimes Against Humanity)

By his acts in relation to the events described in paragraphs 10–19 Georges RUTA-GANDA committed:

> COUNT 1: GENOCIDE, punishable by Article 2(3)(a) of the Statute of the Tribunal; and
>
> COUNT 2: CRIMES AGAINST HUMANITY (extermination) punishable by Article 3(b) of the Statute of the Tribunal.

Counts 3–4

(Crimes Against Humanity)

(Violations of Article 3 common to the Geneva Conventions)

By his acts in relation to the killings at the ETO school, as described in paragraph 14, Georges RUTAGANDA committed:

COUNT 3: CRIMES AGAINST HUMANITY (murder) punishable by Article 3(a) of the Statute of the Tribunal; and

COUNT 4: VIOLATIONS OF ARTICLE 3 COMMON TO THE GENEVA CONVENTIONS, as incorporated by Article 4(a) (murder) of the Statute of the Tribunal.

Counts 5–6

(Crimes Against Humanity)

(Violations of Article 3 common to the Geneva Conventions)

By his acts in relation to the killings at the gravel pit in Nyanza, as described in paragraphs 15 and 16, Georges RUTAGANDA committed:

COUNT 5: CRIMES AGAINST HUMANITY (murder) punishable by Article 3(a) of the Statute of the Tribunal; and

COUNT 6: VIOLATIONS OF ARTICLE 3 COMMON TO THE GENEVA CONVENTIONS, as incorporated by Article 4(a) (murder) of the Statute of the Tribunal.

Counts 7–8

(Crimes Against Humanity)

(Violation of Article 3 common to the Geneva Conventions)

By killing Emmanuel Kayitare, as described in paragraph 18, Georges RUTAGANDA committed:

COUNT 7: CRIMES AGAINST HUMANITY (murder) punishable by Article 3(a) of the Statute of the Tribunal; and

COUNT 8: VIOLATION OF ARTICLE 3 COMMON TO THE GENEVA CONVENTIONS, as incorporated by Article 4(a) (murder) of the Statute of the Tribunal.

Richard J. Goldstone

Prosecutor

The Prosecutor of the Tribunal v. Jean Paul Akayesu

Indictment, Case No. ICTR-96-4-I (12 Feb. 1996)

The Prosecutor of the International Criminal Tribunal for Rwanda, pursuant to his authority under Article 17 of the Statute of the Tribunal, charges:

JEAN PAUL AKAYESU

with GENOCIDE, CRIMES AGAINST HUMANITY and VIOLATIONS OF ARTICLE 3 COMMON TO THE GENEVA CONVENTIONS, as set forth below:

Background

1. On April 6, 1994, a plane carrying President Juvenal Habyarimana of Rwanda and President Cyprien Ntaryamira of Burundi crashed at Kigali airport, killing all on board. Following the death of the two Presidents, widespread killings, having both political and ethnic dimensions, began in Kigali and spread to other parts of Rwanda.

2. Rwanda is divided into 11 prefectures, each of which is governed by a prefect. The prefectures are further subdivided into communes which are placed under the authority

of bourgmestres. The bourgmestre of each commune is appointed by the President of the Republic, upon the recommendation of the Minister of the Interior. In Rwanda, the bourgmestre is the most powerful figure in the commune. His *de facto* authority in the area is significantly greater than that which is conferred upon him *de jure*.

The Accused

3. Jean Paul AKAYESU, born in 1953 in Murehe sector, Taba commune, served as bourgmestre of that commune from April 1993 until June 1994. Prior to his appointment as bourgmestre, he was a teacher and school inspector in Taba.

4. As bourgmestre, Jean Paul AKAYESU was charged with the performance of executive functions and the maintenance of public order within his commune, subject to the authority of the prefect. He had exclusive control over the communal police, as well as any gendarmes put at the disposition of the commune. He was responsible for the execution of laws and regulations and the administration of justice, also subject only to the prefect's authority.

General Allegations

5. Unless otherwise specified, all acts and omissions set forth in this indictment took place between 1 January 1994 and 31 December 1994, in the commune of Taba, prefecture of Gitarama, territory of Rwanda.

6. In each paragraph charging genocide, a crime recognized by Article 2 of the Statute of the Tribunal, the alleged acts or omissions were committed with intent to destroy, in whole or in part a national, ethnical or racial group.

7. The victims in each paragraph charging genocide were members of a national, ethnical, racial or religious group.

8. In each paragraph charging crimes against humanity, crimes recognized by Article 3 of the Tribunal Statute, the alleged acts or omissions were committed as part of a widespread or systematic attack against a civilian population on national, political, ethnic or racial grounds.

9. At all times relevant to this indictment, a state of internal armed conflict existed in Rwanda.

10. The victims referred to in this indictment were, at all relevant times, persons not taking an active part in the hostilities.

11. The accused is individually responsible for the crimes alleged in this indictment. Under Article 6(1) of the Statute of the Tribunal, individual criminal responsibility is attributable to one who plans, instigates, orders, commits or otherwise aids and abets in the planning preparation or execution of any of the crimes referred to in Articles 2 to 4 of the Statute of the Tribunal.

Charges

12. As bourgmestre, Jean Paul AKAYESU was responsible for maintaining law and public order in his commune. At least 2000 Tutsis were killed in Taba between April 7 and the end of June 1994, while he was still in power. The killings in Taba were openly committed and so widespread that, as bourgmestre, Jean Paul AKAYESU must have known about them. Although he had the authority and responsibility to do so, Jean Paul Akayesu never attempted to prevent the killing of Tutsis in the commune in any way or called for assistance from regional or national authorities to quell the violence.

13. On or about 19 April 1994, before dawn, in Gishyeshye sector, Taba commune, a group of men, one of whom was named Francois Ndimubanzi, killed a local teacher, Syl-

vere Karera, because he was accused of associating with the Rwandan Patriotic Front ("RPF") and plotting to kill Hutus. Even though at least one of the perpetrators was turned over to Jean Paul AKAYESU, he failed to take measures to have him arrested.

14. The morning of April 19, 1994, following the murder of Sylvere Karera, Jean Paul AKAYESU led a meeting in Gishyeshye sector at which he sanctioned the death of Sylvere Karera and urged the population to eliminate accomplices of the RPF, which was understood by those present to mean Tutsis. Over 100 people were present at the meeting. The killing of Tutsis in Taba began shortly after the meeting.

15. At the same meeting in Gishyeshye sector on April 19, 1994, Jean Paul AKAYESU named at least three prominent Tutsis—Ephrem Karangwa, Juvenal Rukundakuvuga and Emmanuel Sempabwa—who had to be killed because of their alleged relationships with the RPF. Later that day, Juvenal Rukundakuvuga was killed in Kanyinya. Within the next few days, Emmanuel Sempabwa was clubbed to death in front of the Taba *bureau communal*.

16. Jean Paul AKAYESU, on or about April 19, 1994, conducted house-to-house searches in Taba. During these searches, residents, including Victim V, were interrogated and beaten with rifles and stocks in the presence of Jean Paul AKAYESU. Jean Paul AKAYESU personally threatened to kill the husband and child of Victim U if she did not provide him with information about the activities of the Tutsis he was seeking.

17. On or about April 19, 1994, Jean Paul AKAYESU ordered the interrogation and bearing of Victim X in an effort to learn the whereabouts of Ephrem Karangwa. During the beating, Victim X's fingers were broken as he tried to shield himself from blows with a metal stick.

18. On or about April 19, 1994, the men who, on Jean Paul AKAYESU's instructions, were searching for Ephrem Karangwa destroyed Ephrem Karangwa's house and burned down his mother's house. They then went to search the house of Ephrem Karangwa's brother-in-law in Musambira commune and found Ephrem Karangwa's three brothers there. The three brothers—Simon Mutijima, Thaddee Uwanyiligira and Jean Chrysostome Gakuba—tried to escape, but Jean Paul AKAYESU blew his whistle to alert local residents to the attempted escape and ordered the people to capture the brothers. After the brothers were captured, Jean Paul AKAYESU ordered and participated in the killings of the three brothers.

19. On or about April 19, 1994, Jean Paul AKAYESU took 8 detained men from the Taba *bureau communal* and ordered militia members to kill them. The militia killed them with clubs, machetes, small axes and sticks. The victims had fled from Runda commune and had been held by Jean Paul AKAYESU.

20. On or about April 19, 1994, Jean Paul AYAKESU ordered the local people and militia to kill intellectual and influential people. Five teachers from the secondary school of Taba were killed on his instructions. The victims were Theogene, Phoebe Uwineze and her fiancé (whose name is unknown), Tharcisse Twizeyumuremye and Samuel. The local people and militia killed them with machetes and agricultural tools in front of the Taba *bureau communal*.

21. On or about April 20, 1994, Jean Paul AKAYESU and some communal police went to the house of Victim Y, a 68 year old woman. Jean Paul AKAYESU interrogated her about the whereabouts of the wife of university teacher. During the questioning, under Jean Paul AKAYESU's supervision, the communal police hit Victim Y with a gun and sticks. They bound her arms and legs and repeatedly kicked her in the chest. Jean Paul AKAYESU threatened to kill her if she failed to provide the information he sought.

22. Later that night, on or about April 20, 1994, Jean Paul AKAYESU picked up Victim W in Taba and interrogated her also about the whereabouts of the wife of the university teacher. When she stated she did not know, he forced her to lay on the road in front of his car and threatened to drive over her.

23. Thereafter, on or about April 20, 1994, Jean Paul AKAYESU picked up Victim Z in Taba and interrogated him. During the interrogation, men under Jean Paul AKAYESU's authority forced Victims Z and Y to beat each other and used a piece of Victim Y's dress to strangle Victim Z.

Counts 1–3

(Genocide)

(Crimes Against Humanity)

By his acts in relation to the events described in paragraphs 12–23 Jean Paul AKAYESU is criminally responsible for:

> COUNT 1: GENOCIDE, punishable by Article 2(3)(a) of the Statute of the Tribunal;
>
> COUNT 2: Complicity in GENOCIDE, punishable by Article 2(3)(e) of the Statute of the Tribunal; and
>
> COUNT 3: CRIMES AGAINST HUMANITY (extermination) punishable by Article 3(b) of the Statute of the Tribunal.

Count 4

(Incitement to Genocide)

By his acts in relation to the events described in paragraphs 14 and 15, Jean Paul AKAYESU is criminally responsible for:

> COUNT 4: Direct and Public Incitement to Commit GENOCIDE, punishable by Article 2(3)(c) of the Statute of the Tribunal.

Counts 5–6

(Crimes Against Humanity)

(Violations of Article 3 common to the Geneva Conventions)

By his acts in relation [to] the murders of Juvenal Rukundakuvuga, Emmanuel Sempabwa, Simon Mutijima, Thaddee Uwanyiligira and Jean Chrysostome Gakuba, as described in paragraphs 15 and 18, Jean Paul AKAYESU committed:

> COUNT 5: CRIMES AGAINST HUMANITY (murder) punishable by Article 3(a) of the Statute of the Tribunal; and
>
> COUNT 6: VIOLATIONS OF ARTICLE 3 COMMON TO THE GENEVA CONVENTIONS, as incorporated by Article 4(a) (murder) of the Statute of the Tribunal.

Counts 7–8

(Crimes Against Humanity)

(Violations of Article 3 common to the Geneva Conventions)

By his acts in relation the murders of 8 detained men in front of the *bureau communal* as described in paragraph 19, Jean Paul AKAYESU committed:

> COUNT 7: CRIMES AGAINST HUMANITY (murder) punishable by Article 3(a) of the Statute of the Tribunal; and

COUNT 8: VIOLATIONS OF ARTICLE 3 COMMON TO THE GENEVA CON-
VENTIONS, as incorporated by Article 4(a) (murder) of the Statute of
the Tribunal.

Counts 9–10

(Crimes Against Humanity)

(Violations of article 3 common to the Geneva Conventions)

By his acts in relation [to] the murders of 5 teachers in front of the *bureau communal*
as described in paragraph 20, Jean Paul AKAYESU committed:

COUNT 9: CRIMES AGAINST HUMANITY (murder) punishable by Article 3(a)
of the Statute of the Tribunal; and

COUNT 10: VIOLATIONS OF ARTICLE 3 COMMON TO THE GENEVA CON-
VENTIONS, as incorporated by Article 4(a) (murder) of the Statute of
the Tribunal.

Counts 11–12

(Crimes Against Humanity)

(Violations of Article 3 common to the Geneva Conventions)

By his acts in relation [to] the beatings of Victims U, V, W, X, Y and Z as described in
paragraphs 16, 17, 21, 22 and 23, Jean Paul AKAYESU committed:

COUNT 11: CRIMES AGAINST HUMANITY (torture), punishable by Article 3(f)
of the Statute of the Tribunal; and

COUNT 12: VIOLATIONS OF ARTICLE 3 COMMON TO THE GENEVA CON-
VENTIONS, as incorporated by Article 4(a) (cruel treatment) of the Statute
of the Tribunal.

Richard Goldstone

Prosecutor

Notes

1. Rutaganda and Akayesu were convicted in 1999 and 1998. See also *The Prosecutor
v. Akayesu* in Chapter Ten. Portions of the opinions in these cases appear also in other chapters, *e.g.*, on war crimes, genocide, crimes against humanity.

2. Concerning the Indictment of Rutaganda and trial of persons on "cumulative charges,"
consider:

The Prosecutor v. Rutaganda

Trial Chamber, ICTR-96-3-T (6 Dec. 1999)

Before: Judge Laïty Kama, Presiding

Judge Lennart Aspegren

Judge Navanethem Pillay

109. The Chamber notes, first of all, that the principle of cumulative charges was applied by the Nuremberg Tribunal, especially regarding war crimes and crimes against humanity.

110. Regarding especially the concurrence of the various crimes covered under the Statute, the Chamber, in the *Akayesu Judgement*, the first case brought before this Tribunal, considered the matter and held that:

"[…]it is acceptable to convict the accused of two offences in relation to the same set of facts in the following circumstances: (1) where the offences have different elements; or (2) where the previous creating the offences protect different interests; or (3) where it is necessary to record a conviction for both offences in order fully to describe what the accused did. However, the Chamber finds that it is not justifiable to convict an accused of two offences in relation to the same set of facts where (a) one offence is a lesser included offence of the other, […]or (b) where one offence charges accomplice liability and the other offence charges liability as […]".

111. Trial Chamber II of the Tribunal, in its *Kayishema and Ruzindana Judgement*, endorsed the afore-mentioned test of concurrence of crimes and found that it is only acceptable:

"(1) where offences have differing elements, or (2) where the laws in question protect differing social interests."

112. Trial Chamber II ruled that the cumulative charges in the *Kayishema and Ruzindana Judgement* in particular were legally improper and untenable. It found that all elements including the *mens rea* element requisite to show genocide, "extermination" and "murder" in the particular case were the same, and the evidence relied upon to prove the crimes were the same. Furthermore, in the opinion of Trial Chamber II, the protected social interests were also the same. Therefore, it held that the Prosecutor should have charged the Accused in the alternative.

113. Judge Tafazzal H. Khan, one of the Judges sitting in Trial Chamber II to consider the said case, dissented on the issue of cumulative charges. Relying on consistent jurisprudence he pointed out that the Chamber should have placed less emphasis on the overlapping elements of the cumulative crimes.

"What must be punished is culpable conduct; this principle applies to situations where the conduct offends two or more crimes, whether or not the factual situation also satisfies the distinct elements of the two or more crimes, as proven."

114. In his dissenting opinion, the Judge goes on to emphasized that the full assessment of charges and the pronouncement of guilty verdicts are important in order to reflect the totality of the accused's culpable conduct.

"[…]where the culpable conduct was part of a widespread and systematic attack specifically against civilians, to record a conviction for genocide alone does not reflect the totality of the accused's culpable conduct. Similarly, if the Majority had chosen to convict for extermination alone instead of genocide, the verdict would still fail to adequately capture the totality of the accused's conduct."

115. This Chamber fully concurs with the dissenting opinion thus entered. It notes that this position, which endorses the principle of cumulative charges, also finds support in various decisions rendered by the ICTY. In the case of the *Prosecutor v. Zoran Kupreskic and others*, the Trial Chamber of ICTY in its decision on Defence challenges to form of the indictment held that:

"The Prosecutor may be justified in bringing cumulative charges when the articles of the Statute referred to are designed to protect different values and when each article requires proof of a legal element not required by the others."

116. Furthermore, the Chamber holds that offences covered under the Statute—genocide, crimes against humanity and violations of Article 3 common to Geneva Conventions

and of Additional Protocol II—have disparate ingredients and, especially, that their punishment is aimed at protecting discrete interests. As a result, multiple offenses may be charged on the basis of the same acts, in order to capture the full extent of the crimes committed by an accused.

Section 10
The Statute of the International Criminal Court

In 1948, the United Nations General Assembly invited the International Law Commission (ILC) "to study the desirability and possibility of establishing an international judicial organ for the trial of persons charged with genocide or other crimes over which jurisdiction will be conferred upon that organ by international conventions."[1] After considering the matter, the ILC concluded that the establishment of such an organ was both desirable and possible. As a result, in 1950, the General Assembly set up a Committee on International Criminal Jurisdiction consisting of representatives of seventeen member states.[2] The Committee was charged with preparing concrete proposals on the establishment of an international criminal court that could administer the Code of Crimes Against the Peace and Security of Mankind, which the International Law Commission was simultaneously drafting. The Committee submitted a draft statute in 1951, which was amended by a Second Committee in 1953.[3]

The 1953 Draft Statute was permanently shelved due to the absence of an internationally accepted definition of the crime of "aggression" and the resulting inability to complete the Draft Code of Crimes Against the Peace and Security of Mankind, which was to define the subject matter jurisdiction of the International Criminal Court.[4] The General Assembly adopted a definition of "aggression" in 1974, but it would be almost twenty years before the United Nations would return to the project of creating an international criminal court.[5] There are several reasons why the initial efforts of the United Nations to

---

1. The International Law Commission was established by the General Assembly in 1947 pursuant to its obligation to encourage the codification and progressive development of international law under Article 13, paragraph 1 of the United Nations Charter. The ILC consists of 34 members who are persons of recognized competence in international law. The members are elected by the General Assembly bearing in mind the need to ensure representation of the principal legal systems of the world. *See* United Nations, *The Work of the International Law Commission* 4, 28 (4th ed. 1988).

2. Draft Statute for an International Criminal Court (Annex to the Report of the Committee on International Criminal Jurisdiction), 7 U.N. GAOR, Supp. No. 11, at 21, U.N. Doc. A/2136 (1952).

3. Revised Draft Statute for an International Criminal Court (Annex to the Report of the Committee on International Criminal Jurisdiction), 7 U.N. GAOR, Supp. No. 12, at 23, U.N. Doc. A/2645 (1954). *See* Leila Sadat Wexler, *The Proposed Permanent International Criminal Court: An Appraisal*, 29 CORNELL INT'L L. J. 665 (1996).

4. *See* Report of the Int'l Law Comm'n, 42nd Sess., May 1, 1990–July 28, 1990, 45 U.N. GAOR, Supp. No. 10, at 40, U.N. Doc. A/45/10 (1990).

5. *See* Michael Scharf, *The Jury is Still Out on the Need for an International Criminal Court*, 1 DUKE J. INT'L & COMP. L. 135, 139–40 (1991). During this period, a number of other draft statutes for an international criminal court were proposed. In 1981, the U.N. Human Rights Commission proposed a draft Statute for the Establishment of an International Criminal Jurisdiction to Implement the International Convention on the Suppression and Punishment of the Crime of Apartheid. *Id.* In 1982, the International Law Association adopted a Draft Statute for an International Criminal Court at its conference in Montreal. REPORT OF THE INT'L LAW ASSOC., 60TH CONFERENCE, MONTREAL, AUG. 29, 1982 TO SEPT. 4, 1982 (1983). In June of 1990, a Committee of Experts headed by M. Cherif Bassiouni meeting in Siracusa, Italy, adopted a Draft Statute for an International Criminal Tribunal, which is published in M.C. Bassiouni, *A Comprehensive Strategic Approach on International Cooperation for*

create an international criminal court never got off the ground. First, since World War II, there has not been a repeat of the unique circumstances that made the Nuremberg and Tokyo Tribunals possible; that is, there have been no wars in which a coalition broadly supported by other members of the international community has defeated an aggressor and violator of the laws of war and humanity so decisively as to bring about its complete defeat and subjugation. Second, an international criminal court whose goals included the punishment of aggressive warfare was seen in the context of the cold war as a threat to national sovereignty.[6] For the major powers, in particular, the power to review the legitimacy of the use force or to supersede the criminal jurisdiction of national courts was more than they were willing to cede. Finally, the formulation of the United Nations Draft Statute for an International Criminal Court in 1953 had the paradoxical effect of setting back the effort to create such a court. Once the document was drafted, the debate shifted from whether to establish an international criminal court to whether to adopt the 1953 Draft Statute, which was extremely ambitious in the powers it conferred on the court with respect to states. In addition, the Draft Statute was tied inextricably to the Draft Code of Crimes Against the Peace and Security of Mankind, which was strongly opposed by many countries.[7]

With the end of the cold war in the late 1980s, the United Nations returned to its project to create a permanent international criminal court. In 1989, the issue was reintroduced in the agenda of the General Assembly at the urging of a coalition of sixteen Caribbean and Latin American nations led by Trinidad and Tobago, who saw such a court as a way to solve the difficulties which they encounter in prosecuting or extraditing narco-terrorists.[8] The General Assembly acted on the Trinidadian initiative by requesting the International Law Commission to study the issue and report back with its recommendations.

As requested, at the completion of its forty-second session in 1990, the ILC submitted an interim report to the General Assembly on the issue of establishing an international criminal court.[9] The report surveys previous international efforts concerning the establishment of an international criminal court, and contains a cursory discussion of some of the potential benefits and obstacles to establishing such a court. The interim report was primarily devoted to identifying various issues, namely: (1) the jurisdiction and competence of the court; (2) the structure of the court; (3) the legal force of the court's judgments; (4) other questions relating to, *inter alia*, penalties, implementation of judgments and financing; and (5) possible international trial mechanisms other than an international tribunal.

The General Assembly responded to the interim report by requesting the ILC to further consider the issues raised and to make concrete proposals for resolving them.[10] To this end, during its forty-third session, the ILC formed a working group on the question of

---

the Prevention, Control and Suppression of International and Transnational Criminality, 15 Nova L. Rev. 354 (1991).

6. *See* Robert Rosenstock, *Symposium: Should there be an International Tribunal for Crimes Against Humanity,* 6 Pace Int'l L. Rev. 84 (1994); Benjamin B. Ferencz, *An International Criminal Code and Court: Where They Stand and Where They're Going,* 30 Colum. J. Trans. L. 383–384 (1992).

7. *See* M.C. Bassiouni, *Commentaries on the International Law Commission's 1991 Draft Code of Crimes Against the Peace and Security of Mankind* (1993); *United States Report on the ILC Draft Code of Crimes, reprinted in* 87 Am. J. Int'l L. 607 (1993).

8. See U.N. G.A Res. 44/39, 44 UN GAOR, Supp. No. 49, at 1, U.N. Doc. A/44/49 (1989).

9. *See* United Nations Int'l Law Comm'n Report of the International Law Commission on the Work of its Forty-Second Session: Topical Summary of the Discussion Held in the Sixth Committee, paras. 119–156, U.N. Doc. A/CN.4/L.456 (1991).

10. G.A. Res. 46/54 (1992).

an international criminal jurisdiction, chaired by Abdul Koroma of Sierra Leone. The Working Group produced a more detailed point-by-point analysis of the key issues, in some cases with recommended resolutions and in others with a choice of options.[11] The Report of the Working Group greatly refined the ILC's earlier conception of an international criminal court.[12] The Working Group recommended that the court should be a "flexible and supplementary facility" for states parties to its statute and that it should not have exclusive jurisdiction.[13] As so envisioned, the court would provide a third alternative for states currently faced with only two choices when international criminals are found within their territory—to prosecute the individuals or to extradite them to another state. Parties to the Court's statute would select from a list of international offenses those for which they would be bound to provide assistance to the Court. The Court would not be a full-time body, but rather an established structure which could be called into operation when required. On the basis of the Working Group's proposals, on November 25, 1992, the General Assembly adopted by consensus a resolution calling on the International Law Commission to formally draft a statute for an International Criminal Court "as a matter of urgency."[14]

The steps taken by the Security Council to address the war crimes and other atrocities committed in the former Yugoslavia added a new significance and a sense of urgency to the efforts of the General Assembly to create a permanent international criminal court.[15] The Security Council's establishment of the Yugoslavia Tribunal in May 1993 removed any question as to the political and legal feasibility of creating an international criminal court in the latter half of the twentieth century. Most of the complex legal and practical issues that had been identified as barriers to a permanent international criminal court had been successfully met by the Secretary-General's draft statute, adopted by the Security Council, which had been based on the views and proposals of various states and organizations. Thus, the members of the international community were hard pressed to find any justification for continuing to delay the creation of a permanent court.

At its forty-fifth session, in 1993, the International Law Commission reconvened its Working Group on an international criminal court which, borrowing liberally from the Statute of the newly-established Yugoslavia Tribunal, completed a preliminary 67-article draft statute for a permanent court.[16] At its forty-sixth session, in 1994, the Working Group, under the chairmanship of James Crawford of Australia, refined the draft statute, consisting of 60 articles and an annex enumerating treaty crimes over which the Court would have jurisdiction.[17] Thereafter, the International Law Commission submitted the statute to the General Assembly for consideration, and recommended that an international conference

---

11. Report of the Working Group on the question of an international criminal jurisdiction, *Report of the Int'l Law Comm'n, 44th Sess., May 4, 1992–July 24, 1992*, 47 U.N. GAOR, Supp. No. 10, annex, at 143, U.N. Doc. A/47/10 (1992).

12. *Id.*

13. *Id.* at 162.

14. G.A. Res. 47/33 (November 25, 1992), U.N. Doc. A/47/584. For a discussion of the debate which led to the adoption of this resolution, *see* Virginia Morris & Christianne Bourloyannis, *The Work of the Sixth Committee at the Forty-seventh Session of the UN General Assembly*, 87 Am. J. Int'l L. 306, 314 (1993).

15. Paul D. Marquardt, *Law Without Borders: The Constitutionality of An International Criminal Court*, 33 Colum. J. Trans. L. 73, 92 (1995).

16. *See* Report of the International Law Commission on the Work of its Forty-fifth Session, 48 U.N. GAOR, Supp. No. 10, at 258, U.N. Doc. A/48/10 (1993).

17. *See* Report of the International Law Commission on the Work of its Forty-sixth Session, 49 U.N. GAOR, Supp. No. 10, U.N. Doc. A/49/10 (1994).

be convened to adopt the statute in the form of a treaty.[18] The draft that was submitted represented a compromise between those who would have gone much further, and those who felt that nothing should be done at all.[19]

The final Statute of the International Criminal Court was adopted at a conference in Rome in 1998.[20] Read the Statute of the ICC, in the Documents Supplement.

As Professor Sadat explains, the negotiation and adoption of the International Criminal Court Statute worked an "uneasy revolution" in international law. *See* Leila Nadya Sadat & S. Richard Carden, *The New International Criminal Court: An Uneasy Revolution*, 88 GEORGETOWN L. J. 381 (2000). Consider the following description of the conference.

Leila Nadya Sadat, The International Criminal Court and the Transformation of International Law: Justice for the New Millennium
1–8 (2002)*

From June 15 through July 17, 1998, representatives of 160 countries, closely watched by 250 non-governmental organizations (NGOs), met in Rome to negotiate a Treaty that would establish a permanent international criminal court. The weather was hot, the mood alternated between exhilaration and anxiety, the work was hard. Issues that had been debated for more than two years during the Preparatory Committee meetings leading up to the Rome Conference remained on the table unresolved. The starting point of the negotiations was a complex consolidated text containing 116 articles, including some 1300 phrases in brackets. It was extremely difficult to read, let alone understand.

The Conference was held in the United Nations Food and Agricultural Organization building (*la FAO* in Italian), a large, rather plebeian structure from the Mussolini period, with a splendid view of *Il Palatino* from the top floor terrace. Colorful flags surrounding the building flew high under a brilliant blue sky, as each delegation and many individuals who had been involved in the task of establishing a permanent international criminal court made moving speeches at the opening Plenary Sessions.... Delegates shuttled back and forth between Committee of the Whole meetings, Working Group meetings, and informal consultations, feverishly trying to complete the Statute in the time allotted, while NGO representatives observed, discussed and participated in the negotiations from their Headquarters in the *FAO's* aptly named Sudan room.

As is by now well-known, after five weeks of grueling negotiations, the Diplomatic Conference adopted a Statute for the Court in an emotional vote of 120 to 7, with 21 countries abstaining. The United States, whose delegation was instrumental in the development of the Statute throughout the Preparatory Committee meetings and the Rome Conference, was one of the seven countries voting against the Treaty.[1]

---

18. *Id.*

19. Sadat, *supra* note 3, at 726.

20. For information concerning the formation of the "Rome" Statute or treaty at the Rome Conference and various views and proposals during the sessions, *see, e.g.,* M. Cherif Bassiouni, *Negotiating the Treaty of Rome on the Establishment of an International Criminal Court*, 32 CORNELL INT'L L.J. 443 (1999). *See also* LEILA NADYA SADAT, THE INTERNATIONAL CRIMINAL COURT AND THE TRANSFORMATION OF INTERNATIONAL LAW: JUSTICE FOR THE NEW MILLENNIUM (2002).

* Copyright © 2002 by Transnational Publishers, Inc. Reproduced with permission of Transnational Publishers, Inc.

1. *Id.* at 32 n.156. The United States requested the vote. Because it was unrecorded, it is unclear which States voted no, in addition to the United States, although China, India, Iraq, Israel, Libya,

The adoption of the International Criminal Court Statute is the culmination of a Century of hard work and false starts. As the Preamble to the Treaty notes, the purpose of the Court is to end impunity for the perpetrators of "atrocities that deeply shock the conscience of humanity." ...

Given the unsuccessful history of previous efforts to establish an international criminal court, and the tepid support of many of the major powers during the Preparatory Committee meetings leading up to the Diplomatic Conference, the adoption of the Statute by the Diplomatic Conference came as a surprise. It can be credited, at least in part, to the enormous lobbying and informational efforts of NGOs, which conducted a tireless campaign in support of the Court and came together in a new example of global civil society.... The NGO movement was able to amass its strength through the formation of a coalition, the Coalition for an International Criminal Court (CICC), that originated under the auspices of the World Federalist Movement and ultimately grew from 30 to 800 NGOs from all over the world. The CICC was able to influence the treaty-making process substantially, particularly as it came to form an alliance with the so-called "like-minded" States. This group of States, although individually holding quite divergent views on many issues, were united in their view that the Court's ultimate establishment was a priority, and emerged as an important component of the Conference's ultimate success. Finally, strong support from many European countries and other traditional U.S. allies rallied the West behind the Court despite the opposition of the United States....

The International Criminal Court is the last great international institution of the Twentieth Century. It is no exaggeration to suggest that its establishment could reshape our thinking about international law. For if many aspects of the Rome Treaty demonstrate the tenacity of traditional Westphalian notions of State sovereignty, there are nonetheless elements of supranationalism and efficacy in the Statute that could prove extremely powerful. Not only does the Statute place State and non-State actors side-by-side in the international arena, but the Court will put real people in real jails. Indeed, the establishment of the Court raises hopes that the lines between international law on the one hand, and world order, on the other, are blurring and that the normative structure being created by international law might one day influence or even restrain the Hobbesian order established by the politics of States....

The overwhelming vote of the delegates to the Diplomatic Conference to approve the ICC Treaty opened a window to the future. The substantive law, institutional structure, procedures and foundations of the Court establish an extraordinarily rich and complex legal regime. Indeed, it is arguable that the contribution that the Statute and its adoption have made and will make to international law is separate from the question whether the Court is ultimately successful.... Yet the Revolution wrought by the Diplomatic Conference was in no sense an easy one, and the political will that carried the day in Rome must be translated into financial and logistical support if the Court is to succeed.... The journey from the Hague to Rome was long and arduous; it is to be hoped that the journey back to the Hague will be shorter, less encumbered, and ultimately successful....

Notes and Questions

1. A major difference between the permanent ICC and the ad hoc ICTs for Yugoslavia and Rwanda concerns the method of establishment. Unlike the ad hoc tribunals that were

---

Qatar, and Yemen are among the most likely candidates, according to discussions with delegates and observers at the time.

created by the Security Council under the U.N. Charter, the ICC is established by a separate multilateral treaty. Also, in contrast to the ad hoc tribunals, whose orders can be ignored only at the peril of risking Security Council sanctions, the obligations of states with respect to the ICC are created by the Statute of the ICC and apply directly only to states parties thereto except when the Court is activated per terms of the Statute by the Security Council acting under Chapter VII of the Charter.

2. Under the ILC Draft Statute, the subject matter jurisdiction of the permanent court could have extended to crimes under customary international law, namely genocide, other crimes against humanity, war crimes, and aggression, as well as the fourteen other crimes defined by or pursuant to the treaties listed in the draft annex (many of which also reflect custom or may subsequently develop into customary law). The scope of the Court's jurisdiction had been a matter of contention between the members of the international community, and the United States had taken the position that the Court's jurisdiction should be limited to war crimes, genocide, and crimes against humanity. *See generally, Comments Received Pursuant to Paragraph 4 of General Assembly Resolution 49/53 on the Establishment of an International Criminal Court, Report of the Secretary-General,* U.N. Doc. A/AC.244/1/Add.2, 31 March 1995, at 7–29 (Comments of the Government of the United States of America on Draft Articles for a Statute of an International Criminal Court, March 30, 1995). Why do you think the United States had favored such a significantly limited subject matter jurisdiction for the Court? Is such preferable?

What crimes are now within the jurisdiction of the ICC? See Articles 5–8, 10, 21, 22(2) and (3), 121. When studying Chapters Eight-Nine, consider whether ICC jurisdiction over war crimes and crimes against humanity is limited or expanded in any way by the ICC Statute.

3. In terms of ICC jurisdiction over persons, must the state of nationality of the accused ratify the treaty? Recall Chapter Three, Sections 1 and 2. See Articles 12–15, 17–18, 89–90, 98 of the Statute of the ICC; Paust, *The Reach of ICC Jurisdiction Over Non-Signatory Nationals,* 33 Vand. J. Trans. L. 1 (2000); Michael P. Scharf, *The ICC's Jurisdiction over the Nationals of Non-Party States: A Critique of the U.S. Position,* 64 L. & Contemp. Probs. 67 (2001); Johan D. van der Vyver, *Prosecution and Punishment of the Crime of Genocide,* 23 Fordham Int'l L.J. 286, 337–39, 346, 354 (1999). If the state of nationality has not ratified, what state must under Article 12(1) and (2)? Can the Prosecutor initiate an investigation *proprio motu* or if a case is referred to the Prosecutor by the U.N. Security Council? See Article 13(b)-(c). If neither the state of nationality of the accused nor the state on whose territory an alleged crime has occurred have ratified the treaty, can the Prosecutor proceed with an investigation if the Security Council has referred the matter to the Prosecutor? See Article 13(b).

4. The United States had once taken the position that the Court's jurisdiction over a particular situation should be triggered only by a decision of the Security Council. *Comments Received Pursuant to Paragraph 4 of General Assembly Resolution 49/53 on the Establishment of an International Criminal Court, Report of the Secretary-General,* U.N. Doc. A/AC.244/1/Add.2, 31 March 1995, at 7–29. Why do you think the United States favored such a requirement? Why might other states have opposed this approach? *See also* Bassiouni, *Negotiating the Treaty of Rome, supra.*

5. Textwriters have noted early progress with respect to ICC efforts in 2005. Consider: "As of April 2005, the ICC had been authorized to investigate cases from Central African Republic, Democratic Republic of Congo, Ivory Coast, and the Republic of Uganda. The Uganda referral stemmed from the civil war in northern Uganda that has led to 100,000

dead and 1,500,000 refugees. In February 2005, a spokesperson for the Court announced that arrests warrants would issue for up to a dozen suspects, which would be the first arrest warrants issued by the Court."

"A defining moment for the Court also involved alleged war crimes committed during the crisis in Darfur, Sudan. Reports exist of indiscriminate attacks by Sudanese government forces and militias (including the killing of civilians, genocide, torture, enforced disappearances, destruction of villages, rape and other forms of sexual violence, pillaging and forced displacement) which have produced some 300,000 deaths and left some 2,000,000 persons homeless. A U.N. commission released a report in early 2005 identifying 51 suspects (including members of the Sudanese government) and explaining the evidence against them. In February 2005, Louise Arbour, the U.N. High Commissioner for Human Rights, emphasized that such crimes must be referred to the ICC, explaining that '[t]here is no hope for sustainable peace in Darfur without immediate access to justice.' U.N. Secretary-General Kofi Annan added that '[i]t is vital that these crimes are not left unpunished.' However, the Bush Administration, because of domestic opposition to the ICC, took a different view and advocated the creation of an *ad hoc* international court for Darfur to be established in Arusha, Tanzania (where the ICTR Trial Chambers operate). China and Algeria took a third view, opposing international adjudication, and arguing that Sudan's own courts should try those who have been implicated. In the face of a united European view favoring referral of these cases to the ICC, the U.S. finally abandoned its opposition on March 31, 2005 and agreed not to veto the U.N. Security Council's referral of the Darfur crimes to the ICC. The Council's vote was 11-0, with Algeria, Brazil, China, and the United States abstaining. The United States was persuaded to abstain after it received assurances that any U.S. citizens accused of war crimes in the Sudan would not be handed over to the ICC or to any non-U.S. court. The Acting U.S. Ambassador to the United Nations reiterated that the U.S. still 'fundamentally objects' to the ICC but had abstained because '[i]t is important that the international community speak with one voice in order to help promote effective accountability.'" Jordan J. Paust, Jon M. Van Dyke, Linda A. Malone, International Law and Litigation in the U.S. 35–36 (3 ed. 2005).

On June 1, 2006, the International Criminal Police Organisation (Interpol) issued Red Notices requesting the arrest of five commanders of the Ugandan rebel group Lords Resistance Army. These are the first Red Notices issued by Interpol at the request of the Office of the Prosecutor of the ICC. The five are accused of crimes against humanity and war crimes, including murder, abduction, sexual crimes, rape, and child conscription. The ICC publicly unsealed the warrants of arrest against the five commanders on October 13, 2005.

In March 2009, the ICC issued an arrest warrant for President al-Bashir of the Sudan. Sudan is not a Party to the ICC, but there was an Article 12(b) referral of the matter to the ICC by the U.N. Security Council.

In February 2011, the U.N. Security Council referred the situation in Libya to the ICC for investigation and possible prosecution. Libyan leader Muammar Qadaffi was killed later in Libya that year by a Libyan national near the end of a seven-month war that had involved U.S., NATO, and other forces under an authorization of the use of force for certain purposes in U.N. S.C. Res. 1973 (March 17, 2011).

6. What is the standard adopted regarding the burden of proof before the ICC? See Article 66. Is this standard required by the International Covenant on Civil and Political Rights?

7. What forms of evidence are allowed? See Articles 67–69, 72. Is cross-examination of witnesses guaranteed under the Statute? *See* Articles 67–69.

8. What types of penalties are permissible? See Article 77.

9. Articles 81–82 of the Statute of the ICC allow the Prosecutor and the convicted person to appeal certain decisions, including the decision of acquittal in certain listed circumstances (Article 81(1)(a)). Is appeal of acquittal consistent with the U.S. constitutional prohibition of double jeopardy? With the International Covenant on Civil and Political Rights? Could the U.S. surrender U.S. citizens to an international court that allows the prosecutor to appeal an acquittal? Recall *Hirota v. MacArthur*, 338 U.S. 197, 198 (1948), in Chapter Four, Section 8, and the fact that the U.S. has Executive agreements with the ICTs for surrender of accused to such tribunals. There are two important rationales for the U.S. constitutional prohibition of double jeopardy. One rationale is that the trial itself is a great ordeal, and once the defendant is acquitted, the ordeal must end. *See United States v. Ball*, 163 U.S. 662, 669 (1896). The other is based on the increased risk of an erroneous conviction that may occur if the state, with its superior resources, were allowed to retry an individual until it finally obtained a conviction. *See Green v. United States*, 355 U.S. 184, 187–188 (1957); *United States v. DiFrancesco*, 449 U.S. 117, 130 (1980). Are both of these rationales convincing? Are they relevant to prosecution before an international criminal court? Could Canada surrender Canadians to such a tribunal?

10. Like the Statute of the ICTs for the Former Yugoslavia and Rwanda, the Statute of the ICC avoids using the term "extradition" to the relevant tribunal or court. *See* Statute of the ICC, arts. 89–102. This was intended to allow the Court to circumvent the laws and constitutional provisions in many states that prohibit them from extraditing their own nationals. Do you think the courts of such states would be willing to treat surrender or rendition to a permanent international criminal court as anything other than extradition? This problem does not arise at the international level with respect to the ad hoc tribunals because states cannot plead their domestic law (or even bilateral treaties) as an excuse for noncompliance with the orders of the ad hoc tribunals by virtue of their establishment by the Security Council acting under Chapter VII and the U.N. Charter, articles 25, 39, 41, 48–49, 103. With respect to the ICTs, the U.S. has Executive agreements with the tribunals for the rendering of accused. Recall Chapter Five, Section 1 B.

11. How and when can the treaty be amended? See Article 121. How and when can amendments to "Elements" of crimes be created? See Article 9(2). How are "Elements" of crimes "adopted"? What if the elements are inconsistent with customary international law? *See* Articles 9(3), 10, 21(1)(b) and (3), 22(1) and (3). In June 2010, The Review Conference meeting in Kampala, Uganda adopted a resolution on the Crime of Aggression with Annexes that provide Amendments to the Rome Statue and to the Elements of Crimes. See Chapter Seven and Resolution RC/Res. 6 (2010), in the Documents Supplement.

12. For further reading concerning the ICC, *see, e.g.*, The Statute of the International Criminal Court: A Documentary History (M. Cherif Bassiouni ed. 1999); The International Criminal Court: The Making of the Rome Statute (Roy S. Lee ed. 1999); Commentary on the Rome Statute of the International Criminal Court: Observers' Notes, Article by Article (Otto Triffterer ed.1999); Leila Nadya Sadat, The International Criminal Court and the Transformation of International Law: Justice for the New Millennium (2002); Mahnoush H. Arsanjani, *The Rome Statute of the International Criminal Court*, 93 Am. J. Int'l L. 22 (1999); *The International Criminal Court and National Amnesty Laws*, 93 Proc., Am. Soc. Int'l L. 65 (1999); Bartram S. Brown, *U.S. Objections to the Statute of the International Criminal Court: A Brief Response*, 31 N.Y.U. J. Int'l Law & Pol. 855 (1999); *Complementarity: Reconciling the Jurisdiction of National Courts and International Criminal Tribunals*, 23 Yale J. Int'l L. 383 (1998); Marcella David, *Grotius Repudiated: The American Objections to the*

International Criminal Court and the Commitment to International Law, 20 MICH. J. INT'L L.337 (1999); Jordan J. Paust, *remarks*, 93 PROC., AM. SOC. INT'L L. 73 (1999); Beate Rudolf, *Considérations constitutionnelles à propos de l'établissement d'une justice pénal internationale*, 39 REV. FRAN. DE DROIT CONST. 451 (1999); Leila Nadya Sadat & S. Richard Carden, *The New International Criminal Court: An Uneasy Revolution*, 88 GEORGETOWN L.J. 381 (2000); David J. Scheffer, *The United States and the International Criminal Court*, 93 AM. J. INT'L L. 12 (1999); *The International Criminal Court: The Challenge of Jurisdiction*, 93 PROC., AM. SOC. INT'L L. 68 (1999); Johan D. van der Vyver, *Prosecution and Punishment of the Crime of Genocide*, 23 FORDHAM INT'L L.J. 286, 287–89, 318, 336–50, 354 (1999); Ruth Wedgwood, *Fiddling in Rome: America and the International Criminal Court*, FOREIGN AFF. 20 (Nov.-Dec. 1998); symposium, 32 CORNELL INT'L L. J. (1999) (articles and essays by: Philippe Kirsch, Cherif Bassiouni, Richard Dicker, William Lietzau, Diane Orentlicher, Didier Pfirter, Michael Scharf, David Scheffer, Ruth Wedgwood).

13. For further reading concerning earlier proposals for a permanent international criminal court, *see, e.g.*, Bernhard Graefrath, *Universal Criminal Jurisdiction and an International Criminal Court*, 1 EUR. J. INT'L L. 153 (1990); M. Cherif Bassiouni, *The Time Has Come for an International Criminal Court*, 1 IND. INT'L & COMP. L. REV. 1 (1991); Michael P. Scharf, *The Jury is Still Out on the Need for An International Criminal Court*, 1 DUKE J. COMP. & INT'L L. 135 (1991); M. Cherif Bassiouni & Christopher L. Blakesley, *The Need for an International Criminal Court in the New World Order*, 25 VAND. J. TRANS. L. 151 (1992); Benjamin B. Ferencz, *An International Criminal Code and Court: Where They Stand and Where They're Going*, 30 COLUM. J. TRANS. L. 375 (1992); AMERICAN BAR ASSOCIATION TASK FORCE ON AN INTERNATIONAL CRIMINAL COURT, ESTABLISHMENT OF AN INTERNATIONAL CRIMINAL COURT, *reprinted in* 27 INT'L LAW. 257 (1993); Christian Tomuschat, *A System of International Criminal Prosecutions is Taking Shape*, 50 THE REVIEW 56 (Int'l Comm. of Jurists 1993); Christopher L. Blakesley, *Obstacles to the Creation of a Permanent War Crimes Tribunal*, 18 FLETCHER FORUM OF WORLD AFF. 77 (1994); James Crawford, *The ILC's Draft Statute for an International Criminal Tribunal*, 88 AM. J. INT'L L. 140 (1994); Robert Rosenstock, *Symposium: Should there be an International Tribunal for Crimes Against Humanity*, 6 PACE INT'L L. REV. 84 (1994); Leila Sadat Wexler, *The Proposed Permanent International Criminal Court: An Appraisal*, 29 CORNELL INT'L L. J. 665 (1996); Michael P. Scharf, *Getting Serious About An International Criminal Court*, 6 PACE INT'L L. REV. 103 (1994); Paul D. Marquardt, *Law Without Borders: The Constitutionality of an International Criminal Court*, 33 COLUM. J. TRANS. L. 74 (1995).

14. On the creation of an Ad Hoc Committee and a preparatory committee and their efforts to further the process leading to a permanent court, see Chapter One, Section 1, para. 4.

15. Consider the effect of the following domestic U.S. legislation:

22 U.S.C. § 262-1

Restriction relating to United States accession to any new international criminal tribunal

(a) Prohibition. The United States shall not become a party to any new international criminal tribunal, nor give legal effect to the jurisdiction of such a tribunal over any matter described in subsection (b), except pursuant to—

(1) a treaty made under Article II, section 2, clause 2 of the Constitution of the United States on or after October 21, 1998; or

(2) any statute enacted by Congress on or after October 21, 1998.

(b) Jurisdiction described. The jurisdiction described in this section is jurisdiction over—

(1) persons found, property located, or acts or omissions committed, within the territory of the United States; or

(2) nationals of the United States, wherever found.

(c) Statutory construction. Nothing in this section precludes sharing information, expertise or other forms of assistance with such tribunal.

(d) "New international criminal tribunal defined. The term "new international criminal tribunal" means any permanent international criminal tribunal established on or after October 21, 1998, and does not include—

(1) [the ICTY]; or

(2) [the ICTR].

Other relevant laws include:

Restriction relating to United States accession to the International Criminal Court. P.L. 106-113, Div. B, § 1000(a)(7), 113 Stat. 1536 (Nov. 29, 1999)

(a) Prohibition. The United States shall not become a party to the International Court except pursuant to a treaty made under Article II, section 2, clause 2 of the Constitution of the United States on or after the date of enactment of this Act.

(b) Prohibition. None of the funds authorized to be appropriated by this or any other Act may be obligated for use by, or for support of, the International Criminal Court unless the United States has become a party to the Court pursuant to a treaty made under Article II, section 2, clause 2 of the Constitution of the United States on or after the date of enactment of this Act.

(c) International Criminal Court defined. In this section, the term "International Criminal Court" means the court established by the Rome Statute of the International Criminal Court, adopted by the United Nations Diplomatic Conference of Plenipotentiaries on the Establishment of an International Criminal Court on July 17, 1998.

Prohibition on extradition or transfer of United States citizens to the International Criminal Court. P.L. 106-113, Div. B, § 1000(a)(7), 113 Stat. 1536 (Nov. 29, 1999)

(a) Prohibition on extradition. None of the funds authorized to be appropriated or otherwise made available by this or any other Act may be used to extradite a United States citizen to a foreign country that is under an obligation to surrender persons to the International Criminal Court unless that foreign country confirms to the United States that applicable prohibitions on reextradition apply to such surrender or gives other satisfactory assurances to the United States that the country will not extradite or otherwise transfer that citizen to the International Criminal Court.

(b) Prohibition on consent to extradition by third countries. None of the funds authorized to be appropriated or otherwise made available by this or any other Act may be used to provide consent to the extradition or transfer of a United States citizen by a foreign country to a third country that is under an obligation to surrender persons to the International Criminal Court, unless the third country confirms to the United States that applicable prohibitions on reextradition apply to such surrender or gives other satisfactory assurances to the United States that the third country will not extradite or otherwise transfer that citizen to the International Criminal Court....

16. The United States delegation had been heavily involved in the negotiation of the ICC Statute. President Clinton ultimately signed the Statute on the last day it was open

for signature, December 31, 2000, although he expressed reservations about certain provisions of the treaty. The Bush administration was strenuously opposed to the ICC, going so far as to "unsign" the treaty and to enter into so-called "Article 98" bilateral agreements with various countries, thereby attempting to exempt U.S. personnel from the ICC's jurisdiction. Countries refusing to enter into Article 98 agreements have lost military and other assistance, provoking a strong backlash against the U.S. policy, both from the countries targeted and the European Union in particular. With the referral of the situation in Darfur, Sudan, to the Court in 2005, U.S. opposition appeared to have been waning, but many of the punitive aspects of U.S. policy remain. For a good discussion, *see, e.g.*, Leila Nadya Sadat, *Summer in Rome, Spring in the Hague, Winter in Washington? U.S. Policy Towards the International Criminal Court*, 21 Wis. Int'l L. J. 557 (2003).

Why was the Bush Administration so opposed to the International Criminal Court? Why is U.S. policy so different than the policies of similar democracies? Shortly after the election of President Bush in 2000, the U.S. stopped sending delegates to the Preparatory Commission meetings for the Court that were elaborating many of the ancillary documents important to the Court's establishment and operation, and after the Court's Statute entered into force in 2002, the U.S. did not send any delegates to the Assembly of States Parties meetings held to discuss the Court's operation. Is it in the interest of the U.S. to join the ICC for flexibility with respect to possible prosecution of U.S. nationals held by Iran or Syria?

Professor David Scheffer has noted that under the Obama Administration the United States has assisted the ICC in tracking and apprehending Joseph Kony, head of the Resistance Army in Uganda and others who had been indicted by the ICC for various crimes, has supported the ICC's investigation of alleged crimes in Kenya, facilitated the U.N. Security Council referral of the situation in Libya to the ICC, and has "participated with observer nation status in the periodic meetings of the court's Assembly of States Parties." David Scheffer, *America's Embrace of the International Criminal Court*, in Jurist (Jul 2, 2012), http://jurist.org/forum/2012/06/dan-scheffer-us-icc.php.

Ambassador-at-Large for War Crimes Issues Stephen J. Rapp spoke to the Assembly of States Parties in 2011, stating in part:

> [A]lthough the United States is not a party to the Rome Statute, we are continuing to engage with the ICC and States Parties to the Rome Statute to end impunity for the worst crimes. Over the past several years, we have sent active observer delegations to the [Assembly of States Parties] sessions and the Review Conference in Kampala. We have actively engaged with the [Office of the Prosecutor] and the Registrar to consider specific ways that we can support specific prosecutions already underway, and we have responded positively to a number of informal requests for assistance. We supported the UN Security Council's ICC referral regarding Libya and are working hard to ensure that those charged by the Court there face justice consistent with international standards. From the [Democratic Republic of the Congo] to Cote d'Ivoire, Darfur to Libya, we have worked to strengthen accountability for atrocities because we know, as President Obama has said, that "justice is a critical ingredient for lasting peace."

U.S. Official Describes U.S. Policy Toward International Criminal Court, 106 Am. J. Int'l L. 384 (2012). Does this indicate that the United States will likely become a party to the ICC? *Compare* Prahant Sabharwal, *Manifest Destiny: The Relationship between the United States and the International Criminal Court in a Time of International Upheaval*, 18 New

ENG. J. INT'L & COMP. L. 311 (2012), *with* Megan A. Fairlie, *The United States and the International Criminal Court Post-Bush: A Beautiful Courtship but an Unlikely Marriage*, 29 BERKELEY J. INT'L L. 528 (2011). *See also* Leila Nadya Sadat, *On the Shores of Lake Victoria: Africa and the Review Conference for the International Criminal Court*, 2010(1) AFLA QUARTERLY 10.

Part Three

Offenses

Chapter 7

Offenses Against Peace

Introductory Note

Some have assumed, wrongly, that crimes against peace were not recognizable violations of international law until the post-World War II trials at Nuremberg and Tokyo. As the following material demonstrates, such offenses have a recognizable existence at least since the dawn of the United States. See also Chapter Four and Chapter Six, Section 1 *supra*. Indeed, our Revolution was justified in part as a defensive response to England's "War against the natural rights of all Mankind" and her "cruel and impolitic purpose of enslaving ... by violence" and other acts of "cruel aggression."

Early U.S. cases and opinions had also addressed the precept of "aggression," "acts of hostility" and offenses against "peace," and the "violation of territorial rights." In 1794, Congress passed the Neutrality Act to assure U.S. compliance with the law of nations. As John Jay wrote more generally in The Federalist No. 3, "it is of high importance to the peace of America that she observe the law of nations." And Attorney General Lee wrote in 1797, "That the peace of mankind may be preserved, it is the interest as well as the duty of every government to punish with becoming severity all the individuals of the State who commit this offense." Many of the early prosecutions involved private perpetrators of such crimes against peace.

Individuals had also been prosecuted for initiating an unjust war or for administering territories through acts of cruel oppression threatening the common interest. In 1818, the Congress at Aix-La-Chapelle decided to detain Napoleon for waging wars against the peace of the world. Also in 1818, there occurred the famous trial in America of two Englishmen, Arbuthnot and Ambrister, for incitement of the Creek Indians and the levying of war against the United States in violation of the law of nations and the laws of war. See Chapter Four, Section 7 D. There had also been other examples of trials of persons "for initiating or contributing to the initiation of aggressive war" before the World War II trials. See Q. Wright, *The Law of the Nuremberg Trial*, 41 Am. J. Int'l L. 38, 63 n.102 (1947).

Section 1
Violations of Neutrality

A. General Offenses

Henfield's Case
11 F. Cas. 1099 (C.C.D. Pa. 1793)
[in Chapter Four, Section 2]

Commonwealth v. Schaffer
4 U.S. (4 Dall.) xxvi, xxxi (Mayor's Ct. of Phila. 1797)

(argument of Ingersoll & Thomas)

The prosecution against Henfield, in the circuit court, was for a violation of his duty, as a citizen of the United States, in entering on board a French privateer, and cruising against the subjects of the king of Great Britain, with whom the United States were at peace, under the sanction of a treaty. This was contrary to the law of nations, to the treaty, and against the constitution of the United States. This was not a crime resulting from the regulations of an act of congress.

1 Ops. Att'y Gen.
(1795, 1796, 1797)
[see Chapter Four, Section 2]

The Three Friends
166 U.S. 1, 53 (1897) (Fuller, C.J.)
[see Chapter Four, Section 5]

Talbot v. Janson
3 U.S. (3 Dall.) 133, 155–58 (1795) (Paterson, J.)

The United States are neutral in the present war; they take no part in it; they remain common friends to all the belligerent powers, not favoring the arms of one to the detriment of the others. An exact impartiality must mark their conduct towards the parties at war; for, if they favor one to the injury of the other, it would be a departure from pacific principles, and indicative of an hostile disposition. It would be a fraudulent neutrality. To this rule there is no exception, but what arises from the obligation of antecedent treaties, which ought to be religiously observed. If, therefore, the capture of the Magdalena was effected by Ballard [a U.S. national] alone, it must be pronounced to be illegal, and of course the decree of restitution is just and proper.

This leads us, to consider the capture as having been made by Ballard [U.S.] and Talbot [French]. Talbot commanded the privateer *L'Ami dela Pointa Pitre*. The question is, as the Magdalena struck to and was made prize of by Ballard, and as Talbot, who knew his situation, aided in his equipment, and acted in confederacy with him, afterwards had a sort of joint possession, whether Talbot can detain her as prize by virtue of his French commission? To support the validity of Talbot's claim it is contended, that Ballard had no commission or an inadequate one, and therefore his capture was illegal. That it was lawful for Talbot to take possession of the ship so captured, being a Dutch bottom, as the United Netherlands were at open war and enmity with the French republic, and Talbot was a naturalized French citizen, acting under a regular commission from the governor of Guadaloupe. It has been already observed, that Ballard was a citizen of the United States; that the *L'Ami de la Liberte* of which he had the command, was fitted out and armed as a vessel of war in the United States; that as such she sailed from the United States, and cruised against nations at peace and in amity with the said states. These acts were direct and daring violations of the principles of neutrality, and highly criminal by the law of nations. In effecting this state of things, how far was Talbot instrumental and active? What was his knowledge, his agency, his participation, his conduct in the business? It appears in evidence, that Talbot expected Ballard at Tybee; that he waited for him there several days; that he set sail without him, and in a short time returned to his former station. This indicates contrivance and a previous communication of designs. At length Ballard appeared. On his arrival, Talbot put on board the *Ami de la Liberte*, in Savannah river, and confessedly within the jurisdiction of the United States, four cannon, which he had brought for the purpose. Were these guns furnished by order of the French consul? The insinuation is equally unfounded and dishonorable. They also fired a salute, and hailed Sinclair a citizen of the United States, as an owner. An incident of this kind, at such a moment, has the effect of illumination. Talbot knew Ballard's situation, and in particular aided in fitting out the *L'Ami de la Liberte* by furnishing her with guns. Without this assistance she would not have been in a state for war. An essential part of the outfit, therefore, was provided by Talbot. The equipment being thus completed, the two privateers went to sea. When on the ocean, they acted in concert; they cruised together, they fought together, they captured together. Talbot knew that Ballard had no commission; he so states it in his claim: the facts confirm the statement; for, about an hour after Ballard had captured the Magdalene, he came up, and took a joint possession, hoping to cover the capture by his commission, and thus to legalize Ballard's spoliation. How silly and contemptible is cunning—how vile and debusing is fraud. In furnishing Ballard with guns, in aiding him to arm and outfit, in co-operating with him on the high seas, and using him as the instrument and means of capturing vessels, Talbot assumed a new character, and instead of pursuing his commission acted in opposition to it. If he was a French citizen, duly naturalized, and if, as such, he had a commission fairly obtained, he was authorized to capture ships belonging to the enemies of the French republic, but not warranted in seducing the citizens of neutral nations from their duty, and assisting them in committing depredations upon friendly powers. His commission did not authorize him to abet the predatory schemes of an illegal cruiser on the high seas; and if he undertook to do so, he unquestionably deviated from the path of duty. Talbot was an original trespasser, for he was concerned in the illegal outfit of the *Ami de la Liberte*. Shall he then reap any benefit from her captures, when brought within the United States? Besides, it is in evidence, that Ballard took possession first of the Magdalene, and put on board of her a prizemaster and some hands; Talbot, in about an hour after, came up, and also put on board a prizemaster, and other men. The possession in the first instance was Ballard's; he was not ousted of it; the prey was not taken from him; indeed, it was never intended to deprive him of it. So far from it, that it was an artifice to cover the booty. Talbot's possession was gained by a fraudulent co-operation with Ballard, a citizen of the United States, and was a mere fetch or contrivance in order to secure the capture. Ballard still continued in possession. The Magdalene thus taken and possessed, was carried into Charleston. Can there be a doubt with respect to restoration? Stating the case answers the question. It has been said that Ballard had a commission, and acted under it. This point has already been considered, and, indeed, is not worth debating; the commission, if any, was illegal, and of course the seizures were so. But then what effect has this upon Talbot? Does it make his case better or worse? The truth is, that Talbot knew that Ballard had no commission, and he also knew the precise case and situation of the *Ami de la Liberte*; to whom he belonged, where fitted out, and for what purpose. Talbot gave Ballard guns within the jurisdiction of the United States, and thus aided in making him an illegal cruiser; he consorted and acted with him, and was a participant in the iniquity and fraud. In short, Ballard took the Magdalena, had the possession of her, and kept it; Talbot was in under Ballard by connivance and fraud, not with a view to oust him of the prize, but to cover and secure it; not with a view to bring him into judgment as a transgressor against the law of nations, but to intercept the stroke of justice and prevent his being punished. If Talbot procured possession of the Magdalena through the medium of Ballard, a citizen of the United States, and then brought her within the jurisdiction of the said states, would it not be the duty of the competent authority to order her to be restored? The principle deducible from the law of nations, is plain; — you shall not make use of our neutral arm, to capture vessels of your enemies, but of our friends. If you do, and bring the captured vessels within our jurisdiction, restitution will be awarded. Both the powers in the present instance, though enemies to each other, are friends of the United States; whose citizens ought to preserve a neutral attitude; and should not assist either party in their hostile operations. But if, as is agreed on all hands, Ballard first took possession of the Magdalena, and if he continued in possession and brought her within the jurisdiction of the United States, which I take to be the case, then no question can arise with respect to the legality of restitution. It is an act of justice, resulting from the law of nations, to restore to the friendly power the possession of his vessel, which a citizen of the United States illegally obtained, and to place Joost Jansen, the master of the Magdalena, in his former state, from whence he had been removed by the improper interference, and hostile demeanor of Ballard. Besides, it is right to conduct all cases of this kind, in such a manner, as that the persons guilty of fraud, should not gain by it. Hence the efficacy of the legal principle, that no man shall set up his own fraud or iniquity, as a ground of action or defense. This maxim applies forcibly to the present case, which, in my apprehension, is a fraud upon the principles of neutrality, a fraud upon the law of nations, and an insult, as well as a fraud, against the United States, and the republic of France.

18 U.S.C. § 25

(1794) (now § 960)
[see Chapter Four, Section 2]

United States v. Smith

27 F. Cas. 1192, 1220–21

(argument of counsel and questions of Paterson, J.), 1228–31 (C.C.D.N.Y. 1806) (No. 16,342) (Paterson, J.)

[Editors' note: Col. William S. Smith, son-in-law of former President John Adams, was indicted for violating the Neutrality Act of 1794. He claimed that he had authority to act from President Thomas Jefferson and Secretary of State James Madison in support of an expedition to liberate Venezuela that was interrupted in Caracas. Smith had been raising money, outfitting a merchant ship with weapons, and enlisting recruits for the expedition. See Christopher Stone, " 'Original Intent' and Following Orders," L.A. Times, Jul. 22, 1987, pt. II, at 5.]

[Defense counsel for Smith] It appears then, that the indictment and statute are only pointed against preparatory acts for carrying on an enterprise against a power at peace. Will the counsel for the prosecution offer evidence of the sailing of the Leander, or of any act of hostility? If they do, it must be in order to lay matter of aggravation before the jury, and let them consider how far that is consistent with their denial of our right to prove matter of mitigation in the same way. But as to the acts charged in the indictment, they are only preparatory, and independent of any actual hostility. As to them, the state of the country forms an irresistible justification both of Colonel Smith and of the president. The constitution indeed does not allow the latter to declare war, but does it forbid his providing and preparing the means of carrying it on, while congress are in actual and secret deliberation whether they shall declare war against a nation that is committing and provoking hostilities? Spain, indeed, was technically at peace by the treaty of San Lorenzo, but she was actually at war by the law of nations; she had broken that treaty, plundered our ships, invaded our territories, and carried our citizens from thence as prisoners by military force. Such a nation is not entitled, if I may say so, to the benefits of this act, the object of which is, that so long as any prince of potentate shall act towards us with perfect amity, and not be equivocal or unfriendly conduct, render preparatory measures for war advisable, so long as it shall be forbidden under the penalties of this law, to any individuals to break that amity, and by unauthorized acts to endanger the peace of the two countries. But if the foreign power shall itself have broken that amity, and shall have given just grounds of war, no government ought to omit "providing and preparing the means" for military enterprizes; nor could any law have intended to prevent the preparatory efforts of individuals for subduing the public enemy. The memorable congress that commenced your revolution, did not hesitate to provide and prepare the means of meeting the English before the actual war was declared; nor did in censure or discountenance those patriots, who, unauthorized by any orders, and before the formal declarations of war, possessed themselves of Ticonderoga and Crown Point.

The circumstances of the times, we have shown, justified the president in giving his approbation, and my client, under that approbation, in providing and preparing the means of a military enterprise against Spain. And surely no enterprise could be more useful or effectual for drawing the enemy from our southern and western frontiers; none more worthy of the exalted and philosophic mind of our chief magistrate; none more consonant to the enlightened and philosophic views of society and politics, which he has exhibited to the world, than an expedition to liberate South America; to destroy at once Spanish tyranny and power on our own continent; to enfranchise, by one effort, millions of our fellow creatures from the most frightful bondage; and to lay the foundations, in so large a portion of the globe, for the freedom and the happiness of man!

Paterson, Circuit Justice. You state in the affidavit that it was done with the knowledge and approbation of the president, but it is stated in the affidavit that he authorized the fitting out of the expedition?

[Defense counsel] I conceive it was not necessary; for though I have argued upon the effects of an authorization, it was only to show that the argument of the adverse counsel went much too far, when they contended that the president could not authorize any such measure. For our defence, it will be only necessary to shown that the president was, under the circumstances of the times, warranted to provide and prepare the means for a military expedition; and that, in what he might do, we acted with his knowledge and approbation. "*Qui prohibere potest et non prohibet, jubet.*" The knowledge and approbation of the chief magistrate and heads of departments, if we shall prove them to have been sufficiently express and positive, will amount to justification; but even if we shall fail in establishing them to that extent, they will still afford very powerful inducements for mitigating the punishment. This is denied on the other side; but I would ask, if it could be proved that this enterprise was carried on against the president's express order, would not that be matter of aggravation? If it would, surely the reverse must be matter of mitigation. The mistake into which a defendant may have been led by the approbation of the government, and the innocence of his motives, must surely mitigate a discretionary punishment. In this case we do not rely upon mere general and vague approbation of the measure; we will show that approbation was given to this very defendant's being concerned in it....

Paterson, Circuit Justice. It appears to the court, that James Madison, secretary of state, Robert Smith, secretary of the navy, and Jacob Wagner and William Thornton, who are officers under the department of the secretary of state, have been duly served with subpoenas to attend as witnesses on the part of the defendant, and that they do not attend pursuant to the process of the court.... [Subsequently,] the defendant has come forward with an affidavit stating the material facts, which he conceives he will be able to prove by the evidence of Mr. Madison, Mr. Smith, Mr. Wagner and Mr. Thornton. This part of the affidavit runs in the following words: "And this deponent farther saith, that he hopes and expects to be able to prove by the testimony of the said witnesses, that the expedition and enterprise, to which the said indictment relates, was begun, prepared and set on foot with the knowledge and approbation of the president of the United States, and with the knowledge and approbation of the secretary of state of the United States. And the deponent farther saith, that he hopes and expects to be able to prove, by the testimony of the said witnesses, that if he had any concern in the said expedition and enterprise, it was with the approbation of the president of the United States, and the said secretary of state. And the deponent further saith, that he is informed, and doth verily believe, and hopes and expects to be able to prove, by the testimony of the said witnesses, that the prosecution against him for the said offence charged in the said indictment is commenced and prosecuted by order of the president of the United States. And the deponent farther saith, that he has been informed and doth verily believe, that the said James Madison and Robert Smith are prevented from attending by order or interposition of the president of the United States." ...

The first question is, whether the facts stated in the defendant's affidavit be material, or ought to be given in evidence, if the witnesses were not in court, and ready to testify to their truth? Does the affidavit disclose sufficient matter to induce the court to put off the trial? As judges, it is our duty to administer justice according to law....

The evidence which is offered to a court must be pertinent to the issue, or in some proper manner connected with it.... The defendant is indicted for providing the means, to wit, men and money, for a military enterprise against the dominions of the king of Spain with whom the United States are at peace, against the form of a statute in such case made and provided. He has pleaded not guilty; and to evince his innocence, to justify his infraction of the act of congress, or to purge his guilt, he offers evidence to prove, that this military enterprise was begun, prepared, and set on foot with the knowledge and approbation of the executive department of our government. Sitting here in our judicial capacities, we should listen with caution to a suggestion of this kind, because the president of the United States is bound by the constitution to "take care that the laws be faithfully executed." These are the words of the instrument; and, therefore, it is to be presumed that he would not countenance the violation of any statute, and particularly if such violation consisted in expeditions of a warlike nature against friendly powers. The law, indeed, presumes, that every officer faithfully executes his duties, until the contrary be proved. And, besides the constitutional provision just mentioned, the seventh section of the act under consideration expressly declares, that it shall be lawful for the president of the United States, or such other person as he shall have empowered for that purpose, to employ such part of the land or naval forces of the United States, or of the militia thereof, as shall be judged necessary for the purpose of preventing the carrying on of any such expedition or enterprise from the territories of the United States against the territories or dominions of a foreign prince or state with whom the United States are at peace. 3 Swift's Laws, 91, 92 [1 Stat. 384].

The facts, however, which are disclosed in the defendant's affidavit, we must, in the discussion of the present question, take to be true in the manner therein set forth; and the objection goes to the invalidity, the inoperative virtue, and the unavailing nature of the facts themselves. Are the contents of the affidavit pertinent—are they material—are they relevant? The fifth section of the statute, on which the indictment is founded, is expressed in general, unqualified terms; it contains no condition, no exception; it invests no dispensing power in any officer or person whatever. Thus it reads: "And be it further enacted and declared, that if any person shall, within the territory or jurisdiction of the United States, begin or set on foot, or provide or prepare the means for, any military expedition or enterprise to be carried on from thence against the territory or dominion of any foreign prince or state with whom the United States are at peace, every such person so offending shall, upon conviction, be adjudged guilty of a high misdemeanor, and shall suffer fine and imprisonment at the discretion of the court, in which the conviction shall be had, so as that such fine shall not exceed three thousand dollars, nor the term of imprisonment be more than three years." The section which I have read is declaratory of the law of nations; and, besides, every species of private and unauthorized hostilities is inconsistent with the principles of the social compact, and the very nature, scope, and end of civil government. The statute, which is the basis of the present indictment, was passed the 5th of June, 1794, and was temporary; but congress found it expedient, and, perhaps, necessary, to continue it in force, without limitation of time, which was done on the 24th of April, 1800 [2 Stat. 54]. This fifth section, which prohibits military enterprises against nations with which the United States are at peace, imparts no dispensing power to the president. Does the constitution give it? Far from it, for it explicitly directs that he shall "take care that the laws be faithfully executed." This instrument, which measures out the powers and defines the duties of the president, does not vest in him any authority to set on foot a military expedition against a nation with which the United States are at peace. And if a private individual, even with the knowledge and approbation of this high and preeminent officer of our government, should set on foot such a military expedition, how can he expect to be exonerated from the obligation of the law? Who holds the power of dispensation? True, a nolle prosequi may be entered, a pardon may be granted; but these presume criminality, presume guilt, presume amenability to judicial investigation and punishment, which are very different from a power to dispense with the law.

Supposing then that every syllable of the affidavit is true, of what avail can it be on the present occasion? Of what use or benefit can it be to the defendant in a court of law? Does it speak by way of justification? The president of the United States cannot control the statute, nor dispense with its execution, and still less can he authorize a person to do what the law forbids. If he could, he would render the execution of the laws dependent on his will and pleasure; which is a doctrine that has not been set up, and will not meet with any supporters in our government. In this particular, the law is paramount. Who has dominion over it? None but the legislature; and even they are not without their limitation in our republic. Will it be pretended that the president could rightfully grant a dispensation and license to any of our citizens to carry on a war against a nation with whom the United States are at peace? Ingenious and learned counsel may imagine, and put a number of cases in the wide field of conjecture; but we are to take facts as we find them, and to argue from the existing state of things at the time. If we were at war with Spain, there is an end to the indictment; but, if at peace, what individual could lawfully make war or carry on a military expedition against the dominions of his Catholic majesty? The indictment is founded on a state of peace, and such state is presumed to continue until the contrary appears. A state of war is not set up in the affidavit. If, then, the president knew and approved of the military expedition set forth in the indictment against a prince with whom we are at peace, it would not justify the defendant in a court of law, nor discharge him from the binding force of the act of congress; because the president does not possess a dispensing power. Does he possess the power of making war? That power is exclusively vested in congress; for, by the eighth section of the 1st article of the constitution, it is ordained, that congress shall have power to declare war, grant letters of marque and reprisal, raise and support armies, provide and maintain a navy, and to provide for calling forth the militia to execute the laws of the Union, suppress insurrections, and repel invasions. And we accordingly find, that congress have been so circumspect and provident in regard to the last three particulars, that they have from time to time vested the president of the United States with ample powers.

Thus, by the act of the 28th of February, 1795 (3 Swift's Laws, 188 [1 Stat. 424]), it is made lawful for the president to call forth the militia to repel invasions, suppress insurrections, and execute the laws of the Union. Abstractedly from this constitutional and legal provision, the right to repel invasions arises from self-preservation and defence, which is a primary law of nature, and constitutes part of the law of nations. It therefore becomes the duty of a people, and particularly of the executive magistrate, who is at their head, the commander-in-chief of the forces by sea and land, to repel an invading foe. But to repel aggressions and invasions is one thing, and to commit them against a friendly power is another. It is obvious that if the United States were at war with Spain at the time that the defendant is charged with the offence in the indictment, then he does not come within the purview of the statute, which makes the basis of the offence to consist in beginning or preparing the means to carry on a military expedition or enterprise against a nation with which the United States are at peace. If, indeed, a foreign nation should invade the territories of the United States, it would I apprehend, be not only lawful for the president to resist such invasion, but also to carry hostilities into the enemy's own country; and for this plain reason, that a state of complete and absolute war actually exists between the two nations. In the case of invasive hostilities, there cannot be war on the one side and peace on the other. What! in the storm of battle, and, perhaps, in the full tide of victory, must we stop short at the boundary between the two nations, and give over the conflict and pursuit? Will it be an offence to pass the line of partition, and smite the invading foe on his own ground? No; surely no. To do so would be a duty, and cannot be perverted into a crime. There is a manifest distinction between our going to war with a nation at peace, and a war being made against us by an actual invasion, or a formal declaration. In the former case, it is the exclusive province of congress to change a state of peace into a state of war. A nation, however, may be in such a situation as to render it more prudent to submit to certain acts of a hostile nature, and to trust to negotiations for redress, than to make an immediate appeal to arms. Various considerations may induce to a measure of this kind; such as motives of policy, calculations of interest, the nature of the injury and provocation, the relative resources, means and strength of the two nations, & c. and, therefore, the organ intrusted with the power to declare war, should first decide whether it is expedient to go to war, or to continue in peace; and until such a decision be made, no individual ought to assume an hostile attitude; and to pronounce, contrary to the constitutional will, that the nation is at war, and that he will shape his conduct and act according to such a state of things. This conduct is clearly indefensible, and may involve the nation, of which he is a member, in all the calamities of a long and expensive war. It is a matter worthy of notice on the present occasion, that when the offence laid in the indictment is stated to have been committed, congress were in session; and if, in their estimation, war measures were prudent or necessary to be adopted, they would, no doubt, have expressed their sentiments on the subject, either by a public declaration of their will, or by authorizing the executive authority to proceed hostilely against the king of Spain. But nothing of this kind has been done, or at least appears to have been done. Congress does not choose to go to war; and where is the individual among us who could legally do so without their permission? Whoever violates the law becomes liable to its penalties; nor can the observance of the law be dispensed with, unless it contains a clause authorizing certain persons to dispense with it under specified circumstances or whenever they may think it expedient. In the present case, if war had occurred between the United States and Spain at the time the facts stated in the indictment were committed, they would not amount to an offence within the statute, which relates to a time of tranquility and peace. The defendant in this case would have been out of the statute. War is not pretended; and the law under consideration is absolute, requires universal obedience, and does not vest any officer with a dispensing power, or the extraordinary privilege of authorizing a person to do what it expressly prohibits. In appearing, then, that the testimony of Mr. Madison, Mr. Smith,, Mr. Wagner, and Mr. Thornton, as stated in the defendant's affidavit, is not pertinent to the issue, nor material by way of justification or defence against the facts charged in the indictment, their absence cannot operate as a legal excuse to put off the trial....

[Editors' note: from F. Cas.: "The jury retired, and after an absence of two hours, they returned a verdict of not guilty."]

Dellums v. Smith

577 F. Supp. 1449, 1450–53 (N.D. Cal. 1984), *rev'd on other grounds*, 797 F.2d 817 (9th Cir. 1986)

Plaintiffs filed suit to require the Attorney General to conduct a preliminary investigation as to whether the President, the Secretary of State, the Secretary of Defense and other federal executive officers have violated the Neutrality Act, a federal criminal law, by supporting paramilitary operations against Nicaragua. The Neutrality Act, 18 U.S.C. § 960, declares that:

> Whoever, within the United States, knowingly begins or sets on foot or provides or prepares a means for or furnishes the money for, or takes part in, any military or naval expedition or enterprise to be carried on from thence against the territory or dominion of any foreign prince or state, or any colony, district, or people with whom the United States is at peace, shall be fined not more than $3,000 or imprisoned not more than three years, or both.

Plaintiffs' complaint was founded upon the Ethics in Government Act. 28 U.S.C. §§ 591–598, which directs the Attorney General to conduct a preliminary investigation upon receiving specific information from a credible source that federal criminal law has been violated by any federal official designated in the statute.

The Court found, and the Attorney General has since admitted, that the information presented by plaintiffs was sufficiently specific and that it came from a sufficiently credible source. *Dellums v. Smith*, 573 F. Supp. 1489 at 1504–1505 (N.D. Cal. 1983). The Court also determined that officials covered by the Ethics in Government Act *may* have violated the Neutrality Act. *See id.* at 1502 n.11. For these reasons, the Court ordered the Attorney General to conduct a preliminary investigation as required by the Ethics in Government Act. *Id.* at 1504–1505. Pursuant to the same statute, the Court also ordered that unless the Attorney General makes a determination within ninety days that there are no reasonable grounds to believe that further investigation is warranted, he must apply for the appointment of independent counsel. *Id.* at 1505.

Defendants, in opposing plaintiffs' motion for summary judgment and moving for dismissal of the action, argued that plaintiffs lack standing to sue, that the Ethics in Government Act does not grant a private right of action to plaintiffs, that the ruling sought requires an impermissible advisory opinion, and that the action presents a non-justiciable political question. The Court rejected each of these contentions and granted plaintiffs' motion for summary judgment....

The contention that the Neutrality Act reaches executive officials is at least as persuasive as defendant's claim that it does not. The statute itself contains no exception for any person or official. Thus, the doctrine espoused by defendants finds no support on the face of the statute. Consideration of the English statutes upon which the Neutrality Act was modeled supports the conclusion that the American statute's broad language was chosen purposefully. The English statutes provide express exceptions for acts done with leave or license of the crown, i.e., the executive. *See* Lobel, *The Rise and Decline of the Neutrality Act: Sovereignty and Congressional War Powers in United States Foreign Policy*, 24 Harv. Int'l L.J. 1, 31–33 (1983) (hereinafter cited as "Lobel"). The absence of such provisions from the American Act reflects a decision to retain and protect the Constitution's delegation of war power to the legislative branch. *See* U.S. Const. art. I, § 8. In addition, uncontradicted authority holds that the President cannot aid or authorize private expeditions against foreign nations without the approval of Congress.

In 1806, two civilians were indicted and tried for aiding an attempt to launch an expedition against Spanish America in violation of the Neutrality Act. *United States v. Smith*, 27 F. Cas. 1192 (C.C.N.Y. 1807) (No. 16,342). As part of their defense, they sought to subpoena Secretary of State James Madison and other federal executive officials to prove their claim that their acts had been authorized by President Jefferson. *Id.* at 1228.

The Court declined to issue the requested subpoenas on the ground that such testimony of the cabinet members was immaterial. William Paterson, a Supreme Court Justice and participant in the Constitutional Convention, presided over the trial and handed down the court's opinion. He first examined the Neutrality Act and found that is "is expressed in general, unqualified terms; it contains no condition no exception; it invests no dispensing power in any officer or person whatsoever." Justice Paterson then determined that the Constitution itself does not create such an exception for the President. "This instrument [the Constitution], which measures out the powers and defines the duties of the President, does not vest in him any authority to set on foot a military expedition against a nation with which the United States is at peace." *Id.* at 1229–30. In conclusion, Justice Paterson stated that "the law under consideration is absolute" and "requires universal obedience." *Id.* at 1231.

This conclusion is well-supported by the history of the Neutrality Act. One of its major purposes was to protect the constitutional power of Congress to declare war or authorize private reprisal against foreign states. *See* Lobel, *supra*, at 27–37. This purpose was recognized by early presidents. "[W]hether the interest or honor of the United States requires that they should be made a party to any such struggle, and by inevitable consequence to the war which is waged in its support, is a question which by our Constitution is wisely left to Congress alone to decide. It is by the laws already made criminal in our citizens to embarrass or anticipate that decision by unauthorized military operations on their part." President Martin Van Buren, Second Annual Message to Congress (Dec. 3, 1838), *reprinted in* 3 *Messages & Papers of the Presidents*, 483, 487 (J. Richardson ed. 1896); *see also* Inaugural Address of President John Adams (Marsh 4, 1797), *reprinted in* 1 *Messages & Papers of the Presidents*, *supra*, at 231.

Believing that the Neutrality Act bound the President, congressional opponents of the law attempted unsuccessfully to amend it during the 1800s. For example, in 1854, Senator Slidell introduced a resolution seeking to amend the Neutrality Act by allowing the President to suspend its operation during any recess of Congress for up to 12 months when, "in his opinion, the public interests require" such a suspension. Cong. Globe, 33d Cong., 1st Sess. 1021, 1023–24 (1854). Slidell's proposed amendment failed. Similarly, in 1858, Senator Slidell introduced a resolution to amend the Neutrality Act to permit presidential suspension during recesses. Cong. Globe, 35th Cong., 1st Sess. 462 (1858). This proposal also failed. The Neutrality Act remains today substantially the same as it appeared in the original enactment of 1794. The failure of Senator Slidell's proposed amendments fortifies the view that the Neutrality Act grants no executive discretion to authorize paramilitary expeditions against foreign governments with which this nation is not at war.

To support their claim that the executive officials are immune from the coverage of the act, defendants refer to provisions of the 1794 Act empowering the President to take certain actions to enforce the statute's prohibitions. *See* Act of June 5, 1794, §8, 1 Stat. 381, 384 (1794). The existence of such enforcement powers does not preclude application of the Act to the Executive. For example, Attorney General Robert Jackson rendered the opinion that section 3 of the 1917 reenactment of the Act applied to the President and prevented the President from releasing to the British Government boats then under construction for the United States Navy. 29 Op. Atty. Gen. 484, 494–96 (1940). Attorney General Jackson reached this conclusion even though he acknowledged the provision authorizing presidential enforcement of the prohibition. *See id.* at 494.

Similarly misguided is defendants' reference to the President's powers and duties as "Commander in Chief of the Army and Navy of the United States," and to various military operations conducted by these forces. The paramilitary operations challenged by plaintiffs were not alleged to have been conducted by the armed forces of the United States. The legislative history of the statute indicates that it was not intended to cover the use of regular United States armed forces. *See* Lobel, *supra*, at 31 n. 159. Plaintiffs alleged that the named officials may have violated the Neutrality Act by supporting *private* expeditions. Justice Paterson ruled in *Smith* that such expeditions do not lose the taint of illegality merely because authorized by the Executive. No substantial legal authority contradicts this construction of the Neutrality Act.

The same distinction vitiates defendants' citation to the War Powers Resolution as an illustration of the President's plenary authority to intervene militarily in foreign countries. That resolution is directed to the President's power to introduce the "United States Armed Forces," not paramilitary or other private forces. 50 U.S.C. §§ 1541(a); 1541(c); 1547(c)....

The history of the Neutrality Act and judicial precedent demonstrate the reasonableness of the view that the Act applies to all persons, including the President. The Court reaffirms its original determination that the "Executive actions alleged by plaintiffs, if true, *may* violate federal law." Consequently, in this case, a preliminary investigation may not be refused. . . .

Notes and Questions

1. In one of the footnotes of the *Dellums* opinion it is disclosed: "A memorandum authored by the Department of Justice Office of Legal Counsel has been submitted by defendants as an exhibit to their reply memorandum ... This memorandum deals primarily with another statute that was part of the Neutrality Act, 18 U.S.C. § 959(a), and concludes that the provision is not violated when CIA agents serve in the employ of a foreign military service. 18 U.S.C. § 960 and *Smith* are distinguished as follows:

> We understand this case to stand for the proposition that where an activity is not otherwise within the authority of the Executive Branch, it could not authorize a private individual to engage in it. Since the Executive cannot constitutionally wage war on a nation against which there has been no congressional declaration of war, the President's "authorization" to a private citizen is simply immaterial. By contrast, where an activity is otherwise within the province of the Executive as is the case with intelligence gathering, we think that sovereign authorization would be found a good defense. . . ."

2. In view of the above, do you believe that there are grounds to suspect that Oliver North, Admiral Poindexter and others might have engaged in actions violative of the Neutrality Act and the law of nations? Why were there no prosecutions on such grounds?

3. For further readings in addition to Professor Lobel's article, cited in *Dellums, see,* e.g., Note, *The Iran-Contra Affair, the Neutrality Act, and the Statutory Definition of "At Peace,"* 27 VA. J. INT'L L. 343 (1987); Note, *Nonenforcement of the Neutrality Act: International Law and Foreign Policy Powers Under the Constitution,* 95 HARV. L. REV. 1955 (1982); Paust, *The Link Between Human Rights and Terrorism and Its Implications Concerning the Law of State Responsibility,* 11 HASTINGS INT'L & COMP. L. REV. 41 (1987).

4. Would a pardon of Oliver North and others for violations of the law of nations be constitutionally permissible? See J. Paust, *Contragate and the Invalidity of Pardons for Violations of International Law,* 10 HOUS. J. INT'L L. 51 (1987) (arguing that the pardon power relates to crimes against the United States as such and not to crimes under the laws of the United States, which include international crimes incorporated by reference or otherwise into U.S. law).

5. As recognized by President Washington and Attorney General Bradford in 1795, individuals can be guilty of complicitous involvement in violations of the law of nations, e.g., "aiding, or abetting hostilities." See Chapter Six; see also *Henfield's Case,* 11 F. Cas. at 1103, *passim.* Given such historic prohibition, one can recognize that individuals can be prosecuted under the Neutrality Act for complicitous behavior. See also 18 U.S.C. § 2; *Jacobsen v. United States,* 272 F. 399 (C.C.A. Ill. 1921), *cert. denied,* 256 U.S. 703 (1921); *United States v. Ram Chandra,* 254 F. 635 (D.C. Cal. 1917;) *United States v. Tauscher,* 233 F. 597 (D.C.N.Y. 1916) (conspiracy).

6. On the primacy of federal statutes over presidential orders (that are not within an exclusive Executive power), see also *United States v. Clarke,* 87 U.S. (20 Wall.) 92, 112–13 (1874) ("No power was ever vested in the President to repeal an act of Congress" and presidential proclamations of amnesty did not have such an effect); *Gelston v. Hoyt,* 16 U.S. (3 Wheat.) 246, 330–33 (1818) (statute controls presidential instructions re: seizure of vessels); *The Flying Fish,* 6 U.S. (2 Cranch) 170, 177–79 (1804) (statute prevails over

presidential orders); Paust, *Executive Pans and Authorizations to Violate International Law Concerning Treatment and Interrogation of Detainees*, 43 Columbia J. Transnat'l L. 811, 842 n.114 (2005) (regarding cases addressing congressional power to set limits on presidential war powers); Paust, *Above the Law: Unlawful Executive Authorizations Regarding Detainee Treatment, Secret Renditions, Domestic Spying, and Claims to Unchecked Executive Power*, 2007 Utah L. Rev. 345 (2007).

United States v. Black

685 F.2d 132, 133–34 (5th Cir. 1982), *cert. denied*, 459 U.S. 1021 (1982)

Per Curiam:

The facts of the appeal are unusual. In the spring of 1979, defendant Perdue presented a proposal to the prime minister of Granada that included forming a group of mercenary soldiers to overthrow the Granadan government. The island of Dominica was to serve as a jumping-off spot. This plan was subsequently replaced by one to overthrow the Republic of Dominica. Several parties were brought into the plan, including appellants Hawkins and Black. Perdue's lieutenant Wolfgang Droege, an acquaintance of Hawkins, explained the plan to Hawkins. Hawkins not only joined the group but introduced Perdue to a person who contributed $13,000 to help finance the coup. Black was introduced to the group through one David Duke, an associate of the Ku Klux Klan. Perdue had discussed his plans with Duke from the outset, and Duke suggested that Black might be interested in joining in the coup. After hearing the details, Black stated that he would both join and try to recruit others. Perdue chartered a boat to carry the mercenaries and equipment to Dominica. The captain of the vessel, however, reported him to the Bureau of Alcohol, Tobacco and Firearms, and an undercover agent was assigned to the vessel. The agent was informed by Droege that they hoped to set up a cocaine refining plant on the island. On the night the vessel was to leave for Dominica, ten men, including Black and Hawkins, were arrested with all their military equipment.

All ten were indicted in a seven-count indictment. Seven pleaded guilty to violating the Neutrality Act in exchange for the dropping of the remaining six counts. Black, Hawkins, and a third defendant, Norris, stood trial before a jury. Norris was acquitted, but Black and Hawkins were convicted on two counts: violating the Neutrality Act and conspiracy. They appeal, asserting that their trial was rendered unfair by the admission in evidence of a Nazi flag found on another defendant, of testimony about the cocaine refining plant, of their codefendants' guilty pleas, and by references to Duke and the Klan. We affirm.

David Duke and the KKK

It was at the request of the defense, however, that each individual venireman was examined concerning David Duke and the KKK. All those veniremen who became jurors stated that it would not influence their decision. Pursuant to Rule 24(a), Fed. R.Crim.P., the trial judge is vested with broad discretion in the conduct of voir dire, and absent an abuse of discretion and a showing that the rights of the accused have been prejudiced thereby, the scope and content of voir dire will not be disturbed on appeal. *United States v. Harper*, 505 F.2d 924, 925 (5th Cir. 1974). The only other evidence relating to the Klan was an unsolicited response by a government witness that was not emphasized to the jury. There was no error here.

The Nazi Flag

Appellants contend that the Nazi flag was irrelevant because it was owned and being carried by another defendant at the time of the arrest. Again, the trial court is afforded wide discretion in determining whether evidence is relevant or prejudicial. *United States v. Brown*, 547 F.2d 1264, 1266 (5th Cir. 1977). 18 U.S.C. § 960 states that it is illegal to aid in any "military or naval expedition" against a friendly nation. The Nazi and Confederate flags were introduced, along with military fatigue clothes, canteens, knives, assault rifles, and other military gear to show the military nature of the group, as well as to counter appellants' contention that their motive was to defend America against Communism by joining the Dominica defense forces and putting down a Communist insurgency there. In these circumstances, we cannot say that the court erred in concluding that the flag's relevance outweighed its prejudice to the appellants.

The Cocaine Refining Plant

Appellants claim that they had no interest in producing drugs and therefore that this testimony should have been excluded. Black and Hawkins conspired with others for the common purpose of overthrowing the government of Dominica and of setting up the Nortic Corporation. They admitted that they were each to be granted a percentage of Nortic. The statement by the coconspirator Droege was relevant to show that this was a money-making scheme in order to rebut the argument that appellants were merely fighting Communism. It is not critical whether Black and Hawkins actually knew of the cocaine operation. "The conspirators need not know each other nor be privy to the details of each enterprise comprising the conspiracy ... as long as the evidence is sufficient to show that each defendant possessed full knowledge of the conspiracy's general purpose and scope."

B. Mercenarism

Protocol I Additional to the Geneva Conventions of 12 August 1949, and relating to the protection of victims of international armed conflicts

(1977)

Article 47

MERCENARIES

1. A mercenary shall not have the right to be a combatant or a prisoner of war.

2. A mercenary is any person who:

(a) is specially recruited locally or abroad in order to fight in an armed conflict;

(b) does, in fact, take a direct part in the hostilities;

(c) is motivated to take part in the hostilities essentially by the desire for private gain, and, in fact, is promised, by or on behalf of a party to the conflict, material compensation substantially in excess of that promised or paid to combatants of similar ranks and functions in the armed forces of that Party;

(d) is neither a national of a Party to the conflict nor a resident of territory controlled by a Party to the conflict;

(e) is not a member of the armed forces of a Party to the conflict; and

(f) has not been sent by a State which is not a Party to the conflict on official duty as a member of its armed forces.

Neutrality and Nonbelligerency — Mercenaries

Burmester, *The Recruitment and Use of Mercenaries in Armed Conflicts*
72 Am. J. Int'l L. 37, 43–44, 49–50, 52, 54 (1978)[1]

In the United States, the first law dealing with foreign enlistment was enacted in 1794. Subsequent laws have been passed extending its scope. The present provisions, based on a 1909 law, make it an offense for a person to accept a commission or to enlist in or agree to go abroad with the purpose of enlistment in a foreign force. They also make it an offense to recruit in the United States, but it is necessary to show that some agreement or understanding has been entered into. A mere advertisement is not proscribed. The provisions are applicable to civil as well as international conflicts. But, in contrast to the United Kingdom legislation, the U.S. provisions only apply to acts within the country. Thus, if a person goes abroad voluntarily and enlists in a foreign force, he will not be subject to prosecution.... [in the U.S.]

When the Simba revolt broke out in 1964, Tshombe moved quickly to organize an effective fighting force led by mercenaries. After General Mobutu took over the presidency in November 1965, many of the South African and Rhodesian mercenaries recruited by Tshombe were replaced by largely French-speaking mercenaries. Mercenaries also continued to be involved in plans to restore Tshombe, with Angola apparently being used as a base. Following complaints from the Democratic Republic of the Congo, the Security Council on July 10, 1967 adopted a resolution which condemned any state which persisted "in permitting or tolerating the recruitment of mercenaries ... with the objective of overthrowing the Governments of State Members of the United Nations" and called upon governments to ensure that their territory as well as their nationals were not used for the recruitment, training and transit of mercenaries designed to overthrow the Government of the Democratic Republic of the Congo. This followed an earlier resolution of October 14, 1966, which urged Portugal not to allow foreign mercenaries to use Angola as a base of operations for interference in the domestic affairs of the Congo. The Security Council in a further resolution on November 15, 1967 condemned in particular the failure of Portugal to prevent the mercenaries from using Angola as a base of operations for armed attacks against the Congo. The use of mercenaries in Africa has also been condemned by the Organization of African Unity, which has urged states to take action to prevent their nationals from being used as mercenaries.

The use of mercenaries in the Congo on a large scale provoked considerable opposition. The repeated calls of the Security Council for foreign states to cease assisting mercenaries and for the adoption of measures to prevent their departure and the continued appeals for the end of foreign intervention clearly lend weight to the view that a state has an obligation to control the recruitment of its nationals in situations where a threat to peace and security exists. Such an obligation goes beyond that recognized in traditional customary international law....

In the Declaration on Principles of International Law concerning Friendly Relations and Co-operation among States in accordance with the Charter of the United Nations, the following statement appears under the principle that "States shall refrain in their international relations from the threat or use of force against the territorial integrity or political independence of any State, or in any other manner inconsistent with the purposes of the United Nations":

---

1. Reproduced with permission from 72 AJIL 37 (1978), © The American Society of International Law.

> Every State has the duty to refrain from organizing or encouraging the organization of irregular forces or armed bands, including mercenaries, for incursion into the territory of another State.

This statement continues to limit the obligations of states to control of the actual organization of mercenary and other irregular forces. There is no obligation imposed on states actually to prevent their own nationals from joining a mercenary force. Nor does such an obligation emerge in the definition of aggression adopted by the UN General Assembly in 1974, which provides that "the *sending* by or on behalf of a State of armed bands, groups, irregulars or mercenaries, which carry out armed force against another State" of such gravity as to amount to certain prescribed acts shall qualify as an act of aggression (emphasis added). No longer is the actual organization of such forces clearly proscribed. This merely reflects one of the many shortcomings in the definition, which cannot be seen as a full statement of the relevant law.

While the customary international law may be as set out above, it is necessary to consider whether the maintenance of a peaceful world order does not require an extension of the duties thus far imposed on states. The basis for the obligation of states to control the recruiting and organizing of mercenary and other irregular forces on their territory has traditionally been founded on the duty of impartiality imposed on a neutral state. Any consideration of the problem today cannot ignore, however, the major changes in the legal order that the United Nations Charter has brought about. The right to resort to force and to provide assistance to another state under attack has been severely curtailed in the case of international conflicts. Use of mercenaries in such conflicts may reasonably be regarded as foreign intervention, although no third state may be directly involved or approve of the use of its nationals in a mercenary force. Mercenaries can be seen as private outside forces not under the effective control of any state except that by which they are engaged. If one accepts as a primary goal the minimization of armed conflict, the use of outside private armed force, often in situations where the Charter would prohibit formal state intervention, seems a legitimate matter for concern and legal regulation....

As early as 1968 in a resolution on the Implementation of the Declaration of the Granting of Independence to Colonial Countries and Peoples, the General Assembly declared:

> that the practice of using mercenaries against movements for national liberation and independence is punishable as a criminal act and that the mercenaries themselves are outlaws, and calls upon the Governments of all countries to enact legislation declaring the recruitment, financing and training of mercenaries in their territory to be a punishable offence and prohibiting their nationals from serving as mercenaries.

This paragraph was introduced by the Soviet Union on behalf of a number of East European countries toward the end of debate on the resolution. It is not debated. After the adoption of the resolution as a whole, several Western European countries recorded their reservations on this paragraph. The declaration was, however, reiterated in Resolution 2548 (XXIV) of December 11, 1969 and Resolution 2708 (XXV) of December 14, 1970. In Resolution 3103 (XXVIII) of December 12, 1973 on the "Basic Principles on the Legal Status of Combatants Struggling Against Colonial and Alien Domination and Racist Regimes," the following "basic principle" was proclaimed:

> "5. The use of mercenaries by colonial and racist regimes against the national liberation movements struggling for their freedom and independence from the yoke of colonialism and alien domination is considered to be a criminal act and the mercenaries should accordingly be punished as criminals."

Notes and Questions

1. For further references, *see, e.g., In the Trial of F. E. Steiner: A Court Martial*, (1971) Sudan L.J. & Rpts. 147; Cesner & Brant, *Law of the Mercenary: An International Dilemma*, 6 Capital U.L. Rev. 339 (1977); Note, *The Laws of War and the Angolan Trial of Mercenaries: Death to the Dogs of War*, 9 Case West. Res. J. Int'l L. 323 (1977). *See also* Cotton, *The Rights of Mercenaries as Prisoners of War*, 77 Mil. L. Rev. 143 (1977).

2. Recall *Henfield's Case* (Chapter Four); 1 Ops. Att'y Gen. (1795) & (1797) (Chapter Four); *Talbot v. Janson.* Is it true that mercenaries are not criminally sanctionable under customary international law? Under relevant treaty law? See also Note, *Leashing the Dogs of War: Outlawing the Recruitment and Use of Mercenaries*, 22 Va. J. Int'l L. 589, 604–05, *passim* (1982) ("U.N. resolutions, regional treaties, draft conventions, and criminal trials have encouraged the development of an international legal standard condemning the status of mercenary as a crime of war ... the majority international legal position on the issue").

3. In December of 1989 the U.N. General Assembly approved a new Convention Against the Recruitment, Use, Financing and Training of Mercenaries, U.N. G.A. Res. 44/34 (Dec. 11, 1989), in 29 I.L.M. 89 (1990). Some have suggested that the Convention will contribute to the extradition of "mercenaries" who train private armies of drug lords.

Article 1 (1) of the 1989 Convention substantially retains the definition found in Art. 47 (2) (a), (c)–(f) of the Geneva Protocol. Article 1 (2) of the 1989 Convention adds additional definitional factors. Consider also the nature of the offenses and state duties contained in the extract of the Convention found in the Documents Supplement.

Section 2
Aggressive War and Force

A. Early Recognitions

1 Ops. Att'y Gen.
(1795, 1797)
[see Chapter Four, *supra*]

Trial of *Arbuthnot and Armbrister*
(1818)
[see Chapter Four, Section 7D, *supra*]

B. World War I

Barbara Tuchman, The Guns of August
127, 151–53 (1962)

On a return visit to Brussels in 1910, the Kaiser proved indeed to be most reassuring. Belgium had nothing to fear from Germany, he told van der Elst. "You will have no grounds of complaint against Germany.... I understand perfectly your country's position ... I shall never place her in a false position."

On the whole, Belgians believed him. They took their guarantee of neutrality seriously. Belgium had neglected her army, frontier defenses, fortresses, anything that implied lack of confidence in the protective treaty....

[Aug. 4, 1914]

At three o'clock members reconvened in the Reichstag to hear an address by the Chancellor and to perform the remainder of their duty which consisted first of voting war credits and then adjournment. The Social Democrats agreed to make the vote unanimous, and spent their last hours of parliamentary responsibility in anxious consultation whether to join in a "*Hoch*" for the Kaiser which they satisfactorily resolved by making it a *Hoch* for "Kaiser, People, and Country."

Everyone, as Bethmann rose to speak, waited in painful expectancy for what he had to say about Belgium. A year ago Foreign Minister Jagow had assured a secret session of the Reichstag steering committee that Germany would never violate Belgium, and General von Heeringen, then War Minister, had promised that the Supreme Command in the event of war would respect Belgium's neutrality as long as Germany's enemies did. On August 4 deputies did not know that their armies had invaded Belgium that morning. They knew of the ultimatum but nothing of the Belgian reply because the German government, wishing to give the impression that Belgium had acquiesced and that her armed resistance was therefore illegal, never published it.

"Our troops," Bethmann informed the tense audience, "have occupied Luxembourg and perhaps"—the "perhaps" was posthumous by eight hours—"are already in Belgium." (Great commotion.) True, France had given Belgium a pledge to respect her neutrality, but "We knew that France was standing ready to invade Belgium" and "we could not wait." It was, he said inevitably, a case of military necessity, and "necessity knows no law."

So far he had his hearers, both the right which despised him and the left which mistrusted him, in thrall. His next sentence created a sensation. "Our invasion of Belgium is contrary to international law but the wrong—I speak openly—that we are committing we will make good as soon as our military goal has been reached." Admiral Tirpitz considered this the greatest blunder ever spoken by a German statesman; Conrad Haussman, a leader of the Liberal party, considered it the finest part of the speech. The act having been confessed in a public *mea culpa,* he and his fellow deputies of the left felt purged of guilt and saluted the Chancellor with a loud "*Sehr richtig!*" In a final striking phrase— and before his day of memorable maxims was over he was to add one more that would make him immortal—Bethmann said that whoever was as badly threatened as were the Germans could think only of how to "hack his way through."

A war credit of five billion marks was voted unanimously, after which the Reichstag voted itself out of session for four months or for what was generally expected to be the duration. Bethmann closed the proceedings with an assurance that carried overtones of the gladiators' salute: "Whatever our lot may be, August 4, 1914, will remain for all eternity one of Germany's greatest days!" ...

In Berlin, the British ambassador, Sir Edward Goschen, presented the ultimatum in a historic interview with the Chancellor. He found Bethmann "very agitated." According to Bethmann himself, "my blood boiled at this hypocritical harping on Belgium which was not the thing that had driven England into war." Indignation launched Bethmann into a harangue. He said that England was doing an "unthinkable" thing in making war on a "kindred nation," that "it was like striking a man from behind while he was fighting for his life against two assailants," that as a result of "this last terrible step" England would be responsible for all the dreadful events that might follow, and "all for just a word—'neutrality'—just for a scrap of paper...."

Commission on the Responsibility of the Authors of the War and on Enforcement of Penalties, Report Presented to the Preliminary Peace Conference
March 29, 1919 (*reprinted in* 14 AM. J. INT'L L. 95 (1920))[1]

The Commission was charged to inquire into and report upon the following points:

1. The responsibility of the authors of the war.

2. The facts as to breaches of the laws and customs of war committed by the forces of the German Empire and their Allies, on land, on sea, and in the air during the present war.

3. The degree of responsibility for these offences attaching to particular members of the enemy forces, including members of the General Staffs, and other individuals, however highly placed.

4. The constitution and procedure of a tribunal appropriate for the trial of these offences.

5. Any other matters cognate or ancillary to the above which may arise in the course of the enquiry, and which the Commission finds it useful and relevant to take into consideration....

RESPONSIBILITY OF THE AUTHORS OF THE WAR

On the question of the responsibility of the authors of the war, the Commission, after having examined a number of official documents relating to the origin of the World War, and to the violations of neutrality and of frontiers which accompanied its inception, has determined that the responsibility for it lies wholly upon the Powers which declared war in pursuance of a policy of aggression, the concealment of which gives to the origin of this war the character of a dark conspiracy against the peace of Europe.

This responsibility rests first on Germany and Austria, secondly on Turkey and Bulgaria. The responsibility is made all the graver by reason of the violation by Germany and Austria of the neutrality of Belgium and Luxemburg, which they themselves had guaranteed. It is increased, with regard to both France and Serbia, by the violation of their frontiers before the declaration of war.

I. PREMEDITATION OF THE WAR

A.—Germany and Austria

Many months before the crisis of 1914 the German Emperor had ceased to pose as the champion of peace. Naturally believing in the overwhelming superiority of his army, he openly showed his enmity towards France. General von Moltke said to the King of the Belgians: "This time the matter must be settled." In vain the King protested. The Emperor and his Chief of Staff remained no less fixed in their attitude.

On the 28th June, 1914, occurred the assassination at Sarajevo of the heir-apparent of Austria. "It is the act of a little group of madmen," said Francis Joseph. The act, com-

---

1. Reproduced with permission from 14 AJIL 95 (1920), © The American Society of International Law.

mitted as it was by a subject of Austria-Hungary on Austro-Hungarian territory, could in no wise compromise Serbia, which very correctly expressed its condolences and stopped public rejoicing in Belgrade. If the Government of Vienna thought that there was any Serbian complicity, Serbia was ready to seek out the guilty parties. But this attitude failed to satisfy Austria and still less Germany, who, after their first astonishment had passed, saw in this royal and national misfortune a pretext to initiate war.

At Potsdam a "decisive consultation" took place on the 5th July, 1914. Vienna and Berlin decided upon this plan: "Vienna will send to Belgrade a very emphatic ultimatum and a very short limit of time."

The Bavarian Minister, von Lerchenfeld, said in a confidential despatch dated the 18th July, the facts stated in which have never been officially denied: "It is clear that Serbia cannot accept the demands, which are inconsistent with the dignity of an independent state." Count Lerchenfeld reveals in this report that, at the time it was made, the ultimatum to Serbia had been jointly decided upon by the Governments of Berlin and Vienna; that they were waiting to send it until President Poincare and M. Viviani should have left for St. Petersburg; and that no illusions were cherished, either at Berlin or Vienna, as to the consequences which this threatening measure would involve. It was perfectly well known that war would be the result....

At midday on the 18th Austria declared war on Serbia. On the 29th the Austrian Army commenced the bombardment of Belgrade, and made its dispositions to cross the frontier.

The reiterated suggestions of the *Entente* Powers with a view to finding a peaceful solution of the dispute only produced evasive replies on the part of Berlin or promises of intervention with the Government of Vienna without any effectual steps being taken....

On the 3rd August von Schoen went to the Quai d'Orsay with the declaration of war against France. Lacking a real cause of complaint, Germany alleged, in her declaration of war, that bombs had been dropped by French aeroplanes in various districts in Germany. This statement was entirely false. Moreover, it was either later admitted to be so or no particulars were ever furnished by the German Government.

Moreover, in order to be manifestly above reproach, France was careful to withdraw her troops 10 kilom. from the German Frontier. Notwithstanding this precaution, numerous officially established violations of French territory preceded the declaration of war.

The provocation was so flagrant that Italy, herself a member of the Triple Alliance, did not hesitate to declare that in view of the aggressive character of the war the *casus foederis* ceased to apply.

CONCLUSIONS

1. *The war was premeditated by the Central Powers together with their Allies, Turkey and Bulgaria, and was the result of acts deliberately committed in order to make it unavoidable.*

2. *Germany, in agreement with Austria-Hungary, deliberately worked to defeat all the many conciliatory proposals made by the Entente Powers and their repeated efforts to avoid war.*

II. VIOLATION OF THE NEUTRALITY OF BELGIUM AND LUXEMBURG

A. — *Belgium*

Germany is burdened by a specially heavy responsibility in respect of the violation of the neutrality of Belgium and Luxemburg. Article 1 of the Treaty of London of the 19th April, 1839, after declaring that Belgium should form a "perpetually neutral State," had placed this neutrality under the protection of Austria, France, Great Britain, Russia and Prussia. On the 9th August, 1870, Prussia had declared "her fixed determination to respect

Belgian neutrality." On the 22nd July, 1870, Bismarck wrote to the Belgian Minister at Paris, "This declaration is rendered superfluous by existing treaties."

It may be of interest to recall that the attributes of neutrality were specifically defined by the fifth Hague Convention, of the 18th October, 1907. That convention was declaratory of the law of nations, and contained these provisions—"The territory of neutral Powers is inviolable" (Article 1). "Belligerents are forbidden to move troops or convoys, whether of munitions of war or of supplies, across the territory of a neutral Power" (Article 2). "The fact of a neutral Power resisting, even by force, attempts against its neutrality cannot be regarded as a hostile act" (Article 10).

There can be no doubt of the binding force of the treaties which guaranteed the neutrality of Belgium. There is equally no doubt of Belgium's sincerity or of the sincerity of France in their recognition and respect of this neutrality.

On the 29th July, 1914, the day following the declaration of war by Austria-Hungary against Serbia, Belgium put her army on its reinforced peace strength, and so advised the Powers by which her neutrality was guaranteed and also Holland and Luxemburg....

At Paris the reply was categorical: "The French Government are resolved to respect the neutrality of Belgium, and it would only be in the event of some other Power violating that neutrality that France might find herself under the necessity, in order to assure the defence of her own security, to act otherwise."

On the same day as this reply was made at Paris, the French Minister at Brussels made the following communication to M. Davignon, the Belgian Minister of Foreign Affairs: "I am authorized to declare that, in the event of an international war, the French Government, in accordance with the declarations they have always made, will respect the neutrality of Belgium. In the event of this neutrality not being respected by another Power, the French Government, to secure their own defence, might find it necessary to modify their attitude".

At this point is may be recalled that the pretext invoked by Germany in justification of the violation of Belgian neutrality, and the invasion of Belgian territory, seemed to the German Government itself of so little weight, that in Sir Edward Goschen's conversations with the German Chancellor, von Bethmann Hollweg, and with von Jagow, the Secretary of State, it was not a question of aggressive French intentions, but a "matter of life and death to Germany to advance through Belgium and violate the latter's neutrality," and of "a scrap of paper." Further, in his speech on the 4th August, the German Chancellor made his well-known avowal: "Necessity knows no law. Our troops have occupied Luxemburg, and perhaps have already entered Belgian territory. Gentlemen, that is a breach of international law.... We have been obliged to refuse to pay attention to the justifiable protests of Belgium and Luxemburg. The wrong—I speak openly—the wrong we are thereby committing we will try to make good as soon as our military aims have been attained. He who is menaced, as we are, and is fighting for his all can only consider how he is to hack his way through." To this avowal of the German Chancellor there is added and overwhelming testimony of Count von Lerchenfeld, who stated in a report of the 4th August, 1914, that the German General Staff considered it "necessary to cross Belgium: France can only be successfully attacked from that side. At the risk of bringing about the intervention of England, Germany cannot respect Belgian neutrality."

As for the Austrian Government, it waited until the 18th August to declare war on Belgium, but as early as the middle of the month "the motor batteries sent by Austria have proved their excellence in the battles around Namur, as appears from a proclamation of the German general who at the time was in command of the fortress of Liege, which German troops had seized. Consequently, the participation of Austria-Hungary in the violation of Belgian neutrality is aggravated by the fact that she took part in that violation without any previous declaration of war.

B.—*Luxemburg*

The neutrality of Luxemburg was guaranteed by Article 2 of the Treaty of London, 11 May, 1867, Prussia and Austria-Hungary being two of the guarantor Powers. On the 2nd August, 1914, German troops penetrated the territory of the Grand Duchy. Mr. Eyschen, Minister of State of Luxemburg, immediately made an energetic protest.

The German Government alleged "that military measures have become inevitable, because trustworthy news had been received that French forces were marching on Luxemburg." This allegation was at once refuted by Mr. Eyschen.

CONCLUSION

The neutrality of Belgium, guaranteed by the treaties of the 19th April, 1839, and that of Luxemburg, guaranteed by the treaty of the 11th May, 1867, were deliberately violated by Germany and Austria-Hungary.

III. PERSONAL RESPONSIBILITY

The third point submitted by the Conference is thus stated:

> *The degree of responsibility for these offences attaching to particular members of the enemy forces, including members of the General Staffs and other individuals, however highly placed.*

For the purpose of dealing with this point, it is not necessary to wait for proof attaching guilt to particular individuals. It is quite clear from the information now before the Commission that there are grave charges which must be brought and investigated by a court against a number of persons.

In these circumstances, the Commission desire to state expressly that in the hierarchy of persons in authority, there is no reason why rank, however exalted, should in any circumstances protect the holder of it from responsibility when that responsibility has been established before a properly constituted tribunal. This extends even to the case of heads of states. An argument has been raised to the contrary based upon the alleged immunity, and in particular the alleged inviolability, of a sovereign of a state. But this privilege, where it is recognized, is one of practical expedience in municipal law, and is not fundamental. However, even if, in some countries, a sovereign is exempt from being prosecuted in a national court of his own country the position from an international point of view is quite different.

We have later on in our Report proposed the establishment of a high tribunal composed of judges drawn from many nations, and included the possibility of the trial before that tribunal of a former head of state with the consent of that state itself secured by articles in the Treaty of Peace. If the immunity of a sovereign is claimed to extend beyond the limits above stated, it would involve laying down the principle that the greatest outrages against the laws and customs of war and the laws of humanity, if proved against him, could in no circumstances be punished. Such a conclusion would shock the conscience of civilized mankind.

In view of the grave charges which may be preferred against—to take one case—the ex-Kaiser—the vindication of the principles of the laws and customs of war and the laws of humanity which have been violated would be incomplete if he were not brought to trial and if other offenders less highly placed were punished. Moreover, the trial of the offenders might be seriously prejudiced if they attempted and were able to plead the superior orders of a sovereign against whom no steps had been or were being taken.

There is little doubt that the ex-Kaiser and others in high authority were cognizant of and could at least have mitigated the barbarities committed during the course of the war. A word from them would have brought about a different method in the action of their subordinates on land, at sea and in the air.

We desire to say that civil and military authorities cannot be relieved from responsibility by the mere fact that a higher authority might have been convicted of the same offence. It will be for the court to decide whether a plea of superior orders is sufficient to acquit the person charged from responsibility.

CONCLUSION

All persons belonging to enemy countries, however high their position may have been, without distinction of rank, including Chiefs of States, who have been guilty of offences against the laws and customs of war or the laws of humanity, are liable to criminal prosecution....

Any tribunal appropriate to deal with the other offences to which reference is made might hardly be a good court to discuss and deal decisively with such a subject as the authorship of the war. The proceedings and discussions, charges and counter-charges, if adequately and dispassionately examined, might consume much time, and the result might conceivably confuse the simpler issues into which the tribunal will be charged to inquire. While this prolonged investigation was proceeding some witnesses might disappear, the recollection of others would become fainter and less trustworthy, offenders might escape, and the moral effect of tardily imposed punishment would be much less salutary than if punishment were inflicted while the memory of the wrongs done was still fresh and the demand for punishment was insistent.

We therefore do not advise that the acts which provoked the war should be charged against their authors and made the subject of proceedings before a tribunal.

There can be no doubt that the invasion of Luxemburg by the Germans was a violation of the Treaty of London of 1867, and also that the invasion of Belgium was a violation of the Treaties of 1839. These treaties secured neutrality for Luxemburg and Belgium and in that term were included freedom, independence and security for the population living in those countries. They were contracts made between the high contracting parties to them, and involve an obligation which is recognized in international law.

The Treaty of 1839 with regard to Belgium and that of 1867 with regard to Luxemburg were deliberately violated, not by some outside Power, but by one of the very Powers which had undertaken not merely to respect their neutrality, but to compel its observance by any Power which might attack it. The neglect of its duty by the guarantor adds to the gravity of the failure to fulfil the undertaking given. It was the transformation of a security into a peril, of a defence into an attack, of a protection into an assault. It constitutes, moreover, the absolute denial of the independence of states too weak to interpose a serious resistance, an assault upon the life of a nation which resists, an assault against its very existence while, before the resistance was made, the aggressor in the guise of tempter, offered material compensations in return for the sacrifice of honor. The violation of international law was thus an aggravation of the attack upon the independence of states which is the fundamental principle of international right.

And thus a high-handed outrage was committed upon international engagements, deliberately, and for a purpose which cannot justify the conduct of those who were responsible.

The Commission is nevertheless of opinion that no criminal charge can be made against the responsible authorities or individuals (and notably the ex-Kaiser) on the special head of these breaches of neutrality, but the gravity of these gross outrages upon the law of nations and international good faith is such that the Commission thinks they should be the subject of a formal condemnation by the Conference.

CONCLUSIONS

1. The acts which brought about the war should not be charged against their authors or made the subject of proceedings before a tribunal.

2. On the special head of the breaches of the neutrality of Luxemburg and Belgium, the gravity of these outrages upon the principles of the law of nations and upon international good faith is such that they should be made the subject of a formal condemnation by the Conference.

3. On the whole case, including both the acts which brought about the war and those which accompanied its inception, particularly the violation of the neutrality of Belgium and Luxemburg, it would be right for the Peace Conference, in a matter so unprecedented, to adopt special measures, and even to create a special organ in order to deal as they deserve with the authors of such acts.

4. It is desirable that for the future penal sanctions should be provided for such grave outrages against the elementary principles of international law.

Treaty of Peace with Germany
(Versailles, June 28, 1919)

PENALTIES

Article 227

The Allied and Associated Powers publicly arraign William II of Hohenzollern, formerly German Emperor, for a supreme offence against international morality and the sanctity of treaties.

A special tribunal will be constituted to try the accused, thereby assuring him the guarantees essential to the right of defence. It will be composed of five judges, one appointed by each of the following were: namely the United States of America, Great Britain, France, Italy and Japan.

In its decision the tribunal will be guided by the highest motives of international policy, with a view of vindicating the solemn obligations of international undertakings and the validity of international morality. It will be its duty to fix the punishment which it considers should be imposed.

The Allied and Associated Powers will address a request to the Government of the Netherlands for the surrender to them of the ex-Emperor in order that he may be put on trial.

Article 228

The German Government recognizes the right of the Allied and Associated Powers to bring before military tribunals persons accused of having committed acts in violation of the laws and customs of war. Such persons shall, if found guilty, be sentenced to punishments laid down by law. This provision will apply notwithstanding any proceedings or prosecution before a tribunal in Germany or in the territory of her allies.

The German Government shall hand over to the Allied and Associated Powers, or to such one of them as shall so request, all persons accused of having committed an act in violation of the laws and customs of war, who are specified either by name or by the rank, office or employment which they held under the German authorities.

ARTICLE 229

Persons guilty of criminal acts against the nationals of one of the Allied and Associate Powers will be brought before the military tribunals of that Power.

Persons guilty of criminal acts against the nationals of more than one of the Allied and Associated Powers will be brought before military tribunals composed of members of the military tribunals of the Powers concerned.

In every case the accused will be entitled to name his own counsel.

ARTICLE 230

The German Government undertakes to furnish all documents and information of every kind, the production of which may be considered necessary to ensure the full knowledge of the incriminating acts, the discovery of offenders, and the just appreciation of responsibility.

Treaty of Peace between the Allied and Associated Powers and Austria
(September 10, 1919)

PENALTIES

ARTICLE 173

The Austrian Government recognizes the right of the Allied and Associated Powers to bring before military tribunals persons accused of having committed acts in violation of the laws and customs of war. Such persons shall, if found guilty, be sentenced to punishments laid down by law. This provision will apply notwithstanding any proceedings or prosecutions before a tribunal in Austria or in the territory of her allies.

The Austrian Government shall hand over to the Allied and Associated Powers, or to such one of them as shall so request, all persons accused of having committed an act in violation of the laws and customs of war, who are specified either by name or by rank, office or employment with they held under the Austrian authorities.

ARTICLE 174

Persons guilty of criminal acts against the nationals of one of the Allied and Associated Powers will be brought before the military tribunals of that Power.

Persons guilty of criminal acts against the nationals of more than one of the Allied and Associated Powers will be brought before military tribunals composed of members of the military tribunals of the Powers concerned.

In every case the accused will be entitled to name his own counsel.

ARTICLE 175

The Austrian Government undertakes to furnish all documents and information of every kind, the production of which may be considered necessary to ensure the full knowledge of the incriminating acts, the discovery of offenders and the just appreciation of responsibility.

ARTICLE 176

The provisions of Articles 173 to 175 apply similarly to the Governments of the States to which territory belonging to the former Austro-Hungarian Monarchy has been assigned, in so far as concerns persons accused of having committed acts contrary to the laws and customs of war who are in the territory or at the disposal of the said States.

If the persons in question have acquired the nationality of one of the said States, the Government of such State undertakes to take, at the request of the Power concerned and in agreement with it, all the measures necessary to ensure the prosecution and punishment of such persons.

Notes and Questions

1. Do you agree with the Commission Report with respect to the trial of persons for violations of treaties of neutrality, aggressive war? Was there precedent of some sort for the trial of Kaiser William II of Germany?

2. William II had fled to the Netherlands and was not surrendered for prosecution. Lists of other alleged offenders were compiled by the Allied Governments and presented to Germany in 1920, but Germany proposed to try the accused before its highest court at Leipzig, which proposal was accepted. Of the more than 1,000 persons accused of war crimes, only a few were actually tried. See Chapter Six *supra*.

3. The following Reservation to the Commission Report was made by the members of the Japanese delegation:

> "The Japanese Delegates on the Commission on Responsibilities are convinced that many crimes have been committed by the enemy in the course of the present war in violation of the fundamental principles of international law, and recognize that the principal responsibility rests upon individual enemies in high places. They are consequently of opinion that, in order to re-establish for the future the force of the principles thus infringed, it is important to discover practical means for the punishment of the persons responsible for such violations.
>
> A question may be raised whether it can be admitted as a principle of the law of nations that a high tribunal constituted by belligerents can, after a war is over, try an individual belonging to the opposite side, who may be presumed to be guilty of a crime against the laws and customs of war. It may further be asked whether international law recognizes a penal law as applicable to those who are guilty.
>
> In any event, it seems to us important to consider the consequences which would be created in the history of international law by the prosecution for breaches of the laws and customs of war of enemy heads of states before a tribunal constituted by the opposite party.
>
> Our scruples become still greater when it is a question of indicting before a tribunal thus constituted highly placed enemies on the sole ground that they abstained from preventing, putting an end to, or repressing acts in violation of the laws and customs of war, as is provided in clause (c) of section (b) of Chapter IV."

Do you agree or disagree with these reservations?

4. After World War I, certain treaties recognized the prohibition of certain uses of force. Do these reaffirm prior trends or set new precedent binding only among treaty signatories? Consider the following two examples:

Treaty Providing for the Renunciation of War as an Instrument of National Policy

(Paris, August 27, 1928) (the "Kellogg-Briand Pact"), 46 Stat. 2343, T.S. No. 796, 2 Bevans 732, 94 L.N.T.S. 57

[Germany, United States, Belgium, France, Great Britain, India, Italy, Japan, Poland, Czechoslovakia]

Deeply sensible of their solemn duty to promote the welfare of mankind:

Persuaded that the time has come when a frank renunciation of war as an instrument of national policy should be made to the end that the peaceful and friendly relations now existing between their peoples may be perpetuated;

Convinced that all changes in their relations with one another should be sought only by pacific means and be the result of a peaceful and orderly process, and that any signatory Power which shall hereafter seek to promote its national interests by resort to war should be denied the benefits furnished by this Treaty;

Hopeful that, encouraged by their example, all the other nations of the world will join in this humane endeavor and by adhering to the present Treaty as soon as it comes into force bring their peoples within the scope of its beneficent provisions, thus uniting the civilized nations of the world in a common renunciation of war as an instrument of their national policy: ...

> *Article I.* The High Contracting Parties solemnly declare in the names of their respective peoples that they condemn recourse to war for the solution of international controversies and renounce it as an instrument of national policy in their relations with one another.
>
> *Article II.* The High Contracting Parties agree that the settlement or solution of all disputes or conflicts of whatever nature or of whatever origin they may be, which may arise among them, shall never be sought except by pacific means.
>
> *Article III.* The present Treaty shall be ratified by the High Contracting Parties named in the Preamble in accordance with their respective constitutional requirements, and shall take effect as between them as soon as all their several instruments of ratification shall have been deposited at Washington.
>
> This Treaty shall, when it has come into effect as prescribed in the preceding paragraph, remain open as long as may be necessary for adherence by all the other Powers of the world. Every instrument evidencing the adherence of a Power shall be deposited at Washington and the Treaty shall immediately upon such deposit become effective as between the Power thus adhering and the other Powers parties hereto.

Convention on Rights and Duties of States

(Montevideo, December 26, 1933)
49 Stat. 3097, T.S. No. 881, 3 Bevans 145, 165 L.N.T.S. 19

The Governments represented in the Seventh International Conference of American States [recognize]:

> *Article 8.* No state has the right to intervene in the internal or external affairs of another.

Article 9. The jurisdiction of states within the limits of national territory applies to all the inhabitants.

Nationals and foreigners are under the same protection of the law and the national authorities and the foreigners may not claim rights other or more extensive than those of the nationals.

Article 10. The primary interest of states in the conservation of peace. Differences of any nature which arise between them should be settled by recognized pacific methods.

Article 11. The contracting states definitely establish as the rule of their conduct the precise obligation not to recognize territorial acquisitions or special advantages which have been obtained by force whether this consists in the employment of arms, in threatening diplomatic representations, or in any other effective coercive measure. The territory of a state is inviolable and may not be the object of military occupation nor of other measures of force imposed by another state directly or indirectly or for any motive whatever even temporarily....

Notes and Questions

1. Do either of the above treaties mention duties of individuals, crimes, or criminal sanctions? Did the treaties addressed by the 1919 Commission? Are such necessary?

2. By WWII, 63 states had ratified the Kellogg-Briand Pact.

C. World War II

[recall Chapter Two, *supra*]

Opinion and Judgment, International Military Tribunal at Nuremberg
(1946)

The Common Plan or Conspiracy and Aggressive War

The Tribunal now turns to the consideration of the Crimes against Peace charged in the Indictment. Count One of the Indictment charges the defendants with conspiring or having a common plan to commit crimes against peace. Count Two of the Indictment charges the defendants with committing specific crimes against peace by planning, preparing, initiating, and waging wars of aggression against a number of other States. It will be convenient to consider the question of the existence of a common plan and the question of aggressive war together, and to deal later in this Judgment with the question of the individual responsibility of the defendants.

The charges in the Indictment that the defendants planned and waged aggressive wars are charges of the utmost gravity. War is essentially an evil thing. Its consequences are not confined to the belligerent States alone, but affect the whole world.

To initiate a war of aggression, therefore, is not only an international crime; it is the supreme international crime differing only from other war crimes in that it contains within itself the accumulated evil of the whole.

The first acts of aggression referred to in the Indictment are the seizure of Austria and Czechoslovakia; and the first war of aggression charged in the Indictment is the war against Poland begun on September 1939.

Before examining that charge it is necessary to look more closely at some of the events which preceded these acts of aggression. The war against Poland did not come suddenly out of an otherwise clear sky; the evidence has made it plain that this was a war of aggression, as well as the seizure of Austria and Czechoslovakia, was premeditated and carefully prepared, and was not undertaken until the moment was thought opportune for it to be carried through as a definite part of the pre-ordained scheme and plan. For the aggressive design of the Nazi Government were not accidents arising out of the immediate political situation in Europe and the world; they were a deliberate and essential part of Nazi foreign policy.

From the beginning, the National Socialist movement claimed that its object was to unite the German People in the consciousness of their mission and destiny, based on inherent qualities of race, and under the guidance of the Fuhrer.

For its achievement, two things were deemed to be essential: the disruption of the European order as it had existed since the Treaty of Versailles, and the creation of a Greater Germany beyond the frontiers of 1914. This necessarily involved the seizure of foreign territories.

War was seen to be inevitable, or at the very least, highly probable, if these purposes were to be accomplished. The German people, therefore, with all their resources, were to be organized as a great political-military army, schooled to obey without question any policy decreed by the State....

The Seizure of Austria

The invasion of Austria was a pre-meditated aggressive step in furthering the plan to wage aggressive wars against other countries. As a result Germany's flank was protected, that of Czechoslovakia being greatly weakened. The first step had been taken in the seizure of "Lebensraum"; many new divisions of trained fighting men had been acquired; and with the seizure of foreign exchange reserves, the re-armament program had been greatly strengthened.

On 21 May 1935 Hitler announced in the Reichstag that Germany did not intend either to attach Austria or to interfere in her internal affairs. On 1 May 1935 he publicly coupled Czechoslovakia with Austria in his avowal of peaceful intentions; and so late as 11 July 1936 he recognized by treaty the full sovereignty of Austria.

Austria was in fact seized by Germany in the month of March 1938....

It was contended before the Tribunal that the annexation of Austria was justified by the strong desire expressed in many quarters for the union of Austria and Germany; that there were many matters in common between the two peoples that made this union desirable; and that in the result the object was achieved without bloodshed.

These matters, even if true, are really immaterial, for the facts plainly prove that the methods employed to achieve the object were those of an aggressor. The ultimate factor was the armed might of Germany ready to be used if any resistance was encountered. Moreover, none of these considerations appear from the Hossbach account of the meetings of 5 November 1937 to have been the motives which actuated Hitler. On the contrary, all the emphasis is there laid on the advantage to be gained by Germany in her military strength by the annexation of Austria.

The Seizure of Czechoslovakia

The conference of 5 November 1937 made it quite plain that the seizure of Czechoslovakia by Germany had been definitely decided upon. The only question remaining was the selection of the suitable moment to do it. On 4 March 1938 the Defendant Von Ribbentrop wrote to the Defendant Keitel with regard to a suggestion made to Von Ribbentrop by the Hungarian Ambassador in Berlin, that possible war aims against Czechoslovakia should be discussed between the German and Hungarian Armies. In the course of this letter Von Ribbentrop said:

> "I have many doubts about such negotiations. In case we should discuss with Hungary possible war aims against Czechoslovakia, the danger exists that other parties as well would be informed about this." …

The Invasion of Denmark and Norway

The aggressive war against Poland was but the beginning. The aggression of Nazi Germany quickly spread from country to country. In point of time the first two countries to suffer were Denmark and Norway.

On 31 May 1939 a Treaty of Non-Aggression was made between Germany and Denmark, and signed by the Defendant Von Ribbentrop. It was there solemnly stated that the parties to the Treaty were "firmly resolved to maintain peace between Denmark and Germany under all circumstances." Nevertheless, Germany invaded Denmark on 9 April 1940.

On 2 September 1939, after the outbreak of war with Poland, Germany sent a solemn assurance to Norway.…

From this narrative it is clear that as early as October 1939 the question of invading Norway was under consideration. The defense that has been made here is that Germany was compelled to attack Norway to forestall an Allied invasion, and her action was therefore preventive.

It must be remembered that preventive action in foreign territory is justified only in case of "an instant and overwhelming necessity for self-defense, leaving no choice of means, and no moment of deliberation" (The Caroline Case, Moore's *Digest of International Law*, II, 412). How widely the view was held in influential German circles that the Allies intended to occupy Norway cannot be determined with exactitude.…

Violations of International Treaties

The [I.M.T.] Charter defines as a crime the planning or waging of war that is a war of aggression or a war in violation of international treaties. The Tribunal has decided that certain of the defendants planned and waged aggressive wars against 12 nations, and were therefore guilty of this series of crimes. This makes it unnecessary to discuss the subject in further detail, or even to consider at any length the extent to which these aggressive wars were also "wars in violation of international treaties, agreements, or assurances."

These treaties are set out in Appendix C of the Indictment. Those of principal importance are the following.

Hague Conventions

In the 1899 Convention the signatory powers agreed: "before an appeal to arms … to have recourse, as far as circumstances allow, to the good offices or mediation of one or more friendly powers." A similar clause was inserted in the Convention for Pacific Settlement of International Disputes of 1907. In the accompanying Convention Relative to Opening of Hostilities, Article I contains this far more specific language: "The Contracting Powers recognize that hostilities between them must not commence without a previous and explicit warning, in the form of either a declaration of war, giving reasons, or an ultimatum with a conditional declaration of war." Germany was a party to these conventions.

Versailles Treaty

Breaches of certain provisions of the Versailles Treaty are also relied on by the Prosecution—Not to fortify the left bank of the Rhine (Articles 42–44); to "respect strictly the independence of Austria" (Article 80); renunciation of any rights in Memel (Article 99); and the Free City of Danzig (Article 100); the recognition of the independence of the Czechoslovak State; and the military, naval, and air clauses against German rearmament found in Part V. There is no doubt that action was taken by the German government contrary to all these provisions, the details of which are set out in Appendix C. With regard to the Treaty of Versailles, the matters relied on are:

1. The violation of Articles 42 to 44 in respect of the demilitarized zone of the Rhineland:

2. The annexation of Austria on 13 March 1938, in violation of Article 80:

3. The incorporation of the district of Memel on 22 March 1939, in violation of Article 99;

4. The incorporation of the Free City of Danzig on 1 September 1939, in violation of Article 100;

5. The incorporation of the provinces of Bohemia and Moravia on 16 March 1939, in violation of Article 81:

6. The repudiation of the military, naval, and air clauses of the Treaty, in or about March of 1935.

On 21 May 1935 Germany announced that, whilst renouncing the disarmament clauses of the Treaty, she would still respect the territorial limitations, and would comply with the Locarno Pact. (With regard to the first five breaches alleged, therefore, the Tribunal finds the allegation proved.)

Treaties of Mutual Guarantee, Arbitration, and Non-Aggression

It is unnecessary to discuss in any detail the various treaties entered into by Germany and with other Powers. Treaties of mutual guarantee were signed by Germany at Locarno in 1925, with Belgium, France, Great Britain, and Italy, assuring the maintenance of the territorial *status quo*. Arbitration treaties were also executed by Germany at Locarno with Czechoslovakia, Belgium, and Poland.

Article I of the latter treaty is typical, providing: "All disputes of every kind between Germany and Poland ... which it may not be possible to settle amicably by the normal methods of diplomacy, shall be submitted for decision to an arbitral tribunal...."

Conventions of Arbitration and Conciliation were entered into between Germany, the Netherlands, and Denmark in 1926; and between Germany and Luxembourg in 1929. Non-aggression treaties were executed by Germany with Denmark and Russia in 1939.

Kellogg-Briand Pact

The Pact of Paris was signed on 27 August 1928 by Germany, the United States, Belgium, France, Great Britain, Italy, Japan, Poland, and other countries; and subsequently by other powers. The Tribunal has made full reference to the nature of this Pact and its legal effect in another part of this judgment. It is therefore not necessary to discuss the matter further here, save to state that in the opinion of the Tribunal this Pact was violated by Germany in all the cases of aggressive war charged in the Indictment. It is to be noted that on 26 January 1934 Germany signed a Declaration for the Maintenance of Permanent Peace with Poland, which was explicitly based on the Pact of Paris, and in which the use of force was outlawed for a period of ten years.

The Tribunal does not find it necessary to consider any of the other treaties referred to in the Appendix, or the repeated agreements and assurances of her peaceful intentions entered into by Germany.

The Law of the Charter

The jurisdiction of the Tribunal is defined in the Agreement and Charter, and the crimes coming within the jurisdiction of the Tribunal, for which there shall be individual responsibility, are set out in Article 6. The law of the Charter is decisive, and binding upon the Tribunal.

The making of the Charter was the exercise of the sovereign legislative power by the countries to which the German Reich unconditionally surrendered; and the undoubted right of these countries to legislate for the occupied territories has been recognized by the civilized world. The Charter is not an arbitrary exercise of power on the part of the victorious Nations, but in the view of the Tribunal, as will be shown, it is the expression of international law existing at the time of its creation; and to that extent is itself a contribution to international law.

The Signatory Powers created this Tribunal, defined the law it was to administer, and made regulations for the proper conduct of the Trial. In doing so, they have done together what any one of them might have done singly; for it is not to be doubted that any nation has the right to set up special courts to administer law. With regard to the constitution of the Court, all that the defendants are entitled to ask is to receive a fair trial on the facts and law.

The Charter makes the planning or waging of a war of aggression or a war in violation of international treaties a crime; and it is therefore not strictly necessary to consider whether and to what extent aggressive war was a crime before the execution of the London Agreement. But in view of the great importance of the questions of law involved, the Tribunal has heard full argument from the Prosecution and the Defense, and will express its view on the matter.

[At this point the Tribunal addressed the question of *nullum crimen sine lege*—see Chapter Six, Section 3A, *supra*]

This view is strongly reinforced by a consideration of the state of international law in 1939, so far as aggressive war is concerned. The General Treaty for the Renunciation of War of 27 August 1928, more generally known as the Pact of Paris or the Kellogg-Briand Pact, was binding on 63 nations, including Germany, Italy and Japan at the outbreak of war in 1939. In the preamble, the signatories declared that they were:

> "Deeply sensible of their solemn duty to promote the welfare of mankind; persuaded that the time has come when a frank renunciation of war as an instrument of national policy should be made to the end that the peaceful and friendly relations now existing between their peoples should be perpetuated ... all changes in their relations with one another should be sought only by pacific means ... thus uniting civilised nations of the world in a common renunciation of war as an instrument of their national policy...."

The first two articles are as follows:

> "Article I. The High Contracting Parties solemnly declare in the names of their respective peoples that they condemn recourse to war for the solution of international controversies and renounce it as an instrument of national policy in their relations to one another."

"Article II. The High Contracting Parties agree that the settlement or solution of all disputes or conflicts of whatever nature or whatever origin they may be, which may arise among them, shall never be sought except by pacific means."

The question is, what was the legal effect of this Pact? The nations who signed the Pact or adhered to it unconditionally condemned recourse to war for the future as an instrument of policy, and expressly renounced it. After the signing of the Pact, any nation resorting to war as an instrument of national policy breaks the Pact. In the opinion of the Tribunal, the solemn renunciation of war as an instrument of national policy necessarily involves the proposition that such a war is illegal in international law; and that those who plan and wage such a war, with its inevitable and terrible consequences, are committing a crime in so doing. War for the solution of international controversies undertaken as an instrument of national policy certainly includes a war of aggression, and such a war is therefore outlawed by the Pact. As Mr. Henry L. Stimson then Secretary of State of the United States, said in 1932:

"War between nations was renounced by the signatories of the Kellogg-Briand Treaty. This means that it has become throughout practically the entire world … an illegal thing. Hereafter, when nations engage in armed conflict, either one or both of them must be termed violators of the general treaty law.… We denounce them as law breakers."

But it is argued that the Pact does not expressly enact that such wars are crimes, or set up courts to try those who make such wars. To that extent the same is true with regard to the laws of war contained in the Hague Convention. The Hague Convention of 1907 prohibited resort to certain methods of waging war. These included the inhumane treatment of prisoners, the employment of poisoned weapons, the improper use of flags of truce, and similar matters. Many of these prohibitions had been enforced long before the date of the Convention; but since 1907 they have certainly been crimes, punishable as offenses against the law of war; yet the Hague Convention nowhere designates such practices as criminal, nor is any sentence prescribed, nor any mention made of a court to try and punish offenders. For many years past, however, military tribunals have tried and punished individuals guilty of violating the rules of land warfare laid down by this Convention. In the opinion of the Tribunal, those who wage aggressive war are doing that which is equally illegal, and of much greater moment than a breach of one of the rules of the Hague Convention. In interpreting the words of the Pact, it must be remembered that international law is not the product of an international legislature, and that such international agreements as the Pact of Paris have to deal with general principles of law, and not with administrative matters of procedure. The law of war is to be found not only in treaties, but in the customs and practices of states which gradually obtained universal recognition, and from the general principles of justice applied by jurists and practised by military courts. This law is not static, but by continual adaptation follows the needs of a changing world. Indeed, in many cases treaties do no more than express and define for more accurate reference the principles of law already existing.

The view which the Tribunal takes of the true interpretation of the Pact is supported by the international history which preceded it. In the year 1923 the draft of a Treaty of Mutual Assistance was sponsored by the League of Nations. In Article I the Treaty declared "that aggressive war is an international crime," and that the parties would "undertake that no one of them will be guilty of its commission." The draft treaty was submitted to 29 states, about half of whom were in favor of accepting the text, the principal objection appeared to be in the difficulty of defining the acts which would constitute "aggression," rather than any doubt as to the criminality of aggressive war. The preamble to the

League of Nations 1924 Protocol for the Pacific Settlement of International Disputes ("Geneva Protocol") after "recognising the solidarity of the Members of the international community," declared that "a war of aggression constitutes a violation of this solidarity and is an international crime." It went on to declare that the contracting parties were "desirous of facilitating the complete application of the system provided in the Covenant of the League of Nations for the pacific settlement of disputes between the States and of ensuring the repression of international crimes." The Protocol was recommended to the members of the League of Nations by a unanimous resolution in the assembly of the 48 members of the League. These members included Italy and Japan, but Germany was not then a member of the League.

Although the Protocol was never ratified, it was signed by the leading statesmen of the world, representing the vast majority of the civilized states and peoples, and may be regarded as strong evidence of the intention to brand aggressive war as an international crime.

At the meeting of the Assembly of the League of Nations on 24 September 1927, all the delegations then present (including the German, the Italian, and the Japanese), unanimously adopted a declaration concerning wars of aggression. The preamble to the declaration stated:

"The Assembly:

Recognizing the solidarity which unites the community of nations;

Being inspired by a firm desire for the maintenance of general peace;

Being convinced that a war of aggression can never serve as a means of settling international disputes, and is in consequence an international crime...."

The unanimous resolution of 18 February 1928 of 21 American republics at the Sixth (Havana) Pan-American Conference, declared that "war of aggression constitutes an international crime against the human species."

All these expressions of opinion, and others that could be cited, so solemnly made, reinforce the construction which the Tribunal placed upon the Pact of Paris, that resort to a war of aggression is not merely illegal, but is criminal. The prohibition of aggressive war demanded by the conscience of the world, finds its expression in the series of pacts and treaties to which the Tribunal has just referred.

It is also important to remember that Article 227 of the Treaty of Versailles provided for the constitution of a special Tribunal, composed of representatives of five of the Allied and Associated Powers which had been belligerents in the First World War opposed to Germany, to try the former German Emperor "for a supreme offense against international morality and the sanctity of treaties." The purpose of this trial was expressed to be "to vindicate the solemn obligations of international undertakings, and the validity of international morality." In Article 228 of the Treaty, the German Government expressly recognized the right of the Allied Powers "to bring before military tribunals persons accused of having committed acts in violation of the laws and customs of war." ...

The Law as to the Common Plan or Conspiracy

In the previous recital of the facts relating to aggressive war, it is clear that planning and preparation had been carried out in the most systematic way at every stage of the history.

Planning and preparation are essential to the making of war. In the opinion of the Tribunal aggressive war is a crime under international law. The Charter defines this offense as planning, preparation, initiation, or waging of a war of aggression "or participation in a Common Plan or Conspiracy for the accomplishment ... of the foregoing." The Indictment follows this distinction. Count One charges the Common Plan or Conspiracy. Count Two charges the planning and waging of war. The same evidence has been introduced to support both Counts. We shall therefore discuss both Counts together, as they are in substance the same. The defendants have been charged under both Counts, and their guilt under each Count must be determined.

The "Common Plan or Conspiracy" charged in the Indictment covers 25 years, from the formation of the Nazi Party in 1919 to the end of the war in 1945. The Party is spoken of as "the instrument of cohesion among the Defendants" for carrying out the purposes of the conspiracy—the overthrowing of the Treaty of Versailles, acquiring territory lost by Germany in the last war and "Lebensraum" in Europe, by the use, if necessary, of armed force, of aggressive war. The "seizure of power" by the Nazis, the use of terror, the destruction of trade unions, the attack on Christian teaching and on churches, the persecution of Jews, the regimentation of youth—all these are said to be steps deliberately taken to carry out the common plan. It found expression, so it is alleged, in secret rearmament, the withdrawal of Germany from the Disarmament Conference and the League of Nations, universal military service, and seizure of the Rhineland. Finally, according to the Indictment, aggressive action was planned and carried out against Austria and Czechoslovakia in 1936–1938, followed by the planning and waging of war against Poland; and, successively, against 10 other countries.

The Prosecution says, in effect, that any significant participation in the affairs of the Nazi Party or Government is evidence of a participation in a conspiracy that is in itself criminal. Conspiracy is not defined in the Charter. But in the opinion of the Tribunal the conspiracy must be clearly outlined in its criminal purpose. It must not be too far removed from the time of decision and of action. The planning, to be criminal, must not rest merely on the declarations of a party program, such as are found in the 25 points of the Nazi Party, announced in 1920, or the political affirmations expressed in *Mein Kampf* in later years. The Tribunal must examine whether a concrete plan to wage war existed, and determine the participants in that concrete plan....

[T]he threat of war—and war itself if necessary—was an integral part of the Nazi policy. But the evidence establishes with certainty the existence of many separate plans rather than a single conspiracy embracing them all. That Germany was rapidly moving to complete dictatorship from the moment that the Nazis seized power and progressively in the direction of war, has been overwhelmingly shown in the ordered sequence of aggressive acts and wars already set out in this Judgment.

In the opinion of the Tribunal, the evidence establishes the common planning to prepare and wage war by certain of the defendants. It is immaterial to consider whether a single conspiracy to the extent and over the time set out in the Indictment has been conclusively proved. Continued planning, with aggressive war as the objective, has been established beyond doubt. The truth of the situation was well stated by Paul Schmidt, official interpreter of the German Foreign Office, as follows:

> "The general objectives of the Nazi leadership were apparent from the start, namely the domination of the European Continent, to be achieved first by the incorporation of all German speaking groups in the Reich, and secondly, by territorial expansion under the slogan "Lebensraum." The execution of these basic objectives, however, seemed to be characterized by improvisation. Each succeeding step was apparently carried out as each new situation arose, but all consistent with the ultimate objectives mentioned above."

The argument that such common planning cannot exist where there is complete dictatorship is unsound. A plan in the execution of which a number of persons participate is still a plan, even though conceived by only one of them; and those who execute the plan do not avoid responsibility by showing that they acted under the man who conceived it. Hitler could not make aggressive war by himself. He had to have the cooperation of statesmen, military leaders, diplomats, and business men. When they, with knowledge of his aims, gave him their cooperation, they made themselves parties to the plan he had initiated. They are not to be deemed innocent because Hitler made use of them, if they knew what they were doing. That they were assigned to their tasks by a dictator does not absolve them from responsibility here any more than it does in the comparable tyranny of organized domestic crime.

Count One, however, charges not only the conspiracy to commit aggressive war, but also to commit War Crimes and Crimes against Humanity. But the Charter does not define as a separate crime any conspiracy except the one to commit acts of aggressive war. Article 6 of the Charter provides:

> "Leaders, organizers, instigators, and accomplices participating in the formulation or execution of a common Plan or Conspiracy to commit any of the foregoing crimes are responsible for all acts performed by any persons in execution of such plan."

In the opinion of the Tribunal these words do not add a new and separate crime to those already listed. The words are designed to establish the responsibility of persons participating in a common plan. The Tribunal will therefore disregard the charges in Count One that the defendants conspired to commit War Crimes and Crimes against Humanity, and will consider only the common plan to prepare, initiate, and wage aggressive war.

Notes and Questions

1. Does the Judgment attempt to define "aggression"? Is there sufficient guidance from the Judgment for future prosecutions of those involved in "wars of aggression"?

2. Do you agree with the Tribunal that there was adequate precedent for notice to German leaders that crimes against peace had been proscribed? What sort of precedential matters were identified?

3. Is it likely that one can be prosecuted for engaging in a "war of aggression" without proof of a criminal conspiracy?

4. Do you agree with the Tribunal that Germany had no lawful right to invade Norway and Denmark? Had this sort of claim been raised by Germany before?

5. How would the Judgment of the International Military Tribunal at Nuremberg apply with respect to U.S. intervention in Central America in the 1980s? Materials which follow are also relevant.

6. On the precept of "necessity," see also Arbitration between Russia and Turkey, Scott, Hague Court Reports 297, 317–18 (1916); Oscar Chin Case, P.C.I.J. Ser. A/B, No. 63, at 113 (1934) (Anzilotti, J., sep. op.). *See also* Vienna Convention on the Law of Treaties of May 22, 1969, arts. 60–62, U.N. Doc. A/CONF. 39/27, p. 289.

United States v. von Leeb (The High Command Case)
American Military Tribunal, 1948
XI Trials of War Criminals 462 (1950)

The initiation of war or an invasion is a unilateral operation. When war is formally declared or the first shot is fired the initiation of the war has ended and from then on there is a waging of war between the two adversaries. Whether a war be lawful, or aggressive and therefore unlawful under international law, is and can be determined only from a consideration of the factors that entered into its initiation. In the intent and purpose for which it is planned, prepared, initiated and waged is to be found its lawfulness or unlawfulness.

As we have pointed out, war whether it be lawful or unlawful is the implementation of a national policy. If the policy under which it is initiated is criminal in its intent and purpose it is so because the individuals at the policy-making level had a criminal intent and purpose in determining the policy. If war is the means by which the criminal objective is to be attained then the waging of the war is but an implementation of the policy, and the criminality which attaches to the waging of an aggressive war should be confined to those who participate in it at the policy level.

This does not mean that the Tribunal subscribes to the contention made in this trial that since Hitler was the dictator of the Third Reich and that he was supreme in both the civil and military fields, he alone must bear criminal responsibility for political and military policies. No matter how absolute his authority, Hitler alone could not formulate a policy of aggressive war and alone implement that policy by preparing, planning, and waging such a war. Somewhere between the Dictator and Supreme Commander of the Military forces of the nation and the common soldier is the boundary between the criminal and the excusable participation in the waging of an aggressive war by an individual engaged in it. Control Council Law No. 10 does not definitely draw such a line.

It points out in paragraph 2 of Article II certain fact situations and established relations that are or may be sufficient to constitute guilt and sets forth certain categories of activity that do not establish immunity from criminality. Since there has been no other prosecution under Control Council Law No. 10 with defendants in the same category as those in this case, no such definite line has been judicially drawn. This Tribunal is not required to fix a general rule but only to determine the guilt or innocence of the present defendants.

The judgment of the IMT held that:

> The Charter is not an arbitrary exercise of power on the part of the victorious nations, but in view of the Tribunal, as will be shown, it is the expression of international law existing at the time of its creation; and to that extent is itself a contribution to international law.

We hold that Control Council Law No. 10 likewise is but an expression of international law existing at the time of its creation. We cannot therefore construe it as extending the international common law as it existed at the time of the Charter to add thereto any new element of criminality, for so to do would give it an ex post facto effect which we do not construe it to have intended. Moreover, that this was not intended is indicated by the fact that the London Charter of 8 August 1945, is made an integral part of the Control Council Law.

Since international common law grows out of the common reactions and the composite thinking with respect to recurring situations by the various states composing the family of nations, it is pertinent to consider the general attitude of the citizens of states with respect to their military commanders and their obligations when their nations plan, prepare for and initiate or engage in war.

While it is undoubtedly true that international common law in case of conflict with state law takes precedence over it and while it is equally true that absolute unanimity among all the states in the family of nations is not required to bring an international common law into being, it is scarcely a tenable proposition that international common law will run counter to the consensus within any considerable number of nations.

Furthermore, we must not confuse idealistic objectives with realities. The world has not arrived at a state of civilization such that it can dispense with fleets, armies, and air forces, nor has it arrived at a point where it can safely outlaw war under any and all circumstances and situations. In as much as all war cannot be considered outlawed then armed forces are lawful instrumentalities of state, which have internationally legitimate functions. An unlawful war of aggression connotes of necessity a lawful war of defense against aggression. There is no general criterion under international common law for determining the extent to which a nation may arm and prepare for war. As long as there is no aggressive intent, there is no evil inherent in a nation making itself militarily strong. An example is Switzerland which for her geographical extent, her population and resources is proportionally stronger militarily than many nations of the world. She uses her military strength to implement a national policy that seeks peace and to maintain her borders against aggression.

There have been nations that have initiated and waged aggressive war through long periods of history, doubtless there are nations still disposed to do so; and if not, judging in the light of history, there may be nations which tomorrow will be disposed so to do. Furthermore, situations may arise in which the question whether the war is or is not aggressive is doubtful and uncertain. We may safely assume that the general and considered opinions of the people within states — the source from which international common law springs are not such as to hamper or render them impotent to do the things they deem necessary for their national protection.

We are of the opinion that as in ordinary criminal cases, so in the crime denominated aggressive war, the same elements must all be present to constitute criminality. There first must be actual knowledge that an aggressive war is intended and that if launched it will be an aggressive war. But mere knowledge is not sufficient to make participation even by high ranking military officers in the war criminal. It requires in addition that the possessor of such knowledge, after he acquires it shall be in a position to shape or influence the policy that brings about its initiation or its continuance after initiation, either by furthering, or by hindering or preventing it. If he then does the former, he becomes criminally responsible; if he does the latter to the extent of his ability, then his action shows the lack of criminal intent with respect to such policy.

If a defendant did not know that the planning and preparation for invasions and wars in which he was involved were concrete plans and preparations for aggressive wars and for wars otherwise in violation of international laws and treaties, then he cannot be guilty of an offense. If, however, after the policy to initiate and wage aggressive wars was formulated, a defendant came into possession of knowledge that the invasions and wars to be waged were aggressive and unlawful, then he will be criminally responsible if he, being on the policy level, could have influenced such policy and failed to do so.

If and as long as a member of the armed forces does not participate in the preparation, planning, initiating, or waging of aggressive war on a policy level, his war activities do not fall under the definition of crimes against peace. It is not a person's rank or status, but his power to shape or influence the policy of his state, which is the relevant issue for determining his criminality under the charge of crimes against peace.

International law condemns those who, due to their actual power to shape and influence the policy of their nation, prepare for, or lead their country into or in an aggressive war. But we do not find that, at the present stage of development, international law declares as criminals those below that level who, in the execution of this war policy, act as the instruments of the policy makers. Anybody who is on the policy level and participates in the war policy is liable to punishment. But those under them cannot be punished for the crimes of others. The misdeed of the policy makers is all the greater in as much as they use the great mass of the soldiers and officers to carry out an international crime; however, the individual soldier or officer below the policy level is but the policy makers' instrument, finding himself, as he does, under the rigid discipline which is necessary for and peculiar to military organization....

But however much their failure is morally reprimandable, we are of the opinion and hold that international common law, at the time they so acted, had not developed to the point of making the participation of military officers below the policy making or policy influencing level into a criminal offense in and of itself.

International law operates as a restriction and limitation on the sovereignty of nations. It may also limit the obligations which individuals owe to their states, and create for them international obligations which are binding upon them to an extent that they must be carried out even if to do so violates a positive law or directive of state. But the limitation which international common law imposes on national sovereignty, or on individual obligations, is a limitation self-imposed or imposed by the composite thinking in the international community, for it is by such democratic processes that common law comes into being. If there is no generality of opinion among the nations of the world as to a particular restriction on national sovereignty or on the obligations of individuals toward their own state, then there is no international common law on such matter.

By the Kellogg-Briand Pact 63 nations, including Germany, renounced war as an instrument of national policy. If this, as we believe it is, is evidence of a sufficient crystallization of world opinion to authorize a judicial finding that there exist crimes against peace under international common law, we cannot find that law to extend further than such evidence indicates. The nations that entered into the Kellogg-Briand Pact considered it imperative that existing international relationships should not be changed by force. In the preamble they state that they are:

> Persuaded that the time has come when ... all changes in their relationships with one another should be sought only by pacific means....

This is a declaration that from that time forward each of the signatory nations should be deemed to possess and to have the right to exercise all the privileges and powers of a sovereign nation within the limitations of international law, free from all interference by force on the part of any other nation. As a corollary to this, the changing or attempting to change the international relationships by force of arms is an act of aggression and if the aggression results in war, the war is an aggressive war. It is, therefore, aggressive war that is renounced by the pact. It is aggressive war that is criminal under international law.

The crime denounced by the law is the use of war as an instrument of national policy. Those who commit the crime are those who participate at the policy making level in planning, preparing, or in initiating war. After war is initiated, and is being waged, the policy question then involved becomes one of extending, continuing or discontinuing war. The crime at this stage likewise must be committed at the policy making level.

The making of a national policy is essentially political, though it may require, and of necessity does require, if war is to be one element of that policy, a consideration of matters military as well as matters political.

It is self-evident that national policies are made by man. When men make a policy that is criminal under international law, they are criminally responsible for so doing. This is the logical and inescapable conclusion.

The acts of commanders and staff officers below the policy level, in planning campaigns, preparing means for carrying them out, moving against a country on orders and fighting a war after it has been instituted, do not constitute the planning, preparation, initiation, and waging of war or the initiation of invasion that international law denounces as criminal.

Under the record we find the defendants were not on the policy level, and are not guilty under count one of the indictment. With crimes charged to have been committed by them in the manner in which they behaved in the waging of war, we deal in other parts of this judgment.

D. Post World War II

Principles of the Nuremberg Charter and Judgment

Formulated by the International Law Commission, 5 U.N. GAOR, Supp. No. 12, at 11–14, para. 99, U.N. Doc. A/1316 (1950)[1]

I. Any person who commits an act which constitutes a crime under international law is responsible therefor and liable to punishment.

II. The fact that internal law does not impose a penalty for an act which constitutes a crime under international law does not relieve the person who committed the act from responsibility under international law.

III. The fact that a person who committed an act which constitutes a crime under international law acted as Head of State or responsible Government official does not relieve him from responsibility under international law....

IV. The crimes hereinafter set out are punishable as crimes under international law:

  a. Crimes against peace:

    (i) Planning, preparation, initiation or waging of a war of aggression, or a war in violation of international treaties, agreements or assurances;

    (ii) Participation in a common plan or conspiracy for the accomplishment of any of the acts mentioned under (i)....

VII. Complicity in the commission of a crime against peace, a war crime, or a crime against humanity as set forth in Principle VI is a crime under international law.

Question

1. Can a nation-state lawfully benefit from its own wrong? Consider: *Aboitiz & Co. v. Price*, 99 F. Supp. 602, 612 (D. Utah 1951) (dictum)

> The Japanese occupation was an act of unprovoked aggression. It was an international crime. It was outside and in violation of international law.

> Japan and the United States agreed in the 1907 Hague Convention I for the Pacific Settlement of International Disputes: " ... before an appeal to arms ... to have recourse, as far as circumstances allow, to the good offices or mediation of one or more friendly powers".

---

1. In 1946, the United Nations General Assembly affirmed "the principles of international law recognized by the Charter of the Nuremberg Tribunal and the judgment of the Tribunal." G.A. Res. 95(I), U.N. Doc. A/64/Add. 1 (unanimous). The General Assembly had also requested the International Law Commission to formulate such principles, which it did in 1950.

And, Japan, as well as the United States, signed and ratified the 1907 Hague Convention III, relative to the opening of hostilities, which contains the specific language: "The Contracting Powers recognize that hostilities between themselves must not commence without previous and explicit warning, in the form either of a reasoned declaration of war or of an ultimatum with conditional declaration of war."

We all remember the sneaking and deceitful tactics of Japan's diplomats, Kurusu and Nomura, on the eve of the surprise attack on Pearl Harbor, tactics which the record in the Nurnberg trials shows had Hitler's approval and commendation. The occupation of the Philippines was in violation of at least these two provisions, and, from our point of view, that occupation could have no legitimate purposes which Japan was entitled to realize.

See also Factory at Chorzow Case, 1927 P.C.I.J., Ser. A, No. 9, at 31; Article 5 (3) of the 1974 Definition of Aggression, in the Documents Supplement.

Charter of the United Nations
(June 26, 1945, 59 Stat. 1031)

[read the preamble to the U.N. Charter and Articles 1–2, 24–25, 33, 39–42, 48, 51, 52–53, 55–56, 103]

Notes and Questions

1. What is the use of "armed force ... in the common interest" within the meaning of the preamble to the Charter? See also Articles 1, 55.

2. Are all threats or uses of force prohibited by the language of Article 2, paragraph 4, of the Charter? Or are there only three types? States and textwriters are split. Concerning the express prohibition of merely three types of armed force under Article 2(4) of the Charter, see, for example, Paust, *Use of Armed Force against Terrorists in Afghanistan, Iraq, and Beyond*, 35 Cornell Int'l L.J. 533, 536–37 (2002); see also John Norton Moore, et al., National Security Law 131 (1990); Anthony D'Amato, *The Invasion of Panama Was a Lawful Response to Tyranny*, 84 Am. J. Int'l L. 516, 520 (1990); Michael Reisman & Myres S. McDougal, *Humanitarian Intervention to Protect the Ibos*, in Humanitarian Intervention and the United Nations 167, 177 (Richard B. Lillich ed., 1973); Carsten Stahn, *Enforcement of the Collective Will After Iraq*, 97 Am. J. Int'l L. 803, 816 (2003). *But see* Yoram Dinstein, War, Aggression and Self-Defence 87–88 (4 ed. 2005); Mary Ellen O'Connell, *The Resort to Drones Under International Law*, 39 Denv. J. Int'l L. & Pol'y 585, 589 (2011) (current law is adequate) (preferring that Article 2(4) prohibits all force above a "de minimis" level); Christian J. Tams, *The Use of Force Against Terrorists*, 20 Eur. J. Int'l L. 359, 364–65 (also noting early and decades long disagreement), 375 (2009). If Article 2(4) does not prohibit all uses of armed force by a state in the territory of another state, what might the consequences be with respect to humanitarian intervention to stop massive violations of international criminal law (*e.g.*, genocide and other crimes against humanity)? Which approach to interpretation seems preferable?

3. Is merely "armed" "force" prohibited or regulated under Article 2 (4)? See also Paust & Blaustein, The Arab Oil Weapon (1977); R. Lillich, Economic Coercion and the New International Economic Order (1976). Most states and textwriters believe that merely "armed" force is proscribed, although the word "armed" does not appear in

Article 2 (4) and appears in Article 51. Would a cyber attack on U.S. defense computer systems that closes them down for hours constitute a use of "armed" force?

4. Is preemptive self-defense permissible under Article 51 of the Charter? Is "anticipatory" self-defense (when force is perceived to be necessary just before an armed attack)? What requirements or standards are articulated? How would these have applied in the circumstance of German claims to invade Belgium in the World War I era, to invade Norway and Denmark during World War II? *See also* Mary Ellen O'Connell, The Myth of Preemptive Self-Defense, at http://www.asil.org/taskforce/oconnell.pdf; Paust, *Use of Force against Terrorists*, *supra* at 533–38; Jordan J. Paust, *Responding Lawfully to International Terrorism: The Use of Force Abroad*, 8 WHITTIER L. REV. 711, 716–19, 729–32 (1986). U.N. Security Council Resolution 487 (1981) condemned the Israeli preemptive attack on an Iraqi nuclear reactor as a "clear violation of the Charter of the United Nations and the norms of international conduct." Israel had claimed that Iraq's civil nuclear reactor program might later produce enriched weapons-grade nuclear fuel and that at some later point the fuel might be used to create nuclear weapons which might some day be aimed at Israel and fired at Israel.

In 2002, the Bush Administration's National Security Strategy indicated that a general goal is to prevent "our enemies from threatening us, our allies, and our friends, with weapons of mass destruction" and claimed that the U.S. must "stop rogue states and their terrorist clients before they are able to threaten or use" such weapons, although the U.S. "will not use force in all cases to preempt emerging threats." Nevertheless, it states, the U.S. "has long maintained the option of preemptive actions to counter a sufficient threat to our national security ... even if uncertainty exists as to the time and place of the enemy's attack." National Security Strategy (Sept. 17, 2002), available at http:www.usinfo.state.gov. Would certain effectuations of such a policy be impermissible? Could they be criminal?

5. What is an "armed attack" within the meaning of Article 51 of the Charter? Does it include a process of attack over time? The French version of Article 51 includes the phrase *agression armee*. Would armed "aggression" involve a broader circumstance than armed "attack"? Would some forms of cyber-attack constitute an armed attack?

6. An armed attack on one's military forces abroad or on one's nationals abroad has been considered to be included within Article 51. *Compare* Louis Henkin, The Missile Attack on Baghdad and its Justifications, ASIL Newsletter 3 (June–Aug. 1993) *with* Jordan J. Paust, Response to President's Notes on Missile Attack on Baghdad, ASIL Newsletter 4 (Sept.-Oct. 1993); Paust, *Responding Lawfully*, *supra* at 716, 728–29.

7. Is self-defense under Article 51 limited to defense against armed attacks by states? *See, e.g.*, Harold Hongju Koh, *The Spirit of the Laws*, 43 HARV. INT'L L.J. 23, 25, 28 (2002); Harold Hongju Koh, *The Obama Administration and International Law*, speech before the Am. Soc'y Int'l L., Mar. 25, 2010, pt. B [hereinafter Koh, *Obama Administration*], available at http://www.state.gov/s/1/releases/remarks/139119.htm; Jordan J. Paust, *Use of Armed Force against Terrorists in Afghanistan, Iraq, and Beyond*, 35 CORNELL INT'L L.J. 533, 533–38 (2002). Could the United States lawfully target non-state actor members of al Qaeda in Pakistan (without Pakistani consent) who are directly participating in ongoing armed attacks against the U.S., U.S. embassies, and U.S. nationals abroad?

The vast majority of textwriters have affirmed that non-state actor armed attacks can trigger the right of self-defense addressed in Article 51 of the Charter even if selective responsive force directed against a non-state actor occurs within a foreign country. Nothing in the language of Article 51 restricts the right to engage in self-defense to circumstances of armed attacks by a state and nothing in the language of the Charter requires a conclusion lacking in common sense that a state being attacked can only defend itself within its own borders. Although there is some disagreement, writings cited here demonstrate that if responsive force is directed merely against the non-state actors who are perpetrating ongoing armed attacks, the use of force against them in a foreign state in compliance with Article 51 of the U.N. Charter is not a use of force against the foreign state, an attack "on" or "against" its territory, or a use of force in violation of its territorial "integrity" within the meaning of Article 2(4) of the Charter. Moreover, the two states would not be at war. Whether use of force against the non-state actors creates an armed conflict would depend on the status of the non-state actors (*e.g.*, as a belligerent, peoples, or insurgent—see Chapter Eight).

General patterns of pre-Charter (including the *Caroline* incident, noted below) and post-Charter practice and general patterns of *opinio juris* affirm these points as well as the fact that a state being attacked does not need special express consent of the state from which non-state actor armed attacks emanate and on whose territory a self-defense drone targeting takes place against the non-state actor. Additionally, it would be demonstrably incorrect to claim that a state has no right to defend itself outside its own territory absent (1) attribution or imputation of non-state actor attacks to the foreign state when the foreign state is in control of non-state actor attacks, or (2) the existence of a relevant international or non-international armed conflict. Moreover, the inherent right of self-defense in case of an armed attack is not limited to a circumstance where the state from whose territory a non-state actor armed attack emanates is unwilling or unable to control its territory. *See, e.g.,* Yoram Dinstein, War, Aggression and Self-Defence 184–85, 204–08 (4 ed. 2005); Paust, *Self-Defense Targetings of Non-State Actors and Permissibility of U.S. Use of Drones in Pakistan,* 19 J. Transnat'l L. & Pol'y 237, 241–59, 279–80 (2010) (also documenting U.S. claims for nearly 200 years to use permissible measures of self-defense against various non-state actors, including belligerents, tribes, insurgents, pirates, former slaves, smugglers and privateers, Mexican marauders, marauding mobs in Nicaragua, and al Qaeda. *Id.* at 244–48); Michael N. Schmitt, *Responding to Transnational Terrorism Under the* Jus ad Bellum*: A Normative Framework,* in International Law and Armed Conflict: Exploring the Faultlines: Essays in Honour of Yoram Dinstein 167–68, 176–77 (Michael N. Schmitt & Jelena Pejic eds. 2007); *but see* O'Connell, *The Resort to Drones, supra*; Ashley S. Deeks, *"Unwilling or Unable": Toward a Normative Framework for Extraterritorial Self-Defense,* 52 Va. J. Int'l L. 483 (2012) (claiming without attention to many historic trends that the foreign state must be "unwilling or unable" to stop non-state actor attacks); Paul H. Robinson & Adil Ahmad Haque, *Advantaging Aggressors: Justice & Deterrence in International Law,* 3 Harv. Nat'l Sec. J. 143, 157 (2011) (without attention to many historic trends, claiming that the foreign state must be responsible for the non-state actor attacks). As noted, Article 51 provides that states may use defensive force "if an armed attack occurs" and does not require that the armed attack be directed or controlled by a state. The Taliban provided al Qaeda a safe haven to launch the 911 attacks, but did not exercise effective control over that specific use of force. Does this mean that the removal of the Taliban in Afghanistan did not constitute a legitimate exercise of self-defense under Article 51 of the U.N. Charter?

8. Prior to the U.N. Charter, the famous *Caroline* incident, on December 29, 1837, led to an exchange of letters in 1842 by Lord Ashburton of the U.K. (then in control of Canada) and U.S. Secretary of State Webster. The incident had involved an attack on the *Caroline* (a small steamer that had been used to transport persons and supplies in support of insurgent armed attacks that had been taking place against Canada and had triggered a right of self-defense). The attack on the *Caroline* occurred in U.S. territory by a small force led by a British officer. The attack resulted in the death of one U.S. citizen, the wounding of several others, one person being missing, and the loss of the burning ves-

sel over Niagara Falls. The U.K. denied violating international law with respect to its method of self-defense but apologized for the invasion of U.S. territory. Secretary Webster wrote in response:

> The President sees with pleasure that your Lordship fully admits those great principles of public international law, applicable to cases of this kind, which this government has expressed; and that on your part, as on ours, respect for the inviolable character of the territory of independent states is the most essential foundation of civilization.... [W]hile it is admitted that exceptions growing out of the great law of self-defense do exist, those exceptions should be confined to cases in which the "necessity of that self-defense is instant, overwhelming, and leaving no choice of means, and no moment for deliberation."

Some have argued that the *Caroline* incident supports recognition of the right of self-defense prior to the existence of armed attacks on a state. Since insurgent armed attacks against British rule in Canada had already occurred and had been ongoing, is this correct? Was Webster expressing disagreement about the right of self-defense or the actual measure or means employed? For more detailed consideration of the *Caroline* incident and the right of self-defense against non-state actor armed attacks, *see, e.g.,* Paust, *Self-Defense Targetings, supra* at 241–44, 257 n.48, available at http://ssrn.com/abstract=1520717.

9. Permissible measures of self-defense must comply with general principles of reasonable necessity, distinction (*e.g.,* between lawful targets and ordinary civilians), and proportionality whether or not such measures take place in time of armed conflict or relative peace. *See, e.g.,* Case Concerning Oil Platforms (Islamic Republic of Iran v. United States of America), 2003 I.C.J. 161, 183, para. 43 (Nov. 6); Advisory Opinion, Legality of the Threat or Use of Nuclear Weapons, 1996 I.C.J. 226, 245, para. 41 ("submission of the exercise of the right of self-defense to the conditions of necessity and proportionality is a rule of customary international law"), 246, para. 46 ("belligerent reprisals ... would, like self-defense, be governed *inter alia* by the principle of proportionality") (Jul. 8); Case Concerning Military and Paramilitary Activities in and Against Nicaragua (Nicaragua v. United States of America), 1986 I.C.J. 14, 94, para. 176 (U.N. Article 51 does not mention that "self-defense would warrant only measures which are proportional to the armed attack and necessary to respond to it, a rule well established in customary international law," but this demonstrates the interface that exists between treaty provisions and customary precepts), 103, para. 194 (June 27); Thomas M. Franck, *On Proportionality of Countermeasures in International Law*, 102 Am. J. Int'l L. 715, 719–21 (2008) (noting the I.C.J.'s ability to use the general principle of proportionality first, to determine whether there is a right to use force in self-defense (*jus ad bellum*), and second, "whether the level of countermeasures deployed is permitted by law; whether it is proportionate to the attack itself and to the needs of self-defense (*jus in bello*)"). If any of these principles are violated, the responsive measure of self-defense is unlawful. Would the persons responsible also be subject to prosecution for unnecessary death, injury, or suffering that occurred as perpetrators of offenses against peace? Recall that offenses against peace (such as breaches of neutrality) have occurred at the hands of private perpetrators.

10. How can the U.N. Security Council take action under Article 42? Who decides what is a "threat to peace" under Article 39? Are all decisions of the Security Council binding on members of the U.N.? See Articles 1, 24–25, 48, 55, 56.

11. After the deadlock of the U.N. Security Council during the Korean Conflict, the U.N. General Assembly carved out a special competence to meet threats to the peace and acts of "aggression" in its 1950 Uniting for Peace Resolution. See U.N. G.A. Res. 377A, 5

U.N. GAOR, Supp. No. 20, at 10, U.N. Doc. A/1775 (1951). Such competence was confirmed indirectly by the International Court of Justice. See Certain Expenses of the United Nations, [1962] I.C.J. 150.

12. Is the Judgment at Nuremberg of precedential import with respect to the application of U.N. Charter proscriptions to individuals for criminal sanction purposes? Is there any mention of individual responsibility, crimes, or criminal sanctions in the U.N. Charter? For example, could violations of the U.N. Charter occurring with respect to Iraq's invasion of Kuwait in August 1990 be used during a criminal prosecution of Saddam Hussein for crimes against peace? *See also* U.N. S.C. Res. 678 (29 Nov. 1990) [extracts in Note 20 below].

13. Scholars have been in sharp disagreement whether the U.S. intervention in Vietnam in the 1960s and early 1970s (or whether those of the People's Republic of China and the Soviet Union) was legally permissible. *See, e.g.,* vols. I–IV, The Vietnam War and International Law (R. Falk ed., 1968, 1969, 1972, 1976).

14. In 1967, there occurred two sessions and verdicts of a private International War Crimes Tribunal set up primarily by Bertrand Russell in Stockholm. The Tribunal found the United States to have been guilty of a war of aggression in Vietnam. See Against the Crime of Silence — Proceedings of the International War Crimes Tribunal (J. Duffett ed. 1970). The "governments of Australia, New Zealand and South Korea" were also found to have "been accomplices of the United States in the aggression against Vietnam in violation of international law." See *id.* at 309.

Of what value are such private efforts? See also R. Falk, *Keeping Nuremberg Alive,* in International Law: A Contemporary Perspective 494 (R. Falk, F. Kratochwil, S. Mendlovitz eds. 1985). Of what value are efforts of international tribunals and decisions generally?

See also J. Carey, UN Protection of Civil and Political Rights 63–66, 69 (1970), extract reprinted at R. Lillich & F. Newman, International Human Rights: Problems of Law and Policy 818–21 (1979). If primarily an urgent witnessing, to what end?

15. The 1970 Declaration on Principles of International Law, U.N. G.A. Res. 2625, in the Documents Supplement, provides authoritative clarification of relevant U.N. Charter norms. Read the Declaration, especially concerning the permissibility of use of force, human rights, and self-determination.

16. The norm of nonintervention reflected partly in U.N. Charter article 2 (7) is elaborated upon in the Declaration. In this regard, what is an "affair of" a particular state as opposed to that of the international community? Is "intervention" as such proscribed or are there distinctions to be made between permissible and impermissible intervention? See also Advisory Opinion on Nationality Decrees in Tunis and Morocco (France and Great Britain), 1923 P.C.I.J., Ser. B, No. 4, at 24 (considering art. 15 (8) of the Covenant of the League of Nations); J.N. Moore, *Toward an Applied Theory for the Regulation of Intervention,* in Law & Civil War in the Modern World 3 (J.N. Moore ed. 1974); Moore, *Intervention: A Monochromatic Term for a Polychromatic Reality,* in 2 The Vietnam War and International Law 1061 (R. Falk ed. 1969); McDougal & Reisman, *Rhodesia and the United Nations: The Lawfulness of International Concern,* 62 Am. J. Int'l L. 1 (1968).

17. Is the use of force to overthrow a foreign government absolutely impermissible under the U.N. Charter, as amplified by the 1970 Declaration? See U.N. S.C. Res. 940 (July 31, 1994) (re: Haiti); U.N. G.A. Res. 39/2 (Sept. 28, 1984) (re: illegal regime in South Africa and self-determination assistance, "recognizing the legitimacy of their struggle to eliminate apartheid and establish a society based on majority rule with equal participation by all the people … [and] Urges all Governments and organizations … to assist the oppressed people of South Africa in their legitimate struggle for national libera-

tion...."); U.N. G.A. Res. 3314, Resolution on the Definition of Aggression, art. 7 (noted below); Protocol I to the 1949 Geneva Conventions, art. 1 (4) (in the Documents Supplement); International Convention Against the Taking of Hostages, art. 12 (in the Documents Supplement); African Charter on Human and Peoples' Rights, art. 20 (2) ("oppressed peoples shall have the right to free themselves from the bonds of domination by resorting to any means recognized by the international community"), (3) ("All peoples shall have the right to assistance of the States parties to the present Charter in their liberation struggle against foreign domination, be it political, economic or cultural."), done in Banjul, June 26, 1981, O.A.U. Doc. CAB/LEG/67/3 Rev. 5; panel, *The United Nations Charter and the Use of Force: Is Article 2(4) Still Workable?*, 78 PROCEEDINGS, AM. Soc. INT'L L. 68 (1984); Paust, *The Human Right to Participate in Armed Revolution and Related Forms of Social Violence: Testing the Limits of Permissibility*, 32 EMORY L.J. 545, 560–67 (1983); Paust, *Aggression Against Authority: The Crime of Oppression, Politicide and Other Crimes Against Human Rights*, 18 CASE W. RES. J. INT'L L. 283, 297–98 (1986); W.M. Reisman, *Coercion and Self-Determination*, 78 AM. J. INT'L L. 642 (1984).

18. If the use of force in self-defense and certain forms of armed intervention are permissible — indeed, if even other forms of "self-help" or "self-determination assistance" are permissible — does the 1970 Declaration adequately clarify what constitutes an impermissible "war of aggression" (which "constitutes a crime against peace")? What criteria are discernible? See Paust, *Use of Force against Terrorists, supra* at 547–48.

19. Was NATO's use of force in Kosovo in 1999 to stop genocidal violence against Kosovo Albanians permissible under the U.N. Charter? The Security Council was veto-deadlocked and some argued that the use of force by members of NATO was impermissible under Article 2 (4), not authorized under Article 42, and therefore unlawful. Is that correct? See especially Articles 52–53. Does the duty of states under Article 56 enhance NATO member competence? *Compare* Anthony D'Amato, *International Law and Kosovo*, 33 U.N. L. RPTS. 112 (May 1999) (Article 2(4) prohibits only three types of force and none of the three prohibitions were violated re: Kosovo; and NATO force is permissible humanitarian intervention, especially to secure human rights); Jordan J. Paust, *NATO's Use of Force in Yugoslavia, id.* at 114 (not prohibited by Article 2(4) and is permissible under Articles 52–53, especially since Article 53 merely precludes "enforcement action" "under [the] authority" of the Security Council and not regional action under Article 52 where the Security Council is veto-deadlocked and cannot decide on "enforcement measures" "under its authority." Further, NATO's action was serving of peace, security, self-determination, and human rights); Paul Rutkus, *Licensing of Armed Force: NATO's Attack on Yugoslavia*, at 17 (ICTY Statute requires NATO member states to cooperate with the Prosecutor and Tribunal re: arrests and production of evidence in Kosovo, if requested); Paust, *Use of Force against Terrorists, supra* at 545–47; Abram Chayes, *The Legal Case for U.S. Action in Cuba*, 47 DEP'T STATE BULL. 763, 764 (1962) (O.A.S. General Assembly resolution authorized forceful interdiction of Soviet vessels heading to Cuba); Julie Mertus, *Reconsidering the Legality of Humanitarian Intervention: Lessons from Kosovo*, 41 WM. & MARY L. REV. 1743, 1772 (2000); *cf* YORAM DINSTEIN, WAR, AGGRESSION AND SELF-DEFENCE 310–14 (4 ed. 2005) (missing the point that Article 52 provides for "regional action" when the Security Council is unable to act and to authorize "enforcement action" as such); CHRISTINE GRAY, INTERNATIONAL LAW AND THE USE OF FORCE 113 (2000) (the Cuban missile crisis was authorized as "regional peacekeeping under Chapter VIII of the UN Charter." *But see id.* at 40 (NATO authorization regarding Kosovo without Security Council authorization was supposedly of "doubtful" validity)); editorial comments of Professors Henkin, Wedgwood, Chinkin, Falk, Franck, Reisman, 93 AM. J. INT'L L. 824

(1999) *with* Jonathan I. Charney, *Anticipatory Humanitarian Intervention in Kosovo*, 32 VAND. J. TRANS. L. 1231 (1999) (revised from 93 AM. J. INT'L L. 834 (1999)).

U.N. Security Council Authorizations to Use Force

20. Concerning U.N. Security Council "authorization" of states to use armed force in the Gulf region after Iraq's refusal to comply with Security Council resolutions demanding Iraqi withdrawal from Kuwait, *see, e.g.*, U.N. S.C. Res. 678 (29 Nov. 1990), authorizing states "to use all necessary means to uphold and implement" prior resolutions "and all subsequent relevant resolutions and to restore international peace and security in the area" and requesting "all States to provide appropriate support for the actions undertaken." Had peace and security been restored in the region prior to the U.S. military operations in Iraq in March 2003? Are peace and security restored in the region today?

The War in Iraq (2003—2011)

U.N. Security Res. 1441 (8 Nov. 2002)

The Security Council,

Recalling all its previous relevant resolutions, in particular its resolutions 661 (1990)..., 678 (1990)..., 686 (1991)..., 687 (1991)..., 688 (1991)..., 707 (1991)..., 715 (1991)..., 986 (1995)..., and 1284 (1999) of 17 December 1999, and all the relevant statements of its President,

Recalling also its resolution 1382 (2001) of 29 November 2001 and its intention to implement it fully,

Recognizing the threat Iraq's non-compliance with Council resolutions and proliferation of weapons of mass destruction and long-range missiles poses to international peace and security,

Recalling that its resolution 678 (1990) authorized Member States to use all necessary means to uphold and implement its resolution 660 (1990) of 2 August 1990 and all relevant resolutions subsequent to resolution 660 (1990) and to restore international peace and security in the area,

Further recalling that its resolution 687 (1991) imposed obligations on Iraq as a necessary step for achievement of its stated objective of restoring international peace and security in the area, ...

Deploring also that the Government of Iraq has failed to comply with its commitments pursuant to resolution 687 (1991) with regard to terrorism, pursuant to resolution 688 (1991) to end repression of its civilian population and to provide access by international humanitarian organizations to all those in need of assistance in Iraq, and pursuant to resolutions 686 (1991), 687 (1991), and 1284 (1999) to return or cooperate in accounting for Kuwaiti and third country nationals wrongfully detained by Iraq, or to return Kuwaiti property wrongfully seized by Iraq,

Recalling that in its resolution 687 (1991) the Council declared that a ceasefire would be based on acceptance by Iraq of the provisions of that resolution, including the obligations on Iraq contained therein,

Determined to ensure the full and immediate compliance by Iraq without conditions or restrictions with its obligations under resolution 687 (1991) and other relevant resolutions and recalling that the resolutions of the Council constitute the governing standard of Iraqi compliance, ...

Determined to secure full compliance with its decisions,

Acting under Chapter VII of the Charter of the United Nations,

1. *Decides* that Iraq has been and remains in material breach of its obligations under relevant resolutions, including resolution 687 (1991), in particular through Iraq's failure to cooperate with United Nations inspectors and the IAEA, and to complete the actions required under paragraphs 8 to 13 or resolution 687 (1991);

2. *Decides*, while acknowledging paragraph 1 above, to afford Iraq, by this resolution, a final opportunity to comply with its disarmament obligations under relevant resolutions of the Council; and accordingly decides to set up an enhanced inspection regime with the aim of bringing to full and verified completion the disarmament process established by resolution 687 (1991) and subsequent resolutions of the Council;

3. *Decides* that, in order to begin to comply with its disarmament obligations, in addition to submitting the required biannual declarations, the Government of Iraq shall provide to UNMOVIC, the IAEA, and the Council, not later than 30 days from the date of this resolution, a currently accurate, full, and complete declaration of all aspects of its programmes to develop chemical, biological, and nuclear weapons, ballistic missiles, and other delivery systems such as unmanned aerial vehicles and dispersal systems designed for use on aircraft. including any holdings and precise locations of such weapons, components, sub- components, stocks of agents, and related material and equipment, the locations and work of its research, development and production facilities, as well as all other chemical, biological, and nuclear programmes, including any which it claims are for purposes not related to weapon production or material;

4. *Decides* that false statements or omissions in the declarations submitted by Iraq pursuant to this resolution and failure by Iraq at any time to comply with, and cooperate fully in the implementation of, this resolution shall constitute a further material breach of Iraq's obligations and will be reported to the Council for assessment in accordance with paragraphs 11 and 12 below;

5. *Decides* that Iraq shall provide UNMOVIC and the IAEA immediate, unimpeded, unconditional, and unrestricted access to any and all, including underground, areas, facilities, buildings, equipment, records, and means of transport which they wish to inspect, as well as immediate, unimpeded, unrestricted, and private access to all officials and other persons whom UNMOVIC or the IAEA wish to interview in the mode or location of UNMOVIC's or the IAEA's choice pursuant to any aspect of their mandates; further decides that UNMOVIC and the IAEA may at their discretion conduct interviews inside or outside of Iraq, may facilitate the travel of those interviewed and family members outside of Iraq, and that, at the sole discretion of UNMOVIC and the IAEA, such interviews may occur without the presence of observers from the Iraqi Government; and instructs UNMOVIC and requests the IAEA to resume inspections no later than 45 days following adoption of this resolution and to update the Council 60 days thereafter; ...

8. *Decides* further that Iraq shall not take or threaten hostile acts directed against any representative or personnel of the United Nations or the IAEA or of any Member State taking action to uphold any Council resolution;

9. *Requests* the Secretary-General immediately to notify Iraq of this resolutions, which binding on Iraq demands that Iraq confirm within seven days of the notification its intention to comply fully with this resolution; and demands further that Iraq cooperate immediately, unconditionally, and actively with UNMOVIC and the IAEA;

10. *Requests* all Member States to give full support to UNMOVIC and the IAEA in the discharge of their mandates, including by providing any information related to prohibited programmes or other aspects of their mandates, including on Iraqi attempts since 1998 to acquire prohibited items, and by recommending sites to be inspected, persons to be interviewed, conditions of such interviews, and data to be collected, the results of which shall be reported to the Council by UNMOVIC and the IAEA;

11. *Directs* the Executive Chairman of UNMOVIC and the Director-General of the IAEA to report immediately to the Council any interference by Iraq with inspection activities, as well as any failure by Iraq to comply with its disarmament obligations, including its obligations regarding inspections under this resolution;

12. *Decides* to convene immediately upon receipt of a report in accordance with paragraphs 4 or 11 above, in order to consider the situation and the need for full compliance with all of the relevant Council resolutions in order to secure international peace and security;

13. *Recalls*, in that context, that the Council has repeatedly warned Iraq that it will face serious consequences as a result of its continued violations of its obligations;

14. *Decides* to remain seized of the matter.

Notes and Questions

1. Was the U.S. use of force in Iraq in 2003 permissible under S.C. Resolution 1441? Textwriters and states were split on this issue, although most seem to assume that the U.S. use of force was impermissible. Compare Kirgis, Security Council Resolution 1441 on Iraq's Final Opportunity to Comply with Disarmament Obligations, at http://www.asil.org/insights/insigh92.htm; Mary Ellen O'Connell, Addendum to Armed Force in Iraq: Issues of Legality; with Paust, *Use of Armed Force against Terrorists in Afghanistan, Iraq, and Beyond*, 35 Cornell Int'l L.J. 533, 549–50, 556 (2002), available at http://ssrn.com/abstract=1798582; Yoram Dinstein, remarks, 97 Proc., Am. Soc'y Int'l L. 147–49 (2003).

2. Did S.C. Resolution 1441 (2002) revitalize S.C. Res. 678 (1990)? Were the authorizations to use force in resolution 678 ever terminated? Was the 1991 war ever terminated? What would be the effect with respect to permissibility of the use of force in 2003 if the 1991 war was never terminated?

3. S.C. Res. 687 (1991) adopted a cease-fire (which does not end war but suspends active hostilities), but warfare continued soon thereafter, especially concerning no-fly zones, and intensified in 1993 and 1998. What did S.C. Res. 1441 (2002) declare in connection with resolution 687?

4. S.C. Resolution 687 (1991) recognized the "threat that all weapons of mass destruction pose to peace and security in the area," decided "that Iraq shall unconditionally accept the destruction, removal, or rendering harmless, under international supervision," various chemical and biological weapons and ballistic missiles, and decided "that Iraq shall unconditionally agree not to acquire or develop nuclear weapons or nuclear-usable-material," among others. Was resolution 687 a "relevant" subsequent resolution? No weapons of mass destruction were subsequently found in Iraq. Does that make a difference?

5. S.C. Resolution 688 (1991) condemned the Iraqi regime's "repression of the Iraqi civilian population in many parts of Iraq, including most recently in Kurdish-populated areas, the consequences of which threaten international peace and security in the region." Was

resolution 688 a "relevant" subsequent resolution? Was use of force for a regime change under resolutions 1441 and 688 permissible?

6. How long did Iraq have to comply with Resolution 1441? Who decides?

The Armed Conflict in Libya
(2011)

On March 17, 2011, the United Nations Security Council noted "the escalation of violence and the heavy civilian casualties" that had taken place in Libya and that "widespread and systematic attacks [were] currently taking place" in Libya; condemned "the gross and systematic violation of human rights, including arbitrary detentions, enforced disappearances, torture and summary executions;" and authorized Member States of the U.N. "to take all necessary measures ... to protect civilians and civilian populated areas under threat of attack in the Libyan Arab Jamahiriya, including Benghazi, while excluding a foreign occupation force of any form on any part of Libyan territory." U.N. S.C. Res. 1973, prmbl. and para. 4 (17 March 2011), U.N. Doc. S/RES/1973 (17 Mar. 2011). The Security Council also decided "to establish a ban on all flights in the airspace above the Libyan Arab Jamahiriya in order to help protect civilians." *Id.* para. 6. See also U.N. S.C. Res. 2016 (27 Oct. 2011), prmbl., U.N. Doc. S/RES/2016 (27 Oct. 2011); U.N. S.C. Res. 2009 (16 Sept. 2011), prmbl., U.N. Doc. S/RES/2009 (16 Sept. 2011); U.N. S.C. Res. 1970 (26 Feb. 2011), prmbl. ("[r]ecalling the Libyan authorities' responsibility to protect its population"), U.N. Doc. S/RES/1970 (2011).

On March 24, 2011, the United States and other members of NATO began a campaign using significant military force in Libya to uphold the authorization of the Security Council. Later in 2011, the United States and other members of NATO continued attacks on targets in Libya and the continued use of armed force migrated from protection of civilians as such to include support for rebel forces that led to rebel control of Tripoli and regime change some seven months after the use of armed force by members of NATO had begun.

Notes and Questions

1. Did U.N. S.C. Resolution 1973 merely authorize creation of a no-fly-zone?

2. Was use of force by the U.S. and NATO against the Qaddafi regime in Libya permissible under U.N. S.C. Resolution 1973? Were there other U.N. Charter precepts that can support regime change in Libya?

Professor Paust has written that over a period of months, it had become reasonably necessary to provide support for regime change in Libya in order to effectively protect civilians who were under a series of murderous armed attacks and serious threats of imminent future attacks by the Qaddafi regime. In addition to the U.N. Security Council authorization to use all necessary measures of protective force, which covered the subsequent need for regime change in order to protect civilians from ongoing armed attacks, during later stages of the Libyan armed conflict there was a change in the international legal status of the Libyan rebel-insurgents to belligerents, and they consented to and welcomed U.S. and NATO uses of force. Still later, the Libyan National Transitional Council (NTC) gained recognition as the legitimate representative of the Libyan people, and its consent provided additional independent legitimacy for use of force to support regime change, to provide self-determination assistance to the Libyan people, and to participate in collective self-defense against continuous armed attacks by remnants of the Qaddafi regime. See Jordan J. Paust, *Constitutionality of U.S. Participation in the United Nations-Authorized War in Libya*, 26 EMORY INT'L L. REV. 43, 44–45 (2012); see also Legal Adviser Harold Hongju Koh, Statement Regarding Use of Force in Libya (Mar. 26, 2011) ("U.S. forces have targeted the Qaddafi regime's air defense systems, command and control structures, and other capabilities of Qaddafi's armed forces used to attack civilians and civilian populated areas"), available at http://www.state.gov/s/l/releases/remarks/159201.htm, reprinted in part in 105 AM. J. INT'L L. 605 (2011).

Do you agree?

3. The General in command of NATO's air operation in Libya has noted that selective use of force by NATO involved continual protection of civilians and civilian populated areas from armed attacks by pro-Qaddafi forces (PGF) but that anti-Qaddafi forces (AGF) were not attacked because "[w]e saw when the ... [AGF] entered towns, they liberated the town and the people. They did not indiscriminately attack civilians and in fact, kept the civilians away from any of the fighting between the AGF and PGF." Lieutenant General Ralph J. Jodice II, email to editor (Apr. 20, 2012) (on file with Professor Paust).

4. Concerning recognition in July, 2011 by thirty-two countries (including the U.S.) that the NTC became "the legitimate governing authority in Libya," see Fourth Meeting of the Libya Contact Group Chair's Statement, July 15, 2011, Istanbul, Turkey, para. 4. *See also* Secretary of State Hillary Clinton, remarks during the Istanbul meeting, reproduced in part in *U.S. Measures Related to Libyan Conflict Raise Multiple Legal Issues*, 105 AM. J. INT'L L. 776, 780 (2011); William Wan & William Booth, *Libyan Rebels Given Full U.S. Recognition*, WASH. POST, Jul. 16, 2011, at A9; Stefan Talmon, *Recognition of the Libyan National Transitional Council*, ASIL Insight (June 16, 2011), available at http://www.asil.org/insights110616.cfm. With respect to recognition of the National Transitional Council of Libya (NTCL) and Security Council encouragement of the NTCL (or "the Libyan authorities") to implement its plans, for example, to protect Libya's population, restore governmental services, prevent violations of human rights, and ensure an inclusive political process involving free elections, *see, e.g.*, U.N. S.C. Res. 2009, *supra* paras. 5, 7.

M. Cherif Bassiouni & Benjamin B. Ferencz, *The Crime Against Peace*
in 1 INTERNATIONAL CRIMINAL LAW 167–70 (M.C. Bassiouni ed. 1986)

The notion of aggression was known as far back as the early days of Greece.[2] In the twentieth century, it has been a recurrent theme among international lawyers who have tried to determine the merits of the concept and its usefulness to the development of world order.[3] The term "aggression," as a legal concept in international law, began to develop meaningfully during the era of the League of Nations. The League of Nations sought to control the limits of the legal license to engage in war.[4] These efforts continued to the present in the United Nations where a Special Committee on the Question of Defining Aggression was at work for 20 years to produce in 1974 an internationally agreed-upon definition.[5]

---

2. I. BROWNLIE, INTERNATIONAL LAW AND THE USE OF FORCE BY STATES 1–65 (1963)[hereinafter Brownlie].

3. J. STONE, AGGRESSION AND WORLD ORDER 1 (1958)[hereinafter STONE].

4. *Id.* at 15.

5. *See, e.g.*, B. FERENCZ, DEFINING INTERNATIONAL AGGRESSION [1975] [hereinafter DEFINING AGGRESSION].

The writings of Aristotle, Cicero, St. Augustine and St. Thomas Aquinas in Western civilization set forth the philosophical premise of legitimacy of war in their attempt to distinguish between just and unjust war.[6] The ancient Greek City-States, despite their very high level of civilization, destroyed themselves in the Peloponnesian wars—a pattern that constitutes to threaten humankind. The Romans enacted codes of "natural law" which decreed that wars could be lawful only if they were lawfully declared and had a just cause, such as the protection of territory or in defense of honor. Those who waged war without Senate approval could be handed over to the enemy for punishment.[7] Theologians like Saint Augustine (354–430 A.D.) and Archbishop Isidore of Seville (530–636) revived Roman considerations regarding when a war might justly be fought. The Pope at the Council of Cleremont Ferrand in 1095, proclaimed the "Peace of God" which prohibited warfare on certain religious holidays under penalty of excommunication and anathema.[8] Franciscus de Victoria (1480–1546),[9] a Spanish theologian who is widely regarded as one of the founders of international law, argued that lawful wars had to be morally justifiable, such as in self-defense or to right a wrong received. Unjust aggressors were legally under a duty "to make good the expenses of the war," and no subject was bound to wage an unjust war "even though his sovereign commands." In the writings of Victoria, there can also be found the roots of a definition of aggression, a probing of the parameters of permissible self-defense, the idea of proportionality, the limits of military necessity, the responsibility of heads of state and the unavailability of superior orders as an excuse for acts of aggression.[10] These early doctrines were forerunners of principles of international criminal law that were to be recognized and widely approved four centuries later.[11]

Efforts to control war existed in other earlier civilizations. The Chinese, Hindu, Egyptian and Assyrian-Babylonian civilizations likewise devised norms of legitimacy of war.[12] The Islamic civilization based on the Qu'ran also set forth specific rules as to the legitimacy of war.[13] These rules and practices had some influence on the development of Western civilization by virtue of Islam's contacts in the Middle Ages with the Crusades and

---

6. The distillation of these writings is found in H. Grotius, De Jure Belli ac Pacis (Bk. II, 1625), which is the foundation of Western international law. A similar though somewhat more humanistic reflection of the same classics is found in E. de Vattel, La Droit des Gens (1887). *See also* W. Bellis, The Legal Position of War: Changes in its Practice and Theory from Plato to Vattel (1937). For an interesting survey, *see* von Elbe, *The Evolution of the Concept of Just War in International Law,"* 33 Am. J. Int'l L. 665 (1939). *See also* Q. Wright, A Study of War (1964).

7. *See* Richard Zouche, *An Exposition of Fecial Law and Procedure* (1st ed. 1650), in The Classics of International Law (1911).

8. *See* Georges Goyau, *l'Eglise Catholique et le Droit des Gens*, VI Recueil des Cours 127, 137 (1925).

9. *The Reflectiones in Moral Theology of the Very Celebrated Spanish Theologian, Franciscus de Victoria*, The Classics of International Law (1917), *reproduced in* B.B. Ferencz, Enforcing International Law, Doc. 1, at 95 (1983)[hereinafter referred to as Enforcing International Law].

10. *Id.*

11. *See* Brownlie, *supra* note 2; Stone, *supra* note 3.

12. A. Aymard & J. Auboyer, L'Orient et la Grece Antique (Tome 1, 1953); *see also* A. Nussbaum, A Concise History of the Law of Nations (1947).

13. M. Khadduri, The Islamic Law of Nations (1986); A. Mahmassani, The Principles of International Law in Light of Islamic Doctrine (1966); S. Ramadan, Islamic Law, Its Scope and Equity (1961); H. Hamidullah, Muslim Conduct of State (1981); Reshid, *l'Islam et le Droit de Gens*, Rec. des Cours de L'Academie de Droit Int'l de la Haye 4 (1937); Draz, *Le Droit International Public de l'Islam*, 5 Rev. Egyptienno de Droit Int'l 17 (1949); A. Armanazi, L'Islam et le Droit International (1949); Majid, *The Moslem International Law*, 28 L.Q. Rev. 89 (1912); Bassiouni, *Islam: Concept, Law and World Habeas Corpus*, 1 Rutgers-Camden L.J. 160 (1969); M.C. Bassiouni, The Islamic Criminal Justice System (1982).

with Spain and southern France and southern Italy when these areas were under Muslim control. Such influence appears in writings of certain Canonists.[14] Thus, by the seventeenth century, a strong philosophical foundation had been established particularly in Western civilization for the limitations of war (and its conduct).

Huig von Groot, more commonly known as Hugo Grotius (1583–1645), who is generally considered to be the "father" of international law, wrote in his third book on THE LAWS OF WAR AND PEACE that even in warfare, justice and honor were obligatory. Those who waged war wrongfully would be held personally accountable for their aggression, and even military officers who could have prevented the wars, would be held personally responsible.[15] It was unlawful to wage war against a party that was willing to accept arbitration,[16] and Grotius recalled the dictum of Cicero who said that men settled disputes by argument whereas force was a characteristics of beasts. He called for humane conduct even in warfare "lest by imitating wild beasts too much we forget to be human."[17]

The next historical phase was that of formulating normative prescriptions against these forms of war—forms which have come to be rejected by the shared values of the world community.[18] Since time immemorial, kings and other lesser rulers have entered into bilateral and multilateral treaties as a means of regulating their relations for the prevention of war. Since the Treaty of Westphalia of 1648, the practice of nonaggression treaty-making expanded and contributed to the development of what could be called an emerging world consciousness for the prevention of war.[19] In this context, the control of war is best illustrated by those multilateral undertakings whose goal is to control, regulate, prevent and prohibit war as the reflection of a world community effort based on generally shared community values.

Efforts to outlaw war as an instrument of national policy and to inhibit acts of aggression found expression in a number of plans for restructuring the prevailing international order, or disorder. The Grand Design of King Henry IV (in 1603), the writings of Quaker William Penn (toward the end of that century), proposals by the Abbe de Saint Pierre in 1713, of Rousseau in 1782, and Immanuel Kant in 1795, are illustrative of schemes whereby the lawful use of force would be determined by an international parliament and judiciary backed by an international army to maintain or restore peace. Unfortunately, none of these plans found acceptance, although the basic ideas were incorporated into the constitution of a new confederation of states known as The United States of America.

In more recent times, there have been 49 multilateral treaties from 1899 to date dealing directly with the prohibition of war, and the preservation of peace. Among these, the major treaties are:

    1.   The Hague Conventions of 1899 and 1907 on the Pacific Settlement of International Disputes.[20]

---

14. *See* C. RHYNE, INTERNATIONAL LAW 23 (1971).

15. H. Grotius, *De Jure Belli ac Pacis Libri Tres*, Chap. X, Sec. 4, in THE CLASSICS OF INTERNATIONAL LAW (1925), *reproduced in* II ENFORCING INTERNATIONAL LAW, *supra* note 9, Doc. 6, at 132.

16. *Id.* Chap. XXIII, Sec. VIII.

17. *Id.* Chap. XXV, Sec. II.

18. Bassiouni, *The Proscribing Function of International Criminal Law in the Processes of International Protection of Human Rights*, 9 YALE J. WORLD PUB. ORD. 193 (1982).

19. *See* MAJOR PEACE TREATIES OF MODERN HISTORY 1698–1957 (Israil & Chile eds., with an introduction by Toynbee 1967).

20. The Hague Conventions of 1899 and 1907 are the Convention of the Pacific Settlement of International Disputes, signed at The Hague, 29 July 1899, 25 MARTENS NOUVEAU RECUEIL (2d) 930, 32 Stat. 1799, T.S. No. 392; and the Convention on the Pacific Settlement of International Disputes,

2. The Treaty of Versailles of 1919 which condemned aggressive war.[21]

3. The Covenant of the League of Nations which prohibited war of aggression in 1920.[22]

4. The Kellogg-Briand Paris Pact of 1928 on the renunciation of war as an instrument of national policy.[23]

5. The 1945 London Charter which criminalized aggressive war.[24]

6. The United Nations Charter of 1945 which prohibited aggressive war.[25]

Throughout history, efforts to define and codify aggression have also taken place in official and academic circles. Finally in 1973, the United Nations Special Committee on Defining Aggression produced an agreed definition,[26] which implicitly, and with reference to the historic efforts to prevent and punish aggressive war, could be deemed an international proscription susceptible of criminalization. Yet, there is a need for a more specific convention on the subject similar to existing ones on other aspects of international crimes. This is ostensibly one of the purposes of the Draft Code of Offenses Against the Peace and Security of Mankind, which though before the United Nations since 1954, has since then been tabled but been placed again before the General Assembly in 1978. The efforts of the United Nations in the area of prevention of war have also produced other results,[27] notably the development of peacekeeping forces as a means of curtailing and preventing war.[28]

---

signed at The Hague, 18 October 1907, 3 MARTENS NOUVEAU RECUEIL (3d) 360, 36 Stat. 2199, T.S. No. 536.

21. Signed at Versailles, 11 MARTENS NOUVEAU RECUEIL (3d) 323, III Treaties, Conventions, International Acts, Protocols and Agreements Between the United States of America and Other Powers, 1910–1923, at 3329 (Redmond ed. 1923).

22. Signed at Versailles, 28 June 1919, 11 MARTENS NOUVEAU RECUEIL (3d) 323, Article 10. For text, *see* 12 AM. J. INT'L L. SUPP. 151 (1919).

23. General Treaty for Renunciation of War as an Instrument of National Policy (Kellogg-Briand Pact or Pact of Paris), signed at Paris, 94 L.N.T.S. 57, 46 Stat. 2342, T.S. No. 796; M. HUDSON, 4 INTERNATIONAL LEGISLATION 2522 (1923)[hereinafter cited as Hudson]. It was preceded, however, by the 1923 "Draft Treaty on Mutual Assistance," which was not ratified, and followed by the 1933 London Convention on Defining Aggression, 147 L.N.T.S. 69.

24. Agreement for the Prosecution and Punishment of Major War Criminals of the European Axis (London Charter), signed at London, 82 U.N.T.S. 279, 59 Stat. 1544, E.A.S. No. 472. *See also* 9 Hudson, *supra* note 23, at 659.

25. Signed at San Francisco, 26 June 1945, 59 Stat. 1031, T.S. No. 993, Article 2(4); *see also* Charter of the Organization of American States, signed at Bogota, 119 U.N.T.S. 3, 2 U.S.T., 2394, T.I.A.S. No. 2361, Article 16.

26. *See* "Report of the Special Committee on Defining Aggression," U.N. Doc. A/9519 (XXIX) 12 April 1974; U.N. Doc. A/9890 (XXIX), 6 December 1974. For a discussion of definitional issues, *see* B. FERENCZ, DEFINING AGGRESSION, *supra* note 5. *See also* STONE, *supra* note 3; C. POMPE, AGGRESSIVE WAR: AN INTERNATIONAL CRIME (1953); *Declaration on Principles of International Law Concerning Friendly Relations and Cooperation Among States in Accordance with the Charter of the United Nations,* in this chapter.

27. *See* Draft Code of Offenses Against the Peace and Security of Mankind (International Law Commission), 9 U.N. GAOR, Supp. No. 9, at 11, U.N. Doc. A/2693 (1954).

28. For a comprehensive survey of U.N. peacekeeping activities up to 1973, *see* Agrawala, *Permanent of Temporary Peace-keeping Forces — A World Peace Force,* in 1 M.C. BASSIOUNI & V.P. NANDA, A TREATISE ON INTERNATIONAL CRIMINAL LAW 694 (1973). *See also* D. BOWETT, UNITED NATIONS FORCES (1964).

Resolution on the Definition of Aggression

December 14, 1974

[Read the Resolution on Aggression, in the Documents Supplement]

Notes and Questions

1. Is application of the Definition nearly self-operative? Consider Articles 1, 2, and 3(a), (b), and (d) in connection with the 1986 bombing of Libya by the United States and the 1998 missile attacks on alleged terrorist sites in Afghanistan and the Sudan by the United States in response to al Qaeda bombings of U.S. embassies in Kenya and Tanzania. See also symposium, 8 WHITTIER L. REV. no. 3 (1986). Note that the 1974 Definition is hinged ultimately on whether or not the U.N. Charter has been violated.

2. Is the 1974 definition too limited, for example, with respect to types of actors, types of force, in other ways? See also Articles 4, 6. Are private actors covered?

3. In view of *Ex parte Quirin* (see Chapter Four, *supra*) and the U.S. constitutional issues at stake, is an accused on sufficient notice of what might be labeled a "war of aggression" in every instance? See 1974 Definition of Aggression, Articles 2 and 4. See also *id.*, Arts. 6–8.

4. With respect to then current commentary on the 1974 definition by one involved in the process of its creation, *see, e.g.*, remarks of Rosenstock, 70 U.S. DEP'T STATE BULL. 498 (1974).

5. President Truman, in 1950, had noted that the United States had opposed attempts to define "aggression" during the formation of the U.N. Charter. As the President noted:

> "The United States opposed this proposal. It took the position that a definition of aggression cannot be so comprehensive as to include all cases of aggression and cannot take into account the various circumstances which might enter into the determination of aggression in a particular case. Any definition of aggression is a trap for the innocent and an invitation to the guilty. The United States position prevailed at San Francisco, and the Charter adopted a system whereby the appropriate U.N. organ, in the first instance the Security Council, would determine on the basis of the facts of a particular case whether aggression has taken place."

5 WHITMAN, DIGEST OF INTERNATIONAL LAW 740 (1965).

Do you agree with the former President? See also M. MCDOUGAL & F. FELICIANO, LAW AND MINIMUM WORLD PUBLIC ORDER 61–62 (1961).

6. In 1970, the International Court of Justice recognized that obligations "towards the international community as a whole ... are obligations *erga omnes*. Such obligations derive, for example, in contemporary international law, from the outlawing of acts of aggression, and of genocide, as also from the principles and rules concerning the basic rights of the human person...." Case Concerning the Barcelona Traction, Light and Power Company, Limited (Belgium v. Spain), [1970] I.C.J. 3, paras. 33–34. In the 1976 I.L.C. Draft Convention on State Responsibility, it was also recognized that "an international crime may result ... from" an international obligation "prohibiting aggression."

7. Did the governments of Afghanistan and South Africa meet the standard of legitimacy found in Article 21 of the Universal Declaration of Human Rights? Article 21(3) of the Universal Declaration reads:

"The will of the people shall be the basis of the authority of government; this will shall be expressed in periodic and genuine elections which shall be by universal and equal suffrage and shall be held by secret vote or by equivalent free voting procedures."

Does the 1970 Declaration on Principles of International Law reaffirm this type of standard? See also Western Sahara Advisory Opinion, [1975] I.C.J. 4, 12, 31–33, 36; U.N. S.C. Res. 940 (July 31, 1994) (regarding Haiti); U.N. G.A. Res. 39/2 (Sept. 28, 1984) (regarding the illegal apartheid regime in South Africa).

8. Was the Soviet intervention in Afghanistan in 1980 legally permissible? What provisions of the U.N. Charter, the 1970 Declaration on Principles of International Law, and the 1974 Definition of Aggression are relevant? See also remarks of President Carter, January 4, 1980, in N.Y. Times, Jan. 5, 1980, at 6, col. 1; U.N. G.A. Res. 40/12 (Nov. 13, 1985); U.N. G.A. Res. 41/33 (Nov. 5, 1986); U.N. S.C. draft res., U.N. Doc. S/13729 (1980) (failed because of Soviet veto, vote: 13–2); Reisman, *The Resistance in Afghanistan Is Engaged in a War of National Liberation*, 81 Am. J. Int'l L. 906 (1987); Khan, *A Legal Theory of International Terrorism*, 19 Conn. L. Rev. 945 (1987).

9. Would U.S. support of Afghan rebels against the apartheid regime in the 1980s have been legally permissible? Consider also 1970 Declaration on Principles of International Law; Paust & Blaustein, *War Crimes Jurisdiction and Due Process: The Bangladesh Experience*, 11 Vand. J. Trans. L. 1, 11–12 n. 39, 18–20 & n.69, 30–31 (1978) (self-determination assistance and collective self-defense). *But see* Intentional Commission of Jurists, The Events in East Pakistan, 1971 (Geneva 1972).

10. Would U.S. support of South African rebels have been legally permissible? See also U.N. G.A. Res. 2, 39 U.N. GAOR, Supp. No. 51, at 14–15, U.N Doc. A/39/51 (Sept. 28, 1984) (vote: 133–0–2); panel, *Permissible Measures and Obligations for Outside States and Internal Peoples Toward Minority Rule in South Africa*, 80 Proc., Am. Soc. Int'l L. 308 (1986).

11. In view of your approach(es) to the last four questions, was the continuing U.S. support of the Contras against the government of Nicaragua legally permissible? See also Appraisals of the ICJ Decision: Nicaragua v. United States (Merits), 81 Am. J. Int'l L. 77 (1987); J.N. Moore, *The Secret War in Central America and the Future of World Order*, 80 Am. J. Int'l L. 43 (1986); J. Rowles, *"Secret Wars," Self-Defense and the Charter—A Reply to Professor Moore*, 80 Am. J. Int'l L. 568 (1986). In general, the United States was concerned about Nicaraguan support of insurgents in El Salvador, claiming that such was a violation of prohibitions concerning the use of force, including the general norm of non-intervention, and also constituted an attack within the meaning of Article 51 of the Charter. Nicaragua was concerned about responsive force engaged in by the United States against Nicaragua, including support of the Contras (who were seeking to overthrow the government of Nicaragua).

Portions of the International Court's decision follow.

Case Concerning Military and Paramilitary Activities in and against Nicaragua

(Nicaragua v. United States), [1986] I.C.J. 14

113. The question of the degree of control of the *contras* by the United States government is relevant to the claim of Nicaragua attributing responsibility to the United States for activities of the *contras* whereby the United States has, it is alleged, violated an obligation of international law not to kill, wound or kidnap citizens of Nicaragua. The activities in question are said to represent a tactic which includes "the spreading of terror and

danger to non-combatants as an end in itself with no attempt to observe humanitarian standards and no reference to the concept of military necessity." In support of this, Nicaragua has catalogued numerous incidents....

115. The Court has taken the view ... that United States participation, even if preponderant or decisive in the financing, organizing, training, supplying and equipping of the *contras*, the selection of its military or paramilitary targets, and the planning of the whole of its operation, is still insufficient in itself, on the basis of the evidence in the possession of the Court, for the purpose of attributing to the United States the acts committed by the *contras* in the course of their military and paramilitary operations in Nicaragua. All the forms of United States participation mentioned above, and even the general control by the respondent State over a force with a high degree of dependency on it, would not in themselves mean, without further evidence, that the United States directed or enforced the perpetration of the acts contrary to human rights and humanitarian law alleged by the applicant State. Such acts could well be committed by members of the *contras* without the control of the United States. For this conduct to give rise to legal responsibility of the United States, it would in principle have to be proved that the State had effective control of the military or paramilitary operations in the course of which the alleged violations were committed....

174. In its Judgment of 26 November 1984, the Court ... [c]ontrary to the views advanced by the United States, ... affirmed that it "cannot dismiss the claims of Nicaragua under principles of customary and general international law simply because such principles have been enshrined in the texts of the conventions relied upon by Nicaragua. The fact that the above mentioned principles, recognized as such, have been codified or embodied in multilateral conventions does not mean that they cease to exist and to apply as principles of customary law, even as regards countries that are parties to such conventions. Principles such as those of the non-use force, non-intervention, respect for the independence and territorial integrity of States, and the freedom of navigation, continue to be binding as part of customary international law, despite the operation of provisions of conventional law in which they have been incorporated." (*I.C.J. Reports 1984* p. 424, para. 73.)....

176. As regards the suggestion that the areas covered by the two sources of law are identical, the Court observes that the United Nations Charter, the convention to which most of the United States argument is directed, by no means covers the whole area of the regulation of the use of force in international relations. On one essential point, this treaty itself refers to pre-existing customary international law; this reference to customary law is contained in the actual text of Article 51, which mentions the "inherent right" (in the French text the "droit naturel") of individual or collective self-defence, which "nothing in the present Charter shall impair" and which applies in the event of an armed attack. The Court therefore finds that Article 51 of the Charter is only meaningful on the basis that there is a "natural" or "inherent" right of self-defence, and it is hard to see how this can be other than of a customary nature, even if its present content has been confirmed and influenced by the Charter. Moreover the Charter, having itself recognized the existence of this right, does not go on to regulate directly all aspects of its content. For example, it does not contain any specific rule whereby self-defence would warrant only measures which are proportional to the armed attack and necessary to respond to it, a rule well established in customary international law. Moreover, a definition of the "armed attack" which, if found to exist, authorizes the exercise of the "inherent right" of self-defence, is not provided in the Charter, and is not part of treaty law. It cannot therefore be held that Article 51 is a provision which "subsumes and supervenes" customary international law.

It rather demonstrates that in the field in question, the importance of which for the present dispute need hardly be stressed, customary international law continues to exist alongside treaty law. The areas governed by the two sources of law thus do not overlap exactly, and the rules do not have the same content. This could also be demonstrated for other subjects, in particular for the principle of non-intervention....

In the contention of the United States, the Court cannot properly adjudicate the mutual rights and obligations of the two States when reference to their treaty rights and obligations is barred; the Court would be adjudicating those rights and obligations by standards other than those to which the Parties have agreed to conduct themselves in their actual international relations.

181. The question raised by this argument is whether the provisions of the multilateral treaties in question, particularly the United Nations Charter, diverge from the relevant rules of customary international law to such an extent that a judgment of the Court as to the rights and obligations of the parties under customary law, disregarding the content of the multilateral treaties binding on the parties, would be a wholly academic exercise, and not "susceptible of any compliance or execution whatever" (*Northern Cameroons, I.C.J. Reports 1963*, p. 37). The Court does not consider that this is the case. As already noted, on the question of the use of force, the United States itself argues for a complete identity of the relevant rules of customary international law with the provisions of the Charter. The Court has not accepted this extreme contention, having found that on a number of points the areas governed by the two sources of law do not exactly overlap, and the substantive rules in which they are framed are not identical in content (paragraph 174 above). However, so far from having constituted a marked departure from a customary international law which still exists unmodified, the Charter gave expression in this field to principles already present in customary international law, and that law has in the subsequent four decades developed under the influence of the Charter, to such an extent that a number of rules contained in the Charter have acquired a status independent of it. The essential consideration is that both the Charter and the customary international law flow from a common fundamental principle outlawing the use of force in international relations. The differences which may exist between the specific content of each are not in the Court's view, such as to cause a judgment confined to the field of customary international law to be ineffective or inappropriate, or a judgment not susceptible to compliance or execution.

182. The Court concludes that it should exercise the jurisdiction conferred upon it by the United States declaration of acceptance under Article 36, paragraph 2, of the Statute, to determine the claims of Nicaragua based upon customary international law notwithstanding the exclusion from its jurisdiction of disputes "arising under" the United Nations and Organization of American States Charters.

183. In view of this conclusion, the Court has next to consider what are the rules of customary international law applicable to the present dispute. For this purpose, it has to direct its attention to the practice and *opinio juris* of States; as the Court recently observed.

> "it is of course axiomatic that the material of customary international law is to be looked for primarily in the actual practice and *opinio juris* of States, even though multilateral conventions may have an important role to play in recording and defining rules deriving from custom, or indeed in developing them." (*Continental Shelf (Libyan Arab Jamahiriya/ Malta), I.C.J. Reports 1985*, pp. 29–30, para. 27.)

In this respect the Court must not lose sight of the Charter of the United Nations and that of the Organization of American States, notwithstanding the operation of the multilateral treaty reservation. Although the Court has no jurisdiction to determine whether the conduct of the United States constitutes a breach of those conventions, it can and must take them into account in ascertaining the content of the customary international law which the United States is also alleged to have infringed.

184. The Court notes that there is in fact evidence, to be examined below, of a considerable degree of agreement between the Parties as to the content of the customary international law relating to the non-use of force and non-intervention. This concurrence of their views does not however dispense the Court from having itself to ascertain what rules of customary international law are applicable. The mere fact that States declare their recognition of certain rules is not sufficient for the Court to consider these as being part of customary international law, and as applicable as such to those States. Bound as it is by Article 38 of its Statute to apply, *inter alia*, international custom "as evidence of a general practice accepted as law", the Court may not disregard the essential role played by general practice. Where two States agree to incorporate a particular rule in a treaty, their agreement suffices to make that rule a legal one, binding upon them; but in the field of customary international law, the shared view of the Parties as to the content of what they regard as the rule is not enough. The Court must satisfy itself that the existence of the rule in the *opinio juris* of States is confirmed by practice.

185. In the present dispute, the Court, while exercising its jurisdiction only in respect of the application of the customary rules of non-use of force and non-intervention, cannot disregard the fact that the Parties are bound by these rules as a matter of treaty law and of customary international law. Furthermore, in the present case, apart from the treaty commitments binding the Parties to the rules in question, there are various instances of their having expressed recognition of the validity thereof as customary international law in other ways. It is therefore in the light of this "subjective element" — the expression used by the Court in its 1969 Judgment in the *North Sea Continental Shelf* cases (*I.C.J. Reports 1969*, p. 44) — that the Court has to appraise the relevant practice.

186. It is not to be expected that in the practice of States the application of the rules in question should have been perfect, in the sense that States should have refrained, with complete consistency, from the use of force or from intervention in each other's internal affairs. The Court does not consider that, for a rule to be established as customary, the corresponding practice must be in absolutely rigorous conformity with the rule. In order to deduce the existence of customary rules, the Court deems it sufficient that the conduct of States should, in general, be consistent with such roles, and that instances of State conduct inconsistent with a given rule should generally have been treated as breaches of that rule, not as indications of the recognition of a new rule. If a State acts in a way prima facie incompatible with a recognized rule, but defends its conduct by appealing to exceptions or justifications contained within the rule itself, then whether or not the State's conduct is in fact justifiable on that basis, the significance of that attitude is to confirm rather than to weaken the rule.

187. The Court must therefore determine, first, the substance of the customary rules relating to the use of force in international relations, applicable to the dispute submitted to it. The United States has argued that, on this crucial question of the lawfulness of the use of force in inter-State relations, the rules of general and customary international law, and those of the United Nations Charter, are in fact identical. In its view this identity is so complete that, as explained above (paragraph 173), it constitutes an argument to prevent the Court from applying this customary law, because it is indistinguishable from the multilateral treaty law which it may not apply. In its Counter-Memorial on jurisdiction

and admissibility the United States asserts that "Article 2(4) of the Charter *is* customary and general international law". It quotes with approval an observation by the International Law Commission to the effect that

> "the great majority of international lawyers today unhesitatingly hold that Article 2, paragraph 4, together with other provisions of the Charter, authoritatively declares the modern customary law regarding the threat or use of force" (*ILC) Yearbook*, 1966, Vol. II, p. 247).

The United States points out that Nicaragua has endorsed this view, since one of its counsel asserted that "indeed it is generally considered by publicists that Article 2, paragraph 4, of the United Nations Charter is in this respect an embodiment of existing general principles of international law". And the United States concludes:

> "In sum, the provisions of Article 2(4) with respect of the lawfulness of the use of force *are* 'modern customary law' (International Law Commission, *loc. cit.*) and the 'embodiment of general principles of international law' (counsel for Nicaragua, Hearing of 25 April 1994, morning, *loc. cit.*). There is no other 'customary and general international law' on which Nicaragua can rest its claims."

> "It is, in short, inconceivable that this Court could consider the lawfulness of an alleged use of armed force without referring to the principal source of the relevant international law—Article 2(4) of the United Nations Charter."

As for Nicaragua, the only noteworthy shade of difference in its view lies in Nicaragua's belief that

> "in certain cases the rule of customary law will not necessarily be identical in content and mode of application to the conventional rule".

188. The Court thus finds that both Parties take the view that the principles as to the use of force incorporated in the United Nations Charter correspond, in essentials, to those found in customary international law. The Parties thus both take the view that the fundamental principle in this area is expressed in the terms employed in Article 2, paragraph 4, of the United Nations Charter. They therefore accept a treaty-law obligation to refrain in their international relations from the threat or use of force against the territorial integrity or political independence of any State, or in any other manner inconsistent with the purposes of the United Nations. The Court has however to be satisfied that there exists in customary international law an *opinio juris* as to the binding character of such abstention. This *opinio juris* may, though with all due caution, be deduced from, *inter alia*, the attitude of the Parties and the attitude of States towards certain General Assembly resolutions, and particularly resolution 2625 (XXV) entitled "Declaration of Principles on International Law concerning Friendly Relations and Co-operation among States in accordance with the Charter of the United Nations". The effect of consent to the text of such resolutions cannot be understood as merely that of a "reiteration or elucidation" of the treaty commitment undertaken in the Charter. On the contrary, it may be understood as an acceptance of the validity of the rule or set of rules declared by the resolution by themselves. The principle of non-use of force, for example, may thus be regarded as a principle of customary international law, not as such conditioned by provisions relating to collective security, or to the facilities or armed contingents to be provided under Article 43 of the Charter. It would therefore seem apparent that the attitude referred to expresses an *opinio juris* respecting such rule (or set of rules), to be thenceforth treated separately from the provisions, especially those of an institutional kind, to which it is subject on the treaty-law plane of the Charter....

190. A further confirmation of the validity as customary international law of the principle of the prohibition of the use of force expressed in Article 2, paragraph 4, of the Char-

ter of the United Nations may be found in the fact that it is frequently referred to in statements by State representatives as being not only a principle of customary international law but also a fundamental or cardinal principle of such law. The International Law Commission, in the course of its work on the codification of the law of treaties, expressed the view that "the law of the Charter concerning the prohibition of the use of force in itself constitutes a conspicuous example of a rule in international law having the character of *jus cogens*" (paragraph (1) of the commentary of the Commission to Article 50 of its draft Articles on the Law of Treaties, *ILC Yearbook*, 1966-II, p. 247). Nicaragua in its Memorial on the Merits submitted in the present case states that the principle prohibiting the use of force embodied in Article 2, paragraph 4, of the Charter of the United Nations "has come to be recognized as *jus cogens*". The United States, in its Counter-Memorial on the questions of jurisdiction and admissibility, found it material to quote the views of scholars that this principle is a "universal norm", a "universal international law", a "universally recognized principle of international law", and a "principle of *jus cogens*".

191. As regards certain particular aspects of the principle in question, it will be necessary to distinguish the most grave forms of the use of force (those constituting an armed attack) from other less grave forms. In determining the legal rule which applies to these latter forms, the Court can again draw on the formulations contained in the Declaration on Principles of International Law concerning Friendly Relations and Co-operation among States in accordance with the Charter of the United Nations (General Assembly resolution 2625 (XXV), referred to above). As already observed, the adoption by States of this text affords an indication of their *opinio juris* as to customary international law on the question. Alongside certain descriptions which may refer to aggression, this text includes others which refer only to less grave forms of the use of force. In particular, according to this resolution:

> "Every State has the duty to refrain from the threat or use of force to violate the existing international boundaries of another State or as a means of solving international disputes, including territorial disputes and problems concerning frontiers of states....
>
> States have a duty to refrain from acts of reprisal involving the use of force....
>
> Every State has the duty to refrain from any forcible action which deprives peoples referred to in the elaboration of the principle of equal rights and self-determination of that right to self-determination and freedom and independence.
>
> Every State has the duty to refrain from organizing or encouraging the organization of irregular forces or armed bands, including mercenaries, for incursion into the territory of another State.
>
> Every State has the duty to refrain from organizing, instigating, assisting or participating in acts of civil strife or terrorist acts in another State or acquiescing in organized activities within its territory directed towards the commission of such acts, when the acts referred to in the present paragraph involve a threat or use of force."

192. Moreover, in the part of this same resolution devoted to the principle of non-intervention in matters within the national jurisdiction of States, a very similar rule is found:

> "Also, no State shall organize, assist, foment, finance, incite or tolerate subversive, terrorist or armed activities directed towards the violent overthrow of the regime of another State, or interfere in civil strife in another State."

In the context of the inter-American system, this approach can be traced back at least to 1928 (Convention on the Rights and Duties of States in the Event of Civil Strife, Art. 1 (1)); it was confirmed by resolution 78 adopted by the General Assembly of the Organization of American States on 21 April 1972. The operative part of this resolution reads as follows:

"The General Assembly Resolves:

1. To reiterate solemnly the need for the member states of the Organization to observe strictly the principles of nonintervention and self-determination of peoples as a means of ensuring peaceful coexistence among them and to refrain from committing any direct or indirect act that might constitute a violation of these principles.

2. To reaffirm the obligation of those states to refrain from applying economic, political, or any other type of measures to coerce another state and obtain from it advantages of any kind.

3. Similarly, to reaffirm the obligation of these states to refrain from organizing, supporting, promoting, financing, instigating, or tolerating subversive, terrorist, or armed activities against another state and from intervening in a civil war in another state or in its internal struggles."

193. The general rule prohibiting force allows for certain exceptions. In view of the arguments advanced by the United States to justify the acts of which it is accused by Nicaragua, the Court must express a view on the content of the right of self-defence, and more particularly the right of collective self-defence. First, with regard to the existence of this right, it notes that in the language of Article 51 of the United Nations Charter, the inherent right (or "droit naturel") which any State possesses in the event of an armed attack, covers both collective and individual self-defence. Thus, the Charter itself testifies to the existence of the right of collective self-defence in customary international law. Moreover, just as the wording of certain General Assembly declarations adopted by States demonstrates their recognition of the principle of the prohibition of force as definitely a matter of customary international law, some of the wording in those declarations operates similarly in respect of the right of self-defence (both collective and individual). Thus, in the declaration quoted above on the Principles of International Law concerning Friendly Relations and Co-operation among States in accordance with the Charter of the United Nations, the reference to the prohibition of force is followed by a paragraph stating that:

"nothing in the foregoing paragraphs shall be construed as enlarging or diminishing in any way the scope of the provisions of the Charter concerning cases in which the use of force is lawful".

This resolution demonstrates that the States represented in the General Assembly regard the exception to the prohibition of force constituted by the right of individual or collective self-defence as already a matter of customary international law.

194. With regard to the characteristics governing the right of self-defence, since the Parties consider the existence of this right to be established as a matter of customary international law, they have concentrated on the conditions governing its use. In view of the circumstances in which the dispute has arisen, reliance is placed by the Parties only on the right of self-defence in the case of an armed attack which has already occurred, and the issue of the lawfulness of a response to the imminent threat of armed attack has not been raised. Accordingly the Court expresses no view on that issue. The Parties also agree in holding that whether the response to the attack is lawful depends on observance of the

criteria of the necessity and the proportionality of the measures taken in self-defence. Since the existence of the right of collective self-defence is established in customary international law, the Court must define the specific conditions which may have to be met for its exercise, in addition to the conditions of necessity and proportionality to which the Parties have referred.

195. In the case of individual self-defence, the exercise of this right is subject to the State concerned having been the victim of an armed attack. Reliance on collective self-defence of course does not remove the need for this. There appears now to be general agreement on the nature of the acts which can be treated as constituting armed attacks. In particular, it may be considered to be agreed that an armed attack must be understood as including not merely action by regular armed forces across an international border, but also "the sending by or on behalf of a State of armed bands, groups, irregulars or mercenaries, which carry out acts of armed force against another State of such gravity as to amount to"*(inter alia)* an actual armed attack conducted by regular forces, "or its substantial involvement therein". This description, contained in Article 3, paragraph *(g)*, of the Definition of Aggression annexed to General Assembly resolution 3314 (XXIX), may be taken to reflect customary international law. The Court sees no reason to deny that, in customary law, the prohibition of armed attacks may apply to the sending by a State of armed bands to the territory of another State, if such an operation, because of its scale and effects, would have been classified as an armed attack rather than as a mere frontier incident had it been carried out by regular armed forces. But the Court does not believe that the concept of "armed attack" includes not only acts by armed bands where such acts occur on a significant scale but also assistance to rebels in the form of the provision of weapons or logistical or other support. Such assistance may be regarded as a threat or use of force, or amount to intervention in the internal or external affairs of other States. It is also clear that it is the State which is the victim of an armed attack which must form and declare the view that it has been so attacked. There is no rule in customary international law permitting another State to exercise the right of collective self-defence on the basis of its own assessment of the situation. Where collective self-defence is invoked, it is to be expected that the State for whose benefit this right is used will have declared itself to be the victim of an armed attack....

202. The principle of non-intervention involves the right of every sovereign State to conduct its affairs without outside interference; though examples of trespass against this principle are not infrequent, the Court considers that it is part and parcel of customary international law. As the Court has observed: "Between independent States, respect for territorial sovereignty is an essential foundation of international relations" *(I.C.J. Reports 1949,* p. 35), and international law requires political integrity also to be respected. Expressions of an *opinio juris* regarding the existence of the principle of non-intervention in customary international law are numerous and not difficult to find. Of course, statements whereby States avow their recognition of the principles of international law set forth in the United Nations Charter cannot strictly be interpreted as applying to the principle of non-intervention by States in the internal and external affairs of other States, since this principle is not, as such, spelt out in the Charter. But it was never intended that the Charter should embody written confirmation of every essential principle of international law in force. The existence in the *opinio juris* of States of the principle of non-intervention is backed by established and substantial practice. It has moreover been presented as a corollary of the principle of the sovereign equality of States. A particular instance of this is General Assembly resolution 2625 (XXV), the Declaration of the Principles of International Law concerning Friendly Relations and Co-operation among States. In the *Corfu*

Channel case, when a State claimed a right of intervention in order to secure evidence in the territory of another State for submission to an international tribunal *(I.C.J. Reports 1949,* p. 34), the Court observed that:

> "the alleged right of intervention is the manifestation of a policy of force, such as has, in the past, given rise to most serious abuses and such as cannot, whatever be the present defects in international organization, find a place in international law. Intervention is perhaps still less admissible in the particular form it would take here; for, from the nature of things, it would be reserved for the most powerful States, and might easily lead to perverting the administration of international justice itself." *(I.C.J. Reports 1949,* p. 35.) …

208. In particular, as regards the conduct towards Nicaragua which is the subject of the present case, the United States has not claimed that its intervention, which it justified in this way on the political level, was also justified on the legal level, alleging the exercise of a new right of intervention regarded by the United States as existing in such circumstances. As mentioned above, the United States has, on the legal plane, justified its intervention expressly and solely by reference to the "classic" rules involved, namely, collective self-defence against an armed attack. Nicaragua, for its part, has often expressed its solidarity and sympathy with the opposition in various States, especially in El Salvador. But Nicaragua too has not argued that this was legal basis for an intervention, let alone an intervention involving the use of force.

209. The Court therefore finds that no such general right of intervention, in support of an opposition within another State, exists in contemporary international law. The Court concludes that acts constituting a breach of the customary principle of non-intervention will also, if they directly or indirectly involve the use of force, constitute a breach of the principle of non-use of force in international relations….

211. The Court has recalled above (paragraphs 193 to 195) that for one State to use force against another, on the ground that that State has committed a wrongful act of force against a third State, is regarded as lawful, by way of exception, only when the wrongful act provoking the response was an armed attack. Thus the lawfulness of the use of force by a State in response to a wrongful act of which it has not itself been the victim is not admitted when this wrongful act is not an armed attack. In the view of the Court, under international law in force today—whether customary international law or that of the United Nations system—States do not have a right of "collective" armed response to acts which do not constitute an "armed attack". Furthermore, the Court has to recall that the United States itself is relying on the "inherent right of self-defence" (paragraph 126 above), but apparently does not claim that any such right exists as would, in respect of intervention, operate in the same way as the right of collective self-defence in respect of an armed attack. In the discharge of its duty under Article 53 of the Statute, the Court has nevertheless had to consider whether such a right might exist; but in doing so it may take note of the absence of any such claim by the United States as an indication of *opinio juris.…*

263. The finding of the United States Congress also expressed the view that the Nicaraguan Government had taken "significant steps towards establishing a totalitarian Communist dictatorship". However the regime in Nicaragua be defined, adherence by a State to any particular doctrine does not constitute a violation of customary international law; to hold otherwise would make nonsense of the fundamental principle of State sovereignty, on which the whole of international law rests, and the freedom of choice of the political, social, economic and cultural system of a State. Consequently, Nicaragua's domestic policy options, even assuming that they correspond to the description given of

them by the Congress finding, cannot justify on the legal plane the various actions of the Respondent complained of. The Court cannot contemplate the creation of a new rule opening up a right of intervention by one State against another on the ground that the latter has opted for some particular ideology or political system.

264. The Court has also emphasized the importance to be attached, in other respects, to a text such as the Helsinki Final Act, or, on another level, to General Assembly resolution 2625 (XXV) which, as its name indicates, is a declaration on "Principles of International Law concerning Friendly Relations and Co-operation among States in accordance with the Charter of the United Nations". Texts like these, in relation to which the Court has pointed to the customary content of certain provisions such as the principles of the non-use of force and non-intervention, envisage the relations among States having different political, economic and social systems on the basis of coexistence among their various ideologies; the United States not only voiced no objection to their adoption, but took an active part in bringing it about....

267. The Court also notes that Nicaragua is accused by the 1985 finding of the United States Congress of violating human rights. This particular point requires to be studied independently of the question of the existence of a "legal commitment" by Nicaragua towards the Organization of American States to respect these rights; the absence of such a commitment would not mean that Nicaragua could with impunity violate human rights. However, where human rights are protected by international conventions, that protection takes the form of such arrangements for monitoring or ensuring respect for human rights as are provided for in the conventions themselves. The political pledge by Nicaragua was made in the context of the Organization of American States, the organs of which were consequently entitled to monitor its observance. The Court has noted above (paragraph 168) that the Nicaraguan Government has since 1979 ratified a number of international instruments on human rights, and one of these was the American Convention on Human Rights (the Pact of San José, Costa Rica). The mechanisms provided for therein have functioned. The Inter-American Commission on Human Rights in fact took action and compiled two reports (OEA/Ser.L/V/11.53 and 62) following visits by the Commission to Nicaragua at the Government's invitation. Consequently, the Organization was in a position, if it so wished, to take a decision on the basis of these reports.

268. In any event, while the United States might form its own appraisal of the situation as to respect for human rights in Nicaragua, the use of force could not be the appropriate method to monitor or ensure such respect. With regard to the steps actually taken, the protection of human rights, a strictly humanitarian objective, cannot be compatible with the mining of ports, the destruction of oil installations, or again with the training, arming and equipping of the *contras*. The Court concludes that the argument derived from the preservation of human rights in Nicaragua cannot afford a legal justification for the conduct of the United States, and cannot in any event be reconciled with the legal strategy of the respondent State, which is based on the right of collective self-defence....

292. For these reasons,

THE COURT ...

(3) By twelve votes to three,

Decides that the United States of America, by training, arming, equipping, financing and supplying the *contra* forces or otherwise encouraging, supporting and aiding military and paramilitary activities in and against Nicaragua, has acted, against the Republic of Nicaragua, in breach of its obligation under customary international law not to intervene in the affairs of another State;

IN FAVOUR : President Nagendra Singh; Vice-President de Lacharriére; Judges Lachs, Ruda, Elias, Ago, Sette-Camara, Mbaye, Bedjaoui, Ni and Evensen; Judge ad hoc Colliard;

AGAINST : Judges Oda, Schwebel and Sir Robert Jennings.

(4) By twelve votes to three,

Decides that the United States of America, by certain attacks on Nicaraguan territory in 1983–1984, namely attacks on Puerto Sandino on 13 September and 14 October 1983; an attack on Corinto on 10 October 1983; an attack on Potosi Naval Base on 4/5 January 1984; an attack on San Juan del Sur on 7 March 1984; attacks on patrol boats at Puerto Sandino on 28 and 30 March 1984; and an attack on San Juan del Norte on 9 April 1984; and further by those acts of intervention referred to in subparagraph (3) hereof which involve the use of force, has acted, against the Republic of Nicaragua, in breach of its obligation under customary international law not to use force against another State;

IN FAVOUR : President Nagendra Singh; Vice-President de Lacharriére; Judges Lachs, Ruda, Elias, Ago, Sette-Camara, Mbaye, Bedjaoui, Ni and Evensen; Judge ad hoc Colliard;

AGAINST : Judges Oda, Schwebel and Sir Robert Jennings.

(5) By twelve votes to three,

Decides that the United States of America, by directing or authorizing overflights of Nicaraguan territory, and by the acts imputable to the United States referred to in subparagraph (4) hereof, has acted, against the Republic of Nicaragua, in breach of its obligation under customary international law not to violate the sovereignty of another State;

IN FAVOUR : President Nagendra Singh; Vice-President de Lacharriére; Judges Lachs, Ruda, Elias, Ago, Sette-Camara, Mbaye, Bedjaoui, Ni and Evensen; Judge ad hoc Colliard;

AGAINST : Judges Oda, Schwebel and Sir Robert Jennings.

(6) By twelve votes to three,

Decides that, by laying mines in the internal or territorial waters of the Republic of Nicaragua during the first months of 1984, the United States of America has acted, against the Republic of Nicaragua, in breach of its obligations under customary international law not to use force against another State, not to intervene in its affairs, not to violate its sovereignty and not to interrupt peaceful maritime commerce;

IN FAVOUR : President Nagendra Singh; Vice-President de Lacharriére; Judges Lachs, Ruda, Elias, Ago, Sette-Camara, Mbaye, Bedjaoui, Ni and Evensen; Judge ad hoc Colliard;

AGAINST : Judges Oda, Schwebel and Sir Robert Jennings.

(7) By fourteen votes to one,

Decides that, by acts referred to in subparagraph (6) hereof, the United States of America has acted, against the Republic of Nicaragua, in breach of its obligations under Article XIX of the Treaty of Friendship, Commerce and Navigation between the United States of America and the Republic of Nicaragua signed at Managua on 21 January 1956;

IN FAVOUR : President Nagendra Singh; Vice-President de Lacharriére; Judges Lachs, Ruda, Elias, Oda, Ago, Sette-Camara, Sir Robert Jennings, Mbaye, Bedjaoui, Ni and Evensen; Judge ad hoc Colliard;

AGAINST: Judge Schwebel. . . .

(12) By twelve votes to three,

Decides that the United States of America is under a duty immediately to cease and to refrain from all such acts as may constitute breaches of the foregoing legal obligations;

In Favour : President Nagendra Singh; Vice-President de Lacharriére; Judges Lachs, Ruda, Elias, Ago, Sette-Camara, Mbaye, Bedjaoui, Ni and Evensen; Judge ad hoc Colliard;

Against : Judges Oda, Schwebel and Sir Robert Jennings.

(13) By twelve votes to three,

Decides that the United States of America is under an obligation to make reparation to the Republic of Nicaragua for all injury caused to Nicaragua by the breaches of obligations under customary international law enumerated above;

In Favour : President Nagendra Singh; Vice-President de Lacharriére; Judges Lachs, Ruda, Elias, Ago, Sette-Camara, Mbaye, Bedjaoui, Ni and Evensen; Judge ad hoc Colliard;

Against : Judges Oda, Schwebel and Sir Robert Jennings.

Dissenting Opinion of Judge Schwebel

... I. The Court's Conclusion is Inconsistent with the General Assembly's Definition of Aggression

162. While the conclusion which the Court has reached on this question is inconsistent with the large and authoritative body of State practice and United Nations interpretation to which the Nicaraguan Memorial adverts, the Court is not the first to maintain that acts of armed subversion—of "indirect aggression"—by one State against another cannot be tantamount to armed attack. In the long debates that ultimately culminated in the adoption by the United Nations General Assembly of the Definition of Aggression, opinion on this question was divided. The Soviet Union, a leading proponent of the adoption of a definition of aggression, in its draft definition enumerated among the acts of "*armed* aggression (direct or indirect)":

> "The use by a State of armed force by sending armed bands, mercenaries, terrorists or saboteurs to the territory of another State and engagement in other forms of subversive activity involving the use of armed force with the aim of promoting an internal upheaval in another State ..." (A/8719, p. 8; emphasis supplied.)

Six Powers—Australia, Canada, Italy, Japan, the United Kingdom and the United States—proposed that the use of force in international relations, "overt or covert, direct or indirect" by a State against the territorial integrity or political independence of another State may constitute aggression when effected by means including:

> "(6) Organizing, supporting or directing armed bands or irregular or volunteer forces that make incursions or infiltrate into another State;
>
> (7) Organizing, supporting or directing violent civil strife or acts of terrorism in another State; or
>
> (8) Organizing, supporting or directing subversive activities aimed at the violent overthrow of the Government of another State." (A/8719, pp.11–12)

163. In marked contrast to these approaches of "East" and "West", 13 small and middle Powers put forward a draft definition of aggression which did not include indirect as well as direct uses of force. Their definition spoke only of "the use of armed force by a State against another State". Their list of acts of aggression conspicuously failed to include acts of force effected by indirect means. The Thirteen-Power draft further specified, in a section which did not list acts of aggression, that:

> "When a State is victim in its own territory of subversive and/or terrorist act by irregular, volunteer or armed bands organized or supported by another

State, it may take all reasonable and adequate steps to safeguard its existence and its institutions, without having recourse to the right of individual or collective self-defence against the other State under Article 51 of the Charter". (*Ibid.*, p. 10).

That provision was complementary to a further proviso that:

"The inherent right of individual or collective self-defence of a State can be exercised only in the case of the occurrence of armed attack (armed aggression) by another State ..." (*Ibid.*, p. 9).

164. As Professor Julius Stone—widely recognized as one of the century's leading authorities on the law of the use of force in international relations—concluded in respect of the Thirteen-Power proposals:

"to take away the right of individual and collective self-defence ... was, of course, the precise purpose of the Thirteen Power provision ... It sought to achieve this purpose, both by withholding the stigma of aggression, and by express statement. Acceptance of such a provision would have been at odds with the Charter and general international law as hitherto accepted in a number of respects.

First ... international law imputed responsibility to a State knowingly serving as a base of such para-military activities, and gave the victim State rather wide liberties of self-defence against them.

Second, none of the Charter provisions dealing with unlawful use of force, whether armed or not, offers any basis for distinguishing between force applied by the putative aggressor, or indirectly applied by him through armed bands, irregulars and the like ...

Third ... the General Assembly has more than once included at least some species of "indirect" aggression within its description of "aggression".

Fourth, it may be added that from at least the Spanish Civil War onwards, the most endemic and persistent forms of resorts to armed force ... have been in contexts caught as "aggression" by the Soviet and Six Power drafts, but condoned more or less fully by the Thirteen Power Draft". (*Conflict through Consensus*, 1977, pp. 89–90).

It will be observed that the essential legal rationale of the Judgment of the Court in the current case appears to be well expressed by these Thirteen-Power proposals which Professor Stone characterized as "at odds with the Charter and general international law ...".

165. The Thirteen-Power proposals were not accepted by the United Nations Special Committee on the Question of Defining Aggression. They were not accepted by the General Assembly. On the contrary, the General Assembly by consensus adopted a Definition of Aggression which embraces not all, but still the essence of the proposals of the Six Powers and the Soviet Union. Its list in Article 3 of the acts which shall "qualify as an act of aggression" includes:

"(g) The sending by or on behalf of a State of armed bands, groups, irregulars or mercenaries, which carry out acts of armed force against another State of such gravity as to amount to the acts listed above, *or its substantial involvement therein*". (emphasis supplied)....

166. It has been demonstrated above and in the appendix to this opinion that the Nicaraguan Government is "substantially involved" in the sending of armed bands, groups and irregulars to El Salvador. Nicaragua apparently has not "sent" Nicaraguan irregulars to fight in El Salvador, but it has been "substantially involved" in the sending of leadership of the Salvadoran insurgency back and forth. As has been shown by the admissions

of a principal witness of Nicaragua. Mr. MacMichael, and other evidence, leadership of the Salvadoran insurgency has been established in and operated from Nicaragua, and moved into and out of El Salvador from and to its Nicaraguan bases with the full support of the Nicaraguan Government, a situation which in substance equates with Nicaragua's "sending" of that leadership to direct the insurgency in El Salvador. As Professor Stone concludes, while Article 3 (g) "requires there to have been a 'sending' into the target State, it inculpates the host State not merely when that State did the sending, but also when it has a 'substantial involvement therein'" (*loc. cit.*, pp. 75–76). Nicaragua's substantial involvement further takes the forms of providing arms, munitions, other supplies, training, command-and-control facilities, sanctuary and lesser forms of assistance to the Salvadoran insurgents. Those insurgents, in turn, carry out acts of armed force against another State, namely, El Salvador. Those acts are of such gravity as to amount to the other acts listed in Article 3 of the Definition of Aggression, such as invasion, attack, bombardment and blockade. The many thousands of El Salvadorans killed and wounded, and the enormous damage to El Salvador's infrastructure and economy, as a result of insurgent attacks so supported by Nicaragua is ample demonstration of the gravity of the acts of the insurgents.

167. It accordingly follows not only that the multiple acts of subversive intervention by Nicaragua against El Salvador are acts of aggression, and that those acts fall within the proscriptions of the Definition of Aggression. It is also important to note that the Definition — contrary to the Thirteen-Power proposals — designedly says nothing about prohibiting a State from having recourse to the right of individual or collective self-defence when that State "is a victim in its own territory of subversive and/or terrorist acts by irregular, volunteer or armed bands organized or supported by another State". That prohibitive proposal proved unacceptable to the international community. Rather, it is plain that, under the Definition, and customary international law, and in the practice of the United Nations and of States, a State is entitled in precisely these circumstances to act in individual and collective self-defence. To be entitled to do so, it is not required to show that the irregulars operating on its territory act as the agents of the foreign State or States which support them. It is enough to show that those States are "substantially involved" in the sending of those irregulars on to its territory....

170. The Court's reasoning is open to criticism, in terms of the Definition of Aggression and under customary international law — not to speak of the realities of modern warfare. Article 3 (g) does not confine its definition of acts that qualify as acts of aggression to the sending of armed bands; rather, it specifies as an act of aggression a State's "substantial involvement" in the sending of armed bands. That provision is critical to the current case. As pointed out in paragraph 166 of this opinion, and detailed in its appendix, Nicaragua has been pervasively, not merely substantially, involved in many aspects of the sending of armed groups of insurgents to El Salvador — and especially involved in the sending of the leadership of those insurgents, a leadership based in Nicaragua — even if Nicaragua itself had not simply sent such armed bands from its territory to that of El Salvador. It is one thing to send; it is another to be "substantially involved" in the sending....

K. The Court's Views on Counter-Intervention and Its Implied Support for "Wars of Liberation"

174. When the Court's Judgment comes to deal with questions of intervention, it finds that the United States has committed "a clear breach of the principle of non-intervention" by its support of the *contras*. The Court at the same time finds it possible — re-

markably enough—to absolve Nicaragua of any act of intervention in El Salvador, despite its multiple acts of intervention in El Salvador in support of the Salvadoran insurgents....

175. While this conclusion may be treated as *obiter dictum* in view of the fact that there is no plea of counter-intervention before the Court, it is no more correct because it is unnecessary. In my view, its errors are conspicuous. The Court appears to reason this way. Efforts by State A (however insidious, sustained, substantial and effective), to overthrow the government of State B, if they are not or do not amount to an armed attack upon State B, give rise to no right of self-defence by State B and hence, to no right of State C to join State B in measures of collective self-defence. State B, the victim State, is entitled to take counter-measures against State A, of a dimension the Court does not specify. But State C is not thereby justified in taking counter-measures against State A which involve the use of force.

176. In my view, the Court's reasoning certainly as it applies to the case before the Court, is erroneous for the following reasons: (a) A State is not necessarily and absolutely confined to responding in self-defence only if it is the object of armed attack. (b) Armed attack in any event is not only the movement of regular armed forces across international frontiers; it is not only the sending by State A of armed bands across an international frontier to attack State B or overthrow its government; it is, as the Definition of Aggression puts it, "substantial involvement therein"—for example, the very sort of substantial involvement which Nicaragua's multifaceted involvement in promoting and sustaining the Salvadoran insurgency illustrates. (c) In a case such as the case before the Court, where Nicaragua has carried out and continues to carry out the acts of support of armed insurgency against the Government of El Salvador which El Salvador which El Salvador and the United States have charged and the appendix to this opinion establishes, the Government of El Salvador has had the choice of acting in self-defense or capitulating. Lesser measures of counter-intervention could not suffice. It has chosen to act in self-defence, but it lacks the power to carry the battle to the territory of the aggressor, Nicaragua. (d) In such a case, El Salvador is entitled to seek assistance in collective self-defence. Such assistance may in any event take place on the territory of El Salvador, as by the financing, provisioning and training of its troops by the United States. But, as shown below, contemporary international law recognizes that a third State is entitled to exert measures of force against the aggressor on its own territory and against its own armed forces and military resources.

177. I find the Court's enunciation of what it finds to be the law of counter-intervention as applied to this case unpersuasive for all these reasons. More generally, I believe that it raises worrisome questions. Let us suppose that State A's support of the subversion of State B, while serious and effective enough to place the political independence of State B in jeopardy, does not amount to an armed attack upon State B. Let us further suppose that State A acts against State B not only on its behalf but together with a Great Power and an organized international movement with a long and successful history of ideology and achievement in the cause of subversion and aggrandizement, and with the power and will to stimulate further the progress of what that movement regards as historically determined. If the Court's *obiter dictum* were to be treated as the law to which States deferred, other Great Powers and other States would be or could be essentially powerless to intervene effectively to preserve the political independence of State B and all other similarly situated States, most of which will be small. According to the Court, State B could take counter-measures against State A, but whether they would include measures of force is not said. What is said is that third States could not use force, whether or not the preservation of the political independence—or territorial integrity—of State B depended on

the exertion of such measures. In short, the Court appears to offer—quite gratuitously—a prescription for overthrow of weaker governments by predatory governments while denying potential victims what in some cases may be their only hope of survival....

S. The United States Has not Unlawfully Intervened in the Internal or External Affairs of Nicaragua

241. Relying on the same factual allegations which it has advanced against the United States in respect of the use of force against it, Nicaragua also maintains that the United States stands in breach of its obligations under the Chapter of the Organization of American States, as contained in Articles 18, 19, 20 and 21, and under customary international law. The essence of its claim is that the United States has unlawfully intervened in the internal and external affairs of Nicaragua by attempting to change the policies of its Government or the Nicaraguan Government itself.

242. In view of the comprehensive and categorical injunctions of the OAS Charter against intervention, and the much narrower but significant rules of non-intervention of customary international law, Nicaragua's prima facie case appears to be considerable. On analysis, however, it is inadequate, and for two reasons (in addition to those posed by the multilateral treaty reservation). The first of those reasons goes a long way towards countering Nicaraguan contentions of unlawful intervention. The second vitiates them.

243. It has been shown that, in order to extract from the OAS and its Members their recognition of the Junta of National Reconstruction in place of the Government of President Somoza, the Junta, in response to the OAS resolution of 23 June 1979, gave undertakings to the OAS and its Members to govern in accordance with specified democratic standards and policies (see paras. 8–13 of the appendix to this opinion). It has also been shown that the Nicaraguan Government has failed so to govern, and has so failed deliberately and willfully, as a matter of State policy (ibid.)....

245. The Permanent Court of International Justice in its advisory opinion on *Nationality Decrees Issued in Tunis and Morocco (P.C.I.J., Series B, No. 4,* p. 24) dealt with what is a matter of domestic jurisdiction in classic terms:

> "The question whether a certain matter is or is not solely within the jurisdiction of a State is an essentially relative question; it depends on the development of international relations ... it may well happen that, in a matter which ... is not, in principle, regulated by international law, the right of a State to use its discretion is nevertheless restricted by obligations which it may have undertaken towards other States. In such a case, jurisdiction which, in principle, belongs solely to the State, is limited by the rules of international law".

There is nothing to debar a state—or a revolutionary junta entitled to bind the State—from undertaking obligations towards other States in respect of matters which otherwise would be within its exclusive jurisdiction. Thus, under the Statute of the Council of Europe, every Member of the Council of Europe "must accept the principles of the rule of law and of the enjoyment by all persons within its jurisdiction of human rights and fundamental freedoms" (Art.3). Any Member which has seriously violated Article 3 may be suspended from its rights of representation. The history of the Council of Europe demonstrates that these international obligations are treated as such by the Council; they may not be avoided by pleas of domestic jurisdiction and non-intervention.

246. The Nicaraguan Junta of National Reconstruction, by the undertakings it entered into not only with the OAS but with its Members, among them, the United States (which individually and in consideration of those undertakings treated with the Junta as the Government of the Republic of Nicaragua), has not dissimilarly placed within the domain of

Nicaragua's international obligations its domestic governance and foreign policy to the extent of those undertakings. Thus, what otherwise would be "the right" of Nicaragua "to use its discretion is nevertheless restricted by obligations" which it has undertaken towards those States, including the United States. It follows that, when the United States demands that Nicaragua perform its undertakings given to the OAS and its Members, including the United States, to observe human rights, to enforce civil justice, to call free elections; when it demands that the Junta perform its promises of "a truly democratic government ... with full guaranty of human rights" and "fundamental liberties" including "free expression, reporting" and trade union freedom and "an independent foreign policy of non-alignment" (appendix to this opinion, paras. 8–11), the United States does not "intervene" in the internal or external affairs of Nicaragua. Such demands are not a "form of interference or attempted threat against the personality of the State" of Nicaragua. They are legally well-grounded efforts to induce Nicaragua to perform its international obligations.

247. The Court, however, has found that, by its 1979 communications to the OAS and its Members, Nicaragua entered into no commitments. It may be observed that that conclusion is inconsistent not only with the views of the United States quoted in the Court's Judgment, but apparently with the views of Nicaragua (appendix to this opinion, para. 53). In my view, the commitment of Nicaragua is clear: essentially, in exchange for the OAS and its Members stripping the Somoza Government of its legitimacy and bestowing recognition upon the Junta as the Government of Nicaragua, the Junta extended specific pledges to the OAS and its Members which it bound itself to "implement" (appendix, paras. 8–13, especially para. 10). I am confirmed in that conclusion by the former Director of the Department of Legal Affairs of the OAS, Dr. F.V. Garcia Amador, who has characterized the pledges of the Junta in question as constituting "its formal obligation". In his view:

> "These obligation included the installation of a democratic government to be composed of the principal groups which had opposed the previous regime and the guarantee to respect the human rights of all Nicaraguans, without exception. The requirements imposed by the Meeting [the Seventeenth Meeting of Consultation of the Ministers of Foreign Affairs in 1979] were not unexpected, especially in view of the Resolution of June 23, 1979 which proposed the '[i]mmediate and definitive replacement of the Somoza regime' in order to resolve the situation in Nicaragua". (Loc. cit., p. 40.)

248. It is of course obvious that the Junta did not, by its written undertakings to the OAS and its Members, conclude an international agreement in treaty form. But, as the Vienna Convention on the Law of Treaties recognized (Art. 3), and as the Permanent Court of International Justice held in the *Legal Status of Eastern Greenland, Judgment, 1933 P.C.I.J. Series A/B, No. 53*, page 71, an international commitment binding upon a State need not be made in written, still less particularly formal, form. The question is simply, did the authority of the State concerned give an assurance, or extend an undertaking, which, in the particular circumstances, is to be regarded as binding upon it? When a revolutionary government, soliciting recognition, has given assurances to foreign governments, such assurances have repeatedly been treated by foreign governments as binding the revolutionary government and its successors. I do not see why the assurances of the Junta were not binding, made as they were, not only to the OAS but to its "Member States"; assurances which the Junta affirmed it "ratified", which it characterized as a "decision" which it intimated it took "in fulfillment of the Resolution of the XVII Meeting of Consultation of Ministers of Foreign Affairs of the OAS adopted on 23 June 1979", and which it affirmed it "will immediately proceed ... to Decree, [which] Organic Law ... will

govern the institutions of the State" in pursuance of a Program which the Government of National Reconstruction will "Implement". As the Inter-American Commission on Human Rights recognized, the OAS deprived the Somoza Government of legitimacy. The OAS offered recognition to the Junta on bases which the Junta accepted. The Junta in reply indeed prescribed that, immediately following its installation inside Nicaragua, "the Member States of the OAS ... will proceed to recognize it as the legitimate Government of Nicaragua" and that it in turn "will immediately proceed" to decree its Fundamental Statute and Organic Law and implement its Program (appendix, para. 10). The OAS and its Members performed; the Government of Nicaragua did not. Not only was the creation of an international obligation clear; so was its breach.

249. It does not follow, however, that the United States is entitled to use any means whatever to persuade Nicaragua to perform its international obligations. Under the regime of the United Nations Charter, and in contemporary customary international law, a State is not generally entitled to use force to require another State to carry out its international legal obligations; a State may use force only in response to the lawful injunctions of the United Nations and of regional organizations acting in conformity with the Purposes and Principles of the United Nations, and in individual or collective self-defence.

250. This brings us to the second, and dispositive, consideration. The United States claims that the measures of force which it has exerted, directly and indirectly, against Nicaragua, are measures of collective self-defence. If that claim is good—and, for the reasons expounded above, I believe that it is—it is a defence not only to Nicaraguan charges of the unlawful use of force against it but of intervention against it. That is demonstrated by the terms of the OAS Charter. Articles 21 and 22 provide:

> "Article 21
>
> The American States bind themselves in their international relations not to have recourse to the use of force, except in the case of self-defence in accordance with existing treaties or in fulfillment thereof.
>
> Article 22
>
> Measures adopted for the maintenance of peace and security in accordance with existing treaties do not constitute a violation of the principles set forth in Articles 18 and 20".

As has been shown above, the use of force by the United States comports not only with the United Nations Charter but with the Rio Treaty—one of the "existing treaties" to which Articles 21 and 22 of the Charter of the OAS refer. The "measures adopted for the maintenance of peace and security in accordance with existing treaties" by the United States and El Salvador, in exercise of their inherent right of collective self-defence, thus "do not constitute a violation of the principles set forth in Articles 18 and 20" of the OAS Charter. Nor do they transgress customary international law. If a State charged with intervention actually acted in collective self-defence, its measures are treated not as unlawful intervention but as measures of justified counter-intervention or self-defence.

Notes and Questions

1. Do you agree with the Court's opinion (all of it) or the dissenting opinion (all of it), or what?

2. Would you have made any different claims before the Court on behalf of the United States (which did not appear during ICJ proceedings on the merits), or Nicaragua?

3. Was the Court correct that "sovereignty" or self-determination of a people is equivalent to or consistent with "adherence by a State to any particular doctrine … ideology or political system"? Consider U.N. Charter, arts. 1(2) and (3), 55(c), 56; U.N. G.A. Res. 2625 (XXV), Declaration on Principles of International Law (1970); Universal Declaration of Human Rights, art. 21(3); Western Sahara Advisory Opinion, [1975] I.C.J. 12, 31–33, 36; U.N. S.C. Res. 940 (July 31, 1994) (re: Haiti); U.N. G.A. Res. 39/2 (Sept. 28, 1984) (re: the illegal apartheid regime in South Africa); American Convention on Human Rights, preamble and art. 29(c); American Declaration of the Rights and Duties of Man, art. XX.

4. In view of the majority opinion's dictum concerning use of force to effectuate human rights, can you distinguish NATO's use of force in Kosovo in 1999 to stop genocidal violence?

5. Are there any other current events to which the Judgment of the Court might be relevant? Do you foresee the likelihood of criminal sanctions being employed?

6. In the Court's opinion, one reads that for the United States to have "legal responsibility" with respect to U.S. participation in *Contra* operations implicating human rights violations because of U.S. "financing, organizing, training, supplying and equipping of the *Contras*, the selection of its military and paramilitary targets, and the planning of the

whole of its operation," it would "have to be proved that the State [the U.S.] had effective control of the military and paramilitary operations" of the *Contras* for state responsibility of the U.S. to arise and there was insufficient evidence that the U.S. "directed or enforced the perpetration of the acts" under consideration. *Id.* at 65 (para. 115). See also *id.* at 113 (para. 216), 129 (para. 254). Do you agree? See also Paust, *The Link Between Human Rights and Terrorism and its Implications Concerning the Law of State Responsibility*, 11 Hastings Int'l & Comp. L. Rev. 41, 45–53 (1987).

Later, the International Criminal Tribunal for Former Yugoslavia declared that "in addition to financing, training and equipping or providing operational support," the state should have a "role in organizing, coordinating or planning the military actions of the" non-state group. See The Prosecutor v. Tadic, IT-94-1-T (Trial Chamber Judgment, 7 May 1997), para. 137. *See also* Paust, *Use of Armed Force against Terrorists in Afghanistan, Iraq, and Beyond*, 35 Cornell Int'l L.J. 533, 540–44 (2002). State responsibility leading to political, diplomatic, economic, or juridical sanctions can also arise if a state adopts non-state actor conduct as its own. *See, e.g.,* United States Diplomatic and Consular Staff in Tehran (United States v. Iran), 1980 I.C.J. 3; Responsibility of States for Internationally Wrongful Acts, art. 11 ("if and to the extent that the State acknowledges and adopts the conduct in question as its own"), U.N. G.A. Res. 56/83, U.N. GAOR, 56th Sess., Annex, Supp. No. 10, U.N. Doc. A/56/83 (2001). Even where it exists, state responsibility is not the same as an "armed attack" triggering the right of self-defense, but it could allow use of diplomatic, political, economic, and juridic sanctions.

7. In view of the recognitions in Note 6, was the use of armed force by the United States on October 7, 2001 against the Taliban regime in Afghanistan permissible because the Taliban had "harbored" bin Laden and members of al Qaeda, let them train persons in Afghanistan, and refused to extradite bin Laden to the United States for trial? In answering this question, assume that there is no known evidence that the Taliban regime was aware of pending 9/11 attacks by al Qaeda. See also Paust, *Use of Force against Terrorists in Afghanistan, supra* at 540–44.

8. What level of armed force is required to constitute an "armed attack"? In the *Nicaragua* case, the I.C.J. declared that it is "necessary to distinguish the most grave forms of the use of force (those constituting an armed attack) from other less grave forms" 1986 I.C.J. at 101, para. 191. See also Case Concerning Oil Platforms (Islamic Republic of Iran v. United States of America), 2003 I.C.J., 161, 187, para. 51 (quoting Nicaragua v. United States, at para. 72), 195, para. 72 ("the mining of a single military vessel might be sufficient to bring into play the 'inherent right of self-defense'"). Does Article 51 of the Charter express any distinction with respect to the inherent right of self-defense on the basis of gravity, scale, or effects? Do you think that a state can respond with proportionate force against the "most grave forms" of armed force but must suffer lesser forms of armed aggression? According to some, the use of force in response to "less grave forms" of attack is prohibited and, as the I.C.J. stated per dictum, that a "mere frontier incident" does not constitute an armed attack. 1986 I.C.J. at para. 195. Do you agree? How can a state tell whether the attack against it is of a sufficient scale and effect or is a "mere frontier incident"?

Others disagree. *See, e.g.*, Yoram Dinstein, War, Aggression and Self-Defence 193, 195 ("it would be fallacious to dismiss automatically from consideration as an armed attack every frontier incident," such as when a soldier fires a single bullet across a border or a small military unit is attacked; "'[t]he gravity of an attack may affect the proper scope of defensive use of force…, but it is not relevant to determining whether there is a right of self-defense in the first instance'" (quoting William H. Taft, IV, former Legal Adviser to the U.S. Secretary of State); "'even a small border incident'" can constitute an armed attack (quoting J.L. Kunz)), 202 (cumulative "pin-prick" attacks can be viewed as a process of armed attack), 230–31 (4 ed. 2005); Judith Gardam, Necessity, Proportionality and the Use of Force by States 143, 161 (2004); Christian J. Tams, *The Use of Force Against Terrorists*, 20 Eur. J. Int'l L. 359, 370 & nn.69, 71 (2009) (noting that a gravity threshold articulated in 1986 "remained controversial," citing Dahm, Dinstein, Feder, Gazzini, and Randelzhofer), 379–81 (noting new practice of states). Is there a need to abandon an unrealistic gravity limitation? Professor Paust has written that "some who prefer that an 'armed attack' be of significant gravity before it triggers the inherent right of self-defense may have to change their preference as limited forms of non-state actor armed attacks increase and in reality require immediate and precise responsive uses of force that can be achieved through use of drones, whether or not the non-state actor attacks are terroristic in purpose and effect or amount to measures of asymmetric war across national borders. Restrictivist interpretations can encourage non-state actors to attack across borders and provide functional safe-havens." Paust, chapter 59, Remotely Piloted Warfare as a Challenge to the *Jus ad Bellum*, in Oxford Handbook on the Prohibition of the Use of Force, forthcoming (Marc Weller ed., Oxford Univ. Press. 2013). He adds with respect to the hypothetical that follows, the hypothetical "demonstrates the point that even a few relatively low level rocket attacks by non-state actors across borders will likely be considered by states to constitute armed attacks even if others debate whether they are of significant 'gravity' and effect. For real-world decision makers who see their fellow nationals being killed, injured, and terrorized, a supposed gravity limitation will be simply unavailing."

9. Consider the following hypothetical:

Consider the circumstance where a non-state terrorist group acquires rockets capable of striking short-range targets and starts firing them from Mexico (without the consent of the Government of Mexico or prior foreseeability) into Fort Bliss, a U.S. military base near El Paso, Texas. Must the United States actually obtain a special express consent of the Mexican Government or already be engaged in a war with the terrorist group (if that is even possible) before resorting to a selective use of force in self-defense to silence the terrorist attacks on U.S. military personnel and other U.S. nationals? I doubt that any state under such a process of armed attack would wait while the rocket attacks continue or expect that under international law it must wait to engage in selective self-defense against the attackers. Furthermore, I doubt that any state would expect that it cannot engage in measures of self-defense to stop such rocket attacks if it had not been and cannot be at war with non-state terrorist attackers or that it cannot take such defensive measures if it is not otherwise engaged in a relevant armed conflict.

Certainly the President of the United States would try to communicate as soon as possible with the President of Mexico and others concerning what is occurring and the fact that the United States is not attacking Mexico, but the U.S. President would not have to wait for a formal response while rockets are raining down on U.S. soldiers. Additionally, although it would be polite, the United States would not have to warn Mexican authorities before engaging in selective measures of self-defense to stop continuing attacks. Under various circumstances, a warning can be impracticable, futile, and/or create complications threatening the success of a self-defense response, especially in other contexts if a special operations unit is being used for reconnaissance or to carry out the self-defense action.

From Paust, *Self-Defense Targetings of Non-State Actors and Permissibility of U.S. Use of Drones in Pakistan*, 19 J. TRANSNAT'L L. & POL'Y 237, 255-56 (2010).

10. Recall that in the *Nicaragua* case, the I.C.J. held that "the provision of arms [by one state] to the opposition in another State [does not] constitute ... an armed attack on that State" by the state that merely supplied arms and does not control "the opposition" (so that there is no attribution or imputation of responsibility with respect to the armed attack). 1986 I.C.J. at para. 230. The Court held that "[e]ven at a time when the arms flow was at is peak, and again assuming the participation of the Nicaraguan Government, that would not constitute such armed attack" by Nicaragua on El Salvador. *Id*. Therefore, El Salvador was barred from using armed force against Nicaragua in order to prevent Nicaragua from providing arms to insurgent forces seeking to overthrow its government. What are the implications of the I.C.J.'s ruling? Must states suffering non-state actor armed attacks merely respond to the attacks by the non-state actors?

11. In the *Nicaragua* case, the I.C.J. recognized that the forms of armed attack by one state against another that can trigger the right to use force in self-defense include (but are not necessarily limited to) "action by regular armed forces [of the attacking state] across an international border" and "the sending by or on behalf of a State of armed bands, groups, irregular or mercenaries, which carry out acts of armed force against another State ... or its substantial involvement therein." 1986 I.C.J. at 103, para. 195 (quoting the 1974 Definition of Aggression, art. 3). Therefore, use of armed force by non-state actors constitutes an armed attack by a state if, for example, the non-state actors were sent by the state or the armed force was effectively controlled by the state. Professor Yoram Dinstein proposes that a use of force constitutes an "armed attack" under Article 51 if it causes or risks causing "serious consequences, epitomized by territorial intrusions, human casualties or considerable destruction of property." DINSTEIN, *supra* at 193. Should any illegal armed force that risks serious loss of life or property trigger a state's right of self-defense, subject to the limitations inherent in principles of necessity, distinction, and proportionality?

12. On June 11, 2010 at Kampala, Uganda, the Review Conference of the International Criminal Court (ICC) adopted Resolution RC/Res.6 concerning the Crime of Aggression, by consensus after a lengthy process involving years of negotiation. Annexes I, II & III to the Resolution set forth Amendments to the Rome Statute of the ICC on the Crime of Aggression. See ICC's Definition of Aggression in the Documents Supplement.

Will this Amendment change the definition of aggression recognized in the 1974 Resolution on the Definition of Aggression in any substantial way, especially since Article 8 *bis*, paragraph 2 incorporates the 1974 resolution by using the phrase "[a]ny of the following acts..., shall, in accordance with" the 1974 Resolution, "qualify as an act of aggression"? What is the effect of Article 8 *bis*, paragraph 1, which identifies the crime of aggression with "an act of aggression which, by its character, gravity and scale, constitutes a manifest violation of the Charter of the United Nations"? Necessarily, must there be a violation of the U.N. Charter? Does such a requirement throw the question of interpretation back to issues with respect to interpretation of various articles of the U.N. Charter? Yet, what is the effect of the word "manifest"? What is the effect of the phrase "by its character, gravity and scale"?

See generally Surendran Koran, *The International Criminal Court and the Crime of Aggression: Beyond the Kampala Convention*, 34 Hous. J. Int'l L. 231 (2012); STEFAN BARRIGA, WOLFGANG F. DANSPECKGRUBER, & CHRISTIAN WENAWESER, EDS., THE PRINCETON PROCESS ON THE CRIME OF AGGRESSION: MATERIALS OF THE SPECIAL WORKING GROUP ON THE CRIME OF AGGRESSION, 2003-2009 (2009); Leila Nadya Sadat, *On the Shores of Lake Victoria: Africa and the Review Conference for the International Criminal Court*, 2010(1) AFLA QUARTERLY 10; Noah Weisbord, *Judging Aggression*, 50 COLUM. J. TRANSNAT'L L. 82 (2011); Beth van Schaak, *Negotiating at the Interface of Power & Law: The Crime of Aggression*, *available at* http://works.bepress.com/beth_van_schaack/2 (2010); Claus Kress and Leonie von Holtzendorff, *The Kampala Compromise on the Crime of Aggression*, 8(5) J. INT'L CRIM. JUSTICE 1179 (2010).

Section 3
Aggression Against Authority

Paust, *Aggression Against Authority: The Crime of Oppression, Politicide and Other Crimes Against Human Rights*
18 CASE W. RES. J. INT'L L. 283, 286–90, 294–96 (1986)

The relatively recent effort of the United Nations General Assembly (General Assembly) to define aggression and to reiterate its prohibition under the United Nations Charter (U.N. Charter) is only partly adequate to this task. It is useful in demonstrating certain proscribed actions directed "against the sovereignty, territorial integrity or political independence of another state," but it falls short of providing any further guidance concerning proscribed acts of aggression by a government against its own people. The Resolution on the Definition of Aggression calls upon all states to refrain from "all acts of aggression and other uses of force contrary to the Charter of the United Nations and the Declaration on Principles of International Law, and reaffirms "the duty of States not to use armed force to deprive peoples of their right to self-determination...." It notes that nothing contained in the definition "could in any way prejudice the right to self-determination ... of peoples forcibly deprived of that right ... nor the right of these peoples to struggle to that end and to seek and receive support...," notes that "the question whether an act of aggression has been committed must be considered in the light of all the circumstances," and notes that "acts enumerated ... are not exhaustive...." Moreover, the definition affirms that aggression also includes the use of armed force "in any other manner [than the proscribed attacks against another state, which is] inconsistent with the Charter," but does not provide further clarification. Nonetheless, "[a] war of aggression," the Declaration affirms, "is a crime against international peace". In this sense, the Declaration reaffirms recognition in the authoritative 1970 Declaration on Principles of International Law that "[a] war of aggression constitutes a crime against the peace, for which there is responsibility under international law".

Under the U.N. Charter, "the threat or use of force against the territorial integrity or political independence of any state, or in any other manner inconsistent with the Purposes of the United Nations" is proscribed. As the Declaration on Principles of International Law affirms, "[s]uch a threat or use of force constitutes a violation of international law and the Charter ..." and is tied also to "the duty to refrain from any forcible action which deprives peoples ... of their right to self-determination...." Because article 1, paragraph 2, of the U.N. Charter recognizes respect for self-determination of peoples as a major purpose, and because article 2, paragraph 4, prohibits the threat or use of force in any manner inconsistent with the purposes of the United Nations, it is clear that the threat or use of force against the self-determination of a people entitled to such right is proscribed by the Charter.

Other resolutions of the General Assembly have affirmed this interconnected prohibition and implicitly confirm that the use of force in violation of article 2(4) to deprive a people of self-determination constitutes a crime against peace. In fact, the General Assembly has resolutely condemned "all forms of oppression, tyranny and discrimination ... wherever they occur," and has strongly condemned racism and all "totalitarian" ideologies and practices. The General Assembly stated that such ideologies and practices:

> which are based on terror and racial intolerance, are incompatible with the purposes and principles of the Charter of the United Nations and constitute a gross violation of human rights and fundamental freedoms which may jeopardize world peace and the security of peoples.

With respect to the latter practices, the General Assembly has also called upon all states to prosecute the perpetrators of such violations. More recently, the International Law Commission has made an inviting recognition that "an international crime may result ... from ... a serious breach of an international obligation of essential importance for safeguarding the right of self-determination...." The Commission also noted that "domination" of a people "by force" may constitute a crime against self-determination. This recognition can undoubtedly apply to the use of force by a government to deprive a people of self-determination and thus to engage in acts of "domination" and political oppression.

The right of a given people to political self-determination is also a fundamental human right and is interconnected necessarily with several other important human rights, including the right of individuals freely to participate in the political process. The respect for and observance of human rights is also a major purpose of the U.N., and article 2, paragraph 4, of the Charter prohibits the threat or use of force in any manner "inconsistent with the Purposes of the United Nations". Thus, it is clear that an additional interconnected basis exists for the proscription of the threat or use of force against political self-determination. For a similar reason, aggression against authority is proscribed by the U.N. Charter.

Under international law, the legitimate authority of a government exists on the basis of the "will of the people" expressed through a relatively full, free, and equal participation of individuals in the political process. Such a standard of authority is now entrenched in many interrelated human rights and the precept of self-determination; each is ultimately protected in the U.N. Charter and subsequent authoritative decisions. When force is used to oppress individual or group participation in the political process and is used to change the dynamic outcome of such a process identifiable in an aggregate will of individuals, such a use of force constitutes an aggression against authority, human rights and the process of self-determination. Hence, such a use of force violates articles 1(2), 1(3), 2(4) and 56 of the U.N. Charter. It is among the more odious of violations, posing a threat to several fundamental Charter precepts, and can affect the rights of numerous victims — more numerous in fact than the victims of ordinary violations of international law or many other forms of international crime.

More recently, the General Assembly applied these international precepts while condemning the governmental process of South Africa. The General Assembly reaffirmed the need for the "establishment of a non-racial democratic society based on majority rule, through the full and free exercise of adult suffrage by all the people in a united and unfragmented South Africa;" and recognized the "legitimacy of … [the] struggle [by the oppressed people of South Africa] to eliminate *apartheid* and establish a society based on majority rule with equal participation by all of the people of South Africa." The General Assembly, in its nearly unanimous resolution, also condemned the South African "regime for defying relevant resolutions of the United Nations and persisting with the further entrenchment of apartheid, a system declared a crime against humanity and a threat to international peace and security." Such an oppression of the authority of the people is a form of political slavery that is not only violative of human rights and self-determination, but also constitutes treason against humanity which should increasingly be recognized as a crime of oppression and a crime against humanity.

Crimes Against Humanity Reconsidered

The Principles of the Nuremberg Charter and Judgment recognize that crimes against humanity include:

> [M]urder, extermination, enslavement, deportation and other inhuman acts done against any civilian population, or persecution on political, racial or religious grounds, when such acts are done or such persecutions are carried on in execution of or in connection with any crime against peace or any war crime.

Since the crime includes acts done against any population and persecution on political grounds, aggression against authority and political oppression can constitute a crime against humanity [under the Principles] if done in connection with "any crime against peace or any war crime"....

More generally, however, a crime against peace should also be recognized whenever a violation of international law is of such serious magnitude that it poses a significant threat to peace. The main concern in a post-Nuremberg world is not merely with a war or threat of war between nation-states. Numerous decisions of U.N. bodies and the writings of scholars demonstrate that there is also a pervasive concern of the international community with threats to peace that are posed by non-war actions and events. It is not unusual, for example, to discover a recognized interdependence between peace and human rights, and that significant deprivations of human rights can themselves result in a serious threat to international peace. Where such a threat is reasonably foreseeable as a result of serious violations of international law, as in the case of widespread political oppression and aggression against authority, it is logical and policy-serving to extend recognition of the concept of crimes against peace to such a circumstance. Having done so, one might recognize that such illegality constitutes a crime against humanity as well.

This is not actually a new approach to the problem posed by criminal actions violative of the law of the international community. As early as the 1600s, Grotius recognized that crimes against the law of nations are "offenses which affect human society at large … and which other states or their rulers have a right to deal with." Grotius had also recognized the propriety of a "war" against a ruler who engages in a "manifest oppression" of his or her people, noting that such a military response was "undertaken to protect the subjects of another ruler from oppression" and to assure that they are not further denied "the right of all human society" to freedom from oppression. In that sense, "war" against the oppressor-ruler was a form of sanction strategy in response to acts of oppression that could affect human society at large.…

In their seminal work on *Law and Minimum World Public Order*, McDougal and Feliciano also note that the real question concerns the impermissibility of coercion rather than the "technical characterizations" of phrases such as "war of aggression," "crimes against peace," "threats to the peace," or "threat or use of force," and that "[i]n the framing of the United Nations Charter the deliberate choice was made to keep these technical characterizations as ambiguous as they appear". Instead of precise definitional exercises, they suggest attention be directed to a range of "relevant factors in context which should rationally affect decision".

Finally, in an effort to clarify relevant prohibitions of political oppression under international law, another affinity between the initiation of a war of aggression and aggression against authority should be noted. At Nuremberg, it was recognized that the initiation of a war of aggression is "the supreme international crime" because "it contains within itself the accumulated evil of the whole", including each resulting individual international crime. Similarly, aggression against authority "contains within itself the accumulated evil of the whole", and when peace is affected it is certainly no less dangerous and of no less import to the international community.…

ANNEX

Draft Convention on the Prevention and Punishment of the Crime of Politicide

PREAMBLE

THE CONTRACTING PARTIES,

Having Considered the recognition of the International Law Commission in its 1979 Draft Articles on State Responsibility that actions against self-determination can be criminally sanctioned;

Recognizing that aggression against authority is incompatible with international legal precepts of self-determination and human rights, including the human right of all persons to participate in the political processes of their society and to a governmental process based on the authority of the people as guaranteed in the Universal Declaration of Human Rights;

Considering the obligation of States under the Charter of the United Nations to respect and observe human rights as well as the precept of self-determination;

Recognizing that the individual, having duties to other individuals and to the community to which he or she belongs, is also under a responsibility to respect and observe human rights law;

Being Concerned that serious acts of political oppression continue to thwart the right of peoples to self-determination, the process of legitimate authority of governments, and the interrelated human rights of persons, and that serious crimes of oppression have gone unpunished;

HEREBY AGREE:

Article I

The Contracting Parties confirm that politicide, whether committed in time of peace or in time of war, is a crime under international law which they undertake to prevent and to punish.

Article II

In the present Convention, politicide means, at least, any of the following acts committed with an intent politically to oppress, in whole or in part, any human group, as such:

    (a) Killing members of the group;

    (b) Terrorizing members of the group;

    (c) Kidnapping, incarcerating or arbitrarily restricting the movement of members of the group;

    (d) Torturing or causing other serious bodily or mental harm to members of the group;

    (e) Arbitrarily restricting access of any members of the group to the media;

    (f) Imposing other measures intended to prevent a relatively free participation by members of the group in a political process.

Article III

The following acts shall be punishable:

    (a) Politicide;

    (b) Conspiracy to commit politicide;

    (c) Direct and public incitement to commit politicide;

    (d) Attempt to commit politicide;

    (e) Complicity in politicide.

Article IV

Persons committing politicide or any of the other acts enumerated in Article III shall be punished upon conviction, whether they are constitutionally responsible rulers, public officials or private individuals. There shall be no form of immunity with regard to the prohibited acts.

Article V

The Contracting Parties undertake to enact, in accordance with their respective Constitutions, the necessary legislation to give effect to the provisions of the present Convention and, in particular, to provide severe and effective penalties for persons guilty of politicide or of any of the other acts enumerated in Article III.

Article VI

1. Persons charged with politicide or any of the other acts enumerated in Article III can be tried by a competent tribunal of any State, given the universal nature of jurisdiction over human rights violations, or by such international penal tribunal as may have jurisdiction with respect to those Contracting Parties which shall have accepted its jurisdiction.

2. Any Contracting Party that has within its territory any person reasonably accused of having committed any of the above acts shall, if it does not extradite such person, be obliged, without exception whatsoever, to take such person into custody and submit the case to its competent authorities for the purpose of prosecution. Those authorities shall take their decision in the same manner as in the case of any ordinary offense of a serious nature under the law of that state.

Article VII

1. Politicide and the other acts enumerated in Article III shall not be considered as political crimes for the purposes of extradition.

2. The Contracting Parties pledge themselves in such cases to grant extradition in accordance with their laws and treaties in force.

3. The offenses listed in Article III shall be deemed to be included as extraditable offenses in any extradition treaty existing between Contracting Parties or Parties may, at their option, consider this Convention as the legal basis for extradition for such offenses. Contracting Parties undertake to include the offenses as extraditable offenses in every future extradition treaty to be concluded between them.

Article VIII

The Contracting Parties shall also assure that effective civil remedies are available, in accordance with their respective Constitutions, to the victims of offenses listed in Article III, including effective remedies against the perpetrators of such offenses who may be found within their territory in accordance with the right to an effective remedy guaranteed in Article 8 of the Universal Declaration of Human Rights.

Article IX, and so forth [as appropriately amended from Articles VIII to XIX of the Genocide Convention, if not also from treaties such as the 1971 Convention for the Suppression of Unlawful Acts Against the Safety of Civil Aviation, 24 U.S.T. 564].

Notes and Questions

1. Do you support efforts to adopt the draft convention? The draft has been sponsored by World Habeas Corpus, a private international organization, for consideration. Of further interest is the fact that the United States Senate voted 93–1 in favor of directing the President to seek renewed negotiations concerning inclusion of political groups as such within those protected by the Genocide Convention. See Washington Weekly Report, vol. 12, No. 7, at 3 (UNA-USA Feb. 21, 1986).

2. How would you improve the draft?

3. Note that the ICT for Former Yugoslavia (ICTY) has found that crimes against humanity in addition to genocide need not have a nexus with armed conflict or crimes against peace. See Chapter Six, Section 9. Also see Article 7 of the Statute of the International Criminal Court (ICC), in the Documents Supplement.

4. Would aggression against authority and crimes against self-determination have been appropriate considerations with respect to governmental uses of armed force against their own populations during "the Arab Spring," especially by the Qadaffi Government against the Libya people in 2011? See generally, Paust, *International Law, Dignity, Democracy, and the Arab Spring*, 46 CORNELL INT'L L.J. (2012).

Chapter 8

War Crimes

Introductory Note

War crimes are offenses against the laws of war, more recently termed the laws of armed conflict or humanitarian law which apply during wars or armed conflicts. Although war has never been merely state-to-state, whether a state is at war and it is international in character depends upon the status of opponents (*e.g.,* whether they are states, nations, peoples, belligerents, or insurgents). In general, theorists prefer to separate laws concerning (1) the regulation of methods and means of combat, weaponry, and area controls (*e.g.,* those concerning occupied territory), such as those stressed in the 1907 Hague Convention No. IV, from those laws of armed conflict concerning (2) the protection of human beings, most notably the newer 1949 Geneva Conventions and Protocols thereto (extracts of which are in the Documents Supplement). However, no neat, ever-determinative lines are possible, since the laws of armed conflict ultimately relate to protections of persons or property and the policies of human dignity and of lessening unnecessary death, injury and suffering. For example, the 1863 Lieber Code (which was created to reflect certain customary laws of war at the time) emphasized both strands of the law of war. See the Documents Supplement. Within the 1907 Hague Convention, one also finds norms relating to the protection of persons; and within Geneva law, one finds norms relevant to selection of targets (especially in Protocol I), approaches to combat, and occupied territory. More important is an understanding of what provisions are applicable, in what contexts, to whom, with what sorts of rights and protections, and with what probable consequences.

The history of the law of war and its rich content is much more extensive than our chapter allows.[1] In more modern times, one of the first codifications of what was perceived to be the customary law of war was the 1863 Lieber Code, Instructions for the Government of Armies of the United States in the Field, General Orders No. 100 (April 24, 1863). This document, used during the U.S. Civil War and later by the Germans during the Franco-Prussian War, became an historic base for further codifications such as those portions of the 1899 and 1907 Hague Conventions concerning war on land. As noted in prior chapters, the 1907 Hague Convention No. IV was recognizably customary

---

1. For background, consider M. Cherif Bassiouni, Crimes Against Humanity in International Law 192–234 (1992); Antonio Cassese, The New Humanitarian Law of Armed Conflict (1979); M. Keen, The Law of War in the Late Middle Ages (1965); Myres S. McDougal & Florentino P. Feliciano, Law and Minimum World Public Order: The Legal Regulation of International Coercion (1961); Howard S. Levie, *The Laws of War and Neutrality,* in John N. Moore, Frederick S. Tipson, Robert F. Turner (eds.), National Security Law 307–13 (1990); Jean S. Pictet, I Commentary, Geneva Convention for the Amelioration of the Condition of the Wounded and Sick in Armed Forces in the Field 9–16 (1952); J. Paust, *My Lai and Vietnam: Norms, Myths and Leader Responsibility,* 57 Mil. L. Rev. 99, 108–18, *passim* (1972) (considered partly in Chapter Four, Section 7 D).

international law applicable during World War II. Already, in 1864, the first Geneva Convention had been codified—with ten articles for protection of the wounded and sick. Geneva law was supplemented with new conventions in 1906 and 1929–with extended coverage for wounded and sick at sea and prisoners of war. In 1949, the four Geneva Conventions took form: GWS (Wounded & Sick), GWS at Sea, GPW (Prisoners of War), and GC (Civilians)—the latter providing the first Geneva Convention directed to protections of civilians as such. The 1949 Conventions were supplemented in 1977 with the adoption of two Protocols. Numerous other treaties adopted in the twentieth century have further supplemented normative guarantees, rights, and prohibitions found in the law of the Hague and Geneva law, including the more general law of human rights and several international criminal treaties such as the 1948 Genocide Convention (see Chapter Ten) and customary legal trends, such as those concerning Crimes Against Humanity (see Chapter Nine). As recognized by the Swiss scholar and professor at Heidelberg, Johann Bluntschli, in 1866: "Human rights remain in force during war." Quoted in J. PAUST, INTERNATIONAL LAW AS LAW OF THE UNITED STATES 206 (2 ed. 2003).

Introductory Problem

For purposes of this problem, assume that you are a district judge presiding over the trial of General Fawaz Hussein, the (fictional) cousin of Iraqi President Saddam Hussein. Assume that General Hussein was captured by U.S. forces during the War in Iraq that began in 2003, and is being tried today in a federal district court. The indictment, containing the allegations against General Hussein, is reproduced below. General Hussein has moved for dismissal of any or all of the charges on the grounds that the facts alleged do not constitute a basis for criminal liability under the laws of war. Based on the materials on war crimes contained in this chapter, as well as those in Chapter Two on individual responsibility, you should assess whether each of the charges alleges facts which, if proved, would constitute grounds for criminal liability under the laws of war. In addition, you should address the following defense claims: (a) "lack of knowledge," (b) "obedience to orders," (c) "military necessity," (d) lack of protected status under the Geneva law for Kuwaiti "terrorist" detainees. Consider also other challenges the General might argue (recall Chapter Four).

Indictment of Fawaz Hussein

Background.

1. The defendant, General Fawaz Hussein, was the commander of the Iraqi National Tank and Artillery Battalion. As such, the defendant had 1,000 troops under his command. The defendant answered directly to Saddam Hussein, the President of Iraq and the Commander-in-Chief of the Iraqi army as well as the Iraqi Minister of Defense, Donsni Beersfeld.

2. The crimes charged herein are violations of the laws of war as reflected and codified in the following instruments, among others: (1) the 1949 Geneva Conventions (to which the U.S. and Iraq are parties); (2) Protocols I and II (1977) Additional to the Geneva Conventions (which apply as customary international law); and (3) the opinions and judgments of the trials of Nazi war criminals in the *Dreierwalde* case, the *Von Leeb* case, and the *List* case, among others.

3. Even if the defendant had no actual knowledge of the actions of his troops described below, his personal criminal liability may be grounded on the principle of command responsibility. Nor may he escape liability relying on the defense that he was following Saddam Hussein's orders, since such orders were patently unlawful. Nor may he escape liability

relying on the necessity defense, since the acts described below went beyond what was absolutely necessary for the conduct of military operations.

Count 1.

4. The defendant violated Protocol I of the Geneva Conventions and the customary law of war when, in 1990, he ordered his troops to surround Kuwait City, to cut off all power and water into the city, to bomb it into submission with artillery fire, and to confiscate the city's foodstuffs and medical stores to feed and care for the members of the Iraqi army. The fact that there was a small enemy military garrison in Kuwait City does not absolve defendant of liability.

Count 2.

5. The defendant violated the Geneva Convention Relative to the Protection of Civilian Persons in Time of War when, after the takeover of Kuwait City, troops under his command entered the Kuwait City Hospital and, when they discovered that the hospital personnel were hiding uninjured armed Kuwaiti soldiers there, they destroyed the facility, raped several nurses, and shot several doctors. In addition, the surviving hospital personnel were taken into custody as hostages in order to ensure the cooperation of the subjugated Kuwaiti population during the Iraqi occupation. In a televised broadcast, Saddam Hussein warned that, in accordance with a classified presidential directive and a court order, two of the captured Kuwaiti hospital "terrorist" personnel would be killed for every Iraqi killed by Kuwaiti resistance fighters. Altogether, 50 of the captured hospital personnel were executed by Fawaz Hussein's troops pursuant to this directive.

Count 3.

6. The defendant violated the Geneva Convention Relative to the Treatment of Prisoners of War and the customary law of war when troops under his command seized hundreds of Kuwaiti soldiers and civilians, and placed them in detention near Iraqi command bunkers and military bases as "human shields" so as to ensure that the bunkers and bases would not be subject to attack. Under two written directives from Iraqi Minister of Defense Beersfeld, captured Kuwaiti soldiers and civilians were authorized to be stripped naked and hooded during interrogation, use of dogs were authorized as part of "fear up harsh" interrogation, and the tactic of "water boarding" was authorized (whereby a detainee is made to experience an intense, terroristic fear of drowning). General Hussein ordered his troops to use the interrogation tactics on several detainees.

Count 4.

7. The defendant violated the Geneva Convention Relative to the Protection of Civilian Persons when the troops under his command destroyed Kuwait's seven oil processing plants and set at least 500 Kuwaiti oil wells on fire.

> Wherefor, the Special Prosecutor submits that this court should find the defendant, Fawaz Hussein, guilty of the aforementioned violations of the laws of war and impose such sentence as the Tribunal may deem just and proper.

Sources of International Humanitarian Law

International humanitarian law is not a completely cohesive body of law, but an amalgam of separate legal principles and proscriptions[2] applicable to international and non-

---

2. Hans-Peter Gasser, *International Humanitarian Law, Introduction* to HANS HAUG, HUMANITY FOR ALL 1, 3 (1993). Gasser also lists the sources of international humanitarian law as the 1949 Geneva

international armed conflicts. Hans-Peter Gasser defines international humanitarian law in the following manner:

> previously known as the *law of war* [international humanitarian law] is a special branch of law governing situations of armed conflict—in a word, war. International humanitarian law seeks to mitigate the effects of war, first in that it limits the choice of means and methods of conducting military operations, and secondly in that it obliges the belligerents to spare persons who do not or no longer participate in hostile actions.[3]

These and other proscriptions are also included under the label of international criminal law.[4] Because international criminal law and international humanitarian law have not been completely codified, each proscription generally arises from a different source of law, *i.e.*, international agreements or treaties and customary law, although the two can constantly influence each other and what used to be merely treaty-based law can later reflect customary law (see Chapter One). Thus, it is useful to distinguish the particular source of conventional or customary international law.[5] Yet, distinctions between conventional and customary sources are not necessarily clear-cut, especially when some instruments are meant to reflect custom at the time of their formation (*e.g.*, the 1863 Lieber Code, *infra*) and, as soon as ink is dry on a new instrument, custom can have its influence with respect to the interpretation of printed words. It is widely recognized that the 1949 Geneva Conventions, including common Article 3 and the grave breach provisions, and Articles 11, 48–54, 75, and 85 of Protocol I, in addition to other provisions therein, embody customary international law. Recall the 1993 Report of the Secretary-General, in Chapter Six, Section 9, at para. 35 ("beyond doubt" customary international law includes "the Geneva Conventions of 12 August 1949"). As recognized at Nuremberg, the laws and customs of war include the 1907 Hague Convention and customary law as it

---

Conventions, Protocols I and II, and the rules of international customary law which are *jus cogens*. *Id.* at 18; *see also* Theodor Meron, Human Rights and Humanitarian Norms as Customary Law (1989); M. Cherif Bassiouni, *The Commission of Experts Established pursuant to Security Council Resolution 780: Investigating Violations of International Humanitarian law in the Former Yugoslavia*, 5 Crim. L.F. 279, 321–24 (1994).

3. Gasser, *supra* note 1, at 3.

4. *See* M. Cherif Bassiouni, International Crimes: Digest/Index of International Instruments 1815–1985, at 143–314 (1986); Yves Sandoz, *Penal Aspects of International Humanitarian Law*, in 1 International Criminal Law 201 (M. Cherif Bassiouni ed., 1986) [hereinafter Bassiouni, ICL].

5. For the law of armed conflict applicable to different types of conflicts, *see, e.g.*, G. Abi-Saab, Droit Humanitaire et Conflits Internes (1986); A. Andries, Eléments de Droit Pénal National et International (1992); Michael Bothe, *et al.*, New Rules for Victims of Armed Conflicts (1982); E. David, Principles de Droit des Conflits Armés (1994); The Laws of Armed Conflicts: A Collection of Conventions, Resolutions and Other Documents (Dietrich Schindler & Jiri Toman eds., 1981); The Law of War: A Documentary History (Leon Friedman ed., 1972); Howard S. Levie, The Code of International Armed Conflict (1986); F. Thomas, Debestraffing van Oorlogsmisdaden (1993); Michel Veuthey, Guérilla et Droit Humanitaire (1983); G. Abi-Saab, *War of National Liberation in the Geneva Conventions and Protocols*, 1979 Recueil des Cours D'Academie de Droit Intern'l 411; A. Cassese, *War of National Liberation and Humanitarian Law*, in Mélanges Pictet 319 (1984); F. Ouguergouz, *Guerres de libération nationale en droit humanitaire: quelques classifications*, in Mise en Oeuvre du Droit International Humanitaire 345 (F. Kalshoven & Y. Sandoz eds., 1988); J. Paust & A. Blaustein, *War Crimes Jurisdiction and Due Process: The Bangladesh Experience*, 11 Vand. J. Trans. L. 1 (1978); D. Plattner, *Law répression des violations du droit international humanitaire applicable aux conflits armés non internationaux*, Revue Internationale de Croix-Rouge Sept.-Oct. 1990, at 447; Sandoz, *supra* note 3; Michel Veuthey, *Non-International Armed Conflict and Guerilla Warfare*, in 1 Bassiouni, ICL, *supra* note 3, at 243.

has evolved since then. War crimes, as they emerge from customary laws of war, are criminally punishable.[6] These few distinctions illustrate the separate nature of the applicable sources of law and the overlap of some of their proscriptive norms. Genocide and Crimes Against Humanity are considered part of international humanitarian law even though they apply in time of peace as well as in time of war.

Review: Chapter Six, Sections 1–10, in particular:

Opinion and Judgment, IMT at Nuremberg
[see Chapter Six, Section 3]

Report of General Taylor
[see Chapter Six, Section 3]

Report of the Secretary General
(1993)

[see Chapter Six, Section 9]

Section 1
Applicability

When do the laws of war apply?

U.S. Army Field Manual 27-10, The Law of Land Warfare
(1956)

8. Situations to Which Law of War Applicable

a. Types of Hostilities. War may be defined as a legal condition of armed hostility between States. While it is usually accompanied by the commission of acts of violence, a state of war may exist prior to or subsequent to the use of force. The outbreak of war is usually accompanied by a declaration of war.

Instances of armed conflict without a declaration of war may include, but are not necessarily limited to the exercise of armed force pursuant to a recommendation, decision or call by the United Nations, in the exercise of the inherent right of individual or collective self-defense against armed attack, or in the performance of enforcement measures through a regional arrangement, or otherwise, in conformity with appropriate provisions of the United Nations Charter.

b. Customary Law. The customary law of war applies to all cases of declared war or any other armed conflict which may arise between the United States and other nations, even

---

6. *See generally* J. Pictet, IV Commentary at 583 ("Geneva Conventions form part of what are generally called the laws and customs of war, violations of which are commonly called 'war crimes.'"); FM 27-10, paras. 499 ("Every violation of the law of war is a war crime"), 506b; Howard S. Levie, Terrorism in War: The Law of War Crimes (1993). As noted in other chapters, this is so even though some treaties, like the 1907 Hague Convention, do not expressly refer to criminal sanctions.

if the state of war is not recognized by one of them. The customary law is also applicable to all cases of occupation of foreign territory by the exercise of armed force, even if the occupation meets with no armed resistance.

c. Treaties. Treaties governing land warfare are applicable to various forms of war and armed conflict as provided by their terms. The Hague Conventions apply to "war". Common Article 2 of the Geneva Conventions of 1949 states:

In addition to the provisions which shall be implemented in peacetime, the present Convention shall apply to all cases of declared war or of any other armed conflict which may arise between two or more of the High Contracting Parties, even if the state of war is not recognized by one of them.

The Convention shall also apply to all cases of partial or total occupation of the territory of a High Contracting Party, even if the said occupation meets with no armed resistance.

Although one of the Powers in conflict may not be a party to the present Convention, the Powers who are parties thereto shall remain bound by it in their mutual relations. They shall furthermore be bound by the Convention in relation to the said Power, if the latter accepts and applies the provisions thereof. (*GWS, GWS Sea, GPW, GC, art. 2*)

d. Special Case of Civil Wars. See paragraph 11.

9. Applicability of Law of Land Warfare in Absence of a Declaration of War

As the customary law of war applies to cases of international armed conflict and to the forcible occupation of enemy territory generally as well as to declared war in its strict sense, a declaration of war is not an essential condition of the application of this body of law. Similarly, treaties relating to "war" may become operative notwithstanding the absence of a formal declaration war.

10. When Law of Land Warfare Ceases to Be Applicable

The law of land warfare generally ceases to be applicable upon:

a. The termination of a war by agreement, normally in the form of a treaty of peace; or

b. The termination of a war by unilateral declaration of one of the parties, provided the other party does not continue hostilities or otherwise decline to recognize the act of its enemy; or

c. The complete subjugation of an enemy State and its allies, if prior to a or b; or

d. The termination of a declared war or armed conflict by simple cessation of hostilities.

However, certain designated provisions of the Geneva Conventions of 1949 (see GC, art. 6) continue to be operative, notwithstanding the termination of any antecedent hostilities, during the continuance of military occupation. Insofar as the unwritten law of war and the Hague Regulations extend certain fundamental safeguards to the persons and property of the populations of occupied territory, their protection continues until the termination of any occupation having its origin in the military supremacy of the occupant, notwithstanding the fact the Geneva Convention relative to the Protection of Civilian Persons may have ceased to be applicable.

11. Civil War

a. Customary Law. The customary law of war becomes applicable to civil war upon recognition of the rebels as belligerents.

b. Geneva Conventions of 1949.

[common Article 3]

In the case of armed conflict not of an international character occurring in the territory of one of the High Contracting Parties, each party to the conflict shall be bound to apply, as a minimum, the following provisions:

(1) Persons taking no active part in the hostilities, including members of armed forces who have laid down their arms and those placed *hors de combat* by sickness, wounds, detention, or any other cause, shall in all circumstances be treated humanely, without any adverse distinction founded on race, colour, religion or faith, sex, birth or wealth, or any other similar criteria.

To this end, the following acts are and shall remain prohibited at any time and in any place whatsoever with respect to the above-mentioned persons:

(a) violence to life and person, in particular murder of all kinds, mutilation, cruel treatment and torture;

(b) taking of hostages;

(c) outrages upon personal dignity, in particular, humiliating and degrading treatment;

(d) the passing of sentences and the carrying out of executions without previous judgment pronounced by a regularly constituted court, affording all the judicial guarantees which are recognized as indispensable by civilized peoples.

(2) The wounded and sick shall be collected and cared for.

An impartial humanitarian body, such as the International Committee of the Red Cross, may offer its services to the Parties to the conflict.

The Parties to the conflict should further endeavor to bring into force, by means of special agreements, all or part of the other provisions of the present Convention.

The application of the preceding provisions shall not affect the legal status of the Parties to the conflict. (GWS, GPW, GWS Sea, GC, art. 3)

J. Pictet (ed.), IV Commentary, Geneva Convention Relative to the Protection of Civilian Persons in Time of War
(1958)

[re: common Article 2]

Paragraph 1—Armed Conflicts Involving The Application of The Convention

By its general character, this paragraph deprives belligerents, in advance, of the pretexts they might in theory put forward for evading their obligations. There is no need for a formal declaration of war, or for recognition of the existence of a state of war, as preliminaries to the application of the Convention. The occurrence of *de facto* hostilities is sufficient.

It remains to ascertain what is meant by "armed conflict". The substitution of this much more general expression for the word "war" was deliberate. It is possible to argue almost endlessly about the legal definition of "war". A State which uses arms to commit a hostile act against another State can always maintain that it is not making war, but merely engaging in a police action, or acting in legitimate self-defence. The expression "armed conflict" makes such arguments less easy. Any difference arising between two States and leading to the intervention of members of the armed forces is an armed conflict within the meaning of Article 2, even if one of the parties denies the existence of a state of war. It makes no difference how long the conflict lasts, or how much slaughter takes place.

The respect due to the human person as such is not measured by the number of victims....

1. *Introductory sentence—Field of application of the Article*[common Article 3]

A. *Cases of armed conflict*—What is meant by "armed conflict not of an international character"?

That was the burning question which arose again and again at the Diplomatic Conference. The expression was so general, so vague, that many of the delegations feared that it might be taken to cover any act committed by force of arms—any form of anarchy, rebellion, or even plain banditry. For example, if a handful of individuals were to rise in rebellion against the State and attack a police station, would that suffice to bring into being an armed conflict within the meaning of the Article? In order to reply to questions of this sort, it was suggested that the term "conflict" should be defined or—and this would come to the same thing—that a list should be given of a certain number of conditions on which the application of the Convention would depend. The idea was finally abandoned—wisely, we think. Nevertheless, these different conditions, although in no way obligatory, constitute convenient criteria, and we therefore think it well to give a list drawn from the various amendments discussed: they are as follows:

(1) That the Party in revolt against the *de jure* Government possesses an organized military force, an authority responsible for its acts, acting within a determinate territory and having the means of respecting and ensuring respect for the Convention.

(2) That the legal Government is obliged to have recourse to the regular military forces against insurgents organized as military and in possession of a part of the national territory.

(3) (a) That the *de jure* Government has recognized the insurgents as belligerents; or

(b) That it has claimed for itself the rights of a belligerent; or

(c) That it has accorded the insurgents recognition as belligerents for the purposes only of the present Convention; or

(d) That the dispute has been admitted to the agenda of the Security Council or the General Assembly of the United Nations as being a threat to international peace, a breach of the peace, or an act of aggression.

(4)(a) That the insurgents have an organization purporting to have the characteristics of a State.

(b) That the insurgent civil authority exercises *de facto* authority over persons within a determinate portion of the national territory.

(c) That the armed forces act under the direction of an organized authority and are prepared to observe the ordinary laws of war.

(d) That the insurgent civil authority agrees to be bound by the provisions of the Convention.

The above criteria are useful as a means of distinguishing a genuine armed conflict from a mere act of banditry or an unorganized and short-lived insurrection.

Does this mean that Article 3 is not applicable in cases where armed strife breaks out in a country, but does not fulfill any of the above conditions (which are not obligatory and are only mentioned as an indication)? We do not subscribe to this view. We think, on the contrary, that the scope of application of the article must be as wide as possible. There can be no drawbacks in this, since the Article in its reduced form, contrary to what might be thought, does not in any way limit the right of a State to put down rebellion, nor does it increase in the slightest the authority of the rebel party. It merely demands respect for certain rules, which were already recognized as essential in all civilized countries, and embodied in the municipal law of the States in question, long before the Convention was signed . . .

The obligation resting on the Party to the conflict which represents established authority is not open to question. The mere fact of the legality of a Government involved in an internal conflict suffices to bind that Government as a Contracting Party to the Convention. On the other hand, what justification is there for the obligation on the adverse Party in revolt against the established authority? At the Diplomatic Conference doubt was expressed as to whether insurgents could be legally bound by a Convention which they had not themselves signed. But if the responsible authority at their head exercises effective sovereignty, it is bound by the very fact that it claims to represent the country, or part of the country. The "authority" in question can only free itself from its obligations under the Convention by following the procedure for denunciation laid down in Article 158. But the denunciation would not be valid, and could not in point of fact be effected, unless the denouncing authority was recognized internationally as a competent Government. It should, moreover, be noted that under Article 158 denunciation does not take effect immediately. . . .

PARAGRAPH 4. — LACK OF EFFECTS ON THE LEGAL STATUS OF THE PARTIES TO THE CONFLICT

This clause is essential. Without it neither Article 3, nor any other Article in its place, would ever have been adopted. It meets the fear — always the same one — that the application of the Convention, even to a very limited extent, in cases of civil war may interfere with the *de jure* Government's lawful suppression of the revolt, or that it may confer belligerent status, and consequently increased authority and power, upon the adverse Party. . . .

Consequently, the fact of applying Article 3 does not in itself constitute any recognition by the *de jure* Government that the adverse Party has authority of any kind; it does not limit in any way the Government's right to suppress a rebellion by all the means—including arms— provided by its own laws; nor does it in any way affect that Government's right to prosecute, try and sentence its adversaries for their crimes, according to its own laws.

In the same way, the fact of the adverse party applying the Article does not give it any right to special protection or any immunity, whatever it may be and whatever title it may give itself or claim.

Article 3 resembles the rest of the Convention in that it is only concerned with the individual and the physical treatment to which he is entitled as a human being without regard to his other qualities. It does not affect the legal or political treatment which he may receive as a result of his behaviour.

Paust & Blaustein, *War Crimes Jurisdiction and Due Process: The Bangladesh Experience*
11 VAND. J. TRANS. L. 1, 11–15 (1978)

Customary Law of War

The customary international law of war applied to the armed conflict between Pakistan and the forces of the subsequent state of Bangladesh from the period of belligerency. That period began prior to the formal recognition of Bangladesh by India on December 6, 1971, prior to general armed intervention into the conflict by Indian troops in early December 1971, and after the Bangladesh Proclamation of Independence on April 10, 1971. The forces of the subsequent state of Bangladesh had (1) an armed force with a responsible command structure, (2) the semblance of a government, (3) control of significant amounts of territory in East Pakistan, (4) recognition by others as a belligerent force, ... (5) generally followed the laws of war [and (6) engaged in sustained or protracted hostilities].

The customary law of war includes the principles of the 1907 Hague Convention, No. IV, and numerous additional prescriptions on the conduct of hostilities, the treatment of captives, and the basic protections of the populations involved in armed conflict.

The 1949 Geneva Conventions

Bangladesh considered itself bound by the Geneva Conventions by virtue of the previous ratification by Pakistan which was at all times bound by the Conventions. The remaining questions were: (1) when did certain provisions of those Conventions apply, and (2) who was entitled to what sort of protection?

It is submitted that sometime after the March 25, 1971, actions in Dacca and the April 10th Bangladesh Proclamation of Independence, common article 3 of the 1949 Geneva Conventions applied specifically in the context of emerging independence and generally to the outbreak of armed hostilities within East Pakistan. There is no definitive view on when this jurisdictional event occurs, but several useful criteria for policy-conscious and rational decision-making have been elaborated by the textwriters. More certain is that once the conflict has reached the level of an actual belligerency (as opposed to an insurgency or some lesser form of armed violence), article 2 of the Geneva Conventions, and thus the bulk of Convention provisions, apply to the conflict. Thus, as the conflict intensifies and the insurgent group gains recognition as a belligerent, the application of the Geneva precepts is expanded. The advent of an armed conflict between troops of Pakistan and India, including the exchange of fire across their borders, undoubtedly made the conflict an international armed conflict governed by article 2 of the Conventions.

A determination must be made of who was entitled to what sort of protection at each stage of the conflict, given the expanded applicability of Geneva law. This poses no major difficulty, for under common article 3 of the Conventions the people of East Pakistan were all entitled to protection outlined in the article if they were not directly engaged in combat. When the conflict became an article 2 conflict the people of East Pakistan, in a state of belligerency, were at least entitled to the protection outlined in Part II of the 1949 Geneva Convention Relative to the Protection of Civilian Persons, and a growing body of authority supports the argument that the provisions of common article 3 should have continued to apply as well. When the state of Bangladesh became a reality, the relevant conduct had already occurred, so questions of shifting nationality were not technically relevant. Where the Geneva law seeks to govern the relations of distinct national groups (states or belligerents) under common article 2 and, presumably, more homogeneous entities under common article 3, a policy consideration is raised in contradistinction to the formal language of article 4 of the Geneva Civilian Convention, which would technically preclude the protections of Part III (but expressly not Part II) of that Convention to "nationals" of the offending party. In the context of a belligerency (to which common article 2 applies as well as Part II) where there are substantial differences in group make-up and one of the groups is striving for self-determination, it is both unrealistic and unresponsive to overall community policy and Geneva goal values to continue to treat the populace of such a belligerent as "nationals" of the other belligerent within the meaning of article 4—especially when common interpretation of the word "nation" or "nationals" is not equated with "state" but can refer also to a group of people. Formalistic thinking would otherwise require that the same persons who are entitled to the protection of the customary law of war do not also receive the full protection of Geneva law, which was enacted to increase protection for civilians in times of armed conflict.

In this case, however, the problem may be mooted by the fact that the alleged misconduct would not only be prohibited by common article 3 of the Geneva Conventions (at such a level of conflict), but also by the language of articles 13 and 16 of the Geneva Civilian Convention which prohibits attacks upon, ill-treatment of, or a failure to affirmatively protect all those who are (1) exposed to grave danger in any manner, (2) wounded, (3) sick, (4) infirm, (5) expectant mothers, (6) children under the age of fifteen who were orphans or had been separated from their families as a result of war, or (7) members of a hospital staff protected under article 20 of that Convention.

The Prosecutor of the Tribunal v. Dusko Tadic
in the International Criminal Tribunal for the Former Yugoslavia (Aug. 10, 1995)
[see Chapter Six, Section 9]

Protocol Additional to the Geneva Conventions of 12 August 1949, and relating to the protection of victims of international armed conflicts (Protocol I)
8 June 1977
[Read the preamble and Articles 1, 3 and 4 of Protocol I]

Protocol Additional to the Geneva Conventions of 12 August 1949, and relating to the protection of victims of non-international armed conflicts (Protocol II)
8 June 1977
[Read the preamble and Articles 1–3 of Protocol II]

Notes and Questions

1. Today, it is widely recognized that although common Article 3 of the 1949 Geneva Conventions was designed to apply to an insurgency (the lowest level of armed conflict under the laws of war), the rights, duties and prohibitions reflected in common Article 3 are now part of customary international law applicable "in all circumstances" during any armed conflict. *See, e.g.*, 4 COMMENTARY, *supra* at 14 ("This minimum requirement in the case of a non-international armed conflict, is *a fortiori* applicable in international conflicts."), 58; ICRC, INTERNATIONAL HUMANITARIAN LAW AND THE CHALLENGES OF CONTEMPORARY ARMED CONFLICT 9 (2003); JEAN-MARIE HENCKAERTS & LOUIS DOSWALD-BECK, 1 CUSTOMARY INTERNATIONAL HUMANITARIAN LAW: RULES 299, 306–19 (ICRC 2005) (the prohibitions reflected in common Article 3 are "fundamental guarantees" that apply as "customary international law applicable in both international and non-international armed conflicts"); U.S. Dep't of Army, TJAG School, OPERATIONAL LAW HANDBOOK 8–9 (2003); Derek Jinks, *Protective Parity and the Law of War*, 79 NOTRE DAME L. REV. 1493, 1508–11

(2004); Paust, *Judicial Power to Determine the Status and Rights of Persons Detained Without Trial*, 44 Harv. Int'l L.J. 503, 512 n.27 (2003) [hereinafter Paust, *Judicial Power*]; Paust, *Executive Plans and Authorizations to Violate International Law Concerning Treatment and Interrogation of Detainees*, 43 Columbia J. Transnat'l L. 811, 816 & nn.17, 19 (2005) [hereinafter Paust, *Executive Plans*], available at http://ssrn.com/abstract=903349; *Case Concerning Military and Paramilitary Activities in and Against Nicaragua (Nicaragua v. United States)*, 1986 I.C.J. 4, at 113–14, paras. 218 ("There is no doubt that, in the event of international armed conflicts, these rules also constitute a minimum yardstick, in addition to the more elaborate rules which are also to apply to international conflicts; and they are rules which … reflect …'elementary considerations of humanity'"), 255 (is included in "general principles of humanitarian law … in the context of armed conflicts, whether international in character or not"); *The Prosecutor v. Delalic*, IT-96-21-A, Judgment (Appeals Chamber, International Criminal Tribunal for Former Yugoslavia, 20 Feb. 2001), at paras. 143, 150, *reprinted in* 40 I.L.M. 630 (2001); *The Prosecutor v. Tadic*, Appeals Chamber, *supra* at para. 102 ("The International Court of Justice has confirmed that these rules reflect 'elementary considerations of humanity' applicable under customary international law to any armed conflict, whether it is of an internal or international character. (Nicaragua Case, at para. 218). Therefore, at least with respect to the minimum rules in common Article 3, the character of the conflict is irrelevant."); *The Prosecutor v. Tadic*, Trial Chamber, *supra* at paras. 65, 67, 74; *The Prosecutor v. Naletilic and Martinovic*, IT-98-34, Judgment (Trial Chamber, ICTY, Mar. 31, 2003), para. 228 (common Article 3 "applies regardless of the internal or international character of the conflict"); *The Prosecutor v. Mucic, et al.* (Appeals Chamber, ICTY, Feb. 20, 2001), paras. 140–50; *Abella v. Argentina*, Case 11,137, Inter-Am. C.H.R., paras. 155–56, OEA/ser.L/V.97, doc. 38 (1997); *Hamdan v. Rumsfeld*, 344 F. Supp.2d 152, 162–63 (D.D.C. 2004); *see also* 2004 UK Ministry of Defence, The Manual of the Law of Armed Conflict 5 n.13 (2004) (recognizing that among "important judgments" the I.C.J. "referred to the rules in Common Art. 3 as constituting 'a minimum yardstick' in international armed conflicts"). It is also widely recognized that the same customary and absolute rights and duties are mirrored in Article 75 of Protocol I to the Geneva Conventions, which is applicable during any international armed conflict.

2. What, within the meaning of Article 3(2) of Protocol II, is an "internal or external affair *of*" a particular state (emphasis added)? When an affair is also "of" the international community, does such a phrase not apply? In general, application of human rights law is of concern to the international community and is not simplistically the prerogative of the state in whose territory and/or at whose hands violations occur. The same pertains with respect to application of common Article 3 of the Geneva Conventions to an internal insurgency. See also common Article l; J. Pictet, III Commentary Relative to the Treatment of Prisoners of War 18, 35, 38, 43 (1960); IV Commentary, *supra* at 15, 37–38, 41, 44; *but see id.* at 16.

3. The first major war to which the 1949 Geneva Conventions applied was the Korean Conflict during which some nineteen countries participated under a U.N. flag. Also recall the U.N. Rules in Chapter Six, Section 4.

4. Did the customary laws of war apply to the social violence that occurred in Libya in early 2011 (*e.g.*, were the criteria for an "insurgency" met when Libyan rebels fought Libyan governmental forces under Muammar Qaddafi)? Did Protocol II's provisions apply if Libya was a party to the Protocol? See Article 1 (1) and (2). Did Protocol I? How would you interpret the phrase "armed conflict" in Article 1 (4) of Protocol I? Must such a conflict satisfy the criteria that must be met for the existence of an insurgency? a belligerency?

Clearly, once the United States and NATO forces engaged in the armed conflict in Libya (under U.N. S.C. Res. 1973 (March 17, 2011)) an armed conflict of an international character had occurred.

5. Did the laws of armed conflict apply to the fighting between the Contras and the Government of Nicaragua in the 1980s? Had the Contras met the criteria for an "insurgency"? What facts would you like to know? Did they apply to U.S. involvement? See *Nicaragua v. United States*, [1986] I.C.J. paras. 218–220; Separate Opinion of Judge Ago, *id.* at para. 11; Separate Opinion of Judge Schwebel, *id.* at para. 257. See also discussion below in Note 9.

6. As noted, all of the customary laws of war apply to a belligerency, such as during the U.S. Civil War. In 1949, when the Geneva Conventions first applied certain laws of war to what is strictly an internal insurgency under common Article 3, it was a radical change of the laws of war. Richard R. Baxter, *Modernizing the Law of War*, 78 Mil. L. Rev. 165, 168–73 (1978).

What is the difference between an "insurgency" and a "belligerency" (or "true civil war"), to which all of the customary laws of war apply? Recall FM 27-10, para. 11 a; Paust & Blaustein, *supra.* See also J. Pictet, III Commentary, *supra* at 38 ("For instance, if one Party to a conflict is recognized by third parties as being a belligerent, that Party would then have to respect the Hague rules."); *The Prize Cases*, 67 U.S. (2 Black) 635, 666 ("When the party in rebellion occupy and hold in a hostile manner a certain portion of territory; have declared their independence; have cast off their allegiance; have organized armies; have committed hostilities against their former sovereign, the world acknowledges them as belligerents"), 669 ("Foreign nations acknowledge it as a war by a declaration of neutrality ... recognizing hostilities as existing....") (1862); *The Santissima Trinidad*, 20 U.S. (7 Wheat.) 283, 337 (1822) ("The government of the United States has recognized the existence of a civil war between Spain and her colonies.... Each party is, therefore, deemed by us a belligerent nation"); U.S. Dep't of Army, Pamphlet 27-161-2, 2 International Law 27 (1962) ("If the rebellious side conducts its war by guerrilla tactics it seldom achieves the status of a belligerent because it does not hold territory and it has no semblence of a government."). Note that the belligerent or insurgent remains bound by the treaty obligations of the state of their nationality as well as by any applicable customary laws of war and human rights law. See also *Chacon v. Eighty-Nine Bales of Cochineal*, 5 F. Cas. 390, 394 (No. 2,568) (C.C.D. Va. 1821) (Marshall, C.J.), aff'd in *The Santissima Trinidad*, *supra* ("Whether Buenos Ayres be a state or not, if she is in a condition to make war, and to claim the character and rights of a belligerent, she is bound to respect the laws of war").

One important difference is that during an insurgency the insurgent fighters do not have combatant status and combatant immunity for what would be lawful acts of war. See ICRC, The Relevance of IHL in the Context of Terrorism (2011) (there is no combatant or pow status for fighters during an insurgency). Therefore, they can be prosecuted under relevant domestic law for murder, assault and battery, and so forth, even with respect to conduct that would provide combatant immunity for combatants during a belligerency or other international armed conflict for acts that are lawful under the laws of war (such as the killing of an enemy combatant who has not surrendered or been captured) and that are not otherwise violative of other international laws (*e.g.*, those proscribing aircraft sabotage, aircraft hijacking, forced disappearance, genocide, or other crimes against humanity). An insurgent who kills an enemy fighter can be prosecuted for murder under relevant domestic law, but the murder is not a war crime. If an insurgent intentionally kills civilians who are not directly participating in hostilities, such killings are violations of the customary laws of war that apply today during an insurgency and, therefore, the insurgent can be prosecuted for the war crime of killing such civilians.

The normal test for "combatant" status during an international armed conflict is membership in the armed forces of a party to the conflict. *See, e.g.,* Paust, *War and Enemy Status After 9/11: Attacks on the Laws of War,* 28 YALE J. INT'L L.325, 329–34 (2003) [hereinafter Paust, *Status*]; see also *The Prosecutor v. Kordic & Cerkez,* IT-95-14/2-A (Appeals Chamber, 17 Dec. 2004), para. 51, "members of the armed forces resting in their homes in the area of the conflict, as well as members of the [Territorial Defence forces] residing in their homes, remain combatants whether or not they are in combat, or for the time being armed." Also note: Article 1 of the Annex to the 1907 Hague Convention expressly states that belligerent status during war will "apply ... to armies" and it expressly sets forth additional criteria that are to be met merely by "militia" or "volunteer corps." The customary 1863 Lieber Code also affirmed: "So soon as a man is armed by a sovereign government and takes the soldier's oath of fidelity, he is a belligerent; his killing, wounding, or other warlike acts are not individual crimes or offenses." Therefore, the Lieber Code reflected both the membership test for what we term "combatant" status and the fact that the combatant has what we term "combatant immunity" for lawful acts of war.

During either an insurgency or an international armed conflict, a fighter who does not meet the test for "combatant" status is an "unprivileged" fighter. Such a person can be prosecuted under domestic law for acts of violence engaged in by such person, but the mere act of unprivileged fighting of enemy fighters is not a war crime. The unprivileged fighter lacks combatant immunity for what would otherwise be lawful acts of war by a combatant during an international armed conflict, however such a person has protections once detained, like any civilian who is not directly participating in hostilities. *Cf* IV COMMENTARY, *supra* at 53 (noting while addressing considerations during formation of Article 5: "[t]hose who take part in the struggle while not belonging to the armed forces are acting deliberately outside the laws of warfare," but will nonetheless benefit from the requirement of humane treatment in Article 5). "Outside," that is, with respect to combatant status and combatant immunity, but nonetheless persons who are protected at least under customary law reflected in common Article 3 once detained.

Language in *Ex parte Quirin,* 317 U.S. 1 (1942), can create confusion. In that case, German "enemy belligerents," "who though combatants," were prosecuted for the war crime of engaging in combat activity out of uniform (prior to creation of the 1949 Geneva Conventions). *See* 317 U.S. at 35–37, 44; Hays Parks, *Special Forces' Wear of Non-Standard Uniforms,* 4 CHI. J. INT'L L. 493, 547 n.31 (2003); Paust, *Status, supra* at 331–32. Yet, the Court stated that it was appropriate "to charge all the petitioners with the offense of unlawful belligerency." 317 U.S. at 23 (emphasis added). The Court also stated that participation in combat "without uniform" subjects the individual "to the punishment prescribed by the law of war for unlawful belligerents." 317 U.S. at 37. Even a combatant who is entitled to prisoner of war status could be charged with the war crime of fighting while out of uniform, which was the major war crime addressed. *See also* IV COMMENTARY, *supra* at 53 ("irregular combatants" are "[t]hose who take part in the struggle while not belonging to the armed forces [and] are acting deliberately outside the laws of warfare." Yet, the acts are not labeled as war crimes). Any person (*e.g.,* a combatant or an unprivileged belligerent) can be prosecuted for their conduct that constitutes a war crime.

Perhaps unwittingly, the Bush Administration turned the meaning of "combatant" on its head and has preferred to classify detainees at Guantanamo as "enemy combatants." *See, e.g., Hamdi v. Rumsfeld,* 542 U.S. 507, 510 (2004); *Padilla v. Hanft,* 423 F.3d 386, 388–93 (4th Cir. 2005); *In re Guantanamo Detainee Cases,* 355 F. Supp.2d 443, 445–50 (D.D.C. 2005). It has also used an overly broad definition of enemy combatant that has no support elsewhere. As noted in *In re Guantanamo Detainee Cases,* "[o]n July 7, 2004, nine days after the issuance of the *Rasul* decision, Deputy Secretary of Defense Paul Wolfowitz issued an Order creating a military tribunal called the Combatant Status Review Tribunal (hereinafter "CSRT") to review the status of each detainee at Guantanamo Bay as an 'enemy combatant.' [The document can be found at http://www.defenselink.mil/news/Jul2004/d20040707review.pdf.] That definition is as follows:

> [T]he term 'enemy combatant' shall mean an individual who was part of *or supporting* Taliban *or al Qaeda forces, or associated forces* that are engaged in hostilities against the United States or its coalition partners. This includes any person who has committed a belligerent act *or has directly supported hostilities* in aid of enemy armed forces."

355 F. Supp.2d at 450 (emphasis added).

Contrary to international law, the Bush Administration also made efforts to prosecute unprivileged fighters for merely fighting in an armed conflict as a war crime. As noted, this "unprecedented effort to characterize all direct participation in hostilities [by civilians] as a war crime ... has largely been a failure — yielding only one guilty plea based on a direct attack on a U.S. soldier — after nearly a decade of efforts to prosecute Guantanamo detainees in military tribunals." David J.R. Frakt, *Direct Participation in Hostilities as a War Crime: America's Failed Efforts to Change the Law of War*, 46 VALP. U. L. REV. 729, 762 (2012).

7. What was the status of the U.S. Civil War and what laws of war applied? See the 1863 Lieber Code, which applied the customary laws of war codified therein in the context of the U.S. Civil War (some portions are extracted in the Documents Supplement); Paust, *My Lai and Vietnam: Norms, Myths and Leader Responsibility*, 57 MIL. L. REV. 99, 115–16, 130–31 (1972).

8. Note that some treaties and customary norms apply in all social contexts, *e.g.*, in times of relative peace or times of armed conflict. The customary prohibition of genocide and human rights law (which contains its own set of derogation provisions with respect to derogable rights) are examples. That customary and treaty-based human rights laws apply during war, recall Bluntschli (quoted *supra*) and *see, e.g.*, LOUISE DOSWALD-BECK, HUMAN RIGHTS IN TIMES OF CONFLICT AND TERRORISM (2011); Paust, *Executive Plans, supra* at 820–23, and the many references cited; Protocol Additional to the Geneva Conventions of 12 August 1949, and Relating to the Protection of Victims of International Armed Conflicts, art. 72 ("other applicable rules of international law relating to protection of fundamental human rights during international armed conflict"), 1125 U.N.T.S. 3 (June 8, 1977); Protocol Additional to the Geneva Conventions of 12 August 1949, and Relating to the Protection of Victims of Non-International Armed Conflicts, prmbl. ("Recalling ... that international instruments relating to human rights offer a basic protection to the human person"), 1125 U.N.T.S. 609 (June 8, 1977); In the case Armed Activities on the Territory of the Congo (Dem. Rep. Congo v. Uganda), 2005 I.C.J. paras. 216–20, 345(3); Advisory Opinion, Legal Consequences of the Construction of a Wall in the Occupied Palestinian Territory, 2004 I.C.J. paras. 104–106; Advisory Opinion, Legality of the Threat or Use of Nuclear Weapons, 1996 I.C.J. 95, 226, 239–40, para. 25 ("The protection of the International Covenant on Civil and Political Rights does not cease in times of war, except by operation of Article 4" regarding derogable rights) (July 8); Human Rights Comm., General Comment No. 31, U.N. Doc. CCPR/C/21/Rev.1/Add.13 (May 26, 2004), para. 11 ("the Covenant applies also in situations of armed conflict to which the rules of international humanitarian law are applicable. While ... more specific rules of international humanitarian law my be specially relevant for the purposes of the interpretation

of Covenant rights, both spheres of law are complementary, not mutually exclusive"); Human Rights Comm., General Comment No. 29, paras. 3, 9, 11 & n.6 , U.N. Doc. CCPR/C/21/Rev.1/Add.11 (2001); U.N. Committee Against Torture, *Consideration of Reports Submitted by States Parties Under Article 19 of the Convention: Conclusions and Recommendations of the Committee against Torture, United States of America*, 36th sess., U.N. Doc. CAT/C/USA/CO/2 (18 May 2006), paras. 14 (the U.S. "should recognize and ensure that the Convention applies at all times, whether in peace, war or armed conflict, in any territory under its jurisdiction...."), 15 ("provisions of the Convention ... apply to, and are fully enjoyed by, all persons under the effective control of its authorities, of whichever type, wherever located in the world"), 19 (there exists an "absolute prohibition of torture ... without any possible derogation"), 24 (the U.S. "should rescind any interrogation technique—including methods involving sexual humiliation, 'water boarding,' 'short shackling,' and using dogs to induce fear, that constitute torture or cruel, inhuman or degrading treatment or punishment, in all places of detention under its *de facto* effective control, in order to comply with the Convention."); Human Rights Comm., *Concluding Observations of the Human Rights Committee, United States of America*, 87th Sess., July 10–28, 2006, paras. 10, 16, U.N. Doc. CCPR/C/USA/CO/3/Rev. 1 (18 Dec. 2006); Leila Zerrougui, *et al.*, Report, *Situation of Detainees at Guantánamo Bay*, U.N. Comm. on Human Rights, 62nd sess., U.N. Doc. E/CN.4/2006/120 (15 Feb. 2006), at paras. 15–16 (adding: "The application of international humanitarian law and of international human rights law are not mutually exclusive, but are complementary."), 83; U.N. S.C. Res. 1378, para. 9 (2006) ("violations of international humanitarian and human rights law in situations of armed conflict"); U.N. S.C. Res. 1265, para. 4, U.N. Doc. S/RES/1265 (Sept. 17, 1999); U.N. S.C. Res. 1100, prmbl., U.N. Doc. S/RES/1194 (1998) ("violations of human rights and of international humanitarian law"); U.N. G.A. Res. 63/166, prmbl. (2008), U.N. Doc. A/RES/63/166 (19 Feb. 2009) ("freedom from torture and other cruel, inhuman or degrading treatment or punishment is a non-derogable right that must be protected under all circumstances, including in times of international or internal armed conflict or disturbance"); U.N. G.A. Res. 59/191, Protection of Human Rights and Fundamental Freedoms While Countering Terrorism, para. 1 (2004), in the Documents Supplement; Council of Europe Parliamentary Assembly Resolution 1433, Lawfulness of Detentions by the United States at Guantanamo Bay (26 April 2005), in the Documents Supplement; Chapter 11, sections 1–2.

What types of rights, duties, and prohibitions are contained in common Article 3 of the Geneva Conventions? What types of nonderogable human rights are contained in Article 7 of the International Covenant on Civil and Political Rights (ICCPR)? The rights reflected in Article 7 are customary rights of universal application and are also peremptory rights *jus cogens* (*i.e.*, they prevail in all contexts and preempt any inconsistent international agreements or limitations therein). Note that common Article 3 also incorporates customary rights to due process by reference. Today, it is widely recognized that Article 14 of the ICCPR reflects minimum customary human rights to due process. Recall *Hamdan v. Rumsfeld*, 548 U.S. 557 (2006); and Chapter Six. Thus, they are incorporated by reference through common Article 3. Concerning other relevant customary and treaty-based human rights, see Chapter Eleven.

9. Is the following definition of "armed conflict" too broad? In *The Prosecutor v. Dusko Tadic*, the Appeals Chamber of the ICTY stated in para. 70:

> "We find that an armed conflict exists whenever there is resort to armed force between states or protracted armed violence between governmental authorities and organized armed groups or between such groups within a state."

Does the definition cover armed conflict between organized armed groups across state lines? Under Geneva law, what sort of conflict might the latter be? Does the phrase "armed force" require that traditional criteria for an insurgency be used? Does the phrase "organized armed groups" include U.N. or NATO peacemakers using armed force as part of their mission? Recall the question in this regard in Chapter Two, Section 3; and FM 27-10, *supra* para. 8 a. Does the definition cover armed conflict by organized armed groups on the high seas or in outer space? Are these international armed conflicts under Geneva law? Would this definition cover armed violence between members of al Qaeda and the regime in Iraq? What is the meaning of "protracted" armed violence? What traditional criteria for an insurgency or application of Geneva Protocol II, art. 1(1) are missing?

See also id. (Trial Chamber, Judgment, May 17, 1997), para. 562 ("terrorist activities … are not subject to international humanitarian law"); *The Prosecutor v. Boskoski & Tareulovski*, IT-04-82-T (Trial Chamber, Judgment, Jul. 10, 2008), paras. 175, 177–78 ("the Trial Chamber in *Tadic* interpreted this test … as consisting of two criteria, namely (i) the intensity of the conflict, and (ii) the organization of the parties to the conflict" and "care is needed not to lose sight of the requirement for protracted armed violence…, when assessing the intensity of the conflict. The criteria are closely related"), 185 (regarding "protracted" violence, what matters is whether the acts are perpetrated in isolation or as part of a protracted campaign that entails the engagement of both parties in hostilities," and quoting *The Prosecutor v. Kordic*: "'[t]he requirement of protracted fighting is significant'"), 199–203 (identifying various other factors); *The Prosecutor v. Musema*, ICTR-96-13-T (Trial Chamber, Judgment, Jan. 27, 2000), para. 248 ("The expression 'armed conflicts' introduces a material criterion: the existence of open hostilities between armed forces which are organized to a greater or lesser degree"); Rome Statute of the International Criminal Court, art. 8(2)(d) ("isolated and sporadic acts of violence" are not "armed conflict"), 2187 U.N.T.S. 90. Has al Qaeda ever engaged in a "protracted campaign that entails engagement of … [other] parties in hostilities," "open hostilities," or use "armed forces" in "protracted fighting"? It should be noted that Professor Cassese, as Judge in the Appeals Chamber of the ICTY, wrote the opinion noted above in *Tadic*, and he later recognized that members of al Qaeda are mere civilians engaged in criminal activities. Antonio Cassese, International Law 410 (2 ed. 2005).

In *The Prosecutor v. Rutaganda*, ICTR-96-3-T, at paras. 91–92 (6 Dec. 1999), the Trial Chamber of the ICTR stated:

> 91. It can thence be seen that the definition of an armed conflict *per se* is termed in the abstract, and whether or not a situation can be described as an "armed conflict", meeting the criteria of Common Article 3, is to be decided upon on a case-by-case basis. Hence, in dealing with this issue, the *Akayesu Judgement* suggested an "evaluation test", whereby it is necessary to evaluate the intensity and the organization of the parties to the conflict to make a finding on the existence of an armed conflict. This approach also finds favour with the Trial Chamber in this instance.

> 92. In addition to armed conflicts of a non-international character, satisfying the requirements of Common Article 3, under Article 4 of the Statute, the Tribunal has the power to prosecute persons responsible for serious violations of the 1977 Additional Protocol II, a legal instrument whose overall purpose is to afford protection to persons affected by non-international armed conflicts. As aforesaid, this instrument develops and supplements the rules contained in Common Article 3, without modifying its existing conditions of applicability. Additional Protocol II reaffirms Common Article 3, which, although it objectively characterized internal armed conflicts, lacked clarity and enabled the States to have a wide area of discretion in its application. Thus the impetus behind the Con-

ference of Government Experts and the Diplomatic Conference in this regard was to improve the protection afforded to victims in non-international armed conflicts and to develop objective criteria which would not be dependent on the subjective judgements of the parties. The result is, on the one hand, that conflicts covered by Additional Protocol II have a higher intensity threshold than Common Article 3, and on the other, that Additional Protocol II is immediately applicable once the defined material conditions have been fulfilled. If an internal armed conflict meets the material conditions of Additional Protocol II, it then also automatically satisfies the threshold requirements of the broader Common Article 3.

10. Can a state be at "war" against a non-state actor such as al Qaeda? Or at "war" with a mere tactic of "terrorism"? The Bush Administration so claimed, but most textwriters disagree. *See, e.g.,* Bruce Ackerman, *This Is Not a War,* 113 YALE L.J. 1871 (2004); Michael Byers, *Terrorism, the Use of Force, and International Law After 11 September,* 51 INT'L & COMP. L.Q. 401 (2002); David Cole, *Enemy Aliens,* 54 STAN. L. REV. 953, 958 (2002); Christopher Greenwood, *War, Terrorism, and International Law,* 56 CURRENT L. PROBS. 505, 529 (2004); Joan Fitzpatrick, *Jurisdiction of Military Commissions and the Ambiguous War on Terrorism,* 96 AM. J. INT'L L. 345, 347–48 (2002); Wayne McCormack, *Emergency Powers and Terrorism,* 185 MIL. L. REV. 69, 70 & n.6 (2005); Mary Ellen O'Connell, symposium, "Terrorism on Trial," *The Legal Case Against the Global War on Terror,* 37 CASE W. RES. J. INT'L L. 349, 349–57 (2005); Paust, *Status, supra* at 326–28; Kenneth Roth, *The Law of War in the War on Terror,* FOREIGN AFF. 2 (Jan.-Feb. 2004); Leila N. Sadat, *Terrorism and the Rule of Law,* 3 WASH. U. GLOBAL STUD. L. REV. 135, 140 (2004); Marco Sassoli, *Use and Abuse of the Laws of War in the "War on Terrorism,"* 22 LAW & INEQ. 195 (2004); Warren Richey, *Tribunals on Trial,* THE CHRISTIAN SCIENCE MONITOR, Dec. 14, 2001, at 1 (*quoting* Professor Leila Sadat: not a war); *see also* Leila Zerrougui, *et al.,* Report, Situation of Detainees at Guantanamo Bay, Commission on Human Rights, 62nd sess., items 10 and 11 of the provisional agenda, U.N. Doc. E/CN.4/2006/120 (Feb. 15, 2006), at 36, para. 83 ("The war on terror, as such, does not constitute an armed conflict for the purposes of the applicability of international humanitarian law."); *cf* Norman C. Bay, *Executive Power and the War on Terror,* 83 DENV. L. REV. 335, 337 n.6 (2005); *but see* John C. Yoo & James C. Ho, *The Status of Terrorists,* 44 VA. J. INT'L L. 207 (2003); Curtis A. Bradley & Jack L. Goldsmith, *Congressional Authorization and the War on Terrorism,* 118 HARV. L. REV. 2047, 2068 (2005) ("[D]espite its novel features, the post-September 11 war on terrorism possesses more characteristics of a traditional war than some commentators have acknowledged.... The United States's continuing combat operations and related use of significant military resources against al Qaeda in Afghanistan and other countries also make a war characterization at least plausible."). In *Pan American World Airways, Inc. v. Aetna Casualty & Surety Co.,* 505 F.2d 989, 1013–15 (2d Cir. 1974), the Second Circuit declared that the U.S. could not have been at war with the Palestinian Front for the Liberation of Palestine, despite alleged terrorist attacks.

If not, can members of al Qaeda rightly be prosecuted for "war crimes" with respect to the 9/11 attacks on the U.S. World Trade Center and the Pentagon in 2001? What sort of other international crimes might apply to such events?

11. In any event, the United States has been involved in international armed conflicts in Afghanistan (since October 2001) and Iraq (since 2003), to which all of the customary laws of war apply as well as relevant treaty based laws of war. *See, e.g.,* Paust, *Executive Plans, supra* at 813–20. During such armed conflicts, the Bush Administration claimed a right to deny rights and protections under Geneva law when "military necessity" allegedly prevailed. Is this claim acceptable under the Geneva Conventions? Consider the

following: Common Article 1 of the Geneva Conventions expressly requires that all of the signatories respect and ensure respect for the Conventions "in all circumstances." It is widely recognized that common Article 1, among other provisions, thereby assures that Geneva law is nonderogable, and that alleged necessity poses no exception unless a particular article allows derogations on the basis of necessity. Article 1 also provides that the duty to respect and to ensure respect for Geneva law is not based on reciprocal compliance by an enemy but rests upon a customary *obligatio erga omnes* (an obligation owing by and to all humankind) as well as an express treaty-based obligation assumed by each signatory that is owing to every other signatory whether or not they are involved in a particular armed conflict. Further, Article 1 ensures that reprisals in response to enemy violations are not permissible. Each recognition above assures that, indeed, as expressly mandated in Article 1 the rights and duties set forth in the Geneva Conventions must be observed "in all circumstances." *Id.* at 814–16.

See also U.N. S.C. Res. 1674, para. 6, U.N. Doc. S/RES/1674 (28 Apr. 2006) (the Security Council demanded that all parties to an armed conflict "comply strictly with the obligations applicable to them under international law, in particular those contained in the Hague Conventions of 1899 and 1907 and in the Geneva Conventions of 1949 and their Additional Protocols of 1977").

12. Under the Geneva Conventions, any person (thus, including a civilian, prisoner of war, unprivileged belligerent, terrorist, state or non-state actor) has rights under the Geneva Civilian Convention, including the customary law reflected in common Article 3 and Article 75 of Protocol I. *See, e.g.*, Paust, *Executive Plans*, *supra* at 817–18; IV COMMENTARY, *supra* at 51 ("Every person in enemy hands must have some status under international law: he is either a prisoner of war and, as such, covered by the Third Convention, a civilian covered by the Fourth Convention, or … a member of the medical personnel.… There is no intermediate status; nobody in enemy hands can be outside the law."), 595 ("applying the same system to all accused whatever their status"), 595; J. PICTET, III COMMENTARY, *supra* at 51 n.1, 76, 423; FM 27-10, *supra* at 31, para. 73 (persons who are not prisoners of war are covered under the Geneva Civilian Convention, where applicable: "he is not entitled to be treated as a prisoner of war. He is, however, a 'protected person' within the meaning of Article 4, GC.…"); 2004 UK MANUAL, *supra* at 145, 148, 150, 216, 225; UK War Office, THE LAW OF WAR ON LAND pt. 3, at 96 (1958); The Prosecutor v. Delalic, IT-96-21-T (Trial Chamber, ICTY, Nov. 16, 1998), at para. 271 ("there is no gap between the Third and the Fourth Geneva Contentions"); MICHAEL BOTHE, *ET AL.*, NEW RULES FOR VICTIMS OF ARMED CONFLICTS: COMMENTARY ON THE TWO 1977 PROTOCOLS ADDITIONAL TO THE GENEVA CONVENTIONS OF 1949, at 261–63 (1982); HENCKAERTS & DOSWALD-BECK, *supra* at 389; HILLARE McCOUBREY, INTERNATIONAL HUMANITARIAN LAW: MODERN DEVELOPMENTS IN THE LIMITATION OF WARFARE 137 (2 ed. 1998); Knut Dormann, *The Legal Situation of "Unlawful/Unprivileged Combatants,"* 85 INT'L REV. RED CROSS 849 (2003); Jinks, *supra* at 1504, 1510–11; Derek Jinks, *The Declining Significance of POW Status*, 45 HARV. INT'L L.J. 367, 374 (2004) ("irrespective of whether war detainees are assigned POW status, humanitarian law accords protections that mirror, in most important respects, the rights accorded POWs."); Legal Adviser, U.S. Dep't of State, William H. Taft IV, *The Law of Armed Conflict After 9/11: Some Salient Features*, 28 YALE J. INT'L L. 319, 321–22 (2003) (non-pows "are not 'outside the law'… [and] they do not forfeit their right to humane treatment" under the 1949 Geneva Civilian Convention and "customary law" reflected "in Article 75 of Additional Protocol I to the Geneva Conventions," "safeguards to which all persons in the hands of an enemy are entitled"); Johannes van Aggelen, *A Response to John C. Yoo, "The Status of Soldiers and Terrorists Under the*

Geneva Convention," 3 Chinese J. Int'l L. 1, 5, 8–9 (2004); *see also* Hamdan v. Rumsfeld, 548 U.S. 557, 629–31 & n.63 (2006) (no gaps in coverage exist under the laws of war with respect to detainees of any status and, at a minimum, common Article 3 of the 1949 Geneva Conventions is applicable during an armed conflict); Hamdan v. Rumsfeld, 344 F. Supp.2d at 161 (if a detainee is not a pw, rights and protections exist under common Article 3); U.S. Dep't of Army, Subject Schedule 27-1, The Geneva Conventions of 1949 and Hague Convention No. IV of 1907, at 7–8 ("these rules are embodied in one general principle: treat all prisoners of war, civilians, or other detained personnel *humanely....* To repeat, we must insure that all persons are treated humanely. These persons may not be subjected to murder, torture, corporal punishment, mutilation, or any form of physical or mental coercion.") (Oct. 8, 1970) (emphasis in original); Council of Europe, Parliamentary Assembly Resolution 1433 (2005) ("At no time have detentions at Guantanamo Bay been within a 'legal black hole'"), in the Documents Supplement.

13. During the armed conflicts involving the U.S. in Afghanistan and Iraq, the Bush Administration attempted to deny Geneva protections to members of al Qaeda because al Qaeda "cannot be considered a state party to" them. Does this make sense? Do the Conventions provide protections for captured personnel from Halliburton or other corporations operating in Iraq? Do the rights and duties reflected in common Article 3 apply to any detainee? Is it likely that any member of al Qaeda captured during such conflicts is a national of a state that has ratified the treaties, since every state but Taiwan is a signatory? Additionally, are the rights and duties reflected in the Geneva Conventions that are customary international law (especially common Article 3) of universal applicability? *See* Hamdan v. Rumsfeld, 344 F. Supp.2d 152, 161 (D.D.C. 2004) (the Conventions "are triggered by the place of the conflict, and not by what particular faction a fighter is associated with"); Paust, *Executive Plans, supra* at 829–31; William H. Taft, IV, Memorandum to Counsel to the President, Comments on Your Paper on the Geneva Convention (Feb. 2, 2002), at 2, available at http://www.nytimes.com/packages/html/politics/20040608_DOC.pdf.

In *Hamdan v. Rumsfeld,* 415 F.3d 33, 41 (D.C. Cir.), a panel of the D.C. Circuit Court of Appeals embraced the Bush Administration's view: "Another problem for Hamdan is that the 1949 Convention does not apply to al Qaeda and its members.... Under Common Article 2, the provisions of the Convention apply to 'all cases of declared war or any other armed conflict which may arise between two or more of the High Contracting Parties, even if the state of war is not recognized by one of them.' Needless to say, al Qaeda is not a state and it was not a 'High Contracting Party.'" If the Conventions actually did not apply to members of al Qaeda in Afghanistan, how can they rightly be detained under GC Article 5 or prosecuted for violations?

14. Are certain nationals of a neutral country denied protections under Part III of the Geneva Civilian Convention (although, if not prisoners of war, they would be protected by customary law reflected in common Article 3 and Article 75 of Protocol I, if not also under certain portions of Part II of the Convention)? If the U.S. detains such persons outside U.S. territory, does the narrow exclusion in GC Article 4 with respect to those found "in the territory" of the U.S. apply? Regarding occupied territory, see also IV Commentary, *supra* at 48 ("in occupied territory they are protected persons and the Convention is applicable to them"); U.S. Dep't of Army, Pam. 27-161-2, II International Law 132 (1962) ("If they are in occupied territory, they remain entitled to protection."); 2004 UK Manual, *supra* at 274 ("Neutral nationals in occupied territory are entitled to treatment as protected persons under Geneva Convention IV whether or not there are normal diplomatic relations between the neutral states concerned and the occupying power.").

Professor Paust has stated: "In any event, limitations in Article 4 are obviated once the general rights, duties and protections in the Convention become customary international law of universal application. In a related manner, the International Military Tribunal at Nuremberg ruled that the fact that (1) Germany refused to ratify the 1907 Hague Convention, and (2) the treaty contained a general participation clause in Article 2 that limited the treaty's reach to armed conflicts between contracting parties became irrelevant once the rules mirrored in the treaty became customary international law." Paust, *Executive Plans, supra* at 819 n.28.

15. Note that with respect to the 1949 Geneva Civilian Convention, one can organize inquiry in terms of the following questions (some of which we have begun to address):

(a) when do certain provisions of the Convention apply?

Through Article 2: to an armed conflict of an international character, including a belligerency (see also FM 27-10, para. 8a re: other "international" conflicts).

Through Article 3: to an armed conflict not of an international character (*e.g.,* an insurgency).

(b) who is protected in Article 2 or Article 3 conflicts?

(1) in the case of an Article 2 conflict:

— those protected in common Article 3 (because what is reflected in the article now provides a minimum set of customary protections even during an international armed conflict, by treaty interpretation and/or customary international law); and

— those identified in Article 4, which refers to certain persons and excludes certain others (*e.g.,* co-nationals and certain nationals of a neutral state while "in the territory" of a detaining state) from Part III protections (*i.e.,* protections that are contained in Articles 27–141), but which does not exclude even such persons from the protections contained in Part II (*i.e.,* in Articles 13–26, some of which have been referred to above). This can involve technical differences because of the scheme set forth in Articles 4 and 13 of the Geneva Civilian Convention.

(2) in the case of an Article 3 conflict: those persons protected within common Article 3 (who include those persons of any status who are no longer taking an active part in hostilities).

(c) what sort of protections apply?

(1) in the case of an Article 2 conflict:

— the customary minimum protections reflected in common Article 3 and in Article 75 of Protocol I;

— for some persons, the protections found in Part II; and

— for some persons, also the protections found in Part III.

(2) in the case of an Article 3 conflict: the protections found in common Article 3.

(d) what sort of sanctions are expressed, although others can also pertain?

(1) in the case of an Article 2 conflict: those found in Part IV, Section I (*i.e.,* Articles 142–149), including the "grave breach" provisions (with "grave breaches" set forth in Article 146).

(2) in the case of an Article 3 conflict: (see below).

What human rights protections apply to detainees of any status. See, for example, Articles 6, 7, 9, 14, 26 of the International Covenant on Civil and Political Rights.

16. Under GPW art. 4, who is entitled to prisoner of war status? During the international armed conflict in Afghanistan that began in October, 2001, the Bush Administration denied pw status to members of the armed forces of the Taliban (which had been at least a *de facto* regime and a belligerent involved in a civil war with the Northern Alliance prior to U.S. entry and which was recognized as the *de jure* regime of Afghanistan by at least three other states). The Bush Administration alleged (incorrectly) that the Taliban in general did not carry arms openly during battle or wear distinctive insignia within the meaning of GPW art. 4(A)(2), although all fighters carry their arms in the open during battles and members of the Taliban generally wore distinctive turbans. What should be the test for Taliban pow status? For U.S. military pow status? Consider the following commentary: "The test for combatant or individual belligerent status under the laws of war is straightforward. It is membership in the armed forces of a party to an armed conflict of an international character. Thus, privileged or lawful belligerents include members of the armed forces of a state, nation, or belligerent during an armed conflict. As noted in U.S. military texts, '[a]nyone engaging in hostilities in an armed conflict on behalf of a party to the conflict' is a 'combatant'[7] and '[c]ombatants … include all members of the regularly organized armed forces of a party to the conflict.'[8] Article 1 of the Annex to the 1907 Hague Convention expressly states that belligerent status will 'apply … to armies' and expressly sets forth additional criteria to be met merely by 'militia.' The customary 1863 Lieber Code also affirmed: 'So soon as a man is armed by a sovereign government and takes the soldier's oath of fidelity, he is a belligerent; his killing, wounding, or other warlike acts are not individual crimes or offenses.'

"The 1949 Convention's list of six separate categories involved a clear change of certain prior interpretations of coverage under the 1929 Convention. Under express terms of the treaty, only one category out of six contains criteria limiting prisoner of war status to those belonging to a group that carries arms openly, wears a fixed distinctive sign recognizable at a distance, and conducts operations generally in accordance with the law of war. Under GPW Article 4(A)(2), these limiting criteria expressly apply only to certain 'militias or volunteer corps' or 'organized resistance movements.' They expressly do not apply to '[m]embers of the armed forces of a Party to the conflict, as well as members of militias or volunteer corps forming part of such armed forces' covered under 4(A)(1) or to '[m]embers of regular armed forces who profess allegiance to a government or an authority not recognized by the Detaining Power' covered under 4(A)(3).

"With respect to the armed forces of a party to the armed conflict in Afghanistan (such as those of the Taliban and the United States), the determinative criterion for prisoner of war status is membership. Thus, members of the armed forces of each party qualify as prisoners of war under GPW Article 4(A)(1), if not 4(A)(3), and the authoritative ICRC has expressly recognized combatant and pw status for all members of the armed forces of the Taliban. Moreover, pw status does not inhibit the ability to detain enemy pws for the duration of an armed conflict, whether or not particular pws can also be prosecuted for war crimes or other violations of international law. Indeed, prisoners of war subject to prosecution do not thereby lose their status as a prisoner of war. There is no need to change the laws of war in that regard.

---

7. U.S. Army Judge Advocate General's School, Operational Law Handbook 12 (2002), available at http://www.jagcnet.army.mil.

8. The U.S. Navy, Annotated Supplement to the Commander's Handbook of Naval Operations 296 (Naval War College, Int'l L. Studies vol. 73, 1999).

"A new extension of the four criteria expressly applicable only to one of six categories addressed in GPW Article 4(A), *i.e.* those covered in 4(A)(2), to the 'armed forces' of a party to an armed conflict (who are presently covered by Article 4(A)(1)) would result in a nonsensical, policy-thwarting denial of pw status to all members of the armed forces of a party to an armed conflict whenever several members do not wear a fixed distinctive sign recognizable at a distance or several members violate the laws of war. Such an approach is illogical and contrary to normal approaches to treaty interpretation; would seriously threaten pw status, combat immunity, and protections for soldiers of various countries including U.S. military; and would be inconsistent with general state practice (which is also relevant for treaty interpretation). In Afghanistan and more generally and in conformity with widespread state practice, several types of U.S. soldiers (*e.g.*, special forces) and various regular soldiers at different times have used camouflage and have otherwise attempted to blend in with local flora or geography in an effort to avoid being recognizable at a distance, since they prefer not to be clearly recognizable at all. Indeed, various U.S. soldiers in Afghanistan have not only not met the criterion of wearing distinctive emblems or signs recognizable at a distance, but have also been spotted wearing Afghan civilian clothing and sporting beards to 'blend in.' Thus, under the nonsensical approach, all U.S. soldiers could be denied prisoner of war status during the conflict in Afghanistan and an upgraded war with Iraq." Paust, *Status, supra* at 332–34.

One district court adopted a contrary view. In *United States v. Lindh,* 212 F. Supp.2d 541, 557 n.35 (E.D. Va. 2002), the district court declared: "Lindh asserts that the Taliban is a 'regular armed force,' under the GPW, and because he is a member, he need not meet the four conditions of the Hague Regulations because only Article 4(2)(A), which addresses irregular armed forces, explicitly mentions the four criteria. This argument is unpersuasive; it ignores long-established practice under the GPW and, if accepted, leads to an absurd result. First, the four criteria have long been understood under customary international law to be the defining characteristics of any lawful armed force.... Thus, all armed forces or militias, regular and irregular, must meet the four criteria if their members are to receive combatant immunity. Were this not so, the anomalous result that would follow is that members of an armed force that meet none of the criteria could still claim lawful combatant immunity merely on the basis that the organization calls itself a 'regular armed force.' It would indeed be absurd for members of a so-called 'regular armed force' to enjoy lawful combatant immunity even though the force had no established command structure and its members wore no recognizable symbol or insignia, concealed their weapons, and did not abide by the customary laws of war. Simply put, the label 'regular armed force' cannot be used to mask unlawful combatant status."

What approach is preferable? What is the reason for requiring members of certain militias and other volunteer corps to wear a "fixed distinctive sign recognizable at a distance" as a precondition to being classified as a prisoner of war under GPW, art. 4(A)(2), but not 4(A)(1) or (3)? What is the reason for requiring them to carry arms openly during an attack? Doesn't every group carry arms openly during an attack? Should soldiers be denied pw status because they wear camouflage during missions?

The Geneva Protocols

Note also that the 1977 Protocols supplement this list, with Protocol I applying to Article 2 conflicts and Protocol II applying to Article 3 conflicts. Apparently every state has ratified the l949 Geneva Conventions except Taiwan, but not all (yet most) states have ratified both Protocols. The United States has yet to ratify either Protocol, but considers most of the provisions to reflect customary law or to be relevant to interpretation of the general conventions. This point is addressed only partly in the *Tadic* decision of the Appeals Chamber of the ICT for Former Yugoslavia (below). Professor Scharf has also recognized: "[A] very strong case can be made that Protocol I has ripened into customary international law ... and, in any event, the United States already imposes the rules contained in Protocol I on U.S. military personnel operating abroad.... .155 [214 in 2012] States have ratified Protocol I, making it one of the most widely ratified treaties. With the addition of the United Kingdom this year, its parties include seventeen of the nineteen members of NATO and three of the Permanent Members of the Security Council. The Protocol has been frequently invoked in various conflicts by governments, U.N. investigative bodies, and the International Committee of the Red Cross. Moreover, U.S. soldiers are subject to arrest and prosecution/extradition for breaches of the Protocol when they are present in the territory of any State Party.... [T]he Reagan Administration declared that many of the other provisions of the Protocol (including most, if not all, of the substantive provisions that are referenced in the ICC's Statute) represent customary international law.[9] Reflecting this position, the U.S. Air Force and Navy commanders' handbooks employ the Protocol's language. When U.S. Troops are deployed to the U.N. for a peace-keeping mission they are subject to Protocol I. And, as a matter of policy on the conduct of hostilities during coalition actions (*e.g.*, in the Persian Gulf and Balkans), the United States has implemented the rules of the Protocol because of the need to coordinate rules of engagement with its coalition partners and because, as a Defense Department Report on the Persian Gulf Conflict explained, several provisions of Protocol I are 'generally regarded as codification of the customary practice of nations, and therefore binding on all.'" Michael P. Scharf, *The ICC's Jurisdiction over the Nationals of Non-Party States: A Critique of the U.S. Position*, 64 LAW & CONTEMP. PROBS. 67 (2001).

The applications of common Article 3 and Protocol II are not coextensive, although they are complementary. Application of either to insurgents does not depend on the insurgents being formal parties to the Geneva Conventions.[10] Application of Protocol II in its entirety, however, depends on whether the state involved is a signatory to the Protocol, since (unlike common Article 3) it is not fully customary law. Thus, common Article 3, especially as custom and as the minimum standard in Article 2 conflicts as well, applies to a broader range of conflicts than does Protocol II. Although both apply to "conflict[s] not of an international character," unlike Protocol II, common Article 3 does not provide definitional criteria with respect to identification of such conflicts.

To meet the jurisdictional requirements of Protocol II, there must be a showing that: (1) Protocol I does not apply and an armed conflict is taking place between the armed forces of a party to Protocol II and dissident armed forces; (2) the dissident armed forces are under responsible command; (3) the dissident forces exercise con-

---

9. Message from the President of the United States transmitting Protocol II Additional to the Geneva Conventions, *reprinted in* 26 I.L.M. 561 (1987).

10. *See, e.g.,* J. PICTET, IV COMMENTARY, *supra* at 37 (as reproduced above). For an example of the application of common Article 3 and Protocol II to one aspect of a conflict while applying the grave breaches provisions of the 1949 Geneva Conventions and Protocol I to other aspects, *see* Military and Paramilitary Activities in and against Nicaragua (Nicaragua v. U.S.), [1986] I.C.J. 14, para. 219. Does this make sense? Is it preferable? See also Note 5 above.

trol over a portion of the territory, enabling them to carry out sustained and concerted military operations; and (4) the dissident forces are capable of implementing Protocol II.[11]

Other Aspects of Internal Versus International Armed Conflicts

Under the customary law of war, an otherwise internal armed conflict will be considered international, for example, when the non-state party to the conflict is recognized as a belligerent or when a foreign state participates in the armed conflict. In these cases, the entire body of the international law of armed conflicts applies.[12] Effects of foreign government involvement have led to two general considerations:

A. Under what is perhaps a more traditional approach:

(1) if a foreign state assists an established government, the conflict is classified as internal and the rules of international conflict do not apply because the insurgents have no belligerent or higher status in international law, unless the conflict is governed by Protocol I, Article 1 (4), there is other outside intervention, or the conflict is international in character for some other reason (*e.g.,* because of U.N. Security Council action under Chapter VII);

(2) if a foreign state assists insurgents against an established government, the conflict can be classified as international and the rules of international armed conflict apply at least between the foreign state and the established government because both are subjects of international law and the conflict is also "between" Contracting Parties within the meaning of common Article 2.

Such an approach seems to stress criteria from another area of law, *i.e.,* issues relating to the permissibility of intervention, and, at times, the technical status of parties to the conflict. Under this approach, the relationship between an established government and insurgents is governed at least by the rules applicable to conflicts of a non-international character, and may include additional humanitarian norms in at least the following cases:

(1) the established government recognizes the insurgents as belligerents (an obsolete practice);

(2) outside recognition of the insurgents as belligerents occurs [then all of the customary laws of war apply];

(3) the established government and the insurgents enter into special agreements pursuant to common Article 3 of the Geneva Conventions, bringing into force some or all of the Geneva Conventions and Protocol I;

(4) Article 1 (4) of Protocol I applies; or

---

11. Protocol II, art. 1. For a discussion of the background concerning adoption of common Article 3 and Protocol II, *see, e.g.,* International Committee of the Red Cross, Commentary on the Additional Protocols of 8 June 1977 to the Geneva Conventions of 12 August 1949 1343–56 (Yves Sandoz, *et al.* eds., 1987); *see also* Bothe, *supra*; Sylvie Junod, *Additional Protocol II; History and Scope*, 33 Am. U. L. Rev. 29 (1983); Charles Lysaght, *The Scope of Protocol II and Its Relationship to Common Article 3 of the Geneva Conventions of 1949 and Other Human Rights Instruments*, 33 Am. U. L. Rev. 9 (1983).

12. See the many citations in Note 3 following the extract of the *Tadic* case below.

(5) the insurgents are classified as an organized resistance movement belonging to an intervening state.[13]

Under each of these scenarios, international humanitarian law will apply to all parties, including third party intervenors. Third party states rarely, if ever, recognize an insurgent as a belligerent.[14] One notable example was the recognition of the Confederate States by England as a belligerent during the U.S. Civil War.

B. Another approach focuses more on the general process of armed violence in which parties participate and various internationalizing elements (in addition to the technical status of and relationships between some of the parties). The phrase "armed conflict not of an international character" found in common Article 3 is interpreted with more emphasis on various elements that may be relevant to the character of a general conflict and lead one to a conclusion that it is not "not of an international character" but "international".[15] Both approaches may hinge on orientations to treaty interpretation, but this latter approach may best serve to advance humanitarian purposes (*i.e.,* the general object and purpose of Geneva law) by tending more often to stress various internationalizing elements. For example, would the fact that Soviet military advisers were directly involved in combat missions of a recognized government's armed forces against what otherwise were mere insurgents sufficiently internationalize the conflict to move it beyond the language of common Article 3? If so, would it fit neatly within the language of common Article 2, especially the word "between" used in relation to another set of words—"Contracting Parties"? From a policy-oriented approach, which interpretive orientation would tend best to serve humanitarian law, especially since all of the customary laws of war apply to a "belligerency" and to other international armed conflicts? Might Article 1 (4) of Protocol I apply in some such situations? Is it policy-serving to have common Article 3 no longer technically applicable (*e.g.,* once the insurgency becomes a "belligerency" to which all of the customary laws of war apply), but common Article 2 to be technically not applicable (*e.g.,* because a "belligerent" is not a "Party" to the Geneva Conventions), but a belligerent can be a "Power" within the meaning of common Article 2? When Geneva Civilian Convention provisions become part of the customary laws of war, should the words "Parties" or "Power" become as irrelevant as the "general participation" clause of Article I of the 1907 Hague Convention, as recognized in the Opinion and Judgement of the IMT at Nuremberg, so that customary GC provisions apply whether or not a belligerent is a "Party" to the Convention? Why is it in the interest of U.S. soldiers to be considered combatants in an "international" armed conflict whenever they are deployed abroad to engage in fighting?

Another example demonstrates related differences. During the Vietnam War, Soviet military advisers were aiding North Vietnamese forces; U.S. and other nation-state forces were engaged in the general armed conflict, sometimes fighting what the U.S. considered to be Viet Cong insurgents in South Vietnam; and South Vietnamese forces fought Viet Cong and North Vietnamese forces. Several countries recognized either the North or

---

13. *See also* Dietrich Schindler II, *International Humanitarian Law and Internal Armed Conflicts,* 1982 Int'l Rev. Red Cross 230, 255–64.

14. *See* Evan Luard, *Civil Conflicts in Modern International Relations,* in The International Regulation of Civil Wars 21 (Evan Luard ed., 1972).

15. At times, Pictet uses the word "international" in contradistinction to common Article 3 conflicts. *See, e.g.,* IV Commentary at 14.

South Vietnamese forces as military forces of a state. Was the Vietnam War an Article 2 conflict? Should one be more technical in focus and stress the status of participants—perhaps concluding that any clash between U.S. forces and Viet Cong forces was not part of the general international conflict but merely an armed conflict "not of an international character" (or that the U.S. was merely aiding a recognized government attempt to put down insurgents)? Alternatively, should one focus on the purposes of Geneva law and overall context, concluding that various participants were actually involved in an international armed conflict? *See generally* vols. 1–4, THE VIETNAM WAR AND INTERNATIONAL LAW (R. Falk ed. 1968–1976).

Section 2
Types of War Crimes

A. General

U.S. Dep't of Army Field Manual 27-10,
The Law of Land Warfare
(1956)

498. Crimes Under International Law

Any person, whether a member of the armed forces or a civilian, who commits an act which constitutes a crime under international law is responsible therefor and liable to punishment.

499. War Crimes

The term "war crime" is the technical expression for a violation of the law of war by any person or persons, military or civilian. Every violation of the law of war is a war crime....

502. Grave Breaches of the Geneva Conventions of 1949 as War Crimes

The Geneva Conventions of 1949 define the following acts as "grave breaches," if committed against persons or property protected by the Conventions:

a. *GWS and GWS Sea.*

Grave breaches to which the preceding Article relates shall be those involving any of the following acts, if committed against persons or property protected by the Convention: wilful killing, torture or inhuman treatment, including biological experiments, wilfully causing great suffering or serious injury to body or health, and extensive destruction and appropriation of property, not justified by military necessity and carried out unlawfully and wantonly. (GWS, art. 50; GWS Sea, art. 51.)

b. *GPW.*

Grave breaches to which the preceding Article relates shall be those involving any of the following acts, if committed against persons or property protected by the Convention: wilful killing, torture or inhuman treatment, including biological experiments, wilfully causing great suffering or serious injury to body or health, compelling a prisoner of war to serve in the forces of the hostile power or wilfully depriving a prisoner of war of the rights of fair and regular trial prescribed in this Convention. (GPW, art. 130.)

c. *GC.*

Grave breaches to which the preceding Article relates shall be those involving any of the following acts, if committed against persons or property protected by the present Convention: wilful killing, torture or inhuman treatment, including biological experiments, wilfully causing great suffering or serious injury to body or health, unlawful deportation or transfer or unlawful confinement of a protected person, compelling a protected person to serve in the forces of a hostile Power or wilfully depriving a protected person of the rights of fair and regular trial prescribed in the present Convention, taking of hostages and extensive destruction and appropriation of property, not justified by military necessity and carried out unlawfully and wantonly. (GC, art. 147.)

504. Other Types of War Crimes

In addition to the "grave breaches" of the Geneva Conventions of 1949, the following acts are representative of violations of the law of war ("war crimes"):

a. Making use of poisoned or otherwise forbidden arms or ammunition.

b. Treacherous request for quarter.

c. Maltreatment of dead bodies.

d. Firing on localities which are undefended and without military significance.

e. Abuse of or firing on the flag of truce.

f. Misuse of the Red Cross emblem.

g. Use of civilian clothing by troops to conceal their military character during battle.

h. Improper use of privileged buildings for military purposes.

i. Poisoning of wells or streams.

j. Pillage or purposeless destruction.

k. Compelling prisoners of war to perform prohibited labor.

l. Killing without trial spies or other persons who have committed hostile acts.

m. Compelling civilians to perform prohibited labor.

n. Violation of surrender terms.

Notes and Questions

1. For other lists, recall Chapter Two, Section 1 (1919 List). See also *id.*, Section 3; Chapter Three, Section 1; Chapter Four, Sections 6–9; Chapter Six; *compare* Article 8 of the Statute of the ICC.

2. In the Principles of the Nuremberg Charter and Judgment, formulated by the U.N. International Law Commission in 1950, the following summary appears:

War Crimes:

Violations of the laws or customs of war which include, but are not limited to, murder, ill-treatment of prisoners of war or of persons on the seas, killing of hostages, plunder of public or private property, wanton destruction of cities, towns, or villages, or devastation not justified by military necessity.

See also Charter of the IMT at Nuremberg, art. 6 (b); Charter of the IMT for the Far East, art. 5 (b) ("Namely, violations of the laws and customs of war"); Control Council Law No. 10, art. II (1)(b)–each in the Documents Supplement. Concerning the fact that violations of the Geneva Conventions other than grave breaches are war crimes that must be punished, see Note 2 following the *Tadic* opinion, *infra*.

3. Most war crimes are committed by military personnel, but recall the recognition in FM 27-10, para. 498 that *any* person, including civilians (official or private), can be a perpetrator. Also recall Chapter Two, Section 1; Chapter Three, Section 1; Chapter Four, Sections 6–9; Chapter Six. At the IMT at Nuremberg, editor-in-chief Julius Streicher of *Der Stürmer* was convicted of crimes against humanity "in connection with war crimes" because of his "incitement to murder and extermination at the time when Jews in the East were being killed under the most horrible conditions." 22 Trials of the Major War Criminals Before the International Military Tribunal 549 (1949). Several of the German industrialists were also found guilty of "plunder of property." Chapter Four, Section 8. See also The Prosecutor v. Tadic, Decision on the Defense Motion on Jurisdiction (Trial Chamber, International Criminal Tribunal for Former Yugoslavia, 10 Aug. 1995), para. 61 ("Violations of the laws or customs of war are commonly referred to as 'war crimes.' They can be defined as crimes committed by any person ...'whether committed by combatants or civilians, including the nationals of neutral states'"); 11 Op. Att'y Gen. 297, 299–300 (1865); 4 Commentary, Geneva Convention Relative to the Protection of Civilian Persons in Time of War 13 ("any man or any woman"), 79 ,209–10, 591–94 602 ("all") (ICRC, Jean S. Pictet ed. 1958); U.K. Ministry of Defence, The Manual of the Law of Armed Conflict 428 ("civilians," "any person") (2004); Jordan J. Paust, *After My Lai: The Case for War Crime Jurisdiction Over Civilians in Federal District Courts*, 50 Tex. L. Rev. 6, 12–17 (1971); *Weisshaus v. Swiss Bankers Ass'n*, 225 F.3d 191 (2d Cir. 2000); *Kadic v. Karadzic*, 70 F.3d 232, 239–40, 242–43 (2d Cir. 1995), *cert. denied*, 518 U.S. 1005 (1996); *Presbyterian Church of Sudan v. Talisman Energy, Inc.*, 374 F. Supp.2d 331 (S.D.N.Y. 2005); *Id.*, 244 F. Supp.2d 289, 305, 308–19, 320–25 (S.D.N.Y. 2003); *In re Agent Orange Product Liability Litig.*, 373 F. Supp.2d 7, 58–59 (E.D.N.Y. 2005); *Estate of Rodriquez v. Drummond Co., Inc.*, 256 F. Supp.2d 1250 (N.D. Ala. 2003); *Doe v. Islamic Salvation Front*, 993 F. Supp. 3, 7–8 (D.D.C. 1998); *Ex parte Mudd*, manuscript opinion (1868); The War Crimes Act, 18 U.S.C. §2441(a) ("Whoever"); *see also Linder v. Portocarrero*, 963 F.2d 332, 336–37 (11th Cir. 1992) (crimes of the Contras). Concerning private duties, *see also* Jordan J. Paust, *The Reality of Private Rights, Duties, and Participation in the International Legal Process*, 25 Mich. J. Int'l L. 1229 (2004).

4. In *The Prosecutor v. Alfred Musema*, ICTR-96-13-T (Trial Chamber, 27 Jan. 2000), addressing breaches of Common Article 3 of the Geneva Conventions and of Protocol II, the ICTR recognized that "civilians can be held responsible for violations of international humanitarian law committed in an armed conflict," and that "it is well-established that the post-World War II Trials unequivocally support the imposition of individual criminal liability for war crimes on civilians where they have a link or connection with a Party to the conflict." *Id.* at paras. 268, 274. Is it necessary that civilian perpetrators of any type of war crime have a "link" with a Party? *Musema* stated in para. 285(a): "nor would it be required that the acts [of humiliating or degrading treatment] be committed under state authority." Common Article 3 of the Geneva Conventions states that "each Party to the conflict shall be bound to apply, as a minimum, the following provisions...."

The Trial Chamber in *Musema* set forth a requirement "that there is a link or nexus between the offence committed and the armed conflict for Article 4 of the Statute [of the ICTR] to apply," that the crimes alleged "must be closely related to the hostilities or committed in conjunction with the armed conflict." *Id.* at paras. 259–260. Using this approach, the Trial Chamber in The *Prosecutor v. Rutaganda*, ICTR-96-3-T (6 Dec. 1999),

acquitted Rutaganda regarding three counts of violations of common Article 3. The Appeals Chamber in *Rutaganda* reversed and entered findings of guilt on two of the three counts, but accepted a so-called nexus requirement. ICTR-96-3-A (26 May 2003).
Must all war crimes be committed "in conjunction with ... armed conflict"? Consider war crimes committed by civilians during an occupation. The Trial Chamber in *Musema* added: "In the *Rutaganda* Judgment it was held that the term nexus should not be defined *in abstracto*. Rather, the evidence adduced in support of the charges against the accused must satisfy the Chamber that such a nexus exists. Thus, the burden rests on the Prosecutor to prove beyond a reasonable doubt, that, on the basis of the facts, such a nexus exists between the crime committed and the armed conflict." *Id.* at para. 262, *citing Rutaganda* Judgment, paras. 102–103 (which merely cited *Akayesu* Judgment, paras. 70, 643). Is there any other precedent for such a "nexus" requirement? Does it only apply regarding the reach of Article 4 of the Statute of the ICTR? The *Rutaganda* Judgment added that it was determined in the *Akayesu* Judgment and by the Appeals Chamber of the ICTY in *Tadic* that "the requirements of Common Article 3 and Additional Protocol II apply in the whole territory where the conflict is occurring and are not limited to the 'war front' or to the 'narrow geographical context of the actual theater of combat operations.'" At para. 101, *citing Akayesu* Judgment at paras. 635–636; *Tadic* (2 Oct. 1995), at para. 69. Where it applies, should the burden regarding proof of a "nexus" be "beyond a reasonable doubt"?

The Trial Chamber in *Musema* also noted that its jurisdiction under Article 4 of the Statute of the ICTR was limited to "serious violations" of Common Article 3 of the Geneva Conventions and of Protocol II; that the "Trial Chamber in the *Akayesu* Judgment understood, in line with the Appeals Chamber Decision in *Tadic* that the phrase 'serious violation' means 'a breach of a rule protecting important values which must involve grave consequences for the victim'"; that the list of violations in Article 4 of the Statute was taken from Common Article 3 and Protocol II; and that such violations are "serious" and are also violative of customary international law. *Id.* at paras. 286–288.

5. Do the "grave breach" provisions of the Geneva Conventions apply to situations regulated by common Article 3 of the Conventions? *Compare* M. Cherif Bassiouni, The Law of the International Criminal Tribunal for the Former Yugoslavia 441–632 (1996); O. Gross, *The Grave Breaches System and the Armed Conflict in the Former Yugoslavia*, 16 Mich. J. Int'l L. 783, 825 & n.178 (1995); T. Meron, *War Crimes in Yugoslavia and Developments in International Law*, 88 Am. J. Int'l L. 78, 80–81 (1994); M. Scharf, *Swapping Amnesty for Peace: Was there a Duty to Prosecute International Crimes in Haiti?*, 31 Tex. Int'l L. J. 1, 20(1996); *with* J. Paust, *Applicability of International Criminal Laws to Events in the Former Yugoslavia*, 9 Am. U. J. Int'l L. & Pol. 499, 510–12 & ns.39–42 (1994); Paust & Blaustein, *supra* at 2, 14–15, 28 n.101; J. Pictet, IV Commentary at 591 (citing common Article 3 in connection with discussion of the general section on criminal sanctions); *The Prosecutor of the Tribunal v. Dusko Tadic*, in Chapter Six, Section 9. *See also* T. Meron, *The Continuing Role of Custom in the Formation of International Humanitarian Law*, 90 Am. J. Int'l L. 238, 243 (1996) ("the appeals chamber should have devoted more attention to discussing the possibility that ... the core offenses listed in the grave breaches provisions may have an independent existence as a customary norm applicable also to violations of at least common Article 3.")[hereinafter Meron, *Continuing*]; *International Criminalization of Internal Atrocities*, 89 Am. J. Int'l L. 554 (1995).

The Prosecutor v. Dusko Tadic

Decision on the Defence Motion for Interlocutory Appeal on Jurisdiction, ICTY Appeals Chamber, IT-94-1-AR72 (2 Oct. 1995)

Cassese, J.

79. Article 2 of the Statute of the International Tribunal provides:

"The International Tribunal shall have the power to prosecute persons committing or ordering to be committed grave breaches of the Geneva Conventions of 12 August 1949...."

By its explicit terms, and as confirmed in the Report of the Secretary-General, this Article of the Statute is based on the Geneva Conventions of 1949 and, more specifically, the provisions of those Conventions relating to "grave breaches" of the Conventions. Each of the four Geneva Conventions of 1949 contains a "grave breaches" provision, specifying particular breaches of the Convention for which the High Contracting Parties have a duty to prosecute those responsible. In other words, for these specific acts, the Conventions create universal mandatory criminal jurisdiction among contracting States. Although the language of the Conventions might appear to be ambiguous and the question is open to some debate*(see, e.g.,* [*Amicus Curiae*] Submission of the Government of the United States of America Concerning Certain Arguments Made by Counsel for the Accused in the Case of *The Prosecutor of the Tribunal v. Dusko Tadic,* 17 July 1995, (Case No. IT-94-1-T), at 35–6 (hereinafter, U.S. *Amicus Curiae Brief)),* it is widely contended that the grave breaches provisions establish universal mandatory jurisdiction only with respect to those breaches of the Conventions committed in international armed conflicts [no citations were provided]. Appellant argues that, as the grave breaches enforcement system only applies to international armed conflicts, reference in Article 2 of the Statute to the grave breaches provisions of the Geneva Conventions limits the International Tribunal's jurisdiction under that Article to acts committed in the context of an international armed conflict.

The Trial Chamber has held that Article 2 [of the Statute of the Tribunal]:

"[H]as been so drafted as to be self-contained rather than referential, save for the identification of the victims of enumerated acts; that identification and that alone involves going to the Conventions themselves for the definition of 'persons or property protected....

[T]he requirement of international conflict does not appear on the face of Article 2. Certainly, nothing in the words of the Article expressly require its existence; once one of the specified acts is allegedly committed upon a protected person the power of the International Tribunal to prosecute arises if the spatial and temporal requirements of Article 1 are met....

[T]here is no ground for treating Article 2 as in effect importing into the Statute the whole of the terms of the Conventions, including the reference in common Article 2 of the Geneva Convention [sic] to international conflicts. As stated, Article 2 of the Statute is on its face, self-contained, save in relation to the definition of protected persons and things." (Decision at Trial, at paras. 49–51.)

80. With all due respect, the Trial Chamber's reasoning is based on a misconception of the grave breaches provisions and the extent of their incorporation into the Statute of the International Tribunal. The grave breaches system of the Geneva Conventions establishes a twofold system: there is on the one hand an enumeration of offences that are regarded so serious as to constitute "grave breaches", closely bound up with this enumeration a mandatory enforcement mechanism is set up, based on the concept of a duty and a right of all Contracting States to search for and try or extradite persons allegedly responsible for "grave breaches". The international armed conflict element generally at-

tributed to the grave breaches provisions of the Geneva Conventions is merely a function of the system of universal mandatory jurisdiction that those provisions create. The
international armed conflict requirement was a necessary limitation on the grave breaches
system in light of the intrusion on State sovereignty that such mandatory universal jurisdiction
represents. State parties to the 1949 Geneva Conventions did not want to give other States
jurisdiction over serious violations of international humanitarian law committed in their
internal armed conflicts—at least not the mandatory universal jurisdiction involved in
the grave breaches system.

81. The Trial Chamber is right in implying that the enforcement mechanism has of
course not been imported into the Statute of the International Tribunal, for the obvious
reason that the International Tribunal itself constitutes a mechanism for the prosecution
and punishment of the perpetrators of "grave breaches". However, the Trial Chamber has
misinterpreted the reference to the Geneva Conventions contained in the sentence of Article 2: "persons or property protected under the provisions of the relevant Geneva Conventions". (Statute of the Tribunal, art. 2.) For the reasons set out above, this reference
is clearly intended to indicate that the offences listed under Article 2 can only be prosecuted when perpetrated against persons or property regarded as "protected" by the Geneva
Conventions under the strict conditions set out by the Conventions themselves. This reference in Article 2 to the notion of "protected persons or property" must perforce cover
the persons mentioned in Articles 13, 24, 25 and 26 (protected persons) and 19 and 33
to 35 (protected objects) of Geneva Convention I; in Articles 13, 36, 37 (protected persons) and 29, 24, 25 and 27 (protected objects) of Convention II; in Article 4 of Convention III on prisoners of war; and in Articles 4 and 20 (protected persons) and Articles
18, 19, 21, 22, 33, 53, 57 etc. (protected property) of Convention IV on civilians. Clearly,
these provisions of the Geneva Conventions apply to persons or objects protected only to
the extent that they are caught up in an international armed conflict. By contrast, those
provisions do not include persons or property coming within the purview of common Article 3 of the four Geneva Conventions....

83. We find that our interpretation of Article 2 is the only one warranted by the text
of the Statute and the relevant provisions of the Geneva Conventions, as well as by a logical construction of their interplay as dictated by Article 2. However, we are aware that
this conclusion may appear not to be consonant with recent trends of both State practice
and the whole doctrine of human rights—which, as pointed out below (see paras. 97–127),
tend to blur in many respects the traditional dichotomy between international wars and
civil strife. In this connection the Chamber notes with satisfaction the statement in the
amicus curiae brief submitted by the Government of the United States, where it is contended that:

"the 'grave breaches' provisions of Article 2 of the International Tribunal Statute apply
to armed conflicts of a non-international character as well as those of an international
character." (U.S. Amicus Curiae Brief, at 35.)

This statement, unsupported by any authority, does not seem to be warranted as to the
interpretation of Article 2 of the Statute. Nevertheless, seen from another viewpoint,
there is no gainsaying its significance: that statement articulates the legal views of one of
the permanent members of the Security Council on a delicate legal issue; on this score it
provides the first indication of a possible change in *opinio juris* of States. Were other States
and international bodies to come to share this view, a change in customary law concerning the scope of the "grave breaches" system might gradually materialize. Other elements
pointing in the same direction can be found in the provision of the German Military
Manual mentioned below (para. 131), whereby grave breaches of international human-

itarian law include some violations of common Article 3. In addition, attention can be drawn to the Agreement of 1 October 1992 entered into by the conflicting parties in Bosnia-Herzegovina. Articles 3 and 4 of this Agreement implicitly provide for the prosecution and punishment of those responsible for grave breaches of the Geneva Conventions and Additional Protocol I. As the Agreement was clearly concluded within a framework of an internal armed conflict (see above, para. 73), it may be taken as an important indication of the present trend to extend the grave breaches provisions to such category of conflicts. One can also mention a recent judgement by a Danish court. On 25 November 1994 the Third Chamber of the Eastern Division of the Danish High Court delivered a judgement on a person accused of crimes committed together with a number of Croatian military police on 5 August 1993 in the Croatian prison camp of Dretelj in Bosnia (The Prosecution v. Refik Saric, unpublished (Den. H. Ct. 1994)). The Court explicitly acted on the basis of the "grave breaches" provisions of the Geneva Conventions, more specifically Articles 129 and 130 of Convention III and Articles 146 and 147 of Convention IV (The Prosecution v. Refik Saric, Transcript, at 1 (25 Nov. 1994)), without however raising the preliminary question of whether the alleged offences had occurred within the framework of an international rather than an internal armed conflict (in the event the Court convicted the accused on the basis of those provisions and the relevant penal provisions of the Danish Penal Code. (see *id.* at 7–8)) This judgement indicates that some national courts are also taking the view that the "grave breaches" system may operate regardless of whether the armed conflict is international or internal.

84. Notwithstanding the foregoing, the Appeals Chamber must conclude that, in the present state of development of the law, Article 2 of the Statute only applies to offences committed within the context of international armed conflicts.

Li, J. (concurring in part)

7. Professor Meron states the customary international law of war crimes very correctly and clearly in the following terms:

"Whether the conflicts in Yugoslavia are characterized as internal or international is critically important. The fourth Hague Convention of 1907, which codified the principal laws of war and served as the normative core for the post-World War II war crimes prosecutions, applies to international wars only. The other principal prong of the penal laws of war, the grave breaches provisions of the Geneva Conventions and Protocol I, is also directed to international wars. Violations of common Article 3 of the Geneva Conventions, which concerns internal wars, do not constitute grave breaches giving rise to universal criminal jurisdiction. Were any part of the conflict deemed internal rather than international, the perpetrators of even the worst atrocities might try to challenge prosecutions for war crimes or grave breaches, but not for genocide or crimes against humanity." (Meron, *War Crimes in Yugoslavia and the Development of International Law*, 88 AJIL 78, 80 (1994).)

8. The Final Report of 27 May 1994 of the Commission of Experts established pursuant to Security Council resolution 780 (1992) takes the same view as Professor Meron:

"If a conflict is classified as international, then the grave breaches of the Geneva Conventions, including Additional Protocol I, apply as well as violations of the laws and customs of war. The treaty and customary law applicable to international armed conflict is well-established. The treaty law designed for internal armed conflict is in common [A]rticle 3 of the Geneva Conventions, Additional Protocol II of 1977, and [A]rticle 19 of the 1954 Hague Convention for the Protection of Cultural Property in the Event of Armed Conflict. These legal sources do not use the terms 'grave breaches' or 'war crimes'. Further, the content of customary law applicable to internal armed conflict is debatable. As a result, in general, unless the parties to an internal armed conflict agree otherwise, the only offences committed in internal armed conflict for which universal jurisdiction exists are 'crimes against humanity' and genocide, which apply irrespective of the conflicts' classification." (S/1994/674, p. 13, para. 42.)

9. And the ICRC, an authority on international humanitarian law, in the Preliminary Remarks on the Setting-up of an International Tribunal for the Prosecution of Persons Responsible for Serious Violations of International Humanitarian Law Committed in the Territory of the Former Yugoslavia, "underline[s] the fact that, according to humanitarian law as it stands today, the notion of war crimes is limited to situations of international armed conflict". (DDM/JUR/442 b, 25 March 1993, para. 4.)

10. Now, I may turn to the difference of my opinion from that of the Decision. The Decision asserts that there has been development of customary international law to such an extent that all the various violations of the laws or customs of war as enumerated in lit. (a)–(e) of Article 3 of the Statute of this Tribunal are liable to be prosecuted and punished even if they are committed in internal armed conflict. I cannot agree with this assertion....

12. As regards the interpretative statements of the French, U.S. and U.K. delegates on Article 3 of the Statute in the Security Council when voting on the resolution adopting the Statute, I agree. But these interpretative statements only give grounds for interpreting Article 3 of the Statute as granting the Tribunal the power to prosecute the various violations specified in the two Additional Protocols of 1977 and common Article 3 of the Geneva Conventions of 1949, which interpretation I endorse; they, however, do not maintain that the violations of the laws or customs of war which are enumerated in lit. (a)–(e) and committed in an internal armed conflict should be prosecuted according to Article 3 of the Statute....

Sidhwa, J. (concurring)

117. Article 3 of the Statute lists five offences under paras. (a) to (e), with the condition that "such violations shall include, but not be limited to" the same. The list is therefore illustrative and not limited to the five offences stated. It is clear, therefore, that the 1907 Hague Regulations, the 1949 Geneva Conventions with Additional Protocols I and II, the 1945 Charter of the International Military Tribunal 1945, apart from other conventions, constitute laws of war and that war crimes embodied therein, if they constitute serious violations of international humanitarian law, become offences liable to punishment under Article 3 of the Statute. Likewise, the 1907 Hague Regulations, the 1949 Geneva Conventions with Additional Protocols I and II and the instances given in the decision of the Nurnberg Tribunal, on the authoritative pronouncement of the Secretary-General as contained in para. 44 of his report, constitute, apart from others, the customs of war. There is an overlapping between Articles 2 and 3 of the Statute qua the "grave breaches". Since Article 2 of the Statute specifically deals with the "grave breaches", Article 3 thereof must be taken to cover all other serious violations of the 1949 Geneva Conventions and the Additional Protocols apart from the "grave breaches". Thus, Article 3 of the Statute covers *inter alia* war crimes embodied in the 1949 Geneva Conventions and the two Protocols, excluding the "grave breaches" but including all others, such as Common Article 3 thereof, if they constitute serious violations of international humanitarian law. Article 3 of the Statute would, therefore, cover both international and internal armed conflicts....

Abi-Saab, J. (concurring in part)

One of the merits of the Decision is that by its finding that "grave breaches" are subsumed in the "serious violations of the laws or customs of war" it resituated the Statute firmly within the modern trend recognizing the essential identity of the legal regime of viola-tions of the two strands of the *jus in bello*. But the Decision had to qualify this finding in a manner that would still preserve for Article 2 of the Statute an autonomous field of ap-plication in relation to Article 3, pursuant to the "*effet utile*" principle of interpretation.

While I agree with the way the Decision portrays the relationship between "grave breaches" and "serious violations of the laws or customs of war" as that of species to genus, and I can see some merit in applying them separately "grave breaches" being more con-cretely formulated by reference to the detailed provisions of the Geneva Conventions— I find the "division of labour" between the two Articles of the Statute in the Decision rather artificial. Instead of reaching, as the Decision does, for the acts expressly men-tioned in Article 2 via Article 3 when they are committed in the course of an internal armed conflict, I consider, on the basis of the material presented in the Decision itself, that a strong case can be made for the application of Article 2, even when the incriminated act takes place in an internal conflict.

Admittedly the traditional view, as far as the interpretation of the Geneva Conven-tions is concerned, has been that the "grave breaches" regime does not apply to internal armed conflicts. But the minority view that it does is not devoid of merit if we go by the texts alone and their possible teleological interpretation.

Regardless, however, of the outcome of this initial debate, if we consider the recent developments which are aptly presented in the Decision, we can draw two conclusions from them. The first is that a growing practice and *opinio juris* both of States and international organizations, has established the principle of personal criminal responsibility for the acts figuring in the grave breaches articles as well as for the other serious violations of the *jus in bello*, even when they are committed in the course of an internal armed con-flict. The second conclusion is that in much of this accumulating practice and *opinio juris*, the former acts are expressly designated as "grave breaches" (see Decision para. 83).

This is not a mere question of semantics, but of proper legal classification of this ac-cumulated normative substance, with a view to introducing a modicum of order among the categories of crimes falling within the substantive jurisdiction of the Tribunal.

The legal significance of this substance can be understood in at least two ways other than the one followed by the Decision, in order to bring the acts committed in internal conflicts within the reach of the grave breaches regime in the Geneva Conventions, and consequently of Article 2 of the Statute.

As a matter of treaty interpretation—and assuming that the traditional reading of "grave breaches" has been correct—it can be said that this new normative substance has led to a new interpretation of the Conventions as a result of the "subsequent practice" and *opinio juris* of the States parties: a teleological interpretation of the Conventions in the light of their object and purpose to the effect of including internal conflicts within the regime of "grave breaches". The other possible rendering of the significance of the new nor-mative substance is to consider it as establishing a new customary rule ancillary to the Conventions, whereby the regime of "grave breaches" is extended to internal conflicts. But the first seems to me as the better approach. And under either, Article 2 of the Statute applies—the same as Articles 3, 4 and 5—in both international and internal conflicts.

This construction of Article 2 is supported by the fact that it coincides with the un-derstanding of the parties to the conflict themselves of the legal situation. Thus in their Agreement of 1 October 1992—concerning the implementation of their earlier Agreement of 22 May 1992 which they specifically concluded within the framework of common Ar-ticle 3 of the Geneva Conventions—they excluded from the obligation to release pris-

oners those "accused of or sentenced for, grave breaches ..." (Article 3) . They thus recognized the applicability of the regime of grave breaches in their on-going conflict, which
they had already classified as internal....

Notes and Questions

1. Judge Cassese states that "'persons ... protected under the provisions of the relevant Geneva Conventions'" [see GC art. 147] or "by the Geneva Conventions" do not include persons protected under common Article 3. See *id.* Opinion of Cassese, at para.
81. Does this make sense, especially since common Article 3 applies in all armed conflicts as a minimum standard? Further, he did not mention (but arguably did not exclude) Articles 13 and 16 of Convention IV (Geneva Civilian Convention). *See also id.*,
para. 76. *Cf.* J. Paust, *Applicability of International Criminal Laws to Events in the Former
Yugoslavia, supra* at 512–13, and references cited; *Legal Aspects of the My Lai Incident: A
Response to Professor Rubin*, 50 Ore. L. Rev. 138, 143–49 (1971), reprinted in 3 The Vietnam War and International Law 359 (R. Falk ed., ASIL 1972); Paust & Blaustein,
supra(each demonstrating application of Geneva law even to one's own nationals in certain cases).

How should treaties be interpreted? Customary criteria are reflected in Article 31(1)
of the Vienna Convention on the Law of Treaties, 1155 U.N.T.S. 331, (a treaty must be
interpreted "in accordance with the ordinary meaning to be given to the terms of the
treaty in their context and in light of its object and purpose") and Article 31(3)(b) (and
in accordance with "any subsequent practice in the application of the treaty"). Which interpretation best complies?

2. Was the language quoted from Professor Meron's article by Judge Li (in his para. 7)
correct? Does it ultimately matter whether a violation of common Article 3, which is a
violation of the laws of war and a war crime, is a "grave" breach of the Conventions? FM
27-10, para. 506 b recognizes that "[t]he principles quoted in [, for example, Article 146
of the Geneva Civilian Convention, quoted herein in Chapter Two, Section 3, and addressing grave breaches as well as "all acts contrary to the provisions of the present Convention other than grave breaches"] are declaratory of the obligations of belligerents
under customary international law to take measures for the punishment of war crimes committed by all persons, including members of a belligerent's own armed forces." Recall that
paragraph 499 states that "Every violation of the law of war is a war crime" and that paragraph 507 recognizes "Universality of Jurisdiction" over war crimes. See also Chapter Two,
Section 3 (re: all war crimes), and Chapter Three, Section 1 (same); J. Pictet, I Commentary, *supra* at 367–68 ("the 1929 Convention called for the punishment of *all* acts contrary to the provisions of the Convention ... *all* breaches of the present Convention should
be repressed ... [national legislation] must include a general clause ... providing for the
punishment of other breaches of the Convention."); IV Commentary, *supra* at 583 ("The
Geneva Conventions form part of what are generally called the laws and customs of war,
violations of which are ...'war crimes'"), 587, 590–94 ("must also suppress all other acts
contrary to the provisions of this Convention ... all breaches should be suppressed ...
[and states] should institute judicial or disciplinary punishment for breaches of the Convention."), 597, 602 ("other breaches ... will be punished").

In light of the above, do you find the statements at the end of paragraph 80 of Judge
Cassese's opinion persuasive? Do States have jurisdiction in any event? Do common Articles 1 and 3 of the Geneva Conventions provide another counter to "sovereignty" over
internal armed conflicts? Does universal jurisdiction and responsibility over numerous sorts

of international criminal activity that can occur completely within a State also constitute a counter to such "sovereignty" interests?

Also in light of the above, do you agree with Judges Sidhwa and Abi-Saab that violations of common article 3 of the Geneva Conventions and Protocol II, as part of the laws of war, constitute war crimes? Judge Cassese would also agree. See Cassese opinion, *supra* at paras. 87–127 (adding in para. 89 that Article 3 of the Statute covers, among other war crimes, "violations of common Article 3 and other customary rules on internal conflicts...."); *see also* Meron, *Continuing, supra* at 239, 243; Paust & Blaustein, *supra*. Is a "breach" of common Article 3 a breach of Geneva law?

3. Professor Meron was quoted for the proposition that the customary Hague Convention No. IV of 1907 applies only to "international wars". Do you suspect that a recognized belligerency or true civil war is an "international" war? Recall Paust & Blaustein, *supra*(H.C. IV of 1907, all other customary laws of war, and common Article 2 of the Geneva Conventions apply to a recognized belligerency); U.S. FM 27-10, para. 11 a, *supra*; see also U.S. Dep't of Army Pam. 27-161-2, INTERNATIONAL LAW 27 (1962) ("If a civil war has reached such proportions that the rebellious side is accorded the status of a belligerent the legal effect ... is the same as that of an international war."); 1863 Lieber Code, arts. 149–154; DIG. OPS. OF JAG, ARMY 244 (U.S. 1866) (considered as exemplifying customary international law); BLUNTSCHLI ON THE LAW OF WAR AND NEUTRALITY — A TRANSLATION FROM HIS CODE OF INTERNATIONAL LAW 3–4 (F. Lieber translation) (U.S. Army T.J.A.G. School, ICL library); H. HALLECK, ELEMENTS OF INTERNATIONAL LAW AND LAWS OF WAR 151–53 (1866); I. HYDE, INTERNATIONAL LAW 198 (2 ed. 1947); J. PICTET, III COMMENTARY, *supra* at 38 (quoted above concerning application of the customary laws of war to a belligerency); 2 OPPENHEIM'S INTERNATIONAL LAW 370–72 & n.1 (7 ed. H. Lauterpacht 1948); NATALINO RONZITTI, INTERNATIONAL LAW AND THE USE OF FORCE BY NATIONAL LIBERATION MOVEMENTS (1988); Tom Farer, *The Humanitarian Laws of War in Civil Strife: Toward a Definition of "International Armed Conflict,"* 7 REV. BELGE DE DROIT INT'L 20 (1971); Hans-Peter Gasser, *Der Internationale Strafgerichtshoffür das frühere Jugoslawevien und das "Kriegsrecht und die Kriegagebräuche": Eline Glosse zu Artikel 3 des Statuts,* 2 HUMANITÄREN VÖLKERRECHT INFORMATIONSSCHRIFTEN 60 (1993); Martin Hess, *Die Anwendbarkeit des Humanitären Völkerrechts, insbesondere in gemischten Konflikten,* in 39 SCHWEIZER STUDIEN ZUM INTERNATIONALEN RECHT 150 (1985); Theodor Meron, *War Crimes in Yugoslavia and the Development of International Law,* 88 AM. J. INT'L L. 78 (1994); John E. Parkerson, Jr., *United States Compliance with Humanitarian Law Respecting Civilians During Operation Just Cause,* 133 MIL. L. REV. 31, 35–39 (1991); J. Paust, *Applicability, supra* at 506–10; Yves Sandoz, *Reflexion sur la Mise en Oeuvre du Droit International Humanitaire et sur le Rôle du Comité International de la Croix-Rouge en Ex-Yougoslavie,* 4 REVUE SUISSE DE DROIT INTERNATIONAL ET DE DROIT EUROPÉEN 461 (1993); *see also* Meron, *Continuing, supra* at 242–43 ("I agree that, as a matter of law, some important Hague rules already apply to noninternational armed conflicts....").

The Appeals Chamber in *The Prosecutor v. Dusko Tadic*, at para. 127 (Cassese Op.), had recognized that customary norms applicable to "internal strife" "cover such areas as protection of civilians from hostilities, in particular from indiscriminate attacks, protection of civilian objects, in particular cultural property, protection of all those who do not (or no longer) take active part in hostilities, as well as prohibition of means of warfare proscribed in international armed conflicts and [the] ban of certain methods of conducting hostilities." In *The Prosecutor v. Hadzihasanovic & Kubura*, IT-01-47-AR73.3 (Appeals Chamber, Decision on Joint Defence Interlocutory Appeal of Trial Chamber Decision on Rule 98bis Motions for Acquittal,11 Mar. 2005), the Appeals Chamber found that the war crimes of (1) "wanton destruction of cities, towns or villages not justified by military necessity"; (2) "plunder of public or private property"; and (3) "destruction or wilful damage done to institutions dedicated to religion" apply in internal armed conflicts as well as in international armed conflicts as offenses under customary international law. *Id.* paras. 26–30, 37–38, 44–48.

See also Geneva Protocol II, arts. 4, 13–14, 17; Statute of the ICC, art. 8(2)(e)(i)–(iv), regarding norms other than common Article 3 applicable during an insurgency.

4. It should be noted that Article 38 1(b) of the Statute of the I.C.J. does not include the limiting word "States" with respect to the formation of customary international law through general practice accepted as law.

5. Given the controversial decision in *Tadic* that "grave breaches" of the Geneva Conventions can only occur during an international armed conflict (which is not controversial within the ICTY), the ICTY has had to deal with the issue whether an accused should know that he or she is participating in such an armed conflict when "grave breaches" are charged. In *The Prosecutor v. Naletilic & Martinovic*, IT-98-34-A (Appeals Chamber, 3 May 2006), paras. 113–122, the Appeals Chamber decided that an Appeals Chamber decision in The Prosecutor v. Kordic & Cerkez, IT-95-14/2-A (Appeals Chamber Judgment, 17 Dec. 2004), para. 311, that the accused need not "make a correct legal evaluation as to the international character of the armed conflict," the accused must be "aware of the factual circumstances, *e.g.*, that a foreign state was involved in the armed conflict" [in that case, participation by Croatian troops] (*Kordic & Cerkez* at para. 311) "was correct, and follows logically from the principles established in *Tadic.*" *Naletilic & Martinovic* at para. 113. "The principle of individual guilt requires that an accused can only be convicted for a crime if his *mens rea* comprises the *actus reus* of the crime ... that he knew of the facts that were necessary to make his conduct a crime ... [and] he must have had knowledge of the facts that made his or her conduct criminal." *Id.* para. 114. "The Appeals Chamber concludes that the existence and international character of an armed conflict are both jurisdictional prerequisites (as established in *Tadic*) and substantive elements of crimes pursuant to Article 2 of the Statute.... Thus, the Prosecution's obligation to prove intent also encompasses the accused's knowledge of the facts pertinent to the internationality of an armed conflict.... [T]here has to be a nexus between the act of the accused and the international armed conflict. It is illogical to say that there is such a nexus unless it is proved that the accused has been aware of the factual circumstances concerning the nature of the hostilities.... [T]he Prosecution has to show 'that the accused *knew* that his crimes' had a nexus to an international armed conflict, or at least that he had knowledge of the factual circumstances later bringing the Judges to the conclusion that the armed conflict was an international one.... It is a general principle of criminal law that the correct legal classification of a conduct by the perpetrator is not required. The principle of individual guilt, however, demands sufficient awareness of *factual* circumstances establishing the armed conflict and its (international or internal) character." *Id.* paras. 116–119.

6. The ICTR provided more detail concerning some of the violations of Common Article 3 of the Geneva Conventions, as limited by Article 4 (e) of the Statute of the ICTR (to "serious violations") in *The Prosecutor v. Musema*, ICTR-96-13-T (27 Jan. 2000):

285.... Required elements of Article 4 (e) of the Statute of the Tribunal

a) *Humiliating and degrading treatment*: Subjecting victims to treatment designed to subvert their self-regard. Like outrages upon personal dignity, these offences may be regarded as a lesser forms of torture; moreover ones in which the motives required for torture would not be required, nor would it be required that the acts be committed under state authority.

b) *Rape*: The specific elements of rape are stated in Section 3.3. on Crime against Humanity in the Applicable Law. [see Chapter Nine, Section 5]

c) *Indecent assault*: The accused caused the infliction of pain or injury by an act which was of a sexual nature and inflicted by means of coercion, force, threat or intimidation and was non-consensual.

The violation must be serious

286. Article 4 of the Statute states that "The International Tribunal for Rwanda shall have the power to prosecute persons committing or ordering to be committed serious violations of Common Article 3 and of the Additional Protocol II". The Trial Chamber in the *Akayesu* Judgement understood, in line with the Appeals Chamber Decision in *Tadic* that the phrase "serious violation" means "a breach of a rule protecting important values which must involve grave consequences for the victim".

287. The list of serious violations provided in Article 4 of the Statute is taken from Common Article 3 of the Geneva Conventions and of Additional Protocol II, which outline "Fundamental Guarantees"as a humanitarian minimum of protection for war victims. The list in Article 4 of the Statute thus comprises serious violations of the fundamental humanitarian guarantees which, as has been stated above, are recognised as customary international law.

288. In the opinion of the Chamber, violations of these fundamental humanitarian guarantees, by their very nature, are therefore to be considered as serious.

7. In view of the above, do you think that stripping persons naked and hooding them as an interrogation tactic is "humiliating" and/or "degrading"? Is it "cruel" or "inhuman" treatment? Would the use of snarling dogs to instill intense fear or even terrorism constitute cruel, inhuman, degrading, or humiliating treatment? Would waterboarding (used to instill an intense and terrifying fear of drowning)? Would an interrogation tactic of "the cold cell" (where a naked detainee is kept in a cell cooled to 50 degrees and periodically doused with cold water), "fear up harsh: significantly increasing the fear level in a detainee," or "yelling to create fear" constitute cruel, inhuman, degrading, or humiliating treatment? These interrogation tactics were authorized by members of the Bush Administration for use against persons detained during the wars in Afghanistan and Iraq. *See, e.g.*, Paust, *The Absolute Prohibition of Torture and Necessary and Appropriate Sanctions*, 43 VALP. U. L. REV. 1535, 1553–58 (2009), available at http://ssrn.com/asbtract=1331159; Paust, *Executive Plans*, *supra* at 812, 824–51, adding: in *Ireland v. United Kingdom* [25 Eur. Ct. H.R. (ser. A) at 5 (1971)], the European Court of Human Rights ruled that British interrogation tactics of wall-standing (forcing the detainees to remain for periods of some hours in a "stress position"), hooding, subjection to noise, deprivation of sleep, and deprivation of food and drink "constituted a practice of inhuman and degrading treatment" proscribed under human rights law.[16] In 1996, the European Court recognized that where a detainee "was

---

16. *Id*. at 41, para. 96, 66, para. 167. The court noted that the "techniques were applied in combination, with premeditation and for hours at a stretch; they caused, if not bodily injury, at least intense physical and mental suffering to the persons subjected thereto and also led to acute psychiatric disturbances during interrogation," and, "accordingly," were forms of inhuman treatment. *Id*. at 66, para. 167. The Court concluded that the "techniques were also degrading, since they were such as to arouse in their victims feelings of fear, anguish and inferiority capable of humiliating and debasing them and possibly breaking their physical or moral resistance."

stripped naked, with his arms tied behind his back and suspended by his arms ... [, s]uch treatment amounted to torture."[17] In another case, the European Court stated that treatment was "'degrading' because it was such as to arouse in its victims feelings of fear, anguish and inferiority capable of humiliating and debasing them."[18] The International Criminal Tribunal for Former Yugoslavia has also identified criteria for determining whether certain conduct constitutes criminally sanctionable "torture"[19] or "cruel" or "inhuman" treatment.[20] Moreover, the Committee against Torture created under the Convention Against Torture and Other Cruel, Inhuman or Degrading Treatment or Punishment has condemned the use of the following interrogation tactics as either torture or cruel, inhuman or degrading treatment: (1) restraining in very painful conditions, (2) hooding under special conditions, (3) sounding of loud music for prolonged periods, (4) sleep deprivation for prolonged periods, (5) threats, including death threats, (6) violent shaking, and (7) using cold air to chill [Concluding Observations of the Committee against Torture: Israel, 18th Sess., U.N. Doc. A/52/44 (1997) at paras. 256–257.]. Earlier, a U.S. Army pamphlet addressing Geneva and other law of war proscriptions warned that an illegal means of interrogation of a detainee included "dunking his head into a barrel of water, or putting a plastic bag over his head to make him talk," adding: "No American soldier can commit these brutal acts, nor permit his fellow soldiers to do so."

8. The Army has charged the former head of the interrogation center at Abu Ghraib prison with criminal charges in connection with the abuses at the prison. Ten lower-ranking soldiers who served at the prison outside Baghdad have been convicted for abusing prisoners, including an Army dog handler who was sentenced to incarceration for six

---

17. Aksoy v. Turkey, 6 Eur. Ct. H.R. 2260, 23 EHRR 553, at paras. 60, 64 (18 Dec. 1996). The Court stated that "torture attaches only to deliberate inhuman treatment causing very serious and cruel suffering." *Id.* at paras. 63–64. The victim was detained for some two weeks and had claimed to have been subjected to beatings and had been stripped naked, hooded, and subjected to electric shocks. *Id.* at paras. 60, 64.

18. T & V v. United Kingdom, Judgment of 16 Dec. 1999, at para. 71, 30 EHRR 121 (2000).

19. *See, e.g.,* The Prosecutor v. Kunarac, IT-96-23-T & IT-96-23/1-T (Trial Chamber, International Criminal Tribunal for Former Yugoslavia), para. 497 (22 Feb. 2001) (intentional "infliction, by act or omission, of severe pain or suffering, whether physical or mental"); *Id.* (Appeals Chamber, 12 June 2002), para. 149 (adding "but there are no more specific requirements which allow an exhaustive classification or enumeration of acts which may constitute torture. Existing case law has not determined the absolute degree of pain required for an act to amount to torture"), para. 150 (rape can constitute torture); The Prosecutor v. Naletilic & Martinovic, IT-98-34-A (Appeals Chamber, 3 May 2006), paras. 299–300 (quoted in Chapter Eleven); The Prosecutor v. Furundzija, IT-95-17/1 (Trial Chamber, Judgment), paras. 159–64 (10 Dec. 1998) (sexual violence can constitute torture); The Prosecutor v. Kvocka, IT-98-30/1 (Trial Chamber, Judgment), para. 149 (2 Nov. 2001) (same); William A. Schabas, *The Crime of Torture and the International Criminal Tribunals*, 37 CASE W. RES. J. INT'L L. 349, 362–63 (2006) (addressing decisions of the ICTR and ICTY regarding rape and sexual violence as torture); Johan D. van der Vyver, *Torture as a Crime Under International Law*, 67 ALBANY L. REV. 427 (2003).

20. With respect to "cruel" treatment, a trial chamber of the ICTY declared that "cruel treatment is treatment which causes serious mental or physical suffering and constitutes a serious attack on human dignity." The Prosecutor v. Delalic, IT-96-21-T (Trial Chamber, International Criminal Tribunal for Former Yugoslavia), para. 551 (Nov. 16, 1998). The same decision recognized that "inhuman treatment is an intentional act or omission, that is an act which, when judged objectively, is deliberate and not accidental, which causes serious mental or physical suffering or injury or constitutes a serious attack on human dignity." *Id.* at para. 543. Other ICTY cases confirm the *Delalic* recognitions. *See, e.g.,* KNUT DORMANN, ELEMENTS OF WAR CRIMES UNDER THE ROME STATUTE OF THE INTERNATIONAL CRIMINAL COURT 65 n.72 (re: inhuman), 398–99 ns. 7–8 (re: cruel) (2003).... With respect to torture, see also Zubeda v. Ashcroft, 333 F.3d 463, 472 (3d Cir. 2003) ("[r]ape can constitute torture"); Al-Saher v. I.N.S., 268 F.3d 1143, 1147 (9th Cir. 2001).

months for using his snarling canine to torment Iraqi prisoners. Former Cpl. Charles Graner Jr. received the longest sentence—10 years in prison. Army Reservist Lynndie England, photographed giving a thumbs-up in front of naked prisoners, is serving a three year prison term.

9. Is terrorism unknown to the laws of war? *See, e.g.,* the 1919 List of War Crimes, GC art. 33; United States v. von Leeb, extract *infra.*

B. Conduct of Hostilities and Other Protections

U.S. Dep't of Army FM 27-10, The Law of Land Warfare
(1956)

[para. 3] a. Prohibitory Effect. The law of war places limits on the exercise of belligerent's power ... and requires that all belligerents refrain from employing any kind or degree of violence which is not actually necessary for military purposes and that they conduct hostilities with regard for the principles of humanity and chivalry.

The prohibitory effect of the law of war is not minimized by "military necessity" which has been defined as that principle which justifies those measures not forbidden by international law which are indispensable for securing the complete submission of the enemy as soon as possible. Military necessity has been generally rejected as a defense for acts forbidden by the customary and conventional laws of war inasmuch as the latter have been developed and framed with consideration for the concept of military necessity.

b. Binding on States and Individuals. The law of war is binding not only upon States as such but also upon individuals and, in particular, the members of their armed forces....

25.... [I]t is a generally recognized rule of international law that civilians must not be made the object of attack directed exclusively against them.... [*compare* Article 51(3) of Protocol I]

28. Refusal of Quarter

It is especially forbidden ... to declare that no quarter will be given.

29. Injury Forbidden After Surrender

It is especially forbidden ... to kill or wound an enemy who, having laid down his arms, or having no longer means of defense, has surrendered at discretion.

30. Persons Descending by Parachute

The law of war does not prohibit firing upon paratroopers or other persons who are or appear to be bound upon hostile missions while such persons are descending by parachute. Persons other than those mentioned in the preceding sentence who are descending by parachute from disabled aircraft may not be fired upon.

31. Assassination and Outlawry

[The Hague Convention] provides:

It is especially forbidden ... to kill or wound treacherously individuals belonging to the hostile nation or army.

This article is construed as prohibiting assassination, proscription, or outlawry of an enemy, or putting a price upon an enemy's head, as well as offering a reward for an enemy "dead or alive". It does not, however, preclude attacks on individual soldiers or officers of the enemy whether in the zone of hostilities, occupied territory or elsewhere....

39. Bombardment of Undefended Places Forbidden

The attack or bombardment, by whatever means, of towns, villages, dwellings, or buildings which are undefended is prohibited. (HR, art. 25.) ...

41. Unnecessary Killing and Devastation

Particularly in the circumstances referred to in the preceding paragraph, loss of life and damage to property must not be out of proportion to the military advantage to be gained. Once a fort or defended locality has surrendered, only such further damage is permitted as is demanded by the exigencies of war, such as the removal of fortifications, demolition of military buildings, and destruction of stores.

42. Aerial Bombardment

There is no prohibition of general application against bombardment from the air of combatant troops, defended places, or other legitimate military objectives....

47. Pillage Forbidden

The pillage of a town or place, even when taken by assault, is prohibited. (HR, art. 28.) ...

56. Devastation

The measure of permissible devastation is found in the strict necessities of war. Devastation as an end in itself or as a separate measure of war is not sanctioned by the law of war. There must be some reasonably close connection between the destruction of property and the overcoming of the enemy's army. Thus the rule requiring respect for private property is not violated through damage resulting from operations, movements, or combat activity of the army; that is, real estate may be used for marches, camp sites, construction of field fortifications, etc. Buildings may be destroyed for sanitary purposes or used for shelter for troops, the wounded and sick and vehicles and for reconnaissance, cover, and defense. Fences, wood, crops, buildings, etc., may be demolished, cut down, and removed to clear a field of fire, to clear the ground for landing fields, or to furnish building materials or fuel if imperatively needed for the army....

57. Protection of Artistic and Scientific Institutions and Historic Monuments

The United States and certain of the American Republics are parties to the so-called [1935] Roerich Pact, which accords a neutralized and protected status to historic monuments, museums, scientific, artistic, educational, and cultural institutions in the event of war between such States.

[See also Convention (and Regulations and Protocol) for the Protection of Cultural Property in the Event of Armed Conflict, done at the Hague, May 14, 1954, 249 U.N.T.S. 240.]

58. Destruction and Seizure of Property

It is especially forbidden ... to destroy or seize the enemy's property, unless such destruction or seizure be imperatively demanded by the necessities of war.

59. Booty of War

a. Public Property. All enemy public movable property captured or found on a battlefield becomes the property of the capturing State.

The Declaration of St. Petersburg
(1868) (extract)

... Considering that the progress of civilization should have the effect of alleviating as much as possible the calamities of war;

That the only legitimate object which States should endeavor to accomplish during War is to weaken the military forces of the enemy;

That for this purpose it is sufficient to disable the greatest number of men;

That this object would be exceeded by the employment of arms which uselessly aggravate the sufferings of disabled men, or renders their death inevitable;

That the employment of such arms would therefore be contrary to the laws of humanity;

The Contracting Parties engage mutually to renounce ... the employment by their military or naval troops of any projectile of a weight below 400 grammes [some 14 ounces], which is either explosive or charged with fulminating or inflammable substances....

Hague Declaration No. IV
July 29, 1899, para. 3

The Contracting Parties agree to abstain from the use of bullets which expand or flatten easily in the human body, such as bullets with a hard envelope which does not entirely cover the core, or is pierced with incisions.

Geneva Protocol of 1925 (Protocol prohibiting the use in War of Asphyxiating, Poisonous or other Gases, and of Bacteriological Methods of Warfare)
done in Geneva 17 June 1925,
L.N.T.S. 1929 No. 2138, 26 U.S.T. 571, T.I.A.S. No. 8061

... Whereas the use in war of asphyxiating, poisonous or other gases, and all analogous liquids, materials or devices, has been justly condemned by the general opinion of the civilized world; ...

To the end that this prohibition shall be universally accepted as a part of International Law, binding alike the conscience and the practice of nations;

Declare:

That the High Contracting Parties, so far as they are not already Parties to Treaties prohibiting such use, accept this prohibition, agree to extend this prohibition to the use of bacteriological methods of warfare and agree to be bound as between themselves according to the terms of this declaration....

Hague Convention (No. IV) Respecting the Laws and Customs of War
(1907)

[read the extracts of HC IV in the Documents Supplement]

Notes and Questions

1. Concerning the prohibition of assassination more generally, recall Chapter Three, Section 1 and Chapter Five, Section 5 C.

2. There are many developments concerning the regulation of weaponry. Consider, for example, Convention on the Prohibition of the Development, Production and Stockpiling of Bacteriological (Biological) and Toxin Weapons and on Their Destruction, done in London, Moscow and Washington, April 10, 1972, 26 U.S.T. 583, T.I.A.S. No. 8062; Convention on the Prohibition of Military or Any Other Hostile Use of Environmental Modification Techniques, 1970, 1108 U.N.T.S. 88 (1977); Convention on Prohibitions or Restrictions on the Use of Certain Conventional Weapons Which May be Deemed to Be Excessively Injurious or to Have Indiscriminate Effects, and Protocols I-III, U.N. Doc. A/CONF. 95/15 (1980), in 19 I.L.M. 1523 (1980); Declaration on the Prohibition of Chemical Weapons, Paris, Jan. 11, 1989, in 28 I.L.M. 1020 (1989); Convention on the Prohibition of the Development, Production, Stockpiling and Use of Chemical Weapons and on their Destruction, Jan. 13, 1993, in 32 I.L.M. 800 (1993); Convention on the Prohibition of the Use, Stockpiling, Production and Transfer of Anti-Personnel Mines and their Destruction, in 36 I.L.M. 1507 (1997); Hans-Peter Gasser, *For Better Protection of the Natural Environment in Armed Conflict: A Proposal for Action*, 89 Am. J. Int'l L. 637 (1995); Janet Lord, *Legal Restraints in the Use of Landmines: Humanitarian and Environmental Crisis*, 25 Cal. W.L.J. 311 (1995); Rex J. Zedalis, *The Chemical Weapons Convention Implementation Act: United States Control over Exports*, 90 Am. J. Int'l L. 138 (1996); Special Issue on Disarmament, 28 McGill L. J. 453 (1983). Does the U.S. have the right unilaterally to destroy an Iranian chemical weapons facility? Recall Chapter Seven, Section 2 D. If it is targeted during an armed conflict with Iran?

3. Concerning conventional weaponry, it should be noted that some weapons are prohibited *per se* and, therefore, may never be used, while other weapons are regulated by general principles of necessity and proportionality and more specific customary or treaty-based norms. As noted below, the use of poison for any purpose is absolutely forbidden. Also, the absolute prohibitions of weapons covered by the 1868 St. Petersburg Declaration and the 1899 Hague Declaration No. IV are customary prohibitions, and the Hague Declaration's language appears in the Rome Statute of the ICC, art. 8(2)(ix). Language in the first part of the Geneva Protocol of 1925 appears in the Rome Statute, art. 8(2)(b)(xviii). *See generally* J. Paust, *Does Your Police Force Use Illegal Weapons? A Configurative Approach to Decision Integrating International and Domestic Law*, 18 Harv. Int'l L. J. 19, 29–37 (1977); U.S. FM 27-10, at paras. 34–38; Note 1 *supra*.

4. The French text of Article 23 (e) of the Annex to Hague Convention No. IV does not contain the word "calculated" and it is the authoritative text. The French text retained the wording from the 1899 Hague Convention No. II, July 29, 1899, Annex, Art. 23 (e): "of a nature to cause superfluous injury" ("*propres a causer des maux superflus*"). Under customary law, the words "unnecessary" and "superfluous" are now interchangeable in this regard. *See, e.g.,* Paust, *Does Your Police Force Use Illegal Weapons?, supra* at 30 n.43. *See also* Article 8 (2)(b)(xx) of the Statute of the ICC ("of a nature to cause"). However, there is a limitation in the ICC article which is not a customary limitation (*i.e.,* "provided that such ... are the subject of a comprehensive prohibition and are included in an annex to this Statute" created by an amendment).

5. What is the nature of the prohibition of "poison" and "asphyxiating, poisonous or other gases"? Consider the following: Customary international law reflected in Article 23(a) of the 1907 Hague Convention expressly affirms the *per se* prohibition of poi-

son—that is, it may never be used under any circumstances and, thus, regardless of attempts at justification or claims of military necessity. See also Captain Paul A. Robblee, *The Legitimacy of Modern Conventional Weaponry*, 71 MIL. L. REV. 95, 101–02, 104–05, 110 (1976). It does not matter how poison is employed (*e.g.*, by pellet, liquid or gas, dropped by hand or modern aircraft) and it does not matter against whom the poison is employed (*e.g.*, solely against enemy combatants, against a mixture of enemy combatants and noncombatants, or in areas inhabited merely by noncombatants), since by the plain meaning of Article 23(a) it is prohibited "to employ" poison in any manner. Further, the treaty does not merely prohibit "poisoned weapons," but also prohibits the employment of "poison," *i.e.*, one is prohibited "[t]o employ poison" of any sort in any manner. With respect to poisonous effects of herbicides, in 1945 the Judge Advocate General of the U.S. Army recognized the dynamic reach of the customary prohibition of poison to gases and "crop-destroying chemicals which can be sprayed by airplane." See Major General Myron C. Cramer, Memorandum for the Secretary of War, Subject: Destruction of Crops by Chemicals, SPJGW 1945/164 (Mar. 1945), reprinted in 10 I.L.M. 1304 (1971).

Long ago, the authoritative 1863 Lieber Code recognized that customary laws of war prohibited "the use of poison in any way," even in the face of claims of "military necessity" (Article 16) and that "[t]he use of poison in any manner, be it to poison wells, or food, or arms, is wholly excluded from modern warfare. He that uses it puts himself out of the pale of the law and usages of war" (Article 70). The "[p]oisoning of wells" also appears in a list of customary war crimes recognized by the Commission on the Responsibility of the Authors of the War and on Enforcement of Penalties that was presented to the Preliminary Peace Conference in Paris following World War I. See List of War Crimes, No. 32 (1919). The U.S. Army Field Manual utilized during the Vietnam War (and still today) also recognized that it is a war crime to employ poison. FM 27-10, *supra* at 18, para. 37, 180, para. 504(i). More generally, it was known by the Founders that "poisoners ... by profession" were international criminals. *See, e.g.*, 1 Op. Att'y Gen. 509, 515 (1821), quoting E. DE VATTEL, THE LAW OF NATIONS (1758).

The United Kingdom also recognized prior to the Vietnam War that "using asphyxiating, poisonous or other gases, and all analogous liquids, materials or devices" is a war crime. 1958 UK MANUAL, *supra* at 175, para. 626(r). Importantly, the "[u]se of deleterious and asphyxiating gases" also appears on the 1919 List of War Crimes, No. 26. Thus, prior to adoption of the 1925 Geneva Protocol, use of "deleterious and asphyxiating gases" as well as poison in any form had already been recognized as per se violations of the customary laws of war. An important issue, therefore, is whether use of particular herbicides or other chemicals in spray form or gas was "deleterious" or "asphyxiating" even if use of others would not have reached these customary legal triggers. Further, the customary prohibitions shed light on the meaning of certain phrases in the 1925 Geneva Protocol. When the drafters of the 1925 Protocol affirmed that "use in war of asphyxiating, poisonous or other gases, and of all analogous liquids, materials or devices, has been justly condemned by the general opinion of the civilized world," the drafters recognized and affirmed what we would term today a pattern of general *opinio juris* that recognizably condemned their use. Similarly, when the drafters recognized that "such use has been declared in Treaties to which the majority of Powers of the world are Parties," the drafters were affirming that a general *opinio juris* was extant and reflected also in treaties.

Importantly also, in 1945 the Cramer Memorandum addressed "certain crop-destroying chemicals which can be sprayed by airplane" recognized that "a customary rule of international law has developed by which poisonous gases and those causing unnecessary suffering are prohibited," these include "poisonous and deleterious gases," and customary law requires that "chemicals do not produce poisonous effects upon enemy personnel, either from direct contact, or indirectly from ingestion of plants and vegetables which have been exposed thereto," adding that "[w]hether ... agents ... are toxic ... is a question of fact which should definitely be ascertained." See Cramer, Memorandum, *supra*, reprinted in 10 I.L.M. 1304, 1305–06 (1971). *See also* DOD General Counsel J. Fred Buzhardt, letter to Senator J.W. Fulbright (Apr. 5, 1971) ("chemical herbicides, harmless to man," would not be proscribed per se, but "as poison..., their use against crops intended solely for the consumption by the enemy's forces would clearly have been prohibited by Article 23(a) of the Hague Regulations ... [which], in effect, declares that any use of a lethal substance against human beings is, per se, a use which is calculated to cause unnecessary suffering."), reprinted in 10 I.L.M. 1300, 1302 (1971) (stating that his opinion was also "that of the Judge Advocate Generals of the Army, Navy and Air Force"). "The weight of opinion [in 1970] appears ... to favor the view that customary international law proscribes the use in war of lethal chemical and biological weapons," but a question remained whether it outlawed *per se* any "use of tear gas and herbicides" as opposed to their particular use or effects that violated relevant international law. Richard R. Baxter & Thomas Buergenthal, *Legal Aspects of the Geneva Protocol of 1925*, 64 Am. J. Int'l L. 853, 853–54 (1970). Their study also noted that the U.S. was concerned whether all "irritant chemicals (tear gas) and anti-plant chemicals" fell per se "within the prohibition of the use in war of "'other gases.'" See *id*. at 855, 857 & n.18 (re: U.S. statement to the U.N. General Assembly regarding riot control agents), 859, 861. There were suggestions that the phrase "other gases" that were prohibited per se should only apply "to chemical agents similar to those of asphyxiating or poisonous gases." *Id*. at 856–57.

Was the use of certain herbicides during the Vietnam War a violation of the laws of war? *Cf In re* Agent Orange Litigation, 373 F. Supp.2d 7 (E.D.N.Y. 2005), *aff'd*, 517 F.3d 104 (2d Cir. 2008). Would they be today?

6. What is the nature of "military necessity"? Does this principle allow use of force that is merely beneficial in carrying out a necessary military operation or force that is proportionate to a military advantage? See Paust, *Weapons Regulation, Military Necessity and Legal Standards: Are Contemporary Department of Defense Practices Inconsistent with Legal Norms?*, 4 Den. J. Int'l L. & Pol. 229 (1974), adding:

> it must be emphasized that it has never been an accepted international legal standard in modern times that armed forces can employ any form or intensity of violence which is consistent with or helpful in the attainment of a legitimate military objective. Such an approach is far too broad. It amounts to a military "benefit" test as opposed to a military "necessity" test, and the military benefit or "*Kriegsraison*" theory was expressly repudiated at Nuremberg.

See also *United States v. List*, *infra*; M. McDougal & F. Feliciano, Law and Minimum World Public Order 520 (1961); M. Greenspan, The Modern Law of Land Warfare 297 (1959); U.S. Department of Army Pam. No. 27-161-2, International Law 9–10 (1962).

7. For an analysis of the law of air warfare or aerial bombardment *compare* H. DeSaussure, *The Laws of Air Warfare: Are There Any?*, in The Int'l Lawyer (1971); Law and Responsibility in Warfare: The Vietnam Experience 119–149 (P. Trooboff ed., ASIL 1975); *with* J. Paust, *My Lai and Vietnam, supra* at 140 n.156 and 146–153. See also J. M. Spaight, Air Power and War Rights (3 ed. 1947); M. Greenspan, The Modern Law of Land Warfare 351–353 (1959); M. McDougal & F. Feliciano, Law and

MINIMUM WORLD PUBLIC ORDER 79–80 (1961); II OPPENHEIM'S INTERNATIONAL LAW 516–533 (7 ed. 1952).

Do the 1949 Geneva Conventions apply? *See, e.g.,* common Article 3; Geneva Civilian Convention, Articles 4 ("in the hands of"), 13, 16; Protocol I, Articles 51, 75(1) ("in the power of"), 75(2); IV COMMENTARY at 47 ("'in the hands of' is used in an extremely general sense. It is not merely a question of being in enemy hands directly, as a prisoner is. The mere fact of being in the territory of a Party to the conflict or in occupied territory implies that one is in the power or 'hands' of the Occupying Power").

When U.S. Navy Seals killed Osama bin Laden in his compound in norther Pakistan on May 2, 2011, assuming that he had not surrendered, was bin Laden "in the hands of" or "in the power of" the Seals team? Consider Hague Convention No. IV, Annex, art. 23 (b) ("it is especially forbidden ... [t]o kill or wound treacherously individuals belonging to the hostile nation or army"),(c) ("it is especially forbidden ... [t]o kill or wound an enemy who, having laid down his arms, or having no longer means of defence, has surrendered"); Rome Statute of the ICC, art. 8(2)(b)(vi) (same re: a "combatant" who "has surrendered"), (xi) (Killing or wounding treacherously individuals belonging to the hostile nation or army"); Jordan J. Paust, *Permissible Self-Defense Targeting and the Death of bin Laden*, 39 DENV. J. INT'L L. & POL'Y 569, 578–83 (2011).

8. Recall paragraph 25 of FM 27-10. Geneva Protocol I, arts. 48 and 51 require that parties to an international armed conflict "distinguish between the civilian population and combatants and between civilian objects and military objectives and accordingly shall direct their operations only against military objectives" (art. 48, which articulates the principle of distinction) and that "[t]he civilian population as such, as well as individual civilians, shall not be the object of attack" (art. 51(2)). However, "[c]ivilians shall enjoy the protection afforded ... unless and for such time as they take a direct part in hostilities" (art. 51(3)). When a civilian takes a direct part in hostilities such a person is a DPH and is targetable. This set of customary rules is well-known, but it is not always agreed exactly what forms of civilian participation in hostilities are "direct" and subject a civilian to permissible attack. Consider the following extract from Paust, *Self-Defense Targetings of Non-State Actors and Permissibility of U.S. Use of Drones in Pakistan*, 19 J. TRANSNAT'L L. & POL'Y 237 (2010), available at http://ssrn.com/abstract=1520717 :

An extremely restrictive view of direct and active participation might involve the claim that civilians who are members of a non-state organization engaged in armed attacks can only be targeted during the time that they actually carry out the attacks. *See also* ... Inter-American Commission on Human Rights Report on Terrorism and Human Rights, OEA/Ser.L/v/II.116, Doc. 5, rev. 1 corr. (Oct. 22, 2002), at para. 69, which noted that "[i]t is possible ... [that the fighter "who engaged in hostilities"] cannot ... revert back to civilian status or otherwise alternate between combatant and civilian status"). The more realistic and policy-serving view is that such persons who directly participate in a process of armed attacks over time *are* directly and actively taking a part in hostilities. It is not a question of formal status, but of direct and active participation over time....

Importantly, the International Committee of the Red Cross has recognized that such non-state fighters can be recognized as "members" of "organized armed groups ... [that consist] of individuals whose continuous function is to take a direct part in hostilities ('continuous combat function' [CCF])" or "members of an organized armed group with a continuous combat function" and that they are targetable. *See* ICRC, GUIDANCE ON THE NOTION OF DIRECT PARTICIPATION IN HOSTILITIES UNDER INTERNATIONAL HUMANITARIAN LAW 16, 27, 36, 70–73 (2009). The ICRC adds that "members of organized armed groups ... cease to be civilians ... and lose protection against direct attack." *Id.* at 17. The ICRC would distinguish such member-fighters or "fighting forces" "from civilians who directly participate in hostilities on a merely spontaneous, sporadic, or unorganized basis." *Id.* at 34. The latter are targetable when they directly participate in hostilities. Moreover, direct participation in hostilities by civilians includes their "[m]easures preparatory to the execution of a specific act ... as well as the deployment to and the return from a location of its execution." *Id.* at 17, 65–68. *See also* YORAM DINSTEIN, THE CONDUCT OF HOSTILITIES UNDER THE LAW OF INTERNATIONAL ARMED CONFLICT 27–29 (2004) (preferring that civilians who are directly participating lose civilian status); NILS MELZER, TARGETED KILLING IN INTERNATIONAL LAW 56, 310, 314, 317 (general practice is "to directly attack insurgents" or organized armed groups "even when they are not engaged in a particular military operation," the practice is not internationally condemned, and "members of organized armed groups ... are not regarded as civilians, but as approximately equivalent to State armed forces" for targeting purposes), 319–20, 327–28 (those with "functional 'combatancy'" are targetable), 345 (direct participation is "reached where a civilian supplies ammunition to an operational firing position, arms an airplane with bombs for a concrete attack, or transports combatants to an operational combat area") (2008); *Public Committee Against Torture v. Government of Israel*, HCJ 769/02 (S.Ct. Israel Dec. 14, 2006), para. 39 ("a civilian who has joined a terrorist organization ... and in the framework of his role in that organization he commits a chain of hostilities, with short periods of rest between them, loses his immunity from attack").

A major problem with the ICRC's preference concerning "sporadic" fighters is that military forces engaged in targetings might not be able to tell whether a fighter is a member of an organized group or only joins in sporadically. *See also* MELZER, *supra* at 319 (it may be "problematic in operational reality").

Do you suspect that one who directly finances hostilities is a DPH? *See* ICRC GUIDANCE, *supra* at 51–52, 54 (economic or financial activities engaged in by civilians may be "war-sustaining activities," but not direct participation in hostilities); MELZER, *supra* at 341, 345; *Public Committee Against Torture v. Israel, supra* at para. 35 ("a person who sells food or medicine to an unlawful combatant is not taking a direct part, rather an indirect part in hostilities. The same is the case regarding a person who aids the unlawful combatants by general strategic analysis, and grants them logistical general support, including monetary aid"). *But see* Amos N. Guiora, *Proportionality "Re-Configured,"* in 31 ABA NAT. SEC. L. RPT. 9, 13 (Feb. 2009) (arguing for a change in law to allow targeting of those who are merely "passive supporters" of hostilities). Professor David Luban notes why such an expansive form of targeting is unacceptable. *See* David Luban, *Was the Gaza Campaign Legal?, id.* at 15–16. Note that the 1863 Lieber Code contained two articles that recognized a need to make a distinction—Article 22 ("the distinction between the private individual ... and the hostile country itself, with its men in arms" and "the unarmed citizen is to be spared in person") and Article 23 ("Private citizens ... the inoffensive individual").

Do you agree with the ICRC approach, that persons who are not "combatants," but who are members of an organized armed group and have a continuous combat function (CCF) are targetable?

In 2009, the U.S. used a drone to kill a top Taliban leader inside Pakistan who was directly participating in armed hostilities. The targeting also resulted in the deaths of his wife, his wife's parents, his uncle, a Taliban lieutenant, and seven bodyguards. Was the targeting permissible? Was it in compliance with the principle of proportionality? Would you want to know additional facts? Why?

9. During the 1991 Gulf War, the U.S. used "smart" weaponry to specifically target what it stated was a sophisticated communications and intelligence center located in a bunker near civilian buildings and also misused by civilians as an air raid shelter. The Iraqis claimed that it was an example of unnecessary killing of civilians. Several bodies were seen being lifted out of the targeted bunker, most without clothing (which may be suspicious). Do you suspect that such a targeting was a war crime? Explain. See also Article 51 of Geneva Protocol I (in the Documents Supplement).

10. During the 1991 Gulf War, if Iraq, which had occupied Kuwait, targeted Kuwaiti oil wells when leaving occupied Kuwait, what international norms do you suspect would have been violated? See Articles 53 and 147 of the 1949 Geneva Civilian Convention; Geneva Protocol I, arts. 52, 55; H.C. No. IV, Annex, arts. 23(g), 46, 55. Recall Article 19(3)(d) of the International Law Commission's Draft Convention on State Responsibility, in Chapter Seven, Section 2 C. What human rights might also be implicated with respect to massive environmental pollution? Would the targeting of oil storage tanks of use to the enemy military be impermissible?

11. During the 1999 NATO air strikes in Kosovo, would the targeting of a major bridge in Belgrade, Yugoslavia that was used by the Yugoslavian military have been a proper military target? When it was known that thousands of civilians were on the bridge in the evening during a candlelight procession to protect the bridge?

12. It is expected that there will be an increased use of drones and other robotics during armed conflicts and measures of self-defense within or outside the context of war. Already there have been uses of "remotely piloted" land-based, naval, and air and space robotics. For example, remotely controlled robots are used during war and domestic law enforcement to find and dismantle explosives and some can sniff for chemical or bacteriological/biological weaponry. Some fully autonomous vehicles, mines, and other mechanisms are not "piloted," but are addressed. One publication notes that "[a]utonomous systems are also part of the projected ground forces" and that there will be "a reconfigurable skirmishing vehicle," a "'stealth tank,'" "unmanned supply lorries and mine-clearing vehicles," "a small, tracked robot vehicle that can undertake missions normally done by a single soldier;" and "aerial robots dropping ground robots and using a few special forces to guide them." *Autonomous Vehicles: Robot Wars*, ENGINEER, June 6, 2011, at 20. Concerning various types of military robotics, see Patrick Lin, George Bekey & Keith Abney, *Autonomous Military Robotics: Risk, Ethics, and Design* 1, 5–6, 11–19 (Dec. 20, 2008), available at http://www.ethics.calpoly.edu/ONR_report.pdf. Consider this revised extract from Paust, *Remotely Piloted Warfare as a Challenge to the* Jus ad Bellum, in OXFORD HANDBOOK ON THE USE OF FORCE IN INTERNATIONAL LAW (Marc Weller ed. 2013):

Drones can come in various sizes, and in the future some will predictably be the size of a dragonfly. Some drones and other robotics are also likely to use increasingly sophisticated computerized forms of intelligence gathering and analysis for decision making with respect to identification and engagement of targets during war and self-defense, perhaps even with a completely autonomous decisional, learning, and operational capability. Are there identifiable challenges posed by the foreseeable development and increasing availability and use of drones and other robotics? Will their increased use require changes in that laws of war, especially with respect to the need to adhere to basic legal principles that limit violence and its effects?

Presently, it is not generally expected that use of drones for targeting during war will require a change in the laws of war. However, there are at least two predictable developments in drone technology that raise concerns whether drones will be sufficiently controlled and permit compliance with general principles of necessity, distinction, and proportionality. First, there is concern that some drones will become completely autonomous and will be used to hunt and quickly eliminate human beings and objects within the matrix of programed targets. Presently, drones used for targeting during war and self-defense are operated by human beings, and there are often others who can participate in decisions concerning target identification and whether to engage a particular target. Drones often have the capability to fly over an area for hours, allowing nuanced human choice with respect to all features of context, including those concerning identification of the target; the importance of the target; whether equally effective alternative methods of targeting or capture exist; the presence, proximity, and number of civilians who are not targetable; whether some civilians are voluntary or coerced human shields; the precision in targeting that can obtain; and foreseeable consequences with respect to civilian death, injury, or suffering.

Some foresee a growing use of on-board computers to locate targets, provide valuable contextual input, and coordinate with other drones and aircraft, but assume that human beings will still make needed choices concerning proper application of the principles of distinction and proportionality and whether a target should even be engaged under the circumstances. Others foresee a problematic future use of drones that are completely autonomous and, if they do not kill and destroy needlessly because of computer glitches, they might kill and destroy without adequate consideration of all relevant features of context despite possible increased sophistication in their programing. In fact, some systems can be placed in an autonomous mode by a human decision maker and then hunt for human or material targets in a defensive or offensive manner. Depending on their capabilities, smart autonomous hunting drones and other hunting robots might be blind with respect to the need to comply with customary principles of distinction and proportionality.

Second, it has been reported that research "is headed away from single drones and towards a co-ordinated team or swarm of vehicles with a specified mission and location…, a swarm of robots," and that "inevitably there will be more autonomy; the robots will be required to make more decisions." It is also foreseeable that with respect to swarms, a human can provide the initial order to a swarm, but "drones in the armed swarm would work out between them which element would enact an attack order." Quite possibly, use of a swarm might pose greater danger with respect to computer glitches and the need for nuanced decision making with respect to identification and engagement of particular targets. Nonetheless, the swarm can prove to be valuable with respect to some forms of lawful uses of offensive and defensive force. Basic legal norms do not need to be changed, but efforts should be made to assure the existence of adequate computerized and human controls and the development of rules of engagement (ROE) to restrain their actual use. Wanton and reckless disregard of consequences can lead to criminal and civil sanctions, but these can occur with respect to misuse of any weapons system.

Also see generally, Eyal Benvenisti, *The Legal Battle to Define the Law on Transnational Asymmetric Warfare*, 20 Duke J. Comp. & Int'l L. 339 (2010); Laurie R. Blank, *After Top Gun: How Drone Strikes Impact the Law of War*, 33 U. Pa. J. Int'l L. 675 (2012); Aaron M. Drake, *Current U.S. Air Force Drone Operations and Their Conduct in Compliance with International Humanitarian Law—An Overview*, 39 Denv. J. Int'l L. & Pol'y 629 (2011); Chris Jenks, *Law From Above: Unmanned Aerial Systems, Use of Force, and the Law of Armed Conflict*, 85 N.D. L. Rev. 649 (2009); Michael W. Lewis, *Drones and the Boundaries of the Battlefield*, 47 Tex. Int'l L.J. 293 (2012); Michael A. Newton, *Flying into the Future: Drone Warfare and the Changing Face of Humanitarian Law*, 39 Denv. J. Int'l L. & Pol'y 601 (2011); Mary Ellen O'Connell, *The Resort to Drones Under International Law*,

39 Denv. J. Int'l L. & Pol'y 585 (2011); Michael N. Schmitt, *Drone Attacks Under the* Jus ad Bellum *and* Jus in Bello: *Clearing the "Fog of Law,"* 13 Y.B. Int'l Humanitarian L. 311 (2010); Markus Wagner, *Taking Humans Out of the Loop: Implications for International Humanitarian Law*, 21 J. L., Info. & Sci. _(2011).

13. With respect to the taking of hostages, reprisals, violence against hostages, and the shooting of prisoners—all in connection with the general principles of necessity and proportionality—and all prior to the 1949 Geneva Conventions [which prohibit hostage-taking and reprisals], the 1977 Geneva Protocols, the 1979 Hostages Convention and other legal developments, consider the following:

The Dreierwalde Case
Trial of Karl Amberger (Formerly Oberfeldwebel), Case No. 7
BRITISH MILITARY COURT, WUPPERTAL,
11th—14th March, 1946
from U.N. War Crimes Commission, Law Reports of Trials of War Criminals,
81, 86–87 (1947)

Shooting of unarmed prisoners of war. Plea that they were thought to be trying to escape. Hague Convention No. IV of 1907.

The accused was in charge of a party conducting five allied prisoners of war ostensibly to a Railway Station. On the way, the party, including the accused, began firing on them; all were killed except one, who escaped though wounded. The case for the Prosecution was that since the prisoners of war had made no attempt to escape, the shooting was in violation of the laws and usages of war. The Defence claimed that Amberger had genuinely believed that the prisoners were trying to escape. The Commission found him guilty and sentenced him to death by hanging.

The conventional rule of International Law which protects prisoners of war, whether or not they have surrendered, is now contained in the International Convention relative to the treatment of Prisoners of War, signed at Geneva on 27th July, 1929, and Article 2 states that:

"Prisoners of War are in the power of the hostile Government, but not of the individual or formation which captured them.

"They shall at all times be humanely treated and protected, particularly against acts of violence, from insults and from public curiosity.

"Measures of reprisal against them are forbidden."

This provision develops the principle already contained in Art. 4 of the 1907 Hague Regulations respecting the laws and customs of war on land.

There is no doubt that the allied airmen, who did not surrender to the German armed forces but were captured by German civilians, came under the protection of Art. 2 of the 1929 Convention. It is also safe to say that the killing of prisoners of war constituted a war crime under customary International Law even before the promulgation and ratification of the Conventions of 1907 and 1929....

Concerning the Legality of the Shooting of Prisoners While Attempting to Escape

The Judge Advocate in his summing up made the following statement:

"Gentlemen, war is a cruel thing, and there are certain rules which apply to war. One is that it is the duty of an officer or a man if he is captured to try and escape. The corollary to that is that the Power which holds him is entitled to prevent him from escaping, and in doing so no great niceties are called for by the Power that has him in his control: by that I mean it is quite right if it is reasonable in the circumstances, for a guard to open fire on an escaping prisoner, though he should pay great heed merely to wound him, but if he should be killed though that is very unfortunate it does not make a war crime.... If the accused, Karl Amberger, did see that his prisoners were trying to escape or had reasonable grounds for thinking that they were attempting to escape then that would not be a breach of the rules and customs of war, and therefore you would not be able to say a war crime had been committed."

It follows from this statement that a person who came under the protection of the Hague and Geneva Conventions and the provisions of customary International Law protecting prisoners of war would subsequently lose that protection on the rise of any set of circumstances which caused his captors reasonably to believe that he was attempting to escape. It should be noted that these circumstances need not, apparently, arise due to the acts or omissions of the captive. While it is not enough for the captor to have a merely subjective fear that an attempt to escape is being made, on the other hand the events which give rise to the requisite reasonable apprehension could on the face of the Judge Advocate's statement, be due to other agencies than the volition of the prisoner.

Chapter 3—"Penal Sanctions with regard to Prisoners of War"—of the 1929 Convention makes no mention of the shooting at, or killing of, prisoners attempting to escape.

Under Article 50, escaped prisoners who are recaptured before being able to rejoin their own armed forces or to leave the territory occupied by the armed forces which captured them shall be liable only to disciplinary punishment (*i.e.*, they shall not be liable to judicial proceedings). Under Article 54, imprisonment is the most severe disciplinary punishment which may be inflicted on a prisoner of war. These provisions, however, leave open the question of the procedure which can legally be followed while the prisoner is still in flight.

There is surprisingly little authority on this point. The 6th (Revised) Edition of Volume II of Oppenheim-Lauterpacht's *International Law* contains the following passage: "The conviction became general that captivity should only be the means of preventing prisoners from returning to their corps and taking up arms again" (p. 293). An escaping prisoner, it could be argued, was already potentially in arms again and this circumstance justified his being treated as already once again a member of the opposing forces. At all events, firing upon prisoners who reasonably appear to be attempting an escape seems to be accepted State practice.

United States v. von Leeb, *et al.*

10 Trials of War Criminals 3
11 Trials of War Criminals 528–29, 562–63 (1948) (The High Command Case)

Hostages and Reprisals

In the Southeast Case [Hostage Case], United States vs. Wilhelm List, *et al.*, (Case No. 7), the Tribunal had occasion to consider at considerable length the law relating to hostages and reprisals. It was therein held that under certain very restrictive conditions and subject to certain rather extensive safeguards, hostages may be taken, and after a judicial finding of strict compliance with all preconditions and as a last desperate remedy hostages may even be sentenced to death. It was held further that similar drastic safeguards, restrictions, and judicial preconditions apply to so-called "reprisal prisoners." If so inhumane a measure as the killing of innocent persons for offenses of others, even when drastically safe-guarded and limited, is ever permissible under any theory of international law, killing without full compliance with all requirements would be murder. If killing is not permissible under any circumstances, then a killing with full compliance with all the mentioned prerequisites still would be murder.

In the case here presented, we find it unnecessary to approve or disapprove the conclusions of law announced in said judgment as to the permissibility of such killings. In the instance of so-called hostage taking and killing, and the so-called reprisal killings with which we have to deal in this case, the safeguards and preconditions required to be observed by the Southeast judgment were not even attempted to be met or even suggested as necessary. Killings without full compliance with such preconditions are merely terror murders. If the law is in fact that hostage and reprisal killings are never permissible at all, then also the so-called hostage and reprisal killings in this case are merely terror murders.

The responsibility of defendants for any such acts will be considered in our determination of the cases against the individual defendants....

[food and other property]

Pillage of public and private property — The prosecution relies upon two orders to sustain this charge. The first of these orders is from the 12th Panzer Division on 11 November 1941, directing an operation against certain villages "used by the partisans as a base of operations" with instructions to seize the cattle, horses, and chickens and most of the food, but further directing a small amount of food be left for the population at the direction of the commander of the operations. We cannot say this order was illegal.

Likewise an order of XXXIX Corps issued on 7 December 1941, regarding a forced retreat, called for the destruction of food and fodder that could not be taken along in the retreat. The destruction of these foodstuffs would tend to hamper the advancing enemy and we cannot find it was not justified under the exigency of the situation.

We do not find any criminality under this phase of the case.

[siege warfare]

Criminal conduct pertaining to the siege of Leningrad — Leningrad was encircled and besieged. Its defenders and the civilian population were in great straits and it was feared the population would undertake to flee through the German lines. Orders were issued to use artillery to "prevent any such attempt at the greatest possible distance from our own lines by opening fire as early as possible, so that the infantry, if possible, is spared shooting on civilians." We find this was known and approved by von Leeb. Was it an unlawful order?

"A belligerent commander may lawfully lay siege to a place controlled by the enemy and endeavor by a process of isolation to cause its surrender. The propriety of attempting to reduce it by starvation is not questioned. Hence, the cutting off of every source of sustenance from without is deemed legitimate. It is said that if the commander of a besieged place expels the noncombatants, in order to lessen the number of those who consume his stock of provisions, it is lawful, though an extreme measure, to drive them back so as to hasten the surrender" [quoting HYDE, III INTERNATIONAL LAW 1802–03 (2 ed. 1945) — see also Article 18 of the 1863 Lieber Code, in the Documents Supplement.]

We might wish the law were otherwise but we must administer it as we find it. Consequently, we hold no criminality attached on this charge.

United States v. List, *et al.*

11 Trials of War Criminals 757, 1248–49, 1250, 1252–54, 1270–71 (1948) (The Southeast [Hostages] Case)

The major issues involved in the present case gravitate around the claimed right of the German armed forces to take hostages from the innocent civilian population to guarantee the peaceful conduct of the whole of the civilian population and its claimed right to execute hostages, members of the civil population, and captured members of the resistance forces in reprisal for armed attacks by resistance forces, acts of sabotage and injuries committed by unknown persons....

The question of hostages is closely integrated with that of reprisals. A reprisal is a response to an enemy's violation of the laws of war which would otherwise be a violation on one's own side. It is a fundamental rule that a reprisal may not exceed the degree of the criminal act it is designed to correct. Where an excess is knowingly indulged, it in turn is criminal and may be punished. Where innocent individuals are seized and punished for a violation of the laws of war which has already occurred, no question of hostages is involved. It is nothing more than the infliction of a reprisal. Throughout the evidence in the present case, we find the term hostage applied where a reprisal only was involved....

An examination of the available evidence on the subject convinces us that hostages may be taken in order to guarantee the peaceful conduct of the populations of occupied territories and, when certain conditions exist and the necessary preliminaries have been taken, they may, as a last resort, be shot. The taking of hostages is based fundamentally on a theory of collective responsibility. The effect of an occupation is to confer upon the invading force the right of control for the period of the occupation within the limitations and prohibitions of international law. The inhabitants owe a duty to carry on their ordinary peaceful pursuits and to refrain from all injurious acts toward the troops or in respect to their military operations. The occupant may properly insist upon compliance with regulations necessary to the security of the occupying forces and for the maintenance of law and order. In the accomplishment of this objective, the occupant may only, as a last resort, take and execute hostages.

Hostages may not be taken or executed as a matter of military expediency. The occupant is required to use every available method to secure order and tranquility before resort may be had to the taking and execution of hostages. Regulations of all kinds must be imposed to secure peace and tranquility before the shooting of hostages may be indulged. These regulations may include one or more of the following measures: (1) the registration of the inhabitants, (2) the possession of passes or identification certificates, (3) the establishment of restricted areas, (4) limitations of movement, (5) the adoption of curfew regulations, (6) the prohibition of assembly, (7) the detention of suspected persons, (8) restrictions on communication, (9) the imposition of restrictions on food supplies, (10) the evacuation of troublesome areas, (11) the levying of monetary contributions, (12) compulsory labor to repair damage from sabotage, (13) the destruction of property in proximity to the place of the crime, and any other regulation not prohibited by international law that would in all likelihood contribute to the desired result.

If attacks upon troops and military installations occur regardless of the foregoing precautionary measures and the perpetrators cannot be apprehended, hostages may be taken from the population to deter similar acts in the future provided it can be shown that the population generally is a party to the offense, either actively or passively....

It is essential to a lawful taking of hostages under customary law that proclamation be made, giving the names and addresses of hostages taken, notifying the population that upon the recurrence of stated acts of war treason the hostages will be shot. The number of hostages shot must not exceed in severity the offenses the shooting is designed to deter. Unless the foregoing requirements are met, the shooting of hostages is in contravention of international law and is a war crime in itself. Whether such fundamental requirements have been met is a question determinable by court martial proceedings. A military commander may not arbitrarily determine such facts. An order of a military commander for the killing of hostages must be based upon the finding of a competent court martial that necessary conditions exist and all preliminary steps have been taken which are essential to the issuance of a valid order. The taking of lives of innocent persons arrested as hostages is a very serious step....

That international agreement is badly needed in this field is self-evident.

International law is prohibitive law and no conventional prohibitions have been invoked to outlaw this barbarous practice. The extent to which the practice has been employed by the Germans exceeds the most elementary notions of humanity and justice. They invoke the plea of military necessity, a term which they confuse with convenience and strategical interests. Where legality and expediency have coincided, no fault can be found insofar as international law is concerned. But where legality of action is absent, the shooting of innocent members of the population as a measure of reprisal is not only criminal but it has the effect of destroying the basic relationship between the occupant and the population. Such a condition can progressively degenerate into a reign of terror. Unlawful reprisals may bring on counter reprisals and create an endless cycle productive of chaos and crime. To prevent a distortion of the right into a barbarous method of repression, international law provides a protective mantle against the abuse of the right.... Excessive reprisals are in themselves criminal and guilt attaches to the persons responsible for their commission.

It is a fundamental rule of justice that the lives of persons may not be arbitrarily taken. A fair trial before a judicial body affords the surest protection against arbitrary, vindictive, or whimsical application of the right to shoot human beings in reprisal. It is a rule of international law, based on these fundamental concepts of justice and the rights of individuals, that the lives of persons may not be taken in reprisal in the absence of a judicial finding that the necessary conditions exist and the essential steps have been taken to give validity to such action....

Military necessity has been invoked by the defendants as justifying the killing of innocent members of the population and the destruction of villages and towns in the occupied territory. Military necessity permits a belligerent, subject to the laws of war, to apply any amount and kind of force to compel the complete submission of the enemy with the least possible expenditure of time, life, and money. In general, it sanctions measures by an occupant necessary to protect the safety of his forces and to facilitate the success of his operations. It permits the destruction of life of armed enemies and other persons whose destruction is incidentally unavoidable by the armed conflicts of the war; it allows the capturing of armed enemies and others of peculiar danger, but it does not permit the killing of innocent inhabitants for purposes of revenge or the satisfaction of a lust to kill. The destruction of property to be lawful must be imperatively demanded by the necessities of war. Destruction as an end in itself is a violation of international law. There must be some reasonable connection between the destruction of property and the overcoming of the enemy forces. It is lawful to destroy railways, lines of communication, or any other property that might be utilized by the enemy. Private homes and churches even may be destroyed if necessary for military operations. It does not admit the wanton devastation of a district or the willful infliction of suffering upon its inhabitants for the sake of suffering alone....

... Unless civilization is to give way to barbarism in the conduct of war, crime must be punished. If international law as it applies to a given case is hopelessly inadequate such inadequacy should be pointed out. If customary international law has become outmoded, it should be so stated. If conventional international law sets forth an unjust rule, its enforcement will secure its correction. If all war criminals are not brought to the bar of justice under present procedures, such procedures should be made more inclusive and more effective. If the laws of war are to have any beneficent effective, they must be enforced.

The evidence in this case recites a record of killing and destruction seldom exceeded in modern history. Thousands of innocent inhabitants lost their lives by means of a firing squad, hangman's noose, people who had the same inherent desire to live as do these defendants....

An order, directory or mandatory, which fixes a ratio for the killing of hostages or reprisal prisoners, or requires the killing of hostages or reprisal prisoners for every act committed against the occupation forces is unlawful. International law places no such unrestrained and unlimited power in the hands of the commanding general of occupied territory. The reprisals taken under the authority of this order were clearly excessive. The shooting of 100 innocent persons for each German soldier killed at Topola, for instance, cannot be justified on any theory by the record. There is no evidence that the population of Topola were in any manner responsible for the act. In fact, the record shows that the responsible persons were an armed and officered band of partisans. There is nothing to infer that the population of Topola supported or shielded the guilty persons. Neither does the record show that the population had previously conducted themselves in such a manner as to have been subjected to previous reprisal actions. An order to shoot 100 persons for each German soldier killed under such circumstances is not only excessive but wholly unwarranted. We conclude that the reprisal measure taken for the ambushing and killing of 22 German soldiers at Topola were excessive and therefore criminal. It is urged that only 449 persons were actually shot in reprisal for the Topola incident. The evidence does not conclusively establish the shooting of more than 449 persons although it indicates the killing of a much greater number. But the killing of 20 reprisal prisoners for each German soldier killed was not warranted under the circumstances shown. Whether the number of innocent persons killed was 2,200 or 449, the killing was wholly unjustified and unlawful.

The reprisal measures taken for the Topola incident were unlawful for another reason. The reprisal prisoners killed were not taken from the community where the attack on the German soldiers occurred. The record shows that 805 Jews and gypsies were taken from the collection camp at Sabac and the rest from the Jewish transit camp at Belgrade to be shot in reprisal for the Topola incident. There is no evidence of any connection whatever, geographical, racial, or otherwise between the persons shot and the attack at Topola. Nor does the record disclose that judicial proceedings were held. The order for the killing in reprisal appears to have been arbitrarily issued and under the circumstances shown is nothing less than plain murder....

The defendant List also asserts that he had no knowledge of many of the unlawful killings of innocent inhabitants which took place because he was absent from his headquarters where the reports came in and that he gained no knowledge of the acts. A commanding general of occupied territory is charged with the duty of maintaining peace and order, punishing crime, and protecting lives and property within the area of his command. His responsibility is coextensive with his area of command. He is charged with notice of occurrences taking place within that territory. He may require adequate reports of all occurrences that come within the scope of his power and, if such reports are incomplete or otherwise inadequate, he is obliged to require supplementary reports to apprize him of all the pertinent facts. If he fails to require and obtain complete information, the dereliction of duty rests upon him and he is in no position to plead his own dereliction as a defense. Absence from headquarters cannot and does not relieve one from responsibility for acts committed in accordance with a policy he instituted or in which he acquiesced. He may not, of course, be charged with acts committed on the order of someone else which is outside the basic orders which he has issued. If time permits he is required to rescind such illegal orders, otherwise he is required to take steps to prevent a recurrence of their issue.

Want of knowledge of the contents of reports made to him is not a defense. Reports to commanding generals are made for their special benefit. Any failure to acquaint themselves with the contents of such reports, or a failure to require additional reports where inadequacy appears on their face, constitutes a dereliction of duty which he cannot use in his own behalf....

Notes and Questions

1. Today, does "military necessity" permit the killing of captured "noncombatants" without trial? Consider extracts from the Geneva Civilian and Prisoners of War Conventions (in the Documents Supplement), including common Article 3; and FM 27-10, paragraph 85:

Killing of Prisoners

A commander may not put his prisoners to death because their presence retards his movements or diminishes his power of resistance by necessitating a large guard, or by reason of their consuming supplies, or because it appears certain that they will regain their liberty through the impending success of their forces. It is likewise unlawful for a commander to kill his prisoners on grounds of self-preservation, even in the case of airborne or commando operations, although the circumstances of the operation may make necessary rigorous supervision of and restraint upon the movement of prisoners of war.

This is not a unilateral policy, and even in the absence of specific provisions in the 1949 Geneva Conventions requiring compliance "in all circumstances" and without a military necessity exception unless expressly stated, there exists an exemplification of customary international law which should not be unfamiliar to a war crimes prosecutor. In *United States v. List* the court stated:

Military necessity or expediency do not justify a violation of positive rules. International law is prohibitive law. Articles 46, 47, and 50 of the Hague Regulations of 1907 make no exceptions to its enforcement. The rights of the innocent population therein set forth must be respected even if military necessity or expediency decree otherwise. [11 T.W.C. at 1255]

Furthermore, in actual combat situations it is not necessary to kill prisoners of war or other detainees. Effective alternatives are always available.

2. Assume that you are a military lawyer and your commander wants a decision as to the legality of the following extract from DOD GEN-25/ DA Pam 360-521, Handbook for U.S. Forces in Vietnam (1966) before he issues orders in conformity thereto:

[at p. 97, Section VII. Search and Destroy Operations. 29. General]

a. The primary objectives of search and destroy operations are to find, fix and destroy the enemy; to destroy or seize his equipment, foodstuffs, medical supplies and base areas; and, whenever possible, destroy his political and military infrastructure....

Check also: Hague Convention No. IV (1907), Annex, Article 23 (g); 1949 Geneva Civilian Convention, Articles 13, 16, 23, 53, 57; Protocol I, Article 54.

3. Concerning destruction of food and use of starvation as a weapon today, see Notes and Questions at the end of this chapter. With respect to siege warfare and firing artillery rounds at civilians today, consider Articles 3, 4 ("in the hands of"), 13, 16–17 of the Geneva Civilian Convention. Does GC Article 4 apply to civilians fleeing a besieged area? Consider also Protocol I, arts. 48, 51. Does Article 75(1) of Protocol I apply to such persons? Does Article 75(2)?

4. Early recognitions of violations of the laws of war included:

a. Thomas Jefferson's letter to Virginia Governor Patrick Henry in March 27, 1779 stating that captured enemy troops should be humanely treated and that it "is for the benefit of mankind to mitigate the horrors of war as much as possible." He also wrote to Major General Benedict Arnold, commander of the British force at Portsmouth, that he expected the General to "concur with us in endeavoring as far as possible to alleviate the inevitable miseries of war by treating captives as humanity and natural honor requires."

b. Henry Wheaton's treatise in 1836:

"No use of force is lawful, except so far as it is necessary. A belligerent has, therefore, no right to take away the lives of those subjects of the enemy whom he can subdue by any other means. Those who are actually in arms, and continue to resist, may be lawfully killed: but the inhabitants of the enemy's country who are not in arms, or who, being in arms, submit and surrender themselves, may not be slain, because their destruction is not necessary for obtaining the just ends of war.

"The custom of civilized nations, founded on this principle, has therefore exempted the persons of the sovereign and his family, the members of the civil government, women and children, cultivators of the earth, artisans, labourers, merchants, men of science and letters, and generally all other public or private individuals engaged in the ordinary civil pursuits of life, from the direct effect of military operations, unless actually taken in arms, or guilty of some misconduct in violation of the usages of war by which they forfeit their immunity."

HENRY WHEATON, ELEMENTS OF INTERNATIONAL LAW 250 § 2, 251–52 § 4 (1st ed. 1836).

Wheaton's recognition of the reach of the principle of necessity can be compared with the 1868 Declaration of St. Petersburg's affirmation "[t]hat the only legitimate object which States should endeavor to accomplish during War is to weaken the military forces of the enemy."

c. General Winfield Scott's General Orders No. 20, Head Quarters of the Army, Tampico, 19 Feb. 1847, which prohibited: "2. Assassination; murder; malicious stabbing or maiming; rape; malicious assault and battery; robbery; theft; the wanton destruction of churches, cemeteries or other religious edifices and fixtures, and the destruction, except by order of a superior officer, of public or private property...."

How were these earlier recognitions mirrored or expanded in the 1863 Lieber Code created by Professor Francis Lieber, Major General Halleck and others during the U.S. Civil War in an effort to reflect customary laws of war?

Instructions for the Government of Armies of the United States in the Field
General Orders No. 100 (1863) (the Lieber Code)

[Read the extracts from the Lieber Code in the Documents Supplement]

Geneva Convention Relative to the Protection of Civilian Persons in Time of War of August 12, 1949
75 U.N.T.S. 287

[Read the extracts from the Geneva Civilian Convention]

Geneva Convention Relative to the Treatment of Prisoners of War, 12 August 1949
75 U.N.T.S. 135

[Read Articles 12–14, 18–20, 22–23 of the Geneva Prisoner of War Convention]

Notes and Questions

1. With respect to Geneva Civilian Convention coverage of a state's own nationals from harm perpetrated by state forces or others of the same nationality, *see, e.g.*, GC arts. 1, 3, 4, 13–24; Protocol I, art. 75; J. Paust, *Applicability of International Criminal Laws to Events in the Former Yugoslavia*, 9 AM. U. J. INT'L L. & POL. 499, 510, 512–13 (1994), and references cited.

2. Concerning the Israeli practice of administrative detention of Palestinians (without trial) in the West Bank and Gaza and applicable Hague and Geneva law (including GC arts. 5, 27), *see, e.g., Report of the ICJ Mission of Inquiry Into the Israeli Military Court System in the Occupied West Bank and Gaza*, 14 HAST. INT'L & COMP. L. REV. 1, 52–61 (1990). What is the test or burden of proof regarding detention of persons who are security threats "in the territory of a Party to the conflict," "in occupied territory"? See also Jelena Pejic, *The European Court of Human Rights' Al-Jedda judgment: the oversight of international humanitarian law*, 93 INT'L REV. OF THE RED CROSS 1, 9 (no. 883Sept. 2011) (with respect to "'measures of control' that may be taken by a state with respect to civilians whose activity is deemed to pose a serious threat to its security[, i]t is uncontroversial that direct civilian participation in hostilities falls into that category [and] other civilian behaviour may also meet the threshold of posing a serious security threat to the detaining power," adding: "[e]xamples of activities … are the financing of combat operations, general recruitment for combat, etc." *Id.* at n.38).

Did the U.S. meet this test with respect to detention of persons without trial in Afghanistan, Iraq, and Guantanamo Bay, Cuba and elsewhere during the wars in Afghanistan and Iraq? Are security detainees entitled to a review of the propriety of their detention? See GC arts. 42–43, 78; GPW, art. 5; Paust, *Judicial Power, supra* at 510–14. With respect to human rights at stake, including the right to take proceedings to an independent court of law concerning the propriety of detention, *see, e.g.*, International Covenant on Civil and Political Rights, art. 9; Paust, *Judicial Power, supra* at 503–10 (documenting evidence that the right to judicial review is a customary and nonderogable human right); Hamdi v. Rumsfeld, 542 U.S. 507 (2004); Rasul v. Bush, 542 U.S. 466 (2004); *In re* Guantanamo Detainee Cases, 355 F. Supp.2d 443 (D.D.C. 2005) (especially concerning U.S. military Combatant Status Review Tribunal (CSRT) procedures at Guantanamo); Hamdan v. Rumsfeld, 415 F.3d 33, 33, 41 (D.C. Cir.); Boumediene v. Bush, 553 U.S. 723 (2008) (constitutional habeas applies to aliens located at Guantanamo Bay, Cuba).

3. Read GC, arts. 49, 147. Is it ever lawful to transfer a non-prisoner of war out of occupied territory? Consider the following remarks:

The Bush Administration's claim [concerning the transfer of persons out of occupied territory is] set forth in a previously secret March 19, 2004 draft DOJ memo prepared by Jack L. Goldsmith [which] recognizes that everyone lawfully in Iraq is a protected person under the Geneva Conventions but argues that "protected persons," such as Iraqi nationals, can be transferred "from Iraq to another country to facilitate interrogation, for a brief but not indefinite period," and that persons who are not lawfully in Iraq can be denied protections and transferred.[1] Yet, the denial of protections under common Article 3 with respect to any detainee under any circumstances is a violation of Geneva law and, therefore, a war crime; and the transfer from occupied territory of any "protected person" under the Geneva Civilian Convention who is not a prisoner of war, such as those protected under common Article 3, is a war crime in violation of Article 49 of the Geneva Civilian Convention as well as a "grave breach" of the Convention under Article 147 [see also Article 85(4)(a) of Protocol I]; Sec'y of State v. Rahmatullah, [2012] UKSC 48, paras. 33-36 (Oct. 31, 2012) (U.K. court rejects Goldsmith memo reasoning and finds violation of Article 49). The Charter of the International Military Tribunal at Nuremberg [Article 6(b)] also lists "deportation ... for any other purpose of civilian population of or in occupied territory" as a war crime. [The Charter's use of "of or in" does not distinguish between persons who are nationals or aliens in occupied territory or who are lawfully or unlawfully under domestic law "in" occupied territory.] It also lists "deportation ... committed against any civilian population" as a crime against humanity. [*Id.* art. 6(c)] Additionally, transfer of any "person to another State where there are substantial grounds for believing that he would be in danger of being subjected to torture" is prohibited by the Convention Against Torture and Other Cruel, Inhuman or Degrading Treatment or Punishment. Paust, *Executive Plans, supra* at 850–51. More generally, under human rights law a person must not be rendered to another country where there is a "real risk" of human rights deprivations.

---

1. *See, e.g.*, Jack Goldsmith, Memorandum to William H. Taft, IV, *et al.*, re Draft Memorandum for Alberto R. Gonzales, Counsel to the President, Re: Permissibility of Relocating Certain "Protected Persons" from Occupied Iraq 2–5, 14 (Mar. 19, 2004), available at KAREN J. GREENBERG & JOSHUA L. DRATEL, EDS., THE TORTURE PAPERS: THE ROAD TO ABU GHRAIB 366 (2005). The Goldsmith memo offered a specious claim that to "remove" or "relocate" is not to "transfer" or "deport". See Goldsmith, *supra* at 2–5. However, treaties are to be interpreted with respect to their object and purpose as well as the ordinary meaning of their terms, which clearly encompasses transfer of any sort, for any purpose, and for however long. *See also* 2004 UK MANUAL, *supra* at 293 ("forbidden to *transfer* forcibly ... not *moved* outside occupied territory") (emphasis added). An earlier military pamphlet recognized that the prohibition involves "forced individual or mass *relocation*." U.S. Dep't of Army Pam. No. 20-151, *Lectures of the Geneva Conventions of 1949*, at 19 (28 Apr. 1958) (emphasis added). The only exceptions are specifically addressed in the Geneva Civilian Convention. See GC, art. 49, paragraph 2 (certain types of "evacuation"); IV COMMENTARY, *supra* at 279 ("The prohibition is absolute and allows of no exceptions, apart from those stipulated in paragraph 2.").

4. When does the Geneva Civilian Convention, or portions thereof, cease to apply? See Article 6. In general, the customary laws of war apply until "peace" occurs. See FM 27-10, para. 10 a; *cf. id.* para. 10 d.

5. What sort of protections pertain for prisoners of war? *See, e.g.,* GPW, arts. 7, 13–17, *passim.*

6. Rape is expressly prohibited in Article 27 of the Geneva Civilian Convention, a prohibition based in customary international law. See also the 1919 List of War Crimes; the 1863 Lieber Code, arts. 44, 47. Is rape also impliedly prohibited in common Article 3, in Article 16? Can rape constitute "torture," "violence to … person," "cruel treatment," "outrages upon personal dignity," "humiliating and degrading treatment," exposure to "grave danger," "acts of violence or threats thereof," "inhuman treatment," "great suffering," "serious injury to body or health"? *See also The Prosecutor v. Musema,* ICTR-96-13-T, paras 220–229 (27 Jan. 2000), extract in Chapter Nine, Section 5; and footnote 19 at the end of Section 2 A of this Chapter. Can rape constitute a "grave breach" of the Geneva Conventions? What are the elements of the war crime of "rape" or "sexual violence"? In the Elements of Crimes regarding the ICC?

For further affirmation of rape as a war crime, *see, e.g.,* U.S. Dep't of Army, Subject Schedule 27-1, *The Geneva Conventions of 1949 and Hague Convention No. IV of 1907,* at 8 (8 Oct. 1970) ("rape, or any other form of sexual assault"); William A. Schabas, *The Crime of Torture and the International Criminal Tribunals,* 37 CASE W. RES. J. INT'L L. 349, 362–63 (2006); Theodor Meron, *Rape as a Crime under International Humanitarian Law,* 87 AM. J. INT'L L. 424 (1993); Madeline Morris, *By Force of Arms: Rape, War and Military Culture,* 45 DUKE L.J. 651 (1996); Fionnuala Daibhnaid Ni Aolain, *The Entrenchment of Systematic Abuse—Mass Rape in the Former Yugoslavia,* 8 HARV. H.R.J. 285 (1995); Paust, correspondence, 88 AM. J. INT'L L. 88 (1994); Paust, *Applicability, supra* at 516–17 n.61 (prohibitions under Geneva law (including grave breach provisions), customary law, and other precepts); Cherif Bassiouni & Marcia McCormick, *Sexual Violence: An Invisible Weapon of War in the Former Yugoslavia* (DePaul Occas. Paper No. 1, 1996) (same); symposium, 5 HAST. WOMEN'S L.J. no. 2 (1994) (especially the contributions of Professors Koenig and Copelon); Adrien Katherine Wing & Sylke Merchan, *Rape, Ethnicity, and Culture: Spirit Injury From Bosnia to Black America,* 25 COLUM. H.R.L. REV. 1, 9–12, 20–25 (1993). The Indictments of Karadzic and Mladic and of Tadic (*see also* Chapter Six, Section 9) expressly referred to rape and "sexual assault" as genocide, other crimes against humanity, and/or grave breaches of Geneva law. See also Article 8 (2)(a)(ii)–(iii), (b)(xxii) of the Statute of the ICC.

7. In 2006, the U.N. Security Council affirmed "that deliberately targeting civilians and other protected persons as such in situations of armed conflict is a flagrant violation of international humanitarian law"; reaffirmed "its condemnation in the strongest terms of all acts of violence or abuses committed against civilians in situations of armed conflict in violation of applicable international obligations with respect in particular to (i) torture and other prohibited treatment, (ii) gender-based and sexual violence, (iii) violence against children, (iv) the recruitment and use of child soldiers, (v) trafficking in humans, (vi) forced displacement, and (vii) the intentional denial of humanitarian assistance"; and condemned "in the strongest terms all sexual and other forms of violence committed against civilians in armed conflict, in particular women and children." U.N. S.C. Res. 1674, paras. 3, 5, 19 (28 Apr. 2006). In 2011, the Security Council authorized the use of armed force in Libya in order to protect civilians and civilian populated areas from attacks by the government of Libya. U.N. S.C. Res. 1973 (2011). In March 2011, the U.S., NATO, and other countries participated in an international armed conflict that lasted some seven

months and led to regime change in Libya. By July 2011, thirty-two countries (including the U.S.) had recognized the Libyan National Transitional Council (NTC) as "the legitimate governing authority in Libya.

8. Outside the law of armed conflict, there are few gender-specific international criminal provisions. See J. Paust, *Women and International Criminal Law Instruments and Processes*, in 2 Women and International Human Rights Law 349 (Kelly D. Askin & Dorean M. Koenig eds. 2000); Convention on the Elimination of All Forms of Discrimination Against Women, art. 6, 1249 U.N.T.S. 13. Should there be others? See Chapters Nine and Ten.

9. Note that the Optional Protocol to the Convention on the Rights of the Child prohibits the recruitment and use of children under 18 years of age in armed conflict. However, parties to the Rights of the Child Convention must assure that children under 15 not take a direct part in hostilities. *Id.* art. 38(2). Geneva Protocol I, art. 77 uses a 15 years old test. The first successful prosecution of an accused in a Trial Chamber of the ICC occurred in March 14, 2012, with the conviction of Thomas Lubanga Dyilo (head of the military wing of the Union of Congolese Patriots), as co-perpetrator, of the war crimes of conscripting and enlisting children under the age of 15 and using them to participate actively in hostilities during an internal armed conflict in the Democratic Republic of the Congo in 2002 and 2003. In July, 2012, he received a sentence of 14 years in prison.

10. Note that Article 29 of the Geneva Civilian Convention refers to state and individual responsibility. Such responsibility can be both criminal and civil in nature. Pictet's IV Commentary, *supra* at 209–211 recognizes such dual and "distinct" responsibilities as well as the possibility of both criminal and civil sanctions, Pictet adding: "The principle of State responsibility further demands that a State whose agent has been guilty of an act in violation of the Convention, should be required to make reparation. This already followed from Article 3 of the Fourth Hague Convention of 1907 respecting the Laws and Customs of War on Land, which states that 'a belligerent Party which violates the provisions of the said Regulations [The Hague Regulations] shall, if the case demands, be liable to pay compensation. It shall be responsible for all acts committed by persons forming part of its armed forces.'" *Id.* at 210. Pictet also refers to Article 148 of the Geneva Civilian Convention, which provides that "No ... Party shall be allowed to absolve itself or any other ... Party of any liability incurred by itself or by another ... Party in respect of [grave] breaches...." See Pictet, *supra* at 211, 602–03, adding that the State "remains liable to pay compensation" even if it has prosecuted the individual perpetrators. Concerning money damages for war crimes, recall Chapter Four, Section 7 D; Chapter Six, Section 9 A (Article 106 of the Rules of Procedure and Evidence of the ICT for Former Yugoslavia and Article 24 (3) of the Statute of the Tribunal re: property); Article 75 of the Statute of the ICC; Restatement§ 404, Comment b; *Sosa v. Alvarez-Machain*, 124 S.Ct. 2739, 2783 (2004) (Breyer, J., concurring in part and concurring in judgment); *The Paquete Habana*, 189 U.S. 453, 464 *ff* (1903); *id.*, 175 U.S. 677, 700, 711, 714 (1900); *Weisshaus v. Swiss Bankers Ass'n*, 225 F.3d 191 (2d Cir. 2000); *Kadic v. Karadzic*, 70 F.3d 232, 242–43 (2d Cir. 1995); *Linder v. Portocarrero*, 963 F.2d 332, 336–37 (11th Cir. 1992); *Estate of Rodriguez v. Drummond Co.*, 206 F. Supp.2d 1250, 1259–61 (N.D. Ala. 2003); *Presbyterian Church of Sudan v. Talisman Energy, Inc.*, 244 F. Supp.2d 289, 310–11, 320–25 (S.D.N.Y. 2003); *Mehinovic v. Vuckovic*, 198 F. Supp.2d 1322, 1350–52 (N.D. Ga. 2002); *Iwanowa v. Ford Motor Co.*, 57 F. Supp.2d 41 (D.N.J. 1999); *Doe v. Islamic Salvation Front*, 993 F. Supp. 3, 5, 8 (D.D.C. 1998); *Linder v. Portocarrero*, 963 F.2d 332, 336–37 (11th Cir. 1992); J. Paust, International Law as Law of the United States 226–27, 291, 293, 313 (2 ed. 2003); Paust, *Suing Karadzic*, 10 Leiden J. Int'l L. 91 (1997); *Suing Saddam:*

Private Remedies for War Crimes and Hostage-Taking, 31 Va. J. Int'l L. 351, 360–70, 378 (1991), and references cited; Research in International Law, *The Law of Responsibility of States for Damage Done in Their Territory to the Person or Property of Foreigners* (Harvard Law School), Comment, 23 Am. J. Int'l L., Supp. 167 (1929); U.S. Dep't of Army Pam. 27-161-1, International Law 84–86 (1964).

11. Today, is it a violation of international law to use starvation as a weapon for military purposes? Against noncombatants, against combatants? Should food be considered neutral property (*e.g.*, property not subject to intentional destruction and that should pass freely through enemy lines), such as medicine and medical supplies?

See panel, *The Right to Food*, 69 Proceedings, Am. Soc. Int'l L. 50–51 (1975); J. Paust, *The Human Rights to Food, Medicine and Medical Supplies, and Freedom from Arbitrary and Inhumane Detention and Controls in Sri Lanka*, 31 Vand. J. Trans. L. 617 (1998); E. Rosenblad, *Starvation as a Method of Warfare—Conditions for Regulation by Convention*, 7 Int'l Lawyer 252 (1973); Mudge, *Starvation as a Means of Warfare*, 4 Int'l Lawyer 228 (1970); U.N. G.A. Res. 3102 (XXVIII) (12 Dec. 1973). FM 27-10, at 18, para. 37, affirms that use of poison is unlawful, but it states that efforts "to destroy, through chemical or bacterial agents harmless to man, crops intended solely for consumption by the armed forces (if that fact can be determined)" would be permissible. Nonetheless, the Manual makes clear (1) that the chemicals or bacterial agents used must not be "poison," (2) that they must be "harmless to man," (3) that the crops must be "solely for consumption" by the enemy military, and (4) that it must be "determined" that the crops are *solely* for military consumption. Clearly, crops that cannot be identified as those to be used solely for consumption by the enemy military must not be targeted. Thus, crops that could be used by enemy military as well as noncombatants cannot be targeted under any circumstances. This prohibition is especially important where combatants and civilians are intermingled. Also, if one cannot "determine" that they would be used solely by enemy military, a wanton or reckless targeting would not be compatible with the law of war prohibition. See also Sir Henry S. Maine, International Law: A Series of Lectures Delivered Before the University of Cambridge, 1887, Lecture VII ("The poisoning of water or food is a mode of warfare absolutely forbidden."), reprinted in the Avalon Project at Yale Law School; the 1863 Lieber Code, *supra* art. 70 (poisoning of "wells, or food," is proscribed).

FM 27-10 also recognized that "[p]oisoning of wells or streams" is a war crime. *Id.* at 180, para. 504(i). The Manual attempted to reflect customary law on this point recognized in a number of British texts prohibiting "[t]he contamination of sources of water." See U.S. Dep't of Army, Pam. 27-161-2, *supra* at 41. For example, the 1958 British Manual on The Law of War on Land recognized that "poisoning of wells, streams, and other sources of water supply" were examples of war crimes. 1958 UK Manual, *supra* at 175, para. 626(i). This same customary prohibition is reflected in U.S. Dep't of Army, *The Law of Land Warfare: A Self-Instructional Text* 36 (28 Apr. 1972), and in U.S. Dep't of Army Subject Schedule No. 27-1, *The Geneva Conventions of 1949 and Hague Convention No. IV of 1907*, at 10 (3 Oct. 1970), which also notes that an order to place a dead body in a well is clearly illegal because such conduct "poisons the water and the poisoning of wells and streams is a war crime" (*id.*) and which also identifies as a war crime the killing of "a farmer's water buffalo," *id.* at 5. It was also reflected in U.S. Dep't of Army Subject Schedule 27-1, *The Hague and Geneva Conventions* 24 (20 April 1967) and in MACV Directive 20-4, Inspections and Investigations of War Crimes, para. 3(c) (Headquarters, United States Military Assistance Command, Vietnam, 18 May 1968). That a "poisoning of springs and water courses" is a customary war crime was also recognized in 3 Commentary, Geneva

CONVENTION RELATIVE TO THE TREATMENT OF PRISONERS OF WAR 421 (ICRC, Jean S. Pictet ed. 1960). The customary 1863 Lieber Code was also on point far earlier: "use of poison in any manner, be it to poison wells, or food ... is wholly excluded from modern warfare." Lieber Code, *supra*, art. 70.

Article 54 of Protocol I to the 1949 Geneva Conventions sets forth a newer customary standard. Read Article 54 in the Documents Supplement. *Compare* Article 8 (2)(b)(xxv) of the Statute of the ICC. Concerning the use of food as a weapon and the Statute of the ICC, see Paust, *Content and Contours of Genocide, Crimes Against Humanity, and War Crimes*, in INTERNATIONAL LAW IN THE POST-COLD WAR WORLD: ESSAYS IN MEMORY OF LI HAOPEI (Wang Tieya & Sienho Yee eds. 2000)**, adding:

A policy of denial and neglect involving starvation can also constitute other violations of humanitarian law when used wantonly or in reckless disregard of consequences. The indiscriminate use of food as a weapon is covered under Articles 51 (4) ("[i]ndiscriminate attacks") and 54 (1) ("[s]tarvation of civilians as a method of warfare") and, especially, 54 (2) of Protocol I, as well as under Article 14 (1) of Protocol II. A policy of denial and neglect involving starvation can also result in violations, for example, of Articles 3, 16, 23, 24, and 147 of the Geneva Civilian Convention. Such a policy should also be prosecutable, for example, under Article 8 (2) (a) (ii), (iv), (b) (x), (xi), (xiii), (xvi), (xxi), (c) (i)–(ii), and (e) (v), (ix), (xi), and (xii) of the Rome Statute even if starvation is not intentional. In my opinion, food, like medicine and medical supplies, should always be treated as neutral property during an armed conflict. Starvation, even of enemy combatants, seems necessarily inhumane and to involve unnecessary and lingering death and suffering.

Moreover, Article 8 (2) (b) (xxv), addressing starvation, is too limited for a different reason. Not all means of starvation are addressed, but only starvation perpetuated "by depriving them of objects indispensable to their survival." The latter phrase should at least be interpreted logically and in view of a plain meaning to include starvation by depriving persons of food and any other "object" that in context is indispensable to the survival of civilians. Article 54 (1) and (2) of Protocol I to the Geneva Conventions lists starvation of civilians and the deprivation of objects indispensable to their survival as separate crimes. In any event, "starvation of civilians," by any means, is already proscribed under customary international law.

12. The 1977 Protocol I to the 1949 Geneva Conventions adds important limitations on the actions of combatants, especially targetings involving "indiscriminate" attacks during relevant armed conflicts. Read Articles 51 and 75 of Protocol I, in the Documents Supplement. *Compare* Article 8 (2)(b) of the Statute of the ICC. How would each apply to Yugoslavian military targetings in Kosovo before NATO's intervention in 1999? How would they apply to NATO's use of air power in Kosovo before NATO ground troops arrived?

A press release from the Office of the Prosecutor, Carla Del Ponte, dated 13 June 2000 stated that the Prosecutor of the ICTY decided not to pursue a criminal investigation of "any aspect of NATO's 1999 air campaign" and that "[a]lthough some mistakes were made by NATO, the Prosecutor is satisfied that there was no deliberate targeting of civilians or unlawful military targets by NATO." The Prosecutor relied on a 26 page Final Report to the Prosecutor by the Committee Established to Review the NATO Bombing Campaign Against the Federal Republic of Yugoslavia, available at www.icty.org/x/file/Press/nato061300.pdf. The Report stated that with respect to crimi-

---

** Reproduced with permission of Routledge, Ltd.

nal responsibility for air targetings "[t]he *mens rea* for the offence is intention or recklessness, not simple negligence," adding: "In determining whether or not the *mens rea* requirement has been met, it should be borne in mind that commanders deciding on an attack have duties: a) to do everything practicable to verify that the objectives to be attacked are military objectives, b) to take all practicable precautions in the choice of methods and means of warfare with a view to avoiding or, in any event to minimizing incidental civilian casualties or civilian property damage, and c) to refrain from launching attacks which may be expected to cause disproportionate civilian casualties or civilian property damage." *Id.* para. 28. Is the "expected to cause" standard like a criminal negligence standard, since it entails a lower threshold than wanton, reckless disregard? See also Geneva Protocol I, arts. 35(3), 51(5).

Note that ICC jurisdiction over war crimes involving air or artillery targeting is more limited than the reach of customary international law. *See, e.g.,* Paust, *Content and Contours,** supra*, noting:

… Within Article 8 (2) (b) (iv), concerning attacks, for example, causing "incidental loss of life or injury to civilians or damage to civilian objects," one finds the only provision containing the delimiting phrase "in the knowledge that such attack will cause." This is an improper standard or threshold with respect to all forms of relevant criminal liability and, thus, is another indication of the quite limited jurisdiction of the Court. The phrase "in the knowledge or in wanton disregard that such attack may cause" would have reached other serious war crimes, but was not chosen. Instead, the limiting phrase within Article 8 (2) (b) (iv) assures that an entire area of criminal responsibility attaching to wanton or reckless disregard of consequences will not be addressed by the ICC unless it falls within other sections of Article 8 (2), which is possible depending on the language used in other sections and various features of context. Sometimes the *mens rea* standard concerning customary war crimes is reflected in the words "wilful," "wilfully," or "deliberate," as used in Article 147 of the 1949 Geneva Civilian Convention or used a few times with respect to certain customary war crimes found in the 1919 List of War Crimes prepared by the Responsibilities Commission, but sometimes the standard includes "wanton" or "wantonly," as in Article 147 of the Geneva Civilian Convention and certain crimes in the 1919 List. Both instruments are evidence of the fact that the two standards are different, that their drafters knew how to set higher or lower thresholds of criminal responsibility, and that they chose to set higher thresholds only in certain instances. Indeed, the same points pertain with respect to Article 8 of the Rome Statute.

More generally with respect to wanton or reckless disregard, it is informative that Article 44 of the customary 1863 Lieber Code proscribed "[a]ll wanton violence" and Article 16 addressed "wanton devastation." "Wanton devastation and destruction" was also the standard used in crimes numbers 18 and 20 in the 1919 List prepared by the Responsibilities Commission. With respect to World War II prosecutions, the Report of Robert H. Jackson to the President of the United States identified "wanton destruction" as among the "[a]trocities and offenses against persons or property" to be addressed at Nuremberg. Similarly, *United States v. List, et al.* noted that "military necessity … does not admit the wanton devastation of a district.…" The crime of "wanton destruction of cities, towns or villages" was also expressly recognized in Article 6 (b) of the Charter of the International Military Tribunal at Nuremberg. Thereafter, the Principles of the Nuremberg Charter and Judgment formulated by the International Law Commission and adopted by the

---

* Also reproduced with permission of Routledge, Ltd.

U.N. General Assembly affirmed that "[v]iolations of the laws or customs of war ... include, but are not limited to, ... wanton destruction of cities, towns, or villages...." The same crime was also recognized in Article 3(d) of the Bangladesh International Crimes (Tribunals) Act of 1973. More recently, the Indictment of Radovan Karadzic and Ratko Mladic issued by the International Criminal Tribunal for the Former Yugoslavia addresses crimes involving "wantonly appropriated and looted" property and "wanton and unlawful destruction of" property. The Statute of the International Criminal Tribunal for the Former Yugoslavia has also identified crimes involving "extensive destruction and appropriation of property ... carried out unlawfully and wantonly" and "wanton destruction of cities, towns or villages...." Interestingly, Article 8 (2) (b) (xiii) and (e) (xii) of the Rome Statute assures that the new ICC will be able to address "Destroying or seizing the enemy's property" without limiting words such as "intentionally" or "wantonly." In order to constitute a "grave breach" within the meaning of the Rome Statute, however, Article 8 (2) (a) (iv) requires "Extensive destruction or appropriation of property ... [that is] carried out unlawfully and wantonly."

Article 51 (5) of Protocol I to the Geneva Conventions also provides a standard with perhaps a lower threshold when using the phrase "an attack which may be *expected* to cause incidental loss" (emphasis added). Similarly, the phrase "intended, or may be *expected*, to cause" found in Article 35 (3) of Protocol I (emphasis added) includes a standard of responsibility far less than "in the knowledge that such ... will cause." The "or may be expected" language also appears in the preamble to the Convention on Prohibitions or Restrictions on the Use of Certain Conventional Weapons Which May be Deemed to be Excessively Injurious or to Have Indiscriminate Effects....

A related problem concerning ICC coverage of customary crime involves the oft-repeated phrase "intentionally directing attacks" found in Article 8 (2) (b) (i)–(iii), (ix), (xxiv) and (e) (i)–(iv). For reasons noted above with respect to criminal responsibility for wanton or reckless disregard, the language used in the Rome Statute clearly does not reach all customary criminal responsibility.

13. Concerning application of the principles reflected in Article 51 of Protocol I, which are derived from custom, recall the Indictments of Karadzic and Mladic in Chapter Two, Section 1.

14. Note that Article 51(2) prohibits "[a]cts or threats of violence the primary purpose of which is to spread terror...." Must terror actually be produced? In *The Prosecutor v. Galic*, IT-98-29-T (Trial Chamber Judgment and Sentence, 5 Dec. 2003), Major General Stanislav Galic was convicted with respect to his role as commander of the Bosnian Serb Army's SRK Corps during the "Siege of Sarajevo." The Trial Chamber ruled that a terror outcome is not necessary with respect to a violation of Article 51(2) and stated that three elements of the offense must exist as follows: (1) acts of violence directed against the civilian population or individual civilians not taking direct part in hostilities causing death or serious injury to body or health within the civilian population, (2) the offender wilfully made the civilian population or individual civilians not taking direct part in hostilities the object of those acts of violence, and (3) the offence was committed with the primary purpose of spreading terror among the civilian population. *Id.* paras.133–134. Moreover, military necessity is not an excuse with respect to the crime of targeting of civilians. *Id.* para. 44. Also, indiscriminate attacks "may qualify as direct attacks against civilians" (*Id.* para. 57.) and "certain apparently disproportionate attacks may give rise to the inference that civilians were actually the object of attack (*Id.* para. 60), but the Prosecution must prove that the accused wilfully made the civilian population or relevant individual civilians the object of an attack for the crime of targeting civilians to be

proven. *Id*. paras. 55–56. This is in contrast to the crime of indiscriminate attacks under Article 51(4)–(5), which requires that the Prosecution prove that an "attack was launched wilfully and in knowledge of circumstances giving rise to the expectation of excessive civilian casualties." *Id*. para. 59.

15. Are electrical power works and grids sometimes a lawful military target? During the 1991 Gulf War, it was claimed that the U.S. targeted Iraqi power plants with the result that some water systems in the city of Baghdad did not function. Was such a war crime? What else would you like to know? See also Protocol I, arts. 54, 56.

During the 1999 NATO air strikes in Kosovo, a television transmission tower was targeted. If intentionally targeted, would such a targeting be a war crime? Consider Protocol I, arts. 51–52, 54, 56. Also consider *United States v. Ohlendorf*, IV TRIALS OF WAR CRIMES BEFORE THE NUERNBERG MILITARY TRIBUNALS 466, 467 (1948): during the total warfare in WWII, "communications are to be destroyed, railroads wrecked, ammunition plants demolished, factories razed, all for the purpose of impeding the military. In these operations it inevitably happens that nonmilitary persons are killed." The Final Report to the Prosecutor stated that the NATO bombing of the Serbian TV and Radio Station in Belgrade was "part of a planned attack aimed at disrupting and degrading the C3 (Command, Control and Communications) network" and concluded that "[i]nsofar as the attack was actually aimed at disrupting the communications network, it was legally acceptable." *Id*. paras. 72, 75. Some 10 to 17 persons were estimated to have been killed during the attack. The Report addressed Article 52 of Protocol I and used a two-prong test: "was the station a legitimate military objective and; if it was, were the civilian casualties disproportionate to the military advantage gained by the attack." *Id*. para. 75. Does this "military advantage" test adequately reflect the "military necessity" test?

16. Consider the following hypothetical:

During an international armed conflict, General Mala has told you that he wants to target several "military objectives" whose destruction he claims will be strategically valuable. Would you agree to the destruction of the following:

– a new enemy soccer stadium during the evening when no one would be around, because it symbolizes national pride and its destruction would send an important demoralizing message;

– a military housing complex where enemy officers and their families reside;

– a civilian airliner headed to the enemy capital with its top general and aides among the 200+ passengers on board;

– a truck convoy carrying needed food to enemy military and a few civilians in the enemy capital;

– three civil nuclear reactors that power the electric grid in the enemy capital;

– a factory in the countryside that produces military weapons while the civilian workforce is on their day shift;

– the well-guarded home of the enemy President while he and his family are sleeping.

17. The Final Report to the Prosecutor contained terse consideration of admitted use of "depleted uranium projectiles" by NATO aircraft. The Report admitted that the principle of proportionality is applicable, but seemed to argue merely that use of such projectiles is not *per se* illegal and that its prior analysis concerning effects of NATO bombings on the environment are somehow determinative. What the Report did not address is whether use of such weaponry is violative of customary prohibitions of "poison or poi-

soned weapons," employment of "arms, projectiles or material of a nature to cause unnecessary suffering" (*e.g.*, a lingering death, injury or suffering after a person is taken out
of combat, as in the case of neutron warheads—see Paust, remarks, 72 PROC., ASIL 39,
43–45 (1978)), or employment of radioactive weapons in circumstances where they may
be expected to cause incidental loss to civilian life or injury that would be excessive.

18. Is espionage an international crime? During time of war? Article 30 of the 1907 Hague
Convention, Annex, states: "A spy taken in the act shall not be punished without previous trial." See *United States ex rel. Wessels v. McDonald*, 265 F. 754, 762 (E.D.N.Y. 1920)
("A spy may not be tried under the international law when he returns to his own lines,
even if subsequently captured, and the reason is that, under the international law, spying is not a crime, and the offense which is against the laws of war consists of being found
during the war in the capacity of a spy. *Martin v. Mott*, 12 Wheat. 19….") See also Art. 31
of the 1907 Hague Convention; FM 27-10, THE LAW OF LAND WARFARE 33, para. 77
(1956) ("no offense against international law. Spies are punished, not as violators of the
laws of war…." but as crimes against that state).

Chapter 9

Crimes Against Humanity

Fictional Introductory Problem

For purposes of this problem, assume that you are a judge presiding over the trial of Andre Bagosora, who is being prosecuted in Burundi for committing crimes against humanity and genocide in neighboring Rwanda. The indictment and the Defendant's motion for dismissal are reproduced below. Based on the materials on crimes against humanity and genocide contained in this chapter and Chapter Ten, you should assess the validity of each of the defendant's grounds for dismissal. What other issues might arise or legal policies appear to be at stake?

Burundi v. Bagosora

Indictment # 3-19-97, in the Trial Court of Burundi

1. The Defendant, Andre Bagosora, is a 35 year old Tutsi male of Rwandan citizenship. He is a private businessman who had close ties to the previously ruling governmental elite in Rwanda.

2. The population of the neighboring country of Rwanda is composed primarily of two groups, the majority Hutu and the minority Tutsi. In 1933, the colonial power (Belgium) conducted a census in order to issue identity cards, which labeled every Rwandan as either Hutu or Tutsi. Tribal classifications were determined on a patrilineal basis, taking sole account of the father's ethnicity. Thus, a person whose father was Tutsi was considered a Tutsi, regardless of the mother's ethnic background.

3. The Hutus and Tutsis had been fighting in Rwanda since Rwanda became an independent country in 1959. After the plane carrying the President of Rwanda (a Hutu) was shot down on April 6, 1994, the Hutus launched a genocidal campaign against the Tutsi, killing as many as one million Tutsi during a four month period. Tutsis were targeted because of their ethnic, political, and gender identifications. The genocide was halted when the Tutsis militarily defeated the Hutus and most of the Hutus fled to neighboring Zaire. In December of 1997, two million Hutu refugees returned peacefully to Rwanda.

4. In January of 1997, Radio Milles Collines, which since 1995 has been owned and operated by the defendant, began a campaign of hatred against the returning Hutu refugees. Cassette recordings exist of a speech by the defendant, in which he called on Tutsis "to capture the returning Hutu women, strip them naked, and rape them in order to create Tutsi children."

5. Subsequently, in 1998, thousands of Tutsi civilians undertook a campaign of mass rape against the female Hutu refugees. Amnesty International estimates that 10,000 female Hutu refugees were victims of sexual abuse at the hands of the Tutsis.

6. The defendant was taken into custody during a visit to Burundi. He is charged with committing crimes against humanity and genocide. The Burundi Court has universal jurisdiction over his crimes. There is no statute of limitations.

Motion to Dismiss the Indictment

The Defendant requests a dismissal of the indictment against him on the following grounds:

1. Burundi lacks jurisdiction under international law to prosecute the Defendant, who is a Rwandan citizen and is charged with crimes that occurred in Rwanda.

2. The acts alleged could not constitute crimes against humanity because they occurred during peacetime, not in the course of an armed conflict.

3. Since there has been so much intermarriage between Hutus and Tutsis through the years that ethnographers and historians question whether Hutus and Tutsis are technically distinct ethnic groups, violence against the Hutus cannot constitute a crime against humanity or the crime of genocide.

4. Because the defendant was a non-governmental actor, he cannot be convicted of crimes against humanity or genocide. Further, both types of crime must be committed in the context of a state policy to engage in widespread acts of extermination.

5. Since gender is not one of the protected groups under the Genocide Convention, alleged rapes cannot constitute the crime of genocide. Moreover, the defendant is alleged only to have urged radio listeners to commit rape, not to kill or otherwise destroy a group. Thus, his alleged act does not constitute the crime of genocide. Further, acts of rape are not covered as acts constituting crimes against humanity or genocide.

6. The charges against the Defendant contravene the free speech provisions of the Burundi Constitution (which is identical to the U.S. First Amendment), and the Burundi Constitution must control.

Section 1
Nuremberg and Earlier

One should recall that in the late 1700s and early 1800s there were references to "duties of humanity," "duty of humanity," "crimes against mankind," "crimes against the human family," "enemies of the whole human family" (noted in Chapter Four), which seem related to concepts of laws of humanity, offenses against the laws of humanity, and crimes against humanity. During the 1915 massacres of Armenians by Turks, the governments of Great Britain, France and Russia had condemned the massacres as "crimes against humanity and civilization." See QUINCY WRIGHT, HISTORY OF THE UNITED NATIONS WAR CRIMES COMMISSION 35 (1948); *The Prosecutor v. Akayesu, infra,* paras. 565–566. Some low to mid-level Turkish persons were prosecuted in military commissions after World War I. See www.armeniangenocide.org/genocide.htm. A few years later, a former U.S. Secretary of State wrote that the slave trade had become a "crime against humanity." See Lansing, *Notes on World Sovereignty,* 15 AM. J. INT'L L. 13, 25 (1921). Already in 1874 in the United States George Curtis had labeled slavery a "crime against humanity." See III ORATIONS AND ADDRESSES OF GEORGE WILLIAM CURTIS 208 (C. Norton ed. 1894). *See also* McMullen v. Hodge and Others, 5 Tex. 34, 71 (1849); Norris v. Newton, 18 F. Cas. 322, 324 (C.C.D. Indiana 1850) (No. 10,307) ("There can be no higher offense against the laws of humanity and justice … than to arrest a free man … with the view of making him a slave."); O'Loughlin v. People, 90 Colo. 368, 378, 10 P. 543 (1932) ("rape of a step-daughter is …'a crime against humanity'"), quoting Wilkinson v. People, 86 Colo. 406, 411, 282 P. 257 (1929); State v. Robins, 221 Ind. 125, 46 N.E.2d 691 (1943) (sodomy of a girl is a "crime against mankind"); Toth v. State, 141 Neb. 448, 464, 3 N.W.2d 899 (1942) (re: incest and rape, also quoting *Wilkinson*); State v. Hogan, 63 Ohio St. 202, 214, 58 N.E. 572 (1900) ("piracy and the slave trade were offenses not only against humanity, but against civilization"); Rodriguiz v. State, 20 Tex. Ct. App. 542, 546 (Tex. Crim. App. 1886) (sexual intercourse with a female of severely diminished mental capacity was not covered by state criminal law but is one of the "heinous crimes against humanity"); Compton v. State, 13 Tex. Ct. App. 271, 274 (Tex. Crim. App. 1882) (incest with a stepdaughter is "a crime against humanity"); State v. Lilly, 47 W.Va. 496, 500, 35 S.E. 837 (1900) (dictum re: abortion: "[t]here is no crime more heinous against humanity"); 1 Op. Att'y Gen. 509, 513 (1821) ("crimes against mankind," citing H. GROTIUS, THE LAW OF WAR AND PEACE, Book One, ch. 21, § 3). In 1855, the slave trade was also related to a "crime against mankind." United States v. Darnaud, 25 F. Cas. 754, 760 (C.C. Pa. 1855); see also United States v. Haun, 26 F. Cas. 227, (C.C.S.D. Ala. 1860) (Campbell, J., on circuit) (slave trade is a crime against "human rights" and against "humanity"); Henfield's Case, 11 F. Cas. 1099, 1107 (C.C.D. Pa. 1793) (No. 6,360) (Wilson, J., on circuit) (breaches of neutrality involve violations of the "duties of humanity").

Also recall that in the 1919 Report of the Commission on the Responsibility of the Authors of the War and on Enforcement of Penalties formulated by representatives from several States and presented to the Paris Peace Conference, criminal responsibility was identified in terms such as "offences against … the laws of humanity" and "violations," "breach[es] of," and "outrages against … the laws of humanity." The 1868 Declaration of St. Petersburg also referred to violations of the "laws of humanity" (see Chapter Eight, Section 2 B) and so did the preamble to the 1907 Hague Convention No. IV (in the "Martens clause"). Perhaps the trial of von Hagenbach in 1474 for violations of the "laws of God and man" is relevant, especially in view of the nature of the crimes charged. See Chapter Six, Section 1. Of apparent rhetorical significance was the statement of Charles Darwin in 1881, who opposed limits on "experiments on living animals," and opined "that to retard the progress of physiology is to commit a crime against humanity." Quoted in Penn. Co. for Ins. v. Commissioner, 25 B.T.A. 1168, 1172 (U.S. Bd. Tax App. 1932).

The Prosecutor v. Akayesu

ICTR-96-4-T (2 Sept. 1998)

Before: Judge Laïty Kama, Presiding

    Judge Lennart Aspegren

    Judge Navanethem Pillay

565. Crimes against humanity are aimed at any civilian population and are prohibited regardless of whether they are committed in any armed conflict, international or internal in character. In fact, the concept of crimes against humanity had been recognised long before Nuremberg. On 28 May 1915, the Governments of France, Great Britain and Russia made a declaration regarding the massacres of the Armenian population in Turkey, denouncing them as "crimes against humanity and civilisation for which all the members of the Turkish government will be held responsible together with its agents implicated in the massacres." The 1919 Report of the Commission on the Responsibility of the Au-

thors of the War and on Enforcement of Penalties formulated by representatives from several States and presented to the Paris Peace Conference also referred to "offences against ... the laws of humanity."

566. These World War I notions derived, in part, from the Martens clause of the Hague Convention (IV) of 1907, which referred to "the usages established among civilised peoples, from the laws of humanity, and the dictates of the public conscience." In 1874, George Curtis called slavery a "crime against humanity." Other such phrases as "crimes against mankind" and "crimes against the human family" appear far earlier in human history (see 12 N.Y.L. Sch. J. Hum. Rts. 545 (1995) [extract printed in this chapter, *supra*]).

What is interesting with respect to historic recognitions of "laws of humanity" and "crimes against humanity" is that the reach of these precepts was potentially quite broad, perhaps as far-reaching as human rights. They involved several types of conduct and were not limited to state actors or war contexts. *See generally* J. Paust, *Threats to Accountability After Nuremberg, infra*. It should be noted that the phrase "any civilian population" addressed in *Musema* can include merely civilians as such and that in The Prosecutor v. Tadic, IT-94-1-T (Judgment), para. 634 (7 May 1997), it was recognized that the phrase makes it clear that crimes against humanity can be committed against civilians of the same nationality as the perpetrator or those who are stateless, as well as those of a different nationality.

Justice Robert Jackson in his report to the President of the United States in 1945 concerning crimes addressed at Nuremberg (another extract of which follows) recognized the relevance of the "Martens clause"when stating: "[t]hese principles have been assimilated as a part of International Law at least since 1907. The Fourth Hague Convention provided that the inhabitants and belligerents shall remain under the protection and the rule of 'the principles of the law of nations, as they result from the usages established among civilized peoples, from the laws of humanity and the dictates of public conscience.'"

Report of Justice Robert H. Jackson
to the President of the United States
released June 7, 1945

The Legal Charges [Before the IMT, Nuremberg]

Against this background it may be useful to restate in more technical lawyer's terms the legal charges against the top Nazi leaders and those voluntary associations such as the S.S. and Gestapo which clustered about them and were ever the prime instrumentalities, first, in capturing the German state, and then, in directing the German state to its spoliations against the rest of the world.

(a) Atrocities and offenses against persons or property constituting violations of International Law, including the laws, rules, and customs of land and naval warfare. The rules of warfare are well established and generally accepted by the nations. They make offenses of such conduct as killing of the wounded, refusal of quarter, ill treatment of prisoners of war, firing on undefended localities, poisoning of wells and streams, pillage and wanton destruction, and ill treatment of inhabitants in occupied territory.

(b) Atrocities and offenses, including atrocities and persecutions on racial or religious grounds, committed since 1933. This is only to recognize the principles of criminal law as they are generally observed in civilized states. These principles have been assimilated as a part of International Law at least since 1907. The Fourth Hague Convention provided that inhabitants and belligerents shall remain under the protection and the rule of "the principles of the law of nations, as they result from the usages established among civilized peoples, from the laws of humanity and the dictates of the public conscience."

(c) Invasions of other countries and initiation of wars of aggression in violation of International Law or treaties.

International Military Tribunal at Nuremberg, Indictment Number 1

Count Four—Crimes Against Humanity

[Read the Charter of the I.M.T. at Nuremberg, Article 6 (c), in the Documents Supplement]

Statement of the Offense

All the defendants committed Crimes against Humanity during a period of years preceding 8th May, 1945 in Germany and in all those countries and territories occupied by the German armed forces since 1st September, 1939 and in Austria and Czechoslovakia and in Italy and on the High Seas.

All the defendants, acting in concert with others, formulated and executed a common plan or conspiracy to commit Crimes against Humanity as defined in Article 6(c) of the Charter. This plan involved, among other things, the murder and persecution of all who were or who were suspected of being hostile to the Nazi Party and all who were or who were suspected of being opposed to the common plan alleged in Count One.

The said Crimes against Humanity were committed by the defendants and by other persons for whose acts the defendants are responsible, (under Article 6 of the Charter) as such other persons, when committing the said War Crimes, performed their acts in execution of a common plan and conspiracy to commit the said War Crimes, in the formulation and execution of which plan and conspiracy all the defendants participated as leaders, organizers, instigators and accomplices.

These methods and crimes constituted violations of international conventions, of internal penal laws, of the general principles of criminal law as derived from the criminal law of all civilized nations and were involved in and part of a systematic course of conduct. The said acts were contrary to Article 6 of the Charter.

The prosecution will rely upon the facts pleaded under Count Three as also constituting Crimes against Humanity.

(A) Murder, Extermination, Enslavement, Deportation and Other Inhumane Acts Committed Against Civilian Populations Before and During the War

For the purposes set out above, the defendants adopted a policy of persecution, repression, and extermination of all civilians in Germany who were, or who were believed to, or who were believed likely to become, hostile to the Nazi Government and the common plan or conspiracy described in Count One. They imprisoned such persons without judicial process, holding them in "protective custody" and concentration camps, and subjected them to persecution, degradation, despoilment, enslavement, torture and murder.

Special courts were established to carry out the will of the conspirators; favored branches or agencies of the State and Party were permitted to operate outside the range even of nazified law and to crush all tendencies and elements which were considered "undesirable." The various concentration camps included Buchenwald, which was established in 1933 and Dachau, which was established in 1934. At these and other camps the civilians were put to slave labor, and murdered and ill-treated by diverse means, including those set out in Count Three above, and these acts and policies were continued and extended to the occupied countries after the 1st September, 1939, and until 8th May, 1945.

(B) Persecution on Political, Racial and Religious Grounds in Execution of and in Connection With the Common Plan Mentioned in Count One

As above stated, in execution of and in connection with the common plan mentioned in Count One, opponents of the German Government were exterminated and persecuted. These persecutions were directed against Jews. They were also directed against persons whose political belief or spiritual aspirations were deemed to be in conflict with the aims of the Nazis.

Jews were systematically persecuted since 1933; they were deprived of their liberty, thrown into concentration camps where they were murdered and ill-treated. Their property was confiscated. Hundreds of thousands of Jews were so treated before the 1st September 1939.

Since the 1st September, 1939, the persecution of the Jews was redoubled; millions of Jews from Germany and from the occupied Western Countries were sent to the Eastern Countries for extermination.

Particulars by way of example and without prejudice to the production of evidence of other cases are as follows:

The Nazis murdered amongst others Chancellor Dollfuss, the Social Democrat Breitscheid and the Communist Thaelmann. They imprisoned in concentration camps numerous political and religious personages, for example Chancellor Schuschnigg and Pastor Niemoller.

In November, 1938 by orders of the Chief of the Gestapo, anti-Jewish demonstrations all over Germany took place. Jewish property was destroyed, 30,000 Jews were arrested and sent to concentration camps and their property confiscated.

Under Paragraph VIII A, above, millions of the persons there mentioned as having been murdered and ill-treated were Jews.

Among other mass murders of Jews were the following:

At Kislovdosk all Jews were made to give up their property: 2,000 were shot in an anti-tank ditch at Mineraliye Vodi: 4,300 other Jews were shot in the same ditch.

60,000 Jews were shot on an island on the Dvina near Riga.

20,000 Jews were shot at Lutsk.

32,000 Jews were shot at Sarny.

60,000 Jews were shot at Kiev and Dniepropetrovsk.

Thousands of Jews were gassed weekly by means of gas-wagons which broke down from overwork.

As the Germans retreated before the Soviet Army they exterminated Jews rather than allow them to be liberated. Many concentration camps and ghettos were set up in which Jews were incarcerated and tortured, starved, subjected to merciless atrocities and finally exterminated.

About 70,000 Jews were exterminated in Yugoslavia....

Wherefore, this Indictment is lodged with the Tribunal in English, French and Russian, each text having equal authenticity, and the charges herein made against the above named defendants are hereby presented to the Tribunal.

ROBERT H. JACKSON

Acting on Behalf of the United States of America

FRANCOIS DE MENTHON

Acting on Behalf of the French Republic

HARTLEY SHAWCROSS

Acting on Behalf of the United Kingdom of Great Britain and Northern Ireland

R. A. RUDENKO

Acting on Behalf of the Union of Soviet Socialist Republics

Judgment of the International Military Tribunal at Nuremberg
(1946)

(E) Persecution of the Jews

The persecution of the Jews at the hands of the Nazi Government has been proved in the greatest detail before the Tribunal. It is a record of consistent and systematic inhumanity on the greatest scale....

... Adolf Eichmann, who had been put in charge of this program by Hitler, has estimated that the policy pursued resulted in the killing of 6,000,000 Jews, of which 4,000,000 were killed in the extermination institutions.

(F) The Law Relating to War Crimes and Crimes Against Humanity

[see Chapter Six, Section 3]

Notes

1. Note that the Indictment identifies two types of crimes against humanity. At Nuremberg before the IMT, 16 were convicted of crimes against humanity. See Chapter Six, Section 3.

2. Note also with respect to the Indictment that if the accused had a "common plan ... to commit Crimes against Humanity," obviously a "common plan" was not a necessary element of or subsumed within a crime against humanity. See also Sadat, *The Interpretation of the Nuremberg Principles, infra*; The Rome Statute of the ICC requires that the defendant's action be linked to a "State or organizational policy." *Id.* art. 7(2)(a). Therefore, is this an example of why the ICC only has limited jurisdiction over crimes against humanity. The language of the Rome Statute has generated difficulties at the ICC. See *Situation in the Republic of Kenya*, ICC (2010), *infra*; Leila Nadya Sadat, *Crimes Against Humanity in the Modern Age*, 106 AM. J. INT'L L. _ (2012). *See also* Paust, *The International Criminal Court Does Not Have Complete Jurisdiction Over Customary Crimes Against Humanity and War Crimes*, 43 THE JOHN MARSHALL L. REV. 681, 693–97 (2010).

3. Professor Cherif Bassiouni has written:

> The Tribunal did find that crimes against humanity actually were committed prior to the War; the judgment against defendant Neurath is illustrative of this fact. His offenses under counts three and four were categorized as "Criminal Activity in Czechoslovakia," some of which occurred before the War. However, since the offenses were committed in connection with crimes against peace, that is, the takeover of Czechoslovakia [*i.e.*, acts of aggression–recall Chapter Seven],

they were considered proper subjects of prosecution under the Charter. Thus, it was not the "nature" of the act that was determinative of its punishability but rather the "circumstances" under which it was committed, surely an artificial criterion.

The judgment of acquittal of defendant Streicher further illuminates the curious way in which crimes against humanity were defined. The reasoning supportive of the acquittal was that since the program of extermination of the Jews was initiated before the War, and hence already in progress, Streicher committed no crime connected with the War.

M.C. Bassiouni, *Crimes Against Humanity*, in 3 INTERNATIONAL CRIMINAL LAW 51, 68 (M.C. Bassiouni ed. 1987). See Article 7 of the ICC. Is it different? See also M. CHERIF BASSIOUNI, CRIMES AGAINST HUMANITY: HISTORICAL EVOLUTION AND CONTEMPORARY APPLICATION 14–19 (2011).

Control Council Law No. 10
art. II(1)(c) (1945)

Crimes against Humanity. Atrocities and offenses, including but not limited to murder, extermination, enslavement, deportation, imprisonment, torture, rape, or other inhumane acts committed against any civilian population, or persecutions on political, racial or religious grounds whether or not in violation of the domestic laws of the country where perpetrated.

Telford Taylor, Final Report to the Secretary of the Army on the Nuernberg War Crimes Trials Under Control Council Law No. 10
at 64–65, 69, 224–226 (1949)

Finally, there were the crimes which the average man would think of as most characteristic of the Nazis, and which we may describe as *degradation or extermination of national, political, racial, religious, or other groups*. These crimes cover the vast and terrible world of the Nuernberg laws, yellow arm bands, "Aryanization," concentration camps, medical experiments, extermination squads, and so on. These were the sort of deeds and practices which the provisions of the definition concerning "crimes against humanity" were intended to reach. Actually, when committed in the course of belligerent occupation (whether in the occupied country or elsewhere), these were also "war crimes." But the concept of "crimes against humanity" comprises atrocities which are part of a campaign of discrimination or persecution, and which are crimes against international law even when committed by nationals of one country against their fellow nationals or against those of other nations irrespective of belligerent status....

The fourth and largest category—"crimes against humanity," consisting of atrocities committed in the course or as a result of racial or religious persecutions—played a part in all 12 of the trials. Murderous "experiments," perpetrated in the name of medicine, had been inflicted on Jews, gypsies, and other unfortunate inmates of the concentration camps, as was developed in the "Medical," "Milch,"" and "Pohl" cases (Cases No. 1, 2, 4, respectively). The entire system of concentration-camp administration was explored in the "Pohl case." In the "Justice case" (Case No. 3) the Nazi judges and legal officials were accused of "judicial murder" by perverting the German legal system so as to deny to Poles, Czechs, and others the protection of law. Concentration-camp inmates were among the most miserable victims of the slave-labor program, as was disclosed in the "Krupp," "Far-ben," "Ministries," and "Pohl" cases. The notorious "final solution of the Jewish question," the objective of which was nothing less than the extermination of European Jewry, was the basis of the "Einsatz case" (Case No. 9), and an important facet of the "Ministries case" (Case No. 11). The complicity of the military leaders in the "solution" was dealt with in the "Hostage" and "High Command" cases (Cases No. 7 and 12). In the "RuSHA case" (Case No. 8), the defendants were the principal officials in the so-called resettle-ment program, under which thousands of farmers in eastern Europe and the Balkans were robbed of their land or the benefit for German "settlers," and Germanic-looking children of Polish, Czech, or other eastern European parentage were torn from their par-ents and taken to the Reich for "Germanization."

In two cases, an entire count of each indictment was devoted to the charge that the de-fendants had committed crimes against humanity during the early years of the Third Reich, and before the outbreak of war in 1939. In the "Flick case" the defendants were ac-cused of complicity in the forced "Aryanization" of Jewish industrial and mining prop-erties. In the "Ministries case" a number of the defendants were charged with responsibility for the discriminatory laws and abuses, and the misery and atrocities resulting therefrom, under which German Jewry suffered during those years. In each [such] case [under Con-trol Council Law 10], the Tribunal dismissed the charge as outside its competence....

Crimes Against Humanity

None of the Nuremberg judgments squarely passed on the question whether mass atrocities committed by or with the approval of a government against a racial or religious group of its own inhabitants in peacetime constitute crimes under international law. Such a contention was made by the prosecution before the IMT, but the Tribunal disposed of this charge by holding that the language of the London Charter limited its jurisdiction to such crimes as were committed in the course of or in connection with aggressive war. Again in the "Flick Case" and in the "Ministries Case" the prosecution raised the same question; in each indictment an entire count was devoted to the charge of prewar atroc-ities, chiefly against Jews. Although the language of Law No. 10 defining "crimes against humanity" differed in certain particulars from the comparable definition in the London Charter, the "Flick" and "Ministries" tribunals followed the decision of the IMT and de-clined to take jurisdiction of the charge.

However, in two other Nuremberg cases where the question was raised only collater-ally, the Nuremberg tribunals made significant and important observations on this ques-tion. Thus, in the "Einsatzgruppen Case" the Jewish exterminations of which the defendants were accused occurred during and after 1941, but it was charged that these murders con-stituted not only "war crimes" but also "crimes against humanity." Since no acts prior to 1939 were involved, the Tribunal had no occasion to pass upon the question of con-struction of Law No. 10 which confronted the "Flick" and "Ministries" tribunals. But in convicting the defendants of "crimes against humanity" the court expressly stated that "this law is not limited to offenses committed during war," and observed that—

> Crimes against humanity are acts committed in the course of wholesale and systematic violation of life and liberty. It is to be observed that insofar as international jurisdiction is concerned the concept of crimes against humanity does not apply to offenses for which the criminal code of any well-ordered State makes adequate provision. They can only come within the purview of this basic code of human-ity because the State involved, owing to indifference, impotency or complicity, has been unable or has refused to halt the crimes and punish the criminals.

So, too, in the "Justice Case," where "crimes against humanity" committed after 1939 were also charged against the defendants, the Tribunal stated:

> ... it can no longer be said that violations of the laws and customs of war are the only offenses recognized by common international law. The force of circumstance, the grim fact of worldwide interdependence, and the moral pressure of public opinion have resulted in international recognition that certain crimes against humanity committed by Nazi authority against German nationals constituted violations not alone of statute but also of common international law.

The court proceeded to review a number of incidents extending over a century where nations or their chiefs of state had intervened or protested against religious or racial atrocities in Turkey, Rumania, and elsewhere, and quoted with approval Bluntschli's statement that "states are allowed to interfere in the name of international law if 'human rights' are violated to the detriment of any single race."

The practical importance of this question can hardly be overstated, and the convention recently concluded by the United Nations on the subject of "genocide" is a manifestation of the lively interest which it has awakened. Important as is the concept of "aggressive war," and beneficent as the Hague and Geneva Conventions may be, we can hardly expect much further judicial development and interpretation of "crimes against peace" or "war crimes" except in the unhappy event of another war. The concept of "crimes against humanity," however, if it becomes an established part of international penal law—as it seems to be doing—will be of the greatest practical importance in peacetime. Indeed, it may prove to be a most important safeguard against future wars, inasmuch as large-scale domestic atrocities caused by racial or religious issues always constitute a serious threat to peace.

United States v. Altstoetter, *et al.*

("The Justice Case"), III Trials of War Criminals Before the Nuremberg Military Tribunals Under Control Council Law No. 10, 1946–1949

C.C. Law 10 is not limited to the punishment of persons guilty of violating the laws and customs of war in the narrow sense....

As the prime illustration of a crime against humanity under C.C. Law 10, which by reason of its magnitude and its international repercussions has been recognized as a violation of common international law, we cite "genocide" which will shortly receive our full consideration. A resolution recently adopted by the General Assembly of the United Nations is in part as follows:

> "The General Assembly therefore—
>
> Affirms that genocide is a crime under international law which the civilized world condemns, and for the commission of which principals and accomplices— whether private individuals, public officials, or statesmen, and whether the crime is committed on religious, racial, political or any other grounds—are punishable; ...

The General Assembly is not an international legislature, but it is the most authoritative organ in existence for the interpretation of world opinion. Its recognition of genocide as an international crime is persuasive evidence of the fact. We approve and adopt its conclusions. Whether the crime against humanity is the product of statute or of common international law, or, as we believe, of both, we find no injustice to persons tried for such crimes. They are chargeable with knowledge that such acts were wrong and were punishable when committed....

The very essence of the prosecution's case is that the laws, the Hitlerian decrees and the Draconic, corrupt, and perverted Nazi judicial system themselves constituted the substance of war crimes and crimes against humanity and that participation in the enactment and enforcement of them amounts to complicity in crime. We have pointed out that governmental participation is a material element of the crime against humanity. Only when official organs of sovereignty participated in atrocities and persecutions did those crimes assume international proportions. It can scarcely be said that governmental participation, the proof of which is necessary for conviction, can also be a defense to the charge.

Notes and Questions

1. The 1950 Principles of the Nuremberg Charter and Judgment formulated by the International Law Commission of the United Nations (5 U.N. GAOR, Supp. No. 12, at 11–14, para. 99, U.N. Doc. A/1316, 1950) attached the following phrase to the paragraph on crimes against humanity: "when such acts are done or such persecutions are carried out in execution of or in connection with any act of aggression or any war crime." No such phrase appeared in Control Council Law No. 10. Further, the 1950 Principles did not retain the categories of "imprisonment, torture, rape" found in Control Council Law No. 10, but missing from Article 6(c) of the Nuremberg Charter. Were such words necessary?

Some eighteen years later, the U.N. General Assembly adopted the Convention on the Nonapplicability of Statutory Limitations to War Crimes and Crimes Against Humanity by resolution, article 1(b) of which states:

> "Crimes against humanity whether committed in time of war or in time of peace as they are defined in the Charter of the International Military Tribunal, Nuremberg, of August 8, 1945, and confirmed by resolutions 3(I) of February 13, 1946 and 95(I) of December 11, 1946, of the General Assembly of the United Nations...."

G.A. Res 2391 (XXIII), 23 U.N. GAOR, Supp. (No. 18) 40, U.N. Doc. A/7218 (1968)

Thus, it seems that the phrase added in the 1950 Principles was dropped. Additionally, the 1968 resolution contained the broad phrase "committed in time of war or in time of peace." The Nuremberg Charter (see the Documents Supplement) had utilized a similar phrase, "before or during the war," only in connection with the first category of crimes against humanity, while limiting issues of persecution as such by the phrase "in execution of or in connection with any crime within the jurisdiction of the Tribunal." What differences might attach? Which phrase or set of phrases is most authoritative, those in the 1945 Charter of the IMT (approved generally by the U.N. General Assembly in 1946), the 1950 I.L.C. Principles (approved by the U.N. General Assembly), Control Council Law No. 10, or the 1968 U.N. General Assembly resolution?

2. Article 5(c) of the Tokyo Charter for the I.M.T. for the Far East reads:

> *Crimes against Humanity*: Namely, murder, extermination, enslavement, deportation, and other inhumane acts committed before or during the war, or persecutions on political or racial grounds in execution of or in connection with any crime within the jurisdiction of the Tribunal, whether or not in violation of the domestic law of the country where perpetrated.

3. Does language in any of the abovementioned Charters, Laws, Principles or resolutions require that crimes against humanity be "widespread," "systematic," "serious," "cruel,"

or part of a "state policy," "common plan," or conspiracy? Need such crimes be committed by those acting on behalf of a state? See J. Paust, *Threats to Accountability After Nuremberg: Crimes Against Humanity, Leader Responsibility and National Fora*, 12 N.Y.L.S. J. H.R. 547 (1995); *see also* Article IV of the 1948 Genocide Convention (in Chapter Ten); *but see* language quoted from the Einsatzgruppen Case, *supra*, and *Altstoetter, supra; The Prosecutor v. Akayesu*, ICTR-96-4-T, *infra*.

In The Prosecutor v. Krstic, IT-98-33-A (Appeals Chamber Judgment, 19 Apr. 2004), para. 223, it was declared that the existence of a plan or policy is not required for crimes against humanity or genocide, although such can be relevant concerning an intent to engage in widespread or systematic conduct. Twelve ICTY and four ICTR cases and the Special Court for Sierra Leon have recognized that a plan is not required.

4. Are there two basic types of crimes against humanity identified in those documents?

5. It has been stated that "[t]he Nuremberg Charter applied a customary international law of human rights in charging the Nazi war criminals, inter alia, with 'crimes against humanity'... The U.N. Charter codifies that customary law and renders applicable to all states at least such human rights law as was invoked at Nuremberg." L. HENKIN, R. PUGH, O. SCHACHTER, H. SMIT, INTERNATIONAL LAW 986 (2 ed. 1987). See also HERSCH LAUTERPACHT, INTERNATIONAL LAW AND HUMAN RIGHTS 35–38, 61–62 (1968); RICHARD B. LILLICH, INTERNATIONAL HUMAN RIGHTS 896–99 (2 ed. 1991); MYRES M. McDOUGAL, HAROLD D. LASSWELL, LUNG-CHU CHEN, HUMAN RIGHTS AND WORLD PUBLIC ORDER 354–56, 535–36, 542–46 (1980); FRANK NEWMAN & DAVID WEISSBRODT, INTERNATIONAL HUMAN RIGHTS 663–64, 715–17 (1990); TELFORD TAYLOR, NUREMBERG AND VIETNAM: AN AMERICAN TRAGEDY 79 (1970); M. Cherif Bassiouni, Crimes Against Humanity, in 3 INTERNATIONAL CRIMINAL LAW — ENFORCEMENT 51, 52 (M. Cherif Bassiouni ed. 1987); M. Cherif Bassiouni, *The Proscribing Function of International Criminal Law in the Processes of International Protection of Human Rights*, 9 YALE J. WORLD PUB. ORD. 193, 201 (1982).

6. Would the list of "crimes against humanity" recognized at Nuremberg, if committed during war, also constitute war crimes under then customary international law? Recall Chapter Eight. What is the significance of the International Tribunal's recognition that "from the beginning of the war in 1939 war crimes were committed on a vast scale, which were also crimes against humanity...."? Are war crimes war crimes by any other name? See also *Eichmann, infra; but see* Egon Schwelb, *Crimes Against Humanity*, 23 BRIT. Y.B. INT'L L. 178, 206 (1946). Today, recall Geneva Civilian Convention, arts. 3, 13, 16, *passim* (in Chapter Eight) with respect to the reach of Geneva law to one's own nationals. Also recall the laws of war applicable to a belligerency that were extant prior to 1939.

7. Can crimes against humanity be committed against combatants or, at least, former combatants? The Tokyo Charter did not limit either type of crimes against humanity to civilian victims and other customary documents only limited the first type to civilian victims. In The Prosecutor v. Krstic, *supra*, para. 223, the Appeals Chamber recognized that genocidal intent need not involve an intent to destroy civilians as such and that genocide can occur where a perpetrator seeks to target military personnel at least in part because they are members of a relevant group. Since genocide is a type of crime against humanity, the decision appears to be relevant here as well. In The Prosecutor v. Martic, IT-95-11-A (Appeals Chamber, Judgment) (9 Oct. 2008), the Appeals Chamber held that the term "civilian" means person who are not members of the armed forces. *Id.* para. 297.

Consider also the war crimes listed *supra* in Chapters Two, Six, and Eight. Is it significant that the 1919 list applied to "[a]ll persons ... guilty of offenses against the laws and customs of war or the laws of humanity"? *But see* M.C. Bassiouni, *Crimes Against Humanity*, in 3 International Criminal Law: Enforcement 5, 53–4 (M.C. Bassiouni ed. 1987). The 1919 Commission relied in part on the "Martens clause" to the 1907 Hague Convention No. IV which had referred to the "laws of humanity". See Note 3 below. During the conference, representatives from the U.S. and Japan had objected to use of the phrase "laws of humanity," arguing that it was vague and not a part of positive international law. See Annex to the Report, Memorandum of Reservations presented by the Representatives of the United States to the Report of the Commission. For a critical appraisal, see Lord Wright, *War Crimes Under International Law*, 62 L.Q. Rev. 40, 48–9 (1946); *see also* J. Garner, *Punishment of Offenders Against the Laws and Customs of War*, 14 Am. J. Int'l L. 70 (1920). Clearly, however, it was a part of treaty law and had referred to general and overarching principles. Lord Wright was the Chairman of the United Nations War Crimes Commission established by the Declaration of St. James in 1942 which investigated war crimes during WW II. *See* Quincy Wright, History of the United Nations War Crimes Commission(1948), wherein the prior position of the U.S. was also criticized.

According to Professor Bassiouni: at Versailles in 1919, it did not suit the foreign policy interests of the U.S. government to recognize such a principle. By 1945, however, the concept was revised in order to prosecute Nazi offenders who had committed horrible crimes against their fellow nationals—crimes not covered by the laws of war except in cases of belligerency. The failed attempt of a few years past was transformed by a new political will into a valid precedent and, in this case, the facts drove the law. *See* M. Cherif Bassiouni, *International Law and the Holocaust*, 9 Cal. West. Int'l L. J. 201, 274 (1979); *see also* J. F. Willis, Prologue to Nuremberg: The Politics and Diplomacy of Punishing War Criminals of the First World War(1982); D. Mamas, *Prosecuting Crimes Against Humanity: The Lessons of World War I*, 13 Fordham J. Int'l L. 86 (1990).

8. In 1985, a U.S. Circuit Court has recognized that Israeli law enacted to punish war crimes and "crimes against humanity" committed in 1942 or 1943 reaches "crimes [that are] universally recognized and condemned by the community of nations" and that Israel "has jurisdiction to punish … war crimes and crimes against humanity" committed at such times under the universality principle. *Demjanjuk v. Petrovsky*, 776 F.2d 571, 582–83 (6th Cir. 1985), *cert. denied*, 475 U.S. 1016 (1986). Demjanjuk was subsequently tried and convicted in Israel. See L.A. Times, April 26, 1988, §1, at 1, col. 3. However, he was later released upon proof of mistaken identity and returned to the U.S. in 1993 where lengthy deportation proceedings began.

9. In 2005, a three-judge panel of a Spanish court convicted Adolfo Scilingo, a former Argentinian naval officer, of crimes against humanity, torture, and illegal detention of persons during Argentina's "dirty war" between 1976 and 1983. The Scilingo Case, Judgement No. 16/2005, Audiencia Nacional (National Court) de Madrid (3d Sec., Crim. Div., 19 Apr. 2005). He was sentenced to 21 years in prison for each death of 31 persons and 5 years each for torture and illegal detention for a total of 640 years. During the proceedings, Scilingo admitted to being on board two "death flights" during which detainees were stripped naked, drugged, and thrown to their deaths over the ocean. He also testified about abuses committed at a torture center, the Buenos Aires Navy School of Mechanics. Human rights groups claim that over 30,000 persons were "disappeared" during the "dirty war".

10. Would non-state actor attacks by members of al Qaeda on the World Trade Center in New York on September 11, 2001 be prosecutable as crimes against humanity? Would the attack at that date on the Pentagon? Although not required in the customary World War II instruments, were the 9/11 attacks "widespread" or "systematic"? See M. Cherif Bassiouni, *Legal Control of International Terrorism: A Policy-Oriented Assessment*, 43 Harv. Int'l L.J. 83, 101 (2002) ("the attacks upon the United States of September 11

constitute 'Crimes Against Humanity' as defined in Article 7 of the Statute of'' the ICC); Antonio Cassese, *Terrorism is also Disrupting Some Crucial Legal Categories of International Law*, 12 EUR. J. INT'L L. 993, 994–95 (2011); Jordan J. Paust, *The International Criminal Court Does Not Have Complete Jurisdiction Over Customary Crimes Against Humanity and War Crimes*, 43 THE JOHN MARSHALL L. REV. 681, 691, 694 n.37 (2010) (citing many other authors); Leila Nadya Sadat, *Terrorism and the Rule of Law*, 3 WASH. U. GLOBAL STUD. L. REV. 135, 148–49 (2004); David J. Scheffer, *Staying the Course with the International Criminal Court*, 35 CORNELL INT'L L.J. 47, 49, 50 n.6 (2002); Susan Tiefenbrun, *A Semiotic Approach to a Legal Definition of Terrorism*, 9 ILSA J. INT'L & COMP. L. 357, 386 n.115 (2003) (quoting Professor Michael P. Scharf); *cf* William A. Schabas, *State Policy as an Element of International Crimes*, 98 J. CRIM. L. & CRIMINOLOGY 953 (2008) (arguing that, contrary to trends in decision in the ICTY and a majority viewpoint, "state policy" should be a requirement).

Canadian courts have also recognized private actor complicity or leader responsibility for crimes against humanity committed by the Sri Lanka insurgent group LLTE. *See, e.g.*, Sivakumar v. R, 1997 WL 1913825, 37 Imm. L.R. (2d) 191 (Fed. Ct. Can. 1997) (leader responsibility); Pushpanathan v. Canada, 2002 WL 31918433, 25 Imm. L.R. (3d) 242 (Imm. & Refugee Bd. (App. Div.) 2002) (private actor complicity).

Section 2
Eichmann Trial (Israel)

The Attorney General of the Government of Israel v. Adolf, the Son of Karl Adolf Eichmann
Criminal Case No. 40/61 (1961)

[Editors' note: These excerpts are taken from the opinion and judgment of the 3 judge District Court of Jerusalem, presided over by Mr. Justice Landau]

Our jurisdiction to try this case is based on the Nazis and Nazi Collaborators (Punishment) law, *a statutory law the provisions of which are unequivocal*....

... we have reached the conclusion that the law in question conforms to the best traditions of the law of nations.

The power of the State of Israel to enact the law in question or Israel's right to punish is based, with respect to the offences in question, from the point of view of international law, on a dual foundation: The universal character of the crimes in question and their specific character as being designated to exterminate the Jewish people. In what follows we shall deal with each of these two aspects separately....

The abhorrent crimes defined in this law are crimes not under Israel law alone. These crimes which afflicted the whole of mankind and shocked the conscience of nations are grave offenses against the law of nations itself ('*delicta juris gentium*'). Therefore, so far from international law negating or limiting the jurisdiction of countries with respect to such crimes, in the absence of an International Court the international law is in need of the judicial and legislative authorities of every country, to give effect to its penal injunctions and to bring criminals to trial. The authority and jurisdiction to try crimes under international law are universal....

The 'crime against the Jewish people' is defined on the pattern of the genocide crime defined in the "Convention for the prevention and punishment of genocide' which was adopted by the United Nations Assembly on 9.12.48. The 'crime against humanity' and the 'war crime' are defined on the pattern of crimes of identical designations defined in the Charter of the International Military Tribunal, (which is the Statute of the Nuremberg Court) annexed to the Four-Power Agreement of 8.8.45 on the subject of the trial of the principal war criminals (the London Agreement), and also in Law No. 10 of the Control Council of Germany of 20.12.45. The offence of 'membership of a hostile organization' is defined by the pronouncement in the judgment of the Nuremberg Tribunal, according to its Charter, to declare the organizations in question as 'criminal organizations', and is also patterned on the Council of Control Law No. 10. For purposes of comparison we shall set forth in what follows the parallel articles and clauses side by side....

In the light of the recurrent affirmation by the United Nations in the 1946 Assembly resolution and in the 1948 convention, and in the light of the advisory opinion of the International Court of Justice, there is no doubt that genocide has been recognized as a crime under international law in the full legal meaning of this term, and at that *ex tunc*; that is to say: the crimes of genocide which were committed against the Jewish people and other peoples were crimes under international law. It follows therefore, in the light of the acknowledged principles of international law, that the jurisdiction to try such crimes is universal.

Attorney General of Israel v. Eichmann

Israel, Supreme Court 1962,
36 Int'l L. Rep. 277, 277–78, 287–89, 294–97, 304 (1968)

1. The appellant, Adolf Eichmann, was found guilty by the District Court of Jerusalem of offenses of the most extreme gravity against the Nazi and Nazi Collaborators (Punishment) Law, 1950 (hereinafter referred to as "the Law") and was sentenced to death. These offences may be divided into four groups:

(a) Crimes against the Jewish people, contrary to Section I (a)(1) of the Law;

(b) Crimes against humanity, contrary to Section I(a)(2);

(c) War crimes, contrary to Section I(a)(3);

(d) Membership of hostile organizations, contrary to Section 3.

2. The acts constituting these offences, which the Court attributed to the appellant, have been specified in paragraph 244 of the judgment of the District Court.

The acts comprised in Group (a) are:

(1) that during the period from August 1941 to May 1945, in Germany, in the Axis States and in the areas which were subject to the authority of Germany and the Axis States, he, together with others, caused the killing of millions of Jews for the purpose of carrying out the plan known as "the Final Solution of the Jewish Problem" with the intent to exterminate the Jewish people;

(2) that during that period and in the same places he, together with others, placed millions of Jews in living conditions which were calculated to bring about their physical destruction, for the purpose of carrying out the plan above mentioned with the intent to exterminate the Jewish people;

(3) that during that period and in the same places he, together with others, caused serious physical and mental harm to millions of Jews with the intent to exterminate the Jewish people;

(4) that during the years 1943 and 1944 he, together with others, "devised measures the purpose of which was to prevent births among Jews by his instructions forbidding child bearing and ordering the interruption of pregnancies of Jewish women in the Theresin Ghetto with the intent to exterminate the Jewish people".

The acts constituting the crimes in Group (b) are as follows:

(5) that during the period from August 1941 to May 1945 he, together with others, caused in the territories and areas mentioned in clause (1) the murder, extermination, enslavement, starvation and deportation of the civilian Jewish population;

(6) that during the period from December 1939 to March 1941 he, together with others, caused the deportation of Jews to Nisco, and the deportation of Jews from the areas in the East annexed to the Reich, and from the Reich area proper, to the German Occupied Territories in the East, and to France;

(7) that in carrying out the above-mentioned activities he persecuted Jews on national, racial, religious and political grounds;

(8) that during the period from March 1938 to May 1945 in the places mentioned above he, together with others, caused the spoliation of the property of millions of Jews by means of mass terror linked with the murder, extermination, starvation and deportation of these Jews;

(9) that during the years 1940–1942 he, together with others, caused the expulsion of hundreds of thousands of Poles from their places of residence;

(10) that during 1941 he, together with others, caused the expulsion of more than 14,000 Slovenes from their places of residence;

(11) that during the Second World War he, together with others, caused the expulsion of scores of thousands of gipsies from Germany and German-occupied areas and their transportation to the German-occupied areas in the East;

(12) that in 1942 he, together with others, caused the expulsion of 93 children of the Czech village of Lidice....

(1) Thus, the category of "crime against the Jewish People" is, as the District Court held in paragraph 26 of its judgment, "nothing but the gravest type of 'crime against humanity'". Although certain differences exist between them—for example, the first offence requires a specific criminal intent—these are not differences material to this case....

[The Character of International Crimes]

II. *The first proposition.* Our view that the crimes in question must today be regarded as crimes which were also in the past banned by the law of nations and entailed individual criminal responsibility, is based upon the following reasons:

(a) As is well known, the rules of the law of nations are not derived solely from international treaties and crystallized international custom. In the absence of a supreme legislative authority and international codes the process of its evolution resembles that of the common law; in other words, its rules are fashioned piecemeal by analogy with the rules embedded in treaties and custom, on the basis of the "general principles of law recognized by civilized nations" and having regard to vital international needs that compel an immediate solution. A principle which constitutes a common denominator of the legal systems current in many countries must clearly be regarded as a "general principle of law recognized by civilized nations"....

(c) In view of the characteristic traits that mark the international crimes discussed above and having regard to the organic development of the law of nations—a development that advances from case to case under the impact of the humane sentiments common to civilized nations and by virtue of the needs vital for the survival of mankind and for ensuring the stability of the world order—it definitely cannot be said that, when the Charter of the Nuremberg International Military Tribunal was signed and the categories of "War Crimes" and "Crimes against Humanity" were defined in it, this merely amounted to an act of legislation by the victorious countries. The truth, as the Tribunal itself said, is that the Charter, with all the principles embodied in it—including that of individual responsibility—must be seen as "the expression of international law existing at the time of its creation; and to that extent (the Charter) is itself a contribution to international law." (I.M.T. (1947), vol. I, p. 218.) See also the identical view expressed by Court No. III in the American Zone of Germany concerning two of the types of crimes mentioned in Control Council Law No. 10.

"All of the war crimes and many, if not all, of the crimes against humanity as charged in the indictment ... were ... (not) violative of pre-existing principles of international law. To the extent to which this is true, C.C. law may be deemed to be a codification, rather than original substantive legislation" (*U.S. v. Altstoetter,* T.W.C., vol. 3, p. 966).

It should be added that many of those who voiced criticism of the Charter and of the Judgment of the International Military Tribunal at Nuremberg directed it against the incorporation into the Charter of the "Crime against Peace" but not against the other two categories (see the articles by Finch in *American Journal of International Law,* 41 (1947), pp. 22, 23, and Doman in *Columbia Law Review,* 60 (1960), p. 413). In so far as other writers have criticized the incorporation of "Crimes against Humanity" as being contrary to international law *de lege lata,* they have done so on the ground that the punishment of the Nazi criminals for the commission of such crimes within Germany and against German citizens imported an excessive interference with the domestic competence of the State (see the article by Schick in the same volume of the *American Journal of International Law,* pp. 778–779). The reply to this argument is first that it is possible to trace a direct line to the inclusion of the crimes mentioned from the wording of the provision of Hague Convention No. IV of 1907, above cited, which refers to "the Laws of Humanity" and "the dictates of public conscience". It stands to reason, as Quincy Wright said (see his article, *ibid.*, p. 60), that this wording should apply "to atrocities against nationals as well as against aliens". In the graphic language of Friedmann (*Legal Theory,* 4th ed., p. 316), "it is hardly necessary to invoke natural law to condemn the mass slaughter of helpless human beings. Murder is generally taken to be a crime in positive international law."....
..if any doubt existed as to this appraisal of the Nuremberg Principles as principles that have formed part of the customary law of nations "since time immemorial", two international documents justify it. We allude to the United Nations General Assembly Resolution of December 11, 1946, which "affirms the principles of international law recognized by the Charter of the Nuremberg Tribunal and the Judgment of the Tribunal", and also to the General Assembly Resolution of the same date, No. 96 (I), in which the General Assembly "affirms that Genocide is a crime under international law"....

What is more, in the wake of Resolution 96 (I) of December 11, 1946, the United Nations General Assembly unanimously adopted on December 9, 1948, the Convention for the Prevention and Punishment of the Crime of Genocide. Article I of this Convention provides:

> "The Contracting Parties confirm that genocide, whether committed in time of peace or in time of war, is a crime under international law."

As the District Court has shown, relying on the Advisory Opinion of the International Court of Justice dated May 28, 1951, the import of this provision is that the principles inherent in the Convention — as distinct from the contractual obligations embodied therein — "were already part of customary international law when the dreadful crimes were perpetrated, which led to the United Nations Resolution and the drafting of the Convention — the crimes of Genocide committed by the Nazis" (paragraph 21 of the judgment).

The outcome of the above analysis is that the crimes set out in the Law of 1950, which we have grouped under the inclusive caption "crimes against humanity", must be seen today as acts that have always been forbidden by customary international law — acts which are of a "universal" criminal character and entail individual criminal responsibility. That being so, the enactment of the Law was not from the point of view of international law a legislative act which conflicted with the principle *nulla poena* or the operation of which was retroactive, but rather one by which the Knesset gave effect to international law and its objectives....

We sum up our views on this subject as follows. Not only do all the crimes attributed to the appellant bear an international character, but their harmful and murderous effects were so embracing and widespread as to shake the international community to its very foundations. The State of Israel therefore was entitled, pursuant to the principle of universal jurisdiction and in the capacity of a guardian of international law and an agent for its enforcement, to try the appellant. That being the case, no importance attaches to the fact that the State of Israel did not exist when the offences were committed. Here therefore is an additional reason — and one based on a positive approach — for rejecting the second, "jurisdictional", submission of counsel for the appellant.

Notes and Questions

1. What was the smallest number of direct victims identified in *Eichmann* as an example of a crime against humanity (in Group (b))?

2. In 1984, a nearly unanimous resolution of the U.N. General Assembly condemned the illegal regime in South Africa "for defying relevant resolutions of the United Nations and persisting with the further entrenchment of apartheid, a system declared a crime against humanity and a threat to international peace and security." G.A. Res. 2, 39 U.N. GAOR, Supp. No. 51, at 14–5, § 3, U.N. Doc. A/39/51 (Sept. 28, 1984) (vote: 133–0–2).

A decade earlier, the U.N. General Assembly adopted the International Convention on the Suppression and Punishment of the Crime of Apartheid by resolution, Article 1 of which declares that "apartheid is a crime against humanity" and that relevant acts "are crimes violating the principles of international law, in particular the purposes and principles of the Charter of the United Nations." (see Chapter Eleven).

3. The U.S. Army Field Manual 27-10, THE LAW OF LAND WARFARE (1956), para. 498, recognized that any person who commits a crime against humanity has committed "a crime under international law" and "is responsible therefor and liable to punishment." Crimes against humanity as such are not defined therein. If such crimes are not also war crimes, how might they be prosecuted within or by the United States? Consider also the chapter on genocide, *infra*.

For a recommended addition to Title 18 of the United States Code, *see, e.g.,* 85 PROC., AM. SOC. INT'L L. 16 (1991); Paust, *Threats to Accountability After Nuremberg, supra.*

Section 3
Barbie, Touvier and Papon Trials (France)

Matter of Barbie

France, Court of Cassation (Criminal Chamber) Oct. 6, 1983 and Jan. 26, 1984,
extract from: 78 INT'L L. REP. 125 (1988)

SUMMARY: *The facts:*—Klaus Barbie was head of the Gestapo in Lyons from November 1942 to August 1944, during the wartime German occupation of France. At the end of the war a warrant for his arrest was issued by the French authorities but, although arrested, he later disappeared. He was tried *in absentia* for war crimes and sentenced to death by the *Tribunal Permanent des Forces Armées de Lyon* in two judgments of 29 April 1952 and 25 November 1954.

It was eventually discovered that Barbie had taken refuge in Bolivia. The French Government sought in vain to obtain his extradition. In a judgment of 11 December 1974 the Supreme Court of Bolivia rejected the French extradition request on the ground that there was no extradition treaty between the two countries. Following the election of a new President in December 1982, the Bolivian authorities decided to expel Barbie on the ground that he had used a false identity to obtain Bolivian citizenship.

Meanwhile new proceedings relating to crimes against humanity had been instituted against him in February 1982 in Lyons. Barbie was accused of murder, torture and arbitrary arrests, detentions and imprisonment. In Lyons alone he was alleged to have been responsible for the murder of 4,342 persons, the deportation of 7,591 Jews and the arrest and deportation of 14,311 members of the French Resistance. An arrest warrant was issued by the Examining Magistrate of Lyons on 3 November 1982. On 3 February 1983 he was expelled by the Bolivian authorities and put on board an aircraft bound for French Guiana. On arrival he was apprehended by the airport police and immediately flown to France where he was transferred to the custody of the Examining Magistrate in Lyons.

[extract from decision of Oct. 6, 1983]

Furthermore, reference should be made to the combined provisions of the Preamble and Article 4 of the London Agreement of 8 August 1945, Article 6 of the Charter of the International Military Tribunal of Nuremberg which is annexed to that Agreement, as well as to the recommendations contained in the United Nations Resolution of 13 February 1946. Both the Agreement and the Resolution refer to the Moscow Declaration of 30 October 1943 and are themselves referred to in the [French] Law of 26 December 1964. It results from these provisions that "all necessary measures" are to be taken by the Member States of the United Nations to ensure that war crimes, crimes against peace and crimes against humanity are punished and that those persons suspected of being responsible for such crimes are sent back "to the countries in which their abominable deeds were done in order that they may be judged and punished according to the laws of those countries".

By reason of the nature of those crimes, these provisions are in accordance with the general principles of law recognized by the community of nations, referred to in Article 15(2) of the International Covenant on Civil and Political Rights and Article 7(2) of the European Convention for the Protection of Human Rights and Fundamental Freedoms. The provisions in question arise from international treaties which have been properly integrated into the municipal legal order and have an authority superior to that of laws by virtue of Article 55 of the Constitution of 4 October 1958.

The ground of cassation must therefore be rejected.

[extract from submission of the French Advocate General]

... the *Chambre d'accusation* of Lyons ... did not take account of certain essential factors, which I have endeavoured to specify, and therefore failed to draw the conclusions which ought to have resulted from its examination of the case.

The *Chambre d'accusation* remained aloof from the historic implications of the problem before it.

I also believe that the judgment under appeal, faced with the task of determining the scope of the crimes against humanity with which Klaus Barbie could be charged, adopted an approach which was too restrictive and even altered the definition of such crimes....

The concept of the protection of humanity, the "conscience" of humanity, is very old. I have read much on the subject but will not burden you with my reflections, which are not in place here.

When, in fact, does the first indication appear of the transposition into positive law of this protection of humanity? When do we find that it is translated into an indictment, proceedings or a trial? Curiously I have discovered that a rough outline of the exercise of jurisdiction which goes beyond the strict traditional framework already appeared in the fifteenth century. I hope that I will be excused a short excursion into history! It is rare ... On 9 May 1474 Pierre de Hagenbach, a bailiff of Charles the Foolish responsible for the administration of Alsace which had recently been annexed, was condemned to death and executed for acts which were not all specified or personalized and which included numerous acts of brutality which he had committed on that territory, in violation of the law of nations. His judges were not those who would have had territorial jurisdiction but rather the representatives of a number of free cities including Strasbourg, Colmar and Basle, meeting specially for that purpose. Please excuse this digression which, taking account of the geographical dimensions of the period, allows certain parallels to be drawn.

In fact the idea of the protection of humanity only really came to life in concrete form after the 1914–18 war in an abortive attempt at judgment of Guillaume II, to which I have already referred in previous submissions which I have had the honour to present to you in this case. But it was only the calculated, systematic atrocities of the last war which really caused the world community to react. That reaction came first in the form of the voices of several Heads of State including Churchill who, from 1942 onwards, raised his voice in solemn warning against the "inhuman acts" committed in occupied countries....

... [T]he Charter of the International Military Tribunal, which links procedure and prosecution and forms an integral part of the London Agreements which were formally incorporated into municipal law by the Law of 1964, constitutes the "first stone", which has remained the only source of positive law....

The Charter, in Article 6, contains two definitions with regard to war crimes and crimes against humanity....

Article 6(b) gives the following description of war crimes:

> Murder, ill-treatment or deportation to slave labour ... killing of hostages, plunder ... destruction ... devastation ...

Article 6(c) which deals with crimes against humanity covers specifically:

> Murder, extermination, enslavement, deportation and other inhumane acts ...
> or persecutions ...

The careful choice of each term used surely makes it clear that the intention of those who drafted this text was to make a distinction between brutality which is unfortunately inherent in many wars and a major, orchestrated attack on the very dignity of man.

My second remark constitutes a linchpin in my argument ...

Article 6(c) uses a series of terms defining a certain number of atrocities without making them subject to any particular condition and it is only after the conjunction "or" that political, racial or religious grounds are mentioned and tied, it is true, to the word "persecution".

This break in the sentence is of vital importance because it implies two distinct categories of crimes against humanity, acts which are inhuman in themselves and acts of clearly directed persecution.

One could give an infinite number of glosses but I prefer to rely on the text itself ... because despite the uneasy compromise which influenced its drafting, it is nevertheless the common denominator of the conscience of mankind. Was it not again taken as a reference point by the United Nations in 1968?

How, and according to what lines, was this text applied by the Nuremberg Tribunal?

A constant theme emerges from their deliberations. The exacerbation in the methods used, their systematic nature and the fact that the victims came from all horizons often led to the conclusion that crimes against humanity exceeded the classical notion of war crimes, of which they constituted an aggravated form.

Everyone has in mind the phrase of M. de Menthon which has so often been cited and which so aptly describes the escalating nature of the crime. The striking example which he gave has constantly overshadowed my study of the case. I refer to it again whilst underlining several other passages in his indictment:

> The most frightful aspect of these crimes is perhaps the deliberate moral degradation, the debasement of those detained to the point of making them lose, if that were possible, all character as human beings ...

> The terrible accumulation and confused tangle of crimes against humanity at once includes and surpasses the two more precise legal notions of crimes against peace and war crimes....

Surely these lines constitute a statement of the essential overlap of the different crimes, which the civil parties have criticized the judgment under appeal for failing to perceive.

Since Nuremberg the matter has been clouded over. The courts of several countries have examined, prosecuted and convicted the perpetrators of such acts without finding it necessary to trace the delicate dividing line which this Court is called upon to establish today.

This Chamber has in fact already been required to pronounce on crimes against humanity ... albeit initially in an incidental manner.

In a judgment of 6 February 1975 (*Glaeser v. Touvier*) ... this Chamber allowed the application for designation as a civil party in a case of prosecution for crimes against humanity and stated that such crimes are crimes under ordinary law committed in certain circumstances and for certain reasons "specified in the text which defines them"....

That case concerned the authorization of a private prosecution and in particular the designation of the competent court which was held to be neither the *Tribunal Permanent des Forces Armées* (war crimes) nor the *Cour de Sûreté de l'État* (giving secrets to the enemy) but rather the *Cour d'assises*.

Subsequently in a judgment of this Chamber of 30 June 1976, a first response was given to the problem of the non-application of statutory limitation to the prosecution of crimes against humanity. It should be stressed that the acts at issue in that case had been committed "against persons or groups of persons by reason of their membership of the Resistance or the Jewish community" which, in the view of the eminent Rapporteur Le Gunehec, were capable "of being designated as crimes against humanity"....

Crimes against humanity are not to be confused with genocide which is merely one abominable aspect of such crimes. The only relevant membership, of a victim of action which has reached such a level of horror that it is no more than a mechanism of negation, is his membership of the human race....

But remaining on the plane of ideas, I ask the question whether the notion of a State system or State ideology of which so much has been spoken is not rather too restrictive.

Are there not forces and organizations whose powers might be greater and whose actions might be more extensive than those of certain countries represented institutionally at the United Nations? Care is required because other methods of total abuse of the human condition could equal in horror, albeit from other aspects, those of which we have just spoken. Certain forms of international terrorism are surely in the process of giving us just such an example.

Your judgment, gentlemen, is awaited well beyond the frontiers of France. To my knowledge it is the first occasion when a supreme court anywhere in the world has been called upon to give a precise definition of crimes against humanity....

[extract from decision of the Cour de Cassation, Dec. 20, 1985]

The following acts constitute crimes against humanity within the meaning of Article 6(c) of the Charter of the Nuremberg International Military Tribunal annexed to the London Agreement of 8 August 1945, which are not subject to statutory limitation of the right of prosecution, even if they are crimes which can also be classified as war crimes within the meaning of Article 6(b) of the Charter: inhumane acts and persecution committed in a systematic manner in the name of a State practicing a policy of ideological supremacy, not only against persons by reason of their membership of a racial or religious community, but also against the opponents of that policy, whatever the form of their opposition.

The indictment which is the subject of the judgment under appeal lists various counts of crimes against humanity, arising from a series of acts which are indisputably quite separate from those for which Klaus Barbie was convicted *in absentia* by judgments handed down in 1952 and 1954. These acts, as detailed by the judges of the lower court, consisted in the arrest and illegal imprisonment of numerous persons, followed by brutality and physical torture or deportation to concentration camps normally resulting in the death of the victims. These acts were allegedly committed in 1943 and 1944 by or on the orders of Klaus Barbie, in his capacity as SS Lieutenant and head of the Gestapo of Lyons, which was responsible for the suppression of crimes and political offences. One of the five sections of the Gestapo in Lyons specialized in the fight against communism and sabotage whilst another was responsible for the fight against Jews. The judgment under appeal lists about thirty cases of persons arrested and subsequently tortured to death or deported or, more frequently, persons who died in the course of deportation. That judgment also lists four complete operations carried out on the instructions of the accused and with his participation:

—a raid carried out on 9 August 1944 on the workshops of the SNCF [French Railways] at Oullins, followed by the assassination of one railman and the unlawful imprisonment of ten others;

—a raid on 9 February 1943 at the Lyons headquarters of the Union Generale des Israelites de France, in the course of which eighty-six persons were arrested and brutalized or tortured, before eighty-five of them were deported to the camp of Auschwitz from which only one returned;

—a raid on 6 April 1944 on a reception centre for Jewish children at Izieu, whose forty-four inmates and seven members of staff were also deported to Auschwitz and immediately exterminated in the gas chambers, with the exception of a teacher who was the only person to return from that deportation and the director and two adolescent inmates of the centre, who were transferred to a camp in Lithuania and shot;

—the deportation by the last rail convoy to leave Lyons for Germany on 11 August 1944, of more than six hundred persons who had been held in the three prisons in that city, having been arrested in their capacity, real or presumed, as Jews or resistance fighters and who had been subjected to violence and torture. Following a journey of more than eight days without any supplies, those persons were brought to various concentration camps in Struthof, Dachau, Ravensbruck and Auschwitz. The precise number of persons deported and those who died and those who survived is unknown.

The *Chambre d'accusation*, having analysed Article 6 of the Charter of the Nuremberg International Military Tribunal, stated that

Only the persecution of persons who are non-combatants, committed in furtherance of a deliberate State policy and for racial, religious or political motives, is of such a nature as to constitute a crime against humanity whose prosecution is not subject to statutory limitation. On the other hand a war crime, even if it may be committed by the same means, is characterized, in contrast to a crime against humanity, by the fact that it appears to assist the conduct of the war.

By application of these principles, the *Chambre d'accusation* ordered that an indictment should be drawn up against Klaus Barbie and he should be sent for trial by the *Cour d'assises* for crimes against humanity, but only for those acts established by the examining magistrate which constituted "persecution against innocent Jews", carried out for racial and religious motives with a view to their extermination, that is to say in furtherance of the "final solution" sought by the leaders of the Nazi regime. In this regard, the judgment under appeal is final since no appeal has been lodged against its provisions seising the trial court.

In addition the judgment under appeal, in considering the appeal of the civil parties, confirmed the order of the examining magistrate by which he held that

… the prosecution is barred by statutory limitation to the extent that it relates to the unlawful imprisonment without judgment, torture, deportation and death of combatants who were members of the Resistance, or persons whom Barbie supposed to be members of the Resistance, even if they were Jewish. Even if such acts were heinous and were committed in violation of human dignity and the laws of war, they could only constitute war crimes, whose prosecution was barred by statutory limitation.

It is evident that the combatants in the Resistance were particularly effective in their struggle against the German armed forces, in particular in creating insecurity over the whole of the territory and in neutralizing or destroying entire units. Furthermore the combatants constitute dangerous adversaries requiring elimination and this was the view of all Germans, whether Nazis or not and regardless of any ideology. The security police known as SIPOSD, of which the Gestapo in Lyons directed by Klaus Barbie was a part, fought the combatants by the heinous means which are well known.

The combatants in the Resistance were motivated firstly by the desire to chase out the invader of their country and give freedom to their children. Their political ideology, by comparison with their patriotism, was merely a secondary impetus for their action, inseparable from their patriotism. On the other hand, when the Nazis took into account the political philosophies of their adversaries, they classified them without distinction as "Judeo-Bolsheviks and Communists" in order to render their fight against these "combatants of darkness" more effective.

Finally the judgment under appeal adds that the deportation of persons with regard to whom there was information allowing Barbie to think that they were members of the Resistance was to be considered as a war crime whose prosecution was barred by statutory limitation and not as a crime against humanity, in the absence of the element of intention necessary for the latter crime. With regard to Professor Gompel, a Jewish member of the Resistance, the judgment under appeal states that

> Proof has not been furnished that he was arrested and tortured to death because he was Jewish and the accused was rightly given the benefit of the doubt on this point.

[This Court considers] however that the judgment under appeal states that the "heinous" crimes committed systematically or collectively against persons who were members or could have been members of the Resistance were presented, by those in whose name they were perpetrated, as justified politically by the national socialist ideology. Neither the driving force which motivated the victims, nor their possible membership of the Resistance, excludes the possibility that the accused acted with the element of intent necessary for the commission of crimes against humanity. In pronouncing as it did and excluding from the category of crimes against humanity all the acts imputed to the accused committed against members or possible members of the Resistance, the *Chambre d'accusation* misconstrued the meaning and the scope of the provisions listed in these grounds of appeal.

I.L.R.'s

NOTE. — The *Chambre d'accusation* of the Court of Appeal of Paris, to which the case was remitted by the Court of Cassation, subsequently considered which additional charges should be added to the indictments against Barbie, in the light of the definition of crimes against humanity given by the Court of Cassation. The *Chambre d'accusation* first ordered an additional investigation of the facts (*Barbie*, judgment of 5 March 1986, *Gaz. Pal.* 1986, 1, p. 412).

After examining the results of this investigation the *Chambre d'accusation* held that three additional sets of charges should be added to the indictments as crimes against humanity: the torture and death in prison of Professor Gompel, a Jew who was also a member of the Resistance, in January/February 1944; the arrest and deportation of actual or possible Resistance members in 1943 and 1944; and the deportation and, in many cases, subsequent death of those actual or possible Resistance members taken out of France by the last train to leave Lyons for Germany before the liberation of that city, on 11 August 1944. The *Chambre d'accusation* ordered that *Barbie* should be committed for trial for these additional crimes against humanity and remitted his case to the *Cour d'Assises du Rhône* (*Barbie*, judgment of 9 July 1986, *Gaz. Pal.* 1986, 2, p. 599).

In a later decision the Court of Cassation, explicitly referring to the definition of crimes against humanity given in its judgment of 20 December 1985, quashed a judgment of the *Chambre d'accusation* of the Court of Appeal of Lyons of 25 April 1986. The Court of Cassation held that the torture and deportation of a woman who had belonged to the Resistance, as well as the torture, deportation and murder of her husband and son, by reason of their links with her, could all constitute crimes against humanity. Neither the motives of the victims nor the fact that they might have been detained as hostages were relevant. The case was remitted to the *Chambre d'accusation* of the Court of Appeal of Paris which ordered that further charges should be added to the indictments against Barbie in respect of the crimes committed against all three members of the family in question (*Bogatto, widow of Lesevre,* judgment of 25 November 1986, summarized in *La Semaine Juridique* 1987, IV, p. 42).

The trial of Barbie before the *Cour d'Assises du Rhône* (Judge Cerdini, President) began on 11 May 1987. On 4 July 1987 the Court found him guilty on all 340 counts of the seventeen crimes against humanity with which he was charged. The Court found that there were no extenuating circumstances and he was sentenced to life imprisonment (*Le Monde*, 5–6 July 1987). [Barbie died in prison on Sept. 25, 1991]

Notes and Questions

1. Do you agree with the Court's 1985 opinion? Did the Court merely state that certain acts committed "in a systematic manner in the name of a State practicing a policy of ideological supremacy" can constitute crimes against humanity? Was such a statement merely illustrative of the facts or did the Court state that such crimes must be both "systematic" and "in the name of the State" and that the State must be "practicing a policy of ideological supremacy"? Did the Court expressly approve the statement of the *Chambre d'accusation* concerning the need for a "deliberate State policy"? At the end of the 1985 opinion, what intent was thought to be required–merely an intent to target "politically"? Would even such a requirement be consistent with the customary instruments noted above? Can persecutions other than political persecutions be covered? Are non-state actors immune from prosecution for "crimes against humanity"? Consider also Article IV of the Genocide Convention.

2. Are you convinced by the Advocate General's or the Court's attempt to distinguish "crimes against humanity" from "war crimes," *e.g.,* on the basis of noncombatant status of the victims and/or that war crimes are "characterized ... by the fact that [they appear] to assist the conduct of the war"?

Can crimes against humanity be committed against combatants? Or, at least, former combatants who are captured and are not "civilians"? What types? Can such crimes "assist the conduct" of war in some manner?

3. Are there any international crimes, or any addressed thus far, that can *only* be committed by state officials or "under color of" state authority? Did the Nuremberg Charter, the Tokyo Charter, the Nuremberg Principles, or Control Council Law No. 10 make any reference to a requirement of state official status or actions under state authority?

4. Does anything in the customary World War II instruments support the notion that crimes against humanity require an ideologic or philosophic element?

5. The Court recognized that a series of acts supported "various counts of crimes against humanity." What number of direct victims supported various counts? Consider especially the 1986 decision identified in the I.L.R. note. What appears to be the minimum

number of direct victims with respect to several such crimes? Also recall *Eichmann*, and see *Touvier*, *infra* re: such numbers.

6. The Advocate General rightly recognized that genocide is a type of crime against humanity. Can genocide be committed by non-state actors? Without an ideological motivation or pretext? See Chapter Ten.

7. Note that private suits for money damages with respect to crimes against humanity are recognized in the French cases. Recall Chapter Six, Section 9, with respect to civil claims arising out of atrocities committed in Bosnia-Herzegovina.

Matter of Touvier

[Editors' note: Paul Touvier was the Regional Chief of the Second Division of the Milice (a special paramilitary force formed by the Vichy Government to combat the Resistance and others) at Lyon. In 1989, he was finally arrested. Charges had already been filed and others were added after his arrest—mostly by civil parties. All cases were transferred to Paris and consolidated in 1990.]

Leila Sadat Wexler, *The Interpretation of the Nuremberg Principles by the French Court of Cassation: From Touvier to Barbie and Back Again*

32 COLUM. J. TRANSNAT'L. L. 289, 347–56, 358–62, 366–67, 379–80 (1994)*

The charges were as follows:

(1) Touvier organized the bombing of the Synagogue at Quai Tilsitt in Lyon on December 10, 1943;

(2) Touvier organized and/or participated in a raid by the Milice of Mrs. Vogel's family, and others, which occurred on June 13, 1944;

(3) Touvier participated in the assassination of Victor and Hélène Basch on January 10, 1944;

(4) Touvier, among others in the Gestapo and the Milice, arrested a resister, Jean de Filippis, on January 16, 1944, who was later tortured (in Touvier's presence) and deported;

(5) Touvier arrested and tortured André Laroche on March 29, 1944;

(6) Touvier participated in a raid at the Pré de Foire de Montmelian on April 24, 1944;

(7) Touvier arrested and later assassinated Albert Nathan on August 17, 1944;

(8) Touvier participated in the Milice's arrest and torture of Émile Medina on May 19, 1944;

(9) Touvier participated in the arrest and torture of Robert Nant on May 27, 1944;

(10) Touvier participated in the massacre [of seven Jews] at Rillieux la-Pape on June 29, 1944;

---

(11) Touvier was responsible for the arrest and deportation of Eliette Meyer and Claude Bloch, as well as the assassination of Lucien Meyer, on June 29, 1944.

Judge Getti [*juge d'instruction*] carefully examined the above charges and concluded that Touvier could be prosecuted with respect to five: the attack on the Synagogue at Quai Tilsitt (1); the assassination of Mr. & Mrs. Basch (3); the arrest, torture and deportation of Jean de Filippis (4); the massacre at Rillieux (10); and the arrest and deportation of Eliette Meyer and Claude Bloch, and the assassination of Lucien Meyer (11). With respect to the others, the evidence was inconclusive.

The case was sent to the Indicting Chamber of the Paris Court of Appeals for review. In a 215-page decision that provoked an uproar in France, the Indicting Chamber reversed the *juge d'instruction* and concluded that there was no cause to prosecute Touvier on any of the charges. The appellate court reasoned that either the evidence was insufficient to support the charge in question, or that, even if Touvier's participation in the criminal activity was clear, he could not, as a matter of law, be guilty....

Turning to the third decision in the *Barbie* case, the court found that to be guilty of a crime against humanity, one must intend to take part in carrying out a common plan by systematically committing inhumane acts and illegal persecutions in the name of a state practicing a hegemonic political ideology. To determine whether this was so, the court analyzed the historical record of the Vichy government: its policies toward the Jews and its relationship with the Germans then occupying France. To oversimplify somewhat, although the court agreed that there were certain antisemitic tendencies in the Milice and in the Vichy government, it found that Vichy France simply could not be considered a hegemonic state. Therefore, Touvier could not, as a matter of law, have committed a crime against humanity in carrying out the orders of such a state.... Finally, the court dismissed the idea that Touvier could be guilty due to his work with the Gestapo, finding that Touvier was not carrying out any German plan at Rillieux—it was entirely "*une affaire entre Français*" (a French affair).

It was more the court's revisionist approach to the historical record than its acquittal of Paul Touvier that outraged the public. Seventy-three percent of French men and women reported that they were "shocked" by the decision. A document entitled "*Nous accusons*" (after Zola's *J'accuse*) was signed and published by 188 famous personalities, accusing the three judges of a miscarriage of justice. And, the French National Assembly denounced the verdict. The historical record showed that the Milice specifically excluded Jews from their number and repeatedly targeted them for abuse. Moreover, as the civil parties pointed out in their appeal, the appellate court's own words led one to the conclusion that the Vichy state practiced an ideology of exclusion, hate, and collaboration with the Germans. Finally, Touvier himself admitted that the Milice carried out this assassination under German orders as retaliation for the execution of Philippe Henriot by the Resistance.

An Indictment is Rendered in the *Touvier* case

The decision of the Paris Court of Appeals was brought to the Criminal Chamber, and all waited to see what the High Court would do....

Because none of the parties appealed the six charges that both the *juge d'instruction* and the Court of Appeals dismissed, those charges were not before the Court of Cassation. Thus, only the five incidents for which the *juge d'instruction* had recommended indictment were at issue. As for the four charges that the Court of Appeals had reversed due to insufficient evidence, the Court of Cassation affirmed without much discussion, summarily rejecting the appellants' contention that the Court of Appeals had infected its evaluation of the evidence by systematically discrediting all the witnesses except Touvier. Turning to the massacre at Rillieux, the Court reviewed without editorial comment the "historical" analysis of the Court of Appeals. It then reversed on very narrow grounds: because the criminal acts committed at Rillieux had been accomplished at the instigation of the Gestapo, and because, under Article 6 of the IMT Charter, only those acting "in the interests of the European Axis countries" could be tried under Article 6(c), the Court of Appeals had contradicted itself by finding that Touvier could not have committed a crime against humanity, while conceding that he acted at the instigation of the Gestapo. Thus, the case would be sent to yet another court of appeals for a review of the massacre at Rillieux....

The court of *renvoi* was the Court of Appeals of Versailles, which held on June 2, 1993, that Touvier could be tried for his participation in the massacre at Rillieux, concluding that:

> Touvier actively participated in the criminal acts charged by the prosecution. In this respect, the testimony [to that effect] of the former milicians or former Resistance members is corroborated by own declarations, whether made before or after the start of the judicial investigation.

The court then found that act was a crime against humanity. It was a crime listed in Article 6(c), committed against persons by reason of their membership in a religious group, with the intent of furthering the plan of a state practicing a hegemonic political ideology. Moreover, [Touvier's] French nationality could not protect him; he knowingly and voluntarily associated himself with the Nazis' policy of extermination and persecution that was inspired by political, racial or religious motivations.

Touvier's attorneys pleaded one last defense: duress. They claimed that the pressure of the Gestapo on Touvier was so great that it was a *fait justificatif*, exculpating him from criminal liability. The court summarily rejected this claim, pointing out that Touvier had joined the Milice of his own free will, knowing that its motto included a promise to struggle "against the Jewish leper and for French purity." ...

A Critique of the French Case Law

The jurisprudence of the Court of Cassation in the *Touvier* case leaves one strangely dissatisfied. Touvier was made to stand trial — but only because he was implicated in the murder of the seven men at Rillieux as an accomplice of the Gestapo. Had he carried out the executions, even had they been in the hundreds or thousands, either on his own initiative, or on orders from his superiors at the Milice, the indictment would have failed.

As postulated in the introduction, this uneasiness about the result is due to three problems in the case law. First, the Court misinterprets the spirit of the law it is applying. Second, the Court compounds this with several errors of statutory construction and thereby misinterprets the letter of the law it is applying. Finally, the greatest failure of the jurisprudence was to establish a legal regime to cover the prosecution of crimes against humanity in French law that would not only have applied in this case, but to future cases. Each of these critiques will be set forth in turn.

The Court's Approach to the Case

I will not belabor this point, but feel compelled to point out that at least certain decisions in the *Touvier* case lead one to question the courts' judgment if not impartiality.

Article 6(c) and the Nuremberg Charter, to which the law of 1964 refers, were based on the desire of the Allies to try and to punish the perpetrators of crimes committed during the war. Moreover, the United Nations Resolution of February 13, 1946, to which the law also referred, evinced a desire to try not only the "major" war criminals, but also minor offenders. The former were tried at Nuremberg, the latter in the countries in which their crimes were committed. Paul Touvier was tried and convicted once; the question then simply became, could his case be reopened applying a different, international law, using the 1964 law as a basis?

It is true that in constructing their jurisprudence on crimes against humanity, the French courts had little with which to work. The 1964 law was laconic in its pronouncements (*"un fragment de vide circonscrit"*), leaving the courts with little guidance as to its application. Yet, the message of the French legislature was unmistakable: crimes against humanity should be prosecuted regardless of when and where they were committed. Notwithstanding, it took the courts over ten years and the intervention of the executive branch to agree (in the *Barbie* case) that the legislature meant what it said. Moreover, one might surmise that it was only Barbie's German nationality that made this possible. The most egregious error, by far, however, was the introduction of the requirements of "hegemonic state" and "execution of a common plan" to the long list of elements of the crime against humanity. Neither was justified as a matter of statutory interpretation, as explained below, and both appear to be blatant attempts to exonerate, in advance, the Vichy government from wrong. (Others have suggested that the worry was about possible liability concerning certain "events" in Algeria.) Moreover, these elements shift the focus from Touvier's own individual moral culpability (or lack thereof), which was, after all, one of Nuremberg's greatest legacies, to that of his government. Thus, the introduction of these elements by the Court of Cassation, and its failure to censure the Paris Court of Appeals' misapplication of their meaning, leaves the 1964 law with very few teeth.

Problems of Statutory Construction

The French jurisprudence has also led to the evolution of a definition of crimes against humanity that contradicts the text of Article 6(c). I will address these errors of interpretation in chronological fashion, following the order in which they arose.

> 1. 1975: "crimes against humanity are ordinary crimes (*crimes de droit commun*) committed under certain circumstances and for certain motives specified in the text that defines them"

Distinguishing crimes against humanity both from war crimes and from "ordinary" crimes of murder, rape, etc., has been problematic since the IMT Judgment, which failed to address this issue. The position adopted by the Court of Cassation in the 1975 decisions clearly accepts that crimes against humanity are distinct from war crimes; yet it denies them a special status in French law by assimilating them to "ordinary crimes." Although the Court appeared to depart from this standard in its December 20, 1985 decision in the *Barbie* case, it apparently returned to it in subsequent decisions in the *Touvier* case....

> 2. 1985: "systematically committing inhumane acts and persecutions in the name of a State practicing a hegemonic political ideology"

When articulated by the Court of Cassation in the *Barbie* case, it was unclear what the judges were driving at with this language, which cannot, of course, be found anywhere in Article 6(c) or elsewhere in the IMT Charter or judgment. In the context of the questions presented for decision in the particular case, one could argue that the Court added this simply to show that members of the Resistance as well as Jews were among the members of the "civilian population" protected by Article 6(c). Moreover, in rejecting the notion that it was the victim's intent or activities in an occupied territory that qualified the perpetrator's activities as a crime against humanity or not, the Court is only to be praised. Unfortunately, however, the language of this decision later came to stand for several propositions: first, that the perpetrator must have as his mental intent both an intent to hurt the victim and an intent to attack the group to which the victim belongs (as evidenced by the attack on the victim); second, that only if the perpetrator (i) carried out his crimes on behalf of a State and (ii) that State was one practicing a hegemonic political ideology, could the perpetrator's act or acts be characterized as crimes against humanity. Both propositions are foreign to Article 6(c) and are arguably erroneous.

First, although Article 6(c), in speaking in terms of "humanity" and a civilian "population," implied that one was necessarily speaking of collective victims, the persecution-type crimes (which are based on the victim's membership in a particular group) are separate from the "murder-type" crimes. Thus the text of Article 6(c) would imply that the special intent required by the Court of Cassation is not applicable with respect to this second type of crime. Indeed, if a government (ignoring for now the possibility of private action) wished to engage in random purges as a means to terrorize its population into submission, who would not argue that this constitutes a crime against humanity? With this language the Court of Cassation appears to be equating the crime against humanity to genocide, which proves too much — genocide is merely one form of crime against humanity.

Second, the Court requires state action. So does the majority of the scholarship in this area, but it is worth noting at least two contra-indications. First, the Genocide Convention does not require "state action" but rather states that "persons committing genocide … shall be punished, whether they are constitutionally responsible rulers, public officials or private individuals." This was certainly a possible interpretation of Article 6(c). Second, the Court does not really define what it means by state or government — is it referring to an international or municipal definition? Moreover, what if no "State" or recognized government exists due to a civil war in the country, such as may be true in the former Yugoslavia?

Finally, the Court adds to its requirement that the crimes be perpetrated on behalf of a State, the requirement that the State be one "practicing a hegemonic political ideology." This phrase is one of the Court's own making, although it echoes language used to this effect in the writings [European Scholars] and others [to] … describe[e] Nazi Germany. The first objection one can make to this is, of course, that it is not in Article 6(c) and therefore should not be embroidered thereon by the French courts. Second, the term is impossibly vague.

"Hegemony" may mean the "predominance of one element of a system over others." However, although an ideology is clearly encompassed within the meaning of "hegemony," that ideology need not be either uniform or totalitarian. Thus, to the extent the Court used this phraseology to refer to Nazi Germany, the word may have been accurate; but it is certainly not accurate to say that a state which does not live up to the level of totalitarianism exhibited by Nazi Germany cannot be a hegemonic state. Indeed, the term may simply describe the internal political order of a nation. Thus, as there is a continuum of State behavior that may correctly be characterized as "hegemonic," the term "hegemony" can provide no precise litmus test for a court of law.

3, 1988: "in carrying out a common plan"

In its final word in the *Barbie* case, the Court of Cassation added this requirement to the others: that the defendant must intend to further a "common plan" of a state practicing a hegemonic political ideology. This appears to be an erroneous reading of the third paragraph of Article 6, which included the "common plan or conspiracy" language to add an additional crime to the list of crimes with which the defendants could be charged at Nuremberg. That is, the conspiracy charges were separate from the charges based on the substantive provisions of Articles 6(a), 6(b), and 6(c). This addition may result from the unfamiliarity of continental legal systems with the law of conspiracy, but is nonetheless an unfortunate gloss on Article 6(c).

> 4. 1992: crimes against humanity are restricted to those working "in the interests of the European Axis countries"

This language, which the Court of Cassation presumably added to its 1992 decision in order to find that Touvier could stand trial for his participation in the massacre at Rillieux, also appears to be based on a mistaken reading of the IMT Charter. The language appears in the first paragraph of Article 6, as follows:

> The Tribunal established ... hereof for the trial and punishment of the major war criminals of the European Axis countries shall have the power to try and punish persons who, acting in the interests of the European Axis countries ... committed any of the following crimes.

Like so many other aspects of Article 6 (which is entitled "jurisdiction and general principles") this language appears to be jurisdictional, not a substantive limit on the definition of crimes against humanity in Article 6(c). Thus it was rather disingenuous for the Court to rely on this language as the basis for holding as it did....

Conclusion

"sur une base fragile, on n'édifie rien de solide."

Perhaps reacting to the disarray of the case law, in 1992 the French legislature adopted a new "crimes against humanity" law, codifying the jurisprudence in part, rejecting the jurisprudence in part, and innovating in part.... Although certain aspects of the new law could not be considered an improvement over the jurisprudence to date, its adoption reiterates the commitment of the French legislature to the pursuit and prosecution of perpetrators of crimes against humanity.

The failure of the Court of Cassation to take up the challenge posed by the 1964 law leaves little hope that its approach to the new law will be any more coherent, or more consistent with the spirit of Nuremberg. Like the IMT judgment itself, the French jurisprudence leaves one wishing for more. It also leaves one depressed about the effectiveness of municipal courts as the primary enforcers of international law. Yet, there may be a silver lining....

New French Criminal Code

Title I

Of Crimes against Humanity

Chapter I

Genocide

Art. 211-1. Constitutes genocide the fact, in carrying out a common plan tending to the destruction in whole or in part of a national, ethnic, racial or religious group, or of a group determined by any arbitrary criteria, to commit or cause to be committed, against any members of this group, one of the following acts:

— intentional harm to life;

— causing serious bodily or mental harm;

— inflicting on the group conditions of life of such a nature as to bring about its destruction in whole or in part;

—imposing measures intended to prevent births;

—forcibly transferring children.

Genocide is punishable by life imprisonment....

Chapter II

Other Crimes against Humanity

Art. 212-1. Deportation, enslavement, or the practice of massive and systematic summary executions, the abduction of persons followed by their disappearance, torture or other inhumane acts, inspired by political, philosophical, racial or religious motives and organized in carrying out a common plan against a civil population group are punishable by life imprisonment....

Art. 212-2. When committed in wartime in carrying out a common plan against those fighting the ideological system in the name of which the crimes against humanity are being perpetrated, the acts listed in Article 212-1 are punishable by life imprisonment.

Art. 212-3. Participation in a group formed or a conspiracy (*entente*) established in order to prepare, characterized by one or more acts (*faits matériels*), one of the crimes defined in Articles 211-1, 212-1 and 212-2 is punishable by life imprisonment.

Notes and Questions

1. Do you agree with Professor Sadat or the French legislature or courts? Does the legislature agree with the courts?

2. The legislation ominously deletes "persecution" as such and requires all acts to be "against a civilian population group." Such is quite different than the recognition of two general types of crimes against humanity in the customary World War II instruments. See Paust, *Threats to Accountability After Nuremberg, supra.*

3. Why do you suspect the French legislation is so different?

4. In 2012, France enacted legislation aimed at implementing the complementarity principle of the Rome Statute for the ICC. The French law punishes public, direct incitement to commit genocide; defines the conditions necessary for superior responsibility for crimes against humanity; and extends the definition of crimes against humanity to conform to Article 7 of the Rome Statute. See *Loi 2010-930 du 9 août 2010, portent adaptation du droit pénal à l'institution de la cour pénale internationale* [Law 2010-930 of August 9, 2010 Law to Adapt France's Criminal Code to the International Criminal Court], Journal Officiel de la République Française [J.O.] [Official Gazette of France], Aug. 10, 2010, p. 14678.

5. Compare the French definition of genocide with the customary definition contained in Article II of the Genocide Convention, in Chapter Ten. Since the French legislation is far more restrictive, how will France be able to comply with its obligations under the Genocide Convention? If treaties are superior to the laws by virtue of Article 55 of the French Constitution, should the definition of genocide contained in the 1948 Genocide Convention prevail over the inconsistent legislation?

6. Following the *Touvier* affair, an additional French defendant was prosecuted under the 1964 Law, when Maurice Papon, Secretary-General for the Gironde *Prefecture* was tried in 1997 for his role in the deportation of almost 1600 Jews from the Bordeaux area in France. Unlike Paul Touvier, Papon maintained his innocence, arguing that although his signature did indeed appear on the deportation orders he signed, he was unaware of

the ultimate fate awaiting those deported. Following a highly public and controversial trial, the French Court of Assizes found Papon guilty on charges of arrest and detention, but innocent on the charges of murder. Papon was sentenced on April 2, 1998 to 10 years in prison for "complicity in crimes against humanity." In a bizarre twist to an already unusual case, Papon fled to Switzerland when the verdict was announced, thereby forfeiting his right to an appeal. He thereupon successfully appealed to the European Court of Human Rights, in Strasbourg, which ruled on July 25, 2002, that he was entitled to appeal his conviction even though he had fled. *Affaire Papon v. France*, Case No. 54210/00 (ECHR July 25, 2002). A committee of the French Court of Cassation subsequently held that Papon should have an appeal, but on points of law only arising from the original trial, not on questions of fact. John Lichfield, *Nazi War Criminal Papon wins Right to Appeal*, THE INDEPENDENT, Feb. 27, 2004. In the interim, Papon successfully petitioned to be released from prison on medical grounds, provoking an additional controversy from relatives of his victims and Jewish groups in France. His medical release was unsuccessfully appealed by the government, and he remains free while he pursues his other legal remedies. Pierre-Antoine Souchard, *War criminal Papon Spared Jail Return by Appeal Court*, THE INDEPENDENT, Feb. 14, 2003. For analysis of the indictment and trial in the *Papon* case, see Leila Nadya Sadat, *The Legal Legacy of Maurice Papon*, in MEMORY AND JUSTICE ON TRIAL: THE PAPON AFFAIR (Richard J. Golsan, ed., Routledge, 2000).

Section 4
Mugesera Case (Canada)

Mugesera v. Canada
2005 SCC 40 (S. Ct. Canada 2005), 2 S.C.R. 100

[Editors' note: Mugesera was a permanent resident in Canada who was alleged to have incited murder, genocide, and hate speech and to have committed a crime against humanity in Rwanda before entry into Canada. the Supreme Court ruled that his deportation order was valid and should be reinstated.]

The Elements of a Crime Against Humanity

118. At the time relevant to this appeal, crimes against humanity were defined in and proscribed by ss. 7(3.76) and 7(3.77) of the *Criminal Code* [reproduced in *Finta, supra*]

Sections 7(3.76) and 7(3.77) of the *Criminal Code* have since been repealed. Crimes against humanity are now defined in and proscribed by ss. 4 and 6 of the *Crimes Against Humanity and War Crimes Act*, S.C. 2000, c. 24. Those sections define crimes against humanity in a manner which differs slightly from the definition in the sections of the *Criminal Code* relevant to this appeal. However, the differences are not material to the discussion that follows.

119. As we shall see, based on the provisions of the *Criminal Code* and the principles of international law, a criminal act rises to the level of a crime against humanity when four elements are made out:

1. An enumerated proscribed act was committed (this involves showing that the accused committed the criminal act and had the requisite guilty state of mind for the underlying act);

2. The act was committed as part of a widespread or systematic attack;

3. The attack was directed against any civilian population or any identifiable group of persons; and

4. The person committing the proscribed act knew of the attack and knew or took the risk that his or her act comprised a part of that attack.

120. Despite relying on essentially the same authorities, the lower courts and the tribunal in this appeal were inconsistent in their identification and application of the elements of a crime against humanity under s. 7(3.76) of the *Criminal Code*. We will now briefly review their views on these questions.

121. For the IAD [Immigration & Refugee Board, Appeals Division], Mr. Duquette, relying on this Court's decision in *R. v. Finta*, [1994] 1 S.C.R. 701, found that a crime against humanity must be committed against a civilian population or an identifiable group, must be cruel and must shock the conscience of all right-thinking people (para. 335). He also held that the individual who commits the crime must be aware of the circumstances which render the act inhumane and must be motivated by discriminatory intent (paras. 337–38). To these requirements, he added, relying on *Sivakumar*, that crimes against humanity must occur on a widespread and systematic basis (para. 339).

122. Applying these principles to the facts, Mr. Duquette concluded that counselling murder, even where no murder is subsequently committed, is sufficient to constitute a crime against humanity, particularly where murders have been happening on a widespread and systematic basis (para. 344). In his opinion, Mr. Mugesera had acted with discriminatory intent, and was an educated man who was aware of his country's history, the current political situation and the fact that civilians were being massacred (para. 338). He was therefore aware of the circumstances which rendered his speech a crime against humanity.

123. Nadon J., reviewing the IAD's decision, did not elaborate on the elements of a crime against humanity. He limited his consideration of the issue to finding that Mr. Duquette had erred in law because Mr. Mugesera's counselling of murder and incitement to hatred, absent proof that actual murders had ensued, was not sufficiently "cruel and terrible" to constitute a crime against humanity (paras. 55–56). Nadon J. relied on this Court's decision in *Finta*, at p. 814, to support the proposition that the alleged acts must show an added degree of inhumanity.

124. Decary J.A., for the FCA [Federal Court of Appeals], who apparently also drew on *Finta* and *Sivakumar*, reached an entirely different outcome, both on the law and on its application to the facts. He found that a crime against humanity must occur in the context of a widespread or systematic attack directed against a civilian population with discriminatory intent (para. 57). Having set aside the IAD's findings of fact, he concluded that there was no evidence that the speech had taken place in the context of a widespread or systematic attack, since the massacres which had occurred to that point were not part of a common plan and since there was no evidence that Mr. Mugesera's speech was part of an overall strategy of attack (para. 58).

125. The decisions below leave no doubt as to the existence of a great deal of confusion about the elements of a crime against humanity. Though this Court has commented on the issue in the past, most notably in *Finta*, it is apparent that further clarification is needed.

126. Since *Finta* was rendered in 1994, a vast body of international jurisprudence has emerged from the International Criminal Tribunal for the Former Yugoslavia (ICTY) and the ICTR. These tribunals have generated a unique body of authority which cogently reviews the sources, evolution and application of customary international law. Though the decisions of the ICTY and the ICTR are not binding upon this Court, the expertise of

these tribunals and the authority in respect of customary international law with which they are vested suggest that their findings should not be disregarded lightly by Canadian courts applying domestic legislative provisions, such as ss. 7(3.76) and 7(3.77) of the *Criminal Code*, which expressly incorporate customary international law. Therefore, to the extent that *Finta* is in need of clarification and does not accord with the jurisprudence of the ICTY and the ICTR, it warrants reconsideration....

170. In sum, we have seen that the criminal act requirement for crimes against humanity in ss. 7(3.76) and 7(3.77) is made up of three essential elements: (1) a proscribed act is carried out; (2) the act occurs as part of a widespread or systematic attack; and (3) the attack is directed against any civilian population. The first element means that all the elements of an enumerated act "both physical and moral" must be made out. The second and third elements require that the act take place in a particular context: a widespread or systematic attack directed against any civilian population. Each of these elements has been made out in Mr. Mugesera's case.

171. However, as noted above, making out the criminal act of a crime against humanity will not necessarily imply that there are reasonable grounds to believe that Mr. Mugesera has committed a crime against humanity. Mr. Mugesera must also have had a guilty mind. As a result, we must now go on to consider the mental element of s. 7(3.76) of the *Criminal Code*.

(b) *The Guilty Mind for Crimes Against Humanity*

172. We have seen that an individual accused of crimes against humanity must possess the required guilty state of mind in respect of the underlying proscribed act. We have also underlined that, contrary to what was said in *Finta*, discriminatory intent need not be made out in respect of all crimes against humanity, but only in respect of those which take the form of persecution. This leaves a final question: in addition to the mental element required for the underlying act, what is the mental element required to make out a crime against humanity under s. 7(3.76) of the *Criminal Code*?

173. The question of whether a superadded mental element exists for crimes against humanity was a point of significant contention in *Finta*. Cory J., for the majority, found that the accused must have an awareness of the facts or circumstances which would bring the act within the definition of a crime against humanity (p. 819). La Forest J. penned dissenting reasons suggesting that establishing the mental element for the underlying act was sufficient in itself and thus no additional element of moral blameworthiness was required (p. 754). At the time, there was little international jurisprudence on the question. It is now well settled that in addition to the *mens rea* for the underlying act, the accused must have knowledge of the attack and must know that his or her acts comprise part of it *or* take the risk that his or her acts will comprise part of it: *see, e.g., Tadic*, Appeals Chamber, at para. 248; *Ruggiu*, at para. 20; *Kunarac*, Trial Chamber, at para. 434; *Blaskic*, at para. 251.

174. It is important to stress that the person committing the act need only be cognizant of the link between his or her act and the attack. The person need not intend that the act be directed against the targeted population, and motive is irrelevant once knowledge of the attack has been established together with knowledge that the act forms a part of the attack or with recklessness in this regard: *Kunarac*, Appeals Chamber, at para. 103. Even if the person's motive is purely personal, the act may be a crime against humanity if the relevant knowledge is made out.

175. Knowledge may be factually implied from the circumstances: *Tadic*, Trial Chamber, at para. 657. In assessing whether an accused possessed the requisite knowledge, the court may consider the accused's position in a military or other government hierarchy, public knowledge about the existence of the attack, the scale of the violence and the general his-

torical and political environment in which the acts occurred: *see, e.g., Blaskic*, at para. 259. The accused need not know the details of the attack: *Kunarac*, Appeals Chamber, at para. 102.

176. In *Finta*, the majority of this Court found that subjective knowledge on the part of the accused of the circumstances rendering his or her actions a crime against humanity was required (p. 819). This remains true in the sense that the accused must have knowledge of the attack and must know that his or her acts are part of the attack, or at least take the risk that they are part of the attack.

177. Returning to the case at bar, the findings of the IAD leave no doubt that Mr. Mugesera possessed the culpable mental state required by s. 7(3.76) of the *Criminal Code*. Mr. Duquette found that Mr. Mugesera was a well-educated man who was aware of his country's history and of past massacres of Tutsi (para. 338). He was aware of the ethnic tensions in his country and knew that civilians were being killed merely by reason of ethnicity or political affiliation (para. 338). Moreover, Mr. Duquette found that the speech itself left no doubt that Mr. Mugesera knew of the violent and dangerous state of affairs in Rwanda in the early 1990s (para. 338). These findings of fact clearly show that Mr. Mugesera was aware of the attack occurring against Tutsi and moderate Hutu. Furthermore, a man of his education, status and prominence on the local political scene would necessarily have known that a speech vilifying and encouraging acts of violence against the target group would have the effect of furthering the attack.

178. In the face of certain unspeakable tragedies, the community of nations must provide a unified response. Crimes against humanity fall within this category. The interpretation and application of Canadian provisions regarding crimes against humanity must therefore accord with international law. Our nation's deeply held commitment to individual human dignity, freedom and fundamental rights requires nothing less.

179. Based on Mr. Duquette's findings of fact, each element of the offence in s. 7(3.76) of the *Criminal Code* has been made out. We are therefore of the opinion that reasonable grounds exist to believe that Mr. Mugesera committed a crime against humanity and is therefore inadmissible to Canada by virtue of ss. 27(1)(*g*) and 19(1)(*j*) of the *Immigration Act*.

Note

1. In a prior case, Judge La Forest made the following observation concerning *mens rea*:

In my view, these instructions introduced elements of knowledge of both the *legal* and *moral* status of the conduct, in a way that is not required by either domestic or international law.

It is well established in our domestic criminal law jurisprudence that knowledge of illegality is not required for an accused. Section 19 of the Criminal Code echoes a requirement found in earlier codes (including the one in effect at the time the actions in this case were alleged to have been committed): ignorance of the law by one who commits an offence is not an excuse for committing the offence. At common law the principle is well established....

Nor should it be forgotten that awareness that the act is morally wrong is also immaterial....

The underlying rationale behind the *mens rea* requirement is that there is a lack of sense of personal blame if the person did not in some way even intend to do the action or omission. In finding a war crime or crime against humanity, the trial judge must, of course, look for the normal intent or recklessness requirement in relation to the act or omission that is impugned. However, there is rarely any requirement that the accused knew the legal status or description of his behaviour. This is not part of the rules of our criminal law and, in my view, is not required under international law.

To summarize, then, the correct approach, in my view, is that the accused have intended the *factual* quality of the offence, *e.g.*, that he was shooting a civilian, or that he knew that the conditions in the train were such that harm could occur to occupants. It is not possible to give an exhaustive treatment of which circumstances must have an equivalent knowledge component. Whether there is an equivalent mental element for circumstances will depend on the *particular* war crime or crime against humanity involved. However, in almost if not every case, I think that our domestic definition of the underlying offence will capture the requisite *mens rea* for the war crime or crime against humanity as well. Thus, the accused need not have known that his act, if it constitutes manslaughter or forcible confinement, amounted to an "inhumane act" either in the legal or moral sense....

R. v. Imre Finta, [1994] 28 C.R. (4th) 265 (S. Ct. Canada) (La Forest, dissenting).

Section 5
Newer International Prosecutions

A. The International Criminal Tribunals for the Former Yugoslavia and Rwanda and the Special Court for Sierra Leone

As explored in Chapter Six, *supra*, the Security Council established the International Criminal Tribunal for the Former Yugoslavia in 1993 with jurisdiction over "serious violations of international humanitarian law" committed in the territory of the Former Yugoslavia. ICTY Statute, art. 1. One year later, the Council established the International Criminal Tribunal for Rwanda, which likewise had within its purview "serious violations of international humanitarian law" committed in Rwandan territory or by Rwandan citizens in "neighboring States" in 1994. ICTR Statute, art. 1. Both Statutes included the crime against humanity in their texts, the first international elaboration of the crime since the 1950 Nuremberg Principles. However, confusingly, the definitions of the crime in the Rwanda Statute (article 3) and Yugoslavia Statute (article 5) are different. The differences between the two Statutes, as well as their arguable departure from customary international law, gave rise to certain controversies about the scope and meaning of the crime, difficulties that persist even today after the Tribunals' operation and the adoption of the Rome Statute for the International Criminal Court (ICC), discussed *infra* in Section 5(B). The following excerpt details some of the controversies.

J. Paust, *Threats to Accountability After Nuremberg: Crimes Against Humanity, Leader Responsibility and National Fora*
12 N.Y.L.S. J. H.R. 547 (1995)

Despite the broad historic reach of the concept of crimes against humanity and well-documented definitions in the World War II era, there have been certain recent definitions that might needlessly restrict coverage and accountability. One such definition appears in

Article 5 of the Statute of the International Criminal Tribunal for the Former Yugoslavia. Unlike all of the definitions in the international instruments arising from the World War II era, Article 5 of the Statute fuses the two types together as one, listing "persecutions on political, racial and religious grounds" as merely one form of inhumane acts and requiring that all categories of crimes against humanity be "directed against any civilian population." Article 5 of the Statute also changes the Nuremberg phrase "committed against" (which, in the 1950 ILC Principles, reads "done against") to "directed against," a phrase that may require a slightly higher threshold of *mens rea* (or may involve a shift from an *actus reus* element to a new additional *mens rea* element); and it adds three relevant methods or acts ("imprisonment," "torture" and "rape"), although each is most likely covered by the Nuremberg phrase "other inhumane acts" and each appeared in Control Council Law No. 10. This definitional orientation was adopted despite the fact that the U.N. Secretary-General's Report adopting such a focus had noted that such crimes were recognized in the Nuremberg Charter and Control Council Law No. 10 and that the law "which has beyond doubt become part of international customary law ... is embodied in" the Nuremberg Charter and the Genocide Convention.

Presumably customary definitions contained in those instruments will guide the Tribunal, since they are recognizably those accepted under customary international law and such law was stated to be the law that the Tribunal is required to apply in order to avoid problems connected with "the principle *nullum crimen sine lege*" or *sine jus*.... Certainly customary international law was meant to be the guiding force, a necessary background, the only delimiting criterion, and what the Tribunal is required to apply.

If so, it should not be possible for an accused to escape accountability for criminal persecutions on the ground that they were not "directed against" a "civilian population" as such or in any other way. First, neither the persecution-types of crimes against humanity, nor genocide under customary international law have such a limiting phrase. Second, as the U.N. War Crimes Commission reported in 1948, even when such a phrase is applicable (*i.e.*, to the first type), the words "appear to indicate ... [acts] against civilians" as opposed to a population as such, the Commission also speculating "that single or isolated acts against individuals may be considered to fall outside" the phrase. Thus, it is the commission of an act against (*i.e.*, "committed against" or "done against") civilians that is covered and not merely the intentional targeting of civilians as such (*i.e.*, "directed against"). Even the slightly higher *mens rea* threshold is met, however, when civilians are targeted. With respect to single acts, it is arguable that commission of one act injuring one victim fits the definition if there is an intent thereby to act against or to target other civilians (*e.g.*, as in the case of a terroristic murder or inhumane act against an instrumental target with the object of producing intense fear or anxiety in a primary target involving other civilians). The same double or terroristic-type targeting may also exist with respect to certain persecutions. Moreover, merely because the word persecutions is in the plural does not answer the question whether one persecution is sufficient because the definitions also refer to crimes in the plural (*i.e.*, crimes against humanity, and thus "persecutions" constitute "crimes").

It should be noted that the Report of the U.N. Secretary-General stated that crimes against humanity are "inhumane" and "very serious," but such labels do not appear in Article 5 of the Statute of the International Tribunal, nor are they general elements of the offense or limiting criteria for all types of crimes against humanity. Thus, the Tribunal need not entertain defense claims that some acts were not really "inhumane" or "very serious".

Similarly, the Report noted that some such crimes were part of a "widespread" or "systematic" attack, but these words were not considered to be required elements of the crime that prosecutors must prove and they do not appear in Article 5 of the Statute. Clearly also, the words "serious," "widespread," and "systematic" appear in none of the Charters or formulations noted above, nor do they exist in the definition of genocide contained in the Genocide Convention which, as noted, is a special form of *crimen contra omnes*. Such phrases sometimes appear in judicial opinions or works of textwriters in connection with particular cases or as occasional rhetorical flourish. They are at times descriptive of actual events or partly poetic, but such expressions should not be confused with required elements of the general crime under customary international law. To stress the point, it should not be a defense that an individual's acts were not "systematic" or "widespread".* These are not defenses to genocide, slavery, or more general human rights violations, nor do they appear as elements or defenses in the customary international instruments.

Most unfortunately, however, the newer Rwandan Statute has adopted a restrictive approach that will not serve accountability. Article 3 of the Rwandan Statute also fuses the two basic types and addresses merely those acts that are "part of a widespread or systematic attack against any civilian population. ..." Why this far more limited form of crimes against humanity was utilized is not explained. In any event, it should not be repeated in a more permanent code or statute. Thus, I disagree with certain statements in the 1994 Report of the International Law Commission. While arguing for a similar fusion of the two types recognized at Nuremberg and a severely restrictive definition, the I.L.C. Report stated:

> It is the understanding of the Commission that the definition of crimes against humanity encompasses inhumane acts of a very serious character involving widespread or systematic violations aimed at the civilian population in whole or part. The hallmarks of such crimes lie in their large-scale and systematic nature. The particular forms of unlawful act (murder, enslavement, deportation, torture, rape, imprisonment etc.) are less crucial to the definition that (sic) the factors of scale and deliberate policy, as well as in their being targeted against the civilian population in whole or in part. This idea is sought to be reflected in the phrase "directed against any civilian population" in article 5 of the Yugoslav Tribunal Statute ... The term "directed against any civilian population" should be taken to refer to acts committed as part of a widespread and systematic attack against a civilian population on national, political, ethnic, racial or religious grounds. The particular acts referred to in the definition are acts deliberately committed as part of such an attack.

If adopted, such a codification would fail humanity. Political persecution, religious persecution, and racial persecution should not be less significant than nearly all other in-

---

* In *Attorney General of Israel v. Eichmann*, as few as ninety-three people sufficed in one circumstance. Moreover, in *Matter of Barbie*, sometimes as few as one, three, seven, eleven, thirty, or forty-four victims comprised the number of persons covered. In a later decision of the French Supreme Court in 1986, the Court held that acts against a woman, her husband and son "could all constitute crimes against humanity." In the *Touvier* case, the defendant was convicted of being an accomplice to crimes against humanity involving merely the death of seven persons. In *The Prosecutor v. Akayesu*, ICTR-96-4-T (2 Sept. 1998), paras. 57, 59–63, the number of direct victims were as few as 3, 5, 8, 8, and 8 in various instances, and the Tribunal noted that even under the restrictive Statute of the ICTR (requiring "widespread or systematic attack") the defendant need not directly perpetrate widespread criminal acts if the defendant acted "during" or "as part of" a relevant pattern of crimes against humanity. Relevant acts included murder, torture, rape, and "other inhumane acts." Clearly the number of direct victims need not be large or the crime "widespread." *See also* LYAL S. SUNGA, INDIVIDUAL RESPONSIBILITY IN INTERNATIONAL LAW FOR SERIOUS HUMAN RIGHTS VIOLATIONS 136 (1992) (an attack on one person can suffice); other materials in this chapter.

ternational crimes, and the I.L.C. should not create new thresholds of accountability that are not only missing from customary law reflected in the Charter of the IMT at Nuremberg, but are also not found in connection with the vast majority of international crimes.

Some may argue that it is not practical to convince state elites that they should retain a Nuremberg-oriented prohibition of political or religious persecution, but such a parading of the word "practical," in Orwellian garb, would merely serve political and religious oppression. Surely such a word has lost any redeeming value for the victims of politicide. For them, the word "practical" smacks of an elite or self-oriented view that is partly unreal, socially dangerous and simply outrageous!

Another potentially restrictive definition of crimes against humanity appears in the Canadian Criminal Code. It fuses the two types recognized at Nuremberg into one, requiring that the act or omission be "committed against any civilian population or any identifiable group of persons." Clearly, such a requirement does not comply with customary definitions, since not all types must be committed against a civilian population or group of persons. It appears then that accountability after Nuremberg and uniform application of international criminal law is endangered by imperfect national legislation.

The problem is exacerbated by loose rhetoric found in national judicial opinions. While addressing the Canadian law in 1994, Justice Cory of the Supreme Court of Canada seemed particularly fond of adding phrases or descriptions that should not mistakenly be considered as elements of the general crime. Among the phrases used by Justice Cory that are clearly absent from the customary international instruments and that do not reflect elements or limitations under international law are the following: "so grave that they shock the conscience of all right thinking people," "cruel and terrible actions which are the essential elements," "grievous," "stigma ... must ... [be] overwhelming ... [and have] particularly heavy public opprobrium," "high degree of moral outrage," "untold misery," "immense suffering," "calculated malevolence," "barbarous cruelty," "requisite added dimension of cruelty and barbarism," and the "element of inhumanity must be demonstrated."

Notes and Questions

1. In *The Prosecutor v. Dusko Tadic*, at para. 141, the Appellate Chamber of the ICTY recognized that it is "a settled rule of customary international law that crimes against humanity do not require a connection to international armed conflicts. Indeed, ... customary international law may not require a connection between crimes against humanity and any conflict at all."

2. Did the Statute of the ICTY also define crimes against humanity too narrowly in other ways? See Article 5, in the Documents Supplement.

3. The Trial Chamber in *Nikolic*, IT-94-2-R61 (20 Oct. 1995), para. 26, defined these crimes even more narrowly by requiring: (1) that each type be directed against a civilian population (a limiting element in the Statute); (2) that each be organized and systematic and not the work of isolated individuals; and (3) that the crimes, considered as a whole, must be of a certain scale and gravity. Why do you suspect that certain persons make up limiting elements that are not reflected in the customary instruments and are not called for even in a far too limiting statute? Will these limitations, supposedly made in the name of humanity, actually serve humanity? Who will they tend to serve?

4. Note that, unlike the historic World War II documents, Article 5 of the Statute of the ICTY had required a linkage between crimes against humanity and an "armed conflict, whether of an international or internal character." Neither Article 3 of the Statute of the ICTR nor Article 7 of the Statute of the ICC require such a linkage, and as the tribunal in *Tadic* correctly notes, *supra*, it is not required by customary international law.

Problems concerning crimes against humanity arose perhaps because there has been no general codification in a multilateral convention since the Charters for the I.M.T.s at Nuremberg and for the Far East, although specific subsets are codified in the Genocide Convention and the Apartheid Convention, which are species of crimes against humanity that clearly can occur during times of peace (see Chapters Ten and Eleven). *See* M. Cherif Bassiouni, *"Crimes Against Humanity": The Need for a Specialized Convention*, 31 Colum. J. Trans. L. 457 (1994).

If you were to draft a new Convention on Crimes Against Humanity, what elements and definitions would you include? Earlier, for Professor Bassiouni and others, among the problems to be resolved in the 1990s were: (a) whether there should be a linkage to armed conflict, (b) whether there is a need for a policy of persecution or a policy of systematic harm to a segment of the civilian population, and (c) whether more specific acts which constitute the crime can be enumerated. For Professor Paust and others: (a) today, at least, there is no need for a linkage with an armed conflict;* and (b) there is no need for any such policy, nor should the customary documents be rewritten in order to establish higher thresholds for accountability at the expense of humanity. For Professor Bassiouni, textual phrases such as "other inhumane acts" are too vague and can therefore violate "principles of legality." *See* M. Cherif Bassiouni, Crimes Against Humanity in International Criminal Law 320 *ff.* (1992). For others, they are no more vague than similar human rights provisions, similar provisions in the Hague and Geneva law and the Torture Convention (see Chapter Eleven) and related constitutional provisions applied in various legal systems. Should a Convention on Crimes Against Humanity cover merely what is mirrored in Article 7 of the Rome Statute or should it cover what appears in several of the customary international legal instruments created after World War II? See also Paust, *The International Criminal Court Does Not Have Complete Jurisdiction Over Customary Crimes Against Humanity and War Crimes*, *supra* at 684–700.

5. Recently, a group of nearly 250 distinguished experts drafted a Proposed International Convention on the Prevention and Punishment of Crimes Against Humanity. See Leila Nadya Sadat, *Preface*, in Forging A Convention for Crimes Against Humanity xxvi (Leila Nadya Sadat ed., 2011), stating:

> "The *Proposed Convention* builds upon and complements the ICC Statute by retaining the Rome Statute definition of crimes against humanity but has added robust interstate cooperation, extradition, and mutual legal assistance provisions.... the creative work of the Initiative was to meld these and our own ideas into a single, coherent international convention that establishes the

---

* See early uses of the concept documented above (*e.g.,* including contexts of slavery or the slave trade); Art. II (1)(c) of Control Council Law No. 10; the Genocide Convention; the Apartheid Convention; Art. 1(b) of the Convention on the Nonapplicability of Statutory Limitations to War Crimes and Crimes Against Humanity; Art. 3 of the Statute of the ICTR; *see also* Art. 5(c) of the Charter of the IMT for the Far East (first type of crime against humanity); *Attorney General of Israel v. Eichmann, supra; The Prosecutor v. Dusko Tadic, supra*, in Note 1 above; Paust, *Threats to Accountability*, *supra*.

principle of State Responsibility as well as individual criminal responsibility (including the possibility of responsibility for the criminal acts of legal persons) for the commission of crimes against humanity. The Proposed Convention innovates in many respects by attempting to bring prevention into the instrument in a much more explicit way than predecessor instruments, by including the possibility of responsibility for the criminal acts of legal persons, by excluding defenses of immunities and statutory limitations, by prohibiting reservations, and by establishing a unique institutional mechanism for supervision of the Convention."

6. Should crimes against humanity include gender-specific targeting as a category (even though some such targeting, as part of a mixed targeting otherwise covered by customary definitions, is prosecutable)? *See generally* Rhonda Copelon, *Surfacing Gender: Re-Engraving Crimes Against Women in Humanitarian Law*, 5 HAST. WOMEN'S L. J. 243, 248, 259, 261–63 (1994) (adding: "The expansion of the concept of crimes against humanity explicitly to include gender is ... part of the broader movement to end the historical invisibility of gender violence as a humanitarian and human rights violation."); J. Paust, *Women and International Criminal Law Instruments and Processes*, in 2 WOMEN AND INTERNATIONAL HUMAN RIGHTS LAW 349 (Kelly D. Askin & Dorean M. Koenig eds. 2000); Adrien Katherine Wing & Sylke Merchan, *Rape, Ethnicity, and Culture: Spirit Injury From Bosnia to Black America*, 25 COLUM. H.R.L. REV. 1, 43–44 (1993).

Article 7(1)(h) of the Statute of the ICC includes gender-based persecution among conduct constituting a crime against humanity. See also Brook S. Moshan, *Women, War, and Words: The Gender Component in the Permanent International Criminal Court's Definition of Crimes Against Humanity*, 22 FORDHAM INT'L L.J. 154, 176 (1998).

7. Concerning the fact that Article 7 of the Rome Statute of the ICC does not cover all customary crimes against humanity, see also Jordan J. Paust, *The International Criminal Court Does Not Have Complete Jurisdiction Over Customary Crimes Against Humanity and War Crimes*, 43 JOHN MARSHALL L. REV. 681 (2010), available at http://ssrn.com/abstract=1598440.

The Prosecutor v. Rutaganda
ICTR-96-3-T (6 Dec. 1999)

Before: Judge Laïty Kama, Presiding

Judge Lennart Aspegren

Judge Navanethem Pillay

Crimes against Humanity pursuant to Article 3 of the Statute of the Tribunal

65. Article 3 of the Statute confers on the Tribunal the jurisdiction to prosecute persons for various inhumane acts which constitute crimes against humanity. The Chamber concurs with the reasoning in the *Akayesu Judgement* that offences falling within the ambit of crimes against humanity may be broadly broken down into four essential elements, namely:

(a) the *actus reus* must be inhumane in nature and character, causing great suffering, or serious injury to body or to mental or physical health

(b) the *actus reus* must be committed as part of a widespread or systematic attack

(c) the *actus reus* must be committed against members of the civilian population

(d) the *actus reus* must be committed on one or more discriminatory grounds, namely, national, political, ethnic, racial or religious grounds.

The *Actus Reus* Must be Committed as Part of a Widespread or Systematic Attack

66. The Chamber is of the opinion that the *actus reus* cannot be a random inhumane act, but rather an act committed as part of an attack. With regard to the nature of this attack, the Chamber notes that Article 3 of the English version of the Statute reads "[…] as part of a widespread or systematic attack […]" whilst the French version of the Statute reads "[…] *dans le cadre d'une attaque généralisée et systématique* […]". The French version requires that the attack be both of a widespread *and* systematic nature, whilst the English version requires that the attack be of a widespread *or* systematic nature and need not be both.

The Chamber notes that customary international law requires that the attack be either of a widespread *or* systematic nature and need not be both. The English version of the Statute conforms more closely with customary international law and the Chamber therefore accepts the elements as set forth in Article 3 of the English version of the Statute and follows the interpretation in other ICTR judgements namely: that the "attack" under Article 3 of the Statute, must be either of a widespread or systematic nature and need not be both.

67. The Chamber notes that "widespread", as an element of crimes against humanity, was defined in the *Akayesu Judgement*, as massive, frequent, large scale action, carried out collectively with considerable seriousness and directed against a multiplicity of victims, whilst "systematic" was defined as thoroughly organised action, following a regular pattern on the basis of a common policy and involving substantial public or private resources. The Chamber concurs with these definitions and finds that it is not essential for this policy to be adopted formally as a policy of a State. There must, however, be some kind of preconceived plan or policy.

68. The Chamber notes that "attack", as an element of crimes against humanity, was defined in the *Akayesu Judgement*, as an unlawful act of the kind enumerated in Article 3(a) to (i) of the Statute, such as murder, extermination, enslavement, etc. An attack may also be non-violent in nature, like imposing a system of apartheid, which is declared a crime against humanity in Article 1 of the Apartheid Convention of 1973, or exerting pressure on the population to act in a particular manner may also come under the purview of an attack, if orchestrated on a massive scale or in a systematic manner. The Chamber concurs with this definition.

69. The Chamber considers that the perpetrator must have:

"[…]actual or constructive knowledge of the broader context of the attack, meaning that the accused must know that his act(s) is part of a widespread or systematic attack on a civilian population and pursuant to some kind of policy or plan."

The *Actus Reus* Must be Directed against the Civilian Population

70. The Chamber notes that the *actus reus* must be directed against the civilian population, if it is to constitute a crime against humanity. In the *Akayesu Judgement*, the civilian population was defined as people who were not taking any active part in the hostilities. The fact that there are certain individuals among the civilian population who are not civilians does not deprive the population of its civilian character. The Chamber concurs with this definition.

The Enumerated Acts

76. The Chamber notes that in respect of crimes against humanity, the Accused is indicted for murder and extermination. The Chamber, in interpreting Article 3 of the Statute, will focus its discussion on these offences only.

Murder

77. Pursuant to Article 3(a) of the Statute, murder constitutes a crime against humanity. The Chamber notes that Article 3(a) of the English version of the Statute refers to "Murder", whilst the French version of the Statute refers to "*Assassinat*". Customary International Law dictates that it is the offence of "Murder" that constitutes a crime against humanity and not "*Assassinat*".

78. The *Akayesu Judgement* defined Murder as the unlawful, intentional killing of a human being. The requisite elements of murder are:

(a) The victim is dead;

(b) The death resulted from an unlawful act or omission of the accused or a subordinate;

(c) At the time of the killing the accused or a subordinate had the intention to kill or inflict grievous bodily harm on the deceased having known that such bodily harm is likely to cause the victim's death, and is reckless as to whether or not death ensures;

(d) The victim was discriminated against on any one of the enumerated discriminatory grounds;

(e) The victim was a member of the civilian population; and

(f) The act or omission was part of a widespread or systematic attack on the civilian population.

79. The Chamber concurs with this definition of murder and is of the opinion that the act or omission that constitutes murder must be discriminatory in nature and directed against a member of the civilian population.

Extermination

80. Pursuant to Article 3(c) of the Statute, extermination constitutes a crime against humanity. By its very nature, extermination is a crime which is directed against a group of individuals. Extermination differs from murder in that it requires an element of mass destruction which is not a pre-requisite for murder.

81. The *Akayesu Judgement*, defined the essential elements of extermination as follows:

(a) the accused or his subordinate participated in the killing of certain named or described persons;

(b) the act or omission was unlawful and intentional;

(c) the unlawful act or omission must be part of a widespread or systematic attack;

(d) the attack must be against the civilian population; and

(e) the attack must be on discriminatory grounds, namely: national, political, ethnic, racial, or religious grounds.

82. The Chamber concurs with this definition of extermination and is of the opinion that the act or omission that constitutes extermination must be discriminatory in nature

and directed against members of the civilian population. Further, this act or omission includes, but is not limited to the direct act of killing. It can be any act or omission, or cumulative acts or omissions, that cause the death of the targeted group of individuals.

The Prosecutor v. Musema
ICTR-96-13-T (27 Jan. 2000)

Before: Judge Lennart Aspegren, Presiding

Judge Laïty Kama

Judge Navanethem Pillay

Rape

220. Rape may constitute a crime against humanity, pursuant to Article 3(g) of the Statute. In the *Akayesu* Judgement, rape as a crime against humanity was defined as:

"[…] a physical invasion of a sexual nature, committed on a person under circumstances which are coercive. Sexual violence, which includes rape, is considered to be any act of a sexual nature which is committed on a person under circumstances which are coercive. This act [under the Statute of the ICTR] must be committed:

(a) as part of a widespread or systematic attack;

(b) on a civilian population;

(c) on certain catalogued discriminatory grounds, namely: national, ethnic, political, racial, or religious grounds."

221. The Chamber notes that, while rape has been defined in certain national jurisdictions as non-consensual intercourse, variations on the acts of rape may include acts which involve the insertions of objects and/or the use of bodily orifices not considered to be intrinsically sexual.

222. The Chamber also observes that in defining rape, as a crime against humanity, the Trial Chamber in the *Akayesu* Judgement acknowledged:

"that rape is a form of aggression and that the central elements of the crime of rape cannot be captured in a mechanical description of objects and body parts. The Convention against Torture and Other Cruel, Inhuman and Degrading Treatment or Punishment does not catalogue specific acts in its definition of torture, focusing rather on the conceptual framework of state sanctioned violence. This approach is more useful in international law. Like torture, rape is used for such purposes as intimidation, degradation, humiliation, discrimination, punishment, control or destruction of a person. Like torture, rape is a violation of personal dignity, and rape in fact constitutes torture when inflicted by or at the instigation of or with the consent or acquiescence of a public official or other person acting in an official capacity."

223. The Chamber notes that the definition of rape and sexual violence articulated in the *Akayesu* Judgement was adopted by the Trial Chamber II of the ICTY in its *Delalic* Judgement.

224. The Chamber has considered the alternative definition of rape set forth by Trial Chamber I of the ICTY in its *Furundzija* Judgement, which relies on a detailed description of objects and body parts. In this judgement the Trial Chamber looked to national legislation and noted:

"The Trial Chamber would emphasise at the outset, that a trend can be discerned in the national legislation of a number of States of broadening the definition of rape so that it now embraces acts that were previously classified as comparatively less serious offences, that is sexual or indecent assault. This trend shows that at the national level States tend to take a stricter attitude towards serious forms of sexual assault; the stigma of rape now attaches to a growing category of sexual offences, provided of course they meet certain requirements, chiefly that of forced physical penetration."

225. The *Furundzija* Judgement further noted that "most legal systems in the common and civil law worlds consider rape to be the forcible sexual penetration of the human body by the penis or the forcible insertion of any other object into either the vagina or the anus". Nevertheless, after due consideration of the practice of forced oral penetration, which is treated as rape in some States and sexual assault in other States, the Trial Chamber in that case determined as follows:

"183. The Trial Chamber holds that the forced penetration of the mouth by the male sexual organ constitutes a most humiliating and degrading attack upon human dignity. The essence of the whole corpus of international humanitarian law as well as human rights law lies in the protection of the human dignity of every person, whatever his or her gender. The general principle of respect for human dignity is the basic underpinning and indeed the very *raison d'être* of international humanitarian law and human rights law, indeed in modern times it has become of such paramount importance as to permeate the whole body of international law. This principle is intended to shield human beings from outrages upon their personal dignity, whether such outrages are carried out by unlawfully attacking the body or by humiliating and debasing the honour, the self-respect or the mental well-being of a person. It is consonant with this principle that such an extremely serious sexual outrage as forced oral penetration should be classified as rape."

226. The Chamber concurs with the conceptual approach set forth in the *Akayesu* Judgement for the definition of rape, which recognizes that the essence of rape is not the particular details of the body parts and objects involved, but rather the aggression that is expressed in a sexual manner under conditions of coercion.

227. The Chamber considers that the distinction between rape and other forms of sexual violence drawn by the *Akayesu* Judgement, that is "a physical invasion of a sexual nature" as contrasted with "any act of a sexual nature" which is committed on a person under circumstances which are coercive is clear and establishes a framework for judicial consideration of individual incidents of sexual violence and a determination, on a case by case basis, of whether such incidents constitute rape. The definition of rape, as set forth in the *Akayesu* Judgement, clearly encompasses all the conduct described in the definition of rape set forth in *Furundzija*.

228. The Chamber notes that in the *Furundzija* Judgement, the Trial Chamber considered forced penetration of the mouth as a humiliating and degrading attack on human dignity and largely for this reason included such conduct in its definition of rape even though State jurisdictions are divided as to whether such conduct constitutes rape. The Chamber further notes, as the *Furundzija* Judgement acknowledges, that there is a trend in national legislation to broaden the definition of rape. In light of the dynamic ongoing evolution of the understanding of rape and the incorporation of this understanding into principles of international law, the Chamber considers that a conceptual definition is preferable to a mechanical definition of rape. The conceptual definition will better accommodate evolving norms of criminal justice.

229. For these reasons, the Chamber adopts the definition of rape and sexual violence set forth in the *Akayesu* Judgement.

Questions

1. Are the factors identified in *Rutaganda* concerning "widespread" and "systematic" too limiting? Is "frequent" merely relevant to what is "systematic"? Is "with ... seriousness" really necessary to either? Also recall that in *Akayesu* the number of direct victims were as few as three, five, and eight persons. In The Prosecutor v. Kordic & Cerkez, IT-95-14/2-T (Trial Chamber Judgment, 26 Feb. 2001), para. 179, it was recognized that "widespread" conduct can involve the "cumulative effect of a series of inhumane acts or the singular effect of an inhumane act of extraordinary magnitude." In The Prosecutor v. Naletilic & Martinovic, IT-98-34-T (Trial Chamber Judgment, 31 Mar. 2003), para. 236, it was stated that "systematic" conduct "requires an organized nature of the acts and the improbability of their random occurrence."

Note that *Rutaganda*, in para. 67, did not accept a claim that a state policy must be involved. This is noticeably different than the limit found in French cases in Section 3. Nonetheless, can crimes against humanity be committed in the absence of some "policy"? See other materials in this chapter and Chapter Ten.

Rutaganda cited *Akayesu* concerning a supposed requirement of "widespread" or "systematic" conduct. See ICTR-96-3-T, para. 63 and note 10. *Akayesu* cited nothing for this proposition but the French cases. See ICTR-96-4-T, paras. 567–574 and notes 139–141, arguing that the French cases somehow changed customary international law for the international community. *Id.* at para. 567 ("underwent a gradual evolution in the *Eichmann, Barbie, Touvier* and *Papon* cases.").

2. Regarding "murder," is "intentional killing" the same as an intent to inflict grievous harm knowing that such is "likely" to kill? In the U.S. generally, what factors tend to differentiate "murder 1" from "murder 2"?

3. If "constructive knowledge" of an "attack" on civilian persons suffices, why "must" one "know"? In *The Prosecutor v. Blaskic*, IT-95-14-A (Appeals Chamber Judgment, 29 July 2004), ruled that "knowledge on the part of the accused that there is an attack on the civilian population, as well as knowledge that his act is part thereof" is required. *Id.* para. 126. "The *Blaskic* Appeals Chamber affirmed a number of findings by the Trial Chamber with respect to certain underlying offences as persecutions under Article 5 [of the ICTY Statute]. Although some of these findings reiterate and reaffirm the jurisprudence of the ICTY, the Appeals Chamber succinctly summarized these ... and confirmed the customary nature of these crimes as persecutions.... Thus, the Appeals Chamber concluded that the following offences may constitute persecutions: killing (murder) and causing serious injury; deportation, forcible transfer and forcible displacement; inhumane treatment of civilians; and attacks on cities, towns and villages ... [as well as] destruction and plunder of property." Daryl A. Mundis & Fergal Gaynor, *Current Developments at the Ad Hoc International Criminal Tribunals*, 3 J. Int'l Crim. Justice 268, 274–75 (2005).

Consider also *The Prosecutor v. Naletilic & Martinovic*, IT-98-34-A (Appeals Chamber Judgment, 3 May 2006), paras. 129–130: "in the case of *Kvocka et al*, [the Appeals Chamber stated] 'the discriminatory intent of crimes cannot be inferred directly from the general discriminatory nature of an attack characterised as a crime against humanity. However, the discriminatory intent may be inferred from the context of the attack, provided it is substantiated by the surrounding circumstances of the crime.' [IT-98-

30/1-A, 28 Feb. 2005, para. 366] According to the *Krnojelac* Appeal Judgment, such circumstances include the operation of a prison, in particular the systematic nature of crimes committed against a particular group within the prison, and the general attitude of the alleged perpetrator as seen through his behaviour. [IT-97-25-A, 2 Aug. 2001, para. 184]

[para.] 130. The Appeals Chamber has had occasion to apply this approach in a number of cases. According to the Appeals Chamber in the case of *Kordic and Cerkez*, in the situation in which all the guards belong to one ethnic group and all the prisoners to another, it could reasonably be inferred that the latter group was being discriminated against. [IT-95-14/2-A, 17 Dec. 2004, para. 950] In the *Kvocka et al.* Appeal Judgment, the Appeals Chamber stated that since almost all the detainees in the camp belonged to the non-Serb group, it could reasonably be concluded that the reason for their detention was membership of that group and that the detention was therefore of a discriminatory character." [IT-98-30/1-A, 28 Feb. 2005, para. 366]

With respect to knowledge that ones crimes against humanity are related to an attack on civilians, the Appeals Chamber reiterated a statement in *The Prosecutor v. Tadic*, IT-94-1-A (Appeals Chamber Judgment, 15 July 1999), para. 271, that "'it must be proved that the crimes were *related* to the attack on a civilian population (occurring during an armed conflict) and that the accused *knew* that his crimes were so related.'" *Naletilic & Martinovic*, para. 118. The opinion analogized such a requirement to that contained in Article 2 of the Statute of the ICTY with respect to war crimes and stated that "the Prosecution has to show 'that the accused *knew* that his crimes' had a nexus to an international armed conflict, or at least that he had knowledge of the factual circumstances later bringing the Judges to the conclusion that the armed conflict was an international one.... The perpetrator only needs to be aware of the factual circumstances on which the judge finally determines the existence of the armed conflict and the international (or internal) character thereof. It is a general principle of criminal law that the correct legal classification of a conduct of the perpetrator is not required. The principle of individual guilt, however, demands sufficient awareness of *factual* circumstances establishing the armed conflict and its (international or internal) character." *Id.* paras. 118–119.

The Appeals Chamber in *Naletilic & Martinovic* also recognized that "persecutions may be undertaken by individuals at all levels of a hierarchy; there is no requirement that the individual be a senior figure." *Id.* para. 580.

With respect to alleged cumulative convictions for war crimes of unlawful transfer of persons and plunder of public and private property as well as "conduct underlying these offences [that] also formed part of the basis of the charge of persecutions as a crime against humanity," "the offences ... cannot be said to be consumed within persecutions since the unlawful transfer and plunder were charged as a grave breach of the Geneva Conventions and as a violations of the laws or customs of war while persecutions was charged as a crime against humanity," and "crimes against humanity under Article 5 of the Statute and grave breaches under Article 2 of the Statute contain different elements.... [T]he *Celibici* Appeal Judgment states that the test for permissible cumulative convictions for the same underlying conduct is whether 'each applicable provision contains a materially distinct legal element not present in the other, bearing in mind that an element is materially distinct from another if it requires proof of a fact not required by the other' and [in *Kordic & Cerkez*, para. 1037] '[w]hile Article 5 requires proof that the act occurred as part of a widespread or systematic attack against a civilian population, Article 2 requires proof of a nexus between the acts of the accused and the existence of an international armed conflict as well as the protected persons status of the victims under the

Geneva Conventions.'" *Id.* paras. 561–562, citing The Prosecutor v. Celibici, IT-96-21-A (Appeals Chamber Judgment, 20 Feb. 2001), para. 421.

4. In *The Prosecutor v. Stakic*, IT-97-24-T (Trial Chamber Judgment, 31 July 2003), it was recognized that when a person is accused of having been an indirect perpetrator of an attack conviction can rest on the general discriminatory intent of the accused in relation to an attack committed by direct perpetrators even if the direct perpetrators had no such discriminatory intent if the direct perpetrators were used as an innocent instrument or tool of the indirect perpetrator. *Id.* paras. 737–744.

5. Concerning the difference between murder and extermination, is the word "mass" too limiting? Can a small number of direct victims be "exterminated"? In *The Prosecutor v. Stakic, supra,* a physician, Milomir Stakic, was convicted of extermination, stating that the perpetrator must intend to kill on a massive scale or intend to create conditions of life that lead to the death of a large number of persons or "the annihilation of a mass of people." *Id.* para. 641. Gross negligence or recklessness is not sufficient regarding the *mens rea* required for extermination as a crime against humanity. *Id.* para. 642.

6. Concerning "inhumane" treatment, is the *Rutaganda* approach, requiring "great" suffering or "serious" injury, too limiting? In *The Prosecutor v. Kordic & Cerkez*, IT-95-14/2-A (Appeals Chamber Judgment, 17 Dec. 2004), para. 117, the Appeals Chamber of the ICTY stated that "inhumane" acts as crimes against humanity fulfill the following conditions: (1) the victim must have suffered serious bodily or mental harm, (2) the degree of severity must be assessed on a case-by-case basis with due regard for the individual circumstances, (3) the suffering must be the result of an act or omission of the accused or his subordinate, and (4) when the offence was committed, the accused or his subordinate must have been motivated by the intent to inflict serious bodily or mental harm upon the victim.

7. With respect to the faculty quality of "inhumane," the accused "need not have known that his or her act … amounted to an 'inhumane act' either in the legal or moral sense." Guenael Mettraux, *Crimes Against Humanity in the Jurisprudence of the ICTs for the Former Yugoslavia and for Rwanda*, 43 Harv. Int'l L.J. 237, 297 n.323 (2002).

7. In *The Prosecutor v. Muhimana*, ICTR-95-1B-T (Trial Chamber Judgment, 28 Apr. 2005), para. 546, it was recognized that "coercion is an element that may obviate the relevance of consent as an evidentiary factor in the crime of rape" and "circumstances prevailing in most cases charged under international criminal law, as either genocide, crimes against humanity, or war crimes, will be almost universally coercive, thus vitiating consent." See also Daryl A. Mundis & Fergal Gaynor, *Current Developments at the Ad Hoc International Criminal Tribunals*, 3 J. Int'l Crim. Justice 1134, 1136–37 (2005).

8. An issue concerning rape as a crime against humanity was presented in *The Prosecutor v. Cesic*, IT-95-10/1-S (Trial Chamber Sentencing Judgment, 11 Mar. 2004). "The question arises whether another person could be [an] object or instrument [used for penetrating a person]. In general terms, a person is not considered an object. But you could use another person as an object or an instrument if you depersonalise him, if you take from him what makes him a person; that is, his own free will. Under the circumstances … [where] both detainees [were] instructed to penetrate in the body of the other detainee … [they] were deprived of their own free will." *Id.*, Transcript (8 Oct. 2003), para. 85. Under the circumstances, Cesic "actively participated in the violence inflicted upon the victims before the assault and initiated the assault by ordering it." *Id.*, Sentencing Judgment, para. 36; see also Daryl A. Mundis & Fergal Gaynor, *Current Developments at the Ad Hoc International Criminal Tribunals*, 2 J. Int'l Crim Justice 879, 884 (2004).

9. Concerning "hate speech" as an element of persecution, *The Prosecutor v. Nahimana, et al.*, ICTR-99-52-T (Trial Chamber Judgment and Sentence, 3 Dec. 2003), stated that "hate speech is a discriminatory form of aggression that destroys the dignity of those in the group under attack" and found that newspaper articles in question "created the conditions for extermination and genocide in Rwanda." *Id*. paras. 1072–1074. The Trial Chamber also stated that persecution is "broader than direct and public incitement, including advocacy of ethnic hatred in other forms." *Id*. para. 1078.

The Prosecutor v. Dusko Tadic
IT-94-1-A (Appeals Chamber Judgment, 15 July 1999)

VI. The Third Ground of Cross-Appeal by the Prosecution: The Trial Chamber's Finding that Crimes Against Humanity Cannot be Committed for Purely Personal Motives

238. In the Judgement, the Trial Chamber identified, from among the elements which had to be satisfied before a conviction for crimes against humanity could be recorded, the need to prove the existence of an armed conflict and a nexus between the acts in question and the armed conflict.

239. As to the nature of the nexus required, the Trial Chamber found that, subject to two caveats, it is sufficient for the purposes of crimes against humanity that the act occurred "in the course or duration of an armed conflict". The first caveat was "that the act be linked geographically as well as temporally with the armed conflict". The second caveat was that the act and the conflict must be related or, at least, that the act must "not be unrelated to the armed conflict". The Trial Chamber further held that the requirement that the act must "not be unrelated" to the armed conflict involved two aspects. First, the perpetrator must know of the broader context in which the act occurs. Secondly, the act must not have been carried out for the purely personal motives of the perpetrator....

B. Discussion

247. Neither Party asserts that the Trial Chamber's finding that crimes against humanity cannot be committed for purely personal motives had a bearing on the verdict in terms of Article 25(1) of the Tribunal Statute. [see in Docs. Supp.] Nevertheless this is a matter of general significance for the Tribunal's jurisprudence. It is therefore appropriate for the Appeals Chamber to set forth its views on this matter.

1. Article 5 of the Statute

248. The Appeals Chamber agrees with the Prosecution that there is nothing in Article 5 to suggest that it contains a requirement that crimes against humanity cannot be committed for purely personal motives. The Appeals Chamber agrees that it may be inferred from the words "directed against any civilian population" in Article 5 of the Statute that the acts of the accused must comprise part of a pattern of widespread or systematic crimes directed against a civilian population[1] and that the accused must have *known* that

---

1. [Tribunal's fn. 310] This requirement had already been recognised by this Tribunal in the *Vukovar Hospital* Rule 61 Decision: "Crimes against humanity are to be distinguished from war crimes against individuals. In particular, they must be widespread or demonstrate a systematic character. However, as long as there is a link with the widespread or systematic attack against a civilian population, a single act could qualify as a crime against humanity. As such, an individual committing a crime against a single victim or a limited number of victims might be recognised as guilty of a crime against humanity if his acts were part of the specific context identified above." ("Review of Indictment Pursuant to Rule 61 of the Rules of Procedure and Evidence", *The Prosecutor v. Mile Mrksi) et al.*, IT-95-13-R61 (Trial Chamber I, 3 April 1996), para. 30.

his acts fit into such a pattern. There is nothing in the Statute, however, which mandates the imposition of a *further* condition that the acts in question must not be committed for purely personal reasons, except to the extent that this condition is a consequence or a re-statement of the other two conditions mentioned.

249. The Appeals Chamber would also agree with the Prosecution that the words "committed in armed conflict" in Article 5 of the Statute require nothing more than the *existence* of an armed conflict at the relevant time and place. The Prosecution is, moreover, correct in asserting that the armed conflict requirement is a *jurisdictional* element, not "a substantive element of the *mens rea* of crimes against humanity" (*i.e.*, not a legal ingredient of the subjective element of the crime).

250. This distinction is important because, as stated above, if the exclusion of "purely personal" behaviour is understood simply as a re-statement of the two-fold requirement that the acts of the accused form part of a context of mass crimes and that the accused be aware of this fact, then there is nothing objectionable about it; indeed it is a correct statement of the law. It is only if this phrase is understood as requiring that the motives of the accused ("personal reasons", in the terminology of the Trial Chamber) *not be unrelated to the armed conflict* that it is erroneous. Similarly, that phrase is unsound if it is taken to require proof of the accused's *motives*, as distinct from the intent to commit the crime and the knowledge of the context into which the crime fits.

251. As to what the Trial Chamber understood by the phrase "purely personal motives", it is clear that it conflated two interpretations of the phrase: first, that the act is unrelated to the armed conflict, and, secondly, that the act is unrelated to the attack on the civilian population. In this regard, paragraph 659 of the Judgement held:

> 659. Thus if the perpetrator has knowledge, either actual or constructive, that these acts were occurring on a widespread or systematic basis and does not commit his act for purely personal motives completely *unrelated to the attack on the civilian population*, that is sufficient to hold him liable for crimes against humanity. Therefore the perpetrator must know that there is an attack on the civilian population, know that his act fits in with the attack and the act must not be taken for purely personal reasons *unrelated to the armed conflict.* (emphasis added)

Thus the "attack on the civilian population" is here equated to "the armed conflict". The two concepts cannot, however, be identical because then crimes against humanity would, by definition, *always take place in armed conflict*, whereas under customary international law these crimes may also be committed in times of peace. So the two — the "attack on the civilian population" and "the armed conflict" — must be separate notions, although of course under Article 5 of the Statute the attack on "any civilian population" may be part of an "armed conflict". A nexus with the accused's acts is required, however, *only* for the attack on "any civilian population". A nexus between the accused's acts and the armed conflict is *not* required, as is instead suggested by the Judgement. The armed conflict requirement is satisfied by proof that *there was* an armed conflict; that is all that the Statute requires, and in so doing, it requires more than does customary international law....

2. The Object and Purpose of the Statute

253. The Prosecution has submitted that "the object and purpose of the Statute support the interpretation that crimes against humanity can be committed for purely personal reasons". The Prosecution cites the Tadi? Decision on Jurisdiction, to the effect that "the 'primary purpose' of the establishment of the International Tribunal 'is not to leave unpunished any person guilty of [a] serious violation [of international humanitarian law], whatever the context within which it may have been committed'". This begs the ques-

tion, however, whether a crime committed for purely personal reasons *is* a crime against humanity, and therefore a serious violation of international humanitarian law under Article 5 of the Statute.

254. The Appeals Chamber would also reject the Prosecution's submission concerning the onerous evidentiary burden which would be imposed on it in having to prove that the accused did not act from personal motives, as equally question-begging and inapposite. It is question-begging because if, *arguendo*, under international criminal law, the fact that the accused did not act from purely personal motives was a requirement of crimes against humanity, then the Prosecution would have to prove that element, whether it was onerous for it to do so or not. The question is simply whether or not there is such a requirement under international criminal law.

3. Case-law as Evidence of Customary International Law

255. Turning to the further submission of the Prosecution, the Appeals Chamber agrees that the weight of authority supports the proposition that crimes against humanity can be committed for purely personal reasons, provided it is understood that the two aforementioned conditions—that the crimes must be committed in the context of widespread or systematic crimes directed against a civilian population and that the accused must have *known* that his acts, in the words of the Trial Chamber, "fitted into such a pattern"—are met.

256. In this regard, it is necessary to review the case-law cited by the Trial Chamber and the Prosecution, as well as other relevant case law, to establish whether this case-law is indicative of the emergence of a norm of customary international law on this matter.

257. The Prosecution is correct in stating that the 1948 case cited by the Trial Chamber supports rather than negates the proposition that crimes against humanity may be committed for purely personal motives, provided that the acts in question were knowingly committed as "part and parcel of all the mass crimes committed during the persecution of the Jews". As the Supreme Court for the British Zone stated, "in cases of crimes against humanity taking the form of political denunciations, only the perpetrator's consciousness and intent to deliver his victim through denunciation to the forces of arbitrariness or terror are required".

258. The case involving the killing of mentally disturbed patients, decided by the same court and cited by the Prosecution, is also a persuasive authority concerning the irrelevance of personal motives with regard to the constituent elements of crimes against humanity.

259. The Prosecution's submission finds further support in other so-called denunciation cases rendered after the Second World War by the Supreme Court for the British Zone and by German national courts, in which private individuals who denounced others, albeit for personal reasons, were nevertheless convicted of crimes against humanity.

260. In *Sch.*, the accused had denounced her landlord solely "out of revenge and for the purpose of rendering him harmless" after tensions in their tenancy had arisen. The denunciation led to investigation proceedings by the Gestapo which ended with the landlord's conviction and execution. The Court of First Instance convicted *Sch.* and sentenced her to three years' imprisonment for crimes against humanity. The accused appealed against the decision, arguing that "crimes against humanity were limited to participation in mass crimes and ... did not include all those cases in which someone took action against a single person for personal reasons". The Supreme Court dismissed the appeal, holding that neither the Nuremberg Judgement nor the statements of the Prosecutor be interpreted in such a restrictive way. The Supreme Court stated:

[T]he International Military Tribunal and the Supreme Court considered that a crime against humanity as defined in CCL 10 Article II 1 (c) is committed whenever the victim suffers prejudice as a result of the National Socialist rule of violence and tyranny (*"Gewalt- oder Willkürherrschaft"*) to such an extent that mankind itself was affected thereby. Such prejudice can also arise from an attack committed against an individual victim for personal reasons. However, this is only the case if the victim was not only harmed by the perpetrator—this would not be a matter which concerned mankind as such—but if the character, duration or extent of the prejudice were determined by the National Socialist rule of violence and tyranny or if a link between them existed. If the victim was harmed in his or her human dignity, the incident was no longer an event that did not concern mankind as such. If an individual's attack against an individual victim for personal reasons is connected to the National Socialist rule of violence and tyranny and if the attack harms the victim in the aforementioned way, it, too, becomes one link in the chain of the measures which under the National Socialist rule were intended to persecute large groups among the population. There is no apparent reason to exonerate the accused only because he acted against an individual victim for personal reasons.

261. This view was upheld in a later decision of the Supreme Court in the case of H. H. denounced his father-in-law, V.F., for listening to a foreign broadcasting station, allegedly because V.F., who was of aristocratic origin, incessantly mocked H. for his low birth and tyrannised the family with his relentlessly scornful behaviour. The family members supposedly considered a denunciation to be the only solution to their family problems. Upon the denunciation, V.F. was sentenced by the Nazi authorities to three years in prison. V.F., who suffered from an intestinal illness, died in prison. Despite the fact that H.'s denunciation was motivated by personal reasons, the Court of First Instance sentenced H. for a crime against humanity, stating that "it can be left open as to whether [...] H. was motivated by political, personal or other reasons". Referring to the established jurisprudence of the Supreme Court for the British Zone, the Court of First Instance held that "the motives (*"Beweggründe"*) prompting a denunciation are not decisive (*nicht entscheidend)"*....

265. The Prosecution also refers to the *Eichmann* and *Finta* cases. The *Eichmann* case is inappropriate as the defendant in that case *specifically denied* that he ever acted from a personal motive, claiming that he did what he did "not of his own volition but as one of numerous links in the chain of command". Moreover the court found Eichmann, who was the Head of the Jewish Affairs and Evacuation Department and one of the persons who attended the infamous Wannsee Conference, to be "no mere 'cog', small or large, in a machine propelled by others; he was, himself, one of those who propelled the machine". Such a senior official would not be one to whom the "purely personal reasons" consideration could conceivably apply.

266. The *Finta* case is more on point, not least since the accused was a minor official, a captain in the Royal Hungarian Gendarmerie. He was thus better placed than senior officials to raise an issue as to his exclusively "personal" motives. That case is indeed authority for the proposition that the sole requirements for crimes against humanity in this regard are that:

> [...] there must be an element of subjective knowledge on the part of the accused of the factual conditions which render the actions a crime against humanity.... The mental element of a crime against humanity must involve an awareness of the facts or circumstances which would bring the acts within the definition of a crime against humanity.

267. According to *Finta*, nothing more seems to be required beyond this and there is no mention of the relevance or otherwise of the accused's personal motives.

268. One reason why the above cases do not refer to "motives" may be, as the Defence has suggested, that "the issue in these cases was not whether the Defendants committed the acts for purely personal motives." The Appeals Chamber believes, however, that a further reason why this was not in issue is precisely because motive is generally irrelevant in criminal law, as the Prosecution pointed out in the hearing of 20 April 1999:

> For example, it doesn't matter whether or not an accused steals money in order to buy Christmas presents for his poor children or to support a heroin habit. All we're concerned with is that he stole and he intended to steal, and what we're concerned with ... here is the same sort of thing. There's no requirement for non-personal motive beyond knowledge of the context of a widespread or systematic act into which an accused's act fits. The Prosecutor is submitting that, as a general proposition and one which is applicable here, motives are simply irrelevant in criminal law.

269. The Appeals Chamber approves this submission, subject to the *caveat* that motive becomes relevant at the sentencing stage in mitigation or aggravation of the sentence (for example, the above mentioned thief might be dealt with more leniently if he stole to give presents to his children than if he were stealing to support a heroin habit). Indeed the inscrutability of motives in criminal law is revealed by the following *reductio ad absurdum*. Imagine a high-ranking SS official who claims that he participated in the genocide of the Jews and Gypsies for the "purely personal" reason that he had a deep-seated hatred of Jews and Gypsies and wished to exterminate them, and for no other reason. Despite this quintessentially genocidal frame of mind, the accused would have to be acquitted of crimes against humanity because he acted for "purely personal" reasons. Similarly, if the same man said that he participated in the genocide only for the "purely personal" reason that he feared losing his job, he would also be entitled to an acquittal. Thus, individuals at both ends of the spectrum would be acquitted. In the final analysis, any accused that played a role in mass murder purely out of self-interest would be acquitted. This shows the meaninglessness of any analysis requiring proof of "non-personal" motives. The Appeals Chamber does not believe, however, that the Trial Chamber meant to reach such a conclusion. Rather, the requirement that the accused's acts be part of a context of large-scale crimes, and that the accused knew of this context, was misstated by the Trial Chamber as a negative requirement that the accused not be acting for personal reasons. The Trial Chamber did not, the Appeals Chamber believes, wish to import a "motive" requirement; it simply duplicated the context and *mens rea* requirement, and confused it with the need for a link with an armed conflict, and thereby seemed to have unjustifiably and inadvertently added a new requirement.

270. The conclusion is therefore warranted that the relevant case-law and the spirit of international rules concerning crimes against humanity make it clear that under customary law, "purely personal motives" do not acquire any relevance for establishing whether or not a crime against humanity has been perpetrated....

VII. The Fourth Ground of Cross-Appeal by the Prosecution: The Trial Chamber's Finding that All Crimes Against Humanity Require a Discriminatory Intent

B. Discussion

281. The Prosecution submits that the Trial Chamber erred in finding that all crimes against humanity enumerated under Article 5 require a discriminatory intent. It alleges, further, that because of this finding, the Trial Chamber "restricted the scope of persecu-

tions under subparagraph (h) only to those acts not charged elsewhere in the Indictment rather than imposing additional liability for all acts committed on discriminatory grounds. In doing so, it would appear that the sentence against the accused was significantly reduced." However, the Prosecution does not appeal the sentence imposed by the Trial Chamber in respect of the crimes against humanity counts, or seek to overturn the Trial Chamber's verdict or findings of fact in this regard. Thus, this ground of appeal does not, *prima facie,* appear to fall within the scope of Article 25(1). Nevertheless, and as with the previous ground of appeal, the Appeals Chamber finds that this issue is a matter of general significance for the Tribunal's jurisprudence. It is therefore appropriate for the Appeals Chamber to set forth its views on this matter.

1. The Interpretation of the Text of Article 5 of the Statute

282. Notwithstanding the fact that the ICTY Statute is legally a very different instrument from an international treaty, in the interpretation of the Statute it is nonetheless permissible to be guided by the principle applied by the International Court of Justice with regard to treaty interpretation in its Advisory Opinion on *Competence of the General Assembly for the Admission of a State to the United Nations*: "The first duty of a tribunal which is called upon to interpret and apply the provisions of a treaty is to endeavour to give effect to them in their natural and ordinary meaning in the context in which they occur".

283. The ordinary meaning of Article 5 makes it clear that this provision does not require all crimes against humanity to have been perpetrated with a discriminatory intent. Such intent is only made necessary for one sub-category of those crimes, namely "persecutions" provided for in Article 5(h).

284. In addition to such textual interpretation, a logical construction of Article 5 also leads to the conclusion that, generally speaking, this requirement is not laid down for all crimes against humanity. Indeed, if it were otherwise, why should Article 5(h) specify that "persecutions" fall under the Tribunal's jurisdiction if carried out "on political, racial and religious grounds"? This specification would be illogical and superfluous. It is an elementary rule of interpretation that one should not construe a provision or part of a provision as if it were superfluous and hence pointless: the presumption is warranted that law-makers enact or agree upon rules that are well thought out and meaningful in all their elements.

285. As rightly submitted by the Prosecution, the interpretation of Article 5 in the light of its object and purpose bears out the above propositions. The aim of those drafting the Statute was to make all crimes against humanity punishable, including those which, while fulfilling all the conditions required by the notion of such crimes, may not have been perpetrated on political, racial or religious grounds as specified in paragraph (h) of Article 5. In light of the humanitarian goals of the framers of the Statute, one fails to see why they should have seriously restricted the class of offences coming within the purview of "crimes against humanity", thus leaving outside this class all the possible instances of serious and widespread or systematic crimes against civilians on account only of their lacking a discriminatory intent. For example, a discriminatory intent requirement would prevent the penalization of random and indiscriminate violence intended to spread terror among a civilian population as a crime against humanity. *A fortiori*, the object and purpose of Article 5 would be thwarted were it to be suggested that the discriminatory grounds required are limited to the five grounds put forth by the Secretary-General in his Report and taken up (with the addition, in one case, of the further ground of gender) in the statements made in the Security Council by three of its members. Such an interpretation

of Article 5 would create significant *lacunae* by failing to protect victim groups not covered by the listed discriminatory grounds. The experience of Nazi Germany demonstrated
that crimes against humanity may be committed on discriminatory grounds other than
those enumerated in Article 5(h), such as physical or mental disability, age or infirmity,
or sexual preference. Similarly, the extermination of "class enemies" in the Soviet Union
during the 1930s (admittedly, as in the case of Nazi conduct before the Second World
War, an occurrence that took place in times of peace, not in times of armed conflict) and
the deportation of the urban educated of Cambodia under the Khmer Rouge between
1975-1979, provide other instances which would not fall under the ambit of crimes against
humanity based on the strict enumeration of discriminatory grounds suggested by the
Secretary-General in his Report.

286. It would be pointless to object that in any case those instances would fall under
the category of war crimes or serious "violations of the laws or customs of war" provided
for in Article 3 of the Statute. This would fail to explain why the framers of the Statute
provided not only for war crimes but also for crimes against humanity. Indeed, those
who drafted the Statute deliberately included both classes of crimes, thereby illustrating
their intention that those war crimes which, in addition to targeting civilians as victims,
present special features such as the fact of being part of a widespread or systematic practice, must be classified as crimes against humanity and deserve to be punished accordingly.

2. Article 5 and Customary International Law

287. The same conclusion is reached if Article 5 is construed in light of the principle
whereby, in case of doubt and whenever the contrary is not apparent from the text of a
statutory or treaty provision, such a provision must be interpreted in light of, and in conformity with, customary international law. In the case of the Statute, it must be presumed
that the Security Council, where it did not explicitly or implicitly depart from general
rules of international law, intended to remain within the confines of such rules.

288. A careful perusal of the relevant practice shows that a discriminatory intent is
not required by customary international law for all crimes against humanity.

289. First of all, the basic international instrument on the matter, namely, the London
Agreement of 8 August 1945, clearly allows for crimes against humanity which may be un-
accompanied by such intent. Article 6(c) of that Agreement envisages two categories of
crimes. One of them is that of "murder, extermination, enslavement, deportation, and
other inhumane acts committed against any civilian population", hence a category for
which no discriminatory intent is required, while the other category ("persecutions on political, racial, or religious grounds") is patently based on a discriminatory intent. An identical provision can be found in the Statute of the Tokyo International Tribunal (Article
5(c)). Similar language can also be found in Control Council Law No. 10 (Article II
(1)(c)).

290. The letter of these provisions is clear and indisputable. Consequently, had customary international law developed to restrict the scope of those treaty provisions which
are at the very origin of the customary process, uncontroverted evidence would be needed.
In other words, both judicial practice and possibly evidence of consistent State practice,
including national legislation, would be necessary to show that customary law has deviated from treaty law by adopting a narrower notion of crimes against humanity. Such judicial and other practice is lacking. Indeed, the relevant case-law points in the contrary
direction. Generally speaking, customary international law has gradually expanded the notion of crimes against humanity laid down in the London Agreement. With specific reference to the question at issue, it should be noted that, except for a very few isolated cases

such as *Finta*, national jurisprudence includes many cases where courts found that in the circumstances of the case crimes against humanity did not necessarily consist of persecutory or discriminatory actions.

291. It is interesting to note that the necessity for discriminatory intent was considered but eventually rejected by the International Law Commission in its Draft Code of Offences Against the Peace and Security of Mankind. Similarly, while the inclusion of a discriminatory intent was mooted in the Preparatory Committee on the Establishment of an International Criminal Court (PrepCom), Article 7 of the Rome Statute embodied the drafters' rejection of discriminatory intent.

292. This warrants the conclusion that customary international law, as it results from the gradual development of international instruments and national case-law into general rules, does not presuppose a discriminatory or persecutory intent for all crimes against humanity.

3. The Report of the Secretary-General

293. The interpretation suggested so far is not in keeping with the Report of the Secretary-General and the statements made by three members of the Security Council before the Tribunal's Statute was adopted by the Council. The Appeals Chamber is nevertheless of the view that these two interpretative sources do not suffice to establish that all crimes against humanity need be committed with a discriminatory intent.

294. We shall consider first the Report of the Secretary-General, which stated that the crimes under discussion are those "committed as part of a widespread or systematic attack against any civilian population on national, political, ethnic, racial or religious grounds".

295. It should be noted that the Secretary-General's Report has not the same legal standing as the Statute. In particular, it does not have the same binding authority. The Report as a whole was "approved" by the Security Council (see the first operative paragraph of Security Council resolution 827(1993)), while the Statute was "adopted" (see operative paragraph 2). By "approving" the Report, the Security Council clearly intended to endorse its purpose as an explanatory document to the proposed Statute. Of course, if there appears to be a manifest contradiction between the Statute and the Report, it is beyond doubt that the Statute must prevail. In other cases, the Secretary-General's Report ought to be taken to provide an authoritative interpretation of the Statute.

296. Moreover, the Report of the Secretary-General does not purport to be a statement as to the position under customary international law. As stated above, it is open to the Security Council—subject to respect for peremptory norms of international law (*jus cogens*)—to adopt definitions of crimes in the Statute which deviate from customary international law.[2] Nevertheless, as a general principle, provisions of the Statute defining the crimes within the jurisdiction of the Tribunal should always be interpreted as reflecting customary international law, unless an intention to depart from customary international law is expressed in the terms of the Statute, or from other authoritative sources. The Report of the Secretary-General does not provide sufficient indication that the Security Council did so intend Article 5 to deviate from customary international law by requiring a discriminatory intent for all crimes against humanity. Indeed, in the case under consideration it would seem that, although the discrepancy between the Report and the Statute is conspicuous, the wording of Article 5 is so clear and unambiguous as to ren-

---

2. [Tribunal's fn. 356] For instance, the express requirement in Article 5 of a nexus with an armed conflict creates a narrower sphere of operation than that provided for crimes against humanity under customary international law.

der it unnecessary to resort to secondary sources of interpretation such as the Secretary-General's Report. Hence, the literal interpretation of Article 5 of the Statute, outlined above, must necessarily prevail.

297. Furthermore, it may be argued that, in his Report, the Secretary-General was merely *describing* the notion of crimes against humanity in a general way, as opposed to stipulating a technical, legal definition intended to be binding on the Tribunal. In other words, the statement that crimes against humanity are crimes "committed as part of a widespread or systematic attack against any civilian population on national, political, ethnic, racial or religious grounds" amounts to the observation that crimes against humanity *as a matter of fact usually are* committed on such discriminatory grounds. It is not, however, a legal *requirement* that such discriminatory grounds be present. That is, at least, another possible interpretation. It is true that in most cases, crimes against humanity are waged against civilian populations which have been specifically targeted for national, political, ethnic, racial or religious reasons.

4. The Statements Made by Some States in the Security Council

298. Let us now turn to the statements made in the Security Council, after the adoption of the Statute, by three States, namely, France, the United States and the Russian Federation.

299. Before considering what the legal meaning of these statements may be, one important point may first be emphasised. Although they were all directed at importing, as it were, into Article 5 the qualification concerning discriminatory intent set out in paragraph 48 of the Secretary-General's Report, these statements varied as to their purport. The statement by the French representative was intended to be part of "a few brief comments" on the Statute.[3] By contrast, the remarks of the United States representative were expressly couched as an "interpretative statement"; furthermore, that representative added a significant comment: "[W]e understand that other members of the Council share our view regarding the following clarifications related to the Statute" including the "clarification" concerning Article 5.[4] With regard to the representative of the Russian Federation, his statement concerning Article 5 was expressly conceived of as an interpretative declaration.[5] Nevertheless, this declaration was made in such terms as to justify the proposition that for the Russian Federation, Article 5 "encompasses" crimes committed with a "discriminatory intent" without, however, being limited to these acts alone.

300. The Appeals Chamber, first of all, rejects the notion that these three statements— at least as regards the issue of discriminatory intent—may be considered as part of the

---

3. [fn. 356] He stated the following: "[W]ith regard to Article 5, that Article applied to all the acts set out therein when committed in violation of the law during a period of armed conflict on the territory of the former Yugoslavia, within the context of a widespread or systematic attack against a civilian population for national, political, ethnic, racial or religious reasons" (U.N. Doc. S/PV. 3217, p.11).

4. [fn. 359] On Article 5 the United States representative said that: "[I]t is understood that Article 5 applies to all acts listed in that Article, when committed contrary to law during a period of armed conflict in the territory of the former Yugoslavia, as part of a widespread or systematic attack against any civilian population on national, political, ethnic, racial, gender, or religious grounds" (U.N. Doc. S/PV. 3217, p.16).

5. [fn. 360] He said the following: "While believing that the text of the Statute addresses the tasks that face the Tribunal, and for that reason supporting it, we deem it appropriate to note that, according to our understanding, Article 5 of the Statute encompasses criminal acts committed on the territory of the former Yugoslavia during an armed conflict—acts which were widespread or systematic, were aimed against the civilian population and were motivated by that population's national, political, ethnic, religious or other affiliation" (U.N. Doc. S/PV. 3217, p. 45).

"context" of the Statute, to be taken into account for the purpose of interpretation of the Statute pursuant to the general rule of construction laid down in Article 31 of the Vienna Convention on the Law of the Treaties. In particular, those statements cannot be regarded as an "agreement" relating to the Statute, made between all the parties in connection with the adoption of the Statute. True, the United States representative pointed out that it was her understanding that the other members of the Security Council shared her views regarding the "clarifications" she put forward. However, in light of the wording of the other two statements on the specific point at issue, and taking into account the lack of any comment by the other twelve members of the Security Council, it would seem difficult to conclude that there emerged an agreement in the Security Council designed to qualify the scope of Article 5 with respect to discriminatory intent. In particular, it must be stressed that the United States representative, in enumerating the discriminatory grounds required, in her view, for crimes against humanity, included one ground ("gender") that was not mentioned in the Secretary-General's Report and which was, more importantly, referred to neither by the French nor the Russian representatives in their declarations on Article 5. This, it may be contended, is further evidence that no agreement emerged within the Security Council as to the qualification concerning discriminatory intent.

301. Arguably, in fact, the main purpose of those statements was to stress that it is the existence of a widespread or systematic practice which constitutes an indispensable ingredient of crimes against humanity. This ingredient, absent in Article 5, had already been mentioned in paragraph 48 of the Secretary-General's Report.[6] In spelling out that this ingredient was indispensable, the States in question took up the relevant passage of the Secretary-General's Report and in the same breath also mentioned the discriminatory intent which may, in practice, frequently accompany such crimes.

302. The contention may also be warranted that the intent of the three States which made these declarations was to stress that in the former Yugoslavia most atrocities had been motivated by ethnic, racial, political or religious hatred. Those States therefore intended to draw the attention of the future Tribunal to the need to take this significant factor into account. One should not, however, confuse what happens most of the time (*quod plerumque accidit*) with the strict requirements of law.

303. Be that as it may, since at least with regard to the issue of discriminatory intent those statements may not be taken to be part of the "context" of the Statute, it may be argued that they comprise a part of the *travaux préparatoires*. Even if this were so, these statements would not be indispensable aids to interpretation, at least insofar as they relate to the particular issue of discriminatory intent under Article 5. Under customary international law, as codified in Article 32 of the Vienna Convention referred to above, the *travaux* constitute a supplementary means of interpretation and may only be resorted to when the text of a treaty or any other international norm-creating instrument is *ambiguous or obscure*. As the wording of Article 5 is clear and does not give rise to uncertainty, at least as regards the issue of discriminatory intent, there is no need to rely upon those statements. Excluding from the scope of crimes against humanity widespread or systematic atrocities on the sole ground that they were not motivated by any persecutory or discriminatory intent would be justified neither by the letter nor the spirit of Article 5.

---

6. [fn. 362] The Trial Chamber in its Judgement of 7 May 1997 has also correctly emphasised that the phrases "widespread" and "systematic" are disjunctive as opposed to cumulative requirements (*see* Judgement, paras. 645–648). *See* also the *Nikolic Rule 61 Decision*, ("Review of the Indictment Pursuant to Rule 61 of the Rules of Procedure and Evidence, *The Prosecutor v. Dragan Nikolic*), Case No.: IT-94-2-R61, Trial Chamber I, 20 October 1995) (*Nikolic*) (1995) II ICTY JR 739).

304. The above propositions do not imply that the statements made in the Security Council by the three aforementioned States, or by other States, should not be given interpretative weight. They may shed light on the meaning of a provision that is ambiguous, or which lends itself to differing interpretations. Indeed, in its *Tadic* Decision on Jurisdiction the Appeals Chamber repeatedly made reference to those statements as well as to statements made by other States. It did so, for instance, when interpreting Article 3 of the Statute[7] and when pronouncing on the question whether the International Tribunal could apply international agreements binding upon the parties to the conflict.[8]

C. Conclusion

305. The Prosecution was correct in submitting that the Trial Chamber erred in finding that all crimes against humanity require a discriminatory intent. Such an intent is an indispensable legal ingredient of the offence only with regard to those crimes for which this is expressly required, that is, for Article 5 (h), concerning various types of persecution.

B. The Rome Statute for the International Criminal Court and its Application

As detailed in Chapter Six, in 1998 the Rome Statute for the International Criminal Court was adopted. Crimes against humanity are defined in Article 7 of the ICC Statute, and are one of the three crimes currently falling within the ICC's jurisdiction. Article 7 of the Statute has been criticized by some commentators as being overly restrictive, and, indeed, was the object of long negotiations between delegates, as the following extract suggests:

Leila Nadya Sadat, The International Criminal Court and the Transformation of International Law: Justice for the New Millennium
146–52 (Transnational 2002)*

The Statute adopted by the Diplomatic Conference is a montage of historically-based texts, massaged during difficult political negotiations, that improved the existing law in some respects, but left it either unchanged or more restrictive in other cases. One particularly thorny problem left unresolved by the Statute, for example, is its failure to distinguish jurisdictional from material elements of offenses. By jurisdictional elements, I mean elements that must be established in order for the Court to have jurisdiction over the crime. By material elements, I mean the traditional elements of the underlying crime that render an individual criminally liable, *i.e.*, the *actus reus* and *mens rea* or the *élément materiel* and the *élément moral*. The confusion was no doubt a direct result of the unconscious manner by which theories of universal jurisdiction were converted from international

---

7. [fn. 362] *See Tadic* Decision on Jurisdiction, paras 75, 88 (where reference was also made to the statements of the representatives of the United Kingdom and Hungary).

8. fn. 363] *See ibid.*, para 143 (where reference was made to the statements of the representatives of the United States, the United Kingdom and France).

* Copyright © 2002 by Transnational Publishers, Inc. Reproduced with permission of Transnational Publishers, Inc.

law norms addressing the distribution of competences between States to a norm of international law addressing the negotiation of competence between the international legal order and national legal systems....

Defining crimes against humanity presented one of the most difficult challenges at Rome, for no accepted definition existed, either as a matter of treaty or customary international law.

The disparity in definitions underscores the two major problems in defining the scope of crimes against humanity: first, distinguishing the crime from war crimes and from crimes under domestic law; second, determining which acts are punishable under international law as a matter of individual criminal responsibility, as opposed to State responsibility for violations of human rights. The Rome Statute attempts to address both problems through an extensive *chapeau*. The text is quite restrictive in overall character, although two positive outcomes should be noted. First, the Rome Statute does not require any nexus to an "armed conflict." Although some delegations in Rome repeatedly urged retention of the words "armed conflict," which was a bracketed option in the Zutphen Intersessional Draft and the April Draft Statute, that proposal was properly defeated as contrary to the weight of judicial decisions, national legislation, and other authority.

Second, absent from the *chapeau* is any requirement that the crimes be committed as part of an attack based on political, philosophical, racial, ethnic, religious, or other grounds. Instead, the Statute maintains the historic difference between "murder-type" crimes and "persecution-type" crimes that originated with article 6(c) of the IMT Charter. In this way the Statute tracks the ICTY approach (which was confirmed by the Appeals Chamber in the *Tadic* case) and appears consistent with the weight of authority on this point. The Statute, however, reinserts the linkage later by requiring that the crime of persecution be committed in connection either with another crime against humanity or any other crime within the jurisdiction of the Court.

Article 7 contains four separate preconditions that must be satisfied before jurisdiction attaches in a particular case in which crimes against humanity are charged. Some appear to be purely jurisdictional, meaning that once they have been proved as regards a particular situation, they need not be reestablished *ab initio* with respect to each defendant. Others, however, are material elements of the offense, meaning that they must be committed with intent or knowledge on the part of the defendant, and proven with particularity in each case. The text is essentially a codification of compromises between those who thought the Statute was too innovative in character and too broad in its reach, and those who thought it did not go far enough.... .

Notes and Questions

1. With respect to crimes against humanity prosecutable before the ICC, Article 7(1) begins with the phrase "[f]or purposes of this Statute...." Does Article 7 reach all crimes against humanity identified in customary instruments such as the Charters of the I.M.T.s and Control Council Law No. 10? *See also* Bangladesh International Crimes (Tribunals) Act, art. 3(2)(a) , in the Documents Supplement.

2. Does Article 7(1) of the Statute of the ICC fuse the two general types of crimes against humanity into one and reach crimes of persecution only when committed as part of an attack against a civilian population? Does Article 7(1)(h) further limit the reach of customary crimes of persecution of "persons" by use of the phrase "against any identifiable group or collectivity," thus limiting the reach to exclude ICC jurisdiction over per-

secutions of persons as such, as well as persecution of persons who may not be part of a group or collectivity? *See, e.g.*, Paust, *Content and Contours of Genocide, Crimes Against Humanity, and War Crimes*, in INTERNATIONAL LAW IN THE POST-COLD WAR WORLD: ESSAYS IN MEMORY OF LI HAOPEI (Wang Tieya & Sienho Yee eds. 2000). Professor Paust adds: "Article 7(2)(a) … provides an even more limiting and an illogical definition of 'attack' as 'a course of conduct involving the multiple commission of acts.' Clearly, an 'attack' can otherwise involve a single act. The limitations [of ICC jurisdiction over customary crimes] are compounded by an additional requirement in Article 7(2)(a) that a covered attack be engaged in 'pursuant to or in furtherance of a State or organizational policy.' Thus needlessly excluded are customary crimes against humanity perpetrated by: (a) governmental actors whose crimes are not 'pursuant to or in furtherance of' a State or organizational policy, (b) private unorganized actors, and (c) private actors who do not act pursuant to or in furtherance of a State or 'organizational' policy." *Id*. See also 93 PROC., AM. SOC. INT'L L. 73 (1999); Paust, *The International Criminal Court Does Not Have Complete Jurisdiction Over Customary Crimes Against Humanity and War Crimes*, 43 JOHN MARSHALL L. REV. 681 (2010).

3. Article 7(1) defines the target of crimes against humanity as "any civilian population." Thus under the ICC Statute, non-civilians (*e.g.*, members of the military) are excluded from the class of victims. Any of the prohibited acts enumerated in Article 7(1)(a)–(c), (f)–(i) and (k), if perpetrated against captured combatants, would amount to a war crime or grave breach of the 1949 Geneva Conventions. Does the term "civilian population" include belligerents *hors de combat* who have laid down their weapons, either because they are wounded or because they have been captured? *See* ANTONIO CASSESE, INTERNATIONAL CRIMINAL LAW 93 (2003). As noted in Chapter Eight, combatant status hinges upon membership in the armed forces of a party to an armed conflict and not whether the person is fighting or captured. *See, e.g., The Prosecutor v. Kordic & Cerkez*, IT-95-14/2-A (Appeals Chamber, 17 Dec. 2004), quoted in Chapter Eight.

4. Article 7 both narrows and broadens the customary international law understanding of crimes against humanity. Article 7(2)(a) defines "attack directed against a civilian population" to mean a course of conduct "involving the multiple commission of acts referred to in paragraph 1 against any civilian population, pursuant to or in furtherance of a State or organizational policy to commit such attack." The requirement that an "attack directed against a civilian population" be in furtherance of a State or organizational policy to constitute crimes against humanity significantly narrows the reach of the statute. One commentator who is highly critical of the restrictive definition, posits:

> [I]n the case of murder, or rape, or forced pregnancy, why should it be required that the general practice constitute a policy pursued by a State or an organization? Would it not be sufficient for the practice to be accepted, or tolerated, or acquiesced in by the State or the organization, for those offences to constitute crimes against humanity? Clearly, this requirement goes beyond what is required under international customary law and unduly restricts the notion under discussion.

CASSESE, *supra* at 93.

At the same time, in dealing with persecution-type crimes, Article 7 greatly expands the category of discriminatory grounds. While under customary international law these grounds may be political, racial, ethnic, or religious, Article 7(1)(h) adds "cultural," "gender," and "other grounds that are universally recognized as impermissible under international law."

5. Saddam Hussein has been charged with crimes against humanity for the murder of 148 Shiites from the town of Dujail, north of Baghdad. The victims were killed in re-

sponse to a failed assassination attempt against Saddam. Would the allegations arising from the Dujail, Iraq killings support conviction of Saddam Hussein for crimes against humanity under the definition set forth in Article 5 of the Statute of the ICTY, Article 3 of the Statute of the ICTR, Article 7 of the Statute of the ICC, or Article 13 of the Iraqi High Criminal Court Law?

6. In an historic decision on December 11, 2001, the Special Panel of the Dili District Court in East Timor (consisting of three judges from Brazil, Burundi, and East Timor) convicted ten men of crimes against humanity charges in the Los Palos case. The case was the first involving crimes against humanity to reach trial, and is one of the ten priority cases of the Serious Crimes Unit. (See Chapter Six, *supra*, for a discussion of the East Timor Special Panels). The ten accused received sentences of between 4 years' and the maximum 33 years 4 months' imprisonment. The Special Panel found that there was a widespread and systematic campaign of violence directed at the civilian population during 1999 at the direction of the Indonesian armed forces, and that contrary to many of the claims of the accused, they were aware that their acts (including murder, torture, and forced deportation) were part of that campaign. *See generally* Suzannah Linton, *New Approaches to International Justice in Cambodia and East Timor*, 84 IRRC 93 (March 2002). The Serious Crimes Panel of the District Court of Dili, which heard the case, was applying UNTAET (the United Nations Transitional Administration for East Timor) Regulation 2000/15, which incorporates many provisions from the 1998 Statute for the ICC, including Article 7 (which is section 5 of UNTAET Regulation 2000/15), defining crimes against humanity, with just three differences, each of which are relatively minor. See Kai Ambos & Steffen Wirth, *The Current Law of Crimes Against Humanity*, 13 Crim. L. F. 1 (2002).

7. One of the problems that arises in crimes against humanity cases decided in international courts and tribunals is not only the legal definition of the *chapeaux* elements, but the definition of the predicate crimes (*e.g.*, murder, torture, deportation) as well. Judges and lawyers from different legal systems have a tendency to assume the crimes will be defined internationally as they are in the domestic legal system from whence they come, which is not always true of course. For example, questions have arisen in the Tribunals as to the definition of murder, and particularly whether premeditation is an element the crime, as well as with regard to the definition of extermination and deportation. *See, e.g., The Prosecutor v. Kordic*, IT-95-14/2-T (Trial Chamber Judgement, 26 Feb. 2001); *The Prosecutor v. Blaskic*, IT-95-14-T (Trial Chamber Judgement, 3 Mar. 2000). Obviously, none of the decisions of the ICTY, ICTR, East Timor Special Panels will bind the ICC. However, they may prove instructive to the ICC. The adoption of the Elements of Crimes for the interpretation of the ICC Statute (see the Documents Supplement) by the Assembly of States Parties somewhat ameliorates the ambiguity of these terms in international law, but the ICC will no doubt wrestle with the difficult task of international criminal harmonization.

Decision Pursuant to Article 15 of the Rome Statute on the Authorization of an Investigation into the Situation in the Republic of Kenya
No. ICC-01/09 (31 Mar. 2010)

[Editors' Note: On November 26, 2009, the Prosecutor of the ICC requested authorization to open an investigation into the post-election violence that took place in six out of the eight regions of Kenya, resulting in a reported 1,133 to 1,200 killings of civilians, 900 acts of sexual violence, internal displacement of 350,000, and 3,561 acts causing serious injury.]

II. Whether the Requisite Criteria Have Been Met

A. Whether there is a reasonable basis to believe that crimes against humanity within the jurisdiction of the Court have been committed

70. In the Prosecutor's Request, it is alleged that there is a reasonable basis to believe that the crimes against humanity of murder, rape and other forms of sexual violence, deportation or forcible transfer of population and other inhumane acts were committed and that therefore the Court's material jurisdiction is established. The Prosecutor further submits that these crimes fall under the temporal jurisdiction of the Court since they occurred after the entry into force of the Statute for the Republic of Kenya. Finally, he contends that, since the alleged crimes were committed on Kenyan territory, they fall within the Court's territorial jurisdiction.

71. The Chamber recalls that, to fall under the jurisdiction of the Court, a crime must fulfill the jurisdictional parameters *ratione materiae*, *ratione temporis* and—in the alternative—*ratione personae* or *ratione loci*. In the following sections, the Chamber will address each of these requirements in turn.

1. Jurisdiction *ratione materiae*....

a) Contextual elements of crimes against humanity

(i) The law and its interpretation....

79. The Chamber observes that the following requirements can be distinguished: ...

(aa) An attack directed against any civilian population

80. The meaning of the term "attack," although not addressed in the Statute, is clarified by the Elements of Crimes, which state that, for the purposes of article 7(1) of the Statute, an attack is not restricted to a "military attack." Instead, the term refers to "a campaign or operation carried out against the civilian population."

82. The Chamber need not be satisfied that the entire civilian population of the geographical area in question was being targeted. However, the civilian population must be the primary object of the attack in question and cannot merely be an incidental victim. The term "civilian population" refers to persons who are civilians, as opposed to members of armed forces and other legitimate combatants.

(bb) State or organizational policy

83. Further, article 7(2)(a) of the Statute imposes the additional requirement that the attack against any civilian population be committed "pursuant to or in furtherance of a State or organizational policy to commit such attack." The Elements of Crimes offer further clarification in paragraph 3, in fine, of the Introduction to Crimes against humanity, where it is stated that:

> [it] is understood that "policy to commit such an attack" requires that the State or organization actively promote or encourage such an attack against a civilian population;

and in footnote 6 of the same Introduction to Crimes against Humanity, where it is stated that

> [a] policy which has a civilian population as the object of the attack would be implemented by State or organizational action. Such a policy may, in exceptional circumstances, be implemented by a deliberate failure to take action, which is con-

sciously aimed at encouraging such attack. The existence of such a policy cannot be inferred solely from the absence of governmental or organizational action.

84. The Chamber notes that the Statute does not provide definitions of the terms "policy" or "State or organizational". However, both this Chamber and Pre-Trial Chamber I have addressed the policy requirement in previous decisions. In the case against Katanga and Ngudjolo Chui, Pre-Trial Chamber I found that this requirement:

> […] ensures that the attack, even if carried out over a large geographical area or directed against a large number of victims, must still be thoroughly organised and follow a regular pattern. It must also be conducted in furtherance of a common policy involving public or private resources. Such a policy may be made either by groups of persons who govern a specific territory or by any organisation with the capability to commit a widespread or systematic attack against a civilian population. The policy need not be explicitly defined by the organisational group. Indeed, an attack which is planned, directed or organized—as opposed to spontaneous or isolated acts of violence—will satisfy this criterion.

85. In the "Decision Pursuant to Article 61(7)(a) and (b) of the Rome Statute on the Charges of the Prosecutor Against Jean-Pierre Bemba Gombo," this Chamber also addressed the issue, stating that:

> [t]he requirement of 'a State or organisational policy' implies that the attack follows a regular pattern. Such a policy may be made by groups of persons who govern a specific territory or by any organization with the capability to commit a widespread or systematic attack against a civilian population. The policy need not be formalised. Indeed, an attack which is planned, directed or organised— as opposed to spontaneous or isolated acts of violence—will satisfy this criterion.

86. Regarding the meaning of the term "policy," the Chamber will apply, in accordance with article 21(2) of the Statute, the definitions given in the abovementioned precedents. The Chamber also takes note of the jurisprudence of the ad hoc tribunals, and the work of the International Law Commission (the "ILC").

87. In particular, the Chamber takes note of the judgment in the case against Tihomir Blaskic, in which the ICTY Trial Chamber held that the plan to commit an attack:

> […] need not necessarily be declared expressly or even stated clearly and precisely. It may be surmised from the occurrence of a series of events, inter alia:
>
> > the general historical circumstances and the overall political background against which the criminal acts are set;
> >
> > the establishment and implementation of autonomous political structures at any level of authority in a given territory;
> >
> > the general content of a political programme, as it appears in the writings and speeches of its authors;
> >
> > media propaganda;
> >
> > the establishment and implementation of autonomous military structures;
> >
> > the mobilisation of armed forces;
> >
> > temporally and geographically repeated and co-ordinated military offensives;
> >
> > links between the military hierarchy and the political structure and its political programme;

alterations to the "ethnic" composition of populations;

discriminatory measures, whether administrative or other (banking restrictions, laissez-passer, …);

the scale of the acts of violence perpetrated—in particular, murders and other

physical acts of violence, rape, arbitrary imprisonment, deportations and expulsions or the destruction of non-military property, in particular, sacral sites.

89. With regard to the definition of the terms "State or organizational", the Chamber firstly notes that while, in the present case, the term "State" is self-explanatory, it is worth mentioning that in the case of a State policy to commit an attack, this policy "does not necessarily need to have been conceived 'at the highest level of the State machinery.'" Hence, a policy adopted by regional or even local organs of the State could satisfy the requirement of a State policy.

90. With regard to the term "organizational," the Chamber notes that the Statute is unclear as to the criteria pursuant to which a group may qualify as "organization" for the purposes of article 7(2) (a) of the Statute. Whereas some have argued that only State-like organizations may qualify, the Chamber opines that the formal nature of a group and the level of its organization should not be the defining criterion. Instead, as others have convincingly put forward, a distinction should be drawn on whether a group has the capability to perform acts which infringe on basic human values:

the associative element, and its inherently aggravating effect, could eventually be satisfied by 'purely private criminal organizations, thus not finding sufficient reasons for distinguishing the gravity of patterns of conduct directed by 'territorial' entities or by private groups, given the latter's acquired capacity to infringe basic human values.

92. The Chamber finds that had the drafters of the Statute intended to exclude non-State actors from the term "organization," they would not have included this term in article 7(2)(a) of the Statute. The Chamber thus determines that organizations not linked to a State may, for the purposes of the Statute, elaborate and carry out a policy to commit an attack against a civilian population.

93. In the view of the Chamber, the determination of whether a given group qualifies as an organization under the Statute must be made on a case-by- case basis. In making this determination, the Chamber may take into account a number of considerations, inter alia: (i) whether the group is under a responsible command, or has an established hierarchy; (ii) whether the group possesses, in fact, the means to carry out a widespread or systematic attack against a civilian population; (iii) whether the group exercises control over part of the territory of a State; (iv) whether the group has criminal activities against the civilian population as a primary purpose; (v) whether the group articulates, explicitly or implicitly, an intention to attack a civilian population; (vi) whether the group is part of a larger group, which fulfills some or all of the abovementioned criteria. It is important to clarify that, while these considerations may assist the Chamber in its determination, they do not constitute a rigid legal definition, and do not need to be exhaustively fulfilled.

(cc) Widespread or systematic nature of the attack

110. The supporting material further indicates that, depending on the respective location and the phase of the violence, the attacks were directed against members of specifically identified communities. These communities were targeted on behalf of their ethnicity which was, in turn, associated with the support of one of the two major political parties, PNU and ODM.

111. Accordingly, during the initial phase of the violence. Rift Valley was the scene of attacks specifically targeting the non-Kalenjin community and in particular people of Kikuyu, Kisii, and Luhya ethnicity, perceived as affiliated with the PNU....

112. During the phase of retaliatory violence, the attacks were directed mainly against the non-Kikuyu communities.... @judge: (bb) State or organizational policy

117. Upon examination of the available information, the Chamber observes that some of the violent events which occurred during the period under examination spontaneously arose after the announcement of the election results. Additionally, there were accounts of opportunistic crime which accompanied the general situation of lawlessness. However, the Chamber is of the view that the violence was not a mere accumulation of spontaneous or isolated acts. Rather, a number of the attacks were planned, directed or organized by various groups including local leaders, businessmen and politicians associated with the two leading political parties, as well as by members of the police force.

118. With regard to the initial attacks, the Chamber notes various accounts of meetings of local leaders, businessmen and politicians. Most of these meetings were convened in Rift Valley, with the alleged aims to discuss the eviction of the Kikuyu community, to coordinate violence and to organize funding.

119. The supporting material includes additional accounts of meetings between businessmen or politicians and groups of young people. It is alleged that during these meetings, the youth were given instructions, supplied with weapons and distributed money. Moreover, it is reported that training and oathing in camps or at private residences took place in preparation for the attacks. In some instances, such meetings were directly followed by violent attacks against specific communities.

120. The supporting material further indicates that prior to the elections, some politicians employed inflammatory rhetoric to articulate their aim to evict the Kikuyus. Such statements were publicly disseminated through leaflets or the media. In addition, there are references to warnings given to people in anticipation of the violence.

121. The Chamber also considers that the organized nature of some of the attacks may further be inferred from the strategy and method employed in the attack. In this regard, it is reported that the attacks were well coordinated and organized....

122. The supporting material also highlights phenomena such as the large supply of petrol and the use of sophisticated weaponry. Such phenomena are consistent with allegations that businessmen or politicians financed the violence or directly supplied vehicles, petrol or weapons which were to be used in the attacks.

123. With regard to the entity behind the initial attacks, the supporting material contains references pointing to the involvement of Kalenjin leaders, businessmen and ODM politicians, including cabinet ministers. Finally, several ODM politicians reportedly announced in public their determination to evict the Kikuyu community.

124. Some of the retaliatory attacks showed similar features pointing to forms of organization and planning. In this regard, the Chamber notes a number of references to meetings organized by politicians, local businessmen and local leaders where attacks against communities associated with the ODM were reportedly discussed....

125. There are accounts of politicians employing hate speech against non-Kikuyu communities as well as ethnic propaganda disseminated by religious leaders and local language media. In addition, it is reported that prior to the violence, verbal warnings and leaflets were circulated among the non-Kikuyus.

126.… It is further alleged that PNU politicians financed the violence or supplied weapons, vehicles and petrol.…

127. Groups associated with the planning of the retaliatory attacks included Kikuyu leaders, businessmen and PNU politicians who reportedly planned the attacks against perceived rival communities during their meetings. Furthermore, with regard to the violence which occurred in Naivasha between 27 and 30 January 2008, the Waki Commission claimed it had evidence that "government and political leaders in Nairobi, including key office holders at the highest level of government may have directly participated in the preparation of the attacks." Finally, the supporting material contains a number of contentions to the effect that, especially in Rift Valley and in the slums of Nairobi, Kikuyu leaders enlisted Kikuyu gangs, and in particular the Mungiki gang, to unleash violence on perceived rival communities.

128. With regard to the attacks emanating from the police, it is reported that the killings of the suspected Mungiki members occurred pursuant to a government campaign aimed at the suppression of this gang while the killings of suspected SLDF members and Mt Elgon residents reportedly occurred in the context of a government joint military-police operation.

(cc) Widespread nature of the attack

179. Accordingly, since the requirement of jurisdiction *ratione loci* is fulfilled, the Chamber is under no obligation to examine jurisdiction *ratione personae* under article 12(2)(b) of the Statute.… @judge:Dissenting Opinion of Judge Hans-Peter Kaul

I. Introduction and Main Conclusions

1. The majority concluded, upon examination of the Prosecutor's "Request for authorization of an investigation pursuant to Article 15" (the "Prosecutor's Request") and the facts contained in the supporting material, including the victims' representations, that there is a reasonable basis pursuant to article 15(4) of the Rome Statute (the "Statute") to proceed with an investigation of alleged crimes against humanity on the territory of the Republic of Kenya from 1 June 2005 until 26 November 2009.

2. I regret that I am unable to accept the decision of the majority and the analysis that underpins it.

3. Basing my analysis on the supporting material, including the victims' representations, I am of the considered view that Pre-Trial Chamber II (the "Chamber") should not authorize the commencement of the Prosecutor's *proprio motu* investigation in the situation of the Republic of Kenya.… 6.… The question is not whether or not those crimes have happened. The issue is whether the ICC is the right forum before which to investigate and prosecute those crimes.…

8. As a Judge of the International Criminal Court (the "Court" or the "ICC"), I would like to ask all in the Republic of Kenya who yearn for justice and who support the intervention of the Court in this country for understanding the following: there are, in law and in the existing systems of criminal justice in this world, essentially two different categories of crimes which are crucial in the present case. There are, on the one side, international crimes of concern to the international community as a whole, in particular genocide, crimes against humanity and war crimes pursuant to articles 6, 7, and 8 of the Statute. There are, on the other side, common crimes, albeit of a serious nature, prosecuted by national criminal justice systems, such as that of the Republic of Kenya.

9. There is, in my view, a demarcation line between crimes against humanity pursuant to article 7 of the Statute, and crimes under national law. There is, for example, such a

demarcation line between murder as a crime against humanity pursuant to article 7(l)(a) of the Statute and murder under the national law of the Republic of Kenya. It is my considered view that the existing demarcation line between those crimes must not be marginalized or downgraded, even in an incremental way. I also opine that the distinction between those crimes must not be blurred.

10. Furthermore, it is my considered view that this would not be in the interest of criminal justice in general and international criminal justice in particular.... As a Judge of the ICC, I feel, however, duty-bound to point at least to the following: such an approach might infringe on State sovereignty and the action of national courts for crimes which should not be within the ambit of the Statute. It would broaden the scope of possible ICC intervention almost indefinitely. This might turn the ICC, which is fully dependent on State cooperation, in a hopelessly overstretched, inefficient international court, with related risks for its standing and credibility. Taken into consideration the limited financial and material means of the institution, it might be unable to tackle all the situations which could fall under its jurisdiction with the consequence that the selection of the situations under actual investigation might be quite arbitrary to the dismay of the numerous victims in the situations disregarded by the Court who would be deprived of any access to justice without any convincing justification.

32. I now turn to the Statute of the ICC which seems to follow another route by establishing that a "State or organizational policy" is a legal requirement radiating on the entire chapeau of article 7 of the Statute as it is linked with the element of "attack" and not the component "systematic." This fact compels me to conduct a careful analysis before drawing an analogy with or relying on the jurisprudence of other tribunals. Article 10 of the Statute reinforces the assumption that the drafters of the Statute may have deliberately deviated from customary rules as evinced in the jurisprudence of other courts and tribunals in providing that "[n]othing in this Statute shall be interpreted as limiting or prejudicing in any way existing or developing rules of international law for purposes other than in the Statute."

3. Interpretation of Article 7(2)(a) of the Statute According to Article 31 of the Vienna Convention. 34.... I apply the principles comprised in article 31 of the Vienna Convention on the Law of Treaties (the "VCLT")....

36. An "attack directed against any civilian population" *per definitionem legis* is a course of conduct involving the multiple commission of acts against such population "pursuant to or in furtherance of a State or organizational policy to commit such attack". The Statute suggests that the attack is not any attack that has been directed against any civilian population. Rather, it is qualified by the added features that it is "widespread" or "systematic" and that it was conducted "pursuant to or in furtherance of a State or organizational policy." As the latter qualification represents a point of disagreement with the majority's decision, I shall develop my understanding on this aspect of article 7 of the Statute only.

37. The Statute clarifies that, on the one hand, either a State may adopt such a policy or, on the other hand, that an "organizational policy" may be found to exist. I observe that the Statute does not provide any guidance regarding the notion "organizational policy." Based on the English text of the Statute one might arrive to the conclusion that in this case the policy need only be "organizational," seemingly referring to the nature of such policy as being (only) of an organized, planned or systematic manner, leaving aside the question of attribution to a specific authorship. However, I note that the English text of the Statute is phrased more broadly than other authentic versions of the Statute, leaving some doubt as to its exact meaning. The original of the Statute in Arabic, Chinese, English,

French, Russian and Spanish are equally authentic. A look at the French, Spanish and Arabic text reveals the following.

38. [After reviewing the other authentic texts,] I conclude that while the English text would accept the meaning of a policy to be of a systematic nature but does not necessarily need to be authored by an entity like that of an "organization", the other authentic texts of the Statute clearly refer to the requirement that a policy be adopted by an 'organization'. In case where two or more versions possess equal authority and one appears to have a wider bearing than the other, I shall adopt the interpretation which offers the more limited interpretation and which accords with the intention of the drafters as enshrined in the other texts. I therefore believe that the Statute has opted for the meaning whereby "organizational" shall be construed as meaning to pertain to an organization.... 51. I read the provision such that the juxtaposition of the notions "State" and 'organization' in article 7(2)(a) of the Statute are an indication that even though the constitutive elements of statehood need not be established those 'organizations' should partake of some characteristics of a State. Those characteristics eventually turn the private 'organization' into an entity which may act like a State or has quasi-State abilities. These characteristics could involve the following: (a) a collectivity of persons; (b) which was established and acts for a common purpose; (c) over a prolonged period of time; (d) which is under responsible command or adopted a certain degree of hierarchical structure, including, as a minimum, some kind of policy level; (e) with the capacity to impose the policy on its members and to sanction them; and (f) which has the capacity and means available to attack any civilian population on a large scale.

52. In contrast, I believe that non-state actors which do not reach the level described above are not able to carry out a policy of this nature, such as groups of organized crime, a mob, groups of (armed) civilians or criminal gangs.... For it is not the cruelty or mass victimization that turns a crime into a *delictum iuris gentium* but the constitutive contextual elements in which the act is embedded.

53. In this respect, the general argument that any kind of non-state actors may be qualified as an 'organization' within the meaning of article 7(2)(a) of the Statute on the grounds that it "has the capability to perform acts which infringe on basic human values" without any further specification seems unconvincing to me. In fact this approach may expand the concept of crimes against humanity to any infringement of human rights. I am convinced that a distinction must be upheld between human rights violations on the one side and international crimes on the other side, the latter forming the nucleus of the most heinous violations of human rights representing the most serious crimes of concern to the international community as a whole.

b) Contextual Interpretation.... c) Object and Purpose

56. The restricted interpretation of this contextual requirement is also warranted by a teleological interpretation of article 7(2)(a) of the Statute, i.e., in light of its object and purpose.... What is the object and purpose of crimes against humanity? What is in fact the underlying rationale or raison d'être of crimes against humanity? What makes it different from other common crimes which fall solely under the jurisdiction of States? ...

V. General Conclusions

148. On a general note, I observe that the information available does not lead to the conclusion of 'one' "attack" during the time frame under examination but a series of numerous incidents, as suggested by the Prosecutor. Numerous violent acts were launched at different times by different groups and against different groups throughout the coun-

try. The violence was at the occasion of the as rigged perceived presidential elections in December 2007. The reasons for the violence appear to go beyond allegations of manipulated elections. Information in the supporting material and the victims' representations suggests that the cause of the violence may be found in long-lasting and unresolved issues, such as land distribution, poverty, unemployment, rental issues, inter-ethnic tensions, xenophobia, disenfranchisement, perceived discrimination, desire for ethnically homogenous neighbourhoods, organized crime, retaliation and anger over the support of the opposing political party. The origin of such issues may sometimes date back to colonial times. Albeit the motives of the perpetrators are not decisive and may vary, it nevertheless sheds light on the question of the existence of a possible policy....

150. While I accept that some of the violence appears to have been organized and planned in advance, I fail to see the existence of an 'organization' behind the violent acts which may have established a policy to attack the civilian population within the meaning of article 7(2)(a) of the Statute. I find indications in the supporting material that some local leaders, some local businessmen, some local politicians, some religious leaders, some journalists at local vernacular radio stations, some chiefs of communities and some civic and parliamentary aspirants were involved in the preparation of the violence. But I do not see an 'organization' meeting the prerequisites of structure, membership, duration and means to attack the civilian population. To the contrary, the overall assessment of the information in the supporting material, including the victims' representations leads me to conclude that several centres of violence in several provinces existed which each do not rise to the level of crimes against humanity.

151. In the event that those centres of violence was to be considered as 'one' attack, the unifying element would be the policy implemented by an 'organization' at the national level. As I don't have information available indicating that such policy was adopted at the national level, I fail to see how those crimes and centres of violence could be assessed in light of article 7(1) of the Statute.

152. A different aspect involves the conduct of law enforcement agencies and the military. The reactions of the police during the "post-election violence" range from being mere passive observers, assisting civilians, being overwhelmed with the situation to actively engaging in the violence. In many areas of Kenya, the police had to be assisted by the military to re-gain control. Another distinct aspect of police involvement concerns its participation in addressing organized crime and combating movements which do not necessarily relate to the events surrounding the "post-election violence." In sum, I have not found any information in the supporting material, including the victims' representations, suggesting that a State policy existed pursuant to which the civilian population was attacked.

153. In total, the overall picture is characterized by chaos, anarchy, a collapse of State authority in most parts of the country and almost total failure of law enforcement agencies.In light of all of the above, I feel unable to authorize the commencement of an investigation in the situation in the Republic of Kenya.

Notes and Questions

1. Which opinion is the more persuasive, the majority or the dissent? For a discussion of each side's persuasiveness and precedential value, *see* Leila Nadya Sadat, *Crimes Against Humanity in the Modern Age*, 106 AM. J. INT'L L. _ (2012). *See also* Charles C. Jalloh, *Situation in the Republic of Kenya*, 105 AM. J. INT'L L. 540 (2011); Claus Kress, *On the Outer Limits of Crimes Against Humanity: The Concept of Organization within the Policy Re-*

quirement: Some Reflections on the March 2010 ICC Kenya *Decision*, 23 LEIDEN J. INT'L L. 855 (2010); Darryl Robinson, *Essence of Crimes Against Humanity Raised by Challenges at ICC*, EJIL Talk, Sept. 27, 2011, http://www.ejiltalk.org/essence-of-crimes-against-humanity-raised-by-challenges-at-icc/#more-3782; William A. Schabas, *Prosecuting Dr. Strangelove, Goldfinger, and the Joker at the International Criminal Court: Closing the Loopholes*, 23 LEIDEN J. INT'L L. 847 (2010).

2. The Pre-Trial Chamber in the Kenya case adopted the factors articulated in *Prosecutor v. Blaskic*, No. IT-9Fli5-14-T (Trial Chamber Judgement, 3 March 2000), as relevant and probative in deciding whether there was a "policy" to commit an attack against the Kenyan civilian population. Consider the list of factors in paragraph 87 of the opinion. Which of these factors are most probative as to whether there was a policy to commit an attack against a civilian population?

In earlier ICTY and ICTR cases, the policy element was considered to be a requisite element of crimes against humanity. *See, e.g., Prosecutor v. Tadic*, Case No. IT-94-1-T (Trial Chamber Judgement, 7 May 1997), para. 653; *Prosecutor v. Akayesu*, Case No. ICTR-96-4-T (Trial Chamber Judgment, 2 Sept. 1998), para. 653; *Prosecutor v. Rutaganda*, Case No. ICTR-96-3-T (Trial Chamber Judgement, 6 Dec. 1999), para. 69; *Prosecutor v. Musema*, Case No. ICTR-96-13-T (Trial Chamber Judgement, 27 Jan. 2000), para. 204; *Prosecutor v. Kayishema and Ruzindana*, Case No. ICTR-95-1-T (Trial Chamber Judgement, 21 May 1999), paras. 123–25, 581. However, the policy requirement was abandoned by the *Kunarac* Appeal Judgement, which held that the attack need not be supported by any form of "policy" or "plan." *See Prosecutor v. Kunarac*, et al., Case No. IT-96-23 & IT-96-23/1-A (Appeal Chamber Judgement, 12 June 2002), para. 98. This conclusion was affirmed in *Prosecutor v. Vasiljevic*, Case No. IT-98-32-T (Trial Chamber Judgement, 29 Nov. 2002), para. 36; *Prosecutor v. Naletilic and Martinovic*, Case No. IT-98-34-T (Trial Chamber Judgement, 31 March 2003), para. 234; *Prosecutor v Semanza*, Case No. ICTR-97-20-T (Trial Chamber Judgement, 15 May 2003), para. 329.

3. In the case of a "State" policy to commit an attack, the policy "does not necessarily need to have been conceived 'at the highest level of the State machinery.'" *Prosecutor v. Blaskic*, Case No. IT-95-14-T (Trial Chamber Judgement, 3 March 2000), para. 205. A policy adopted by regional or local governmental agencies could satisfy the requirement of a State policy. Must the "organizational policy" be established, endorsed or condoned at the highest policy-level of the "organization"?

4. The Pre-Trial Chamber in the Kenya case maintained that a distinction should be drawn on whether a group has the capability to perform acts which "infringe on basic human values." Para. 90. Is this standard too vague? Does the Chamber's definition of "organizational" risk expanding the concept of crimes against humanity to any infringement of human rights?

Judge Kaul's dissent stated that the juxtaposition of the notions of "State" and "organization" in Article 7(2)(a) of the ICC statute require that the "organization" possess some characteristics of a State. Para. 51. For Judge Kaul, this means that criminal organizations and syndicates would not qualify as "organizations" under Article 7(2)(a). However, what about more sophisticated criminal enterprises such as violent drug cartels or terrorist organizations? Do these groups possess State-like characteristics? Should their members be prosecuted for crimes against humanity? Review the opinion of the French Advocate General in the *Barbie* case, *supra* Section 3. Would he agree with Judge Kaul? The preamble of the ICC statute accentuates the gravity of the crimes subject to the jurisdiction of the ICC. The preamble states:

Mindful that during this century millions of children, women and men have been victims of unimaginable atrocities that deeply shock the conscience of humanity,

Recognizing that such grave crimes threaten the peace, security and well-being of the world,

Affirming that the most serious crimes of concern to the international community as a whole must not go unpunished and that their effective prosecution must be ensured by taking measures at the national level and by enhancing international cooperation, ...

Determined to these ends and for the sake of present and future generations, to establish an independent permanent International Criminal Court in relationship with the United Nations system, with jurisdiction over the most serious crimes of concern to the international community as a whole.

Would the prosecution of members of organized crime for crimes against humanity be consistent with the fundamental principles set forth in the preamble to the ICC statute? Concerning claims that organized criminal activities can be covered, see, for example, Sonia Merzon, *Extraterritorial Reach of the Trafficking Victims Protection Act*, 39 Geo. Wash. Int'l L. Rev. 887, 913 (2007), *citing* Tom Obokata, *Trafficking of Human Beings as a Crime Against Humanity: Some Implications for the International Legal System*, 54 Int'l & Comp. L.Q. 445 (2005); Paust, *The International Criminal Court Does Not Have Complete Jurisdiction Over Customary Crimes Against Humanity and War Crimes*, *supra* at 694; Jennifer M. Smith, *An International Hit Job: Prosecuting Organized Crime Acts as Crimes Against Humanity*, 97 Geo. L.J. 1111, 1122–24, 1126–28 & nn.148–149, 1129–30, 1139–52 (2009) (adding: national courts and the ICTY have "recognized that private actors could commit crimes against humanity" and "state policy" is not required; and since the Appeals Chamber decision in *The Prosecutor v. Kunarac* "explicitly held that a policy or plan is not even an element of crimes against humanity under customary international law, ... other ICTY and ICTR judgments have consistently reaffirmed that a plan or policy is not a requisite legal element.... [listing 12 ICTY cases and 4 ICTR cases] For example, the ICTR Appeals Chamber in *Semanza v. Prosecutor* reaffirmed that the existence of a plan or policy is not" required "and rejected the defendant's contention that crimes against humanity require 'the existence of a political objective' and 'the implication of high level political and/or military authorities in the definition and establishment of [a] methodical plan'"); Bruce Zagaris, *U.S. International Cooperation Against Transnational Organized Crime*, 44 Wayne L. Rev. 1401, 1462 (1998) ("genocide and crimes against humanity by transnational organized crime groups").

5. Consider the following hypothetical:

The dictatorial President of country Z, Ur R. Ong, has been publicly accused of a crime against humanity involving a successful bomb attack on the elite of his political opposition during their annual meeting, at which all three hundred or so of the conferees were killed. Ong claims that he, with the aid of a few of his most loyal colonels, planned this on his own in self-defense and in order to save the civilian population from political extremists who were plotting a terrorist campaign. When asked about the Nuremberg Charter, On said that it only applied during war, that it has been replaced by the Rome Statute of the ICC, and that the killing of the terrorists occurred during peace, was the internal affair of country Z, and was certainly not a crime against humanity under customary international law? Is Ong correct?

6. For further discussion of crimes against humanity in the Rome Statute, *see, e.g.,* Kelly Dawn Askin, *Crimes within the Jurisdiction of the International Criminal Court*, 10 Crim. L. F. 33 (1999); Kai Ambos & Steffen Wirth, *The Current Law of Crimes Against*

Humanity, 13 Crim. L. F. 1 (2002). *See also generally* M. Cherif Bassiouni, Crimes Against Humanity in International Criminal Law (2d ed. 1999); David Luban, *A Theory of Crimes Against Humanity*, 29 Yale J. Int'l L. 85 (2004).

Chapter 10

Genocide

Section 1
The Convention

Convention on the Prevention and Punishment
of the Crime of Genocide
78 U.N.T.S. 277*

[Read the Genocide Convention, in the Documents Supplement]

Article II of the Genocide Convention, which defines genocide, arguably has certain flaws. One problem is that the protected "group" is limited to "national, ethnical, racial or religious" and does not directly include social, cultural, or political groups as such.[2] The latter two were part of the original draft definition of Article II, but were opposed by the U.S.S.R. and thus not included in the approved text. Nevertheless, the negotiating history of the Convention reveals that the drafters intended the definition to be flexible and progressive to meet evolving exigencies.[3] This was needed because the definition was essentially reactive to the Nazi practices between 1932–1945, but was never intended to be limited to events during the Holocaust. In a 1992 authoritative interpretation, the Final Report of the Commission of Experts Established Pursuant to Security Council Resolution 780 (1992) to Investigate Violations of International Humanitarian Law in the Former Yugoslavia, the Commission took the position that

---

* This Convention was adopted by the U.N. General Assembly on December 9, 1948 (G.A. Res. 2670), 3 GAOR, Part 1, U.N. Doc. A/810, p. 174); entered into force on January 12, 1951. There are more than 141 state parties.

2. Note, however, that these might be factors relevant to the determination of other groupings (like ethnic, national or religious). Cultural groups are not directly included within the customary definition of genocide, but cultural characteristics might similarly relate to conclusions whether other groups exist.

3. *See* United Nations Report on the Study of the Question of the Prevention and Punishment of the Crime of Genocide, E/CN.4/Sub. 2/416, 4 July 1978, pp. 13–24, particularly paras. 46–91; *reprinted in* 1 INTERNATIONAL CRIMINAL LAW 389–97 (M. Cherif Bassiouni ed. 1986). *See also* Revised and Updated Report on the Question of the Prevention and Punishment of the Crime of Genocide Prepared by Mr. B. Whitaker, Review of Further Developments in Fields with which the Sub-Commission has been concerned, U.N. ESCOR, Human Rights Sub-Commission on the Prevention of Discrimination and Protection of Minorities, 38th Sess., U.N. Doc. E/CN.4/Sub. 2/1985, 16, 2 July 1985. For a distinction between intent and motive, *see, e.g.,* WAYNE R. LAFAVE & AUSTIN W. SCOTT, JR., CRIMINAL LAW 216 (2d ed. 1986). For an approach to "specific intent," *see, e.g., Michalic v. Cleveland Taubers,* 346 U.S. 325 (1960); *Holland v. United States,* 348 U.S. 121 (1954).

the definition of the crime of genocide is not static.[4] Further, the definition encompasses not merely a "group" in its entirety, but also a "part" thereof, like the intellectual elite or women who are targeted because they are members of a relevant group.[5] Moreover, a given group can be defined on the basis of its localized or regional existence, as opposed to an all-inclusive concept encompassing all members wherever they may be.

According to Professor Bassiouni:

> A second flaw in the Convention is the element of intent which requires "specific intent." While this type of intent is more readily identifiable in leaders or decision-makers, it is not always easily demonstrated with respect to the different layers or levels of executors of the policy. Thus, proving specific intent of lower level executors can be difficult. Yet it would be unfair, for example, to convict a prison guard who kills a prisoner of the crime of genocide without the specific intent to carry out the policy of genocide. That crime would also be a "war crime" if committed during an armed conflict. [see Chapter Eight] When the accused are other than decision-makers, the mental element should include at least knowledge by the executor that he is carrying out a genocidal policy. The major difference between "genocide" and "crimes against humanity" is that the former requires a specific intent to "destroy, in whole or in part" a given "group," while the latter does not.[6]

According to others, there is no such flaw in the Convention. There is merely the need to prove a specific intent to commit one of the acts defined in Articles II and III. Further, there is no unfairness in prosecuting any person, of any rank, who in fact has the "intent to destroy, in whole or in part," within the meaning of Article II, or who has been reasonably accused of conspiracy, incitement, attempt, or complicity within the meaning of Article III. It is not necessary that there be a "policy" of genocide or some further specific intent unspecified in the customary definition of genocide contained in Article II.

Questions

1. Under the Convention, is there a duty to prosecute those reasonably accused of genocide? See Articles I ("undertake to prevent and to punish"), IV ("Persons committing ... shall be punished"), and V; 1993 Report of the Secretary-General, in Chapter Six,

---

4. U.N. SCOR, U.N. DOC. S/1994/674, 27 May 1994, para. 96. *See also* M. Cherif Bassiouni, *The Commission of Experts Established Pursuant to Security Council Resolution 780: Investigating Violations of International Humanitarian Law in the Former Yugoslavia*, 5 Crim. L.F. 279 (1994); M. Cherif Bassiouni, *Current Developments: The United Nations Commission of Experts Established Pursuant to Security Council Resolution 780 (1992)*, 88 Am. J. Int'l L. 784 (1994).

5. Annex to the Final Report (*supra*), U.N. SCOR, Annex IV, "The Policy of Ethnic Cleansing" and Annex "Prijedor", U.N. DOC. S/1994/674/Add. 2 (Vol. I) (Dec. 28, 1994), and Annex IX, "Rape and Sexual Assault", U.N. DOC. S/1994/674/Add. 2 (Vol. V) (May 31, 1995). *See also* M. Cherif Bassiouni & Marcia McCormick, *Sexual Violence: An Invisible Weapon of War in the Former Yugoslavia* (Occasional Paper No. 1 International Human Rights Law Institute, DePaul University College of Law 1996); Lawrence J. LeBlanc, *The Intent to Destroy Groups in the Genocide Convention: The Proposed U.S. Understanding*, 78 Am. J. Int'l L. 369 (1984); materials that follow in this chapter.

6. *See, e.g.*, M. Cherif Bassiouni, Crimes Against Humanity in International Criminal Law (1992).

Section 9, at para. 45 ("shall be tried and punished"). Given the fact that the crime of genocide is a violation of customary international law over which there is universal jurisdiction, is there also a universal duty to initiate prosecution or extradite? Recall Chapter Two, Section 3; *Eichmann*, in Chapter Nine, Section 2.

2. Under the Convention, is there a duty to prevent genocide? See Articles I, VIII. Professor Schabas has written: "The Outcome Document, adopted at the United Nations summit in September 2005, affirms that 'each individual state has the responsibility to protect its populations from genocide, war crimes, ethnic cleansing and crimes against humanity.'... It is uncontroversial to maintain that the duty to prevent genocide is one of customary international law.... Perhaps the Outcome Document will help to lay to rest a controversy ... whether or not the 'ethnic cleansing' that has been an ugly feature of the civil war in Darfur [Sudan] constitutes the crime of genocide." William A. Schabas, *Genocide, Crimes Against Humanity, and Darfur: The Commission of Inquiry's Findings on Genocide*, 27 Cardozo L. Rev. 1703 (2006). In response partly to U.S. claims that conduct in Darfur amounts to genocide, the U.N. Security Council created a Commission of Inquiry in 2004 to address the issue. The 2005 Report of the Commission concluded that "genocidal intent" appeared to be lacking with respect to a Sudanese "policy of attacking, killing and forcibly displacing members of some tribes," which did not prove "a specific intent to annihilate, in whole or in part" but rather "that those who planned and organized attacks on villages pursued the intent to drive the victims from their homes, primarily for purposes of counter-insurgency warfare." See U.N. Secretary-General, Report of the International Commission of Inquiry on Violations of International Law and Humanitarian Law and Human Rights Law in Darfur, para. 518, U.N. Doc. S/2005/60 (31 Jan. 2005); Schabas, *supra* at 1705–06, adding that the Commission nonetheless "characterized the behaviour of the pro-government Janjaweed paramilitaries as 'crimes against humanity'" and that the Security Council has referred "'the situation in Darfur since 1 July 2002' to the International Criminal Court."

In one example investigated, the Darfur Commission Report concluded that instead of genocidal intentions, the intention was to murder all those men they considered as rebels, as well as [to] forcibly expel the whole population so as to vacate the villages and prevent rebels from hiding among or getting support from the local population" and in some instances "populations surviving attacks on villages are not killed outright in an effort to eradicate the group; rather, they are forced to abandon their homes and live together in areas selected by the Government." Report, *supra* at paras. 514–515.

3. What constitutes genocide within the meaning of Article II?

4. What is the specific intent required? With respect to specific acts covered in Article II (a)—(e), are there additional *mens rea* requirements concerning the specific acts or methods? In *Prosecutor v. Niyitegeka*, ICTR-96-14-A (Appeals Chamber Judgement, 9 July 2004), the Appeals Chamber held that the term "as such" in the definition of genocide does not prohibit a conviction for genocide where the perpetrator was also driven by other motivations. The Court stated that term "as such" means that the proscribed acts were committed against the victims *because of* their membership in the protected group, but not *solely* because of such membership.

5. In order to commit genocide, as opposed to an attempt to commit genocide under Article III (d), must the perpetrator destroy a relevant group "in whole or in part" or must the perpetrator merely intend to do so while committing one or more of the listed acts?

Must there be an intent to destroy the group in whole or in part or merely its identity? In *The Prosecutor v. Milosevic*, IT-02-54-T (Decision on Motion for Judgment of Acquittal, 16 June 2004), the Trial Chamber declared that "[i]t is the material destruction of the group which must be intended and not the destruction of its identity." *Id.* para. 124. Is the "intent to destroy" requirement limited to the intent to "physically" or "biologically" destroy members of the protected group? In *Prosecutor v. Krajisnik*, IT-00-39-T (Trial Chamber Judgement, 27 Sept. 2006), the Trial Chamber indicated that the "intent to destroy" can encompass more than physical or biological destruction:

> It is not accurate to speak of "the group" as being amenable to physical or biological destruction. Its members are, of course, physical or biological beings, but the bonds among its members, as well as such aspects of the group as its members' culture and beliefs, are neither physical nor biological. Hence the Genocide Convention's "intent to destroy" the group cannot sensibly be regarded as reducible to an intent to destroy the group physically or biologically, as has occasionally been said.

6. Could al Qaeda attacks on the World Trade Center and the Pentagon in the U.S. on September 11, 2001 constitute acts of genocide under Article II? Near the end of this chapter, consider whether those involved in conspiracy or complicity to commit such attacks could be prosecuted under the U.S. genocide legislation (especially 18 U.S.C. §§ 1091, 1093(8)).

7. If U.S. military personnel targeted armed Iraqi military personnel during the Iraq war because they were Iraqi soldiers, would such targetings involve the killings of a national group with the intent to destroy that group "in part"? Is it relevant that such conduct is permissible under the laws of war? *Cf* The Prosecutor v. Krstic, IT-98-33-A (Appeals Chamber Judgment, 19 Apr. 2004), para. 226, genocide can be committed against military personnel if they are killed because they are part of a relevant group with the intent to destroy in whole or in part members of that group.

8. If Serbian military units intentionally killed Muslim persons in Bosnia-Herzegovina in order to "ethnically cleanse" areas of Muslims by causing those left alive to flee, were the killings genocide? Does it depend on one's definition of "ethnically cleanse"? Consider ANTONIO CASSESE, INTERNATIONAL CRIMINAL LAW 98–100 (2003) ("It would seem that Article IV does not cover the conduct currently termed in non-technical language 'ethnic cleansing,' that is the forcible expulsion of civilians belonging to a particular group from an area, a village, or a town.").

9. What do you think is meant by the phrase "ethnic cleansing"? Like the former President of the Appeals Chamber of the ICTY, Antonio Cassese, Judge Lauterpacht has stated that this phrase encompasses "the forced migration of civilians." See Application of the Convention on the Prevention and Punishment of the Crime of Genocide (Bosnia and Herzegovina v. Yugoslavia (Serbia and Montenegro)), 1993 I.C.J. 325, 431 (separated op., Judge Elihu Lauterpacht). Is this all that the phrase might encompass? See also John Quigley, *State Responsibility for Ethnic Cleansing*, 32 U.C. DAVIS L. REV. 341 (1999) ("It is an umbrella term that covers a variety of delictual acts aimed at driving members of an ethnic group from their home area"); Final Report of the Commission of Experts Established Pursuant to Security Council Resolution 780 (1992), U.N. SCOR, Annex 1, at 33, U.N. Doc. E/CN.4/1995/176 (1995) ("a purposeful policy designed by one ethnic or religious group to remove by violent and terror-inspiring means the civilian populations of another ethnic or religious group from certain geographic areas").

A. Prosecutions Before the International Criminal Tribunal for Rwanda

The Prosecutor v. Jean-Paul Akayesu

ICTR-96-4-T (2 Sept. 1998)

Before: Judge Laïty Kama, Presiding

Judge Lennart Aspegren

Judge Navanethem Pillay

12. Before rendering its findings on the acts with which Akayesu is charged and the applicable law, the Chamber is of the opinion that it would be appropriate, for a better understanding of the events alleged in the Indictment, to briefly summarise the history of Rwanda. To this end, it recalled the most important events in the country's history, from the pre-colonial period up to 1994, reviewing the colonial period and the "Revolution" of 1959 by Gregoire Kayibanda. The Chamber most particularly highlighted the military and political conflict between the Rwandan Armed Forces (RAF) and the Rwandan Patriotic Front(RPF) and its armed wing, from 1990. This conflict led to the signing of the Arusha Peace Accords and the deployment of a United Nations peacekeeping force, UNAMIR.

13. The Chamber then considered whether the events that took place in Rwanda in 1994 occurred solely within the context of the conflict between the RAF and the RPF, as some maintain, or whether the massacres that occurred between April and July 1994 constituted genocide. To that end, and even if the Chamber later goes back on its definition of genocide, it should be noted that genocide means, as defined in the Convention for the Prevention and Punishment of the Crime of Genocide, as the act of committing certain crimes, including the killing of members of the group or causing serious physical or mental harm to members of the group with the intent to destroy, in whole or in part, a national, ethnical, racial or religious group, as such.

14. Even though the number of victims is yet to be known with accuracy, no one can reasonably refute the fact that widespread killings took place during this period throughout the country. Dr. Zachariah, who appeared as an expert witness before this Tribunal, described the piles of bodies he saw everywhere, on the roads, on the footpaths and in rivers and, particularly, the manner in which all these people had been killed. He saw many wounded people who, according to him, were mostly Tutsi and who, apparently, had sustained wounds inflicted with machetes to the face, the neck, the ankle and also to the Achilles' tendon to prevent them from fleeing. Similarly, the testimony of Major-General Dallaire, former Commander of UNAMIR, before the Chamber indicated that, from 6 April 1994, the date of the crash that claimed the life of President Habyarimana, members of FAR and the Presidential Guard were going into houses in Kigali that had been previously identified in order to kill. Another witness, the British cameraman, Simon Cox, took photographs of bodies in various localities in Rwanda, and mentioned identity cards strewn on the ground, all of which were marked "Tutsi".

15. Consequently, in view of these widespread killings the victims of which were mainly Tutsi, the Trial Chamber is of the opinion that the first requirement for there to be genocide has been met, to wit, killing and causing serious bodily harm to members of a group. The second requirement is that these killings and serious bodily harm be committed with the intent to destroy, in whole or in part, a particular group targeted as such.

16. In the opinion of the Chamber, many facts show that the intention of the perpetrators of these killings was to cause the complete disappearance of the Tutsi people. In this connection, Alison DesForges, a specialist historian on Rwanda, who appeared as an expert witness, stated as follows: "on the basis of the statements made by certain political leaders, on the basis of songs and slogans popular among the interahamwe, I believe that these people had the intention of completely wiping out the Tutsi from Rwanda so that—as they said on certain occasions—their children, later on, should not know what a Tutsi looked like, unless they referred to history books". This testimony given by Dr. DesForges was confirmed by two prosecution witnesses, who testified separately before the Tribunal that one Silas Kubwimana said during a public meeting chaired by the Accused himself that all the Tutsi had to be killed so that someday Hutu children would not know what a Tutsi looked like. Dr. Zachariah also testified that the Achilles' tendons of many wounded persons were cut to prevent them from fleeing. In the opinion of the Chamber, this demonstrates the resolve of the perpetrators of these massacres not to spare any Tutsi. Their plan called for doing whatever was possible to prevent any Tutsi from escaping and, thus, to destroy the whole group. Dr. Alison DesForges stated that numerous Tutsi corpses were systematically thrown into the River Nyabarongo, a tributary of the Nile, as seen, incidentally, in several photographs shown in court throughout the trial. She explained that the intent in that gesture was "to send the Tutsi back to their origin", to make them "return to Abyssinia", in accordance with the notion that the Tutsi are a "foreign" group in Rwanda, believed to have come from the Nilotic regions.

17. Other testimonies heard, especially that of Major-General Dallaire, also show that there was an intention to wipe out the Tutsi group in its entirety, since even newborn babies were not spared. Many testimonies given before the Chamber concur on the fact that it was the Tutsi as members of an ethnic group who were targeted in the massacres. General Dallaire, Doctor Zachariah and, particularly, the Accused himself, unanimously stated so before the Chamber.

18. Numerous witnesses testified before the Chamber that the systematic checking of identity cards, on which the ethnic group was mentioned, made it possible to separate the Hutu from the Tutsi, with the latter being immediately arrested and often killed, sometimes on the spot, at the roadblocks which were erected in Kigali soon after the crash of the plane of President Habyarimana, and thereafter everywhere in the country.

19. Based on the evidence submitted to the Chamber, it is clear that the massacres which occurred in Rwanda in 1994 had a specific objective, namely the extermination of the Tutsi, who were targeted especially because of their Tutsi origin and not because they were RPF fighters. In any case, the Tutsi children and pregnant women would, naturally, not have been among the fighters. The Chamber concludes that, alongside the conflict between the RAF and the RPF, genocide was committed in Rwanda in 1994 against the Tutsi as a group. The execution of this genocide was probably facilitated by the conflict, in the sense that the conflict with the RPF forces served as a pretext for the propaganda inciting genocide against the Tutsi, by branding RPF fighters and Tutsi civilians together through the notion widely disseminated, particularly by Radio Television Libre des Mille Collines (RTLM), to the effect that every Tutsi was allegedly an accomplice of the RPF soldiers or "Inkotanyi". However, the fact that the genocide occurred while the RAF were in conflict with the RPF, obviously, cannot serve as a mitigating circumstance for the genocide.

20. Consequently, the Chamber concludes from all the foregoing that it was, indeed, genocide that was committed in Rwanda in 1994, against the Tutsi as a group. The Chamber is of the opinion that the genocide appears to have been meticulously organized. In fact, Dr. Alison Desforges testifying before the Chamber on 24 May 1997, talked of "cen-

trally organized and supervised massacres". Some evidence supports this view that the genocide had been planned. First, the existence of lists of Tutsi to be eliminated is corroborated by many testimonies. In this respect, Dr. Zachariah mentioned the case of patients and nurses killed in a hospital because a soldier had a list including their names.

21. The Chamber holds that the genocide was organized and planned not only by members of the RAF, but also by the political forces who were behind the "Hutu-power", that it was executed essentially by civilians including the armed militia and even ordinary citizens, and above all, that the majority of the Tutsi victims were non-combatants, including thousands of women and children....

37. Having made its factual findings, the Chamber analysed the legal definitions proposed by the Prosecutor for each of the facts. It thus considered the applicable law for each of the three crimes under its jurisdiction, which is all the more important since this is the very first Judgement on the legal definitions of genocide on the one hand, and of serious violations of Additional Protocol II of the Geneva Conventions, on the other. Moreover, the Chamber also had to define certain crimes which constitute offences under its jurisdiction, in particular, rape, because to date, there is no commonly accepted definition of this term in international law.

38. In the opinion of the Chamber, rape is a form of aggression the central elements of which cannot be captured in a mechanical description of objects and body parts. The Chamber also notes the cultural sensitivities involved in public discussion of intimate matters and recalls the painful reluctance and inability of witnesses to disclose graphic anatomical details of the sexual violence they endured. The Chamber defines rape as a physical invasion of a sexual nature, committed on a person under circumstances which are coercive. Sexual violence, including rape, is not limited to physical invasion of the human body and may include acts which do not involve penetration or even physical contact. The Chamber notes in this context that coercive circumstances need not be evidenced by a show of physical force. Threats, intimidation, extortion and other forms of duress which prey on fear or desperation may constitute coercion.

39. The Chamber reviewed Article 6 (1) of its Statute, on the individual criminal responsibility of the accused for the three crimes constituting *ratione materiae* of the Chamber. Article 6(1) enunciates the basic principles of individual criminal liability which are probably common to most national criminal jurisdictions. Article 6(3), by contrast, constitutes something of an exception to the principles articulated in Article 6(1), an exception which derives from military law, particularly the principle of the liability of a commander for the acts of his subordinates or "command responsibility". Article 6(3) does not necessarily require the superior to have had knowledge of such to render him criminally liable. The only requirement is that he had reason to know that his subordinates were about to commit or had committed and failed to take the necessary or reasonable measures to prevent such acts or punish the perpetrators thereof.

40. The Chamber then expressed its opinion that with respect to the crimes under its jurisdiction, it should adhere to the concept of notional plurality of offences (cumulative charges) which would render multiple convictions permissible for the same act. As a result, a particular act may constitute both genocide and a crime against humanity.

41. On the crime of genocide, the Chamber recalls that the definition given by Article 2 of the Statute is echoed exactly by the Convention for the Prevention and Repression of the Crime of Genocide. The Chamber notes that Rwanda acceded, by legislative decree, to the Convention on Genocide on 12 February 1975. Thus, punishment of the crime of genocide did exist in Rwanda in 1994, at the time of the acts alleged in the In-

dictment, and the perpetrator was liable to be brought before the competent courts of Rwanda to answer for this crime.

42. Contrary to popular belief, the crime of genocide does not imply the actual extermination of a group in its entirety, but is understood as such once any one of the acts mentioned in Article 2 of the Statute is committed with the specific intent to destroy "in whole or in part" a national, ethnical, racial or religious group. Genocide is distinct from other crimes inasmuch as it embodies a special intent or *dolus specialis*. Special intent of a crime is the specific intention, required as a constitutive element of the crime, which requires that the perpetrator clearly seek to produce the act charged. The special intent in the crime of genocide lies in "the intent to destroy, in whole or in part, a national, ethnical, racial or religious group, as such".

43. Specifically, for any of the acts charged under Article 2(2) of the Statute to be a constitutive element of genocide, the act must have been committed against one or several individuals, because such individual or individuals were members of a specific group, and specifically because they belonged to this group. Thus, the victim is chosen not because of his individual identity, but rather on account of his being a member of a national, ethnical, racial or religious group. The victim of the act is therefore a member of a group, targeted as such; hence, the victim of the crime of genocide is the group itself and not the individual alone.

44. On the issue of determining the offender's specific intent, the Chamber considers that intent is a mental factor which is difficult, even impossible, to determine. This is the reason why, in the absence of a confession from the Accused, his intent can be inferred from a certain number of presumptions of fact. The Chamber considers that it is possible to deduce the genocidal intent inherent in a particular act charged from the general context of the perpetration of other culpable acts systematically directed against that same group, whether these acts were committed by the same offender or by others. Other factors, such as the scale of atrocities committed, their general nature, in a region or a country, or furthermore, the fact of deliberately and systematically targeting victims on account of their membership of a particular group, while excluding the members of other groups, can enable the Chamber to infer the genocidal intent of a particular act.

45. Apart from the crime of genocide, Jean-Paul Akayesu is charged with complicity in genocide and direct and public incitement to commit genocide.

46. In the opinion of the Chamber, an Accused is an accomplice in genocide if he knowingly aided and abetted or provoked a person or persons to commit genocide, knowing that this person or persons were committing genocide, even if the Accused himself lacked the specific intent of destroying in whole or in part, the national, ethnical, racial or religious group, as such.

47. Regarding the crime of direct and public incitement to commit genocide, the Chamber defines it mainly on the basis of Article 91 of the Rwandan Penal Code, as directly provoking another to commit genocide, either through speeches, shouting or threats uttered in public places or at public gatherings, or through the sale or dissemination, offer for sale or display of written material or printed matter in public places or at public gatherings or through the public display of placards or posters, or by any other means of audiovisual communication. The moral element of this crime lies in the intent to directly encourage or provoke another to commit genocide. It presupposes the desire of the guilty to create, by his actions, within the person or persons whom he is addressing, the state of mind which is appropriate to the commission of a crime. In other words, the person who is inciting to commit genocide must have the specific intent of genocide: that

of destroying in whole or in part, a national, ethnical, racial or religious group, as such. The Chamber believes that incitement is a formal offence, for which the mere method used is culpable. In other words, the offence is considered to have been completed once the incitement has taken place and that it is direct and public, whether or not it was successful....

51. With regard to count one on genocide, the Chamber having regard, particularly, to the acts described in paragraphs 12(A) and 12(B) of the Indictment, that is, rape and sexual violence, the Chamber wishes to underscore the fact that in its opinion, they constitute genocide in the same way as any other act as long as they were committed with the specific intent to destroy, in whole or in part, a particular group, targeted as such. Indeed, rape and sexual violence certainly constitute infliction of serious bodily and mental harm on the victims. See above, the findings of the Trial Chamber on the Chapter relating to the law applicable to the crime of genocide, in particular, the definition of the constituent elements of genocide, and are even, according to the Chamber, one of the worst ways of inflicting harm on the victim as he or she suffers both bodily and mental harm. In light of all the evidence before it, the Chamber is satisfied that the acts of rape and sexual violence described above, were committed solely against Tutsi women, many of whom were subjected to the worst public humiliation, mutilated, and raped several times, often in public, in the Bureau Communal premises or in other public places, and often by more than one assailant. These rapes resulted in physical and psychological destruction of Tutsi women, their families and their communities. Sexual violence was an integral part of the process of destruction, specifically targeting Tutsi women and specifically contributing to their destruction and to the destruction of the Tutsi group as a whole.

52. The rape of Tutsi women was systematic and was perpetrated against all Tutsi women and solely against them. A Tutsi woman, married to a Hutu, testified before the Chamber that she was not raped because her ethnic background was unknown. As part of the propaganda campaign geared to mobilizing the Hutu against the Tutsi, the Tutsi women were presented as sexual objects. Indeed, the Chamber was told, for an example, that before being raped and killed, Alexia, who was the wife of the Professor, Ntereye, and her two nieces, were forced by the Interahamwe to undress and ordered to run and do exercises "in order to display the thighs of Tutsi women". The Interahamwe who raped Alexia said, as he threw her on the ground and got on top of her, "let us now see what the vagina of a Tutsi woman tastes like". As stated above, Akayesu himself, speaking to the Interahamwe who were committing the rapes, said to them: "don't ever ask again what a Tutsi woman tastes like".

53. On the basis of the substantial testimonies brought before it, the Chamber finds that in most cases, the rapes of Tutsi women in Taba, were accompanied with the intent to kill those women. Many rapes were perpetrated near mass graves where the women were taken to be killed. A victim testified that Tutsi women caught could be taken away by peasants and men with the promise that they would be collected later to be executed. Following an act of gang rape, a witness heard Akayesu say "tomorrow they will be killed" and they were actually killed. In this respect, it appears clearly to the Chamber that the acts of rape and sexual violence, as other acts of serious bodily and mental harm committed against the Tutsi, reflected the determination to make Tutsi women suffer and to mutilate them even before killing them, the intent being to destroy the Tutsi group while inflicting acute suffering on its members in the process.

54. The Chamber has already established that genocide was committed against the Tutsi group in Rwanda in 1994, throughout the period covering the events alleged in the Indictment. Owing to the very high number of atrocities committed against the Tutsi,

their widespread nature not only in the commune of Taba, but also throughout Rwanda, and to the fact that the victims were systematically and deliberately selected because they belonged to the Tutsi group, with persons belonging to other groups being excluded, the Chamber is also able to infer, beyond reasonable doubt, the genocidal intent of the accused in the commission of the above-mentioned crimes; to the extent that the actions and words of Akayesu during the period of the facts alleged in the Indictment, the Chamber is convinced beyond reasonable doubt, on the basis of evidence adduced before it during the hearing, that he repeatedly made statements more or less explicitly calling for the commission of genocide. Yet, according to the Chamber, he who incites another to commit genocide must have the specific intent to commit genocide: that of destroying in whole or in part, a national, ethnical, racial, or religious group, as such.

55. In conclusion, regarding Count One on genocide, the Chamber is satisfied beyond reasonable doubt that these various acts were committed by Akayesu with the specific intent to destroy the Tutsi group, as such. Consequently, the Chamber is of the opinion that the acts alleged in paragraphs 12, 12A, 12B, 16, 18, 19, 20, 22 and 23 of the Indictment, constitute the crimes of killing members of the Tutsi group and causing serious bodily and mental harm to members of the Tutsi group. Furthermore, the Chamber is satisfied beyond reasonable doubt that in committing the various acts alleged, Akayesu had the specific intent of destroying the Tutsi group as such.

56. Regarding Count Two, on the crime of complicity in genocide, the Chamber indicated *supra* that, in its opinion, the crime of genocide and that of complicity in genocide were two distinct crimes, and that the same person could certainly not be both the principal perpetrator of, and accomplice to, the same offence. Given that genocide and complicity in genocide are mutually exclusive by definition, the accused cannot obviously be found guilty of both these crimes for the same act. However, since the Prosecutor has charged the accused with both genocide and complicity in genocide for each of the alleged acts, the Chamber deems it necessary, in the instant case, to rule on Counts 1 and 2 simultaneously, so as to determine, as far as each proven fact is concerned, whether it constituted genocide or complicity in genocide....

Notes and Questions

1. The *Akayesu* Judgment also recognized that "[t]he Genocide Convention is undeniably ... customary international law...." *Id.* at para. 495. The Chamber also recognized that bodily or mental harm "does not necessarily mean ... permanent and irremediable" harm (*id.* at para. 502); that an "ethnic group is generally defined as a group whose members share a common language or culture" (*id.* at para. 513); that, according to the *travaux préparatoires* concerning the Convention, groups covered include "any group which is stable and permanent like the said four groups ... and [if] membership is by birth" (*id.* at para. 516); and that with respect to *mens rea* there should be a "clear intent to destroy, in whole or in part," and the "offender is culpable because he knew or should have known that the act committed would destroy, in whole or in part, a group" (*id.* at para. 520).

2. In *The Prosecutor v. Karemera, Ngirumpatse, and Nzirorera*, ICTR-98-44-AR73(C) (Appeals Chamber, 16 June 2006), the Appeals Chamber ruled that Trial Chambers of the ICTR must henceforth take judicial notice of the following: (1) the existence of Twa, Tutsi and Hutu as protected groups falling under the Genocide Convention; (2) between 6 April and 17 July 1994 there were throughout Rwanda widespread or systematic attacks against a civilian population based on Tutsi ethnic identification, during the attacks some Rwandan citizens killed or caused serious bodily injury or mental harm to persons per-

ceived to be Tutsi, as a result there were a large number of deaths of persons of Tutsi ethnic identify; and (3) between 6 April and 17 July 1994 there was genocide in Rwanda against the Tutsi ethnic group.

3. In *Akayesu*, the Trial Chamber held that "the crime of genocide and that of complicity in genocide were two distinct crimes" with different mental elements. *Id.* at para. 56. The Trial Chamber stated:

> In the opinion of the Chamber, an Accused is an accomplice in genocide if he knowingly aided and abetted or provoked a person or persons to commit genocide, knowing that this person or persons were committing genocide, even if the Accused himself lacked the specific intent of destroying in whole or in part, the national, ethnical, racial or religious group, as such.

Id. at para. 46.

Therefore, according to the Trial Chamber in *Akayesu*, "complicity," "accomplice," and "aided and abetted" reflect basically the same type of responsibility and in order to convict a person of complicity in genocide the prosecutor is not required to prove that the accused acted with genocidal intent. The prosecutor is only required to prove that the accused knowingly assisted persons to commit genocide, knowing that such persons were committing genocide.

The *Akayesu* Trial Chamber's view of complicity in genocide has been rejected by other Trial Chambers and affirmed by others. Apparently, one question exists whether "complicity in genocide" (which is the phrase found in Article III (e) of the Genocide Convention and in some parts of the Statutes of the ICTY and ICTR) should be treated differently than complicity to commit other international crimes, since genocide as such requires a special criminal intent. Does complicity in genocide also require a special *mens rea*? In *Prosecutor v. Karemera, et al.,* ICTR-98-44-T (Trial Chamber Judgement, 18 May 2006), the Trial Chamber held that "complicity is one of the forms of criminal responsibility that is applicable to the crime of genocide, and not a crime itself." *Id.* at para. 7. The Trial Chamber in *Karemera* further stated:

> Whereas the genocide is the crime, joint criminal enterprise and complicity in genocide are two modes of liability, two methods by which the crime of genocide can be committed and individuals held responsible for this crime.... Complicity can only be pleaded as a form of liability for the crime of genocide.

Id. at para. 8. Therefore, according to *Karemera*, in order to convict an accused of genocide under a theory of complicity, the prosecution must prove genocidal intent. *But see Prosecutor v. Semanza*, ICTR-97-20-T, at 394 (Trial Judgement, 15 May 2003), at para. 394 (finding no material distinction between aiding and abetting and complicity in genocide).

The *Karemera* Trial Chamber's construction of complicity in genocide seems at odds with the Statute of the ICTY. Article 4(3) provides:

> The following acts shall be punishable:
>
> (a) genocide;
>
> (b) conspiracy to commit genocide;
>
> (c) direct and public incitement to commit genocide;
>
> (d) attempt to commit genocide;
>
> (e) complicity in genocide.

Article 4(3) lists different genocide-related crimes, including complicity in genocide. Article 7(1) sets forth a list of different forms of liability, different ways in which the crimes within the jurisdiction of the ICTY can be committed, including the acts of genocide proscribed in Article 4(3). Article 7(1) provides:

> A person who planned, instigated, ordered, committed or otherwise aided and abetted in planning, preparation or execution of a crime referred to in articles 2 to 5 of the present Statute, shall be individually responsible for the crime.

Complicity as such is not mentioned in the different methods of criminal responsibility set forth in Article 7(1), although the Statute authorizes individual criminal liability for aiding and abetting. As noted in *Akayesu* and *Semanza*, are they basically the same forms of responsibility? Recall Chapter Two, Section 1. C. The Statute of the ICTR is similarly structured. *See* Statute of the ICTR, arts. 2(3) and 6(1).

Which position do you prefer? Should complicity in genocide be construed as a separate crime or merely a method by which genocide can be committed? For articles discussing the inconsistent application of complicity in genocide by the ICTY and ICTR, *see* Grant Dawson & Rachel Boynton, *Reconciling Complicity in Genocide and Aiding and Abetting Genocide in the Jurisprudence of the United Nations Ad Hoc Tribunals*, 21 Harv. Hum. Rts. J. 241 (2008); Daniel M. Greenfield, *The Crime of Complicity in Genocide: How the International Criminal Tribunals for Rwanda and Yugoslavia Got It Wrong, and Why It Matters*, 98 J. Crim. L. & Criminology 921 (2008). Professor Elies van Sliedregt of the University of Amsterdam has written that under the case law of the ICTY and ICTR "the content and meaning of complicity in genocide remains unclear and contested" and the fact that the Statutes of the tribunals both contain separate parts with respect to complicity in genocide and aiding and abetting "has given rise to contradictory rulings." Elies van Sliedregt, *Complicity to Commit Genocide*, in The UN Genocide Convention: A Commentary 162, 163, 169 (Paola Gaeta ed. 2009), adding: "it is by now accepted that the reason for this coexistence [of the two phrases] in the Statutes is bad drafting." *Id.* at 167 (citing *Krstic, Semanza*, and G. Mettraux, International Crimes and the Ad Hoc Tribunals 257 (2006). He also notes: "At the ICTY, it is by now a well-established rule that the *mens rea* for aiding and abetting is knowledge of the intent of the principal and the awareness that one's acts or conduct will assist the principal in the commission of the crimes. The aider and abettor need not share the principal's *mens rea*.... Eventually, the ICTR Appeals Chamber in *Ntakirutimana* brought the ICTR law in harmony with ICTY case law.... [But] the *ad hoc* Tribunal's case law remains unclear as to what the appropriate mental standard for complicity in genocide is." *Id.* at 170–71.

4. In *Prosecutor of Kalimanzira*, ICTR-05-88-A (Appeals Chamber Judgement, 20 Oct. 2010), the Appeals Chamber distinguished the crime of direct and public incitement to commit genocide (which is punishable under Article 2(3)(c)) from instigating genocide (punishable under Article 6(1)). The most important difference is that the acts constituting incitement must be "direct" and unequivocally "public." The Appeals Chamber observed that "all convictions before the Tribunal for direct and public incitement to commit genocide involve speeches made to large, fully public assemblies, messages disseminated by the media, and communications made through public address system over a broad public area." *Id.* at para. 156. The Chamber held that public incitement to genocide pertained to mass communications, and that private incitement such as private conversations, meetings or messages, was specifically excluded. *Id.* at para. 158.

5. In the Rome Statute of the ICC, the offense of direct and public incitement to commit genocide has been eliminated as a separate offense. "Direct and public incitement" is

recast under Article 25(3)(e) as a mode of individual criminal responsibility. Should "direct and public incitement" to commit genocide be treated as a separate crime, as it is under Articles 2(3)(c) and 4(3)(c), respectively, of the ICTR and ICTY statutes, or merely as a form of individual criminal liability, the position embraced by Article 25(3)(e) of the Statute of the ICC? *See* Chile Eboe-Osuji, *"Complicity in Genocide" versus "Aiding and Abetting Genocide": Construing the Difference in the ICTR and ICTY Statutes*, 3 J. Int'l Crim. Just. 56, 60 n. 15 (2005) (arguing that "direct and public incitement" should be a separate crime).

The Prosecutor v. Rutaganda
ICTR-96-3-T (6 Dec. 1999)

Before: Judge Laïty Kama, Presiding

Judge Lennart Aspegren

Judge Navanethem Pillay

48. The Chamber accepts that the crime of genocide involves, firstly, that one of the acts listed under Article 2(2) of the Statute be committed; secondly, that such an act be committed against a national, ethnical, racial or religious group, specifically targeted as such; and, thirdly, that the "act be committed with the intent to destroy, in whole or in part, the targeted group".

The Acts Enumerated under Article 2(2)(a) to (e) of the Statute

49. Article 2(2)(a) of the Statute, like the corresponding provisions of the Genocide Convention, refers to "*meurtre*" in the French version and to "killing" in the English version. In the opinion of the Chamber, the term "killing" includes both intentional and unintentional homicides, whereas the word "*meurtre*" covers homicide committed with the intent to cause death. Given the presumption of innocence, and pursuant to the general principles of criminal law, the Chamber holds that the version more favourable to the Accused should be adopted, and finds that Article 2(2)(a) of the Statute must be interpreted in accordance with the definition of murder in the Criminal Code of Rwanda, which provides, under Article 311, that "Homicide committed with intent to cause death shall be treated as murder".

50. For the purposes of interpreting Article 2(2)(b) of the Statute, the Chamber understands the words "serious bodily or mental harm" to include acts of bodily or mental torture, inhumane or degrading treatment, rape, sexual violence, and persecution. The Chamber is of the opinion that "serious harm" need not entail permanent or irremediable harm.

51. In the opinion of the Chamber, the words "deliberately inflicting on the group conditions of life calculated to bring about its physical destruction in whole or in part", as indicated in Article 2(2)(c) of the Statute, are to be construed "as methods of destruction by which the perpetrator does not necessarily intend to immediately kill the members of the group", but which are, ultimately, aimed at their physical destruction. The Chamber holds that the means ... include subjecting a group of people to a subsistence diet, systematic expulsion from their homes and deprivation of essential medical supplies below a minimum vital standard.

52. For the purposes of interpreting Article 2(2)(d) of the Statute, the Chamber holds that the words "measures intended to prevent births within the group" should be construed as including sexual mutilation, enforced sterilization, forced birth control, forced

separation of males and females, and prohibition of marriages. The Chamber notes that measures intended to prevent births within the group may be not only physical, but also mental.

53. The Chamber is of the opinion that the provisions of Article 2(2)(e) of the Statute, on the forcible transfer of children from one group to another, are aimed at sanctioning not only any direct act of forcible physical transfer, but also any acts of threats or trauma which would lead to the forcible transfer of children from one group to another group.

Potential Groups of Victims of the Crime of Genocide

55. The Chamber notes that the concepts of national, ethnical, racial and religious groups have been researched extensively and that, at present, there are no generally and internationally accepted precise definitions thereof. Each of these concepts must be assessed in the light of a particular political, social and cultural context. Moreover, the Chamber notes that for the purposes of applying the Genocide Convention, membership of a group is, in essence, a subjective rather than an objective concept. The victim is perceived by the perpetrator of genocide as belonging to a group slated for destruction. In some instances, the victim may perceive himself/herself as belonging to the said group.

56. Nevertheless, the Chamber is of the view that a subjective definition alone is not enough to determine victim groups, as provided for in the Genocide Convention. It appears, from a reading of the *travaux préparatoires* of the Genocide Convention, that certain groups, such as political and economic groups, have been excluded from the protected groups, because they are considered to be "mobile groups" which one joins through individual, political commitment. That would seem to suggest *a contrario* that the Convention was presumably intended to cover relatively stable and permanent groups.

57. Therefore, the Chamber holds that in assessing whether a particular group may be considered as protected from the crime of genocide, it will proceed on a case-by-case basis, taking into account both the relevant evidence proffered and the political and cultural context as indicated *supra*....

60. The *dolus specialis* is a key element of an intentional offence, which offence is characterized by a psychological nexus between the physical result and the mental state of the perpetrator. With regard to the issue of determining the offender's specific intent, the Chamber applies the following reasoning, as held in the *Akayesu Judgement*:

> " [...] intent is a mental factor which is difficult, even impossible, to determine. This is the reason why, in the absence of a confession from the accused, his intent can be inferred from a certain number of presumptions of fact. The Chamber is of the view that the genocidal intent inherent in a particular act charged can be inferred from the general context of the perpetration of other culpable acts systematically directed against that same group, whether these acts were committed by the same offender or by others. Other factors, such as the scale of atrocities committed, their general nature, in a region or a country, or furthermore, the fact of deliberately and systematically targeting victims on account of their membership of a particular group, while excluding the members of other groups, can enable the Chamber to infer the genocidal intent of a particular act."

61. Similarly, in the *Kayishema and Ruzindana Judgement*, Trial Chamber II held that:

> "[...] The Chamber finds that the intent can be inferred either from words or deeds and may be determined by a pattern of purposeful action. In particu-

lar, the Chamber considers evidence such as […] the methodical way of planning, the systematic manner of killing. […]"

62. Therefore, the Chamber is of the view that, in practice, intent can be, on a case-by-case basis, inferred from the material evidence submitted to the Chamber, including the evidence which demonstrates a consistent pattern of conduct by the Accused.

The Prosecutor v. Musema
ICTR-96-13-T (27 Jan. 2000)

Before: Judge Lennart Aspegren, Presiding

Judge Laïty Kama

Judge Navanethem Pillay

Conspiracy to Commit Genocide

195.… [T]he Chamber raised the question as to whether an accused could be convicted of both genocide and conspiracy to commit genocide.

196. Under Civil Law systems, if the conspiracy is successful and the substantive offence is consummated, the accused will only be convicted of the substantive offence and not of the conspiracy. Further, once the substantive crime has been accomplished and the criminal conduct of the accused is established, there is no reason to punish the accused for his mere *résolution criminelle* (criminal intent), or even for the preparatory acts committed in furtherance of the substantive offence. Therefore an accused can only be convicted of conspiracy if the substantive offence has not been realized or if the Accused was part of a conspiracy which has been perpetrated by his co-conspirators, without his direct participation.

197. Under Common Law, an accused can, in principle, be convicted of both conspiracy and a substantive offence, in particular, where the objective of the conspiracy extends beyond the offences actually committed. However, this position has incurred much criticism. Thus, for example, according to Don Stuart:

> "The true issue is not whether evidence has been used twice to achieve convictions but rather whether the fundamental nature of the conspiracy offence is best seen […] as purely preventive, incomplete offence, auxiliary offence to the principal offence and having no true independent rationale to exist on its own alongside the full offence. On this view it inexorably follows that once the completed offence has been committed there is no justification for also punishing the incomplete offence."

198. In the instant case, the Chamber has adopted the definition of conspiracy most favourable to Musema, whereby an accused cannot be convicted of both genocide and conspiracy to commit genocide on the basis of the same acts. Such a definition is in keeping with the intention of the Genocide Convention. Indeed, the "*Travaux Préparatoires*" show that the crime of conspiracy was included to punish acts which, in and of themselves, did not constitute genocide. The converse implication of this is that no purpose would be served in convicting an accused, who has already been found guilty of genocide, for conspiracy to commit genocide, on the basis of the same acts.

Notes and Questions

1. Can conspiracy to commit genocide amount to more than an "incomplete offence," involving a greater threat or evil than acts of genocide because of the conspiratorial agree-

ment to commit genocide? Does the evil of acts of genocide relate more to the intent of the perpetrator (*i.e.*, to target persons because they are thought to be members of a certain group(s)) than the acts of killing, etc., that are also elements of the offense and numbers of direct victims? If so, is the evil intent that is connected with acts of genocide magnified when there is a conspiracy as opposed to lone, ad hoc acts of genocide by one perpetrator?

Professor Jens David Ohlin has noted that "conspiracy is an inchoate offence, and a completed genocide need not occur for a conviction to obtain." He adds: "The Trial Chamber's view [in *Musema*] was rejected by other trial chambers in several cases which allowed convictions for both genocide and conspiracy to commit genocide," citing *The Prosecutor v. Nahimana*, ICTR-99-52-T (3 Dec. 2003), at para. 1043; *The Prosecutor v. Niyitegeka*, ICTR-96-14-T (16 May 2003), at para. 502. Jens David Ohlin, *Incitement and Conspiracy to Commit Genocide* in The Genocide Convention: A Commentary 218, 220 (Paola Gaeta ed., 2009).

2. In *The Prosecutor v. Niyitegeka*, ICTR-96-14-T (May 15, 2003), *aff'd* (Appeals Chamber July 9, 2004), the Trial Chamber used circumstantial evidence of intent to find a broadcaster guilty of conspiracy to commit genocide and direct and public incitement of genocide. The Trial Chamber stated that conspiracy to commit genocide is "defined as an agreement between two or more persons to commit the crime of genocide. *Id.* para. 423. *The Prosecutor v. Nahimana, Barayagwiza, and Ngeze*, ICTR-99-52-T (Dec. 3, 2003), found defendants guilty of conspiracy to commit genocide and direct and public incitement to commit genocide on the basis of circumstantial evidence, citing the Trial Chamber in *Niyitegeka*. In *The Prosecutor v. Semanza*, ICTR-97-20-T (May 15, 2003), the Trial Chamber found the defendant guilty of complicity to commit genocide and crimes against humanity.

3. In *Prosecutor v. Nahimana, et al.*, ICTR-99-52-A (Appeals Chamber Judgement, 28 Nov. 2007), the Appeals Chamber held that a concerted agreement may be inferred from the alleged conspirators' conduct, in particular their "concerted or coordinated action," but that the existence of a concerted agreement "must be the only reasonable inference based on the totality of the evidence" for the *actus reus* to be satisfied. The Appeals Chamber, by a 4-1 majority, set aside the convictions of Nahimana, Barayagwizq and Ngeze for conspiracy to commit genocide, finding that the existence of a conspiracy was not the only reasonable inference from the appellants' concerted activities. What is the legal authority for requiring that the existence of a conspiratorial agreement "must be the only reasonable inference" to be drawn for the appellants' concerted action? Does this standard impose an unreasonable burden on the prosecution seeking to convict for conspiracy to commit genocide?

4. Concerning rape or sexual violence as a means of committing genocide, as an *actus reus*, also see Karen Engle, *Feminism and Its (Dis)contents: Criminalizing Wartime Rape in Bosnia and Herzegovina*, 99 Am. J. Int'l L. 778 (2005); Johan D. van der Vyver, *Prosecution and Punishment of the Crime of Genocide*, 23 Fordham Int'l L.J. 286, 300–01, 310–12 (1999), also offering an expanded conceptualization of *dolus directus* versus *indirectus* and *eventualis. Id.* at 307–08. Also recall the extract from *Musema* in Chapter Nine.

5. The ICTY and ICTR have used two approaches to define the notion of a national, ethnic, racial, or religious group: objective and subjective. In accordance with the objective approach, "the group should be regarded as a social fact, a reality regarded as stable and permanent. Individuals are members of the group automatically and irreversibly by way of being born within the group." Agnieszka Szpak, *National, Ethnic, Racial, and Re-*

ligious Groups Protected Against Genocide in the Jurisprudence of the Ad Hoc International Criminal Tribunals, 23 Eur. J. Int'l L. 155, 173 (2012). "The subjective approach presupposes in turn that the group exists as much as its members perceive themselves as belonging to that group (self-identification) or are as such perceived by the perpetrators of the genocide (identification by others)." *Id.* Which is the better approach, the objective or subjective? Should a hybrid objective/subjective approach be used to identify whether the victims were members of a protected group?

6. Concerning the "extension" of groups listed in Article II of the Convention in *Akayesu* and *Rutaganda* and claims that genocide under customary international law includes a broader reach with respect to targeted groups, *see, e.g.,* van der Vyver, *supra* at 304–06, 318 ("jurisprudence of international tribunals exceeds the bounds ... by extending the protection afforded to target groups to include all institutional groups (those whose membership are not exclusively determined by voluntary entry into and exit from the group), such as gay and lesbian communities."), 355 ("provided only that one is ... born into the social group"); Schabas, *supra* at 1713 (The Darfur Commission Report "went too far in suggesting that the interpretive expansion of the four groups enumerated in the Genocide Convention 'has become part and parcel of international customary law.'"). The Trial Chamber in *Akayesu* declared that the prohibited targetings reach "'stable' groups, constituting in a permanent fashion and membership ... which is determined by birth, with the exclusion of the more 'mobile' groups which one joins through individual voluntary commitment, such as political and economic groups." ICTR-96-4-T, para. 510 (2 Sept. 1998). Recall para. 56 in *Rutaganda, supra.*

Should the crime of genocide punish killings committed with the "intent to destroy in whole or part" "stable" groups, but exempt from coverage killings committed with the same intent directed against "mobile" groups? What is the justification for this distinction? How do you determine whether someone is a member of a "stable" or "mobile" group? Is gender a "stable" group? Should genocide be extended to include gender killings committed with genocidal intent?

7. The 2005 Darfur Commission of Inquiry Report recognized that "various tribes that have been the object of attacks and killings ... do not appear to make up ethnic groups distinct from the ethnic group to which persons or militias that attack them belong. They speak the same language (Arabic) and embrace the same religion (Muslim)" and "objectively the two sets of persons at issue do not make up two distinct protected groups," but there has grown "a self-perception of two distinct groups," one "African" and the other "Arab" and what is important in this context is that the perpetrator and victim "see each other and themselves as constituting distinct groups." See Report, *supra* at paras. 508–509, 511. The Report adds: "What matters from a legal point of view is the fact that the interpretive expansion of one of the elements of the notion of genocide (the concept of protected group) by the two International Criminal Tribunals is in line with the object and scope of the rules on genocide (to protect from deliberate annihilation essentially stable and permanent human groups), ... which are no longer identified only by their objective connotations but also on the basis of the subjective perceptions of members of groups." *Id.* para. 501.

What is critical under the Convention, that targetings actually be made against the types of human groups listed in Article II or that there be a genocidal intent to destroy such a human group in whole or in part? Could a mistaken genocidal targeting constitute genocide or merely an attempt? Note that the Darfur Commission Report accepts both an expansion of groups to include "stable and permanent human groups" and a subjective approach to genocidal targetings based primarily on intent as opposed to objective features of context. Professor Schabas is critical of both of these approaches, but notes acceptance of the "subjective approach" in other ICTR cases. Schabas, *supra* at 1712–14, citing *The Prosecutor v. Semanza*, ICTR-97-20-T (Judgement and Sentence, May 15, 2003), para. 317; *The Prosecutor v. Kajelijeli*, ICTR-98-44A-T (Judgment and Sentence, Dec. 1, 2003), para. 811. Which approaches do you prefer?

8. Concerning claims that the reach of customary prohibitions of genocide include targetings of political groups as such, *see, e.g.*, U.N. G.A. Res. 96(I) (1946); Matthew Lippman, *The Convention on the Prevention and Punishment of the Crime of Genocide: Fifty Years Later*, 15 Ariz. J. Int'l & Comp. L. 415, 464 (1998); Beth Van Schaack, *The Crime of Political Genocide: Repairing the Genocide Convention's Blind Spot*, 106 Yale L.J. 2259 (1997); van der Vyver, *supra* at 355; materials in Section 3. Recall from Chapter Nine that political "persecution" can constitute a crime against humanity.

9. In *The Prosecutor v. Rwamakuba*, ICTR-98-44-AR72.4 (Appeals Chamber, Decision on Interlocutory Appeal Regarding Application of Joint Criminal Enterprise to the Crime of Genocide, 22 Oct. 2004), the Appeals Chamber found that customary international law prior to 1992 criminalized the intentional participation in a common plan to commit genocide and recognized application of the doctrine of joint criminal enterprise to the crime of genocide, noting that the doctrine of "joint criminal enterprise does not create a separate crime of participating through the means identified in that doctrine ... [and] is only concerned with the mode of liability of committing crimes within the jurisdiction of the Tribunal." *Id.* paras. 14, 30–31. The drafting history of the Convention, the Chamber declared, makes "clear that the Contracting Parties sought to ensure that all persons involved in a campaign to commit genocide, at whatever stage, were subject to criminal responsibility ... [although i]t is not clear whether the drafters viewed criminal responsibility through intentional participation in a common plan as a form of commission of genocide, complicity in genocide, or conspiracy to commit genocide." *Id.* paras. 26–28.

10. In April, 2001, four Rwandan nationals (Messrs. Ntezimana and Higaniro, and two nuns, Mukangango, and Mukabutera) appeared before Belgium's Cour d'Assises. They were accused of genocide and crimes against humanity with respect to several homicides in the Butare region of Rwanda. It was the first prosecution under a 1993 Belgian law allowing prosecution for war crimes, human rights violations, and related crimes. The two nuns were found guilty in 2001. In June, 2005, two Rwandans (Nzabonimana and Ndashyikirwa) were found guilty of war crimes and murder in connection with genocidal massacres. The Belgian law was amended in 2003, limiting jurisdiction to cases involving Belgian citizens and residents.

11. Regarding domestic prosecutions, see also Wolfgang Kaleck, *From Pinochet to Rumsfeld: Universal Jurisdiction in Europe 1998-2008*, 30 Mich. J. Int'l L. 927, 932–33 (four convicted in Belgium), 935 (Belgian conviction of Rwandan Major), 938 (French cases), 939 (Swiss conviction and some cases transferred to the ICTR), 944 (case in the Netherlands), 946–47 (in Denmark, case against former official dropped because of insufficient evidence), 948 (investigations in Norway), 957 (investigations in Spain) (2009); Máximo Langer, *The Diplomacy of Universal Jurisdiction: The Political Branches and the Transnational Prosecution of International Crimes*, 105 Am. J. Int'l L. 1, 8–9, 13–14 (current proceedings in Germany), 22–23 (pending cases in France), 28, 32 (convictions in Belgium), 42 (trials in Belgium, Canada, the Netherlands, and Switzerland) (2011); BBC, Rwandan Genocide Conviction, May 23, 2009 (conviction in Canada), available at http://www.bbc.co.uk/worldservice/africa/2009/05/090523_rwanda_canada.shtml; Edmund Kagire, *Another Genocide Fugitive Arrested in Belgium*, N.Y. Times, Apr. 21, 2011; Matti Huuhtanen, *Ex-Pastor Jailed for Life in Finland Genocide Conviction*, The Star,

June 11, 2010; Jordan J. Paust, *Genocide in Rwanda, State Responsibility to Prosecute or Extradite, and Nonimmunity for Heads of State and Other Public Officials*, 34 Hous. J. Int'l L. 57, 58–62 (2011) (also addressing prosecutions in Rwanda).

B. Prosecutions Before the International Criminal Tribunal for Former Yugoslavia

Crimes against humanity, including genocide, were committed on a vast scale in Rwanda in 1994 and have led to prosecutions within Rwanda and in an International Criminal Tribunal for Rwanda (ICTR) that was created by the United Nations Security Council in November 1994. By August 2011, there had been eighty-two cases before the ICTR that resulted in fifty-seven convictions or cases pending appeal, one case awaiting trial, ten cases in progress, eight acquittals, two detainees released, two detainees deceased before judgment, and two cases transferred to national jurisdiction in France.

Prosecutions of genocide before the Trial Chambers of the ICTY demonstrated a problem concerning proof beyond a reasonable doubt of genocidal intent to destroy a group in whole or in part when circumstantial evidence of such an intent is utilized.

In *The Prosecutor v. Jelisic*, IT-95-10-T (Trial Chamber, Dec. 14, 1999 and Appeals Chamber, Judgment, July 5, 2001), Goran Jelisic, a low ranking policeman who tortured and killed detainees in concentration camps in 1992 in Brcko, was convicted of 31 counts of war crimes and crimes against humanity but acquitted of genocide. The Trial Chamber ruled that there was insufficient evidence to establish beyond a reasonable doubt that he had the requisite intent to destroy a group of Muslims in whole or in part, although he chose victims because they belonged to such a group. The Trial Chamber stressed that the prosecution had not proven that his conduct was engaged in as part of a larger plan to destroy such a group and that the number of direct victims was not a substantial number of the overall group, which presumably would aid in the use of circumstantial evidence to prove genocidal intent.

In *The Prosecutor v. Sikirica*, IT-95-8-T (Trial Chamber, Judgment on Defence Motions to Acquit, Sept. 3, 2001), the same problem of proof was evident. Dusko Sikirica was the commander of a concentration camp at Prijedor where hundreds of Bosnian Muslims and Croats were tortured and killed. The Trial Chamber ruled that the prosecution had not proven genocidal intent beyond a reasonable doubt when the existence of large numbers of victims might have been the result of random killings as opposed to genocidal killings, especially when they were not simply exterminated soon after capture, the victims did not seem to have any special significance to their community except that most were young men who could be used for military service, and the Bosnian Serb leaders in the area had transferred women, children and elderly Muslims and Croats out of the area instead of killing them.

In *The Prosecutor v. Krstic*, IT-98-33-T (Trial Chamber, Aug. 2, 2001), the Trial Chamber found General Radislav Krstic guilty of genocide during his Bosnian Serb Drina Corps capture of Srebrenica in 1995 where thousands were massacred. General Krstic was also a member of the Bosnian Serb Army's Main Staff. The Trial Chamber also found him guilty of persecution, cruel and inhumane treatment, terrorizing a civilian population, forcible transfer of persons, and destruction of property as crimes against humanity, as well as murder as a war crime. *See, e.g.*, Mark Drumbl, *ICTY Authenticates Genocide at Srebrenica and Convicts for Aiding and Abetting*, 5 Melbourne J. Int'l L. 434, 435 n.5 (2004). The prosecution proved that genocide had occurred in the area of Srebrenica, since the widespread and systematic killings could not have occurred without a genocidal plan even though women and children had been transferred out of the area. Moreover, the Trial Chamber used a "joint criminal enterprise" aspect of criminal responsibility that had been established in *The Prosecutor v. Tadic*, IT-94-1-A and IT-94-1-A*bis* (Jan. 26, 2000), whereby guilt can be established when one knowingly participates in acts to advance the goal of a joint criminal enterprise (which "embraces actions perpetrated by a collectivity of persons in furtherance of a common criminal design." *Tadic* at paras. 193, 220). However, his conviction was reduced by the Appeals Chamber from genocide and complicity in genocide (under Article 4(3)(e) of the Statute of the ICTY) to aiding and abetting genocide under Article 7(1) of the Statute. The Appeals Chamber found that evidence supported the conclusion that General Krstic was aware of the intent to commit genocide by troops under his command, but that this alone did not prove that he had a genocidal intent. IT-98-33-A, at paras. 129, 134, 140 (Appeals Chamber, judgment, Apr. 19, 2004). Nonetheless, at a later time he became clearly involved as an aider and abettor of genocide committed by others and he participated in a criminal enterprise in that fashion, *i.e.*, he knowingly aided others who had genocidal intent as they engaged in acts of genocide.

Confusion exists with respect to the statement of the Appeals Chamber in *Krstic* that "[i]t is well established that where a conviction of genocide relies on the intent to destroy a protected group 'in part,' the part must be a substantial part of that group," since there is no such requirement in the Genocide Convention or in the Statute of the ICTY. Was this a statement as to elements of the crime or merely a statement concerning use of circumstantial evidence as proof of genocidal intent? Adding to the confusion, the Appeals Chamber set forth circumstantially-based elements of a supposed "substantial" part requirement, including the number of persons targeted, the prominence of the targeted part (especially men of military age) within the overall group, the area of targetings, the likely impact of the targetings on the survival of the group (*e.g.*, killing of Muslim men of military age could have "severe procreative implications for the Srebrenica Muslim community, potentially consigning the community to extinction." Moreover, the killing of more than 7,000 men of military age was, "assuredly, a physical destruction [in part], and given the scope of the killings, the Trial Chamber could legitimately draw the inference that their extermination was motivated by genocidal intent." *Id.* para. 27. *See also* Trial Chamber, Judgment, para. 91: "the elimination of virtually all the men [from Srebrenica] has made it almost impossible for the Bosnian Muslim women ... to successfully re-establish their lives"), and the fact that Muslim women and children were removed because their "transfer completed the removal of all Bosnian Muslims from Srebrenica, thereby eliminating even the residual possibility that the Muslim community in the area could reconstitute itself." The Appeals Chamber "found a causal connection between the murder of 7,000 men and the intent to destroy the Srebrenica Bosnian Muslims; it then found a further causal link between the intended destruction of the Srebrenica Bosnian Muslims as a targeted group and the intended destruction of the protected group, namely Bosnian Muslims as a whole." Drumbl, *supra* at 440.

The Appeals Chamber also ruled that the existence of a plan or policy to commit genocide is not required, although if it exists such a plan or policy can aid in recognition of genocidal intent of a perpetrator or aid in demonstrating that an attack on a civilian population was widespread or systematic. *Id.* para. 223.

In *The Prosecutor v. Blagojevic & Jokic*, IT-02-60-T (Trial Chamber, Judgment, Jan. 17, 2005), the Trial Chamber found Colonel Vidoje Blagojevic, a commander of an infantry brigade within the Bosnian Serb Drina Coprs, guilty of complicity in genocide by aiding and abetting genocide within the meaning of Articles 4(3)(e) and 7(1) of the Statute of the ICTY. Aiding and abetting genocide occurs when the person (1) carried out an act which consisted of practical assistance, encouragement or moral support to the principal that had a "substantial effect" on the commission of the crime, (2) had knowledge that his or her own acts assisted in the commission of the specific crime by the principle offender, and (3) knew that the crime was committed with specific intent. *Id.* para. 782.

Importantly, "forcible transfer of a population" can constitute an act or method of genocide—in particular, the term "destroy" "can encompass the forcible transfer of a population." *Id.* para. 665. *Compare* Article II(e) of the Convention. The Trial Chamber added: "the physical or biological destruction of a group is not necessarily the death of the group members. While killing large numbers of a group may be the most direct means of destroying a group, other acts or series of acts, can also lead to the destruction of the group. A group is comprised of its individuals, but also of its history, traditions, the relationship between its members, the relationship with other groups, the relationship with the land. The Trial Chamber finds that the physical or biological destruction of the group is the likely outcome of a forcible transfer of the population when this transfer is conducted in such a way that the group can no longer constitute itself—particularly when it involves the separation of its members.... [this] reasoning and conclusion are not an argument for the recognition of cultural genocide, but rather an attempt to clarify the meaning of physical or biological destruction." *Id.* para. 666. "The forcible transfer of the women, children and elderly is a manifestation of the specific intent to rid the Srebrenica enclave of its Bosnian Muslim population. The manner in which the transfer was carried out—through force and coercion, by not registering those who were transferred, by burning the houses of some of the people, sending the clear message that they had nothing to return to, and significantly, through its targeting of literally the entire Bosnian Muslim population of Srebrenica, including the elderly and children—clearly indicates that it was a means to eradicate the Bosnian Muslim population from the territory where they had lived." *Id.* para. 675. "Bosnian Serb forces not only knew that the combination of the killings of the men with the forcible transfer of the women, children and elderly, would inevitably result in the physical disappearance of the Bosnian Muslim population of Srebrenica, but clearly intended through these acts to physically destroy this group." *Id.* para. 677.

In *The Prosecutor v. Brdanin*, IT-99-36-T(Trial Chamber, Judgment, Sept. 1, 2004), the Bosnian Serb entity's regional Vice President and later President in the region of Krajina was charged with genocidal deaths of Bosnian Muslims and Croats. Although the Trial Chamber did not accept the charges of genocide (with a high *mens rea* requirement) based on a joint criminal enterprise (with a lower standard of reasonable foreseeability of the criminal acts of others), the Appeals Chamber reversed this decision because, although Brdanin intended that Bosnian Muslims and Croats would be forcibly transferred out of the region, he was also responsible for resultant genocide that was a foreseeable outcome of the criminal enterprise of forced removal. On remand, the Trial Chamber (9 Sept. 2004) found him not guilty of genocide because circumstantial evidence of genocidal intent must provide an inference that could be the only reasonable inference under the circumstances. In context, the forced removal of persons did not support an intent to destroy the group in whole or in part and, supposedly, the acts or methods of genocide listed in the Convention "prohibit only the physical or biological destruction of a human group."

In *The Prosecutor v. Plavsic*, IT-00-39&40/1-S (Sentencing Judgment, Feb. 27, 2003), former President of the Bosnian Serb group Biljana Plavsic plead guilty to one count of persecutions on political, racial, and religious grounds, a crime against humanity, in ex-change for dismissal of a charge of genocide.

Notes and Questions

1. Was the Trial Chamber in *Brdanin* correct that only acts involving "physical or bi-ological destruction" are covered in Article II(a)–(e) of the Convention? Is "bodily ... harm" "destruction"?, Is "mental harm"?, Are "conditions of life"?, Is "forcibly transfer-ring children"? Moreover, is the intent to destroy through these and other acts or meth-ods of primary significance?

2. Professor Schabas has written that ICTY cases have recognized "that an individual, acting alone, may commit genocide." Schabas, *supra* at 1710, citing *Jelisic*, Trial Chamber Judgment at para. 100; Appeals Chamber Judgment, at para. 48. However, he prefers that a "state plan or policy" be "an essential ingredient of the crime." *Id.* at 1711. Do you agree? Again, is the primary evil involved a genocidal intent by the perpetrator or numbers or a state plan (which does not appear in the Convention as a limitation)?

3. The ICTR and ICTY have consistently held that the existence of a state policy is not an element of genocide. *See Prosecutor v. Popovic, et al.*, IT-05-88-T (Trial Chamber Judge-ment, 10 June 2010) (citing cases); *Prosecutor v. Simba*, ICTR-01-76-A (Appeals Chamber Judgement, 18 March 2010). *See also Prosecutor v. Nchamihigo*, (ICTR-2001-63-A (Appeals Chamber Judgement, 18 March 2010) (a high-level plan is not required for genocide).

Section 2
Application in Bangladesh

Paust & Blaustein, *War Crimes Jurisdiction and Due Process: The Bangladesh Experience*
11 Vand. J. Trans. L. 1 (1978)

Genocide

Since Pakistan had ratified the Genocide Convention prior to the period during which the conduct in violation of the Convention is alleged to have occurred, it clearly applied to the accused. Furthermore, since article 1 of the Genocide Convention states that "geno-cide, whether committed in time of peace or in time of war, is a crime under interna-tional law," it clearly applies during both peace and war times....

Article 6 requires that persons charged with genocide be tried "by a competent tri-bunal of the State in the territory of which the act was committed, or by such international penal tribunal as may have jurisdiction." It seems reasonable to interpret this provision as granting jurisdictional competence to the new government with authority over the same territory in which the acts were committed.[7] Furthermore, there is no stated re-striction as to when such a state should have come into legal existence, and Bangladesh is "the State in the territory of which the act was committed."

---

7. *See generally* Genocide Convention, *supra*, preamble; *id.* art. 1. Nothing in article 6 states that persons charged with genocide *must* be tried in such a state and no other.

The United Nations General Assembly has declared that the crime of genocide as defined in the 1948 Genocide Convention also constitutes a crime against humanity, "even if such acts do not constitute a violation of the domestic law of the country in which they were committed."[8] Thus, Bangladesh has jurisdiction over such acts when they are committed in connection with either crimes against peace or war crimes, even though there is no implementing legislation in Pakistan or in Bangladesh. Two days after the surrender of Pakistani troops to India and Bangladesh the General Assembly additionally affirmed "that refusal by States to co-operate in the arrest, extradition, trial and punishment of persons guilty of war crimes and crimes against humanity is contrary to the purposes and principles of the Charter of the United Nations and to generally recognized norms of international law."[9]

It is also relevant that the early code of Bluntschli on the law of war contained the following declaration:

> Inter-necine wars and wars of annihilation against nations or races susceptible of existence and culture constitute a violation of the law of war.
>
> 1. The war of extermination against the idolatrous inhabitants of Palestine, which the ancient Jews regarded as a holy duty, is today condemned as an act of barbarity, and can no longer be praised as an example worthy of imitation.[10]

There is ample evidence of a customary, inherited expectation that genocide was actually prohibited as a violation of the customary international law of war.[11]

Notes

1. Recall the definition of genocide in the 1973 Bangladesh International Crimes Act (see Chapter Six, Section 6). What was added?

2. Concerning the fact that jurisdiction over genocide under customary international law is not territorially limited, also see *Case Concerning Application of the Convention on the Prevention and Prosecution of the Crime of Genocide* (Bosnia and Herzegovina v. Yugoslavia), 1996 I.C.J. 595, 616; *Attorney General of Israel v. Eichmann*, 36 INT'L L. RPT.

---

8. G.A. Res. 2391, at 3 (formally adopting the Convention on the Non-Applicability of Statutory Limitations to War Crimes and Crimes Against Humanity (in force Nov. 11, 1970). *See also* G.A. Res. 2583, 24 U.N. GAOR (1834th plen. mtg.), U.N. Doc. A/RES/2583 (1970); Miller, *The Convention on the Non-Applicability of Statutory Limitations to War Crimes and Crimes Against Humanity*, 65 AM. J. INT'L L. 476 (1971).

9. G.A. Res. 2840, at 2. Those purposes and principles would include the obligation to take action to assure "universal respect for, and observance of," international human rights and fundamental freedoms (including human rights in times of armed conflict). *See* U.N. CHARTER, preamble; *id.* arts. 1(2)–(3), 55(c), 56.

10. BLUNTSCHLI, at 15. The current example of such fanatically barbarous misdeeds can come under the heading of a terroristic *Jihad* or holy war.

11. See G.A. Res. 96, *supra*; Lemkin, *Genocide as a Crime Under International Law*, 41 AM. J. INT'L L. 145 (1947); Schwelb, *Crimes Against Humanity*, 23 BRIT. Y.B. INT'L L. 178 (1946). *Cf.* Kunz, *The Genocide Convention*, 43 AM. J. INT'L L. 738 (1948) (considering the effect of the Convention on prior law). For authoritative comment on the customary nature of the crime of genocide, see *Attorney General of Israel v. Eichmann*, 36 INT'L L. REP. 18, §§ 17–20. ("According to an Advisory Opinion of the International Court of Justice of May 28, 1951, given at the request of the United Nations General Assembly on the question of the reservations to the convention, the principles inherent in the convention are acknowledged by the civilized nations as binding on the country even without conventional obligation").

18, 39 (Dist. Ct. Jerusalem 1961) ("The reference of Article 6 to territorial jurisdiction, apart from the jurisdiction of the non-existent international tribunal, is not exhaustive. Every sovereign State may exercise its existing powers within the limits of customary international law...."); van der Vyver, *supra* at 287, 319–20; Chapter Two, Section 3; Chapter Three, Section 1.

Section 3
Genocide and Politicide

Paust, *Aggression Against Authority: The Crime of Oppression, Politicide and Other Crimes Against Human Rights*
18 Case W. Res. J. Int'l L. 283, 292–94, 304–05 (1986)

Genocide and Political Oppression

Acts of genocide directed against "a national, ethnical, racial or religious group, as such,"[1] may be motivated by, or result in, the political oppression of members of such groups and impermissibly interfere with the process of authority and self-determination. To that extent, the customary prohibition of genocide, with concomitant universal enforcement jurisdiction, can be useful in opposing aggression against authority and political oppression. Additionally, it does not matter that such attacks happen to coincide with attacks on "political" groups.[2] Attacks on the groups specified in the treaty and which are motivated by, or result in, political oppression of such persons can be criminally sanctioned. Moreover, today it can be recognized that whether or not attacks on "political" groups as such involve acts of genocide, such attacks are necessarily violative of the precept of self-determination and fundamental human rights. As such, they constitute aggression against

---

1. I share the viewpoint that the prohibition of genocide now at least is customary. *See* Case Concerning The Barcelona Traction, Light and Power Co., Ltd., (Belgium v. Spain), 1970 I.C.J. 3, paras. 33–34 (Judgment of February 5); G.A. Res. 96, 1 U.N. GAOR at 189, U.N. Doc. A/64/Add. 1 (1946) *reprinted in* [1946–1947] U.N. Y.B. 255 (unanimously affirming that genocide already "is a crime under international law"); Genocide Convention, *supra,* at preamble ("genocide *is* a crime under international law"), art. 1 ("The Contracting parties confirm that genocide ... *is* a crime under international law") (emphasis added); M. McDougal, H. Lasswell & L. Chen, Human Rights and World Public Order 215, 355–56 (1980); Edwards, *Contributions of the Genocide Convention to the Development of International Law,* 8 Ohio N.U.L. Rev. 300, 305–06, 308–09 (1981); Paust & Blaustein, *supra* at 22–23, ns. 76–77; Comment, *The United States and the 1948 Genocide Convention,* 16 Harv. Int'l L.J. 683 (1975). *But see* Starkman, *Genocide and International Law: Is There a Cause of Action?,* 8 A.S.I.L.S. Int'l L.J. 1, 13–21 (1984). The new Restatement also adopts this view. Restatement of the Foreign Relations Law of the United States §404 and Reporters' Note 1 thereto, §702(a) and Comment d and Reporters' Note 3 thereto (3 ed. 1987).

2. *See* M. C. Bassiouni, International Criminal Law — A Draft International Criminal Code 72 (1980); P. Drost, II The Crime of State: Genocide 62 (1959); L. Sohn & T. Buergenthal, International Protection of Human Rights 929 (1973). Although the United States favored inclusion of an express category of "political" group within article 2 of the Genocide Convention, and such was included in the 1946 General Assembly resolution on Genocide, such a category was dropped later in order to gain a quicker and more widespread ratification. Comment, *Genocide: A Commentary on the Convention,* 58 Yale L.J. 1142, 1145 (1949). Early in 1986, the U.S. Senate voted 92 to 1 in favor of a resolution directing the President to seek renewed negotiations concerning inclusion of political groups within those specified in the Genocide Convention. *See* Washington Weekly Report, vol. 12, No. 7, at 3 (UNA-USA Feb. 21, 1986).

authority, a violation of the U.N. Charter, the crime of oppression, and what the International Law Commission has recognized as a crime against self-determination. To the extent that violations of relevant human rights are criminally sanctioned, any gap in coverage by the Genocide Convention will prove to be of little import.

Nevertheless, it may be important to emphasize these recognitions in a new international instrument, if only to further sanctify criminal proscription and to provide additional guidance concerning the contours of present prohibitions. For that purpose, a draft Convention on the Prevention and Punishment of the Crime of Politicide is offered in the annex to this article [see the Draft Convention, in Chapter Seven, Section 3]. Politicide, as a useful rallying term, can encompass more odious forms of aggression against authority, the crime against self-determination, the crime of political oppression, and so forth, while providing a logically related focus in supplementation of the Genocide Convention.

Hurst Hannum, *International Law and Cambodian Genocide: The Sounds of Silence*
11 HUMAN RIGHTS Q. 82 (1989)*

This article examines the feasibility of bringing an application to the International Court of Justice, under the terms of Article IX of the Genocide Convention or Article 36 of the Statute of the Court. It concludes that such an application would be legally feasible and politically desirable and that the failure of any state thus far to institute proceedings before the Court is an indefensible abdication of international responsibility.

The first part of this article considers in some detail the factual evidence of genocide in Cambodia, countering the view expressed by some that, however deplorable they might have been, the Khmer Rouge killings were not technically "genocide." The second part outlines the elements of a successful application under the Genocide Convention, including questions of the Court's jurisdiction, the existence of a dispute between an applicant state and Democratic Kampuchea and whether the killings of Cambodians themselves by the Khmer Rouge leadership constitute genocide against a "national" group within the meaning of the convention. The third part considers the application under the Court's compulsory jurisdiction, charging Democratic Kampuchea with violations of customary international law and crimes against humanity, *i.e.*, mass arbitrary killings and widespread systematic torture....

Killings

Three distinct categories of deliberate killings occurred in Democratic Kampuchea: waves of massacres; individual executions following imprisonment and interrogation; and arbitrary and summary executions. To an extent, similar patterns can be seen in all three methods of state-sponsored murder, and all were directed to the same goal: the relentless purge from the Cambodian nation of elements deemed tainted and corrupted.

The first groups to be identified, isolated, and executed were the officer corps and the defeated army, the higher ranking civil servants of the previous two regimes, and, in some instances, their entire families. In 1976, corresponding to what the Khmer Rouge identified as an intensification of the class struggle, the more highly educated professional classes were targeted. Later, to advance the progress of the new social order, the Khmer Rouge leadership decided to purge the Cambodian nation of those they described as hav-

---

* Reprinted by the permission of the Johns Hopkins University Press © 1989.

ing lingering attitudes of "privateness" or "propertyism"—attitudes that should have disappeared with the abolition of markets and private property and the dissolution of the capitalist classes. This was the theoretical foundation for waves of massacres directed against Khmer Rouge cadres and elements of the Cambodian peasantry.

The most thoroughly documented regional purge occurred in the Eastern Zone in 1978, in which an estimated minimum of 100,000 people were executed in a six-month period. While some of those executed in the Eastern Zone belonged to a recognizable political group judged disloyal by Democratic Kampuchea's central leadership, far larger numbers of people were killed because they were deemed to be tainted merely by having lived under the jurisdiction of the presumedly disloyal political faction. The overwhelming number of those massacred were simple peasants or urban evacuees without any particular political affiliation, who were not members of any "political group" in the common sense meaning of those words.

In addition to those destroyed in the expanding massacres directed against successive segments of the populace, scores of thousands were individually executed, usually following interrogation and torture, in a nationwide system of prison-execution centers. The apex of this nationwide prison-execution system was S.21, the central prison-execution facility in Phnom Penh. S.21, now known as "Tuol Sleng," was an extermination facility operating under the direct control of Democratic Kampuchea's highest leadership. Only seven prisoners, whose skills were useful to the prison authorities and the leadership, are known to have survived; twenty thousand died. One of the last acts of the Democratic Kampuchea prison officials before fleeing in January 1979 was to slit the throats of the prisoners then chained to their interrogation cots; when Tuol Sleng was discovered, pools of blood were still coagulating beneath their bodies.

Execution schedules recorded each day's work, and the highest daily figure was 582 people executed on 27 May 1978. The composition of a particular day's execution schedule usually reflected the mix of prisoners at that time, but particular days were occasionally reserved to kill certain types of prisoners. For example, 1 July 1977 was devoted to executing the imprisoned wives and children of those killed previously; 22 July 1977 was devoted to "smashing" people from the Ministry of Public Works. Because the victims' names are identified by occupation and place of arrest, the daily arrest and execution schedules make it possible to reconstruct the patterns of killings by Democratic Kampuchea, as waves of victims washed through the prison to their deaths....

Finally, refugee and survivor accounts contain innumerable references to killings by lower-level Khmer Rouge cadres, often intended as punishments for minor infractions or "bad" attitudes, which served to ensure Khmer Rouge control through indiscriminate terror. As a Khmer Rouge slogan noted, *tuk meun chamnenh, dak meun khat*: "there is no profit in keeping them; there is no loss in removing them." These arbitrary and summary executions also are "killings" within the meaning of Article II(a) of the Genocide Convention and contributed to the partial destruction of the Cambodian national group itself....

... There is no statute of limitations on crimes against humanity, including genocide. So long as those persons responsible for planning, directing or committing acts of genocide have not been punished, "whether they are constitutionally responsible rulers, public officials, or private individuals," Democratic Kampuchea is in violation of its obligations under Article IV....

The meaning of the phrase "national group"

The fundamental rule of treaty interpretation is set forth in Article 31 of the Vienna Convention of the Law of Treaties:

A treaty shall be interpreted in good faith in accordance with the ordinary meaning to be given to the terms of the treaty in their context and in the light of its object and purpose....

The first clause of Article II of the Genocide Convention identifies "a national, ethnical, racial or religious group" as within its scope. Applying the principles set forth immediately above, it is clear that a national group such as the Khmer people of Kampuchea, falls within the ambit of Article II of the Genocide Convention, whether or not such a group constitutes a majority or a minority within a particular state.

That the Khmer people decimated by the government of Democratic Kampuchea constitutes a "national group" within any generally accepted definition of that term cannot be doubted. The Khmers have a distinct language and a political and social history that spans centuries, and they are ethnically distinct from neighboring peoples. Whether or not they also constitute an ethnical or racial group within the meaning of Article II does not detract from their status as a national group as well. Indeed, under the injunction by the Court in the *Anglo-Iranian Oil Co.* case, the word "national" must be given a different meaning than the other adjectives utilized in the text, or it would be merely superfluous.

The term "national minority" was widely understood by the drafters of the Convention, as demonstrated in greater detail below, and the absence of the term "minority" from the Convention must be presumed to be intentional. Any interpretation which seeks to equate "national group" with "national minority" is inconsistent with the plain language chosen by the drafters and cannot be sustained....

If the Khmer national group falls within the ambit of Article II even when it constitutes a majority in a given state, the question then becomes whether the group allegedly committing or tolerating genocide must be nationally, ethnically, racially, or religiously distinct from its intended victims. A search of the text of the treaty reveals no such requirement; indeed, there is no reference whatsoever to the nature of the "persons" liable for punishment under Articles IV, V, and VI, nor is there any limitation on the "state" responsible for implementing the treaty. As stated in the 1985 United Nations *Study on Genocide*, "[i]t is noteworthy that the definition [of genocide] does not exclude cases where the victims are part of the violator's own group." ...

A careful survey of the preparatory work of the Genocide Convention—including the meetings of the Ad Hoc Committee on Genocide established by the Economic and Social Council in 1948, and the debates in the Economic and Social Council, Sixth Committee of the General Assembly, and the General Assembly itself—reveals no specific vote or consensual decision with respect to the term "national". There are, however, general references to the terms "national" and "ethnical" and to the phrase "as such," as well as discussions of cultural genocide and general consideration of those persons who should be protected under the Convention....

The concept of cultural genocide was ultimately excluded from the Convention by a vote of the Sixth Committee. While there were undoubtedly many different reasons for the votes of various delegations, the identification of "cultural genocide" with "minority" rights by some delegations supports the interpretation put forward herein that the concept of "national" and other groups is not limited to minorities....

The debate over a Swedish amendment to add the term "ethnical" to the list of protected groups supports a broad interpretation of the word "national." As noted by the Soviet representative, "An ethnical group was a sub-group of a national group; it was a smaller collectivity than the nation, but one whose existence could nevertheless be of benefit to humanity." Some believed that there was no difference between an "ethnical" and a "national" group or between "ethnical" and "racial" group. Nevertheless, "ethnical" was added to the list of protected groups by narrow margin.

Despite a request early in the debate on Article II for a definition of the term "national group," the full committee did not judge further definition to be required. In the context of the present application, however, nothing in the *travaux préparatoires* is contrary to or incompatible with the proposition that the Khmer people of Kampuchea constitute a national group within the meaning of Article II....

The contention that groups such as the Buddhist monkhood or Cham were primarily political groups and that their destruction therefore is not covered by the Genocide Convention cannot be sustained. Even if political motives coincided with the hatred of religion, "foreigners," and ideological deviance, the targeted destruction of religious and ethnical groups by the government of Democratic Kampuchea is precisely the kind of "odious scourge" the Genocide Convention is intended to prohibit.

With respect to the Khmer national group, there was obviously no intention on the part of the Democratic Kampuchean authorities to destroy the Khmer group "in whole," as this would have implied their own demise. Nevertheless, there was a clear intent to destroy the national group "in part," which becomes apparent when one analyses the scope and scale of the destruction visited upon the Khmer people by the Khmer Rouge government. The wholesale massacres of families, villages, and other subgroups of the Khmer people provide persuasive evidence that the aim of the Democratic Kampuchean government was not merely the elimination of political opponents or reform of the socioeconomic structure of the country, but rather the wholesale remaking of the Khmer people according to a deliberately imposed vision. If the Genocide Convention means anything, it means that a state cannot destroy those parts of its own people that do not conform sufficiently to the government's own view of social, racial, or ideological purity....

In the only official analysis under UN auspices of the massive human rights violations in Democratic Kampuchea, the Chairman of the UN Sub-Commission on Prevention of Discrimination and Protection of Minorities concluded that the destruction of Kampuchean society by the government of Democratic Kampuchea amounted to "nothing less than auto-genocide." While "auto-genocide" as a term has no legal status, the terrible reality it describes is what the Genocide Convention defines as the destruction "in part" of a "national group"....

It is difficult to imagine a more persuasive "series of facts linked together" than the evidence of murder and partial destruction of religious and ethnical groups and the Cambodian national group itself than is presently available with respect to the period of Khmer Rouge rule in Democratic Kampuchea from 1975 to 1979. The single conclusion required by this evidence is that Democratic Kampuchea has violated its obligations under the Genocide Convention not to commit or tolerate genocide.

Questions

1. Do you agree with Professor Hannum? What types of persons were targets and why were they targeted?

2. Is "auto-genocide" covered by Article II? Whether or not it is, would it constitute a crime against humanity?

3. What was the probable intent of perpetrators? Who was targeted and why? Were Cambodians or Khmer people targeted because they were Cambodians or Khmer people as such? What does Article II of the Genocide Convention require?

4. If Spanish nationals were targeted by the Pinochet regime in Chile because they were Spanish, would such targetings constitute genocide? What if they were targeted because they were "liberal"?

5. Should the Genocide Convention be amended to include gender-based targeting as such? See J. Paust, *Women and International Criminal Law Instruments and Processes*, in 2 WOMEN AND INTERNATIONAL HUMAN RIGHTS LAW 349 (Kelly D. Askin & Dorean M. Koenig eds. 2000); Berta Esperanza Hernandez-Truyol, *Women's Rights as Human Rights — Rules, Realities and the Role of Culture: A Formula for Reform*, 21 BROOK. J. INT'L L. 605, 649–50 (1996).

6. Consider also the following hypotheticals involving mixed motives. If a group of women is targeted because the women are Muslim and because they are women, is the targeting genocidal in purpose? If the same mixed motives exist but the women killed or seriously bodily injured are not in fact Muslim, is the targeting genocidal? Besides the specific intent, what do you need to know? Must there be an impact on the relevant group (*i.e.*, the group covered in Article II of the Convention)? If a genocidal intent exists, can some impacts be indirect as where an instrumental target (*e.g.*, a group of women) is not part of a covered group, but the covered group is the primary target of the perpetrators and the primary group suffers certain effects? Consider Article II and prohibited acts (b) and (d). What about acts (a), (c), or (e)?

In *The Prosecutor v. Niyitegeka*, ICTR-96-14-A (Appeals Chamber Judgment, 9 July 2004), the Appeals Chamber ruled that the phrase "as such" (reflected in Article II of the Convention) does not require that the intent of the perpetrator be merely or "solely" to target a relevant group and that the perpetrator can have other motivations but still be responsible for genocide. *Id*. para. 53. The Appeals Chamber upheld the conviction of Niyitegeka (who had been a Minister of Information in Rwanda in 1994) for genocide, conspiracy to commit genocide, direct and public incitement to commit genocide, murder, extermination, and other inhumane acts as crimes against humanity.

Section 4
U.S. Implementation

Senate Committee on Foreign Relations, International Convention on the Prevention and Punishment of the Crime of Genocide
S. Exec. Rept. No. 92-6, 92d Cong., 1st Sess. 1–18 (4 May 1971)

The Committee on Foreign Relations, to which was referred the International Convention on the Prevention and Punishment of the Crime of Genocide (Ex. O, 81st Cong., first sess.), having considered the same, reports favorably thereon with three understandings and one declaration and recommends that the Senate advise and consent to ratification thereof....

Since the treaty, in article I, specifically refers to "time of war," the possible effect of the Genocide Convention on U.S. military forces abroad, especially when in combat, was carefully considered. This is particularly relevant since the word "genocide" has been loosely applied to the incidents at My Lai. However, as will be seen in the discussion of article II below where genocide is defined, whatever occurred at My Lai — and the committee does not prejudge the matter — it was not genocide, as defined in the treaty. Combat actions do not fall within the meaning of the Genocide Convention. They are subject to other international and national laws....

Acts Constituting Genocide ...

The testimony and discussion of article II turned on the alleged vagueness of certain of its terms — "in whole or in part," "group", "as such," and "mental harm." While the committee had no particular problem with the meaning of these words, in order to allay any misconceptions, it recommends to the Senate two understandings to this article:

"(1) That the U.S. Government understands and construes the words 'intent to destroy, in whole or in part, a national, ethnical, racial, or religious group, as such' appearing in article II to mean the intent to destroy a national, ethnical, racial, or religious group by the acts specified in article II in such a manner as to affect a substantial part of the group concerned.

"(2) That the U.S. Government understands and construes the words 'mental harm' appearing in article II(b) to mean permanent impairment of mental faculties."

The first of these understandings serves to emphasize the importance which the committee attaches to the word "intent." Basic to any charge of genocide must be the *intent* to destroy an entire group because of the fact that it is a certain national, ethnical, racial, or religious group, in such a manner as to affect a substantial part of the group. There have been allegations that school busing, birth control clinics, lynchings, police actions with respect to the Black Panthers, and the incidents at My Lai constitute genocide. The committee wants to make clear that under the terms of article II none of these and similar acts is genocide unless the *intent* to destroy the group as a group is proven. Harassment of minority groups and racial and religious intolerance generally, no matter how much to be deplored, are not outlawed per se by the Genocide Convention. Far from outlawing discrimination, article II is so written as to make it, in fact, difficult to prove the "intent" element necessary to sustain a charge of genocide against anyone....

The second of the understandings was suggested by the executive branch in 1949 and while the executive branch no longer considers this understanding to be necessary, the committee thinks it will be helpful to eliminate any doubt as to what is meant by "mental harm.".…

Punishable Acts ...

The principal question about the meaning of article III concerned the relationship of the words "direct and public incitement to commit genocide" to the freedom of speech guarantees of the first amendment.

The 1969 case of *Brandenburg v. Ohio* was cited by several witnesses as the most recent reaffirmation of the line drawn by the Supreme Court between protected speech and prohibited direct and immediate incitement to action. In that case, the Court said: " ... the constitutional guarantees of free speech and free press do not permit a State to forbid or proscribe advocacy of the use of force or of law violation except where such advocacy is directed to inciting or producing imminent lawless action and is likely to incite or produce such action." (395 U.S. 444.) This is a 1969 per curiam decision of the Supreme Court and there is no reason to expect any reversal of this doctrine, with which the language of the Genocide Convention is consistent....

Punishment of Persons ...

While most of the testimony on [article IV] attempted to establish that governments, as well as individuals, could be held responsible for commission of genocidal acts, the committee believes that this argument is somewhat strained. The article clearly refers to "persons." The government's responsibility is to punish such persons, whether they are constitutionally responsible rulers, public officials, or private individuals....

Implementing Legislation ...

[Article V] makes clear that the convention is construed not [to] be self-executing and that implementing legislation is required to give effect to its provisions. Indeed, the committee regards Senate approval of the convention as the first in a two-step procedure. The Department of State is already on record as proposing to recommend to the President that the instrument of ratification of the convention not be deposited until the implementing legislation has been enacted. This statement by the Department has been incorporated into a declaration to be included in the resolution of ratification as follows:

"4. That the United States Government declares that it will not deposit its instrument of ratification until after the implementing legislation referred to in article V has been enacted." ...

Trial of Persons Charged With Genocide ...

[Article VI] provoked considerable discussion, not because of its language but because of the means suggested for its implementation. Executive branch and other testimony brought out that the negotiating history of the convention makes it clear that the courts of the country in which the accused has citizenship can likewise have jurisdiction over the crime. This theory of concurrent jurisdiction—jurisdiction based on the site of the alleged offense and jurisdiction based on the nationality of the offender—was thoroughly explored during the hearings. It was pointed out that a number of nations, particularly colonial powers, have consistently asserted the right to try their own nationals for crimes committed outside their territory. Even the United States in certain limited areas—counterfeiting, theft of Government property, treason, antitrust violations—has exercised jurisdiction over its citizens for acts committed abroad. This concept of concurrent jurisdiction no doubt will be closely examined during consideration of the implementing legislation. However, the U.S. Government should make it clear to the other contracting parties that it intends to construe article VI so as to permit it to try its own nationals for punishable genocide acts whether committed at home or abroad. For this reason, the committee recommends to the Senate the following understanding:

"(3) That the U.S. Government understands and construes article VI of the convention in accordance with the agreed language of the report of the Legal Committee of the United Nations General Assembly that nothing in article VI shall affect the right of any State to bring to trial before its own tribunals any of its nationals for acts committed outside the State...."

Role of the United Nations

In the discussion of [article VIII], the question was raised whether it would broaden or enlarge the powers of the United Nations. Genocide, as the term is accepted by the committee, namely, mass murder on a broad scale, would pose a threat to world peace and it would clearly be within the powers of the United Nations to discuss it. The article itself moreover refers to "action under the Charter of the United Nations" which limits its scope to that document, including the article 2(7) proscription against intervention "in matters which are essentially within the domestic jurisdiction of any state...."

As a practical matter, whether we are a party to the Genocide Convention or not, the United Nations can discuss alleged genocide in the United States or anywhere else any time it so chooses. The committee moreover is quite certain that for propaganda and other purposes spurious charges of this nature will continue to be made in the United Nations, whether we do or do not ratify the Genocide Convention, if only because our position in the world makes us a visible target of discontent. Indeed, we lend more color to such charges by not being a party to the Genocide Convention. This being the case, the question whether article VIII gives the United Nations greater scope to discuss genocide seems relatively immaterial. It is important, moreover, in this connection to bear in mind that such enforcement powers as the United Nations has are lodged in the Security Council, subject to the veto power, which the United States now has demonstrated it will not hesitate to exercise.

Settlement of Disputes ...

The jurisdiction of the Court [under article IX] will extend to disputes relating to the interpretation, application, or fulfillment of the convention, including those relating to the responsibility of a state for genocide. It must be noted that such cases will fall under article 36(1) of the Court's statute which provides:

"1. The jurisdiction of the Court comprises all cases which the parties refer to it and all matters specially provided for in the Charter of the United Nations or *in treaties and conventions in force.*" [emphasis added.]

Cases arising under the Genocide Convention will not be covered by the Connally amendment under which the United States reserves to itself the right to determine which cases it considers to be within its domestic jurisdiction and therefore outside the jurisdiction of the Court. The Connally amendment applies only to article 36(2) — the so-called compulsory jurisdiction clause....

THE CONVENTION AND THE CONSTITUTION

Discussion of the Genocide Convention during the hearings renewed the debate over whether a treaty can authorize what the Constitution prohibits. The Supreme Court, in its own words, "has regularly and uniformly recognized the supremacy of the Constitution over a treaty" (*Reid v. Covert*). It is therefore fallacious to claim that the Genocide Convention will supersede or set aside the Constitution of the United States. It will not and cannot do so.

A related argument was raised by some witnesses to the effect that the Congress would have no power to enact legislation making genocide a crime if the convention were not approved. The power of Congress to do so rests on article I, section 8, clause 10, of the Constitution: "The Congress shall have the Power ... To Define and Punish Piracies and Felonies committed on the high Seas, and Offences against the Law of Nations.... ," as well as on the necessary and proper clause. The fact that the Congress enacts a statute pursuant to a treaty, as would be the case in the Genocide Convention, does not alter its competence to enact such legislation in any event....

Questions

1. Do you agree the "whatever occurred at My Lai" was not genocide? What would the prosecutor have to prove?

2. Can genocide occur in time of armed conflict? Recall Chapter Six, Sections 6 and 9.

3. Does Article II of the Convention require that the intent of the perpetrator to destroy in whole or in part be an intent "in such a manner as to affect a substantial part of the group concerned"? Does Article II require that the acts of the perpetrator "affect a substantial part of the group concerned"?

4. Must there be an "intent to destroy the group as a group"?

1986 Lugar/Helms/Hatch Provisos as Approved by the Foreign Relations Committee

Resolved (two-thirds of the Senators present concurring therein), That the Senate advise and consent to the ratification of the International Convention on the Prevention and Punishment of the Crime of Genocide, adopted unanimously by the General Assembly of the United Nations in Paris on December 9, 1948 (Executive O, Eighty-first Congress, first session), Provided that—

I. The Senate's advice and consent is subject to the following reservations:

(1) That with reference to Article IX of the Convention, before any dispute to which the United States is a party may be submitted to the jurisdiction of the International Court of Justice under this article, the specific consent of the United States is required in each case.

(2) That nothing in the Convention requires or authorizes legislation or other action by the United States of America prohibited by the Constitution of the United States as interpreted by the United States.

II. The Senate's advice and consent is subject to the following understandings, which shall apply to the obligations of the United States under this Convention:

(1) That the term "intent to destroy, in whole or in part, a national, ethnical, racial, or religious group as such" appearing in Article II means the specific intent to destroy, in whole or in substantial part, a national, ethnical, racial, of religious group as such by the acts specified in Article II.

(2) That the term "mental harm" in Article II(b) means permanent impairment of mental faculties through drugs, torture, or similar techniques.

(3) That the pledge to grant extradition in accordance with a state's laws and treaties in force found in Article VII extends only to acts which are criminal under the laws of both the requesting and the requested state and nothing in Article VI affects the rights of any state to bring to trial before its own tribunals any of its nationals for acts committed outside a state.

(4) That acts in the course of armed conflicts committed without the specific intent required by Article II are not sufficient to constitute genocide as defined by this Convention.

(5) That with regard to the reference to an international penal tribunal in Article VI of the Convention, the United States declares that it reserves the right to effect its participation in any such tribunal by a treaty entered into specifically for that purpose with the advice and consent of the Senate.

III. The Senate's advice and consent is subject to the following declaration:

That the President will not deposit the instrument of ratification until after the implementing legislation referred to in Article V has been enacted.

Extract: Vol. XII-7 UNA/USA Washington Weekly Report 1-3
(21 Feb. 1986)

Senate Lends Consent To Genocide Convention

By a vote of 83 ayes to 11 noes, the Senate has given its advice and consent to the ratification of the Genocide Convention....

Senate Leadership Seeks to Bridge Gap

Sen. Richard Lugar (R-IN), Chairman of the Committee on Foreign Relations, opened debate on the treaty by acknowledging the thirty-six year stalemate between those who have believed that ratification has strong symbolic value and those who have sought a definition of precise obligations under the treaty and its impact on U.S. sovereignty. He explained that the eight provisos seek to delineate those obligations. To reaffirm our commitment to human rights and rule of law, to prevent the United States from being unfairly criticized and to recall the Holocaust—these are the reasons why I believe the Senate should approve the Genocide Convention," said Lugar. Added Sen. Claiborne Pell (D-RI), ranking minority member of the Committee on Foreign Relations, "By making genocide a crime under international law, the convention is a powerful instrument for the protection of life and the advancement of human rights throughout this planet."

Sen. Jesse Helms (R-NC), the principal advocate of treaty obligation clarifications in the Foreign Relations Committee, argued that, "From the very beginning my chief object with regard to the Genocide Convention has been to see that the independent sovereignty of the United States is protected from interference by an international regime of law." Helms termed inclusion of the eight provisions the 'sovereignty package' since it is designed to protect this nation's sovereignty from the intrusion of the United Nations into the domestic matters of the United States, and the people of this country. Sen. Orrin Hatch (R-UT), another proponent of the reservations package, commented that, "While it is time to resolve these issues, we must not compromise our constitutional form of government in the process. Participation in world affairs need not and should not result in any diminution of liberty in the United States." Although Hatch eventually voted in favor of Senate consent, Helms announced early in the debate that he would be unable to vote for the treaty with the attached reservations. "I think that the United States should be moving away from entangling alliances, not moving toward more in an uncertain future," he said.

Reservations Package Clarifies U.S. Obligations

As consented to by the Senate, the United States expresses eight reservations to the convention. The two most contentious provisions require the specific consent of the United States for any appearance before the International Court of Justice on a legal question involving genocide and assert the sovereignty of the U.S. Constitution. In the second case, no provision of the convention could authorize or permit legislation, executive conduct or legal action contrary to the U.S. Constitution as interpreted by the United States. Other reservations include a statement that armed conflict, by itself, does not constitute genocide; a prohibition on the extradition of American citizens for crimes not in violation of U.S. law; a stricter definition of the mental state necessary to commit genocide; clarification of mental harm through the use of drugs and torture; the requirement for a specific treaty for U.S. involvement in any international genocide penal tribunal; and a declaration preventing the President from depositing the instrument of ratification until Congress passes implementing legislation. This last reservation prevents the treaty's provisions from becoming self-executing. Implementing legislation would make the convention part of the U.S. legal code; Congress is expected to act on it shortly.

Attachment of the reservations package to the treaty caused considerable controversy during Foreign Relations Committee deliberations in May 1985. Most of the Democratic members of the Committee argued that several of the reservations weakened the treaty and made it meaningless. Committee Chairman Lugar, however, insisted that the eight conditions be attached to the convention to overcome conservative concerns that the treaty would supersede the authority of the U.S. Constitution and threaten the rights of U.S. citizens. Lugar reinforced his commitment to including the conditions by threatening to suspend Committee markup of the treaty if the package was not accepted. At that time, the panel voted 9 ayes to 8 noes to include the most contentious reservations in the treaty. Restating his position on the Senate floor, Lugar noted that, "These provisos delineate and qualify the U.S. obligations under the convention; they in no way detract from the symbolic value that will inhere from ratification." Sen. Christopher Dodd (D-CT), an opponent of the reservations package who tried to weaken the World Court reservation in Committee, noted on the Senate floor that, "If it comes to the question of voting on the treaty with the present conditions or putting off this issue once again, I will vote for ratification."

Symms Rebuffed on "Killer Amendment"

By a vote of 31 ayes to 62 noes, Sen. Steven Symms (R-ID) was defeated in his attempt to amend the treaty to include political groups among those listed for protection in the convention. Amendment of the convention in any form would have effectively nullified it; the President would find it necessary to gain the assent of the ninety-six other signatories to such an amendment before he could ratify it on behalf of the United States. Lugar argued that the Symms amendment " ... is effectively a killer amendment. It is the same as a vote against the treaty." The Senate later voted 93 ayes to 1 no on a resolution directing the President to seek renewed negotiations on the treaty with a view to including political genocide in the convention....

U.S. Legislation
Genocide, 18 U.S.C. §§ 1091–1093

(as amended 2007)

§ 1091. Genocide

(a) **Basic offense.**—Whoever, whether in time of peace or in time of war, in a circumstance described in subsection (d) and with the specific intent to destroy, in whole or in substantial part, a national, ethnic, racial, or religious group as such—

(1) kills members of that group;

(2) causes serious bodily injury to members of that group;

(3) causes the permanent impairment of the mental faculties of members of the group through drugs, torture, or similar techniques;

(4) subjects the group to conditions of life that are intended to cause the physical destruction of the group in whole or in part;

(5) imposes measures intended to prevent births within the group; or

(6) transfers by force children of the group to another group; or attempts to do so, shall be punished as provided in subsection (b).

(b) **Punishment for basic offense.**—The punishment for an offense under subsection (a) is—

(1) in the case of an offense under subsection (a)(1) where death results, by death or imprisonment for life and a fine of not more than $1,000,000, or both; and

(2) a fine of not more than $1,000,000 or imprisonment for not more than twenty years, or both, in any other case.

(c) **Incitement offense.**—Whoever in a circumstance described in subsection (d) directly and publicly incites another to violate subsection (a) shall be fined not more than $500,000 or imprisoned not more than five years, or both.

(d) **Required circumstance for offenses.**—The circumstance referred to in subsections (a) and (c) is that—

(1) the offense is committed in whole or in part within the United States;

(2) the alleged offender is a national of the United States (as that term is defined in section 101 of the Immigration and Nationality act (8 U.S.C. 1101));

(3) the alleged offender is an alien lawfully admitted for permanent residence in the United States (as that term is defined in section 101 of the Immigration and Nationality Act (8 U.S.C. 1101));

(4) the alleged offender is a stateless person whose habitual residence is in the United States; or

(5) after the conduct required for the offense occurs, the alleged offender is brought into, or found in, the United States, even if that conduct occurred outside the United States.

(e) Nonapplicability of certain limitations.— Notwithstanding section 3282 of this title, in the case of an offense under subsection (a)(1), an indictment may be found, or information instituted, at any time without limitation.

[§ 3282 provides a 5 year statutory limitation regarding "offenses not capital"]

§ 1092. Exclusive remedies

Nothing in this chapter shall be construed as precluding the application of State or local laws to the conduct proscribed by this chapter, nor shall anything in this chapter be construed as creating any substantive or procedural right enforceable by law by any party in any proceeding.

§ 1093. Definitions

As used in this chapter—

(1) the term "children" means the plural and means individuals who have not attained the age of eighteen years;

(2) the term "ethnic group" means a set of individuals whose identity as such is distinctive in terms of common cultural traditions or heritage;

(3) the term "incites" means urges another to engage imminently in conduct in circumstances under which there is a substantial likelihood of imminently causing such conduct;

(4) the term "members" means the plural;

(5) the term "national group" means a set of individuals whose identity as such is distinctive in terms of nationality or national origins;

(6) the term "racial group" means a set of individuals whose identity as such is distinctive in terms of physical characteristics or biological descent;

(7) the term "religious group" means a set of individuals whose identity as such is distinctive in terms of common religious creed, beliefs, doctrines, practices, or rituals; and

(8) the term "substantial part" means a part of a group of such numerical significance that the destruction or loss of that part would cause the destruction of the group as a viable entity within the nation of which such group is a part.

U.N. Human Rights Commission, Res. 1987/25, Status of the Convention on the Prevention and Punishment of the Crime of Genocide

The Commission on Human Rights,

Recalling General Assembly resolutions 40/142 of 13 December 1985 and 41/147 of 4 December 1986,

Also recalling its resolution 1986/18 of 10 March 1986,

Further recalling General Assembly resolution 260 A (III) of 9 December 1948, in which the Assembly approved the Convention on the Prevention and Punishment of the Crime of Genocide and proposed it for signature and ratification or accession,

Reaffirming its conviction that genocide is a crime which violates the norms of international law and runs counter to the spirit and aims of the United Nations,

Expressing its conviction that strict observance by all States of the provisions of the Convention is necessary for the prevention and punishment of the crime of genocide,

1. *Strongly condemns once again* the crime of genocide;

2. *Affirms* the necessity of international co-operation in order to liberate mankind from this odious crime....

Notes and Questions

1. Is Genocide now (whether or not it had been in 1948) a violation of customary international law? See text *supra*; RESTATEMENT OF THE FOREIGN RELATIONS LAW OF THE UNITED STATES § 404 and Reporters' Note 1, § 702, Comments d and n and Reporters' Note 3 (3 ed. 1987); Chapter Six, Section 9, especially the 1993 Report of the Secretary-General, at paras. 35, 45; Paust, *Congress and Genocide: They're Not Going to Get Away With It*, 11 MICH. J. INT'L L. 90, 90–92 (1989). The latter article contains a survey of numerous textwriters on the status of the prohibition of genocide as customary international law (*id.* at 90–91 and n.1) and as *jus cogens* (*id.* at 92–93 & n.3). Newer affirmations include: Johan D. van der Vyver, *Prosecution and Punishment*, *supra* at 287, 319–20.

2. Does Article II of the Convention define that which is prohibited under customary international law, with a possible exception regarding extended groups? See Paust, *id.* at 93–4; RESTATEMENT, § 702, Comment d; Statute of the ICTY, art. 4; Statute of the ICTR, art. 2; Statute of the ICC, art. 6; questions in Section 1. If so, has the U.S. attempt to redefine "genocide" come too late? Note that in 2004 a concurrent resolution of the U.S. House and Senate used the customary definition of genocide when declaring "the actions in Darfur, Sudan, are genocide." H.R. Concurrent Res. 467, 108th Cong.; S. Concurrent Res. 133 (2004). Consider also:

Paust, *Congress and Genocide*...

First, the attempted "understanding" [regarding "substantial" part] is fundamentally incompatible with the object and purpose of the treaty and will thereby be legally unacceptable. Second, the attempt to redefine genocide in such a radical manner has been obviated by the development of a customary international law independent of a long, abnegative effort of the Senate to allow the United States to participate in the treaty process.

Part of the radical effort to gut the Convention of any functional criminal effect hinged upon a blatant attempt to unilaterally rewrite article II of the Convention. In particular, the treaty phrase "with intent to destroy, in whole or in part," appears in the Senate's 1986 "understanding" as [with] the specific intent to destroy, in whole or in *substantial* part...." The phrase "specific intent" actually is appropriate under the circumstances, but the threshold element of the crime of genocide would be shifted by the last portion of such language from the treaty's lower threshold of intent to destroy a relevant group "in part" to the Senate's nearly impossible threshold of intent to destroy a relevant group "in substantial part."

One can imagine the type of defenses that the Senate's "understanding" might permit. For example, is a nuclear incineration of all of the Jews in and around the state of Israel to be excused under such an "understanding" merely because a "substantial part" of the Jews of the world were not targeted? If Hitler himself had been prosecuted under the Senate's present version, a defense to what the world knows as acts of genocide might have been: "Yes, I attempted to exterminate Jews as such and thousands, even millions, of Jews, but I never had the specific intent to destroy a 'substantial' part of such a group, nor could I or my followers have done so—we never had control of even half the Jews of the world." Or take the putative defense of a member of the KKK in the United States: "Sure, I intended to exterminate as many blacks as I could get my sights on, but I never had more than 2,000 in my gun sights and never had the intent to destroy a 'substantial' part of such group, nor could I physically do so." Even nationwide conspirators in the KKK, each responsible for the known acts of co-conspirators, might defend: "We never intended to kill more than six million blacks and thus never intended to kill a 'substantial' part of the blacks in the U.S., much less in the world." It is evident, therefore, that U.S. prosecutors (under the Senate's present "understanding") would have a nearly impossible burden in proving an intent to destroy a relevant group "in substantial part." When half the persons within a large group were not even targeted by an accused, how could a prosecuting attorney prove that there was an intent to destroy a "substantial part" of such a group? Even if the phrase "substantial part" could theoretically include just more than one third, one fourth or ten percent, why would we want such threshold quotas set against what the world still knows as acts of genocide? The significant evil involved (and the fundamental difference between murder and genocide) hinges not upon percentages of group extermination but upon the singling out of victims of a certain group because they are members of such a group—the targeting of members of a group as such. That evil is not merely against a particular group or its members. In the long run it involves an attack upon our common dignity, an attack upon us all.

The Senate also attempted to rewrite section b of article II of the treaty. The treaty prohibition of an intent to cause "serious ... mental harm to members" of a relevant group would be changed by the present Senate "understanding" to an intent to cause "*permanent* impairment of mental faculties through drugs, torture or similar techniques." Thus, it would be possible for alleged terrorists or Nazi war criminals to defend their actions with proof of the fact that intense fear or anxiety produced in the primary victims was not intended to be "permanent" but temporary. Indeed, how would prosecutors meet the even more difficult burden of proving beyond a reasonable doubt that an intent existed not merely to cause "serious" but "permanent" mental harm? It might also be alleged by an accused that specific terroristic tactics utilized did not equate with "torture or similar techniques" because the primary victims were never captured or under the control of the accused. Here again, U.S. prosecutors would be at a serious disadvantage and the object and purpose of the Convention would be needlessly thwarted.

Even more incredible was a 1987 bill in the House of Representatives designed supposedly "to implement" the Genocide Convention. A definitions portion of H.R. 807 would have redefined "substantial part" to mean "a part of a group of such numerical significance that the destruction or loss of that part would cause the destruction of the group as a viable entity...." How would a U.S. prosecutor prove such an element? If ninety-five percent of a group of thirty-five million men, women and children was brutally and systematically exterminated at the hands of some nationwide conspirators, would a defense be that the remaining five percent, now even more unified in its group identification and determination, was never targeted and still constitutes a viable entity? Under such a definition, must "the group as a viable entity" be exterminated or an intent to do so be proven beyond a reasonable doubt before genocide recognizably exists? Hitler's defense under such a definitional scheme would have been even stronger, and so would that of any future exterminators of racial, religious, national, or ethnic groups as long as they intend to leave some "viable" portion of the group or as long as it cannot be proven that they did not. Frankly, I've never heard of a more ludicrous, if not egregious, effort at drafting an "Implementation Act." There can be no doubt that adoption of the putative definition of "substantial part" in H.R. 807 would be fundamentally incompatible with the object and purpose of the Genocide Convention and leave the United States effort at meaningful adherence to the treaty and customary international law a laughable disgrace....

From the above, it is evident that the Senate's 1986 "understanding" should be changed. The present understanding would clash so seriously with the ordinary meaning of the terms of the treaty as well as its object and purpose that it could not survive a good faith, legally appropriate interpretation of the treaty. As an attempted "reservation," the Senate's "understanding" would be legally unacceptable since it is incompatible with the object and purpose of the Convention. Further, such an "understanding" cannot be legally operative in the case of a contrary *jus cogens*, which is the case here.

Questions

1. On October 14, 1988, S.1851 (which followed H.R. 807) was passed by the U.S. Senate. The House also passed its version of S.1851 on October 19th. President Reagan signed the legislation on November 4, 1988, and deposited the U.S. instrument of ratification of the Convention with the U.N. on November 25, 1988. Is the treaty thus "last in time" for the United States as opposed to U.S. legislation? Did the 2007 amendment to the legislation make it last in time? What differences exist? What statutory provisions would not prevail under the "last in time" rule, especially if some of the "understandings" concerning the treaty are void because they are incompatible with the object and purpose of the treaty? If the legislation is trumped entirely under the last-in-time rule, can prosecutors use the treaty directly for prosecution of genocide or, alternatively, use customary international law as the basis for prosecution? Recall Chapter Four, Section 5. Also see Johan D. van der Vyver, *Prosecution and Punishment, supra* at 353.

2. Under the legislation, can the U.S. prosecute members of al Qaeda for genocide in connection with the attacks on the World Trade Center and the Pentagon on September 11, 2001? Within the meaning of Section 1091(d), was "the offense" committed by bin Laden (the leader of al Qaeda) "committed within the United States"? Would Section 1093(8) fit? Do Sections 1091 and 1098(3) require the actual destruction of the group as a viable entity or an intent to destroy "a part of a group of such numerical significance that the destruction or loss of that part would cause the destruction of the group as a viable entity"?

3. Could the U.S. have prosecuted the former Iraqi dictator Saddam Hussein under the U.S. legislation for his widespread attacks on Iraqi Kurds in Northern Iraq after numerous Kurds engaged in armed violence against his regime? Would such attacks fit within Article II of the Genocide Convention?

4. If the United States does not have adequate legislation to prosecute all acts of genocide, is the U.S. in violation of Articles I, IV and V of the Convention? Also see Lee A. Steven, *Genocide and the Duty to Extradite or Prosecute: Why the United States is in Breach of Its International Obligations*, 39 Va. J. Int'l L. 425 (1999); *see also* van der Vyver, *supra* at 352. What legislation would you recommend now to adequately implement U.S. obligations under the Genocide Convention? Under customary international law? Would your legislation incorporate the Convention by reference?

5. Presently, can the U.S. prosecute some acts of genocide that are not covered by the 1988 legislation? as violations of customary international law? With respect to war crimes, recall 18 U.S.C. § 2441 and 10 U.S.C. §§ 818, 821; hostage-taking, 18 U.S.C. § 1203; U.S. national victims of murder or serious bodily harm, 18 U.S.C. §§ 2331–2332.

6. Section 1092 of the U.S. statute expressly does not preempt state jurisdiction. Can states within the United States exercise universal jurisdiction over acts of genocide committed outside their territory? There have been state prosecutions of war crimes, piracy, and other infractions of the law of nations. Assume that you have been requested by a state legislator to draft a criminal statute to cover genocide under the Convention and/or customary international law. Draft the statute.

7. Note that Section 1092 merely states that it does not create a "substantive or procedural right". It does not preclude use of direct incorporation of customary international law or use of other federal statutory bases for incorporation such as the Alien Tort Claims Act, 28 U.S.C. § 1350, and the Torture Victim Protection Act — both of which execute relevant treaty law. *See, e.g.,* J. Paust, International Law as Law of the United States 10, 14–15, 63–66, 284, 311, 373–74 (2 ed. 2003). Congressional intent to override the treaty, not even mentioned, would have to be clear and unequivocal. *See, e.g., id.* at 99, 107–08, *passim*. Even then, there would be exceptions to the last in time rule protecting rights under treaties and customary law. *See id.* at 86–100, *passim*.

8. When humans come, the extermination of species has been a common consequence for at least ten thousand years. Intended, negligent, unintended, it has still been a result. Should the intentional extermination of a life species be regulated by international law? What of new but threatening species we encounter in the future? Are we really prepared for space exploration? More generally, see M. Scharf & L. Roberts, *The Interstellar Relations of the Federation: International Law and "Star Trek: The Next Generation,"* 25 Toledo L. Rev. 577 (1995).

Are the following relevant or earth-bound? Convention on International Trade in Endangered Species of Wild Fauna and Flora, 27 U.S.T. 1087, T.I.A.S. No. 8249, in 12 I.L.M. 1085 (1973); Convention on Biological Diversity (With Annexes), done at Rio de Janeiro, 5 June 1992, in 31 I.L.M. 818 (1992).

Chapter 11

Human Rights

Section 1
General Human Rights

[recall Chapter Three, Section 1]

Human rights are at stake with respect to most international crimes. The reach of human rights law is so broad that many of the chapters on types of offenses could be placed as sections in this chapter. As noted in Chapter Eight, human rights law also applies during any armed conflict as well as in times of relative peace. Consider what types of human rights are at stake with respect to abductions, assassinations, certain breaches of neutrality, war crimes, genocide, other crimes against humanity, slavery, impermissible terrorism, and piracy. In *United States v. Haun*, 26 F. Cas. 227 (C.C.S.D. Ala. 1860) (No. 15,329), Justice Campbell, sitting on circuit, ruled that congressional legislation to suppress the slave trade was supported by several treaties and was valid. He also quoted President Jefferson's Message to Congress in 1806 concerning private duties with respect to human rights, recognizing that Congress "'might interpose their authority constitutionally to withdraw the citizens of the United States from all further violations of human rights which have been so long continued on the unoffending inhabitants of Africa.'" *Id.* at 231.

In this chapter we emphasize the prohibitions of torture and other cruel, inhuman, and degrading acts; race-based discrimination, including apartheid; hostage-taking; secret detention and the "disappearance" of persons. Also recall Article 19(3)(b) and (c) of the I.L.C.'s Draft Convention on State Responsibility, in Chapter Seven, Section 2 C, addressing crimes against self-determination and crimes against obligations "of essential importance for safeguarding the human being...."

A. The United Nations Charter

More generally, all states have a duty under Articles 55(c) and 56 of the United Nations Charter to take joint and separate action to achieve "universal respect for, and observance of, human rights" and, thus, not to authorize their violation or to violate them in any location with respect to any person. See also U.N. G.A. Res. 59/195, Human Rights and Terrorism, preamble (2004); U.N. G.A. Res. 59/191, Protection of Human Rights and Fundamental Freedoms While Countering Terrorism, preamble and para. 1 (2004), both in the Documents Supplement; Declaration on Principles of International Law Concerning Friendly Relations and Co-Operation Among States in Accordance With the Charter of the United Nations, U.N. G.A. Res. 2625 (Oct. 24, 1970), 25 U.N. GAOR, Supp.

No. 28, at 121, U.N. Doc. A/8028 (1971) ("Every State has the duty to promote through joint and separate action universal respect for and observance of human rights and fundamental freedoms in accordance with the Charter.").

One uses evidences of the content of customary human rights to identify those rights "guaranteed to all by the Charter." See Filartiga v. Pena-Irala, 630 F.2d 876, 882 (2d Cir. 1980), adding: "the guarantees include, at a bare minimum, the right to be free from torture. This prohibition has become part of customary international law as evidenced and defined by the Universal Declaration of Human Rights.... Charter precepts embodied in this Universal Declaration 'constitute basic principles of international law.' G.A. Res. 2625 (XXV) (Oct. 24, 1970)." *Id.* In addition to the prohibition of torture, Article 5 of the Universal Declaration prohibits "cruel, inhuman or degrading treatment or punishment." U.N. G.A. Res. 217A, art. 5, 3 U.N. GAOR, U.N. Doc. A/810, at 71 (1948). As a matter of customary international law, these prohibitions are absolute. The more general right to human dignity is mirrored in Article 1. *Id.* art. 1. Concerning the status of the Universal Declaration and its use as an authoritative interpretive aid, *see, e.g.*, MCDOUGAL, LASSWELL, CHEN, HUMAN RIGHTS AND WORLD PUBLIC ORDER 274, 302, 325–27 (1980); see also Paust, *Executive Plans and Authorizations to Violate International Law Concerning Treatment and Interrogation of Detainees*, 43 COLUMBIA J. TRANSNAT'L L. 811, 822 n.40 (2005) (Executive recognition of Article 5, among others, as customary international law) [hereinafter Paust, *Executive Plans*]. The same absolute prohibitions are found in the Resolution on Torture and other Cruel, Inhuman or Degrading Treatment or Punishment, G.A. Res. 59/182, U.N. Doc. A/RES/59/182 (2004), and the 1975 Declaration on the Protection of All Persons from Being Subjected to Torture and Other Cruel, Inhuman or Degrading Treatment or Punishment, U.N. G.A. Res. 3452, 30 U.N. GAOR, Supp. No. 34, at 91, U.N. Doc. A/1034 (1976). Article 2 of the 1975 Declaration affirms that each form of prohibited conduct violates human rights under the U.N. Charter. The 1975 Declaration was also used in *Filartiga* to identify U.N. Charter-based and customary human rights prohibitions. 630 F.2d at 882–83. *See also* Kadic v. Karadzic, 70 F.3d 232, 240 (2d Cir. 1995), *cert. denied*, 518 U.S. 1005 (1996); *In re* Estate of Marcos Human Rights Litig., 978 F.2d 493, 499 (9th Cir. 1992), *cert. denied*, 508 U.S. 972 (1993).

The 1988 Body of Principles for the Protection of All Persons Under Any Form of Detention or Imprisonment also affirms that "[a]ll persons under any form of detention ... shall be treated in a humane manner and with respect for the inherent dignity of the human person." U.N. G.A. Res. 43/173, 43 U.N. GAOR, Supp. No. 49, at 297, U.N. Doc. A/43/49 (1988). *See also* Kane v. Winn, 319 F. Supp.2d 162, 197–99 (D. Mass. 2004) (use of the Body of Principles as evidence of customary law).

B. The International Covenant on Civil and Political Rights

The International Covenant on Civil and Political Rights (ICCPR), 999 U.N.T.S. 171 (1966), contains articles relevant to detention of individuals (*e.g.*, art. 9), treatment of persons (*e.g.*, art. 7), minimum rights to due process (*e.g.*, art. 14), and other rights relevant to international criminal law responsibilities and enforcement. Article 7 expressly prohibits torture and cruel, inhuman, or degrading treatment or punishment and Article 4(2) assures that such prohibitions are absolute and non-derogable even in time of national emergency.

Does the ICCPR apply anywhere that U.S. government personnel or agents detain individuals? Consider the following commentary: the ICCPR applies wherever a person is subject to the jurisdiction or effective control of a party to the treaty. *See, e.g.*, ICCPR, *supra* art. 2(1); Advisory Opinion, Legal Consequences of the Construction of a Wall in the Occupied Palestinian Territory, 2004 I.C.J. paras. 108–111 (The ICCPR "is applicable in respect of acts done by a State in the exercise of its jurisdiction outside its own territory"); Human Rights Committee, General Comment No. 31, at para. 10 (applies "to all persons subject to their jurisdiction. This means ... anyone within the power or effective control of that State party, even if not situated within the territory of the State.... [The ICCPR applies] to all individuals ... who may find themselves in the territory or subject to the jurisdiction of a State Party.... [It] also applies to those within the power or effective control of the forces of a State Party acting outside its territory, regardless of the circumstances in which such power or effective control was obtained), para. 11 ("the Covenant applies also in the situation of armed conflict to which the rules of international humanitarian law are applicable."), U.N. Doc. CCPR/C/21/Rev.1/Add.13 (2004); General Comment No. 24, at paras. 4, 12 ("all those under a State party's jurisdiction"), U.N. Doc. CCPR/C/21/Rev.1/Add.6 (1994); Coard, *et al.* v. United States, Case No. 10.951, Report No. 109/99, Annual Report of the Inter-Am. Comm. H.R. (Sept. 29, 1999); Alejandre, *et al.* v. Cuba, Case No. 11.589, Annual Report of the Inter-Am. Comm. H.R. (Sept. 29, 1999); Human Rights Comm., Concluding Observations on Croatia, 28/12/92, U.N. Doc. CCPR/C/79/Add.15 (1992), § 9; Leila Zerrougui, *et al.*, Report, *Situation of Detainees at Guantanamo Bay*, Commission on Human Rights, 62nd sess., items 10 and 11 of the provisional agenda, U.N. Doc. E/CN.4/2006/120 (Feb. 15, 2006), at 8–9, para. 11; Paust, *Executive Plans, supra* at 822 n.40. More specifically, there is no territorial limitation set forth with respect to the absolute rights and duties contained in Article 7 of the ICCPR. The authoritative decisions and patterns of *opinio juris* noted above are part of subsequent practice and expectation relevant to proper interpretation of the treaty. *See* Vienna Convention on the Law of Treaties, art. 31(3)(b), 1155 U.N.T.S. 331 (1969) [hereinafter Vienna Convention]. Treaties must also be interpreted in light of their object and purpose (*see, e.g., id.* art. 31(1)), which in this instance is to assure universal respect for and observance of the human rights set forth in the treaty. *See* ICCPR, *supra* preamble (recognizing "equal and inalienable rights of all," recognizing that "everyone ... [should] enjoy" human rights, and "[c]onsidering the obligation of States under the Charter of the United Nations to promote universal respect for, and observance of, human rights"). The preamble to the treaty must also be used for interpretive purposes (*see, e.g.*, Vienna Convention, *supra* art. 31(2)), which in this instance reflects the object and purpose of the ICCPR to achieve universal respect for and observance of the human rights set forth in the treaty. More generally, human rights treaties are presumptively universal in reach in view of the general and preemptive duty of States under the United Nations Charter to achieve universal respect for and observance of human rights. *See, e.g.*, U.N. Charter, arts. 55(c), 56; ICCPR, *supra* preamble; Vienna Convention, *supra* art. 31(3)(c) ("any relevant rules of international law" (such as the preemptive human rights duties under the U.N. Charter) are to be taken into account when interpreting a treaty (such as the ICCPR). Further, the Supreme Court has recognized that treaties are to be interpreted in a broad manner in order to protect express and implied rights. *See, e.g.*, Paust, *Executive Plans, supra* at 832 n.76.

Article 50 of the treaty also assures that orders, authorizations, conspiracies, complicitous conduct (including memos that abet violations), and other acts within the territory of a Party that are in violation of the treaty are proscribed "without any limitations or exceptions."

Concerning the invalidity of an attempted reservation to Article 7's reach to *all* forms of torture, cruel, inhuman, and degrading treatment, *see, e.g., id.* at 823 n.42; Concluding Observations of the Human Rights Committee: United States of America, U.N. Doc. CCPR/C/79/Add.50, para. 14 (1995); Human Rights Committee, General Comment No. 24, para. 8, U.N. Doc. CCPR/C/21/Rev.1/Add.6 (1994). Article 7 is also expressly among the nonderogable articles in the treaty. See ICCPR, *supra* art. 4(2). Moreover, the rights and duties reflected in Article 7 are part of customary and *jus cogens* international law of a nonderogable and universal reach regardless of attempted treaty reservations or understandings. *See, e.g.*, Paust, *Executive Plans, supra* at 821–23.

When interpreting Article 7 of the ICCPR, the Human Rights Committee created by the Covenant declared: "Complaints about ill-treatment must be investigated.... Those found guilty must be held responsible, and the alleged victims must themselves have effective remedies at their disposal, including the right to obtain compensation." General Comment No. 7, para. 1, Report of the H.R. Comm., 37 U.N. GAOR, Supp. No. 40, Annex V, U.N. Doc. E/CN.4/Sub.2/Add.1/963 (1982). General Comment No. 20 (1992) replaced No. 7 and recognized that "it is not sufficient" merely to make violations "a crime" (para. 8), states should report "the provisions of their criminal law which penalize torture and cruel, inhuman and degrading treatment or punishment, specifying the penalties applicable to such acts, whether committed by public officials or other persons acting on behalf of the State, or by private persons. Those who violate article 7, whether by encouraging, ordering, tolerating or perpetrating prohibited acts, must be held responsible" (para. 13), states have a duty to afford protection against such acts "whether inflicted by people acting in their official capacity, outside their official capacity or in a private capacity" (para. 2), and "[a]mnesties are generally incompatible with" such duties and "States must not deprive individuals of the right to an effective remedy...." (para. 15), in International Human Rights Instruments, U.N. Doc. HRI/GEN/1 (4 Sept. 1992), at 29–32. Note that this General Comment is merely one of a number of instruments and decisions that have recognized private duties under human rights law and that the existence of private duties is often expressed or implied in human rights treaties. *See, e.g.*, Jordan J. Paust, *The Reality of Private Rights, Duties, and Participation in the International Legal Process*, 25 MICH. J. INT'L L. 1229, 1241–45 (2004).

C. The American Declaration and O.A.S. Charter

Many of the same rights, duties and prohibitions apply to conduct within the Americas through the Charter of the Organization of American States and the American Declaration of the Rights and Duties of Man, O.A.S. Res. XXX (1948), arts. I ("Every human being has the right to life, liberty and the security of person."), XXV (" ... Every individual who has been deprived of his liberty ... has the right to humane treatment"), O.A.S. Off. Rec. OEA/Ser. L/V/I.4, Rev. (1965). As a party to the Charter of the Organization of American States, the U.S. is bound by the American Declaration, which is a legally authoritative indicia of human rights protected through Article 3(k) of the O.A.S. Charter [*see also id.* arts. 44, 111]. *See, e.g.*, Advisory Opinion OC-10/89, I-A, Inter-Am. Court H.R., Ser. A: Judgments and Opinions, No. 10, paras. 45, 47 (1989); Inter-Am. Comm. H.R., Report on the Situation of the Inhabitants of the Interior of Ecuador Affected by Development Activities, Chapter VIII (1996), OEA/Ser.L/V/II.96, doc. 10 rev. 1 (Apr. 24, 1977) ("The American Declaration ... continues to serve as a source of international obligation for all member states"); The "Baby Boy" Opinion, Case 2141, Inter-Am. Comm. H.R. 25, OEA/Ser.L/V/II.54, doc. 9 rev. 1 (1981), at para. 15 ("As a consequence of Article 3j, 16, 51e, 112 and 150 of [the Charter], the provisions of other instruments and resolutions of the OAS on human rights acquired binding force. Those instruments and resolutions of the OAS on human rights approved with the vote of the U.S. Government" include the American Declaration of the Rights and Duties of Man. That Declaration affirms several human rights, now protected through the O.A.S. Charter, including the right to "resort to the courts to ensure respect for ... [one's] legal rights" documented in Article XVIII); Roach Case, No. 9647, Inter-Am. Comm. H.R. 147, OEA/Ser.L/V/II.71, doc. 9 rev. 1 (1987), at para. 48; *see also* RICHARD B. LILLICH & HURST HANNUM, INTERNATIONAL HUMAN RIGHTS 802–04 (3 ed. 1995); DAVID WEISSBRODT, JOAN FITZPATRICK, FRANK NEWMAN, INTERNATIONAL HUMAN RIGHTS 598–600 (3 ed. 1996); MCDOUGAL, LASSWELL, CHEN, *supra* at 198, 316.

Within the Americas, the United States is also bound to take no action inconsistent with the object and purpose of the American Convention on Human Rights, 1144 U.N.T.S. 123 (1969), which would necessarily include orders, authorizations, complicity, and more direct acts in violation of the human rights protected in the Convention. This obligation arises because the U.S. has singed the treaty while awaiting ratification. *See, e.g.*, Vienna Convention, *supra* art. 18. Article 5 of the American Convention requires:

(1) Every person has the right to have his physical, mental, and moral integrity respected.

(2) No one shall be subjected to torture or to cruel, inhuman, or degrading punishment or treatment. All persons deprived of their liberty shall be treated with respect for the inherent dignity of the human person....

Section 2
Torture and Other Inhumane Acts

Convention Against Torture and Other Cruel, Inhuman or Degrading Treatment or Punishment
Dec. 10, 1984, 1465 U.N.T.S. 85
[Read the Torture Convention, in the Documents Supplement]

Questions

1. As of January, 2012, there are 147 signatories to the Convention. How is torture defined in Article 1 of the treaty? One textwriter and former President of the Appeals Chamber of the ICTY has noted that torture thus defined has the following elements: (1) an act that causes severe pain or suffering, whether physical or mental; (2) intentionally inflicted; (3) for a purpose listed or some other purpose; (4) inflicted by or at the instigation of or with the consent or acquiescence of a public official or other person acting in an official capacity; and (5) such pain or suffering does not arise "only from" nor is it "inherent in or incidental to lawful sanctions." *See* ANTONIO CASSESE, INTERNATIONAL CRIMINAL LAW, 119–20 (2003). Thus, the *actus reus* requires an "act" that causes severe pain or suffering, whether physical or mental. Under the Convention, torture does not involve every act that causes pain or suffering. The pain or suffering caused must be "severe." The CAT, however, does not elaborate on the key aspect of "severe." *See also* Notes 13–14 *infra*.

Thus also, there are two *mens rea* requirements. First, the act that causes severe pain and suffering must be "intentionally" inflicted on a person (not recklessly or negligently). The second aspect is not entirely clear. It is stated that the infliction of severe pain or suffering must be done for a purpose, such as for the purpose of: (1) obtaining from the victim or a third person information or a confession, (2) punishing the victim for an act he or a third person committed or is suspected of committing, (3) intimidating or coercing the victim or a third person; or (4) for any reason based on discrimination of any kind. However, the list of purposes is illustrative and not exhaustive, as noted by the phrase "for such purposes as". Moreover, paragraph 2 of Article 1 adds that the definition contained therein "is without prejudice to any international instrument ... which does or may contain provisions of wider application." Since most human rights instruments and the Geneva Conventions prohibit "torture" for any purpose and two of the major human rights instruments are addressed in the preamble as instruments that prohibit torture regardless of purpose, it is logical that the CAT did not attempt to restrict relevant purposes to those that are expressly listed in Article 1. *See also* Article 2(2); The Prosecutor v. Delalic, IT-96-21-T (Trial Chamber Judgment, 16 Nov. 1998), para. 470 ("there is no requirement that the conduct must be solely perpetrated for a prohibited purpose. Thus, ... the prohibited purpose must simply be part of the motivation behind the conduct and need not be the predominating or sole purpose."). Must the relevant purpose be more than a mere purpose to torture, *i.e.*, more than use of torture as an end in itself?

2. Are rape and other sexual offenses covered in Article 1? in Article 16? Recall the recognitions of the ICTR and ICTY in Chapter Eight that rape and other forms of sexual violence can constitute torture.

3. Can members of al Qaeda be prosecuted for violations of the Convention? Under this Convention, can there be some private perpetrators? See J. Paust, *The Other Side of Right: Private Duties Under Human Rights Law,* 5 HARV. H.R.J. 51, 61 (1992). See also para. 2 of Article 1. Other human rights treaties proscribe torture and cruel, inhuman or degrading treatment and punishment without mention of the status of perpetrators. *See, e.g.*, ICCPR, art. 7; *see also id.* art. 5(1) (implied duties of groups and persons). The CAT Committee has noted that the phrase "other persons acting in an official capacity" can include some non-state actors in Somalia with quasi-governmental authority. Elmi v. Australia, Comm. No. 120/1998, U.N. Doc. CAT/C/22/D/120/1998 (1999).

4. In the U.S., the Violence Against Women Act (VAWA), 42 U.S.C. § 13,981, which provides civil remedies for "a crime of violence motivated by gender," was enacted in part to protect human rights of women from private acts of violence. *See, e.g.*, Paust, *Human Rights Purposes of the Violence Against Women Act and International Law's Enhancement of Congressional Power*, 22 HOUS. J. INT'L L. 209 (2000).

5. Do obligations of a Party to the treaty apply merely in the territory of the Party? See preamble and arts. 2(1), 4(1), 5(1) and (2), 16. See Committee Against Torture, *Consideration of Reports Submitted by States Parties Under Article 19 of the Convention: Conclusions and Recommendations of the Committee against Torture, United States of America*, 36th sess., U.N. Doc. CAT/C/USA/CO/2 (18 May 2006), paras. ("The State party should recognize and ensure that the Convention applies at all times, whether in peace, war or armed conflict, in any territory under its jurisdiction"), 15 ("provisions of the Convention expressed as applicable to 'territory under the State party's jurisdiction' apply to, and are fully enjoyed by, all persons under the effective control of its authorities, of whichever type, wherever located in the world."), 17 (detention "in any secret detention facility under its *de facto* effective control ... constitutes, *per se*, a violation of the Convention"), 18 ("enforced disappearance in any territory under its jurisdiction ... constitutes, *per se*,

a violation of the Convention"), 24 ("in all places of detention under its *de facto* effective control"), 26 ("eradicate all forms of torture and ill-treatment of detainees by its military or civilian personnel, in any territory under its jurisdiction") [hereinafter U.N. CAT Report].

6. With respect to Article 2, para. 1 ("territory under its jurisdiction"), *see also Loizidou v. Turkey*, 310 Eur. Ct. H.R., Ser. A (23 Mar. 1995) (portions of Cyprus were occupied territory under the jurisdiction of Turkey), examined in J. Kokott & B. Rudolf, International Decisions, 90 Am. J. Int'l L. 98, 98–100 (1996).

7. Under Article 2, para. 3, can a superior order be used in mitigation? Recall that customary international law concerning the reach of individual responsibility with respect to superior orders can be read into any treaty.

8. With respect to money damages, *compare* Article 14, para. 1, *with id.*, para. 2 and Article 16, paras. 1 and 2. See also U.N. CAT Report, *supra* at paras. 28 ("full redress, compensation and rehabilitation"), 32 ("redress, including appropriate compensation"). With respect to U.S. cases addressing civil liability for torture, cruel, inhuman, and/or degrading treatment, *see, e.g.*, Cabello v. Fernandez-Larios, 402 F.3d 1148 (11th Cir. 2005) (Fernandos Larios, who served as a bodyguard to the general in command of a death squad during Pinochet's regime in Chile, was found liable for crimes against humanity, extrajudicial killing, torture, and cruelty with respect to massacres in 5 Chilean cities); Kadic v. Karadzic, 70 F.3d 232 (2d Cir. 1995); Filartiga v. Pena-Irala, 630 F.2d 876 (2d Cir. 1980); Presbyterian Church of Sudan v. Talisman Energy, Inc., 244 F. Supp.2d 289, 305–06, 326 (S.D.N.Y. 2003); Mehinovic v. Vuckovic, 198 F. Supp.2d 1322, 1347–49 (N.D. Ga. 2002) ("Cruel, inhuman, or degrading treatment is a discrete and well-recognized violation of customary international law and is, therefore, a separate ground for liability," adding: "cruel, inhuman, or degrading treatment includes acts which inflict mental or physical suffering, anguish, humiliation, fear and debasement, which do not rise to the level of 'torture'" and that being "forced to observe the suffering of their friends and neighbors ... [is] another form of inhumane and degrading treatment"); Estate of Cabello v. Fernandez-Larios, 157 F. Supp.2d 1345, 1360–61 (S.D. Fla. 2001); Daliberti v. Republic of Iraq, 97 F. Supp.2d 38, 45 (D.D.C. 2000); Cicippio v. Islamic Republic of Iran, 18 F. Supp.2d 62, 65–69 (D.D.C. 1998); Xuncax v. Gramajo, 886 F. Supp. 162, 187 (D. Mass. 1995); Forti v. Suarez-Mason, 672 F. Supp. 1531 (N.D. Cal. 1987) (torture and summary execution). See also Note 14 below concerning inhumane and degrading treatment.

9. Article 37 of the Convention on the Rights of the Child, 1577 U.N.T.S. 3 (1989), similarly requires that signatories "shall ensure that: (a) No child shall be subjected to torture or other cruel, inhuman or degrading treatment or punishment" and adds: "Neither capital punishment nor life imprisonment without possibility of release shall be imposed for offences committed by persons below 18 years of age."

This treaty also requires signatories to "take all appropriate measures ... to protect children from the illicit use of narcotic drugs and psychotropic substances" (art. 33); "to protect the child from all forms of sexual exploitation and sexual abuse, ... [including taking] all appropriate national, bilateral and multilateral measures to prevent: (a) The inducement or coercion of a child to engage in any unlawful sexual activity; (b) The exploitative use of children in prostitution or other unlawful sexual practices; (c) The exploitative use of children in pornographic performances and materials" (art. 34); and to "take all appropriate national, bilateral and multilateral measures to prevent the abduction, the sale of or traffic in children for any purpose or in any form" (art. 35). The treaty also requires that signatories "take all appropriate measures to promote physical and psychological recovery and social re-integration of a child victim of: any form of neglect, exploitation, or abuse; torture or any other form of cruel, inhuman or degrading treatment or punishment; or armed conflicts...." *Id.* art. 39.

10. Article 6 of the Convention on the Elimination of All Forms of Discrimination Against Women, 1249 U.N.T.S. 13 (1979), mandates that all signatories "shall take all appropriate measures, including legislation, to suppress all forms of traffic in women and exploitation of prostitution of women."

11. The U.S. statute proscribing torture is 18 U.S.C. §2340 *et seq.* Section 2340A(a), Torture, states: "Whoever outside the United States commits or attempts to commit torture shall be fined under this title or imprisoned not more than 20 years, or both, and if death results to any person from conduct prohibited by this subsection, shall be punished by death or imprisonment for any term or years or for life." The U.N. Committee Against Torture found the legislation lacking: "sections 2340 and 2340 A of the United States Code limit federal criminal jurisdiction over acts of torture to extraterritorial cases. The Committee also regrets that, despite the occurrence of cases of extraterritorial torture of detainees, no prosecutions have been initiated under the extraterritorial torture statute.... [The U.S.] should enact a federal crime of torture consistent with article 1 of the Convention ... to prevent and eliminate acts of torture ... in all its forms.... [The U.S.] should ensure that acts of psychological torture ... are not limited to 'prolonged mental harm' as set out in the State party's understandings lodged at the time of ratification of the Convention, but constitute a wider category of acts, which cause severe mental suffering, irrespective of their prolongation or its duration." U.N. CAT Report, *supra* at para. 13. The Committee also stated that the U.S. "should promptly, thoroughly, and impartially investigate any responsibility of senior military and civilian officials authorizing, acquiescing or consenting, in any way, to acts of torture committed by their subordinates." *Id.* para. 19.

12. During the wars in Afghanistan and Iraq, the Bush Administration attempted to interpret "torture" in a very narrow way that was not consistent with Article 1 of the Convention. *See, e.g.,* Jay S. Bybee, Memorandum for Alberto R. Gonzales, Counsel to the President, Re: Standards of Conduct for Interrogation under 18 U.S.C. §§2340-2340A (Aug. 1, 2002) (claiming that torture must involve death or organ failure and that mental suffering must be permanent), available at http://news.findlaw.com/wp/docs/doj/bybee80102mem.pdf; Jeffrey Smith, *Memo Offered Justification for Use of Torture*, WASH. POST, June 8, 2002, at A1; Paust, *Executive Plans, supra* at 834–36. A second Bybee memo argued that water-boarding and putting a person in a closed box was not torture). Is only "torture" prohibited under the CAT, arts. 1, 16, the ICCPR, art. 7; GC art. 3, and customary international law reflected therein? The Administration also claimed that a U.S. reservation to the treaty and an understanding limited the reach of the treaty. *See* Reservation No. 1, available at CONG. REC. S17486-01 (daily ed., Oct. 27, 1990) ("the United States considers itself bound by the obligation under Article 16 to prevent 'cruel, inhuman or degrading treatment or punishment,' only insofar as the term 'cruel, inhuman or degrading treatment or punishment' means the cruel, unusual and inhumane treatment or punishment prohibited by the Fifth, Eighth, and/or Fourteenth Amendments to the Constitution of the United States."). Professor Paust has remarked: Clearly, the attempted reservation would be incompatible with the object and purpose of the Convention, since application of the reservation would preclude coverage of all forms of cruel, inhuman and degrading treatment as required under the Convention. As such, it is void *ab initio* as a matter of law. *See* Vienna Convention on the Law of Treaties, *supra* art. 19(c). It was claimed recently by Alberto Gonzales that the pu-

tative reservation not only sought to limit the type of treatment proscribed (*i.e.*, that the phrase "cruel, inhuman, or degrading" set forth in a multilateral treaty "means" merely that which is recognized under U.S. constitutional amendments), but also sought to limit the treaty's reach overseas (*i.e.*, "means" treatment or punishment prohibited by the amendments and, if they don't apply overseas, such treatment or punishment overseas is o.k.). *See* Sonni Efron, *Torture Becomes a Matter of Definition: Bush Nominees Refuse to Say What's Prohibited*, N.Y. Times, Jan. 23, 2005, at A1. Such an attempted reservation would be doubly incompatible with the object and purpose of the treaty and void as a matter of law. [*See also* Note 5 above] In any event, the customary prohibitions reflected in the treaty are universally applicable and have no such limitations. Paust, *Executive Plans*, *supra* at 823 n.43. See also Leila Zerrougui, *et al.*, Report, *Situation of Detainees at Guantanamo Bay*, Commission on Human Rights, 62nd sess., items 10 and 11 of the provisional agenda, U.N. Doc. E/CN.4/2006/120 (Feb. 15, 2006) [hereinafter U.N. Experts' Report], at 45 n.48, quoting Conclusions and Recommendations of the Committee against Torture: United States of America, 15/05/2000, U.N. Doc. A/55/44, paras. 179–180 (2000). See also The United States and Torture (Marjorie Cohn ed. 2011); M. Cherif Bassiouni, The Institutionalization of Torture by the Bush Administration (2010); Christopher L. Blakesley, Terror and Anti-Terrorism: A Normative and Practical Assessment (2006); Marjorie Cohn, Cowboy Republic: Six Ways the Bush Gang Has Defied the Law (2007); Mark Danner, Abu Ghraib and the War on Terror (2004); John W. Dean, Worse Than Watergate: The Secret Presidency of George W. Bush (2004); Amos N. Guiora, Constitutional Limits on Coercive Interrogation (2008); Seymour M. Hersh, Chain of Command: The Road From 9/11 to Abu Ghraib (2004); Peter Jan Honigsberg, Our Nation Unhinged: The Human Consequences of the War on Terror (2009); Joseph Margulies, Guantánamo and the Abuse of Presidential Power (2006); Thomas Michael McDonnell, The United States, International Law, and the Struggle Against Terrorism 47–57, 60 (2009); Jordan J. Paust, Beyond the Law: The Bush Administration's Unlawful Responses in the "War" on Terror (2007); Philippe Sands, Torture Team: Rumsfeld's Memo and the Betrayal of American Values (2008); Michael P. Scharf & Paul R. Williams, Shaping Foreign Policy in Times of Crisis 129–30, 181–95 (2010); Diane Marie Amann, *Abu Ghraib*, 153 U. Pa. L. Rev. 2085, 2086, 2094 (2005); Karima Bennoune, *"To Respect and to Ensure": Reconciling International Human Rights Obligations in a Time of Terror*, 97 Proc., Am. Soc'y Int'l L. 23, 24 (2003); Jordan J. Paust, *The Bush-Cheney Legacy: Serial Torture and Forced Disappearance in Manifest Violation of Global Human Rights Law*, 18 Barry L. Rev. (2013), available at http://ssrn.com/abstract=1989099 (concerning nine false claims of the Bush-Cheney Administration, "there has been notable rejection of their false claims that (1) relevant human rights law that is binding on the United States and its nationals does not apply outside United States territory; (2) human rights law does not apply during war or armed conflict; (3) alleged necessity can allow deviation from the absolute prohibitions of torture and cruel, inhuman, and degrading treatment under the laws of war and human rights law; (4) certain detained persons have no rights under applicable laws of war; (5) attempted U.S. reservations to two human rights treaties (which are facially and were known to be void *ab initio* as a matter of law) precluded their full reach regarding absolute and peremptory prohibitions of all forms of torture, cruel, inhuman, and other unlawful treatment; (6) certain interrogation tactics that had already been recognized as torture were not torture; (7) non-prisoners of war could be lawfully transferred from occupied territory to secret detention sites and to Guantanamo Bay for coercive interrogation or even lawful interrogation or detention; (8) the President and his entourage are not bound by the laws of war and, more generally, that they were above the law; and (9) through such manifestly unacceptable ploys members of the Administration could avoid criminal prosecution for authorizing or aiding and abetting international criminal conduct.").

13. With respect to authorizations within the Bush Administration, including the military, to strip persons naked and use of hooding as interrogation tactics, to use dogs to strike fear during interrogation and for terroristic purposes, to use water-boarding (which induces a significant fear of drowning), to use "fear up harsh: significantly increasing the fear level of a detainee," and to use other interrogation tactics not previously approved in U.S. military interrogation manuals, *see, e.g.*, Paust, *Executive Plans, supra* at 812, 824–51; Note 12 above.

In October 2006, former President Bush admitted that he had a "program" of secret detention and "tough" interrogation. *See, e.g.*, GEORGE W. BUSH, DECISION POINTS 170 (2010) (Bush admitted authorizing waterboarding, which is decidedly torture); JANE MAYER, THE DARK SIDE: THE INSIDE STORY OF HOW THE WAR ON TERROR TURNED INTO A WAR ON AMERICAN IDEALS 150 (noting an early 2002 meeting of Yoo, Gonzales, Addington, Flanigan, and Haynes discussing "what sorts of pain" to inflict), 185 (noting conflicts between Addington and Bellinger), 198–99 (noting that Addington, Gonzales, Haynes, Goldsmith, and others had flown to Guantanamo in September 2002 to discuss and observe use of patently unlawful SERE [Survival Evasion Resistance and Escape] tactics on detainees who were still held in secret detention or forced disappearance), 304, 307, 311–2 (noting the facilitating role of Gonzales) (2008); JOSE RODRIGUEZ, HARD MEASURES (2012) (admissions regarding waterboarding and other coercive tactics by former Deputy Director of Operations (Nov. 16—Dec. 2004) and Director, National Clandestine Service (Dec. 2004—Nov. 30, 2007), CIA); JOHN YOO, WAR BY OTHER MEANS ix, 35, 39–40, 43, 171–72, 187, 190–92, 200, 231 (2006); Jens David Ohlin, *The Torture Lawyers*, 51 HARV. INT'L L.J. 193 (2010); Jordan J. Paust, *The Absolute Prohibition of Torture and Necessary and Appropriate Sanctions*, 43 VALPARAISO U. L. REV. 1535, 1544–45, 1559–69 (2009) (also noting certain facilitating and abetting roles of Cheney, Addington, Gonzales, Rice, Rumsfeld, Tenet, Ashcroft, Yoo, Bybee, Haynes, Bradbury, Rizzo, Feith, Philbin, Flanigan, Goldsmith, and others), available at http://ssrn.com/abstract=1331159; Report, *Senate Armed Services Committee Inquiry Into the Treatment of Detainees in U.S. Custody*, Dec. 20, 2008; Majority Staff Report, House Committee on the Judiciary, *Reining in the Imperial Presidency: Lessons and Recommendations Relating to the Presidency of George W. Bush*, Jan. 13, 2009, at 110–46 (also noting: "in Secretary Powell's view, Mr. Bush was 'complicit' in those abuses." *Id.* at 136).

Would any of these tactics amount to cruel, inhuman, or degrading treatment, if not torture? See Paust, *The Absolute Prohibition, supra* at 1553–58 (water-boarding or a related inducement of suffocation, use of dogs to create intense fear, threatening to kill the detainee or family members, and the cold cell or a related inducement of hypothermia are each manifestly forms of torture. For example, there were 29 U.S. federal and state court cases, 7 U.S. Dep't of State Human Rights Country Reports, a decision of the European Court of Human Rights, and 2 decisions of the Inter-American Court of Human Rights that had recognized that water-boarding and related conduct is torture. *Id.* at 1553–54 n.69); U.N. CAT Report, *supra* at para. 24 (the U.S. "should rescind any interrogation technique, including methods involving sexual humiliation, 'water boarding,' 'short shackling' [*e.g.*, shackling a detainee to a hook in the floor], and using dogs to induce fear, that constitute torture, cruel, inhuman or degrading treatment or punishment, in all places of detention under its *de facto* effective control, in order to comply with its obligations under the Convention."); U.N. Experts' Report, *supra* Note 12, at 9–10, paras. 12–14,

21–22, paras. 41–45, 24–25, paras. 51–52, 37, para. 87; Council of Europe, Parliamentary Assembly, Res. 1433, *Lawfulness of Detentions by the United States in Guantanamo Bay*, paras. 7(i)–(vi), 8(i)–(iii), (vii) (2005), in the Documents Supplement; International Committee of the Red Cross, *ICRC Report on the Treatment of Fourteen "High Value Detainees" in CIA Custody* (Feb. 2007), quoted in Mark Danner, *Voices from the Black Sites*, 56 The N.Y. Rev. of Bks. no. 6 (Apr. 9, 2009), available at http://www.nybooks.com/articles/22530. See also Evan Wallach, *Drop by Drop: Forgetting the History of Water Torture in U.S. Courts*, 45 Columbia J. Transnat'l L. 468 (2007) (also noting early uses of waterboarding and related inducement of suffocation during World War II and convictions); M. Cherif Bassiouni, *The Future of Human Rights in the Age of Globalization*, in Perspectives on International Law in an Era of Change 22, 31 (2012).

14. What constitutes torture or cruel, inhuman or degrading treatment? See Convention, art. 1; recall Notes 8 and 13 above, and consider: In *Ireland v. United Kingdom*, 25 Eur. Ct. H.R. (ser. A) at 5 (1978), the European Court of Human Rights ruled that British interrogation tactics of wall-standing (forcing the detainees to remain for periods of some hours in a "stress position"), hooding, subjection to noise, deprivation of sleep, and deprivation of food and drink "constituted a practice of inhuman and degrading treatment" proscribed under human rights law.[1] In 1996, the European Court recognized that where a detainee "was stripped naked, with his arms tied behind his back and suspended by his arms ... [, s]uch treatment amounted to torture."[2] In another case, the European Court stated that treatment was "'degrading' because it was such as to arouse in its victims feelings of fear, anguish and inferiority capable of humiliating and debasing them."[3] The International Criminal Tribunal for Former Yugoslavia has also identified criteria for determining whether certain conduct constitutes criminally sanctionable "torture"[4] or

---

1. *Id.* at 41, para. 96, 66, para. 167. The court noted that the "techniques were applied in combination, with premeditation and for hours at a stretch; they caused, if not bodily injury, at least intense physical and mental suffering to the persons subjected thereto and also led to acute psychiatric disturbances during interrogation," and, "accordingly," were forms of inhuman treatment. *Id.* at 66, para. 167. The Court concluded that the "techniques were also degrading, since they were such as to arouse in their victims feelings of fear, anguish and inferiority capable of humiliating and debasing them and possibly breaking their physical or moral resistance." *Id.*

2. Aksoy v. Turkey, 6 Eur. Ct. H.R. 2260, 23 EHRR 553, at paras. 60, 64 (18 Dec. 1996). The Court stated that "torture attaches only to deliberate inhuman treatment causing very serious and cruel suffering." *Id.* at paras. 63–64. The victim was detained for some two weeks and had claimed to have been subjected to beatings and had been stripped naked, hooded, and subjected to electric shocks. *Id.* at paras. 60, 64.

3. T & V v. United Kingdom, Judgment of 16 Dec. 1999, at para. 71, 30 EHRR 121 (2000).

4. *See, e.g.*, The Prosecutor v. Kunarac, IT-96-23-T & IT-96-23/1-T (Trial Chamber, International Criminal Tribunal for Former Yugoslavia), para. 497 (22 Feb. 2001) (intentional "infliction, by act or omission, of severe pain or suffering, whether physical or mental"); *Id.* (Appeals Chamber, 12 June 2002), para. 149, adding "but there are no more specific requirements which allow an exhaustive classification or enumeration of acts which may constitute torture. Existing case law has not determined the absolute degree of pain required for an act to amount to torture"), para. 150 (rape can constitute torture); Johan D. van der Vyver, *Torture as a Crime Under International Law*, 67 Albany L. Rev. 427 (2003). In The Prosecutor v. Naletilic & Martinovic, IT-98-34-A (Appeals Chamber, 3 May 2006), paras. 299–300, the Appeals Chamber used the test stated in *Kunarac* and added: "while the suffering inflicted by some acts may be so obvious that the acts amount *per se* to torture, in general allegations of torture must be considered on a case-by-case basis so as to determine whether, in light of the acts committed and their context, severe physical or mental pain or suffering was inflicted. Similar case-by-case analysis is necessary regarding the crime of wilfully causing great suffering." Para. 299. In the case before the tribunal, "the Appeals Chamber agrees that telling prisoners falsely that they will be executed, in a "brutal context that makes the statement believable, can amount to wilfully causing great suffering. In addition, severe physical abuse in the course of interrogation ... also generally

"cruel" or "inhuman" treatment.[5] Moreover, the Committee against Torture created under the Convention Against Torture and Other Cruel, Inhuman or Degrading Treatment or Punishment has condemned the use of the following interrogation tactics as either torture or cruel, inhuman or degrading treatment: (1) restraining in very painful conditions, (2) hooding under special conditions, (3) sounding of loud music for prolonged periods, (4) sleep deprivation for prolonged periods, (5) threats, including death threats, (6) violent shaking, and (7) using cold air to chill.[6] Earlier, a U.S. Army pamphlet addressing Geneva and other law of war proscriptions warned that an illegal means of interrogation of a detainee included "dunking his head into a barrel of water, or putting a plastic bag over his head to make him talk," adding: "No American soldier can commit these brutal acts, nor permit his fellow soldiers to do so."[7] Paust, *Executive Plans*, *supra* at 845–46.

15. For discussion of why the threat of administering truth serum can constitute torture whereas the administration of such does not, see Linda M. Keller, *Is Truth Serum Torture?*, 20 Am. U. Int'l L. Rev. 521 (2005).

16. The authors of the U.N. Experts' Report, *supra* Note 12, maintain that force-feeding to deter Guantanamo detainees from carrying out long-term hunger strikes to protest their incarceration constitutes "torture" as defined by CAT. *Id.* paras. 54 & n.73, 70, 82. Do you agree; would you prefer more facts? Does force-feeding of detainees rise to the level of the infliction of "severe" pain or suffering? If so, was the infliction of severe pain or suffering committed for the purpose of obtaining information or a confession (short term or long term, *e.g.*, to keep detainees alive in order to obtain information later)? To punish the victim? To intimidate or coerce the victim? For an unlawful discriminatory purpose? Does force-feeding constitute "other acts of cruel, inhuman or degrading treatment or punishment" within the meaning of Article 16 of CAT?

17. The U.N. Committee Against Torture has also recognized that "secret detention … constitutes, *per se*, a violation of the Convention" and that "enforced disappearance … constitutes, *per se*, a violation of the Convention." U.N. CAT Report, *supra* at paras. 17–18. The Committee also declared that "detaining persons indefinitely without charge, constitutes *per se* a violation of the Convention." *Id.* para. 22. With respect to U.S. attempts to deny *habeas corpus* review of the propriety of detention, the Committee warned that the U.S. "should ensure that independent, prompt and thorough procedures to review the circumstances of detention and the status of detainees are available to all detainees as required

---

amounts to wilfully causing great suffering, particularly when combined with acts designed to cause psychological torment, such as falsely informing a prisoner that his father had been killed or firing guns at prisoners so as to create an atmosphere of terror." Para. 300.

5. With respect to "cruel" treatment, a trial chamber of the ICTY declared that "cruel treatment is treatment which causes serious mental or physical suffering and constitutes a serious attack on human dignity." The Prosecutor v. Delalic, IT-96-21-T (Trial Chamber, International Criminal Tribunal for Former Yugoslavia), para. 551 (Nov. 16, 1998). The same decision recognized that "inhuman treatment is an intentional act or omission, that is an act which, when judged objectively, is deliberate and not accidental, which causes serious mental or physical suffering or injury or constitutes a serious attack on human dignity." *Id.* at para. 543. Other ICTY cases confirm the *Delalic* recognitions. *See, e.g.*, Knut Dormann, Elements of War Crimes under the Rome Statute of the International Criminal Court 65 n.72 (re: inhuman), 398–99 ns. 7–8 (re: cruel) (2003). With respect to torture, see also Zubeda v. Ashcroft, 333 F.3d 463, 472 (3d Cir. 2003) ("[r]ape can constitute torture"); Al-Saher v. I.N.S., 268 F.3d 1143, 1147 (9th Cir. 2001).

6. Concluding Observations of the Committee against Torture: Israel, 18th Sess., U.N. Doc. A/52/44 (1997) at paras. 256–257.

7. U.S. Dep't of Army Subject Schedule 27-1, *The Geneva Conventions of 1949 and Hague Convention No. IV of 1907*, at 7 (8 Oct. 1970).

by article 13 of the Convention." *Id.* para. 27. With respect to Guantanamo Bay, the Committee stated that the U.S. "should cease to detain any person at Guantanamo Bay and close this detention facility, permit access by the detainees to judicial process or release them as soon as possible, ensuring that they are not returned to any State where they could face a real risk of being tortured." *Id.* para. 22. With respect to a U.S. claim that its obligation under Article 3 does not extend to persons detained outside U.S. territory, the Committee declared that the U.S. "should apply the *non-refoulement* guarantee to all detainees in its custody, cease the rendition of suspects, in particular by its intelligence agencies, to States where they face a real risk of torture, in order to comply with its obligations under article 3 of the Convention. The State party should always ensure that suspects have the possibility to challenge decisions of *refoulement*." *Id.* para. 20. *See also* Leila Nadya Sadat, *Ghost Prisoners and Black Sites: Extraordinary Rendition Under International Law*, 57 Case W. Res. J. Int'l L. _ (2006); Diane Marie Amann, *The Committee Against Torture Urges an End to Guantanamo Detention*, ASIL Insight (June 8, 2006), available at http://www.asil.org/insights/2006/06/insights060608.html.

18. In *The Prosecutor v. Furundzija*, ICTY-95-17/1, at paras. 153–155 (10 Dec. 1998), it was recognized that the prohibition of torture "has evolved into a peremptory norm or *jus cogens*, that is, a norm that enjoys a higher rank in the international hierarchy than treaty law and even 'ordinary' customary rules. The most conspicuous consequence of this higher rank is that the principle at issue could not be derogated from by States.... [para. 154] an absolute value from which nobody must deviate. 155. The fact that torture is prohibited by a peremptory norm of international law has other effects at the inter-state and individual levels. At the inter-state level, it serves to internationally de-legitimise any legislative, administrative or judicial act authorizing torture. It would be senseless to argue, on the one hand, that on account of the *jus cogens* value of the prohibition against torture, treaties or customary rules providing for torture would be null and void *ab initio*, and then be unmindful of a State say, taking national measures authorising or condoning torture or absolving its perpetrators through an amnesty law. If such a situation were to arise, the national measures, violating the general principles and any relevant treaty provision, would produce the legal effects discussed above and in addition would not be accorded international legal recognition...." *See also* remarks of U.N. Secretary-General Kofi Annan: "[t]orture is an atrocious violation of human dignity. It dehumanizes both the victim and the perpetrator. The pain and terror deliberately inflicted by one human being upon another leave permanent scars.... Freedom from torture is a fundamental human right that must be protected under all circumstances. Growing awareness of international legal instruments and protection mechanisms gives hope that the wall of silence around this terrible practice is gradually being eroded." Freedom from Torture "Fundamental Right," Says Secretary-General, SG/SM/7855, OBV/223 (June 26, 2001), available at www.unis.unvienna.org/unis/pressrels/2001/sgsm7855.html.

19. In addition to Article 25 of the American Declaration (requiring "humane treatment") and Article 5 of the American Convention, other regional human rights instruments recognize the absolute prohibition of torture and cruel, inhuman, and degrading treatment. *See, e.g.*, African Charter of Human and Peoples' Rights, art. 5; Arab Charter on Human Rights, art. 8 (which also requires that "[t]he commission of, or participation in, such acts shall be regarded as crimes"); and the European Convention, art. 3.

20. Foreign prosecutions of individuals for torture include: (1) in June, 2005, a French trial in absentia of Ould Dah, a Mauritanian military officer, accused of torturing two other officers in 1991, led to a 10 year prison sentence ("universal jurisdiction" was used in connection with a 1994 law implementing the Torture Convention and Dah was de-

tained in Montpellier, France while participating in a training course); (2) the Spanish conviction of Adolfo Scilingo of crimes against humanity, torture, and illegal detention in connection with the Argentinian "dirty war" between 1976 and 1983, admitting that he was on board two "death flights" during which detainees were mistreated and thrown to their deaths over the ocean (Third Section of the Criminal Division of the Audiencia Nacional (National Court) (19 April 2005); and (3) the Rotterdam District Court judgment of April 7, 2004, against one Sebastien Nzapali in Prosecutor v. N, who "in or around October 1996, in Matadi, jointly and in conjunction with others … as head of the Garde Civile for the province of Bas-Zaire" in the Congo during the reign of Mobutu, engaged in "complicity in torture, repeatedly committed" within the meaning of the Dutch Torture Convention Implementation Act and Section 8 of the International Crimes Act. The case proceeded on the basis of universal jurisdiction and the crime of torture involved Nzapali's use of his bodyguards to against a harbor official who did not clear a car of a friend through customs. Nzapali had the victim beaten "'as a punching bag'" while defendant watched from a balcony. The court found that "the acts of the accused, whereby he abused his position, and seriously affected the physical and mental integrity of the victim, acting in violation of the universal respect for human rights and the fundamental freedoms, show a complete lack of respect for the dignity of a fellow human being." See Ward Ferdinandusse, Comment on *Prosecutor v. N.*, Case No. AO7178, 99 Am. J. Int'l L. 686 (2005). See also Jones v. Saudi Arabia (Ct. App., U.K. 2004) (allowing civil suit by 4 U.K. citizens against several Saudi officials for alleged torture and denying claims to immunity).

Section 3
Race Discrimination

A. General Discrimination

International Convention on the Elimination of All Forms of Racial Discrimination
660 U.N.T.S. 195

[Read Article 4 of the Race Discrimination Convention, in the Documents Supplement]

Question

1. When the United States ratified this convention in 1994 it attached a reservation to the effect that nothing in the Convention shall require the United States to authorize legislation or other action incompatible with the U.S. Constitution, including those provisions relating to free speech. The reservation saves the United States from violating the treaty if it does not, in accordance with the Constitution, enact legislation to criminalize racist speech and organizations. Does the reservation guarantee a specific interpretation of the First Amendment of the U.S. Constitution? See J. Paust, International Law as Law of the United States 313 *ff.* (1996).

B. Apartheid

International Convention on the Suppression and Punishment of the Crime of "Apartheid"

done in New York, Nov. 30, 1973, 1015 U.N.T.S. 243

[Read the Apartheid Convention, in the Documents Supplement]

Notes and Questions

1. In 1984, the U.N. General Assembly passed a resolution recalling that the Security Council had rejected "the so-called 'new constitution' [of the apartheid regime in South Africa] and declared it null and void," commended "the united resistance of the oppressed people of South Africa ... and recogniz[ed] the legitimacy of their struggle to eliminate apartheid and establish a society based on majority rule with equal participation by all the people of South Africa...," urged "all Governments and organizations ... to assist the oppressed people of South Africa in their legitimate struggle for national liberation;" and condemned "the South African racist regime for ... persisting with the further entrenchment of apartheid, a system declared a crime against humanity and a threat to international peace and security". G.A. Res. 39/2 (28 Sept. 1984) (vote: 133–0–2 abstentions).

2. Is mere membership a crime under Article III?

3. Is leader responsibility (noted in Chapter Two, Section 1), as part of customary law, impliedly covered in Article IV (b), or is it limited to circumstances noted in Article III?

Section 4
Hostage-Taking

International Convention Against the Taking of Hostages
1316 U.N.T.S. 205 (1979)

[Read the Hostage-Taking Convention, in the Documents Supplement]

Questions

1. Is asylum or amnesty possible under Article 15 of the Convention if the accused has not been subject to initiation of prosecution under Article 8 (1)? See also preamble ("either be prosecuted or extradited").

2. Is hostage-taking covered if a U.S. perpetrator takes a foreign tourist hostage, within the meaning of Article 1 (1), in a convenience store in Texas? See also Article 13.

3. Can a member of al Qaeda who engages in hostage-taking of European victims in Iraq be prosecuted for a violation of the Convention?

Security Council Resolution Condemning Hostage-Taking
U.N. S.C. Res. 579 (1985)

The Security Council,

Deeply disturbed at the prevalence of incidents of hostage-taking and abduction, several of which are of protracted duration and have included loss of life,

Considering that the taking of hostages and abductions are offences of grave concern to the international community, having severe adverse consequences for the rights of the victims and for the promotion of friendly relations and co-operation among States,....

1. *Condemns unequivocally* all acts of hostage-taking and abduction;

2. *Calls for* the immediate safe release of all hostages and abducted persons wherever and by whomever they are being held;

3. *Affirms* the obligation of all States in whose territory hostages or abducted persons are held urgently to take all appropriate measures to secure their safe release and to prevent the commission of acts of hostage-taking and abduction in the future;

4. *Appeals* to all States that have not yet done so to consider the possibility of becoming parties to [various Conventions listed] ... ;

5. *Urges* the further development of international co-operation among States in devising and adopting effective measures which are in accordance with the rules of international law to facilitate the prevention, prosecution and punishment of all acts of hostage-taking and abduction as manifestations of international terrorism.

United States v. Alvarez-Machain
504 U.S. 655 (1992)
[see Chapter Five, Section 4 B]

United States v. Yunis
681 F. Supp. 896 (D.D.C. 1988)
[see Chapter Three, Sections 1 and 2]

United States v. Yunis
924 F.2d 1086 (D.C. Cir. 1991)
[see Chapter Twelve, Section 4 C]

Section 5
Disappearances

Section 702 (c) of the RESTATEMENT notes that "causing the disappearance of individuals" is a violation of the customary international law of human rights. U.S. cases have addressed civil remedies for such a violation, and one such case has offered a definitional orientation: It has "two essential elements: (1) abduction by state officials or their agents;

followed by (2) official refusals to acknowledge the abduction or to disclose the detainee's fate." *Forti v. Suarez-Mason,* 694 F. Supp. 707, 711 (N.D. Cal. 1988); see also *id.* at 710. The court noted that the Organization of American States "has also denounced 'disappearance' as 'an affront to the conscience of the hemisphere and … a crime against humanity'", *id.* at 710, citing O.A.S. Inter-Am. Comm. H.R. "General Assembly Resolution 666 (November 18, 1983)." Also see *The Prosecutor v. Kupreskic,* IT-95-16-T (ICTY Trial Chamber, Judgment, 14 Jan. 2000); *In re Estate of Marcos, Human Rights Litigation,* 25 F.3d 1467, 1475 (9th Cir. 1994); *Bowoto v. Chevron Corp.,* WL 2349336 at *29 (N.D. Cal. 2007); *Tachiona v. Mugabe,* 234 F. Supp.2d 401, 406 (S.D.N.Y. 2002); *Xuncax v. Gramajo,* 886 F. Supp. 162, 184–85 (D. Mass. 1995).

In 1992, the United Nations General Assembly also adopted the Declaration on the Protection of All Persons from Enforced Disappearance, U.N. G.A. Res. 47/133 (8 Dec. 1992), reprinted in 32 I.L.M. 904 (1993). In Article 1 of the Declaration, it was stated: "Any act of enforced disappearance is an offence to human dignity. It is condemned as a denial of the purposes of the Charter of the United Nations and as a grave and flagrant violation of the human rights and fundamental freedoms proclaimed in the Universal Declaration of Human Rights and reaffirmed in international instruments in this field." Article 4, paragraph 1, declares: "All acts of enforced disappearance shall be offences under criminal law punishable by appropriate penalties which shall take into account their extreme seriousness." Article 5 also declares that such acts render "perpetrators and the State or State authorities which organize, acquiesce in or tolerate such disappearances liable under civil law.…" In 2006, the U.N. adopted the International Convention for the Protection of All Persons from Enforced Disappearance, read the Convention in the Documents Supplement. Article 7(1)(i) of the Rome Statute of the International Criminal Court lists enforced disappearance of persons as a crime against humanity and paragraph (2)(i) thereof contains a definition of enforced disappearance for purposes of ICC prosecution — see the Documents Supplement. See also Note 17 in Section 1 above.

Inter-American Convention on the Forced Disappearance of Persons
done in Belen, Brazil, June 9, 1994

[Read the Disappearance of Persons Convention, in the Documents Supplement]

Questions

1. Is amnesty possible in view of Articles I (a), (b), (c), III ("mitigating" circumstances), VI, IX (no "immunities" or "special dispensations")? Should amnesty ever pertain with respect to international crime? Recall Chapter Two, Section 3. The preamble to the U.N. Convention on Enforced Disappearance expresses the determination "to prevent enforced disappearance and to combat impunity for the crime of enforced disappearance."

2. More generally, are criminal sanctions for human rights violations appropriate? Should greater attention be paid to the concept of crimes against human rights? See Paust, *Applicability of International Criminal Laws to Events in the Former Yugoslavia,* 9 AM. U.J. INT'L L. & POL. 499, 518–21 (1994); *Aggression Against Authority: The Crime of Oppression, Politicide and Other Crimes Against Human Rights,* 18 CASE W. RES. J. INT'L L. 283, 290–92 (1986), and references cited; Chapter Nine.

3. Since the preamble to the Inter-American Convention reaffirms that systematic disappearance is a crime against humanity, could General Pinochet of Chile have been rightly

prosecuted for such acts committed during his regime? *See also* Articles I (b), IX. Could he have been extradited to countries within the Americas? See Article V.

4. Is the prohibition derogable? See the preamble and Article X.

5. During the wars in Afghanistan and Iraq, the Bush Administration had detained numerous individuals there; at Guantanamo Bay, Cuba; and in many other places without disclosing the whereabouts of all persons detained or their names. As noted above, in 2006 former President Bush admitted that he had a "program" of secret detention. Are such forms of secret detention violations of the prohibition of forced disappearance? *See, e.g.,* Statute of the ICC, art. 7(2)(i); Inter-American Convention on the Forced Disappearance of Persons, art. II; Council of Europe Parliamentary Assembly, Res. 1433, *Lawfulness of Detentions by the United States in Guantanamo Bay*, paras. 7(vi), 8(vii)–(viii), in the Documents Supplement; Maureen R. Berman, Roger C. Clark, *State Terrorism: Disappearances*, 13 Rutgers L.J. 531 (1982); Jordan J. Paust, *Post-9/11 Overreaction and Fallacies Regarding War and Defense, Guantanamo, the Status of Persons, Treatment, Judicial Review of Detention, and Due Process in Military Commissions*, 70 Notre Dame L. Rev. 1335, 1352–56 (2004); Sadat, *Ghost Prisoners, supra*; Xuncax v. Gramajo, 886 F. Supp. 162, 184–85 (D. Mass. 1995); Forti v. Suarez-Mason, 694 F. Supp. 707, 710–12 (N.D. Cal. 1988); see also U.N. CAT Report, *supra* at paras. 17–18 (quoted above). Are they violations of the Geneva Conventions? *See* Geneva Civilian Convention, arts. 5, 25, 71, 106–07; IV Commentary, Geneva Convention Relative to the Treatment of Civilian Persons in Time of War 56–58 (ICRC, J. Pictet ed. 1958).

6. If a member of al Qaeda engages in hostage-taking of some European nationals in Iraq and the location of the hostages is otherwise unknown, can the member of al Qaeda be prosecuted for forced disappearance of the hostages?

7. Article 8(2) of the European Convention for the Prevention of Torture and Inhuman or Degrading Treatment or Punishment requires signatories to provide the European Committee for the Prevention of Torture and Inhuman or Degrading Treatment or Punishment full information on all places where persons deprived of their liberty are held. Eur. T.S. No. 126 (1987), art. 8(2). The European Court of Human Rights has held that a state violates Article 2 of the European Convention for the Protection of Human Rights and Fundamental Freedoms if the authorities fail to take reasonable measures to prevent the disappearance of a person with respect to whom there is a particular risk of disappearance. *See* Mahmut Kaya v. Turkey, 28 EHRR 1 (28 Mar. 2000); Gongadze v. Ukraine, judgment of (8 Nov. 2005). Further, Articles 2 and 13 are violated by the failure of authorities to carry out an investigation of disappearances. *See* Cyprus v. Turkey, 35 EHRR 30 (10 May 2001); Kurt v. Turkey, 27 EHRR 373 (25 May 1998), adding that Article 5 requires the authorities to take effective measures to safeguard against a risk of disappearance and to conduct prompt and effective investigations.

8. Note that Article 1(2) of the U.N. Convention on Enforced Disappearance expressly states that "[n]o exceptional circumstances whatsoever, whether a state of war or a threat of war, internal political instability or any other public emergency, may be invoked as a justification." This recognition of the absolute nature of the prohibition of forced disappearance is mirrored in Article X of the Inter-American Convention. Necessarily, secret detention is a *per se* crime that is never justifiable.

9. Note that Article 13 of the U.N. Convention expressly precludes consideration of forced disappearance as a political offense for purposes of extradition. This is mirrored in Article V of the Inter-American Convention.

Chapter 12

Terrorism

Section 1
The Problem of Definition

Introductory Problem

In sweeping language in 1985, the United Nations General Assembly "[u]nequivocally" condemned, "as criminal, all acts, methods and practices of terrorism wherever and by whomever committed." Nearly every year thereafter, subsequent resolutions have contained the same or similar language. *See, e.g.,* Human Rights and Terrorism, U.N. G.A. Res. 59/195, para. 1 (2004); Protection of Human Rights and Fundamental Freedoms While Countering Terrorism, U.N. G.A. Res. 59/191, preamble (2004); Declaration on Measures to Eliminate International Terrorism, U.N. G.A. Res. 49/60, para. 1 (1994); U.N. G.A. Res. 46/51, para. 1 (1991), all in the Documents Supplement. See also Terrorist Attacks on Internationally Protected Persons, U.N. G.A. Res. 66/12 (18 Nov. 2011), para. 1 ("Reiterates its strong and unequivocal condemnation of terrorism in all its forms and manifestations, committed by whomever, wherever and for whatever purposes, as it constitutes once of the most serious threats to international peace and security"); Protection of Human Rights and Fundamental Freedoms While Countering Terrorism, G.A. Res. 66/171 (19 Dec. 2011), prmbl.; same title, G.A. Res. 63/185 (Dec. 18, 2008); Measures to Eliminate International Terrorism, G.A. Res. 63/129 (Dec. 11, 2008).

The Security Council also "resolutely" condemned "'all acts of terrorism'... in all its forms, wherever and by whomever committed," while endorsing a similar statement of the Secretary-General that same year. In 2004 and 2005, three Security Council resolutions affirmed the illegality of all forms of terrorism. In Resolution 1566, the Council condemned "in the strongest terms all acts of terrorism irrespective of their motivation, whenever and by whomever committed." U.N. S.C. Res. 1566 (8 Oct. 2004) (this resolution also reaffirmed the need for States to "ensure that any measures taken to combat terrorism comply with all their obligations under international law ... in particular international human rights, refugee, and humanitarian law." *Id.* prmbl.). In Resolution 1617, the Council reaffirmed "that terrorism in all its forms and manifestations constitutes one of the most serious threats to peace and security and that any acts of terrorism are criminal and unjustifiable regardless of their motivations, whenever and by whomever committed." U.N. S.C. Res. 1617 (29 July 2005). These phrases were repeated in Resolution 1822 (June 30, 2008). Resolution 1526 reiterated the Council's "unequivocal condemnation of all forms of terrorism and terrorist acts." U.N. S.C. Res. 1526 (30 Jan. 2004). In 2011, the Security Council reiterated these points and reiterated "its unequivocal condemnation of Al-Qaida and other individuals, groups, undertakings and entities associated with it, for ongoing and multiple criminal terrorist acts aimed at causing the deaths of innocent civilians and other victims, destruction of property and greatly undermining stability. U.N. S.C. Res. 1989 (17 June 2011), prmbl. The Security Council also reaffirmed "that terrorism cannot and should not be associated with any religion, nationality or civilization." *Id*. Therefore, it is clear that all acts of terrorism, committed in any context, by any person of any status, for any purpose, are proscribed. Nonetheless, none of the General Assembly or Security Council resolutions actually or fully defined that which is so resolutely condemned.

For years, the international community has tried unsuccessfully to arrive at a common definition of terrorism. Proposals have repeatedly been made to convene an international conference to draft a convention defining terrorism. See Marcello Di Fillippo, *Terrorist Crimes and International Co-Operation: Critical Remarks on the Definition and Inclusion of Terrorism in the Category of International Crimes*, 19 Eur. J. Int'l L. 533, 539–40 (2008) (discussing the lack of progress by the U.N. General Assembly in completing a draft comprehensive convention on international terrorism); Mahmoud Hmoud, *Negotiating the Draft Comprehensive Convention on International Terrorism, Major Bones of Contention*, 4 J. Int' Crim. Just. 1031 (2006) (same).

Come to class prepared to participate in a simulated U.N. Conference to adopt a definition of terrorism. Students will be assigned to four groups. Members of Group A will represent Australia, Germany, the United Kingdom, or the United States (countries vulnerable to terrorist acts abroad). Members of Group B will represent Iraq, Israel, Russia, or Peru (countries with active insurgent groups in their territory or nearby). Members of Group C will represent China, Cuba, Iran, North Korea, or Syria (countries that have been accused of participating in state-sponsored terrorism or terroristic oppression); Group D will represent Human Rights Watch and Amnesty International, NGOs with observer status and an ability to lobby in the halls at the conference. Bring to class a draft text for an international definition of terrorism that would be acceptable to your assigned country given its unique interests. Be prepared to explain your approach, argue for adoption of your text as well as the elements contained in your definition, and critique likely counter proposals or elements of a definition that you did not adopt. The following reading materials and questions will help you approach this problem.

Michael P. Scharf, Symposium: "Terrorism on Trial:" *Defining Terrorism as the Peacetime Equivalent of War Crimes: Problems and Prospects*
36 Case W. Res. J. Int'l L. 359, 360–63 (2004)

The International Quest for a General Definition of Terrorism

In 1987, the United Nations General Assembly adopted Resolution 42/159, recognizing that the effectiveness of the struggle against terrorism could be enhanced by the establishment of a generally agreed definition of international terrorism. The issue was initially assigned to the U.N. Sixth (Legal) Committee, which had over the years drafted a number of conventions addressing specific crimes committed by terrorists, although none of these conventions ever used the word "terrorism" let alone provided a definition of the term. When the Sixth Committee failed to make progress in reaching a consensus definition of terrorism, the General Assembly in 1996 established an ad hoc committee to develop a comprehensive framework for dealing with international terrorism.

Foremost among its accomplishments, the ad hoc committee developed the International Convention for the Suppression of the Financing of Terrorism, which defined terrorism as (1) any activity covered by the twelve anti-terrorism treaties; and (2) "any other act intended to cause death or serious bodily injury to a civilian, or to any other person not taking an active part in the hostilities in a situation of armed conflict, when the purpose of such act, by its nature or context, is to intimidate a population, or to compel a Government or an international organization to do or to abstain from doing any act." 129 States have so far ratified this multilateral treaty. This was as close as the international community has ever come to adopting a widely accepted general definition of terrorism.

Immediately after the events of September 11, 2001, the General Assembly established a working group to develop a comprehensive convention on international terrorism. In the spirit of cooperation that marked the early days after the September 11 attacks, the members of the working group nearly reached consensus on the following definition of terrorism:

> [Terrorism is an act] intended to cause death or serious bodily injury to any person; or serious damage to a State or government facility, a public transportation system, communication system or infrastructure facility ... when the purpose of such act, by its nature or context, is to intimidate a population, or to compel a Government or an international organization to do or abstain from doing an act.

The effort hit a snag, however, when Malaysia, on behalf of the 56-member Organization of the Islamic Conference (OIC), proposed the addition of the following language:

> Peoples' struggle including armed struggle against foreign occupation, aggression, colonialism, and hegemony, aimed at liberation and self-determination in accordance with the principles of international law shall not be considered a terrorist crime.

According to Nicholas Rostow, General Counsel to the U.S. Mission to the United Nations, the OIC's proposal intended to exempt acts against Israel over the occupied territories and acts against India over Kashmir from the definition of terrorism, and to brand violations of the laws of war by State military forces such as the Israel Defense Forces as terrorist acts. When neither side was willing to compromise on this issue, the project was shelved indefinitely.

With work on a general definition of terrorism once again stalled in the General Assembly, the U.N. Security Council stepped in to the fray. Acting under Chapter VII of the U.N. Charter, the Council adopted Resolution 1373, which in essence transformed the Terrorism Financing Convention into an obligation of all U.N. member States, requiring them to prohibit financial support for persons and organizations engaged in terrorism. The Council missed an opportunity, however, to adopt a universal definition of terrorism when it decided not to include the Terrorism Financing Convention's definition of terrorism in Resolution 1373, but rather to leave the term undefined and to allow each State to ascertain its own definition of terrorism. Further, the Council created a committee (The Counter-Terrorism Committee) to oversee the implementation of the resolution, but it did not give the Committee the mandate to promulgate a list of terrorists or terrorist organizations to whom financial assistance would be prohibited under the resolution.

The Security Council's most recent statement on terrorism came in response to a bloody terrorist attack at an elementary school in Russia in October 2004. Upon Russia's insistence, the Security Council adopted Resolution 1566, which provides:

> [para. 3. Recalls that] criminal acts, including against civilians, committed with the intent to cause death or serious bodily injury, or taking of hostages, with the

purpose to provoke a state of terror in the general public or in a group of persons or particular persons, intimidate a population or compel a government or an international organization to do or to abstain from doing any act, which constitute offenses within the scope of and as defined in the international conventions and protocols relating to terrorism, are under no circumstances justifiable by considerations of a political, philosophical, ideological, racial, ethnic, religious, or other similar nature, and calls upon all States to prevent such acts and, if not prevented, to ensure that such acts are punished by penalties consistent with their grave nature.

At first blush this clause seems to be a general definition of terrorism, similar to that contained in the Terrorist Financing Convention. But due to the inclusion of the italicized language (which was required to gain consensus), this clause actually does no more than reaffirm that there can be no justification for committing any of the acts prohibited in the twelve counter-terrorism conventions; a sentiment that was expressed in numerous past General Assembly and Security Council resolutions.

Editors' note: In the following Notes and Questions there are several points worth considering as you attempt to identify elements that you prefer to include in an acceptable definition of terrorism. There are sub-headings for clusters of Notes and Questions that may be useful for organizing inquiry. More generally, there are issues presented whether a definition is preferable; what purposes would be served by an acceptable definition; whether prior definitions in international instruments or domestic U.S. legislation are preferable, realistic, or skewed; whether, contrary to the continual condemnation of all acts of terrorism by the U.N. General Assembly and Security Council, there should be a definitional exclusion of certain actors (*e.g.*, state actors who terrorize their own population or others) or contexts (*e.g.*, any sort of terrorism during war, revolution or other self-determination struggles); and whether related definitional exclusions should be used (*e.g.*, by identifying "terrorist organizations" and thereby excluding other groups and actors, *e.g.*, states, that might use a tactic of terrorism). The Editors apparently disagree on some of these points. You might consider whether attempts to exclude certain actors or contexts are manipulative and can inhibit consensus. Some states seem to prefer exclusions of their conduct and overly broad inclusion of conduct against them as if to affirm "what we do is not 'terrorism,' what you do is."

Notes and Questions

Is there a Need for an International Definition?

1. In 1991, a U.S. Representative to the United Nations (who is one of the co-authors of this book) explained the United States Government's continuing objection to the convening of an international conference to define terrorism and distinguish it from the legitimate struggle for self-determination. See Statement of Michael P. Scharf, United States Adviser to the Forty-Sixth General Assembly, in the Sixth Committee, on Item 125, Terrorism, October 21, 1991, Press Release USUN 63-(91).

2. Thirteen years later, Professor Scharf wrote:

There are significant gaps in the regime of the anti-terrorism conventions. For example, assassinations of businessmen, engineers, journalists and educators are not covered, while similar attacks against diplomats and public officials are prohibited. Attacks or acts of sabotage by means other than explosives against a passenger train or bus, or a water supply or electric power plant, are not covered;

while similar attacks against an airplane or an ocean liner would be included. Placing anthrax into an envelope would not be covered; nor would most forms of cyber-terrorism. Additionally, acts of psychological terror that do not involve physical injury are not covered, even though placing a fake bomb in a public place or sending fake anthrax through the mails can be every bit as traumatizing to a population as an actual attack.

Michael P. Scharf, Symposium: "Terrorism on Trial": *Defining Terrorism as the Peacetime Equivalent of War Crimes: Problems and Prospects*, 36 Case W. Res. J. Int'l L. 359 (2004). The several anti-terrorism Conventions are reproduced in the Documents Supplement. What other "terrorist" acts can you think of that are not covered by these treaties?

3. Professor Paust considers the statement above to at times beg the question at stake, *i.e.*, what is "terrorism"? For example, he considers that a realistic and objective definition must include the elements of an intent to produce terror and a "terror" outcome (*i.e.*, the creation of intense fear or anxiety in a targeted individual or group). Some assassinations are merely for the purpose of elimination with no intent to produce "terror" and no noticeable terror outcome, whether or not particular elimination targetings are otherwise criminal. Is the mere elimination of a lawful military target during war, such as a military engineer, necessarily "terrorism"? Is the self-defense targeting of a non-state, non-combatant actor, like bin Laden, in or outside the context of war necessarily "terrorism"? What train, bus, or airplane is an attack directed against—an enemy military vehicle or aircraft during war? What is "cyber-terrorism"? Is the disruption of an enemy defense computer network during war, with no intent to produce terror, "terrorism"? When a civilian hacker destroys computer files in a government computer system to prove his prowess, is that "terrorism," whether or not such is criminal?

4. Alex Schmid, the Senior Crime Prevention and Criminal Justice Officer at the U.N.'s Terrorism Prevention Branch in Vienna, has suggested eight reasons why it is important to have an internationally accepted general definition of terrorism:

—Developing an effective international strategy requires agreement on what it is we are dealing with, in other words, we need a definition of terrorism.

—International mobilization against terrorism ... cannot lead to operational results as long as the participants cannot agree on a definition.

—Without a definition, it is impossible to formulate or enforce international agreements against terrorism.

—Although many countries have signed bilateral and multilateral agreements concerning a variety of crimes, extradition for political offences is often explicitly excluded, and the background of terrorism is always political.

—The definition of terrorism will be the basis and the operational tool for expanding the international community's ability to combat terrorism.

—It will enable legislation and specific punishments against those perpetrating, involved in, or supporting terrorism, and will allow the formulation of a codex of laws and international conventions against terrorism, terrorist organizations, states sponsoring terrorism, and economic firms trading with them.

—At the same time, the definition of terrorism will hamper the attempts of terrorist organizations to obtain public legitimacy, and will erode support among those segments of the population willing to assist them (as opposed to guerrilla activities).

—Finally, the operational use of the definition of terrorism could motivate terrorist organizations, due to moral and utilitarian considerations, to shift from terrorist activities to alternate courses (such as guerrilla warfare) in order to attain their aims, thus reducing the scope of international terrorism.

Alex Schmid, Symposium: "Terrorism on Trial": *Terrorism — The Defninitional Problem*, 36 CASE W. RES. J. INT'L L. 375 (2004). Which reasons do you find the most compelling? Which do you find least compelling?

5. The absence of an internationally accepted definition of terrorism has led some U.S. courts to dismiss civil claims and criminal charges in terrorist-related cases. In the concurring opinion dismissing plaintiffs' tort actions against certain alleged terrorists responsible for an attack on a bus in Israel in *Tel-Oren v. Libyan Arab Republic*, 726 F.2d 795 (D.C. Cir. 1984), Judge Harry Edwards stated:

> While this nation unequivocally condemns all terrorist attacks, that sentiment is not universal. Indeed, the nations of the world are so divisively split on the legitimacy of such aggression as to make it impossible to pinpoint an area of harmony or consensus. Unlike the issue of individual responsibility, which much of the world has never even reached, terrorism has evoked strident reactions and sparked strong alliances among numerous nations. Given this division, I do not believe that under current law terrorist attacks [outside of those prohibited by international conventions] amount to law of nations violations.

See also *id.* at 807 (Bork, J., concurring) (otherwise misleadingly citing claims and viewpoints of Professor Paust in *"Nonprotected" Persons or Things,* in LEGAL ASPECTS OF INTERNATIONAL TERRORISM 341, 354–58 [Bork citing 355–56] (A. Evans & J. Murphy eds. 1978). Note that one year later the U.N. General Assembly and Security Council began to unequivocally condemn, as criminal, all acts of terrorism in all contexts.

More recently, in the case of *United States v. Yousef*, 327 F.3d 56 (2003), the U.S. Court of Appeals for the Second Circuit, dismissed extraterritorial terrorism charges based on "universal jurisdiction," and concluded:

> We regrettably are no closer now than eighteen years ago to an international consensus on the definition of terrorism or even its proscription; the mere existence of the phrase "state-sponsored terrorism" proves the absence of agreement on basic terms among a large number of States that terrorism violates public international law. Moreover, there continues to be strenuous disagreement among States about what actions do or do not constitute terrorism, nor have we shaken ourselves free of the cliche that "one man's terrorist is another man's freedom fighter." We thus conclude that the statements of Judges Edwards, Bork, and Robb remain true today, and that terrorism — unlike piracy, war crimes, and crimes against humanity — does not provide a basis for universal jurisdiction.

In view of the consensus reached in the U.N. General Assembly and Security Council over the last many years, do you agree with the statement that by 2003 there was no consensus regarding the proscription of terrorism? In any event, what has been the main problem at the international level?

Competing Prior International and Domestic U.S. Definitions

6. The first international attempt to define terrorism was undertaken by the League of Nations, which in 1937 drafted a Convention for the Prevention and Punishment of Terrorism. The League of Nations Convention defined terrorism as "criminal acts directed against a State and intended or calculated to create a state of terror in the minds of par-

ticular persons, or a group of persons or the general public." League of Nations Convention, Art. 1(2), League of Nations Doc. C.547 M.384 1937 V (1937). The League of Nations Convention never entered into force as only one nation, India, ratified it before the outbreak of World War II and the demise of the League of Nations. *See* Geoffrey Levitt, *Is "Terrorism" Worth Defining?*, 13 Ohio N.U.L. Rev. 97, 98 n.3 (1986). What acts would the League of Nations Convention cover? Does it require a political purpose and use of violence or a weapon? Is the Convention's definition too broad or too narrow? Does it cover targetings of non-state victims? Does the word "criminal" beg an important question?

7. The United States government employs multiple definitions of terrorism:

— United States House of Representatives Permanent Select Committee on Intelligence (2002): "Terrorism is the illegitimate, premeditated violence or threat of violence by subnational groups against persons of property with the intent to coerce a government by installing fear amongst the populace."

— State Department: "Terrorism means premeditated, politically motivated violence perpetrated against noncombatant targets by subnational groups or clandestine agents, usually intended to influence an audience." 22 U.S.C. § 2656 f(d) (requiring an annual report on "terrorism").

— FBI: "Terrorism is defined as the unlawful use, or threatened use, of force or violence by a group or individual ... committed against persons or property to intimidate or coerce a government, the civilian population, or any segment thereof, in furtherance of political or social objectives." 18 U.S.C. § 2332 (providing extraterritorial criminal jurisdiction over a "terrorist" act directed at U.S. citizens).

— FBI/NSA: The Foreign Intelligence Surveillance Act, which authorizes procedures for electronic surveillance of terrorist suspects, defines international terrorism as "activities that (1) involve violent acts or acts dangerous to human life that are a violation of the criminal laws of the United States or of any State, or that would be a criminal violation if committed within the jurisdiction of the United States or any State; (2) appear to be intended—(a) to intimidate or coerce a civilian population; (b) to influence the policy of a government by intimidation or coercion; or (c) to effect the conduct of a government by assassination or kidnapping."

— Office of Foreign Assets Control: The financing of terrorism is prohibited by 18 U.S.C. § 2339C. Within the context of § 2339C, "terrorism"is defined by reference to nine international conventions on terrorism listed in § 2339C(e)(7). In other words, it is a federal offense to provide or collect funds with the intention that such funds be used to carry out any of the conduct prohibited by the enumerated terrorism conventions. Terrorism is further defined in § 2339C as "any other act intended to cause death or serious bodily injury to a civilian, or to any other person not taking an active part in the hostilities in a situation of armed conflict, when the purpose of such act ... is to intimidate a population, or to compel a government or an international organization to do or to abstain from doing any act." 18 U.S.C. § 2339C(a)(1)(B).

— DOD (2000): "Terrorism is the calculated use of violence or threat of violence to inculcate fear; intended to coerce or to intimidate governments or societies in the pursuit of goals that are generally political, religious or ideological."

Why do you think the U.S. Government employs so many different definitions instead of a uniform definition of terrorism? In what ways are the above definitions different?

What elements appear in some that are lacking in others (*e.g.*, intent, political or other purpose, means used, types of targets, terror outcome)? What is the significance of the differences in these U.S. definitions of terrorism? Consider also the elements contained in the 1994 Declaration on Measures to Eliminate International Terrorism, para. 3 (*e.g.*, intent, political purpose, terror outcome). Are they reflected in each form of domestic legislation? Would some legislation include the use of armed force, even when permissible under the U.N. Charter? Can covert warfare involve premeditated and politically motivated violence?

8. Different countries also employ divergent definitions of terrorism. Consider:

— The United Kingdom's 1999 Prevention of Terrorism Act, defines terrorism as follows: "Terrorism means the use or threat of action where the action falls within subsection (2) (*i.e.* violence, serious damage, endangering life, etc.) and (b) the use or threat is designed to influence the government or to intimidate the public or a section of the public, and (c) the use or threat is made for the purpose of advancing a political, religious or ideological cause."

— The French Criminal Code defines terrorism as:"Acts are terrorist acts when they are intentionally committed by an individual entity or by a collective entity in order to seriously disturb law and order by intimidation or by terror. Article 421-1 of the French Criminal Code lists the following acts as terrorist acts: Attempted murder, assault, kidnapping, hostage-taking on airplanes, ships, all means of transport, theft, extortion, destructions, and crimes committed during group combat, the production or ownership of weapons of destruction and explosives including the production, sale, import and export of explosives, the acquisition, ownership, transport of illegal explosive substances, the production, ownership, storage, or acquisition of biological or chemical weapons, and money laundering.

— Canadian law defines a "terrorist activity" in the Criminal Code as an action that takes place either within or outside of Canada that "is an offense under one of the ten United Nations anti-terrorism conventions and protocols; or is an action": "taken or threatened for political, religious, or ideological purposes and threatens the public or national security by killing, seriously harming or endangering a person, substantial property damage that is likely to seriously harm people or by interfering with or disrupting an essential service, facility or system."

See Susan Tiefenbrun, *A Semiotic Approach to a Legal Definition of Terrorism*, 9 ILSA J. INT'L & COMP. L. 357 (2003).

9. A UN High-Level Panel on Threats, Challenges and Change, A More Secure World: Our Shared Responsibility, UN Doc. A/59/565 (2004), at 52 [hereinafter, "High-Level Panel Report"], recommended that the General Assembly should rapidly complete negotiations on a comprehensive convention on terrorism, defining terrorism to include:

... any action, in addition to actions already specified by the existing conventions on aspects of terrorism, the Geneva Conventions and Security Council resolution 1566 (2004), that is intended to cause death or serious bodily harm to civilians or non-combatants, when the purpose of such an act, by its nature or context, is to intimidate a population, or to compel a Government or an international organization to do or abstain form doing any act.

What acts and elements are covered in the various definitions set forth above? What acts and elements are left out? Do some appear to be manipulative? What terms are vague or otherwise problematic? Which definitions are the most expansive, and which are the most narrow?

State Terrorism

10. Unlike the consistent condemnation of all acts of terrorism by the U.N. General Assembly and Security Council since the mid-1980s, should the definition of terrorism exclude acts committed by government or military personnel undertaken "in the exercise of their official duties," even if they are terroristic in purpose and effect? What about a North Korean, Cuban, or Syrian governmental use of terroristic tactics to control portions of the country's civilian population? What about use of terroristic tactics by those governments abroad? In the context of armed conflicts, is such conduct sufficiently protected or regulated by international humanitarian law. Recall Article 33 of the Geneva Civilian Convention, Article 51(2) of Protocol I, and the 1919 List of War Crimes (addressed in Chapter Eight). Is the use of dogs during interrogation of detainees for the purpose of creating extreme fear a terroristic interrogation tactic? Is the use of an interrogation tactic involving a threat of imminent death to members of a detainee's family a terroristic tactic? In any event, are these tactics prohibited under common Article 3 of the Geneva Conventions, among others? See Chapter Eight.

11. The European Union adopted a *Framework Decision on Combating Terrorism* in June, 2002 which defined terrorism as a series of enumerated acts undertaken with the intent of either "seriously intimidating a population," "unduly compelling a Government or international organization to perform or abstain from performing any act," or "seriously destabilizing or destroying the fundamental political, constitutional, economic or social structure of a country or an international organization." Is this approach too limiting in terms of actors, too inclusive in terms of its potential reach? How would you define "seriously intimidating" and "unduly compelling"? Does this approach require elements of an intent to produce terror or the outcome of terror? Borrowing language from the Terrorist Bombings Convention, the preamble to the Framework Decision excludes the actions of armed forces during an armed conflict, which are governed by international humanitarian law.

12. What are the essential elements of such a definition? Are the definitions appropriate or flawed? Are there any lurking dangers in overly broad phrases such as "intimidate" or "compel"? Should U.S. use of armed force against Iranian nuclear facilities in order to induce the Iranian regime to comply with an internationally approved program of development of peaceful nuclear material constitute "terrorism"? Would the use of force resulting in serious bodily injury of some persons in order to overthrow an illegal regime in a foreign country, in one's own country, or as part of a U.N. Security Council or NATO authorized mission be "terrorism"? Would use of cruel or inhuman interrogation tactics in front of a number of other detainees constitute "terrorism"? Should the outcome of "terror" be a necessary criterion with respect to any objective definition of "terrorism" and should that outcome be intended?

Non-Combatants Verses Lawful Military Targets

13. In 1992, Alex Schmid, the Senior Crime Prevention and Criminal Justice Officer at the U.N.'s Terrorism Prevention Branch in Vienna, proposed a novel approach to the problem of defining terrorism which would draw on the existing consensus of what constitutes a war crime. See Alex P. Schmid, The Definition of Terrorism, A Study in Compliance with CTL/9/91/2207 for the U.N. Crime Prevention and Criminal Justice Branch, Dec. 1992. After circulating without much interest through the United Nations during the last decade, Schmid's proposal suddenly gained world-wide attention in April 2004, when

it was cited by the Supreme Court of India as a way around what the Court characterized as the "Gordian definitional knot." In *Singh v. Bihar*, 2004 SOL Case No. 264, April 2, 2004, para. 16, the Indian Supreme Court explained: "If the core of war crimes-deliberate attacks on civilians, hostage-taking and the killing of prisoners is extended to peacetime, we could simply define acts of terrorism veritably as peacetime equivalents of war crimes." What benefits or problems do you see with Schmid's proposal? In this regard, consider that although it cited Alex Schmid's definitional approach with approval, the Indian Supreme Court cautioned that "if terrorism is defined strictly in terms of attacks on non-military targets, a number of attacks on military installations and soldiers' residences could not be included," since they can be legitimate military targets during armed conflict (recall Chapter Eight).

14. Should the definition of terrorism apply only to acts against civilians and noncombatants, and exclude attacks on military personnel? What about military personnel who are outside of the area of armed conflict? What about military personnel who are unarmed and off duty? What about police forces? What about Government officials? What about military installations, headquarters, vessels, aircraft, or vehicles during an armed conflict? Were the attacks on the USS Cole in 2000 in Yemen and the Pentagon in 2001 by members of al Qaeda acts of terrorism? See also *Regina v. Gul*, [2012] 1 Cr. App. R. 37, ¶ 47 ("[W]e conclude that, although international law may well develop through state practice or *opinio juris* a rule restricting the scope of terrorism so that it excludes some types of insurgent attacking the armed forces of government from the definition of terrorism, the necessary widespread and general state practice or the necessary *opinio juris* to that effect has not yet been established.").

15. Under Geneva law, terroristic targetings of noncombatants to which the Conventions or Protocols apply are prohibited. *E.g.*, 1949 Geneva Civilian Convention, art. 33 ("all measures of … terrorism"); Protocol I, art. 51 (2) (acts or threats of violence "the primary purpose of which is to spread terror among the civilian population"); Protocol II, art. 4 (2) ("acts of terrorism" against noncombatants and others "who do not take a direct part … in hostilities"); 1919 Responsibilities Commission List of War Crimes, crime no. 1. In The Prosecutor v. Galic, IT-98-29-T (Trial Chamber Judgment and Sentence, 5 Dec. 2003) the Trial Chamber of the ICTY declared that three elements need to be proven with respect to this crime: (1) acts of violence directed against the civilian population or individual civilians not taking a direct part in hostilities causing death or serious injury to body or health within the civilian population, (2) the offender wilfully made the civilian population or individual civilians not taking a direct part in hostilities the object of those acts of violence, and (3) the offence was committed with the primary purpose of spreading terror among the civilian population. *Id.* para. 133; but see *id.* para. 134 ("The Majority rejects the Parties' submissions that actual infliction of terror is an element of the crime of terror. The plain wording of Article 51 (2), as well as the *travaux préparatoires* of the Diplomatic Conference exclude this from the definition of this offense.").

During an armed conflict, terror outcomes are not unusual and are even foreseeable on the battlefield or near and around hostilities. For this reason, should a definition of terrorism include an intent to produce terror? Is there and should there be an exclusion from what is considered impermissible terrorism of terroristic tactics directed against combatants and lawful military targets during an armed conflict? See J. Paust, *An Introduction to and Commentary on Terrorism and the Law*, 19 CONN. L. REV. 697, 705–10 (1987); *Terrorism and the International Law of War*, 64 MIL. L. REV. 1, 27–31 (1974). This latter approach avoids the problem of exclusion by definition (*i.e.*, the terroristic tactics during war that are not otherwise violative of the laws of war are terrorism) but recognizes that during war one form of terrorism appears to be permissible in view of actual patterns of practice and legal expectation with respect to the laws of war.

16. If peacetime attacks against military personnel and installations are not considered terrorist, should the international humanitarian law "collateral damage doctrine" apply, such that loss of innocent civilian life is not considered a crime so long as the target, its timing and the means employed were legitimate and proportionate and reasonable steps were taken to avoid unnecessary civilian casualties? Should the international humanitarian law "obedience to superior orders defense" apply to such acts? For a criticism of application of such international humanitarian law doctrines to peacetime acts of terrorism, see Michael P. Scharf, Symposium: "Terrorism on Trial": *Defining Terrorism as the Peacetime Equivalent of War Crimes: Problems and Prospects*, 36 CASE W. RES. J. INT'L L. 359 (2004).

17. After the al Qaeda attacks on September 11, 2001, the Bush Administration adopted the terminology "war on terrorism." Subsequently, the Obama Administration adopted the phrase "war against al Qaeda." Can a state be in a "war" with a terroristic tactic? Can the United States even be at "war" with al Qaeda as such? Recall Chapter Eight concerning the minimal levels of war or armed conflict.

In testimony before the Senate Judiciary Committee, Scott Silliman, the Executive Director of the Center on Law, Ethics and National Security at Duke University School of Law, explained that since the United States was not in a state of armed conflict with al Qaeda on the morning of September 11, 2001, the attacks by the non-state actor al Qaeda could not be considered violations of the laws of war. *See On DOJ Oversight: Preserving Our Freedoms While Defending Against Terrorism: Hearing on Review of Military Terrorism Tribunals Before Congress*, 107th Cong. (2001), *available at* 2001 WL 26187921. Although al Qaeda had been responsible for a few prior sporadic attacks against the United States, including the bombings of the U.S. embassies in Kenya and Tanzania in 1998 and the attack on the U.S.S. Cole in 2000, and the United States had attacked al Qaeda's Afghan training bases with cruise missiles in 1998, Silliman concluded that these did not rise to the level of protracted armed violence between governmental authorities and organized armed groups as required to trigger the laws of war. Some of the Editors have reached similar conclusions, *i.e.*, that the U.S. cannot be at "war" with al Qaeda as such although the laws of war apply in actual wars in Afghanistan and Iraq and the U.S. has the right to engage in self-defense under Article 51 of the U.N. Charter against non-state actor armed attacks. Recall Chapters Seven and Eight.

Nevertheless, in promulgating the instruments governing the prosecution of al Qaeda members before U.S. military commissions, the Bush Administration made clear that in its view, ongoing mutual hostilities were not required to qualify the attacks of September 11 as an armed conflict. Rather, "[a] single hostile act or attempted act may provide sufficient basis for the nexus [between the conduct and armed hostilities] so long as its magnitude or severity rises to the level of an armed attack'... or the number, power, stated intent or organization of the force with which the actor is associated is such that the act or attempted act is tantamount to an attack by an armed force." Department of Defense Military Commission Instruction No. 2, Crimes and Elements for Trials by Military Commission, § 5(C) (April 30, 2003), *available at* http://www.defenselink.mil/news/May2003/d20030430milcom instno2.pdf. Applying this novel definition which reduces the armed conflict threshold to require merely a single severe terrorist act, the Military Commissions have charged several members of al Qaeda with committing war crimes in relation to the attacks of September 11. *See* Press Releases, U.S. Department of Defense, Two Guantanamo Detainees Charged

(Feb. 24, 2004), Additional Military Commission Charges Referred (Jul. 14, 2004) *available at* www.defenselink.mil/releases/2004. Recalling Chapter Eight, do you agree with this approach?

Human Rights Violations

18. Would most forms of terrorism violate human rights law? Which human rights might be at stake? See also Restatement §§ 404, Comm. a, 702 (c), (d), (e), (g); Ireland v. United Kingdom, 25 Eur. Ct. H.R. (Ser. A), para. 149 (1978) (dictum: "terrorist activities … of individuals or of groups … are in clear disregard of human rights."); Paust, *The Link Between Human Rights and Terrorism and Its Implications for the Law of State Responsibility*, 11 Hast. Int'l & Comp. L. Rev. 41 (1987); Paust, *An Introduction, supra.* Concerning the relation of terroristic tactics and terror outcomes to human rights violations, see also the 1994 Declaration on Measures to Eliminate International Terrorism, preamble and paras. 2–3; Protection of Human Rights and Fundamental Freedoms While Countering Terrorism (2004); Human Rights and Terrorism (2004), all in the Documents Supplement. With respect to private individual and group duties under human rights law, see, e.g., International Covenant on Civil and Political Rights, prmbl. and art. 5(1); Chapter 11.

Terrorists Verses Freedom Fighters

19. The UN High-Level Panel Report (*supra* at 51) notes that "the search for an agreed definition [of terrorism] usually stumbles on two issues":

> The first is the argument that any definition should include States' use of armed forces against civilians. We believe that the legal and normative framework against State violations is far stronger than in the case of non-State actors and we do not find this objection to be compelling. The second objection is that peoples under foreign occupation have a right to resistance and a definition of terrorism should not override that right. The right to resistance is contested by some. But it is not the central point: the central point is that there is nothing in the fact of occupation that justifies the targeting and killing of civilians.

Do you agree with the statement of the High-Level Panel that no matter the legitimacy of the cause (*e.g.*, trying to overthrow a tyrannical and repressive regime or occupying power) nothing can justify the targeting and killing of civilians? With respect to the issue of national liberation struggles or resistance to occupation, one commentator has stated: "While the struggles themselves may be legitimate, the means adopted can be regarded as terrorist offences if they do not conform to the requirements of international law." Tal Becker, Terrorism and the State: Rethinking the Rules of State Responsibility 113 (2006). Indeed, isn't the main point worth stressing that one must distinguish issues concerning the permissibility of the use of force or violence and issues concerning use of certain tactics? Terrorism is a tactic and in any legitimate armed conflict or struggle there are certain tactics that are illegal regardless of the legitimacy of the conflict or struggle. Recall Chapter Nine. Confusion between the two can also inhibit objective and policy-serving choice concerning definitions of the tactic of "terrorism."

Two more recent regional conventions (namely those adopted by the Organization of African Unity and Organization of the Islamic Conference) contain a provision according to which struggles waged by peoples for their liberation or self-determination shall not be considered terrorist. Article 3 of the Organization of African Unity Convention on the Prevention and Combating of Terrorism provides: "the provisions of Article 1, the struggle waged by peoples in accordance with the principles of international law for their liberation or self-determination, including armed struggle against colonialism, occupation, aggression and domination by foreign forces shall not be considered as terrorist acts." Article 2 of the Convention of the Organization of the Islamic Conference on Combating International Terrorism recognizes a similar exclusion of overall struggles from the strategy or tactic of terrorism as such.

20. For some, the major problem in defining terrorism has been distinguishing "terrorists" from "freedom fighters" or "revolutionaries." During the 1980s, the U.S. Government labeled the rebels in El Salvador "agents of subversion," while referring to the Afghan guerrillas as "resisters" and the Contras in Nicaragua as "freedom fighters" who in President Reagan's words were "the moral equivalent of the Founding Fathers." *Newsweek*, January 6, 1986, at 39. Do these labels reflect a double standard or are the distinctions justified? According to one author:

> To make the struggle with terrorism more successful, we should at least attempt to distinguish between "terrorists" and "revolutionaries." Although there is no unanimity among writers on international law concerning the right to fight against the constituted government, one argument should be spelled out more clearly. The very essence of democracy provides for the power of the majority, the protection of the rights of the minority, and legally recognized, nonviolent methods for the exchange of ruling teams. To recognize a right to the violent change of the legally constituted government as inherent in democracy would undermine the sense of democracy itself.

Rett R. Ludwikoski, *Political and Legal Instruments in Supporting and Combating Terrorism: Current Developments*, 11 TERRORISM 197, 206 (1988). Do you agree with this distinction? Does it confuse two separate questions: the legitimacy of an overall struggle or process and that of particular tactics utilized? Is, for example, a member of a revolutionary group in a country with a non-democratic regime who blows up a school bus full of children with the intent to terrorize others any less a "terrorist" than one who commits the same act with the same intent in a democracy? Further, is the perpetrator of such a tactic any less a terrorist if he/she happens to be an official in a dictatorial or democratic process? Do all democracies provide full protection with respect to the rights of minorities? Consider, for example, the United Kingdom's treatment of members of the IRA in Northern Ireland during the 1970s and 1980s and Israel's treatment of the Palestinians in the occupied territories. Would an objective focus on terrorism as a strategy or tactic help to avoid confusion between the legitimacy of a general struggle and that of a terroristic tactic? Are not even "freedom fighters" bound to refrain from war crimes, acts of genocide, and impermissible strategies of terrorism? Recall the 1919 list of war crimes in Chapter Two, Section 1 and the Documents Supplement.

Critiquing Elements of the Various Definitions

21. Professor Susan Tiefenbrun has remarked with respect to the need to objectively identify various elements:

"Semiotics is the science of signs. A semiotic approach to the meaning of the term 'terrorism' includes an investigation of its hidden meanings, its connotations as well as denotations. A semiotic approach is designed to uncover the basic structural elements of the meaning of a term, and each element acts as a sign for the identification of a terrorist act. The elements of the definition are either necessary or sufficient for the act to be deemed a terrorist act."

Susan Tiefenbrun, *A Semiotic Approach to a legal Definition of Terrorism*, 9 ILSA J. INT'L & COMP. L. 357, 358–59 (2003). She suggested "five basic structural elements: (1) The perpetration of violence by whatever means; (2) The targeting of innocent civilians;

(3) With the intent to cause violence or with wanton disregard for its consequences; (4) For the purpose of causing fear or intimidating an enemy; [and] (5) In order to achieve some political, military, ethnic, ideological, or religious goal." *Id.* at 360–61. However, she admits that "[t]here is no agreement as to who is actually included in" the category of "innocent civilian." *Id.* at 362. Does any international crime hinge on the innocence of the victim(s)? Some philosophers argue that, on a relative scale, no one is "innocent."

Interestingly, she also identified, among others, an interesting definition in the Arkansas Criminal Code: "a person commits the offense of terroristic threatening if, with the purpose of terrorizing another person, he threatens to cause death or serious physical injury or substantial property damage to another person." Ark. Code Ann. § 5-13-301. How is the Arkansas definition different?

22. Use of intent and political purpose elements in defining terrorism now seems common (*i.e.*, that the actions must be intentional and engaged in for a political purpose). See also Gerhard Hafner, *The Definition of the Crime of Terrorism*, in INTERNATIONAL COOPERATION IN COUNTER-TERRORISM 34, 36–37 (Giuseppe Nesi ed. 2006) (also addressing some points considered in the 2002 Report of the U.N. Working Group, U.N. Doc. A/C.6/57/L.9 (6 Oct. 2002)). Indeed, "terrorism" should be viewed as a strategy or tactic — thus, one intentionally engaged in for certain political purposes. *See, e.g.*, Declaration on Measures to Eliminate International Terrorism, U.N. G.A. Res. 49/60, para. 3 (1994). Consider whether the following would thereby be excluded:

– the conduct of a serial killer rapist who randomly or selectively targets female victims and enjoys the notoriety he achieves as one who tortures his victims before killing them and who spreads significant fear in the community.

– the crash of an eighteen wheeler gasoline tanker in a city tunnel caused by reckless driving of the truck driver and causing a catastrophic explosion and fire in the tunnel, death and serious injury to numerous persons, and terror among several survivors.

23. Should the threat of violence against persons also be covered, *e.g.*, a bombing of a building (an instrumental target) coupled with an intentional threat of future terroristic violence against persons (the primary terroristic target)? Is the word "violence," or even the phrase "politically motivated violence," too broad? Is such necessary or too limiting? Consider the case where alleged terrorists release nerve gas, a deadly chemical, or a biologic agent in a subway in order to induce terror within a sector of a city? Would the phrase "use of violence or a weapon" cover such conduct? Should the definition of terrorism include certain computer crimes ("cyber-terrorism") and attacks against the environment ("eco-terrorism") committed with the intention to intimidate a population or compel a government to act or refrain from acting? or merely when the intent is to produce terror and use of the tactic actually produces "terror"?

24. U.N. Security Council Resolution 1566 (2004), para. 3 declared that the Council:

Recalls that criminal acts, including against civilians, committed with the intent to cause death or serious bodily injury, or taking of hostages, with the purpose to provoke a state of terror in the general public or a group of persons or particular persons, intimidate a population or compel a government or an international organization to do or to abstain from doing any act, which constitute offences within the scope of an as defined in the international conventions and protocols relating to terrorism are under no circumstances justifiable by considerations of a political, philosophical, ideological, racial, ethnic, religious or other similar nature....

Was this an attempt to define "terrorism"? If so, what would be the *mens rea* that must be proven under the Security Council definition of terrorism? What would be the *actus reus*? Does such an *actus reus* include any of the criminal acts prohibited by the 14 major international legal instruments and additional amendments dealing with terrorism? Further, under this Security Council resolution would terrorism be limited to serious acts of violence directed at civilians or merely "serious bodily injury"? Finally, would you prefer to define "terrorism" by using this paragraph of the resolution?

25. To be realistic, descriptive and not dangerously overly broad, should a definition of "terrorism" necessarily involve a "terror" outcome? Would such an element involve creation of intense fear or anxiety in a primary target? *See, e.g.*, Paust, *An Introduction, supra* at 703–05. Also recall the elements contained in Article 51 (2) of Protocol I to the Geneva Conventions (in Chapter Nine) ("Acts or threats of violence the primary purpose of which is to spread terror among the civilian population....") and the 1994 Declaration on Measures to Eliminate International Terrorism, para. 3 ("Criminal acts intended or calculated to provoke a state of terror ... for political purposes"). The same language in paragraph 3 of the 1994 Declaration appears in 2008 G.A. resolution. Measures to Eliminate International Terrorism, G.A. Res. 63/129, at para. 4 (Dec. 11, 2008). See also U.N. S.C. Res. 1566 (2004) (quoted in Note 24 above). "Terror" has been defined as "[t]he state of being terrified or greatly frightened; intense fear, fright or dread." II THE COMPACT EDITION OF THE OXFORD ENGLISH DICTIONARY 3268 (1971). Why is a dictionary definition relevant to the interpretation of international agreements or customary international norms? *See, e.g.*, Vienna Convention on the Law of Treaties, art. 31(1) (interpret in view of "the ordinary meaning to be given to the terms"); Chapter One, Sections 1 and 2. Why are creators of dictionaries generally able to define terrorism while governments seem unable to agree amongst themselves?

26. For extensive criticism of some of the abovementioned definitional elements as being overly broad, under inclusive, and/or insufficiently related to an objective or realistic definition that can capture a wider consensus, *see, e.g.*, Paust, *supra*, at 701–09, and references cited. Consider, for example, such terms or phrases as "involve," "acts dangerous," "appear to be intended," "intimidate," "coerce," "influence," "effect," "retaliate". Is the word "intimidate" logically the equivalent of "terrorize"?

27. With respect to the label "terrorist" for an entire group or organization, what interpretation do you prefer with respect to the word "practicing"? Should the practice be intended by the group and should it be fairly systematic or common as opposed to circumstances where use of terroristic tactics is merely by certain members of the group or at infrequent times? Is a "terrorist organization," unit, or cell one that primarily uses terrorism as a tactic? Is a self-determination struggle "terroristic" merely because such tactics might be engaged in by certain elements of the movement? *See* Paust, *supra*, at 705–10. The term "foreign terrorist organization" is broadly defined under U.S. law. Pursuant to 8 U.S.C. § 1189(a), the U.S. Secretary of State is authorized to designate an organization as a "foreign terrorist organization" if the organization satisfies three elements: (1) the organization is a foreign organization; (2) that engages in terrorist activity or terrorism as defined by federal statute; and (3) the terrorist activity or terrorism threatens the security of United States nationals or the national security of the United States. Designating an organization a "foreign terrorist organization" has serious legal consequences. It is a federal felony to provide "material support" to a foreign terrorist organization punishable by 15 years imprisonment, and, if the death of any person results, imprisonment for any term of years or life.

28. In 1987, Professor Paust suggested the following as a descriptive and objective definition:

"'terrorism' involves the intentional use of violence, or the threat of violence, by a precipitator (the accused) against an instrumental target in order to communicate to a primary target a threat of future violence, so as to coerce the primary target through intense fear or anxiety in connection with a demanded political outcome."

Paust, *An Introduction, supra,* at 701. Professor Michael Reisman at Yale had been of great help in formulating this definition. Do you agree with this approach? If not, what would you change? He adds that it should not be determinative whether instrumental or primary targets are "innocent" or the tactic is used in an armed conflict or any other social context, and the two questions of what is "terrorism" and whether any particular use of the tactic is "legitimate" should definitely be considered separately. *See, e.g.,* Paust, *An Introduction, supra,* at 701–10, and references cited. Today, he would change "violence" to "a weapon" or use the phrase "violence or a weapon" in order to cover non-violent weapons such as use of biological and bacteriological weapons and possibly even cyber weapons. See Paust, *Terrorism's Proscription and Core Elements of an Objective Definition,* 8 Santa Clara J. Int'l L. 51 (9010), available at http://ssrn.com/abstract=1583437; Paust, *Terrorism as an International Crime,* in International Cooperation in Counter-Terrorism 25 (Giuseppe Nesi ed. 2006). He might also drop the element of "political" outcome, because it might not cover ideological, religious, ethnic, or race-based purposes as such. See also Beth Van Schaack, *Finding the Tort in Terrorism in International Law,* 28 Rev. Litig. 382, 411, 435, 447 n.295 (2009).

Professor Bassiouni has stated that terrorism "is a strategy of violence designed to instill terror in a segment of society in order to achieve a power-outcome, propagandize a cause, or inflict harm for vengeful political purposes." M. Cherif Bassiouni, *Legal Control of International Terrorism: A Policy Oriented Assessment,* 43 Harv. Int'l L.J. 83, 84 (2002). See also M. Cherif Bassiouni, International Terrorism: Multilateral Conventions (1937-2011) 16–17 (2001) ("Terrorism is an ideologically motivated strategy of internationally proscribed violence designed to inspire terror within a particular segment of a given society in order to achieve a power-outcome or to propagate a claim or grievance, irrespective of whether its perpetrators are acting for and on behalf of themselves, or on behalf of a state"); Antonio Cassese, International Law 449 n.25, 450 ("must be aimed at spreading terror" and "[a]s for *mens rea,* there must be a criminal intent to perpetrate the acts … as well as the special intent (*dolus specialis*) to spread terror") (2 ed. 2005); Tiefenbrun, *supra* at 381 ("Bassiouni uses the word 'terror' rather than fear to define 'international terrorism,' thereby preserving the original denotation of the Latin word "terrore" (fear producing)); Van Schaack, *supra* at 412, 415, 419, 427; Declaration on Measures to Eliminate International Terrorism, G.A. Res. 49/60, at para. 3 (Dec. 9, 1994) ("intended or calculated to provoke a state of terror in the general public, a group of persons or a particular person"); Measures to Eliminate International Terrorism, G.A. Res. 63/129, at para. 4 (Dec. 11, 2008) (same); U.N. S.C. Res. 1566 (2004) (quoted in Note 24 above).

Alternative Approaches

29. If it is not possible to ever reach international consensus on a general definition of terrorism, would it make sense instead to agree on an international process for identifying "terrorist organizations"?

At the Club of Madrid International Summit on Democracy, Terrorism and Security, 8–11 March 2005, the Working Group on Legal Responses to Terrorism made the following proposal in paragraph 2.6 of its report: "In order to help States identify terrorist organizations to whom financial support is prohibited by the Convention on the Suppression of Terrorist Financing and Security Council Resolution 1373 (2001), the Counter Terrorism Committee (CTC) established by the Security Council should develop a core list of organizations that the CTC determines to be involved, directly or indirectly, with acts of financing of terrorism. In developing this list, the CTC should employ procedural safeguards to ensure that organizations and individuals associated with them which are not so involved are not erroneously included. States would thereafter be bound to subject organizations included in the list to the sanctions enumerated in resolution 1373 (2001). States would also remain free to impose sanctions on non-listed organizations that the State determines to be involved in terrorism."

Michael P. Scharf, Symposium: "Terrorism on Trial": *Defining Terrorism as the Peacetime Equivalent of War Crimes: Problems and Prospects*, 36 Case W. Res. J. Int'l L. 359 n. 12 (2004). What benefits or problems do you see with this approach?

30. Another alternative is to include with the definition of terrorism a list of exclusions, defining what "terrorism" is not. Such a "negative definition" might include provisions:

— Excluding mere acts of property damage as well as acts of sabotage like interrupting the flow of an oil pipeline even when the saboteurs are engaging in acts of terrorism on other occasions.

— Excluding attacks on military installations, aircraft, navy vessels, barracks which are guarded even when those who attack military installations or personnel are otherwise also engaging in acts of terrorism.

— Excluding attacks on police stations and armed police on patrol in situations of armed conflict;

— Excluding cases of collateral damage where the targeting of civilians was not deliberate (*e.g.* when an attack on a police station misfires and civilians are (also) victims.

— Excluding cases of attacks on secular or religious symbols unless it is combined with the victimization of people (an attack on a knowingly empty church would not qualify, an attack on a full church would).

— Excluding certain types of assassinations, *e.g.* when the direct victim is the only target, as opposed to de-individuated murder where the victim serves only as message generator to reach a wider audience.

— Excluding acts of war which do not qualify as war crimes.

— Excluding guerrilla warfare activities which are not war crimes.

— Excluding acts of legal use of force by legitimate authorities to impose public order when acting within the boundaries of the rule of law.

— Excluding acts of (collective) political violence which are spontaneous, as in riots, demonstrations, revolts.

Alex Schmid, Symposium: "Terrorism on Trial": *Terrorism — The Definitional Problem*, 36 Case W. Res. J. Int'l L. 375 (2004). Should there be any such exclusions? Which of these exclusions do you think make the most and least sense? Which countries do you think would favor the various exclusions? Do any of these approaches fall into the trap of "what I do is not 'terrorism,' what you do is"?

The Appeals Chamber of the Special Tribunal for Lebanon's Definition

30. The Special Tribunal for Lebanon ("STL"), established in 2007 by the United Nations Security Council to prosecute those responsible for the 2005 bombings that killed

former Lebanese Prime Minister Rafiq Hariri and twenty-two others, is the world's first international court with jurisdiction over the crime of terrorism. See Statute of the Special Tribunal for Lebanon, *appended to* S.C. Res. 1757, U.N. Doc. S/RES/1757 (May 30, 2007). On January 17, 2011, the Tribunal's Prosecutor, Daniel Bellemare, submitted a sealed indictment for the pre-trial judge to confirm. The pre-trial judge, in turn, requested that the Appeals Chamber resolve fifteen questions relating to the substantive criminal law to be applied by the STL, the applicable modes of criminal responsibility, and guidance regarding whether the STL should charge crimes cumulatively or in the alternative. In response, the STL Appeals Chamber handed down a landmark ruling on February 16, 2011. See Interlocutory Decision on the Applicable Law: Terrorism, Conspiracy, Homicide, Perpetration, Cumulative Charging, Special Tribunal for Lebanon Appeals Chamber, Case No. STL-11-01/I (Feb. 16, 2011). The Appeals Chamber judgment is summarized in the following excerpt:

Michael P. Scharf, INTRODUCTORY NOTE TO THE DECISION OF THE APPEALS CHAMBER OF THE SPECIAL TRIBUNAL FOR LEBANON ON THE DEFINITION OF TERRORISM, 50 I.L.M. 509 (2011).

Although the STL's Statute stipulates that the court is to apply the crime of terrorism as defined by Lebanese law, the Appeals Chamber held that the STL is authorized to construe Lebanese law defining terrorism with the assistance of international treaty and customary law. Interlocutory Decision, paras 45, 62. This was a departure from the traditional approach of treaty interpretation, as reflected in Article 32 of the Vienna Convention on the Law of Treaties, in which the Tribunal would apply the "ordinary meaning" of the terms of the Statute unless the text was found to be either ambiguous or obscure or would lead to an interpretation which is manifestly absurd or unreasonable. Since the Statute of the STL clearly stated that the Court was to apply the Lebanese domestic law on terrorism outside of violations of the laws of war (which contain provisions against terrorism), under the traditional approach, resort to supplementary means of interpretation would be appropriate only if the Court had found that there was an inconsistency or gap in the applicable Lebanese law.

In diverging from the traditional approach, the Appeals Chamber stated that "the old maxim *in claris non fit interpretation* (when a text is clear there is no need for interpretation) is in truth fallacious," explaining that "it overlooks the spectrum of meanings that words, and especially a collection of words, may have and misses the truth that context can determine meaning." Interlocutory Decision, para. 19. Instead, the Appeals Chamber adopted a "semiotic" approach to interpretation. Semiotics begins with the assumption that terms such as "terrorism" are not historic artifacts whose meaning remains static over time. Rather, the meaning of such terms changes along with the interpretative community or communities. As the STL Appeals Chamber explained, this interpretative approach "recognizes the reality that society alters over time and interpretation of a law may evolve to keep pace." Interlocutory Decision, para. 21.

The Appeals Chamber thus held that it was appropriate to read the Lebanese law in the context of "international obligations undertaken by Lebanon with which, in the absence of very clear language, it is presumed any legislation complies." Interlocutory Decision, paras. 19–20. This interpretive approach opened the door for the Appeals Chamber to determine whether a defined offense of terrorism exists under customary international law. To that end, the Appeals Chamber found that "although it is held by many scholars and other legal experts that no widely accepted definition of terrorism has evolved in the world society because of the marked difference of views on some issues, closer scrutiny reveals that in fact such a definition has gradually emerged." Interlocutory Decision, paras. 83 and 102.

Based on its review of state practice and indicators of *opinio juris*, the Appeals Chamber declared that the customary international law definition of terrorism consists of

> the following three key elements: (i) the perpetration of a criminal act (such as murder, kidnapping, hostage-taking, arson, and so on), or threatening such an act; (ii) the intent to spread fear among the population (which would generally entail the creation of public danger) or directly or indirectly coerce a national or international authority to take some action, or to refrain from taking it; (iii) when the act involves a transnational element. Interlocutory Decision at para 85.

Reading the Lebanese law on terrorism together with the definition of terrorism under customary international law, the Appeals Chamber concluded that the particular means used in an attack were not dispositive in determining whether an attack was terrorism or simply murder. Intelocutory Decision at para. 147. In other words, contrary to Lebanese case law, the Appeals Chamber opined that attacks committed by rifles or handguns, which are not likely per se to cause a danger to the general population, are nevertheless within the jurisdiction of the STL. Interlocutory Decision at paras. 59, 138, 145.

Yet, the significance of this aspect of the Appeals Chamber opinion is far broader than its application to the case before the STL. This is the first time in history that an international tribunal has authoritatively confirmed the crystallization of a general definition of terrorism under customary international law. The decision will almost certainly spark a debate about whether the STL's conclusion is correct in light of the conventional view that the international community has not yet reached consensus on a general definition of terrorism. Since the decision has been issued by an international tribunal, and penned by a highly respected jurist, it is possible that the decision itself will be seen as "a Grotian moment," crystallizing a customary international law definition of terrorism. If so, the decision will have a momentous effect on the decades-long effort of the international community to develop a broadly acceptable definition of terrorism

Questions

1. In view of prior materials in this Chapter, is the definition adopted by the Special Tribunal objective, adequate, preferable? Is there a requirement of a terroristic purpose (*i.e.*, that the perpetrator intend to produce terror)? What does "or ... indirectly coerce" mean? Is "coerce" the same as terrorize? Is there a requirement of a terror outcome? How can any conduct that is not intended to produce terror and that does not produce terror realistically and objectively constitute terrorism?

2. What test is proposed concerning whether an act is "criminal"? Should the reach of an international legal prohibition of terrorism hinge upon the reach of whatever is covered by domestic law of one of some 195 countries?

3. Should there be an exception for purely domestic terrorism?

4. Should there be a new international convention on "terrorism"? If so, what definition would you prefer and why?

Section 2
The Multilateral Legal Framework

Introductory Note

Prior to the 21st Century, outside developments in the law of war, progress in countering terrorism through application of the rule of law was blocked by a seemingly inexorable international disagreement over whether violent acts committed in furtherance of national liberation struggles should be encompassed within the definition of terrorism. As an alternative to the debate over a general definition of terrorism, the international community has concluded over the last twenty years a series of individual conventions that identify specific acts which all Parties agree are inherently unacceptable. By agreeing that the offenses enumerated in these instruments are criminal regardless of motivation or context, this approach avoids the controversy over who is a "terrorist" and who is a "freedom fighter."

A. U.N. Terrorism Resolutions

Reproduced in the Documents Supplement are the 1991, 1994, and 2004 United Nations General Assembly resolutions, each of which follows a pattern of the 1991 resolution: "unequivocally condemns, as criminal and unjustifiable, all acts, methods and practices of terrorism wherever and by whoever committed." (A nearly identical resolution was adopted by the United Nations by consensus in 1985, 1989 and 1993). Rather than attempt to define terrorism, the 1991 resolution simply lists the "existing international conventions relating to various aspects of the problem of international terrorism." These international "anti-terrorist" conventions require States Parties to criminalize specified conduct, to either initiate prosecution of or to extradite the transgressors, and to cooperate with other States for effective implementation. However, as noted above, the 1994 resolution identified certain elements of "terrorism," including intent, political purpose, and terror outcome. Check each resolution; see also in particular:

U.N. G.A. Resolution 46/51
9 Dec. 1991, U.N. Doc. A/46/654

[Read the 1991 Resolution on Terrorism, in the Documents Supplement]

Notes and Questions

1. The General Assembly's 1991 resolution does not define the term "terrorism." It does, however, refer to human rights and it refers to the acts covered by the several international conventions and protocols listed in the preamble. Those conventions prohibit the following: aircraft hijacking, aircraft sabotage, attacks against ships and fixed platforms in the ocean, attacks at airports, violence against officials and diplomats, hostage-

taking, theft of nuclear material, and use of unmarked plastic explosives. Would resort to other forms of terror-violence not covered by those conventions such as placing a bomb in a market place or attacking a school bus with a machine gun for political purposes and with an intent to produce a terror outcome fit within the resolution's unequivocal condemnation of terrorism? Today, the 1997 International Convention for the Suppression of Terrorist Bombings fills a gap for signatories and their nationals.

2. Paragraph 3 of the 1991 resolution states that it is a violation of international law for states to organize, instigate, assist or participate in terrorist acts in other States, or acquiesce in or encourage activities within their territory directed towards the commission of such acts. Would the mere act of providing financial assistance to a terrorist organization be a violation of international law? Today, the 1999 International Convention for the Suppression of the Financing of Terrorism provides broader coverage among signatories and their nationals. What about the provision of other forms of logistical support such as passports and weapons? Would permitting a terrorist organization to maintain a headquarters or training facility in a State's territory be a violation of international law? Also recall Chapter Seven, Sections 1 and 2, concerning norms of nonintervention and breach of neutrality laws. Would refusing to extradite a person charged with acts of terrorism on the basis of the political offense exception to extradition (discussed in Chapter Five, Section 1) be a violation of international law? In answering these questions, consider the International Court of Justice's opinion in *the Case of Military and Paramilitary Activities in and Against Nicaragua (Nicaragua v. United States of America)* in Chapter Seven, Section 2. In that case, the ICJ held that, by arming, training, and directing the Contras, the United States violated the customary international law principle of the non use of force by "organizing or encouraging the organization of irregular forces or armed bands ... for incursion into the territory of another State." *Id.* at para. 228. The Court stressed, however, that neither Nicaragua's provision of arms to the opposition in El Salvador nor the United States' provision of funds to the Contras in Nicaragua, by themselves, amounted to a prohibited use of force. *Id.* at paras. 228, 230. *But see* Chapter Seven, Sections 1 and 2, concerning impermissible intervention and violations of neutrality laws; JOHN F. MURPHY, PUNISHING INTERNATIONAL TERRORISTS: THE LEGAL FRAMEWORK FOR POLICY INITIATIVES 59 (1985), quoting I.L.C. resolution on International Terrorism: "'No situation could be envisaged in which state support for persons or groups engaged or preparing to engage in the acts ... of international terrorism would not violate basic rules of international law.'"

3. In 1986, the United States bombed targets in Tripoli, the capital of Libya, partly in response to a series of terrorist attacks in Europe culminating in the bombing of a Berlin disco in which two Americans were killed and over 100 people injured. The United States justified its action on the basis of evidence that the persons responsible for the terrorist attacks had traveled on Libyan passports and that Libya was likely to continue to support acts of terrorism against the United States unless something was done. At the time, the President of the United States, Ronald Reagan, stated that these were the latest in a series of attacks "with support and direction" by Libya and added: "By providing material support to terrorists groups which attack U.S. citizens, Libya has engaged in armed aggression against the United States under established principles of international law, just as if it had used its own armed forces." Secretary of State George Shultz elaborated:

> "A nation attacked by terrorists is permitted to use force to prevent or preempt future attacks, to seize terrorists, or to rescue its citizens when no other means is available. The law requires that such actions be necessary and proportionate. But this nation has consistently affirmed the rights of states to use force in ex-

ercise of their right of individual or collective self-defense. The U.N. Charter is not a suicide pact."

Abraham D. Sofaer, *International Law and the Use of Force*, THE NATIONAL INTEREST 53, 57 (Fall 1988). See also Sofaer, *Terrorism, the Law, and National Defense,* 126 MIL. L. REV. 89 (1989). Do you agree? Was the 1986 bombing in Tripoli consistent with the International Court of Justice's holding in the Nicaragua Case? More generally, is "preemptive" self-defense permissible and was the armed conflict, however short, nonetheless permissible under international law? *Compare* Paust, *Responding Lawfully to International Terrorism: The Use of Force Abroad,* 8 WHITTIER L. REV. 711 (1986) *with* Boyle, *Preserving the Rule of Law in the War Against Terrorism, id.*

4. Does the last paragraph of the 1991 resolution preserve the right of peoples struggling against alien or colonial domination to resort to acts of "terrorism"? Does the phrase "the right of these peoples to struggle *legitimately* to this end" mean that resort to terrorism can never be justified since "terrorism" is not a legitimate means? Can some terrorist acts be legitimate and distinguished from acts that are unacceptable under any circumstances? With respect to terroristic tactics utilized against combatants and other lawful military targets during an armed conflict, see Paust, *An Introduction, supra,* at 705–10, and references cited. Recall the notes on law of war documents in Section 1 of this chapter.

5. In 1994, the General Assembly adopted the *Declaration on Measures to Eliminate International Terrorism*, contained in the annex to resolution 49/60. The Declaration states, *inter alia*, that "criminal acts intended or calculated to provoke a state of terror in the general public, a group of persons or particular persons for political purposes are in any circumstances unjustifiable, whatever the considerations of political, philosophical, ideological, racial, ethnic, religious or any other nature that may be invoked to justify them." Does this constitute an internationally agreed upon definition of terrorism? What acts would fall within this definition? What acts would the definition exclude? Would the fact that this definition only covers "criminal acts" exempt violence committed as part of a struggle for national liberation or pursuant to concerted activities designed to achieve self-determination?

6. On September 18, 2001, the Security Council, acting pursuant to its Chapter VII authority, adopted Resolution 1373. Paragraphs 1 and 2 of the resolution requires all states (not merely members of the U.N.) to engage in various actions. What conduct is required? See Resolution 1373 in the Documents Supplement. Does Resolution 1373 constitute an authorization to use military force?

B. The Anti-Terrorism Conventions

John F. Murphy, *The Future of Multilateralism and Efforts to Combat International Terrorism*

25 COLUM. J. TRANS. L. 35, 41–53 (1986)*

The Major Multilateral Conventions

The world community has responded to international terrorism in a number of ways. The most formal legal response has been the conclusion of international agreements de-

---

signed to combat various manifestations of international terrorism. Less legal in form, although raising legal issues, is the imposition of sanctions upon states that support international terrorism. Such sanctions have been applied in accordance with informal political consensus....

To date [1986], the world community has adopted [eight] global antiterrorist conventions: the Convention on Offenses and Certain Other Acts Committed on Board Aircraft (Tokyo Convention), the Convention for Suppression of Unlawful Seizure of Aircraft (Hague Convention), the Convention for Suppression of Unlawful Acts Against the Safety of Civil Aviation (Montreal Convention), the Convention on Prevention and Punishment of Crimes Against Internationally Protected Persons, Including Diplomatic Agents (Convention on Protected Persons), the International Convention Against the Taking of Hostages (Hostages Convention), [the Protocol for the Suppression of Unlawful Acts of Violence at Airports Serving International Civil Aviation (Airport Security Protocol), the IMO Convention for the Suppression of Unlawful Acts against the Safety of Maritime navigation (Maritime Terrorism Convention), and the Protocol for the Suppression of Unlawful Acts against the Safety of Fixed Platforms located on the Continental Shelf (Fixed Platforms Protocol).]

These conventions seek to suppress international terrorism by establishing a framework for international cooperation among states. To accomplish this goal, the Convention on Protected Persons, for example, requires states parties (1) to cooperate in order to prevent, within their territories, preparations for attacks on diplomats within or outside their territories, (2) to exchange information, and (3) to coordinate administrative measures against such attacks. If an attack against an internationally protected person takes place and an alleged offender has fled the country where the attack occurred states parties are to cooperate in the exchange of information concerning the circumstances of the crime and the alleged offender's identity and whereabouts. Any state party where the alleged offender is found is obliged to take measures to ensure his presence for purposes of extradition or prosecution and to inform interested states and international organizations of the measures taken. Finally, parties are to cooperate in assisting criminal proceedings brought for attacks on internationally protected persons. This imposes, *inter alia*, an obligation on the state party to supply all relevant evidence at its disposal.

A key feature of these conventions is the requirement that a state party that apprehends an alleged offender in its territory either extradite him or submit his case to its own authorities for purposes of prosecution. Strictly speaking, none of these conventions alone creates an obligation to extradite; by requiring the submission of alleged offenders for prosecution if extradition fails, they contain an inducement to extradite. Moreover, legal basis for extradition is provided either in the convention or through incorporation of the offenses mentioned in the convention into existing or future extradition treaties between the parties. To varying degrees, the conventions also obligate the parties to take the important practical step of attempting to apprehend the accused and hold him in custody.

The most important goal of these provisions is to ensure prosecution of the accused. To this end, the conventions state quite strongly the alternative obligation either to extradite or to submit the accused for prosecution. The obligation, however, is not to try the accused, much less to punish him, but to submit the case to be considered for prosecution by the appropriate national prosecution by the appropriate national prosecuting authority. If the prosecuting state's criminal justice system lacks integrity, the risk of political intervention in the prosecuting or at trial exists. Such intervention may prevent the trial or conviction of the accused, or act as a mitigating influence at the sentencing stage.

Even if the prosecuting state's criminal justice system functions with integrity, it may be very difficult to obtain the evidence necessary to convict the accused when the alleged offense was committed in another country. This very practical impediment to conviction can be removed only by patient and sustained efforts to develop and expand "judicial assistance" and other forms of cooperation between the law enforcement and judicial systems of different countries. The conventions create an obligation to cooperate in this regard but, as will be demonstrated in greater detail later in this article, this obligation is often difficult for countries with different types of legal systems to meet, even assuming that they act in complete good faith.

The Hostages Convention adds a new dimension to existing international legal measures to combat terrorism. The convention seeks to ensure that international acts of hostage-taking will be covered either by the Hostages Convention itself or by one of the applicable conventions on the law of armed conflict. The Hostages Convention also constitutes a partial rejection of the contention that acts of terrorism are permissible if committed as part of a war of national liberation.

Two other multilateral conventions, while not directed expressly against terrorism, serve a similar purpose. The Convention on the Prohibition of the Development, Production and Stockpiling of Bacteriological (Biological) and Toxic Weapons and on Their Destruction prohibits the development, production or stockpiling of microbiological and biological agents (weapons) that are of potential use to terrorists. Similarly, the recently concluded Convention on the Physical Protection of Nuclear Materials (Convention on Nuclear Material) prevents parties from exporting or importing or authorizing the export or import of nuclear material used for peaceful purposes, unless they give assurances that such material will be protected at prescribed levels during international transport. The Convention on Nuclear Material also provides a framework for international cooperation in the recovery and protection of stolen nuclear material, and requires that states parties make certain serious offenses involving nuclear material punishable, and that they extradite or prosecute offenders.

The effectiveness of these global conventions as antiterrorist measures is questionable. Even if fully implemented, the limited and piecemeal solutions of these conventions would be of little use in combating the many manifestations of terrorism. For example, they do not cover attacks on international business persons, a common tactic of international terrorism. Similarly, they do not criminalize bombings and other violent attacks against civilians, an increasingly prevalent stratagem of international terrorists. Moreover, existing global conventions have not been effectively implemented.

The early returns on the Hostages Convention are not encouraging. On October 7, 1985, four gunmen seized the Italian cruise ship *Achille Lauro* and shot hostage Leon Klinghoffer, a U.S. citizen. On October 10, after having surrendered to Egyptian authorities, the hijackers were flown out of Egypt on an Egyptian jet. U.S. Navy fighters intercepted the jet over international waters and forced it to land in Sicily. On the jet, along with the four hijackers, was Mohammed Abbas, the leader of the Palestine Liberation Front, who had reportedly masterminded the hijacking. On October 11, the U.S. Government asked Italy to keep Abbas in custody. Two days after this request Italy released Abbas, claiming that the evidence was insufficient to justify holding him any longer. It did so although the United States, in accordance with the terms of the U.S.-Italy extradition treaty, had requested the provisional arrest of Abbas based on an arrest warrant and other documentation demonstrating his complicity in the hijacking and charging him with hostage-taking and piracy under U.S. law. In order to obtain the arrest warrant from the U.S. federal judge, the United States had already been forced to show probable cause that Abbas had committed the crime charged.

At the time of Abbas's release, Italy had signed but had not yet ratified the Hostages Convention. Thus it did not violate that Convention. However, in releasing Abbas, Italy acted in a way that defeated the object and purpose of the Hostages Convention, contrary to article 18 of the Vienna Convention on the Law of Treaties. Moreover, Italy acted contrary to the terms of the bilateral U.S.-Italy extradition treaty.

Yugoslavia, where Abbas flew after leaving Italy, is a party to the Hostages Convention and has a bilateral extradition treaty with the United States. On October 12, the United States presented the Yugoslavian authorities with more evidence of Abbas's complicity in the crime and asked Yugoslavia to hold him. Nonetheless, on October 13, Yugoslavian officials informed the United States that they would not hold Abbas. Apparently, Yugoslavia had never taken Abbas into custody, despite the U.S. request for provisional arrest based on the same arrest warrant presented to Italian officials and additional documentation in full compliance with the U.S.-Yugoslavia extradition treaty. There is no evidence that the Yugoslavian judiciary was involved in any way in this decision.

Under the Hostages Convention, Yugoslavia had an obligation either to extradite Abbas or to submit him to its authorities for the purpose of prosecution. Even assuming that the evidence originally presented by the United States was insufficient under Yugoslavian law to detain Abbas for the purpose of possible extradition or prosecution, at a minimum Yugoslavia had a duty to comply in good faith with its international obligations, and thus to detain him for a period of time that would give the United States a reasonable opportunity to offer additional evidence in an effort to meet the Yugoslavian standard.

Five days after allowing Abbas to leave, Yugoslavia explained that it viewed him as having diplomatic immunity as an official of the PLO. Italy hinted at the possibility of immunity as well, either because of Abbas's position in the PLO or because he reportedly carried an Iraqi diplomatic passport.

These claims are patent nonsense. As a representative of the PLO, Abbas enjoyed no diplomatic immunity because the PLO is not a country. Nor did his Iraqi diplomatic passport afford him any protection, since a diplomat enjoys immunity from criminal prosecution only in the country to which he has been assigned or if in transit between diplomatic assignments. Neither of these circumstances applied to Abbas.

Sanctions Against the Harboring of Aircraft Hijackers. The Bonn Declaration

Most of the global antiterrorist conventions have relatively strong dispute settlement provision that allow for binding arbitration or adjudication, however, some of them permit a party to "opt out" in accordance with a reservation made at the time it became a party. The United States relied in part on such a dispute settlement provision in the Convention on Protected Persons in bringing its action against Iran before the International Court of Justice. Yet none of these conventions provides for economic or other sanctions against states that offer haven or other assistance to terrorists.

The first efforts in September, 1973 to conclude an independent sanctions convention for the International Civil Aviation Organization (ICAO) [Aircraft hijacking and sabotage] Conventions at the Rome Security Conference and at the ICAO Extraordinary Assembly were unsuccessful. Other efforts to conclude a sanctions convention have met with a similar fate. Efforts in the ICAO having failed, an initiative outside the United Nations was undertaken. On July 21, 1978, the heads of state and government participating in the Bonn Economic Summit (Canada, France, the Federal Republic of Germany, Italy, Japan, the United Kingdom, and the United States—known as the Summit Countries) agreed upon a declaration which has come to be known as the Bonn Declaration on Hijacking. The declaration provides:

The Heads of State and Government, concerned about terrorism and the taking of hostages, declare that their governments will intensify their joint efforts to combat international terrorism. To this end, in cases where a country refuses extradition or prosecution of those who have hijacked an aircraft/and or does not return such aircraft, the Heads of State and Government are jointly resolved that their governments shall take immediate action to halt all in-coming flights from that country, or from any country of the airlines of the country concerned. They urge other governments to join them in the commitment.

Although there is some disagreement on this point, most commentators agree that the Bonn Declaration is not a binding legal instrument, but rather a statement of policy which expresses the intent of the Summit Countries to take action when, subsequent to a hijacking, other states have failed to live up to their obligations with regard to it. Follow-up efforts have succeeded in obtaining widespread support for the declaration and in inducing additional countries to become parties to the ICAO Conventions.

The first test of the Bonn Declaration came on July 20, 1981. At that time, the heads of state and government meeting at the Ottawa Economic Summit considered the hijacking in March, 1981 of a Pakistan International Airlines aircraft to Afghanistan. Recalling and reaffirming the principles set forth in the 1978 Bonn Declaration, the heads of state and government stated that the action of the Afghan regime, both during the incident and subsequently (in giving refuge to the hijackers), "was and is a flagrant breach of its international obligations under the Hague Convention to which Afghanistan is a party and constitutes a serious threat to air safety." Accordingly, the heads of state and government proposed to "suspend all flights to and from Afghanistan in implementation of the Bonn Declaration unless Afghanistan immediately takes steps to comply with its obligations." They also called upon "all states which share their concern for air safety to take appropriate action to persuade Afghanistan to honor its obligations." The United States favored an immediate application of the Bonn Declaration sanctions. However, France, the Federal Republic of Germany, and the United Kingdom, which were the only countries among the seven to whose territories Ariana Afghan Airlines flew, were of the opinion that they could not employ sanctions without violating the terms of their bilateral air transit agreements with Afghanistan. Accordingly, these states instead gave Afghanistan a year's notice of their intent to terminate the air transit agreements. On November 30, 1982, all three implemented the Bonn Declaration by terminating all air traffic with Afghanistan

Notes and Questions

1. Several anti-terrorism treaties contain nearly identical language, with the exception of the provisions defining the various offenses and providing for jurisdiction. Consider the Montreal Aircraft Sabotage Convention and the relevant provisions of U.S. domestic law implementing the Convention, and thereafter the provisions defining offenses and providing for jurisdiction contained in the Airport Security Protocol to the Sabotage Convention, the Hague Aircraft Hijacking Convention, the Internationally Protected Persons Convention, the Hostage-Taking Convention, and the Maritime Terrorism Convention and its Fixed Platform Protocol. The earlier Tokyo Hijacking Convention was different. Newer treaties in the Documents Supplement include: the International Convention for Suppression of Terrorist Bombings; International Convention for Suppression of Financing of Terrorism. Note that the Convention for Suppression of Terrorist Bombings excludes "activities undertaken by military forces of a state in the exercise of their official duties"

(art. 19 (2)) or, in certain cases, when the offense is committed within a single state (art. 3). Would acts undertaken by military forces of a state that are in violation of their official duties be covered?

2. The U.S. Dep't of State, COUNTRY REPORTS ON TERRORISM 2005, 42–44 (April 2006), lists thirteen treaties as those directly related to terrorism, many of which are in the Documents Supplement: 1963 Tokyo Convention on Offences and Certain Other Acts Committed on Board Aircraft (180 Parties), 1970 Convention for the Suppression of Unlawful Seizure of Aircraft (181 Parties), 1971 Convention for the Suppression of Unlawful Acts Against the Safety of Civil Aviation (183 Parties), 1973 Convention on the Prevention and Punishment of Crimes Against Internationally Protected Persons, including Diplomatic Agents (159 Parties), 1970 International Convention Against the Taking of Hostages (153 Parties), 1979 Convention on the Physical Protection of Nuclear Material (116 Parties), 1971 Protocol for the Suppression of Unlawful Acts of Violence at Airports Serving International Civil Aviation, Supplementary to the Convention for the Suppression of Unlawful Acts against the Safety of Civil Aviation (156 Parties), 1988 Convention for the Suppression of Unlawful Acts Against the Safety of Maritime Navigation (134 Parties), 1988 Protocol for the Suppression of Unlawful Acts Against the Safety of Fixed Platforms Located on the Continental Shelf (123 Parties); 1991 Convention on the Making of Plastic Explosives for the Purpose of Detection (123 Parties), 1997 International Convention for the Suppression of Terrorist Bombings (145 Parties), 1999 International Convention for the Suppression of the Financing of Terrorism (150 Parties), 2005 International Convention for the Suppression of Acts of Nuclear Terrorism (100 signatures, no ratifications).

There are currently fourteen major international instruments dealing with terrorism. See 2010 Convention on the Suppression of Unlawful Acts Relating to International Civil Aviation (24, signatures, no ratifications). For a brief summary of each of the fourteen counterterrorism conventions and protocols see International Legal Instruments to Counter Terrorism, *available at* http://www.un.org/terrorism/instruments.shtml (last visited June 4, 2012).

Tokyo Convention on Offences and Certain Other Acts Committed on Board Aircraft
704 U.N.T.S. 219, 20 U.S.T. 2941, T.I.A.S. No. 6768 (1963)

[Read the Tokyo Convention, in the Documents Supplement]

1971 Montreal Convention for the Suppression of Unlawful Acts Against the Safety of Civil Aviation
974 U.N.T.S. 177, 1973 Can. T.S. No. 23, 24 U.S.T. 564, T.I.A.S. No. 7570

[Read Articles 1–3, 5–9, 11, 14, in the Documents Supplement]

18 U.S.C. § 32, Destruction of Aircraft or Aircraft Facilities
(Implementing the Montreal Convention)

(a) Whoever willfully—

(1) sets fire to, damages, destroys, disables, or wrecks any aircraft in the special aircraft jurisdiction of the United States or any civil aircraft used, operated, or employed in interstate, overseas, or foreign air commerce;

(2) places or causes to be placed a destructive device or substance in, upon, or in proximity to … any such aircraft … if such placing or causing to be placed is likely to endanger the safety of any such aircraft; …

(5) performs an act of violence against or incapacitates any individual on any such aircraft, if such act of violence or incapacitation is likely to endanger the safety of such aircraft; …

shall be fined not more than $100,000 or imprisoned not more than twenty years or both.

(b) Whoever willfully—

(1) performs an act of violence against any individual on board any civil aircraft registered in a country other than the United States while such aircraft is in flight, if such act is likely to endanger the safety of that aircraft;

(2) destroys a civil aircraft registered in a country other than the United States while such aircraft is in services or causes damage to such an aircraft which renders that aircraft incapable of flight or which is likely to endanger that aircraft's safety in flight;

(3) places or causes to be placed on a civil aircraft registered in a country other than the United States while such aircraft is in service, a device or substance which is likely to destroy that aircraft, or to cause damage to that aircraft which renders that aircraft incapable of flight or which is likely to endanger that aircraft's safety in flight; …

shall, if the offender is later found in the United States, be fined not more than $100,000 or imprisoned not more than twenty years, or both.

49 U.S.C. App. § 1301, Definitions

(38) The term "special aircraft jurisdiction of the United States" includes—

(a) civil aircraft of the United States;

(b) aircraft of the national defense forces of the United States;

(c) any other aircraft within the United States;

(d) any other aircraft outside the United States—

(i) that has its next scheduled destination or last point of departure in the United States, if that aircraft next actually lands in the United States.

(ii) having "an offense," as defined in the Convention for the Suppression of Unlawful Seizure of Aircraft, committed aboard, if that aircraft lands in the United States with the alleged offender still aboard; or

(iii) regarding which an offense as defined in subsection (d) or (e) of article 1, section 1 of the Convention for the Suppression of Unlawful Acts against the Safety of Civil Aviation (Montreal, September 23, 1972) is committed if the aircraft lands in the United States with an alleged offender still on board; and

(e) other aircraft leased without crew to a lessee who has his principal place of business in the United States, or if none, who has his permanent residence in the United States;

while that aircraft is in flight, which is from the moment when all external doors are closed following embarkation until the moment when one such door is opened for disembarkation or in the case of a forced landing, until the competent authorities take over the responsibility for the aircraft and for the persons and property aboard.

Protocol for the Suppression of Unlawful Acts of Violence at Airports Serving International Civil Aviation, Supplementary to the Convention for the Suppression of Unlawful Acts Against the Safety of Civil Aviation

signed at Montreal on 24 February 1988, International Civil Aviation Organization Doc. 9518

[Read Articles I–III, in the Documents Supplement]

1970 Hague Convention on the Suppression of Unlawful Seizure of Aircraft (Hijacking)

860 U.N.T.S. 105, 1972 Can. T.S. No. 23, 22 U.S.T. 1641, T.I.A.S. No. 7192

[Read the Hague Hijacking Convention, in the Documents Supplement]

1973 Convention on the Prevention and Punishment of Crimes Against Internationally Protected Persons, Including Diplomatic Agents

1977 Can. T.S. No. 43, 28 U.S.T. 1975, T.I.A.S. No. 8532

[Read the Convention on Internationally Protected Persons, in the Documents Supplement]

1979 International Convention Against the Taking of Hostages

[see the Documents Supplement and Chapter Eleven, Section 4]

Convention for the Suppression of Unlawful Acts Against the Safety of Maritime Navigation

done at Rome on 10 March 1988, International Maritime Organization Doc. SUA/CON/15/Rev.1, 1993 Can. T.S. No. 10

[Read the extracts, in the Documents Supplement]

Protocol for the Suppression of Unlawful Acts Against the Safety of Fixed Platforms Located on the Continental Shelf

done at Rome on 10 March 1988, International Maritime Organization Doc. SUA/CONF/15/Rev.1

[Read the extracts, in the Documents Supplement]

Notes and Questions

1. Most of the anti-terrorism conventions have been ratified by large numbers of states. Recall Note 2 following the extract of Professor Murphy's article. Does such widespread ratification of the treaties necessarily mean that they now reflect customary international law? What two elements must be generally conjoined to create customary law? Recall Chapter One. *See also* the language of the D.C. and Second Circuits

quoted in Section 1, Note 4, above. Today, most states and textwriters consider that at least the Tokyo, Hague Hijacking, Montreal Aircraft Sabotage, Internationally Protected Persons, and Hostages Conventions reflect customary international law of universal applicability.

2. Can a state that has ratified one of these treaties use the jurisdictional provisions of the treaty to prosecute a national of a state that has not ratified the treaty if the national is found within the ratifying state's territory? Clearly yes if the treaty reflects customary international law (recall Chapter Three, Section 1, with respect to universal jurisdiction) since universal jurisdiction is appropriate with respect to customary international crimes. Recall also that Germany had refused to ratify the 1907 Hague Convention No. IV, which contained a participation clause limiting its application to wars between parties to the treaty, but that by 1939 the treaty had reflected customary international law of universal application binding also German nationals. Consider the remarks in the following extract from Professor Scharf's article, whether you agree, and whether something is missing. You might also reconsider the extract of *United States v. Yunis* in Chapter Three, Section 1. Michael P. Scharf, *Application of Treaty-Based Universal Jurisdiction to Nationals of Non-Party States*, 35 New England L. Rev. 363 (2001):

> The question of the application of universal jurisdiction under the anti-terrorism treaties with respect to nationals of Non-Party States was addressed by the D.C. Circuit Federal Court of Appeals in the case of *United States v. Yunis*. The United States had indicted, apprehended and prosecuted Fawaz Yunis, a Lebanese national, for hijacking from Beirut airport a Jordanian airliner with two U.S. citizens as passengers. The United States asserted jurisdiction in the first instance on the basis of the International Convention Against the Taking of Hostages, a treaty which provides jurisdiction over hostage-takers, despite the fact that Lebanon was not a party to the treaty and did not consent to the prosecution of Yunis in the United States. The Court [of Appeals] upheld its jurisdiction based on the domestic legislation implementing the Convention which had conferred upon it universal and passive personality jurisdiction over this type of terrorist act. As Counsel to the State Department's Counter Terrorism Bureau at the time, I recall that U.S. government officials in the Departments of Justice and State perceived this confirmation that the anti-terrorism conventions could provide the basis for the United States to prosecute the nationals of Non-Party States as an important precedent in the fight against terrorism.
>
> The *Yunis* precedent was ... reaffirmed in *United States v. Ali Rezaq*, where the United States apprehended and prosecuted a Palestinian national for hijacking an Egyptian airliner, despite the fact that Palestine (his claimed country of nationality) is not party to the Hague Hijacking Convention. The principle has also been applied in a series of recent cases in which the United States has asserted jurisdiction pursuant to the hostage-taking Convention over Chinese nationals who smuggled foreign citizens into the United States and held them captive until their relatives living in the United States paid ransom to secure their release. In these cases the defendants unsuccessfully challenged the court's jurisdiction on equal protection grounds because only non-U.S. nationals in U.S. territory could be convicted of violating the domestic criminal statute implementing the Hostage Taking Convention, which carries with it a higher sentencing range than mere kidnapping. In non of these cases did the courts exhibit concern that China was not a party to the Convention, at the time of the acts in question, which served as the basis for U.S. jurisdiction over the defendants.

The United States is not the only country that has asserted treaty-based jurisdiction over the nationals of Non-Party States. In a case similar to *Rezaq*, a Dutch court confirmed that it had jurisdiction pursuant to the Hijacking Convention and the Aircraft Sabotage Convention over a Palestinian defendant who claimed to be a resident of East Jerusalem.

3. In 1988, Pan Am Flight 103 exploded over Lockerbie Scotland, killing all those aboard. The plane took off from Germany, where the bomb hidden in a suitcase was loaded into its cargo hold; the plane's destination was New York City; the plane was registered to the United States; the passengers included American, German, British, and French nationals; the suspected perpetrators were two Libyan nationals; and the suspects have taken refuge in Libya. Which countries have permissive jurisdiction (*e.g.*, victim theory or universal by treaty jurisdiction) over the alleged perpetrators under the Montreal Sabotage Convention? Which country has mandatory jurisdiction under the Convention? Now examine the jurisdiction provisions of the Hostage Taking Convention and the Maritime Sabotage Convention. How do they differ from those contained in the Montreal Sabotage Convention? By special agreement, an ad hoc court was set up in the Netherlands to try two Libyan accused rendered to the tribunal. The trial began May 3, 2000 and one person was convicted and one was not proven guilty. See Chapter Two, Section 3.

4. The several anti-terrorism conventions are said to contain an initiate prosecution or extradite requirement based on the formula contained in Articles 6(1) and 7 of the Montreal Aircraft Sabotage Convention. What loopholes does this formula contain that can be used to frustrate the requirement? *See, e.g.*, Article 8(2).

5. Does the Montreal Aircraft Sabotage Convention only apply to bombs placed aboard aircraft, or would it also apply to the downing of an aircraft by a surface to air missile? Iran had brought suit against the United States before the International Court of Justice for the downing of an Iranian Airbus by a missile fired by the U.S. Vincennes. *See Aerial Incident of 3 July 1988 (Islamic Republic of Iran v. United States)*. Iran claimed that the United States violated the Montreal Sabotage Convention by refusing to prosecute or extradite the servicemen responsible for the "accident." In its briefs, the United States argued that the Montreal Aircraft Sabotage Convention should not apply to acts committed by the armed forces of a State. Do you agree? What would be the implications if the Court accepted this argument? Iran and the United States settled the controversy in a Settlement Agreement of Feb. 9, 1996. See 90 AM. J. INT'L L. 278 (1996).

6. If a state submitted a case falling within the Montreal Sabotage Convention to its courts for extradition proceedings, and the courts determined that the offense was a non-extraditable political offense, would the Convention require the state to then submit the case for domestic prosecution? The United States and United Kingdom have issued indictments for the two Libyan officials accused of planting the bomb on Pan Am Flight 103. The two countries thereafter demanded that Libya surrender the suspects. Libya refused to surrender the suspects and stated that it was investigating the matter, and then later asserted that its own investigation indicated that domestic prosecution was not warranted. Was Libya's response permissible in view of the terms of the Montreal Aircraft Sabotage Convention? Libya then requested the United States and United Kingdom to turn over any evidence they possessed in order to determine if domestic charges were warranted. The United States and United Kingdom declined, asserting that such action would be inappropriate since the Government of Libya itself was behind the bombing. Was the response of the United States and United Kingdom consistent with their obligations under the Convention?

7. The anti-terrorism conventions do not work well in situations in which the State with custody over the alleged offender is itself apparently implicated in the offense. The United States and United Kingdom, therefore, took the Pan Am 103 issue to the U.N. Security Council which, acting under Chapter VII of the U.N. Charter, issued a resolution (1) requiring Libya to surrender the suspects to the United States or United Kingdom, and (2) imposing international sanctions on Libya pending its compliance with the resolution. *See* Resolution 748 (31 March 1992). Relying on Article 14 of the Montreal Aircraft Sabotage Convention, Libya requested arbitration and when the United States and United Kingdom refused, it immediately brought a case against the United States and United Kingdom before the International Court of Justice, claiming that it had a right under the Montreal Sabotage Convention to decline to extradite so long as it had submitted the case to its competent authorities for the purpose of deciding whether there were sufficient grounds for a prosecution. Under Article 14 of the Sabotage Convention, should Libya have been required to wait six months after requesting arbitration before bringing suit before the World Court? In his opinion in the case, Judge Oda of Japan, the acting president of the World Court, stated that he was satisfied that the Court possessed jurisdiction, despite the six-month rule in Article 14(1) of the Montreal Convention, since the circumstances had appeared to leave no room to negotiate the organization of an arbitration. Judge Ni of China, on the other hand, opined that Libya's request should be denied on the sole ground of the non-fulfillment of the six-month period requirement, without having to decide at the same time the merits of the case.

8. On April 14, 1992, the International Court of Justice ruled by a vote of 11 to 5 that under Articles 25 and 103 of the U.N. Charter, the binding Security Council resolution takes precedence over any other treaty commitments and therefore supersedes Libya's right to prosecute in lieu of extraditing under the Montreal Sabotage Convention. In favor: Vice-President Oda (Japan), Acting President, President Sir Robert Jennings (UK), Judges Lachs (Poland), Ago (Italy), Schwebel (USA), Ni (China), Evenmen (Norway), Tarassov (Russia), Guillaume (France), Shahabuddeen (Guyana), and Aguilar (Venezuela). Against: Judges Bedjaoui (Algeria), Weeramantry (Sri Lanka), Ranjeva (Madagascar), Ajibola (Nigeria), and Judge ad hoc El-Kosheri (Libya). Most of the judges opined, however, that but for the adoption of Resolution 748, Libya would have been in the right in refusing to extradite.

9. Would the United States be obligated under the Tokyo or Hague Hijacking Conventions (if it does not initiate prosecution) to return to China a former political prisoner who hijacked an aircraft to Hawaii in order to avoid the death sentence imposed for taking part in a pro-democracy demonstration? Should it be? *Cf. United States v. Tiede*, in Chapter Four, Section 8. Consider Articles 7 and 8 (2) of the Hague Convention (which are the same as those in the Montreal Convention). See also Paust, *Extradition and United States Prosecution of the* Achille-Lauro *Hostage-Takers: Navigating the Hazards,* 20 Vand. J. Trans. L. 235, 244–49 (1987); Williams, *International Law and Terrorism: Age-Old Problems, Different Targets,* 26 Can. Y.B. Int'l L. 87 (1988). European states have adopted a special treaty denying the political offense exception to extradition in the case of a violation of these and several other listed treaties. See European Convention on the Suppression of Terrorism, E.T.S. No. 90, reprinted in 15 I.L.M. 1272 (1976). Is such preferable? Recall Chapter Five, Section 1 E.

10. Is it an offense under the Tokyo or Hague Hijacking Conventions to "hijack" an airplane which is sitting empty on the runway or in a hanger? See 1970 Hague Convention, art. 3(1). This situation has arisen on several occasions with respect to refugees trying to flee from repressive governments from the Eastern Bloc and Cuba.

11. Would the murder by persons under the command of Somali warlord Mohamed Aideed of 24 Pakistani U.N. peacekeeping troops in 1993 or the execution of 12 Belgian U.N. peacekeeping troops by radical Hutu forces in Rwanda in 1994 constitute an offense under the Internationally Protected Persons Convention? Who is an "agent" of the United Nations? Would the 1949 Geneva Conventions or 1977 Protocols thereto apply? Human rights law? The 1979 Hostages Convention? Consider Chapters Eight and Eleven, Sections 1 and 4. The issue of criminal responsibility for attacks on United Nations and associated personnel has led to adoption of a new convention. See Convention on the Safety of United Nations and Associated Personnel, in the Documents Supplement.

12. On June 9, 1987, the Summit Seven Countries issued a *Joint Statement on International Terrorism*, the annex to which expanded the policy announced in the Bonn Declaration on Hijacking (discussed in John Murphy's article above) to other forms of terrorism against civil aviation. To provide further inducement to countries to abide by their obligations to extradite or to initiate prosecution of offenders of the international anti-terrorism conventions, the United States has enacted legislation authorizing the imposition of economic sanctions against countries that provide support to terrorists, including those that provide sanctuary from prosecution. By far the most important statute in this area is the Anti-Terrorism and Arms Export Amendments Act of 1989, P.L. 101-222, codified at 22 U.S.C. 1732, 2364, 2371, 2753, 2776, 2778, 2780; 10 U.S.C. 2327; and 50 U.S.C. 2405. This act creates a uniform scheme of sanctions that are automatically triggered against countries that the Secretary of State has determined have "repeatedly provided support for acts of international terrorism." Such sanctions include the prohibition of military sales, export of munitions items, foreign aid, and tax credits. In addition to these automatic sanctions, various statutes authorize restrictions on exports to and imports from countries that are included in the Secretary of State's so-called "terrorist list." The 1987 terrorist list is reproduced at 55 Fed. Reg. 37790; others are available through the U.S. Dep't of State website: http://wwww.state.gov. 49 U.S.C. § 1514 also authorizes the President to suspend air services to certain safe haven states.

Section 3
Domestic Legislation

Introductory Note

The United States has several different criminal statutes under which it can exercise jurisdiction over most types of terrorism affecting U.S. interests. These range from general statutes such as the Civil War era sedition law and the Racketeer Influenced and Corrupt Organizations Act (RICO), to criminal legislation specifically targeted at terrorists such as the statutes implementing the several international anti-terrorism conventions. These implementing statutes elaborate the offenses, create U.S. criminal jurisdiction over offenders, and specify appropriate penalties. One such statute is noted above in connection with the Montreal Convention.

The most ambitious and unique anti-terrorism criminal statute is Section 1202 of the Omnibus Diplomatic Security and Antiterrorism Act of 1986, 18 U.S.C. § 2331 *et seq.*, as amended. This legislation, which is sometimes referred to as the "terrorist long arm statute," fills a gap present in the patchwork of international anti-terrorism conventions and their implementing statutes by extending United States criminal jurisdiction to cover "terrorists" and many other persons who kill, assault or make any violent attack upon U.S. nationals abroad. Consider what perpetrators and what victims would be covered under various portions of the legislation. In particular, could § 2332 be used to prosecute Usama bin Laden with respect to his direction of the use of aircraft against the World Trade Center on September 11, 2001?

18 U.S.C. § 2332. Criminal penalties

(a) Homicide.—Whoever kills a national of the United States, while such national is outside the United States, shall—

(1) if the killing is a murder as defined in section 1111(a) of this title, be fined under this title or imprisoned for any term of years or for life, or both so fined and so imprisoned;

(2) if the killing is a voluntary manslaughter as defined in section 1112(a) of this title, be fined under this title or imprisoned not more than ten years, or both; and

(3) if the killing is an involuntary manslaughter as defined in section 1112(a) of this title, be fined under this title or imprisoned not more than three years, or both.

(b) Attempt or conspiracy with respect to homicide.—Whoever outside the United States attempts to kill, or engages in a conspiracy to kill, a national of the United States shall—

(1) in the case of an attempt to commit a killing that is a murder as defined in this Chapter, be fined under this title or imprisoned not more than 20 years, or both; and

(2) in the case of a conspiracy by two or more persons to commit a killing that is a murder as defined in section 1111(a) of this title, if one or more of such persons do any overt act to effect the object of the conspiracy, be fined under this title or imprisoned for any term of years or for life, or both so fined and so imprisoned.

(c) Other conduct.—Whoever outside the United States engages in physical violence—

(1) with intent to cause serious bodily injury to a national of the United States; or

(2) with the result that serious bodily injury is caused to a national of the United States;

shall be fined under this title or imprisoned not more than five years, or both.

(d) Limitation on prosecution.—No prosecution for any offense described in this section shall be undertaken by the United States except on written certification of the Attorney General or the highest ranking subordinate of the Attorney General with responsibility for criminal prosecutions that, in the judgment of the certifying official, such offense was intended to coerce, intimidate, or retaliate against a government or a civilian population.

Legislative History, P.L. 99-199

International Criminal Jurisdiction Over Terrorist Conduct

The Senate Amendment (sec. 714) includes a provision extending jurisdiction over certain crimes by terrorists against American citizens abroad.

The House bill contains no comparable provision.

The conference substitute (sec. 1202) establishes extraterritorial jurisdiction over serious violent attacks by terrorists upon U.S. nationals.... As in the Senate amendment, there is no requirement that the U.S. Government prove during the criminal prosecution the purpose of the murder. The elements are (1) the murder (2) of a U.S. national (3) outside the territorial jurisdiction of the United States.

The conspiracy paragraph of the conference substitute incorporates two conspiracy provisions from the Senate amendment and reaches terrorist conspiracies or attempts abroad to kill a U.S. national whether that national is outside the United States or within the United States. Paragraph (c) of the conference substitute is designed to provide jurisdiction over violent attacks against property, including but not limited to bombings and arson, as well as violent attacks against persons. In any case, the attack must be one that is intended to, or does, result in serious bodily injury to a U.S. national. The maximum prison sentence is set at 5 years.

The committee of conference does not intend that chapter 113A reach nonterrorist violence inflicted upon American victims. Simple barroom brawls or normal street crime, for example are not intended to be covered by this provision. To ensure that this statute is used only for its intended purpose, the conference substitute requires that the Attorney General certify that in his judgment such offense was intended to coerce, intimidate, or retaliate against a government or civilian population.

This paragraph also limits the authority to make the necessary certification for prosecution under this statute to the Attorney General or "the highest ranking subordinate of the Attorney General with responsibility for criminal prosecutions." The quoted language refers either to the Deputy Attorney General or the Associate Attorney General depending on their respective responsibilities. Although the Deputy Attorney General is the second highest ranking official of the Department of Justice, if the Associate Attorney General has primary responsibility for criminal prosecutions, he/she is the appropriate certifying official in addition to the Attorney General.

The determination of the certifying official is final and not subject to judicial review.

The term "civilian population" includes a general population as well as other specific identifiable segments of society such as the membership of a religious faith or of a particular nationality, to give but two examples. Neither the targeted government nor civilian population, or segment thereof, has to be that of the United States.

Notes and Questions

1. Subsequently § 2332a addressed an offense where "[a] person ... uses, or attempts or conspires to use, a weapon of mass destruction — (1) against a national of the United States while such national is outside the United States; (2) against any person within the United States; or (3) against any property that is owned, leased or used by the United States or by any department or agency of the United States, whether the property is within or outside of the United States...." § 2332a (c) includes among definitions of "weapon of mass destruction": "(B) any weapon that is designed or intended to cause death or serious bodily injury through the release, dissemination, or impact of toxic or poisonous chemicals, or their precursors; (C) any weapon involving a disease organism; or (D) any weapon that is designed to release radiation or radioactivity at a level dangerous to human life." As noted, § 2333 also provides limited civil remedies. Would § 2332a cover the Oklahoma City bombing of a federal building? *See also United States v. McVeigh*, 153 F.3d 1166 (10th Cir. 1998). Would it cover the use of bacteriological or biological weapons in the subways of New York as part of a terroristic tactic that led to the death of hundreds of persons? Would § 2332a, b, or c cover the Sept. 11, 2001 attacks on or the prior bombing of the World Trade Center? Consider *United States v. Salameh*, 261 F.3d 271 (2d Cir.

2001); *id.*, 152 F.3d 88 (2d Cir. 1998); *United States v. bin Laden, et al.*, 92 F. Supp.2d 225 (S.D.N.Y. 2000).

2. Is the reach of these statutes too broad or appropriate under principles of international law concerning jurisdiction to prescribe? See Chapter Three, Sections 1 and 2. Consider human rights law and the universality principle, *e.g.*, Universal Declaration of Human Rights, arts. 1, 2, 3, 5, in the Documents Supplement; Paust, *The Other Side of Right, supra.* Also recall *United States v. Yunis,* in Chapter Three.

3. While many countries have legislation implementing the several anti-terrorism conventions to which they are party, no other country has anything like the U.S. terrorist long arm statute. Is this surprising in view of only minority acceptance of the victim theory of jurisdiction to prescribe? Recall Chapter Three, Section 2. Might other states protest? Most of the countries responding to the Counsel of Europe Survey of National Law and Practices with Respect to Terrorism, May 7, 1991, COE Doc. PC-TE (91) 1, including Austria, Canada, Belgium, Denmark, France, Greece, Iceland, Luxembourg, Malta, the Netherlands, Norway, Spain, Switzerland, and Sweden indicated that they have no special anti-terrorism legislation on their books. Other countries, such as Germany, Italy, Portugal, and Turkey have legislation that makes it a crime to belong to a "terrorist" organization or to provide support for or recruit for a "terrorist" organization. What do you suspect the functional reach of "terrorist" organization is in Turkey? Under human rights law, can mere membership be a crime? Consider the Universal Declaration of Human Rights, arts. 2, 3, 9, 11, 18–20, 29(2), 30. Also recall Chapter Two, Sections 1 and 2. *See also* symposium, *Security of the Person and Security of the State: Human Rights and Claims of National Security,* 9 Yale J. World Pub. Ord. 1 (1982).

Similarly, the United Kingdom's Prevention of Terrorism (Temporary Provisions) Act of 1989 makes it a crime to provide support to "proscribed organizations" in Northern Ireland. The United States adopted this approach when, on January 23, 1995, pursuant to the International Economic Emergency Powers Act (IEEPA), 50 U.S.C. 1702(b)(3) and (4), the President of the United States issued Executive Order No. 12,947, which prohibits any transaction by a United States national or within the United States with a person or organization designated by the Secretary of State as "terrorist." Do you think this approach might run afoul of the First Amendment of the U.S. Constitution? Of human rights more generally? Is the proscription too vague?

4. In *A (FC) and Others (FC) v. Secretary of State for the Home Department* (House of Lords, U.K. 16 Dec. 2004), the House of Lords held that section 23 of the Anti-terrorism, Crime and Security Act 2001 is incompatible with articles 5 and 14 of the European Convention on Human Rights insofar as it is disproportionate and permits detention of suspected international terrorists in a way that discriminates on the ground of nationality or immigration status.

5. The original U.S. Senate proposal for the terrorist long arm statute would have required proof at trial that the accused acted with a specified "terrorist" intent. Terrorism, for this purpose, would have been defined by reference to the definition contained in the Foreign Intelligence Surveillance Act, which authorizes the Attorney General to order electronic surveillance to acquire foreign intelligence information (see note 7 below). However, recognizing that such a requirement would inadvertently render convictions of terrorists more difficult than ordinary criminals and could turn trials into political forums for the defendants, the final version of the legislation merely provides that the Attorney General must certify that the accused appeared to have a terrorist intent as a

prerequisite to prosecution. As the legislative history stresses, such intent is not an element of the offense to be proved at trial. Is this preferable?

6. § 2332 of the terrorist long arm statute is unique in that it allows the prosecutor (the Attorney General), rather than the court, to determine the question of federal jurisdiction (and the determination is supposedly non-reviewable). Do you think this aspect of the statute is vulnerable to a constitutional challenge on separation of powers grounds? Consider also RESTATEMENT § 431, Comm. a; Chapter Three.

7. There has been scholarly debate over whether § 2332 is based on the protective principle or the passive personality principle, which has traditionally been described as anathema to U.S. policy (see Chapter Three, Section 2). In introducing the legislation, Senator Specter asserted that the statute's basis is the protective principle:

> International law also recognizes broad criminal jurisdiction. If an alleged crime occurs in a foreign country, a nation may still exercise jurisdiction over the defendant if the crime has a potential adverse effect upon its security or the operation of its governmental functions. This basis for jurisdiction over crimes committed outside the United States has been applied by the Federal courts in contexts ranging from drug smuggling to perjury. Clearly, then, the exercise of U.S. criminal jurisdiction is also justified to prosecute the terrorist who assaults or murders American nationals abroad as a means of affecting U.S. policy. Such attacks undoubtedly have an adverse effect upon the conduct of our Government's foreign affairs, and potentially threaten the security interest of the United States as well.

See Statement of Senator Specter, Congressional Record, July 22, 1985. Based on the broad language of the statute, including section (d), what is the flaw in Senator Specter's statement? *See also United States v. Yunis*, 681 F. Supp. at 903 n.14, in Chapter Three, Section 2. Nonetheless, in view of human rights law can universal jurisdiction provide a basis? Recall Chapter Three, Sections 1 and 2; Paust, *An Introduction, supra*, at 700–02, 715–17, 749; *The Link Between Human Rights and Terrorism, supra*. *See also United States v. bin Laden, et al.*, 92 F. Supp.2d 189 (S.D.N.Y. 2000), addressed in Chapter Three, and *United States v. Yunis*, 924 F.2d 1086 (D.C. Cir. 1991), addressed *infra*.

8. 18 U.S.C. § 2339A(a) criminalizes the provision of "material support or resources" knowing or intending that such will "be used in preparation for or in carrying out" a violation of statutorily enumerated crimes. § 2339B(a)(1) criminalizes conduct when one "knowingly provides material support or resources to a foreign terrorist organization." One commentator notes: "To convict a defendant under … [2339A] the government must prove that the defendant provided material support or resources that were used for a *particular* act of terrorism…. Section 2339B, in the other hand, has been a mainstay of post-9-11 terrorism prosecutions … because its prohibitions are susceptible to broad interpretation; persons who traveled to Afghanistan and trained with al Qaeda can be convicted of providing personnel (themselves) to a designated terrorist group." Tung Yin, *Ending the War on Terrorism One Terrorist at a Time: A Noncriminal Detention Model for Holding and Releasing Guantanamo Bay Detainees*, 29 HARV. J. L. & POL. POL'Y 149, 179–80 (2005), citing among examples *United States v. Goba*, 220 F. Supp.2d 182 (W.D.N.Y. 2002); *United States v. Lindh*, 212 F. Supp.2d 541 (E.D. Va. 2002). He cautions: "Yet its potential for broad interpretation has resulted in a number of successful constitutional vagueness challenges." *Id.* at 180–81, addressing *United States v. Khan*, 309 F. Supp.2d 789, 821 (E.D. Va. 2004) (although fighting with the Taliban could indirectly benefit al Qaeda, such indirect support does not provide "material support or resources" *United States v. Sat-*

tar, 272 F. Supp.2d 348, 359 (S.D.N.Y. 2003) ("these terms and concepts applied to the prohibited provision of personnel provide no notice to persons of ordinary intelligence" *Cf United States v. Assi*, 414 F. Supp.2d 707 (E.D. Mich. 2006)). In 2010, the U.S. Supreme Court in *Holder v. Humanitarian Law Project*, 130 S. Ct. 2705 (2010), upheld the constitutionality of the material support statute, 18 U.S.C. § 2339B, and rejected plaintiffs' First Amendment freedom of association and freedom of speech claims, and a Fifth Amendment due process vagueness argument.

9. Section 1021 of the National Defense Authorization Act (NDAA), Pub. L. 112-81, 125 Stat. 1298 (Dec. 31, 2011) "affirms that the authority of the President to use all necessary and appropriate force pursuant to the (AUMF) includes the authority of the Armed Forces of the United States to detain covered persons (as defined in subsection (b)) pending disposition under the laws of war" and would permit detention without trial of "a person who was a part of or substantially supported al-Qaeda, the Taliban, or associated forces that are engaged in hostilities against the United States or its coalition partners, including any person who has committed a belligerent act or has directly supported such hostilities in aid of such enemy forces." § 1021(b)(2), (c)(1). Note that this statute incorporates the laws of war by reference. Also recall the *Charming Betsy* rule that federal statutes are to be interpreted consistently with international law. Of course, international law can enhance presidential power and provide limits thereto. *See, e.g.*, Paust, *In Their Own Words: Affirmations of the Founders, Framers, and Early Judiciary Concerning the Binding Nature of the Customary Law of Nations*, 14 U.C. Davis J. Int'l L. & Pol'y 205, 240–45 (2008); Chapter Eleven, Section 2. What might those powers and limits be? Recall Chapter Eight on the reach of the laws of war.

In May, 2012, this provision was found to be unconstitutionally vague in *Hedges v. Obama*, _ F. Supp2d _ (S.D.N.Y. 2012). In *Hedges*, Judge Katherine Forrest issued a preliminary injunction and ruled that "the statute at issue places the public at undue risk of having their speech chilled for the purported protection from al-Qaeda, the Taliban, and 'associated forces' — *i.e.*, 'foreign terrorist organizations.' The vagueness of § 1021 does not allow the average citizen, or even the Government itself, to understand the type of definiteness to which our citizens are entitled, or what conduct comes within its scope" and the Government could not offer a specific example of what is meant by "substantially supported" or "directly supported." *Id*. Moreover, "the Government conceded that the statute lacks a scienter or *mens rea* requirement of any kind.... Thus, an individual could run the risk of substantially supporting or directly supporting an associated force without even being aware that he or she was doing so." *Id*. Judge Forrest distinguished 18 U.S.C. § 2339B regarding "material support" to a foreign terrorist organization and the Supreme Court decision in *Holder v. Humanitarian Law Project*, 130 S.Ct. 2705 (2010), because of the latter statute's definitions and the fact that the Supreme Court stressed that they had been narrowed and clarified over time, "the very definitions and the knowledge requirement that are missing from this statute." *Id*.

What do you think "substantially supported" might mean? Would the phrase cover advocating the ideological views of al Qaeda or the Taliban? Should the phrase be given the same meaning as "material support" that is defined in 18 U.S.C. § 2339B? Judge Forrest noted several reason why this would not be preferable, including the need to avoid violating the separation of powers and the conclusion that to import meaning from other statutes "would [be to] ignore the differences between those two statutes that this Court is required to assume are intentional." *Id*.

10. The United States has enacted a variety of statutes to facilitate the prosecution of terrorists under the terrorist long arm statute and the statutes implementing the anti-ter-

rorism conventions. One such statute is the Foreign Intelligence Surveillance Act of 1978 (FISA), 50 U.S.C. §§ 1801–1811. The Act authorizes the government to conduct wire taps in aid of protecting the United States against attack by foreign governments or international terrorist groups after obtaining approval for such during a secret "probable cause" hearing before a secret Foreign Intelligence Surveillance Court (§ 1805(a)(3) & (6)), with the possibility of appeal and possible review by the Supreme Court. In *United States. v. Rahman*, 861 F. Supp. 247 (S.D.N.Y. 1994), the court held that FISA can be used to gather evidence for a criminal case. For a comprehensive discussion of the procedures for obtaining a FISA warrant and legal challenges to FISA see Jimmy Gurule & Geoffrey S. Corn, Principles of Counter-Terrorism Law 205–241 (West Publ. 2011).

In late 2005, a significant controversy arose over previously secret domestic surveillance by the National Security Agency without compliance with congressional requirements set forth in the FISA. The Bush Administration claimed sweeping power under the commander in chief clause of the Constitution to violate any inhibiting congressional legislation. *See* DOJ memorandum, Legal Authorities Supporting the Activities of the National Security Agency Described by the President, Jan. 19, 2006, at 3, 35, available at http://rawstory.com/other/justicerawstory.pdf; Charlie Savage, *Bush Challenges Hundreds of Laws: President Cites Powers of His Office*, Boston Globe, Apr. 30, 2006, at 1. Many have claimed that the commander in chief power is subject to certain congressional controls, that the President is not above the law, and that FISA must be complied with. *See, e.g.*, ABA res., Feb. 13, 2006, and Report, ABA Task Force on Domestic Surveillance in the Fight Against Terrorism, available at http://www.abanews.org/docs/domsurvrecommendationfinal.pdf; Paust, *Not Authorized By Law: Domestic Spying and Congressional Consent*, JURIST, Dec. 2005, available at http://jurist.law.pitt.edu/forumy/2005/12/not-authorized-by-law-domestic-spying.php. Regarding some of the cases recognizing congressional power to limit certain commander in chief functions, *see, e.g.*, Paust, *Executive Plans and Authorizations to Violate International Law Concerning Treatment and Interrogation of Detainees*, 43 Columbia J. Transnat'l L. 811, 842 n.114 (2005), available at http://www.columbia.edu/cu/jtl/Vol_43_3_files/Paust.pdf.

11. Another important statute in this category is the Rewards for Terrorism Information Act, Pub.L. 99-399, 22 U.S.C. § 2708, which authorizes the Secretary of State to pay up to two million dollars to any individual who furnishes information leading to the arrest or conviction, in any country, of a person committing or conspiring to commit an act of international terrorism. The two million in federal funds is matched by a parallel program sponsored by the Air Transport Association, representing the U.S. airline industry, and the Air Line Pilots Association, representing U.S. commercial pilots, bringing the total available for terrorist information to four million dollars. In 1990, the Department of State launched a world-wide campaign with television and radio announcements featuring several motion picture stars (Charlie Sheen, Charlton Heston, and Charles Bronson), which encouraged viewers with any information about an act of terrorism to "be a hero" and contact authorities in their country, the nearest U.S. Embassy, or a post office box in Washington, D.C.

Index